AMERICAN SONGWRITERS

Biographical Dictionaries from The H. W. Wilson Company

American Reformers
Greek and Latin Authors 800 B.C.–A.D. 1000
European Authors 1000–1900
British Authors Before 1800
British Authors of the Nineteenth Century
American Authors 1600–1900
Twentieth Century Authors
Twentieth Century Authors: First Supplement
World Authors 1950–1970
World Authors 1970–1975
World Authors 1975–1980

The Junior Book of Authors
More Junior Authors
Third Book of Junior Authors
Fourth Book of Junior Authors and Illustrators
Fifth Book of Junior Authors and Illustrators

Great Composers: 1300–1900
Composers Since 1900
Composers Since 1900: First Supplement
Musicians Since 1900
American Songwriters

World Artists 1950–1980

AMERICAN SONGWRITERS

An H.W. Wilson Biographical Dictionary

---

by
DAVID EWEN

THE H.W. WILSON COMPANY

NEW YORK

1987

Library of Congress Cataloging-in-Publication Data

Ewen, David, 1907–
  American songwriters.

  Bibliography: p.
  Includes index.
  1. Composers—United States—Biography.
2. Lyricists—United States—Biography. I. Title.
ML390.E825 1987   784.5'0092'2 B]   86–24654
ISBN 0–8242–0744–0

PRINTED IN THE UNITED STATES OF AMERICA

CONTENTS

SONGWRITERS

INTRODUCTION

As a replacement for *Popular American Composers* (1962) and *Popular American Composers: First Supplement* (1972), *American Songwriters* is neither a mere revision nor a simple updating of the two earlier publications. It is a total reorganization, representing an overhaul of editorial values and yielding a work of much greater scope than its predecessors.

American Songwriters consists of 146 biographies, about 90 of which are of composers, with the remainder devoted to lyricists and composer-lyricists who were omitted from the earlier books, which dealt exclusively with composers. Too often, the lyricist has been the orphan of the songwriting business, receiving far less attention than his music-composing partner. Yet the wordsmith's contribution is a crucial one, and *American Songwriters* attempts to illuminate this comparatively shadowy area in popular music by highlighting the achievements not only of tunesmiths, but of those who write the words that sit beneath the notes as well. In giving lyricists the same in-depth treatment as composers, this volume provides information not readily available elsewhere.

Moreover, as in *Popular American Composers* and its *Supplement*, biography is emphasized over criticism, though biographical coverage has been greatly expanded in *American Songwriters*. But a dramatically important dimension has been added to this volume: the performance history of individual songs, together with notes on how and why many of the artists' standards came to be written. Supplementing the songs mentioned in each biography, the medium in which they first appeared is identified, as are the performer or performers who introduced them. The later performance history of each song is also provided, including a listing of the films and stage musicals into which it has been interpolated and of early recordings and selected later ones. For Broadway and Off Broadway musicals, where so many of America's best-loved songs are incubated, the text is briefly summarized. Because some 5,600 compositions are mentioned in the biographies, an index is included that lists each song and locates it by page number.

Attention is paid, too, to the performance history of major stage musicals, including information on significant revivals, awards, mention of original cast or soundtrack recordings, and the performance run of most productions. In regard to the length of a musical's stage run, a word of caution is in order. In different eras the number of consecutive performances spelling success has varied greatly. Early in the 20th century, musicals with an initial Broadway run of less than 100 performances were money-makers, inasmuch as a Broadway production launched the series of out-of-town runs that would earn the show its profits. Through the 1920s, when production costs were low, a run of about 200 performances meant box-office success. But as costs mounted, the number of performances required for a musical's success increased from about 300 shows in the 1930s, to some 500 in the '40s and '50s and more than 600 or 700 in following decades.

In selecting subjects for inclusion in a book spanning two centuries, I have chosen only those men and women who, in my estimation, have a durable place in the history of the American popular song through sustained creative achievement over an extended period of time; those whose most memorable numbers have become standards, entering into the permanent repertory of American popular music. Scrupulously avoided have been composers or lyricists whose meteoric careers only momentarily lit up the musical skies, producing but a handful of hit songs or bestselling recordings. Nor have I included composers or lyricists, however gifted, whose work failed to achieve popularity with a mass audience.

As its title indicates, this book is devoted wholly to Americans, whether by birth or by naturalization. Distinguished foreign songwriters, even if they established residence in this country and worked here as popular composers, have been excluded. Also, this book deals exclusively with compositions intended for the voice, combining words *and* music. Thus, none of the splendid music by Americans within instrumental formats is taken into account—be it ragtime, jazz, folk, country and western, pop, rock or the background music for films or television shows. However, compositions originating as instrumentals to which lyrics were added later are discussed in this volume.

A note on the organization of dual and individual biographies. Lyricists who have worked productively with several different composers are assigned separate articles. On the other hand, the careers of lyricists identified solely with one composer, as Lorenz Hart was with Richard Rodgers, are discussed within the biography of that composer. Thus the repetition of facts, awards and achievements is avoided. Accordingly, when a lyricist is treated in his own biography, the performance history of his songs can be found in the biographies of the composers with whom he worked. In each instance, a cross-reference within the lyricist's biography directs the reader to the relevant composers.

To insure thoroughness, I have tried to enlist the assistance of the songwriters themselves in compiling this material. In most instances, the composer or lyricist was invited to read the first draft of his biography for any necessary factual alterations. The cooperation of several songwriters proved invaluable, and my gratitude is profound. I thank Sammy Fain in particular for his help in assembling an article that I hope does justice to him and his long and distinguished career.

In preparing this volume I made use of the resources of numerous musical organizations and music publishers. I also tapped my own personal files, gathered over half a century, which contain a storehouse of invaluable materials. A final bow goes to my wife, Hannah, who undertook the laborious task of typing this manuscript and helped to shepherd it through its various stages of progress.

Throughout *American Songwriters* certain acronyms, abbreviations and nicknames have been used. They are:

ABC. American Broadcasting Company.

ASCAP. American Society of Authors, Composers and Publishers.

BBC. British Broadcasting Corporation.

BMI. Broadcast Music Inc.

CBS. Columbia Broadcasting System.

Emmy. Annual awards presented by the National Academy of Television Arts and Sciences.

Gold record, platinum record. Awards presented by the Recording Industry Association of America for albums selling 500,000 units or a single disc selling one million copies (gold record); or one million album units and two million singles (platinum record).

Grammy. Annual awards presented by the National Academy of Recording Arts and Sciences.

MGM. Metro-Goldwyn-Mayer.

NBC. National Broadcasting Company.

Oscar. Annual awards presented by the Academy of Motion Picture Arts and Sciences.

RCA. Radio Corporation of America.

Tony. The Antoinette Perry Awards presented each year by the American Theatre Wing for distinguished achievements in the Broadway theater.

David Ewen
Boca Raton, 1985
(November 26, 1907–December 28, 1985)

AMERICAN SONGWRITERS

AMERICAN SONGWRITERS

ADAMS, LEE. *See* **STROUSE, CHARLES** and **ADAMS, LEE**

ADAMSON, HAROLD (December 10, 1906–August 17, 1980). Harold Adamson's career as a lyricist spanned more than three decades and his credits include songs for 45 motion pictures and 12 Broadway shows. He worked with some of Hollywood and Broadway's most successful composers. Nineteen of his songs were featured on *Your Hit Parade* and five were nominated for Academy Awards.

Harold Campbell Adamson was born in Greenville, New Jersey. His father, James Harold Adamson, was a building contractor and his mother, Marion (Campbell) Adamson, was of Scottish descent. Harold was raised in Brooklyn, New York, where he attended public schools and began taking piano lessons. At the age of ten, he became a victim of poliomyelitis, but the affliction did not interfere with his education. In 1923 he entered the Hackley School, a preparatory school in Tarrytown, New York, where he wrote poetry for school publications and sketches for school shows. He also developed a lifelong interest in baseball, but because he was unable to participate as a player, he served as manager of the school team. At the same time, his father was amassing a small fortune, and the family moved to a beautiful estate he built on a private island adjacent to the Yacht Club in Larchmont, New York.

After graduating from Hackley, Adamson pursued his ambition to become a thespian at the University of Kansas. There he contributed song lyrics to school shows and acted in summer stock productions. He transferred to Harvard University, where he wrote sketches and lyrics for Hasty Pudding Club Shows and contributed the libretto and lyrics for *Close-Up*, a satire on Hollywood. *Close-Up* was the first musical produced by the Harvard Dramatic Club, and the cast included Henry Fonda and Margaret Sullavan. While at Harvard, Adamson also contin-

HAROLD ADAMSON

ued to act in the summer productions of the University Players Guild at the Old Silver Beach Theatre in Falmouth, Massachusetts. A local critic reported that "Mr. Adamson seems always to fall into the most difficult of character roles, but he does these with such consummate art that we can applaud the casting director for his unerring good judgment."

Adamson's theatrical activities at Harvard came to the attention of Vincent Youmans, then near the end of his long and successful career on Broadway. As a result, following Adamson's graduation in 1930, Florenz Ziegfeld engaged him to contribute lyrics to a new Youmans musical, *Smiles* (November 18, 1930). Though the book had been written by William Anthony McGuire (after Noël Coward), and Fred and Adele Astaire and Marilyn Miller led the cast, *Smiles* was a box-office failure, closing after only 92 performances. But for Adamson, the cloud had a silver lining: with Youmans and Mack Gordon he had created the classic, "Time on My Hands."

After *Smiles*, Adamson joined forces with

3

composer Burton Lane, who was still a teenager when they met. Together they composed "Say the Word" for *The Third Little Show* (June 1, 1931) and collaborated on their first important Broadway assignment, songs for the seventh edition of *Earl Carroll's Vanities* (August 27, 1931). The show was unpopular with the critics, but achieved a solid run of 278 performances.

In 1933 Adamson and Lane accepted an offer from Metro-Goldwyn-Mayer to write songs for *Dancing Lady* (1933), starring Joan Crawford. They contributed three songs to the film, including the memorable "Everything I Have is Yours." The following year, they composed songs for the Spencer Tracy film, *Bottoms Up,* and the popular "Your Head on My Shoulder" for *Kid Millions,* a United Artists' vehicle for Eddie Cantor. In 1935 "Ev'rything's Been Done Before" from *Reckless* became the first of their songs heard on the new radio program, *Your Hit Parade.*

The year 1935 also brought major changes in Adamson's private life. He married Judy Crisfield on November 26; the marriage ended in divorce in 1941. Their daughter, Eve, later distinguished herself Off Broadway as producer and artistic director of the Jean Cocteau Repertory Theatre.

Adamson and Lane parted company, and for a brief period, Adamson worked with Walter Donaldson, one of the most successful and highly sought after Hollywood composers. They produced songs for *The Great Ziegfeld* (1936), including "You," which achieved first position on *Your Hit Parade* on April 18, and "Did I Remember?" for the Jean Harlow film *Suzy* (1936); the latter song earned Adamson his first Academy Award nomination.

At the same time, Adamson began a long and productive collaboration with Jimmy McHugh, a veteran of both Broadway and Hollywood musicals. Their first film was *Banjo on My Knee* (1936), followed by *Hitting a New High* (1937), starring the coloratura soprano, Lily Pons. For Universal Studios, they composed songs for the George Murphy films *You're a Sweetheart* (1937) and *Top of the Town* (1937), among them "Where Are You?" Two Deanna Durbin films came next: *Mad About Music* (1938) and *That Certain Age* (1938) which included the Oscar nominee, "My Own."

During the next few years, Adamson continued to contribute occasional songs to motion pictures, but he also participated in the composition of several independent hits. With Johnny Watson and Jan Savitt he wrote "Seven Twenty in the Books" and "It's a Wonderful World." Both were introduced by Savitt and his orchestra in

1939, and the latter was adopted as the orchestra's theme song.

In the same period, Adamson returned to the Broadway stage contributing lyrics to *Banjo Eyes,* which opened on Christmas day in 1941 less than three weeks after the bombing of Pearl Harbor. The book was an adaptation of the John Cecil Holm and George Abbott play *Three Men on a Horse* (1935), and the production starred Eddie Cantor. One of the high points of the evening was Adamson's song, "We're Having a Baby," written with the composer Vernon Duke. But what might have been a long and successful run was cut short by the departure of Cantor after only 126 performances.

In 1942 Adamson turned to writing lyrics for instrumental compositions. The first of these was *Manhattan Serenade,* a sentimental tribute to the sights and sounds of New York City composed by Louis Alter in 1928. The original version had been made popular by Paul Whiteman and his orchestra in a recording that sold over a million copies, and it was heard on radio for more than 15 years as the theme song for the weekly comedy series, *Easy Aces.* Adamson's new version, promoted by the orchestras of both Dorsey brothers, also became quite popular. He also wrote lyrics for the "Mardi Gras" section of Ferde Grofe's *Mississippi* (1926); the result was "Daybreak," a hit recorded by Tommy Dorsey and his orchestra with Frank Sinatra, and sung by Kathryn Grayson in the MGM extravaganza *Thousands Cheer* (1943).

In 1943 Adamson found himself back in Hollywood. He collaborated with Jule Styne on songs for *Hit Parade of 1943* from which "Change of Heart" brought him his third Oscar nomination. He also renewed his partnership with Jimmy McHugh, and the pair now produced some of their best songs, including several standards. Inspired by the war, they published in 1943 "Comin' in on a Wing and a Prayer," and continued to compose songs for motion pictures. Among their successes were *Higher and Higher* (1943), which starred Frank Sinatra and included "I Couldn't Sleep a Wink Last Night" (for which they received an Oscar nomination), "A Lovely Way to Spend an Evening," and "The Music Stopped"; *Four Jills in a Jeep* (1944), which included "How Blue the Night" and "Dig You Later (A Hubba-Hubba-Hubba)" from *Doll Face* (1945). Their collaboration was also revived briefly after the war for "It's a Most Unusual Day" from *A Date with Judy* (1948) and the Broadway musical *As the Girls Go* (November 13, 1948). Based on the premise that the United States had just elected its first woman president, it starred Irene Rich and Bobby Clark as her husband.

In addition to his professional engagements, Adamson made various contributions to the war effort and received citations from the U. S. Treasury Department and the Hollywood Canteen. After the war he married Broadway actress Gretchen Davidson (on December 18, 1947) and they moved to North Alpine Drive in Beverly Hills. Both brought offspring from previous marriages: Adamson, his daughter, and Gretchen, a daughter, Gretchen, and a son, Andrew D. Amerson, who later held the post of Deputy Attorney General for the State of California.

In the 1950s Adamson found several new partners, among them Hoagy Carmichael. "My Resistance is Low" was introduced by Carmichael and Jane Russell in *The Las Vegas Story* (1953); the team also composed "When Love Goes Wrong" for *Gentlemen Prefer Blondes* (1953) and songs for *Three for the Show* (1955).

Adamson also collaborated with Harry Warren and Leo McCarey on the title song of *An Affair to Remember* (1957), which brought him his fifth Academy Award nomination, and with Victor Young on the title song for *Around the World in Eighty Days* (1956). This became a bestseller in recordings by Victor Young and his orchestra, Jane Morgan, Eddie Fisher, Bing Crosby, and Nat King Cole, among many others. It reached first position on *Your Hit Parade* in 1957. Michael Todd, the producer of the film, insisted that this song be played during intermission wherever the motion picture was shown. Adamson later adapted the song from the film and added new ones (with Sammy Fain, composer) for a stage production in 1964.

In the 1960s Adamson continued working for motion pictures, though only intermittently. Among his last projects were *A Ticklish Affair* (1963) with George Stoll and Robert Vaneps, *Island of Love* (1963) and the comedic Don Knotts vehicle, *The Incredible Mr. Limpet* (1964), with Sammy Fain.

Adamson suffered a stroke in 1971 and formally retired five years later. In recognition of his contribution to popular music, he received an award from ASCAP in 1976, and Beverly Hills proclaimed March 28, 1979 "Harold Adamson Day" in celebration of his being chosen to receive an Aggie Award from the American Guild of Authors and Composers.

In July 1980 Adamson fell into a coma and died in Los Angeles five weeks later on August 17, 1980. The memorial service on September 22, held at All Saints' Episcopal Church in Beverly Hills, included the reading of a poem by Robert Nathan, written in Adamson's memory.

ABOUT: Stambler, I. Encyclopedia of Popular Music, 1965; Craig, W. Sweet and Lowdown: America's Popular Song Writers, 1978; Craig, W. The Great Songwriters of Hollywood, 1980.
Periodicals—Variety August 27, 1980.

ADLER, RICHARD (August 3, 1921–), composer-lyricist, was born in New York City, the son of Clarence and Elsa Adrienne (Richard) Adler. Since Clarence Adler was a prominent pianist and teacher, Richard grew up in a household where great music was a way of life. He received some piano instruction from his father, but before long he dropped its study for good. After that, he was self-taught in music. His academic education took place at Columbia Grammar School, New York City, from which he graduated in 1939. At the University of North Carolina he took a course in playwriting with Paul Green and received a B.A. degree in 1943.

During World War II, Adler served in the United States Navy (1943–46), aboard a YP-PC boat in the Pacific, holding the rank of lieutenant junior grade. Returning to civilian life he worked for the advertising branch of the Celanese Corporation (1946–50). His avocation was songwriting, initially only the lyrics. Most of his earliest efforts were recognizably amateurish. But "Teasin'," (1950, music by Philip Springer) was published and also successfully recorded by Connie Haines. In England, in a recording by the Beverly Sisters, it reached the number one spot on the charts.

Frank Loesser, the famous songwriter and head of the publishing house of Frank Music Inc., introduced Adler to Jerry Ross in 1950. Ross, too, was a songwriting novice. Born Jerold Ross in New York City on March 9, 1926, he made several boyhood appearances in singing roles on the Yiddish stage and in a Yiddish-language motion picture. Having written his first song while attending high school, he continued to write at New York University, where he took courses in music. After graduating from NYU, he wrote songs for productions in the summer hotels of the Catskill Mountains, the so-called borscht belt. There he met and befriended Eddie Fisher, who introduced him to several publishers, none of whom showed any interest in his work. Undaunted, Ross kept on writing songs. His meeting with Adler was the turning point in his own career as well as in that of Adler.

Adler and Ross struck up both a friendship and a writing partnership. Before long, they marketed special material to Jimmy Durante, Marlene Dietrich and Eddie Fisher, as well as to the popular weekly television program *Stop the Music!* They were also a team while writing their

RICHARD ADLER

songs, a unique kind of team since both were involved equally in writing lyrics as well as music. "It's impossible to say who does what and when," Adler explained after their first song successes. "But we've set rules. If I come in with what I think is a beautiful idea, and he says, 'I don't like it,' I can scream, I can rave, but it's out. It obviates arguments. There has to be unanimity in our operation."

With Frank Music Inc. as their publisher, they achieved a modest success in 1951 with "Strange Little Girl," which was popularized by several recordings, notably one by Eddie Howard. They also made their bow on Broadway with four songs in a revue, *John Murray Anderson's Almanac* (December 10, 1953). The best was "Acorn in the Meadow," introduced by Harry Belafonte, which he later recorded.

In 1953, with Dave Kapp's assistance, Adler and Ross wrote "Even Now," recorded by Eddie Fisher. That same year they had their first major hit song, "Rags to Riches," inspired by Eddie Fisher's career and a chance remark by Adler that Fisher had progressed from "rags to riches." Recorded by Tony Bennett, it sold two million discs in 1953–54. The sheet music sold more than a million copies. The song achieved first position on *Your Hit Parade* on November 14, 1953, one of nine presentations. A year later, Adler and Ross composed "True Love Goes On and On," recorded by Burl Ives with the Gordon Jenkins Orchestra.

George Abbott, the esteemed stage director, took note of their talent and contracted Adler and Ross to write their first full-length score for a Broadway musical. That project, *The Pajama Game* (May 13, 1954), was an adaptation by Abbott and Richard Bissell of Bissell's novel, *7½ Cents*. Its theme was labor-management relations in the Sleep-Time Pajama Factory in Cedar Rapids, Iowa, and the plot revolves around a strike by the employees against management and the romance of Babe Williams, head of the Union grievance committee, and Sid Sorokin, the factory superintendent. Opening a new musical in late spring usually spelled box-office disaster, since it had to face the summer doldrums before the run could gain momentum. But the projected musical seemed doomed for other reasons as well. Its songwriters were novices in the theater, and so were the producers (Griffith and Prince) and the choreographer (Bob Fosse). Also, the subject of a labor dispute, and the unromantic settings of a factory and a union headquarters, were hardly the wool from which successful musicals were spun, at least not in 1954. Nevertheless all elements came together to make for stunning entertainment, enhanced by Abbott's skillful, fast-moving direction. One critic gushed that *The Pajama Game* was "a delirious daffy delight, . . . a royal flush and a grand slam rolled into one." The show had a run of 1,063 performances, becoming only the eighth musical in Broadway history to reach the magic 1,000 circle. It captured the Tony and the Donaldson Awards as the season's best musical. It returned to Broadway in 1957, just six months after the termination of its original run, and in 1973 it was revived again on Broadway, with Adler as coproducer. A successful motion picture adaptation in 1957 starred Doris Day with a cast largely culled from the original stage production. In 1958, how *The Pajama Game* came to be written and produced was the subject of a new musical, *Say, Darling,* music by Jule Styne.

The songs of Adler and Ross were winners. *New York Times* critic Brooks Atkinson said that "[Adler and Ross] have written an exuberant score in any number of good American idioms without self-consciousness. . . . Mr. Adler and Mr. Ross wrote like musicians with a sense of humor." Two songs were successful both in and outside the theater. "Hey, There," was a one-man duet in which John Raitt sang the number into a dictaphone before playing it back; while listening, he sang contrapuntal comments. He repeated this performance in the motion-picture version. This song's offstage popularity was greatly enhanced by Rosemary Clooney's recording, which sold about 2,500,000 copies. "Hey, There" had 17 appearances on *Your Hit Parade,* ten times in first position. "Hernando's Hideaway" was a tango (or a mock tango) introduced by Raitt and Carol Haney on the stage and sung by Haney in the film. It made 14 appearances on *Your Hit Parade,* reaching first position on June 12, 1954. It was a bestselling recording in a performance by Archie Blyer and his orchestra. Other numbers from this score had greater impact on the stage than away from it. "Steam Heat" was a show-stopper. This dance routine, choreographed by Bob Fosse, was performed with hissing and other vocal sounds in which Carol Haney (in her Broadway debut) appeared as a gamin dressed in a derby and tight-fitting male attire, flanked by two men similarly dressed. This performance made her a star. "There Once Was a Man" was a Western-style ballad performed by Raitt and Janis Paige on the stage and by Doris Day in the film.

Adler and Ross's second musical came a year later: *Damn Yankees* (May 5, 1955). This, too, was directed by Abott; had a run of more than 1,000 performances; was honored with the Tony and the Donaldson Awards as the year's best musical; and was made into a motion picture in 1958 with Gwen Verdon and Ray Walston reprising their stage roles. *Damn Yankees* was the adaptation by Abbott and Douglas Wallop of Wallop's novel, *The Year the Yankees Lost the Pennant.* The story centers on the fortunes of a baseball team, a theme treated as a modern-day version of the Faust legend. Joe Boyd, a middle-aged baseball fanatic, makes a pact with the devil, trading his soul for a pennant for his beloved, luckless Washington Senators, with himself as star player. When he is tempted to renege on the bargain, a bewitching siren, Lola, is recruited by the devil to keep Joe to the terms of his covenant. With astute direction and stellar performances, *Damn Yankees* became the most successful Broadway musical ever on a sports subject. Brooks Atkinson described it in *The New York Times* "as shiny as a new baseball. . . . The music had the spirit and brass you'd expect to find at the ball park." The leading songs were "Whatever Lola Wants" and "Heart." "Whatever Lola Wants" profited from Gwen Verdon's infectious performance both on the stage and on the screen. The song also enjoyed considerable success in Sarah Vaughan's recording. "Heart," with which the manager of the Senators hopes to instill courage in his team, was introduced on the stage by Russ Brown, Jimmie Komack, Nathaniel Frey and Albert Linville and was sung on the screen by Ray Walston, Rae Allen, Jimmie Komack and Albert Linville; It sold more than a million discs in Eddie Fisher's recording. "Whatever Lola Wants" and "Heart" had seven representations each on *Your Hit Parade.* The music of *The Pajama Game* and *Damn Yankees* was released in original and soundtrack recordings.

With two giant stage successes, Adler and Ross

had become the most highly esteemed new songwriters on Broadway since World War II. The partnership ended suddenly on November 11, 1955, when Jarold Ross died in New York of chronic bronchiectasis after years of illness.

In 1958, with Robert Allen as composer, Adler wrote the lyrics to "Everybody Loves a Lover" and "The Girl on Page 44." Doris Day made the former famous in her recording which sold two million copies and reached the number one spot on many foreign charts. The Four Lads made a bestselling recording of "The Girl on Page 44." From this point on, Adler avoided collaboration by writing his own lyrics. He first did so for two television musicals in 1959, which he coproduced with David Susskind: *Little Women* on October 16 and *The Gift of the Magi* on December 9, their music recorded on soundtrack albums.

On January 3, 1958, Adler married Sally Ann Howes, a British actress. This was Adler's second marriage. The first had been to Marion Hart on September 4, 1951; they were divorced not long before Adler's marriage to Howes. From his first marriage, Adler had two sons, one of whom, Christopher, became a song lyricist; he died in 1984 at the age of 30. After divorcing Howes in 1966, Adler married Ritchey Farrell Banker on December 27, 1968, but they, too, were divorced, in 1976.

While Sally Ann Howes was still his wife, she starred in *Kwamina* (October 23, 1961), with which Adler returned to Broadway as lyricist and composer. The musical is set in a newly independent African nation where a white woman, Eve, becomes emotionally involved with Kwamina, a black African doctor—a relationship that ends in separation. "We were more interested in showing the conflicts between the old and the new Africa than with a love affair," Adler explained. "There's no physical manifestation of the friendship between the hero, who is an English-educated Negro, and Eve, the white African girl, because we're just showing one aspect of African society." *Kwamina* lasted just 32 performances but its short run was not the fault of the score. "In its dances and chanting," wrote Howard Taubman, the drama critic of *The New York Times,* "*Kwamina* summons up the mysterious spirit of a remote corner of an unknown continent." "Another Time, Another Place," a ballad introduced by Sally Ann Howes, was recorded by Robert Goulet. "The Cocoa Bean Song," performed by the ensemble to open the production, had an evocative, African-cum-Broadway flavor. The original cast album was recorded and released after the show closed—a rare occurrence—and became a bestseller within two months.

In the early 1960s, Adler took a recess from Broadway to produce shows honoring the administrations of Presidents Kennedy and Johnson. In 1962, he produced and staged the White House Presidential Corps and Photographers Show for President Kennedy and the English Prime Minister Harold MacMillan in Washington, D. C. The same year he also produced the New York City salute to Kennedy at Madison Square Garden. Adler produced and directed the Inaugural Anniversary Salute to President Kennedy in the nation's capital on January 18, 1963. On January 14, 1964, at the request of President and Mrs. Johnson, he directed and was master-of-ceremonies at the new administration's first state dinner and, in 1965, he produced the Inaugural Gala for President Johnson. In addition to these productions, he was trustee of the John F. Kennedy Center in Washington from 1964 to 1977 and consultant on the arts for the White House from 1965 to 1969. In 1977 he was appointed head of the then recently established American Musical Theatre Center at Duke University.

Adler returned to the theater in 1968 with unhappy results. *A Mother's Kisses* was a musical that opened and closed out of town. After that came *Music Is,* a stage musical with book by George Abbott based on Shakespeare's *Twelfth Night.* Here Adler fulfilled the functions of composer and coproducer, with Will Holt supplying the lyrics. Though it had been well received at the Kennedy Center, the show closed in New York after the eight performances attendant upon its December 20, 1976 opening. The best songs were the ballad "Should I Speak of Loving You?" (introduced by Catherine Cox) and the comic and lightly salacious "I Am It" which was introduced by Christopher Hewitt.

"I got so depressed after *Music Is,*" Adler later confided, "that I decided I wouldn't write any more shows." Nevertheless, he was soon writing words and music to *Roman Holiday,* with book by Robert Anderson. On the strength of Adler's score, NBC financed the show. But Adler's streak of bad luck on Broadway continued; the production fell apart before going into rehearsal.

In 1966 Adler wrote lyrics and music, and was producer, for a television special, *Musical Olympus 7-0000,* presented on the Stage 67 program of the ABC-TV network. Its score was released in a soundtrack recording. In 1976 Adler produced Richard Rodgers's penultimate Broadway musical, *Rex,* and that, too, was a failure.

Through the years, Adler has been a highly esteemed creator of musical commercials, writing for such brand names as Newport Filter and Kent cigarettes, Hertz, Bon Ami, Willys Oakland, Lucky Lager Beer, Colgate and Eastman Kodak. The National Advertising Association chose his commercial for Newport Filter cigarettes as the best of the year.

In the late 1970s Adler turned from popular to concert music. *Memory of Childhood,* for full symphony orchestra, was premiered by the Detroit Symphony on October 6, 1978 and later performed by other major American orchestras. Adler was commissioned by the Soviet Emigré Orchestra to write a composition for its festival of music at Carnegie Hall on July 10, 1979. He responded with *Retrospectrum,* for chamber orchestra. After that came *Yellowstone Overture,* which originated in 1980 as a composition for brass and had been introduced in New York City by the Metropolitan Brass. On a commission from the American Philharmonic Orchestra in New York, Adler rewrote it for symphony orchestra; as such, it had its first hearing on November 2, 1980, in New York. *Wilderness Suite* was later written under a special arrangement with the Department of Interior and the National Park Service and was premiered and recorded by the Utah Symphony. *The Lady Remembers,* a symphonic suite honoring the centenary of the Statue of Liberty, was first performed by the Detroit Symphony in Washington, D. C. on October 28, 1985.

In 1981 Adler was presented the Distinguished Alumnus Award by the University of North Carolina, his alma mater.

ABOUT: Rigdon, W. (ed.) The Biographical Encyclopedia and Who's Who of the American Theatre, 1966. *Periodicals*—New York Times Magazine June 19, 1955; Washington Star February 2, 1982.

AGER, MILTON (October 6, 1893 – May 6, 1979). Among his many hit songs in Tin Pan Alley, in the Broadway theater and for motion pictures, his best known is "Happy Days Are Here Again," the traditional theme song of the Democratic Party from the time of Franklin Delano Roosevelt.

Composer Milton Ager was born in Chicago, the sixth of nine children of Lithuanian emigrants Simon and Fanny Ager. Simon was the owner of a livery stable in Chicago and a dealer in horses and cattle. Milton's older sister, Anne, who loved to sing and play the piano, was an important influence in his musical development. Soon after the turn of the century she acquired a piano which Milton, not yet ten, learned to play without instruction. Before long, he had begun improvising tunes. Though musically illiterate, he devised a system of notation to get his melodies on paper.

MILTON AGER

Because of a chronic throat ailment, he did not begin public school until he was eight. One of his teachers encouraged him to borrow texts on music from the library. Thus he taught himself to read and write music. At the same time he improved his piano technique by trial and error. At high school, where he worked on the school magazine, he composed several songs. His mother, noting his devotion to music, convinced the manager of a local silent movie theater to hire him as pianist. In 1910, after his third year in high school, Ager turned his back on formal schooling to work full time in a movie theater, performing the popular tunes of the day during intermissions. His next job was for the Chicago branch of the publishing firm of Waterson, Berlin and Snyder, plugging its songs in shops in the Southwest. In 1913–14 he worked as piano accompanist for several performers touring the Orpheum vaudeville circuit.

Ambitious to make headway in the song business, Ager left Chicago for Manhattan in 1914 to become a staff pianist for the home office of Waterson, Berlin and Snyder. One of his duties was to devise a workable piano part or orchestration for "lead" sheets, a sheet which contained the melodic line (and occasionally the lyrics as well) and sometimes suggestions for the harmonies. On his own, he completed several instrumental pieces for the piano, in collaboration with Pete Wendling, which he sold to Waterson, Berlin and Snyder for $25 each.

During World War I, Ager served in the army morale division entertaining troops stationed at Fort Greenleaf, Georgia. After the war, he worked as piano demonstrator and songwriter

for the publishing house of William Jerome Music Company, which was soon absorbed by Leo Feist, Inc. At Feist, Ager met the veteran lyricist, Grant Clarke, whom he hounded to produce workable lyrics that he, Ager, would set to music. In desperation, Clarke threw at Ager the line, "Everything's peaches down in Georgia," and told him to try developing a melody around the idea. Ager quickly wrote music for a possible chorus, and Joseph W. Meyer provided the musical setting for a possible verse; Grant Clarke then wrote the lyrics. "Everything is Peaches Down in Georgia" was published by Leo Feist in 1918. Al Jolson introduced it at one of his Sunday evening Winter Garden concerts and helped to popularize it. Ager, Meyer and Clarke then went on to write "Anything is Nice if It Comes From Dixieland," published by Feist in 1919.

In 1920, John Murray Anderson, the Broadway producer of revues, contracted Ager to compose his first score for a Broadway production, *What's In a Name?* (March 19, 1920). With Jack Yellen hired to write the lyrics, a successful partnership was now formed. "A Young Man's Fancy" (lyrics written with John Murray Anderson) was introduced by Rosalind Fuller.

In 1921, the year before Ager and Yellen's first song success, Ager had composed "I'm Nobody's Baby" (lyrics by Benny Davis and Lester Santly). It proved such a favorite with female singers in vaudeville in the early 1920s that a million copies of sheet music were sold. The song was recorded by Ruth Etting and revived for Judy Garland in the motion picture *Andy Hardy Meets a Debutante* (1940). Also in 1940 it made 11 appearances on *Your Hit Parade.*

In 1922 Ager and Yellen formed the publishing firm of Ager, Yellen and Bornstein, launching it with two Ager-Yellen hits. "Who Cares?" was eventually interpolated by Al Jolson into his Winter Garden extravaganza, *Bombo.* "Lovin' Sam, the Sheik of Alabam'" was introduced in vaudeville by Sophie Tucker and recorded by Nora Bayes and Isabella Patricola. In 1922 "Lovin' Sam" was interpolated into two Broadway musicals: for Grace Hayes in *Bunch and Judy* and for Eddie Cantor in *Make It Snappy.* Twenty-eight years later, this song was revived for Hoagy Carmichael and Kirk Douglas in the motion picture *Young Man With a Horn.*

"Louisville Lou, the Vampire Lady," of 1923, was introduced in vaudeville by Sophie Tucker and recorded that year by Arthur Gibbs. A year later, Ager and Yellen (with Bob Bigelow and Charles Bates assisting with the lyrics) wrote "Hard-Hearted Hannah, the Vamp of Savannah," which was recorded that year by Dolly Kay. Frances Williams introduced "Hannah" in vaudeville and interpolated it into her Broadway musical, *Innocent Eyes* (1924). Subsequently, this song was popularized by Margaret Young in vaudeville and, in the 1950s, in recordings by Peggy Lee and Ray Charles. Ella Fitzgerald sang it in the motion picture *Pete Kelly's Blues* (1955).

In 1924 Ager and Yellen had another million-copy sheet music sale with "I Wonder What's Become of Sally?" It was recorded by Joe Schenck, Al Jolson, Dick Todd and Ted Lewis and his orchestra. Jack Yellen revealed that this number had been written as a "counter-seller"—a song not plugged professionally but performed by salesmen behind music counters on the urging of song salesmen. "But I had the feeling that we had written something more than a counter seller. I rushed to Pennsylvania Station for a train to Philadelphia where Gus Van and Joe Schenck were appearing as vaudeville headliners. . . . I sang the song for Schenck just once. The following Monday he featured it at the Palace Theater in New York. Within a week our professional offices were jammed with vaudevillians waiting to rehearse." This ballad was interpolated into the Cole Porter screen biography *Night and Day* (1946), where it was sung by Ginny Simms.

Three Ager-Yellen hit songs blossomed in 1927. "Ain't She Sweet?" was introduced by Paul Ash and his orchestra at the Oriental Theatre in Chicago. Eddie Cantor, Sophie Tucker and Lillian Roth were some of the stars fitting it into their repertories. Gene Austin, Harry Richman, Lee Morse, Johnny Marvin and Ben Bernie and his orchestra were among those who recorded it originally, with Frank Sinatra reviving it in a later release. In time, the sheet-music sale exceeded a million copies. The song was subsequently featured in several motion pictures. In *You Were Meant for Me* (1948) it was sung by Dan Dailey and Jeanne Crain. It was also heard on the soundtrack of the nonmusical film *Picnic* (1956), starring Kim Novak and William Holden. With "Forgive Me," Ruth Etting had a best selling recording. In 1942 this song was interpolated into the nonmusical film *Bells of Capricorn*; in 1946, into *Margie*; and in 1956 into the *Eddy Duchin Story*. In 1962, after Eddie Fisher's revival of this song in a bestselling recording, the song appeared three times on *Your Hit Parade*. "Crazy Words, Crazy Tune" was recorded in 1927 by (Ernie) Jones and (Billy) Hare, Frank Crumit and the Irving Aaronson Commanders.

Ager and Yellen's only success in the Broadway musical theater was in 1928 with *Rain or Shine* (February 9, 1928), which had a then substantial run of 360 performances. (Their three earlier musicals had all been box-office failures: *What's in a Name* in 1920, *Zig Zag* in 1922 and *Ted Lewis Frolic* in 1923.) In *Rain or Shine,* comedian Joe Cook took center stage as the proprietor of a bankrupt circus who, when the troupe goes on strike, takes over the entire performance by juggling, doing a balancing act, catching lighted matches in his mouth, singing, dancing, telling stories and manipulating mammoth, quixotic contraptions. Of special musical interest were the title song and "Forever and Ever," both introduced by Frances Shelley and Warren Hull.

The last Broadway musical to which Ager and Yellen contributed songs was *John Murray Anderson's Almanac* (August 14, 1929), which lasted only 69 performances.

In 1929, when the silent screen learned to speak, many leading Broadway and Tin Pan Alley songwriters were lured to the movie capital. Ager and Yellen were among the earliest arrivals. Their first assignment was *Honky Tonk* (1929), tailormade for its star, Sophie Tucker, who sang the two leading songs, "I'm the Last of the Red Hot Mammas" and "He's a Good Man to Have Around," both of which she also recorded. For *King of Jazz* (1930), Ager and Yellen wrote "A Bench in the Park" and "Happy Feet," among other numbers. The former was introduced by the Brox Sisters, Paul Whiteman and his orchestra, the Rhythm Boys (whose lineup included Bing Crosby) and George Chiles; the latter song was introduced by the Sisters G. and recorded by the Revelers. Both were used for spectacular production sequences devised by John Murray Anderson. *Chasing Rainbows* (1930) included among its four Ager-Yellen songs the historic "Happy Days Are Here Again."

Chasing Rainbows was in its last weeks of production when Ager and Yellen received a hurried call to write a choral number to be sung by a group of World War I soldiers. They complied with "Happy Days Are Here Again." When this song was filmed, it received only a hurried perfunctory treatment. The studio regarded this motion picture so adversely that for a long time it was not released. Meanwhile, the firm of Ager, Yellen and Bornstein published the song. A song plugger brought an orchestration to George Olsen, whose orchestra was then performing at the Hotel Pennsylvania in Manhattan. "It was on Black Thursday of the Big Depression," Yellen recalled in a letter to this author. "In the big dining room at the hotel, a handful of gloom-stricken diners were feasting on gall and wormwood. Olsen looked at the title of the orchestration and passed out the parts. 'Sing it for the corpses, perhaps they'll come back to life,' he instructed the vocalist. After a couple of choruses, the 'corpses' joined in sardonically, hysterically, like doomed prisoners on their way to a firing squad. Before the night was over, the hotel lobby resounded with what would soon become the theme song of ruined stock speculators as they leaped from hotel windows." As desperation deepened in the first months of the Great Depression, the song came to represent the hopes of a people eager to believe that the worst was over, that economic recovery was truly just around the corner.

George Olsen and his orchestra brought the song to the Roosevelt Hotel in Hollywood. One evening, Irving Thalberg, the legendary head of MGM, and some of his studio executives, were in the audience. When the crowd noisily picked up the refrain of "Happy Days Are Here Again," Thalberg asked why a song like this was not being used in an MGM picture, only to be told that it had, indeed, been written for the studio and that the motion picture in which it was featured was still in the can. The next day, the studio summoned stars and extras to reshoot the entire scene giving more prominence to the song, whose refrain was now sung several times. Because of this classic song, *Chasing Rainbows* was finally released but the film was rejected by the public.

In 1932, the then Governor Franklin D. Roosevelt chose "Happy Days Are Here Again" as his presidential campaign song. From then on, this song, in addition to becoming the one which invoked memories of the Depression-era 1930s, was the anthem of the Democratic party. It was first recorded in 1929 by George Olsen and his orchestra and by Charles King. Contributing to this song's popularity was its use by Lucky Strike cigarettes as a theme song for one of the radio shows it sponsored. Fred Allen sang it in the motion picture *Thanks a Million* (1935); it was sung by a busload of tourists in *The Night of the Iguana* (1964), starring Richard Burton and Ava Gardner; it was interpolated into the film biography of New York's Mayor James J. Walker, *Beau James* (1957); and it was heard on the soundtrack of *Paper Moon* (1973), whose setting was the Midwest during the Depression. In 1963 Barbra Steisand took an important step toward superstardom with her recording of "Happy Days."

In 1930, Ager and Yellen ended their collaboration. Yellen sold out his interest in his publishing firm and devoted himself mainly to producing and writing film scripts for 20th-Century–Fox. Ager withdrew from publishing in 1944 when the firm of Ager, Yellen and Bornstein was sold to Advanced Music Corporation.

Ager continued to write songs for another two decades. These were the best known: "Auf Wiedersehn, My Dear," (c. 1931, written with Al Hoffman, Ed Nelson and Al Goodheart) was recorded by Morton Downey and Russ Columbo.

"Trust in Me" (1934, lyrics by Ned Wever, music written with Jack Schwartz) was represented five times on *Your Hit Parade* in 1937, following successful recordings by Mildred Bailey and by Abe Lyman and his orchestra. The song was revived in 1961 in Etta James's recording.

"Seein' is Believin'" (1935, lyrics by Stanley Adams) was popularized in a recording by Rudy Vallee. It received four presentations on *Your Hit Parade*.

Written in 1936 with Charles Newman and Murray Mencher, "You Can't Pull the Wool Over My Eyes" was recorded by Ted Weems and his orchestra and presented nine times on *Your Hit Parade*.

"West Wind" (1936, lyrics by Charles Newman, music written with Murray Mencer) was recorded by Joe Moss and heard twice on *Your Hit Parade*.

"Ten Pins in the Sky" (1939, lyrics by Joseph McCarthy) was introduced in the film *Listen Darling* (1938) by Judy Garland, who also recorded it.

Ager spent his last years in a modest apartment on Wilshire Boulevard in Los Angeles with his wife, Cecilia Ager, a former movie critic and newspaper columnist. They had been married on February 2, 1922 in New York's City Hall with Mayor John J. Walker officiating. They had two daughters, the elder of whom is Shana Alexander, the noted author and liberal political columnist. The infant, Shana, was thought to have been the inspiration for "Ain't She Sweet?"

Ager received a plaque in 1969 commemorating his 50-year affiliation with ASCAP. He died in Los Angeles on May 6, 1979.

ABOUT: ASCAP Biographical Dictionary, 4th ed. 1980; Craig, W. Sweet and Lowdown: America's Popular Song Writers, 1978.

AHLERT, FRED E. (September 19, 1892–October 20, 1953), composer, was born in New York City, the son of Henry Ahlert, a businessman, and Julia (Polachek) Ahlert. Fred began to play the piano when he was 14, and he continued more intensive music training while attending Townsend Harris Hall high school in Manhattan. There he made his first attempts at performing and writing popular songs. For two summers he worked in an ice cream parlor with

FRED E. AHLERT

Ben Bernie (who later became a famous band-leader), entertaining the clientele for a salary of seven dollars a week.

After graduating from Townsend Harris Hall, Ahlert entered the College of the City of New York, and from there went on to Fordham Law School. Though he graduated from Fordham, he never practiced law. Intending to make the music business his career he found a job at the publishing house of Waterson, Berlin and Snyder. At the same time, he made arrangements for the Irving Aaronson Commanders and the first arrangements used by Fred Waring. Ahlert also wrote special material for the Avon Comedy Four, Fields and Seeley and the Watson Sisters. The first of his compositions to be published was *Beets and Turnips,* a piano piece written in collaboration with Cliff Hess in 1914.

On August 2, 1915 he married Mildred Goldberg. They had three sons, one of whom, Richard, became a professional songwriter, and another, Fred E. Ahlert Jr., a music publisher.

Though he was constantly writing songs, popular recognition did not come to Ahlert until 1919 when "Who Played Poker With Pocahontas When John Smith Went Away?" (lyrics by Sam M. Lewis and Joe Young) was published. A year later, two more of his songs were published by Waterson, Berlin and Snyder, each of which had a substantial sheet music sale. "I'd Love to Fall Asleep and Wake Up in My Mammy's Arms" (lyrics by Lewis and Young) became a favorite of "mammy" singers in vaudeville. The second was "You Ought to See My Baby" (lyrics by Roy Turk). In 1922 came "I Gave You Up Just Before You Threw Me Down" (lyrics by Bert

Kalmar and Harry Ruby) which was recorded that year by Joseph Knecht. "Put Away a Little Ray of Golden Sunshine for a Rainy Day" (lyrics by Lewis and Young) followed in 1926 and "There's a Cradle in Caroline" (lyrics by Lewis and Young) in 1927.

Ahlert's first major hit song and his first standard, "I'll Get By" (lyrics by Turk), appeared in 1928. It was originally popularized by Ruth Etting, with whom it was henceforth identified, following which it entered the repertories of many other ballad singers of the late 1920s. It sold more than a million copies of sheet music and several million discs in various recordings including those by Dick Haymes, Billie Holiday, Nick Lucas, Aileen Stanley and the orchestras of Ben Bernie and Gus Arnheim. It was first heard in motion pictures in *Puttin' On the Ritz* (1930), starring Harry Richman. After that it was heard as a recurring theme on the soundtrack of *A Guy Named Joe* (1943), starring Spencer Tracy. In 1944 it was interpolated into *Follow the Boys,* the year in which the song was heard on *Your Hit Parade* 22 times. Dan Dailey sang and danced to it in *You Were Meant for Me* (1948). It was also part of "Born in a Trunk," an extended song sequence performed by Judy Garland in *A Star Is Born* (1953), and was sung by Gogi Grant (dubbing for Ann Blyth) in *The Helen Morgan Story* (1958). "I'll Get By" also provided the title for a 1950 motion picture starring Dennis Day and June Haver; it was played under the opening credits by Harry James and his orchestra and, within the film, was sung by Gloria De Haven and June Haver. The recording by Ben Bernie and his orchestra was used on the soundtrack for the closing scene of the Woody Allen film *Zelig* (1983).

Having realized his first million-copy sheet-music sale with "I'll Get By," Ahlert became convinced in 1928 that the time had come for him to publish his own songs. Founding the firm of Fred E. Ahlert Inc., he himself published his next standard, "Mean to Me" (lyrics by Roy Turk) in 1929, when it was recorded by Ruth Etting, Ben Bernie and his orchestra and the orchestra of the Dorsey brothers. Later recordings were made by Helen Morgan, Etta James, Billie Holiday, Kay Starr and the Andrews Sisters. In 1984 Linda Ronstadt revived it on her album, *Lush Life.* Since Ruth Etting was largely responsible for popularizing it, it was interpolated into the Ruth Etting film biography, *Love Me or Leave Me* (1955), where it was sung by Doris Day. In Billie Holiday's screen biography, *Lady Sings the Blues* (1972), it was sung by Diana Ross, and in the Robert Altman film, *California Split* (1974), it was sung by Phyliss Shotwell.

In 1929 Ahlert was in the vanguard of Broadway and Tin Pan Alley composers and lyricists who beat a track to Hollywood in California to write songs for motion pictures in the wake of *The Jazz Singer* (1927). With Roy Turk as lyricist, Ahlert contributed three songs to the film *Marianne* (1929). A year later Ramon Novarro introduced "Into My Heart" in *Gay Madrid*. "It Must Be You" was introduced by Robert Montgomery in *Free and Easy* (1930), whose title song was sung by Buster Keaton in his debut in talking pictures.

Ahlert's subsequent song successes were more the products of Tin Pan Alley than Hollywood, though he did contribute occasional numbers to films. As a composer-publisher he wrote most of the songs without contractual commitments to either stage or screen, plugging them to success in the time-honored tradition of Tin Pan Alley, and only then occasionally finding a place for them in a motion picture.

"Walkin' My Baby Back Home" (1930, lyrics by Roy Turk) was written for Harry Richman, who introduced and popularized it in vaudeville and recorded it. It was later recorded by Nick Lucas, Lee Morse, Dean Martin and Jo Stafford. In the early 1950s it was revived by Johnnie Ray and Nat King Cole in their respective bestselling recordings with the result that, in 1952, the song appeared 12 times on *Your Hit Parade*, three times in first position. Donald O'Connor and a chorus sang it in a 1953 motion picture bearing the song title.

In 1931 "I Don't Know Why" (lyrics by Turk) became a favorite in vaudeville. It was recorded by the Tommy Dorsey orchestra (with Frank Sinatra performing the vocal), Kate Smith, Russ Columbo and the Andrews Sisters. It was interpolated into the film *Faithful in My Fashion* in 1946, the year in which it made a single appearance on *Your Hit Parade*. "Where the Blue of the Night Meets the Gold of the Day" (1931, lyrics by Turk) was interpolated into the film *The Big Broadcast* (1932) for Bing Crosby in his first screen appearance in a major role. Crosby then made it his theme song and his recording was a bestseller. It was also successfully recorded by Nat King Cole.

Other Ahlert successes in the 1930s were "Love You Funny Thing" (1932, lyrics by Turk), which was recorded by Bing Crosby; "I Wake Up Smiling" (1934, lyrics by Edgar Leslie); "The Moon was Yellow" (1934, lyrics by Edgar Leslie), recorded by Carmen Cavallero and by the Bob Grant Orchestra. "I'm Gonna Sit Right Down and Write Myself a Letter" (lyrics by Joe Young) followed in 1935. It was recorded and popularized by Fats Waller and was also re-corded by the Boswell Sisters, Johnny Mercer and Nat Brandwynne and his orchestra. It made 16 appearances on *Your Hit Parade*. In 1956–57 it was revived in bestselling recordings by Bill Haley and the Comets and by Billy Williams. "Life is a Song" (1935, lyrics by Joe Young) was introduced by Frank Parker and that year appeared 11 times on *Your Hit Parade*, twice in first position. "Take My Heart" (1936, lyrics by Joe Young) was recorded by Nat Brandwynne and his orchestra. It was represented 11 times on *Your Hit Parade*, twice in first position.

Ahlert composed songs for the musical stage twice. In 1937 he contributed six numbers (lyrics by Joe Young) to *The Riviera Follies*, a nightclub act. His only involvement with the Broadway musical theater came on October 10, 1940 with *It Happens on Ice*, an ice extravaganza produced by Sonja Henie and starring Joe Cook. For this production he wrote two numbers with lyrics by Al Stillman.

Ahlert did little songwriting after "Where Do You Keep Your Heart?" (1940, lyrics by Stillman), which Frank Sinatra recorded as vocalist for the Tommy Dorsey orchestra. After 1940 Ahlert devoted himself to executive duties at ASCAP, serving as director from 1933 to 1953 and as president from 1948 to 1950. He died in New York City in 1953.

ABOUT: Craig, W. Sweet and Lowdown: America's Popular Song Writers, 1978.

ARLEN, HAROLD (February 15, 1905–April 23, 1986), was one of the great popular composers of the 20th century. Of the 500-odd songs for which he wrote the music, more than three dozen became standards, including such classics as "Over the Rainbow," "Get Happy," "Stormy Weather," and "One for My Baby (and One for the Road)." According to the *New York Times* writer John S. Wilson, "The distinctive Arlen touch was the jazz-bassed, blues-rooted quality of his music. Such songs as 'Stormy Weather' and 'Blues in the Night' place him, as a composer, alongside Duke Ellington rather than Richard Rodgers or Jerome Kern or Irving Berlin. [But Arlen's songs] cover such a range of style and content . . . that almost any singer can find a number of songs that suit his or her style."

He was born Hyman Arluck in Buffalo, New York, the older of two sons of Samuel and Celia (Orlin) Arluck. His father was a cantor, whose synagogue choir Harold joined when he was seven. At this time Arlen responded to two musical forms, Hebraic religious chants and jazz.

Arlen studied classical piano for about four

HAROLD ARLEN

years, until he was 12. "My father gave me piano lessons so I could be a teacher and not have to work on *shabbas* (the Sabbath)," he told Max Wilk, the author of *They're Playing Our Song.* These piano lessons and the records he heard at home introduced Arlen to concert and operatic music, but his first love always was popular music. The first popular piece he learned to play on the piano was a ragtime number, "Indianola," and as he entered his teens Arlen began collecting ragtime and jazz records.

In Buffalo's elementary and secondary public schools, Alren showed no interest in scholarship, but his musical talent was unmistakable. He played piano in his elementary school orchestra and later played the piano in local amateur bands.

After dropping out of Technical High School at the age of 15, Arlen earned a living by playing piano in a silent movie theater and performing in a vaudeville act. With two other 15-year-olds, he formed the Snappy Trio, a band that performed in Buffalo's red-light district. When this group added two musicians and became the Southbound Shufflers, it was hired to play on a lake steamer. Arlen then joined the Yankee Six. Growing to 12 pieces and renamed the Buffalodians, this band became popular through engagements at college and society events and at a downtown ballroom restaurant. In all of these groups, Arlen served as singer and arranger as well as pianist. "I could always improvise," he recalled, "and I loved to invent unconventional tunes for the men in the band who couldn't do anything but follow the written melody. I wanted them to get off it and sound like somebody

in New York." The Buffalodians soon received bookings in Cleveland and Pittsburgh and, in 1925, in Manhattan, at the Palace Theatre and a club called the Monte Carlo.

At this time Arlen's consuming ambition was to become a singer rather than a composer. Nevertheless in 1926 a bluesy piano piece, "Minor Gaff"(written with Dick George), became Arlen's first published song.

Arnold Johnson, an eminent jazz bandleader, hired Arlen as an arranger and singer for his group's appearances on Broadway and in the orchestra pit of the *George White Scandals of 1928.* When Arlen left Johnson's band in 1928, he tried to make it as a singer in vaudeville. Within a year he had concluded that the harsh demands of a singing career were "something my temperament couldn't take." Now concentrating on songwriting, he published three numbers in 1929. One of these, "The Album of My Dreams" (lyrics by Lou Davis), was introduced and recorded by Rudy Vallee, and earned Arlen a royalty of $900.

Vincent Youmans engaged Arlen as a rehearsal pianist for *Great Day!* in 1929. During a break, Arlen amused himself by improvising a vamp that caught the ear of Will Marrion Cook, the conductor of the chorus, who encouraged Arlen to work it up as a popular song. With Ted Koehler as lyricist, Arlen turned his piano ditty into "Get Happy," a "hallelujah" number that has become a standard. Ruth Etting introduced it in the Broadway musical, *9:15 Revue,* on February 11, 1930. Although that show closed after just seven performances, Remick published "Get Happy" and George Gershwin praised it. On the strength of this song, a Remick subsidiary gave Arlen a songwriting job, temporarily enabling him to devote himself solely to composition. He initially earned $50 a week, but the salary was soon doubled.

"Get Happy" was memorably recorded by Judy Garland, who sang it in the 1950 motion picture *Summer Stock.* It was also recorded by the orchestra of Harry James and, as a piano solo, by Art Tatum. In the Jane Froman film biography, *With a Song in My Heart* (1950), she sang it on the soundtrack, dubbing for Susan Hayward.

Beginning in 1930, with Ted Koehler as his lyricist, Arlen wrote songs for revues mounted at Harlem's legendary Cotton Club. To *Brown Sugar,* a Cotton Club revue of 1930, Arlen and Koehler contributed two numbers, and of the eight songs they composed for *Rhythmania* (1931), two became standards. "Between the Devil and the Deep Blue Sea" was introduced by Aida Ward and recorded by Ella Fitzgerald, Bob

Crosby, Kate Smith and the orchestra of Eddy Duchin. "I Love a Parade" was recorded by the Arlen-Ohman Orchestra and by Harry Richman. "I Love a Parade" was interpolated into the 1932 movie *Manhattan Parade* and was popularized in vaudeville and nightclubs by Harry Richman, who also recorded it.

From the *Cotton Club Parade of 1932*, came "I've Got the World on a String"; introduced by Aida Ward, it was first recorded by Bing Crosby and later by Frank Sinatra, Lena Horne, and the orchestra of Woody Herman. This song was revived for June Haver and Gloria De Haven in the film, *I'll Get By* (1950). "Minnie the Moocher's Wedding Day" also came from the *Cotton Club Parade of 1932*. The song paid homage to Cab Calloway, composer of "Minnie the Moocher," and Calloway himself introduced Arlen's song.

Arlen's most important song from the Cotton Club Parade of 1933 was "Stormy Weather," the most celebrated blues number ever written by a white composer. Arlen and Koehler had intended "Stormy Weather" as a vehicle for Calloway, but he was unavailable for that revue. Consequently Ethel Waters was asked to join the cast so that she might introduce it. In her autobiography Waters called the singing of "Stormy Weather" the turning point in her career. "When I got out there in the middle of the Cotton Club floor . . . I was singing the story of my misery and confusion, . . . the story of the wrongs and outrages done to me by people I loved and trusted. . . . I sang 'Stormy Weather' from the depths of my private hell in which I was being crushed and suffocated." As guest vocalist with the Leo Reisman orchestra, in 1933 Arlen himself made the first successful recording of "Stormy Weather." The song became Lena Horne's signature, and it was also recorded by Ethel Waters, Frank Sinatra, Peggy Lee, Adelaide Hall, Frances Langford, Connie Boswell and the orchestras of Duke Ellington, Guy Lombardo and Eddy Duchin. Horne sang it in the 1934 film *Stormy Weather*, and it was the highlight of her one-woman Broadway show of 1981–82. Connie Boswell sang it in *Swing Parade of 1946* and also recorded it.

In 1930 five of Arlen and Koehler's non-Cotton Club songs were used in the eighth edition of *Earl Carroll's Vanities*. The best was "The March of Time," introduced by Harry Stockwell and John Hale. A year later, with Jack Yellen as lyricist, Arlen wrote the score for the Broadway musical *You Said It* (January 19, 1931), which had a 168-performance run. The book was by Sid Silvers and Jack Yellen and the production starred Lou Holtz as Pinkie Pincus, an enterpris-

ing freshman at Kenton College. When the dean's daughter is caught bootlegging, Pinkie clears up her good name by stealing the evidence against her. The title song, introduced by Mary Lawlor and Stanley Smith, was recorded by the orchestra of Red Nicholas with Arlen doing the vocal. The swinging "Sweet and Hot" was introduced by Lyda Roberti and recorded in 1931 by the orchestras of Fletcher Henderson and Ben Pollack.

"Satan's Li'l Lamb" (1932) was the first song that Arlen wrote with the lyricist E. Y. ("Yip") Harburg. It was interpolated into the Broadway revue *Americana* for Francetta Malloy and the Musketeers, and was recorded by Ethel Merman. Arlen's first blues classic, "I Got a Right to Sing the Blues" (lyrics by Koehler), was interpolated into the tenth edition of *Earl Carroll's Vanities* in 1932. Introduced by Lillian Shade, it was recorded by Lena Horne, Billie Holiday, Ethel Merman and Judy Garland.

In *The Great Magoo (1932)*, a nonmusical Broadway play by Ben Hecht and Gene Flower, "If You Believe in Me" (lyrics by Billy Rose and E. Y. Harburg) was introduced by Claire Charlton. With the title changed to "It's Only a Paper Moon," it was heard in the 1933 film *Take a Chance* (1933), in which it was sung by June Knight and Buddy Rogers. "Paper Moon" was recorded by the Mills Brothers, Nat King Cole, Ella Fitzgerald, Cliff Edwards and Benny Goodman. It made just one appearance on *Your Hit Parade*, on December 8, 1945, but Tennessee Williams used it in *A Streetcar Named Desire* on Broadway two years later. This song was revived 25 years later in the acclaimed Peter Bogdanovich film, *Paper Moon* (1973), and it was interpolated for Barbra Streisand into *Lucky Lady* (1975), the sequel to *Funny Girl*, Fanny Brice's screen biography.

In 1934, with the title number and two other songs for *Let's Fall in Love*, Arlen and Koehler fulfilled their first Hollywood assignment. The movie starred Ann Sothern, who reprised the title song after it had been introduced by Arthur Jarrett. In 1933 this song was recorded by Phil Regan; in 1934 by the orchestra of Eddy Duchin and by radio's "Street Singer," Arthur Tracy; and decades later by Paul Anka. In subsequent films Don Ameche and Dorothy Lamour sang it in *Slightly French* (1949), Robert Cummings in *Tell it to the Judge* (1949), Judy Holliday and Jack Lemmon in *It Should Happen to You* (1954), and Bing Crosby in *Pepe* (1960). Carmen Cavallero played it on the soundtrack of *The Eddy Duchin Story* (1956).

In 1932 Arlen returned to the vaudeville stage as a vocalist-pianist in an act starring Ethel Merman. Arlen himself was the star of a vaudeville act called *Stormy Weather*, in which he performed his own blues compositions and brought the show to a climax by doing the title song with the support of a black chorus. *Stormy Weather* opened at the Radio City Music Hall on May 19, 1933 before touring the Loew vaudeville circuit. On records, Arlen was the vocalist for numerous jazz groups' renditions of his songs.

The *Cotton Club Parade of 1934* was the last such production for which Arlen and Koehler wrote the songs. By then, Arlen was one of America's leading songwriters, and he was much in demand on both coasts. For Broadway he composed the complete score for *Life Begins at 8:40* (lyrics by Ira Gershwin and E. Y. Harburg), a Winter Garden revue starring Bert Lahr and Ray Bolger that opened on August 27, 1934 and had a run of 237 performances. "I proved that I could come out of the Cotton Club," Arlen remarked. "It was an interesting road to travel." Four songs from *Life Begins* were of special interest: "What Can You Say in a Love Song?" introduced by Josephine Houston and Barlett Simmons; "You're a Builder-Upper," by Ray Bolger and Dixie Dunbar; "Let's Take a Walk Around the Block," by Earl Oxford and Dixie Dunbar; and "Fun to Be Fooled" by Frances Williams and Barlett Simmons. "Fun to Be Fooled" was recorded by Anita Ellis. In the Winter Garden revue *The Show Is On* (1936), Bert Lahr praised wood and its vast usefulness in "Song of the Woodman" (lyrics by Harburg), one of three Arlen songs in that production.

Horray for What! (December 1, 1937), with a 200-performance run, had a complete score by Arlen and Harburg. In Howard Lindsay and Russel Crouse's book, based on a Harburg scenario, Ed Wynn starred as Chuckles, a horticulturist who, experimenting with ways of poisoning insects, invents a gas that is lethal to humans. The efforts of international spies and agents of the League of Nations to acquire Chuckles's formula add to the show's comic proceedings. Its principal ballad, "I've Gone Romantic on You," was introduced by Jack Whiting and June Clyde. Here, too, were heard "Moanin' in the Mornin'", introduced by Vivian Vance, and a patriotic number, "God's Country," introduced by Whiting and the Five Reillys. "God's Country" was performed on the screen by Judy Garland and Mickey Rooney in *Babes in Arms* (1939).

For motion pictures in the later 1930s Arlen composed songs for *Strike Me Pink*, starring Eddie Cantor and Ethel Merman (1936); *The Singing Kid*, starring Cantor (1936); *Stage Struck* and *Gold Diggers of 1937* (both 1936), both starring Dick Powell and Joan Blondell; *Artists and Models* (1937); and *Love Affair*, starring Irene Dunne and Charles Boyer (1939). In *Stage Struck* Dick Powell introduced, and later recorded, "Fancy Meeting You" (lyrics by Harburg).

Arlen's finest screen song of these years was never used in a movie. "Last Night When We Were Young" (1935, lyrics by Harburg) had been intended for the motion picture *Metropolitan*, but was deleted as a vocal number and used instrumentally as background music. Judy Garland heard Laurence Tibbett's recording of this song, recorded it herself and tried unsuccessfully to have it interpolated for her into the screen musical *In the Good Old Summertime*. Sinatra sang "Last Night" in the film *Take Me Out to the Ball Game* (1945), but the song was again left on the cutting-room floor by film editors. Nevertheless it became an Arlen-Harburg classic and a particular favorite of both men. The song has become known through Sinatra's recording and as Alec Wilder wrote in *American Popular Song*, "Once you have heard the Sinatra version, you can't imagine anyone else singing it." As for "Last Night" itself, Wilder said, "It is one [song] which has gone far beyond the boundaries of popular music. For me, it is a concert song, without a trace of trying to be."

On January 8, 1937 Arlen married Anya ("Annie") Taranda. She was a Powers model and show girl who had appeared in the chorus of the 1932 edition of *Earl Carroll's Vanities*, to which Arlen had contributed songs. They acquired a house on Lookout Mountain Road in Laurel Canyon, Los Angeles, which they occupied for two decades.

In 1938 the MGM producer Arthur Freed, just two months before filming was scheduled to begin, called upon Arlen and Harburg to compose the score for *The Wizard of Oz*, a star-studded extravaganza serving as a vehicle for the studio's 16-year-old singing star, Judy Garland. Released in 1939, *The Wizard of Oz* had an unforgettable cast—Judy Garland (as Dorothy), Ray Bolger (as the Scarecrow), Bert Lahr (as the Cowardly Lion) and Jack Haley (as the Tin Man). Three Arlen-Harburg songs became standards from a score that was released in a soundtrack recording. "We're Off to See the Wizard" was introduced by Garland, Lahr, Haley and Bolger, and "Ding-Dong the Witch is Dead" was performed by a chorus of "Munchkins." "Over the Rainbow" was the song that became Judy Garland's signature and brought its authors an Oscar. When, following emotional upheavals and professional disasters that would have ended almost any other entertainer's career, Garland made her comeback at New York's Palace Theatre in 1967, it was "Over the Rainbow" that lent drama and poignancy to the moment. She sang it while seated on the apron of the stage, her feet dangling over the orchestra pit, a single spotlight on her tear-stained face. In addition to her recording, there were others by Sinatra, Fred Waring's Pennsylvanians, Jo Stafford, and Louis Prima.

The melody of "Over the Rainbow" had come to Arlen as he and his wife were driving down Sunset Boulevard. She stopped the car and Arlen hastily jotted down the notes, completing the song's music the following day. When Harburg heard it, he objected to its solemnity, thinking the melody more suitable for a Nelson Eddy ballad than a Judy Garland. Seeking Ira Gershwin's counsel, Arlen and Harburg were advised to use a more modest harmonic texture and a faster tempo, suggestions they heeded without hesitation.

At MGM, "Over the Rainbow" encountered strong resistance. Garland loved the song, but on three different occasions the decision to drop it was reached, and only Arthur Freed's support kept "Over the Rainbow" in the production. Even the song's publisher was critical, objecting to the vocal difficulty of negotiating the octave leap in the chorus on the word "somewhere" and considering the release in the chorus jejune. But Arlen made no changes and "Over the Rainbow," like the film, became an instant classic. In 1939 bestselling recordings were made by Garland, Bing Crosby and the orchestra of Horace Heidt. Rosemary Clooney later recorded it with Harry James and his orchestra. Of the song's 15 representations on *Your Hit Parade*, seven were in first position. Eileen Farrell sang it on the soundtrack of *Interrupted Melody* (1955) and Elizabeth Hartmann hummed it in the nonmusical film *A Patch of Blue* (1965).

Arlen's collaboration with the lyricist Johnny Mercer began in 1941 with the motion picture *Blues in the Night*. The producer had wanted to call the film *Hot Nocturne* and make it a realistic treatment of jazz and jazz musicians. This in mind, Arlen and Mercer wrote "Blues in the Night" with Arlen adhering to traditional blues structure but combining it with the arched melody (here expanded to 58 measures) that was characteristic of Arlen compositions. Before *Hot Nocturne* was released, "Blues in the Night" was popularized in recordings by Jimmie Lunceford and Dinah Shore (her first to sell a million copies) and the film title was changed. Other recordings were made by Peggy Lee, Johnny Mercer, Ella Fitzgerald, Jo Stafford with the Pied Pipers, Fred Waring's Pennsylvanians, and the orchestras of Benny Goodman, Woody Her-

man and Harry James. "Blues in the Night" made 13 appearances on *Your Hit Parade*, twice in first position. In the film the number was sung by William Gillespie. Another notable Arlen-Mercer song from *Blues in the Night* was "This Time the Dream's on Me," introduced by Priscilla Lane.

"Blues in the Night" lost out in the Oscar competition to Jerome Kern's "The Last Time I Saw Paris." However, Kern felt that Arlen's blues was the more deserving of an Academy Award, and used his influence to change the Academy bylaws governing the nomination of songs. Henceforth only songs written specifically for the screen could be candidates for an Oscar; interpolations like "The Last Time I Saw Paris" became ineligible. More than 40 years after it had been written "Blues in the Night" provided the title for a Broadway revue that opened on June 2, 1982. A stunning second-act opener, the title song was delivered by Leslie Uggams and Debbie Shapiro.

"That Old Black Magic," composed by Arlen and Mercer for *Star-Spangled Rhythm* (1942), was introduced by Johnny Johnston and danced to by Vera Zorina. The song was originally popularized through Billy Daniels's recording, which sold over two million copies, and by 1943 it had been recorded by the orchestra of Charlie Barnet, Judy Garland, Frank Sinatra, Margaret Whiting, Glenn Miller and Fred Waring's Pennsylvanians. In 1943 "That Old Black Magic" had 15 representations on *Your Hit Parade*. A standard, it has been performed in numerous motion pictures. In *Here Come the Waves* (1944) Bing Crosby sang it as a sardonic comment on the craze for pop singers like himself and Sinatra. Sinatra sang it in *Meet Danny Wilson* (1952) and Marilyn Monroe in *Bus Stop* (1956). In 1958 the Louis Prima–Keely Smith recording won a Grammy.

Arlen and Mercer composed "One for My Baby (and One for the Road)" for Fred Astaire in the movie *The Sky's the Limit* (1943). Tony Bennett enjoyed one of his earliest recording successes with this number, which was also recorded by Sinatra (three times), Harry Belafonte, Astaire, Johnny Mercer, and Lena Horne, who made it one of her specialties. Sinatra sang it in the 1950 film, *Young at Heart*. Also from the score for *The Sky's the Limit*, "My Shining Hour" was introduced by Astaire and Sally Sweetland (the latter dubbing on the soundtrack for Joan Leslie). It was recorded by the orchestra of Glen Gray and by Fred Waring's Pennsylvanians. "My Shining Hour" had two hearings on *Your Hit Parade*.

"Ac-cent-tchu-ate the Positive" (1944) had 13

representations on *Your Hit Parade*, four in first position. The idea for this song came to the writers during an automobile ride when, to relieve the monotony, Arlen began humming a tune that had the flavor of a spiritual. Mercer then tried to fit to the melody the words "ac-cent-tchu-ate the positive," a phrase he remembered from public school. Arlen and Mercer developed this idea into a song for Bing Crosby for the motion picture *Here Come the Waves* (1944), in which Crosby sang it in a duet with Sonny Tufts. Crosby, performing with the Andrews Sisters, popularized it in a bestselling recording. Mercer himself recorded it as well.

In *Here Come the Waves* Bing Crosby and Betty Hutton introduced "Let's Take the Long Way Home" and "I Promise You." The former was recorded by Cab Calloway in 1944 and on April 7, 1945, the song had its one hearing on *Your Hit Parade.* "I Promise You" was recorded by Jo Stafford and by the orchestras of Horace Heidt and Sammy Kaye.

In 1945 Arlen and Mercer composed the title song and "June Comes Around Every Year" for *Out of This World.* Bing Crosby introduced both on the soundtrack, and his recording of "Out of This World" was represented on *Your Hit Parade* on July 14, 1945.

Harburg was Arlen's lyricist for "Happiness is a Thing Called Joe," which Ethel Waters introduced in the motion picture adaptation of Vernon Duke's Broadway musical, *Cabin in the Sky* (1943). This ballad became a favorite of female singers, including Judy Garland, who recorded it. It was also recorded by Woody Herman and his orchestra, and Susan Hayward sang it in the film, *I'll Cry Tomorrow* (1955).

Arlen composed one more song classic for the screen. It was a bluesy ballad for Judy Garland in the 1953 remake of *A Star is Born*, "The Man That Got Away" (lyrics by Ira Gershwin). This number, which Garland recorded, became another signature for her, second in importance in her repertory only to "Over the Rainbow." A year after *A Star Is Born* was released, Arlen and Ira Gershwin wrote five songs for *The Country Girl* (1954), the motion picture adaptation of Clifford Odets's Broadway play of the same name. The film starred Bing Crosby and Grace Kelly, with Crosby singing "The Search Is Through" and "Dissertation on the State of Bliss" (the latter also known as "Love and Learn").

After a seven-year absence, Arlen returned to the Broadway musical theater with *Bloomer Girl* (October 5, 1941), with Harburg as lyricist. With a text by Fred Saidy and Sid Herzig, *Bloomer Girl* was a period piece set in the town of Cicero, Illinois in 1861. Its heroine, Evelina, is a feminist who wears bloomers instead of hoop skirts and goes to jail with her aunt, Dolly Bloomer, for aiding an escaped slave. Arlen's showstopper here was "I Got a Song," a blues performed by Richard Huey. Other notable Arlen-Harburg songs from the show were "Evelina," which Bing Crosby recorded; "Right as Rain," introduced by Celeste Holm and David Brooks; "T'morra, T'morra," introduced by Joan McCracken; and "The Eagle and Me," a slave song about freedom introduced by Dooley Wilson and recorded by Bing Crosby. With its 654-performance run, *Bloomer Girl* was Arlen's greatest box-office success on Broadway. An original cast recording was released.

With Johnny Mercer as his lyricist, Arlen next composed the score for the Broadway musical *St. Louis Woman* (March 30, 1946). It was originally planned as a folk play with an all-black cast. However, when rewritten, *St. Louis Woman* became a familiar melodrama, concentrating on the affair between Little Augie, a jockey, and Della Green, the "St. Louis woman" for whose love he is driven to murder his rival. Much of the emotion generated by the show came less from the predictable plot than from the best musical numbers: "Any Place I Hang My Hat is Home"; "Legalize My Name" and "A Woman's Prerogative," both introduced and recorded by Pearl Bailey; and "Come Rain or Come Shine," a ballad shared by Ruby Hill and Harold Nicholas. The last of these was recorded by Tommy Dorsey, Dick Haymes and Helen Forrest, Margaret Whiting, Jo Stafford and Ray Charles. The Ray Charles version was heard again on the soundtrack of the nonmusical film, *The King of Comedy* (1983), starring Jerry Lewis and Robert De Niro. Though the initial run of *St. Louis Woman* was only 113 performances, an original cast album was released.

Convinced that their score had artistic merit, Arlen and Mercer expanded *St. Louis Woman* into an opera, which they initially retitled *Blues Opera.* New material was added, and two older Arlen-Mercer standards were interpolated, "That Old Black Magic" and "Blues in the Night." *Blue Opera* was produced in Minneapolis on August 28, 1957. An orchestral suite from that score (orchestrated by Samuel Matlowsky) was performed by the New York Philharmonic (conducted by André Kostelanetz) on November 2, 1957. Retitled *Free and Easy*, this blues opera opened in Amsterdam in December 1959 for what was planned as the start of a European tour that would culminate in a Broadway show. But it closed down permanently after playing to half-empty houses in Amsterdam and then in Paris.

Arlen's next two Broadway musicals had West Indian settings. The first was *House of Flowers* (December 30, 1954). Arlen's collaborator was the novelist Truman Capote, writing for the first time the text of a musical play and song lyrics. The House of Flowers is a bordello in Haiti run by Mme. Fleur, each of whose girls is named after a different flower. The young lovers here are Mme. Fleur's innocent ward, Ottilie, and Royal, a barefoot boy from the hills, a love affair Mme. Fleur is unable to thwart. Pearl Bailey was cast as Mme. Fleur and Diahann Carroll (in her Broadway debut) played Ottilie. Carroll introduced "A Sleepin' Bee" and "I Never Has Seen Snow," and Ada Moore and Enid Mosier introduced "Two Ladies in de Shade of de Banana Tree."

The House of Flowers was a failure (165 performances) on Broadway, as it was when revived Off Broadway in 1968. *Jamaica* (October 31, 1957), book by Fred Saidy and Yip Harburg, however, had a respectable run of 557 performances. Arlen's lyricist once again was Harburg, and *Jamaica* featured Lena Horne in her first Broadway appearance in a starring role. The setting is Pigeon Island, near Kingston, where Savannah (Horne) dreams of leaving the island for New York City. These dreams lead her to reject the love of a humble fisherman, Koli. But when he proves himself a hero during a ferocious hurricane, Savannah is reconciled to spending the rest of her days with him on the island. Lena Horne was heard in a lighthearted parody of torch songs, "Take it Slow, Joe," and in an amusing dream picture of New York and its mechanical wonders, "Push de Button." Adelaide Hall joined her in singing the lullaby, "Coconut Sweet," and "Savannah" is a love ballad that Koli sings to Savannah. The complete scores of *House of Flowers* and *Jamaica* were released on original cast albums.

Arlen's Broadway career ended with a failure, *Saratoga* (December 7, 1959), lyrics by Johnny Mercer, book by Morton da Costa based on Edna Ferber's novel, *Saratoga Trunk*. Despite the presence of Howard Keel and Carol Lawrence as the stars, *Saratoga* was a lavish but ponderous production that survived only 80 performances. "Love Held Lightly," introduced by Odette Myrtil, and "Goose Never Be a Peacock," introduced by Carol Brice, were the leading numbers in a fine score that also included "Petticoat High," a production number in the manner of early New Orleans jazz.

In the early 1960s, Arlen was ill, and his work schedule suffered. By the end of the decade he had written just a few random songs, and contributed nothing new to the stage or the screen.

His wife, Anya, died
extinguish Arlen's ci

On February 25,
salute to Arlen starri
Arlen himself makin
appearances. When
Fame had been org
one of the first ten n
In 1977 a two-album
standards was release
and 1976. In 1984, w
shared the second an
gers Award for disti
the musical theater.

The Arlens had cha
Beverly Hills to a dup
tan's Upper East Side
ings reflected two c
books and artworks. (
as well as a collector c
pastimes was watchin

Asked by Max Wil
creativity, Arlen repli
comes from. Everytim
self says, 'Jesus, how w
part of myself says, '(
Brother, you have to
that you're a writer, to
'Go, do it.'"

"Watching Arlen in
substantiates the *mysti*
wrote Edward Jablonsk
songwriter. "He will clc
furrow his brow in dee|
powerful yet sensitive f
seven white and five
worth keeping, And whc
songs, something many
better than anyone else
performance as he i
an . . . impassioned del
mor, certainly one of tl
personality, he takes b
maintains a level of in
music."

Arlen died at his Man|
age of 81. He was surviv
len.

ABOUT: Jablonski, E. Harolc
Blues, 1961; Wilder, A. Ame
Wilk, M. They're Play
Periodicals—New York Tim
24, 1986; Stereo Review l
April 30, 1986.

IARACH, BURT (May 12, 1929–)
DAVID, HAL (May 25, 1921–). In the
few songwriters could rival Burt Bach's success as composer. With Hal David
lyricist, his songs received 20 gold records
l as an Oscar, a Tony and several Gram-
His television specials, some of which
ht him Emmys, and his appearances in
lubs and concert halls have ranked him
; the most successful performers of his
Yet such success was never purchased at
ice of pursuing superficial trends, or slant-
ngs for a given market. His songs are mus-
sophisticated, sometimes complex, and
y unconventional in structure and content,
n identity unmistakably Bacharach's own.
only son, Burt Bacharach was born in Kan-
cy, Missouri, on May 12, 1929. At the time
birth, his father, Bert Bacharach, worked
partment store. He later turned to journal-
id had a column, *Now See Here,* which
ndicated for 19 years by King Features. In
50s he published two books, *Book for Men
ight Dress.* Burt's mother, Irma (Freeman)
rach, was a portrait painter and an ama-
inger who devoted herself completely to
mily after her son's birth.
en Burt was two, the family moved to Kew
ns in Queens, where he attended school.
gan studying music early; first the cello,
he drums, and then the piano, which be-
his prime instrument. Though intensely
al, he disliked practicing since it kept him
playing touch football with his friends. His
ion was to become a football star, but at
. Hills High School he could not make the
because he was too small. "To be the life
party," he recalled, "I played piano in a
y night dance band and suddenly I was
a real group of musicians, practicing to-
, meeting people. Music made me be-

on graduating from Forest Hills High, he
l piano at a resort in the Catskills during
mmer and, in winter, he toured army hos-
for the USO. He studied piano and compo-
at the Mannes School of Music in New
City, at the Berkshire Music Center with
s Milhaud and Henry Cowell during the
er, and at McGill University in Canada.
opular rather than concert music absorbed
terest. Bacharach was beginning to com-
popular songs, one of which, "The Night to
n," was published.
m 1950 to 1952 he served in the military,
ties being largely musical: playing the pi-
the officer's club on Governors Island and
concerts at Fort Dix. Since he had no rep-

BURT BACHARACH

ertory, his performances consisted of improvisations, of medleys of popular tunes of the day,
and scraps of melody he invented spontaneously.
In Germany he did arrangements for a dance
band.

While in uniform in Germany he met Vic Damone, the popular singer. Once Bacharach was
discharged from the army, Damone engaged
him as piano accompanist. Various jobs followed
playing the piano in nightclubs and restaurants,
and working as accompanist for the Ames Brothers, Imogene Coca, Polly Bergen, Paula Stewart
and other performers. Paula Stewart became his
first wife on December 22, 1953, a marriage
ending in divorce in 1958.

Working as accompanist for the Ames Brothers during a Las Vegas engagement convinced
Bacharach he could write songs as good or better
than those the Ames Brothers were featuring. As
a potential songwriter, Bacharach rented an office in New York's Brill Building and spent the
next ten months composing songs while supporting himself as piano accompanist for Joel Grey,
Georgia Gibbs and Steve Lawrence. Only one of
these songs, recorded by Patti Page, was published and its title Bacharach has forgotten because the number was "so awful."

At Famous Paramount Music Company, in
1957, he met Hal David, a young lyricist who by
then had already produced several successful
lyrics for songs recorded by Frank Sinatra and
Teresa Brewer, among others. Bacharach and
David decided to join forces as songwriters.

One of three sons of Gedalier David and Lina
(Goldberg) David, Hal was born in Brooklyn, on
May 25, 1921. His father was the proprietor of

HAL DAVID

a kosher delicatessen on Pennsylvania Avenue, and the David family lived in an apartment above the restaurant. Hal's older brother, Mack, nine years his senior, was a productive song lyricist whose career became the northern star by which Hal David guided his own course in the songwriting business.

While attending public school Hal worked part-time as a busboy in his father's restaurant. His boyhood interests were sports and the use of words. At school he contributed short stories and poems to its magazine. By the time he graduated from Thomas Jefferson High School he knew he wanted to become a professional writer. David entered the School of Journalism at New York University and remained there two years. A summer job writing promotional material for Publishers Service so intrigued him that, after his sophomore year, he dropped out of school.

During World World II he served in the Special Services Division in Hawaii under Major Maurice Evans, the celebrated British actor. David wrote sketches and his first song lyrics for army productions. On the basis of these songs, and while still in uniform, he became a member of ASCAP in 1943.

After the war, Evans gave David several leads to Broadway projects, but nothing came of them. Nor was David more successful in peddling songs to publishers. Though still incapable of making a living from his art, he married Anne Rauchman on December 24, 1947. They made their home in an attic apartment in Lynbrook, Long Island, with David subsisting for a time on his wife's salary as a schoolteacher.

Soon after his marriage, David sold a song to Sammy Kaye, the bandleader, on the strength of which Kaye hired him to write special material for Kaye's radio show. With Don Rodney as composer, David wrote "The Four Winds and Seven Seas" in 1959, which Kaye and his orchestra introduced and helped make a moderate success. Guy Lombardo liked the song so much he hired David as a songwriter for $50 a week.

Gradually, songs with David's lyrics began being heard in successful recordings. "American Beauty," written in 1950 with Red Evans and Arthur Altman, was recorded by Frank Sinatra; "Bell Bottom Blues" (music by Leon Carr), in 1953, by Teresa Wright; "My Heart is a Fool" (music by Frank Weldon), in 1954, by Val Anthony; "My Heart is an Open Book" (music by Lee Pockriss), in 1956, by Carl Dobbins Jr. One of David's songs even found a place in motion pictures: "Wonderful Wasn't It?" (music by Don Rodney) in *Rainbow 'Round My Shoulder* (1952), starring Frankie Laine.

By 1957 Hal David had worked well with various composers, but never on any sustained basis with any single one. His meeting with Bacharach brought him a permanent partner at last. In 1957 they wrote "Magic Moments" and "The Story of My Life," both published by Famous Paramount Music Company. "Magic Moments" was recorded by Perry Como, and "The Story of My Life" by Marty Robbins and by Mitch Miller. All these recordings had strong sales.

Between 1958 and 1961 the Bacharach-David partnership had to mark time as Bacharach was employed during those years as musical director for Marlene Dietrich in her appearances in Europe and the United States. During this period he did not altogether abandon songwriting. Two of his songs were recorded in 1961. Gene McDaniel performed "Tower of Strength" (lyrics by Bob Hilliard) and the Shirelles recorded "Baby, It's You" (lyrics by Mack David and Barney Williams). One of Bacharach's most popular songs among rock and rollers, "Baby, It's You" was recorded by the Beatles in the mid-1960s and the British pop stars Elvis Costello and Nick Lowe performed it as a duet in 1984. Two songs with Hal David's lyrics were heard in motion pictures: in *Wonderful to Be Young* (1961) and *Forever My Love* (1962). In 1962 Bacharach's song "Any Day Now" (lyrics by Bob Hilliard) was recorded by the soul singer Chuck Jackson.

All this while Hal David worked with other composers as well as with Bacharach. Sarah Vaughan recorded and popularized "Broken-Hearted Melody" (music by Sherman Edwards) in 1959. In 1960 David provided English words to a popular Italian song, "Il Nostro Concerto" (music by Umberto Bindi), which Al Martino popularized in his recording as "Our Concerto." Patti Page recorded "You'll Answer to Me" (music by Sherman Edwards) in 1961 and Joanie Sommers recorded "Johnny Get Angry" (music by Edwards) in 1962. Also in 1962, "A Whistling Tune" (music by Edwards) was interpolated into *Kid Galahad,* starring Elvis Presley, who sang it on the EP soundtrack recording.

In 1962, Bacharach's commitments to Marlene Dietrich ended temporarily. For the next decade he worked exclusively with Hal David and the songs they wrote made them the most successful American words-and-music team of the 1960s.

Inspired by a motion picture starring Jimmy Stewart and John Wayne, and appropriating its title, they wrote "The Man Who Shot Liberty Valance" in 1962. Gene Pitney's recording reached fourth place on the charts, where it remained 14 weeks. Pitney also made a bestselling recording of "Only Love Can Break a Heart" (1962) and Jerry Butler followed suit with "Make It Easy on Yourself" (1963).

In 1962 Bacharach and David were supervising a recording session when Bacharach took note of a young black singer, Dionne Warwick. She was then a student at the Hartt College of Music and a member of the Gospelaires, which was providing the backup vocal accompaniment in the studio. A few months later he called on her to make a demonstration record of his song "Don't Make Me Over" (the title and subject for which came from Warwick herself when she angrily replied to one of Bacharach's criticisms). That demonstration record brought Warwick a contract from Scepter Records, and another one with Bacharach and David to provide her with songs and to supervise her recording sessions. "Don't Make Me Over" was Warwick's first commercial recording as a solo performer, and in 1962 became her first record to reach the top ten on the charts. From then on, her ascent to stardom was made on the steps of songs by Bacharach and David. No singer before her or since has been so closely identified with a single pair of songwriters as Warwick was in the 1960s and early 1970s. She recorded much of Bacharach and David's oeuvre; many of these songs were tailored to fit Warwick's singing style and personality. By 1975, when the Bacharach-David affiliation with Warwich ended for a decade, she had sold over 15 million discs of Bacharach's songs, bringing her numerous gold records and Grammys.

Dionne Warwick was not the only performer to have hits with songs by Bacharach and David.

For "Wives and Lovers" (1963), inspired by, but not heard in, the motion picture of the same title, Jack Jones won a Grammy. This song was also recorded by Steve Lawrence. In 1965 Gene Pitney had another Bacharach winner with "Twenty-four Hours From Tulsa," and so did Bobby Vinton ("Blue on Blue") and Dusty Springfield ("Wishin' and Hopin'"). Dionne Warwick's first two gold records came for "Anyone Who Had a Heart" (1963) and "Walk on By" (1964). Warwick's string of bestsellers included the following Bacharach-David songs: "A Message to Michael" (1963), "Reach Out for Me" (1963), "Trains and Boats and Planes" (1964), "A House is Not a Home" (1964), and "Do You Know the Way to San José?" (1967). "A House is Not a Home" was inspired by, but not used in, a 1964 motion picture of the same name starring Shelley Winters.

"What the World Needs Now is Love" (1965) became a gold record for Jackie De Shannon, and was also recorded by Michele Lee. This song had originally been assigned to Dionne Warwick, who felt it did not suit her singing style, though she later included it on one of her albums. A recording of this song was used ironically in the final scene of director Paul Mazursky's *Bob and Carol and Ted and Alice* (1969). Jackie De Shannon also had a hit with her recording of "Trains and Boats and Planes."

Many other distinguished singers recorded songs by Bacharach and David: Sandi Shaw ("With Always Something to Remind Me"); Aretha Franklin ("I Say a Little Prayer"); Sergio Mendes and Brasil '66 ("The Look of Love"); Herb Alpert ("This Guy's in Love With You"); Tony Bennett ("Make It Easy on Yourself"); Jack Jones ("The Look of Love"); Johnny Mathis ("I Say a Little Prayer"); Robert Goulet ("This Guy's in Love With You"); Ed Ames ("Close to You"); Vikki Carr ("One Less Bell to Answer"); Jane Morgan ("A Message to Michael"); Gene Pitney ("Only Love Can Break a Heart").

Some Bacharach and David's songs originated in motion pictures. Before she recorded it, Doris Day introduced "Send Me No Flowers" in the 1964 film of that title. In 1968's *What's New Pussycat?,* starring Peter Sellers, Tom Jones, then still a novice as a singer, performed the title number on the soundtrack before making it into a bestselling record. In the same picture, "Here I Am" and "My Little Red Book" were also introduced, the former becoming a bestseller in Dionne Warwick's recording, the latter recorded by a short-lived rock group called Love. In *Alfie* (1966), starring Michael Caine, Cher sang the title number on the soundtrack. She also recorded it, but the most successful recordings of this song were by Dionne Warwick and Cilla Black. Bacharach's own recording in 1967 of music from *Alfie* brought him a Grammy for best instrumental arrangement. The title song of *The April Fools* (1969), starring Jack Lemmon, was not sung within the film itself, but was performed on the soundtrack by Percy Faith and his orchestra.

The high watermark of the career in motion pictures of Bacharach and David came in 1969. Having previously received several Oscar nominations they finally won it with "Raindrops Keep Fallin' on My Head" which became a standard almost overnight after being heard in *Butch Cassidy and the Sundance Kid* (1969), starring Paul Newman and Robert Redford. Individually, Bacharach received an Oscar as well as a Grammy for his scoring of the film. "Raindrops Keep Fallin' on My Head" was introduced by B. J. Thomas on the soundtrack, and his recording sold more than three million discs. The song was also recorded by Andy Williams.

The partnership of Bacharach and David was unusual in its operations. Because David's home was on the East Coast, and Bacharach's in the West, much of their work was done by telephone. When ideas were crystallized, David would spend three or four weeks of intensive work sessions with Bacharach in California, or Bacharach would go to New York. Outside their work, mainly due to geography, they did not mingle socially, preferring to confine their relationship to their professional duties. "The system works well," Bacharach told an interviewer. "The separation keeps our outlooks fresh. . . . If we spent more time with each other socially, we'd have less to bounce off each other."

Bacharach does not work at the piano. When he composes, he has his ideas fully realized before putting notes on paper. He can work well almost anywhere, anytime, and under any conditions. Usually the writing of the music preceded the lyrics. Bacharach and David worked harmoniously, respecting each other's foibles and idiosyncrasies, suggestions and criticisms. They would argue their respective points of view until one accepted the validity of the other's ideas. Bacharach found David always to be "kind and gentle, which is important when you have to stay in a room with him all day." For his part, David thought Bacharach was thoroughly cooperative, and a professional to the tips of his fingers.

David's working method was to have a lyric firmly in mind before he began to write. He devoted a full day to his labors (with time off for lunch), working not at a desk but in a soft chair while thinking for hours at a stretch. It took him several days to conceive the first line to "Alfie" but the rest of the lyric came in an hour. David reveals that writing the complete "What the World Needs Now is Love" required not days or months but more than a year. The whole chorus section came to him quickly, but the verses took many months to germinate.

In May 1965 Bacharach married Angie Dickinson, the film and television star. Initially they settled in a rented house in Beverly Hills where their daughter, Nikki, was born in 1966. They later acquired a Beverly Hills home of their own while Bacharach maintained his former bachelor apartment on East 61st Street in Manhattan, which he had used for years as his hideout whenever he visited New York. When Angie Dickinson and their daughter joined him in New York, the three would occupy a hotel suite.

Bacharach and David's only score for the Broadway musical theater was for *Promises, Promises* (December 1, 1968), which had a run of 1,281 performances. It transferred to the stage *The Apartment,* a popular film starring Jack Lemmon and Shirley MacLaine and directed by Billy Wilder. The top executive of an insurance company uses the bachelor apartment of one of his employees for his extramarital dalliances. The employee, Chuck, is a hapless innocent attracted to Fran, a waitress at the company restaurant. One of the executive's paramours, she is eventually discarded and subsequently attempts suicide in Chuck's bed. Rescued by the next-door physician, Fran finds solace, then true love, with Chuck. "The whole piece," reported Clive Barnes in *The New York Times,* "has a sad and wry humanity [and] the Burt Bacharach music excitingly reflects today." The principal song was the ballad "I'll Never Fall in Love Again," introduced by Jerry Orbach, and Jill O'Hara, which Dionne Warwick successfully recorded. It was also recorded by André Kostelanetz. The title song, which was recorded by Arthur Fiedler's Boston Pops Orchestra, was introduced by Orbach and "Whoever You Are" by O'Hara. *Promises, Promises* received the Tony as the season's best musical and a Grammy for its original cast recording.

The success of *Promises, Promises* in 1968 and *Butch Cassidy and the Sundance Kid* in 1969 was the peak of Bacharach and David's careers as songwriters. A precipitous decline in their professional fortunes followed. They composed the score for *Lost Horizon* (1973), a musical film adaptation of James Hilton's novel which had been made into a popular nonmusical film in 1937. The new musical film version was a box-office and critical disaster. However, one of its numbers, "The World is a Circle," was recorded by the Sandpipers while the complete score was released in a soundtrack recording.

More setbacks followed. In 1975 the artistic liaison between Dionne Warwick and Bacharach and David was shattered when she sued them for an alleged violation of an agreement to produce her next album for Warner Brothers. One year later, Bacharach and Angie Dickinson were permanently separated (with divorce coming in 1981). And not long after the fiasco of *Lost Horizon,* the collaboration of Burt Bacharach and Hal David ended. It took Bacharach several years before he could find a winning combination with another lyricist.

Though his career was temporarily at ebbtide, Bacharach stayed in the limelight as a performer. He had made his nightclub debut at Harrah's Club in Lake Tahoe in a 60-minute production in which he starred as an informal commentator, orchestral arranger, conductor of the orchestra, singer, pianist and composer of hit songs all in a single neat package. In May 1970 he sold out five performances at the Westbury Music Fair in New York; two months later he made eight appearances in one week at the Greek Theatre in Los Angeles, breaking all the box-office records of that auditorium in its 18-year history. He was also the host of television specials, beginning with 1970's *The Sound of Bacharach* on NBC which brought the show's director an Emmy. *The First Bacharach Special* of 1971 also garnered an Emmy as the year's best musical variety program. Bacharach continued to be popular both in nightclubs and television even though, as a composer of hit songs, he had been temporarily sidetracked.

In addition to his vast earnings as performer and songwriter, Bacharach has numerous far-flung financial investments. He has owned a publishing company, two restaurants, a car-washing service in New York, real estate in Georgia, a stable of race horses and a herd of cattle.

Bacharach began finding himself again as a composer in the late 1970s through a personal and artistic partnership with Carol Bayer Sager, a noted lyricist who became his wife on April 3, 1982. She shared center stage with him at nightclub and concert apperances and on television specials, including the *Burt Bacharach and Carole Sager Salute* in 1983. She also became his lyricist. With Bacharach, the country-pop singer and songwriter Christopher Cross and with Paul Allen, she helped to write "Best That You Can Do" (also known as "Arthur's Theme"), which was introduced by Cross on the soundtrack of the motion picture *Arthur* (1981), a comedy star-

ring Dudley Moore. This song, Bacharach's first hit in 11 years, won both an Oscar and a Golden Globe Award.

Sager collaborated with Bacharach on the LP *Sometimes Late at Night,* which Bacharach produced in 1982 while serving as composer and arranger. Here, Sager was vocalist as well as Bacharach's lyricist. With Sager as lyricist, Bacharach's songs were heard in the comic film *Night Shift* (1982).

In 1982 Bacharach recorded one of his most innovative albums in a decade, a collection mostly of orchestral pieces performed by the Houston Symphony. Called *Woman,* this album included several novel, attractive numbers, notably the title song, "New York Lady," and "Summer of '77."

Bacharach's "Heartlight" (music written with Neil Diamond, lyrics by Sager), recorded by Neil Diamond, was selected as one of the most frequently performed songs of 1983 in the BMI catalogue. "Maybe" (music written with Marvin Hamlisch, lyrics by Sager) was introduced by Roberta Flack on the soundtrack of the film *Romantic Comedy* (1983), starring Dudley Moore. "Sleep With Me" (lyrics by Sager) was included on Diamond's 1984 album *Primitive.*

In 1984, after a decade, Bacharach was reunited with Dionne Warwick. "Finders of Lost Loves" (lyrics by Sager) was Bacharach's theme for a prime-time television series which Warwick sang as a duet with Luther Vandross. One year later, Warwick recorded Bacharach's "Extravagant Gestures" (lyrics by Sager). This song was inspired by Sager's 1985 novel of the same title, the first theme song ever composed for a novel.

Following his breakup with Bacharach, Hal David wrote the lyrics to Henry Mancini's music for the motion picture *Oklahoma Crude* (1973), starring George C. Scott and Faye Dunaway. He has written several songs to the music of other composers after that, including "America Is" in 1985 (music by Joe Raposto), the official song for the centenary of the Statue of Liberty in 1986, which B. J. Thomas introduced on the Merv Griffin TV program in October 1985. But he has devoted himself primarily to executive duties at ASCAP, having become a member of its board of directors in 1974, vice president in 1979, and, in 1980, Stanley Adams's successor as president.

The Hal Davids reside in Roslyn, New York. His wife, Anne, who has distinguished herself as a painter and sculptor, works in various civic enterprises and is the author of *A Guide to Volunteer Services.* They have two sons. David's interests include boating, skiing, playing tennis, community affairs and baseball; for several

years he coached a local little league baseball
team on Long Island.

ABOUT: Current Biography, 1970; Ewen, D. Great Men
of American Popular Song, 2d ed. 1972;
Periodicals—ASCAP Today August 1970;
Newsweek November 22, 1970; Washington Post
November 10, 1969.

BALL, ERNEST R. (July 21, 1878–May 3,
1927), composer of Irish and love ballads, was
born in Cleveland, Ohio. Precocious in music, he
received his training at the Cleveland Conservatory, where he studied piano and composition.
By the age of 13, he was giving piano lessons,
and at 15, he composed his first piece of music,
a march for the piano.

Ball went to New York as a young man, to further his career in music. For six months, he
worked as relief pianist at Keith's Union Square
Theatre, a vaudeville house. He then was hired
as piano demonstrator for the publishing house
of M. Witmark & Sons in Tin Pan Alley, at a salary of $20 a week. "At Witmark's," he later re-
called, "when I was not busy demonstrating
songs, I used to play over airs that came to me,
and it was here, in odd moments, that I did my
first composing." His first adult effort was "In
the Shadow of the Pyramids" (lyrics by Cecil
Mack) in 1904. Though it was introduced that
year on the Broadway stage by the dynamic May
Irwin in *Miss Black is Back*, the song was a failure.

But success soon arrived. A year later, he composed "Will You Love Me in December As You
Do in May?" to lyrics by James J. ("Jimmy")
Walker, then state senator and later mayor of
New York City. In *American Magazine*, Ball recounted how he came to write it: "One night in
New York . . . I met Senator James J. Walker. . . . He handed me some verses for a song.
They were scribbled on a piece of paper. I read
them over. . . . I put the bit of paper in my
pocket and for the next two months carried these
scribbled lines around with me. . . . Bit by bit,
I worked out a tune that somehow seemed to fit,
and finally, I wrote the music to the words."
Walker also recalled the first time Ball played
the melody for him: "Ernie Ball ran his magical
fingers over the keyboard, plucking the tune he
was improvising, note by note. He finally swept
both hands over the keys in broad chords of the
finished melody and I knew that a hit had been
born. I clasped Ernie around his shoulders and
kissed his cheek." Janet Allen, of the vaudeville
team of Allen and McShane, introduced this
song in vaudeville. (She later became Walker's

ERNEST R. BALL

first wife.) Hundreds of thousands of copies of
sheet music were sold and the Knickerbocker
Serenaders made one of the earliest recordings.
This song also provided Ball with the opportunity to gain a foothold in vaudeville as a performer. In 1905, he made his debut as pianist-
composer, and for the rest of his life, he was a
headliner in an act featuring his hit ballads.

In addition, "Will You Love Me in December
As You Do in May?" became identified with the
personal and political life of Jimmy Walker. It
was played when he married Janet Allen (1912)
and when he first took office as mayor of New
York City (1926). In 1935, when he returned to
New York after a self-imposed exile abroad, the
song greeted him on his arrival, and at his death
in 1946, it was sung and played on radio as a final tribute. Inevitably, "Will You Love Me in
December?" was heard in his motion picture biography, *Beau James* (1957), starring Bob Hope,
and it was also interpolated into the film musical, *The Eddie Cantor Story* (1953).

The success of this song led Ball to reevaluate
himself as a composer. He realized that he had
been writing songs with the sole aim of catering
to current fashion and producing hits; those
songs had been failures. But "Will You Love Me
in December?" was composed for his own satisfaction and not a potential audience: "Then and
there, I determined that I would write honestly
and sincerely of the things I knew about and that
folks generally knew about and were interested
in."

He enjoyed an even greater success in 1906
with "Love Me and the World is Mine" (lyrics by
Dave Reed, Jr.). It was received coolly at Proc-

tor's Fifth Avenue Theatre that year, but became successful when Maude Lambert (Ball's second wife) and Truly Shattuck used it in their vaudeville acts. Sheet music sales exceeded one million copies; this convinced the Witmark to sign Ball to a 20-year contract as staff composer with a large annual guarantee in 1907, the first time a composer in Tin Pan Alley had been given such terms. When the contract expired, it was renewed for an additional 10 years, but Ball did not live to complete it.

"Love Me and the World is Mine" also entered the concert hall when Irish opera tenor John Mc-Cormack incorporated it into his recital repertory and recorded it. Among the motion pictures in which it has been heard are *San Francisco* (1936), where it was sung by Jeanette MacDonald; *The Strawberry Blonde* (1941), starring James Cagney and Rita Hayworth; and *The Eddie Cantor Story*.

The first of Ball's classic Irish ballads was "Mother Machree" (lyrics with Rida Johnson Young), written in 1910 in collaboration with Chauncey Olcott. Olcott was a composer and singer-actor known particularly for his renditions of Irish ballads, and Ball continued to be associated with him in many capacities through the years. Olcott introduced "Mother Machree" in the Broadway play, *Barry of Ballymore* (January 30, 1910) and it became so inextricably identified with him that it was used prominently in the Olcott film biography, *My Wild Irish Rose* (1947). Charles Harrison recorded it in 1914; later recordings include those made by John Mc-Cormack, Helen Clark, Richard Crooks, and James Melton.

Ball continued to collaborate with Olcott, and in 1913, he composed music to the lyrics of Olcott, Young and others for the musical, *Isle o' Dreams* (January 27, 1913). In it, Olcott introduced the classic, "When Irish Eyes Are Smiling" (lyrics by Olcott and George Graff, Jr.). It was recorded that year by Harry MacDonough and subsequently became such a staple in the repertory of Morton Downey, radio's beloved tenor in the 1920s and 1930s, that, in addition to recording it, he is said to have performed it at least 1,000 times. It was also recorded by Bing Crosby, Kate Smith, and John McCormack, among others; Betty Grable sang it in the motion picture, *Coney Island* (1943), and it was also heard in the films, *Let Freedom Ring* (1939), *Doughboys in Ireland* (1942) and *Top o' the Morning* (1949).

In 1914, Ball became a charter member of AS-CAP, the performing rights organization. At that time, he also composed songs for the Olcott vehicles, *The Heart of Paddy Whack* (1914), which included "A Little Bit of Heaven" (lyrics by J. Keirn Brennan), and for *Macushla* (*Pulse of My Heart*; 1915). "A Little Bit of Heaven" continued to be popular into the 1930s and 1940s with recordings by Harry James and Kate Smith, and it became the title song of a motion picture (1940) starring Gloria Jean. Ball's last song, "Rose of Kilarney" (lyrics by William Davidson) composed in 1927, was also an Irish ballad.

Though he was becoming famous for his Irish ballads, Ball also composed others, particulary about love: "In the Garden of My Heart" (1908) set lyrics by opera singer and popular song composer Caro Roma; "Till the Sands of the Desert Grow Cold" (lyrics by George Graff, Jr.) became a hit in 1911 when it was recorded by Wilfred Glenn; "Goodbye, Good Luck, God Bless You" and "Turn Back the Universe and Give Me Yesterday" (lyrics by J. Keirn Brennan) of 1916, owed their great popularity to frequent use by ballad singers in vaudeville, and Ball himself recorded "Goodbye, Good Luck, God Bless You" in 1916, as did Henry Burr and Will Oakland; "Dear Little Boy of Mine" (lyrics by Brennan) followed in 1918.

One of Ball's greatest successes, "Let the Rest of the World Go By" (1919; lyrics by Brennan), first appeared to be a failure. When initial attempts to have it performed on the stage yielded no results, Julius Witmark used his influence to induce various performers to try it out: Elizabeth Spencer (with Charles Hart) recorded it (1919) and other performers incorporated it into their vaudeville acts. The ballad eventually caught on and more than three million copies of the sheet music were sold.

Ball continued to appear in vaudeville, sharing his act in later years with his wife, Maude Lambert. After a benefit performance at the Yost Theater in Santa Ana, California on May 3, 1927, where he offered a medley of his leading hit songs, Ball suffered a fatal heart attack in his dressing room. It has been estimated that, at the time of his death, more than 25 million copies of sheet music of his songs had been sold.

In 1944, 20th-Century-Fox released a musical romance, *Irish Eyes Are Smiling*, loosely based on the life of the composer. The cast included Dick Haymes as the composer, June Haver, and Leonard Warren and Blanche Thebom from the Metropolitan Opera. The musical numbers included such favorites as "Let the Rest of the World Go By," "Dear Little Boy of Mine," "A Little Bit of Heaven," "Love Me and the World is Mine" and "Mother Machree."

ABOUT: Gilbert, D. Lost Chords, 1942; Witmark, I. The Story of the House of Witmark: From Ragtime to Swingtime, 1939.

BERGMAN, ALAN, (September 11, 1925–   )
and BERGMAN, MARILYN (November 10,
1929–   ). Alan and Marilyn Bergman are partners both as lyricists and in their private lives.
They have become the most important husband-
and-wife lyric-writing team in American popular music, with three Oscars and several Golden
Globe awards and Emmys.

Alan Bergman was born in Brooklyn, the son
of Samuel and Ruth (Margulies) Bergman. The
father was a clothing salesman. Alan attended
the Ethical Culture School and the Abraham
Lincoln High School in his native borough, graduating high school in 1942. After leaving Brooklyn he attended the University of North Carolina
in Chape Hill, where he majored in music and
theater arts. During World War II, he served in
the Army, writing and directing shows for the
Special Services (1943–45). Upon his discharge,
he returned to Chapel Hill, receiving his B. A.
degree in 1948. He then left North Carolina to
attend UCLA (1948–49), where he earned a
master's degree. Settling in Philadelphia in 1949,
he worked for the next four years as a television
director for CBS in charge of televised baseball
games, musical shows and other primetime features. He was also writing songs, music as well
as words. Johnny Mercer was so impressed with
some of them that he advised Bergman to consider songwriting as a profession.

In 1953 Bergman moved back to Los Angeles
where he wrote special material for the *Shower
of Stars* and other primetime television programs. He met Marilyn Keith through a mutual
collaborator, the composer Lew Spence. Keith,
too, was a native of Brooklyn. Her father, Albert
A. Katz, like Bergman's, was in the clothing business. Marilyn's childhood ambition was to become a concert pianist, and she studied with
private teachers. In 1945 she graduated from the
High School of Music and Art in New York, a
school for talented young art students. She enrolled in New York University as a premedical
student, but soon decided to major in English,
emphasizing creative writing and the study of
psychology, and amassed credits for degrees in
both English and psychology. In the early 1950s
Marilyn fell down a flight of steps, breaking one
shoulder and dislocating another. To recuperate,
she moved to Los Angeles to live with her family, which had settled there in 1949. To keep herself busy, she began writing songs at the urging
of a friend, Bob Russell, a lyricist; her first song
was recorded by Peggy Lee.

Soon after they met, Bergman and Marilyn
Keith decided to write song lyrics together while
leaving the music composition strictly to others.
With this in mind, they came to New York to
consult with the noted composer-publisher

ALAN and MARILYN BERGMAN

Frank Loesser. It was during this trip that
friendship and creative collaboration ripened
into romance. "It was the best thing Loesser ever
did, maybe even better than *Guys and Dolls*,"
Marilyn Bergman commented.

They were married on February 9, 1958, and
in 1960 their daughter Julie was born. By then,
husband and wife had already begun to make
their mark as lyricists, having had their first major success in 1957 with "Yellow Bird." This was
a West Indian folk tune that Norman Luboff
had adapted into an American popular song for
which the Bergmans wrote the words. After being introduced by the Norman Luboff Choir in
their album *Songs of the Caribbean*, "Yellow
Bird" gained popularity through recordings by
Arthur Lyman and by Roger Williams. The
Mills Brothers and Lawrence Welk also contributed to its popularization. Since then, it has become a standard both in the United States and
abroad, with more than 150 international recordings in many tongues. This song is thought
to have been the last piece of music heard by
President Kennedy, inasmuch as the record was
found on his phonograph turntable in his Fort
Worth hotel, where he stayed the day before he
traveled to Dallas.

Working with various composers, the Bergmans soon began tailoring songs for individual
performers and motion pictures. In 1960, with
Lew Spence as composer, they wrote "Nice 'n'
Easy" for Frank Sinatra as the title song for one
of his albums. That year, with Spence, they also
contributed the title song to the motion picture
The Marriage-Go-Round (1961). Tony Bennett
sang it on the soundtrack, then popularized it in

a recording and in public appearances. Other songs for which the Bergmans wrote lyrics to Spence's music included "I Never Left Your Arms," introduced by Dinah Shore in a recording; "Sleep Warm," written for and introduced by Sinatra; and "That Face," written for and featured by Fred Astaire in a television special.

The Bergmans made their bow in the Broadway musical theater with *Something More* (November 10, 1964), for which Sammy Fain was the composer. It was a box-office failure, lasting only 15 performances. In Hollywood, they were called upon to write title numbers and principal songs for many major screen productions. In 1967 they wrote "Make Me Rainbows" (music by John Williams) which was heard in the film *Fitzwilly* and was successfully recorded by Jack Jones and by Vic Damone. With Quincy Jones composer, they contributed the title song to *In the Heat of the Night* starring Sidney Poitier (1967), introduced on the soundtrack by Ray Charles, whose recording became a bestseller.

When the Bergmans wrote the theme song for *The Thomas Crown Affair* (1968) they initiated a highly productive collaboration with Michel Legrand, the French-born composer who became one of Hollywood's most important composers of screen songs. For "The Windmills of Your Mind," introduced in *The Thomas Crown Affair,* Legrand composed eight different melodies. When he met with the Bergmans to complete the song, all of the principals made the same melody their final choice. Noel Harrison sang it on the soundtrack and Dusty Springfield's recording was a hit. This song won an Oscar as well as a Golden Globe Award, and has since become a standard.

The second Oscar for the Bergmans, together with two Grammys and a Golden Globe, came for the title song of *The Way We Were* (1973), introduced by its star Barbra Streisand who also recorded it. Here the Bergmans collaborated with the composer Marvin Hamlisch, with whom they also wrote "The Last Time I Felt Like This" for *Same Time, Next Year* (1978), which Johnny Mathis and Jane Oliver introduced as a duet on the soundtrack and recorded.

The collaboration of Legrand and the Bergmans yielded many more songs after "The Windmills of Your Mind." "What Are You Doing the Rest of Your Life?" was written for the motion picture, *The Happy Ending* (1966), in which it was introduced on the soundtrack by Michael Dees. "Summer Me, Winter Me" was a song adapted from the main instrumental theme from the motion picture, *The Picasso Summer* (1969). It was initially recorded by Barbra Streisand, and later by Johnny Mathis and by Frank Sinatra. "The Summer Knows," introduced in *Summer of '42* (1971), was included by Barbra Streisand on her album *Barbra Jean* and was also recorded successfully by Andy Williams and Sinatra. "The Hands of Time" came from the motion picture *Brian's Song* (1971). "Pieces of Dreams" was heard in *Little Boy Lost* (1971) and has become popularly known by the movie title. "How Do You Keep the Music From Playing" was the song highlight from *Best Friends* (1982) and Tony Bennett has featured it in concert. Legrand and the Bergmans also composed all the songs for *Yentl* (1983), directed by Barbra Streisand; its soundtrack recording became a platinum record in 1985. The two principal numbers from *Yentl* were "The Way He Makes Me Feel" and "Papa, Can You Hear Me?"; each was nominated in 1984 for an Oscar. But when the Oscars were distributed, the Bergmans and Legrand won it not for one of their songs but for the overall score. "Something New in My Life," by Legrand and the Bergmans, was introduced by Stephen Bishop in the film *Micki and Maude* (1984).

Speaking of his collaboration with the Bergmans, Legrand once said: "Incredible things happen. Their words say exactly what my music says—always." Such creative empathy exists when the Bergmans work with other noted Hollywood composers. The ability of these two lyricists to "pitch" their words to the differing styles of different composers make them among the most versatile lyricists of our time.

Henry Mancini was their composer when they wrote "All His Children" for *Sometimes a Great Notion* (1971), a song the country-and-western singer Charley Pride helped to popularize. With Mancini, the Bergmans also wrote "Where Do You Catch the Bus for Tomorrow?" for *A Change of Season* (1980), which Kenny Rankin recorded; "Ask Me No Questions," sung by Sue Ramey in *Back Roads* (1981); and the theme song for *The Man Who Loved Women* (1983), starring Burt Reynolds and based on one of François Truffaut's Antoine Daniel films.

With the composer Maurice Jarre, the Bergmans wrote "Marmalade, Molasses and Honey" for the Paul Newman film *The Life and Times of Judge Roy Bean* (1972), a song successfully recorded by Andy Williams. With the composer David Shire, they wrote the title song for *The Promise* (1978), recorded by Melissa Manchester. With composer Dave Grusin they wrote "Something Funny Going On" for *And Justice for All* (1979), starring Al Pacino; the recurrent theme in *The Champ* (1979), which Kenny Rankin recorded; "Comin' Home to You" for *Author! Author!* (1982); and "It Might Be You," introduced in the Dustin Hoffman film *Tootsie* (1982), in which it was sung by Stephen Bishop. The last-named number was selected as one of the most frequently performed songs of 1983 in the BMI catalogue. With John Williams as their composer, the Bergmans wrote "If We Were in Love" for Luciano Pavarotti's screen debut in *Yes, Giorgio* (1982), the only new song in that film.

To Sergio Mendes's music, the Bergmans wrote the lyrics for the title song of *Look Around,* the hit album by Sergio Mendes and Brasil 66. Neil Diamond, as composer, collaborated with them on "Don't Bring Me Flowers," which had been intended as a theme for a television series but was never used. Barbra Streisand and Neil Diamond recorded it separately and together in three releases that were bestsellers. Barbra Streisand also helped popularize "I Believe in Love" (music by Kenny Loggins), written by the Bergmans for the third screen remake of *A Star Is Born* (1970), starring Streisand and Kris Kristofferson. On Streisand's bestselling *Wet* album (1979) she included "On Rainy Afternoons" (music by Lalo Schifrin) and "After the Rain" (music by Legrand), for which the Bergmans prepared the lyrics.

The Bergmans have also written the theme songs of television series including the Norman Lear–produced situation comedies *Maude* and *Good Times* and the Sandy Duncan Show, all three to Dave Grusin's music. "The World Goes On" (music by Quincy Jones) became the title theme song for a TV special after it had won a prize at the 1967 International Song Festival in Rio de Janeiro. The Bergmans were awarded two Emmys in 1974 for the score of *Queen of the Stardust Ballroom,* music by Billy Goldenburg, starring Maureen Stapleton, and, in 1976, for the songs to *Sybil* (music by Leonard Rosenman). *Queen of the Stardust Ballroom* was rewritten as a Broadway musical, *Ballroom* (December 14, 1978), with book by Jerome Kass and direction and choreography by Michael Bennett, and with Dorothy Loudon starring in the role of the widow who finds romance in a Bronx ballroom. On TV and on Broadway, one of its most popular numbers was "I Love to Dance Like They Used to Dance."

The Bergmans told Stephen Holden of *The New York Times*: "Our experiences in the theater and film have shown us that the two require entirely different writing. They speak to different parts of the brain. Theater is a long-shot medium in which people are listening first and looking second. . . . But in the movie theater, with larger than life images, they are looking first and listening secondarily. . . . We found we must be more abstract when writing for film, because film really speaks more to the preconscious part of the brain, the part of us that dreams."

The Bergmans' lyrics are generally written after the music has been composed because, as they explained, "The composer needs the freedom to write the strongest possible melody to be a leitmotif for the spine of the score." When writing lyrics for the screen, "First we see the movie, then the isolated sequence, which is usually a hole that has been deliberately left to be filled. . . . The actual process of writing the lyric is like two potters passing the clay back and forth. At the end of the song, we rarely know who wrote what."

For the motion picture *From Noon to Three* (1976), Alan Bergman not only wrote the lyrics with his wife, but also made his debut as an actor. He was seen in the role of a songwriter. That same year, while Alan was working as an actor, Marilyn Bergman was making her debut as a director. She became one of ten women chosen by the American Film Institute to receive a grant to direct films for the Institute's Directing workshop for Women and for the Institute's continuing program to help develop female directors.

Both Alan and Marilyn Bergman are politically active, and have been involved in many liberal civic causes. On June 1, 1980 "A Tribute to Alan and Marilyn Bergman" was held at the Dorothy Chandler Pavilion of the Los Angeles Music Center; the event helped raise more than $150,000 for the American Civil Liberties Union. At that time, songs by the Bergmans were performed by a roster of stars that included Barbra Streisand (in her first public appearance in six years), Neil Diamond, Michel Legrand and many others.

The Bergmans live in an English country house in Beverly Hills. Apart from their creative and civic interests, Alan enjoys tennis, reading, photography and the collection of art, and Marilyn collects antiques.

ABOUT: *Periodicals*—ASCAP in Action Fall 1980; New York Times December 24, 1982.

BERLIN, IRVING (May 11, 1888–), composer-lyricist, dominated American popular music for more than half a century. He has composed more than 1,000 songs, at least a dozen of which have become classics, as well as the scores for 20 Broadway musicals and 17 movie musicals. Among his standards are "God Bless America," "Oh, How I Hate to Get Up in the Morning," "Alexander's Ragtime Band," and "White Christmas."

IRVING BERLIN

He was born Israel Baline in Temun, in Siberian Russia, on May 11, 1888, the youngest of the eight children of Moses and Leah (Lipkin) Baline. The father was an impoverished cantor in a small synagogue. In addition to poverty, the Balines suffered persecution at the hands of Cossacks. When Israel was four, the town of Temun was victimized by a pogrom. The family was saved by hiding under blankets in the forest until the slaughter was over. The Balines subsequently sold their possessions so that they could make their way across the ocean by steerage to America.

Their first home was a dank basement apartment on Monroe Street on New York's Lower East Side. A few weeks later they moved nearby to Cherry Street, Israel's home for his first years in America. His father became an inspector of kosher meats, gave Hebrew lessons to children, and occasionally substituted as a cantor in the synagogue. Four of the Baline children went to work in sweatshops.

When Israel began his schooling, his teachers regarded him as an indifferent, even lazy, student. He preferred playing games on city streets, running with gangs of boys his age, and going swimming with friends in the East River at the foot of Cherry Street, to attending school. His other interest, singing, was a heritage from his father, and he became a member of the synagogue choir. Berlin has recalled: "I suppose it was singing with my father that gave me my musical background. It was in my blood."

The death of Moses Baline in 1896 aggravated the family's financial problems. All eight children had to take jobs, with Israel earning a few daily pennies by hawking the *Evening Journal* in the streets after school. When he was 14, Israel decided to break with home, family and school and try to earning his living by singing popular ballads in cafés and on street corners. He slept in hallways, in basements and occasionally in the streets, spending the daytime searching for professional singing opportunities. He worked with "Blind Sol," a peripatetic New York street minstrel, and as a solo performer he sang at such cafés as Callahan's in Chinatown and the Chatham on Doyer Street.

One day a passerby, impressed by his singing, introduced him to Harry von Tilzer, the prominent songwriter and publisher. At a salary of five dollars a week, Israel Baline plugged songs from the balcony of Tony Pastor's Music Hall on 14th Street. One act he plugged for was the Three Keatons, from whose ranks came the great comedian of the silent screen, Buster Keaton.

In 1906 Baline was hired as a singing waiter at Pelham's Café in Chinatown, where for a dollar a day he entertained patrons with renditions of currently popular songs and then helped clean up after closing time. It was here that he taught himself to play the piano by ear and began writing songs. At first he only wrote parodies of hit songs and topical events, setting them to familiar melodies. Baline's introduction to "talk of the town" publicity was the result of a visit to the café by Prince Louis Battenberg and his entourage. After Baline had sung some of his parodies, the Prince tipped him five dollars. Israel, with an aristocratic flourish, declined to accept, explaining that singing for the Prince had itself been sufficient compensation. The following day this incident was reported in the New York *World* by Herbert Bayard Swope, who had been a member of the prince's party.

It was at Pelham's Café that Baline composed his first published song. He wrote it at the request of Pelham's proprietor, who envied the recent publication of a song composed by the employees of a rival café. With Michael Nicholson, the Pelham Café pianist, as composer, Baline wrote the words for "Marie From Sunny Italy," which was published by Joseph W. Stern on May 8, 1907. On the sheet music Baline was identified as "I. Berlin," and he began to call himself "Irving Berlin." Though he earned just 37 cents from his first publication, he now considered himself a professional songwriter.

In 1908 Berlin wrote his first song with his own music, "The Best of Friends Must Part." He also wrote words and music for a song that found its way into a Broadway musical, "She was a Dear Little Girl," heard in *The Boys and Betty*, which starred Marie Cahill and opened on November 2, 1908. In 1909 Berlin had a modest success with "Dorando," a novelty song in Italian dialect inspired by the long distance runner Dorando's defeat in the 1908 Olympic games. It was published by Ted Snyder, who had recently formed the Seminary Music Company.

By 1909 Berlin had left Pelham's to work as a singing waiter at Jimmy Kelly's, a café near Union Square. Mendelssohn's *Spring Song* inspired him to compose words and a syncopated melody for "That Mesmerizing Mendelssohn Tune," which was recorded in 1909 by Billy Murray and by Arthur Collins with Byron G. Harlan. Another Berlin song of 1909—"Next to Your Mother, Who Do You Love?"—was sung at Carey Walsh's saloon on Coney Island by the young and still unknown Eddie Cantor. It was in 1909, too, that Berlin composed the music for the first of several songs in Yiddish dialect, "Sadie Salome Go Home" (lyrics by Edgar Leslie), which altered Fanny Brice's destiny as a performer. In 1910 she was a ragtime singer at the Columbia Theatre, a burlesque house. Invited to do a specialty number at a benefit, Brice asked Berlin to provide her with material, and he complied with "Sadie Salome Go Home." Though she had never before done a comedy number, let alone one with a Yiddish accent, she brought down the house with Berlin's number. When, later in 1910, she graduated from burlesque to the Ziegfeld Follies, one of her debut songs was another humorous Yiddish-inflected number, "Goodbye, Becky Cohen" (words and music by Berlin), which established Brice's reputation as a comedienne with a gift for "Yiddish" comedy songs. In this same edition of the Follies she delivered another Berlin song, one with no ethnic overtones, "Doing the Grizzly Bear," which she later recorded, as did Sophie Tucker and Billy Murray with the American Quartette. It was revived in the movie *Wharf Angel* (1934).

In addition to writing his own music, at this time Berlin was contributing lyrics to music composed by Ted Snyder. One of their songs, "Oh! How That German Could Love," was introduced by Sam Bernard in the Casino Theatre musical *The Girl and the Wizard* in 1909, the year Berlin recorded it (it was the only recording he ever made as a singer). "My Wife's Gone to the Country" (lyrics by Berlin and George Whiting) became Berlin's first song success. After Eddie Cantor had featured it in his vaudeville act, it was heard so often on the stage and in a 1909 recording by Arthur Collins with Byron G. Harlan that the New York *Evening Journal* commissioned Berlin to write additional lyrics for publication in 1910. Sheet-music sales were in excess of several hundred thousand copies, and

Berlin's royalties amounted to the then substantial sum of $7,000.

The success of "My Wife's Gone to the Country" brought Berlin a partnership in Ted Snyder's publishing firm, whose name was changed to Snyder, Waterson and Berlin. (Berlin remained with the company until 1919, and his songs contributed immeasurably to its prosperity.) The music of Berlin and Snyder was receiving increasing attention on the Broadway stage. In 1910 Sam Bernard introduced "Bring Back My Lena to Me" in *He Came from Milwaukee* at the Casino Theatre; May Irwin popularized "That Opera Rag" in *Getting a Polish*; and Nora Bayes made "Stop That Rag" a sensation in *The Jolly Bachelors*. Berlin and Snyder themselves became performers when they were featured in the cast of the revue *Up and Down Broadway* (July 19, 1910). Dressed in collegiate sweaters, tennis racquets under their arms, they sauntered across the stage of the Casino Theatre introducing two of their new songs, "Oh, That Beautiful Rag" and "Sweet Italian Love."

In songs like "That Opera Rag" and "Oh, That Beautiful Rag," Berlin, like so many of his colleagues in Tin Pan Alley, revealed his indebtedness to ragtime. With "Alexander's Ragtime Band" (1916, words and music by Berlin), still another syncopated number billed as a ragtime, Berlin became a national celebrity. He wrote it as a new member of New York's Friar's Club when he was asked to contribute a song to the *Friar's Frolics* of 1911. The song was not performed at the Friar's Club but it was introduced by Eddie Miller and Helen Vincent at the Garden Café in Manhattan. Emma Carus, a strong-voiced ragtime singer, created a sensation when she used it in her vaudeville act in Chicago in 1911. Among the many vaudeville stars who featured it in their acts were Sophie Tucker, Helen Vincent and Ethel Levey. Al Jolson performed it with Lew Dockstader's Minstrels, and it was recorded by Arthur Collins. The song caught on quickly, becoming an American standard almost overnight. Within a few months of publication, more than a million copies of sheet music had been sold.

Though "Alexander's Ragtime Band" is considered the most popular ragtime to have come from Tin Pan Alley, it is not a true ragtime. Except for the title and the use of syncopation on the word "just" in the chorus, it is a march tune with interpolations of bugle calls and a brief quotation from Stephen Foster's "Swanee River." It has been recorded successfully many times—by Al Jolson and Bing Crosby (individually and in duet), Eddie Cantor, the Andrews Sisters, the Boswell Sisters, Benny Goodman, and

Kid Ory's Creole Band, among others. It was heard in the 1938 movie *Alexander's Ragtime Band,* starring Alice Faye and Tyrone Power. It was also used for an extended production number featuring Ethel Merman, Dan Dailey, Mitzi Gaynor, Donald O'Connor and Johnny Raye in *There's No Business Like Show Business* (1954), demonstrating how "Alexander's Ragtime Band" would be performed in different countries. At this time the song was recorded by Merman and Dailey. The melody has also been heard in the symphony hall, quoted in John Alden Carpenter's symphonic suite *Adventures in a Perambulator* (1915).

Berlin continued to write successful ragtime-derived numbers. "Everybody's Doin' It" (words and music by Berlin) appeared in 1911 and helped to make the Turkey Trot a popular dance. This number was recorded that year by Arthur Collins with Byron G. Harlan, and by the Columbia Quartette. It was revived in *Alexander's Ragtime Band* for Alice Faye and Wally Vernon, in *Easter Parade* (1948) for Judy Garland and chorus and in *The Fabulous Dorseys* for Tommy Dorsey and his orchestra. Berlin himself introduced his "That Mysterious Rag" (music by Ted Snyder) and "The Ragtime Jockey" (words and music by Berlin) when he starred in *The Passing Show of 1912* (July 22, 1912), a Winter Garden revue. "Ragtime Sextette" was Berlin's ragtime parody of the sextet from *Lucia di Lammermoor;* he wrote it for Al Jolson, who featured it in the Winter Garden extravaganza, *The Whirl of Society* in 1912.

In 1913, at the Hippodrome in London, billed as "the ragtime king," Berlin sang many of his ragtime hits, including one number written especially for this occasion, "The International Rag." Convinced that Berlin had written every popular ragtime song, British audiences, at encore time when he invited them to request their favorites from his repertory, would call for every ragtime tune with which they were familiar.

As the "king of ragtime," Berlin was engaged to write his first complete Broadway score for the revue *Watch Your Step* (December 8, 1914), which was described in the program as "a syncopated musical." It starred Vernon and Irene Castle, then America's favorite dance team, for whom Berlin wrote *Watch Your Step* as a showcase. It had a run of 175 performances. One of Berlin's best numbers in the show was "The Syncopated Walk," which the Castles introduced and which the Peerless Quartette recorded.

Berlin's second complete Broadway score was for *Stop! Look! Listen!* (December 25, 1915), a musical comedy which ran for 105 performances. A flimsy plot (book by Harry B. Smith)

takes a chorus girl and her partner to various locales in the continental United States, Hawaii and Europe. For the first-act finale, Berlin composed "Everything in America is Ragtime," a production number introduced by Gaby Deslys.

Not all of Berlin's numbers in *Watch Your Step* and *Stop! Look! Listen!* were syncopated. The score for the former included "Play a Simple Melody," introduced by Charles King and Sallie Fisher. This was Berlin's first song to combine two contrapuntal melodies (one in simple quarter notes, the other syncopated) with two different sets of lyrics, each sung separately, then simultaneously as the song reached its climax. In 1950 "Play a Simple Melody" was revived by Bing Crosby in a duet with his son, Gary, in a million-selling recording that gave the song almost a dozen hearings on *Your Hit Parade.* Later recordings were made by Dinah Shore and by Jo Stafford. Ethel Merman and Dan Dailey sang it in *There's No Business Like Show Business* and recorded it. One of the irresistibly charming numbers in *Stop! Look! Listen!* was "I Love a Piano," which is one of Berlin's personal favorites in his prodigious repertory. Arthur Collins with Byron G. Harlan and Billy Murray recorded it first, and Blossom Seeley covered it later. Judy Garland and Fred Astaire revived it in *Easter Parade* (1948).

Even before writing "Play a Simple Melody" and "I Love a Piano," Berlin had demonstrated his mastery of idioms other than ragtime. "Woodman, Woodman Spare That Tree" was one of the songs that made Bert Williams a star of the *Ziegfeld Follies of 1911.* He recorded it two years later. "When the Midnight Choo Choo Leaves for Alabam'" was a hit song in 1912. Alice Faye revived it in *Alexander's Ragtime Band* and Ethel Merman, Dan Dailey, Mitzi Gaynor and Donald O'Connor in *There's No Business Like Show Business.* In 1913 Berlin composed the ballad "When I Lost You," an enormous success with sheet music sales of more than two million copies. The initial recordings were made by Manuel Romain, Henry Burr and Bessie Smith, with later ones by Frank Sinatra, Bing Crosby, Kay Starr and Kate Smith. "When I Lost You" was Berlin's first successful ballad and his first hit song with autobiographical connotations. It was born in tragedy. On February 13, 1913 Berlin had married Dorothy Goetz, the sister of the Broadway producer E. Ray Goetz. They honeymooned in Cuba, and then took up residence on Manhattan's Upper West Side, on Riverside Drive. Two weeks later Dorothy died of typhoid fever. Berlin tried to flee his grief by traveling to Europe. That proved futile, and he sublimated his sorrow in the writing of his first ballad.

In 1915 Berlin composed a sentimental ballad that had a curious origin. It was inspired by a newspaper account of how Charles Lounsberry, a lawyer, bequeathed to his children "the dandelions in the field, and the daisies thereof . . . the days to be merry in." This story so moved Berlin that he composed (words and music) "When I Leave the World Behind" and dedicated it to Lounsberry's memory. The song was popularized by an Al Jolson recording. Decades later it was revived in a recording by Teresa Brewer. (Years after the ballad's composition, Berlin learned that Charles Lounsberry and his will were fictitious, that the entire story had been a journalist's hoax.)

From 1916 to 1918 Berlin worked primarily in the musical theater. He collaborated with Victor Herbert on the score for *The Century Girl* (November 6, 1916), a Ziegfeld-produced revue starring Elsie Janis, Sam Bernard and Leon Erroll. One of the highlights of the show was a ragtime number by Berlin that was sung in counterpoint to Victor Herbert's waltz, "Kiss Me Again." In the *Cohan Revue of 1918* (December 13, 1917), featuring Nora Bayes, Berlin shared the score with George M. Cohan. In the flag-waving *Ziegfeld Follies of 1918* (June 18, 1918) "Blue Devils of France" (words and music by Berlin) was introduced by Lillian Lorraine and "I'm Gonna Pin a Medal on the Girl I Left Behind" was introduced by Frank Carter; the latter was recorded by the Peerless Quartette.

In 1918, shortly after the United States declared war, Berlin was inducted into the Army. Stationed at Camp Upton, New York, a temporary station for troops embarking on overseas duty, Berlin saw the need for entertaining the troops, and he conceived the idea of writing and producing an all-soldier show. The Army encouraged him because the show would raise money for a much needed Service Center. With a cast of 350 uniformed men, and all textual and musical material written by Berlin, *Yip, Yip, Yaphank* opened in New York City on August 19, 1918, where it played to capacity audiences for four weeks before traveling to Boston, Philadelphia and Washington, D. C.

Two classic Berlin songs came from this show. "Oh, How I Hate to Get Up in the Morning" was introduced by Berlin himself, appearing in his soldier's uniform. "Mandy," sung by Private John Murphy, became popular when it was interpolated for Marilyn Miller into the *Ziegfeld Follies of 1919* (June 16, 1919). Jack Haley sang it in *Alexander's Ragtime Band.* "Oh, How I Hate to Get Up in the Morning" was recorded in 1918 by Arthur Fields, "Mandy" by Van and Schenck in 1919 and later by Eddie Cantor and

by Bing Crosby with Danny Kaye. Cantor revived "Mandy" in the film *Kid Millions* (1934), and the song was later interpolated into *Blue Skies* (1946), whose score consisted of 19 other Berlin songs, and Vera-Ellen and John Brescia sang it in *White Christmas* (1954). Both songs also appeared in the 1943 movie *This Is the Army.*

After the war Berlin solidified his position as America's leading songwriter. From the *Ziegfeld Follies of 1919* emerged two more Berlin standards. "You'd Be Surprised" was introduced by Eddie Cantor, and his recording in 1919 became his only disc to sell a million copies. San Juan sang it in *Blue Skies* and Dan Dailey in *There's No Business Like Show Business.* "A Pretty Girl is Like a Melody" was introduced in the *Follies* by John Steel in a lavish production number in which each of the female dancers represented a classical composition. The first successful recordings of "A Pretty Girl" were made in 1919 by John Steel and by Ben Selvin's Novelty Orchestra. Since 1919 this ballad has provided theme music for countless fashion shows and beauty pageants, and for many years it served as the unofficial theme song of the *Ziegfeld Follies.* The song was used for an Oscar-winning production number in the movie *The Great Ziegfeld* (1936), in which it was sung by Dennis Morgan. Alice Faye sang it in *Alexander's Ragtime Band,* Fred Astaire and chorus in *Blue Skies* and Ethel Merman and Dan Dailey in *There's No Business Like Show Business.*

In 1919 an "Irving Berlin Week" was celebrated throughout the United States to mark the opening of the composer's own New York publishing house, Irving Berlin Inc. His songs were heard in auditoriums around the country, and Berlin himself headlined as a vaudeville entertainer at Manhattan's Palace Theatre.

In 1921, in partnership with Sam H. Harris and Joseph Schenck, Berlin helped to finance the building of the Music Box Theatre on West 45th Street. To ensure its success, Berlin produced and wrote the score for an annual musical, *The Music Box Revue.* The first edition opened on September 22, 1921 and ran for 440 performances. It was a lavish production starring Sam Bernard, Joseph Santley, Ivy Sawyer and the Brox Sisters, and was filled with "ravishingly beautiful tableaux, . . . gorgeous costumes . . . a wealth of comedy and spectacular freshness," according to Arthur Hornblow of *Theatre Magazine.* Three more editions of this revue followed on October 23, 1922, (330 performances), September 22, 1923 (273 performances) and December 1, 1924 (184 performances). To all four productions Berlin contributed significant songs. In 1921 "Everybody Step," a syncopated number, was sung by the Brox Sisters while "Say It With Music" was a ballad shared by Wilda Bennett and Paul Frawley. "Everybody Step" was recorded by Ted Lewis's orchestra and by Paul Whiteman, whose orchestra also recorded "Say It With Music." Ethel Merman sang "Everybody Step" in *Alexander's Ragtime Band* and Bing Crosby did it in *Blue Skies*. Alice Faye revived "Say it With Music" in *Alexander's Ragtime Band*.

In the 1923 editions, two of Berlin's loveliest ballads were featured: "All Alone" and "What'll I Do?" Both were performed by a singer who was still an unknown but who would soon emerge as a glamorous prima donna—Grace Moore. Neither ballad had been written for the *Music Box Revue*. "What'll I Do?" was introduced by Grace Moore at a benefit performance at the Metropolitan Opera earlier in 1923; after being sung on the radio by Frances Alda, it was added to the already running *Music Box Revue*. Al Jolson recorded "All Alone" in 1924 (and again in 1947) with later recordings made by Bing Crosby, Frank Sinatra, Connie Boswell, Dinah Shore and Georgia Gibbs. In *Alexander's Ragtime Band* it was sung by Alice Faye, who also performed "What'll I Do?" Among the first to record "What'll I Do?" were Jolson, Frances Alda, and the orchestras of Paul Whiteman and Paul Specht. Harry Nilsson included it on his bestselling album *A Little Bit of Schmilsson in the Night* (1973) and Linda Ronstadt revived it in a recording of 1982. Danny Thomas sang it in the movie *Big City* (1947), and in 1974 it was used as a recurrent theme in *The Great Gatsby*, starring Mia Farrow, Bruce Dern and Robert Redford.

A third ballad of frustrated love had no affiliation with the *Music Box Revue*. "All By Myself" was composed in 1921 and introduced that year at the Palace Theatre by Jolson, who also recorded it. Additional recordings were released by Frank Crumit, Charles King, Aileen Stanley, Ted Lewis and, much later, by Bobby Darin, Glen Gray and the Casa Loma Orchestra and the McGuire Sisters.

In 1924 Berlin fell in love with Ellin Mackay, the socialite daughter of Clarence H. Mackay, the head of Postal Telegraph. Berlin and Ellin were from vastly different social and religious worlds, and her father used his wealth and power in a fruitless attempt to discredit Berlin in his daughter's eyes. Berlin and she were married in New York City on January 4, 1926. Their courtship received so much publicity that it inspired a popular song, "When a Kid Who Came From

the East Side Found a Sweet Society Rose" (lyrics by Al Dubin, music by Jimmy McHugh). The Berlins have three daughters.

Berlin's love for Ellin inspired him to write other love ballads, including "Remember" and "Always" (both 1925). Ruth Etting made "Remember" one of her specialties and it was recorded by Al Jolson, Kenny Baker, Connie Boswell and Andy Williams. Alice Faye sang it in *Alexander's Ragtime Band*, Kathryn Grayson in *So This Is Love* (1953), the movie biography of opera singer Grace Moore, and a chorus performed it in *There's No Business Like Show Business*. "Always" was recorded in 1925 by the orchestra of Vincent Lopez, and later recordings were made by Al Jolson, Grace Moore, Dinah Shore and Frank Sinatra. In 1944 the song had nine hearings on *Your Hit Parade*, and two years later it was revived as a choral number in *Blue Skies*.

After the 1924 edition of the *Music Box Revue*, Berlin composed the score for *The Cocoanuts* (December 8, 1925), which, starring the Marx Brothers, had a 375-performance run on Broadway. With a farcical text by George S. Kaufman, *Cocoanuts* is set in Florida, where Henry W. Schlemmer, played by Groucho Marx, is the shady proprietor of a hotel and a real estate swindler. He and the other Marx Brothers (Chico, Harpo and Zeppo) make a shambles of Kaufman's plot with their riotous, anarchic shenanigans. Berlin's best song was "When My Dreams Come True," introduced by Mary Eaton and Oscar Shaw. It was recorded by Paul Whiteman and by Fred Waring's Pennsylvanians.

To *Betsy*, a Rodgers and Hart musical produced by Flo Ziegfeld in 1926, Berlin contributed "Blue Skies," in which it was sung by the show's star, Belle Baker. The first recordings of the song were made by the orchestras of Sam Lanin, George Olsen and Jimmy and Tommy Dorsey; later recordings were by Bing Crosby, Perry Como, Mel Tormé, Ella Fitzgerald, Tommy Dorsey's orchestra (vocal by Frank Sinatra), Dinah Shore and Harry Richman. In 1978 a recording by Willie Nelson reached first place on the country music charts. Al Jolson sang it when he made his screen debut in *The Jazz Singer* (1927), and he included "Blue Skies" on the soundtrack of his film biography, *The Jolson Story* (1947). "Blue Skies" was interpolated into *Glorifying the American Girl* (1930), was sung by Alice Faye in *Alexander's Ragtime Band*, provided the title for a 1946 Bing Crosby movie, and served as a duet for Bing Crosby and Danny Kaye in *White Christmas*.

On August 16, 1927 the *Ziegfeld Follies of*

1927 (168 performances) opened, its complete score the work of Berlin, the first of the *Follies* for which one man wrote all the songs. Eddie Cantor introduced "Learn to Sing a Love Song" and "It All Belongs to Me." Ruth Etting introduced (then recorded) "Shaking the Blues Away," which was revived for Doris Day in *Love Me or Leave Me* (1955), the movie biography of Ruth Etting.

With the advent of sound, Berlin began to write for the screen. "Marie," the theme song of *The Awakening* (1928), was recorded by the orchestras of Tommy Dorsey and Louis Armstrong. Janet Blair, Stuart Foster and Tommy Dorsey's band performed it in *The Fabulous Dorseys* (1947) and it was interpolated for a trio in *There's No Business Like Show Business.* "Coquette," the theme song and title of a 1929 Mary Pickford movie, was recorded by the Dorsey Brothers orchestra. "Where is the Song of Songs for Me?" was the theme song of *Lady of the Pavements* (1928), and was sung by its star, Lupe Velez, who also recorded it. For the 1929 movie version of *The Cocoanuts,* Berlin wrote a new ballad, "When My Dreams Come True," introduced as a duet for Mary Eaton and Oscar Shaw and recorded by Hal Kemp and his orchestra, Paul Whiteman, and Fred Waring's Pennsylvanians.

For Jolson in *Mammy* (1930), Berlin composed "Let Me Sing—and I'm Happy," which Jolson introduced, recorded and revived in his two movie biographies, *The Jolson Story* and *Jolson Sings Again* (1950). "Let Me Sing" was also recorded by Gene Austin and by Ruth Etting. To *Reaching for the Moon* (1930), starring Douglas Fairbanks Sr., Berlin contributed the title song, heard instrumentally on the soundtrack. It was interpolated into *Top Speed* (1931) and recorded by Ruth Etting and Kate Smith.

"Puttin' on the Ritz" became the musical trademark of Harry Richman after he introduced it in the 1930 movie of the same name, in which Richman made his screen debut. Richman recorded it in 1930 and again in 1947, and it was also recorded by Judy Garland. Clark Gable, in one of his rare attempts at singing and dancing, performed it in *Idiot's Delight* (1938), in which he was paired with Norma Shearer. With new lyrics, the song was reintroduced in *Blue Skies* by Fred Astaire, who danced to its music in a scene using a series of split screens to create the effect of eight dancing Astaires. Astaire also recorded it. "Puttin' on the Ritz" became an international disco hit in 1982–83, when a campy version of the song was recorded by the Austrian singer Falco. It was the first appearance of a Berlin song on the American charts since 1954.

In 1927, as if anticipating the writer's block that would grip him a few years later, Berlin composed "The Song is Ended," a ballad recorded by Ruth Etting, by Nick Lucas and by Louis Armstrong with the Mills Brothers, and interpolated into *Blue Skies.* From 1930 to 1932, Berlin wrote nothing, and he feared that his creativity was gone. However the unexpected success of two of his older ballads ended Berlin's dry spell. "Say it Isn't So" had never been published because Berlin thought it inferior, but in 1932 Rudy Vallee introduced it on his radio program and recorded it, as did Connie Boswell. Also that year, Bing Crosby enjoyed a hit with his recording of Berlin's "How Deep is the Ocean?" Crosby sang it again in *Blue Skies* and Sinatra performed it in *Meet Danny Wilson* (1952). Ethel Merman and Dick Haymes, among others, also recorded it.

Berlin's self-confidence now restored, he composed the score of *Face the Music* (February 17, 1932). This Broadway musical (book by Moss Hart) was about a police sergeant being investigated for the possession of illicit funds. Desperately trying to get rid of the money, he finances a Broadway musical produced by a showman with a long resumé of stage fiascos. But the musical turns out to be a blockbuster, and the fortunes of the sergeant, who had been ruined financially by the investigation, are reversed. Though it received good reviews, *Face the Music* lasted only 165 performances. Berlin's score yielded two hit songs "Soft Lights and Sweet Music" and "Let's Have Another Cup o' Coffee," both introduced by Katherine Carrington and J. Harold Murray. Like "Paper Moon," "Let's Have Another Cup o' Coffee" is one of the songs by which the early years of the Great Depression are remembered. This song later served as theme music for the popular radio program, the Maxwell House Show Boat, and it was sung by Ethel Merman in *There's No Business Like Show Business.*

A great Broadway success, with 400 performances, was Berlin's revue *As Thousands Cheer* (September 30, 1933; book by Berlin and Moss Hart). From this production came "Easter Parade," the standard which was introduced by the revue's stars, Marilyn Miller and Clifton Webb. "Easter Parade's" melody, though, had been composed by Berlin in 1917 for another lyric, a song called "Smile and Show Your Dimple" which was recorded that year by Samuel Ash. The song was a failure and it lay forgotten until 1933, when Berlin needed a melody for a Fifth Avenue Easter Parade scene for *As Thousands Cheer.* "Easter Parade" was first recorded in 1933 by the orchestra of Freddy Martin, and thereafter by Al Jolson, Clifton Webb, Perry

Como and Kate Smith. Recordings by Harry James in 1942 and Guy Lombardo in 1947 each sold more than a million discs. Between 1944 and 1958 the song was heard ten times on *Your Hit Parade* during Easter. Don Ameche sang it in *Alexander's Ragtime Band*, Bing Crosby in *Holiday Inn* (1942) and Judy Garland in the movie musical *Easter Parade* (1948), in which she was starred with Fred Astaire and Ann Miller.

There were two other Berlin classics in the score of *As Thousands Cheer*. "Heat Wave" was sung by Ethel Waters and danced to by Letita Ide, José Limon and the Weidman Dancers. It was recorded by Waters, by Mildred Bailey and by the Boswell Sisters. Alice Faye sang it in *Alexander's Ragtime Band*; Olga San Juan sang it, and Fred Astaire and Joan Caulfield danced to it, in *Blue Skies*; Bing Crosby and Danny Kaye performed it as a duet in *White Christmas*; and Marilyn Monroe gave it a sultry rendition in *There's No Business Like Show Business*. "Not for All the Rice in China" was introduced by Marilyn Miller, Clifton Webb and ensemble; it was recorded by Webb and revived by Bing Crosby in *Blue Skies*.

In the six-year hiatus between *As Thousands Cheer* and his next Broadway production, Berlin wrote primarily for the screen. His score for *Top Hat* (1935), the greatest of the Fred Astaire–Ginger Rogers movies, was highlighted by the ballad "Cheek to Cheek," which Astaire sang to Rogers and later in the film was used as background music for one of their celebrated dance routines. Astaire made the first recording, and he was followed by Frank Sinatra, Hildegarde, Morton Downey, "Buddy" Rogers, Bing Crosby and the Boswell Sisters. In 1935 the song had 12 hearings on *Your Hit Parade*, five times in first position. It achieved the greatest commercial success of any Berlin song up to that time, with more than a million copies of sheet music sold. Other memorable songs in *Top Hat* were "Isn't it a Lovely Day?," sung by Astaire and danced to by him and recorded by Astaire and by Hildegarde; it had nine hearings on *Your Hit Parade*. "The Piccolino," used for an Astaire-Rogers dance number after she had sung it, was recorded by Astaire and by "Buddy" Rogers. "No Strings (I'm Fancy Free)," which had three hearings on *Your Hit Parade*, was introduced in the film by Astaire, who recorded it. "Top Hat, White Tie and Tails" was introduced and recorded by Astaire (and by the Boswell Sisters and by Louis Armstrong), and had nine representations on *Your Hit Parade*.

One year later another Astaire-Rogers song-and-dance musical, *Follow the Fleet* (1936), fea-

tured a Berlin score. It was a dramatically altered remake of a property that had served in 1927 as the basis for the Vincent Youmans Broadway musical, *Hit the Deck*. Berlin's best numbers were "Let's Face the Music and Dance," sung by Astaire and danced to by Astaire and Rogers; it had eight hearings on *Your Hit Parade*. "I'm Putting All My Eggs in One Basket," introduced by Astaire and Rogers, appeared nine times on *Your Hit Parade*. "Let Yourself Go," sung by Rogers, had 11 hearings on *Your Hit Parade*. Astaire recorded "Let's Face the Music and Dance" and "Let Yourself Go," as did Ray Nobles's orchestra, and Guy Lombardo and His Royal Canadians and the Boswell Sisters covered "I'm Putting All My Eggs in One Basket."

In *On the Avenue* (1937) Dick Powell introduced Berlin's "I've Got My Love To Keep Me Warm," heard six times on *Your Hit Parade* in 1937 and 11 times in 1949. It was recorded by Dick Powell, Mildred Bailey and Aileen Stanley and was interpolated into the film *The Way We Were* (1973), starring Barbra Streisand and Robert Redford. Alice Faye sang "This Year's Kisses" in *On the Avenue*; the song was performed eight times on *Your Hit Parade*, three times in first position. "Slumming on Park Avenue," introduced and recorded by Alice Faye, and "You're Laughing at Me," introduced by Dick Powell, each had a single representation on *Your Hit Parade* in January 1937.

Carefree (1938) was another vehicle for Astaire and Rogers. They introduced "Change Partners" and "The Yam," each recorded by Astaire with the former receiving nine hearings on *Your Hit Parade*.

Alexander's Ragtime Band (1938), starring Don Ameche, Ethel Merman, Alice Faye and Tyrone Power, was the first movie musical to assemble the hit songs of a single composer—in this case, 26 all-time Berlin favorites. One was a new number, "Now It Can Be Told," introduced by Ameche and reprised by Faye. Recorded by Bing Crosby, it had nine hearings on *Your Hit Parade*.

From *Second Fiddle* (1939), came Berlin's popular ballad "I Poured My Heart Into a Song." Tyrone Power introduced it and it was reprised by Rudy Vallee. Recorded by Jimmy Dorsey and by the orchestra of Artie Shaw (vocal by Helen Forrest), it had nine hearings on *Your Hit Parade*.

In 1938 Berlin went on a European holiday. Returning to America with a deep loathing of fascism and his patriotism intensified, Berlin was asked by Kate Smith for a patriotic song that she might perform on her popular radio show. Failing to come up with a melody that satisfied him, he revived one he had written for *Yip, Yip, Yaphank's* flag-waving finale but then discarded. With new lyrics, it became "God Bless America," which Kate Smith introduced on the CBS radio network on Armistice Eve, in November 1938. Reflecting the mood of the times, Smith's recording became a huge bestseller. "God Bless America" was sung at the presidential nominating conventions of both major parties in 1940. As the war in Europe raged on, the song was heard in theaters and other public places throughout the United States, and many Americans wanted "God Bless America" made the national anthem. Many other recordings followed Smith's, by Bing Crosby, Deanna Durbin, Margaret Whiting, Fred Waring's Pennsylvanians and Horace Heidt and his Musical Knights. On the screen, Deanna Durbin sang it in *Hers to Hold* (1943) and Kate Smith in *This Is the Army*. At the conclusion of the Oscar-winning film *The Deer Hunter* (1978), starring Robert De Niro, Meryl Streep and John Cazale, it was sung or chanted like a dirge by a group of friends from a small industrial town in western Pennsylvania, their lives having been irreparably altered by the American involvement in the Vietnam War.

Although Berlin discouraged those who wanted to replace "The Star-Spangled Banner" with "God Bless America," his song has become America's second national anthem. On February 18, 1955 President Eisenhower presented Berlin with a gold medal, authorized by Congress, largely because he had written "God Bless America." The song's royalties of several hundred thousand dollars were donated by Berlin, who refused to exploit his patriotism, to the Boy and Girl Scout associations and to the Campfire Girls.

After Pearl Harbor, Berlin's songwriting focused increasingly on the war effort. To promote the sale of war bonds he wrote "Any Bonds Today?" which was recorded by the Andrews Sisters, by Kay Kyser's orchestra and by Jimmy Dorsey's band (vocal by Helen O'Connell). "Arms for the Love of America," recorded by Kay Kyser, was for the U.S. Army, and "I Paid My Income Tax Today," recorded by Dick Robertson, for the Treasury Department. For the Red Cross, Berlin composed "Angels of Mercy," recorded by Fred Waring's Pennsylvanians and by Glen Miller. For the U. S. Navy he wrote "I Threw a Kiss in the Ocean," which Kate Smith recorded, as did the orchestras of Jimmy Dorsey, Benny Goodman and Horace Heidt. Earnings from these numbers were turned over to government agencies.

Meanwhile, on May 28, 1940, after a six-year absence, Berlin returned to the Broadway musical theater. *Louisana Purchase* (444 performances) had a book by Morrie Ryskind (based on a story by B. G. De Sylva) and starred William Gaxton and Victor Moore. Senator Oliver P. Logansberry is sent from Washington to New Orleans to investigate the corrupt Louisiana Purchase Company and its shady lawyer, Jim Taylor. The Senator is briefly silenced when Taylor contrives to use three seductive women to compromise Logansberry's honor. This scheme fails, and the Senator manages to prove his innocence and triumph over the slick crooks. Two new ballads were heard in this score. "Tomorrow is a Lovely Day" was introduced by Irene Bordoni and recorded by Bea Wain and Tommy Dorsey (vocal by Frank Sinatra). "You're Lonely and I'm Lonely" was a duet for Irene Bordoni and Victor Moore; it was recorded by Tommy Dorsey (vocal by Sinatra), Tony Martin and Mary Martin, and had two hearings on *Your Hit Parade*. When *Louisiana Purchase* was made into a movie in 1941 starring Bob Hope and Vera Zorina, "It's a Lovely Day Tomorrow" was heard on the soundtrack under the credits, while "You're Lonely and I'm Lonely" was retained as a principal song.

Berlin's greatest contribution to the war effort came with his next stage musical, *This Is the Army* (July 4, 1942). Like *Yip, Yip, Yaphank*, this was an all-soldier show, produced, directed and written by Berlin to raise money for the Army Emergency Relief. Making his temporary home once again in the barracks of Camp Upton, Berlin found firsthand material for his sketches and production numbers set in the mess hall, the PX, the canteen, the service club and the training field. *This Is the Army*, with a cast of 300, opened at Manhattan's Century Theatre on Independence Day for a four-week run that had to be extended to 12. This was followed by a national tour, and performances for troops in Europe, the Near East and the Pacific. In 1942 the score was released in an original cast album, and in 1943 the revue was filmed in Hollywood. *This Is the Army* earned more than ten million dollars for the Emergency Relief and another $350,000 for British relief agencies. For this achievement, Berlin was decorated with the Medal of Merit by General George C. Marshall. More than two decades later, in 1977, Berlin was awarded the Medal of Freedom by President Gerald R. Ford.

Berlin's score, consisting mostly of new material, had a rousing, humorous opening number in "This is the Army, Mr. Jones," sung by a male chorus. The ballad "I Left My Heart at the Stage Door Canteen," introduced by Karl Oxford and company, was popularized in recordings by the orchestras of Sammy Kaye and Charlie Spivak. It had a dozen hearings on *Your Hit Parade*. "I'm Getting Tired So I Can Sleep," introduced by Kenny Baker and recorded by Jimmy Dorsey's orchestra (vocal by Bob Eberle), was heard twice on *Your Hit Parade*. But it was an older Berlin song, a carry-over from World War I, that regularly stopped the show—"Oh, How I Hate to Get Up in the Morning" from *Yip, Yip, Yaphank*, delivered in New York by Berlin himself, dressed in Army regalia and singing in his small, piping voice.

In 1942, while *This Is the Army* was being prepared, Berlin's score for *Holiday Inn* could be heard on the screen. It starred Bing Crosby and Fred Astaire in a production in which each song represented a different holiday. "Easter Parade," sung by Astaire, was revived, and for the Christmas holidays Berlin composed a new ballad, "White Christmas," possibly his most popular song. It was introduced by Crosby and Marjorie Reynolds, and in 1942 it was recorded by Crosby and the orchestras of Gordon Jenkins and Charlie Spivak. It has since been recorded by Crosby (a second time), the Ames Brothers, Eddy Arnold, Vic Damone, Frank Sinatra (three times), Eddie Fisher and, in a violin transcription, by Jascha Heifetz. It has become in America a Yuletide classic, probably second only to "Silent Night, Holy Night" in seasonal repetitions. From 1942, when it was heard 15 times (ten in first position) on *Your Hit Parade*, to 1955, "White Christmas" was performed on that program every year. The song reached the popular top-ten charts in 1955 and the top-40 charts in 1962. When "White Christmas" celebrated its 20th birthday, 30 new recordings were released, including renditions by Pat Boone, Paul Anka, Steve Lawrence, Peggy Lee and Ella Fitzgerald. By 1982, almost 142 million recordings of "White Christmas" had been sold, with Bing Crosby's total alone in excess of 25 million. In 1954 the song provided the title for the movie starring Bing Crosby, Danny Kaye and Rosemary Clooney.

In *Holiday Inn* Berlin's new song for St. Valentine's Day was "Be Careful, It's My Heart," introduced by Crosby, who also recorded it in 1942, as did Kate Smith, Dinah Shore and Tommy Dorsey (vocal by Sinatra). The song made 15 appearances on *Your Hit Parade*. *Holiday Inn's* score was released in a soundtrack recording.

Berlin's first postwar Broadway production became his most spectacular theatrical success—*Annie Get Your Gun* (May 16, 1946), which had an initial run of 1,147 performances and has been revived many times. A movie adaptation starring Betty Hutton and Howard Keel was released in 1950.

Produced by Rodgers and Hammerstein, *Annie Get Your Gun* had been planned as a starring vehicle for Ethel Merman, with music by Jerome Kern and lyrics by Dorothy Fields. When Kern died suddenly in 1945, the producers persuaded Berlin to write the score. With book by Dorothy Fields and her brother, Herbert, *Annie Get Your Gun* is about Annie Oakley, the star of Buffalo Bill's Wild West Show, a brash backwoods girl who is handier with a rifle than with romance or book l'arnin'. When she falls in love with Frank Butler, the head of the rival Pawnee Bill show, she does not know how to win her man. In time, Frank succumbs to her charm, even though his preference had always been for petite, well-bred, docile women.

As Annie Oakley, Ethel Merman gave one of her most dynamic performances, and she was handsomely supported by Ray Middleton as Frank Butler. For them, Berlin fashioned a score remarkable for the range of styles and moods it encompassed and for the inventiveness of its melody and lyrics. Romance was spelled out in "They Say it's Wonderful," a ballad shared by Merman and Middleton, and recorded in 1946 by Merman and by Sinatra. Subsequently it was recorded by Sinatra (two more times), Bing Crosby and Perry Como. "They Say It's Wonderful" was heard 22 times on *Your Hit Parade* in 1946, four times in first position. Two comedy numbers were assigned to Ethel Merman: "You Can't Get a Man With a Gun," which she and Judy Garland recorded, and "Doin' What Comes Natur'lly," recorded by Merman, Dinah Shore, and the orchestras of Jimmy Dorsey and Freddy Martin. The latter song appeared 14 times on *Your Hit Parade*. Ethel Merman also introduced (and recorded) "I Got the Sun in the Morning," a number heard 12 times on *Your Hit Parade* after being recorded by the orchestras of Artie Shaw, Leo Reisman and Les Brown. Merman and Middleton shared "Anything You Can Do" as a duet; Bing Crosby recorded it with Dick Haymes and the Andrews Sisters. The sentimental waltz, "The Girl That I Marry," introduced by Middleton, was recorded three times by Sinatra, with other recordings made by Eddie Fisher and by Dick Haymes. "There's No Business Like Show Business," introduced by William O'Neal, Middleton, Marty Ray and Merman, has become the unofficial anthem of the American theater. A standard, it has been memorably recorded by Ethel Merman, Frank Sinatra, Mel Tormé, and the orchestra of Artie Shaw. In the 1954 movie of the same name, it was sung by Ethel Merman, Marilyn Monroe, Donald O'Connor, Johnny Ray and Mitzi Gaynor.

In the film version of *Annie Get Your Gun*,

"They Say it's Wonderful" was sung by Betty Hutton and Howard Keel; "You Can't Get a Man With a Gun," "Doin' What Comes Natur'lly" and "I Got the Sun in the Morning," by Betty Hutton; "Anything You Can Do," by Hutton and Keel; "The Girl That I Marry," by Keel; and "There's No Business Like Show Business," by Hutton, Keel, Keenan Wynn and Louis Calhern.

In 1957 *Annie Get Your Gun*, starring Mary Martin, toured the United States, a production also seen that year as a prime-time special on network television. In 1966, when *Annie Get Your Gun* was revived at New York City's Lincoln Center Berlin added a new song, "An Old-Fashioned Wedding," which was introduced by Ethel Merman and Bruce Yarnell. The music of *Annie Get Your Gun* was released in both an original cast and a soundtrack recording.

For Berlin's next musical, *Miss Liberty* (July 15, 1959), which had a run of 308 performances, Robert Sherwood, the dramatist and three-time winner of the Pulitzer Prize, wrote his first libretto. Set in New York and Paris in 1885, *Miss Liberty* described the efforts to raise money for the base of the Statue of Liberty, with subplots involving the rivalry between New York's two powerful newspapers, the *Herald* and the *World*, and the romance of a breezy newspaper reporter, Horace Miller, and Dominique, a Parisian girl he thinks was the model for the Statue of Liberty. In this score appeared an inspirational song, "Give Me Your Tired, Your Poor"; the music was Berlin's but the lyrics came from the words by Emma Lazarus inscribed on the base of the statue. It was sung by Allyn McLerie and the ensemble in the final scene, and was recorded by Fred Waring's Pennsylvanians and by Tony Martin. "Let's Take an Old-Fashioned Walk" was a number Berlin had written in 1940 for the movie *Easter Parade*, but it had been dropped from the production. It appeared in *Miss Liberty* as a duet for McLerie and Eddie Albert, was recorded by Frank Sinatra with Doris Day, and was represented on *Your Hit Parade* nine times. "Just One Way to Say I Love You," another duet for Albert and McLerie, was recorded by Al Jolson, Perry Como, Frank Sinatra and Patti Page, and received nine hearings on *Your Hit Parade*. "Paris Wakes Up and Smiles" was introduced by McLerie and Johnny Thompson and was recorded by Al Jolson and by Margaret Whiting. The entire score of *Miss Liberty* was recorded in an original cast album.

Call Me Madam (October 12, 1950), book by Russel Crouse and Howard Lindsay, was a starring vehicle for Ethel Merman, who portrayed Mrs. Sally Adams, the American ambassador to the little duchy of Lichtenburg. (The character was modeled after the true-to-life Perle Mesta, America's ambassador to Luxembourg and a noted Washington, D. C. hostess.) Sally Adams has her eye on Cosmo Hamilton, the Prime Minister of Lichtenburg. As this romance unfolds and comes to a happy resolution, the action moves swiftly from Washington to Lichtenburg and back, the plot complicated by domestic and international political intrigue.

The hit song from this score was the ballad, "You're Just in Love," whose chorus had two different melodies and two different sets of lyrics, first sung separately then contrapuntally by Ethel Merman and Russell Nype. It was recorded by Louis Armstrong with Velma Middleton, by Perry Como with the Fontaine Sisters, by Rosemary Clooney with Guy Mitchell and by Ethel Merman with Dick Hayman. "You're Just in Love" appeared 13 times on *Your Hit Parade*, three times in first position. "The Best Thing for You" was a duet for Merman and Paul Lukas. It was recorded by Merman, Perry Como, Bing Crosby and Eddie Fisher. "It's a Lovely Day Today" was shared by Russell Nype and Galina Talva and was recorded by Perry Como with the Fontaine Sisters. "They Like Ike" was a hymnlike homage to General Dwight D. Eisenhower, who used the song two years later to promote his presidential candidacy. This song was introduced by Pat Harrington, Ralph Chambers and Jay Velie.

Call Me Madam had a Broadway run of 644 performances, and was made into a movie in 1959, with Merman repeating her stage role. "You're Just in Love" was sung by Merman, George Sanders and Donald O'Connor, and "The Best Thing for You" by Merman, Sanders and O'Connor. When *Call Me Madam* was produced as a television special in the fall of 1968, the title of the Eisenhower song was changed to "We Still Like Ike." The score of *Call Me Madam* was released in an original cast album.

Mr. President (October 20, 1962; 265 performances) was Berlin's last score for Broadway. Here international diplomacy and Washington politics were combined with a behind-the-scenes glimpse at the life of an American president's family in the White House, romanticized by a love affair between the President's daughter, Leslie, and Pat Gregory, a former secret service man. Berlin's score, recorded in an original cast album, provided a duet for the young lovers in "Empty Pockets Filled With Love." This, too, was a contrapuntal number with two contrasting melodies and two different sets of lyrics sung separately, then together. "Meat and Potatoes" was a more conventional duet, for Jack Haskell and Stanley Grover, and "Is He the Only Man in the World?" was a duet for Nanette Fabray and

Anita Gillette. "This is a Great Country" made it possible for Robert Ryan, in the role of the president, to sing a hymn of praise to America.

After World War II, Berlin's involvement with movies continued to be a happy one, and the formula followed by Hollywood producers was the one established in 1938 with *Alexander's Ragtime Band*. In each instance the plot, usually a diverting story about show people, was little more than a frame for the performance of Berlin's hit songs (mostly older numbers, though some were written for the film score). Each of the four movies that appeared between 1946 and 1954 bore the title of a Berlin song. The new number in *Blue Skies* (1946) was "You Keep Coming Back Like a Song," which was introduced by Bing Crosby and had 11 hearings on *Your Hit Parade*. In addition to the many old Berlin favorites in *Easter Parade* (1948) were two significant new numbers. "A Couple of Swells" was introduced by Fred Astaire and Judy Garland. (Their routine was included in *That's Entertainment Part II* [1976], and Garland often featured the song in her personal appearances.) "It Only Happens When I Dance With You," introduced by Astaire and danced to by him and Ann Miller, was recorded by Frank Sinatra, Perry Como and Vic Damone.

In *White Christmas* (1954) the leading new songs were "The Best Things Happen While You're Dancing," sung by Danny Kaye (who recorded it) and chorus and danced to by Kaye and Vera-Ellen, and "Count Your Blessings Instead of Sheep," a ballad introduced by Bing Crosby, reprised by Crosby and Rosemary Clooney, and recorded by Crosby with Kaye and by Eddie Cantor and Eddie Fisher. Fisher's recording in 1954 took a Berlin song to the number five spot on the pop charts, and "Count Your Blessings" had 13 hearings on *Your Hit Parade*. The music from *Blue Skies, Easter Parade, White Christmas* and *There's No Business Like Show Business* was recorded in soundtrack albums.

Berlin's contribution to the nonmusical film, *Sayonara* (1957), starring Marlon Brando, was the title song, which he had composed four years earlier under the title "Sayonara, Sayonara." In the film the song was heard as a recurring theme in the background music and was sung under the opening titles. It was popularized by Eddie Fisher's bestselling recording.

By the late 1960s Berlin's creative years were behind him. In 1966 he wrote "An Old-Fashioned Girl," and two years later, when the *Ed Sullivan Show* honored Berlin on his 80th birthday, Berlin composed and introduced for the occasion "I Used to Play by Ear." In 1974 he

presented his old upright piano, on which so many of his songs had been written, as a gift to the Smithsonian, a gesture signifying the end of his songwriting career. He discouraged attempts to honor him on his 90th and 95th birthdays, either in the form of a national celebration or on a television special.

Except for his years as an apprentice, Berlin always wrote both the music and the lyrics for his songs. That he rose so high as composer with so little musical training—he can play the piano by ear only in the key of F-sharp major, and uses a piano with a special lever under the keyboard that transposes any music he plays to the desired key—has been much discussed. It is remarkable too that, despite just a few years of public schooling, his ability to express gracefully any sentiment in his lyrics make him one of America's most gifted lyricists as well. With Berlin, words and music flow together so seamlessly that it is as though they were conceived simultaneously. Yet, as he has explained "I usually get the phrase first—words. I keep repeating it over and over, and the first thing I know I begin to get a sort of rhythm, and then a tune. I don't say all my songs are written that way. Sometimes I hear the tune first, and then I start trying to fit words to it. In recent years, I've worked away from the piano. Often a phrase of a melody comes to me and I work it out mentally. My keyboard is in my mind."

Alec Wilder, in *American Popular Song*, wrote: "Berlin . . . has never deviated from his purpose of writing songs which stem from the music of the people, whether it be ragtime, swing music, country music, or the work of his contemporaries. . . . Anything . . . he liked he absorbed and recreated in his own uniquely singing fashion. . . . Let it be said that he is the best all-around, over-all songwriter America has ever had. . . . I can speak of only one composer as the master of the entire range of popular song—Irving Berlin."

Berlin owns an apartment at Gracie Square in New York City and a 50-acre farm in Livingston Manor, in New York's Catskill Mountains. As he got older, his main diversion was painting.

The most comprehensive anthology of Irving Berlin's recorded music was released in 1979 by the Book-of-the-Month Club. Entitled *There's No Business Like Show Business: The Magical Songs of Irving Berlin*, the album contained 52 songs arranged chronologically from 1911 to 1953. Most of the renditions were distinguished recordings which dated from the period when Berlin had composed them.

ABOUT: Ewen, D. The Story of Irving Berlin, 1950;

Freedland, M. Irving Berlin, 1976; Wilder, A. American Popular Song, 1972; Wilk, M. They're Playing Our Song, 1973.

BERNSTEIN, LEONARD (August 25, 1918–). The protean Leonard Bernstein has had a career virtually unparalleled in 20th-century music. He has distinguished himself as a composer of concert music and music for the popular musical theater. He has acquired international fame as a conductor and his stature as pianist, teacher, lecturer and author is imposing. This biography will focus on his accomplishments in the Broadway musical theater, with only passing reference to his other achievements.

Born in Lawrence, Massachusetts, he was the first of three children of Samuel Joseph and Jennie (Resnick) Bernstein. The father ran a thriving establishment providing supplies to beauty parlors and barber shops. He was a Hebraic scholar who subscribed to egalitarian values and had enlightened, tolerant attitudes towards other religions and cultured traditions which he transmitted to Leonard.

A sickly child, Leonard grew into boyhood unhappy and lonely, because his introverted personality and sense of inferiority stemming from his slight physical stature made it hard for him to make friends. The only music he heard at home was the Hebraic chants and Jewish folk songs his father sang, and some popular hit songs of the day on the family phonograph. Away from home, he heard little else but the music of religious services in the synagogue. Sometimes, while visiting friends or relatives, he would try to pick out tunes on the piano.

When he was 11, his aunt deposited an old, weather-beaten upright piano in the Bernstein household. "I made love to it right away," Bernstein recalled, and he began scouting the neighborhood for a piano teacher. His first two were unsatisfactory, but the third, Helen Coates, was the right teacher at the right time. In addition to giving him a strict technical training, she encouraged him to listen to concert music on the radio, to study musical scores borrowed from the library, and to try his hand at compositon. She remembers Bernstein as "frighteningly gifted. He could read, sing and memorize anything. He absorbed in one lesson an arrangement that took most of my pupils five or six lessons to learn."

Music helped him to become extroverted, transforming a frail and sickly child into a vigorous, athletic one. As he put it: "One day I was a scrawny little thing that anybody could beat up, and the next time I looked around I was the biggest boy in class. I could run faster, jump higher,

LEONARD BERNSTEIN

dive better than anybody." He now made friends easily, particularly among those who liked to hear him play jazz and popular tunes on the piano. He gained even more popularity in school as a soloist with the public school orchestra in Boston.

His academic education, begun in Boston grammar schools, was continued at the Boston Latin School, which he attended from his 11th to his 17th years as a brilliant student. He graduated in 1935 with honors, in the top ten percent of the class, and he composed the graduating class song.

From 1935 to 1939 Bernstein attended Harvard College, taking courses in harmony, counterpoint and music history with Walter Piston and Edward Burlingame Hill, among others. At Harvard his involvement with music was constant. He composed the scores for, helped produce, and acted in several college-day japes; played piano accompaniments for the school film club, much of it improvised; and performed contemporary music, including some of his own pieces, at meetings and concerts of the Harvard Music Club, of which he was a member. For the Harvard Classical Club production of Aristophane's *The Birds* in 1939, he both composed the accompanying music and served as conductor, his first effort with the baton. That year, at Harvard, he produced and played the piano accompaniments for Marc Blitzstein's *The Cradle Will Rock*.

Away from campus, he continued to study the piano with Heinrich Gebhard. Upon his graduation in June 1939 (cum laude in music) he went to New York. He played the piano for the Revuers, a Greenwich Village nightclub act made up of Adolph Green and Betty Comden (later famous as song lyricists and authors of musical comedy texts) and Judy Holliday (later star of stage and screen). This assignment paid him nothing. Not yet eligible to join the musicians' union, he was unable to find jobs in music that could support him.

He left New York in the fall of 1939 to enter the Curtis Institute of Music in Philadelphia, where he remained until June 1941, studying conducting with Fritz Reiner and piano with Isabelle Vengerova. The summers of 1940 and 1941 were spend at the Berkshire Music Center at Tanglewood where he started out as Serge Koussevitzky's pupil in conducting and became his assistant.

After leaving the Curtis Institute, Bernstein performed various musical chores in New York. He played the piano at concerts of modern music and arranged popular songs for a publisher. He was also composing concert music, most importantly his first symphony, *Jeremiah* (1942).

On August 25, 1943 he was named by Artur Rodzinski as the assistant conductor of the New York Philharmonic, an unprecedented development since he had never before conducted a professional orchestra. The following November 14, Bernstein made a spectacular debut as professional conductor as a last-minute replacement for Bruno Walter at a Sunday afternoon concert of the New York Philharmonic. His performance was reported on the front pages of *The New York Times* and the New York *Herald Tribune* and was commented on in several other newspapers. Thus began the career that brought him worldwide fame as a conductor of both orchestras and opera companies. In 1953 Bernstein became the first American-born conductor to perform in Milan's historic La Scala Opera House. From 1958 to 1969 he was the music director of the New York Philharmonic, the first native-born American to hold that post.

Not long after his conducting debut he realized his first success as composer of concert music when *Jeremiah Symphony* was introduced by the Pittsburgh Symphony, with Bernstein conducting, in 1944. It soon made the rounds of other major American orchestras, and received the New York Music Critics Circle Award as the year's best symphonic work. Bernstein continued writing major concert and operatic works, as well as ballet scores. These included two more symphonies, *Age of Anxiety* (1949) and *Kaddish* (1963); three ballets, *Fancy Free* (1944), *Facsimile* (1946) and *Dybbuk* (1976); the one-act operas *Trouble in Tahiti* (1950) and *A Quiet Place* (1983) which were later conflated into a single full-length opera; *Serenade,* for violin solo, strings and percussion (1954); *Chichester Psalms,* for chorus (1965); *Mass,* a theater piece for singers, players and dancers (1971); *Songfest,* a cycle of American poems for six singers and orchestra (1977); and *Halil,* a nocturne for solo flute, string orchestra and percussion.

Bernstein's first score for Broadway was *On the Town* (December 28, 1944). This musical, with book and lyrics by Betty Comden and Adolph Green (who were also seen in the cast) was a spinoff of Bernstein's first ballet, *Fancy Free,* whose subject was three American sailors on leave and on the prowl for "girls." *Fancy Free*'s choreographer had been Jerome Robbins (in his first such assignment) and he filled a similar role in *On the Town.* Enlarging on the ballet's scenario, Comden and Green developed a story line in which three sailors, on 24-hour shore leave in Manhattan, go "on the town." One of them comes upon a photograph of Miss Turnstiles in the subway and resolves to find her. The three sailors embark on this expedition, the trail leading them from Times Square to Coney Island. They finally encounter her in a Carnegie Hall studio taking vocal lessons. During the search, the second sailor becomes enamored of a lady taxi driver while the third falls for an anthropology student. Under George Abbott's briskly paced direction, the musical proved to be high-voltage entertainment. Bernstein's songs evoked a range of feeling from the sentimental to the lighthearted. The score, recorded in an original cast album, opened with a paean to the metropolis, "New York, New York," introduced by the three sailors (performed by John Battles, Adolph Green and Chris Alexander). (This song is not to be confused with a standard by John Kander and Fred Ebb, first heard as the title number of the movie *New York, New York.*) The principal ballads were "Lucky to Be Me" and "Lonely Town," each introduced by Battles. "I Can Cook, Too" and "I Get Carried Away" were satirical, the former introduced by Betty Comden and Adolph Green, the latter by Nancy Walker. Horace Heidt and his orchestra recorded "Lucky to Be Me."

With an initial run of 463 performances, *On the Town* was a box-office success. With the Page One Award from the Newspaper Guild, it was recognized as the season's best musical. In 1949 this musical starred Frank Sinatra and Gene Kelly in a movie adaptation that had all of the stage production's zest and energy. In this film most of Bernstein's score was dropped in favor of songs by others. But "New York, New York" was retained, sung by Sinatra, Kelly and Jules Munshin. A decade later, *On the Town* received two revivals on Off Broadway, and in 1973 it returned briefly to Broadway.

Before returning to musical comedy, Bernstein composed four songs and two choruses (to his own lyrics) as incidental music for Sir James M. Barrie's *Peter Pan* (April 25, 1950). Bernstein's second musical was *Wonderful Town* (February 23, 1953), based on stories by Ruth McKenney of two young females who come from Ohio to New York to make their fortunes, one as a writer (Ruth), the other an actress (Eileen). These stories had previously been used for the Broadway play *My Sister Eileen* (1940), in an adaptation by Joseph Fields and Jerome Chodorov, and in a 1942 motion picture with that same title. However familiar the characters and story had now become, *Wonderful Town* was a consistently energetic and at times hilarious musical comedy libretto, the work once again of Fields and Chodorov. In the musical, as in earlier versions, Eileen and Ruth make their home in a basement apartment in Greenwich Village. There they mingle with a farrago of eccentrics, among them a landlord whose hobby is abstract painting, and members of the Brazilian navy on leave. The girls are beset by minor annoyances and major mishaps, not the least of which are the blasting for a new subway line under their apartment, nocturnal interruptions by men seeking favors from a courtesan who had been the previous occupant of their apartment, and Eileen's incarceration for causing a riot. But the two young women survive, and realize their ambitions. Bernstein's resilient score (to the agile lyrics of Comden and Green) included a haunting ballad, "A Quiet Girl," introduced by George Gaynes. But the song from his score that grew popular outside the theater in 1953 was "O-H-I-O," a duet shared by Rosalind Russell and Edith Adams. It had originally been intended as a takeoff of nostalgic songs about home and hometowns, but acquired popularity as a sentimental ballad. "My Darlin' Eileen," introduced by Edith Adams, Delbert Anderson and a male chorus, is a parody of Irish balladry, and "One Hundred Easy" is a catalogue of the ways a woman is sure to lose her man, introduced by Rosalind Russell.

The Broadway run of *Wonderful Town* exceeded that of *On the Town* by 100 performances. It also outdistanced the earlier musical in gathering awards, capturing the Drama Critics Circle and the Donaldson awards and a Tony as the season's best musical. Other Tony awards came for Bernstein's score and Robbins's choreography, and other Donaldson awards for the score, the book, and the lyrics. A national company toured the country; the songs were recorded in an original cast album; and the production came to television as a CBS special in 1959. It was revived in New York in 1957, 1962 and 1963. In each instance critics agreed that both story and music had dated hardly at all. When *Wonderful Town* was made into a motion picture musical bearing the title of *My Sister Eileen* (1955), the Bernstein score was replaced by one by Jule Styne.

In 1954 Bernstein won an award from *Downbeat,* the influential jazz magazine, for his only original score for motion pictures, the background music for *On the Waterfront* (1954), starring Marlon Brando. Bernstein adapted this score into *Symphonic Suite from On the Waterfront* (1955), whose world premiere he conducted in 1955 at the Berkshire Music Festival, Tanglewood.

When first produced, Bernstein's third Broadway musical, *Candide* (December 1, 1954), was praised by the critics but a box-office failure (73 performances). Voltaire's satirical tale was adapted for the musical stage by Lillian Hellman with lyrics mainly by Richard Wilbur. In this musical, as in Voltaire, the resourceful Candide is disenchanted to discover from his misadventures that all is not the best in this best of all possible worlds. Aged, weary and wizened, he decides to settle down and cultivate his own garden. Meeting the demands of a text that covered many locales, some of them exotic, Bernstein's score encompassed a wide range of styles, from a gavotte, a mazurka and a tango to music hall tunes, popular American song styles and jazz idioms. "None of his previous theater music has had the joyous variety, humor and richness of this score," reported Brooks Atkinson in *The New York Times.* The opera-buffa-like overture has become a repertory number at "pop" concerts and can often be heard on symphony programs as well. Most of the songs are so inextricably tied up to the text that, by themselves, they lack popular appeal. Two are exceptions: the aria "Glitter and Be Gay" (lyrics by Richard Wilbur), introduced by Barbara Cook, and the ballad "Eldorado" (lyrics by Lillian Hellman), introduced by Robert Rounseville. Though *Candide* was not successful, its original cast recording became a collector's item.

Following a brief stay on Broadway, *Candide* embarked on a national tour and, in 1971, was revived on Broadway. In 1973–74 it reappeared in a new version, first in Brooklyn, then on Broadway, with a new book by Hugh Wheeler still loosely based on Voltaire, additional lyrics by Stephen Sondheim, and imaginative staging by Harold Prince. It now finally achieved its deserved critical acclaim and box-office returns (741 performances). In 1977 *Candide* entered the opera house with a production by the Minnesota Opera and, in 1982, with another revised version, it was produced by the New York City

Opera and billed as "the world premiere of the operatic version."

Less than a year after *Candide*'s Broadway debut, Bernstein was the musical participant in a theatrical event of the first rank, the opening night of *West Side Story* on September 26, 1956. The show's basic idea was conceived by Jerome Robbins, who was also responsible for the choreography. Arthur Laurents wrote the text and Stephen Sondheim, in his first contribution to the American musical theater, the lyrics. The text carries the story of Shakespeare's *Romeo and Juliet* to 1950s New York, where two teenage gangs are bitter rivals—the Puerto Ricans and the white street kids. In the main plot, Maria, a Puerto Rican girl and sister of a gang leader, and Tony, a member of the rival white gang, are in love. As in the Shakespeare tragedy, the lovers are doomed by the hatred of opposing clans.

Rarely before in the American musical theater was a social problem—juvenile delinquency in this instance—depicted with such realism. Brooks Atkinson in *The New York Times* called *West Side Story* "a major achievement . . . a profoundly moving show . . . that is pathetic, tender and forgiving." To another critic, this musical moved "with the speed of a switchblade knife-thrust." Ballet here became an integral part of the overall context, sometimes commenting on the dramatic action, sometimes advancing it. As the dance critic John Martin noted, the theatrical substance of *West Side Story* was realized "not in the talked plot but in moving bodies. . . . The cast acts and reacts in terms of movement, and that is the most direct medium that exists for the conveying of inner states of feeling."

The tension, the conflicts, even the sardonic overtones of the text are caught and fixed in Bernstein's songs and dynamic ballet music. "Tonight," the ballad in which Maria and Tony pledge eternal love on a tenement fire escape, was introduced by Carol Lawrence and Larry Kert. "Maria," introduced by Larry Kert, became a bestseller in a recording by Johnny Mathis; it was subsequently also recorded by the eminint opera tenor, Placido Domingo. "I Feel Pretty," introduced by Carol Lawrence, and "Somewhere," sung offstage by Reri Grist for a ballet sequence, are two more memorable songs; the latter was later revived by Barbra Streisand in a recording. The music for the dance episodes was developed by Bernstein into *Symphonic Dances from West Side Story* (1960), its premiere taking place in 1961 in a performance by the New York Philharmonic with Lukas Foss conducting.

Following its inital run of 734 performances at the Winter Garden, *West Side Story* toured the United States before returning to Broadway on April 27, 1960 for an additional run of 249 performances. It has often been revived since then, most significantly at New York's Lincoln Center in 1968 and on Broadway in 1980. In 1961 the movie adaptation, starring Natalie Wood and Richard Beymer, proved a cinematic tour de force, acknowledged by Hollywood when the film won ten Oscars, including the one for the year's best motion picture. In the film, "Tonight" and "I Feel Pretty" were sung on the soundtrack by Marni Nixon dubbing for Wood. The soundtrack recording, the recipient of a Grammy, was on the top-ten charts for nearly two years and by 1970 five million albums had been sold, supplementing the previous sale of more than two million copies of the Broadway original cast recording, which had stayed on the charts for 186 weeks. Still another bestselling album of the complete score was released by Deutsche Grammophon in 1985. The cast included stars from the world of opera (Kiri Te Kanawa, José Carreras, Tatiana Troyanos, Marilyn Horne), and Leonard Bernstein conducted.

To commemorate the American bicentennial, Bernstein composed the music for *1600 Pennsylvania Avenue,* for which Alan Jay Lerner provided both the text and the music. En route to Broadway, *1600 Pennsylvania Avenue* encountered production difficulties which required heavy rewriting and doctoring. It limped to Broadway on May 4, 1976, collapsing after seven performances. Bernstein salvaged some of the material from his score for an orchestral compositon, *Slava!,* written to honor the world-famous cellist-conductor, Mstislav Rostropovich, which was premiered by the National Symphony Orchestra of Washington, D. C., Rostropovich conducting, in 1977. One of the songs from the stage score, "Take Care of This House," was sung at the inaugural concert for President Carter at the Kennedy Center on January 19, 1977.

Bernstein's career in popular music and his near-iconic status in American culture have been enhanced by his television lecture-concerts. These include discussions of "The World of Jazz" on October 16, 1955, and "The American Musical Comedy" on March 16, 1957, both on the Omnibus program and the latter the recipient of an Emmy. His "Jazz in Serious Music" was aired on November 30, 1958 on the Lincoln Center President's program. These three scripts were reprinted in Bernstein's first book, *The Joy of Music* (1959). His other books are: *Leonard Bernstein's Young People's Concerts for Reading and Listening* (1962), *The Infinite Variety of Music* (1966) and *Findings* (1982).

On September 9, 1951 Bernstein married Felicia Montealgre Cohn, a native of Costa Rica who had come to the United States to pursue a career in the theater. They raised three children while occupying a 16-room complex on the top two floors of a Park Avenue residence and a summer house in Fairfield, Connecticut. Felicia Bernstein died in East Hampton, New York, in 1978. In her memory Bernstein established scholarships at Columbia University, New York University and the Juilliard School.

Many and varied are the honors accorded Bernstein for his contributions to music. In America these included 15 honorary degrees awarded in the years 1957–76, nine Grammy awards, eleven Emmys, the Albert Einstein Commemorative Award, the International Education Award (presented by President Nixon), the Kennedy Center Honors and in 1985 the National Academy and Recording Arts and Sciences Lifetime Achievement Award. Festivals of Bernstein's music, which included his stage music, were heard in Israel and Austria in 1977, the University of Massachusetts at Amherst in 1978, and in Kansas City, Missouri, in 1979.

ABOUT: Bernstein, B. Family Matters, 1982; Briggs, J. Leonard Bernstein: The Man, His Work and His World, 1961; Ewen, D. Leonard Bernstein, 2d. ed. 1967; Gottlieb, J. (ed.) Leonard Bernstein: A Complete Catalogue of His Works, 1978; Bernstein on Broadway, 1981; Gruen, J. and Heyman, K. The Private World of Leonard Bernstein, 1968. *Periodicals*—New York Times Magazine December 19, 1979; New Yorker January 11, 1959, January 18, 1959.

BERRY, CHUCK (January 15, 1926–   ). Composer-lyricist Chuck Berry was a pioneer of the rock movement, sometimes described as the "song laureate" of the decade of the 1950s. The sound Berry developed has been widely imitated; indeed it was a source for the rejuvenation of rock music in the mid-1960s. In *Rock Encyclopedia* Lillian Roxon spoke of Berry as "maybe the single most important name in the history of rock. . . . there is not a rock musician working today [the late 1960s] who has not consciously or unconsciously borrowed from his sound, the sound that was to become the definitive sound of '50s rock."

He was born Charles Edward Anderson Berry in San Jose, California, the son of a carpenter who provided his family of six children (three girls and three boys) with the basic comforts of middle-class life. In Chuck's infancy the family moved to Missouri, finally settling in a comfortable house in a well-groomed area.

CHUCK BERRY

Berry received his initial music instruction from a fellow chorister of St. Louis's Antioch Baptist Church. His formative musical influences were gospel (which he performed with a gospel quartet), country music, and the ballads of Nat King Cole and Frank Sinatra. He began piano study when he was eight, and at 13, while attending the Simmons Grammar School, acquired a guitar which he learned to play without instruction. At Sumner High School he was encouraged by his music teacher, Julia Davis.

Despite the support he seems to have been given at home and at school, Berry took part in an amateurish robbery attempt in 1944, was caught, tried, and sentenced to three years in a reformatory. After that he worked on an assembly line at the General Motors Fisher Body plant and, having completed the study of cosmetology at night at the Poro School of Beauty Culture, as a hairdresser.

By the early 1950s, Berry was married and the father of two children. To supplement his income he did some gigs as a guitarist and, in 1952, formed a trio with pianist Johnny Johnson and drummer Ebby Harding, playing weekend engagements at a popular black club, the Cosmopolitan in East St. Louis. In music, Chuck discovered Louis Jordan, master of the blues, whose comedic routines also made a great impression on Berry, who was now beginning to write songs that combined country music and pop balladry with the idiom of rhythm and blues. The humor in these songs also showed the influence of Jordan, and their irreverent, have-a-good-time message was an expression of Berry's own puckish nature.

In 1955 Berry visited Chicago to find a market for his songs. There he met Muddy Waters, the legendary urban blues singer, at whose performances Chuck sat in on the guitar. Impressed with Berry's guitar playing, Waters arranged an audition with Leonard Chess, president of Chess Records, for whom Berry performed such original songs as "Ida Red," a satirical takeoff on country songs, and "Wee Wee Hours," a blues. Berry's own preference was "Wee Wee Hours" but Chess liked "Ida Red" and decided to promote it as a single with "Wee Wee Hours" the flip side. A strong rhythm-and-blues beat was added and the title "Ida Red" was changed to "Maybelline." Berry's recording, with Johnny Johnson on piano, was released by Chess in 1955 to become one of the first giant hits of the rock era.

Having signed a contract with Chess that brought him $400 in cash, Berry returned to St. Louis and quit the hairdressing business to devote himself entirely to music. "Maybelline," heavily plugged by Alan Freed, the influential disc jockey, on his New York radio show, reached number one on *Billboard*'s rhythm and blues chart. Shortly thereafter it shot to number one in the country-and-western ratings and number five in pop.

When "Maybelline" was published, two disc jockeys, Russ Fratto and Alan Freed, were credited as coauthors, although neither contributed significantly to its writing. Describing how these two came to receive royalties from his hit, Berry told one interviewer that "Alan Freed grabbed a third. Actually there were two grabbers. Russ Fratto . . . was on it, too. I got it back from Fratto but I didn't get it from Freed. It went to his estate—and they still get a third. Freed actually didn't sit down with me at all or write anything." The consensus in the music industry is that the authorship ascribed to Fratto and Freed was compensation for their radio promotion of the song. After "Maybelline" all music and lyrics for his songs were attributed to Berry alone.

According to Robert Christgau in his *Newsday* article, Berry's innovation lay in his adaptation of "country guitar lines [to] blues-style picking. . . . Berry's limited but brilliant vocabulary of guitar riffs was quickly recognized as the epitome of rock and roll." In his lyrics Berry tapped the experiences of teenagers who, in the 1950s, were beginning to dominate the record-buying market. In his paeans to adolescence, Berry spoke of teen crushes, dancing at DJ hops, autograph hunters, juke boxes and soda fountains, parties, the hassles at school and work, frustrated love and sex. Developing his subjects with a wry wit rarely encountered in rock, and

producing one hit song after another, Berry set the rock revolution into motion. In 1956 came "Roll Over, Beethoven," a clever sneer at snobbish high culture, as well as "No Money Down," "Brown-Eyed Handsome Man" and "Too Much Monkey Business." The next year saw the appearance of "School Day," "Oh Baby Doll," and "Rock and Roll Music," the last being the number that helped to popularize the term "rock 'n' roll." In 1958 he wrote and recorded the semiautobiographical "Johnny B. Goode," about a country boy who becomes a rock star, and "Sweet Little Sixteen" and "Carol." In 1959 his hits included "Almost Grown" and the much-covered "Memphis, Tennessee." Almost all of these, in Berry's own recordings for Chess, sold in the vicinity of one million copies.

The iconography of the American popular culture of the 1950s, or at least that part which was consumed by teenagers, is enshrined in Berry's lyrics. His musical narratives were also the first to espouse a rock 'n' roll myth which would be powerfully restated two decades later in the songs of Bruce Springsteen—that rock music can be a form of personal salvation.

"Chuck Berry epitomizes the folk artist of the rock idiom," Carl Belz wrote in *The Story of Rock*. "His style did not change because it did not have to; from the beginning, it unconsciously expressed the responses of the artist and his audience to the ordinary realities of their world. . . . The keynote of Chuck Berry's style is its open endorsement of happiness, fun, and good times. . . . The frankness, honesty and naivete of Chuck Berry's songs give them a continuing significance. . . . Its meaning is in the spontaneous, vital pleasure of creating music."

The success of "Maybelline" had launched Chuck Berry's career as a public performer. On his first tour, in 1956, he made 101 appearances in as many evenings. At the Paramount Theatre in New York City he unveiled the "duck walk"—a sitting walk or waddle with knees bent that he executed while playing the guitar. (To an interviewer Chuck insisted that he devised the walk spontaneously one evening to detract attention from his shabby attire.) The audience howled its approval, and the duck walk became a trademark of Berry's stage act. In 1958 Berry made the first of many appearances on Dick Clark's *American Bandstand* television show. He was also featured in numerous movies of the early rock era, including *Rock, Rock, Rock* (1956), in which Alan Freed appeared with other rock notables; *Mr. Rock and Roll* (1957); and *Jazz on a Summer's Day* (1959), a documentary filmed at the Newport Jazz Festival of 1958. In 1973 he would appear in *Let the Good Times Roll,* a documentary of his tour with other 1950s rock stars in a series of concerts called "Rock and Roll Revival." In 1978 he made a cameo appearance in *American Hot Wax*, loosely based on the career of Alan Freed.

From his public and screen appearances and the mounting sales of his singles and albums (the first two albums being *After School Sessions* and *One Dozen Berrys*, both released in October 1958), Berry became a millionaire. He acquired a mansion in St. Louis and a thriving entertainment emporium called Chuck Berry's Club Bandstand. The rising generation of rock stars in the closing years of the 1950s regarded him as the innovator who paved the way for them, and they recorded his compositions.

Then Berry's world collapsed around him. In 1959 he fired an Apache Indian hatcheck girl who had been working in his nightclub. In retaliation, she alleged that, when she was 14, Berry had discovered her in New Mexico and then had taken her to St. Louis as his mistress. Berry was charged with having violated the Mann Act, which forbids the transportation of minors across state lines for immoral purposes. The two trials that followed lasted two years. Though it was established that the girl had been a prostitute and had traveled with Berry of her own free will, he was found guilty. In February 1962 he was committed to the Federal Penitentiary in Terre Haute for two years.

Berry left prison in 1964 a bitter man. His family had deserted him; Club Bandstand had closed down; his income was sharply reduced, for he had written no new songs, made no fresh recordings, and had not been able to tour. But he was not forgotten. It was publicized that Elvis Presley had been influenced not only by Berry's songs but by his performing style as well. The so-called British rock invasion initiated by the Beatles in 1964 consisted largely of music inspired by the 1950s sounds of Berry, Presley, Buddy Holly, and Little Richard. None of the songs of these rock artists was covered more often than Berry's. The Beatles revived "Roll Over, Beethoven" in 1964 and "Rock and Roll Music" the following year, with George Harrison becoming something more than a glorified rhythm guitarist by copying almost note for note Berry's riffs. The Rolling Stones regarded Berry as their patron saint. They revived "Carol" and "Around and Around"; their quintessential hard-rock guitarist, Keith Richards, patterned his style closely after Berry's. In 1963 the Beach Boys achieved stardom with "Surfin' U. S. A.," whose melody was Berry's "Sweet Little Sixteen" joined to new lyrics by Brian Wilson. Between 1963 and 1964 Lonnie Mack and Johnny Rivers each released

hit recordings of "Memphis"; Mack's was an instrumental version. The country star, Buck Owens, had a mid-1960s success with "Johnny B. Goode." In the early 1970s the Rolling Stones popularized Berry's "Little Queenie" (composed about 1958). Later that decade Linda Ronstadt had a top-ten hit with her cover of "Back in the U. S. A.," a Berry song from about 1961 to which the Beatles paid homage in 1968 with "Back in the U. S. S. R.," composed by Lennon and McCartney. In 1985 Bruce Springsteen made "Bye Bye Johnnie" (1960) the B side of his hit single, "I'm on Fire."

Released in 1964, Berry's *Greatest Hits* was able to do well on the charts. Before that year was over he had written and recorded two classics, "Nadine" and "No Particular Place to Go," as well as "You Never Can Tell." In 1965 he wrote "Reelin' and Rockin'," which later became a bestseller for the Dave Clark Five. Additionally, Berry's return to the stage in the United States and in a successful tour of Europe proved his audience had not deserted him. His London concert was released as a live album in May 1965. In the late 1960s he settled in Wentzville, Missouri, where he opened Berry Park, an amusement park and country club complex. For about five years he recorded with Mercury Records but by 1970 he was back with Chess.

In the years 1965–70 Berry wrote no songs of consequence. His greatest record success since the late 1950s came in 1972 with a risqué song he had composed two decades earlier. Originally called "My Ding-a-Ling," it had been recorded by Dave Bartholomew in 1954. Mercury refused to allow Berry to record the song until he changed its title to "My Tambourine," which he did in 1968. But reissued in 1972 as "My Ding-a-Ling," with the sing-along chorus of "Won't you play with my ding-a-ling," it became a gold record, selling more than two million copies worldwide.

Berry has continued to be a scintillating stage performer into the 1980s. After he appeared in a New York nightclub in 1983, a reviewer for *Variety* called him "the true sovereign of rock music. . . . Berry is still a consummate crowd-pleasing trooper [whose performance] summed up the essence of old-time rock 'n' roll."

In 1976, Berry received the National Music Award from the American Music Conference and in 1980 BMI awarded him four Special Commendations for his achievements in rhythm and blues, rock 'n' roll, country, and pop. This was the first time four commendations in as many categories had been bestowed on one person. In 1984, at ceremonies attending the Grammy awards, the National Academy of Recording

Arts and Sciences presented him with its Life-time Achievement Award. Meanwhile, in 1982, Chess Records released the first six albums planned as a comprehensive anthology of classic urban blues songs. That first volume was devoted entirely to Chuck Berry's best songs. In the 1970s Chess had also released Berry's *Golden Decade, Golden Decade Volume 2* and *Golden Decade Volume 3.*

ABOUT: De Witt, H. B. Chuck Berry: Rock and Roll Music, 1978; Jahn, M. The Story of Rock from Elvis Presley to the Rolling Stones, 1973; Roxon, L. Rock Encyclopedia, 1971; Stambler, I. Encyclopedia of Pop, Rock and Soul, 1974; Tobler, J. Guitar Heroes, 1978; Yorke, R. The History of Rock 'n' Roll, 1976. *Periodicals*—Newsday October 22, 1971; New York Post June 10, 1969; Washington Post September 17, 1970.

EUBIE BLAKE

BLAKE, EUBIE (February 7, 1883–February 12, 1983) and **SISSLE, NOBLE** (July 10, 1889–December 18, 1975). In the course of his 100 years, the legendary composer Eubie Blake became one of America's most beloved entertainers. Starting out as a pianist in a bordello, he became a leading exponent of ragtime, and with the lyricist Noble Sissle he wrote the music and starred in *Shuffle Along*, the first successful all-black production on Broadway to appeal to white audiences.

The son of former slaves, Eubie Blake was born James Hubert Blake in Baltimore, Maryland in 1883. He was the only one of the family's 11 children to survive infancy. His father, John Summer Blake, a Civil War veteran, was a stevedore; his mother, the devoutly religious Emily (Johnson) Blake, was a domestic. Eubie's interest in music was revealed when, age six, he clambered up to an organ in a department store and begain picking out tunes. For six years, he took piano lessons from a neighbor, Margaret Marshall, a church organist. Further music instruction came from Llewellyn Wilson, the conductor of the Baltimore Colored Orchestra. By the time he was 12 Blake had joined a vocal quartet that performed popular tunes outside of saloons. He was already a devotee of ragtime, which, proscribed at home by his fundamentalist mother, he performed whenever he could on an organ at school.

A fight over a girl led to Blake's expulsion from the eighth grade, permanantly ending his formal education. At the age of 15 he found work as a pianist in a Baltimore bordello which paid him a salary of three dollars a week for seven nights of work but earned him nightly tips of about ten dollars. When his mother discovered where he was working, she insisted that her husband make him quit. However, when the practical father, who earned nine dollars a week, was apprised of his son's sizable weekly income, he allowed Eubie to continue with his job. While working there for the next three years, Blake composed his first song "Charleston Rag" (1889), a piano piece. Because Blake could not read or write music, the song was not transcribed until many years later and remained unpublished until 1919, when it was brought out by M. Witmark & Sons.

Blake's career in show business began on July 4, 1901 in Fairfield, Pennsylvania, when he was hired to play the melodeon (a small reed organ) for Dr. Frazier's Medicine Show. A year later, Blake joined a traveling minstrel show, *In Old Kentucky*, doing a buck and wing dance. *In Old Kentucky* took Blake to New York City for the first time. By 1903 he was back in Baltimore, where for the next four years he played the piano in a saloon, a brothel, and other night spots frequented by the local demimonde. From 1907 to 1910 he held a regular and comparatively well-paying job at Baltimore's newly opened Goldfield Hotel, which was owned by Joe Gans, the lightweight boxing champion of the world. During the summers, Blake worked as a pianist in such Atlantic City hotels as the Belmont, the Boathouse and Kelly's.

In July 1910, in Baltimore, Blake married Avis Lee, a classical pianist. They had no children.

In 1914 Blake's first publications appeared, "Chevy Chase" and "Fizz Water," piano pieces issued by Joseph W. Stern & Company. A turning point in Blake's career came in 1915 when

NOBLE SISSLE

he was hired as the pianist for Joe Porter's Serenaders at River View Park in Baltimore. The band's vocalist was Noble Sissle, who became Blake's lyricist.

Noble Lee Sissle was born in Indianapolis, Indiana in 1889, the first son of George A. Sissle, a minister, and Martha Angeline Sissle, a schoolteacher. Noble became interested in music through listening to his father play hymns on the organ. "My father hoped I would go into the ministry," he recalled. "In fact, my first public appearance was as a minister in a Tom Thumb wedding [when I was five years old]." However, Sissle's ambition was to become a singer. As a boy, he sang in the choir of his father's church and in the assembly of the public school he attended.

In 1906 the Sissle family moved to Cleveland, where Noble attended Central High School. He played on the football and baseball teams and sang in the school's glee club, of which he later became the director. In 1908, while still in school, he got his first professional singing job, performing hymns and spirituals with the Edward Quartette, which toured the Midwest on the Chautauqua evangelical concert circuit. After graduating from Central High in 1910, he continued to work as a singer, traveling as far west as Denver and as far east as New York City. He enrolled in De Pauw University in Greenville, Indiana in 1913, but, preferring to sing in movie houses and with dance orchestras, he dropped out after one semester. When such random engagements as these were unavailable, he supported himself by working menial jobs. While working as a waiter at the Severin Hotel

in Indianapolis early in 1915, Sissle was hired by the hotel's manager to organize a 12-piece band. Later that spring, he was taken on as the vocalist for Joe Porter's Serenaders in Baltimore, where he met Eubie Blake.

The first song on which Blake and Sissle collaborated—Blake's first composition that was not a piano instrumental—was "It's All Your Fault," written in 1915 with the assistance of Eddie Nelson. Sophie Tucker introduced it in her vaudeville act at the Maryland Theatre in Baltimore the week the song was written. Also in 1915, and again with Eddie Nelson's help, Blake and Sissle composed "See America First," which was followed by "At the Pullman Porter's Ball," for which they received no assistance from Nelson. Lou Clayton introduced "America First" in 1916 in vaudeville.

Between 1915 and 1916, Blake and Sissle worked independently of one another in various bands in Baltimore, Palm Beach and New York City. In the spring of 1916, Sissle joined Jim Europe's famous Society Orchestra, the first all-black band to play often at exclusive society parties, and he persuaded Europe to hire Blake. Temporarily reunited, Blake and Sissle composed "Good Night, Sweet Angeline" (written with James Reese "Jim" Europe) and "Mammy's Little Choc'late Cullud Chile," both in 1916 and both recorded by Sissle and Blake. In the summer of 1916, Sissle and Blake worked as a two-man singer-pianist team, performing at weddings, parties and other social events.

Sissle and Blake were again separated during World War I, when Sissle and Jim Europe enlisted in the Army. Sissle and Europe organized a regimental band at Camp Wadsworth, South Carolina, with Sissle as drum major. While serving with the American Expeditionary Forces and holding the rank of lieutenant Sissle wrote the lyrics for several Blake-composed war songs: "To Hell With Germany," "What a Great Day" and "On Patrol in No Man's Land." All became hits in France through performances by Europe's regimental jazz band.

After the Armistice was signed, Jim Europe and his 369th U.S. Infantry Jazz Band toured America. As the vocalist, Sissle was billed as "the greatest singer of his race." On May 9, 1919 at Mechanics Hall in Boston, Jim Europe was murdered by the band's drummer. Europe's agents then asked Sissle and Blake to complete the Jazz Band's bookings by touring the Keith vaudeville circuit as a two-man singing act. Backed by a small jazz combo, "The Dixie Duo," as Sissle and Blake were called, opened in Bridgeport, Connecticut and went on to the Harlem Opera House in New York before appearing at the Palace Theatre. Thus were they able to introduce to America older songs like "Good Night, Angeline"; "Mammy's Little Choc'late Cullud Chile"; "What a Great Day"; "To Hell With Germany" and "On Patrol in No Man's Land." Between 1919 and 1920, they wrote and introduced "Gee! I'm Glad That I'm From Dixie"; "Ain'tcha Comin' Back, Mary Ann, to Maryland"; "He's Always Hanging Around"; "Gee, I Wish I had Someone to Rock Me in the Cradle of Love"; "You've Been a Good Little Mammy to Me"; "Pickaninny Shoes" and "Good Fellow Blues." "Gee, I Wish I Had Someone to Rock Me," "Ain'tcha Comin' Back" and "Pickaninny Shoes" were also recorded by Sissle and Blake.

For their act, they appeared in formal evening dress as they had with the Society Orchestra, rejecting the outlandish costumes and makeup hitherto required of black performers. Robert Kimball and William Bolcom described their act in *Reminiscing with Sissle and Blake*: "Sissle and Blake entered the stage from the opposite sides, while the band played their opener, 'Gee, I'm Glad that I'm from Dixie.' The piano bench would be set at right angles to the piano. Blake on the piano end, Sissle on the singing end, but neither stayed in place very long at a time—the two managed to turn the piano into a trench, a dance floor, whatever would fit the needs of the number. There would be close harmony in 'Good Night, Angeline,' then a pin spot on Noble for 'Pickaninny Shoes.' . . . Following this, there might be a piano solo by Blake, then the big finale—the Sissle-Europe 'On Patrol in No Man's Land,' with Sissle sliding across the floor on one shoe . . . dodging the Very light, and hitting the ground with every rocket, bombardment, and fusillade from Blake's piano."

While Sissle and Blake were touring the Keith vaudeville circuit, Sissle married Harriet Toye on December 25, 1919 in Montclair, New Jersey.

While performing in Philadelphia in 1920, Sissle and Blake met Flournoy E. Miller and Aubrey Lyles, partners in a comedy dancing act. Eager to expand their routine into a full-scale production, Miller and Lyles enlisted both the songwriting and performing services of Sissle and Blake. The four men quickly assembled a production that combined the talents of both teams of performers. The unifying device was a sketch Miller and Lyles had featured in their vaudeville act—a campaign for mayor of Jim Town pitting "Steve Jenkins" against "Sam Peck," partners in a grocery store.

With help from John Cort, a theater owner who gave them used costumes from shows that had recently closed and provided rehearsal space in what had been a lecture hall on 63rd

Street in Manhattan, the four men prepared their musical, *Shuffle Along*. After tryouts before black audiences in New Jersey, Washington, D. C. and Philadelphia the show opened at the 63rd Street Theatre on May 23, 1921. Although no critics attended the debut of *Shuffle Along*, audience enthusiasm and positive "word of mouth" brought them in droves to later performances. "How [the performers] pranced and cavorted and wriggled and laughed," gushed Alan Dale in the New York *American*. "These people made pep seem something different [than] the tame thing known further downtown. Every sinew in their bodies danced; every tendon in their frame responded to their extreme energy." Within a few weeks, the show had grown so popular with white audiences that 63rd Street itself had to be changed into a one-way thoroughfare to accommodate the flow of traffic to and from the theater. Special midnight performances were given on Wednesdays to accommodate the theatrical trade. The show remained on the boards for a run of 504 performances, an outstanding run in those days. Three road companies went on tour.

More important, *Shuffle Along* broke the color barrier on Broadway. The road shows broke color barriers in previously all-white theaters in cities in the American heartland. And the production, to quote *Current Biography*, "in style and form set the pattern for further Broadway musicals." In addition to starring with Sissle, Miller, and Lyles, Blake had written the music and led the orchestra. One of the enduring hits from *Shuffle Along* was "I'm Just Wild About Harry," which President Truman used as his campaign song in 1948.

In addition to songs that Sissle and Blake carried over from their vaudeville act, they wrote new numbers. "I'm Just Wild About Harry" was new, and so was "Bandana Days," which Sissle and Blake wrote in a phone conversation when Sissle was in Boston and Blake in New York. Arthur Porter and the company introduced it within the context of a plantation scene. Another popular new number was "Love Will Find a Way," a love duet sung by Lottie Gee and Roger Matthews. This song disproved the notion that white audiences would not accept a love song exchanged by black performers. Lottie Gee and a group called the Jim Sunflowers introduced "I'm Just Wild About Harry." Blake composed it as a slow, sentimental waltz, but Lottie Gee induced him to speed up the tempo and that is how it is known.

Blake himself recorded "Bandana Days" and "I'm Just Wild About Harry" as piano solos. "I'm Just Wild About Harry" was recorded by Paul

Whiteman, Marion Harris, Vaughn de Leath and Judy Garland, and many others. In motion pictures it was sung by Alice Faye in *Rose of Washington Square* (1939); by Judy Garland and Mickey Rooney in *Babes in Arms* (1939); by Ted Lewis and his orchestra in *Is Everybody Happy?* (1943) and by Al Jolson on the soundtrack of *Jolson Sings Again* (1949).

Among the cast of *Shuffle Along* were many unknown performers who later achieved fame. Florence Mills, who replaced Gertrude Saunders in the show, stole the limelight with her version of "I'm Craving for That Kind of Love." Josephine Baker and Paul Robeson sang in the chorus. William Grant Still, who became one of America's renowned composers of concert music and operas, played in the orchestra. Hall Johnson, who went on to found and lead the Hall Johnson Choir, was the chorus master.

In 1923 Sissle and Blake rehearsed "You Were Meant for Me" for interpolation into a Boston production of *Shuffle Along*. André Charlot, the English producer, purchased the rights to the song for his London revue. "You Were Meant for Me" (not to be confused with the 1929 standard composed by Arthur Freed and Nacio Herb Brown) was introduced in 1923 by Noel Coward and Gertrude Lawrence in *London Calling*, their first singing appearance together in the revue, *London Calling*. The following year Gertrude Lawrence and Jack Buchanan made it a hit on the other side of the Atlantic, performing it on Broadway in *André Charlot's Revue of 1924.*

Success for Sissle and Blake was often followed by failure. *Shuffle Along*'s successor was *Elsie* (April 2, 1923), which lasted on Broadway just 40 performances. *The Chocolate Dandies* (September 1, 1924), a dream fantasy that Sissle and Blake performed as well as wrote, survived 96 performances.

When *The Chocolate Dandies* closed in May 1925, Sissle and Blake returned to vaudeville. Later that year they left for an eight-month tour of Europe. In London they contributed two numbers to Charles B. Cochran's *Revue of 1926*. Cochran asked Sissle and Blake to write all the songs for his next London production, but he was turned down because Blake was eager to return to the United States. When Sissle went back to Europe in the summer of 1927, Blake stayed behind, interrupting their partnership for several years.

Sissle played English music halls and theaters then organized a band in Paris and toured Europe. Returning to New York in 1931, he led his own orchestra at the Park Central Hotel and was also heard with the band on the CBS radio network. At the same time, Blake toured the Keith-Albee Orpheum circuit in vaudeville in 1928–29 with the singer Broadway Jones in an act called *Shuffle Along, Jr.* In 1929 he opened on the Balaban-Katz vaudeville circuit for the headlining act of Fanchon and Marco.

As a songwriter, Blake found a new lyricist in Andy Razaf, to whom he was introduced by Lew Leslie. Planning to mount a Broadway successor to his all-black revue *Blackbirds of 1928*, Leslie wanted Razaf and Flournoy E. Miller to write the book and the lyrics and Blake to contribute some of the music.

"Andy's working method is like no one else's I have ever seen," Blake recalled. "He will hear a tune once through, sit right down and write out the lyric in one sitting. In all the time we worked together . . . I never saw him change a line with me."

Blake and Razaf wrote the hit song that came out of Lew Leslie's *Blackbirds of 1930* (October 27, 1930), "Memories of You." Minto Cato, for whom it was written introduced it; Ethel Waters recorded it, as did Glen Gray and the Casa Loma Orchestra. This song became so popular that Blake adopted it as his signature music. Benny Goodman revived "Memories of You" in *The Benny Goodman Story* (1956), and it was interpolated into *The Gene Krupa Story* (1959).

Two other notable songs from *Blackbirds of 1930* were sung by Ethel Waters, "My Handy Man Ain't Handy No More" which she introduced, and "You're Lucky to Me," which she reprised after it had been introduced by John Bubbles and Neeka Shaw. Despite the strong score and the superb production, *Blackbirds of 1930* lasted just 62 performances.

Trying to recapture some of their former glory, Sissle and Blake were reunited with *Shuffle Along of 1933* (December 24, 1932). Starring Sissle and Blake with Flournoy Miller, it stayed on the boards less than two weeks. Then in a truncated version, they toured with the show as an opening act for films in silent movie houses.

Sissle left the road show in February 1933 to become the bandleader at the Park Central Hotel once again. From 1938 to 1942, he and his orchestra appeared at Billy Rose's Diamond Horeshoe in New York City. During World War II, Sissle joined the U.S.O. and put together an updated version of *Shuffle Along*. At this time he married his second wife, Ethel, with whom he had two children. He also helped found the Negro Actors Guild, serving as its first president, and opened a managing bureau for young performers.

Eubie Blake, however, was soon to enter into semiretirement. The only way he could mount his new musical, *Swing It* (July 27, 1937), in the Broadway vicinity was as a modest, and unsuccessful, WPA production. (Joshua Milton Reddie was his lyricist for that show.) In 1939 his wife, Evis, died. In the early 1940s, with Razaf again his lyricist, Blake composed the music for *Tan Manhattan*, which closed during a tryout in Washington, D. C.

During the Second World War Blake, too, toured the U.S.O. circuit with his own band. On December 27, 1945, Blake married Marion Tyler, a dancer. They lived in her house in the Bedford-Stuyvesant section of Brooklyn, Blake's home for the rest of his life.

Feeling out of touch with music and show business, Blake, now about 64 years old, enrolled in New York University to study the the the difficult Schillinger method of composition. He completed the four-year course in two and a half years, and began to write down old songs he had composed years before and committed to memory. He also continued to compose new songs.

His professional fortunes reached their nadir in 1952, when he and Sissle were reunited for the last time bringing to Broadway an updated version of *Shuffle Along*. They had been encouraged by the revival of "I'm So Wild About Harry" by President Truman in the presidential campaign of 1948. But *Shuffle Along of 1952* (May 8, 1952), expired after four performances. "If by any remote chance they ever put on the show again," wrote the critic George Jean Nathan, "what they had best do is throw away all the many variations and present it exactly as it was in 1921. It is, if anything a nostalgic show, and you can't work up an nostalgia by dressing up a favorite old aunt like a bobby soxer." Much truer to the spirit of the 1921 production was the revival of *Shuffle Along* on Off Broadway in February 1978, when it was booked into a small theater for a two-week engagement.

By the 1960s, if Eubie Blake was remembered at all, it was as a relic of a bygone musical and theatrical era. Then a new generation discovered ragtime, and a 1954 recording Blake had made of his early piano rags, which went unnoticed at the time, suddenly became popular. As a result, in 1969 Columbia Records reissued some of Eubie Blake's old masters in the form of a two-record album, *The 86 Years of Eubie Blake*. It sold well, and by 1973 four more albums of Blake's music had been issued by a company Blake himself formed in 1972. One of these, *Sissle and Blake's Early Rare Recordings*, was a bestseller. Even some of Blake's old piano rolls were being reproduced on discs by the ORS Music Rolls Company.

Just before his 87th birthday, Blake found himself once again in the public eye. He appeared at the New Orleans Jazz Festival in June 1969 and received a thunderous ovation, and his performance on March 1, 1972 at New York's Town Hall attracted a huge audience. In October 1972, Yale University presented Blake and Sissle its Ellington medal in a ceremony in which the two troopers recreated some of their old vaudeville routines. And on December 3, 1972 Blake performed a full-length concert at the Lincoln Center. "He was just remarkable, regardless of age," reported John S. Wilson in *The New York Times*. "He played with unabashed assurance and unfailing precision. . . . His singing voice was sure and firm with no quavers or hesitations."

Blake's 90th birthday was celebrated by ASCAP on February 7, 1973. Later that year Robert Kimball and William Bolcom published, *Reminiscing with Sissle and Blake*, the biography of the two men. Sissle died two years later.

The Eubie Blake revival reached its climax on September 20, 1978 at the Ambassador Theatre on Broadway with the staging of *Eubie*, an all-black revue. Blake was present at the opening and received a rousing hand. Having neither plot nor dialogue, *Eubie* consisted of 23 of Blake's songs (lyrics by Sissle, Razaf, Johnny Brandon, Flournoy Miller and Jim Europe), performed to dance. The production was conceived and directed by Julianne Boyd and staged by Billy Wilson. "Any production that marches swiftly with unabated zest from one eye-dazzling song-and-dance number to the next has nothing to fear from the accusation that it is out of the past," wrote Brendan Gill in *The New Yorker*. "Time passing is the best of critics; trash vanishes with a welcome celerity, and what is of value survives, diamond-hard, indestructible." After 13 weeks of out-of-town tryouts, *Eubie* ran on Broadway for 439 performances before going on tour. The score was released as an original cast LP.

Though somewhat enfeebled, Blake continued to pursue his professional career almost until he attained the age of one hundred. At public appearances he played the piano and sang his songs, and he appeared on television programs like the *Johnny Carson Show*. In Chicago on October 5, 1979, Blake and Frank Sinatra became the first performers to be inducted into the newly formed American Music and Entertainment Hall of Fame. On October 9, 1981 he was presented the Presidential Medal of Honor by President Reagan at the White House. Blake's last public appearance came on January 31, 1982, when the "Eubie Blake Celebration Concert" was staged at the Eastman Theatre in Rochester, New York. He played "Memories of You."

The death of his wife, Marion, in June 1982 dealt Blake a painful blow, but it did not keep him from attending ceremonies at the Kennedy Center in Washington, D. C. on February 6, 1983 at which a dozen stars of show business and the music industry celebrated his 100th birthday. This performance, "Eubie Blake: A Century of Music," debuted on television through the facilities of the Public Broadcasting Service on May 7, 1983, several months after Blake's death.

On February 7, 1983 pneumonia prevented Blake from attending a salute to him at St. Peter's Lutheran Church in New York on his 100th birthday; nor was he able to participate that same day at a private party at the Shubert Theatre in his honor which was attended by 1,500 of his admirers and friends. However, a special phone set up at the theater transmitted these festivities to his home in Brooklyn, where Blake died five days later.

ABOUT: Current Biography, 1974; Kimball, R. and Bolcom, W. Reminiscing with Sissle and Blake, 1973. *Periodicals*—ASCAP Today Spring 1978; Ebony July 1973; New York Times February 13, 1983; Stereo Review November 1972; Time December 18, 1972; Washington Post August 12, 1972.

JAMES A. BLAND

BLAND, JAMES A. (October 22, 1854–May 4, 1911) composer-lyricist, was the first black man to receive credit for having made significant contributions to American popular music. Born in Flushing, New York in 1854 he was the descendant of free blacks. His father, Allen A. Bland, was one of the first blacks in America to complete a college education, and a few years after James's birth, Allen Bland became the first black man to be appointed an examiner in the United States Patent Office. In Washington, D.C. James attended public schools. As a boy he liked to sing his own compositions while accompanying himself on the banjo, which he had taught himself to play. He worked as a page in the House of Representatives, which qualified Bland for membership in the Manhattan Club, made up of black clerks employed by government agencies. With other members, Bland formed a glee club that entertained for prominent Washingtonians and visitors to the capital. On these occasions he would perform his own songs, one of which, "Christmas Dinner," has survived.

After graduating from high school, he enrolled at Howard University together with his father, who was studying law. At college, James majored in a general liberal arts program. Though not a superior student he was a popular entertainer, and performed often at clubs, private parties, weddings and other social affairs, for both black and white audiences.

Bland's ambition was to go on the stage and, specifically, to become a star of the minstrel show, then the principal form of theatrical entertainment. Leaving Howard University when he was 19, he was unable to join a minstrel-show troupe because at that time minstrels were white performers impersonating blacks. Not until 1875 did Bland find employment as a minstrel, when he was hired by an all-black minstrel company headed by Billy Kersands. At this time black minstrel performers, like their white counterparts, darkened their faces with burnt cork and whitened a large area around the mouth. Black minstrels also donned the characteristic minstrel-show attire of the period—a frock coat with a large flower in the lapel, striped pants, calico shirt, a high silk hat and white gloves—and imitated their white rivals' exaggerated mimicry of so-called Negroid gestures and speech patterns.

Bland's first success as performer came with Callender's Original Georgia Minstrels, a touring company which advertised itself as "the great Southern slave troupe." When Jack Haverly acquired the Original Georgia Minstrels, the troupe was renamed Haverly's Genuine Colored Minstrels. Under Haverly's management, the company appeared at Niblo's Gardens in New York City in the spring of 1879. With Haverly's troupe Bland performed many of his own songs for which he always wrote words as well as music.

The songs for which Bland is remembered were published between 1878 and 1880, all introduced and popularized in minstrel shows. His first standard, "Carry Me Back to Old Virginny," (1878), was introduced by George Primrose and his minstrels and was soon taken up by other companies, including the Original Georgia Minstrels. This ballad is believed to have been inspired by the sight of a plantation in an idyllic setting on the banks of the James River in the Tidewater section of Virginia near Williamsburg. While gazing upon this peaceful scene, Bland is supposed to have recalled a dream described to him by a girl at Howard University in which she saw her ancestral homestead, which reminded her of "old Virginny." In Bland's ballad, the girl's dream has become a black man's wish to be home again in Virginia. In 1940 "Carry Me Back to Old Virginny" was adopted as the official song of the state of Virginia. In the early 1910s, a recording of this ballad by Alma Gluck, the distinguished concert singer, sold an unprecedented two million copies. Later recordings were made by Frances Langford and the Mills Brothers with Louis Armstrong. The song has been heard in numerous movies, including *In Old Chicago* (1938), *Golden Girl* (1951) and the screen biography of Jane Froman, *With a Song in My Heart* (1952).

Golden Girl also revived another Bland classic, the title song from the minstrel show *Oh, Dem Golden Slippers* (1879). Bland composed it as a "walk around" for the Original Georgia Minstrels, after which it became a staple in the repertory of all minstrel troupes. For over 50 years, "Dem Golden Slippers" was the theme music for the Mummers' New Year's Day parade in Philadelphia. In *Golden Girl* it was sung under the titles, then performed in the opening sequence by Mitzi Gaynor and Guy Robertson, with James Barton performing a buck-and- wing dance.

"In the Evening by the Moonlight" (1879) was inspired by the same plantation setting on the James River that is thought to have inspired "Carry Me Back to Old Virginny." Bland himself introduced "In the Evening" with the Original Georgia Minstrels. The instant popularity of this ballad led Bland to write a companion piece called "In the Morning by the Bright Light," also published in 1879. Bland wrote this song after having seen blacks in the rural South sitting outside their cabins strumming on banjos. Bland published two other songs in 1880 that became minstrel show favorites, "De Golden Wedding" and "Hand Me Down My Walking Stick."

In 1881 Bland, dispensing with blackface makeup, toured England with the all-black Callender-Haverly Minstrels, who opened at His Majesty's Theatre in London in July. After having toured England with this popular troupe for about two years, Bland decided to remain in Europe. Abandoning all the accoutrements of the minstrel show, and appearing instead in the fashions of the day, he toured England and Germany, performing his own songs. He became one of England's most popular performers, and was known as "the Prince of Negro songwriters." He gave command performances for Queen Victoria and the Prince of Wales. In Germany he was considered a leading American songwriter and his popularity rivaled that of Stephen Foster and John Philip Sousa. Bland's annual income exceeded $10,000 and was supplemented by his royalties, but he was careless in handling money, and when the popularity of the minstrel show declined he was left penniless.

In 1901 Bland returned to the United States, where a friend in Washington, D. C. secured him a menial desk job. Bland wrote the songs for a stage musical, *The Sporting Girl*, which was a box-office disaster and earned him no money. He moved to Philadelphia, where he spent his last few years in poverty. When he passed away in the spring of 1911, no newspaper carried an account of his death. Bland was buried in an unmarked grave in a secluded corner of a black cemetery in Merion, Pennsylvania.

In 1939, through the efforts of ASCAP, his grave was found and landscaped and a headstone was erected. An inscription on that headstone notes that he wrote 600 songs, though it is impossible to say how many he actually wrote, because most of his songs were not copyrighted and were often expropriated by minstrel-show performers who passed them off as their own creations, a common practice in those days. Only 53 Bland songs are listed in the Library of Congress, and the Library possesses copies of only 38. In addition to songs already mentioned, Bland composed "Close Dem Windows;" "Tapioca"; "Pretty Little Carolina Rose"; "Listen to the Silver Trumpets"; "Way Up Yonder"; "Traveling Back to Alabam'" and "Gabriel's Band."

"Various writers have attempted to trace Bland's style to the folk music of Southern blacks," wrote Charles Hamm in *Yesterdays*. "But the musical environment that shaped his style was the minstrel stage, not the plantation." Robert C. Toll described the content of Bland's songs in *Blacking Up: The Minstrel Show in Nineteenth Century America*: "His nostalgic Old Darkies expressed great love for their masters and mistresses; his plantation songs were free from antislavery protests and from praise of freedom; his religious songs contained many stereotyped images of flashy dressers and overindulgent parties; and his Northern Negros strutted, sang, danced, and had flapping ears, huge feet and gaping mouths."

ABOUT: Hamm, C. Yesterdays: Popular Song in America, 1979; Toll, R. C. Blacking Up: The Minstrel Show in the Nineteenth Century, 1974.

BOCK, JERRY (November 23, 1928–). With Sheldon Harnick as his lyricist, composer Jerry Bock wrote the songs for *Fiorello!*, one of three Broadway musicals to receive the Pulitzer Prize in drama, and for *Fiddler On the Roof*, perhaps the most successful musical in the history of the American theater.

He was born Jerrold Lewis Bock in New Haven, Connecticut, the son of George Joseph Bock, a traveling salesman of automotive parts, and Rebecca (Alpert) Bock, who played the piano by ear. Bock has recalled that his father "was uncommonly fair in letting me pursue all sorts of musical dreams, and never exerted a modicum of pressure on me to try a more substantial craft. [My mother] encouraged me all the way, though she wanted me to work harder at the piano than I did, but never ended up by forcing me. Both my folks' unpressured point of view gave me room to stretch, and I think that very freedom I enjoyed was a healthy influence. It was a fine line, neither permissive nor regimented, and it seems to have worked for me."

When Bock was two his family moved to New York, living first in the Bronx, then in the Flushing section of Queens. At P.S. 32 in Flushing, he began taking piano lessons when he was nine. However, Bock was impatient with exercises and scales and did not like to practice, preferring instead to spend his time improvising at the piano. His piano teacher was sympathetic to Bock's approach, but her attempts to discipline his creativity with instruction in harmony were unsuccessful.

Bock gave up piano lessons for good when he entered Flushing High School, but he continued to play the piano and entertained ideas of becoming a composer. He would perform at parties, trying out songs he was now beginning to write. But at high school he had interests other than music. He edited the school paper and contributed poems to small literary journals. In his last year at Flushing High he wrote an original score for a musical called *My Dream* (1945) and assisted in writing the lyrics. Bock also played piano in the orchestra when *My Dream* was staged in the Flushing area to raise money for recreational equipment on a U.S. Navy hospital ship. He recalled: "It was my first taste of theatrical excitement and may have influenced me to begin thinking about that special field of music."

After high school, Bock's plan was to major in journalism in college as a preliminary to finding

JERRY BOCK

work in advertising. In 1945 he enrolled in the University of Wisconsin. During registration week, he impulsively decided to try and gain admission to the School of Music, even though it had been five years since he had taken his last piano lesson and there was nothing in the classical literature he could perform. At the audition, he failed dismally at an attempt to sight-read a few simple hymns and had to confess he was a musical novice with more enthusiasm than training. He then offered to perform something in a popular vein—an arrangement he had made of army bugle calls that segued into kitsch variations in the style of Bach, Beethoven and Rachmaninoff, and ended in a jazz flourish. "They seemed amused," Bock said. "Finally one spoke and said I showed signs of inventiveness, but that I needed basic training. Would I be willing to start at the beginning? I was willing, and they accepted me into the school."

At the university, Bock repeated the approach to music of his adolescent years. His response to the formal study of harmony, counterpoint and violin was lackadaisical, and he spent his time writing for literary magazines, working in college theatrical productions, improvising at the piano and writing songs. Indeed, the subjects he studied were outside the periphery of music: English, philosophy, and political science. Then, as in high school, he wrote 17 songs for an original musical, *Big as Life*, which was produced by the University's Haresfoot Club, an all-male dramatic society. The book for the show was a fanciful treatment of the Paul Bunyan legend and *Big as Life* toured Wisconsin, was mounted in Chicago, and then had a week-long run in Madison.

The score was entered in an annual BMI-sponsored competition among college students, and it won. One of the prizes was the publication of four of his songs in professional sheet-music form, Bock's first sheet-music publications. The most successful of these numbers was "Logger Beer" (lyrics by Jack Royce).

A fellow student at the university, Larry Holofcener, hoped to parlay his talent for lyric-writing into a career in the theater, and after the run of *Big as Life* Bock and Holofcener became a words-and-music team. Their first effort was a narrative poem describing the birth of a potato *latke* (potato pancake), for which Bock provided the background music. When listeners found themselves charmed by the tune, Bock and Holofcener were encouraged, and decided to try and market their songs in New York. They left school in 1949 and, in Manhattan, auditioned for Max Liebman, the producer of *The Admiral Broadway Revue*, which was hosted by Sid Caesar on the NBC television network. Liebman signed Bock and Holofcener to a contract calling for them to write songs for his television show. In February 1950 *The Admiral Broadway Revue* was renamed *Your Show of Shows*, a classic from television's Golden Age of comedy starring Sid Caesar and Imogene Coca, and Bock and Holofcener wrote for the show for three years. They also worked in the summers of 1950, 1951 and 1953 at Camp Tamiment, an adult camp in the Pocono Mountains where, each Saturday night, a revue was staged with sketches, songs, sets and costuming all prepared by a resident company. Affiliated with Camp Tamiment since 1939, Leibman used his influence to get Bock and Holofcener hired as songwriters. "The type of songs we wrote for Tamiment spanned the revue gamut," Bock said. "Openings, finales, middle production numbers, ballads, ballet-ballads, boy and girl numbers, comedy trios and quartets, a multiple range of infinite variety. I found it the most exciting apprenticeship. It was a never-ending learning process."

On May 28, 1950, a year after having left Wisconsin and a few months after signing on as a songwriter for *The Admiral Broadway Revue*, Bock married Patti Faggen. They had met in 1947 at the university, where Patti, a speech major, also had been involved in the school's dramatic activities. They raised two children, a son and a daughter.

At this time Bock encountered a series of professional setbacks. By 1952, television producers were increasingly reluctant to pay for original songs for their shows, preferring to rely on the standard repertory of current hits. Their songwriting efforts rejected, Bock and Holofcener were forced to earn their living writing sketches, continuity, dialogue and special material for television stars, including Mel Tormé and Kate Smith, and for nightclub acts.

In 1955 a New York music publisher, Tommy Valando, became interested in their songs. In return for awarding exclusive rights to their work to Valando, he signed Bock and Holofcener to a modest weekly stipend. This initiated a 30-year professional relationship between Valando and Bock. "He was," declared Bock, "an outstanding critic, an outstanding supporter, and best of all, a dear friend." Through Valando, Bock and Holofcener began working in Tin Pan Alley. By the end of 1955, they had written four songs for a film travelogue about New York called *Wonders of Manhattan*, which earned an honorable mention at the 1956 Cannes Film Festival. On September 7, 1955 they made their bow in the Broadway musical theater with three numbers that were interpolated into *Catch a Star*, a revue whose basic score was by Sammy Fain and Phil Charig. The revue lasted on Broadway just three weeks and is remembered only because it was the occasion of Neil Simon's debut in the Broadway musical theater with sketches written in collaboration with his brother, Danny. "Fly Little Heart," one of the songs by Bock and Holofcener, drew praise from Richard Rodgers.

With *Mr. Wonderful* (March 22, 1956), Bock and Holofcener had their first Broadway success. This musical was a vehicle for Sammy Davis, Jr., making his Broadway debut. The libretto by Joseph Stein and Will Glickman cast Davis as Charlie Welch, an obscure New Jersey song-and-dance man who is encouraged by his fianceé and his best friend to try for the big time. At their urging he puts together a nightclub act in Miami Beach that makes him a star. The second-act nightclub scene, in which Sammy Davis, Jr. stunned audiences with his singing and dancing, made *Mr. Wonderful* a resounding success. It stayed on Broadway for 383 performances and would have had a much longer run if Sammy Davis, who was indispensable, had not left the production. The show produced two hit songs for Bock and Holofcener (lyrics written in collaboration with George Weiss). The title song, introduced by Olga James, was recorded by Peggy Lee and was represented on *Your Hit Parade* on April 28, 1956. "Too Close for Comfort," introduced by Sammy Davis, Jr., was made into a hit record by Eydie Gormé and became a jazz standard. The entire score was issued in an original cast recording.

If the year of 1956 represented an important step forward for Bock, that of 1957–58 was two steps backwards. Still with Holofcener as his lyricist, Bock contributed three songs to the *Ziegfeld Follies* (March 1, 1957), which failed utterly in its effort to reinvigorate the old Ziegfeld formula, folding after 123 performances despite the presence of Beatrice Lillie, who was in top form, and Tallulah Bankhead as its stars.

Bock's second complete score for the Broadway theater was *The Body Beautiful* (January 23, 1958). With book by Joseph Stein and Will Glickman, it dealt with the trials and tribulations of a professional boxer. *The Body Beautiful* collapsed after just 60 performances. Bock called the failure "a major heartbreak," and even his songs failed to survive this disaster, though one love ballad, "Gloria" (introduced by Jack Warden), is not deserving of neglect. However, *The Body Beautiful* did bring Bock together with a new lyricist, Sheldon Harnick. (Bock and Holofcener had parted ways before the *Body Beautiful* fiasco.)

The actor Jack Cassidy, an alumnus from the Camp Tamiment shows, had introduced Bock to Harnick in a restaurant after the opening-night performance of *Shangri-La*, a musical in which Harnick had helped out with the lyrics. "It was simply a quick exchange, and it was over," Bock noted. "The next time Sheldon and I met, which was not long after our first encounter, it was to discuss the possibility of our working together, on an idea strongly suggested to both of us by Joe Stein, who was about to embark on the book of *The Body Beautiful* with Will Glickman. He thought we'd make the right team to do the score. It was love at first write."

The producers Robert E. Griffith and Hal Prince had liked the songs from *The Body Beautiful*, and they contracted Bock and Harnick to write the score for their next production *Fiorello!*. One year to the day after *The Body Beautiful* had folded, Bock and Harnick started work on the new score for Prince and Griffith. "It was truly a labor of love. It was a difficult, stimulating, challenging, provocative but never painful effort. All our egos were in tune, all our temperaments in harmony." In Harnick, Bock found not only a lyricist with a gift for fresh imagery and a neat turn of phrase, but also a lyric writer with extensive formal music training.

Fiorello! (November 23, 1959), with book by Jerome Weidman and George Abbott, traced the career of the diminutive, reformist mayor of New York, Fiorello H. La Guardia, popularly known as "the little flower." That career had begun in 1914 when La Guardia practiced law in Greenwich Village and championed the rights of the underprivileged. The musical carried him through his election to Congress as a friend of the working man, his service in World War I, up to his election as mayor of New York on the progressive Fusion ticket.

But *Fiorello!* was more than a portrait of an individual; it was a colorful depiction of an era in New York spanning the years 1914 to 1932, from the war through the Jazz Age to the Great Depression. "It captures a fabulous political firebrand and a breezy period in the life of New York," reported *The New York Times* critic Brooks Atkinson. "Jerry Bock has set it to a bouncy score that has a satiric line as well as a wonderful waltz of that period." The satiric line was fully developed in two numbers. "Politics and Poker" found a striking parallel between these two pursuits, sung by a male chorus and Howard da Silva, playing the leader of the City Republican Party. "Little Tin Box" was a delightfully humorous tune about investigations of graft and corruption in city politics. The "wonderful waltz" was "Til Tomorrow," introduced by Ellen Hanley as farewell to La Guardia as he was about to leave for the army. Hanley also introduced another memorable ballad, "When Did I Fall in Love?"

Fiorello!, which had a run of 795 performances, made theater history in 1960 by becoming the third musical to capture the Pulitzer Prize in drama (the other recipients were *Of Thee I Sing!* and *South Pacific*). It also received the New York Drama Critics Circle Award and shared the Tony with the Rodgers and Hammerstein musical, *The Sound of Music*. The original cast album of *Fiorello!* was a bestseller.

Some of the principals involved in the making of *Fiorello!* joined forces again to provide another slice of New York's past life and social history. With Jerome Weidman and George Abbott again serving as librettists, and with songs by Bock and Harnick, *Tenderloin* was brought to Broadway on October 17, 1960 for a run of 216 performances. "Tenderloin" was a disreputable section of New York in the 1890s. Maurice Evans, in his bow in the American musical theater, assumed the role of Reverend Brock, a crusading Presbyterian clergyman out to clean up the neighborhood. Efforts to discredit him prove futile, and the Tenderloin district is finally cleaned up. Though the musical boasted satire, nostalgia and sentiment, it lacked the excitement and the consistency of point of view of *Fiorello!*. But the songs, recorded in an original cast album, were a strong asset, as Howard Taubman wrote in *The New York Times*: "The songwriters . . . have supplied material that has the color and flavor in its own right and that makes possible some sprightly production numbers. Sheldon Harnick's lyrics and Jerry Bock's music are the best excuse for *Tenderloin*." One song stood out,

"Artificial Flowers," introduced by Ron Hussmann and chorus and recorded by Bobby Darin.
"My Miss Mary," also sung by Hussmann with
choral support, was in the style of an 1890s song.

Bock and Harnick were next represented on
Broadway by *She Loves Me* (April 23, 1963),
which ran for 301 performances. Based on the
1940 film, *The Shop Around the Corner*, a sentimental comedy directed by Ernst Lubitsch and
starring Margaret Sullavan and James Stewart,
She Loves Me was set in Budapest in 1933. Amelia Balash and George Nowack are co-workers in
a shop called "Parfumerie" and are always at
odds with each other. Both, however, embody
compassion and tenderness in anonymous letters
that they exchange with "pen pals," whom they
fall in love with. When their epistolary identities
are finally revealed, Amelia and George discover that they have been in love with one another
all along. The charm and winning sentimentality of the text were enhanced by a superior score
that earned Bock the designation of "composer
of the year" in a poll of New York drama critics
and a Grammy for the original cast recording.
"The songs," wrote Howard Taubman in *The
New York Times*, "not only capture the gay,
light spirit of the story but also add an extra dimension of magic to it." "Dear Friend" and
"Will He Like Me?," both introduced by Barbara Cook, "Days Gone By," introduced by Lud-
wig Donath, and the title song, introduced by
Daniel Massey, were the score's highlights. Even
years after this musical was first produced the
songs carried charm and conviction. When, in
1979, *She Loves Me* was presented on network
television John J. O'Conner of *The New York
Times* wrote that "the score is exceptionally
good. . . . Mr. Bock's music, carefully suggesting a pronounced Hungarian flavor, is beguiling." One year later, a revival of *She Loves Me*
mounted by Playwrights Horizon in Queens
prompted another *New York Times* critic to remark, "The tunes are winning, sweet and
catchy. . . ."

Though the box-office returns for both
Tenderloin and *She Loves Me* were disappoint-
ing, the next Bock-Harnick Broadway musical
was *Fiddler on the Roof*. Opening on September
22, 1964, *Fiddler on the Roof* quickly became
known as one of the most successful productions
in the history of the American musical theater,
a success of international scope. Based on stories
by Sholom Aleichem that were adapted into a libretto by Joseph Stein, it dealt with the experience of East European Orthodox Jews in the
Russian village of Anatevka in the year of 1905.
The story is a simple one: Teyve, an Old World
Jew, humble and devoutly religious, an uncomplicated soul who must come to terms with the

modern world, is a poor dairyman with five
daughters. He wants to have proper marriages,
but each of the young women has her own ideas
about life. One scandalizes her father by falling
in love with a gentile. Teyve, who does not hesitate to make conversation with God, to argue
with Him and even confront Him with a very
earthly form of logic, eventually convinces himself that his daughters have chosen their husbands wisely. But the play does not end on a
happy note. Persecuted by anti-Semitic Cossacks, Teyve and his wife are forced to flee and
leave behind the good, simple life they have
known.

Every facet of the production had ethnic au-
thenticity: the performances of Zero Mostel as
Teyve, Maria Karnilova as his wife, and Beatrice
Arthur as Yente; the choreography of Jerome
Robbins; Boris Aronson's settings and Bock and
Harnick's songs. Without trying to replicate
Jewish music, or even quoting from Jewish folk
or religious music, Bock managed to infuse his
melodic writing with a Jewish inflection, as Har-
rick did in his lyrics. Yet for all their Old World
overtones, the songs remained solid Broadway
show tunes. Introduced by Mostel and
Karnilova, "Sunrise, Sunset," in which Teyve
and his wife contemplate the irretrievable passage of time while attending the wedding ceremony of one of their daughters, has become a
standard. Mostel also sang "If I Were a Rich
Man"—the only song Bock and Harnick ever tailored to fit a specific performer—and he joined
Michael Granger in singing "To Life." Joanna
Merlin, Linda Ross, Julia Migenes and Tanya
Everett introduced "Matchmaker, Matchmaker."

When, on July 2, 1972, *Fiddler on the Roof*
gave the last performance of its initial Broadway
run, it had been on the boards almost eight years
for the then record run of 3,242 performances.
The show earned 20 million dollars in New York,
and another 15 million from road shows
throughout the United States. Moreover, *Fiddler
on the Roof* captured nine Tony awards, including one for best musical. In addition *Fiddler on
the Roof* has been a resounding international
success. It won hearts everywhere because, as
Howard Taubman noted in *The New York
Times*, it was filled "with laughter and tenderness. It catches the essence of a moment in history with sentiment and radiance. Compounded
of the familiar materials of the musical theater . . . it combines and transcends them to arrive at an integrated achievement of uncommon
quality." *Fiddler on the Roof* has been revived
several times on Broadway, and in 1976, when
Mostel returned as Teyve, the critic Clive Barnes
wrote: "The book, the music, the lyrics are abso-

lutely perfect. There is not a song . . . that you could consider being changed. . . . Come to think of it, the show should never have left New York. It should be a fixture, like the Empire State Building. Or motherhood."

In 1971 *Fiddler on the Roof* was made into a successful motion picture, and the first of several televised versions was aired on the ABC network in 1974. The original Broadway cast album made the bestseller charts just ten days after its release and stayed there for 186 weeks. The soundtrack recording also sold more than a million copies. Numerous foreign-language recordings of the score have been released as well, and the production history of *Fiddler on the Roof* was chronicled in a book by Richard Altman and Mervyn Kaufman, *The Making of a Musical* (1973).

Their next musical, *The Apple Tree* (October 18, 1966), was Bock and Harnick's most experimental production, and it had a substantial Broadway run of 463 performances. For *The Apple Tree*, an ambitious attempt to create a new form for the popular American musical theater, Bock and Harnick wrote the book as well as the score. Each of the three acts was a self-contained whole, and each was based on a well-known story (one by Mark Twain, the others by Frank R. Stockton and Jules Feiffer). The overall theme was Woman: in "The Story of Adam and Eve" with Eve in the Garden of Eden; in "The Lady or the Tiger?" with Princess Barbara in a kingdom in the distant past; and in "Passionella" with a celluloid sex goddess. All three female leads were played by Barbara Harris, who sang the score's three principal songs: "Forbidden Love" (a duet with Alan Alda), a parody of songs about exotic, faraway places; "I've Got What You Want," a satire of come-hither sex songs; and "What Makes Me Love Him?" An original cast album was released.

Bock and Harnick's next score was for *The Rothschilds* (October 18, 1970), with a book by Sherman Yellen. *The Rothschilds* traced the banking empire of the House of Rothschild from its origins to its establishment as one of Europe's most powerful and dynastic of financial institutions. The emphasis was not on the ways that the Rothschild family secured a great fortune but on overtones of modern European attitudes toward Jews. "Mr. Bock's music," said Clive Barnes, "makes a neat nod in the direction of the 18th century, but blends period pastiche with a gentler, more cultivated version of those Jewish folk melodies that were so successful in *Fiddler on the Roof*. The fiddle has become a violin, but it still sounds pretty sweet." Bock has explained that most of his music for this score was "in the

classic tradition of the 18th and 19th century European music." (In the first act, for example, a baroque trumpet is used in the orchestration to create an 18th-century instrumental sound, and brass instruments are stressed in the second act to simulate a 19th-century sound.) The score yielded no hit songs, but there were some very pleasant numbers: "I'm in Love! I'm in Love!" was introduced by Timothy Jerome; "One Room" by Hal Linden and Leila Martin; and "In My Own Lifetime" by Linden. The entire score was released in an original cast album. *The Rothschilds* had a 505-performance run on Broadway.

In addition to his work on Broadway, in the 1950s Bock composed 31 children's songs published and recorded under the title *Sing Something Special.* In 1964 Bock and Harnick fashioned a panorama of the American musical theater called *To Broadway with Love,* for presentation at the New York World's Fair. A year later he and Harnick wrote the music for a Ballantine Ale commercial on television, and in 1966 wrote the songs for a television musical, *The Canterville Ghost.*

After *The Rothschilds,* Bock decided that the time had come for him to be his own lyricist. Consequently he experimented with the "concept" LP format, a series of songs that explore a theme or point of view. His first such venture was the autobiographical *Album Leaves* (1972), a song series in which Bock dealt impressionistically with memories of his earlier years. His second conceptual album was released in 1974, *Trading Dreams.* From 1972 to 1974, Bock also worked on a musical, a murder mystery called *Caper.* "I spent 18 months hammering out a score to what resulted in an unproduced musical," Bock said. "It was an enterprise that gave me enormous satisfaction in the effort to write by myself, and it ended with a few regrets and many rewards that came from the work process."

Since 1975 Bock has not written for the Broadway musical theater. However, he has given assistance to a New York workshop for new writers of the musical theater called The Musical Theatre Lab, founded and directed by Stuart Ostrow.

According to Ostrow, Bock is "almost Rabbinical in his understanding of other people and critical situations. He is a happy, confident personality. His optimism is catching. . . . He makes people better at their job because he [can do his own work] and still have time to be concerned about yours. He never talks about his music; never seems to be looking for some sign from you [that he has] written a beautiful melody. . . . Jerry is a composer, he composes; and when you're having a drink with him he is anything you want him to be: buddy, critic, gin rummy partner, debater, philosopher or brain surgeon. He collects owl figurines and friends."

Bock and his wife make their home not far from the Broadway scene, in Pound Ridge, New York.

ABOUT: Green, S. The World of Musical Comedy, 4th ed. 1980; Rigdon, W. (ed.) The Biographical Encyclopedia and Who's Who of the American Theatre, 1966.

BRAHAM, DAVID (1838–April 11, 1905) and **HARRIGAN, NED**, (October 26, 1844–June 6, 1911). In the 1870s and 1880s, the team of Harrigan and Hart, soon to be known as "Harriganandhart," took New York theatergoers by storm. The appeal of their shows, which were written by Ned Harrigan, was explained by a contemporary critic, Richard Harding Davis: "He has been reproducing New York, so that New Yorkers can come and look at themselves . . . doing the humorous or patriotic or commonplace things he sees them do in the markets and on the stoops and at the street corners." A third equally important, but often less visible, member of the team was David Braham, who composed songs to Harrigan's lyrics, many of which became as popular as the shows for which they were written. But the importance of these shows goes beyond the fact that they were extremely successful and profitable in their own time; for many historians, these productions mark the true beginning of American musical comedy.

Edward "Ned" Harrigan was born on New York's Lower East Side in a tough waterfront neighborhood known as "Cork Row." His father, William, was a shipbuilder and sea captain who later worked as a caulker in an East River shipyard. His mother, Ellen Ann (Rogers), loved many kinds of music and taught her son to appreciate it too; as part of his musical education, he learned many spirituals and also to play the banjo.

From the time he was a boy, Harrigan aspired to be an entertainer. In the cellar of their house, he performed minstrel-show routines with his sister, as well as "Ned Harrigan's One-Man Shows," in which he sang, danced and played several instruments. But his father, a firm believer in the work ethic, planned a career as a longshoreman for his son. Harrigan left P. S. 31 at the age of 14, working first as an errand boy, then as a printer's devil; two years later, he was an apprentice caulker.

But William Harrigan could not prevent his son from spending his spare time at Niblo's Gardens, the Bowery Theatre and other nearby variety halls. At the Bowery, young hopefuls were permitted to perform between acts; when he was 16, Harrigan availed himself of the opportunity one night to deliver (between the routines of Pierce's Original Campbell Minstrels) to deliver a parody of political speeches he had written. The management offered him a contract, but his father forbade him to sign it.

Two years later, Harrigan's parents divorced, and his father married a dour Methodist whose stern approach matched his own. Harrigan found life with them intolerable, so he went to sea, serving as a steward on the clipper, *Fearnaught*, and working on ships sailing along the Gulf coast to and from New Orleans. By a circuitous route, he reached California in 1866, where he earned his living working on the docks.

That year, Harrigan also played his first engagement in San Francisco at the Olympic Theatre. Billed as "Irish Comic Singer—Ed. Harrigan," he opened on October 21; his act ran until the end of the year. This was followed by a number of brief stints in California and Nevada variety houses (including a one-night stand sponsored by the Dashaway Society in San Francisco), in which he sang topical songs he had written, danced, did impersonations, and appeared in sketches and minstrel routines, sharing the stage with well-known performers such as Maggie Moore, Joseph Murphy and Lotta Crabtree.

While in San Francisco, Harrigan met vaudevillian Sam Rickey, with whom he came east in 1870, performing an act in which he played an Irishman to Rickey's stock black role. They opened in New York at the Globe Theatre on November 21, 1870 with a German dialect sketch (Rickey's specialty) entitled "The Little Fraud," built around the song of the same name. Though they were well-received, Rickey proved to be an unreliable partner and Harrigan was forced to split up the act.

With Manning's Minstrels, Harrigan returned to Chicago, where he met Anthony J. Cannon at a shoe-shine stand. Cannon was a delinquent youth with theatrical aspirations who had been performing as "Master Antonio." Harrigan thought Tony might be a suitable "fraulein" in "The Little Fraud," and as "The Nonpareils— Ned Harrigan and Tony Hart," they opened at Chicago's Winter Garden Theatre. With an expanded repertory of sketches, they then went to Boston, officially adopting the billing "Harrigan and Hart"; from Boston, they took the act to New York, opening at the Globe Theatre on October 14, 1871. They also made appearances at other New York variety houses, including a one-week stint filling in at the Union Square Theatre, where David Braham was conducting the house orchestra.

The Brahams were quite influential in musical theater circles; many members of this large family either conducted or played in theater orchestras, and some also composed songs. In Boston Harrigan had recently met David Braham's nephew, John, who had given Harrigan a letter of introduction to the elder Braham.

Little is known about David Braham's background or his early life. He was born in London in 1838, and, as a boy, he studied the harp, an instrument he discovered to be impractical when, on one occasion, a stagecoach driver refused to allow him to board with it. He then took up the more compact violin and soon became proficient enough to concertize in London.

In 1856, with his brother Joseph, Braham came to the United States, where he settled permanently. He found employment in the orchestra of Pony Moore's Minstrels, and during the next few years, he played in the orchestra pits of New York's many minstrel theaters and variety houses; he also conducted Robinson's Military Band. In 1859 he married Annie Hanley from Dublin; six years later he was appointed music director at Henry Wood's Minstrel Hall (later to be taken over by Harrigan and Hart and renamed the Theatre Comique).

By the late 1860s, Braham had begun to compose songs and ballads, using English music hall favorites as models and drawing on his experiences in American theaters. With the help of various lyricists, he produced a repertory of popular songs, which were sung by such performers as Mrs. Annie Yeamans (then child star "Little Jeannie"), P. T. Barnum's circus attraction, Major Tom Thumb, and many minstrels and comedians. Among these songs were "Adolphus Morning Glory," (1868; words by J. B. Murphy), "You're the Idol of My Heart" (1874; words by Gordian K. Hyde), "To Rest, Let Him Gently Be Laid" (1876; words by George Cooper), and "Sway the Cot Gently for Baby's Asleep" (1876; words by Hartley Neville). With George L. Stout, he composed "The Eagle" (1875) for the United States Centennial, "Emancipation Day" (1876) for Josh Hart, and "Eily Machree" (1876), which was popularized by minstrel George Coes. But one of his most successful songs was "Over the Hills to the Poor-House" (1874; words by George L. Catlin), the lament of a sick old man who has been turned out by his children, which was introduced by character actor James W. McKee. The sentimental ballads that were all the

rage in the 1880s and 1890s had their roots in songs such as this by Braham.

Braham and Harrigan got on well together from the start, and their successful collaboration began several months after they met when Harrigan sent Braham a set of lyrics, "The Mulligan Guard," for perusal. Braham decided to set them to music, and Harrigan persuaded William A. Pond to purchase publication rights for $50.

Harrigan and Hart introduced "The Mulligan Guard" at the Academy of Music in Chicago in May 1873. In the sketch, "the Guard" was a sorry three-man army poking fun at the numerous civilian military organizations that paraded in uniform through the city streets. Harrigan appeared at the head in a gold-braided fez and a highly decorated but oversized uniform with a sword hanging from his hip (and over which he constantly tripped); Hart, as the army, followed in a moth-eaten shako and a uniform that was too short and too tight with a musket slung over his shoulder; bringing up the rear was a young black boy, clumsily towing a target.

The routine and the song were both big successes; strains of "The Mulligan Guard" could be heard everywhere, and, according to E. J. Kahn, Jr.: "Throughout America, children, who in other areas might have chanted 'Ten Little Indians,' could be found chanting a variation on that theme called 'Ten Little Mulligan Guards.'" "The Mulligan Guard" also made an impression in Europe; Viennese operetta composer Carl Millöcker used the tune in the Act I finale of *The Beggar Student* (1882), and it is mentioned in Rudyard Kipling's *Kim* (1901) as a favorite of the English Tommies in India. Because of the popularity of "The Mulligan Guard," Pond agreed to publish other songs by Braham and Harrigan, and he later issued a collection of their songs. Braham, Harrigan and Hart capitalized further on this success by introducing a similar song mocking recruiting practices entitled "The Regular Army, O!" (1874).

Harrigan became a constant presence in the Braham household. Though he worked almost continuously with David Braham on new songs, he also found time to pursue Braham's oldest daughter, Annie, whom he married on November 18, 1876. Following the marriage, the Brahams and the Harrigans lived under one roof until the ever-growing number of progeny (the Brahams raised a family of eight) forced the Harrigans (who eventually had ten children) to find separate quarters nearby.

In addition to performing in New York, Harrigan and Hart toured the country in 1874 and 1875, presenting plays written by Harrigan as well as a variety of skits and musical numbers, most of which had been composed by Braham and Harrigan. These sketches often included characters modeled on the people he had known while he was growing up: "Born in the Seventh Ward—the leading downtown New York ward of that day—I was raised among these very Irish, German and colored people, and an instinctive recognition of their humorous side early led me to meditate upon their peculiarities, and at times to give imitations of well-known ward types." When Harrigan and Hart appeared in New York, Braham was in the the pit, conducting the overtures he had composed for the shows (which always included the tune of "The Mulligan Guard"), as well as incidental music and all of the musical numbers.

In 1876, Harrigan and Hart became the proprietors of the Theatre Comique at 514 Broadway. Now that he was spending most of his time in New York, Harrigan began to look increasingly to his roots for material. According to his youngest daughter (and granddaughter of David Braham), Nedda Harrigan (Mrs. Joshua) Logan: "He would ride the streetcars . . . He would go and sit in Battery Park. He'd follow people around, learn their walks, see where they lived. He would buy clothes off people's backs to use for costumes, so they would look authentic." Such characters had already made their debuts in various "Mulligan" and "Skidmore" sketches and songs and also in the hit, *Old Lavender*, presented during the 1877–78 season. Harrigan derived great satisfaction from faithfully characterizing his fellow man; other aspects of playwriting were bothersome: "I wish a fellow could make a play without a plot," Harrigan later remarked. "When I find a bit of poor human nature and place it among its lowly surroundings, it grieves me to make him talk plot."

But because "The Mulligan Guard" had been such a big success, Harrigan wrote an expanded sketch, "The Mulligan Guard Picnic," which he first presented with Hart in the fall of 1878. It caught on, and before long, Harrigan had created an entire cast of characters for a popular series of full-length productions tracing the escapades of the Mulligan family and their neighbors.

The Mulligans, like Harrigan and Hart, were Irish. Harrigan became intimately identified with the role of sturdy Dan Mulligan; Mrs. Annie Yeamans played the role of his wife, Cordelia, and Hart, who assumed several roles during each performance, was Mrs. Welcome (Rebecca) Allup, their black maid. The Mulligan's neighbors were the German Lochmuller family and the black Skidmore family; other associates came from various ethnic backgrounds. Harrigan also

assembled a troupe of regular cast members that included Annie Mack, Harry A. Fisher, Johnny Wild, Michael Bradley and Billy Gray.

The Mulligans and their cohorts returned in *The Mulligan Guard Ball* (January 13, 1879), which ran for an unusual 153 performances (and had the good fortune of opening the night *before* the American premiere of Gilbert and Sullivan's *H.M.S. Pinafore*), and subsequently in *The Mulligan Guard Chowder* (August 11, 1879), *The Mulligan Guard's Christmas* (November 17, 1879), *The Mulligan Guard's Surprise* (February 16, 1880), *The Mulligan Guard Nominee* (November 22, 1880) and *The Mulligan's Silver Wedding* (February 21, 1881), the only one of these shows that ran for fewer than 100 performances. These productions touched on the subjects of political corruption and racial tension; often, one ethnic group was pitted against another. But in spite of the ever-present satirical edge, most of Harrigan's characters were treated sympathetically. The humor, sometimes earthy though not obscene, came primarily from the speech patterns, personal mannerisms, and idiosyncratic behavior Harrigan heard and observed around him.

Braham's songs also contributed to the success of these shows, and, according to E. J. Kahn, Jr., in the 1870s and 1880s, "it would have been a rare experience to stroll past a row of tenement houses on a summer night without hearing one or another of [Braham's] melodies being soothingly intoned within." Among the songs which could be heard was "The Babies on Our Block," which quoted several Irish tunes and may have inspired "The Sidewalks of New York" 15 years later, as well as "The Pitcher of Beer" and "The Skidmore Fancy Ball" from *The Mulligan Guard Ball* (1879). Other hits included a march, "The Skids Are Out Tonight" and "The Little Widow Dunn" from *The Mulligan Guard Chowder* (1879); "The Mulligan Braves," "Down in Gossip Row" and "The Skidmore Masquerade" from *The Mulligan Guard Nominee* (1880); and "South Fifth Avenue" from *The Mulligan's Silver Wedding* (1881).

For Harrigan, these and other songs were essential to the Harrigan and Hart productions: "The short-lived bits of music, coming and going with the freedom and irresponsibility of wild flowers, helped to lighten the toil of the working people . . . admitting sunshine into many a darkened life. Virtue, disguised as music, enters the home of poverty, and holds temptation at bay with the gentle weapon called the popular song. Make songs for the poor, and you plant roses among the weeds." In 1891 Braham, "a bespectacled, professorial-looking man with a floppy mustache and . . . red hair," explained to the New York *Herald* (July 12, 1891) how these "roses" came into being: "After [Harrigan] gives [the words] to me I read them all over a number of times until I get a good idea of the time and the style of the music each calls for . . . On my way downtown on the elevated train I take out Ned's manuscript, hold my paper over it so that I can see just one line. Then I hum that line over until I get something that suits me and jot it down on the paper. If I can't find any air I like, I skip it and go to the next line."

With the advent of the "Mulligan" series, the Harrigan and Hart shows began to receive serious attention from the press. Braham and Harrigan were thought to rival England's Gilbert and Sullivan; Harrigan was also compared to Molière and John Gay, while Braham was likened to Jacques Offenbach and Mozart. The distinguished novelist and poet William Dean Howells felt that Harrigan's plays represented the birth of an authentic American theater, and in an 1886 essay, he christened Harrigan "the Dickens of America." While discussing his own work, Harrigan told *Pearson's Magazine*: "I have sought above all to make my plays like pages from actual life. I have depicted some painful types, I am well aware, and some that may have been shockingly realistic in their unconventional fidelity to a stratum of human society . . . which was rather an unknown country to the playwrights and even to the storytellers of my Mulligan, Old Lavender and Leather Patch days. My slum and beggar types, my tramps, are not the burlesque caricatures that appeal to the mirth of spectators by absurd and implausible exaggeration of rags and makeup. I examine the general effect of every character with the closest scrutiny, just as I watch the general gestures and movements and 'color,' so to speak, of the part."

In 1881 Harrigan and Hart refurbished the old Globe Theatre at 728 Broadway and christened it the New Theatre Comique. Their first production there, *The Major* (August 29, 1881), in which Harrigan played a flamboyant scalawag not above double-crossing his friends, was extremely successful (150 performances) even though it completely abandoned the Mulligans. During the second half of the season, the even more profitable *Squatter Sovereignty* (January 9, 1882) was at the Comique. The show centered on the conflict of landowners and squatters near the East River, and the score produced two hits, "Paddy Duffy's Cart," a nostalgic song ("Oh, I Love to Talk of Old New York") introduced by George Merritt, and "The Widow Nolan's Goat."

Because the loyal patrons of the Comique were unaccustomed to the portrayal of Jewish characters in even Harrigan and Hart's productions, the opening of *Mordecai Lyons* (October 26, 1882) came as a shock. The critics found the plot contrived, and the show barely survived long enough for a new one to be prepared. Its replacement was *McSorley's Inflation* (November 27, 1882), which was closer in spirit to the Mulligan tradition. The show achieved a respectable run, and several of its songs, "I Never Drink Behind the Bar," "McNally's Row of Flats," "The Old Feather Bed" and "The Charleston Blues" (which referred to a black military band) immediately became popular.

After the disastrous experience of the previous season, Harrigan decided to bring back the Mulligans in *Cordelia's Aspirations* (November 5, 1883), thought by some to be his best work and certainly one of his most successful (176 performances). In it, the Mulligans move uptown to posh Madison Avenue because Cordelia's relatives, believing her to be wealthy, are coming from Ireland to visit, and she does not want her deception to be discovered. Complications ensue, and Cordelia becomes so distraught that, in a melodramatic scene, she attempts suicide, drinking what she believes to be "Roach Poison." Before the final curtain, it is revealed that she has succeeded only in stumbling unwittingly upon the maid's reserve supply of booze. Cordelia realizes that she was much happier in her former surroundings, and later in the season, in *Dan's Tribulations* (April 7, 1884), the Mulligans returned to their old friends and neighbors in the familiar downtown setting.

On December 23, 1884, the New Theatre Comique was completely destroyed by fire. This was a staggering financial blow, as the theater had not been insured. Harrigan and Hart then leased the New Park Theatre (later the Herald Square) on Broadway at 35th Street, where they opened with *McAllister's Legacy* (January 5, 1885). When the show did poorly, they moved to the 14th Street Theatre, hoping for better business there. But the financial losses incurred by the fire and the failure of the new show at the box office brought the increasingly strained personal and professional relationship of Harrigan and Hart to the breaking point. *McAllister's Legacy* was their last show together.

For Tony Hart, this spelled the end of a successful career. He tried to make it on his own as an actor, but because his health and mental condition were deteriorating, these attempts were ineffectual. A victim of paresis, he came to a tragic end in a mental hospital in Worcester, Massachusetts, where he died on November 4, 1891.

After the split with Hart, Harrigan and

Braham continued to work together. On August 31, 1885, they mounted a revival of *Old Lavender* with several new songs, including the hit "When Poverty's Tears Ebb and Flow" (Will Oakland made an early recording of this in 1910). Other revivals followed (Dan Collyer often assumed Tony Hart's roles), and interspersed with these were original productions such as *The Leather Patch* (1886), *The O'Reagans* (1886), *McNooney's Visit* (1887), and *Waddy Googan* (1888), which were moderately successful.

In 1890 Harrigan's Theatre opened at 63 West 35th Street (near Sixth Avenue), featuring what was to be the greatest success of Harrigan and Braham's career. *Reilly and the 400* (December 29, 1890) further explored how one becomes a member of high society and also the unwritten rules that govern it. Pawnbroker Wily Reilly will never belong to the upper crust, but his son, a lawyer who is to marry into a wealthy family because of his father's efforts on his behalf, will gain entrée. Ada Lewis, as Kittie Lynch, the first of her "tough girl" roles, quickly became one of the audience's favorites, and the show's best song was the memorable waltz "Maggie Murphy's Home," introduced by the 15-year-old Emma Pollock. With a spectacular run of 202 performances, *Reilly and the 400* was Harrigan and Braham's longest-running show.

The Last of the Hogans (December 21, 1891) was the last successful show on which Harrigan and Braham collaborated; it is remembered because one of its songs, "Danny By My Side," whose opening line is "The Brooklyn Bridge on Sunday is known as lover's lane," was sung by Governor Alfred E. Smith during the celebration of the Brooklyn Bridge's 50th anniversary. *The Woolen Stocking* (1893) and *Notoriety* (1894) came next, but when they failed, Harrigan's was leased to Richard Mansfield, who soon renamed it the Garrick Theatre.

As their fortunes continued to decline, Harrigan and Braham began to work independently of one another. Braham composed the score for *The Finish of Mr. Fresh* (1898), but he no longer had the luxury of writing for a cast of regulars he knew intimately, and the result was a fiasco. However, he continued to conduct and was engaged at Wallack's at the time of his death. In his last years, he suffered from a fatal kidney condition, and he died in New York City on April 11, 1905.

Harrigan toured on the Keith & Proctor vaudeville circuit from 1897 to 1899, performing excerpts form various Harrigan and Hart shows, and in 1901 he published a book entitled *The Mulligans.* His last show, *Under Cover* (music by Braham's son George) opened in New

York in 1903 (90 performances), and he also accepted engagements as an actor. Harrigan's final performance took place on May 9, 1909 at the annual gambol of the Lambs Club; he had presented a medley of his best-known songs, and while waiting to participate in the show's finale, he suffered a stroke. Harrigan was despondent during the last two years of his life; he suffered from chronic heart disease and believed that he had been completely forgotten by the public. He died in New York City on June 6, 1911.

Later generations in the theater owe much to the shows of Harrigan, Hart and Braham, a debt that George M. Cohen was among the first to acknowledge in his song, "Harrigan" ("H-A-Double R-I-G-A-N Spells Harrigan"). As Samuel G. Freedman pointed out in *The New York Times* (January 27, 1985): "Beyond the importance of his themes, Harrigan also laid the groundwork for what would become American musical comedy, particularly in his use of songs to advance the stage action . . . The variety circuit that spawned Harrigan and Hart would metamorphose into vaudeville, burlesque and silent films, the training ground for such comedians as Bob Hope and Milton Berle, and the influence on such modern theater artists as the mime Bill Irwin."

Many of Braham and Harrigan's songs were revived in a Broadway musical entitled *Harrigan 'n' Hart* (January 31, 1985), starring Harry Groener as Ned Harrigan and Mark Hamill as Tony Hart. The book, written by Michael Stewart, was based on *The Merry Partners: The Age and Stage of Harrigan and Hart* by E. J. Kahn, Jr., with additional material provided by Nedda Harrigan Logan.

ABOUT: Hamm, C. Yesterdays: Popular Song in America, 1979; Kahn, E. J., Jr. The Merry Partners: The Age and Stage of Harrigan and Hart, 1955; Moody, R. Ned Harrigan: From Corlear's Hook to Herald Square, 1980. *Periodicals*: American Mercury February 1929; New York Herald July 12, 1891; New York Times January 27, 1985.

BROWN, LEW (December 10, 1893–February 5, 1958), lyricist, was a member of the songwriting team of De Sylva, Brown and Henderson. Of this trio, Brown was the most prolific, with more than 100 successful songs to his credit. He was born Louis Brownstein in Odessa, Russia to Jacob and Etta (Hirsch) Brownstein. In 1889 the family immigrated to the United States, settling in New Haven, Connecticut, where Brown attended elementary school. The Brownstein family moved to New York City, where Lew attended DeWitt Clinton High School. He was no

LEW BROWN

scholar, but did attract attention with his parodies of current hit songs. Even while working as a lifeguard at Rockaway Beach on Long Island during his summer, he was busy jotting down verses.

Determined to make his way as songwriter, Brown left high school without a diploma. For the next few years he attempted unsuccessfully to market his verses in Tin Pan Alley. Albert von Tilzer, already an experienced hand at writing hit songs, volunteered to set some of Brown's verses to music. They completed five songs in 1912, including "I'm the Lonesomest Gal in Town"—Brown sold the lyrics to a publisher for a flat fee of seven dollars—and "Please Don't Take My Lovin' Man Away."

Within a few years, with Albert von Tilzer as composer, Brown was an established Tin Pan Alley lyricist. In 1917 they wrote the popular World War I ballad, "I May Be Gone for a Long, Long Time," which was interpolated into the Broadway revue *Hitchy Koo of 1917*. Two other von Tilzer–Brown songs in that edition of *Hitchy Koo* were "Au Revoir, But Not Goodbye, Soldier Boy" and "Give Me the Moonlight, Give Me the Girl." Their "Oh, By Jingo," a nonsense song, became popular in 1919, and the von Tilzer–Brown hit of 1920 was "I Used to Love You But It's All Over."

In 1922 Louis Bernstein, of the music publishing firm of Shapiro-Bernstein, suggested that Brown work with a young employee of his company, Ray Henderson, who showed promise as a composer. This fledgling songwriting partnership scored immediate successes with "Georgette" and "Humming," both of 1922.

Their "Annabelle" was interpolated into the *Ziegfeld Follies of 1923*, the year in which they also wrote "Counterfeit Bill From Louisville." The melody of "Why Did I Kiss That Girl?" (1924) was composed by Henderson in collaboration with Robert King, and in 1925 Billy Rose collaborated with Brown in writing the lyrics to Henderson's music for "Don't Bring Lulu."

While working with Henderson, Brown also collaborated with other composers. In 1923, with James Kendis, he wrote "When It's Nighttime in Italy." Kendis, a popular performer in the early days of radio, introduced and popularized it on his radio show. In 1923 Eddie Cantor introduced "Seven or Eleven" (music by Walter Donaldson). "S-H-I-N-E" (1923, lyrics written with Cecil Mack, music by Fred Dabney), was popularized by Louis Armstrong, and it became one of Armstrong's signature songs. "S-H-I-N-E" was revived in the movie *Cabin in the Sky* (1943), in which it was sung by John Bubbles, and it was revived again in 1948 in a bestselling recording by Frankie Laine. In 1923 Brown joined Sidney D. Mitchell in writing the lyrics to Seymour Simons's music for "Ain't You Ashamed?" That year Brown also lampooned the national craze for the nonsense song "Yes, We Have No Bananas" by writing the lyrics for "I've Got the Yes! We Have No Bananas Blues" (music by James F. Haley), which was recorded by Belle Baker with vocal backing by the Virginians. Still another Lew Brown song became a hit in 1923, "Last Night on the Back Porch" (music by Carl Schraubsder), which Winnie Lightner introduced in *George White's Scandals of 1923* and which Paul Whiteman recorded. In 1926 "I'd Climb the Highest Mountain" (music by Sidney Clare) was popularized in vaudeville by Sophie Tucker and by Lillian Roth; it was recorded by Al Jolson, Art Gillham, the Ink Spots and the orchestra of Roger Wolfe Kahn. In 1945 it was interpolated into the motion picture, *Billy Rose's Diamond Horseshoe*.

In 1925 B. G. De Sylva, an established lyricist, joined Brown and Henderson to form the songwriting trio that was to dominate the Broadway musical theater for the next decade. Their first team effort was also their first Broadway musical score, *George White's Scandals of 1925*, in which "I Want a Lovable Baby" was heard. To *George White's Scandals of 1926* De Sylva, Brown and Henderson contributed two of their song classics, "Black Bottom" and "The Birth of the Blues." "Lucky Day" and "The Girl is You" were also introduced in the 1926 revue. For *George White's Scandals of 1928* they wrote "I'm on the Crest of a Wave," "What D'Ya Say?" and "An Old-Fashioned Girl."

Moving from revues to musical comedy, the three songwriters contributed complete scores for the musicals *Good News* (1927); *Manhattan Mary* (1927); *Hold Everything* (1928); *Follow Thru* (1929) and *Flying High* (1930). For motion pictures they wrote songs for *The Singing Fool* (1928), starring Al Jolson; *Sunny Side Up* (1929); *Just Imagine* (1930); *Happy Days* (1930) and *Indiscreet* (1931). (The success of *Good News* prompted De Sylva, Brown and Henderson to form their own publishing firm in 1927.)

From these stage and screen productions came many hit songs. From Broadway's *Good News* came "The Best Things in Life Are Free"; "The Girls of Pi Beta Phi"; "The Varsity Drag" and the title song; from *Hold Everything* came "You're the Cream in My Coffee"; from *Follow Through*, "Button Up Your Overcoat"; "I Want to Be Bad"; "My Lucky Star" and "Don't Hold Everything"; and from *Flying High*, "Good for You, Bad for Me"; "Wasn't it Beautiful While it Lasted?"; "Without Love" and "Thank Your Father." It was for the movie *The Singing Fool* that the team wrote its greatest hit song, "Sonny Boy." From the film *Sunny Side Up* came "I'm a Dreamer, Aren't We All?"; "If I Had a Talking Picture of You" and the title song; from *Just Imagine*, "An Old-Fashioned Girl" and "You Are the Melody"; and from *Indiscreet*, "Come to Me."

De Sylva, Brown and Henderson also composed hit songs that were not intended for scores for the stage and the screen. These were "It All Depends on You" (1926), "Just a Memory" (1927), "Together" (1928) and "You Try Somebody Else" (1931).

The partnership of De Sylva, Brown and Henderson ended with *Indiscreet,* a separation that was finalized when they sold their publishing house. De Sylva became a producer of films and Broadway musicals and worked occasionally as librettist. For a time, Brown and Henderson worked together in the Broadway musical theater. They wrote the complete score for the *George White Scandals of 1931,* which contained five hit songs—"Life is Just a Bowl of Cherries"; "This is the Missus"; "My Song"; "The Thrill is Gone" and "That's Why Darkies Are Born." They went on to write both the libretto and songs for the Broadway musicals *Hot Cha* (1932), starring Bert Lahr, and *Strike Me Pink* (1933), starring Jimmy Durante, both of which were produced by Brown and Henderson. "You Can Make My Life a Bed of Roses" came from *Hot Cha,* "Let's Call it a Day" from *Strike Me Pink.*

In 1931 Brown began working with composers other than Henderson, both for Broadway and

Hollywood. With Jay Gorney as composer, he wrote "Baby Take a Bow" for *Stand Up and Cheer* (1933), the Brown-produced film that made the four-year-old Shirley Temple a star. Sammy Fain composed the music to Brown's lyrics for "That Old Feeling," which was introduced in the Brown-produced film *Vogues of 1938* (1937) and has become a standard. Brown used a popular Czech melody by Jaromir Vejvoca for his "Beer Barrel Polka," which was interpolated into the Broadway musical *Yokel Boy* (1939), which Brown produced. Brought into that faltering show two months after it had opened on July 6, "Beer Barrel Polka" was introduced by the Minute Men from Lexington. It became one of the season's biggest hit songs—26 hearings on *Your Hit Parade* in 1939—through recordings by the Andrews Sisters and by the orchestra of Sammy Kaye. The Andrews Sisters sang it in the movie *Follow the Boys* (1946), and in 1954 "Beer Barrel Polka" was revived as a piano interlude on the soundtrack of the nonmusical film classic, *From Here to Eternity* (1954).

Except for "Beer Barrel Polka," *Yokel Boy's* songs were composed by Sam H. Stept and Lew Brown wrote the lyrics with Charles Tobias. "Comes Love" was introduced by Judy Canova and then danced to by Dixie Dunbar. It was recorded by Harry James and his orchestra and had seven hearings on *Your Hit Parade* in 1939. "Let's Make Memories Tonight" (for which Al Sherman became a fourth collaborator) was introduced by Lois January. "Don't Sit Under the Apple Tree" (a melody previously used for a song called "Anywhere the Bluebird Goes") was used for a farmyard scene. Early in World War II, the song became a favorite of G. I.'s stationed overseas. Kay Kyser and his orchestra with the vocal by the Andrews Sisters performed it in the screen musical *Private Buckaroo* (1942). Bestselling recordings by the Andrews Sisters and by the orchestras of Kay Kyser and Glenn Miller helped this standard to achieve 12 representations on *Your Hit Parade,* five times in first place.

"I Dug a Ditch in Wichita" and "Madame, I Love Your Crepe Suzette," (both 1943, lyrics written with Ralph Freed, music by Burton Lane) were the last new lyrics Brown was to write for the screen. The former was heard in *As Thousands Cheer,* the latter in the film version of *Du Barry Was a Lady.* However, these were not the last of Brown's songs to be featured prominently in films. *Good News* became a motion picture in 1947, and in 1956 Brown's principal songs were revived in *The Best Things in Life Are Free,* the screen biography of De Sylva, Brown and Henderson (Brown was portrayed by Ernest Borgnine). By the time that movie was released Brown had been in near retirement for a decade. With Ray Henderson as composer, he had written "An Old Sombrero" in 1947 and in 1950, to Mabel Wayne's music, "On the Outgoing Tide," the latter popularized in a recording by Perry Como.

Brown died of a heart attack in his apartment at the Navarro Hotel in New York City. He was survived by his second wife, June, and two daughters from his previous marriage.

(For additional information about Lew Brown see the biographies of Sammy Fain, Jay Gorney, Ray Henderson, and Albert von Tilzer.)

ABOUT: Craig, W. Sweet and Low Down: America's Popular Songwriters, 1978; Green, S. The World of Musical Comedy, 4th ed. 1980.

ARTHUR FREED

BROWN, NACIO HERB (February 22, 1896–September 28, 1964) and **FREED, ARTHUR** (September 9, 1894–April 12, 1973). Nacio Herb Brown was the first composer to owe his success to talking pictures. With Arthur Freed as his lyricist, he composed the songs for the first "all talking, all singing, all dancing" screen production, *The Broadway Melody* (1929). This was the first time in motion-picture history that a new score, rather than an adapted one, was used. During the ensuing decade, Brown remained one of the most productive contributors of hit songs to the screen, inaugurating an era in which the motion-picture musical enjoyed its first heyday.

He was born Ignacio Herb Brown in Deming, New Mexico. His father, a former stagecoach driver, was the town sheriff. Nacio's mother, an amateur pianist, gave him his first music lessons; a local musician was later recruited to teach him the violin.

In 1902 the family moved to Los Angeles where he was raised and spent the rest of his life. At Manual Arts High School he made his first attempts at composing. After graduating from high school, he studied business administration for less than a year at the University of California at Los Angeles. He left UCLA to work as a piano accompanist for Alice Doll on the vaudeville circuit. After that, he entered the business world. In Hollywood, he opened a menswear shop that became a thriving establishment. By 1930 Brown had turned his accumulated profits into investments in Southern California real estate. This proved so profitable that he was able to sell his menswear firm to concentrate on real estate. The land boom in and around Beverly Hills made him a millionaire.

While acquiring wealth, Brown regarded composing as a hobby. In collaboration with Zany King (pseudonym for Jack Doll), Brown composed "Coral Sea" in 1920, which Paul Whiteman and his orchestra introduced at the Alexandria Hotel in Los Angeles. This was Brown's first published composition.

At about this time, Brown met and befriended Arthur Freed, a song lyricist, and a collaboration was soon agreed upon. When Freed first became acquainted with Brown, he was 26. The oldest child of Max and Rose (Grossman) Freed, he was born in Charleston, South Carolina in 1894. His father had emigrated from Budapest to Charleston, where he opened a furniture store which did so well that by 1910 he was able to retire to Seattle with his family. One of his other children was Ralph Freed (Arthur Freed's junior by 13 years) who also became a lyricist for motion pictures.

In Seattle, Arthur Freed studied the piano with private teachers, having received his first lessons when he was six. His academic education took place at the Philips Exeter Academy, an exclusive private school, from which he graduated in 1914. At school, his favorite diversion was writing poetry and song lyrics. By the time he graduated he had become determined to become a professional songwriter. Rejecting his father's advice that he continue his education at the University of Washington in Seattle, Freed headed for Chicago. He found employment as a piano demonstrator at the Chicago branch of Waterson, Berlin and Snyder. To these offices, one day, came the mother of the Marx Brothers seeking song material for her sons. Meeting Freed, she encouraged him to leave his job and join the Marx Brothers act in vaudeville as a sing-

NACIO HERB BROWN

er. After one summer with the Marx Brothers, he left for New York, finding a place for himself for two years with the Gus Edwards schoolboy act. After that, Freed wrote songs that were heard in revues for restaurants and nightclubs in New York.

During World War I, Freed served in the army, holding the rank of sergeant in an assignment requiring him to produce shows at Camp Lewis in Washington State. After the war, in Seattle, he wrote several more songs (music by Oliver Wallace), among which "Louisiana" and "Cairo" circulated in theaters. In Seattle, Freed and Wallace ran a music shop that was a financial failure, following which they went separate ways.

Los Angeles was Freed's next and final destination. He and Nacio Herb Brown wrote "When Buddha Smiles" (music written with Jack Doll) which was recorded by Eddie Elkins and by Rudy Wiedoeft. Before Freed and Brown could hit their full stride as collaborators, however, Freed enjoyed a substantial success with "I Cried for You" (music by Gus Arnheim and Abe Lyman). Abe Lyman and his orchestra introduced it in 1923. Recordings by Cliff Edwards, Glen Gray and his Casa Loma Orchestra, and later by Mildred Bailey, Connie Boswell, Kate Smith and Billie Holiday, helped to establish it as a standard. Judy Garland sang it in the screen musical, *Babes in Arms* (1939) with which Freed made his debut as producer. That year (1939) the song made three appearances on *Your Hit Parade*. Harry James and his orchestra (vocal by Helen Forrest) performed it in *Bathing Beauty* (1944) and Doris Day sang it in the Ruth Etting screen

biography, *Love Me or Leave Me* (1955). The song was interpolated into *Somebody Loves Me* (1952) and in the Joe E. Lewis screen biography, *The Joker Is Wild* (1957). Since the song became a Billie Holiday specialty, Diana Ross (playing the role of Billie Holiday) sang it in *The Lady Sings the Blues* (1972).

On March 14, 1923 Freed married Renée Klein; they raised one child, a daughter. After touring the vaudeville circuit as piano accompanist for the singer Frances Williams, Freed took over the management of the Grand Avenue Theatre in Los Angeles (later renamed Orange Grove Theatre) where for four years he produced spoken drama together with musicals in which songs by Freed and Nacio Herb Brown were occasionally heard. In one of these, a revue called *The Picklings,* Bing Crosby made his stage debut.

Freed's next theatrical venture in Los Angeles was a series of musicals collectively entitled *Hollywood Music Box Revue* where more songs by Freed and Nacio Herb Brown were heard. One of Brown's instrumental compositions, *Doll Dance,* was here interpolated for Doris Eaton, after which it was popularized in recordings by the orchestras of Vincent Lopez, Guy Lombardo and Frankie Carle.

When MGM launched its program to produce sound films, Irving Thalberg, its producer, planned a lavish screen musical requiring newly written songs. To realize this project, he contracted Freed and Nacio Brown to supply them. That production, *The Broadway Melody* (1929), ushered in the first significant era in the history of screen musicals. It broke new ground not only by using songs written expressly for that production but also by using a backstage story as a framework for song, dance and production numbers. Charles King sang the title number and the love ballad, "You Were Meant for Me." "The Wedding of the Painted Doll," which had previously been written for and tried out in the *Hollywood Music Box Revue,* became the background music for a spectacular production number after having been sung by James Burrows. "The Broadway Melody" and "You Were Meant for Me" were also recorded by Ben Selvin and his orchestra; "You Were Meant for Me," by Ted Straeter and his orchestra; and "The Wedding of the Painted Doll," by Frankie Carle and his orchestra. As standards, these songs were revived in later screen musicals. "The Broadway Melody" was sung by Gene Kelly in *Singin' in the Rain* (1952). Charles King's voice was dubbed in on the soundtrack of *The Hollywood Revue* (1929) for "You Were Meant for Me." That song was later sung by Bull Montana and Winnie

Lightner in *The Show of Shows* (1929), by Frank Morgan in *Hullabaloo* (1942) and by Gene Kelly (and danced to by Debbie Reynolds) in *Singin' in the Rain*. It was also interpolated into *Penny Serenade*, starring Cary Grant (1941). The title, "You Were Meant for Me" was used for that of a motion picture musical (1948) in which it was the recurring theme and where it was sung by Dan Dailey in the final scene. This song again served as a theme for the nonmusical motion picture, *Let's Make It Legal* (1951), starring Claudette Colbert. "The Wedding of the Painted Doll" returned to the screen in *Singin' in the Rain* and again, in 1976, in a truncated rendition by Arthur Freed himself in *That's Entertainment, Part II.*

With *The Broadway Melody* a giant box-office draw, as well as the first musical ever to win an Oscar as the year's best film, MGM followed suit with similar productions while utilizing the songwriting talents of Freed and Nacio Brown. The next MGM lavish screen musical was *The Hollywood Revue* (1929), which dispensed with plot and fictional characters in favor of a revue with an all-star cast, the first time a film had employed a revue format. Here "You Were Meant for Me" was reprised on the soundtrack by Charles King (dubbing for Conrad Nagel). This score also included a new Freed-Brown song classic in "Singin' in the Rain," which had originally been composed and performed in the *Hollywood Music Box Revue*. In 1929, this song was recorded by the orchestras of the Dorsey brothers, Duke Ellington and Gus Arnheim. In *The Hollywood Revue* it was sung by Cliff Edwards, the Brox Sisters and The Rounders. This marked the beginning of an affiliation between this song and motion pictures that continued long after 1929. The song was interpolated for Judy Garland in *Little Nellie Kelly* (1940), after which it entered her permanent repertory. In 1952, the song inspired and provided the name for a screen musical starring Gene Kelly, Debbie Reynolds and Donald O'Connor. This film, in turn, was made into a stage musical, also named *Singin' in the Rain*, produced in London on June 30, 1983. Both were vehicles for the song hits Freed and Nacio Herb Brown had previously composed for the MGM studio. In the motion picture, Kelly did an extended dance sequence to the title song in a rain-drenched street which became such a screen classic that from then on the song and Gene Kelly became inextricably associated with each other. *That's Entertainment* (1974), an anthology of musical and dance highlights from MGM musicals, presented a montage of the many ways in which "Singin' in the Rain" had been used on the screen through the years. The

entire score from *Singin' in the Rain* was released in a soundtrack recording.

"Pagan Love Song," introduced by Ramon Novarro in *The Pagan* (1930), was interpolated into the film *Night Club Girl* (1944) and was performed in the 1950 film *Pagan Love Song* by Esther Williams and Howard Keel. "Chant of the Jungle" was introduced by Joan Crawford in the film *Untamed* (1930). "Pagan Love Song" was recorded by Ramon Novarro and by James Melton, and "Chant of the Jungle" by Melton and by Kate Smith. "Blondy" came out of *Marianne* (1930). The only rewards from *Lord Byron of Broadway* (1930) were the Freed-Brown songs. The film itself suffered such a setback at the box office that it brought about a precipitous end to the screen careers of its two stars, Charles Kaley and Ethelind Terry. But three songs survived. "Should I?" was introduced by Kaley and Terry and revived for Debbie Reynolds (then danced to by Donald O'Connor) in *Singin' in the Rain*. "A Woman in the Shoe" was sung by Ethelind Terry and "A Bundle of Letters" by Kaley. In *Montana Moon* (1930), "The Moon is Low" was sung by Cliff Edwards and recorded by the orchestras of Guy Lombardo, George Olsen and Roger Wolfe Kahn.

For "I'll Still Belong to You," one of Brown's song successes in 1930, the lyricist was not Freed but Edward Eliscu. Eddie Cantor introduced it into the movie adaptation of the stage musical *Whoopee.*

By 1931 movie audiences had grown tired of stereotyped screen musicals. The studios began to cut down severely on their musical productions. Under such circumstances, Nacio Brown left Hollywood for Broadway. With Richard E. Whiting collaborating with him on the music, and B. G. De Sylva, as lyricist, Brown composed some of the songs for the stage musical, *Take a Chance* (November 26, 1932), which had a run of 243 performances. This was a backstage story involving the production of a musical in which Ethel Merman starred. Though much of this score was the work of Vincent Youmans, the song that regularly stopped the show was "Eadie Was a Lady," by De Sylva–Nacio Brown–Richard Whiting, introduced by Ethel Merman. Its success proved so immediate that duing the musical's first week run *The New York Times* published all of its lyrics, and Ethel Merman recorded it on both sides of a single disc. Lillian Roth sang it in the film adaptation of the musical (1933). After that, the song contributed its title to, and was heard again in, a 1945 movie starring Ann Miller. Two other important songs by De Sylva, Brown and Whiting appeared in the stage production: "You're an Old Smoothie," sung by

Ethel Merman and Jack Haley, and "Turn Out the Light," by Jack Haley, Jack Whiting, June Knight and Sid Silvers. "You're an Old Smoothie" was recorded by Carmen Cavallero and became the theme song of Del Courtney's orchestra. Phyllis Shotwell sang it in the Robert Altman film *California Split* (1974), starring Elliot Gould. "Turn Out the Light" was heard again in the movie adaptation of *Take a Chance.*

Despite the now limited demand for songs in Hollywood, Nacio Herb Brown managed to contribute at least one major hit song to motion pictures in 1932. It was "Paradise" (lyrics by Gordon Clifford and Nacio Herb Brown). Pola Negri sang it in *A Woman Commands* (1932) with recordings made by Russ Columbo (who made it his theme song), Frances Langford, Carmen Cavallero and the orchestras of Guy Lombardo and Kay Kyser. In later motion pictures, it was sung by Belita in *The Gangster* (1947), Gloria Grahame in *A Woman's Secret* (1949), Valentine Cortessa in *Malaya* (1949) and Bob Crosby in *The Five Pennies* (1959).

The Hollywood studios were once again busy filming screen musicals in 1933. With MGM in the vanguard of those producing such films, the services of Freed and Brown were again in demand.

One of the major MGM productions of 1933 was *Going Hollywood* in which Bing Crosby first emerged as a screen star. Freed influenced the studio to hire Crosby because he wanted him to sing "Temptation." It became one of Crosby's earliest bestselling recordings; other discs were later made by Perry Como, Jo Stafford, Gertrude Niesen, Tony Martin and Artie Shaw and his orchestra. The song reappeared in *A Date with Judy* (1948), *Malaya* (1949) and *Seven Hills of Rome* (1958). *Going Hollywood* had other memorable songs. Bing Crosby introduced (then recorded) "After Sundown," "Our Big Love Scene," "Beautiful Girl," and "We'll Make Hay," the last of these in a duet with Marion Davies. "After Sundown" was recorded by Richard Himber and his orchestra. In *Singin' in the Rain*, "Beautiful Girl" was sung by Jimmie Thompson.

In 1933 Freed and Brown composed the title song for *Hold Your Man*, where it was introduced by its star, Jean Harlow. Before that year ended, this song reappeared in *Dancing Lady*, starring Joan Crawford and Clark Gable, where it was sung by Winnie Lightner. Don Bestor and his orchestra recorded it. "Love Songs of the Nile," which Ramon Novarro introduced in *The Barbarian* (1933), was recorded by Wayne King and his orchestra and by the Merry Macs.

A year later, Freed and Brown composed another standard, "All I Do is Dream of You"

which Gene Raymond introduced in *Sadie McKay* (1934). The orchestras of Henry Busse, Jan Garber and Freddy Martin recorded it. Chico Marx plucked it on the piano with an extended forefinger in *A Night at the Opera* (1935); Debbie Reynolds sang it in *Singin' in the Rain* and again (this time in a duet with Bobby Van) in *The Affairs of Dobie Gillis* (1953). Twiggy, in her motion picture debut, sang it in *The Boy Friend* (1971) and Liza Minnelli in *Lucky Lady* (1975).

Out of *The Broadway Melody of 1936*, one of the most successful screen musicals of 1935–36, came several more Freed-Brown standards. "You Are My Lucky Star" was introduced by Frances Langford. During the year this film was released, the song appeared nine times on *Your Hit Parade*, three times in first place. Through the years, "You Are My Lucky Star" was repeatedly revived in motion pictures. Betty James sang it in *Babes in Arms* (1939), Gene Kelly and Debbie Reynolds in *Singin' in the Rain*, Phil Regan in *The Boy Friend* (1971), and Liza Minnelli in *New York, New York* (1972). It was used as a recurrent theme in *The Stratton Story* (1949), starring James Stewart, and was interpolated into the Harry Ruby movie biography, *Three Little Words* (1950). Among those who recorded it were Eleanor Powell, Hildegarde, Louis Armstrong, Nat Brandwyne and his orchestra and Carmen Cavallero.

"Sing Before Breakfast," "On a Sunday Afternoon," "I've Got a Feelin' You're Foolin'" and "Broadway Rhythm" were other strong numbers in *The Broadway Melody of 1936*. The first two were introduced by Vilma and Buddy Ebsen, the latter with the participation of Eleanor Powell. "I've Got a Feelin' You're Foolin'" was introduced by Robert Taylor and June Knight (reprise by Francis Langford). It was heard nine times on *Your Hit Parade*, was recorded by Eleanor Powell, was revived by Jane Froman on the soundtrack of her motion picture biography, *With a Song in My Heart* (1952), and was used recurrently in *Singin' in the Rain*. "Broadway Rhythm" was introduced by Frances Langford and Eleanor Powell and had three appearances on *Your Hit Parade*. Eleanor Powell reprised it in *The Broadway Melody of 1938* (1937), Judy Garland sang it in *Babes in Arms*, and it was interpolated into *Presenting Lily Mars* (1943) and *Singin' in the Rain*. Richard Himber and his orchestra recorded "Sunday Afternoon" and "Broadway Rhythm."

"Alone," which Allan Jones and Kitty Carlisle introduced in the Marx Brothers extravaganza *A Night at the Opera* (1935) where it was reprised by Harpo Marx on the harp, had 16 appearances on *Your Hit Parade*, five times in first position. Hal Kemp and his orchestra recorded it. Judy Garland sang it in *Andy Hardy Meets Debutante* (1940) and it was interpolated into *Born to Dance* (1942).

The Freed-Brown song hit of 1936 was "Would You" (16 times on *Your Hit Parade*). First sung by Jeanette MacDonald in *San Francisco* (1936), it was revived for Debbie Reynolds in *Singin' in the Rain*. MGM assembled another group of its stars for *The Broadway Melody of 1938* (1937), and for it Freed and Brown composed three solid numbers. "Yours and Mine," introduced by Judy Garland and reprised by Eleanor Powell, had two appearances on *Your Hit Parade*. Judy Garland also sang "Everybody Sing" and Eleanor Powell and George Murphy, "I'm Feelin' Like a Million." Jan Garber and his orchestra recorded "Yours and Mine" and "I'm Feelin' Like a Million."

In *Babes in Arms* (1939), Freed emerged for the first time as producer while continuing to serve as Brown's lyricist. To Judy Garland and Mickey Rooney "Good Morning" was assigned which was recorded by Jan Savitt and his orchestra. Thirteen years later, it was revived by Debbie Reynolds, Gene Kelly and Donald O'Connor in *Singin' in the Rain*.

With Freed setting his sights on producing, Nacio Herb Brown soon had to seek out other lyricists for his screen songs. "You Stepped Out of a Dream" (lyrics by Gus Kahn) was introduced by Tony Martin in Freed's second production, *Ziegfeld Girl* (1941), and was recorded by Tony Martin and the orchestras of Guy Lombardo and Glenn Miller. *Ziegfeld Girl* also introduced "Love is Where You Find It" (lyrics by Earl K. Brent), sung in the film and recorded by Kathryn Grayson. "Later Tonight" (lyrics by Leo Robin) was performed by Woody Herman and his orchestra in *Wintertime* (1943). "If I Steal a Kiss" (lyrics by Edward Heyman) was heard in *The Kissing Bandit* (1948) where it was sung by Frank Sinatra. Both Sinatra and Vaughn Monroe recorded it.

Nacio Herb Brown's career as a songwriter for Hollywood ended in the 1940s. He retired in 1950. Two years later, he witnessed a cavalcade of his foremost songs march through the film musical, *Singin' in the Rain*, a Freed production that looked back nostalgically to the early years of talking pictures; some of its story was actually based on the early experiences of Freed and Brown at MGM. Betty Comden and Adolph Green wrote the scenario. One new song by Freed and Brown joined the old hits. It was "Make 'Em Laugh," custom-tailored for Donald O'Connor to allow him to display his versatile

repertory as a clown in what has since become one of the high points of his screen career.

With his songwriting days now well behind him, Brown, a victim of cancer in his last 18 months, died in San Francisco in the fall of 1964. He was survived by his third wife, Georgeana, two sons and a daughter.

For Freed the breakup of his partnership with Brown meant the flowering of a new and greater career at MGM, as producer of some of the most successful musicals ever filmed. As assistant producer of *The Wizard of Oz*, he insisted that the then-little-known Judy Garland assume a starring role planned for Shirley Temple and he fought to keep the song "Over the Rainbow" in the production. Freed brought Gene Kelly to star with Judy Garland in *For Me and My Gal*, thereby having a hand in the making of a new singing-dancing screen star. Freed knew that Colette's story *Gigi* belonged on the screen, purchased the rights, and contracted Lerner and Loewe to write its songs. Freed was the motivating force in the making of an extended 15-minute ballet sequence in *An American in Paris* in which Gene Kelly and Leslie Caron danced to the music of Gershwin's tone poem, thereby opening new horizons for ballet within screen stories. In 1951 and 1958, respectively, *An American in Paris* and *Gigi* each won the Oscar as the year's best film (together with an armful of other Oscars in various departments). Other never-to-be-forgotten Freed productions of screen musicals were *Cabin in the Sky*, *The Harvey Girls*, *Till the Clouds Roll By*, *Easter Parade*, *Words and Music*, *Show Boat*, *On the Town*, *Annie Get Your Gun*, *The Band Wagon*, *Brigadoon*, and *Bells Are Ringing*. At a time when movies rarely grossed more than ten million dollars, Freed's 45 productions grossed a total of 300 million dollars. From three of his musicals came Oscar winning songs: "Over the Rainbow" (lyrics by E. Y. Harburg, music by Harold Arlen) in *The Wizard of Oz*; "On the Atchison, Topeka and the Santa Fe" (words by Johnny Mercer, music by Harry Warren) in *The Harvey Girls*; and the title song from *Gigi* (lyrics by Alan Jay Lerner, music by Frederic Loewe).

In recognition of his achievements as a producer the American Academy of Motion Picture Arts and Sciences (of which he was president from 1963 to 1967) twice honored him: with the Irving Thalberg Award in 1961 and a special award in 1968.

By 1968 Freed's career as producer was at an end. MGM, in a financial decline, was now unwilling to gamble large sums of money on new musicals. Freed had two more projects up his sleeve. One was *Say It with Music* that would have been the screen biography of Irving Berlin, using Berlin's songs with Frank Sinatra and Julie Andrews as stars. Long on the planning schedule at MGM, it was finally scrapped. A second Freed project, a musical based on *Huckleberry Finn*, did not even reach the drawing board.

Freed spent his last years in retirement, severely handicapped by arthritis in his last months. He died of a heart attack at his home in Bel Air, California in 1973.

ABOUT: Burton, J. The Blue Book of Tin Pan Alley, 1950.

BRYANT, BOUDLEAUX (February 13, 1920–) and **BRYANT, FELICE** (August 7, 1925–). When Boudleaux Bryant was elected to the Georgia Music Hall of Fame in September 1982, he was being recognized for his contributions to country music in the 1950s and 1960s. Working by himself, and sometimes in collaboration with his wife, Felice, he has produced more than 700 songs which have had a worldwide record distribution of some 300 million discs. Their best-known numbers—"Rocky Top," "Wake Up, Little Susie," "All I Have to Do is Dream" and "Bird Dog"—were enormous hits on the popular as well as country charts.

Boudleaux Bryant was born in Shellman, Georgia, the son of Daniel Green Bryant and Louise (Farham) Bryant. His father was a small-town lawyer who moved his family to Moultrie, Georgia when Boudleaux was an infant. There Boudleaux began studying the violin at the age of five. With his father's encouragement he continued violin study for 13 years, with the ambition of becoming a concert virtuoso. That goal was never realized, but in 1938 he played the violin for one season with the Atlanta Symphony in Georgia, with the Carl Pathé Concert Orchestra, and with the Charlie Jarrett Little Symphony.

The transition from concert to popular music took place in 1939. In a violin maker's shop he met a representative from radio station WSB, Atlanta, who was looking for a violinist to play on the radio in a "hillbilly" ensemble. Bryant asked for and got the job. During the next decade he played the violin in, and sang with, various bluegrass and jazz groups, in clubs and hotels throughout the United States. In the early 1940s he also performed with Penny Radio's Cowboy Band, a group popular in the South.

In 1945 Boudleaux Bryant was playing at Schroeder Hotel in Milwaukee, whose elevator operator was Felice Scaduto. The daughter of Salvatore and Katherine (Loverdi) Scaduto, she

BOUDLEAUX and FELICE BRYANT

was born in Milwaukee, Wisconsin, on August 7, 1925. While attending Centerstreet Public School, the St. Casmir Catholic School and the North Division High School, all in Milwaukee, she received vocal training. She intended to make her way as a folksinger, but while waiting for an opening she accepted any available job. Boudleaux Bryant and Felice Scaduto began dating, and after a whirlwind three-week courtship, were married in Milwaukee on September 5, 1945. They spent their honeymoon at the Gibson Hotel in Cincinnati, where Boudleaux Bryant was booked for an engagement of several months'.

Up to this time, Boudleaux Bryant had been writing songs mainly as a hobby, though several of them had been recorded by obscure "swing" bands in Texas. Encouraged by his wife, he began taking songwriting more seriously. Moreover, he and his wife frequently worked together on both words and music. The Bryants composed about 80 numbers before one was published and recorded. Then, through the efforts of a singer, Rome Johnson, who was then affiliated with the Acuff-Rose Publishing Company in Nashville, the Bryants met Fred Rose, who purchased "Country Boy," a joint effort by the Bryants. It became their first success when a recording by Little Jimmie Dickens sold more than 350,000 copies.

In 1950 the Bryants moved to Nashville, becoming the first songwriters to settle in what would soon become the capital of country music. There they were employed as representatives of Tannen Music, a New York City-based publisher. In their four years in this post, several of their songs established the Bryants as songwriters. Some were solo efforts by Boudleaux, others were husband-and-wife collaborations. Together they wrote "Have a Good Time," published in 1952 by Acuff-Rose, which Tony Bennett and Billy Eckstine each recorded successfully. In 1962 it was revived in a recording by Sue Thompson, of "Sad Movies (Always Make Me Cry)" fame. Without the help of his wife, Boudleaux Bryant wrote "It's a Lovely, Lovely World" (1952), which Carl Smith (then at the start of his career as a country-and-western singer-guitarist) made into one of his first record hits. Thirty years later it was revived in a recording by Gail Davies and received an award from BMI. "Just Wait Till I Get You Alone," written by Boudleaux and Felice, was popularized by Carl Smith in 1953. "Hey, Joe," a "hillbilly" hoedown of 1953 which Boudleaux wrote alone, became the first of his songs to sell a million discs (in Carl Smith's recording). It also crossed over to the pop charts when Frankie Laine covered it; it was later revived in recordings by Joe Stampley and Moe Bandy. Carl Smith was also responsible for the initial sucess of "Back Up Buddy" (1954, a solo effort by Boudleaux Bryant). "I've Been Thinking" (a collaboration) became a top seller in 1955 in Eddy Arnold's recording.

The Bryants left the Tannen publishing house in 1954 to form Showcase Music, Inc., their own publishing company. Two years later, however, they signed a ten-year contract as songwriters for Acuff-Rose. This ushered in a period of even greater success for the Bryants. When their Acuff-Rose contract ran out, the Bryants organized a new firm of their own, Bryant Publications, with offices in Henderson, a suburb of Nashville. Ultimately this firm was renamed The House of Bryant and, in November 1983, its headquarters transferred to Gatlinburg, Tennessee.

It was through Bryant-composed songs that the young singing duo, the Everly Brothers, crossed over from country music to rock and achieved stardom in the 1950s. Don and Phil Everly were unknowns from the rural south when the influential publisher, Wesley Rose, took them under his managerial wing and arranged a contract for them with Cadence Records. In 1957 their professional recording career was launched when "Bye Bye Love," written by both Bryants, sold a million discs. After that, songs written either by Boudleaux Bryant or by Bryant and his wife, and recorded by the Everly Brothers, accumulated sales of over 11 million discs. "Wake Up, Little Susie," written by both Bryants, was released by the Everlys in 1957. The Everly Brothers' next Boudleaux-composed million-seller was "All I Have to Do

is Dream" (1958, subsequently recorded by Andy Gibb and Victoria Principal). The Everlys followed this with "Bird Dog," which was backed by their recording of "Devoted to You," the latter revived in the 1970s through a recording by Carly Simon and James Taylor. The Everlys then released "Problems" and, in 1959, "Take a Message to Mary." "Problems" and "Message to Mary" were composed by both Bryants, but "Dream," "Devoted" and "Bird Dog" were solo efforts by Boudleaux.

"Bye Bye Love" was revived in 1970 by Simon and Garfunkel, who included a live version of the song on their 1970 *Bridge Over Troubled Water* LP. It was also recorded successfully in 1957 by Webb Pierce. In the 1970s it was further popularized in a bestselling recording by Donny Osmond, and in 1980 it was interpolated into the Bob Fosse film, *All that Jazz.*

Songs by the Bryants, in performances by other top recording artists, invaded not only the country music charts but also those of rock and easy listening "pop." Frankie Laine recorded "Hawk Eye" in 1955; Eddie Arnold, "The Richest Man in the World" in 1955; Christy Lane, "Tryin' to Force You" in 1956; Jim Reeves, "Blue Doll" in 1957; and Bob Luman, "Let's Think About Living" in 1960. All of these were composed solely by Boudleaux. On the other hand, Felice was the solo composer-lyricist of "We Could" in 1955, which was a hit for Al Martino and for the country-and-western artists Charley Pride and Tammy Wynette. Hit songs written by both husband and wife included "Raining in My Heart," which was recorded by Buddy Holly in 1959 and revived in 1970 by Anne Murray. "Love Hurts" (1960) was initially popularized by Roy Orbison and in the 1970s became a top-ten hit in a recording by the rock group Nazareth. In 1964 "I Love to Dance" was recorded by Ernest Ashforth and "Baltimore" was released by Sonny James. "Rocky Top," which both Bryants composed in 1967, became a classic in rockabilly music following Roy Orbison's bestselling release. This number was named the University of Tennessee's official football song and, in 1982, the official song of the state of Tennessee. That same year the Bryants opened the Rocky Top Village Inn, a motel in downtown Gatlinburg, where 15 years earlier they had composed the song while staying in a local motel.

In the 1960s, Boudleaux Bryant branched out into instrumental music with "Mexico." In addition to being a hit in the United States, this number sold more than a million records in West Germany, and within a few years accumulated a disc sale in excess of six million copies in various recordings, including a notable one by Herb

Alpert's Tijuana Brass. More ambitious in structure, though not as successful, is Boudleaux's *Polynesian Suite,* a tonal portrait of the South Sea Islands.

In 1970 Boudleaux Bryant collaborated with the famed guitarist Chet Atkins in writing *Country Gentleman.* As performed by the Nashville Brass it won a Grammy as the best instrumental recording of country music. Later song successes by both Bryants included "Come Live With Me" (1973); "All the Time" (1976); "Sweet Deceiver" (1977); "Penny Arcade" (1977); and "I Can Hear Kentucky Calling." (1980). Christy Lane recorded "Penny Arcade" and "Sweet Deceiver"; Roy Clark, "Come Live With Me"; the Osborne Brothers and Chet Atkins each, "I Can Hear Kentucky Calling"; and Eddy Arnold, "All the Time."

In 1978 the Bryants moved from Nashville to Gatlinburg. They have raised two sons, each of whom works in the music industry.

ABOUT: Stambler, I. and Landon, G. Encyclopedia of Folk, Country and Western Music, 1974. *Periodicals*—BMI: The Many Worlds of Music no. 4, 1982.

BURKE, JOHNNY (October 3, 1908–February 25, 1964). Working successively with three composers—Arthur Johnston, James Monaco and James Van Heusen—Johnny Burke was for 18 years one of the most prolific and successful lyricists in Hollywood. Some of his most memorable screen songs were introduced and popularized by Bing Crosby, who starred in almost half of the 40 or more films, mostly of 1930s and 1940s vintage, in which Burke's lyrics were heard.

He was born John Francis Burke in Antioch, California on October 3, 1908. His father, William Earl Burke was a structural engineer; his mother, Mary Agnes (Mungovan) Burke, a schoolteacher.

While still a child, Johnny Burke was brought by his family to Chicago where he received his education. At the age of five, he began a 12-year period of piano study with Martha Dahn. Between 1921 and 1925 he studied drama and acting with William Madden. While being trained in music and theater, he received his academic education at Lindblom High School from which he graduated in 1924. He then attended Crane College in 1924–25, and, from 1925 to 1927, the University of Wisconsin in Madison where he played the piano in the university orchestra.

In 1926, Burke was hired as piano demonstrator for the Chicago firm of Irving Berlin, Inc. He

JOHNNY BURKE

then went on to New York to work for the same company. As an employee in Tin Pan Alley he supplemented his salary by selling special material to performers and by working as a vocal coach. He was also writing song lyrics, but it was not until 1933 that he enjoyed his first success. It came with "Annie Doesn't Live Here Anymore" (music by Harold Spina). Fred Waring's Pennsylvanians introduced it and popularized it in public appearances and in a recording. By the end of 1934, Burke and Spina had composed several more song hits. "Beat o' My Heart" was introduced by Paul Whiteman and his orchestra and recorded by the orchestras of Leo Reisman and Ben Pollack. "It's Dark on Observatory Hill," was recorded by Ozzie Nelson and his orchestra (vocal by Harriet Hilliard). "You're Not the Only Oyster in the Stew" became a hit recording in a release by Fats Waller. In 1935, Burke and Spina wrote "My Very Good Friend, the Milkman," which Fats Waller introduced.

These successes brought Burke a contract from the Paramount studios in Hollywood in 1936 with which, for the most part, he remained affiliated for almost two decades. The first composer with whom he worked there was Arthur Johnston. Their initial film was *Pennies from Heaven* which came from the Columbia studios rather than Paramount because its star, Bing Crosby, a contract performer at Paramount, was temporarily on loan. The main strength of this motion picture rested in its star and in the songs he introduced. The title song was heard on *Your Hit Parade* 13 times, four times in first position. Crosby's recording was a bestseller, but it was also recorded that year by Hal Kemp and his orchestra. Dick Haymes sang it in *Cruisin' Down the River* (1953); it was interpolated into the nonmusical films, *From Here to Eternity* (1954) and *Picnic* (1956); Bing Crosby sang it again in a guest appearance in the motion picture *Pepe* (1960). In 1981, it was sung by Vermel Begneris in a new movie calling itself *Pennies from Heaven* which, except for the use of the title song, had no further connection with the early Bing Crosby film.

While the title song was the musical highlight of the 1936 *Pennies from Heaven* it was not the only song Crosby introduced there and later recorded. There were three others: "One, Two, Button Your Shoes," "So Do I," and "Let's Call a Heart, a Heart." Hal Kemp and his orchestra recorded "So Do I."

Johnny Burke and Arthur Johnston returned to the Paramount studios with *Go West, Young Man* (1936) which starred Mae West. In *Double or Nothing* (1937), Burke and Johnston were again writing songs for Bing Crosby who introduced "The Moon Got in My Eyes," "It's the Natural Thing to Do" and "All You Want to Do is Dance," all three of which he recorded. "The Moon Got in My Eyes" appeared seven times on *Your Hit Parade*.

Between 1938 and 1940, Johnny Burke shared songwritng credits mainly with the composer James Monaco. They composed songs for seven motion-picture musicals starring Bing Crosby, including *Road to Singapore* which launched the Crosby–Bob Hope "road" series in 1940. Out of these came another handful of hit songs: "I've Got a Pocketful of Dreams" and "On the Sentimental Side" from *Doctor Rhythm* (1938); "An Apple for Teacher," "A Man and His Dreams" and "Go Fly a Kite" from *The Star Maker* (1939); "Only Forever" and "That's for Me" from *Rhythm on the River* (1940); "Too Romantic" from *Road to Singapore* (1940).

For "Scatterbrain," a hit song in 1939, Burke worked with composers Frankie Masters, Kahn Keene and Carol Bean. It was first performed by Frankie Masters and his orchestra before becoming his theme song. Benny Goodman and his orchestra recorded it. It was interpolated into the motion picture, *That's Right—You're Wrong* (1939) for Kay Kyser and his orchestra and, in 1939, had thirteen appearances on *Your Hit Parade*, six times in first position. In 1940, this song provided its title for that of a motion picture starring Judy Canova in which it was used as the background music for a production number.

While still Monaco's collaborator, Burke began a working arrangement with James Van Heusen, composer. Their first song was "Oh,

You Crazy Moon," in 1939, which was followed that year by "Imagination." One year later, they wrote several songs for *Love Thy Neighbor*, starring Jack Benny and Fred Allen. Burke and Monaco contributed the songs for the Bing Crosby film, *Road to Zanzibar* (1941). After that, they became permanently established as songwriting partners for the screen, composing songs for about twenty films in the 1940s. Many of these songs were heard on *Your Hit Parade*, as follows: "Humpty Dumpty Heart" from *Playmates* (1941); "It's Always You," from *Road to Zanzibar* (1941); "Moonlight Becomes You" from *Road to Morocco* (1942); "If You Please" and "Sunday, Monday and Always" from *Dixie* (1943); "It Could Happen to You" from *And the Angels Sing* (1944); "Sleighride in July" from *Belle of the Yukon* (1944); the Oscar-winning "Swinging on a Star" from *Going My Way* (1944); "Aren't You Glad You're You" from *The Bells of St. Mary's* (1945); "Personality" from *Road to Utopia* (1945); "A Friend of Yours" from *The Great John L.* (1945); "But Beautiful" from *Road to Rio* (1947). Also on *Your Hit Parade*, though not from any film, was "Devil May Care" in 1947.

Several other screen songs by Burke and Van Heusen, though not on *Your Hit Parade* deserve mention: the title song from *Road to Morocco*; "Put it There, Pal" from *Road to Utopia*; "You Don't Have to Know the Language" from *Road to Rio* (1947); "Sunshine Cake" from *Riding High* (1950). "Polka Dots and Moonbeams," a song hit in 1940, however, was a number published independently without any screen affiliation. Some of these songs were published by Burke-Van Heusen, Inc., a publishing house founded in 1944.

John Burke and Van Heusen were less fortunate on the Broadway stage. *Nelly Bly* (January 3, 1946) and *Carnival in Flanders* (September 8, 1953), to which they contributed complete scores, had runs of sixteen performances and six performances respectively.

The collaboration of Van Heusen and Burke ended with *Carnival in Flanders*. Though Burke's successful affiliation with motion pictures was now over, his songwriting career continued with two successful numbers intended neither for screen or stage. For "Wild Horses," in 1953, he was both composer and lyricist (using the pen-name of K. C. Bogan for the composer credit), lifting his melody from *Wild Horseman*, a piece in Robert Schumann's *Album for the Young*, for piano. Perry Como popularized the song on radio and in a recording. In 1955, Burke wrote lyrics for "Misty," an instrumental by Erroll Garner made famous in 1954 in a recording by the Garner Trio. As a song with lyrics, it was popularized in 1956 in bestselling recordings by Mitch Miller and his orchestra and by Johnny Mathis, the latter recording realizing a million-disc sale. This song was the inspiration for, and was basic to the plot of, the motion picture *Play Misty for Me* (1971), starring Clint Eastwood.

(For additional material on songs written with James Monaco and James Van Heusen consult the biographies of these composers.)

On May 18, 1961, Burke returned to Broadway with songs (music as well as words) for *Donnybrook!* in which Robert E. McEnroe's text was based on the 1952 John Ford motion-picture classic, *The Quiet Man.* A run of sixty-eight performances for the stage musical marked the termination of Burke's songwriting career. Its score was issued in an original cast album.

After that, Burke lived in retirement in New York with his third wife, Mary (Marisse) Mason, an actress he had married on December 11, 1961. Both former marriages had ended in divorce. He had married Bess Patterson on June 10, 1939 and Pat Stanley on July 4, 1955.

ABOUT: Craig, W. Sweet and Lowdown: America's Popular Song Writers, 1978; Rigdon, W. (ed.) The Biographical Encyclopedia and Who's Who of the American Theatre, 1966.

CAESAR, IRVING (July 4, 1895–   ). Lyricist-composer Irving Caesar was born Isidore Caesar in New York City, the son of Morris Caesar, a teacher and book dealer, and Sofia (Selinger) Caesar. As a boy, Irving received his musical training at the Music School Settlement in downtown Manhattan. His primary schooling took place at the Chautauqua (New York) Mountain Institute in 1908–09, and in 1914 he graduated from Townsend Harris Hall, a New York high school for superior students which compressed the four-year curriculum into three. For a single year (1914–15) he attended the College of the City of New York.

In 1915 Caesar was employed as the official stenographer of the Henry Ford Peace Ship, which the industrialist Henry Ford dispatched to Europe in a futile attempt to bring World War I to an end. After that, Caesar went to work for the Ford Motor Company as a press correspondent. Ford prevailed upon him to work as a mechanic in the Ford automobile plant so that he might acquire the know-how in the manufacture of automobiles to run a branch of Ford's export division.

Caesar's job was filling grease in rear axles on the conveyer belt. But his ambition lay in writ-

IRVING CAESAR

ing song lyrics. Invading Tin Pan Alley to try selling his ware, he became acquainted with George Gershwin, then a young piano demonstrator at the publishing house of Jerome H. Remick. Between late 1916 and early 1917, Caesar often visited Remick's to listen to Gershwin play the piano. Before long, the young Gershwin began setting Caesar's lyrics to music. Their first song was "You-oo, Just You," which Remick published in 1918. It was soon followed by "There's More to the Kiss Than the X-X-X" and "I Was So Young." Since "You-oo, Just You" was introduced in *Hitchy-Koo of 1918,* and "There's More to the Kiss Than the X-X-X" and "I Was So Young" were interpolated into *Good Morning, Judge* (1919), Caesar's career in the Broadway musical theater had begun. In 1919 two other Caesar songs, this time with music by Walter Donaldson, were heard in the Broadway musical *The Lady in Red.*

Besides being collaborators, Caesar and Gershwin had become fast friends who went to the theater and concerts together, played billiards, and were members of a social club which met regularly in a restaurant on Fifth Avenue and 16th Street. Gershwin visited Caesar one day at the Ford plant and, while Caesar was busy at the conveyer belt, they discussed song ideas. Caesar became so engrossed in conversation that he allowed ten rear axles to go by without applying grease, and the axles all later burned out. This prompted the plant foreman to shift Caesar to a desk job, where he remained until 1919. Then, confident that he could make a living through writing songs, he left the factory to devote himself exclusively to the music business.

It was with Gershwin as his musical partner that Caesar realized his first giant song hit, "Swanee." It was first heard in the stage show that opened the Capitol Theatre in New York on October 24, 1919, then was promoted by Al Jolson. Caesar's first-year royalties amounted to the then substantial sum of $10,000, and the song kept on earning money for many years.

During the early 1920s, Caesar made further inroads into the Broadway musical theater. With the collaboration of Eddie Cantor, Caesar wrote "I Love Her, She Loves Me," which Cantor introduced in the revue *Make It Snappy* in 1922 and recorded the same year. To Louis Hirsh's music, and with John Murray Anderson collaborating on the lyrics, Caesar contributed several numbers to two major revues in 1922. "Sixty Seconds Every Minute, I Think of You" was introduced by Carl Randall and Marjorie Peterson in the *Ziegfeld Follies of 1922* and "Nightingale, Bring Me a Rose" was introduced by Lucille Chalfant in the *Greenwich Village Follies of 1922*. For *Poppy*, in which W. C. Fields was starred in 1923, Caesar fitted new American lyrics to a famous Viennese song, "Wien, du Stadt der Lieder," calling it "Someone Will Make You Smile." "What Do You Do Sunday?" (music by Stephen Jones), sung by Luella Gear and Robert Woolsey, was also heard in *Poppy*. In addition to these songs, Caesar wrote the words to Gershwin's music for "The Yankee Doodle Blues" in 1922 and "Nashville Nightingale" in 1923. The former was interpolated in the revue *Spice of 1922* and the latter in *Nifties of 1923*.

Caesar's greatest success in the Broadway theater came two years later with songs for *No, No, Nanette* (September 16, 1925), for which Vincent Youmans was the composer. From that musical, Caesar's greatest song hit since "Swanee" came with "Tea for Two" and "I Want to Be Happy."

Over the next few years, Caesar's lyrics had additional hearings in the Broadway theater. To the successful Vincent Youmans musical *Hit the Deck* (1927) Caesar contributed the lyrics to "Sometimes I'm Happy," one of the show's top numbers. With Joseph Meyer and Roger Wolfe Kahn as composer, Caesar wrote the lyrics to *Here's Howe* (May 1, 1928), which lasted on Broadway for only 71 performances. "Crazy Rhythm" was introduced there by Ben Bernie, Peggy Chamberlain and June O'Dea and recorded that year by Harry Reser and his orchestra. Harry James and his orchestra later recorded it; Dan Dailey sang it in the film *You Were Meant for Me* (1948) as did Patrice Wymore in *Tea for Two* (1950); and it was included on the soundtrack of the Francis Ford Coppola film, *Cotton Club* (1984).

In *Whoopee* (1928), a Ziegfeld production starring Eddie Cantor in one of his most successful book musicals, Cantor sang "My Blackbirds Are Bluebirds Now" (lyrics by Caesar and music by Cliff Friend), an interpolation. George Jessel sang it in *Lucky Boy* (1928), in which he made his debut in talking pictures.

Wonder Bar (March 17, 1941) was a successful Austrian musical adapted for the Broadway stage for Al Jolson (here appearing in white face). For it Caesar wrote both the American libretto and the lyrics. In spite of Jolson's drawing power, the production ran for only 86 performances. "Oh, Donna Clara" (music by Beda Fritz Löhner) was sung in that production by Jolson, who also recorded it. When *Wonder Bar* was made into a motion picture for Jolson in 1943, it had a new score by Al Dubin and Harry Warren.

On September 9, 1943 Caesar appeared on Broadway in the triple role of producer, librettist and lyricist for *My Dear Public*, a revue starring Willie Howard. Sam Lerner assisted with the lyrics while Gerald Marks provided the music. This show lasted 44 performances.

During this period several of Caesar's songs became successful without the benefit of exposure in the Broadway theater. "Satisfied" (music by Cliff Friend) was introduced in 1929 by Rudy Vallee at his nightclub and then popularized by him on radio and in a recording. In 1930, "Just a Gigolo" (music by Leonello Casucci) was an Austrian song for which Caesar prepared new lyrics. Vincent Lopez and his orchestra first popularized it on radio and in a recording, and it was subsequently recorded by Harry Richman and by Tony Martin. "Gigolo" was interpolated into the motion picture *Lover, Come Back* (1946) and was revived for Marlene Dietrich in the film *Just a Gigolo* (1981). Still in 1930, "Lady, Play Your Mandolin" became the only successful song Oscar Levant ever composed. With Caesar's lyrics it was introduced by Nick Lucas, was recorded by Ben Selvin and his orchestra, and then became identified with Blossom Seeley, who featured it in her vaudeville act. For "If I Forget You" (1933) Ceasar composed his own music. James Melton made it popular in vaudeville and on radio, and Frank Sinatra later recorded it.

In the 1930s and 1940s Caesar also wrote songs for motion pictures. Two had music by Ray Henderson: "Hasty Man" (lyrics written in collaboration with Jack Yellen), heard in *George White's Scandals* (1934), and "Animal Crackers in My Soup," from *Curly Top* (1935), starring Shirley Temple. Gerald Marks provided the music for "Count Your Blessings" and "That's What I Want for Christmas." The former, with Caesar's lyrics which were based on verses by Edgar A. Guest, had its initial hearing in the 1934 film *Palooka*. The latter was sung by Shirley Temple in *Stowaway* (1936). "Umbriago" (music by Jimmy Durante) was a specialty number which Durante introduced in the film *Music for Millions* (1944).

With Gerald Marks as composer, and Sammy Lerner providing an assist in the writing of the lyrics, Caesar wrote "Is it True What They Say About Dixie?" in 1936. After Rudy Vallee had popularized it on radio, it was heard that year 14 times on *Your Hit Parade*, five times in first position. Jolson then made it one of his specialties, and sang it on the soundtrack of *Jolson Sings Again* (1949). Iris Adrian and Robin Raymond sang it as a duet in the film *His Butler's Sister* (1943) and Frances Langford recorded it. Again collaborating with Gerald Marks and Sammy Lerner, Caesar wrote "Saskatchewan," which was popularized in 1936 by the popular violinist Dave Rubinoff and after that by Rudy Vallee.

In 1938 Caesar's songwriting career moved away from the worlds of the theater, movies and Tin Pan Alley towards the schoolroom. "Sing a Song of Safety," for which Gerald Marks wrote the music, gained wide circulation in public schools. Its success impelled Caesar to write words and music for other message-bearing children's songs. Thus he composed "Sing a Song of Friendship," "Songs of Health" and, in 1979, "Songs of Manners," all of which were used in schools throughout the United States.

With the classroom still in mind, Caesar also provided a musical setting for "The Pledge of Allegiance," which, by an official resolution of Congress, was accepted as a government document. A different kind of song, but still outside the boundaries of commercial music, is "Your U. S. Mail Gets Through," adopted as the official song of the National Association of Postmasters of the United States. *Pilgrims of 1940* is a concert work for piano, chorus and orchestra.

Caesar, a bachelor, has for many years maintained a residence at the Hotel Park Sheraton in New York City, while conducting his music business at an office nearby in the Brill Building. At intermittent periods he has appeared on television (most importantly on the Ed Sullivan Show), seated at the piano providing a nostalgic retrospective of his hit songs. His diversions include going to the Turkish bath, swimming, betting on horses, and reading.

ABOUT: Craig, W. Sweet and Lowdown: America's Popular Song Writers, 1978; Green, S. Encyclopedia of Theatre Music, 1976; Jablonski, E. The Encyclopedia of American Music, 1981.

CAHN, SAMMY (June 18, 1913–), lyricist, was born Samuel Cohen in a tenement on New York's Lower East Side, the second of five children and the only son of Abraham Cohen and the former Elka Reis. The parents, who had emigrated from Galicia, Poland, operated a small restaurant. The family's financial condition was marginal, but there was always plenty of food on the table and money to provide the children both academic schooling and music lessons. All four daughters studied the piano, while Sammy, because he was a boy, was given violin lessons. "As a kid," Cahn recalled in his autobiography, *I Should Care,* "I was very slight and wore glasses and always carried a violin case." He was derided as a "sissy" by his peers, but at P. S. 147 Cahn won the approval of his schoolmates by pulling mischievous pranks. At public school, and later at Seward Park High School, he was also a chronic truant who would check in to class at 8:30 in the morning and, an hour later, be employed as a rack-up boy at the Seward Park Poolroom for ten cents an hour, working long enough to earn the admission for an afternoon at the movies. "The movies taught me everything," he said, and he was also infatuated with vaudeville shows.

At his own bar mitzvah party Cahn was astonished to discover that playing the violin could be lucrative when his mother paid the band $25. The following summer Cahn began playing the violin at Catskill Mountains resorts. He then became a member of The Pals of Harmony, a small Dixieland band that performed at bar mitzvahs, weddings and other social events.

Convinced that their son was not destined to become a doctor or a lawyer, the Cohens allowed Sammy to drop out of Seward Park High to make his own way. He initially went from job to job—usher in a movie house, tinsmith, operator of a freight elevator, restaurant cashier, porter in a looseleaf bindery plant and, finally, for three years a "candle boy" at the United Dressed Beef Company. All the while he was playing the violin with The Pals of Harmony, for which his mother now served as booking agent.

When he was 16, Cahn went to a vaudeville show where the headliner, Jack Osterman, received an ovation for one of his own songs. This sparked Cahn's ambition to become a songwriter, and that day he wrote his first song lyric, "Like Niagara Falls, I'm Falling for You." After that, while playing the violin in a Bowery burlesque house and on the borscht belt in the Catskills, he discovered he had a facility for writing topical, and sometimes ribald, parodies of popular songs.

In 1933 Cahn wrote the only song for which he produced both words and music, a shimmy

SAMMY CAHN

called "Shake Your Head From Side to Side." It was also his first published song. Thereafter, Cahn concentrated solely on lyric writing. He recruited Saul Kaplan (better known as Saul Chaplin), the pianist in his band, to serve as composer. Renting an office on West 44th Street, they completed ten songs a day as well as special material for Milton Berle, Bob Hope, Phil Silvers, Danny Kaye and Frank Sinatra, among others. In 1935 Cahn and Chaplin composed "Rhythm is Our Business" for the Jimmie Lunceford band, which introduced, recorded, and then adopted it as its theme song. Also in 1935, Jimmie Lunceford introduced, recorded and popularized another Cahn-Chaplin song, "Rhythm in My Nursery Rhymes," whose publication credits Don Raye's help with the lyrics and Lunceford's assistance with the music. This is the song with which, in 1936, Cahn made his first appearance on *Your Hit Parade* with five representations.

In 1936, for the first appearance of Glen Gray and the Casa Loma Orchestra at the New York Paramount, Cahn and Chaplin wrote "The Glen Gray Casa Loma Corporation." Collaborating with Alberta Nichols and L. B. Freemanlyr, that year they composed "Until the Real Thing Comes Along" for Andy Kirk whose recording started his successful performing career. For a recording by Ella Fitzgerald, they wrote "If You Should Ever Leave." Their biggest hit came with "Shoe Shine Boy" in 1936, composed for Louis Armstrong, who introduced it in a nightclub revue at Connie's Inn in New York City. It was recorded by Bing Crosby and by the Mills Brothers.

By the late 1930s Cahn and Chaplin were writing songs and special material at the Vitaphone studios in Brooklyn where motion-picture "shorts" were produced. "We wrote," explained Cahn, "for almost every entertainer known or unknown . . . songs of every type—songs for bands, songs for acrobats, songs for ice-skaters." One of these numbers, "Please Be Kind," introduced by Mildred Bailey, became the first song from a movie "short" to be heard on *Your Hit Parade* where it appeared 13 times, once in first position on March 19, 1938. Also of this period was "I'm a Musical Magical Man," written for Georgie Price and first seen in a cinematic "short" featuring dancing trumpets. Ted Lewis used it in his act for years, recorded it, and interpolated it into one of his films.

While working for Vitaphone in 1936, Cahn and Chaplin, with their friend, Lou Levy, visited the Apollo Theatre in Harlem, famous for its presentations of great black entertainers. One of the acts was a duo that sang a borscht belt Yiddish song called "Bei mir bist du schoen." When the black audience roared its approval without having understood a single word, Cahn instantly grasped the number's potential. Acquiring a copy of the sheet music, he learned that the composer was Sholom Secunda and the lyricist, Jacob Jacobs, who had written it in 1933 for a Yiddish musical produced in Brooklyn. Within a few weeks of the Yiddish show's opening in Brooklyn, the song became a favorite at religious ceremonies and at Catskill Mountains resorts. Guy Lombardo and His Royal Canadians recorded it as an instrumental.

A copy of this sheet music, reposing on the rack of Cahn's piano in the apartment-office which he shared with Lou Levy on 57th Street and Sixth Avenue, attracted the interest of the Andrews Sisters, who were managed by Levy. The Andrews Sisters were not yet a famous singing trio. After Cahn sang "Bei mir bist du schoen" to them in Yiddish, they persuaded Jack Kapp of Decca Records to allow them to record it. Kapp insisted on English lyrics and within half an hour, Cahn wrote them while Chaplin adapted the melody. Only after the Andrews Sisters had recorded it did Cahn and Chaplin clear all the rights with the J. & J. Kamen Company, which now held the copyright. Bearing the Yiddish title of "Bei mir bist du schoen," the new English adaptation became one of the biggest hits of 1938. The recording by the Andrews Sisters sold more than a million copies and catapulted them to stardom. Benny Goodman performed it in a swing version and Ella Fitzgerald in a "hot" rendition. Judy Garland, Kate Smith, Belle Baker, Rudy Vallee and Steve Lawrence with Eydie Gorme were among the performers who did it as a ballad. When Benny Goodman performed it in Carnegie Hall on January 16, 1938, "The audience burst into rhythmic shouts and hand claps, which momentarily produced more decibels than the instruments on the stage," according to a press report. The song appeared nine times on *Your Hit Parade* in 1938, twice in first position. Priscilla Lane sang it in the film *Love, Honor and Behave* (1938) and the Andrews Sisters in *Follow the Boys* (1944). In 1974, when the two surviving Andrews Sisters starred on Broadway in the nostalgic musical *Over Here,* they inspired an ovation with their rendition of it. The only ones who failed to profit from this song's enormous success were Secunda and Jacobs. However, in the early 1960s, the arrangement with the publishers was renegotiated and Secunda and Jacobs were at last enabled to share in the royalties. But by then the song was no longer a money-earner. From their victory, Secunda and Jacobs derived more personal satisfaction than actual cash.

In 1938 Cahn and Chaplin adapted a second Yiddish song for the Andrews Sisters, "Joseph, Joseph" (words and music originally by Nellie Casman and Samuel Steinberg), with the unfulfilled hope of repeating the success of "Bei mir bist du schoen." Two years later, they wrote "You're a Lucky Guy."

When the Brooklyn Vitaphone studios closed down in 1940, its operators, the Warner brothers, dispatched Cahn and Chaplin to California to write songs for talking pictures. Though for two years they collected weekly salaries, no assignments came their way, and they were forced to contribute songs to the grade B motion pictures produced by Republic. The ensuing discouragement brought to an end their songwriting partnership. Chaplin became a noted movie producer and musical supervisor of film musicals.

Feeling he had hit bottom in his profession, Cahn tried to enlist in the armed forces after Pearl Harbor, but was turned down because he suffered from ulcers. Then his luck changed dramatically when Republic asked him to write the lyrics for *Youth on Parade,* a 1942 film for which Jule Styne was the composer. "I've Heard That Song Before" became a smash success after being introduced in the movie by Frank Sinatra. This led to a five-picture deal at Columbia for Cahn and Styne, a collaboration that soon brought to Hollywood and the Broadway stage some of the most successful popular songs of the 1940s and early 1950s.

Cahn and Styne followed the success of "I've Heard That Song Before" with "As Long as There's Music" from *Step Lively* (1944). One of the enduring ballads of the World War II years, "I'll Walk Alone" was introduced in *Follow the Boys* (1944). This was followed by a long procession of film songs: "There Goes That Song Again" and "Poor Little Rhode Island" from *Carolina Blues* (1944); "I Fall in Love Too Easily" and "The Charm of You" from *Anchors Aweigh* (1945); "Anywhere" from *Tonight and Every Night* (1946); "Five Minutes More" from *The Sweetheart of Sigma Chi* (1946); "Time After Time" and "Song's Gotta Come From the Heart" from *It Happened in Brooklyn* (1947); and "It's Magic" from *Romance on the High Seas* (1948). In 1948 Cahn and Styne ended their partnership because Styne preferred Broadway and Cahn wished to remain in Hollywood. Temporarily reunited in 1954, they composed the title song for *Three Coins in a Fountain,* which brought Cahn his first Oscar. Of these songs "I'll Walk Alone," "It's Been a Long, Long Time," "Five Minutes More," "Time After Time," "It's Magic," and "Three Coins in a Fountain" were all represented on *Your Hit Parade.*

Cahn and Styne also brought their songs into the musical theater. Their first stage effort was a failure, *Glad to See You!,* which opened in Philadelphia and closed in Boston in 1944. Above and beyond introducing a fine song in "I Guess I'll Have to Hang My Tears to Dry," this show was particularly significant for Cahn. When the production's star was injured in a car accident, Cahn was hastily recruited to take on the leading role, which he did for several performances in Philadelphia.

Their next musical, however, reached Broadway and stayed there two years. It was *High Button Shoes* (October 9, 1947) starring Phil Silvers. Its two best songs were the polka, "Papa, Won't You Dance With Me?" and "I Still Get Jealous."

Some of Cahn and Styne's hit songs were popularized in recordings rather than on stage or screen. Among these were "Saturday Night is the Loneliest Night in the Week" (1944), "It's Been a Long, Long Time" (1945), "Let it Snow! Let it Snow! Let it Snow!" (1945) and "The Things We Did Last Summer" (1946), all represented on *Your Hit Parade.*

During the period of the Cahn–Styne partnership, Cahn also worked with other composers. To the music of Alex Stordahl and Paul Weston, he wrote the lyrics for "I Should Care," the title Cahn appropriated for his autobiography. Introduced by Robert Allen in the movie *Thrill of Romance* (1945), it became a hit in recordings by Tommy Dorsey and his band (vocal by Frank Sinatra), Shirley Bassey, the Lettermen, and had seven presentations on *Your Hit Parade.* "Day by

Day" (1945), again to the music of Stordahl and Weston, was introduced by Jo Stafford and popularized by Sinatra. It had 13 hearings on *Your Hit Parade*. With Nicolas Brodszky Cahn wrote "Be My Love" for Mario Lanza in the film *Toast of New Orleans* (1950). Lanza's recording was his first million-seller. He reprised it in his next motion picture, *Because You're Mine* (1952), and Connie Francis sang it in *Looking for Love* (1964). With Brodszky, Cahn also wrote "Wonder Why" for Jane Powell in *Rich, Young and Pretty* (1950); the title song for *Because You're Mine,* sung by Mario Lanza and heard 15 times on *Your Hit Parade*; and, for Doris Day, "I'll Never Stop Loving You" in *Love Me or Leave Me* (1959). Sammy Fain was the composer for "Face to Face," which Jane Powell and Gordon MacRae introduced in *Three Sailors and a Girl* (1953), a motion picture which Cahn also produced. To Gene de Paul's music, Cahn wrote "Teach Me Tonight" (1953), successfully recorded by the De Castro Sisters and by Jo Stafford. It had ten presentations on *Your Hit Parade,* holding down first position on November 27, 1954. During this period Cahn also teamed up in the movies with Vernon Duke for *April in Paris* (1953), but *not* for the famous title song; with Arthur Schwartz for *You're Never Too Young* (1955); and with Bronislau Kaper for *Forever Darling* (1956).

On September 5, 1945, Cahn married Gloria Delson, a movie actress. Their first home was an apartment at the Sunset Towers in Hollywood. The Cahns soon acquired a house on Mapleton Drive in Holmby Hills. Later on they had Monte Vista, a house in Palm Springs, and an apartment in Manhattan. They raised a son and a daughter.

Another sustained period of productivity and success took place when Cahn collaborated with the composer James Van Heusen. Cahn first worked with Van Heusen in 1955, writing special material for Bing Crosby's appearance at the Paramount Theatre in New York. Their first film assignment, and their first hit song, was the title number for *The Tender Trap* (1955). Soon after that Cahn and Van Heusen composed songs for a musical adaptation of Thornton Wilder's *Our Town,* which aired on NBC-TV. From that production came "Love and Marriage," which was heard on *Your Hit Parade* and won an Emmy. Cahn and Van Heusen were awarded a second Emmy a decade later for their songs for the 1966 television special, *Jack and the Beanstalk,* starring Gene Kelly. Other television productions to which Cahn and Van Heusen contributed were: four Frank Sinatra specials in 1959–60 that they produced; songs for *Potomac Madness* (1960) starring Bob Hope; the title song of *Hazel,* the sit-com series starring Shirley

Booth, which began in 1961; and songs for two more television specials, *The Legend of Robin Hood* (1958) and *Journey Back to Oz* (1971).

For their songs for motion pictures, they were awarded three Oscars: for "All the Way" from *The Joker Is Wild* (1957), "High Hopes" from *A Hole in the Head* (1959) and "Call Me Irresponsible" from *Papa's Delicate Condition* (1963). "All the Way" was represented on *Your Hit Parade.* Other outstanding Cahn-Van Heusen songs for the screen were: "To Love and Be Loved" from *Some Came Running* (1958); the title song for *Indiscreet* (1958); "The Second Time Around" from *High Time* (1960); the title songs for *Pocketful of Miracles* (1961) and *Where Love Has Gone* (1964); "My Kinda Town" from *Robin and the Seven Hoods* (1964); and the title songs for *Thoroughly Modern Millie* (1967) and *Star!* (1968).

For recordings, they composed the title songs for the Frank Sinatra albums *Come Fly With Me* (1958), *Come Dance With Me* (1959), *No One Cares* (1959), *Ring-a-Ding-Ding* (1961) and *September of My Years* (1965). Cahn once remarked: " . . . I'm considered to have put more words into Frank Sinatra's mouth than any other man."

Cahn-Van Heusen songs were also heard on Broadway. From *Skyscraper* (November 13, 1965) came "Everybody Has a Right to Be Wrong" and "I Only Miss Her When I Think of Her." *Walking Happy* (November 26, 1966) yielded the excellent title song. In sum, their Broadway ventures added little to their prestige, or to their bank accounts, inasmuch as *Skyscraper* ran only 241 performances and the latter lasted just two weeks.

When success again came to Cahn on Broadway it took place in an unexpected area. In 1972 he appeared at the New York YMHA in a series dedicated to song lyricists, singing his own hits while accompanying himself on the piano and embellishing them with witty commentary. Cahn always had a flair for performing his own songs, though his raspy voice was once described as that of "a vain duck with a hangover" and he is no Horowitz at the piano (he can perform only in the key of F major). Nevertheless, his charm in delivering his own numbers woos and wins audiences. His success at the YMHA led Alexander H. Cohen, the Broadway producer, to bring Cahn to Broadway in a one-man show entitled *Words and Music.* It opened on April 16, 1974 and with assisting artists provided not only a showcase for Sammy Cahn's songs but also for his puckish humor and nostalgic recollections. The critic, Richard Watts, called him "brilliant, charming and humorous" and Clive Barnes of

The New York Times called *Words and Music* "a lovely fun show." It had a Broadway run of four months and brought Cahn an Outer Circle Critics Award. This show also did well in Los Angeles in September 1974 and in London in 1976 (where it was called *Sammy Cahn's Song Book*). In 1976 Cahn appeared in a segment of the motion picture anthology *That's Entertainment, Part II.*

Cahn is famous not only for his skill as a lyricist but also for the facility with which he writes. Some of his best lyrics were written in half an hour or less. He is the consummate professional, meticulous about meeting deadlines and all sundry demands, and always rising to every occasion. He is one of the highest-paid lyricists in the trade. Yet most of his writing, particularly during the past decade or so, has been done for free. He is the unofficial poet laureate of Broadway and Hollywood, frequently called upon by his famous friends and colleagues to provide special material for their parties, benefit shows and special celebrations; he never charges a fee. He is also his own best customer, producing self-deprecating, tongue-in-cheek and sometimes sentimental verses to familiar melodies about himself, his career, his voice, his family. He wrote parodies for himself, and for all his guests, at the testimonial dinner given to him at the Hilton Hotel in Manhattan on April 26, 1968. He also concocted his own self-delivered parodies at a 60-hour party at Caesar's Palace in Las Vegas honoring him on his 60th birthday, and for his wife when the Friar's Club celebrated his 61st birthday. "I like to write, " he explained. "Doodling with words on a typewriter is one of my greatest pleasures."

In 1964 Cahn and his wife were divorced. He married Virginia ("Tita") Basile, a fashion consultant and former actress, on August 4, 1970. They live in Cahn's former bachelor quarters on Canon Drive in Beverly Hills. ("It took me almost half a lifetime and three thousand miles to take me from Cannon Street on the East Side to Cannon Drive," he once quipped.) On their visits to Manhattan they occupy an apartment on East 55th Street.

Cahn is president of the National Academy of Popular Music in New York which he helped to found. Besides his autobiography, he is the author of *The Songwriter's Rhyming Dictionary* (1984). Apart from his work, he enjoys watching baseball games, attending parties, and engaging in verbal duels with witty friends and colleagues.

ABOUT: Cahn, S. I Should Care, 1974; Ewen, D. Great Men of American Popular Song, 2d ed. 1972; Wilk, M. They're Playing Our Song, 1973.

CARMICHAEL, HOAGY (November 22, 1899–December 20, 1981), was not only one of the popular and successful songwriters of his day, but according to Alec Wilder, he was "the most talented, inventive, sophisticated, and jazz-oriented of all the great craftsmen." Though many of the songs Carmichael wrote for Tin Pan Alley and Hollywood films have since become standards, he will always be best-known for his immortal "Star Dust." Carmichael's songs were heard frequently on *Your Hit Parade*, and he won an Oscar for "In the Cool, Cool, Cool of the Evening." He also appeared in many films and on television, and composed the music for one Broadway show.

Hoagland Howard Carmichael was born in Bloomington, Indiana, the son of Howard Clyde and Lida Mary (Robison) Carmichael. The Carmichael family was poor, and it was periodically uprooted for brief periods as Howard Carmichael continued to search for a steady livelihood. When the family would return to Bloomington, Lida Carmichael, a trained pianist, supplemented its income by playing at social functions and in silent movie houses.

The popular tunes his mother played made an indelible impression on Hoagy, but he was unaware of his own musical gifts until the age of 12, when one afternoon he heard "Indiana Frangipani" emanating from the nearby university belltower. He correctly reproduced the tune, and from that moment on, as he has written, "the piano had me." With assistance from his mother, he taught himself to play quite well.

In 1915 the family moved to Indianapolis. Uninterested in academic pursuits, Carmichael left high school to work at various jobs, including one as a cement mixer on a twelve-hour night shift. What did fascinate him was jazz, whose first strains were coming north from New Orleans. He spent his days at the piano, either at home or with Reggie Duval, a black pianist who played in Indianapolis dives. Duval taught Carmichael about New Orleans jazz and also gave him valuable pointers on playing ragtime and "hot piano."

Homesick and determined to make something of himself, Carmichael returned to Bloomington in 1919 to complete his high school education. That year, he booked Louie Jordan's band to play at a high school fraternity dance. Hearing a black jazz band for the first time was an experience Carmichael found "soul-shattering." He identified totally with the music because "it was (never) the music of nice comfortable well-bred people . . . (it was) new, disjointed, unorganized music, full of screaming blue notes and a solid beat . . . Jazz maniacs were being born

HOAGY CARMICHAEL

and I was one of them." Carmichael then began to play jazz himself in small groups, some of which included professionals who were drifting north from New Orleans.

Following his graduation in 1922, Carmichael enrolled at Indiana University to study law. While at the university, he cultivated an audience for the new jazz through the efforts of his own bands and those he engaged to play at the university's social functions, among them Bix Beiderbecke and the Wolverines. He was a great admirer of Beiderbecke, the legendary cornetist, and the two became close friends. Carmichael also seized every opportunity to hear other jazz musicians such as Joseph "King" Oliver, Louis Armstrong, and Paul Whiteman.

During his college days, Carmichael spent most of his leisure time at a campus hangout dubbed "The Book Nook" for its lack of literary pretensions. It was there, on a broken-down piano, that he composed his earliest instrumental pieces, among them "Free Wheeling" (1924) and "Washboard Blues" (1925). "Free Wheeling," renamed "Riverboat Shuffle," was recorded by the Wolverines on the historic label Gennett (produced by the Starr Piano Company, Richmond, Indiana), one of the few whose offerings included a large selection of jazz. When Dick Voynow brought his recording to the attention of Irving Mills, Carmichael received his first publishing contract, but to his surprise, he shared the credit for the piece with his two "collaborators." "Riverboat Shuffle" was also recorded by Paul Whiteman with Carmichael singing lyrics by Mitchell Parish; this was the first time his raspy delivery was heard on discs. "Washboard Blues"

was also a success. It was first recorded in 1925 by Curtis Hitch's Harmonists with Carmichael at the piano, and again in 1927 by Red Nichols and the Five Pennies.

Carmichael completed his L.L.B. in 1926 and joined a law firm in West Palm Beach, Florida. En route, he stopped in New York to interest Irving Mills in publishing "Washboard Blues," but he declined Mills's offer of a position as staff pianist. Not long after arriving in Florida, Carmichael heard Nichols's recording of "Washboard Blues" quite by accident. In his excitement, he realized he was not suited for the legal profession, so he resigned from the firm and returned to Bloomington in 1927.

For the next two years, Carmichael worked with a number of musicians including Don Redman, and during a brief stint with the Jean Goldkette band, he learned to read music. He also continued to compose, and his most famous and successful song, "Star Dust," was written in this period.

One evening in 1927, Carmichael was sitting on the "spooning wall" at Indiana University fondly recalling a previous romantic entanglement when a melody came to him. At the "Book Nook" he expanded the melody into a ragtime piece, which a former schoolmate baptized "Star Dust" because "it sounded like dust from the stars drifting down through the summer sky." Carmichael later remarked: "I had no idea what the title meant, but I thought it was gorgeous."

The first recording of "Star Dust" was made in 1927 by Don Redman and the McKinney Cotton Pickers, a black jazz ensemble, who performed it as ragtime. It made little impression. Jimmy Dale, an arranger, suggested that the piece might be more effective at a slower tempo. Emile Seidel and his orchestra recorded it as a ballad with Carmichael at the piano in 1927, and during the playback at this recording session, Carmichael first became aware of the song's potential: "This melody was bigger than I," he recalled in *The Stardust Trail*. "It didn't seem a part of me. Maybe I hadn't written it at all. It didn't sound familiar even. . . . To lay my claims, I wanted to shout back at it, 'Maybe I didn't write you, but I found you!'" According to Alec Wilder, in *American Popular Song*, it was "absolutely phenomenal" for its time because of its unconventional structure and unusual key changes.

Carmichael's publisher, Irving Mills, also recognized the makings of a hit. With Carmichael's consent, he asked Mitchell Parish to provide lyrics in 1929, and the new "Star Dust" was introduced at the Cotton Club in Harlem. Now, singers and bandleaders began to add it to their reportories, and it was plugged by Walter Winchell. But it was the 1930 recording by Isham Jones and his orchestra with a sentimental violin solo by Victor Young which finally established "Star Dust" as a hit. Successful recordings were also made by Tommy Dorsey, Artie Shaw, Bing Crosby, Louis Armstrong, Dinah Shore, Guy Lombardo, Dick Haymes, Glenn Miller, André Kostelanetz, and Frank Sinatra. "Star Dust" has since become one of the greatest American song successes. It has been recorded more than 500 times in 46 different arrangements; the lyrics have been translated into 40 languages; and it was the first song to be recorded on both sides of the same disc, one side featuring a performance by Tommy Dorsey, the other a performance by Benny Goodman.

In 1928, Carmichael went to California to work in motion pictures, now that silent films had been replaced by "talkies." "Star Dust" was still little-known and his other compositions had not yet attracted a large following. Consequently, the doors of the studios remained closed to him. He hitched a ride to New York with the Whiteman orchestra, where he found work as a song plugger for Mills Music. In 1930, RCA Victor invited Carmichael to make a series of recordings, and for the occasion, he organized an ensemble which included the Dorsey brothers, Jack Teagarden, Gene Krupa, Benny Goodman, Joe Venuti and Bix Beiderbecke. An album including some of these performances was released by Historical Records in 1982; in a review of it, Stereo Review cites Carmichael as "one of the handful of true jazz creators of the 1920s."

The early 1930s were productive years. Mildred Bailey introduced several of Carmichael's songs, notably "Rockin' Chair" (1930) and "Georgia on My Mind" (1931). The first of these became her theme song and was so completely identified with her that she was known as "the rockin' chair lady." "Georgia on My Mind" was popularized by the recordings of Fats Waller, Frankie Laine, Ethel Waters, and Frankie Trumbauer, and in 1935, it became the first of Carmichael's songs to be aired on Your Hit Parade. The Hoagy Carmichael orchestra introduced "Lazy River" (1931), which was then successfully recorded by Benny Goodman and the Mills Brothers, and again in 1961 by Bobby Darin and Si Zentner. Carmichael also collaborated for the first time with the lyricist Johnny Mercer on "After Twelve O'Clock" (1931) and "Thanksgivin'" (1932). The following year, Mercer provided lyrics for "Washboard Blues," which became popular under the title "Lazybones." Other songs from this period include "Old Man Harlem" (lyrics by Rudy Vallee) and "Snowball" (introduced by Louis Armstrong) from 1933, and "One Morning in May" (lyrics by Parish), "Moon Country" (lyrics by Mercer) and "Judy" (lyrics by Sammy Lerner) from 1934.

The year of 1936 was an eventful year for Carmichael in several ways. On March 14th he married Ruth Mary Meinardi, a model with whom he raised two sons. It also marked the first time one of his songs was heard on Broadway. "Little Old Lady" (lyrics by Stanley Adams) was introduced by Mitzi Mayfair and Charles Walter in The Show Is On (December 25, 1936). The song had almost been cut because the producer felt it was inappropriate in a sophisticated revue. But E. Y. Harburg, an established lyricist, who was contributing to the show, was so taken with the song that he devised a special scene for it. "Little Old Lady" went on to become one of the highlights of the production; it gained a wide circulation and appeared on Your Hit Parade in first position.

Carmichael returned to Hollywood in 1936, where he signed a contract with Paramount Studios. There he composed "Moonburn" (lyrics by Edward Heyman) for Bing Crosby in Anything Goes (1936), and Gladys Swarthout sang the popular "The Nearness of You" (lyrics by Ned Washington) in Romance in the Dark (1938). He also collaborated with Frank Loesser on a number of hit songs including "Small Fry," introduced by Bing Crosby, Fred MacMurray and Donald O'Connor (who was making his screen debut) in Sing, You Sinners (1938); "Two Sleepy People," sung by Bob Hope and Shirley Ross in Thanks for the Memory (1938); the independent number, "Heart and Soul" (1938); and "We're the Couple in the Castle" from the Walt Disney animated feature, Mr. Bugs Goes to Town (1941).

Carmichael also continued to write songs for Tin Pan Alley, and his "I Get Along Without You Very Well" (1939) had an unusual history. Many years earlier in Bloomington, Carmichael had been given a poem which he decided to set in 1938. Before the song could be published, it was necessary to identify the poet. In his search, Carmichael enlisted the aid of Walter Winchell, then at the height of his fame as a newspaper columnist and radio personality. On one of his broadcasts, Winchell read the opening line of the poem, then asked his listeners to identify the author. Forty-eight people claimed credit, each proving to be a fraud. Further research revealed that the poem had been published in Life magazine over the initials "J. B." who was then discovered to be Mrs. Jane Brown Thompson of Philadelphia. Unfortunately, she died the night before the song was introduced on radio by Dick

Powell on January 19, 1939. A recording was made by Dick Todd that year, and Carmichael later sang it with Jane Russell in *Las Vegas Story* (1952).

Carmichael also produced several other hit songs during the next few years. "Blue Orchids" (1939), recorded by Glenn Miller, was a bestseller, and "Hong Kong Blues" (1939) and "Skylark" (1942) were also quite popular in the many recordings by Bing Crosby, Earl Hines, Billy Eckstine, Bunny Berigan, and the orchestras of Glenn Miller, Gene Krupa and Harry James.

In the same period, Carmichael, with Johnny Mercer as lyricist, composed his only complete score for Broadway. *Walk with Music* (June 11, 1940), text by Guy Bolton, Parke Levy and Alan Lipscott, starred Mitzi Green, Kitty Carlisle and Betty Lawford as three farm girls who go to Palm Beach to snare wealthy husbands. Though many of Carmichael's songs were appealing, the show barely survived 55 performances. "I Walk With Music" was introduced by Kitty Carlisle and Jack Whiting, and Bob Chester and his orchestra recorded it.

In spite of this failure on Broadway, Carmichael continued to accumulate successes as a songwriter on both Tin Pan Alley and in Hollywood, and as an actor in films. In *To Have and Have Not* (1944), Lauren Bacall was introduced on the screen, and Carmichael made his début as Cricket, the piano-player in a Martinique saloon. Two of his songs were heard in the film, "Hong Kong Blues" (introduced by Carmichael) and "How Little We Know" (lyrics by Mercer). He went on to play similar roles in nine other motion pictures; these characters usually resembled Carmichael himself: a gawky, easy-going fellow with a sense of integrity, a strong Hoosier accent and a grating voice. He sometimes introduced new songs in his films, which included "Memphis in June" (lyrics by Paul Francis Webster) in *Johnny Angel* (1945), the hit song "Ole Buttermilk Sky" (written with Jack Brooks) in *Canyon Passage* (1946), *The Best Years of Our Lives* (1946), and *Young Man With a Horn* (1950), which was loosely based on the life of Beiderbecke, and "My Resistance is Low" (lyrics by Harold Adamson) in *Las Vegas Story* (1952).

Carmichael's songs were also featured in other films. "Doctor, Lawyer, Indian Chief" (lyrics by Paul Francis Webster) was sung by Betty Hutton in *The Stork Club* (1945) and was recorded both by her and by Les Brown and his orchestra. "Ivy" (lyrics by Carmichael) was the recurring theme in a motion picture of the same name (1947), popularized in recordings by Dick Haymes, Vaughn Monroe, Vic Damone and Zig-

gy Elman and his orchestra. With Harold Adamson as lyricist, Carmichael composed "When Love Goes Wrong," which was introduced by Marilyn Monroe in *Gentlemen Prefer Blondes* (1953). But Carmichael captured his only Oscar in 1951 for "In the Cool, Cool, Cool of the Evening" (lyrics by Mercer), It was introduced by Bing Crosby in *Here Comes the Groom* (1951), and he later recorded it. It was also heard three times on *Your Hit Parade*.

In addition to his songs for films, Carmichael, with Paul Francis Webster as lyricist, also published several notable independent numbers in the 1940s and early 1950s. Of special interest are "The Lamplighter's Serenade," which was sung by Frank Sinatra in his solo recording debut (1942); "No More Toujours l'amour" (1945); "Bubble-boo, Bubble-boo" (1948); "Follow the Swallow" and "The Three Rivers" (1949); and "Watermelon Weather." These songs were recorded by such well-known performers as Glenn Miller, Tommy Dorsey, Margaret Whiting, Vera Lynn, Perry Como, and Eddie Fisher, as well as Carmichael himself.

In the mid-1940s, Carmichael's voice and personality grew familiar to millions through radio. He was star of *Open House at Hoagy's*, a Sunday evening show, and *Tonight at Hoagy's*, on the Mutual Network in 1944. He was also the host of *The Hoagy Carmichael Show* on CBS in 1946, and made frequent guest appearances on other programs.

Though he continued to compose, Carmichael's late songs are of less interest. Nevertheless, he continued to act in films, the last of which was *Timberjack* (1955). He also appeared on television, initially as a host of *Saturday Night Revue* (1950–54), a variety show on NBC and later assumed the role of "Jonesy," the ranch-hand cook, on the weekly western series, *Laramie* (1959–63). He was also a frequent guest star on other television shows including Ed Sullivan, Milton Berle and Perry Como, as well as at many charitable affairs and benefit shows.

Carmichael was one of ten composers elected to the Songwriter's Hall of Fame when it was first established in 1971. On June 27, 1979, a tribute to Hoagy Carmichael called "The Star Dust Trail" was presented in New York at Carnegie Hall by the Newport Jazz Festival with Bob Crosby, master-of-ceremonies. It offered a restrospective of his songwriting career and included a new piece, *Piano Pedal Rag,* composed for the occasion.

Carmichael was in attendance on January 14, 1981 at the Mark Taper Forum in Los Angeles for the opening of the musical, *Hoagy, Bix and Wolfgang Beethoven Bunkhaus,* a stage adaptation of Carmichael's autobiography, *The Star Dust Trail*. With the use of flashbacks, the musical dramatized Carmichael's years at Indiana University and explored his friendship with Bix Beiderbecke. Twenty-six of Carmichael's songs were represented, including many which have become standards.

In 1955, Carmichael and his wife, Ruth Mary, were divorced. His second marriage, to the actress Dorothy Wanda McKay, took place on June 20, 1977. Carmichael spent his last years in Beverly Hills and Palm Springs; his hobbies included golf and collecting coins.

Hoagy Carmichael died of a heart attack at the Eisenhower Medical Center in Rancho Mirage, California on December 20, 1981.

ABOUT: The Annual Obituary, 1981; Carmichael, H. Sometimes I Wonder, 1965; Carmichael, H. The Stardust Road, 1946; Current Biography, 1941; New Grove Dictionary of American Music, 1986; Wilder, A. American Popular Song, 1972. *Periodicals*—Coronet November 1954; Metronome January 1947; New York Times June 27, 1979; New York Times December 28, 1981; Newsweek June 4, 1945; Songwriter's Review January 1948.

CASH, JOHNNY, (February 26, 1932–). When Johnny Cash was elected to the Country Music Hall of Fame on October 15, 1980, the Country Music Association of Nashville gave official recognition to the preeminent position Cash has occupied for two decades not only as composer-lyricist but also as a performer.

John R Cash (as in Harry S Truman, the "R" does not stand for a name) is one-fourth Cherokee Indian. He was born in a shack in Kingsland, in the backwoods country of Arkansas, the fourth of seven children. His mother, Carrie (Rivera) Cash, played the piano. The father, Ray Cash, was a sharecropper who, in 1926, acquired through a federal land grant 20 acres with shack, barn and mule in Dyess, 200 miles from Kingsland, and it was there that Johnny Cash was raised.

As a boy he helped farm the land, plowing fields, picking cotton (about 350 pounds a day), and going rabbit hunting to help feed his family. While growing up he would sing at work and at home. Music was a heritage from his maternal grandfather, J. L. Rivers, who, despite his own poverty, had owned several musical instruments. The Rivers household was always alive with music-making, with neighbors dropping by to join in the singing of Baptist hymns. These musical fests made a deep impression on young Cash.

Though they could little afford to do so, the

JOHNNY CASH

Cashs acquired a piano with which the mother would lead her family in hymnals. Johnny doted on these religious tunes and also enjoyed listening to country singers on the radio, particularly the performances of Hank Williams and the Carter Family. Cash began composing songs and writing poems and stories when he was 12. By the time he attended high school, he was performing at school functions and on KCLN, a small radio station in Blytheville, Arkansas.

At 14 Cash helped with the family finances by working as a water boy for river gangs at a salary of $2.50 a day. Work was hard and life for him was made even harder when a flood damaged the family farm and home, requiring several months for repair. Tragedy also came when one of his brothers was accidentally killed in the school workshop.

Upon graduating from high school, Cash worked in a factory in Detroit. He was soon back home though, holding various menial positions in town while continuing to pursue his musical interests. When he was 17 he won the first prize of five dollars in a local amateur singing contest. He also received lessons in guitar from his mother and singing lessons from a local teacher, the latter paid for by Mrs. Cash who took in wash to raise the money.

Cash enlisted in the United States Air Force in July 1959. Stationed at Scott Air Force in Belleville, Illinois, he was trained in the radio operating school, completing these studies in San Antonio, Texas. There he met and fell in love for the first time. This romance, with Vivian Liberto, was interrupted when Cash was sent to Germany, where for three years he served as a radio intercept operator.

In Germany, Cash spent his off-hours writing poems, some of which were published in *Stars and Stripes*. He bought his first guitar (for five dollars) and was soon accompanying himself in singing hymns and the songs he composed to entertain his friends at the base. He also performed in German nightclubs.

On July 4, 1954 Cash was honorably discharged with the rank of staff sergeant. A month later, on August 7, he and Vivian Liberto were married by her uncle, a Catholic priest. Their first home was a modest four-room furnished apartment in a poor section of Memphis, Tennessee. Taking advantage of the G. I Bill of Rights, he spent his evenings at Memphis's Keegan Broadcasting School learning to become a disc jockey. During the day, he supported his wife (now pregnant with the first of the four daughters they were to have, two of whom grew up to become country-rock recording stars) by going door-to-door selling electrical appliances. According to Cash, he was "the world's worst salesman."

After five months, he dropped out of Keegan Broadcasting School and tried making headway as a professional singer. An audition for Sam Phillips, head of Sun Records, was a failure because Cash preferred only hymns. "When you have a different kind of song," Phillips told him, "let me hear you again."

Cash's early musical career recieved a boost through his friendships with Luther Perkins and Marshall Grant. Both were full-time mechanics who played music in their spare time: Luther on an amplified guitar, and Marshall on a bass. They joined musical forces, baptized as Johnny Cash and the Tennessee Two. Their first public appearance took place on a Sunday evening in 1954 at a church in north Memphis, where Cash sang several hymns, including one of his own inventions ("Belshazar"). After that they played engagements in and around Memphis.

One day Perkins and Grant suggested that Cash set to music some of the poems he had written in Germany. Cash responded with "Hey, Porter," a railroad ballad which the trio auditioned for Sun Records. Phillips agreed to record it on the condition that Cash provide another song for the "flip" side. That night he composed "Cry, Cry, Cry." Both songs, performed by Cash, were released by Sun in June 1955. With frequent hearings on radio programs in the South and Southwest, both songs climbed to the top ten on the country-and-western charts and remained there several weeks. More than 100,000 copies of the record were sold.

Cash's first public appearance following the release of "Hey, Porter"/"Cry, Cry, Cry" was at a show in an armory in Covington, Tennessee in 1955 headlined by Sonny James, the country singer. That summer, Cash appeared as a guest artist at an Elvis Presley concert at the Overton Park Shell in Memphis. He brought down the house with his renditions of "Hey, Porter" and "Cry, Cry, Cry." Impressed, Bob Neal, Presley's manager at that time, took him under his own managerial wing, and arranged Cash's first tour, which took him through Louisiana, Texas and Mississippi.

Under an exclusive contract to Sun Records, Cash achieved stardom in 1956 with his first recording to earn a gold record, "Folsom Prison Blues." He had written it in 1954 aboard a plane after having seen the motion picture *Inside the Walls of Folsom Prison*. With this number, Cash emerged as a musical spokesman for the downtrodden and the defeated, sentimental material he would frequently tap in later song successes.

A second gold record came that year with "I Walk the Line," still Cash's most beloved song, the one he is invariably urged to sing at his concerts, that is his trademark. In it he recalled his unhappy experiences as a door-to-door salesman and his determination to toe the straight line in life because he had found his true soul mate, a redemptive love. As Cash explained in his autobiography, he had sought to write "a song with something to say. A song . . . that says I'm going to be true not only to those who believe in me and depend on me, but to myself and to God, . . . a song that might give courage to others as well as to myself." He added: "The song came easily. . . . There was no wringing the mind or biting the pencil. The lyrics came as fast as I could write, and in 20 minutes I had it finished." The record remained on the top ten of the country-and-western list for 44 weeks, and entered the pop charts as well. In 1970 "I Walk the Line" was the title of a picture starring Gregory Peck, with the background music consisting of Cash singing the title song and several of his other original numbers.

Recordings of Cash's "So Doggone Lonesome" and "There You Go" and the release of Cash's first successful album, *Johnny Cash Sings the Songs He Made Famous*, all in 1956, helped make Cash one of the most valuable properties in the recording industry—and Sam Phillips's most important "find" since Elvis Presley. Cash's concert performances won him even greater popularity. In addition to his extended tours, he was regularly heard at the Grand Ole Opry in Nashville. In 1957 country music publications singled him out as country music's top star. Between 1956 and 1959, each of his records reached the top ten on the country charts. Many were recordings of his own songs, the most significant of which were "Train of Love"; "Next in Line"; "Ballad of a Teenage Queen"; "Guess Things Happen That Way"; "Five Feet High and Risin'"; "Luther Played the Boogie"; "The Man on the Hill" and "Big River." The last of these was inspired by the flood that had almost ruined his family, but the immediate stimulus came from a line in an article saying that "Johnny Cash has the Big River blues in his voice." He had the whole song—words and music—conceived by the time he finished reading the article. Cash's bestselling records that were songs by other composers included "In the Jailhouse" (by Jimmie Rodgers), "It Ain't Me Babe" (by Bob Dylan) and "The Ballad of Ira Hayes" (by Peter La Forge).

Now a part of the entertainment-world aristocracy, Cash acquired an attractive house on the outskirts of Memphis, an expensive car, and a lavish wardrobe for himself and his wife.

In August 1958 Cash left Sun Records for Columbia. His first Columbia release—his own song, "Don't Take Your Guns to Town"—became an instant bestseller. Three smash Johnny Cash albums followed in rapid succession: *Fabulous Johnny Cash, Ride This Train,* and *The Sound of Johnny Cash.* His affiliation with Columbia would result in sales of more than 20 million Johnny Cash records, making him one of Columbia's three bestselling performing artists, surpassed only by Barbra Streisand and Johnny Mathis.

As a star, Cash was heard throughout the United States, including a sold-out performance at New York's Carnegie Hall in 1961. He also toured Europe, Australia and the Orient. In addition, he appeared in several Hollywood Westerns and was a guest artist on major network television programs. Two managers were now required to supervise his financial interests which, beyond recordings and public appearances, included the administration of two publishing houses (Johnny Cash Music and Saline Music) and various real-estate speculations. He also hired a press agent.

For his public appearances and television performances he donned the costume that earned him the sobriquet of "the man in black"—a long black frock coat, gray striped trousers, a white ruffled shirt beneath a vest, and a black hat. He looked like, in the words of his biographer, Albert Govoni, "a riverboat gambler, a raffish person, a card shark out of the Old West, a post-Civil War Southern dandy, a New Orleans rakehell on his way to a duel over a woman." At public appearances his opening salutation was simply, "Hello, I'm Johnny Cash."

But Cash paid a heavy price for his fame. His long absences from home while on tour caused domestic friction and worsening marital squabbles provoked him to find bachelor quarters in Memphis. Domestic problems were compounded by the tensions and pressures of his high-powered professional life. By the end of the 1950s he was seeking relief in alcohol. In 1959 he was jailed for public drunkenness in Nashville when he tried to break down a door to a night-club that was closed. He also sought solace in drugs: Dexamul, Dexedrine, tranquillizers, amphetamines, barbiturates. "By 1965," Cash confessed, "I was taking more pills than I could find doctors to supply." Between 1959 and 1965 he was arrested seven times, sometimes jailed overnight for wandering about town dazed on pills and booze. One night, in 1965, he was arrested in El Paso for carrying Dexadrine tablets across the Mexican border. His incarcerations, however brief, intensified his lifelong sympathy for prison inmates. "I don't see anything good come out of a prison," he told an interviewer in 1969. "You put them in like animals and tear the souls and guts out of them and let them out worse than when they came in."

His involvement with drugs, combined with poor health, seriously affected Cash's professional life. Though he enjoyed a resounding success in 1963 with his recording of "Ring of Fire" (by Merle Kilgore and June Carter), his greatest recording success since "I Walk the Line," the first half of the 1960s were lean years for Cash. As he began missing professional dates, the engagements grew fewer and fewer. And there was an attendant paucity of hit records to bolster either his ego or his income.

The slow process of rehabilitation was brought about by two forces. One was his love for June Carter. She was a singer-composer who had been a member of the Carter Family of country bluegrass music renown, and had joined Cash's performing troupe in 1961. She used that love, and strength of will rooted in her profound religious faith, to wean Cash from drugs, though this was not achieved without a struggle. After Cash and his first wife were divorced in 1968, he married June Carter on March 1 of that year in Franklin, Kentucky. He recalled: "In 1968 many changes came about . . . but through it all, June and I lived the happiest years of our lives. We stuck together like glue." Their first home was in Hendersonville, near Nashville, where their son, John Carter Cash, was born in 1970.

The second redemptive force in Cash's life at this time was his return to religion. After a week-long visit to Israel in 1967, where he retraced the odyssey of Jesus and visited holy shrines, Cash became a born-again Christian, nourished by his wife's own religious beliefs. That visit prompted Cash to record his *The Holy Land* album in 1968. Religious ardor led him in 1973 to finance and produce *Gospel Road,* a motion picture about the life of Christ, filmed in Israel, with Cash singing hymns on the soundtrack and serving as narrator. Distributed by the Reverend Billy Graham's World Wide Pictures (the first not produced by Graham himself) the film reached Christians everywhere.

Rehabilitation renewed Cash's creativity. In 1967 Columbia had released *Johnny Cash's Greatest Hits,* an LP which was a bestseller for 71 weeks. That same year "Jackson," a recording Cash made with his wife (words and music by Gaby Rodgers and Billy Edd Wheeler) won a Grammy as best country performance by a group. In February 1968 Cash and his troupe performed for the inmates of Folsom Prison, a concert recorded live and released as an LP, *Johnny Cash at Folsom Prison.* In that album, sounds are heard of clanging jail doors, the conversation of prisoners, announcements over the public address system. The record sold almost six million copies and brought Cash a Grammy for the year's best country music performance. At the same time, one of its cuts, the live version of "Folsom Prison Blues," was released as a single and zoomed to the top of the charts.

A second live recording of a prison concert, *Johnny Cash at San Quentin* (1969), brought Cash another gold record. One of its numbers, "A Boy Named Sue" (words and music by Shel Silverstein), sold more than two million copies as a single and brought Cash still another Grammy. His recording of "A Boy Named Sue" also won the first award ever presented by the Country Music Association of Great Britain which selected him as the year's leading singer on records and the foremost country music entertainer.

In the fall and winter of 1968, Cash's appearances at Carnegie Hall and at Madison Square Garden broke all existing box-office records for those venues. Reviewing one of Cash's performances, John S. Wilson said in *The New York Times:* "Mr. Cash, a brilliantly controlled showman, kept his low-keyed delivery just at the throttle's edge—strong enough to rouse his listeners to cheers but never letting it get beyond a warm, easygoing feeling. . . . Mr. Cash . . . made that huge Garden seem intimate and managed to project a feeling of neighborly visiting that is the core of his professional career." By virtue of these and other appearances in sold-out auditoriums, Cash was named "Entertainer of the Year" by the Country Music Association in 1969. Also that year, he and Bob Dylan sang

"Girl From the North Country" as a duet in Dylan's *Nashville Skyline* LP.

On March 16, 1969, *Cash!,* a 90-minute documentary, was telecast by National Education Television. In a slightly altered form, this film was also released to movie houses in 1970 under the title *Johnny Cash: The Man, His World, His Music.* "The movie was fine on television," reported a *New York Times* writer, " and it seems to me even better in the theater, where the color is truer, the visual detail finer and the audience situation more properly theatrical."

On June 7, 1969 Cash became the star of *The Johnny Cash Show,* a 60-minute primetime production on the ABC-TV network taped at the Grand Ole Opry, university campuses and other locales. Supported by other country stars, including his wife and the Tennessee Two, he presented a program of songs he had made famous. On this program, in 1971, he introduced two new songs whcih instantly became standards in his repertory: "The Man in Black," wherein he identified his black outfit as the costume of mourning for victims of persecution and injustice, and "Flesh and Blood."

On an invitation from President and Mrs. Richard M. Nixon, Cash appeared at the White House on April 17, 1970. Brushing aside the numbers the President had requested, which included "Welfare Cadillac," he offered his own old favorites and performed a new number called "What is Truth?," which was sympathetic to the younger generation of the 1960s and their doubts about the wisdom of conducting the Vietnam War. Cash later explained he had refused to perform "Welfare Cadillac," which he had neither written nor recorded, because the song made light of poor people and that he himself had grown up in circumstances that were decidedly not affluent.

With his album *The Johnny Cash Show* (1970), recorded live at the Grand Ole Opry, he scored yet another bestseller. That year he sang his own songs on the soundtrack of two films, *I Walk Alone* and *Little Fauss and the Big Halsey,* the latter starring Robert Redford. A year later he appeared as an actor in *Gunfight,* starring Kirk Douglas, for which he wrote and sang the title number. His *The World of Johnny Cash* album brought him a gold record in 1971. For his varied activities he was earning an annual income in excess of two million dollars.

Since the early 1970s Cash has continued to be both prolific and creative. Among his later albums are *Any Old Wind That Blows* (1973), *Rockabilly Blues* (1980), *Johnny Cash and the Baron* (1981), *The Adventures of Johnny Cash* (1982) and *Johnny 99* (1982). "His voice now is, if anything, richer than ever," wrote Noel Coppage in a review of *Rockabilly Blues* for *Stereo Review* (January 1981). "It has more tones and more texture than it did in the Sun days, and it stays on key better. . . . He is still interested in making his own way." Reviewing *Johnny 99* in *Stereo Review* (March 1984), Alanna Nash said: "It's an elegant, exquisite testament to the staying power—and growth—of one of country music's genuine legends." (The song "Johnny 99" was written by Bruce Springsteen, who included it on his own *Nebraska* album which, in turn, had been influenced by Johnny Cash's country-folk ballads.)

Cash has also continued to hold the limelight with public appearances and as a guest artist on television shows, where he has sometimes performed in dramatic roles, as he once did on an episode of *Columbo*, starring Peter Falk. On May 9, 1980, his 25th anniversary as songwriter-performer was commemorated with a country music special on the CBS television network.

To relieve muscle spasms from surgery in the early 1980s, Cash returned to drugs for relief. Again determined to free himself of drug dependency, he entered the Betty Ford Center, an alcohol and drug rehabilitation program in Rancho Mirage, California in December 1983. "I've heard of people feeling so bad from drugs that they thought they were going to die," Cash told a young audience after he had been cured. "I felt so bad during my hospitalization that I was afraid I was going to live."

Cash and his family reside in a cliff-edge mansion in Hendersonville, Tennesse. When he is not composing or performing, he relaxes by fishing, hunting, waterskiing and practicing shooting with a Colt .45. His daughter Roseanne Cash, from his first marriage, is a popular country/rock singer in her own right.

In 1971 Cash received an honorary doctorate of humanities from Gardner-Webb College in Boiling Springs, North Carolina, and in 1976 an honorary doctorate of humane letters from the National University in San Diego.

ABOUT: Cash, J. Man in Black, 1975; Govoni, A. A Boy Named Cash, 1970. *Periodicals*—BMI: Many Worlds of Music No. 4, 1980; Look April 29, 1968; New York Times March 16, 1969; Time June 9, 1969.

COHAN, GEORGE M. (July 3 or 4, 1878–November 5, 1942), composer-lyricist, a towering figure among the leading songwriters for the musical stage in the early 20th century. Until the Jazz Age, he dominated the American musical theater not only as a composer but also as an au-

GEORGE M. COHAN

thor of musical comedy texts, producer, director, actor, singer and dancer. He helped create a thoroughly American type of show musical that was independent of European traditions and influences.

George Michael Cohan was born in Providence, Rhode Island in early July 1878. Though his birth certificate gives the date of July 3, Cohan himself insisted that he had been born on Independence Day. His father in a diary dated July 3, 1882, noted; "Got a little present for Georgie's birthday tomorrow," but reference books have accepted the date on Cohan's birth certificate as correct.

He was the last of the three children of Jeremiah ("Jerry") and Helen ("Nellie") Frances (Costigan) Cohan, both of whom were vaudevillians. The first of the Cohan children died in infancy. The second, Josephine, was George's elder by two years.

Jerry and Nellie Cohan toured the vaudeville circuit in an act for which Jerry wrote all the material and served as stage director and general manager. By the time George was born, they were a minor attraction, poorly paid and always on the move to fulfill bookings. They lived out of valises, with overnight stops in shabby boarding-houses or sleazy hotels. The two infant children would sleep in dressing rooms while their parents performed. Living like show business nomads made formal schooling virtually impossible for the Cohan children. George attended public school in Providence for just six weeks in 1884 and in music his sole instruction was two weeks of lessons on the violin. Thereafter his musical education was acquired in the theater.

Cohan made his stage debut as an infant, serving as a human prop in *The Two Dans*, a sketch starring his parents. He joined the Cohan act more officially when he was nine in *The Two Barneys*, delivering a few lines of dialogue and playing *The Blue Danube* on the violin. His sister joined the Cohan act in 1888 as a dancer. By then, George's role had been enlarged to include buck and wing dances, recitations and singing. Now known as the Four Cohans, they toured the vaudeville circuit for several years, eventually as headliners earning a thousand dollars a week. The family act became so popular that in 1892 a two-week booking at Robinson's Theatre in Buffalo, New York was extended to a full year. When he was 11, George began writing material for the act, and at 13 he was composing songs.

The first songs Cohan submitted to a publisher were returned with a terse notice of rejection: "Your songs are not publishable. Please do not send any more." His first published song was "Why Did Nellie Leave Her Home?" which M. Witmark and Sons purchased in 1893. About one year later his second published song, "Venus, My Shining Love," entered the repertory of café-house orchestras. "Hot Tamale Alley" (1895) was popularized in vaudeville by May Irwin. "I Guess I'll Have to Telegraph My Baby," the first popular song about wireless telegraphy, though written when he was 14, was not published until 1898. His first success, it was popularized in vaudeville by Ethel Levey and was recorded by Frank Luther much later.

In his autobiography, *From Ragtime to Swingtime*, Isidore Witmark described the young Cohan as a "self-opinionated youngster with implicit faith in his gifts. . . . When he was not arguing with theater folk, he was tramping the streets of New York with unrecognized masterpieces under his arm. He was no more afraid of publishers than he was of managers. . . . Everybody in those days was swellheaded to Georgie, . . . He would pass the Witmark offices and [call] the brothers 'big stiffs'— to himself. 'Just goes to show how smart those babies there are, publishing all that bum material written by a lot of hams, and here am I, the best songwriter, walking right by their door with four or five big sure hits under arm.'"

In addition to writing songs, Cohan now succeeded his father as manager and presiding genius of the Four Cohans, writing their songs and sketches and tending to their business affairs. He even stole the final bow from the rest of his family after the final curtain by making the speech that became his trademark: "My mother thanks you, my father thanks you, my sister thanks you, and *I* thank you."

At this time Cohan was also writing songs and special material for other vaudevillians which he sold for an outright cash fee. "The orders came in so fast," he said, "that I found it impossible to supply the demand. With parodies in every pocket and sketches under my arm, I was soon the envy of all the pencil pushers in the variety branch of the theatrical game." In a three-year period he turned out more than 150 sketches and monologues as well as a handful of songs.

In July 1899 Cohan married Ethel Levey in Atlantic City. Their daughter, Georgette, was born in the summer of 1900. With Ethel Levey, the Four Cohans now expanded to Five.

By this time Cohan was beginning to look beyond the vaudeville stage to the legitimate theater. He realized this ambition with *The Governor's Son*, an expansion of one of his vaudeville sketches. It opened with the Five Cohans at New York's Savoy Theatre on February 25, 1901. Though well received by critics, audiences rejected the show and it closed after 32 performances. Its best songs were "Nothing New Under the Sun," a satire of Broadway musical cliches, and "Push Me Along in My Pushcart," which was revived in the 1968 Broadway musical *George M!*

Leaving New York, *The Governor's Son* toured the country from 1901 to 1903. During this time Cohan turned another of his vaudeville sketches, *Running for Office*, into a vehicle for Broadway. It opened at the 14th Street Theatre on April 17, 1903, and did little better than its predecessor, lasting 48 performances. Its best song was "If I Were Only Mr. Morgan."

Despite the flaws of Cohan's initial ventures into full-length musical production, both *Running for Office* and *The Governor's Son* contain elements of Cohan's later theatrical style. Each was set in a totally American milieu and peopled with recognizably American characters whose speech was urban-contemporary, slangy and colloquial. The songs were simplistic effusions, humorous or sentimental, bearing the hallmarks of the commerical style then in vogue on the American musical stage.

These early Cohan musicals also established Cohan's stage persona—the brash American who wore his hat rakishly low on the forehead, jauntily brandished a bamboo cane, and dressed flamboyantly right down to his ultrafashionable spats. He sang in a nasal twang that twisted out of the corner of his mouth, and danced in a kangaroo strut that became his trademark. Driving home a message, he would point an eloquent forefinger at the audience. In every way Cohan exuded supreme self-confidence and limitless energy. He also flaunted his patriotism in *The*

Governor's Son by waving an American flag while singing "Yankee Doodle Doings." "Never was a plant more indigenous to a particular part of the earth," Oscar Hammerstein II once remarked, "than was George M. Cohan to the United States of his day."

In June 1901 Josephine Cohan retired from the stage and married Fred Niblo. And when the Four Cohans made their next foray into the legitimate theater, George M. broke permanently with his vaudeville past. Instead of expanding one of his sketches, he wrote a full-length book for a musical whose principal character, Tod Sloan, was the real-life American jockey who had ridden in the Derby for the King of England in 1903. Cohan fitted Sloan to his Cohanesque image by calling him Johnny Jones and naming the musical *Little Johnny Jones*. The hero is falsely accused by a disreputable gambler of having thrown a recent Derby race. When Jone's friends sail for home, he remains behind to clear himself with the aid of a very comic detective. Vindicated, he returns to San Francisco and the woman he loves.

Little Johnny Jones opened in New York at the Liberty Theatre on November 7, 1904. Though it had an initial run of only 52 performances and received little praise from the critics, *Johnny Jones* became Cohan's first popular musical through its success on the road. It returned to New York on May 8, 1905 (for a three-and-a-half-month run), on November 13, 1905 (a five-week run) and April 1907 (two weeks). However, when it was revived on Broadway on March 21, 1982 in a production starring Donny Osmond, a *Variety* critic described it as "an embarrassing anachronism with almost no relevance to the modern musical stage."

Cohan's first two song classics came from *Johnny Jones*, both introduced by Cohan himself. With "The Yankee Doodle Boy" he made his first song entrance, and with "Give My Regards to Broadway" he sings farewell at the Southampton pier to his friends about to sail for America. "The Yankee Doodle Boy" was recorded in 1910 by Billy Murray and in later years by the orchestras of Horace Heidt and Fred Waring. It made the first of many appearances on the screen in *The Broadway Melody* (1929). Eddie Buzzell sang it next in the motion picture adaptation of *Little Johnny Jones* (1929), and Jimmy Cagney in Cohan's screen biography, *Yankee Doodle Dandy* (1942). To its strains, Cagney, once again impersonating Cohan, did a buck-and-wing with Bob Hope in *The Seven Little Foys* (1955).

"Give My Regards to Broadway" was also sung by Eddie Buzzell in *Little Johnny Jones* and by

Cagney in *Yankee Doodle Dandy*. It was also interpolated into *The Big Broadcast* (1940) and the Jane Froman screen biography, *With a Song in My Heart* (1952); in *Give My Regards to Broadway* (1948) it was sung by Tom Dailey, Charles Winninger and Fay Bainter. In the 1929 screen adaptation of *Little Johnny Jones* only "Yankee Doodle Boy" and "Give My Regards to Broadway" were retained from the stage score. The other songs were the work of various composers.

Two Cohan routines in later musicals originated in *Little Johnny Jones*. One was a homespun, sentimental, rhymed sermon, which Cohan delivered in "Life's a Funny Proposition After All," half-sung and half-recited to the accompaniment of an orchestra melody. In 1911, "Life's a Funny Business" became one of Cohan's earliest recordings. The second Cohan routine, which had been anticipated in *The Governor's Son*, was to drape the American flag around his body and flounce about the stage, with or without the benefit of an appropriate song.

For his next Broadway musical, *Forty-Five Minutes From Broadway* (January 1, 1906), Cohan did not use the services of any of the Cohans. He wrote it for Fay Templeton, who was making the transition from burlesque to the Broadway musical theater. It was set in the Westchester town of New Rochelle. A lost will of one of the town's deceased millionaires leads his only living relative, Tom Bennett, to claim the fortune. But the fortune belongs to Mary Jane, the millionaire's housemaid, as is proved when the will is found in a suit of clothes. She is in love with Kid Burns, a principled man who refuses to marry her for her money, which causes Mary Jane to destroy the will.

The principal songs were the title number, introduced by Victor Moore and chorus, and two songs about its heroine, Mary Jane. Fay Templeton introduced "Mary's a Grand Old Name" and Donald Brian and chorus introduced "So Long Mary." "Mary's a Grand Old Name," which was recorded by Bing Crosby and by Fred Waring's Pennsylvanians, was interpolated into the film, *Babes on Broadway* (1942). Irene Manning sang it in *Yankee Doodle Dandy* and in *The Seven Little Foys* it served as the background music for a tap dance by Cagney and Hope. "Forty-Five Minutes From Broadway" was sung by Cagney in *Yankee Doodle Dandy*, where Irene Manning was heard in "So Long Mary." The show's Broadway run consisted of just 90 performances.

In *George Washington, Jr.* (February 12, 1906), Cohan again took the starring role, and once again cast his parents and his wife. As in *Little Johnny Jones*, he fashioned the principal character to suit his own personality. His George Washington, Jr., like Cohan himself, is an American chauvinist who hails from Providence, Rhode Island. The hero takes the name of the father of his country to defy his own Anglophile father, who wants him to marry a titled English woman instead of his Southern girlfriend. The idea for the musical came from a song. Meeting up one day with a Civil War veteran who had participated in Pickett's Gettysburg charge, Cohan noticed a folded American flag in his lap. "She's a grand old rag," the veteran observed. The phrase struck Cohan as the basis for a patriotic march for one of his popular flag-waving routines. Cohen then decided to showcase this march in a patriotic musical comedy extravaganza.

At George Washington, Jr.'s first-night performance, the song was called "You're a Grand Old Rag," but when patriotic societies objected to the term "rag," Cohan made the change to "flag." Cohan's spirited delivery of this song, as he ran up and down the stage draped in the stars and stripes, was matched half a century later by Cagney's performance in Yankee Doodle Dandy. Cohan used this song again for a flag-waving routine in The Phantom President, his debut in talking pictures. Billy Murray recorded it in 1910, and a later recording was made by Fred Waring's Pennsylvanians. This was Cohan's first song to sell a million copies of sheet music.

Cohan's score for George Washington, Jr. contained the popular "I Was Born in Virginia," so effectively introduced by Ethel Levey that henceforth she was known as "Ethel Levey of the Virginia song." Cagney and Walter Huston revived it in Yankee Doodle Dandy. After an 81-performance run in New York, George Washington, Jr. went on an extended road tour. When Ethel Levey abruptly left the production in Cleveland in December 1906, it marked the end of her professional and personal relationship with Cohan. They were divorced the following April, and on June 29, 1907 Cohan married Agnes Nolan, an actress who had been in the chorus of Little Johnny Jones. They had three children, and divided their time for many years between residences on Central Park West and after 1914 in Great Neck, Long Island.

In 1906 Cohan and Sam H. Harris founded Cohan and Harris, a theater production firm. They produced Popularity (October 1, 1906), Cohan's first Broadway play without music, and it was a failure, but Cohan's successful plays and musicals made his firm a force to be reckoned with on Broadway for a decade and a half. In fact, subsequent nonmusical Cohan plays, in

which he was cast in the starring role, were to prove more successful than his later musicals, and in their time were regarded as important contributions to the American theater. The best of these were Get Rich Quick Wallingford (September 19, 1910), 424 performances; The Little Millionaire (September 19, 1911), 192 performances; Broadway Jones (September 23, 1912; with Cohan's parents appearing with him for the last time), 178 performances; and Seven Keys to Baldpate (September 22, 1913), 320 performances. Many Cohan-Harris productions by playwrights other than Cohan also did well. By the early 1910s, the expanding activities of Cohan and Harris made necessary the acquisition of interests in seven Broadway theaters, including two houses solely their own, the Cohan and Harris Theatre and the George M. Cohan Theatre.

Several of Cohan's musicals deserve mention. The Talk of the Town (December 3, 1907) reprised Victor Moore in the role of Kid Burns, a character he had portrayed in Forty-Five Minutes from Broadway. In The Yankee Prince (April 20, 1908), a box-office failure, the four Cohans, including Josephine, were reunited. Fifty Miles from Boston (February 3, 1908) starred Edna Wallace Hopper. The Man Who Owns Broadway (October 11, 1909) was a musical version of the ill-fated play, Popularity. Broadway Jones (September 23, 1912), too, was noteworthy. The Cohan Revue of 1916 (February 9, 1916) and The Cohan Revue of 1918 (December 31, 1918) anticipated the sophisticated intimate revues of the 1920s in their satiric outlook on people and events in the news and in their amusing takeoffs of performers.

Only one song classic emerged from any of these productions, "Harrigan," a spelling song ("H-A-double-R-I-G-A-N spells Harrigan") introduced by James C. Marlow in Fifty Miles from Boston. Though ostensibly in praise of the musical's leading character, this song paid tribute to Ned Harrigan, of the popular Harrigan and Hart burlesque team, whom Cohan idolized and who attended the opening-night performance. Cagney and Joan Leslie revived it in Yankee Doodle Dandy. Notable songs from other Cohan musicals were "When a Fellow's on the Level With a Girl Who's on the Square" and "When We Are M-A-double-R-I-E-D," both from The Talk of the Town; "Come on Downtown" from The Yankee Prince; and "There's Something About a Uniform" from The Man Who Owns Broadway". "When We Are M-A-double-R-I-E-D" was recorded in 1915 by Jack Northworth.

The most famous song Cohan ever composed,

"Over There," was not written for musicals. It was composed on the evening of April 8, 1917, the spontaneous response of a patriot to President Wilson's declaration of war against Germany. The following morning, in his Manhattan apartment, Cohan gathered the members of his family. "He said that he had just finished a new song and he wanted to sing it to us," his daughter Mary recalled. "He put on a big tin pan from the kitchen on his head, used a broom for a gun on his shoulder, and he started to mark time like a soldier singing, 'Johnnie get your gun, get your gun, get your gun.' . . . Then he started to walk up and down, swinging one arm vigorously and singing even more loudly: 'Over there, over there, Send the word, send the word, over there.' We kids had heard, of course that the United States was at war, and now here was Dad acting just like a soldier. So I began to sob, and I threw myself down, hanging for dear life to his legs as he marched, begging, him pleading with him not to go to war."

Cohan himself introduced the song to American troops at Fort Myers, near Washington, D. C., but the response was apathetic. Success first came when Charles King sang it at a Red Cross benefit at the Hippodrome Theatre in New York. Nora Bayes was so taken with it that she used it in her vaudeville act, with which she regularly brought down the house, and recorded it. The publishing house of Leo Feist, sensing a giant hit in the making, purchased the publication rights for $25,000, realizing a major coup since the sheet-music sale exceeded two million copies by the time the war ended. President Wilson called "Over There" "a genuine inspiration to all American manhood." In 1917 singers and bands competed to record it with such opera stars as Enrico Caruso and Schumann-Heink. (Caruso's recording, sung in a broken American English accent, has become a collector's item.) As the song by which the First World War will ever be identified, "Over There" is invariably featured in motion pictures with a World War I setting. A quarter of a century after it had been written, Congress authorized President Roosevelt to present Cohan with the congressional Medal of Honor "in belated recognition of his authorship of 'Over There' and 'You're a Grand Old Flag.'" "Over There" was the zenith of Cohan's songwriting career, but two later songs are revived from time to time: "Nellie Kelly I Love You" and "You Remind Me of My Mother," both from the musical *Little Nellie Kelly* (November 13, 1922). The former was introduced by Charles King, was revived for Judy Garland and Gordon MacPhail in the film *Little Nellie Kelly* (1940), and was interpolated into *Yankee Doodle Dandy.* "You Remind Me" was introduced by Charles King and Elizabeth Hines.

By 1919 Cohan had become one of the most powerful men in the Broadway theater, his influence felt in every area of the industry. That year he used his influence to thwart the Actors Equity Association in their bid for recognition as a bargaining agent for its members. Cohan felt there was no place for a union in the theater and that his employees least of all needed no union protection. When a strike of performers was called by Actors Equity, stagehands and musicians walked out in sympathy, and 23 Broadway productions were shut down, including some produced by Cohan and Harris. An infuriated Cohan regarded his friends' and colleagues' support of Equity as a personal betrayal. He now saw the struggle with Equity not as one between management and labor but between Cohan and disloyal friends and ungrateful associates. Refusing to compromise, he vowed to fight to the bitter end.

When Equity emerged victorious, a triumph that was inevitable, normalcy had returned to the Broadway theater by Labor Day, but Cohan's belligerence did not cool. He continued to try to discredit Equity, and when his campaign proved futile he announced that he was through with the theater. He closed down the firm of Cohan and Harris in 1920, dropped his membership in theatrical organizations like The Lambs and Friars Club, and left for Europe.

Upon his return to the United States, Cohan started a new firm, George M. Cohan Productions, and mounted *Genius and the Crowd.* A play by other writers, it was a dismal failure in 1920. His own play, *The Tavern* (September 27, 1920), a personal favorite of Cohan's, had a run of 252 performances but was jeered at by critics. Successful Cohan productions in 1920 were *The Meanest Man in the World,* a play by Augustin MacHugh, and a musical, *Mary,* with a score by Louis Hirsch. However, on May 23, 1921, a revival of *The Tavern* starring Cohan was received so poorly by the public and by critics that Cohan vowed once again that he was through with the theater. At its 27th and last performance, after the final curtain, he told the audience, "I am going away with great regret. I have done nothing but what I have been forced into doing. If at any time anyone can show me how I can return to the theater and retain my self-respect, I hope it will be pointed out to me. When labor no longer has a stranglehold on the profession, I may come back."

He was back on Broadway sooner than expected. On October 3, 1920 the firm of George M. Cohan produced *The O'Brien Girl,* a new musical with a Louis Hirsch score. And over the next decade Cohan continued to produce the works of others as well as his own plays and musicals.

His *Little Nellie Kelly* (1922) ran for 248 performances. (It was in the latter production that Cohan appeared on Broadway for the last time as a singing and dancing star in one of his own musicals.) Most of the shows he mounted, however, were failures. These included Cohan's nonmusical play, *The Song and Dance Man* (December 3, 1923), in which Cohan played the title role, and his last musical, *Billie* (October 1, 1928). The simple homilies, one-dimensional characters, corny sentiments and fervid patriotism that Cohan had dispensed so successfully before were outdated and shopworn in the 1920s. "It's getting too much for me, kid," he told a friend. "I guess people don't understand me anymore and I don't understand them. It's got so that an evening's entertainment just won't do. Give an audience an evening of what they call realism and you've got a hit. It's getting too much for me, kid."

These failures were a bitter pill for Cohan, particularly in the wake of his defeat by Equity. He suffered further humiliation in Hollywood, where he went in 1932 to make his debut in talking pictures. Having been the star of the silent *Broadway Jones* (1917) and *Hit-the-Trial Holiday* (1918), he was now costarred with Claudette Colbert and Jimmy Durante in *The Phantom President*, to which Rodgers and Hart provided the songs. Here Cohan played a dual role, as candidate for the presidency and as the politician's look-alike, a medicine-show man. If Cohan expected to be received in Hollywood as theatrical royalty he was quickly disappointed. Many of his screen colleagues either did not know who he was or regarded him as quaint anachronism. Moreover, his car was always stopped at the studio gate while others were permitted to pass through freely; he was scolded by a 19-year-old superior for submitting his revision ideas on yellow paper in pencil; he was called to the set early each morning though he did not appear before the camera until hours later. The greatest offense of all came in rehearsals, when the filmmakers tried to teach him how to sing, how to speak his lines and even how to execute his flag-waving routine. "If I had my choice between Hollywood and Atlanta," he remarked bitterly, "I'd take Leavenworth." Nevertheless he returned to the screen once more as the star of his own play, *Gambling* (1934), which he produced on Broadway in 1929.

However, the old showman was not yet washed up. He won accolades from critics and ovations from audiences in the starring role of the father in a 1933 stage revival of Eugene O'Neill's comedy, *Ah Wilderness*. And in 1937 he again captured the hearts of critics and audiences by playing President Franklin D. Roosevelt in the Rodgers and Hart musical *I'd Rather Be Right*. That the name of George M. Cohan had once again proved to be magic on Broadway brought him little solace, however. Never satisfied by mouthing dialogue written by others, Cohan made a last pathetic attempt to recapture his former theatrical glory by writing and starring in *The Return of the Vagabond* (May 17, 1940), which closed after seven performances. He observed: "They just don't want me anymore."

Late in his life, in 1941, Cohan received the Congressional Medal of Honor, and one year later New York Mayor La Guardia proclaimed George M. Cohan Day on his birthday. His greatest satisfaction, though, was the filming of *Yankee Doodle Dandy*, which won James Cagney the Academy Award for best actor. The movie featured ten Cohan songs, including most of his standards, and the flag-waving routine that had been Cohan's trademark. At a private showing of *Yankee Doodle Dandy* at his country estate in Monroe, New York, he remarked to his son, "My God, what an act to follow!"

Cohan underwent a successful abdominal operation on October 19, 1941, and spent the next year recuperating at his apartment on Fifth Avenue. But by the time *Yankee Doodle Dandy* had opened he was growing visibly weaker. Just before his death, he asked his nurse to take him by taxi to Broadway, past the corner of 43d Street where once stood the George M. Cohan Theatre, then to the Hollywood Theatre to watch a scene or two from *Yankee Doodle Dandy*. It was his farewell to the street of which he had once been lord and master. He died at his Manhattan apartment with "look after Agnes" his last spoken words.

Cohan left behind a record of achievement unique in the American theater. Some 50 of his 64 years had been spent on the stage. He had written 40 plays, collaborated on 40 others, and shared in the production of 150 more. He had made thousands of appearances as an actor and had composed more than 500 songs, some of them the greatest hits of their time. Gene Buck, the Broadway producer, songwriter and former president of ASCAP, when told of Cohan's death, referred to him as "the greatest single figure the [American] theater had produced."

In 1959 Cohan's statue was unveiled at Duffy Square on Broadway. A decade later, *George M!* (April 8, 1968), a stage musical based on his life with a score of about 20 Cohan songs, opened on Broadway. Despite Joel Grey's portrayal of Cohan the show was not successful, though it did reach a nationwide audience as a television special. In a review of the show's original cast recording, John S. Wilson of *The New York Times* said, "[Cohan's songs] are part of our [American] musical bloodstream. It is virtually impossible not to respond to the vigor and spirit of Cohan's melodies, even those that are tied to his outdated, flag-waving lyrics. His tunes have such a graceful life, such a jaunty air, so much sheer enthusiasm . . . that they survive and flourish, despite the sentiments and the sentimentality that keep cropping up in the lyrics. Cohan's songs are period pieces. No one is even trying to write songs like that these days and no one is likely to."

In 1978 the U.S. Postal Service issued a 15-cent postage stamp to commemorate the centenary of Cohan's birth.

ABOUT: Cohan, G. M. Twenty Years on Broadway, 1925; McCabe, J. George M. Cohan: The Man Who Owned Broadway, 1980; Morehouse, W. George M. Cohan, Prince of the American Theatre, 1972. *Periodicals*—New York Times Magazine May 5, 1967.

CAROLYN LEIGH

COLEMAN, CY (June 14, 1929–) and **LEIGH, CAROLYN** (August 21, 1926– November 19, 1983), Composer Cy Coleman was born Seymour Kaufman in the Bronx, the son of Max and Ida (Prizent) Kaufman. At the age of four, he could reproduce by ear on the piano any tune he heard. He began formal piano study about this time with a local teacher. When he was six, he performed publicly at Steinway Hall and Town Hall in Manhattan. His talent was recognized by the Music Education League, which awarded him the Interborough Prize three consecutive years (1934–37).

He received his academic education in New York elementary schools and at the High School of Music and Art, and took a diploma from the New York College of Music in 1948. His music teachers included Rudolph Gruen and Adele Marcus (piano) and Bernard Wagenaar (composition).

As a teenager during World War II, Coleman played the piano in servicemen's clubs, an assignment that gradually shifted his interest from concert to popular music. After graduating from high school in 1947, he formed a trio that made its debut at New York's Little Club and later performed at various night spots. In 1947 Coleman's affiliation with television began when he served as composer for the DuPont Hour. During the next few years his most important television assignments were the *Date in Manhattan* program on NBC (1948–51) and the Kate Smith show on NBC (1951–52).

He first made his mark as a composer of popular songs in the early 1950s by collaborating with the lyricist Joseph A. McCarthy. Their first hit song was "Why Try to Change Me Now," which Frank Sinatra introduced in 1952. A year later Coleman and McCarthy composed "Tin Pan Alley," with which Coleman entered the Broadway musical theater when the song was used for a first-act finale in *John Murray Anderson's Almanac*. In 1959 Nat King Cole introduced and made a successful recording of the Coleman-McCarthy song, "I'm Gonna Laugh You Out of My Life."

With Bob Hilliard as lyricist, Coleman composed the music for "The Autumn Song," which Tony Bennett popularized in a 1956 recording. Between 1957 and 1958, Coleman composed the music for *Art Ford's Village Party*, a weekly radio feature on station WNEW in New York. For *Compulsion*, a 1957 nonmusical Broadway drama, Coleman composed the incidental music and served as conductor.

In 1957 Coleman initiated a collaboration with lyricist Carolyn Leigh that lasted five years and yielded about 20 published songs (many of them hits), scores for two successful Broadway musicals, and several numbers for motion pictures.

Carolyn Leigh was born Carolyn Paula Rosenthal in the Bronx, the daughter of Henry and Sylvia Rosenthal. While attending Hunter College High School, she began writing verses. She later studied at Queens College and at New York University. She worked as a copywriter for radio and for an advertising firm, and in 1951 was hired by a music publisher to write song lyrics. That year, in collaboration with Henry Glover and Lucky Millinder, she wrote "I'm Waiting

CY COLEMAN

Just for You," which was recorded by Millinder and revived in 1957 in a recording by Pat Boone. "Just Because You're You" (1952, music by Nacio Peter Brown) was recorded by Jo Stafford.

Leigh's popular success dates from 1954, when she wrote the words for "Positively No Dancing" (music by Martin Roman), "Young at Heart" (music by Johnny Richards from the melody for "Moonbeams," which he had composed in 1939) and, to the music of Mark Charlap, nine songs for the Broadway production of *Peter Pan* (October 20, 1954), starring Mary Martin. "Young at Heart" became Leigh's first standard. Frank Sinatra introduced it, recorded it three times and sang it in the final scene of the motion picture *Young at Heart* (1955). One of Sinatra's versions of the song was used in the nonmusical film set in the 1950s, *The Front* (1967), starring Woody Allen. This song was also recorded by Rosemary Clooney, and it had 18 hearings on *Your Hit Parade* in 1954, twice in first position. In *Peter Pan*, Mary Martin introduced "I Won't Grow Up" and "I've Gotta Crow." Leigh's hit songs in 1956 were "How Little We Know" (music by Philip Springer), which Sinatra introduced and recorded, and "Spring in Maine" (music by Steve Allen), introduced and recorded by Margaret Whiting.

Coleman knew Carolyn Leigh only casually when, in 1957, he suggested that they work together. They completed their first song two days later, "A Moment of Madness," which was recorded by Sammy Davis Jr. Later that year they wrote "Good Intentions," "I Walk a Little Faster," and "My How the Time Goes By." Their runaway hit song was "Witchcraft," introduced

in 1957 by Gerry Matthews in Jules Monk's nightclub revue, *Take Five*, before it became a bestseller in a recording by Frank Sinatra. This was the only Coleman song to be represented on *Your Hit Parade*, with two appearances in 1957.

Their second hit song was "Firefly" (1958), which Tony Bennett made into a bestselling recording. In his public appearances and recordings Tony Bennett popularized numerous Coleman-Leigh songs: "Now I Lay Me Down to Sleep" and "It Amazes Me" in 1958; "The Best is Yet to Come" and "Marry Young" in 1959; and "Rules of the Road" in 1961. Numbers popularized by other performers included: "Hibiscus," introduced in 1959 in a recording by Jo Stafford; "You Fascinate Me So," introduced by Jean Arnold in the Julius Monk nightclub revue, *Demi-Dozen* (1959). "The Tempo of the Times" received its first hearing in a 1959 nightclub revue, *Medium Rare,* and in 1960 "Playboy Theme" was written for the television series *Playboy Penthouse Party.*

Coleman and Leigh's first full score for a Broadway musical was for *Wildcat* (December 16, 1960). This musical's book by N. Richard Nash had been tailored for Lucille Ball's return to the Broadway stage following her enormous success as a comedienne on the *I Love Lucy* television show. Dressed in dirty dungarees and blue shirt, Lucy played Wildcat Jackson, an oil wildcatter in Centavo City in 1912. Having acquired oil leases, she becomes so discouraged at her failure to strike oil that she dynamites the works only to have the explosion produce an oil gusher. Her first number was the production's standout song, "Hey, Look Me Over," sung with Paula Stewart. Coleman and Leigh had originally written a more sophisticated number to introduce Lucy's character but decided that something cornier was needed for the homespun Wildcat Jackson. "Hey, Look Me Over" henceforth became Lucille Ball's musical trademark. (The song was also used by young Edward Kennedy in his successful bid for the Democratic nomination for U.S. Senator in the 1962 Massachusetts primary.) The musical itself depended so completely on its star that, when Lucille Ball withdrew after 171 performances, the final curtain had to be drawn. The score was recorded in an original cast album.

Coleman and Leigh returned to the Broadway theater with *Little Me* (November 17, 1962), another musical largely dependent for its success on a star. (It was also the first Broadway musical for which Neil Simon wrote the book.) The star was Sid Caesar in his return to Broadway after a 14-year absence, during which he became one of the superstars of the Golden Age of television comedy. In *Little Me* he played several roles: a nightclub singer who considers himself the world's greatest entertainer; a World War I private; an imperious prince; an autocratic German film director; and a character named Noble Egellsworth, who starts out as a 16-year-old snob and self-proclaimed genius, becomes a World War I daredevil aviator, and ends up a shriveled miser. All these characters become enamored of Belle Poitrine, a lady of questionable virtue whose life and loves are traced from her days of poverty to her reign as a movie queen.

In this production Swen Swenson delivered an effective song-and-dance routine in "I've Got Your Number." Another song in this score became a standard, "Real Live Girl," introduced by Sid Caesar, then used as a dance sequence for World War I soldiers in the trenches. Jack Jones recorded it. "Here's to Me," introduced by Nancy Andrews and chorus, so affected Judy Garland that it was one of the numbers played at her funeral. In another song, "The Other Side of the Tracks," introduced by Virginia Martin, Belle Poitrine recalled her humble early years. All the numbers in this score were recorded in an original cast album.

The initial run of *Little Me* was 257 performances. When it was revived on Broadway on January 21, 1982, Frank Rich of *The New York Times* wrote: "Every song in *Little Me* is tuneful, literate, dexterously crafted." For this revival, the Coleman-Leigh collaboration, which had ended 20 years earlier, was temporarily renewed as they contributed two new songs to the score.

Little Me was the last Broadway musical for which Coleman and Leigh joined talents. Their last successful songs were "When in Rome," which became a bestseller in Barbra Streisand's 1964 recording, and "Pass Me By." The latter was sung by Digby Wolfe on the soundtrack of the motion picture *Father Goose* (1964), starring Cary Grant, and was popularized in Peggy Lee's recording.

While at work, Coleman and Leigh lived near one another in separate houses in East Hampton, Long Island—Carolyn Leigh with her husband, the attorney David Wyn Cunningham Jr., whom she had married in 1959 but subsequently divorced. Coleman and Leigh songs were composed only after much discussion, argument and sometimes vitriolic disagreement. "It's the best way for me," Carol Leigh told an interviewer. "He writes a song and plays it for me and I don't like it and I say, 'Cy, no, I won't write for *that*.'" On the other hand, if Leigh brought Coleman lyrics he found unsuitable he would say: "I've known you to do much better on a bad day for creation. Try again, poet, try again. I wouldn't

link eight notes to that if it were the last lyric on earth." What followed was considerable rewriting and polishing by both composer and lyricist.

The wear and tear of collaboration destroyed the partnership in the early 1960s. Coleman found his next lyricist in the veteran Dorothy Fields. They composed the score for the Broadway musical *Sweet Charity* (January 29, 1966), in which Neil Simon adapted his book from the Federico Fellini film, *Nights of Cabiria* (1957). In the film, the main character had been a simpleminded Roman prostitute, but in Simon's book she is an ingenuous, good-hearted New York dance-hall hostess named Charity, ever sentimentally seeking true love only to find frustration and disenchantment time and again. In preparing his book, Simon assigned wry comments and laugh-provoking asides to lines flashed on an electric signboard while scene shifts were made, thereby focusing sentiment and compassion on his characters. Gwen Verdon played Charity and she regularly brought down the house with "If My Friends Could See Me Now." Wearing a top hat slightly askew over one eye, a cane thrust jauntily under her arm, she made this song-and-dance routine a tour de force. It remained such when Shirley MacLaine assumed the role of Charity in the 1969 motion picture adaptation of the musical, which Coleman scored. Since 1969, MacLaine has used "My Friends" in her nightclub act and on television; Coleman later wrote a television special for her entitled *If My Friends Could See Me Now*. Broadcast in 1974, it won MacLaine two Emmys. She also performed "If My Friends" at the "America Salutes the Queen" program at the London Palladium, which was attended by the royal family and telecast in the United States on NBC on November 29, 1977.

Though it was the musical highlight, "If My Friends Could See Me Now" did not overwhelm the show's other musical numbers. "Big Spender" was sung on the stage by Helen Gallagher, Thelma Oliver and others, while Chita Rivera, Paula Kelly and others presented it in the motion picture. Peggy Lee's recording was a bestseller. Gwen Verdon introduced "There's Gotta Be Something Better Than This" on the stage, MacLaine and Rivera performed it in the film. On the stage, "Baby, Dream Your Dream" was a duet for Gallagher and Oliver, and "Where Am I Going?" a trio for Gallagher, Oliver and Verdon. The last-named song became a bestseller for Barbra Streisand.

With a run of 603 performances, *Sweet Charity* turned out to be Coleman's greatest box-office success on Broadway. Following its long run, it toured the country in a national company.

The music of *Sweet Charity* was issued in both original cast and soundtrack recordings.

Dorothy Fields again was the lyricist when Coleman composed the music for Broadway's *Seesaw* (March 18, 1973). Here Michael Bennett, serving as librettist, director and choreographer, adapted William Gibson's two-character play, *Two for the Seesaw*, retaining the basic plot. An erratic and at times turbulent relationship develops between Jerry Ryan, a proper WASP attorney from Nebraska who deserts a wealthy, shrewish wife to seek a new destiny in New York, and Gittel, a Jewish girl from the Bronx who refers to herself as a "hot-blooded Biblical broad." The musical had a cast of more than 50 and included elaborate dance sequences and production numbers. *Seesaw* was described by Walter Kerr in *The New York Times* as "a love of a show that knows just when to keep the pressure low and when to open up, that in fact knows precisely where its true pressure is." At it turned out, with 296 performances, *Seesaw* barely survived more than one season. The best musical numbers, from a score released in an original cast album, were the title number, presented by the full company in the opening scene and reprised at the end by Michele Lee; "It's Not Where You Start," introduced by Tommy Tune with the company; and "Nobody Does it Like Me," introduced by Michele Lee, a song Shirley Bassey popularized in her Las Vegas nightclub act and made into a bestselling recording.

The writing partnership of Coleman and Fields ended with *Seesaw*, for this was Dorothy Fields's swan song. She died of a heart attack on the evening of March 28, 1974, after having sat through a rehearsal for a road company production of *Seesaw*.

Coleman's next collaborator was Michael Stewart, who wrote both book and lyrics for the Broadway musical, *I Love My Wife* (April 17, 1977), which ran for 864 performances. Adapted from a French comedy by Luis Rego, *I Love My Wife* was a satire on wife-swapping, with two couples (one of the men a sophisticate, the other an innocent) landing in bed for group sex, but never achieving their hoped-for illicit fulfillment. Coleman here fashioned a versatile score, released in an original cast album, which, as Clive Barnes noted in *The New York Times*, "runs the gamut from blues to barrel house, from country and western to marching band. But it is always tuneful, infectious and slightly impish." The only song from the score to gain wide popularity was "Hey, Good Times," introduced by Michael Mark, John Miller, Joseph Saulter and Ken Bichel.

Even before he had started work on *I Love*

My Wife, Coleman joined forces with Betty Comden and Adolph Green in writing numbers for an Off Broadway workshop revue. Enjoying their collaboration, they decided to write the score for a Broadway musical. The subject they chose was *Twentieth Century*, a fast-paced Broadway farce by Ben Hecht and Charles MacArthur which George Abbott had directed on Broadway in 1932 and which became an acclaimed motion picture starring John Barrymore and Carole Lombard in 1934. Most of the action takes place in the 1930s aboard the Twentieth Century Limited, an express train en route from Chicago to New York. Among the assortment of zany characters are a flamboyant producer, Oscar Jaffe, now on the professional skids, and Lily Garland, a movie star whom Jaffe had discovered years before and who had been his mistress. The wily Jaffe schemes to persuade Lily to star in a religious epic which he hopes will restore his lost glory in Hollywood. At the same time he wants to lure her to his bed once again. He accomplishes both missions, but not before a series of comic misadventures transpire. The presence of Imogene Coca as an eccentric religious fanatic contributed to the picaresque proceedings.

For *On the Twentieth Century* (February 19, 1978) the adaptors wrote the musical numbers in a style different from anything Coleman had yet composed. As Comden and Adolph Green told *The New York Times*: "We didn't want to write a 1930s musical, nor did we want a contemporary sound like rock. . . . We talked about characters . . . and soon we realized we were thinking in terms of an overblown, bravura musical style." This score more nearly approached an American-style opera buffa than musical comedy, calling for trained voices, ensemble numbers, and songs and duets that stressed the comic and parodistic more than the romantic and sentimental. In a humorous vein was "Our Private World," introduced by John Cullum and Madeline Kahn. *On the Twentieth Century*, which had a run of 460 performances, won the Tony as the year's best musical and an original cast album of the show's music was released.

Both *I Love My Wife* and *On the Twentieth Century* were commercially successful. But *Home Again*, a Coleman musical with book by Russell Baker and lyrics by Barbara Fried, closed during out-of-town tryouts in 1979.

In composing the score for his next Broadway musical Coleman turned to Michael Stewart for the lyrics while Mark Bramble prepared the text. *Barnum* (April 30, 1980) was a lavish, old-fashioned circus musical spotlighting events from the life of P. T. Barnum in the years 1835 to 1880. All biographical episodes were presented as if they were ring attractions in a Barnum production. The story deals with the relationship between the showman, who carries the unrealities of his business into his daily life, and his wife, Chairy, a practical woman who would have been happy if her husband had worked in a factory. All of the spectacle of a circus was presented on stage—a Ringmaster, clowns, jugglers, tightrope walkers, freaks, and animal acts.

Coleman's music for *Barnum* echoed the popular music of a century ago—marches, ragtime, sentimental ballads, and Tin Pan Alley pop. Jim Dale and Glenn Close introduced "The Colors of My Life," a ballad, and Marianne Tatum was heard on "Love Makes Such Fools of Us All." "Come Follow the Band" was redolent of Sousa. Coleman's score was described by Douglas Watt in *The New Yorker* as "a high spirited affair . . . admirably tailored to its subject as it proceeds on its now rousing, now sentimental, now thoughtful and always straightforward ways." The complete score was recorded in an original cast album. A major box-office attraction, *Barnum* ran for 854 performances.

Coleman's involvement with the musical theater did not preclude him from working in either motion pictures or television. After writing "Pass Me By" for *Father Goose* and the screen adaptation of *Sweet Charity*, he composed either the background music, the theme music or individual songs for *The Art of Love* (1965), *Walk, Don't Run* (1966), *The Heartbreak Kid* (1972) and *Garbo Talks* (1984). The title song of *Walk, Don't Run* was popularized in a recording by Peggy Lee. In 1975 he helped write and coproduced a second Shirley MacLaine TV special, *Gypsy in My Soul*, which won an Emmy for the years best television musical. Among Coleman's varied professional activities is his presidency of the Notable Music Company publishing house.

In 1961 Coleman had been awarded the La Guardia Medal from the City of New York for his contributions to entertainment. For his accomplishments in the musical theater his Broadway colleagues and friends gathered at Lincoln Center on November 15, 1981 to honor him with a production called *Hey, Look Me Over*, a celebration of his music.

After ending her partnership with Coleman, Carolyn Leigh wrote the lyrics for "Stay with Me," a melody adapted by Jerome Moross from the theme music he had written for a 1963 film, *The Cardinal*. Elmer Bernstein composed the music to Leigh's music, and Max Shulman the book, for *How Now, Dow Jones*, which opened on Broadway on December 7, 1967 for a run of 220 performances. Its hero, Charley, promises to marry Kate when the Dow breaks a thousand. Kate, who works on Wall Street, makes a futile attempt to win Charley by issuing a false report that the thousand mark has been reached, thereby wreaking havoc in the financial world. The most noteworthy song in this score was "Step to the Rear," performed by a female chorus. Other songs included "Just for the Moment" and "Big Trouble," each introduced by Marilyn Mason and Brenda Vaccaro. All the music from *How Now, Dow Jones* was collected in an original cast album. Leigh's last musical was *Smiles*, music composed by Marvin Hamlisch.

Leigh made several appearances as a performer of her songs. One of the last of these took place at Michael's Pub in Manhattan in November 1980. Carolyn Leigh died of a heart attack at New York's Lenox Hill Hospital on November 19, 1983.

ABOUT: Rigdon, W. (ed.) The Biographical Encyclopedia and Who's Who of the American Theatre, 1966.

COMDEN, BETTY (May 3, 1915–) and **GREEN, ADOLPH** (December 2, 1915–). During a professional life that has spanned more than four decades, Comden and Green have been inseparable collaborators. As librettists and lyricists for Broadway musicals and as writers of scenarios and lyrics for motion pictures

Betty Comden was born in Brooklyn on May 3, 1915, the daughter of Leo and Rebecca (Sadvoransky) Comden. She revealed an interest in writing and acting at an early age while attending the Ethical Culture School (Brooklyn) and Erasmus Hall High School. At New York University, she majored in and received the Bachelor of Science degree in 1938. After graduation, she made the rounds of theatrical agents trying to find work as an actress. At this time, she was introduced by a mutual friend to a contemporary who was similarly frustrated in his attempts to break into the theater. His name was Adolph Green.

Adolph Green was born in the Bronx on December 2, 1915, the son of Daniel and Helen (Weiss) Green. He, too, had an early history of creativity, writing poetry and acting in plays at De Witt Clinton High School from which he graduated in 1934. He then worked as a runner on Wall Street while searching for an opportunity to reveal his talents as writer and performer. In the summer of 1937, he played the part of "the Pirate King" in a production of Gilbert and Sullivan's *The Pirates of Penzance* at Camp Onata, a resort where young Leonard Bernstein

ADOLPH GREEN   BETTY COMDEN

was employed as music counselor. They became fast friends, and when Bernstein came to New York in 1939 to look for a job, he stayed in Adolph Green's furnished room on East Ninth Street. At another summer resort, Green met and befriended Judy Tuvim, a would-be actress who later became famous on stage and screen as Judy Holliday.

With seemingly no place to go in their respective theatrical careers, Betty Comden, Adolph Green and Judy Holliday decided to join forces. With Alvin Hammer and John Frank, they formed The Revuers, doing shows consisting of topical and satirical songs and sketches, for which Leonard Bernstein occasionally served as accompanist. In 1938, Max Gordon, owner of The Village Vanguard in Greenwich Village, hired them to perform on a single Sunday evening for a fee of $5 each. Because they could not afford to buy material, Comden and Green wrote it themselves. Their first production was *Where To Go in New York* and their first song "The Subway Opening," a history of the Sixth Avenue line. The show went over so well that Gordon engaged them five nights a week at $22 each on a regular basis. Their brand of wit and malice was applied to subjects ranging from Joan Crawford to Freud, from advertising to *The Reader's Digest*, from Scarlett O'Hara (*Gone with the Wind*) to Jean Valjean (*Les Misérables*). New York's cognoscenti, including those from the theater, were drawn to the Village Vanguard to catch their act. One of these early shows, *The Girl with the Two Left Feet*, was recorded on the Musicraft label.

From The Village Vanguard, the Revuers

moved uptown to the Rainbow Room atop the RCA Building, where they began a five-week engagement in September 1939. After that, they also began making weekly appearances on the NBC radio network and performed at Café Society, the Blue Angel, Radio City Music Hall and Loew's State Theatre. "We turned into a New York institution," Betty Comden recalled. They received an offer to appear in a motion picture, *Duffy's Tavern*, but the deal eventually fell through. While in Hollywood, the Revuers were featured at the Trocadero and they performed in the 20th Century-Fox production of *Greenwich Village* (1944); however, most of this footage ended up on the cutting room floor.

By the mid-1940s, Leonard Bernstein had begun to establish himself as an influential musical personality, both as a conductor and composer. He was planning to develop his popular ballet, *Fancy Free* (choreography by Jerome Robbins), into a stage musical for Broadway. Needing collaborators for both book and lyrics, he called upon his friends, Comden and Green.

On the Town (December 28, 1944) was an immediate critical and box-office success that instantly established the reputation of Comden and Green as writers for the musical theater. Their book was a fast-moving frolic with a fresh point of view and considerable vitality. Their best comic lyrics ("I Get Carried Away" and "I Can Cook, Too") had the pungency they had previously brought to their topical songs with the Revuers. But in *On the Town*, they also effectively sounded a poetic note in ballads such as "Lonely Town," "Lucky to Be Me" and "Some Other Time." "I must say," Green told an interviewer, "that Mr. Bernstein inspired us to write in veins we never dreamed we had in us." *On the Town* also marked the debut of Comden and Green as performers on Broadway; Green assumed the role of Ozzie, one of three sailors on a 24-hour pass in Manhattan, and Comden as Claire de Loon, an anthropology student and Ozzie's love interest.

A year later, Comden and Green wrote book and lyrics for *Billion Dollar Baby* (December 21, 1945) to music by Morton Gould. Described in the program as "a musical play of the Terrific Twenties," this Broadway musical recalled many of the fads and foibles of that era: Prohibition, speakeasies, gangsters, bathing-beauty parades, dance marathons, the stock market boom. The plot was incidental, and the music lacked distinction. The book of Comden and Green and the choreography of Jerome Robbins helped carry this show to a modest seven-month run.

Having made a name for themselves on Broadway, Comden and Green were brought to the MGM studios in Hollywood. Retaining their base in Manhattan, they shuttled back and forth from New York to California to meet commitments for both stage and screen. Their first film assignment was to write a new scenario for the 1947 motion picture remake of the De Sylva, Brown and Henderson stage musical, *Good News* (1927). Here, Comden and Green interpolated "The French Lesson" (music by Roger Edens), a song introduced by June Allyson and Peter Lawford poking fun at a rhyming French primer.

Their next screen assignment was *The Barkleys of Broadway* (1949), Fred Astaire and Ginger Rogers's last musical together. Songs for the film had been provided by Harry Warren and Ira Gershwin, which allowed Comden and Green to concentrate on the scenario. Many of the wittiest lines were assigned to Oscar Levant in the supporting role of Ezra Millar.

In 1949, Comden and Green also wrote the scenario for the film adaptation of *On the Town*, which starred Frank Sinatra, Gene Kelly and Jules Munshin as sailors on the make in Manhattan. Comden and Green were also required to write the lyrics for several new songs with music by Roger Edens. One, "Prehistoric Man," was a specialty dance number set in an anthropology museum and introduced by Ann Miller and Jules Munshin. For their lyrics, Comden and Green received the Screenwriters Award (WGA) in 1949.

For their next film, *Take Me Out to the Ball Game* (1949), Comden and Green prepared a scenario involving two baseball players at the turn-of-the-century played by Frank Sinatra

and Gene Kelly. Working again with Roger Edens as composer, Comden and Green wrote lyrics for the songs, which included "Right Girl for Me" (introduced by Sinatra) and "Strictly U. S. A.," a production number with a flag-waving routine worthy of George M. Cohan.

Comden and Green returned to Broadway in 1951 to contribute sketches and lyrics to *Two on the Aisle* (July 19, 1951), a revue starring Bert Lahr and Dorothy Gray. It was the first time they had collaborated with composer Jule Styne, and their songwriting partnership continued for the next three decades. The revue's best songs were "If You Hadn't, But You Did," and "Give a Little, Get a Little Love," introduced by Miss Gray, and "Hold Me–Hold Me–Hold Me."

Before resuming their collaboration with Styne, Comden and Green worked again with Leonard Bernstein, this time as lyricists for his new Broadway musical, *Wonderful Town* (February 25, 1953), which starred Rosalind Russell and Edith Adams. The Comden-Green lyrics, with characteristic sharpness, effectively deflated many pretensions and cliches in songs such as "One Hundred Easy Ways to Lose a Man," "Pass That Football," "Ohio," and "My Darlin' Eileen." Of the ballads, the best was "A Quiet Girl," introduced by George Gaynes. For their lyrics, Comden and Green received the Tony and a Donaldson Award.

From the mid-1950s well into the early 1970s, Comden and Green worked with Jule Styne on Broadway. To a new production of *Peter Pan* (October 20, 1954), starring Mary Martin, Comden and Green contributed lyrics to six numbers (the remainder of the score was by Mark Charlap and Carolyn Leigh). The best remembered of these are "Captain Hook's Waltz" and "Never Never Land."

Comden and Green also wrote the books and lyrics for a number of Styne's subsequent musicals. *Bells Are Ringing*, (November 29, 1956) starring Judy Holliday became Comden and Green's greatest box-office success on Broadway, with a run of 924 performances preceding a nationwide tour and the motion picture adaptation (1960) for which Comden and Green also wrote the scenario. The best satirical numbers were "It's a Simple Little System," a *Schnitzelbank* based on *The Racing Form* and "Drop That Name," a parody on the guests at swank parties. Comden and Green also wrote the words for two ballads which have become standards, "The Party's Over" and "Just in Time."

Next came *Fade Out–Fade In* (May 26, 1964), a minor effort starring Carol Burnett for which Comden and Green wrote the text and lyrics. In the musicals that followed, Comden and Green concentrated exclusively on the lyrics. *Say, Darling* (April 3, 1958) and *Subways are for Sleeping* (December 27, 1961) were also of little consequence. Out of *Do Re Mi* (December 26, 1960) came the standard, "Make Someone Happy," and *Hallelujah, Baby* (April 26, 1967) won a Tony as the season's best musical. *Lorelei* (January 27, 1974) had a run of 754 performances mainly due to the box-office appeal of its star, Carol Channing, who was recreating the role of Lorelei Lee from *Gentlemen Prefer Blondes* (1949). However, the songs by Leo Robin and Jule Styne retained from the earlier production overshadowed the numbers by Comden, Green and Styne.

While thus engaged on Broadway, Comden and Green were also in demand in Hollywood. In 1950, Arthur Freed, producer of musicals at MGM (with whom Comden and Green had previously worked on *The Barkleys* and *On the Town*) wanted to involve the team in a new project in which the story would serve as the frame for the series of song hits for the screen that he and composer Nacio Herb Brown had written during the early years of sound. The Comden-Green scenario for *Singin' in the Rain* (1952) was a satirical comedy about the early days of talking pictures. "The writing of the screenplay," recalled Comden and Green in *Saturday Review*, "gushed in a relatively exuberant flow. We tapped the roots of our memories and experience without editing ourselves when our ideas got wild, satirical and extravagantly nonsensical." Starring Gene Kelly, Donald O'Connor and Debbie Reynolds, *Singin' in the Rain* has become a classic among screen musicals; Pauline Kael said of it: "This exuberant and malicious satire of Hollywood in the late Twenties is perhaps the most enjoyable of all movie musicals—just about the best Hollywood musical of all time."

The Band Wagon (1953), starring Fred Astaire, was Arthur Freed's next major contribution at MGM. Songs by Arthur Schwartz (composer) and Howard Dietz (lyricist) from the Broadway production of the same name (1931) were retained, and Comden and Green conceived a behind-the-scenes look at a debonair silent-movie star who tries to recapture his onetime success with a Broadway musical written for him by a pair of his friends, a pair obviously modeled on Comden and Green themselves.

Two years later, Comden and Green received a second Screenwriters Award for the scenario of MGM's *It's Always Fair Weather* (1955). This was a cynical story about three ex-G.I.'s who arrange to meet ten years after their demobilization, only to discover they have outgrown one other and now have little in common. The trio appears on television in a satire of the program *This Is Your Life*. André Previn composed music for Comden and Green's lyrics, including "I Like Myself," rendered on roller skates by Gene Kelly, "Time for Parting," introduced by Kelly, Dan Dailey and Michael Kidd; and "Thanks a Lot, But No Thanks," sung by Dolores Gray.

Following *It's Always Fair Weather*, Comden and Green wrote the screenplays for *Auntie Mame* (1958), *Bells Are Ringing* (1960), and *What a Way to Go* (1964), and in the 1970s, Comden and Green enjoyed two further successes on Broadway. They won a Tony for their libretto for *Applause* (March 20, 1970); Charles Strouse and Lee Adams collaborated on the score. For *On the Twentieth Century* (February 19, 1978) they wrote both libretto and lyrics (music by Cy Coleman); its best song was "Our Private World," and the team received Tonys for both the show's book and lyrics.

In 1982, Comden and Green expanded their range with a sober subject of serious intent and purpose, a musical sequel to Ibsen's *A Doll's House*. *A Doll's Life* (September 23, 1982), for which they wrote book and lyrics (music by Larry Grossman) traced Nora's life after she leaves her husband and children in a move toward emancipation. "This show," explained Betty Comden, "is closer to the kind of thing we want to be doing, having arrived at this stage of our lives. It examines things we hadn't gone into very much in other works–human relationships and sexuality." But the critics rejected it in no uncertain terms; the show closed after five performances with a loss of $4 million.

On December 23, 1958, Comden and Green first appeared in *A Party With Betty Comden and Adolph Green* in which they performed their hit songs and routines. They gave 82 performances Off Broadway, went on tour, and returned to New York on April 16, 1959, where they won an Obie and recorded the show. With a greatly expanded repertory, they revived the act at the Loeb Center at Harvard University in 1975 and brought the production to New York on February 10, 1977, where it was televised. After seeing the show in 1977, Clive Barnes wrote in *The New York Times*: "As writers, the two of them [Comden and Green] are unusually gifted. They have a manic dexterity with words, a gift for rhyme and an ear for reason. As performers they have this dazzling charm, which makes them the kind of people you would really like to invite into your home."

In describing Comden and Green in *Stereo Review* Paul Kersh wrote: "In the old days, Betty was a rather maternal figure in Adolph's life. She used to see to it that he had carfare in his pocket, kept appointments, and didn't get run over (he's the sort of fellow who reads a book while crossing Times Square)." About Comden, Green told Kersh: "She invariably appears at, say, a producer's conference with our latest work of dialogue or lyrics typed and arranged in readable form. I ultimately show up with a few blank memo papers and some envelopes covered with hastily scribbled telephone numbers. . . . " According to Comden, Green stores up everything he has ever read in his Fernandel-shaped head and is an incurable game player, his favorite being to recite the first or last line of a play or book and challenge his victim to identify the quotation. He is also a voracious record collector.

When at work, they meet daily and keep going from one to five in the afternoon. "We meet daily on the great theory that nothing is wasted," Comden explained. "Somehow it adds up." She also revealed that "I usually sit at the typewriter with a carbon in the machine for Adolph to take home. Sometimes we just sit staring at each other for hours without saying a word. When we're writing lyrics, of course, there are long sessions with the composer, and then further work periods without him. Then, when we go into rehearsals, it's practically around the clock. Every assignment brings its own problems and has to be taken in its own way."

Betty Comden and Adolph Green both live in New York. Comden married designer Steven Kyle on January 4, 1942; they have a son and a daughter. Adolph Green married singer-actress Phyllis Newman on January 31, 1960; they, too, have a son and a daughter.

In 1978, Betty Comden received the New York City Mayor's Award in Art and Culture and the Woman of Achievement Award from New York University's Alumnae Association. Both she and Green were selected in 1981 by the nation's drama critics for induction into the Theater Hall of Fame in New York. In 1984, Betty Comden assumed a speaking role in the New York Playwrights Horizons production of *Isn't It Romantic?* and Adolph Green appeared with Phyllis Newman in *The New Yorkers* at the Trinity School.

ABOUT: Current Biography, 1945; Engel, L. Their Words Are Music, 1975; Wilk, M. They're Playing Our Song, 1973. *Periodicals*—New York Times February 6, 1977; New York Times Magazine December 11, 1960; Stereo Review April 1973.

CONRAD, CON (June 18, 1891–September 28, 1938), composer, was born Conrad S. Dober in New York City to Jewish immigrants who had come to America seeking the prosperous New World. Instead they were impoverished, working long hours for starvation wages and living in a crowded, poorly ventilated tenement on Grand Street on Manhattan's Lower East Side. Still, they never lost their love of culture nor their respect for education, and managed to acquire a used piano on which Conrad received lessons. They also planned to provide him a good academic education, but on both counts were frustrated. Though Dober was talented and enjoyed inventing tunes at the piano, he disliked submitting to the discipline of formal training. Left to himself, he learned to play the piano by ear. After graduating from elementary school, he briefly attended a military academy before enrolling in public high school. There, too, he was undisciplined, refusing to do any schoolwork and often playing truant.

While attending school, Dober helped support his family by working as a page in a Wall Street brokerage house and as an usher in a local movie house and by distributing programs at the Grand Opera House. When he was 16 he quit high school and found work as a pianist at the Variety Fair Theatre on 125th Street. Before long, he had moved from the pit to the stage by serving as a piano accompanist for several acts. After that, he joined Jay Whidden in an act that toured the Keith vaudeville circuit and was featured in a revue that was mounted in London.

In 1912 Con Conrad wrote and published his first song, "Down in Dear New Orleans" (lyrics by Joe Young), which enjoyed modest success after being interpolated for Rae Samuels in the *Ziegfeld Follies of 1912.* He then used his savings to finance the production of a Broadway musical, *Honeymoon Express* (1912), starring Al Jolson.

Now successful both as a producer and as a vaudevillian, Conrad nonetheless wanted to make his way as a songwriter. The amatory adventures of American soldiers in France during World War I was the inspiration for his "Oh! French" (1918, lyrics by Sam Ehrlich). A quarter of a century later, it was revived in the film, *The Dolly Sisters* (1945), in which it was performed by a male chorus. The Original Dixieland Jazz Band introduced three Conrad numbers in 1920: "Singin' the Blues (Till My Daddy Comes Home)" (lyrics by Sam H. Lewis and Joe Young, music written with J. Russel Robinson); "Palesteena," written with J. Russel Robinson; and "Margie" (lyrics by Benny Davis, music written with J. Russel Robinson).

CON CONRAD

The Original Dixieland Jazz Band recorded both "Palesteena" and "Margie" in 1920 while "Palesteena" was recorded that year by Frank Crumit and somewhat later by the orchestra of Nat Brandwyne. The inspiration for "Margie" was Eddie Cantor's young daughter, Margie. This song was popularized by Cantor, who recorded it and interpolated it into the revue, *The Midnight Rounders of 1921*. In 1938 the song became one of the jazz trombonist James "Trummy" Osborne's most successful recordings in a release made with the Jimmie Lunceford orchestra. "Margie" was interpolated into the film *Stella Dallas* (1937) and the movie revue *Hit Parade of 1941*. It also provided the title for two motion pictures, one released in 1940, in which it was sung by Tom Brown and reprised by Joy Hodges, and the other in 1946, in which it was performed in the opening scene. Betty Hutton sang it in *Incendiary Blonde* (1945) and Eddie Cantor on the soundtrack of *The Eddie Cantor Story* (1953).

In 1921 Conrad composed "Ma! He's Making Eyes at Me" (lyrics by Sidney Clare), which, like "Margie," became one of Eddie Cantor's best-known numbers. He introduced it in *The Midnight Rounders of 1921*, recorded it, and sang it on the soundtrack of his screen biography. It was also recorded by Pearl Bailey and by the Merry Macs, and in 1940 it provided the title for a motion picture. "Don't Send Your Wife to the Country" (lyrics by B. G. De Sylva and Harold Atteridge), a novelty song of 1921, was interpolated by Al Jolson into his Winter Garden extravaganza, *Bombo*.

In the early 1920s, Conrad began working with the lyricist Billy Rose. In 1923 they composed "Barney Google" for Eddie Cantor, who introduced it. Ernie Hare and Billy Jones ("The Happiness Boys") and Georgie Price each recorded it in 1923, but "Barney Google" was popularized by Olsen and Johnson. They featured it in a vaudeville act in which they capered up and down the theater aisle in a horse costume ridden by a jockey who was dressed up to resemble Barney Google. Trying to capitalize on this success, Conrad and Rose write a sequel, "Come on Spark Plug," but it failed to duplicate its predecessor's popularity. More successful was "You've Gotta See Mama Ev'ry Night" (1923), introduced in vaudeville by Sophie Tucker and recorded by Dolly Kay and by Kay Starr.

In 1922 Conrad married the eminent actress, Francine Larrimore; they were divorced three years later.

Conrad's first complete Broadway theater score was for *Moonlight* (January 30, 1924), with W. B. Friedlander providing the lyrics. It had a 174-performance run. After that, to lyrics by Friedlander and Isabel Leighton, Conrad composed the score for *Mercenary Mary* (April 13, 1925), which despite a New York run of only 136 performances, became a major box-office attraction in London. *Kitty's Kisses* (May 6, 1926), for which Gus Kahn wrote the lyrics, had a New York run of 170 performances.

Conrad's most important songs of the 1920s, however, were not composed for the theater. "Memory Lane" (1924, lyrics by B. G. De Sylva and Larry Spier) was recorded by Kate Smith and revived in the Abbott and Costello film farce, *In Society* (1944). "Miami" (1925, lyrics by B. G. De Sylva and Al Jolson) was interpolated by Jolson into his Winter Garden show, *Big Boy*, and was recorded by Jolson and by the orchestra of George Olsen. "Lonesome and Sorry" (1926, lyrics by Benny Davis) was introduced and popularized in vaudeville by Benny Davis and recorded by Ruth Etting.

The mid- to late 1920s was a stormy period for Conrad. He had married the actress Francine Larrimore in 1922, but they were divorced just three years later. Moreover, Conrad had invested unwisely in numerous stage productions, and was forced to declare bankruptcy in 1928.

With motion pictures having recently entered the era of sound, Conrad was in the vanguard of New York songwriters who moved to Southern California to compose for the screen. He established permanent residence there in 1928 and his fortunes underwent a happy reversal. His first assignment was the score for the *Fox Movietone Follies* (1929), one of the first screen musicals with a backstage story. To lyrics by Sidney D.

Mitchell and Archie Gottler, Conrad composed for that production "Big City Blues," introduced by Lola Lane and recorded by the orchestras of George Olsen and Arnold Johnson.

In 1929 Conrad wrote the songs for *Broadway* and *The Cockeyed World* and, in 1930, *Let's Go Places* and *Movietone Follies of 1930.* "Crazy Feet" (lyrics by Mitchell and Gottler) was sung by Dixie Lee in *Happy Feet* (1930). "Bend Down, Sister" (lyrics by Ballard MacDonald and Dave Silverstein) was introduced by Charlotte Greenwood in *Palmy Days* (1931) and recorded by Buddy Campbell. For Nino Martini in *Here's to Romance* (1935) Conrad composed the title song and "Midnight in Paris" (lyrics by Herb Magidson). "Here's to Romance" was recorded by the David Rose orchestra, the George Shearing Quartet and the Boston Pops Orchestra and became Conrad's first song to be heard on *Your Hit Parade*, with four appearances in 1935.

In 1934 Conrad made popular music history by winning the first Oscar presented for the year's best screen song. "The Continental" (lyrics by Magidson) was introduced in the 1934 motion picture, *The Gay Divorcee*, adapted from Cole Porter's stage musical, *The Gay Divorce.* There it was introduced by Ginger Rogers before it was danced to by Fred Astaire and Rogers and served as the background music for a spectacular dance finale. Tommy Dorsey and his orchestra (vocal by Frank Sinatra), Kate Smith, and Gertrude Niesen recorded it. In *The Gay Divorcee* Astaire also sang another number by Conrad and Magidson, "A Needle in a Haystack."

Apart from music for motion pictures, Conrad composed two songs in 1931 that were introduced, recorded and made famous by Russ Columbo, who was then being managed by Conrad. "Prisoner of Love" (lyrics by Leo Robin, music written with Clarence Gaskill) was successfully revived twice in recordings: by Perry Como in 1946 and by James Brown and the Famous Flames in 1963. The song had 16 appearances on *Your Hit Parade* in 1946. "You Call it Madness" (lyrics by Gladys Du Bois and Paul Gregory), was further popularized in recordings by Mildred Bailey, Kate Smith, Tony Martin, Fred Rich and his orchestra and the King Cole Trio. In 1932 Conrad's "Lonesome Me" (lyrics by Andy Razaf, music written with Fats Waller) was successfully introduced by the orchestra of George Hall.

Con Conrad died in Van Nuys, California in 1938. His last new song for the screen was "Only When You're in My Arms" (lyrics by Harry Ruby and Bert Kalmar), which was interpolated into the Rogers-Astaire musical, *The Story of Vernon and Irene Castle* (1939).

ABOUT: Craig, W. Sweet and Lowdown: America's Popular Song Writers, 1978. *Periodicals*—Musical America October 10, 1938.

COOTS, J. FRED, (May 2, 1897–April 8, 1985), composer, was born in Brooklyn, the son of William Jerome Coots, a shipping inspector, and Annie (Dent) Coots. Despite the family's poverty, there was a piano in the house, a remnant of more prosperous times. His mother's playing was Coots's first important musical experience: "Mother would come in from her job peddling pins and needles, and instead of complaining would sit down at the piano and play," he later recalled. "Or again, on Saturday nights, I would come home from my own job at Schwab's butcher shop, Mama used to sit down and play. She would tell me: 'There are ways to rise above the poor.'"

As a boy, Coots contracted inflammatory rheumatism which left him an invalid for five years. As he grew stronger, his mother gave him piano lessons to exercise his fingers. "To my surprise," he says, "I discovered a real joy in music. As spring came and I was able to be about, mother had to plead with me to go out and play in the streets instead of sitting all the time at the piano."

Coots graduated from P.S. 118 in the Bay Ridge section of Brooklyn in 1912 after which he was employed as a bond salesman at the Farmers Loan and Trust Company on Wall Street at a salary of $130 a month including lunches. But Coots also found the time to frequent the cubicles for song plugging in the offices of Tin Pan Alley publishers. There, he improvised on the pianos and wrote songs for amateur theatrical productions. In 1917, one of his songs was published: "Mr. Ford, You've Got the Right Idea" (lyrics by Ray Sherwood) inspired by Henry Ford's plans to send a "peace ship" to Europe to try to bring World War I to an end. For this maiden effort, Coots earned a royalty of $5 which he shared with his lyricist. When he sold a second song, "When I Dream of the Girl of My Dreams," Coots abandoned his career on Wall Street to become a composer.

Coots spent the next several years breaking into the music business. He played piano on tour with vaudevillian Frederick Bowers, and upon returning to New York, he worked at the Columbia Theatre, a burlesque house. In 1918, he began working as a song plugger and stock boy at the New York branch of Chicago's McKinley Music Company, where he continued to write songs. He also appeared in nightclubs such as the Silver Slipper and the Club Alamo Wigwam.

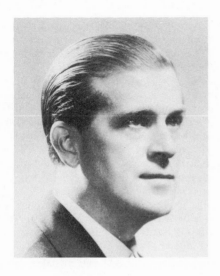

J. FRED COOTS

Before long, Coots was beginning to sell some of his songs, as well as other material, to vaudevillians, including such headliners as the team of Van and Schenck, and the inimitable Sophie Tucker, who introduced "There's a Little Bit of Devil in Your Angel Eyes" (written with vaudevillian Jack Little) at the Palace Theatre in 1920. Savoy and Brennan used some of his material in the *Greenwich Village Follies* of 1920 and 1922, and "In My Little Red Book" (lyrics by McElbert Moore) was introduced by Georgie Price in the Broadway revue, *Spice of 1922.*

Coots saved enough money to join the Friars Club, the haunt of Broadway actors, where he met Eddie Dowling, and together they wrote that year's *Friar's Frolic.* Dowling also had plans to expand (with Cyrus Wood) one of his vaudeville acts into a full-length Broadway musical, but when Victor Herbert and Rudolf Friml were unavailable for the score, Dowling engaged Coots to work with lyricist Raymond Klages. *Sally, Irene, and Mary* (September 4, 1922) had a Broadway run of 318 performances, then toured the country before returning to New York in 1925 for an additional 16 performances. From Coots's first complete Broadway score came his first successful song, "Time Will Tell," introduced by the show's stars, Eddie Dowling and Edna Morn; appealing numbers such as "Jimmie," "I Wonder Why" and "Do You Remember the Days?" further established his reputation.

The success of *Sally, Irene and Mary* brought Coots a contract from the Shuberts to provide music, sometimes complete scores, but more often functional songs and individual numbers for their various Broadway productions. During the next five years, Coots was busily engaged in a succession of Broadway revues beginning with two editions of *Artists and Models* (1924, 1925; composed with Sigmund Romberg), *Gay Paree* (1925), *June Days* (1926), *A Night in Paris* (1926), and *White Lights* (1927). His most important song from these productions was "Promenade Walk" (composed with Al Goodman and Maurice Rubens; lyrics by Clifford Grey), introduced by Frances Williams in *Artists and Models of 1925* and recorded by Johnny Hamp.

He had also married his wife, Margie, on February 18, 1924 and they began raising a family of five children.

At the time Coots's contract with the Shuberts expired, a new minimum basic agreement was adopted by the Authors League of America. The new agreement was unacceptable to the Shuberts; consequently, many contracts were not renewed, and Coots found himself unemployed. For awhile, he played cocktail piano in clubs and speakeasies, and in 1928, he made a comeback with "Doin' the Racoon" (lyrics by Klages), popularized by the George Olsen orchestra and The Knickerbockers. "A Precious Little Thing Called Love" (lyrics by Lou Davis) was introduced by Nancy Carroll in the motion picture, *A Shopworn Angel* (1929); Davis also wrote other lyrics for this melody including "There's a Girl in Caroline" and "If I Ever Fall in Love." "Pal of My Sweetheart" (1929; lyrics by Benny Davis) was promoted in vaudeville by its lyricist. Also popular were "Moonlight Madness" and "A Tale of Alsace-Lorraine."

Meanwhile, Coots was composing his last complete Broadway musical score for *Sons o' Guns* (November 26, 1929). On the boards for 295 performances, it was his most successful show since *Sally, Irene, and Mary*. The libretto, a nostalgic look at the World War I days written by Fred Thompson and Jack Donahue, traces the misadventures of a wealthy socialite drafted into the army. The show's principal songs (lyrics by Arthur Swanstrom and Benny Davis) were "Cross Your Fingers," introduced by Milton Watson and Shirley Vernon, and "Why?" and "It's You I Love," introduced by Jack Donahue and Lily Damita.

While pursuing his songwriting career on Broadway and in Tin Pan Alley, Coots also toured the vaudeville circuit between 1928 and 1930 with Waite Hoyt, the New York Yankees pitcher, and in 1934, he went back on the road with Eddie Dowling and Ray Dooley.

The 1930s were Coots's most productive songwriting years, and many of the songs he composed during this decade have since become standards. In 1930, "I Still Get a Thrill" (lyrics by Benny Davis) was introduced in a broadcast performance by Hal Kemp and his orchestra at the Hotel Taft in New York; it was popularized further in recordings by Bing Crosby, Lee Morse, Johnny Marvin, Dick Haymes and Guy Lombardo and his Royal Canadians. Coots wrote a melody for "Love Letters in the Sand" (lyrics by Nick and Charles Kenny) in 1931 after reading Nick Kenny's poem in *The Mirror*. It was introduced at the Taft Hotel by the George Hall orchestra (Dolly Dawn, vocalist) and was recorded by the Radiolites, the Three Suns, Ross Columbo, and Sam Lanin and his orchestra. The song's popularity continued to grow when the George Hall orchestra adopted it as a signature theme for its regular appearances on the Mutual Broadcasting Company network. A quarter of a century later, "Love Letters" again became a big hit when Pat Boone revived it in a 1957 recording that reached first position on *Your Hit Parade* and sold over a million discs; that year, he also sang it in the motion picture, *Bernardine*.

Several more hits followed in rapid succession: "I Wouldn't Trade the Silver in My Mother's Hair," written with Jack Little in 1932, was introduced by Little in his vaudeville act. The following year, "Two Tickets to Georgia" (lyrics by Joe Young and Charles Tobias) was introduced by the Ted Lewis band at the Paramount Theatre in New York and was further popularized by the Pickens Sisters and the orchestras of Victor Young and Ben Pollack; "I Want to Ring Bells" (lyrics by Maurice Sigler) was introduced by Guy Lombardo and His Royal Canadians (vocal by Carmen Lombardo) and recorded by Joe Venuti and his orchestra; "One Minute to One" (lyrics by Sam H. Lewis) became a specialty of Harry Richman, and it served as the theme song for Gray Gordon and his orchestra. After Morton Downey introduced "For All We Know" (lyrics by Sam M. Lewis) on his radio program in 1934, it was recorded by Kay Kyser, Guy Lombardo and Isham Jones. In 1934, Coots also composed "Santa Claus is Coming to Town" (lyrics by Haven Gillespie), one of the most successful Yuletide songs to come out of In Pan Alley. George Olsen and his orchestra introduced it. Coots was writing special material for Eddie Cantor's weekly radio show at that time, and he showed his Christmas song to him. Cantor initially turned it down, feeling it was a "kiddie song" that had no place in his show; but Cantor's wife, Ida, intervened and at her request, Cantor sang it on his program a week before Thanksgiving in 1934. He made it an instant success and recordings by Bing Crosby with the Andrews Sisters, Perry Como, and Tommy Dorsey then established it as a standard.

From 1936 to 1938, Coots composed songs with Benny Davis as lyricist for revues at Harlem's Cotton Club. The cream of the crop were "The Suzie-Q" (the Suzie-Q was a popular social dance), "Copper-Colored Gal," "Tall, Tan and Terrific," "Alabama Barbeque" and "The Boogie Woogie." In 1938, Coots was also represented by three songs on *Your Hit Parade*: "There's Honey on the Moon Tonight" (lyrics by Haven Gillespie and Mack David), "Summer Souvenirs" (lyrics by Charles Newman), and "You Go to My Head" (lyrics by Haven Gillespie), which was introduced and recorded by Glen Gray and the Casa Loma Orchestra. Subsequent recordings were made by Larry Clinton and his orchestra (vocal by Bea Wain), Billie Holiday, Frank Sinatra, Doris Day and Marlene Dietrich, and it later became the theme song of Mitchell Ayres and his orchestra.

On December 17, 1941, eleven days after the Japanese attack on Pearl Harbor, Coots composed both words and music of one of the earliest songs inspired by World War II, "Goodbye, Mama, I'm Off to Yokohama." Another wartime hit, "A Beautiful Lady in Blue" (lyrics by Sam M. Lewis) had been published in 1935, but it did not become popular until Jan Peerce revived it on radio's Chevrolet Hour several years later.

Coots's career took a new turn in the 1950s, when he began to compose "kiddie" songs to his own lyrics. The first was "When the Teddy Bears Go Marching on Parade" (1952), introduced by Jack Arthur on a children's show on NBC. A year later, "Me and My Teddy Bear" launched Rosemary Clooney's singing career on records and television; she then recorded several more of Coots's songs: "Who'll Tie the Bell on the Old Cat's Tail?," "Ozzie the Ostrich," "Little Sally One-Shoe," and "Little Johnny Chickadee." These and other songs were published by Toy Town Tunes, Inc., a publishing house owned and controlled by Coots. From 1952 to 1961, Coots also appeared throughout the United States in a series of lecture-recitals that included songs and stories entitled "Melodies and Memories," "Fun in Tin Pan Alley," "Broadway Is My Home," and for children, "Toytown on Parade." He retired in 1974.

ABOUT: Craig, W. Sweet and Lowdown: America's Popular Song Writers, 1978; Notable Names in the American Theatre, 1976. *Periodicals*—New York Times April 6, 1930.

DAVID, HAL. *See* **BACHARACH, BURT** and **DAVID, HAL**

DE KOVEN, REGINALD (April 3, 1859–January 16, 1920), America's first significant composer of operetta, was born Henry Lewis Reginald De Koven in Middletown, Connecticut, the son of Dr. Henry and Charlotte (Le Roy) De Koven. His father, uncle and brother were all highly esteemed clergymen in the Protestant Episcopal Church; his father was also professor of theology at Wesleyan University.

Reginald De Koven began studying music when he was seven, but he proved more precocious in languages and was able to translate Latin texts by the time he was eight. When he was 11, his father moved to England, where he received his education and he graduated from St. John's College, Oxford, with a bachelor's degree in 1879. While at Oxford, he periodically visited Stuttgart to study the piano with Wilhelm Speidel. He decided to pursue a career as a professional musician, so he remained in Europe, where he studied the piano with Siegmund Lebert and Pruckner in Stuttgart, composition with Johann Christian Hauff in Frankfurt, and voice with Luigi Vannuccini in Florence.

In 1882 he returned to the United States, settling in Chicago. The necessity of earning a living precluded the possibility of total involvement in music and compelled him to work for several years as a bank teller and clerk in a brokerage house. On May 1, 1884 in Lake Forest, Illinois, he married Anna Farwell, daughter of United States Senator Charles B. Farwell, who was also the proprietor of J. V. Farwell & Co., a prosperous Chicago dry goods firm. The De Kovens had a daughter, Ethel.

De Koven joined his father-in-law's business establishment, and when the State of Texas sold three million acres of land at a nominal price to raise money for a new state capital, De Koven handled the transaction; this made De Koven a millionaire. Financially secure, he now left the business world to devote himself exclusively to composing art songs and sundry works for the concert hall.

While visiting Minneapolis in 1887, De Koven met Henry B. Smith, a Chicago newspaperman who wrote a daily column of light verse and humor. His primary interest, however, was the musical theater, and he had written texts for two "comic operas" that had been produced unsuccessfully by the Chicago Ideals. Smith encouraged De Koven to compose music for his new lyrics and libretti, and one of their first collaborative efforts was *The Begum,* produced by the McCaull Opera Company starring De Wolf Hopper and Jefferson de Angelis in Philadelphia on November 7, 1887. *The Begum* was little more than a clone of Gilbert and Sullivan's *The*

REGINALD DE KOVEN

Mikado, set in India rather than Japan, and it failed. To master his craft, De Koven went to Europe to study opera composition with Richard Genée and Franz von Suppé in Vienna in 1888 and with Léo Delibes in Paris in 1889. While in Vienna, he collaborated with Smith on another operetta, *Don Quixote,* which was first produced in Boston by The Boston Ideal Opera Company ("The Bostonians") on November 18, 1889.

At last, with *Robin Hood,* introduced by The Bostonians at the Chicago Opera House on June 9, 1890, De Koven and Smith not only achieved the major success which had been eluding them, but they also composed the work generally considered to be the most important operetta written in America before Victor Herbert. After its successful run in Chicago, it was performed widely around the country and opened on Broadway in a refurbished production at the Standard Theatre on September 28, 1891 (revivals took place in 1912, 1929, 1932, and 1944); it was also the first American operetta to be mounted on the London stage.

Smith's book closely followed the Robin Hood legend with its escapades of the hero (played by Tom Karl) and his merry band, Maid Marian (Caroline Hamilton), Friar Tuck, the Sheriff of Nottingham, and Guy of Gisborne. The success of *Robin Hood* can also be attributed to De Koven's refined and appealing songs, such as "Brown October Ale," a drinking song introduced by W. H. MacDonald as Little John, and "The Tailor and the Crow," sung to a background of humming voices by Eugene Cowles in his debut as Will Scarlet.

But *Robin Hood* is remembered today because of its most popular song, "Oh, Promise Me," which, ironically, De Koven had not composed for this production—it was an art song, setting music to verses by Clement Scott, published by G. Schirmer in 1889. During rehearsals, it was decided that a sentimental number was needed for Alan-a-Dale to sing preceding the impending marriage of Guy and Maid Marian. De Koven suggested using "Oh, Promise Me," but the idea was immediately rejected by all involved. One day, in her dressing room, contralto Jessie Bartlett Davis (who played Alan-a-Dale), was humming the tune, when the producer told her: "If you sing that song as you are now doing, in a lower key, it will make your reputation." Only then did she consent to sing it, and in addition to becoming the highlight of the evening, "Oh, Promise Me" made Jessie Bartlett Davis one of The Bostonians's biggest stars. Since then, it has been recorded by many opera and concert performers as well as popular singers, notably Nelson Eddy and Conrad Thibault. Nearly a century after its composition, it still has a life of its own as one of several preludes used in conventional wedding ceremonies.

Though the critics praised *Robin Hood* and The Bostonians's production, they were not always kind to De Koven, finding his music to be not only uninspired, but also derivative. De Koven's only response to such criticism and also to stronger insinuations was that the music of all composers is "imitative" to a certain degree; he preferred to discuss other aspects of his work.

After the success of *Robin Hood*, De Koven continue to compose new operettas, all but a few with Harry B. Smith, who had become one of Broadway's most prolific authors and lyricists. During the next two decades, more than 20 of these works were produced, the most noteworthy being *The Fencing Master* (1892), *Rob Roy* (1894), *The Highwayman* (1897), *The Little Duchess* (1901), *Maid Marian* (1902), *Happyland* (1905), and *The Beauty Spot* (1909).

During the 1892–93 season, the touring Bostonians brought two new De Koven-Smith operettas to New York. The first was *The Fencing Master* (November 14, 1892), which featured Marie Tempest in a "trouser role"; the story takes place in 15th-century Italy, and the score included tarantellas, barcaroles, serenades and other evocative musical numbers. The troupe also presented Jessie Bartlett Davis in *The Knickerbockers* (May 29, 1893); in spite of the work's setting in colonial New York, it was popular neither with the critics nor the public, and closed after a one-week run.

Rob Roy (October 29, 1894) was the biggest hit of the 1894–95 season and also De Koven's longest running show (235 performances in two engagements). Though *Rob Roy* is no longer familiar, in its day, it was often favorably compared to *Robin Hood*. The production starred William Pruette and Juliette Corden in a story blending romance and court intrigue in Scotland during the reign of George II. Though none of the songs achieved lasting popularity, "The Merry Miller" (sung by Corden) is reputed to have been given three encores on opening night, and "My Home is Where the Heather Blooms" and "Dearest, Heart of My Heart" were also well-received.

Critics had continued to find De Koven's music "reminiscent" and were beginning to find Smith's books predictable, when the team scored a much-needed success with *The Highwayman* (December 13, 1897). Joseph O'Hara and Hilda Clark were cast as the romantic leads, and introduced songs including "Do You Remember Love?" and "Moonlight Song." But it was a droll, yet shrewd and conniving minor character, Constable Foxy Quiller (played by Jerome Sykes), who brought down the house. He was so popular that "foxy quiller" became a slang expression for anyone with a similar turn of mind, and in 1900, De Koven and Smith were commissioned to write a sequel, *Foxy Quiller*, for Sykes.

De Koven was also associated with the successful *The Little Duchess* (October 14, 1901), produced by Flo Ziegfeld for his wife, Anna Held. The libretto (by Smith) was based on the almost gratuitous plot of the French vaudeville, *Niniche* (1879), in which an actress, hoping to elude her creditors, poses as a duchess. Though Held lacked the appeal of the French star, Anna Judic, the chorus of girls in titillating costumes insured the success of the American adaptation. It was also in this production that child star Willie Howard, who, as an adult, was one of the stage's leading comedians, made his debut.

The reign of The Bostonians was nearing an end, and they commissioned De Koven and Smith to compose *Maid Marian* (January 27, 1902), hoping to recapture the magic of *Robin Hood*. Davis, Barnabee, and MacDonald returned to recreate their original roles; Grace van Studdiford assumed the title role and Frank Rushworth was Robin Hood. On opening night, the audience demanded encores of all of the solo numbers, which included "True Love is Not for a Day" and "Tell Me Again, Sweetheart." In 1902, George P. Upton wrote in *The Standard Light Operas* that he considered the score of *Maid Marian* to be "of a higher order" than that of *Robin Hood*, and "[it] occasionally approaches grand opera in its breadth and earnestness."

Two of De Koven's late operettas achieved

long runs on Broadway, but this was probably due more to the magnetism and drawing power of the performers than to any particular fondness for De Koven's music. *Happyland* (October 2, 1905), with a libretto by Frederic Ranken, was carried to a run of 136 performances by De Wolf Hopper as King Ecstaticus of Elysia; Jefferson De Angelis and his company offered 137 performances of *The Beauty Spot* (April 10, 1909; book by Joseph Herbert). However, the public, having discovered Victor Herbert 10 years earlier, was now becoming acquainted with newcomer Jerome Kern, and displayed increasing indifference to many of De Koven's latest efforts. His last operetta, *Her Little Highness* (October 13, 1913), which opened two weeks after a revival of *Rob Roy*, was forced to close after 16 performances.

De Koven realized that the operettas he had been composing were now going out of fashion, so he turned his attention to grand opera. *The Canterbury Pilgrims* (libretto by Percy MacKaye, after Chaucer) was first staged by the Metropolitan Opera Company in New York on March 8, 1917, and *Rip Van Winkle* (libretto by MacKaye, after Washington Irving) was mounted by the Chicago Opera Company on January 2, 1920. De Koven's compositions also include more than 400 art songs, and various works for piano solo and chorus.

De Koven was seized by a stroke while attending a dinner party given in his honor in Chicago on January 16, 1920. Ten minutes later, it proved fatal.

In addition to his many endeavors in the musical theater, De Koven had also served as music critic on the Chicago *Evening Post* (1889–90), the New York *World* (1892–97; 1907–12), *Harper's Weekly* (1895–97), the New York *Journal* (1898–1900), and in later years, on the New York *Herald*. In this capacity, he was an ardent supporter of native composers and musical life and also a strong advocate of performing opera in English in America. In 1902 he had also founded the Philharmonic Orchestra in Washington, D. C., which he conducted until 1905.

De Koven had lived the life of a *grand seigneur*: for many years, he and his wife resided at 1025 Park Avenue in New York City, a mansion whose furnishings included tapestries and many objets d'art from European palaces and art galleries (as a memorial, De Koven's studio and bedroom were left untouched until the building was demolished in the 1940s). He dressed in sartorial elegance, from his top hat and monocle down to his gold-tipped cane, and he cultivated an Oxford accent. His table was always laden with delicacies imported from around the world,

and he was a connoisseur of fine wine. Fastidious about his appearance, he was continually alternating between overindulgence and spartan diets.

ABOUT: Dictionary of American Biography, 1932; De Koven, A. A Musician and His Wife, 1926.

DENVER, JOHN (December 31, 1943–   ), became a superstar in the 1970s as a performer and composer of wholesome songs that were derived from pop, folk and country music. "The music I make," he has explained, "is my way of trying to share the joy I get from living. I see too many people around me who are unhappy. I want people to hear my songs and walk away with a smile, with a little sunshine on their faces."

He was born Henry John Deutschendorf Jr. in Roswell, New Mexico, the older of two sons of Lieutenant Colonel Henry John Deutschendorf, an Air Force pilot, and Erma Louise (Swope) Deutschendorf. Because the military transferred Colonel Deutschendorf from one post to another, both in the United States and abroad, his family moved often and his elder son made few friends and had what he called a "lonely childhood."

When he was in the seventh grade, his grandmother gave him an acoustic Gibson guitar. He took lessons for a year before losing interest in the instrument. Later, though, his admiration for Elvis Presley made Denver want to learn to play the guitar. "I just started playing again and just got deeper and deeper into it," he recalled. Before long the self-taught teenager was a good enough guitarist to play in local bands and at school functions.

At Arlington Heights High School in Fort Worth, Texas and at the church where he sang in the choir, he made friends through his music and his interest in sports. But, as he has said, "It was the music that really worked for me. It was the thing that I always did that was easy and made me feel good. I liked singing for people."

Disagreements with his parents about the value of receiving a formal education led Denver to quit school in his senior year and run off to California. His father tracked him down, brought him back to Texas and persuaded him to complete high school. His graduation present from his parents was a new electric guitar, a Fender Jazzmaster.

Denver enrolled at Texas Tech University in Lubbock and elected to major in architecture. There he played guitar in a blues band, formed a folk music trio with two fraternity brothers

JOHN DENVER

and also performed as a vocal soloist. The music he paid closest attention to was the folk of Joan Baez, Peter, Paul and Mary, the New Christy Minstrels and the Chad Mitchell Trio. During his junior year, Denver decided to drop out of college. His parents objected, but gave him $250 and said he was free to seek his own destiny.

Early in 1964, he made his way to California, where he found work as a draftsman in Los Angeles and tried to find bookings as a singer at area nightclubs. During his second year in Los Angeles, Denver received a booking to perform solo at a coffeehouse in Westwood for a single weekend, but was kept on for 26 weeks. A producer at Capitol Records had him cut a demonstration record, and, though nothing came of the demo, Henry John Deutschendorf Jr. now changed his name to John Denver.

In 1965, while still in Los Angeles, Denver decided to audition with the Chad Mitchell Trio as a replacement for the departing Mitchell. At the audition in New York City, Denver at first did poorly, partly because he had a cold, and in part because he tried too hard to imitate Mitchell. But after a couple of hours he began to sing his own style. Some days later, in Phoenix, he was informed that he had been chosen from among 250 applicants for the job. Now called the Mitchell Trio, the three men (David Boise, Mike Johnson and Denver) rehearsed for six days before opening at the Cellar Door in Washington, D. C. Later in 1965 the Mitchell Trio released its first album with Denver as lead singer, *The Mitchell Trio: That's the Way It's Gonna Be.* Robert Shelton, reviewing it for *The New York Times*, said that Denver, "although not as versatile a vocalist

[as Mitchell], is a strong instrumental addition, on guitar and banjo, and has the sort of freely projected personality that keeps this lively group very much alive."

While on a concert tour of college campuses with the Mitchell Trio, in November 1966 Denver met Ann Martell, a student at Gustavus Adolphus College in St. Peter, Minnesota. They were married on June 9, 1967, and lived briefly in Chicago before settling in Aspen, Colorado. In the spring of 1975 they adopted a son, Zachary.

Urged by friends to release a tape of songs he was unable to perform with the Mitchell Trio, Denver, in 1967, made a 250-copy pressing of a Christmas album of 13 songs which he presented as a Christmas gift to his family and friends. One of the variety LP's numbers was "Babe, I Hate to Go," which he had written in a hotel room one lonely evening in Washington, D.C. while on tour with the Mitchell Trio. Peter, Paul and Mary recorded it in 1969 on their *Album 1700,* changing the title to "Leaving on a Jet Plane." Released as a single, it reached first position on the *Billboard* pop charts and stayed in the top 100 listings for four months, eventually earning a gold record. Now a standard, "Leaving on a Jet Plane" has been recorded by Liza Minnelli, who included it on her albums *Come Saturday* and *The Liza Minnelli Four Sider,* Andy Williams, Eddy Arnold, and Bobby Darin, and United Airlines used it as theme music for a television commercial.

By the later 1960s traditional folk music had been superseded in the pop music field by rock 'n' roll, and the Mitchell Trio disbanded in November 1968. Denver, however, immediately launched his career as a solo performer. He had a successful one-month engagement at the Leather Jug in Snowmass, Colorado, and then undertook a nationwide tour, appearing in coffeehouses, on college campuses, and at clubs like the Sheraton-Ritz in Minneapolis and the Troubadour in Hollywood.

Denver was proving that he could appeal to younger audiences even though he had none of the flamboyance, charisma or capacity to shock of rock idols like Mick Jagger, Bob Dylan or John Lennon. In fact, with his boyish, all-American good looks, simple country-boy attire and air of innocent naivety, his image was the antithesis of that of rock superstars like Jagger and Jim Morrison. But when the show business manager Jerry Weintraub heard him in 1969 at the Troubadour, he predicted that Denver would some day become "the biggest star in America" and added: "He'll be able to appeal both to young people and to an older audience that usually refused to listen to contemporary acts. They will listen to

John—and let him into their homes on television—because they feel comfortable with him. And John will reach out for them."

Later that year Weintraub became his manager, and groomed Denver for guest spots on network TV programs like the *Merv Griffin Show* and the *Tonight Show*. Before affiliating himself with Weintraub, Denver had signed a two-year recording contract with RCA Victor. On his first album, *Rhymes and Reason* (1969), he included songs by other composers as well as several of his own numbers, including "Leaving on a Jet Plane." The title track, which mourned the loss of youth and beautiful innocence, was characteristic of the tender sentiment songs that would later make him famous. The album enjoyed only moderate commercial success, as did Denver's next three LPs. *Take Me to Tomorrow* and *Whose Garden Was This* were released in 1970. The former album contained several new compositions of his own, the most significant of which were the title song, "Aspenglow," the first of his tributes to Colorado, and "Follow Me," a ballad. Mary Travers, of Peter, Paul and Mary, performed "Follow Me" on her solo album, *Mary*, and a country-western version of the song was recorded by June Carter Cash. On his fourth album, *Poems, Prayers and Promises*, Denver introduced the country-pop standard, "Take Me Home, Country Roads" (words and music by Bill Taffy Danoff). Released as a single, "Take Me Home (West Virginia, Mountain Mama)," had sales of more than one million and established Denver as one of the leading performers of folk-pop-country-western music of the 1970s. "Take Me Home, Country Roads" has become the unofficial song of the state of West Virginia. The album *Poem, Prayers and Promises* which included two other bestselling Denver songs, "Sunshine on My Shoulders" and "I Guess I'd Rather Be in Colorado," earned a platinum record.

Denver recorded two new albums in 1972: *Aerie*, which earned a gold record, and *Rocky Mountain High*, which went platinum. The most popular number on the latter album was its title song, which has become a standard. It took Denver eight months to write "Rocky Mountain High," a quasi-religious paean to the awesome beauty of the Colorado landscape. The Rocky Mountain High LP also contained one of Denver's better autobiographical songs, "Goodbye Again," about the singer's desire to stay home with his wife when professional commitments force him to go on tour.

Denver was now so popular that, in June 1972, he substituted for Johnny Carson as host of the *Tonight Show*, and in November of that year he was the host of an ABC-TV special featuring top rock groups on a program that urged younger Americans to vote in the 1972 presidential election. His public concerts in 1972 included sold-out appearances at the Greek Theatre in Los Angeles, the Universal Amphitheatre in Hollywood, the Blossom Music Center near Cleveland, the Capital Centre near Washington, D. C., Madison Square Garden in New York and, on September 30, 1972, at Carnegie Hall. Reviewing Denver's Carnegie Hall concert, a critic for *Billboard* wrote: "The composer-singer displayed a disarming exuberance throughout his 70-minute set, obviously relishing the fact that a boy from Colorado had finally made it in New York's prestigious Carnegie Hall." In 1975 he undertook what was called a nationwide "six-million-dollar tour." Apart from this 29-city tour, that same year he appeared at Harrah's in Lake Tahoe, Nevada, where he was booked back-to-back with Frank Sinatra, Denver performing for the dinner show and Sinatra for the late-night show. In 1975 Denver also toured Australia, and, a year later, England, which included an appearance at London's Palladium.

Denver continued to appear often on television, in Great Britain as well as the United States, and his hit song "Sunshine on My Shoulders" was the theme music for the dramatic series *Sunshine*. In 1974 he had featured roles in episodes of three dramatic series, *Owen Marshall*, *Marcus Welby, M. D.* and *McCloud*. On March 11, 1974 the first of four specials called *The John Denver Picture Show* debuted on the ABC-TV network. In March 1976 he costarred with Frank Sinatra in a television special called *John Denver and Friend*, and later that year Denver and Mary Tyler Moore were the hosts of the annual Emmy Awards telecast.

The capstone of Denver's acting career came with the movie *Oh, God!* (1977), in which he played a simple, guileless supermarket manager selected by God (George Burns) to bring a message of goodwill to the modern world.

Since 1972, his accumulation of gold and platinum records has made Denver RCA Victor's most valuable property since Elvis Presley. On the *Farewell Andromeda* LP, a gold record of 1973, he introduced the title song and "I'd Rather Be a Cowboy." *John Denver's Greatest Hits* also went gold in 1973. A gold record in 1973, and voted album of the year by the Academy of Country Music, *Back Home Again* included "Annie," an expression of undying love for his wife. As a single, it received a platinum record in 1974. *Back Home Again* also contained "This Old Guitar," about the Gibson his grandmother had given Denver when he was a boy. The cuts from this album that became gold records when released as singles in 1974 were the title number and "Thank God, I'm a Country Boy." Also that year, Denver collected three more gold records for the albums *An Evening with John Denver*, a live recording of one of his concerts, *Rocky Mountain Christmas*, a recording of one of his ABC-TV specials, and *Windsong*. "I'm Sorry," a cut from *Windsong*, earned a gold record in 1974. His album *I Want to Live* (1978) and *John Denver* (1979) went platinum and his *Spirit* (1976) and *Some Days Are Diamonds* (1981) LPs earned gold records. *Spirit*'s leading songs were "How Can I Leave You Again?" and "It Amazes Me." The album *It's About Time* (1984) included the song, "Gold and Beyond," Denver's tribute to the Olympic Games which were held that year in Los Angeles.

In November 1984 Denver became the first American entertainer in many years to tour the Soviet Union, where he was enthusiastically received by large audiences. In 1985 Denver denounced attempts by an organization of concerned parents to compel the recording industry to lable albums according to their "pornographic" content, in the manner of the coding of motion pictures as "G-GP-R-X." Denver claimed that the policing of LPs would prove to be counterproductive, that adolescents would be titillated by records with an "X" rating, and thus more inclined to purchase them.

ABOUT: Current Biography, 1975; Zanderbergen, G. Made for Music, 1976. *Periodicals*—New York Times July 15, 1973; Stereo Review September 1975; Time September 17, 1973; Washington Post May 5, 1974.

DE SYLVA, B. G. (January 27, 1895–July 11, 1950). B. G. ("Buddy") De Sylva, librettist-lyricist, is most often remembered as a member of the songwriting triumvirate of De Sylva, Brown and Henderson, which created songs for some of the most successful stage and screen musicals of the 1920s and early 1930s. However, he was also lyricist for such composers as George Gershwin and Joseph Meyer. De Sylva later went on to become an important producer on Broadway and in Hollywood.

"Buddy" De Sylva, whose official name was George Gard De Sylva, was born in New York on January 27, 1895 to Aloysius Joseph and Georgetta Gard De Sylva. His father was a vaudevillian who had toured the circuit under the name of Hal de Forest, when he met and married Georgetta Gard. After his marriage, Aloysius De Sylva studied and practiced law.

When Buddy was two, the De Sylva family

B.G. DE SYLVA

moved to Los Angeles. Buddy's show business career began at the age of four when he appeared in a song-and-dance act for a benefit at the Los Angeles Grand Opera House where he was billed as "Baby Gard." This appearance was so successful he was engaged to tour the Keith vaudeville circuit. But his grandfather (the sheriff of Azusa, California) insisted that Buddy be allowed to pursue a normal childhood. After graduating from Citrus Union High School, where his play, *Nobody Loves a Fat Man*, had been produced, he attended the University of Southern California for about a year. At the university, he helped produce college shows and, at night, appeared with a Hawaiian band, for which he was paid $60 per week. He was also writing song lyrics.

Al Jolson became interested in De Sylva and introduced some of his songs in the extravaganza at the Winter Garden Theatre, *Sinbad* (1918). Jolson himself is credited with providing the music to De Sylva's lyrics for "n' Everything" (the first of De Sylva's songs to be recorded by Jolson), "I'll Say She Is" (lyrics written with Gus Kahn), "By the Honeysuckle Vine," "You Ain't Heard Nothin' Yet," "Chloe," "I Gave Her That" and "They Can't Fool Me," which were all sung by Jolson in the show. Still one other song by De Sylva was interpolated into *Sinbad*: "Dixie Rose," with music by a young songwriter named George Gershwin. Jolson also recorded "I'll Say She Is" in 1918 and "You Ain't Heard Nothin' Yet," "Chloe" and "I Gave Her That" in 1919.

When De Sylva received his first royalty check of $16,000 for these efforts, he knew his future was in New York. He moved there from

Los Angeles in 1919 and was hired as songwriter by the publisher, J. H. Remick. While at Remick, De Sylva (and Arthur Jackson) wrote lyrics for George Gershwin's first Broadway musical, *La, La, Lucille* (May 26, 1919). The show's most important song was "Nobody But You" (lyrics by De Sylva). De Sylva's songs were also used in other Broadway shows. "I'm the Boy" was heard in *Good Morning, Judge* (1919), and "Snap Your Fingers" was introduced by Frank Crumit in *Greenwich Village Follies of 1920*; the music for both was composed by Louis Silvers. But De Sylva's first hit song came in 1920. To Jerome Kern's music, he wrote lyrics for the standard, "Look for the Silver Lining," and also for "Whip-poor-will," introduced in the musical, *Sally.* He collaborated with Kern again on "You Must Come Over" for the *Ziegfeld Follies of 1921*; his "Four Little Girls With a Past" (music by operetta composer Rudolf Friml) was also used in the production. Jolson continued to introduce De Sylva's songs in his shows at the Winter Garden, and in 1921, he made "April Showers" (music by Silvers) a big hit. Introduced in *Bombo* (October 6, 1921), after the show had opened on Broadway, Jolson recorded it in 1921, as did Ernie Harie, Charles Harrison and Gene Rodemich. Twenty-five years later, Jolson sang "April Showers" in his film biography, *The Jolson Story* (1946) and his new recording for Decca (1946) was such a giant seller (more than one million discs) that the song became a hit all over again and appeared on *Your Hit Parade* in 1947. Jeanne Crain sang it in *Margie* (1946), and in 1948, it was the title song of a Warner Brothers musical in which it was performed in the final scene by Ann Sothern, Jack Carson and Bobbie Ellison.

Jolson also used several other songs by De Sylva in *Bombo,* including "Yoo-Hoo" (music by Jolson), and "Give Me My Mammy" (music by Walter Donaldson), not to be confused with Jolson's specialty, "My Mammy" (1918; lyrics by Sam M. Lewis and Joe Young, music by Walter Donaldson). While touring with *Bombo* in 1924, Jolson introduced another favorite in his repertory, "California, Here I Come" (lyrics written with Jolson, music by Joseph Meyer); it was then heard in the film *Lucky Boy* (1929), starring George Jessel. Jolson also sang it in the Hollywood musical, *Rose of Washington Square* (1930) and again in *The Jolson Story* (1946) and *Jolson Sings Again* (1949). Like "April Showers" his new recording of "California, Here I Come" in 1946 sold more than one million copies. Jane Froman included it in her screen biography, *With a Song in My Heart* (1952), and both the Abe Lyman orchestra and the California Ramblers adopted it as a theme song.

Jolson used another armful of De Sylva's songs during the run of his next show, *Big Boy* (January 7, 1925). "If You Knew Susie" (music by Joseph Meyer), though generally identified with Eddie Cantor, was first sung by Jolson in *Big Boy.* When Cantor recorded it the same year and made it successful, Jolson is reputed to have told him: "You dirty dog. If I'd known that his song was *that* good, you'd never have gotten it from me." For "As Long as I've Got My Mammy" and "Born and Bred in Old Kentucky," Joseph Meyer and James F. Hanley collaborated on the music. Jolson also introduced De Sylva's "Keep Smiling at Trouble" (lyrics written with Jolson, music by Lewis E. Gensler), "Miami" (written with Jolson and Con Conrad) and "Hello Tuckey" (music by Joseph Meyer).

In the early 1920s, De Sylva again collaborated with George Gershwin. They contributed songs to *George White's Scandals* revues from 1922 to 1924, among them "I'll Build a Stairway to Paradise" (lyrics written with Ira Gershwin), "I Found a Four-Leaf Clover," "The Life of a Rose," and "Somebody Loves Me" (lyrics written with Ballard MacDonald). Gershwin and De Sylva's one-act opera, *Blue Monday* (later retitled *135th Street*) was also given a single performance (August 20, 1922) as part of the *Scandals of 1922.* Gershwin and De Sylva also composed "Do it Again" for *The French Doll* (1922); "The Yankee Doodle Blues" (lyrics written with Irving Caesar), for the revue, *Spice of 1922.* "I Won't Say I Will But I Won't Say I Won't" (lyrics written with Ira Gershwin) was used in *Little Miss Bluebeard* (1923) and "Someone Who Believes in You" and "Virginia" in *Sweet Little Devil.* In 1925, De Sylva contributed lyrics to the title song and "Why Do I Love You?" for the George and Ira Gershwin musical, *Tell Me More.*

Among other composers for whom De Sylva wrote lyrics in the early 1920s was Victor Herbert. Their waltz, "A Kiss in the Dark," was the principal song in the operetta, *Orange Blossoms* (1922), and it is a collaboration of which De Sylva was particularly proud. He also worked with James F. Hanley on "Just a Cottage Small by a Waterfall" (1925), which was introduced and popularized by the Irish tenor John McCormack on his concert programs.

By 1925, the success of De Sylva's songs had brought him great wealth. "His prosperity," noted *The New York Times*, "has not made a bookkeeper of him; his round, almost Mongoloid features, are not marked by the lines of a man who has worried a great deal. His mouth curls easily into a smile, the smile easily becomes a chuckle." On April 11, 1925, in New York, De Sylva married Marie Wallace, a *Ziegfeld* girl.

They did not have children, but De Sylva raised his stepson, David Shelley.

Another significant event changed the course of De Sylva's life. In 1925, George Gershwin ended his five-year career as composer for the *George White Scandals*. Ray Henderson, a composer who had previously written some successful songs to Lew Brown's lyrics, was chosen as his successor. Because De Sylva had been associated with the *Scandals* in the preceding years, he was asked to join Henderson and Brown in providing songs for future editions of the *Scandals*. This was a natural turn of events because De Sylva had already worked with Henderson and lyricist Bud Green on "Alabama Bound" (1925). That year, too, De Sylva, Brown and Henderson's first published song, "It All Depends on You" was incorporated into *Big Boy* by Jolson.

The new songwriting team of De Sylva, Brown and Henderson composed the complete score for the *George White Scandals of 1925* (June 22, 1925), whose most important song was "I Want a Lovable Baby." This was followed by a steady stream of songs which have become standards for some of Broadway's most successful productions of the decade. From *George White's Scandals of 1926* (June 14, 1926), which firmly established the trio's reputation, came "The Birth of the Blues," "Black Bottom," "Lucky Day" and "The Girl is You and the Boy is Me." They also composed songs for the 1928 and 1931 editions of the *Scandals*; the latter included "Life is Just a Bowl of Cherries." *Good News* (September 6, 1927) brought the title song, and "The Best Things in Life Are Free," "The Varsity Drag," "Just Imagine" and "Lucky in Love." For *Manhattan Mary* (September 26, 1927) they wrote "Broadway," and for *Hold Everything!* (October 10, 1928), "You're the Cream in My Coffee" and "Don't Hold Everything." In *Follow Thru* (January 9, 1929), "Button Up Your Overcoat," "My Lucky Star," "I Want to Be Bad" and the title song were heard, and in *Flying High* (March 3, 1930), "Wasn't it Beautiful While it Lasted?", "Thank Your Father," and "Good for You, Bad for Me."

In 1928, the team expanded its range by writing for Hollywood musicals. For *The Singing Fool* (1928), starring De Sylva's longtime friend and associate, Al Jolson, they composed "Sonny Boy," commercially the most successful song of their entire career, and their score for a subsequent Jolson vehicle, *Say It With Songs* (1929), included "I'm in Seventh Heaven," "Little Pal," and "Why Can't You?" In *Sunny Side Up* (1929), which starred Janet Gaynor and Charles Farrell and for which De Sylva also served as producer, new hit songs were introduced: the title song,

"Aren't We All?," and "If I Had a Talking Picture of You." Other films also included songs written by De Sylva, Brown and Henderson. Among them were "My Sin" (1929) in *Show Girl in Hollywood* (1930); "An Old-Fashioned Girl" in *Just Imagine (1930);* "You Are the Melody" in *Holy Terror* (1931); and "Come to Me" in *Indiscreet* (1931).

To profit fully from the sheet-music sales of their songs, the songwriters formed the publishing house of De Sylva, Brown and Henderson in 1927. In addition to their show tunes and motion-picture songs, they also published independent numbers. In 1928, the firm released "Together," "The Song I Love" and "For Old Times' Sake"; in 1930, "Don't Tell Her What's Happened to Me"; in 1931, "You Try Somebody Else." With the advent of sound in film, and the insatiable need for songs that accompanied it, the De Sylva, Brown and Henderson Company was acquired by Warner Brothers in the early 1930s.

The songwriting collaboration of De Sylva, Brown and Henderson ended in 1931, when Henderson and Brown decided to return to New York. De Sylva remained in Hollywood, where he occasionally wrote song lyrics, film scenarios and scores for the Fox Studios. But most significantly, he produced five of Shirley Temple's most successful films, including *The Little Colonel (1935)* and *Poor Little Rich Girl* (1936) and screen adaptations of Broadway musicals with which he had been involved. He then went to Universal, where he produced *The Rage of Paris* (1938), the American film début of French actress Daneille Darrieux; *Bachelor Mother* (1939) with Ginger Rogers, and *Love Affair* (1939), starring Irene Dunne followed at RKO. "Wishing" (1924, words and music by De Sylva), from *Love Affair* was recorded by Glenn Miller and reached the top of *Your Hit Parade*.

Though he had not been a failure in Hollywood, De Sylva also went back to New York in 1939. His most recent Broadway venture had been *Take a Chance* (1932), which he coproduced with Lawrence Schwab, and to which he contributed lyrics for music by Richard Whiting, Nacio Herb Brown and Vincent Youmans. Ethel Merman's rendition of "Eadie Was a Lady" (music by Whiting and Nacio Herb Brown) had stopped the show. Upon his return, De Sylva founded B. G. De Sylva Theatrical Enterprises, under whose auspices he produced Cole Porter's *Du Barry Was a Lady* (1939) and *Panama Hattie* (1940), and Irving Berlin's *Louisiana Purchase* (1940), becoming in 1940, the first producer since Ziegfeld to have three hit musicals running simultaneously on Broadway.

His success was due, no doubt to his ability to assemble high-caliber collaborators and casts; in addition to Berlin and Porter, the shows also displayed the talents of Ethel Merman, comedians Victor Moore and William Gaxton, dancer Vera Zorina and choreographer George Balanchine, and librettist Herbert Fields, with whom De Sylva wrote the books for the Cole Porter musicals he produced.

Following this phenomenal success, Hollywood's interest in De Sylva was renewed. In 1941, Paramount appointed him Executive Producer for the studio. Among the films he produced there were *Caught in the Draft* (1941), starring Bob Hope and Dorothy Lamour; Bing Crosby's *Birth of the Blues* (1941), *For Whom the Bell Tolls* (1943) and *The Stork Club* (1945), for which he also wrote the screenplay.

In addition to his contributions to Tin Pan Alley, the theater and to motion pictures, De Sylva founded Capitol Records with Johnny Mercer and Glenn Wallichs in Hollywood in 1942. B. G. "Buddy" De Sylva died of a heart attack in Los Angeles on July 11, 1950. Six years later, 20th Century-Fox released a motion picture musical based on the careers of De Sylva, Brown and Henderson, *The Best Things in Life Are Free,* in which De Sylva was portrayed by Ernest Borgnine.

ABOUT: Current Biography, 1943; Ewen, D. Great Men of American Popular Song, 2d ed. 1972. *Periodicals*—Collier's August 21, 1943; Life December 30, 1940; New York Times July 12, 1950.

DIAMOND, NEIL (January 24, 1941–), composer-lyricist, was born to a middle-class family in Coney Island, Brooklyn. He is the son of Kieve Diamond, the proprietor of a dry goods store, and Rose Diamond.

During his childhood his family moved frequently from one Brooklyn neighborhood to another. Diamond had attended nine different public schools by the time he was 16, and he found it hard to sustain friendships. "I was a solitary child," Diamond recalled, rather awkward, "with ears that were too big and a nose that was too long." His loneliness was intensified by feeling that he was an outsider in a family of achievers. "I grew up in a family where everyone else seemed to be something special. A cousin was the smartest kid in school. My brother was an electronics genius, and so forth. I was a sort of black sheep."

From infancy on, he was drawn to music. "I think I was born with the ability to love music. I remember pushing a girl on a swing and sing-

NEIL DIAMOND

ing to her. It was the only song I knew, the theme song of a cowboy show on TV." When he was three, Diamond won a contest by making theatrical gestures and pretending to sing music from Mozart's *The Marriage of Figaro,* but his first music idols were singing cowboys in Western movies. Later on, working after school in his father's store, he listened to the pop idols of the early 1950s, particularly Frank Sinatra and Eddie Fisher. The songs he then enjoyed most were the show tunes of the Gershwins, Jerome Kern and Lerner and Loewe. Singing popular songs, Diamond said, "was the first real interest I had shown in anything up until that time." In the classroom, he escaped from boredom by scribbling verses, and when he was ten serenaded passersby in the streets with a group of youngsters calling themselves the Memphis Backstreet Boys.

In addition to feeling like an outsider in his family, Diamond's parents were too busy running their store to raise him, leaving that task to his grandparents. When he was 13, Diamond ran away from home. In the Midwest, he organized the Roadrunners, a folk group that performed in coffee houses. Returning home, he entered Erasmus Hall High School, Brooklyn, where he sang in a chorus with Barbra Streisand, though they did not get acquainted at this time.

Aged 16, Diamond acquired a nine-dollar guitar and he had soon taught himself the elementary chord progressions. He learned to play and sing folk numbers he heard performed on the radio by the Weavers. He wrote his first song after hearing Pete Seeger give a talk on the craft of musical composition. Recalling his first song,

"Hear Them Bells," Diamond said: "It just came out. I had a melody and a lyric, a beginning and an end. It was a real song. I wrote it down. It was an outlet for a great deal of frustration." It was also satisfying because it was "something . . . no one [in] my family had done." The songs now came pouring out of him, songs in all popular styles and idioms, influenced by what he heard and loved on the radio—music by Fats Domino, Chuck Berry, and Carole King. "I never really chose songwriting," he explained. "It just absorbed me and became more important in my life as the years passed."

While trying, unsuccessfully, to market his songs in Tin Pan Alley, he graduated from Erasmus Hall High and entered New York University on a fencing scholarship. A premed major, he cut classes and avoided homework, concentrating instead on advancing his career in music. In 1962 he accepted a 16-week job with the Sunbeam Music Company in the Brill building, writing songs for $50 a week. He dropped out of NYU only to discover that he disliked having to tailor songs to dictated specifications. Unhappy and unsuccessful, he was dropped by Sunbeam and for the next three years worked for a string of small publishing houses.

By 1965, Diamond realized he was on a treadmill. He rented an office of his own near the Brill building which became home and work space. He rented a piano, had a pay telephone installed, lived a Spartan existence, and produced song after song. He supported himself by managing to get an advance of $100 every couple of weeks for his songs. It paid the rent and the price of sandwiches at the lunch counter at Woolworth's.

Before the end of 1965, one of his songs was published and successfully marketed, "Sunday and Me," for which he wrote both the music and lyrics. Jay and The Americans recorded it that year and it became a bestseller, reaching 18th place on the *Billboard* listing of the year's top 100 records. "Writing "Sunday and Me',", Diamond said, "was like taking your finger out of the dike. I wrote night and day on anything I could find, shopping bags, scraps of paper."

With Fred Weintraub as his manager, Diamond began performing his songs in public. An engagement at a Greenwich Village nightclub owned by Weintraub attracted the interest of Bert Berns, a producer for Atlantic Records who was then organizing a company of his own, Bang Records. He signed Diamond to a recording contract. In 1966 Diamond's first releases on the Bang label were three of his own songs: "Solitary Man," "Cherry, Cherry" and "I Got the Feeling," each of which became a bestseller. His hit re-

cordings for Bang in 1967 were "Girl, You'll Be a Woman Soon," "I Thank the Lord for the Nighttime" and "Kentucky Woman." A hard rock version of "Kentucky Woman" by Deep Purple was a bestseller in 1968, the year that Diamond's *Velvet Gloves and Spit* became his first LP to earn a gold record.

For the Monkees, an American pop band that modeled itself after the Beatles, Diamond wrote "I'm a Believer," which shot to the top of the charts in 1967 and sold more than a million discs. That same year Diamond composed another number one hit for the Monkees, "A Little Bit Me, a Little Bit You," and a *Cashbox* poll of radio disc jockeys ranked Diamond and Frank Sinatra as the most popular singers of 1967.

Diamond's first hit songs had been aimed directly at the teenage market, but by 1968 he had begun to write songs in which he addressed personal frustrations and inner conflicts. Such an autobiographical number was "Shiloh" (1968), describing Diamond's childhood loneliness and his unfulfilled longing for friendship. When Bang refused to release "Shiloh," insisting that it was unacceptable for the pop market, Diamond broke with the company.

At this time Diamond was also beset with personal problems. When he was about 21, he married his boyhood girlfriend. They had had two daughters and the marriage was floundering. "I realized that this wasn't what I wanted at all and things began to deteriorate from that point. I just decided to split and leave it all behind. In a sense, it was running away." He left New York for Los Angeles in 1968. There he signed a $250,000 contract with Uni Records and obtained a divorce.

With the freedom to write the music he wanted, Diamond produced, in 1968, "Brooklyn Roads," "Sunday Sun," and "Brother Love," and, in 1969, "Brother Love's Traveling Show," "Sweet Caroline" and "Holly Holy." His recordings of "Sweet Caroline" and "Holly Holy," released in 1969, earned gold records. Over the next four years, Diamond produced a series of gold-record-winning albums—*Gold* (1970), *Touching You, Touching Me* (1970), *Taproot Manuscript* (1971), *Stones* (1972), *Moods* (1972) and *Hot August Night* (1972). The singles "Crackling Rose" (1971) and "Song Sung Blue" (1972) went gold as well. The *Hot August Night* LP was a live recording of a performance at the Greek Theatre in Hollywood. It became the first double-record album ever to generate more than two million dollars in sales, and within a few years of its release, *Hot August Night* had sold more than eight million copies.

Many of Diamond's songs of the early 1970s

dealt with autobiographical concerns. In "Brooklyn Roads" he reaffirmed the truth of Thomas Wolfe's "you can't go home again" theme. Another angst-ridden song was "I Am . . . I Said," which described Diamond's isolation and alienation from others. Other songs, however, were more positive. "Song Sung Blue" and "Play Me" expressed the joy he found in artistic creativity. The single "I Am . . . I Said" was Diamond's last recording for Uni.

Backed by a seven-piece band, he gave a concert in the summer of 1972 at the Saratoga (New York) Arts Center, a program billed as *Diamond's Greatest Hits*. He took this production to Broadway for a two-week engagement at the Winter Garden in October. "Up front," reported Grace Lichtenstein in *The New York Times*, "Diamond is totally in command, belting out the tunes in a rich baritone, with a nice, sincere ache to it, swaying gracefully but not graphically. Call him an urban Elvis, a *hamish* Tom Jones. He's a rock singer a girl can take her parents to see." With *Greatest Hits*, Diamond became the first rock star to give a concert on Broadway and the first popular singer since Jolson to be booked at the Winter Garden.

After his Broadway success, Diamond withdrew from public appearances. He spent the next three years examining his life and his career as a composer, a period of introspection that was intensified by four years of psychoanalytic therapy. In 1969 he had married the former Marcia Murphy, with whom he raised two sons, Jesse and Micah. Diamond's years of virtual seclusion were spent with his family at their homes in Malibu Beach and Beverly Hills, as he "retired" from songwriting to fish, ride his motor bike, play chess, read books on philosophy and religion, and go to movies with his wife and children. "I had been going for seven, eight years playing about 100 cities a year," he explained. "It was very good for me to learn to relax. I had no idea it would go on for years. I think that the sabbatical improved my writing."

In 1972 Diamond signed a five-million-dollar contract with Columbia Records, whose first release was Diamond's orchestral score for the motion picture *Jonathan Livingston Seagull*. His most ambitious project, it was, instead of background or "filler" music, a 48-minute score of symphonic scope that took ten months to write. When the film was released in 1973, only part of the music was used on the soundtrack forcing Diamond to go to the courts to have the parts that had been deleted restored. That complete soundtrack earned a platinum record. Diamond's subsequent LPs on the Columbia label—*Twelve Greatest Hits* and *Serenade* (both

1974) and *Beautiful Noise* (1976)—were bestsellers as well. *Beautiful Noise* was a concept album about the history of Tin Pan Alley on which Diamond simulated many of the popular song styles of the past.

He emerged from seclusion in February 1976 with a concert in Utah that kicked off a world tour. His appearance at Hollywood's Greek Theatre was released as *Live at the Greek* in 1977. For the unprecedented fee of $650,000 for five performances, Diamond made his Las Vegas debut in July 1976, opening the New Theatre for the Performing Arts at the Hotel Aladdin. On Thanksgiving 1977 Diamond appeared at the Winterland in San Francisco, where he performed with the Band at their farewell concert, which was released in 1978 as a documentary feature film *The Last Waltz*, directed by Martin Scorcese.

His first television show, *The Neil Diamond Special*, was telecast on NBC on February 21, 1977. This was only his second television appearance, the first having been a 1968 guest appearance on Ed Sullivan's variety show. Later that year *I'm Glad You're Here With Me Tonight*, his second television special, was aired. It became the inspiration for an album of the same title, one of whose cuts was "You Don't Bring Me Flowers" (lyrics written with Alan and Marilyn Bergman). On a 1976 Neil Diamond album titled *You Don't Bring Me Flowers*, he had sung that song as a duet with Barbra Streisand. It was released as a single and earned a gold record. The albums *September Morn* (1980), *On the Way to the Sky* (1982), and *Neil Diamond's Greatest Hits* (1982) were all platinum records, while the album *Rainbow* (1981) and *Heartlight* (1982) became gold records. The title number from *Heartlight* (lyrics by Carole Bayer Sager, music by Diamond and Burt Bacharach) and "I'm Alive" (lyrics by David Foster) were selected as two of the most frequently performed songs in the BMI catalogue in 1983. The album *Primitive* was released in 1984.

In 1980 Diamond made his cinematic acting debut in the starring role of *The Jazz Singer*, a remake of the classic Al Jolson film. Though it received poor reviews from critics, Diamond's performance was praised. As Larry Kart remarked in the Chicago *Tribune*, "Acting may not be the right word for what Diamond does on the screen, but his ability to convey a sense of power-in-reserve, to delineate a character whose emotions are always simmering under the surface, is rare enough to suggest that he has a full-blown movie career ahead of him." In additon to acting, Diamond wrote and introduced the film's songs. "America," an immigrant's tribute to his adopted country, opened and closed the film. Two other songs became popular, "Love on the Rocks" and "Hello, Again," the former as a single as well as a cut on the soundtrack recording, which went platinum and grossed more than the film itself. By the early 1980s, Diamond's worldwide sale of records exceeded fifty million copies.

ABOUT: O'Regan, S. Neil Diamond, 1975. *Periodicals*—ASCAP Today January 1972; Chicago Tribune Magazine December 14, 1980; People January 22, 1979; New York Times October 1, 1972; US February 17, 1981.

DIETZ, HOWARD. *See* **SCHWARTZ, ARTHUR and DIETZ, HOWARD**

DOMINO, FATS (February 26, 1928–), composer-lyricist, was one of the first performers of rhythm and blues to become popular with both black and white audiences. His distinctive singing and piano playing exerted such a powerful influence on early rock stars that his music may be said to have marked the beginning of the rock 'n' roll era. In *Rock Encyclopdia,* Lillian Roxon speaks of him as "the undisputed emperor of the pre-Elvis rock and roll scene."

He was born Antoine Domino in New Orleans, Louisiana in 1928, one of nine children. His father was an amateur violinist and one of Fats's uncles played with several eminent New Orleans jazz bands. A relative gave the Domino family a battered piano on which the five-year-old Antoine began picking out popular blues and ragtime tunes. Noticing the boy's interest, his uncle taught him how to form the basic chords, which was to be his only formal musical instruction. By the age of ten Domino had taught himself to play blues and ragtime well enough to perform on weekends at local roadhouses and honkytonks. The rest of the week he helped support his family by working in a bed-spring factory where his piano playing almost came to an end when his hand was crushed. For hours each day Domino exercised his fingers until mobility and flexibility were restored.

In 1947 Domino married. To support his wife and children, he worked in a lumbermill. He also joined a jazz band but was dropped two weeks later. He then formed a band of his own which played three nights a week at the Hideaway Bar in New Orleans, a gig that earned Domino three dollars a week. He also played piano in a band led by Dave Bartholomew, who introduced him to Lew Chudd, head of the newly

FATS DOMINO

formed Imperial Records. Chudd signed Domino to make rhythm-and-blues records for the black market. Domino's first recording was "Fat Man," a number the 250-pound Domino had written with Dave Bartholomew. This song, a composite of ragtime, blues and boogie-woogie styles, was sung by Domino in a high, rasping, nasal voice as he pounded out a heavy beat accompaniment on the piano and tapped his foot in rhythm. Originally promoted as a "race" recording, "Fat Man" crossed over to white-oriented radio stations. Released in 1950, "Fat Man" had sold more than a million copies by 1953.

Often in collaboration with Bartholomew, but sometimes writing both lyrics and music himself, Domino became the leading exponent of rhythm and blues and early rock 'n' roll in the years before the ascendancy of Chuck Berry and Elvis Presley. Domino's string of annual gold records began in 1952 with "Goin' Home" (written with Alvin E. Young). In 1953 his million sellers were "Going to the River," "You Said You Love Me," "I Lived My Life" (all written with Bartholomew) and "Please Don't Leave Me" (music and lyrics by Domino); in 1954, "Love Me," and "Don't Leave Me This Way" (with Bartholomew); in 1955 "Ain't it a Shame" and "All by Myself" (with Bartholomew); in 1956, "Boll Weevil" (based on the American folk song of the same name), "I'm in Love Again" and "Blue Monday" (with Bartholomew); in 1957, "I'm Walkin'," "It's You I Love" and "I Still Love You" (with Bartholomew); in 1958, "Whole Lotta Lovin'" (with Bartholomew); in 1959, "Be My Guest" (written with John Marascalo and Tom

Boyce); in 1960, "Walkin' to New Orleans" (written with Bartholomew and R. Gundry) and "Don't Come Knockin'" (Domino).

"Ain't it a Shame" was Domino's first number to cross over instantly from rhythm and blues to pop success. In 1956 Domino recorded one of his most memorable numbers, "Blueberry Hill," a country song written by Al Lewis, Larry Stock and Vincent Rose. Other pop hits by Domino were his version of Walter Donaldson's 1927 song, "My Blue Heaven," and "When My Dream Boat Goes Home," which had been composed by Cliff Friend and Dave Franklin in 1936.

By the later 1950s white pop performers began recording Domino's music. Pat Boone's first significant success on the charts was a cover of "Ain't it a Shame" (changing the title to "Ain't That a Shame"). And Ricky Nelson, from the popular television situation comedy, *The Adventures of Ozzie and Harriet*, made his singing debut on that series with "I'm Walkin'." His recording of this number became Nelson's first hit record and made him a teen idol.

Domino had hit albums as well as singles, beginning in the early 1950s with two LPs each entitled *Rock & Rollin'*, featuring his hit songs. Among Domino's most successful albums on the Imperial label were *This Is Fats* and *Fabulous Mr. D.* (both 1958) and *12,000,000 Records* (1959). In 1963 Domino left Imperial for ABC Records, which released his hit albums *Here Comes Fats Again* (1963), *Fats on Fire* (1965) and *Getaway With Fats Domino* (1966). From Warner Brothers/Reprise Records came the bestselling album *Fats Is Back* (1968).

In 1956 Domino began appearing regularly in nightclubs, hotels and on television. He became an annual attraction at the Flamingo Hotel in Las Vegas, and he frequently toured the resort hotels circuit at Lake Tahoe. He also appeared in the film *The Girl Can't Help It* (1956), starring Jayne Mansfield and Tom Ewell, and sang "Blue Monday."

By the early 1960s Domino's career as a composer and performer of hit songs was over, but he continued to draw large audiences to his public appearances. Before the decade ended, however his rhythm-and-blues classics were enjoying a revival of interest both in England and the United States, and Domino's concerts at such large arenas as the Brooklyn Paramount and the Fillmore East in Manhattan drew capacity audiences. Nevertheless by the early 1970s Domino was appearing in concert infrequently so that he could spend more time with his wife and family of eight at his palatial home in New Orleans. The music of the early rock era became fashionable once again in the 1970s and early 1980s, and

Domino's hits were featured as evocative background music in scenes from the films *American Graffiti* (1973), directed by George Lucas, and *Diner* (1982), starring Mickey Rourke.

ABOUT: Hershey, G. Nowhere to Run: The Story of Soul Music, 1984; Stambler, I. Encyclopedia of Pop, Rock and Soul, 1977.

DONALDSON, WALTER (February 15, 1893–July 15, 1947), composer, was born in Brooklyn. His mother, a piano teacher, tried to give her son music lessons, but he resisted formal instruction and taught himself to play the piano by ear. While in high school, he composed the music for school ceremonies and plays. Instead of going to college he went to work for a brokerage house on Wall Street and then found a $15-a-week job as a piano demonstrator in Tin Pan Alley. Dismissed when he was found composing songs on company time, Donaldson began peddling his songs in Tin Pan Alley, and in 1915 sold "Back Home in Tennessee" (lyrics by William Jerome), "We'll Have a Jubilee in Old Kentucky" (lyrics by Coleman Goetz) and "You'd Never Know the Old Town of Mine" (lyrics by Howard Johnson). Arthur Collins recorded these songs in 1915, and all three were popular on the vaudeville circuit. Though written long before Donaldson had ever visited the South, "Back Home in Tennessee" became the unofficial state song of Tennessee.

In 1918 Donaldson composed "The Daughter of Rosie O'Grady" (lyrics by Monty C. Brice), which became a kind of signature for Pat Rooney, who introduced it in his vaudeville act at the Palace Theatre in 1919, accompanying his rendition with a waltz clog that became his stage trademark. "The Daughter of Rosie O'Grady" provided the title for a 1950 motion picture in which it was sung by Gordon MacRae. It was also interpolated into the films *Show Business* (1944), starring Eddie Cantor, and *When My Baby Smiles at Me* (1947), starring Betty Grable.

During World War I, Donaldson was employed for 18 months as an entertainer for American troops at Camp Upton, New York, where Irving Berlin was writing his all-soldiers' show *Yip, Yip, Yaphank*. Because some of Donaldson's songs had been published by the firm of Waterson, Berlin and Snyder, Donaldson and Berlin were acquainted, and at Camp Upton they became close friends.

Two songs of lesser consequence marked Donaldson's initial foray into the Broadway musical theater in 1918. "I Love the Land of Old Black Joe" (lyrics by Grant Clarke) was introduced by

WALTER DONALDSON

Marion Davies in the *Ed Wynn Carnival* and "My Little Bimbo Down in Bamboo Isle" (lyrics by Clarke) was introduced in *Silks and Satins* by Aileen Stanley, who also recorded it.

In 1919 Waterson, Berlin and Snyder published two Donaldson songs inspired by World War I, "Don't Cry, Frenchy, Don't Cry" and "How Ya Gonna Keep 'Em Down on the Farm," lyrics to both by Sam M. Lewis and Joe Young. The latter was recorded in 1919 by Nora Bayes and popularized first by Sophie Tucker in vaudeville and later by Eddie Cantor, who featured it in his public appearances and sang it on the soundtrack of *The Eddie Cantor Story* (1954). Judy Garland sang it in *For Me and My Gal* (1942). Two other Donaldson hit songs of 1919 were "I'll Be Happy When the Preacher Makes You Mine," recorded by Van and Schenck, and "You're a Million Miles From Nowhere" (lyrics to both by Lewis and Young).

When Irving formed his own publishing company in 1919, he hired Donaldson as staff composer. While working at Irving Berlin Inc. Donaldson, over the next decade, wrote the songs that made him one of the most popular composers of the 1920s.

In 1921 Al Jolson interpolated "My Mammy" (lyrics by Lewis and Young) into his Winter Garden extravaganza, *Bombo*. Earlier that year "Mammy" had been sung and plugged on the vaudeville circuit by Bill Frawley, but it was Jolson who made it one of the most memorable numbers of the century. Down on bended knee, his arms outstretched, he declaimed as well as sang it. Jolson recorded it in 1921 and 1928, and performed it in the 1928 motion picture adapta-

tion of *The Jazz Singer*. He again sang "Mammy" in the 1935 film *Rose of Washington Square*, and on the soundtrack of *The Jolson Story* (1946). His 1946 recording of "Mammy" sold more than a million discs.

Donaldson's collaboration with the lyricist Gus Kahn began in 1922. Their first successes that year were "My Buddy" and "Carolina in the Morning," both sung by Al Jolson at his Winter Garden concerts. "Carolina in the Morning" was recorded in 1922 by Ernie Hare, and in 1940 by Kate Smith. It provided the title for a nonmusical film of 1944 in which it was sung by Donald Barry. Doris Day sang it in Gus Kahn's screen biography, *I'll See You in My Dreams* (1952), and the orchestra of Buddy Rogers adopted it as its theme song. Bill Frawley introduced "Carolina in the Morning" in vaudeville, and Jolson sang it on the soundtrack of *Jolson Sings Again* (1946). June Haver and Betty Grable performed it in the movie musical *The Dolly Sisters* (1945); Robert Alda and Ann Sothern in *April Showers* (1948); and Patrice Wymore in *I'll See You in My Dreams*. It was interpolated into *Look for the Silver Lining* (1949), the screen biography of Marilyn Miller.

Written by Kahn and Donaldson in 1923, "Beside a Babbling Brook" was recorded by Georgie Price, by Marion Harris and by Van and Schenck. "My Best Girl" (1924) was recorded by Georgie Price. Written and published in 1924, "I'll See You in My Dreams" was introduced and recorded by the orchestra of Isham Jones. In Kahn's screen biography it was sung by Doris Day and then reprised as a choral number in the final scene. In earlier movies it had been crooned by Bob Crosby in *Pardon My Rhythm* (1944) and sung by Jeanette MacDonald in *Follow the Boys* (1944). "I'll See You in My Dreams" was crucial to the plot of the 1946 movie *Margie*.

The idea for "Yes, Sir, That's My Baby" was conceived at Eddie Cantor's home in Great Neck, Long Island. There Gus Kahn was amused by a toy pig with movable parts that was treasured by Cantor's preadolescent daughter. The rhythm of the toy when it moved inspired Kahn to improvise the lines, "Yes, sir, that's my baby, no sir, don't mean maybe." Cantor introduced the completed Donaldson/Kahn song, and years later sang it on the soundtrack of his screen biography. In 1925, it was popularized in a bestselling recording by Gene Austin, and in 1949 its title was appropriated for a motion picture in which it was sung by Donald O'Connor and Gloria De Haven. Danny Thomas and Doris Day performed it in *I'll See You in My Dreams*, and it was revived for Barbara Harris in the nonmusical film farce *Movie, Movie* (1979).

"I Wonder Where My Baby is Tonight?"; "My Sweetie Turned Me Down"; "The Midnight Waltz and "That Certain Party" were all composed by Donaldson and Kahn in 1925. Popularized in the mid-1920s by Eddie Cantor, "That Certain Party" was revived in 1948 in a bestselling recording by the orchestra of Benny Strong. Donaldson and Kahn followed these popular successes with "Sing Me a Baby Song" and "He's the Last Word" in 1927.

The only complete score composed by Donaldson and Kahn for the Broadway theater was for *Whoopee* (December 4, 1928), a Florenz Ziegfeld production. In a text by William Anthony McGuire based on *The Nervous Wreck*, a comic play, Eddie Cantor was starred as Henry Williams, a hypochondriac who tries to recover from his many ailments on a California ranch. Cantor's principal song, "Makin' Whoopee," became his signature. It was recorded by him and by Harry Richman in 1928. Cantor sang it again in the 1930 motion picture adaptation of *Whoopee* (his screen debut) and on the soundtrack of *The Eddie Cantor Story*, and "Makin' Whoopee" provided the occasion for a Danny Thomas–Doris Day duet in *I'll See You in My Dreams*. In the stage production Frances Upton and Paul Gregory introduced another of *Whoopee*'s highlights, "I'm Bringing a Red, Red Rose," which Ruth Etting recorded. Paul Whiteman and his orchestra recorded both "Makin' Whoopee" and "I'm Bringing a Red, Red Rose."

Then a newcomer to the stage, Ruth Etting was a featured performer in *Whoopee*, and to her Donaldson and Kahn assigned "Love Me or Leave Me," which she recorded and then reprised in the 1930 Broadway musical *Simple Simon*. Dinah Shore revived it in a recording in 1941, and in 1955 "Love Me or Leave Me" provided the title for Ruth Etting's screen biography, in which it was sung by Doris Day. Patrice Wymore sang it in *I'll See You in My Dreams*, and it was interpolated into *Tell It to a Star* (1945) and the Italian-made film *The Basileus Quartet* (1983).

For the screen adaptation of *Whoopee* Donaldson and Kahn composed "My Baby Just Cares for Me" for Cantor. It was interpolated into the nonmusical film *Big City Blues* (1932).

Whoopee, which had a run of 379 performances in 1928–29, returned to Broadway on February 14, 1979. The Donaldson score included not only the three principal numbers from the original stage production and "My Baby Just Cares for Me" from the screen version, but also several other Donaldson standards. Whatever interest the revival generated came from the "superabundance of songs," as *The New York Times*

reviewer observed. "There is not a poor song in it and the best ones . . . are magnificent."

While collaborating with Kahn, Donaldson was also writing music with other lyricists. George Whiting wrote the words for one of Donaldson's best-known ballads, "My Blue Heaven," which Whiting introduced in his vaudeville act in 1924. One of the most celebrated of popular songs about marital bliss, "My Blue Heaven" was not published until Eddie Cantor sang it in the *Ziegfeld Follies of 1927*, and added to the lyrics some lines of his own about the "blue heaven" he had known with his wife Ida and their five daughters. In 1927 Tommy Lyman adapted it as his orchestra's signature, and Gene Austin's recording sold millions of copies. A standard, "My Blue Heaven" has been heard many times on the screen. It was sung by Frances Langford in *Never a Dull Moment* (1943); by Betty Grable and Dan Dailey in the film *My Blue Heaven* (1950); by Doris Day in *Love Me or Leave Me*; and by Bob Crosby and his orchestra in *The Five Pennies* (1959). Fats Domino gave the song a churning rhythm and blues underpinning in a bestselling recording of the 1950s. The song was heard orchestrally on the soundtrack of the nonmusical film *Julia* (1977) starring Jane Fonda and Vanessa Redgrave.

In 1922, to Howard Johnson's lyrics, Donaldson composed "Georgia," which has been adopted as the official song of that state. Lew Brown was the lyricist for "Seven or Eleven," which Cantor introduced on the stage in *Make It Snappy* (1922) and which Sophie Tucker recorded. Edgar Leslie was the lyricist for "On the 'Gin, 'Gin, 'Ginny Shore" in 1923, and one year later Donaldson composed "Let it Rain, Let it Pour" (lyrics by Cliff Friend), which Earl and Bell interpolated into the Broadway revue *The Grab Bag* (1924). With Billy Rose as lyricist, Donaldson wrote "In the Middle of the Night" and "Swanee Butterfly" in 1925. In 1926 Donaldson collaborated with Abe Lyman in writing both words and music for "What Can I Say After I Say I'm Sorry?," which Lyman's orchestra introduced and, years later, was sung by Doris Day in *Love Me or Leave Me*. Ballard MacDonald was the lyricist for the songs Donaldson composed for *Sweetheart Time* (January 19, 1926; 143 performances), the first of his two scores for the Broadway theater.

Donaldson sometimes served as his own lyricist. His "At Sundown" was introduced by Cliff Edwards at the Palace Theatre in New York City in 1927, and Ruth Etting, the Clicquot Club Eskimos and the Arden-Ohman orchestra recorded it in that year. However, the most successful recordings of "At Sundown" were released in the early 1930s by the orchestras of Tommy and Jimmy Dorsey. In motion pictures it was sung by Marsha Hunt in *Music for the Millions* (1944), by the Bobby Brooks Quartet in *This is the Life* (1944) and by Doris Day in *Love Me or Leave Me*. Paul Whiteman's orchestra, with the Dorsey brothers, performed it in *The Fabulous Dorseys* (1947). In addition, it was interpolated into *Glorifying the American Girl* (1929), *Margie* (1946) and *The Joker is Wild* (1957).

"Sam, the Old Accordion Man," composed by Donaldson in 1927, was popularized in vaudeville by Ruth Etting and by the Williams Sisters. It was interpolated into *Glorifying the American Girl* and was sung by Doris Day in *Love Me or Leave Me*. Donaldson's "Just Like a Melody" was popularized in recordings by Gene Austin and by Nick Lucas.

In 1930 Donaldson wrote words and music for three songs recorded and introduced by Guy Lombardo and His Royal Canadians. "You're Driving Me Crazy" was interpolated for Adele Astaire and Eddie Foy Jr. in the 1930 Broadway musical *Smiles*, and was recorded that year by Rudy Vallee and by Lee Morse. In 1955 it was heard in the film *Gentlemen Prefer Brunettes*. "Little White Lies" was recorded in 1930 by Ted Wallace, by Johnny Marvin and by Lee Morse, and later by the orchestra of Tommy Dorsey (vocal by Frank Sinatra). It was interpolated into the 1946 movie *Lover Come Back,* and in 1948 a recording by Dick Haymes sold more than a million copies. Consequently, "Little White Lies" was heard seven times on *Your Hit Parade* in 1948. Donaldson's "Sweet Jennie Lee" (1930) was recorded by the orchestra of Isham Jones and by Guy Lombardo and His Royal Canadians.

In 1931 Helen Morgan and Harry Richman introduced Donaldson's "I'm With You" in the *Ziegfeld Follies of 1931*. That year, Maurice Chevalier popularized Donaldson's "Hello, Beautiful" in a recording.

In 1928 Donaldson had terminated his affiliation with Irving Berlin Inc. to form his own publishing house, Donaldson, Douglas and Gumble. Beginning with *The Prize Fighter and the Lady* (1933), his most important songs were written for motion pictures. With Gus Kahn as his lyricist he composed the songs for *Kid Millions* (1934), starring Eddie Cantor and Ethel Merman. In that movie Cantor introduced "When My Ship Comes In" and "Okay Toots" and Merman, "An Earful of Music," all three were recorded by Cantor. Kahn served as Donaldson's lyricist for "Sleepy Head," which was composed for the Mills Brothers and was recorded by the

orchestra of Vincent Lopez. Kahn also wrote the lyrics for "Once in a Lifetime," introduced by Marion Davies in *Operator 13* (1934); and for "I've Had My Moments," which Jimmy Durante and Eddie Quillan introduced in *Hollywood Party* (1934) and which was recorded in 1934 by the orchestras of Will Osborne and Paul Hamilton. To lyrics by Howard Dietz, Donaldson wrote "Feelin' High," introduced by Shirley Ross and Harry Barris in *Hollywood Party*.

Harold Adamson was Donaldson's lyricist for two hit songs of 1935–36. "Did I Remember?" was introduced by Virginia Bruce and Harry Stockwell in *Here Comes the Band* (1935). In *Suzy* (1936) this song was performed on the soundtrack by Virginia Verrill (dubbing for Jean Harlow) while Cary Grant sang it in the film. Dick Powell, Billie Holiday and Tommy Dorsey all recorded it in 1936. This song was heard 15 times on *Your Hit Parade* that year, six times in first position. "You," introduced by a chorus in *The Great Ziegfeld* (1936), had 12 hearings on *Your Hit Parade*, holding first position on April 18, 1936.

In the later 1930s, Donaldson wrote songs to Johnny Mercer's lyrics, none of which profited from motion picture exploitation. "Could Be," recorded by the orchestra of Mitchell Ayres, was heard eight times on *Your Hit Parade* in 1939. "Got to Get Some Shut Eye" was recorded by Kay Kyser's orchestra and had five representations on *Your Hit Parade* in 1939. Also that year, Benny Goodman recorded "Cuckoo in the Clock." In 1940 Donaldson and Mercer composed "Master Meadowbrook," which Artie Shaw and his orchestra recorded.

"Tonight" (lyrics by Kermit Goell) was Donaldson's last song to be introduced on the screen, in *Big Town* (1947). For the last decade and a half of his life Donaldson, who never married, made his home in Los Angeles. His health failing, in 1946 he retired. Donaldson died in Santa Monica in the summer of 1947.

ABOUT: Craig, W. Sweet and Lowdown: America's Popular Composers, 1978; Jablonski, E. The Encyclopedia of American Music, 1981; Stambler, I. Encyclopedia of Popular Music, 1965.

DRAKE, ERVIN (April 3, 1919–), composer-lyricist, was born Ervin Maurice Druckman in New York City, the third of four children. His father, Max Druckman, had immigrated to the United States from Rumania in 1911. He married a fellow Rumanian emigrant, Pearl Cohen, and established a successful wholesale furniture business in New York. His wife had made brief

ERVIN DRAKE

appearances in two films, but left show business when they married.

Ervin attended New York public schools, graduated from Townsend Harris Hall, a high school for superior students, in 1935 and acquired a bachelor of social science degree from the College of the City of New York in 1940. At CCNY he studied drawing, painting, and lithography, and published cartoons and illustrations in the college humor magazine, *Mercury*, of which he became art editor, then editor-in-chief, and in various national-circulation magazines as well.

"One could reasonably conclude," Drake reminisced, "that having prepared for a life in the graphic arts, I would pursue that career. No. I opted for the life of a songwriter instead. It was absolutely illogical. Musically, I was academically unprepared. All I had to offer was a strong desire, self-conviction and a fairly limited and self-taught pianistic ability." He had contributed songs and sketches to school productions and, while still an undergraduate, even managed to sell several songs to a publisher.

After college, he went to work in his father's furniture business. "I used to cheat on dad by moonlighting in Tin Pan Alley where I tried to peddle my songs," Drake recalled. He had his first song success in 1942 with "Tico-Tico," setting his own words to a popular Brazilian melody by Zequinha Abreu. Drake's English version was introduced in an animated Walt Disney film, *Saludos Amigos* (1943), in which it was sung by Aloysia Oliviera. A year later "Tico-Tico" was recorded by the Andrews Sisters and by Xavier Cugat and his orchestra. The Cu-

gat orchestra performed it in the 1943 motion picture *Bathing Beauty*, starring Esther Williams. The song was interpolated into the films *Kansas City Kitty* (1944) and the Groucho Marx extravaganza, *Copacabana* (1947). Ethel Smith, the popular organist, adopted it as her theme music.

In 1944 Drake, in collaboration with H. J. Lengsfender, wrote "Perdido," a jazz-flavored number set to Juan Tizol's music. In 1942 Duke Ellington recorded it as an instrumental, a version that made "Perdido" a jazz classic. The song, with Drake's lyrics, was revived on Broadway in the 1981 Ellington musical, *Sophisticated Ladies*, where it was sung, and danced to atop a concert grand piano, by Hinton Battle, Greg Burge and Judith Jamison.

Drake scored even greater success in 1943 with "The Rickety Rickshaw Man," for which he worte both words and music. Eddy Howard's 1945 recording sold more than a million copies. "When I got my first royalty check," Drake recalled, "it was so big, the room spun. The song pulled Majestic Records out of the red and me into the music business for good."

In 1946 Drake helped write "Good Morning Heartache" and "Sonata," and, in 1947, "Come to the Mardi Gras" and "Made for Each Other." "Good Morning Heartache" (music by Irene Higginbotham and Dan Fisher) was introduced by Billie Holiday on the first recording in which she worked with a string section, and it entered her nightclub repertory. It was also recorded by such jazz giants as Ella Fitzgerald, Billy Eckstine and Joe Williams. Nevertheless, this song did not become popular with the general public until Diana Ross, in the role of Billie Holiday, sang it in the film, *Lady Sings the Blues* (1972).

"Sonata" (lyrics written with Jimmy Shirl, music by Alex Alstone) was popularized in a million-selling recording of 1947 by Perry Como. For "Come to the Mardi Gras," Shirl was again Drake's co-lyricist in an adaptation of a Brazilian melody by Max Bulhoes. Freddy Martin and his orchestra successfully recorded it, as did Mary Martin with instrumental backing by Guy Lombardo and His Royal Canadians. "Made for Each Other" (lyrics by Drake and Shirl) was adapted from a melody by René Touzet. It was popularized through a recording by Xavier Cugat and his orchestra, vocal by Buddy Clark.

Several Drake songs of the 1940s were introduced in motion pictures. "Can You Guess?" and "Kiss With Your Heart" (music to both by Paul Misraki) were heard in *Heartbeat* (1944) and introduced by Ginger Rogers. "Yo Te Amo Mucho" and "That's That" (music by Sammy Sept and Xavier Cugat) were sung by Cugat to a tiny

Chihuahua dog in *Holiday in Mexico* (1945). "Texas, Brooklyn and Heaven" (words and music written with Shirl) was performed in *Texas, Brooklyn and Heaven* (1948); "Long After Tonight" (lyrics with Shirl, music by Rudy Polk) was used as a recurrent theme in *Arch of Triumph* (1948). When Jane Froman sang "Let's Keep it That Way" (written with Abner Silver and Milton Berle) in the revue *Artists and Models* (1944), Drake made his songwriting debut in the Broadway musical theater.

On May 28, 1947, Drake married Ada Sax, then a secretary, later the head of the copyright division of the Bregman-Vocco-Coon Music Company. They made their home in Great Neck, Long Island, and raised two daughters. Ada died in 1975.

Television, even more than songwriting, engaged Drake's activity from 1948 to 1962. He served in various capacities, as writer, composer, associate producer and producer. In those 14 years he was involved with some 700 telecasts, most of them weekly series. About 40 were specials, starring Steve Lawrence, Eydie Gorme and Gene Kelly, among others. Drake wrote both the script and the song for *To Mamie with Music*, a birthday salute to Mrs. Dwight D. Eisenhower, broadcast in 1956 by both the CBS and NBC television networks. *The Bachelor*, (1956) starring Hal March, Carol Haney and Jayne Mansfield, earned Drake Sylvania Awards both as songwriter and producer. *Yves Montand on Broadway* (1961), for which he was both writer and producer, was nominated for an Emmy, and the Drake-produced Timex Comedy Hour, hosted by Johnny Carson, received the top audience rating in 1962 for a variety special.

While working in television, Drake, in collaboration with Shirl, Al Stillman and Irvin Graham, composed one of his most celebrated standards, "I Believe," a song of religious affirmation. It was written in 1952 for Jane Froman to sing on the television series *U.S.O. Canteen*. With American troops still fighting in Korea, the producer felt that this song, with its inspirational message might help to rehabilitate the career of Jane Froman, who had been absent from the public eye since being injured in an airplane accident during World War II. Froman introduced "I Believe" on Thanksgiving Day 1952, and it proved so popular that she sang it again one month later on her nationally broadcast Christmas show. A recording by Frankie Laine sold more than a million copies in 1953. Other recordings were made by Froman and by Mahalia Jackson, and "I Believe" had 20 hearings on *Your Hit Parade* in 1953, three times in first position. The song has been recorded many times

over the years, and its total sales exceed 20 million discs.

Other songs by Drake from the early 1950s that deserve mention are: "Beloved, Be Faithful" (written with Shirl), which was popularized by Russ Morgan and his orchestra in 1950. "Across the Wide Missouri" (1951) was an adaptation by Drake and Shirl of the American folk ballad, "Shenandoah," with hit recordings made by the Weavers and the orchestra of Hugo Winterhalter. "My Friend" (1954, written with Shirl) was popularized in the United States by Eddie Fisher's recording and in Great Britain by Frankie Laine's. "Weather Pains" (words and music by Drake) was introduced on the Broadway stage by Jane Morgan in the *Ziegfeld Follies of 1957*. "Intrigue" and "At the Beaux Arts Ball" (music by Paul Durant) were introduced in the film *Intrigue* (1957), starring Robert Mitchum.

In 1956 the partnership of Drake and Shirl was dissolved, with Drake now composing music as well as writing lyrics. He also composed his first complete score (words and music) for a Broadway musical, *What Makes Sammy Run?* (February 27, 1964). It was Drake's idea to make a stage musical from Budd Schulberg's bestselling novel of the same name about a ruthless Hollywood tycoon, and he induced Schulberg and his brother, Stuart, to write the show's book. The musical, like the novel, traces the career of Sammy Glick, a monomaniac whose lust for success and power carries him from a job as a copy boy for a New York City newspaper to the heights of success as a Hollywood movie producer. As he schemes his way to the top, he brings tragedy to those nearest him, yet he feels no remorse for those whose lives he has damaged. As Sammy Glick, Steve Lawrence made his first appearance in the Broadway theater. For him, Drake composed the show's best songs, "A Room Without Windows" (sung as a duet with Sally Ann Howes) and "My Hometown." Sally Ann Howes introduced "Something to Live For" and Bernice Massi, "The Friendliest Things"; both songs were recorded by Eydie Gormé. *What Makes Sammy Run?* was a box-office success, lasting 540 performances. Its music was recorded in an original cast album.

A second Broadway musical, *Her First Roman* (October 20, 1968), for which Drake wrote the book as well as words and music, survived just 17 performances. This musical adaptation of Bernard Shaw's *Caesar and Cleopatra* starred Richard Kiley and Leslie Uggams as the famous lovers. "Just for Today" and "I Cannot Make Him Jealous" were popularized through Bobby Short's recordings.

Drake produced pop songs in various genres

that were independent of either the Broadway or television media. "The Old Oaken Bucket" (1960) was a rock-swing version of the American folk favorite with new lyrics. It was successfully recorded by Tommy Sands. In 1961 Drake also wrote new English lyrics for "Al Di La," an Italian pop tune by C. Donida. Drake's Americanized version was popularized in recordings by Connie Francis, the Ray Charles Singers and Jerry Vale. Drake also provided English lyrics for "Quando, Quando" in 1961 and that year composed words and music for "It Was a Very Good Year," which the Kingston Trio featured on their album *Goin' Places*. Though over the next three years the song was recorded by Chad and Jeremy, the Modern Folk Quartet and the Johnny Mann Singers, its popularity was limited to folk performances in coffeehouses. In 1965 Frank Sinatra heard the song on the radio and recorded it for his album, *September of My Years*, celebrating his 50th birthday. When he sang it on a CBS-TV special, *Sinatra: A Man and His Music*, the viewer response was so overwhelming that Sinatra decided to release it as a single. "It Was a Very Good Year" became Sinatra's first release to make the Top Ten in a decade and brought him a Grammy in 1966 for the year's best male vocal performance. This song enjoyed further success in 1966 when Herb Alpert recorded it in a version that sold more than a million copies.

Drake's "The Father of Girls" (1963) also had to wait several years before becoming popular. He wrote the words and music as a deeply felt response to having raised one of his two daughters when she turned 13. Though recorded in England in 1963 by Anthony Newley, it languished for five years, until Perry Como performed it to great acclaim on a television special in 1968. He subsequently recorded it, and "The Father of Girls" became one of his giant sellers. Other fathers of girls, including Paul Anka, Mike Douglas and Pat Boone, have recorded it.

In 1969 Drake composed several pop songs, including "Widows' Weeds," which was introduced in a recording by Carol Channing and also recorded by Pearl Bailey. "Ukulele Talk," a campy song with lyrics and syncopation recalling musical styles of the 1920s, has become a Hawaiian standard through Don Ho's recording.

Drake at last undertook the formal study of music in 1963, entering the Juilliard School of Music where he studied composition with Jacob Druckman. From 1965 to 1968 he studied composition and orchestration with Tibor Serly, and perfected his piano technique through lessons with Bernard Spencer and the jazz pianist David Frank.

From 1973 to 1982, Drake was president of the American Guild of Authors and Composers (AGMA), an organization formed in 1931 to protect its members in their dealings with publishers and users of music. The Guild was instrumental in having legislation for a new copyright law passed in 1976. For his role in securing passage of this legislation, Drake received the Guild's highest award, an Aggie, in Los Angeles in April 1981.

On November 19, 1982, Drake married Edith Berman, whom he had known when she was attending high school and and he was an undergraduate at CCNY. Edith Drake is the owner of Germaine, a successful beauty salon and boutique on Long Island's North Shore. She and her husband live on the Island, in Great Neck, where Drake pursues the hobbies of painting and golf. He also maintains a workshop in Manhattan on West 57th Street.

ABOUT: ASCAP Biographical Dictionary, 4th ed. 1980.

DRESSER, PAUL (April 21, 1857–January 30, 1906). In the late 1880s and 1890s, Paul Dresser's sentimental ballads dominated the American popular music scene. He was born John Paul Dreiser Jr. in Terre Haute, Indiana, on the banks of the Wabash River, the oldest of 12 children, one of whom was Theodore, the celebrated novelist. His father, John Paul Dreiser, had emigrated from Germany, and his mother, Sarah Maria (Schanab) Dreiser was of Czech ancestry. Until his factory burned down, John Dreiser had been a manufacturer of wool; after that, his sporadic attempts to find jobs as a wool sorter, spinner or day laborer left the family impoverished and in debt.

John Dreiser ruled his large family with tyrannical discipline and religious ardor. As W. A. Swanberg notes in his biography of Theodore Dreiser: "Each morning, the family knelt around the father as he asked a blessing for the day, and each evening a similar blessing for the night. His earnest German prayers were a household ritual." Intent on having his oldest son become a priest, he sent Paul away to school at St. Meinrad's Seminary near Evansville, where he spent most of his time writing verses and composing tunes rather than on his religious studies. In a final rebellion against the rigid discipline, he ran away when he was 16, making his way to Indianapolis on foot. There, he joined a traveling medicine show marketing Dr. Hamlin's Wizard Oil; in it, he appeared in blackface and performed some of his own songs. He left the show in Cincinnati and joined a stock company in Louisville, Kentucky, where he was billed as

PAUL DRESSER

"the sensational comique." From there, he proceeded to New York to perform minor roles at Harry Minor's Bowery Theatre, then to serve as blackface end man for the Thatcher, Primrose and West Minstrels. It was at this time that he changed his name from Dreiser to Dresser because he felt it would be more easily remembered by the audience. He returned to Evansville, where he became a leading man at the Apollo Theater and wrote a humorous column for the *Evansville Argus*: while in Evansville, Dresser resided with his mistress, Sallie Walker, in her successful brothel.

Meanwhile, he continued to write songs. "Wide Wings" was published by a small firm in Evansville, and many were gathered in *The Paul Dresser Songster* which he hawked for ten cents a copy in theaters where he performed.

In 1885, Dresser joined the Billy Rice Minstrels as "Mr. Banjo." For these shows, he composed his first successful ballad, "The Letter That Never Came" (1886) which is said to have been inspired by his own amatory frustrations. Dresser introduced it with the Billy Rice Minstrels in Brooklyn, New York in 1886 and sold it to T. B. Harms for publication. May Howard, the burlesque queen who later became his wife, used it in her act and was largely responsible for popularizing it.

Pat Howley, an employee at the publishing firm of Willis Woodward, thought so highly of "The Letter That Never Came" that, in 1887, he purchased and published Dresser's next ballad, "The Outcast Unknown," dedicated to the popular singer and composer, Chauncey Olcott, who featured it widely at his concerts. Convinced by

Howley to give up performing for composing, Dresser became the staff composer for the Willis Woodward Company, where he wrote, among others, two ballads with impressive sheet music sales, "The Convict and the Bird" (1888) and "The Pardon Came Too Late" (1891), a favorite with vaudeville tenors.

In 1894, Howley, in partnership with F. B. Haviland, established the publishing house of Howley and Haviland with Dresser as its staff composer. His songs were extremely popular in an era that glorified the sentimental ballad. In 1894, the firm published Dresser's "Once Ev'ry Year" and "Take a Seat, Lady," and the following year, one of Dresser's giant successes, the ballad "Just Tell Them That You Saw Me." The last of these was inspired by a newspaper story describing the meeting of a lady with a man she had known many years earlier in happier times. She tries to ignore him, but when he pleads with her to speak to him, she replies that some day she will come home, but until that happens, "just tell them that you saw me." This ballad became so popular that, according to Theodore Dreiser, "Comedians on the stage, newspaper photographers, bank tellers and tailors, even staid business men wishing to appear up-to-date, used it ["just tell them that you saw me"] as a parting salute"; lapel buttons bearing this phrase were also to be seen.

Dresser's songs now came thick and fast: in 1895, "Jean" and "We Were Sweethearts for Many Years"; "Don't Tell Her That You Love Her," "He Brought Home Another," "I Wish That You Were Here Tonight" and "I Wonder if She'll Ever Come Back to Me" in 1896; and, in 1897, Dresser's masterpiece, "On the Banks of the Wabash, Far Away."

Theodore Dreiser has claimed credit for suggesting that his brother write a song about the Wabash and helping Dresser to sketch some of the lyrics, but Dresser seems not to have mentioned this. Max Hoffman, orchestrator for the publishing house of M. Witmark & Sons, was with Dresser in Chicago when the ballad was composed: "I went to his room in the Auditorium Hotel," recalled Hoffman, "where instead of a piano there was a small camp organ Paul always carried with him. All the windows were open and Paul was mulling a melody that was practically in finished form. But he did not have the words. So he had me play the full chorus over and over again at least for two or three hours, while he was writing down the words, changing a line here and a phrase there, until the lyric suited him. . . . I have always felt that Paul got the idea from glancing out of the window and seeing the lights glimmering. . . . During the

whole evening Paul made no mention of anyone's having helped him with the song." Within
three months of the song's publication, it was
heard in vaudeville theaters around the country;
in the streets, the melody was played by barrel
organs, and in homes, it was sung at the piano.
During the Spanish-American War it became a
favorite of American soldiers, and on March 4,
1913, it was adopted as the official song of the
state of Indiana, and the Mills Brothers revived
it in 1940. It was also interpolated into motion
pictures, most significantly in Dresser's film biography, *My Gal Sal* (1942) where it was used
for an elaborate production number, and also in
The Jolson Story (1946), *Wait Till the Sun Shines
Nellie* (1952), and *The Monte Carlo Story*
(1957), sung by Marlene Dietrich.

Dresser's fertile creativity kept Howley and
Haviland both busy and prosperous in the late
1890s. Each year, Dresser produced an armful
of ballads about love and its frustrations, some
inspired by his stormy marriage to burlesque
queen, May Howard. Among the best of these
were "Come Tell Me Your Answer, Yes or No,"
"Every Night, There's a Light," and "The Old
Flame Flickers and I Wonder Why" from 1898;
and in 1899, "I Wonder Where She is Tonight,"
"There's Where My Heart is Tonight" and "The
Curse of a Dreamer," which was written when
his wife deserted him and their child for another
man. He first composed "The Curse," which he
regarded as an expression of bitterness so personal that he withdrew it from publication but he
did use it as a weapon with which to win back
his wife, apparently with some temporary success. But when the desertion became permanent,
Dresser rewrote the ballad, providing it with a
happy ending, retitling it "The Curse of the
Dreamer."

Because of Dresser's continuing success, Howley and Haviland made him a partner in the
firm in 1901. That year, as Howley, Haviland
and Dresser, it published the following songs by
Dresser: "In the Great Somewhere," "Mr. Volunteer," "My Heart Still Clings to the Old First
Love," "There's No North or South Today" and
"When the Birds Have Sung Themselves to
Sleep."

Dresser was now at the height of his fame and
prosperity. He was a huge man, six feet tall,
weighing 300 pounds; sentimentality and gener-
osity emanated from every ounce of his being.
He lived in baronial splendor in New York at the
Gilsey House on 29th Street or at the Marlbor-
ough on 36th Street, where he maintained regal-
ly appointed suites. Though he did assist
colleagues, friends and acquaintances who were
in need, the half million dollars he is reputed to

have earned during his songwriting career was
squandered on the good life and all its accoutrements.

After the turn of the century, success turned
to adversity. His new ballads failed to interest a
public that had found new composers to admire
and other ballads to sing. Following the precipitous decline in the sale of Dresser's songs, Pat
Howley abandoned the publishing house in
1904. A year later, Haviland and Dresser were
forced to close shop. Dresser then opened the
Paul Dresser Publishing Co., on 28th Street,
which was soon to be baptized Tin Pan Alley.
But the songs it issued, such as "The Day That
You Grew Older," "Jim Judson—From the
Town of Hackensack" and "The Town Where I
Was Born" were all failures, sinking Dresser deeper into debt.

He made the pathetic gesture of keeping up
the false pretense that he was still prosperous,
still successful, still the public's favorite. Each
day, he arrived at his office dressed in a frock
coat and high silk hat, and among colleagues, he
maintained that the songs he was now writing
were better than ever, that new successes of the
first magnitude were close at hand. But friends
(many of whom had profited from his generosi-
ty), competitors in the song business, and performers who had once sought him out for his
latest hits all turned away from him, often in de-
rision. Though he was in abject poverty, no one
offered to help.

Dresser suffered a heart attack at his sister's
home in New York on January 30, 1906. Describing Dresser's last moments, Theodore Dreiser wrote: "When I arrived, he was already cold
in death, his soft hands folded over his chest, that
indescribable sweetness of expression about his
eyes and mouth."

Though he died a pauper, Dresser proved he
still had one more trick up his sleeve. His last
published song was "My Gal Sal," a belated tribute to Sallie Walker. He predicted it would be
a big hit, but he had been unable to promote it
properly. After his death, the song took wing and
soared in sheet music sales that reached millions
of copies and realized a fortune. "My Gal Sal"
had first been introduced in vaudeville in 1905
by Louise Dresser, a young performer whom
Dresser had discovered who, in gratitude, had
assumed his name. She used the song so consistently in her act that by 1906 it caught on. In the
1930s, it was revived in recordings by the Claude
Hopkins orchestra, the Mills Brothers and Tommy Reynolds and was heard in the motion picture, *The Jazz Singer* (1927). In 1942, "My Gal
Sal" provided the title for Dresser's motion picture biography, which starred Victor Mature as
the composer.

ABOUT: Ewen, D. Great Men of American Popular
Song, 2d ed., 1972; Hamm, C. Yesterdays: Popular
Song in America, 1979; Swanberg, W. A., Dreiser,
1965.

DUBIN, AL (June 10, 1891–February 11,
1945), was born Alexander Dubin in Zürich,
Switzerland, the first of two sons of Simon and
Minna Dubin. The Dubins were emigrés from
Eastern Europe who met in Switzerland; Simon
had come to study medicine and Minna, to pursue a career as a chemist and teacher. The family
came to the United States in the summer of
1896, settling in Philadelphia, where Dr. Dubin
went into practice at his home on Pine Street. By
1900, he was serving on the gynecological staff
of Mount Sinai Hospital (now the Albert Einstein
Medical Center); Mrs. Dubin resumed her career as a chemist.

Al Dubin attended public school in Philadelphia and the Northeast M. T. High School for
one semester. As a boy, he wrote verses which
were published in the *St. Nicholas Magazine*, a
monthly journal for the young that presented
him with a gold medal for one of his efforts. He
loved to listen to popular songs demonstrated by
pluggers in a local music shop, which led him to
try his hand at writing song lyrics. He frequently
played hooky from school to attend vaudeville
shows and musicals in New York City and to
make the rounds in Tin Pan Alley to sell his lyrics. When he was 14, a vaudevillian he had met
in Tin Pan Alley used some of his material; several years later, another vaudevillian bought one
of his numbers for $5.

Dubin was intimidated by his parents' high
expectations of him; his father hoped that he,
too, would be a surgeon, and his dreams of becoming a lyricist (for which he had already
shown talent) only served to anger them. But his
father succeeded in persuading Dubin to return
to the school of his choice; Dubin chose Perkiomen Seminary, a private school in Pennsburg,
where he enrolled in 1909. He distinguished
himself in athletics (football, basketball, track)
and as a writer. He was editor of the school
newspaper and yearbook, for which he wrote
short stories and verses, and he composed one of
the school songs. Though he was an excellent student, his erratic behavior and lackadaisical response to school discipline brought him into
constant conflict with the school's director. "He
really has a remarkable ability along a great
many different lines, chiefly, however, along literary lines," the director wrote to Dr. Dubin in
December 1910. "He has originality and re-
sourcefulness. If the boy would spend half as

AL DUBIN

much time on his studies as most students are
obliged to do, he would probably make perfect
marks in almost every subject that he has, and
still have plenty of time for outside work—for
general reading and diversions." Because of his
mature appearance at an early age, he was able
to partake of the pleasures offered by saloons,
gambling and women, which soon became lifelong addictions. Twice, he was suspended from
school because of his irresponsible actions, and
in December 1911, he was expelled.

Soon after leaving Perkiomen Seminary, Dubin met young composer Joe Burke, with whose
family he lived in Philadelphia for a short period. Lured by the hope of better prospects, Dubin
and Burke moved to New York where they lived
at the Beacon Hotel. The Tin Pan Alley publisher, M. Witmark & Sons, had issued two of Dubin's songs, "Prairie Rose" (music by Morris
Siltmitzer) and "Sunray" (music by Charles P.
Shisler) in 1909; in 1911, they brought out "Oh,
You Mister Moon" (music by Burke). During the
next four years, Witmark published 25 of Dubin's songs to music by various composers. This
did little to advance him financially; to support
himself, he worked as a singing waiter. In 1916,
he had a modest hit with "Twas Only an Irishman's Dream" (lyrics written with John O'Brien,
music by Rennie Cormack); and the following
year, "All the World Will Be Jealous of Me" (music by Ernest R. Ball) established his songwriting
reputation.

During World War I, Dubin served overseas
with the 305th Field Artillery of the 77th Division. He wrote several patriotic songs, some with
good friend, Jimmy Monaco. While on duty at

the front, he was gassed, causing permanent damage to his lungs. Honorably discharged in 1918, he returned to writing lyrics on a full-time basis. Among the songs he completed in the postwar years were "Tripoli" (music by Irving Weill), which was recorded in 1920 by Charles Harrison, and "In the Land of School Days" (music by Gus Edwards) in 1920; in 1921, "Crooning" (words with Herbert V. Veise, music by William Caesar) and "Sundown Brings Back Memories of You" (written with Charles Edmonds; music by Paul Cunningham). The last of these became Dubin's first song to be heard on Broadway: it was interpolated into the *Greenwich Village Follies of 1921*, for which Dubin also wrote special material.

On March 19, 1921, Dubin married Helen McClay, a beautiful show girl. Because Helen was a devout Catholic, Dubin converted to Catholicism for the nuptials in the Church of St. Elizabeth in New York (a civil ceremony had taken place much earlier). Following a brief honeymoon, the family (which included stepdaughter Marie) settled in Manhattan; the Dubin's daughter, Patricia, was born on November 26, 1922. Dubin found domestic life to be more confining than he'd anticipated. He was unable to curb his appetite for alcohol, gambling and women, indulgences that caused him to neglect his financial obligations to his family and to leave home for extended periods of time.

But Dubin did not neglect his career. He convinced publishers Jack and Irving Mills to allow him to write lyrics for some of the instrumental standards ("Humoresque," "O Sole Mio," "Cielito Lindo," "Song of India") in its catalogue; the venture was a great success. 1924 was a particularly prolific year. "What Has Become of Hinky Dinky Parley Voo?" (words with Irving Mills, music by Jimmy McHugh and Irwin Dash) was introduced and popularized on radio by "The Happiness Boys," Ernie Jones and Billy Hare, and he also wrote "Chattachoochee" (lyrics with Billy Rose; music by Sammy Fain), "My Kid" (music by McHugh and Dash) and "I Don't Care What You Used to Be, I Know What You Are Today" (music by McHugh). The following year, "The Lonesomest Gal in Town" also became popular on radio, where it was sung by its composers, Jimmy McHugh and Irving Mills, who were then being featured on the air as "The Hotsy Totsy Boys."

Dubin was also hired to work on several Broadway musicals. "A Cup of Coffee, a Sandwich and You" (words with Billy Rose, music by Joseph Meyer), composed in 1925, was interpolated into *Charlot's Revue of 1926* (November 10, 1925) for Jack Buchanan and Gertrude Lawrence; they also recorded it and it became one of the hits of the year. His first complete Broadway score (with music by Fred Coots) was *White Lights* (October 11, 1927); it ran for only 35 performances. He also contributed "Ham and Eggs in the Morning" (music by Con Conrad and Abner Silver) to the successful musical, *Take the Air* (November 22, 1927), and published a small book, *The Art of Songwriting* (1928).

As a lyricist with impressive credits both in Tin Pan Alley and on Broadway, Al Dubin joined the songwriters who went to Hollywood with the advent of sound in motion pictures and the vogue for screen musicals. In 1926, he had written "My Dream of the Big Parade" (music by McHugh) for promotion of the film *The Big Parade*, and he had contributed songs (with J. Russel Robinson) to Paramount's *The First Kiss* (1928). After he arrived in Hollywood, Dubin continued to work with many composers, most significantly Joe Burke and Harry Warren.

His first screen successes came with Joe Burke. At the Warner Brothers studio, they were assigned to write the songs for *Gold Diggers of Broadway* (1929), one of the first "Technicolor" films and a memorable early screen musical. For it, they composed "Tip Toe Through the Tulips" and "Painting the Clouds with Sunshine," both introduced by Nick Lucas and recorded by him, as well as by Smith Ballew and the Jean Goldkette orchestra. "Painting the Clouds" was also heard in the film version of George M. Cohan's stage musical, *Little Johnny Jones* (1929), and it became the title of a 1951 remake of *Gold Diggers of Broadway*; "Tip Toe Through the Tulips" was heard again on the screen in the film, *Confidential Agent* (1945), and in 1968, it was revived by Tiny Tim in a bestselling recording.

Between 1929 and 1930, Dubin completed the lyrics for approximately 50 published songs. With Burke, he contributed songs to several Warner Brothers productions, including the screen version of Jerome Kern's *Sally* (1929), in which the title song was introduced by Alexander Gray, and they wrote complete scores for *In the Headlines* (1929; "Love Will Find a Way," introduced by Grant Withers and Marian Nixon), *She Couldn't Say No* (1930; "Watching the Dreams Go By," introduced by Winnie Lightner) and *Hold Everything* (1930). "Dancing With Tears in My Eyes" had been dropped from the film *Dancing Sweeties* (1930), but it was recorded by the orchestras of Ben Selvin and Joe Venuti in 1930 and popularized on radio by Rudy Vallee; John Payne sang it in *Kid Nightingale* (1939). In 1931, "For You" was successfully introduced and recorded by Glen Gray and the Casa Loma Orchestra (vocal by Kenny Sargent) and inserted into the film, *Holy Terror* (1931); it appeared on *Your Hit Parade* in 1948, and in the 1950s, it was recorded by Rosemary Clooney and Nat King Cole and by Rick Nelson in 1964.

Dubin reached the apex of his songwriting career with composer Harry Warren. Between 1932 and 1937, they wrote approximately 100 songs (some were among the screen's most successful) for more than two dozen films. After contributing "Three's a Crowd" (lyrics with Irving Kahal) to *The Crooner* (1932), they were assigned to write the songs for *Forty-Second Street* (1933), one of the most successful Hollywood musicals of the 1930s. Four hit songs came from that film: the title song, "Shuffle Off to Buffalo," "You're Getting to Be a Habit With Me" and "Young and Healthy." Next came *Gold Diggers of 1933*, which included "We're in the Money," "I've Got to Sing a Torch Song," "Remember My Forgotten Man" and "Shadow Waltz." Busby Berkeley's *Footlight Parade* (1933) brought "Shanghai Lil" and "Honeymoon Hotel"; the team also worked with Berkeley on *Moulin Rouge* (1934; "Coffee in the Morning, Kisses at Night" and "The Boulevard of Broken Dreams") and on *Gold Diggers of 1935*, which included "The Words Are in My Heart" and Dubin's only Oscar-winning song, "Lullaby of Broadway." For *Roman Scandals* (1933), starring Eddie Cantor, they composed the torchy "No More Love," introduced by Ruth Etting, and "Keep Young and Beautiful," and they provided songs for the Al Jolson films *Wonder Bar* (1934; "Why Do I Dream Those Dreams?" and "Don't Say Goodnight") and *Go Into Your Dance* (1935; "She's a Latin From Manhattan" and "About a Quarter to Nine").

The team's songs were also heard in a number of motion pictures starring Dick Powell and various leading ladies including Ginger Rogers, Joan Blondell and Ruby Keeler; among these were *Twenty Million Sweethearts* (1934; "I'll String Along With You" and "Fair and Warmer"), *Dames* (1934; the classic "I Only Have Eyes for You"), *Broadway Gondolier* (1935; "The Rose in Her Hair" and "Lulu's Back in Town"), *Shipmates Forever* (1935; "Don't Give Up the Ship") and *Gold Diggers of 1937* (1936; "With Plenty of Money and You").

After the introduction of the weekly radio show, *Your Hit Parade*, in 1935, Dubin and Warren's songs were featured frequently. In addition to many of the songs mentioned above, listeners also heard "Where Am I?" from *Stars Over Broadway* (1935), "I Know Now" from *The Singing Marine* (1937), and "How Could You?"

from *San Quentin* (1937), starring Humphrey Bogart and Ann Sheridan. Songs reaching the top position were "I'll Sing You a Thousand Love Songs" from *Cain and Mabel* (1936), starring Clark Gable and Marion Davies, and "Remember Me?" from *Mr. Dodd Takes the Air* (1937), starring Kenny Baker and Jane Wyman.

Dubin's last important collaborations with Harry Warren were the scores for *Gold Diggers in Paris* (1938; "A Stranger in Paree" and "I Wanna Go Back to Bali") and Berkeley's *Garden of the Moon* (1938) which contained the title song, "Confidentially" and "Love is Where You Find It" (lyrics written with Johnny Mercer).

In 1939, Dubin worked again with Jimmy McHugh on Olsen and Johnson Broadway revues, writing "South American Way" for *The Streets of Paris* (June 19, 1939) and songs for *Keep Off the Grass* (May 23, 1940), the best of which was "Clear Out of This World." Using a melody from a piano piece composed by Victor Herbert in 1919, he also wrote "Indian Summer," made popular by Tommy Dorsey with Frank Sinatra; it reached first position on *Your Hit Parade*. "Along the Santa Fe Trail" (music by Will Grosz) was introduced in the film, *The Santa Fe Trail* (1940), starring Errol Flynn and Olivia De Haviland, it was then made into a bestselling recording by Glenn Miller with Ray Eberle. In 1940, "I Never Felt This Way Before" (music by Ellington) was introduced and recorded by Duke Ellington, and "Where Was I?" (music by W. Frank Harling) was first heard in the film *'Til We Meet Again* (1940); it was successfully recorded by the orchestras of Charlie Barnet and Jan Savitt. "We Mustn't Say Goodbye" (music by James Monaco), introduced by the Vaughn Monroe orchestra, was written for the film, *Stage Door Canteen* (1943), and it was nominated for an Academy Award. With the Olsen and Johnson stage extravaganza, *Laffing Room Only* (1944), Dubin was represented on the Broadway stage for the last time with a substantial hit song, "Feudin' and Fightin'," for which he had conceived the title; Burton Lane wrote both the lyrics and the music.

That Dubin published more than 100 songs after 1933 is remarkable in view of his increasingly self-destructive lifestyle. His hedonistic excesses were transformed into gluttony (he soon weighed 300 pounds) and drug addiction. At the end of his life, in spite of his huge earnings, he was often without funds to pay his bills, and was forced to call on ASCAP for advances on future earnings.

His behavior eventually brought his marriage to an end after a long period of separation. On February 23, 1943, Dubin married Edwina Coolidge, a young and ambitious actress; they were divorced a few months later.

Dubin collapsed on the street in New York on February 8, 1945, and was rushed to the Roosevelt Hospital, where the last rights were administered by a Catholic priest; Dubin died there on February 11, 1945. The cause of death given on the death certificate was pneumonia, but the autopsy revealed it to be barbiturate poisoning.

Dubin was inducted posthumously into the Songwriters Hall of Fame in 1971. On August 25, 1980, David Merrick's *Forty-Second Street*, an adaptation of the Hollywood musical, opened on Broadway; it has been extremely successful and has helped to revive the popularity of Dubin's greatest hit songs.

ABOUT: McGuire, P. D. Lullaby of Broadway: Life and Times of Al Dubin, 1983.

VERNON DUKE

DUKE, VERNON (October 10, 1903–January 16, 1969). For many years the composer Vernon Duke assumed dual identities. As Vladimir Dukelsky (his name at birth) he composed concert music, operas and scores for ballets which were performed by some of the world's most prestigious artists and musical organizations. As Vernon Duke he composed popular songs and scores for the Broadway musical stage and the screen. In 1955 he abandoned his given and family names, assigning the name "Vernon Duke" to both his concert music and his popular songs.

Vladimir Dukelsky was born on October 10, 1903 in a railroad station at Parfianovka, Russia, where his mother was seized by labor pains while traveling by train. Duke was of mixed ancestry. He was Russian by birth and Viennese and Spanish on his mother's side. His paternal forebears were Lithuanian and Georgian.

Vernon Duke was the older of two sons of Alexander and Anna (Kopyloff) Dukelsky. The father was a civil engineer who specialized in railroad construction; his mother was Princess Daria Toumanov. Both of Duke's grandmothers were trained pianists, as was his mother; his father was an amateur singer who enjoyed performing gypsy songs. Duke revealed a gift for music early in life. Even in infancy he responded to music; he was also accustomed to hearing his mother play the piano, and at night he was lulled to sleep with the singing of opera arias. When he was seven, his mother gave him piano lessons. It was not long before he had composed a waltz for the piano, a full-length piano sonata, and had attempted a ballet score and an opera. He later received intensive piano training from Lubomirsky (who also began teaching him theo-

ry) and Josephine Leskevich. He was as precocious in his academic studies as in music. About the age of three, he learned to read and write; at four he began studying foreign languages. In high school, as he recalled, "I was good in history, languages and geography." He also showed a talent for writing poetry and drawing caricatures.

His father entertained plans for his son to have a career in diplomacy or in the navy and had enrolled Vladimir's name at birth in the St. Petersburg Naval Academy. When the father died in 1913, the family moved from St. Petersburg to Kiev, where music became Vladimir's preoccupation. He attended the Kiev Conservatory, studying composition with Glière and piano with Marian Dombrosky. He was constantly writing music, imitating the romantic style of Glière and Glazunov. Duke's string quartet and some of his piano pieces and songs were performed at the Conservatory. "Music became my only life," he recalled.

With the outbreak of the Civil War in 1919 Duke's family left Kiev for Odessa. At that city's Conservatory, Duke studied composition with Malishevsky. When the fighting spread to Odessa, the Dukelsky family again took flight coming to Constantinople for a two-year stay. There Duke helped support his family, by arranging concerts for refugees at the local Y.M.C.A. and by playing the piano in movie theaters, cabarets and other public halls. He now became acquainted with American popular songs; those of Irving Berlin and George Gershwin fascinated him particularly. He started writing songs in a similar vein, using the pen names of Ivan Ivin and Alan Lane. "My tunes of the Constantinople vintage . . . sounded as if they were in the authentic American jazz idiom," he remarked, though Duke also conceded that they were obviously derivative of songs by Gershwin and Jerome Kern.

Duke came to the United States in 1921, making his home in New York, first in an uptown basement, then in an apartment in Washington Heights. He found jobs playing piano accompaniments for the "ersatz gypsies who entertained at Second Avenue restaurants. He also wrote music for vaudevillians, performed the piano in an act on the circuit of vaudeville theaters operated by B. F. Keith, and conducted a five-man orchestra in a burlesque house. Writing in a popular idiom, Vernon Duke composed two numbers—"Spooning in a Crowded Bus" and "Don't Waste Your Time Wasting Your Time on Me"—neither of which interested any publishers or performers. "They were not good songs," Duke recalled, "and the lyrics, concocted by myself with the aid of a Russian-English dictionary, were deplorable." He also composed art songs, two of which were performed by Eva Gautier at an International Composers Guild concert in Manhattan. These songs attracted the interest of George Gershwin, who later advised the young songwriter to adopt the American pseudonym of Vernon Duke for his popular efforts and to retain Vladimir Dukelsky for his concert music. Gershwin brought Duke to his publisher, Max Dreyfus of Harms, Inc., but Duke's affiliation with Harms was not consummated until much later.

On the advice of Arthur Rubinstein, for whom Duke composed a piano sonata which the virtuoso liked but never performed, Duke decided in 1924 to leave for Paris to advance his career as composer of concert music. Gershwin found some additional jobs for Duke which provided him with the $800 he needed for his passage and living expenses.

The next five years in Paris and London were to prove providential. The impresario Serge Diaghilev commissioned Duke to compose music for a ballet, Zéphyr et Flore, a huge success when the Ballet Russe introduced it in London. Serge Koussevitzky, the much-admired conductor of the Concerts Koussevitzky in Paris, became Duke's patron, publishing his piano sonata and introducing his Symphony No. 1 (1927) in Paris on June 14, 1928.

Though Vladimir Dukelsky was beginning to flourish, Vernon Duke was stumbling badly. His first popular tune to be published, "Try a Little Kiss," the first piece written under the Vernon Duke pseudonym, went unnoticed, even though

it was interpolated into a London musical, Katja, The Dancer. In 1926 Duke contributed some nine numbers to a London operetta, Yvonne, a critical disaster whose fate was sealed when Noël Coward dubbed it "Yvonne, the terrible." The London musical The Yellow Mask, book by Edgar Wallace and music by Duke, did somewhat better. Duke's song, "For Goodness Sake," was interpolated into the 1927 London revue Bow-Wows and attracted some interest. Other Duke songs were used in Two Little Girls in Blue (1928) and Open Your Eyes (1929). But in Europe in the late 1920s, Duke was known only as a successful composer of concert works.

Returning to the United States in 1929, Duke spent the next year writing background music for motion pictures filmed in studios on Long Island. "I invested in an alarm clock and a stopwatch, bought a business suit, ready-made but comfortable, and learned enough slang to exchange pleasantries with stagehands and orchestra musicians and not be thought pompous. I was given a freshly scrubbed cubbyhole of an office with my name in modest letters on the door, a tiny upright, a writing desk, a music cabinet and a telephone and told to write whatever music Paramount needed. I enjoyed turning out a song for a two-reel short in the morning and a few pages of emotional background music for a dramatic feature in the afternoon." All this time he continued to produce ambitious concert works in his spare time.

Duke's "breakthrough" American popular song, the one he described as his "passport to Broadway," was "I Am Only Human After All" (lyrics by E. Y. Harburg and Ira Gershwin). Accepted for the 9:15 Revue on Broadway in 1930 but never used, it found a place in the Garrick Gaieties of 1930. The first Duke song to be heard in the Broadway musical theater, it was sung by James Norris, Velma Vavra and Imogene Coca. The New Yorker singled out "Only Human" as the "best of the new show numbers" and there was a successful recording by the Colonial Club Orchestra. This song brought Duke a composer's contract from Harms. There were two lesser Duke songs in the same revue—"Too Too Divine" (lyrics by E.Y. Harburg) and "I'm Grover" (lyrics by Newman Levy). Other Duke songs used in Broadway revues were: "Talkative Toes" (lyrics by Howard Dietz) in Three's a Crowd (1930); "Muchacha" (lyrics by E. Y. Harburg) in Shoot the Works (1930); and "Let Me Match My Private Life With Yours" (lyrics by E. Y. Harburg) in Americana (1932), the last of these sung by Albert Carroll.

Duke's song classic, "April in Paris" (lyrics by Harburg), appeared in the first Broadway musical for which Duke composed the complete score, *Walk a Little Faster* (December 7, 1937), a revue starring Beatrice Lillie and Clark and McCullough. Duke explained that this song was something of an afterthought, that it was brought into the revue after the production had gone into rehearsal. "Evelyn Hoey . . . was to be entrusted with the singing chores in the new musical. After several double Scotches, we all got pretty sentimental, the Scotch reminding us of Miss Hoey's tartan shirt in her Paris number, and the mention of the number inevitably leading to Paris, how wonderful it was in the spring and how vile was Manhattan at that time of year. I can't think whether it was Benchley or Woolley who cried out: 'Oh, to be in Paris now that April's here.' The rest went off in true Class B musical picture fashion. "'April in Paris,'" said I melodramatically. "What a title! My kingdom for a piano!" Duke was instantly informed that a piano was available on the second floor. "The piano was wretched indeed, but it made appropriate sounds when persuaded and, using the title 'April in Paris' for what they call the 'front phrase' in the trade, I soon completed the reasonably immortal refrain. I then proceeded to 'ham it up,' telling all and sundry that I had just given birth to a masterpiece that was certain 'to make the show.' The lyrics were written a week later by Harburg."

During the Boston tryouts of *Walk a Little Faster*, "April in Paris" was used for a scene depicting the Left Bank. Evelyn Hoey's delivery of the song was well received, but when the show arrived in New York her performance completely missed the mark, probably because she was suffering from laryngitis and sang it in a whisper that was at times inaudible. The eminent Boston writer, Isaac Goldberg, distressed that the song had been neglected by New York critics, wrote in *The New York Times* that "'April in Paris' is one of the finest musical compositions that ever graced an American production. If I had my way, I'd make the study of it compulsory in all harmony courses."

Walk a Little Faster had only a modest run of 119 performances and "April in Paris" seemed destined to follow it into oblivion. But the song was kept alive by singers in nightclubs catering to sophisticated audiences, and the society chanteuse Marian Chase's recording on the Liberty label was responsible for establishing it as a standard. Subsequent recordings, the best of which were those by the orchestras by Eddy Duchin and Paul Weston, by the popular vocalist Hildegarde, and by two opera stars, Lily Pons and Dorothy Kirsten, further popularized the song. In 1955 it received a jazz treatment in a recording by Count Basie. In the motion picture *April in Paris* (1952) it was sung by Doris Day.

There were two other noteworthy numbers in the *Walk a Little Faster* score (lyrics by Harburg). "Where Have We Met Before?" was introduced by John Hundley, Sue Hicks, Donald Burr and Patricia Dorn, and "Speaking of Love," by Donald Burr and Dave and Dorothy Fitzgibbon.

Having rhapsodized about April in Paris, Duke soon grew sentimental over autumn in Manhattan. In the intimate revue *Thumbs Up* (December 2, 1934), "Autumn in New York" (lyrics and music by Duke) was introduced by J. Harold Murray in the show's finale, then was popularized in a recording by Louella Hogan.

With Harburg as his lyricist, Duke contributed several songs to the *Ziegfeld Follies of 1934* and, with Ira Gershwin as lyricist, to the *Ziegfeld Follies of 1936*. The former was the first edition since 1907 not produced by Ziegfeld himself (he had died in 1932). With Ziegfeld's widow, Billie Burke, replacing him, the 1934 *Follies* starred Fanny Brice, Jane Froman and Eugene and Willie Howard. Jane Froman introduced Duke's "What Is There to Say?" and "Suddenly" (the lyrics of the latter a collaboration of Ira Gershwin and Billy Rose). "Water Under the Bridge" was introduced by Everett Marshall and danced to by Patricia Bowman and "I Like the Likes of You" was shared vocally by Brice Hutchins and Judith Barron and was danced to by Vilma and Buddy Ebsen. Hildegarde recorded both "What is There to Say?" and "Suddenly."

Duke composed the complete score for the *Ziegfeld Follies of 1936* (January 30, 1936) which starred Fanny Brice, Bob Hope and Josephine Baker. Its best song was "I Can't Get Started," heard as a duet by Hope and Eve Arden. This was the song that paved Hope's path to Hollywood and screen success; he was first signed for films after two scriptwriters for the *Big Broadcast of 1936* heard him perform this number. "I Can't Get Started" also became the trademark of Bunny Berigan, who made it his theme song and whose celebrated 1936 jazz recording was years later chosen by the National Academy of Recording Arts and Sciences for the Recording Hall of Fame. This same Berigan jazz recording was used as a recurrent theme on the soundtrack of the dramatic film *Save the Tiger* (1973), starring Jack Lemmon in an Oscar-winning performance. Billie Holiday, Hildegarde, Dinah Shore and the Artie Shaw and Hal Kemp bands are among those who successfully recorded the song.

Four other Duke numbers in the 1936 *Ziegfeld Follies* merit attention. Fanny Brice introduced "He Hasn't a Thing Except Me"; "Island in the West Indies" was sung by Gertrude Niesen and danced to by Josephine Baker; "Words and Music" was assigned to Niesen, who was joined by Rodney McLennan in the performance of "That Moment of Moments." The *Ziegfeld Follies of 1936* had a run of 227 performances.

After the *Ziegfeld Follies of 1936*, Duke contributed "Now" (lyrics by Ted Fetter) to the Broadway revue *The Show Is On* (1936). It was introduced by Grace Barrie and Robert Shafter, then was interpreted in a dance by Paul Haakon and Evelyn Thawl.

In 1937 Hollywood called upon Duke to complete George Gershwin songs for *The Goldwyn Follies* (1938), left unfinished by the composer's untimely death. Duke composed the music for the verses of three Gershwin songs, where only the choruses had been written. He also wrote the music for two ballet sequences choreographed by George Balanchine, and he contributed a complete song of his own, "Spring Again" (lyrics by Ira Gershwin), which was introduced by Kenny Baker.

Duke returned to the Broadway theater with the music for a ballet sequence in the unsuccessful revue *Keep Off the Grass* (May 23, 1940). Before the year of 1940 was over he had also composed the complete score for his most distinguished stage musical, *Cabin in the Sky* (October 25, 1940). With book by Lynn Root, lyrics by John Latouche, choreography by Balanchine, it had an all-black cast headed by Ethel Waters, Todd Duncan and Katherine Dunham. *Cabin in the Sky* was set in the rural South of a mythic black community. The central character is Little Joe, a humble man for whose soul Lucifer Jr. and the Lord's General are in competition. Though Little Joe has a gift for getting into trouble, he manages to reach heaven, largely through efforts of good Petunia and in spite of the temptations offered by Georgia Brown. For this racial libretto, Duke fully exploited his gift for expressive melodies. On opening night Ethel Waters had to repeat the chorus of "Taking a Chance on Love" (lyrics by Ted Fetter and Latouche) half a dozen times before the audience was satisfied, and after that the song regularly stopped the show. George Jean Nathan in his review of *Cabin in the Sky* called it the year's best song. In his autobiography Duke revealed how it came to be written: "We needed a heart-warming song to put the first act over. . . . I reached for the trunk—three days before the opening—and stumbled on 'Fooling Around with Love,' a song Ted Fetter and I had written for an unproduced show. I tried it out on Latouche; he fell for the tune, but thought the title not sufficiently 'on the nose' for the dramatic production. An after-

noon's work, with an assist from Fetter, followed, and what emerged was 'Taking a Chance on Love' . . . an immediate hit, and a solid standard today." When Duke tried out the song for Ethel Waters she needed to listen only to the first eight measures before exclaiming: "Mister, our troubles are over. This is it." Waters also sang it in the 1943 motion-picture adaptation of the stage show. The song was also interpolated into the film *I Dood It* (1943) and was sung by June Haver and Gloria De Haven in the screen musical *I'll Get By* (1943). Having been recorded in 1943 by the Benny Goodman and Sammy Kaye bands, the song had 17 representations on *Your Hit Parade*.

"Taking a Chance on Love" was not the only memorable song in *Cabin in the Sky*. The title song was yet another tour de force for Waters. In the movie adaptation of the stage musical she shared it with Eddie "Rochester" Anderson. The bands of Benny Goodman and Sammy Kaye recorded it and so did the vocalists Ella Fitzgerald and Sarah Vaughan. In the stage musical Ethel Waters also introduced "Savannah." "Hone in the Honeycomb" was assigned to Katherine Dunham on Broadway and to Ethel Waters and Lena Horne on the screen. In the stage musical, Katherine Dunham and Dooley Wilson presented "Love Me Tomorrow."

Cabin in the Sky did better with the critics than at the box office, lasting only 156 performances. An Off Broadway revival in January 1964 ran for just 47 performances. For it, Duke composed a new song, "Living it Up" (lyrics by the composer). From this revival came an original cast album.

Duke's next Broadway assignment was *Banjo Eyes* (December 25, 1941), starring Eddie Cantor. This was a musical stage adaptation of the Broadway comedy *The Men on a Horse* by Cecil Holm and George Abbott, with book by Joe Quillan and Izzy Ellison. Cantor played the part of Erwin, a meek, self-effacing writer of greeting-card verse who (in the musical) gets information about race horses in a dream and learns to pick winners by talking to the horses in the stable. In the process, he becomes involved with gamblers, finally extricating himself from their clutches and returning to his peaceful profession and to his neglected wife. Only one of Duke's songs was a standout, "Nickel to My Name" (lyrics by John Latouche). It was introduced by Bill Johnson before serving as background music for a dance performed by the De Marcos. Eddie Cantor's best number, which had been written specially for him, was "We're Having a Baby" (lyrics by Harold Adamson), which he performed with June Clyde; he was also heard in

"Who Started the Rhumba?" Cantor's box-office appeal insured sold-out houses. But *Banjo Eyes* closed suddenly after only 126 performances when the star had to have a serious operation.

Duke's next few musicals did poorly, with those that reached Broadway folding quickly. *The Lady Comes Across* (January 9, 1942) was an unhappy attempt to star the nightclub comedian, Joe E. Lewis, in a book musical. It closed after three performances. *Jackpot* (January 13, 1944), with Allan Jones and Nanette Fabray, limped on through 67 performances. *Sadie Thompson,* a musical version of Somerset Maugham's *Rain* with June Havoc in the title role, opened on November 16, 1944 and expired after 60 performances. *Dancing in the Streets,* starring Mary Martin, opened and closed in Boston in March 1943. From these musicals, one song was memorable, "The Love I Long For" (lyrics by Howard Dietz), which June Havoc and James Newill introduced in *Sadie Thompson.* It was successfully recorded in 1944 by Vaughn Monroe, by the Three Suns and by Harry James and his orchestra.

During World War II Duke enlisted in the Coast Guard where he attained the rank of lieutenant colonel. He served from August 1942 to September 1945. While in uniform he wrote the music for *Tars and Spars,* a Coast Guard revue starring the then still-unknown Sid Caesar. It was filmed in 1946 with Caesar but with Duke's music completely replaced by Jule Styne and Sammy Cahn songs. While in service Duke also composed "The Silver Shield," a song for the Coast Guard, and music for a war documentary, *Battle Station*; he also led a band at the Brooklyn Barracks.

After the war Duke lived in Paris for two years. In 1949 he returned to the States and settled in California, acquiring a house in Pacific Palisades. It was here that he was to live with his wife, Kay McCracken, a young concert singer whom he married on October 30, 1957. They had no children.

Notwithstanding his West Coast address, Duke was soon back in the musical theater with songs (lyrics by Ogden Nash) for a revue, *Two's Company* (December 15, 1952), starring Bette Davis in her return to Broadway. The show was a failure (91 performances) and a nondescript score recorded in an original cast album was distinguished only by "Out of the Clear Blue Sky," performed by Peter Kelly and Sue Night, and "Just Like a Man," sung by Bette Davis. Once again with Ogden Nash as lyricist, Duke provided the songs for an Off Broadway revue, *The Littlest Revue* (May 22, 1956), in which Tammy Grimes sang "Madly in Love." For *Time*

Remembered (December 12, 1947), a Broadway play by Jean Anouilh, Duke composed the incidental music and two songs. His last contributions to the theater never reached Broadway: *The Pink Jungle* (1959) starring Ginger Rogers and Agnes Moorehead and with lyrics by the composer, and *Zenda* (1963), lyrics by Martin Charnin.

In addition to the many popular songs composed by Vernon Duke, Vladimir Dukelsky composed a library of concert music and ballet scores. Jascha Heifetz introduced a violin concerto of 1942 and Gregor Piatigorsky a cello concerto of 1942 while both musicians were soloists with the Boston Symphony under Serge Koussevitzky. The oratorio *The End of St. Petersburg* (1938) was introduced by the Schola Cantorum of New York City. Leonard Bernstein conducted in New York the premiere of *Ode to the Milky Way* (1945). With Dukelsky scores, the San Francisco Ballet mounted *Emperor Norton* in 1957 and Roland Petit produced *Lady Blue* in 1961.

From 1949 on, Duke was the president of the Society for Forgotten Music he had founded to record neglected music of the past. He wrote an autobiography, *Passport to Paris* (1955), an amusing collection of essays in *Listen Here!* (1963) and a volume of poetry in Russian which was published in Munich in 1962. Just before his death, Duke translated the lyrics of American popular songs into Russian for transmission to the Soviet Union on Radio Liberty. He also completed the score for a never-produced musical based on the life of Mark Twain.

Duke was operated on for a tumor on the lung on January 8, 1969. He died of cardiac arrest in Santa Monica, California after a second operation.

ABOUT: Duke, V. Passport to Paris, 1955; Ewen, D. American Composers: A Biographical Dictionary, 1982.

DYLAN, BOB (May 24, 1941–   ). In the early 1960s Bob Dylan became a cult figure with folk ballads and protest songs for which he wrote both words and music. He decried poverty, social injustice, racial discrimination and war, becoming a hero of the underprivileged and a symbol of rebellion to the dissident youth of the 1960s. But in 1964 Dylan shifted from his emphasis on folk ballads to a hybrid of folk, blues, country and western and rock 'n' roll. Within two years he had become a rock idol in the manner of John Lennon, Paul McCartney and Mick Jagger. Since then Dylan, like his mentor Woody

BOB DYLAN

Guthrie, has become an American folk hero and musical legend in his own lifetime.

Robert Allen Zimmerman, as Bob Dylan originally was named, was born in Duluth, Minnesota to a middle-class Jewish family, the older of two sons of Albert Zimmerman, the proprietor of an appliance store, and Betty (Stone) Zimmerman. Bob was still a child when his family moved farther north to Hibbing. There his father opened another appliance shop and Bob attended public school.

At the age of 11, he met Big Joe Williams, whose blues singing deeply impressed young Zimmerman. He was also listening to the standard popular music of the day on the radio and at the local record store. What moved him was the country blues of Hank Williams, which led him to the rhythm and blues of B. B. King, Muddy Waters and Howlin' Wolf. About 1955 he discovered the rock 'n' roll of Bill Haley and Little Richard. Later he would listen to Elvis Presley and Buddy Holly, but the greatest influence on the teenager was the wild, falsetto-shrieked, gospel-influenced music of Little Richard, the most distinctive black vocalist of the early rock era. Performing at high school dances and local talent shows, young Zimmerman played piano and sang Little Richard songs, imitating his hero's frenzied approach to the new music known as rock.

Dylan's all-consuming preoccupation with music caused friction at home with his father, a practical businessman who worried that his son was neglecting schoolwork and who disapproved of his ambition to become a musician. At school, which he detested, Dylan was an outsider who rebelled against the constraints of small-town life. Emulating his idol, the then recently deceased actor James Dean, he purchased a Harley-Davidson motorcycle and hung out with the "greaser" crowd from the wrong side of the tracks, wearing a black leather jacket and dangling a cigarette from the corner of his mouth. Years later Dylan, the mythmaker, would reinvent his adolescence, saying that he had periodically run away from home and traveled as far west as California, portraying himself as a road bum, carnival hand, and itinerant musician. In fact, his most exotic travels were taken with his parents' permission to Dinkytown, the bohemian quarter of Minneapolis, where he could buy rhythm and blues records and meet black musicians.

The summer before his senior year in high school he adopted the stage name of Bob Dylan. On a state scholarship, he entered the University of Minnesota in Minneapolis in September 1959. As he recalled in a poem entitled "My Life in a Stolen Moment," "I sat in science class 'n flunked out for refusin' to watch a rabbit die. I got expelled from English class for using four-letter words in a paper describing the English teacher." After six months he stopped attending classes at the university and devoted himself to music. On weekends Dylan performed folk and some country songs at The Scholar, a Dinkytown coffee house, and 1960 he became familiar with the folk ballads of Woody Guthrie. He also came under the influence of Dinkytown's resident nonconformists, or "beatniks" as they were called, who introduced him to the mix of Marxist-anarchist ideas that later culminated in the political program of the New Left. They also provided him an intellectual rationale for his increasingly "existential" life-style and hand-to-mouth, the "only-moment-that-matters-is-now" existence. But he expressed himself through music. Guthrie's autobiography, Bound for Glory, became his Bible and Dylan even began to affect Guthrie's "Okie" accent and slightly nasal vocal style. Though Dylan's social consciousness was nascent, Guthrie's music was soon to carry him into the world of protest.

When Dylan arrived in New York City late in January 1961, carrying only a guitar and a knapsack, his first mission was to seek out Guthrie who was confined to a hospital in New Jersey, a virtually immobilized victim of Huntington's Chorea. Though Guthrie was visibly wasting away, Dylan visited him several times a week. Bob was beginning to write original material and to rework old folk and country standards, and he would serenade his handicapped idol with his own songs mixed in with some of Guthrie's. Guthrie began to look forward to these visits, and Dylan's own ballad, "Song to Woody," gave Guthrie much pleasure. Guthrie told some of his friends that "Pete Seeger's a singer of folk songs, not a folksinger. Jack Elliott is a singer of folk songs. But Bobby Dylan is a folksinger. Oh, Christ, a folksinger, all right."

Dylan was now performing at various Greenwich Village folk clubs and coffee houses. The kindness of strangers was his sole support. "I just jumped right to the bottom of New York," he later recalled. "I bummed around. I dug it all—the streets and the snows and the staring and the five-flight walkups and sleeping in rooms with ten people. I dug the trains and the shadows the way I dug ore mines and coal mines." Though he was hungry and cold, his spirit soared. When he could not "crash" at a home of an acquaintance, he slept in the subway. And as a folksinger his ambition was to become the "new Guthrie."

Slowly, Dylan's style was beginning to evolve. In public, as in private, he wore the same threadbare and often dirty uniform, the simple work shirt and jeans of a day laborer. His long curly hair was unkempt, his cherubic face made women want to "mother" him. He sang in a gruff voice filled with emotion, accompanying himself on guitar. Sometimes he performed on the guitar and the harmonica simultaneously (the harmonica was suspended at mouth level on a wire connected to a brace he wore around his neck). He often indulged in onstage "talkin' blues," rambling commentaries on various subjects, speaking with a slow drawl in the vernacular of a "primitive," horrendous syntax and all. Jack Elliott, himself an emulator of Guthrie, described Dylan's early performing style in Scaduto's book: "He was trying to sound like an old man who bummed around 85 years on a freight train, and you could see this kid didn't even have fuzz on his face yet. But I was charmed by it. He was a rough little pixie runt with a guitar. He was [very rough but] headed in the right direction—the words he was singing, the gestures and the mannerisms."

On April 11, 1961, Dylan opened a two-week engagement (for no pay) at Gerde's Folk City on West 4th Street, famous for its Monday night hootenannies. This stint brought no public acclaim, but Dylan now became a name to Gerde's regulars, including such established folk musicians as Dave Van Ronk, who influenced and encouraged him. Dylan was also booked for two additional weeks at Folk City in September. In addition to his repertory of Guthrie songs and other folk ballads like "House of the Risin' Sun," he included new songs of his own, such as "Song to Woody," "Talkin' Bear Mountain" and "Talkin' New York"—all markedly influenced by Guthrie. At his opening night performance at Folk City on September 25, Robert Shelton of The New York Times heard him. A few days later he wrote a review under a four-column heading reading, "Bob Dylan: A Distinctive Folk-Song Stylist." "A bright new face in folk music is appearing at Gerde's Folk City," said Shelton. "Although only 20 years old, Bob Dylan is one of the most distinctive stylists to play in a Manhattan cabaret in months. . . . There is no doubt that he is bursting at the seams with talent. . . . His music has the mark of originality and inspiration, all the more noteworthy for his youth. Mr. Dylan is vague about his antecedents and birthplace, but it matters less where he has been than where he is going and that would seem straight up."

That upward direction was not at first a soaring ascent. When Dylan gave his first public concert at the Carnegie Chapter Hall on November 4, 1961, only about 50 were in attendance, with Dylan earning a fee of $20. John Hammond, the now-legendary recording producer who had discovered Billy Holiday, signed Dylan to a contract with Columbia Records after hearing "Talkin' New York." The first album, Bob Dylan, was released early in March 1962. It contained much of what he had been singing at Folk City, including "Talkin' New York" and "Song to Woody." In its first year the record sold only five thousand copies, in part because Dylan's unusual, and at times grating, voice was not instantly likable. Columbia thought of dropping Dylan but reconsidered when Hammond protested and summoned Johnny Cash to testify to Dylan's talent.

Not discouraged, Dylan became increasingly prolific as a songwriter as the year 1962 progressed. The social and political dislocations of the era—the recognition of poverty and suffering amid affluence, the systematic maltreatment of American blacks and the threat of nuclear holocaust—all served as grist for Dylan's creative mill. "I don't sit around and write songs with the newspapers, like a lot of people do, spread newspapers all around and pick something to write about. It's usually right there in my head before I start," he told Pete Seeger in a radio interview. "The song was there before I came along. It just sort of came and I just sort of took it down with a pencil, and it was all there before I came around."

Nevertheless many newspaper stories grew into Bob Dylan songs. Late in January 1962 he composed "The Ballad of Emmett Till" (with music adapted from a tune previously used by Len Chandler). Till was a young black man who was lynched for having whistled at a white woman. The following April Dylan composed the now-classic anthem that would make him famous, "Blowin' in the Wind," a folk ballad asking questions about racial bigotry, war and hunger, but finding the answer only "blowin' in the wind." This song was born one day in a Greenwich Village coffee house where Dylan and his friends were discussing the civil rights movement and the failure of American society to treat blacks as first-class citizens. "The idea came to me that you were betrayed by your silence," he explained to Scaduto, "that all of us in America who didn't speak out were betrayed by our silence. Betrayed by the silence of the people in power. They refuse to look at what is happening. And the others, they ride the subways and read the *Times*, but they don't understand, and they don't know. They don't even care, that's the worst of it."

Early in 1962, just before his first album was released, Dylan acquired an apartment of his own on West Fourth Street. He shared it with Suze Rotolo, an aspiring artist who stimulated his creativity and encouraged him in his songwriting. (She is the young woman walking arm in arm with him on the cover of the *Freewheelin' Bob Dylan* LP.) That apartment was the sanctuary where Dylan became a prolific writer, sometimes producing several songs in a single day. In 1963 he turned out such protest songs as "Only a Pawn in Their Game," inspired by the murder of civil rights activist Medgar Evars, and "The Ballad of Hollis Brown," about the tragedy of a man driven by poverty to murder his wife and five children before committing suicide. War and all those who summon God as an ally for institutionalized murder were excoriated in "With God on Our Side" (the melody was borrowed from Dominic Behan's "Patriotic Game"). The danger of nuclear annihilation was pointed out in "A Hard Rain's Gonna Fall" and "Talkin' World War III Blues." "Masters of War" attacked manufacturers of munitions in particular and war profiteers in general. Fears for the future were expressed in "When the Ship Comes In." The sexual revolution of the 1950s and early 1960s inspired the writing of "Don't Think Twice, It's All Right," which Peter, Paul and Mary, a folk trio, later recorded in a bestselling release. What later in the decade was to be called the "generation gap" was the theme of "Times They Are A-Changin'."

"Dylan," wrote Burt Korall in the *Saturday Review* (November 16, 1968), "caught the tenor of the times. Innocence was a thing of the past. . . . He realized that isolation from true reality was as unbearable as the reality itself. Yet this did not prohibit him from immersing himself in a surrealistic pessimism. After clearly indicting the world in his 'Blowin' in the Wind' he turned to an inverted mode of writing, couching his point of view within a rush of words and images, oblique and abstract, often approaching hallucination: dreams more frightening than reality."

Bob Dylan's self-appraisal was modest and revealing insofar as he defined himself as a writer rather than a "spokesman" or "leader": "I just have thoughts in my head and I write them. I'm not trying to lead any causes for anyone."

The first indication that Bob Dylan was on the threshold of stardom came when his concert packed Town Hall in New York on April 12, 1963. In *The New York Times* Shelton now described him as a "folk musician who breaks all the rules except those of having something to say and saying it stunningly." In May 1963 Dylan's second album, *Freewheelin' Bob Dylan*, was released. Here he sang "Blowin' in the Wind" for the first time, together with "Hard Rain's Gonna Fall," which had been composed during the 1962 Cuban missile crisis, "Masters of War," and "Don't Think Twice, It's All Right," among other numbers. It sold 10,000 copies a month for an initial total sale of 200,000 copies, bringing Dylan a royalty of about $5,000 a month. Within a few weeks of the release of *Freewheelin'*, a recording of "Blowin' in the Wind" was released by Peter, Paul and Mary. In its first two weeks, their record sold over 300,000 copies and soon achieved sales of more than one million, becoming the largest seller in the history of the Warner Brothers record company up to that date. It earned Grammys in 1964 as the year's best folk recording and as best performance by a vocal group. In their public appearances Peter, Paul and Mary always preceded their performance of "Blowin' in the Wind" with the simple announcement: "Now [we'd] like to sing a song written by the most important folk artist in America today." Sixty other performers recorded it, including Duke Ellington, the Chad Mitchell Trio, Stevie Wonder, Jackie De Shannon, the Kingston Trio, Marlene Dietrich, and the New Christy Minstrels. When Dylan performed it at the 1963 Newport summer music festival, he brought down the house. Joan Baez and Pete Seeger, who were in the audience, leaped on the stage to join him in its performance. After that the song entered Joan Baez's repertory. The civil rights movement made it its anthem, second in importance only to "We Shall Overcome." In his acclaimed documentary history of the civil rights movement, *Portrait of a Decade*, Anthony Lewis opened the book by quoting several lines from this ballad.

By the end of 1963 Dylan's songs were being

heard on college campuses throughout the Unites States. Twice in 1963, however, Dylan was embroiled in controversy. The first incident occurred in the spring, when he was scheduled to appear on the Ed Sullivan Show and sing his "Talkin' John Birch Society Blues," a funny tune about paranoid anticommunism. Network censors thought it too controversial and refused to allow its performance, even over Sullivan's strong objection. As a result, Dylan refused to appear on this popular TV entertainment program. Then in December Dylan shocked the country when, as recipient of the Thomas Paine Award from the Emergency Civil Liberties Committee, he made a rambling speech in which he expressed sympathy for Lee Harvey Oswald, the alleged assassin of President John F. Kennedy.

Dylan's third album, released in January 1964, was *Times They Are A-Changin'*, another bestseller on which he continued to deliver a social message. In addition to the anthemic title song, the record contained the first recordings of "Ballad of Hollis Brown"; "With God on Our Side"; "When the Ship Comes In"; "Only a Pawn in Their Game"; and "The Lonesome Death of Hattie Carroll," among other numbers. Dylan was now the unofficial troubadour of the civil rights movement and the voice of the emerging generation of young Americans whose social activism was to make them vastly different from the 1950s generation of "Young Men in a Hurry."

Recordings, public appearances at colleges, concerts and folk festivals, performances on television, and European tours all now combined to make Dylan a cult figure to devotees of folk music and to political activists. Success and sudden wealth, however, did not change him. He continued to dress in the garb of the young rebel: blue jeans, a turtleneck sweater or blue work shirt, worn-out jacket and boots. Apparently indifferent to the luxuries money could buy, he never really knew how much he was earning, nor did he care. He avoided accumulating possessions or, for that matter, living in any one place for any length of time. His favorite mode of transportation was a motorcycle. For all his fame, Dylan remained as restless, lonely, and introverted as he had been in obscurity.

Nevertheless Dylan suffered a personal setback when his love affair with Suze Rotolo ended. He became involved romantically with Joan Baez, with whom he toured and sang at concerts. Love and its frustrations were largely responsible for drawing him away from songs of protest to inward-looking and poetically autobiographical music. These songs did not condemn a complacent society but spoke of Dylan's hunger for personal freedom, his loneliness, his search for identity. "I went inside to write from, inside me," he explained.

This new songwriting was evident in his fourth album, *Another Side of Bob Dylan*, released in August 1964. Many of these songs were inspired by Suze, especially "Ballad in Plain D," a moving and somewhat bitter account of the disintegration of their love affair. Three songs in particular revealed a new side of Bob Dylan: "All I Really Want to Do," "My Back Pages," and "It Ain't Me, Babe," all of which foreshadowed a new idiom, folk rock. In "All I Really Want to Do" Dylan professed to want nothing more from the women in his life than friendship; he had no wish to subdue or destroy them. Both Sonny and Cher and the Byrds made successful records of this number. In "It Ain't Me, Babe," a song popularized in recordings by Johnny Cash and the Turtles, he lamented that he could not live up to the romantic image of idealized love or lover. In "My Back Pages" Dylan looks upon himself with disdain as an impotent fighter in false social battles aimed at changing the world. It became a bestseller in a recording by the Byrds.

In the early 1960s, when Dylan had taken up folk and country blues, rock 'n' roll had softened into pabulum for teenagers. Elvis Presley was serving in the Army; Little Richard had embraced religion; Chuck Berry was sentenced to prison; Buddy Holly was dead. But one day in 1964 Dylan was driving through Colorado listening to the car radio. Eight of the top ten songs were by the Beatles, whose new sound was to reinvigorate rock music and transform the entire pop scene. "They were doing things nobody was doing," Dylan told Scaduto. "Their chords were outrageous . . . and their harmonies made it all valid. You could only do that with other musicians. . . . I knew [the Beatles] were pointing the direction of where music had to go. . . . And it started me thinking about other people."

By 1965 Dylan, whose ambition as a teenager had been to be a rock 'n' roller, was working with such rock/blues musicians as the guitarist Mike Bloomfield, the keyboards player Al Kooper, and the guitarist/songwriter Robbie Robertson of the Hawks (later known as The Band). For the next two years, Dylan was off "chasing the legend of Elvis Presley," to quote the critic Greil Marcus.

The transformation from folk balladeer to folk rocker was completed with the album *Bringing It All Back Home* (March 1965). He recorded *Highway 61 Revisited* (August 1965) with a full rock band. On the former LP was "Mr. Tambourine Man," Dylan's greatest song success since "Blowin' in the Wind," a plea for "Mr. Tambourine Man" to play Dylan a song to take him through "the smoke rings of [his] mind" so that he can "forget about today until tomorrow." This song was misconstrued as an evocation of a drug trip, with Mr. Tambourine symbolizing drugs, but Dylan disputed the validity of such an interpretation. "Mr. Tambourine Man" became the Byrds' first hit song, a recording that sold over one million discs. Kris Kristofferson sang it in the nonmusical motion picture *Blume in Love* (1973). *Bringing It All Back Home* also included "She Belongs to Me," which Rick Nelson revived in 1969 on a successful live album; "It's All Over Now, Baby Blue," which Dylan sang in the documentary film *Don't Look Back* (1967); "On the Road Again"; "Subterranean Homesick Blues"; "Bob Dylan's 115th Dream"; "Gates of Eden"; and "It's Alright, Ma, I'm Only Bleeding." The best cuts on *Highway 61 Revisited* were the title song; the 1960s rock anthem of revenge, "Like a Rolling Stone," which became Dylan's first bestselling single; "It Takes a Lot to Laugh, It Takes a Train to Cry"; "Desolation Row"; "Ballad of a Thin Man" and "Queen Jane Approximately."

Many folk purists and political activists felt betrayed by Dylan's shift to folk rock, and he was denounced for "selling out" to commercial rock 'n' roll. Onstage at the Newport Folk Festival on July 25, 1965, he revealed an altogether shocking new image: no longer dressed like a Dustbowl emigrant, he wore the black leather jacket, black stovepipe pants, white dress shirt, and high-heeled black boots of a punk dandy who had been groomed on Carnaby Street. His one-time followers booed when, backed by a rock/blues band, he sang "Maggie's Farm," and the hostile crowd drove him from the stage when he tried to play "Like a Rolling Stone." To his new critics, Dylan had this reply: "I can't sing 'With God on Our Side' for 15 years. I was doing fine, you know, singing and playing my guitar. It was a sure thing. . . . I was getting bored with that. . . . I was thinking of quitting."

But if he had lost the segment of his audience that had made him famous, he now gained a mass following, the younger generation whose music was Beatles-influenced rock. *Bringing It All Back Home* became the first Dylan album to generate a million dollars in sales, and the harder rock 'n' roll LP, *Highway 61 Revisited,* was even more popular. His next album of personalized songs in a rock idiom, the Symbolist-influenced *Blonde on Blonde* (May 1966), established him as a rock superstar. *Blonde on Blonde* contained his hauntingly lovely tribute to Joan Baez, "Visions of Johanna"; "Rainy Day Women, No. 12 & 35"; "Just Like a Woman"; "I Want You";

"Memphis Blues Again"; and "Sad-Eyed Lady of the Lowlands." The singles "Positively Fourth Street" and "Can You Please Crawl Out of Your Window" were climbing the bestseller charts before the end of the year 1965. In 1967 *Blonde on Blonde, Highway 61 Revisited* and *Bringing It All Back Home* became the first three Dylan albums to be certified as gold records. That same year a film documentary of his 1965 tour of England, entitled *Don't Look Back,* which presented Dylan off-stage as well as on, was a critical and commercial success. It was re-released in 1983.

Although Dylan's public image was that of the messianic rock star, the prophet of the youth counterculture, he was beginning to achieve a measure of emotional stability in his personal life. On November 22, 1965, he married Sarah Lowndes, a former model and devotee of Eastern mysticism. He subsequently acquired two houses, a brownstone in Greenwich Village and a country place in Woodstock, New York. These were Dylan's first permanent homes since leaving Minnesota. He and Sarah raised five children before their marriage was dissolved in 1977.

It was on July 30, 1966, when Dylan's musical genius and his influence over a mass audience were at their peak, that disaster struck. Riding his Triumph 500 motorcycle at top speed near his Woodstock home, he lost control and suffered a broken neck. After months of recuperation he went into seclusion. During this period Columbia released a collection called *Bob Dylan's Greatest Hits,* which earned a gold record in 1968, but Dylan did not record in the studio for the next 18 months. Instead he spent time in Woodstock playing music with Robbie Robertson and the Hawks, who soon became famous as The Band. In the summer of 1967, using an inexpensive tape recorder in the basement of Dylan's house, he and The Band recorded what is now known as *The Basement Tapes.* Here could be found several Dylan compositions that were popularized in recordings by other artists such as the Byrds (who covered "Nothing Was Delivered" and "You Ain't Goin' Nowhere"); Manfred Mann ("The Mighty Quinn"); and The Band ("I Shall Be Released," "Tears of Rage," and "This Wheel's on Fire"). The tape was illegally pressed into a "bootleg" record called *Great White Wonder,* and for several years enjoyed an underground reputation as one of Dylan's finest creations. In 1975 Columbia released the tapes in the form of an album by Bob Dylan and The Band entitled *The Basement Tapes.* Critics hailed it as one of the most important record releases of the 1970s.

In 1968 Dylan returned to public life with a

critically acclaimed folk-rock album with country-and-western overtones, *John Wesley Harding*. Released in January, it quickly earned him another gold record. "He hammers on several themes: I am simple; I am kind; I am lonely; I have been misunderstood; I am not my image," wrote one reviewer. Another critic called this album "Dylan's supreme work." *John Wesley Harding* included "I'll Be Your Baby Tonight," which was later recorded by Linda Ronstadt; "All Along the Watchtower," which the Jimi Hendrix Experience made into a rock classic; "Dear Landlord"; "I Am a Lonesome Hobo"; the country-pop song "Down Along the Cove"; and "As I Went Out One Morning."

A follow-up to the country rock of "Cove" and "Baby Tonight" was *Nashville Skyline* (April 1969), also a gold record. "Girl From the North Country," which Dylan had written a half-dozen years earlier, appeared here as a duet with Johnny Cash. Among the other song highlights were "Lay, Lady, Lay," which became Dylan's first top-ten hit since "Positively Fourth Street"; "To Be Alone With You"; "I Threw it All Away"; "Tonight I'll Be Staying Here With You"; and "Tell Me That it Isn't True."

Dylan also resumed making concert appearances in 1968 to larger audiences than ever before. That year he appeared at Carnegie Hall for a memorial concert honoring Woody Guthrie. In 1969, returning to England for the first time in four years, he drew 16,000 to the Earl Court in London and almost 200,000 from all parts of Europe to the Isle of Wight. Exploring other media, he composed songs for the motion picture *Pat Garrett and Billy the Kid* (1973) and published a book of poems and prose pieces, *Tarantula* (1971), which had been written years earlier. Princeton University conferred an honorary doctorate of music on him in 1970. Dylan alluded to this ceremonial occasion in the song "Day of the Locusts" from his *New Morning* LP (1970).

Most of Dylan's albums in the 1970s and 1980s earned gold records. They included *Self-Portrait* (June 1970); *New Morning* (October 1970); *Bob Dylan's Greatest Hits, Volume 2* (1971); *Dylan* (1973); *Planet Waves* (1974); *Before the Flood* (1974); *Blood on the Tracks* (1975); *Desire* (1976); *Street Legal* (1978); *Slow Train Coming* (1979); *Infidels* (1983); *Real Live* (1984) and *Empire Burlesque* (1985). One of the strongest Dylan albums of the 1970s, and one of the most melodic of his career, was *New Morning*, which brought "Day of the Locusts" together with two love songs for his wife, "The Man in Me" and "If Not for You"; the last-mentioned was popularized in recordings by George Harrison and Olivia Newton John. Other popular numbers on this LP were "Went to See the Gypsy" and "Time Passes Slowly," which were covered by Judy Collins, and "Sign on the Window."

Dylan launched his first American concert tour in eight years in 1974. Backed by The Band, he opened in Chicago on January 3 and closed in Los Angeles on February 14, performing 40 concerts in 21 cities. Recorded on the Elektra/Asylum label, *Planet Waves* was released while Dylan's heralded return to the concert stage was in progress. With solid backing by The Band, the LP contained such numbers as "The Wedding Song," Bob's tribute to his wife; "On a Night Like This"; "Going, Going Gone"; the anthem, "Forever Young"; and "Hazel." *Before the Flood*, a two-disc LP, consists of live outtakes by Dylan and The Band from the 1974 tour.

Returning to the Columbia label in 1975, Dylan released *Blood on the Tracks*. Widely considered his best album since the late '60s, it contains such major songs as "Tangled Up in Blue," "Idiot Wind," "Shelter From the Storm," and "A Simple Twist of Fate," which was recorded by Joan Baez. Dylan's follow-up to *Tracks* was *Desire*, another critically acclaimed album. Among its stellar numbers are "The Ballad of Hurricane Carter," "Lilly, Rosemary and the Jack of Hearts," "Sister," and "One More Cup of Coffee." That same year Dylan formed an ensemble of old friends from the 1960s, including Joan Baez, the playwright Sam Shepard and the poet Allen Ginsburg, and toured with them under the name "Rolling Thunder Review," appearing mostly in middle-sized towns in the East and Midwest. The live *Hard Rain* LP commemorated the "Rolling Thunder" tour.

Dylan appeared in two motion pictures in the 1970s, as a supporting actor in *Pat Garrett and Billy the Kid* (1973), which was directed by Sam Peckinpah and starred Kris Kristofferson, and as the central character in *Renaldo and Clara* (1978), a rambling, stream of consciousness narrative that was also produced by Dylan. In 1973 a second book, *Writings and Drawings*, and, in 1975, an anthology of his lyrics was published, the latter reappearing in 1985 in an expanded edition entitled *Lyrics, 1962–1985*.

In 1979 Dylan was converted to fundamentalist Christianity. As a born-again Christian he emphasized religious subjects on *Slow Train Coming*, whose principal songs were "Gotta Serve Somebody," "Slow Train," "Precious Angel," and "I Believe in You." Although *Slow Train Coming* went platinum in 1979, Dylan's next LP, *Saved* (1981), with its insistent, even hortatory, religious message, had relatively poor sales, as did his next LP, the critically underrated

Shot of Love (1982). Moreover, many critics and devout fans now considered Dylan a fallen idol, whose moralistic exhortations were irrelevant to their lives. Responding to their criticisms, Dylan pointed out that his lyrics had always been infused with religious imagery and that a deep spiritual commitment had been at the heart of his earlier, ostensibly secular songs.

But with *Infidels,* his 1983 LP, the born-again phase was, if not entirely forgotten, assimilated to larger musical concerns. With the backup playing of such outstanding musicians as the guitarists Mark Knopfler and Mick Taylor and the Jamaican rhythm-section team of Sly Dunbar (drummer) and Robbie Shakespeare (bassist), the album was considered Dylan's strongest since *Desire.* Stephen Holden wrote in *The New York Times* that the best songs on *Infidels* "blend the surreal lyric imagery of Mr. Dylan's most colorful mid-1960s records with the hellfire and damnation rhetoric of his recent Christian period into elliptical pop prophecy." Here Dylan sang songs with political messages—"Union Sundown," "Neighborhood Bully," and "License to Kill"—as well as romantic ballads ("Don't Fall Apart on Me Tonight" and "Sweetheart Like You"). *Infidels,* wrote Steve Simels in *Stereo Review* (January 1984), "gives us an overwhelming sense of a living, breathing, thinking human being at work. . . . That this particular real person should turn out to be an aging bard whom most of us had long since written off as completely irrelevant is merely another of the album's pleasures, one of life's little ironies."

Empire Burlesque (1985) was the first of his 29 albums to be produced by Dylan himself. Here Dylan ceased his proselytizing for Christianity to explore again the themes of love, sex, death and war. "He sounds more human than he has in many years," wrote Jon Pareles in his review in *The New York Times.* Here the best songs include "Dark Eyes," "Never Gonna Be the Same Again," "I'll Remember You," "When the Night Comes Falling From the Sky," "Tight Connection to My Heart," "Clean Cut Kid" and "Trust Yourself." *Empire Burlesque,* wrote Kurt Loder in *Rolling Stone* (July 4, 1985), "puts the snarl back in Bob Dylan's music. This is not a case of mere pop-radio playability; Dylan achieved that amid the burnished, lushly roiling rhythms of 1983's *Infidels.* . . . No, [this] LP is something else: a blast of real rock and roll . . . that affords Dylan more street-beat credibility than he has aspired to since . . . well, pick your favorite faraway year."

Bob Dylan gave his first in-depth interview for national radio on November 17, 1984, a three-hour discussion conducted by Bert Klein-man and featuring the principal songs from 25 Dylan albums. The year of 1985 was one of triumph for the now-44-year-old Dylan. Along with Ray Charles, Michael Jackson, Bruce Springsteen, and Stevie Wonder, he was a featured vocalist on the phenomenally successful hit song, "We Are the World," a plea for aid to victims of poverty and famine. This anthem was composed by Michael Jackson and Lionel Richie, produced by Quincy Jones, and performed by a host of music superstars under the group name of "USA for Africa." All royalites and proceeds from this song, which amounted to several million dollars, went to a fund for famine relief. In July 1985 rock musicians the world over joined together for Live AID in a day-long telethon to raise money for victims of starvation and poverty. The British rock stars gathered at a stadium in London, the Americans at one in Philadelphia where a throng of 90,000 had assembled. There, at about 11:00 P.M. EST, the show came to a climax when Dylan took the stage, accompanied by Keith Richards and Ron Wood, guitarists for the Rolling Stones. To a tumultuous ovation from the crowd, and before a worldwide television audience of approximately one billion, Dylan and friends performed three numbers, the last being with "Blowin' in the Wind." Worldwide Aid brought in more than 50 million dollars from this event.

Late in 1985 Columbia Records released a major retrospective, *Biograph,* a five-record set of 53 songs from all phases of Dylan's career. Included on the album were nine songs Dylan had recorded but never released—"I'll Keep it With Mine," "Percy's Song," "Jet Pilot," and "Caribbean Wind," among others—three previously unreleased studio versions of well-known Dylan songs; six unreleased live cuts, including a live acoustic version of "Visions of Johanna" from 1966; and four songs that had been issued as singles but had never before been included on an LP. In his *New York Times* review of *Biograph,* John Rockwell spoke of Dylan as our "national poet laureate." And in *Rolling Stone,* Tim Holmes wrote that *Biograph* "tells the story of a man's complex and inexhaustible romance with his mentors, influences and heroes; rustic minstrels; . . . romantic, visionary and hipster poets; . . . roots, rock cats and media superstars. . . ."

In the summer of 1986 Dylan launched his most ambitious tour since 1974, playing before large audiences in Japan, Australia and throughout the United States. He received strong rock backing from the popular West Coast band, Tom Petty and the Heartbreakers. Also that summer, Dylan released his fifth album in four years, *Knocked Out Loaded.* Its principal songs were "Brownsville Girl," "Drifting Too Far From Shore" and "Maybe Someday." Written in collaboration with Sam Shepard, "Brownsville Girl" was an 11-minute narrative about a girl and old Gregory Peck movies.

ABOUT: Beal, K. Bob Dylan, 1974; Cable, P. Bob Dylan: His Unreleased Works, 1978; Dowley, T. Bob Dylan: From a Hard Rain to a Slow Train, 1981; Gray. M. Song and Dance Man: The Art of Bob Dylan, 1981; Gross, M. Bob Dylan: An Illustrated History, 1978; Hoggard, S. Bob Dylan: An Illustrated Discography, 1978; Kramer, D. Bob Dylan, 1968; Mellers, W. A Darker Shade of Pale: A Backdrop to Bob Dylan, 1984; Pickering, S. Bob Dylan Approximately: A Portrait of the Jewish Poet in Search of God; a Midrash, 1975; Ribakove, S. Folk-Rock: The Bob Dylan Story, 1966; Rinzler, H. Bob Dylan: The Illustrated Record, 1978; Scaduto, A. Bob Dylan, 1971: Shelton, R. N. Direction Home: The Life and Music of Bob Dylan, 1986; Shepard, S. Rolling Thunder Logbook, 1978; Sloman, L. On the Road with Bob Dylan: Rolling With the Thunder, 1978; Thompson, T. Positively Main Street: An Unorthodox View of Bob Dylan, 1972; Thomson, E. M. Conclusions on the Wall: New Essays on Bob Dylan, 1980; Williams, P. Dylan: What Happened?, 1980. Periodicals—New York Times Magazine November 28, 1971; Rolling Stone July 4, 1985, January 16, 1986; Saturday Review May 30, 1970.

EBB, FRED. *See* **KANDER, JOHN** and **EBB, FRED**

EDWARDS, GUS (August 18, 1879– November 7, 1945), a composer whose songwriting and performing career was developed in vaudeville, was born Augustus Edwards Simon in the German province of Hohenzollern, to Morris and Johanna Simon. The family immigrated to the United States in 1887, settling in the Williamsburg section of Brooklyn.

While attending night school, Edwards worked during the day as a tobacco stripper in his uncle's shop. He frequently played hooky from school to tour the theaters of Manhattan and Brooklyn in search of jobs as a boy soprano, and he regularly entertained his coworkers at the shop and his fellow students at school with his renditions of old-world folk songs. He attracted the interest of Lottie Gilson, the vaudeville star who, in 1888, engaged him to join her act as a "singing stooge." For two dollars a week, Edwards would sit in the balcony and rise, as if spontaneously, from his seat to repeat a song she had just performed. Working with Gilson at Tony Pastor's Music Hall on 14th Street and other nearby theaters, Edwards aroused so much interest that he made the singing stooge a fixture

GUS EDWARDS

in vaudeville, and was the inspiration for a popular tune of the period called "A Song in the Gallery." He worked for other stars as well, for Emma Carus, Helene Mora, Maggie Cline and Imogene Comer at Tony Pastor's, at the Bowery Theatre and at Koster and Bial's, and found singing engagements in saloons, on ferryboats, at lodge halls and between boxing bouts at athletic clubs. The publishing house of M. Witmark & Sons hired him as a plugger to promote the firm's songs from balcony seats. Edwards also sold sheet music at the Circle Theatre on Columbus Circle, the same theater which, some years later, he purchased and renamed the Gus Edwards Music Hall.

Edwards graduated from a seat in the balcony to the stage proper in 1896. The vaudeville agent James Hyde, of Hyde and Behman, heard him at Palmer's Gayety Saloon in Brooklyn, and developed an act for him in which Edwards and several other youths appeared as newsboys in ragged dress, their faces smeared with dirt and papers under their arms. As the Newsboy Quintet, this act performed for years in vaudeville theaters in and around New York. It proved so successful at the Hyde and Behman Music Hall that, in 1896–97, George M. Cohan hired the Newsboy Quintet to tour with the Four Cohans, and in 1898 Edwards's act toured the United States with John L. Sullivan, the heavyweight boxing champion of the world. It was with this act that Edwards introduced, in 1898, his first song, "All I Want is My Black Baby Back" (lyrics by Tom Daly), which Charles Previn had to commit to paper for him because Edwards could neither read nor write music.

During the Spanish-American War, Edwards was engaged to entertain the troops when he met the lyricist Will D. Cobb, with whom he formed a songwriting partnership. In 1899 they wrote "I Couldn't Stand to See My Baby Lose," "The Singer and the Song" and "You Are the Only Girl I'll Ever Care About." In 1900 their "I Can't Tell Why I Love You But I Do, Do, Do" brought them, from Howley and Haviland, one of the largest advances ever given by an American music publisher up to that time. This song was revived in the movies *The Belle of Yukon* (1944), *In Old Sacramento* (1946) and *Somebody Loves Me* (1952). "I'll Be With You When the Roses Bloom Again" was widely heard in vaudeville in 1901. In 1902 they composed "Louisiana Louise," "Could You Be True to Eyes of Blue" and "In the Sweet Bye and Bye."

In 1901 Edwards became an American citizen, legally changing his name to Gus Edwards the following year. In 1903 he started a cabaret, at the Cadicall Hotel in Manhattan, where he himself performed and where he helped to promote the career of the young singer Nora Bayes. Also in 1903, Edwards and Cobb made their songwriting debut in the Broadway musical theater, when "I Love Only One Girl in the Wide, Wide World" and "Rosalie" were interpolated into the successful musical extravaganza, *The Wizard of Oz*, starring Montgomery and Stone. That same year "Billy Grey, U. S. A." was interpolated into the stage musical *Mr. Bluebeard*, starring Eddie Foy. In 1904 "In Zanzibar" was heard in *The Medal and the Maid*, starring Emma Carus, who also recorded it. More successful, however, were two songs not used in a stage musical but which, published in Tin Pan Alley, became popular in vaudeville: "Goodbye, Little Girl, Goodbye" (1904) and "If a Girl Like You Loved a Boy Like Me" (1905), the former composed to satisfy the Tin Pan Alley fad for "goodbye" songs.

With Vincent P. Bryan as his lyricist, Edwards composed two hit songs in 1905; both were published by M. Witmark & Sons, where Edwards was working as a staff pianist. They were "Tammany" and "In My Merry Oldsmobile." The former was composed for a party at the Democratic Club in New York for which Edwards had been engaged as toastmaster. This song had been intended by Bryan and Edwards as a takeoff on the American Indian numbers then so popular in Tin Pan Alley; it also satirized some of the political indiscretions of the Democratic Party machine in New York. Nevertheless, the song proved so popular with party leaders that it was adopted by Tammany Hall as its unofficial theme song.

"In My Merry Oldsmobile" was Tin Pan Alley's first song about an automobile. Its writing was inspired by a newspaper account of the first transcontinental automotive trip (two Oldsmobiles that were driven from Detroit to the Lewis and Clark Exposition in Portland, Oregon, taking 44 days for the journey). This song was revived in the movies, *The Merry Malones* (1944), in which it was sung by Donald O'Connor, Jackie Oakie and Peggy Bryant, and *One Sunday Afternoon* (1948).

On November 28, 1905 Edwards married Lillian Boulanger in New York; they had no children. That same year he formed his own publishing house, the Gus Edwards Music Company, on West 28th Street. His firm was launched with two Edwards-Cobb hits. The company's first song release was their "Sunbonnet Sue" in 1906, which was widely heard in vaudeville and become Edwards's first song to sell a million copies of sheet music. When Edwards composed the score for a musical that toured the vaudeville circuit in 1923, starring Olga Cook and Fred Hildebrant, he called it *Sunbonnet Sue*, and the title number, now a standard, was the show's most popular song. This song was recorded by Bing Crosby, and contributed its title to a 1946 movie whose score included several Edwards standards. "Sunbonnet Sue" was sung by Gail Storm and Phil Regan. This song was also interpolated into Gus Edwards's screen biography, *The Star Maker* (1938).

For *A Parisian Model* (1906), a musical produced by Florenz Ziegfeld as a vehicle for the singer Anna Held, Edwards and Cobb composed "I Just Can't Make My Eyes Behave," a provocative number which remained permanently in Held's repertory. So closely was this song identified with Anna Held that when vaudevillians featured it in their acts in the mid-1900s they invariably affected Held's French accent. The song was interpolated into the movie musical *Strike Up the Band*, starring Judy Garland and Mickey Rooney. For the bevy of beautiful women with which Ziegfeld surrounded his star in *A Parisian Model*, Edwards and Cobb composed "I'd Like to See More of You," for which the girls began undressing until, by a trick stage effect, they finally appeared nude.

In 1908 Edwards extended his influence in show business by becoming a producer of stage musicals. His first project was *Merry Go Round*, for which he bought the Circle Theatre, where he staged many more productions. With Cobb as his lyricist, Edwards placed two songs in the historic Broadway revue produced by Flo Ziegfeld, called simply *Follies*. (Not until several years later was this revue renamed the *Ziegfeld*

Follies.) The Edwards-Cobb songs were "Bye, Bye, Dear Old Broadway" and "On the Grand Old Sand."

In 1908 Edwards composed his best-known song, "School Days" (lyrics by Cobb). It was written for a vaudeville act entitled *School Days*, in which Edwards played a teacher in a classroom filled with some 40 talented children who sang, danced, and did special routines. The song "School Days" sold more than three million copies of sheet music and has become an American song classic. Gail Storm and Phil Regan revived it in the movie *Sunbonnet Sue*, and it was interpolated into *The Star Maker*.

As a vaudeville act, *School Days* was so popular that, over the next two decades, Edwards wrote and starred in similar revues, each with new material, each with a fresh crop of gifted youngsters. For these acts, Edwards scouted the country in search of new talent so intensively that a popular saying was born: "Pull your kids in, here comes Edwards." Among Edwards's discoveries were such future stars as Eddie Cantor, George Jessel, Groucho Marx, Lila Lee, Eddie Buzzell, Georgie Price, the Duncan Sisters, Jack Pearl and Mae Murray. Hit songs by Edwards also came from these revues. Georgie Price introduced "By the Light of the Silvery Moon" (lyrics by Edward Madden) in 1909, singing it from a seat in the audience as a stooge for an act called *School Boys and Girls*. "Silvery Moon" was brought into the *Ziegfeld Follies of 1909* for Lillian Lorraine, who performed it frequently after that. When, in 1933, Edwards was a performer on the stage of the Ziegfeld Theatre, he invited Lorraine from her seat in the audience to mount the stage and sing "By the Light of the Silvery Moon." She complied, but midway through her performance was overcome by emotion and could not continue. "By the Light of the Silvery Moon" provided the title for a 1953 movie musical in which it was performed as a duet by Doris Day and Gordon MacRae. The song has been heard in many other films—in *Ruggles of Red Gap* (1935), starring Charles Laughton; in *The Story of Vernon and Irene Castle* (1939) starring Fred Astaire and Ginger Rogers; in *The Birth of the Blues* (1942); *Hello, Frisco, Hello* (1943); *The Jolson Story* (1946); *Always Leave Them Laughing* (1949); *Two Weeks With Love* (1950); and *Sunbonnet Sue*.

Other Edwards songs that came from these vaudeville "Kiddie" revues were "If I Were a Millionaire" (1910, lyrics by Cobb), which was revived in the movie musical, *The Eddie Cantor Story* (1954), and "Look Out for Jimmy Valentine" (1911, lyrics by Madden), revived in *The Star Maker*. Both songs were recorded by Bing Crosby.

Apart from vaudeville, Edwards composed songs for Broadway musicals. In the *Ziegfeld Follies of 1909* Lillian Lorraine introduced "Up, Up in My Aeroplane" (lyrics by Madden), while soaring high above the audience in a contrived flying machine. One of Tin Pan Alley's first successful songs about flying, it was recorded in 1909 by the Hayden Quartette. For this same Ziegfeld production, Edwards and Madden composed "Come On and Play Ball With Me" and interpolated their "My Cousin Carus." "My Cousin Carus" had been introduced in 1908 in the Broadway musical *Miss Innocence*, starring Lillian Lorraine, and in 1909 it was recorded by Billy Murray. With Edgar A. Smith as his lyricist, Edwards composed the complete score for the Weber and Fields extravaganza, *Hip, Hip, Hooray!* (October 10, 1907).

With the advent of talking pictures, Edwards left the Broadway scene for Hollywood in 1928. Working with Joe Goodwin as his lyricist, he contributed songs to the MGM production, *The Hollywood Revue of 1929*, the screen's first lavish all-star revue. There "Your Mother and Mine" was introduced by Charles King. This song was used in another screen revue, *The Show of Shows* (1929), in which it was performed by Beatrice Lillie, Frank Fay, Louise Fazenda and Lloyd Hamilton. In *Hollywood Revue of 1929*, King sang "Orange Blossom Time" and Cliff "Ukulele Ike." Edwards was heard in "Nobody But You" (not to be confused with an early George Gershwin song of the same title). Edwards also appeared in several film "shorts" produced by MGM.

He returned to vaudeville with a new kiddie act in 1930, appearing at Manhattan's Palace Theatre. Among his new "finds" were Ray Bolger, Hildegarde, and the three Lane sisters. With vaudeville rapidly being eclipsed by radio in the 1930s, Edwards retired in 1938. A year later his movie biography, *The Star Maker*, with Bing Crosby appearing as Edwards, was released by Paramount.

Edwards spent his last years with his wife in Los Angeles, where he died in 1945, in chronic poor health in his last six years.

ABOUT: Ewen, D. Great Men of American Popular Song 2d ed. 1972. *Periodicals*—New York Times Magazine March 23, 1941.

ELLINGTON, DUKE (April 29, 1899–May 24, 1974). As a composer of instrumental compositions and songs, and as a performing artist (pianist as well as conductor of his own orchestra), Duke Ellington shaped jazz history. He was born

DUKE ELLINGTON

Edward Kennedy Ellington in Washington, D. C. the son of James Edward Ellington, a former butler and caterer who had become a draftsman at the Navy Yard, and Daisy (Kennedy) Ellington. The Ellingtons' was a musical household, since the mother was a trained pianist and the father played the piano by ear and enjoyed singing opera arias. Edward began piano study when he was seven, but early on he preferred baseball to music. Hearing Harvey Brooks play jazz on the piano during a visit to Philadelphia awakened his interest in music. While attending public school by day, and working after school at D. C.'s Poodle Dog Café, Ellington composed his first musical piece, a piano instrumental called "Soda Fountain Rag." Amenable now to formal training, Ellington received piano instruction from Oliver "Doc" Perry, a jazz musician whom Ellington later described as his "piano parent." Ellington also took lessons in harmony from Henry Grant while attending Armstrong High School.

One of his friends, a meticulous dresser, took to calling Ellington "Duke." "I think," Ellington explained, "that . . . in order for me to be eligible for his constant companionship [he thought] I should have a title."

When Ellington graduated from Armstrong High School in 1917, he received a scholarship to the Pratt Institute in Brooklyn, having won first prize in a drawing competition sponsored by the NAACP. Ellington never took advantage of this opportunity. Instead, during World War I, he earned his living as a messenger for the Navy and the State Department. He also played the piano in bands and later on started an agency

booking bands for social functions; all the while he also operated a sign-painting business which provided the signs for these engagements. On July 2, 1918, Ellington married Edna Thompson, with whom he had a son, Mercer Kennedy Ellington, destined to become a famous musician who took over the leadership of the Ellington band after his father's death. The Duke Ellington marriage ended in divorce, and his second marriage, to Mildred Dixon, terminated in permanent separation. From 1939 until his death, Ellington lived in a common-law marriage with Beatrice ("Evie") Ellis.

Ellington formed his first band in 1919 and it filled engagements in the Washington area for four years. When he was 23, Ellington moved to New York City where, for a time, he played the piano with Wilbur Sweatman's band. In 1923 Ellington composed his first popular song, "Blind Man's Bluff" (lyrics by Jo Trent). That year Ellington organized a five-man jazz band heard regularly at Barron's, then at the Hollywood, both Harlem clubs. At the Hollywood, later renamed the Kentucky Club, Ellington and his band appeared for four and a half years. It was then that he developed the improvisational style and his individual approach to the blues that would become the hallmarks of the Ellington jazz style. With Jo Trent as his lyricist, he was also writing more popular songs. "Jig Walk," "Jim Dandy" and "With You" were introduced in 1924 in *Chocolate Kiddies,* an all-black revue produced in Berlin, Germany.

Impressed by Ellington's talent and popular appeal, the music publisher Irving Mills signed him to an artist's contract. Mills provided Ellington with the money to expand his band to 12 musicians and also negotiated a booking for the group at Harlem's famed Cotton Club, which began on December 11, 1927, and lasted four years. He also arranged for a recording contract. Ellington's first record with his orchestra was "Jig Walk."

During the Cotton Club years, Ellington's unique jazz style came into its own. "We came in with a new style," Ellington recalled. "Our playing was stark and wild and tense. . . . We tried new effects. One of our trombones turned up one night with an ordinary kitchen pot for a sliphorn. It sounded good. We let him keep it until we could get him a handsome gadget that gave him the same effect. We put the Negro feeling and spirit in our music." As a composer of instrumentals, Ellington wrote "Black and Tan Fantasy," "East St. Louis Toodle-Oo," and "The Mooche," all recorded by his orchestra in 1927. *East St. Louis Toodle-Oo* (composed in collaboration with Bubber Miles) became the signature of the Ellington orchestra on the radio in the 1930s. It was included on *Pretzel Logic* (1974), an album by the rock group Steely Dan. *The Mooche* was written with Irving Mills.

Ellington's music was steadily reaching out to new and larger audiences. In addition to his successful nightclub appearances and recordings he was being heard nightly on radio broadcasts emanating from the Cotton Club. In 1929 Ellington and his orchestra were featured in the George and Ira Gershwin Broadway musical *Show Girl,* produced by Florenz Ziegfeld. The following year Ellington and his band made their first motion-picture appearance in *Check and Double Check*. Ellington's song, "Ring Dem Bells" (written with Irving Mills), was introduced by the Ellington orchestra, which also recorded it. In 1931 Ellington composed the hit song "Mood Indigo," which had originated a year earlier as an instrumental and had been recorded by Ellington and his orchestra under the title of "Dreamy Blues." With lyrics added by Irving Mills and Albany Bigard and the change of title, "Mood Indigo" became Ellington's first hit song. It was originally recorded by the Ellington orchestra before being popularized in recordings by Cab Calloway and his orchestra, Gene Austin, Dinah Shore and the Boswell Sisters. "Mood Indigo" was also performed by the Ellington orchestra on the soundtrack of *Paris Blues* (1961). During the early 1930s Ellington began to compose jazz instrumentals in structures more expansive than the three-or-four-minute items he had thus far created. His first extended number was *Creole Rhapsody* (1931), which took up both sides of a 12-inch record.

Ellington made his first foreign appearances in London in 1933. In addition to public concerts he was invited to Buckingham Palace for a command performance. He made his first transcontinental American tour in 1934, and his first extensive tour of Europe in 1939.

Ellington's next standard, "It Don't Mean a Thing if it Ain't Got That Swing" (lyrics by Irving Mills), appeared in 1932. In Ellington's recording Ivie Anderson made her debut as a vocalist with the Ellington orchestra. It was also recorded by the Mills Brothers. This song represents one of the earliest uses of the term "swing" in popular music, several years before swing became a widely known jazz style.

"Sophisticated Lady" (lyrics by Mitchell Parish and Irving Mills) was recorded in 1933 by the Ellington orchestra and the Washboard Rhythm Kings and later by the orchestras of Bunny Berigan, Lionel Hampton and André Kostelanetz, and by Sophie Tucker and Dinah Shore. It was revived in 1984 by Linda Ronstadt in her album

Lush Life. The Ellington orchestra performed it on the soundtrack of *Paris Blues*. "Solitude" (1934, lyrics by Eddie De Lange and Irving Mills) received the $2,500 ASCAP award as the year's best popular song. The Ellington orchestra, Adelaide Hall, Billie Holiday and the Mills Brothers all recorded it. "In a Sentimental Mood" (lyrics by Irving Mills and Manny Kurtz) appeared in 1936 and a year later was recorded by Ben Pollack and his orchestra.

Ellington's first song to reach *Your Hit Parade* was "I Let a Song Go Out of My Heart" (1938, lyrics by Henry Nemo, John Redmond and Irving Mills) where it was heard 12 times, in first position on May 28, 1939. Mildred Bailey and the orchestras of Ellington and Jimmy Dorsey recorded it.

Other Ellington songs that became popular in 1938 were "Prelude to a Kiss" and "Please Forgive Me" (lyrics to both by Irving Gordon and Irving Mills) and "Pyramid" (lyrics by Gordon and Mill, music written with Juan Tizol). In 1939 came "Something to Live For," Ellington's first collaboration with Billie Strayhorn, "Grievin'" (lyrics by Strayhorn) and, with Strayhorn collaborating on the music, "I'm Checking Out Goodbye." Ellington and his orchestra recorded "Pyramid" in 1938.

In the 1930s Ellington and his orchestra appeared in the motion pictures *Murder at the Vanities* (1934) and *The Hit Parade* (1937). In the former, the orchestra introduced the Ellington instrumental *Ebony Rhapsody*. Ellington's first score for the musical stage was for *Jump for Joy* (August 4, 1941), an all-black revue starring Dorothy Dandridge and Ivie Anderson which was produced in Los Angeles. From this show came "I Got it Bad" (lyrics by Paul Francis Webster), which Ivie Anderson introduced and later recorded with the Ellington orchestra. Other notable recordings were made by Frank Sinatra, Dinah Shore and the orchestras of Bunny Berigan and Earl Hines. This song was revived in the movie *This Could Be the Night* (1957). It made a single appearance on *Your Hit Parade* on January 24, 1942. In 1982 Carly Simon included it on her album *Torch*. The title song of *Jump for Joy* (lyrics by Paul Francis Webster) was introduced by Herb Jeffries. In the early 1960s three separate record albums bore the title *Jump for Joy,* those by Peggy Lee, Joe Williams and "Cannonball" Adderly.

Songs by Ellington reappeared on *Your Hit Parade* four times in the years 1942–44. "Don't Get Around Much Anymore" (lyrics by Bob Russell) was adapted from a 1942 Ellington instrumental, *Never No Lament*. After being recorded in 1942 by Benny Goodman it was heard 16 times on *Your Hit Parade*, three times in first position. "Do Nothin' Till You Hear From Me," of 1943, originated as the Ellington instrumental *Concerto for Cootie*. Bob Russell adapted the lyrics to its melody and as such it was represented on *Your Hit Parade*, once on June 14, 1944. In 1943 it became a bestseller in a jazz recording by Stan Kenton and his orchestra. "I'm Beginning to See the Light" (1944, written with Harry James, Johnny Hodges and Don George) became a hit in recordings by Harry James and his orchestra (vocal by Kitty Kallen) and by Ella Fitzgerald with the Ink Spots. This number had 11 appearances on *Your Hit Parade*, twice in first position. "Don't You Know I Care" (lyrics by Mack David) appeared on *Your Hit Parade* a single time on January 27, 1945.

Other Ellington songs of the late 1940s included "I Ain't Got Nothin' But the Blues" (1944, lyrics by Don George); "I'm Just a Lucky So-and-So" (1945, lyrics by Mack David); and, in 1946, "Just Squeeze Me," for which Lee Gaines wrote the lyrics to the melody of Ellington's instrumental, *Subtle Slough*. All were introduced in recordings by Ellington.

Ellington first brought his music to the Broadway musical stage in *Beggar's Holiday* (December 26, 1946), a modern jazz adaptation of the John Gay ballad opera, *The Beggar's Opera*. Book and lyrics were by John Latouche and its cast included Alfred Drake and Zero Mostel. Here "Take Love Easy" was introduced by Bernice Parks and later recorded by Lena Horne. "Maybe I Should Change My Ways," "Tomorrow Mountain," and "I've Got Me" were sung by Alfred Drake. *Beggar's Holiday* ran for 108 performances.

On January 23, 1943, Ellington made the first of eight annual appearances at Carnegie Hall, New York. For this eventful debut he composed *Black, Brown and Beige*, a one-hour symphonic jazz work portraying the history of American blacks. For Ellington's other appearances at Carnegie Hall he again composed ambitious works. The most significant were *New World a' Comin'* (1943), *The Deep South Suite* (1946), *Liberian Suite* (1947) and *The Tattooed Bride* (1948).

Recognition of Ellington's eminence in jazz came from *Downbeat*, the distinguished jazz magazine, whose 1946 readers' poll ranked him tops among jazz artists as did the magazine's critics' poll two years later. *Esquire* presented him with its Gold Award in 1945, 1946 and 1947, and Wilberforce University in Ohio awarded Ellington his first honorary degree in 1949.

For the remainder of his life, Ellington continued to be a prolific composer. He wrote new music for the concert hall, as well as scores for the ballet, screen, television and the nonmusical theater. Among his major symphonic works were *Harlem* (1951), *Night Creature* (1955), *Festival Suite* (1956), *Sweet Thursday* (1960), *My People* (1963), and *Golden Broom and Green Apple* (1964). For the ballet he composed the score for *The River* (1970), produced by the American Ballet Theatre on June 29, 1971. Another ballet, *The Black Kings*, presented by the Alvin Ailey American Theatre on August 13, 1976, used various Ellington compositions as background music. For motion pictures, Ellington's music was heard on the soundtracks of *Anatomy of a Murder (1959), Paris Blues, Assault on a Queen* (1966) and *Change of Mind* (1969). In 1957 Ellington wrote the music for *A Drum Is a Woman*, produced on television for the U.S. Steel Hour, and five years later for the television series, *The Asphalt Jungle*, an ABC-TV production of 1961. His "I Want to Love You" (lyrics by Marshall Barer) was based on *The Asphalt Jungle* score's main theme. For the Shakespearean Festival Theatre at Stratford, Ontario, Ellington contributed incidental music for a 1963 production of *Timon of Athens*. His return to the Broadway musical stage came with *Pousse Café* (March 18, 1966). This was an adaptation by Jerome Weidman of the celebrated film, *Blue Angel* (1930), but set in New Orleans instead of Weimar Germany. This musical, for which he wrote the entire score, lasted only three performances.

Between 1962 and 1965 Ellington made five foreign tours with his orchestra. The one in 1963 was sponsored by the American State Department and took him for the first time to the Middle East, Ceylon, India and Japan. This visit to exotic places inspired the writing of such concert works as *The Far East Suite, Isfahan* and *Mount Marissa*. In 1964 Ellington and his orchestra gave their first concert at New York's Lincoln Center, when *Golden Broom and Green Apple* was introduced. Before the year's end, he and a sextet of musicians from his orchestra, returned to Lincoln Center for the "Great Performer" series where he introduced *A Blue Mural from Two Perspectives*. He completed an 11-month tour of Europe, Bangkok, New Zealand and Australia in 1970, and in 1971 he and his orchestra met with acclaim for a series of performances in the Soviet Union.

Ellington essayed a new form of musical expression when he presented a "jazz-sacred" concert at the Grace Cathedral in San Francisco on September 16, 1965, for which he composed a score for choir. In his music with religious overtones he sought, as he said, to preach "musical sermons" and make "statements of eternal truths." *In the Beginning*, as this production was called, derived its principal subject matter from the opening words of Genesis. The choir sang and a tap dancer performed before the altar. This event met with such approval that Ellington and his performers were called upon to appear in other houses of worship, always with Ellington providing a new musical score for each occasion—at the Cathedral Church of St. John the Divine in New York; St. Sulpice in Paris; Santa Maria del Mar in Barcelona; Coventry Cathedral and Westminster Abbey in England; and in several synagogues where the text was sung in Hebrew.

Between 1960 and 1973 Ellington received 15 honorary degrees from institutions of learning, including those from Yale, Brown and Columbia Universities. In 1969 the cities of New York and Chicago awarded him with gold medals, and city council President Paul Screvane presented him with the New York City Bronze Medal. During 1965 he was awarded a Grammy for the year's best instrumental jazz performance, and another in 1968 for his composition *Far East Suite* as the best recording. The President's Gold Medal was given to him in 1966 in the name of President Lyndon B. Johnson. The Presidential Medal of Freedom, the highest civilian award bestowed by the United States government, came in 1969 to honor his 70th birthday. In 1970 Ellington was elected to membership in the National Institute of Arts and Letters and a year later to the American Academy of Arts and Letters. Yale University established a Duke Ellington fellowship program in 1972 to further the traditions of jazz, blues and gospel music. On February 11, 1972 the CBS-TV network presented a 90-minute panorama of a half-century of Ellington's music. On his 75th birthday, 35 jazz groups and many renowned artists honored him at Carnegie Hall with performances of his works. The U. S. Post Office honored him posthumously in 1986 with a commemorative stamp.

His foreign awards included a gold medal from the city of Paris in 1965; the use of his portrait on the postage stamp of two African nations in 1967; election to membership in the Royal Swedish Academy of Music in 1971 (Ellington was the first popular American composer to receive this honor); and the Legion of Honor decoration from France in 1973.

However, in 1965 an incident occurred that made front-page news and aroused considerable controversy. Ellington was recommended by the Pulitzer Prize Committee for a special citation in recognition of the "vitality and originality of his total productivity." But a Pulitzer official dissented, and the citation was never given. In protest, two members of the committee resigned (Winthrop Sargeant and Robert F. Eyer), and this final decision was denounced by many musical authorities and organizations. Ellington's response was merely, "Fate is being kind to me. Fate doesn't want me to be famous too young."

On March 25, 1974, Ellington was admitted to the Presbyterian Hospital in Manhattan for treatment of cancer of both lungs. He had an electric piano installed in his room so that he could work on an opera. It was never completed. A fatal pneumonia set in, and Duke Ellington died on May 24. Four days later, ten thousand mourners crowded the Episcopal Cathedral Church of St. John the Divine in New York for the funeral services. Many celebrated jazz artists performed his music and delivered eulogies; another 2,500 heard the services by loudspeaker in front of the Cathedral entrance. Ellington was buried at Woodlawn Cemetery in the Bronx, next to the grave of his parents.

Ralph J. Gleason, the eminent jazz critic, described Ellington as "American's most important composer . . . the greatest the American society has produced. . . . Ellington has created his own musical world which has transcended every attempt to impose category upon it and has emerged as a solid body of work unequalled in American music. His songs have become a standard part of the cultural heritage, his longer compositions, a part of the finest art of our times, and his concerts and personal appearances among the most satisfying for an audience of those of any artist."

Nat Hentoff, another distinguished jazz authority, has spoken of Ellington as "the most original composer in the history of American music so far. I would rank Charles Ives second. Both of these composers exulted in the very act of sounding their imagination. And each, out of different memories and experiences in and against the American grain, especially savored the extraordinary variety of liveliness of American life forms which they transmuted into equally energizing musical forms. I did not know Ives. I knew Ellington from the time I was a boy. He was one of the most valuable teachers I ever had, his particular expertise, in and out of his music, having been the continual exploration and stretching of possibility."

Ellington's only success in the Broadway musical theater came posthumously with *Sophisticated Ladies.* When it opened at the Lunt-Fontanne Theatre on March 1, 1981, where it remained for 767 performances, it was thought to have been the most expensive show mounted in New York to that time. Though called a revue, it actually was a grandiose cabaret show, conceived by Donald McKayle, with choreography by McKayle, Henry Le Tang and Michael Smuin, and musical direction by Ellington's son, Mercer. Gregory Hines and Judith Jamison were the stars, but the production's show-stopper was Ellington's music, represented by 36 songs and numerous short instrumentals recorded in an original cast album. Another revival of Ellington's music in 1981 was an adaptation of some of his works for the background music in the nonmusical motion picture *Rough Cut,* starring Burt Reynolds.

ABOUT: Dance, S. The World of Duke Ellington, 1970; Ellington, D. Music Is My Mistress, 1973; Ellington, M. and Dance, S. Duke Ellington in Person, 1978; George, D. The Real Duke Ellington, 1982; Jewell, D. Duke: A Portrait of Duke Ellington, 1977; Ulanov, B. Duke Ellington, 1946. *Periodicals*—Esquire December 1975; High Fidelity November 1974; New Yorker June 25, July 1, July 8, 1944; New York Times Magazine January 17, 1943, September 12, 1965; Stereo Review December 1969, November 1974.

EMMETT, DAN (October 29, 1815–June 28, 1904), composer-lyricist known as "the father of the minstrel show," was born Daniel Decatur Emmett in Mt. Vernon, Ohio, the oldest of four children of Abraham Emmett, a blacksmith, and Sarah (Zerick) Emmett, a music lover. Their ancestors were emigrants from Ireland who settled in Ohio, which was then part of America's western frontier. Daniel's brother, Lafayette, became the first chief justice of the Minnesota judiciary.

Emmett's first experience with music was listening to his mother sing. As a boy, he taught himself to play the violin, on which he was soon inventing tunes. He received no formal academic training, and his early years were spent working in his father's blacksmith shop. After acquiring rudimentary reading and writing skills, he was apprenticed to a printer. When Emmett was 13, he worked for the *Huron Reflector,* a Norwalk, Ohio newspaper, and later with the *Western Aurora* in Mt. Vernon. It was in his four years of newspaper work that he became educated.

When he was 17, Emmett left home for Cincinnati. On May 2, 1834, he enlisted in the U.S. Army, serving as fifer for the 6th U.S. Infantry stationed at Jefferson Barracks in Missouri. There, he took music lessons from the bandmaster, became an adept drummer, and prepared an instruction manual on drumming that was never published.

The disclosure that he was underage, combined with his father's objection to his being in the military ended Emmett's army career on

DAN EMMETT

July 8, 1935. He returned home but soon left for Cincinnati, where he joined a circus. Having become interested in the 19th-century American black experience as a subject for songs, he composed "Bill Crowder" for Frank Whitaker, a black singer. The lyrics were Emmett's, but the melody was borrowed from a popular tune of the 1830s, "Gumbo Chaff." The lyrics described a black man in Cincinnati who picks a fight with a Jewish seller of old clothing. Emmett's interest in the Negro inspired him to learn to play the banjo, which he performed, in blackface, with the Cincinnati Circus in its tour of Ohio, Indiana, Virginia and Kentucky in 1840. About 1841 Emmett worked with the Raymond and Waring Circus and in 1842 with Spalding's North American Circus.

In 1842 Emmett, as banjoist, teamed up with Frank Brower, a singer, dancer and "bone" player. Joined by a third member, a young black dancer known as Master Pierce, this trio appeared at the Franklin Theatre on New York's Chatham Square in November 1842. Their act featured songs, dances and banjo solos. Thereafter Emmett and Brower worked regularly as performers with a circus on the Bowery, with Emmett adding dancing to his performance repertory. Newspapers described him as "the great Southern banjoist" and Brower as "the perfect representation of Southern Negro characters."

The economic depression of 1842 crippled the emerging public entertainment business as theaters closed and performers everywhere found bookings few and far between. Out-of-work solo actors began to form troupes, and in January 1843, Emmett and Brower formed an act with two other unemployed performers, Billy Whitlock and Dave Pelham. In Emmett's rented room on Catherine Street in New York City, they worked out a musical routine, named themselves the Virginia Minstrels, and booked a trial engagement at a pool hall. On February 6, 1843, the Virginia Minstrels presented "a Negro concert" at the Bowery Amphitheatre for one week. The New York *Herald* described their show: "[They are a] novel, grotesque, original and surprisingly melodious Ethiopian band, entitled the Virginia Minstrels, . . . an exclusively musical entertainment combining the banjo, violin, bone castinets, and tambourine, and entirely exempt from the vulgarities and other objectional features which have hitherto characterized Negro extravaganzas." (The term "Ethiopian" was used in the 19th century to characterize black forms of entertainment.)

The Virginia Minstrels performed on a bill with other acts at the Cornucopia on Park Row on February 6, and from February 17 to March 1 at the Olympic Circus at the Park Theatre in New York. But on March 7, at the Masonic Temple in Boston, they were the entire program for what was advertised as an "Ethiopian concert, . . . a complete evening of instrumental and choral music, and comedy." On this occasion they wore blue swallowtail coats, striped calico shirts and white pantaloons, which became the standard costume of minstrel performers. Wearing blackface, they sang, danced and exchanged light banter. Though not yet identified as such, this was the first true minstrel show, and the imitators of the Virginia Minstrels soon began to spring up around the country.

At the Boston debut two now-well-known songs by Emmett were introduced, "Boatman's Song" and "Old Dan Tucker," both sung by a minstrel chorus. In the program, the former was described as a "much-admired song in imitation of Ohio Boatmen" and the latter as a "Virginian Refrain in which is described the ups and downs of Negro life." "Boatman's Dance" became the favorite of minstrel companies in show scenes of black boatmen plying their trade on the Ohio River.

Emmett's inspiration for writing "Old Dan Tucker" was a ne'er-do-well friend. Now a standard, the song's melody was used by both Henry Clay and James K. Polk in the presidential election of 1844, for their campaign songs "Clay and Frelinghuysen" and "Polk, Dallas and Texas." In 1860 the song "Get Out of the Way," adapting the melody of "Old Dan Tucker," promoted the presidential candidacy of John Bell. The melody was also used by antislavery agitators, most significantly by the singing Hutchinson Family in their song, "Get Off the Track." And in a mid-century anti-rent uprising in New York State, tenant farmers sang their version of "Old Dan Tucker" to protest the sharecropperlike conditions imposed on them by landowners. Years later, the melody of "Old Dan Tucker" became popular as a "call" at square dances.

In 1843 Emmett composed and introduced "My Old Aunt Sally," a minstrel-show standard. Later that year the Virginia Minstrels became the first American minstrel troupe to perform in England. Audiences in Liverpool and Manchester showed no enthusiasm for this new form of entertainment, but the response in London prompted the publication there of an album of 13 songs from the group's repertoire.

After the tour of England the Virginia Minstrels broke up, but Emmett and Frank Brower formed a new troupe. Emmett also became a popular solo performer and often appeared in theaters with minstrel troupes that copied the style of his original band. About 1846 he wrote "Blue Tail Fly," also known as "Jimmy Crack Corn." A minstrel-show classic, it is thought to have been a favorite of President Lincoln's. The modern folksinger Burl Ives has made it a staple in his repertory, and it is Ives who is credited with having given the song its alternative title of "Jimmy Crack Corn." Ives has explained that Emmett's lyric "was 'give me cracked corn and I won't care.' Cracked corn was field corn that cracked when you heated it. That didn't mean much to me so I changed it to 'Jimmy Crack Corn'. . . . It still doesn't mean anything. It's a nonsense syllable."

The melody of Emmett's song "Jordan is a Hard Road to Travel" (1953) suggests a Negro spiritual. In addition to being popularized in minstrel shows, the song entered the repertory of the Hutchinson Family, who used it to arouse antislavery sentiment.

In 1858 Emmett became a member of Bryant's Minstrels, starring in and writing comedy skits and playing the banjo. One of his musical pieces was intended as a walk-around, a rousing finale involving the entire company. For this walk-around, Emmett composed "Dixie," originally titled "I Wish I Was in Dixie Land." According to Emmett, it was written one rainy Sunday afternoon in 1859 in the room on 197 Elm Street, New York City, where he and his wife lived. "At first, when I went at the song", Emmett recalled, "I couldn't get anything. But a line, 'I wish I was in Dixie,' kept repeating itself in my mind, and I finally took it for my start. Suddenly I jumped up and sat down at the table to work. When my wife returned I sang it to her. 'It's all about finished now, except the name.

What shall I call it?' 'Why, call it 'I Wish I Was in Dixie Land,' she said. And so it was." Emmett also explained that the phrase "I wish I was in Dixie" came to him one exceptionally cold New York winter day.

"I Wish I Was in Dixie Land" was introduced by Bryant's Minstrels at Mechanics Hall, New York City, on April 4, 1859. The music highlighted a scene expressing the joyousness of blacks in the South. The first part of the song was shared by several comedians; the second part was sung by the entire company. "It made a tremendous hit," noted Emmett, "and before the end of the week everybody in New York was whistling it." By August 10, 1861 the *New York Clipper* was calling "Dixie" "one of the most popular compositions ever produced. . . . [It has] been played, whistled and sung in every quarter of the globe." In 1860 "Dixie's" melody was adapted for the song "Union Dixie," which promoted the campaign of John Bell, the candidate of the Constitutional Union Party. (The Constitutional Union Party attempted to sidestep the slavery issue, but called for adherence to the "constitution of the country, the union of the states and the enforcement of the laws.")

After the start of the Civil War, the Confederacy—disregarding the song's northern origin—dressed the melody with new martial lyrics and "Dixie" became the South's cri de coeur during the war. Just before General Pickett ordered the charge at Gettysburg, he asked that "Dixie" be played to uplift the troups' morale. "It is marvelous with what wildfire rapidity this tune, 'Dixie', has spread over the whole South," wrote Henry Hotze in *Three Months in the Confederate Army*. The day after General Lee surrendered at Appomattox, a band serenaded President Lincoln outside the White House. At the close of a short speech he requested that "Dixie" be played, calling it "one of the best tunes I ever heard."

In the North, Emmett suffered considerable opprobium because he had composed the song that had become the war anthem of the Confederacy. To offset the attacks against him in the northern press, Emmett composed new lyrics for the melody, urging Union troops "to meet those Southern traitors with iron."

In motion pictures "Dixie" became the musical signifier of the antebellum South and of the Civil War period. For instance, the highlight of *Golden Girl* (1951), starring Mitzi Gaynor as a singer during the Civil War, was her performance of "Dixie." How "Dixie" came to be written, and its subsequent history, was dramatized in the motion picture *Dixie* (1943), in which Emmett was portrayed by Bing Crosby. Other films in which "Dixie" was heard were *With a Song in My Heart* (1952); the Sousa biography *Stars and Stripes Forever* (1952), in which it received a rousing Sousa-band treatment; and in the screen biography *Elvis* (1979), in which it was heard in the finale.

Other compositions by Emmett during the Civil War period were "The Road to Richmond," "Walk Along John" and "Here We Are" (also known as "Cross Over Jordan"). In the late 1840s and 1850s he had written "jig" songs, or banjo dance tunes, which Hans Nathan, the author of *Dan Emmett and the Rise of Early Negro Minstrelsy*, considers "among the best and best known of their kind." One of Emmett's most famous jigs is "Root Hog or Die."

Emmett's success both as a composer and as a star of minstrel shows ended with the Civil War. Nevertheless he continued to perform with minstrel troupes, including one of his own, in the years 1865 to 1878. Between 1868 and 1888 he made his home in Chicago. When his voice was gone, he appeared on the stage as a fiddler. He also wrote humorous "Negro sermons" for *The Clipper*, and from 1872 to 1874 he owned and managed a saloon.

In 1888 Emmett returned to Mt. Vernon, where he spent his last years in retirement. There he raised chickens and tended a garden on his small farm. In 1895 Al G. Field, who managed a minstrel troupe, persuaded the 80-year-old Emmett to tour with his company in Ohio from August 21 until April 1896. At each performance the climax of the show was a rendition of "Dixie" by Emmett. As one writer noted, "Dan was not in his best voice, but every time he appeared before the footlights to sing 'Dixie' the audience went wild."

Emmett died at the age of 89 and was buried in an unmarked grave in the Mt. Vernon cemetery. A memorial tablet for Emmett was unveiled in Fletcher, North Carolina in 1927, and in 1931 a boulder inscribed to his memory was unveiled at the Knox County Memorial building in Mt. Vernon.

Emmett was married two times, to Catherine Rivers in about 1852 and to Mary Louise Brower Bird in 1879, four years after the death of his first wife.

ABOUT: Nathan, H. Dan Emmett and the Rise of Early Negro Minstrelsy, 1962.

EVANS, RAY. *See* **LIVINGSTON, JAY** and **EVANS, RAY**

FAIN, SAMMY (June 17, 1902–   ). Composer Fain (originally Feinberg) was born in New York City, the son of Abraham and Manya (Glass) Feinberg. Willie and Eugene Howard, famous stage comedians, were his first cousins. His father was a prominent rabbi and cantor, and both Sammy and his brother, Harry, later a violinist, often sang in the synagogue with their father. Early in Sammy's boyhood, his family moved to a farm in the Catskill Mountains. Sammy taught himself to play the piano and to write music, and while in grammar school, he composed popular songs, which he tried unsuccessfully to market by mail.

On leaving high school, Fain returned to New York, where he became a staff pianist and composer for Jack Mills, Inc. Fain's first song to attract interest was "Nobody Knows What a Red-Headed Mama Can Do" (1925, lyrics by Irving Mills and Al Dubin), which was introduced and recorded by Sophie Tucker. That year, Fain's songs were also heard for the first time on Broadway, when "Keep on Crooning a Tune" (written in collaboration with Irving Weil and Jimmy McHugh) was used in *Sky High,* a musical in which his cousin Willie Howard was the star, and when "In a Little French Café" (lyrics by Mitchell Parish) was interpolated into a "revised" edition of *Chauve Souris,* a Russian song-and-dance revue imported from Paris, which was extremely popular throughout the 1920s.

For several years, Fain earned his living as a vaudevillian with Artie Dunn in an act billed as "Fain and Dunn." In 1927, the team introduced Fain's first hit song, "Let a Smile Be Your Umbrella" (lyrics by Irving Kahal and Francis Wheeler). This number was then sung in a film musical, *It's a Great Life* (1929); it was recorded by the Andrews Sisters and Perry Como.

"Let a Smile Be Your Umbrella" inaugurated a songwriting partnership between Fain and lyricist Irving Kahal that lasted until Kahal's death 17 years later. They composed "I Left My Sugar Standing in the Rain," "There's Something About a Rose That Reminds Me of You" (1928, lyrics by Kahal and Wheeler), and "Wedding Bells Are Breaking Up That Old Gang of Mine" (1929; lyrics by Kahal and Willie Raskin).

With the advent of the "talkies," Fain and Kahal began to write for the movies, but did not move to Hollywood until 1933. Their first screen song was "You Brought a New Kind of Love to Me" (lyrics by Kahal and Pierre Norman), which Maurice Chevalier introduced in *The Big Pond* (1930) and which both he and Ethel Waters recorded that year. This song was interpolated into the Marx Brothers farce, *Monkey Business* (1931), and more than 30 years later it was used

SAMMY FAIN

as a recurrent theme in *New Kind of Love* (1963), where it was sung by Frank Sinatra. "When I Take My Sugar to Tea" (lyrics by Kahal and Norman), composed in 1931, was also interpolated into *Monkey Business* and recordings of it were made by the King Cole Trio and the Boswell Sisters. Fain and Kahal's "Satan's Holiday" was sung by Ethel Merman in the film, *Follow the Leader* (1930).

Throughout the 1930s, Fain and Kahal contributed songs to more than a dozen motion pictures. In *Footlight Parade* (1933), Dick Powell and Ruby Keeler introduced "By a Waterfall" and "Sittin' on a Backyard Fence" (later recorded by Freddy Martin's orchestra) and "Ah, the Moon is Here." Dick Powell introduced "Lonely Lane" in *College Coach* (1933) and Kay Francis, "When Tomorrow Comes" in *Mandalay* (1933). The radio program *Your Hit Parade* first featured a song by Fain and Kahal in 1935; this was "Ev'ry Day," which Rudy Vallee sang in *Sweet Music* (1935), and which he and Will Osborne each recorded that year. For Mae West, the team composed "Now I'm a Lady" (lyrics by Kahal and Sam Coslow) for the motion picture, *Goin' to Town* (1935).

Fain also composed many songs in the 1930s with lyricists other than Kahal. The lyrics for "Was That the Human Thing to Do?" (1930) were written by Joe Young, and "There's a Little Bit of You in Every Love Song," heard in *Moonlight and Pretzels* (1933), was written in collaboration with E. Y. "Yip" Harburg.

In 1937, with Lew Brown as his lyricist, Fain composed "That Old Feeling," one of his most famous ballads and his first song to receive an

Academy Award nomination. After Virginia Verrill introduced it in the motion picture musical, *Walter Wanger's Vogues of 1938* (1937), it was heard 12 times in first position on *Your Hit Parade*. Peggy Lee later recorded it, as did Adelaide Hall and the orchestras of Count Basie, Jan Garber and Lennie Hayton. Brown was also Fain's lyricist for "Our Penthouse on Third Avenue" and "Love is Never Out of Season," which were introduced in *New Faces of 1937* by Harriet Hilliard and William Brady. For the Broadway revue, *George White's Scandals of 1939-40* (August 28, 1939), which starred his cousins, Willie and Eugene Howard, Fain collaborated with Jack Yellen. Together they wrote the score "Are You Havin' Any Fun?" and "Something I Dreamed Last Night" (lyrics by Yellen and Herb Magidson). "Are You Havin' Any Fun?" was featured seven times on *Your Hit Parade*. Ella Logan introduced both songs on the stage and recorded them.

Though Fain was very busy in Hollywood, he also found time to compose scores for four Broadway shows during the 1930s; three were box-office failures. With Kahal he composed the score for *Everybody's Welcome* (October 13, 1931). It starred the Ritz brothers and the Jimmy Dorsey orchestra but it played to half-empty houses for most of its 139 performances. Kahal and Fain fared even worse at the box office with *Right This Way* (January 4, 1938), to which they contributed three songs. Though it left Broadway after 19 performances, two of Fain's songs, "I'll Be Seeing You" and "I Can Dream, Can't I?," both introduced by Tamara, have become standards. "I Can Dream, Can't I?" was an immediate success, and was revived in 1949 with a million-selling record by the Andrews Sisters. "I'll Be Seeing You" was not accepted by the public until recordings by Tommy Dorsey (vocal by Frank Sinatra), Bing Crosby, Billie Holiday, Hildegarde and Dinah Shore made this song one of the most frequently heard ballads during World War II. The song appeared 24 times on *Your Hit Parade* in 1944, 10 times in first position (only two songs ever appeared first more often); and it became the title song of a motion picture starring Ginger Rogers and Joseph Cotton (1940).

With Charles Tobias as lyricist, Fain realized the greatest Broadway success of his career with *Hellzapoppin'* (Septmeber 22, 1938), described in the program as a "screamlined revue designed for laughing." It starred the vaudevillians Olsen and Johnson, in a madcap melange of parody, satire, stunts and outlandish humor, some of it improvised. In this world of absurdity, however, the score seemed lost in the general commotion. But one song had merit: "It's Time to Say Aloha," introduced by Bettymae and Beverly Crane.

Hellzapoppin' broke all existing records for the Broadway run of a musical (1,404 performances) with the help of plugs from columnist and radio personality Walter Winchell. Its successor, again with Olsen and Johnson, was *Sons o' Fun* (December 1, 1941), for which Fain composed the score with lyrics by Jack Yellen and Irving Kahal. Its success was more modest than that of its preedecessor, but it nevertheless ran for 742 performances. Its most prominent song, "Happy in Love" (lyrics by Yellen), was introduced by Ella Logan.

Fain's fourth Broadway venture was the score for the final editon of the *George White Scandals [George White Scandals of 1939-40]* (August 28, 1939), on which he collaborated with Jack Yellen. The show starred Willie and Eugene Howard. Its best songs were "Are You Havin' Any Fun?" and "Something I Dreamed Last Night" (lyrics written with Herb Magidson), both introduced by Ella Logan. Though the whole show was solid, it ran for only 120 performances.

Fain and Yellen also wrote the score of *Boys and Girls Together* (October 1, 1940), a vehicle for comedian Ed Wynn, who dominated the evening. The show had a run of 191 performances.

After Irving Kahal's death in 1942, Fain continued to work with different lyricists during the 1940s in providing songs for stage and screen, as well as independent numbers. With Ralph Freed, he composed "Please Don't Say No," which was introduced by Tommy Dorsey (with the King Sisters) in *Thrill of a Romance* (1945), and "All the Time," which Guy Lombardo and His Royal Canadians played in *No Leave, No Love* (1946). To Howard Dietz's lyrics, he composed "The Dickey Bird Song," sung by Jeanette MacDonald, Ann E. Todd, Jane Powell, and Eleanor Donahue in *Three Daring Daughters* (1948) and made into a hit record by Freddy Martin and his orchestra. "Violins From Nowhere" (lyrics by Herb Magidson) was the hit of *Michael Todd's Peep Show* (1950). Fain's score for Walt Disney's *Alice in Wonderland* (1951), featured the March Hare's "I'm Late" (lyrics by Bob Hilliard). Sammy Cahn provided the lyrics in Fain's scores for Walt Disney's *Peter Pan* (1952) and *Three Girls and a Sailor* (1953), which featured the ballad "Face to Face."

During the late 1940s, Fain also composed several notable independent songs: "The Secretary Song" (1947; lyrics by Jackie Barnett) was introduced in a recording by Ted Weems and his orchestra; "The Wildest Gal in Town" (1947; lyrics by Yellen) became identified with Duke Ellington and Billy Eckstine. "Dear Hearts and

Gentle People" (1949; lyrics by Bob Hilliard) became a smash hit in recordings by Bing Crosby (which sold more than one million discs) and Dinah Shore. It was heard 15 times on *Your Hit Parade,* seven times in first position.

Fain failed to achieve new successes with two Broadway musicals in 1946 and 1951. *Toplitzky of Notre Dame* (December 26, 1946) was a fantasy in which angels assist the Notre Dame football team in its contest with Army. Neither the book nor the score met with favor, though there was some pleasant music, and the show closed after 60 performances. *Flahooley* (May 14, 1951) also had a brief existence (40 performances). This, too, was a fantasy, about a laughing doll and a genie. *Flahooley* had been planned by Fred Saidy and E. Y. Harburg (authors of the book) to be a successor to their earlier musical, *Finian's Rainbow.* Three songs (lyrics by Harburg) had charm: "The World is Your Balloon," "He's Only Wonderful," and "Here's to Your Illusions," all introduced by Barbara Cook (in her Broadway debut) and Jerome Courtland. A revised version, entitled *Jollyanna,* opened in Los Angeles starring Bobby Clark. In 1950, Fain also contributed several songs to the Broadway revue, *Alive and Kicking,* and, in 1955, to the revue *Catch a Star!,* neither one of which was able to survive more than a few weeks. Paul Francis Webster was his lyricist.

In 1955, with Dan Shapiro as lyricist, Fain turned to Broadway with *Ankles Aweigh* (April 18, 1955), an old-fashioned musical comedy with a book by Guy Bolton and Eddie Davis in which a Hollywood starlet and a Navy flier are honeymooning in the Mediterranean. It achieved a modest run of 178 performances.

In 1960 Fain and Paul Francis Webster composed the score for the short-lived *Christine* (book by Pearl Buck and Charles K. Peck), but Fain also reached the high point of his Hollywood career in the score he wrote with Webster for *Calamity Jane* (1953), from which "Secret Love," introduced and recorded by Doris Day, won an Oscar and sold more than a million discs. They won a second Oscar for the title song of *Love is a Many Splendored Thing* (1955). The recording by the Four Aces sold more than one million copies and reached the top of *Your Hit Parade;* other bestselling versions were made by Eddie Fisher, Doris Day, Frank Sinatra, Richard Tucker, Nat "King" Cole and Don Cornell. For this song, Fain received awards at European popular music festivals: the Agosto Massinese Gold Award in Messina, Italy, and the Diploma di Benemerenza in Nice, France.

Many other screen songs by Fain and Webster were also successful and some were nominated for Oscars. "I Speak to the Stars" was introduced by Doris Day in *Lucky Me* (1955). "A Little Love Can Go a Long, Long Way" was interpolated into the motion picture *Ain't Misbehavin'* (1955) and became a bestseller in a recording by the Dream Weavers. In 1957, the title song for *April Love* was sung by Pat Boone, whose recording of it went on to sell more than one million copies. "A Very Precious Love" was introduced in *Marjorie Morningstar* (1958) by Gene Kelly; Doris Day recorded it and received the motion picture industry's Laurel Award.

Title songs provided subsequent hits. "A Certain Smile" (1958), from the motion picture starring Joan Fontaine and Rossano Brazzi, was popularized by Johnny Mathis's bestselling release; "The Gift of Love" (1958), from the film starring Lauren Bacall, was recorded by Vic Damone; and "Tender is the Night" was introduced by Earl Grant in the film starring Jason Robards and Jennifer Jones (1961), and Johnny Mathis's single became such a giant seller that he used the song title for the name of an album.

In 1959, Fain and Webster provided songs for *A Diamond for Carla,* a musical for television starring Anna Maria Alberghetti and Johnny Desmond, who introduced its two best songs, "Fountain of Dreams" and "For the Love of You." *Around the World in Eighty Days,* a musical based on the book by Jules Verne for which Fain wrote music to lyrics by Harold Adamson, was produced by the St. Louis Municipal Opera in 1962; it was then mounted at the Marine Theatre at Jones Beach in New York during the summers of 1963 and 1964. In the fall of 1964, *Something More!* (lyrics by Alan and Marilyn Bergman), a production which starred Barbara Cook, failed to survive two weeks on Broadway. Fain also contributed songs to the films *The Incredible Mr. Limpet* (1964), *Joy in the Morning* (1965), and more recently, *The Rescuers* (1977) and *Just You and Me, Kid* (1979)

On June 18, 1941, Sammy Fain married Sally Fox; they were divorced eight years later. Their son, Franklin J. Fain, has been involved in various theatrical enterprises. Sammy Fain joined ASCAP in 1926 and was elected to its Board of Directors in 1979. He was elected to the Songwriters Hall of Fame in 1969.

ABOUT:ASCAP Biographical Dictionary, 4th ed. 1980; Craig, W. The Great Songwriters of Hollywood, 1980; Notable Names in the American Theatre, 1976. *Periodicals*—Billboard August 18, 1958; Saturday Review January 23, 1950; Time January 23, 1950.

FIELDS, DOROTHY (July 15, 1905–March 28, 1974). Over four and a half decades, Dorothy Fields, in collaboration with a dozen of America's most prestigious composers, wrote the lyrics for some 400 songs and participated in the writing of 19 Broadway shows and more than a dozen screen musicals. She was the foremost woman song lyricist of her generation.

She was born in Allenhurst, New Jersey on July 15, 1905, the youngest of Lewis and Rose (Harris) Fields's four children. Her father was the stage comedian Lew Fields, of the celebrated burlesque team of Weber and Fields. When that partnership broke up, Fields continued to work on Broadway as a producer and actor. Both Fields and his wife were determined to keep their children from the professional stage, although, in addition to Dorothy, both of their sons achieved distinction on Broadway: Joseph as a playwright, producer and director, and Herbert as a librettist (often in collaboration with his sister).

Dorothy Fields received her academic education from private tutors and, later, at the Benjamin School for Girls in New York City. She received piano instruction from private teachers. She was proficient at the piano and as a singer, had a gift for writing verse and displayed a quick lively intelligence, but her poor aptitude for mathematics kept her out of college. While attending the Benjamin School, the teenaged Fields had been romantically involved with Richard Rodgers, then a student at Columbia University.

After finishing her studies at the Benjamin School, Fields taught dramatic arts there. She also worked as a laboratory technician and, with a friend, opened a school in New York where she played piano and her friend taught dancing. On March 6, 1920 she appeared at Manhattan's Plaza Hotel as a singer in an amateur show for which Rodgers and Hart wrote the songs. All this while she was writing poetry, some of which was published in the popular column, "The Conning Tower," in the *New York World.*

Fields eventually met the composer J. Fred Coots at the Woodmore Country Club, where Coots was performing a medley of his song hits and Dorothy a selection of Rodgers and Hart songs. Coots suggested to Fields that she channel her poetry writing into song lyrics, and provided her with one of his own tunes for her maiden effort. "The music was good," Fields recalled, "but the lyrics were terrible." Nevertheless Coots saw her talent, and attempted to interest publishing houses in her. But publishers gave them the cold shoulder, assuming that, if she had any songwriting talent, her influential father would have pro-

DOROTHY FIELDS

moted her career. Her father's attitude, however, was: "Ladies don't write lyrics."

In 1927, through Coots, Fields met Jimmy McHugh, then a composer and professional manager at the publishing house of Mills Music Inc. McHugh introduced her to his boss, Jack Mills, who commissioned her to write the words for "The American Girl," about the aviatrix Ruth Elder, who was planning a transoceanic flight. Fields completed the lyrics in a single evening and was paid 50 dollars. Elder never crossed the ocean by plane, and the Fields lyrics were never published, but the 50-dollar fee made her a professional composer at last.

Then composing songs for revues produced at Harlem's famous Cotton Club, McHugh asked Fields to write lyrics for two or three of those shows. Although no hit songs came out of this, the Cotton Club provided Fields her first experience in the theater. As she told Maurice Wilk, the author of *They're Playing Our Song,* "The curious thing about the Cotton Club was that they had their openings on Sunday nights so that all the stars would come. Big celebrity night. The night that our show, our first, was to open, they also had Duke Ellington and his orchestra—the first time he appeared in New York. We'd rehearsed [some of our songs] with a woman. . . . Opening night, Walter Winchell was there [and at a] huge family table . . . my mother, my father, my first husband, Joe, . . . and [my brother Herbert]. [The woman] came out after the intermission, and she sang three of the dirtiest songs you ever heard in your life. . . . My father looked at me and asked, 'Did you write those lyrics?' and I was green. I said, 'Of course, I didn't.' So Winchell said, 'You'd better do something about it Lew'. So Pop went to the owner and said, 'If you don't make an announcement that my daughter Dorothy didn't write these lyrics, I'm going to punch you right on the floor.' So they made an announcement: 'These lyrics . . . were not written by Dorothy Fields. Music was not written by Jimmy McHugh.' That was my first experience in the theatre."

Also in 1927, Harry Delmar commissioned Fields and McHugh to write a song for his Broadway revue, *Delmar's Revels,* but on opening night he announced he was not using their number. That song, "I Can't Give You Anything But Love, Baby," became McHugh and Fields's first standard. When Fields and McHugh were contracted by Lew Leslie to provide a score for the Broadway musical, *Blackbirds of 1928* (May 9, 1928), they used the number Delmar had rejected and saw it become the show's musical highlight. Other distinctive songs in that score, McHugh and Fields's first for Broadway, were "Digga, Digga Doo," "Doin' the New Low-Down" and "I Must Have That Man."

Fields and McHugh were now in demand for other Broadway shows. *Hello, Daddy* (December 26, 1928) was a Fields family affair. It was produced by Dorothy's father, who also starred; Dorothy wrote the lyrics, and her brother, Herbert, prepared the text. Its best songs were "Futuristic Rhythm," "Let's Sit and Talk About You," "In a Great Big Way" and "Out There Where the Blues Begins." In 1930 Fields and McHugh contributed songs to Lew Leslie's *International Revue* and to his *The Vanderbilt Revue*. Both productions were box-office failures, but out of the *International Revue* came two more standards: "On the Sunny Side of the Street" and "Exactly Like You." "Button Up Your Heart" and "Blue Again" were first heard in *The Vanderbilt Revue*. For *Singin' the Blues,* a 1931 Broadway play with music, they composed the title song and "It's the Darndest Thing."

The next Fields-McHugh standard, "Don't Blame Me," was introduced in *Clowns in Clover,* a Chicago revue of 1932. In 1933, when the Radio City Music Hall was opened as Manhattan's newest and most glittering Art Deco motion picture cathedral, Fields and McHugh contributed three songs for a stage show there in which Fields appeared as a singer. In 1934 another of their standards, "Thank You for a Lovely Evening," was introduced at a Manhattan nightclub, the Palais Royale, while "Lost in the Fog" was introduced at the Riviera nightclub.

Fields and McHugh traveled to Hollywood in 1929. Over the next few years their songs were heard in eight motion pictures produced at MGM. Their first songs for the screen were "Go Home and Tell Your Mother" and "One More Waltz" (for *Love in the Rough,* 1930). Their most important motion picture songs were: the title song for *Cuban Love Song* (1931), the music written in collaboration with Herbert Stothart; "My Dancing Lady" from *Dancing Lady* (1933), starring Joan Crawford; "Lucky Fella" from *The Prizefighter and the Lady* (1933); "I'm in the Mood for Love," "Speaking Confidentially" and "I Feel a Song Comin' On" from *Every Night at Eight* (1935); the title song for *You're an Angel* (1935); "I'm Livin' in a Great Big Way" from *Hooray for Love* (1935); and "Music in My Heart" from *Nitwits* (1935).

After nine years of working with McHugh, Fields had helped write three of the most memorable standards of the era, and now she turned to other composers, including some of the most venerated songwriters in Hollywood and Broadway. In 1934 Jerome Kern's 1933 Broadway musical, *Roberta,* was being made into a movie. For the Hollywood production Kern composed a new number and Fields was asked to write the lyrics. She responded with "Lovely to Look At," which was nominated for an Academy Award and was heard often on *Your Hit Parade*. A year later Kern was contracted to write the music for *I Dream Too Much* (1935), starring Lily Pons, and he asked Fields to be the lyricist for the entire score. From *I Dream Too Much* came the title song; "The Jockey on the Carousel"; "I Got Love" and "I'm the Echo." For the 1936 Fred Astaire–Ginger Rogers movie, *Swing Time,* Kern and Fields wrote "The Way You Look Tonight," which won both composers their first Oscar. Other notable Kern-Fields songs from *Swing Time* were "A Fine Romance," which was heard on *Your Hit Parade*, "Pick Yourself Up" and "Bojangles of Harlem." *Joy of Living,* (1938) starring Irene Dunne, for which Dorothy Fields was coauthor of the screenplay, featured such delightful Kern-Fields tunes as "You Couldn't Be Cuter," which made *Your Hit Parade,* and "Just Let Me Look at You."

Working with Arthur Schwartz, Dorothy Fields returned to the Broadway theater to write the score of *Stars in Your Eyes* (February 9, 1939), starring Ethel Merman and Jimmy Durante. Its principal song, "It's All Yours," was heard on *Your Hit Parade.*

In the early 1940s Fields collaborated with her brother Herbert in writing the texts for four successful Broadway musicals to which she contributed no lyrics. These were *Let's Face It* (October 29, 1941), *Something for the Boys* (January 7,

1943), *Mexican Hayride* (January 26, 1944)—all three with music and lyrics by Cole Porter—and *Annie Get Your Gun* (May 16, 1946), music and lyrics by Irving Berlin.

As a lyricist for the Broadway theater, Dorothy Fields collaborated with the composer Sigmund Romberg on the musical comedy, *Up in Central Park* (January 27, 1945), for which she and her brother were coauthors of the book. From this production came "Close as Pages in a Book" and "April Snow." For two Broadway musicals of the next decade, Fields wrote lyrics to melodies composed by Arthur Schwartz: *A Tree Grows in Brooklyn* (April 19, 1951) and *By the Beautiful Sea* (April 8, 1954). The latter's text was by Dorothy and Herbert Fields. "Love is the Reason," "I'll Buy You a Star" and "Make the Man Love Me" were introduced in *A Tree Grows in Brooklyn;* "More Love Than Your Love" and "Alone Too Long" in *By the Beautiful Sea.*

Arms and the Girl (February 2, 1950) was a Broadway musical adaptation by Dorothy and Herbert Fields of *The Pursuit of Happiness,* a Theatre Guild play set during the Revolutionary War period. The heroine, Jo Kirkland, disguises herself as a man to fight against the Redcoats, and ultimately uncovers a spy and wins the love of Franz, a Hessian. Fields and Morton Gould wrote the music, and one of the show's songs, "There Must Be Something Better Than Love," which was introduced by Pearl Bailey, proved popular with audiences, but *Arms and the Girl* folded after only 134 performances. The complete score was recorded with the original cast.

For *Redhead* (February 5, 1959), book by Herbert Fields, Sidney Sheldon and David Shaw, Albert Hague composed the music and Fields the lyrics. Gwen Verdon was the show's star as Essie, a simple girl who spins elaborate fantasies while working in a London wax museum. Fantasy turns into reality when she falls in love with Tom Baxter, who also works at a mundane job, and helps him solve a murder. With Gwen Verdon's star turn and Bob Fosse's stunning dance routines, *Redhead* was a box-office success (452 performances) and the winner of six Tony Awards. The score, recorded in an original cast album, had two very memorable numbers: "Just for Love," introduced by Verdon, Richard Kiley and Leonard Stone, and "Two Faces in the Dark," introduced by Bob Dixon.

The composer Cy Coleman worked with Fields on two musicals. *Sweet Charity* (January 30, 1966) starred Gwen Verdon and had a score that contained three hit songs: "If My Friends Could See Me Now," "Big Spender" and "There's Gotta Be Something Better Than This." *Two for*

the Seesaw (March 18, 1973), starring Michele Lee, was a musical adaptation of a two-character play by William Gibson. Its most popular songs were the title number, "It's Not Where You Start" and "Nobody Does it Like Me."

Two for the Seesaw was Dorothy Fields's 19th Broadway musical, and, it turned out, her last. After attending an afternoon rehearsal for a road company production of *Seesaw,* she had a coronary and died at her home that evening, March 28, 1974.

In November 1978, 43 of her songs were gathered for *A Lady Needs a Change,* a stage production conceived and directed by Bill Gils and presented at the Manhattan Theatre Club's Cabaret. "By the end of the show," reported Mel Gussow in *The New York Times,* "it is clear that the lyricist's range is as broad as the distance between Broadway and Hollywood."

(More information on the songs and stage productions discussed in this article can be found in the biographies of Cy Coleman, Jerome Kern, Jimmy McHugh, Sigmund Romberg and Arthur Schwartz.)

"When I'm working on songs," Dorothy Fields told Maurice Wilk, "I'm still a book-writer. I'm not out to write popular song hits, thought I've written songs that have become popular. I'm writing a song to fit a spot in the show, to fit a character, to express something about him or her, to move the story line forward. . . . You have to keep thinking of the situation of the play. . . . Other times the sheer pressure of knowing that you need something will draw it out of you."

Dorothy Fields was married twice. In 1925, when she was just 20, she was wed to Dr. J. J. Weiner, a surgeon, for seven months. On July 14, 1938 she married Eli Lahm, a dress manufacturer, with whom she had two children, David, who became a jazz pianist, and Eliza, who pursued a career in the visual arts. Lahm died in 1958. Dorothy made her home in an apartment on Central Park West, and spent her summers on Long Island. Apart from the theater and her family, Fields's interests included listening to opera and symphonic music and looking at paintings by old masters. She also played tennis and took an active interest in such public service organizations as the Girl Scouts and the Federation of Jewish Philanthropies.

ABOUT: Engel, L. Their Words Are Music, 1975; Wilk, M. They're Playing Our Song, 1973. *Periodicals*—ASCAP Today January 1974.

FISHER, FRED (September 30, 1875–January 14, 1942), composer-lyricist, was born Alfred Breitenbach in Cologne, Germany. His early life was adventurous. At the age of 13 he is thought to have ran away from home to join the German Navy. A few years later, or so Fisher claimed, he became a member of the French Foreign Legion, a permanent reminder of which, he was fond of saying, was the saber cut on his jaw.

In 1900 Fisher immigrated to the United States, arriving on a cattle boat. Settling in Chicago, he received his first piano lessons from a black saloon musician. He then developed his piano playing on his own, without benefit of instruction. His first published song was "Ev'ry Little Bit Helps" (1904, lyrics by George Whiting), followed two years later by "I've Said My Last Farewell," which credits J. Helf, the song's publisher, as a collaborator. "If the Man in the Moon Were a Coon," for which Fisher wrote his own lyrics, realized a sheet-music sale of a million copies in 1906. The last of these was a "coon song," an indelicate term then applied to ragtime numbers that were shouted rather than sung, a style which had been popular since the 1880s.

Over the next two decades, Fisher wrote many of Tin Pan Alley's most popular songs. Though Fisher spoke with a weighty German accent that was redolent of Weber and Fields, he assimilated popular American music idioms as if they were in his native musical tongue. In 1910 "Come Josephine in My Flying Machine" (lyrics by Alfred Bryan) was one of Tin Pan Alley's earliest songs about aviation. Blanche Ring introduced it and popularized it in vaudeville; she recorded it in 1910, and so did Harry Talley. It was interpolated into the movie musical, *The Story of Vernon and Irene Castle* (1939), starring Fred Astaire and Ginger Rogers. "Any Little Girl That's a Nice Little Girl is the Right Little Girl for Me" (lyrics by Thomas J. Gray) was also published and recorded in 1910—the recording made by Billy Murray with the American Quartette—and "When I Get You Alone Tonight" (by Alfred Bryan) followed in 1912.

The Broadway play *Peg o' My Heart* (1912), starring Laurette Taylor, was Fisher's inspiration for one of his standards, "Peg o' My Heart" (lyrics by Alfred Bryan). Composed in 1913, it was interpolated for José Collins in the *Ziegfeld Follies of 1913* and was recorded that year by Charles W. Harrison. This song provided the title for a 1933 movie starring Marion Davies. Ann Blyth sang it in the film *Babes on Swing Street* (1944). Revived in 1947 by the Harmonicats in a recording that sold a million copies, it was also successfully recorded by Peggy Lee and by the Three Suns.

FRED FISHER

"Who Paid the Rent for Mrs. Rip Van Winkle When Rip Van Winkle Went Away?" (lyrics by Alfred Bryan) was a novelty number of 1914. Gaby Deslys introduced it in the Broadway musical, *The Belle of Bond Street* (1914), and Al Jolson incorporated it into his repertory. In 1914 Fisher also wrote "There's a Little Spark of Love Still Burning" (lyrics by Joe McCarthy), which Henry Burr recorded, and in 1915, "There's a Broken Heart for Every Light on Broadway." Recorded that year by Edna Brown and in 1916 by Manuel Romain, "There's a Broken Heart" became a favorite of ballad singers in vaudeville. In 1916 Fisher turned to Irish balladry with "Ireland Must Be Heaven" (lyrics by McCarthy and Howard Johnson), which Charles Harrison recorded. "There's a Little Bit of Bad in Every Good Little Girl" (1916, lyrics by Grant Clarke) was recorded by Irving Kaufman and by Billy Murray, and "They Go Wild Simply Wild Over Me" (1917, lyrics by McCarthy) by Marion Harris. The latter was revived in 1942 in the movie musical *For Me and My Gal,* which starred Judy Garland and Gene Kelly, and in 1973 it was interpolated into the Broadway stage revival of *Irene.*

In 1918 World War I inspired the writing of "Lorraine, My Beautiful Lorraine" (lyrics by Alfred Bryan) and "Oui, Oui, Marie." The former became a featured number for Marion Sunshine in her singing career. "Oui, Oui, Marie" (lyrics by Bryan and McCarthy) was interpolated into the Broadway revue, *Star and Guitar.* Betty Grable sang it in the movie musical *When My Baby Smiles At Me* (1948). In the nonmusical film *What Price Glory* (1952), "Oui, Oui, Marie" was sung in French by Corinne Calvet and in English by a male chorus.

The greatest song success of Fisher's career was "Dardanella" of 1919, but in this instance he wrote only the lyrics. "Dardanella" originated as a syncopated fox-trot for piano by Johnny S. Black, called *Turkish Tom Tom*. Fisher acquired the rights to this piece and wrote lyrics for it. After Fisher published the number as "Dardanella," a vaudevillian, Felix Bernard, came forward with a provable claim that he, not Black, had composed the melody and that he had turned it over to Black for a small fee. To avoid further complications, Fisher purchased Bernard's rights for $100. The first recording of "Dardanella," by the orchestra of Ben Selvin, is believed to have sold a million copies. When other recordings became bestsellers, Bernard went to the courts, claiming he had been tricked into disposing of his rights. He lost his case. Two years later, Fisher started litigation of his own against Jerome Kern in which "Dardanella" was involved. Fisher claimed that Kern had appropriated from "Dardanella" the repetitive rhythmic pattern in the bass for Kern's "Ka-luia." The court decided in favor of Fisher, but with damages of only $250. "Dardanella" was heard as a piano selection in the motion pictures *Baby Face* (1933) and *Stella Dallas* (1937).

Fisher's greatest song success after "Dardanella" was "Chicago (That Toddling Town)," the song most often associated with the Windy City. In 1922, the year "Chicago" was published, Paul Whiteman and his orchestra and the Georgians each recorded it. Blossom Seeley popularized it in vaudeville, then sang it in the Blossom Seeley screen biography, *Somebody Loves Me* (1952). "Chicago" was heard in several nonmusical motion pictures, including *Beyond the Forest* (1949), starring Bette Davis and Joseph Cotton, and *Roxie Hart* (1943), starring Ginger Rogers and Adolphe Menjou. In *Beyond the Forest* it was used as a recurring melody, and in *Roxie Hart* it was played under the titles and used in the closing scene. In *The Story of Vernon and Irene Castle* it was sung by a chorus and danced to by Fred Astaire and Ginger Rogers, and it was sung by Jane Froman on the soundtrack of her movie biography, *With a Song In My Heart* (1952), starring Susan Hayward.

Some of Fisher's other hit songs in the 1920s were: "Daddy, You've Been a Mother to Me" (1920, lyrics by Fisher); "I Found a Rose in the Devil's Garden" (1921, lyrics by Willie Raskin); "When the Honeymoon Was Over" (1921, lyrics by Fisher); "I Want You to Want Me to Want You" (1925, lyrics by Bob Schafter and Alfred Bryan); "50 Million Frenchmen Can't Be Wrong" (1927, lyrics by Billy Rose and Willie Raskin), which was recorded by Sophie Tucker; "When the Morning Glories Wake Up in the Morning" (1927, lyrics by Billy Rose), recorded by Don Voorhees and his orchestra; and "Happy Days and Lonely Nights" (1930, lyrics by Billy Rose), which was interpolated for Ruth Etting in the 1930 Broadway musical, *Simple Simon*.

In the mid-1920s, Fisher went to California to write background music for silent films. After the advent of talkies, he contributed songs to some of the earliest film musicals. Fanny Brice introduced "I'd Rather Be Blue Over You" (lyrics by Billy Rose) in *My Man* (1928). Brice recorded it and Barbra Streisand revived "I'd Rather Be Blue" in *Funny Girl* (1968). "I Don't Want Your Kisses" (lyrics by Fisher) was introduced in *So This Is College* (1929), and "Ich Liebe Dich" (lyrics by Martin Broones) in *Wonder of Women* (1929). For the *Hollywood Revue of 1929*, one of the screen's first all-star revues, Fisher provided music for three production numbers: "Strike Up the Band," "Tambourines" and "Tableaux of Jewels." "Blue is the Night" (lyrics by Fisher) was introduced by Norma Shearer in *Their Own Desire* (1930). In *Children of Pleasure* (1930), Lawrence Gray introduced "Girl Trouble" (lyrics by Fisher) and May Boley introduced "Dust" (lyrics by Andy Rice).

Fisher composed little after 1930, but two numbers deserve attention. "Your Feet's Too Big" (1936, lyrics by Ada Benson) was introduced and popularized by Fats Waller. "Whispering Grass," a novelty number, was written in 1940 in collaboration with his daughter, Doris, who composed the music to Fisher's lyrics. It became popular in London in 1941 and was a bestseller in America in a recording by the Ink Spots. Doris Fisher has since had a successful career as a popular song composer, and her brothers, Marvin and Dan, are also professional songwriters.

In his last three years, Fred Fisher was incapacitated by a chronic disease. He committed suicide by hanging in New York City on January 14, 1942. The last song lyric he wrote was: "There's a ranch way up in heaven, that's where I'll soon be found."

Fisher's screen biography, *Oh, You Beautiful Doll*, more fiction than fact, was released in 1949 with S. Z. Sakall portraying the composer. Its untrue premise was that Fisher, a struggling composer of serious concert music, was induced by a song plugger to turn to popular music. He became extremely successful and used the pen name of "Fred Fisher" to conceal his identity. The film's score, though, is a treasury of Fisher's most appealing songs.

ABOUT: Craig, W. Sweet and Lowdown: America's Popular Song Writers, 1978. *Periodicals*—Metronome February 1942; Newsweek January 26, 1942.

FORREST, GEORGE (July 31, 1915–) and **WRIGHT, ROBERT** (September 25, 1914–), have written librettos and songs for Broadway musicals and lyrics or background music for motion pictures as a team since the beginning of their professional careers. George Chichester Forrest Jr., professionally known as George Forrest (and as "Chet" Forrest during his years in Hollywood), was born in Brooklyn in 1915. He was the son of George Chichester Forrest, a vice president of Manufacturer's Trust Company, a New York banking concern, and Isabel Clifton Paine Forrest. George attended Florida elementary schools and Miami Senior High School before being graduated from Palm Beach High in 1930. Between 1928 and 1933, he studied piano with Marian André and Fanny Green and organ with Lew White. From 1930 to 1934 Forrest earned a living as a pianist for dance orchestras, by playing the piano on cruise ships, as a piano accompanist for nightclub performers, and as an entertainer in nightclubs, where he performed a song for which he had written both words and music, "Little Boy Blue."

George Forrest had met Robert Wright in 1929 while both were students at Miami High. Wright was 15, Forrest a year younger. That year they completed their first collaboration, *Hail to Miami High*, a football march.

Robert C. Wright was born in Daytona Beach, Florida in 1914, the son of James August Schleffel Wright, a pharmacist, and Mona Long (Leatherman) Wright. The "Schleffel" was inherited from Viktor von Schleffel, a paternal granduncle who was poet laureate of Germany and author of the romantic novel, *Der Trompeter von Sakkingen*. While in high school, Wright composed the words and music for his first song, "Ship of Defense" (1929). Though never published it was introduced on network radio by Ralph Kirberry, the NBC "Dream Singer." For years Kirberry used "Ship of Defense" as his radio show's musical signature.

After collaborating on their football song, Forrest and Wright joined forces in 1933 to write their first professional song, "I Gave You a Break." It was introduced that summer by Glen Gray and the Casa Loma Orchestra (with Kenny Sargent as vocalist) at the Long Island Casino. In 1936 Forrest and Wright composed "I Stumbled Over Love" for *New Shoes*, an MGM movie short, in which it was sung by Arthur Lake. Performances by Jo Stafford with the Stafford Sis-

GEORGE FORREST

ters and a recording by Guy Lombardo popularized the song.

In 1936 Forrest and Wright went to Hollywood, where, for seven years, they worked mainly for MGM. "MGM offered us what we considered to be staggering salaries in those days," Wright recalled. "We wrote two songs every week and submitted them to [the studio]. We used to come to work every morning at 9 a.m. until we were told that we were embarrassing other people because nobody comes in until 11 a.m." For MGM productions, Forrest and Wright provided several lyrics, for which they received due credit, but they adapted the works of other composers for more than two dozen films for which they received no credit. Of their adaptations, the most important was of the Sigmund Romberg operetta, *Maytime,* a 1937 film for which they composed a completely new score without being identified. Their most successful song during their Hollywood years was "The Donkey Serenade," for which they wrote new lyrics for a Rudolf Friml melody adapted by Herbert Stothart. It was first heard in the 1937 screen adaptation of Friml's operetta, *The Firefly*. Other notable Forrest and Wright songs for the screen were "Always and Always" (music by Edward Ward), which was introduced by Joan Crawford in *Mannequin* (1938) and used by Meredith Willson as the theme music for his radio hour, and "At the Balalaika," a George Posford melody adapted by Stothart with new lyrics by Forrest and Wright. In the film *Balalaika* (1939) it was introduced by Ilona Massey and the Russian Art Choir. "It's a Blue World," for which Forrest and Wright wrote both lyrics and music,

ROBERT WRIGHT

was introduced by Tony Martin in *Music in My Heart* (1940). In the 1950s it was revived by the Four Freshmen and in the 1970s by Robert Goulet.

During their Hollywood years, Forrest and Wright contributed songs to such major NBC radio productions as the Vicks *Radio Hour* in 1936, the Maxwell House *Good News Hour* in 1937, and *Tune Up Time* in 1940. During World War II they wrote the material for the United States Treasury Department's radio program, *Star Parade*.

Forrest and Wright's first stage musical, *Thank You Columbus*, was produced at the Hollywood Playhouse on November 15, 1940. In 1941 Forrest and Wright wrote the lyrics for new musical material interpolated into the stock company shows *Naughty Marietta* and *Rio Rita*, which were produced in Los Angeles and San Francisco. In August 1941 *Fun for the Money*, for which they wrote the complete score, was mounted at the Hollywood Playhouse.

Before leaving Hollywood in 1941 Forrest and Wright wrote the score for the screen adaptation of the Rodgers and Hart Broadway musical, *I Married an Angel*. They spent the summer of 1942 at Camp Tamiment, an adult resort in the Pocono Mountains, where they wrote material for, and served as producers and stage directors of, 11 revues starring Imogene Coca, Betty Garrett, and Lawrence Brooks, all of whom were just breaking into show business. Over the next few years Forrest and Wright wrote songs for nightclub revues in New York and Hollywood, and provided special material for Jane Froman, Marlene Dietrich, Rosemary Clooney, Celeste Holm and Robert Sterling, among others.

Their initiation into the Broadway musical theater took place with special material for the *Ziegfeld Follies of 1943*. In June 1944, their operetta, *Song of Norway*, was mounted by the Los Angeles Civic Opera Company, and on November 21, 1944 it moved to the East and started a run of 860 performances on Broadway. Its text, which Milton Lazarus derived from a play by Homer Curran, was loosely based on the life of the Norwegian composer Edvard Grieg. The story focuses on his early years and his romance with the singer Nina Hagerup, whom he temporarily deserts for a prima donna. When Grieg's lifelong friend, Rikard Nordraak, dies, Grieg marries Nina and fulfills his destiny, becoming Norway's greatest composer. In the operetta, Grieg was played by Lawrence Brooks and Nina Hagerup by Helena Bliss. Drawing freely from Grieg's melodies, Forrest and Wright fashioned popular songs which became their greatest successes to date. The best known was "Strange Music," melody taken from *Wedding Day in Troldhaugen* and *Nocturne* from Grieg's *Lyric Pieces* for piano. Introduced by Brooks and Bliss, it was recorded by Bing Crosby, by the orchestra of Freddy Martin, and had a single appearance on *Your Hit Parade* on November 11, 1944. "I Love You," sung by Helena Bliss and chorus, was derived from the Grieg song of the same title which he had composed for Nina. "Freddy and His Fiddle," derived from one of Grieg's *Norwegian Dances*, was performed by Kent Edwards, Gwen Jones and chorus. "Now," taken from a Grieg waltz and a violin sonata, was introduced by Irra Petina. "Midsummer's Eve," from a scherzo in E minor and the song "Twas on a Lovely Eve in June," were shared by Irra Petina and Robert Shafer.

After closing in New York, *Song of Norway* toured America for three years. Since than it has often been revived by professional, semiprofessional and amateur companies. Guy Lombardo produced it on Long Island at Jones Beach in 1958 and 1959, and the New York City Opera included it in its repertory in 1981. Extensively revised, *Song of Norway* was made into a lavish motion picture in 1970. In addition to the film's soundtrack recording, albums were released of both the original cast performance in 1944 and Lombardo's 1959 revival.

Following their successful practice of adapting the music of another composer, Forrest and Wright used the music from two Victor Herbert's operettas, *The Fortune Teller* and *Serenade*, for *Gypsy Lady* (September 17, 1946), which survived only 79 performances. *Magdalena* (September 20, 1948), which had a run of 68 performances, quoted from the music of Heitor Villa-Lobos. *The Great Waltz*, which opened in Los Angeles in 1949 before going on tour, borrowed the music of the waltz kings, Johann Strauss, both father and son. In this adaptation Forrest and Wright were assisted by Erich Wolfgang Korngold. *Gypsy Lady* appeared in London under the title of *Romany Lady* in 1947, and *The Great Waltz* was mounted there in 1970.

Not until 1953 did Forrest and Wright score another a box-office success on Broadway. It came with *Kismet* (December 3, 1953), which had a run of 583 performances. Adapting the music of Alexander Borodin, *Kismet* was an extravaganza described in the program as a "musical Arabian night." Charles Lederer and Luther Davis adapted a Broadway play by Edward Knobbok from the early 1910s. The setting was ancient Baghdad, and the protagonist was a young caliph who marries Marsinah, the daughter of the poet Hajj. Alfred Drake, Richard Kiley and Doretta Morrow were starred respectively as Hajj, the caliph and Marsinah.

The show's most popular ballad was "Stranger in Paradise," taken from one of Borodin's *Polovtzian Dances* from *Prince Igor.* In 1953–54, it was represented 17 times on *Your Hit Parade,* six times in first position. Bestselling recordings were made by Tony Bennett, the Four Aces and Caterina Valente. In *Kismet* it was sung by Kiley and Morrow. "And This is My Beloved," the melody taken from the *Nocturne* in String Quartet in D major, was a ballad introduced by Kiley, Morrow, Alfred Drake and Henry Calvin. "Baubles, Bangles and Beads" (the scherzo movement from String Quartet in D major) was introduced by Doretta Morrow. Peggy Lee recorded it, and in 1958 it was revived in a recording by the Kirby Stone Four. "Sands of Time" (derived from *In the Steppes of Central Asia*) was sung by a trio, Drake, Morrow and Richard Oneto. "Night of My Nights" (from Borodin's *Serenade,* for piano) was a romantic solo for Kiley, and "Fate" (from the Symphony in B minor) a duet for Drake and Morrow.

Kismet earned a Tony and an Outer Circle Award as the season's best musical with separate Tonys going to Forrest and Wright for the music and lyrics. In 1953 *Kismet* was released as a motion picture starring Howard Keel, Ann Blythe and Vic Damone. These three sang "And This is My Beloved" while Blythe and Damone shared "Stranger in Paradise." In 1963 Kismet was revived at New York's Lincoln Center for a six-week run before embarking on a 20-week tour. In 1971 *Kismet* again toured the United States, and seven years later it was mounted as an all-black Broadway musical and renamed *Timbuktu!* The setting was moved to a mythical African town, Timbuktu, and the Borodin-derived score was infused with African folk music. Despite having Eartha Kitt as it star, *Timbuktu!* was only moderately successful. Both the original cast recording of the 1953 production of *Kismet* and the soundtrack recording of the motion picture were issued.

Subsequent Forrest-Wright musicals were unsuccessful at the box office and with the critics. Inspired by Moliere's comedies, *The Carefree Heart,* for which Forrest and Wright wrote the book as well as the songs, opened and closed out of town in 1957. Two years later the same fate awaited *At The Grand,* the musical stage version of the motion picture *Grand Hotel. Kean,* a Broadway musical based on the life of the 19th-century English actor, Edmund Kean, was adapted from Jean-Paul Sartre's play. It opened on Broadway on November 2, 1961 and ran for just 92 performances. Two of *Kean's* songs deserved mention: "Sweet Danger," which was introduced by Alfred Drake and Joan Weldon and recorded by Judy Garland, and "The Fog and the Grog," sung by Drake, Christopher Hewett, Robert Penn and Arthur Rubin and recorded by the Mitch Miller Singers. *Anya,* with music taken from Rachmaninoff, had a two-week stay on Broadway after it opened on November 29, 1965. Nevertheless some of *Anya's* songs became popular through recordings. Jimmy Rosselli recorded "This is My Kind of Love," and "If This is Goodbye" was recorded by Margaret Whiting and by Jane Kennedy. "Little Hands" was recorded by Jane Morgan, Sarah Vaughan and Tony Messina. "Snowflakes and Sweethearts" was recorded by Leroy Holmes. The original cast album found a much larger audience than the show. Extensively revised, and retitled *I, Anatasia, Anya* was produced at the New World Festival of the Arts in Miami on June 8, 1982.

For *Dumas and Son,* based on the lives of the celebrated French authors, Forrest and Wright adapted the music of Saint-Saëns. It tried out at the Dorothy Chandler Pavilion in Los Angeles on August 1, 1967, but never reached Broadway. *A Song for Cyrano,* a musical stage version of *Cyrano de Bergerac,* had an out-of-town debut in 1971 but was revived at the University of Alabama in 1982.

Forrest and Wright have been artists-in-residence at Boston University (1959), Hope College (1972) in Holland, Michigan and the University of Alabama (1982). In 1981 they conducted a master class in musical theater at the University of Miami in Florida. Neither Forrest nor Wright ever married. They maintain residences together in Coconut Grove, Brooklyn Heights and London. They also share interests in travel, opera, the theater, swimming, gourmet dining, reading and caring for their giant mastiff, the Duchess of Chichester.

ABOUT: Rigdon, W. (ed.) The Biographical Encyclopedia and Who's Who of the American Theatre, 1966. *Periodicals*—New York Times August 23, 1981.

FOSTER, STEPHEN (July 4, 1826–January 13, 1864), composer-lyricist, was born Stephen Collins Foster in Lawrenceville, Pennsylvania, near Pittsburgh, the ninth of ten children of Colonel William Barclay Foster and Eliza Clayland (Tomlinson) Foster. However, four of their brood died in infancy. The father was a merchant who served two terms in the Pennsylvania legislature and earned the title "colonel" through service as a quartermaster for the United States Army in the War of 1812. Aged five, Stephen was enrolled in a private school in Lawrenceville, Pennsylvania, and continued his education at Rev. Joseph Stockton's Academy in Allegheny, where his family had moved when Stephen was six. He was, though, a poor student, impatient with class discipline and the procedures of formal learning. A moody, introspective boy, he liked to wander about the countryside, daydreaming. From his early years, Foster was drawn to music, and had begun picking out simple, pleasant harmonies on the guitar when he was about two. At the age of six, he would march around his home singing at the top of his voice while beating out rhythms on a drum. "There . . . remains something perfectly original about him," his mother reported to one of Stephen's brothers in 1832. Two years later he began teaching himself to play the flute and the piano.

Through Olivia Pise, a household slave, he became acquainted with the music of American blacks. She sang spirituals to Foster and even took him to black church services, where he was spellbound by the sound of the choir. He would later quote from the melodies of gospel songs in his own music. When he was nine, Foster put on a minstrel show for an audience of relatives and neighbors, singing the popular show tunes of the day. "Child as he was, he was greeted with uproarious applause and called back again and again every night the company gave an entertainment, which was three times a week," wrote Stephen's brother, Morrison.

In spite of his early involvement with music, Foster never received any formal instruction. His father considered music suitable only as an avocation for women, and permitted no one in the family to study music.

STEPHEN FOSTER

When Foster was 14, he moved in with one of his brothers, who was working as an engineer in Towanda, in eastern Pennsylvania. Briefly, in 1840, Stephen attended the Athens Academy in Tioga Point, near Towanda. One of his classmates described him: "His complexion was rather dark; his face and head . . . of uniform width, neither wide nor narrow, but well proportioned. He had a tall, large head which was covered with fine nearly black hair that lay flat upon his scalp, and if I recollect correctly his jaws were somewhat square—indicating firmness. . . . [He] kept much to his room and did not join the boys in sports. . . . Foster evidently was rather delicate in health, mainly, I think, because of lack of physical exercise."

At the academy, Foster composed the first piece of music that he committed to paper. Called "Tioga Waltz," it seems to have been written for commencement exercises on April 1, 1841 and was arranged for four flutes, with Foster performing one of them. "Its performance was very satisfactory," recalled Morrison Foster, "and was rewarded with much applause and an encore."

In July 1841 Foster left the academy and enrolled in Jefferson College in Canonsburg, Pennsylvania. He was there just seven days, when he fell ill and dropped out, putting an end to his formal education. From this point on, he devoted himself to writing songs.

About this time, Foster composed his first published song, "Open Thy Lattice, Love" (1844). This song was dedicated to Susan Portland, a 12-year-old girl who lived next door to Foster and with whom he seems to have been in love. The sheet music is a curiosity because Foster's name was listed as "L. C. Foster." However, his name was properly listed on his second song, "There's a Good Time Coming" (lyrics by Charles Mackey), which was published in Cincinnati in 1846.

Several of Foster's songs, for which he now wrote words as well as music, were composed for a men's club called The Knights of S. T. that, in 1845, gathered twice a week at Foster's home and enlivened their meetings with singing. These Foster compositions were influenced by minstrel music. When the first, "Lou'siana Belle," was sung at his club, it "elicited unanimous applause," as Robert Peebles Nevin wrote in the *Atlantic Monthly* in 1867. The club members encouraged Foster to write another for their next meeting, and he produced "Old Uncle Ned," his first song about blacks. "Old Uncle Ned" was a work-weary old man who laid down his shovel and hoe and went to the place "where all good darkies go." It is likely that Foster wrote "Oh, Susanna" for The Knights of S. T. According to Nevin, the acclaim these songs received at club meetings "opened . . . a wide field, [with] each member acting as an agent of dissemination outside, so that in the course of a few nights they were sung in almost every parlor in Pittsburgh. Although limited to one of the slow processes of communication—from mouth to ear— they were introduced into . . . concert halls, and there became known to W. C. Peters who at once addressed letters requesting copies for publication. These were cheerfully granted by the author." For the publication rights to "Lou'siana Belle" and "Old Uncle Ned" Foster received no payment, but "Oh, Susanna" was purchased for $100. "The two 50-dollar bills," Foster once reminisced, "had the effect of starting me on my present vocation as a songwriter."

"Oh, Susanna" was first performed in public at Andrews' Eagle Ice Cream Saloon in Pittsburgh on September 11, 1847, sung by a group called the Vocalists. It soon found its way into the repertories of minstrel shows, where blackface performers sang it to a banjo accompaniment. This song, together with "Lou'siana Belle" and "Old Uncle Ned," became such a fixture in the repertory of the Sable Harmonists that when W.C. Peters published the three numbers, he used the heading "Songs of the Sable Harmonists" on each of the title pages. During the California gold rush of 1849, "Oh, Susanna" was sung so often by prospectors heading west that the melody became an emblem of the movement. It was also a favorite of pioneers and homesteaders on their way through the American West. "It is a glorious bit of nonsense," John Tasker Howard wrote in his biography of Foster. "Here is a love

of boisterous fun, of rollicking good humor that . . . shows a wealth of jovial spirits. . . . The very tilt of the song is catching, so contagious that almost everyone in America was singing it before he realized what he was singing. The song also traveled to foreign lands. The Germans sang '*Ich komm von Alabama, mit der Banjo auf dem knie*' and many other nations have their version of this song. Bayard Taylor, writing in 1853, tells how he heard a wandering Hindu minstrel singing 'Oh, Susanna' in Delhi." In 1936 the melody of "Oh, Susanna" was used as a campaign song for Alf Landon, the presidential nominee of the Republican party.

Foster's father was disturbed that his son was writing songs instead of pursuing a more "practical" occupation. About 1847, his father prevailed on Foster to take a job as a bookkeeper in a commission house in Cincinnati where Stephen's brother was employed. His bookkeeping career proved to be short-lived. By 1848 Foster had left Cincinnati and returned to Pittsburgh to devote himself exclusively to songwriting. He negotiated a contract with a leading New York publishing house, Firth, Pond & Company, which in 1849 released Foster's first two songs under their imprint, "Nelly Was a Lady" and "My Brudder Gum." Foster's sole payment for each of these was 50 copies of sheet music. But, with "Dolcy Jones," his third song for Firth, Pond, a royalty arrangement was established, a payment of two cents per copy sold after expenses. Though Foster's returns from "Dolcy Jones" amounted only to $21.46, the royalty arrangement enabled him to earn a regular yearly income.

Foster published 11 songs in the six months of 1850. The two that were successful were in the humorous manner of "Oh, Susanna." They were "Nelly Bly" and "Camptown Races" (the latter originally published under the title of "Gwine to Run All Night"). As in the case of "Oh, Susanna," both songs were popularized by the Christy Minstrels, the leading minstrel troupe of the time. A favorite of miners and prospectors during the California gold rush was "Camptown Races," the melody of which was used as the basis of Abraham Lincoln's campaign song in the election of 1860.

Though the income from his songs was not enough to support a family, Foster married Jane Denny McDowell, the daughter of a Pittsburgh physician, on July 22, 1850. She was the "Jeanie" who inspired several of his ballads, the most famous of which is "Jeanie With the Light Brown Hair" (1854). Foster won her hand in marriage from a rival suitor, a handsome, prosperous lawyer. The young couple moved in with Foster's brother, whom he paid a weekly rent of $5.

The marriage was doomed, for Foster was a dreamer with little regard for the material things of life and Jane a practical woman who cared little for music and resented her husband's refusal to work a steady job. These problems were compounded by the birth of their only child, Marion, on April 18, 1851. Moreover, the self-centered and withdrawn Stephen lived increasingly in a private world that excluded everyone except his daughter, whom he adored. And Jane, a devout Methodist, was mortified by his heavy drinking and his friendships with show business performers. Nevertheless Foster loved his wife even if only in his own peculiar and inadequate way.

In the decade before the Civil War, Foster affiliated himself and his music with the minstrel show, already the primary market for his songs. By early 1850, Foster was making it a practice to submit his new songs, sometimes before publication, to Ed Christy, of the popular Christy Minstrels. "I wish to unite with you in every effort to encourage a taste for this style of music, so cried down by opera mongers," Foster wrote on February 23, 1850, when he submitted "Camptown Races" and "Dolly Day" for Christy's consideration.

In 1851 Ed Christy asked Foster for a new number about blacks, Foster gave him "Old Folks at Home," or "Suwanee River," his recently completed composition. Originally, in his search for a river with a two-syllable name, he had planned to write about the Pedee or the Yazoo. Rejecting both as insufficiently euphonious, he discovered the Swanee River in northern Florida, and shortened the name to "Swanee."

Foster sold "Old Folks at Home" to Christy for a sum of about $25. Not only did he assign Christy first performing rights but even permitted him to pass himself off as the song's composer, while retaining for himself the royalties from the sheet-music sales. The alacrity with which he served as a ghost composer for Christy derived from the low opinion accorded popular songs about blacks, which were then termed "Ethiopian" songs, and from the fact that Foster regarded his folk numbers and ballads as a truer measure of his abilities. In 1851 the Christy Minstrels introduced "Old Folks at Home" and Firth, Pond published the sheet music as an "Ethiopian melody sung by the Christy Minstrels, written and composed by Ed Christy."

"Old Folks at Home" enjoyed immediate success. It entered the repertories of minstrel companies throughout the country, and in its first year had sheet-music sales of 40,000, earning Foster a royalty of $1,500, the largest amount of money he had ever made at one time. In Sep-

tember 1852 the *Musical World* reported that it was "one of the most successful songs that has ever appeared in any country. The publishers keep two presses running on it, and sometimes three; yet they cannot supply the demand." The *Albany State Register* observed that "Old Folks at Home" was "on everybody's tongue. . . . Pianos and guitars groan with it, night and day; sentimental ladies sing it; sentimental young gentlemen warble it in midnight serenades; volatile young bucks hum it in the midst of their business and pleasures; boatmen roar it out stentorially at all times; all bands play it; amateur flute players agonize over it every spare moment; and singing stars carol it on theatrical boards and at concerts." Success invited imitation. In the early 1850s many songs were published that tried to exploit the popularity of "Old Folks at Home." Among them were George F. Root's "The Old Folks Are Gone," Hattie Livingston's "Young Folks at Home" and H. Craven Griffith's "Young Folks at Home."

Christy's name continued to appear on the sheet music of "Old Folks at Home" until 1879, when the original copyright expired. By then its sheet-music sales had passed the 200,000 mark (its sheet-music sales are now estimated at 20 million copies, making it one of the most profitable songs ever composed by an American). By legislative action it was named the official song of the state of Florida.

The success of "Old Folks at Home" caused Foster to revalue his feelings about the quality of "Ethiopian songs" and brought home to him the folly of crediting Christy with the composition of some of his songs. On May 25, 1852 Foster wrote Christy: "As I once intimated to you, I had the intention of omitting my name on my Ethiopian songs, owing to the prejudice against them by some, which might injure my reputation as a writer of another style of music. But I find that by my efforts I have done a great deal to build up a taste for Ethiopian songs among refined people by making the words suitable to their taste. . . . Therefore, I have concluded to reinstate my name on my songs and to pursue the business without fear or shame and lend all my energy in making the business live, at the same time that I will now wish to establish my name as the best Ethiopian songwriter."

Foster continued to write so-called "Ethiopian songs," selling only the prepublication rights, for about ten dollars a song, to Ed Christy, and acknowledged his own authorship on the sheet music. In 1852 he composed, and Ed Christy introduced, "Massa's in De Cold, Cold Ground," which sold 75,000 copies of sheet music in its first two years of publication, earning Foster a royalty of more than $1,000. In 1853 he wrote "My Old Kentucky Home," his first song about blacks to be derived from personal experience. In 1852 Foster had set foot on southern soil for the first time, when he visited Federal Home, a mansion in Bardstown, Kentucky. This home, now a musuem run by the state of Kentucky, bears an inscription that Foster composed his ballad there, but this is untrue. "My Old Kentucky Home" has been adopted as Kentucky's official song, and it is the anthem for the Kentucky Derby.

Foster's last classic about blacks, and the only one in which the lyrics are not in 19th-century dialect, is "Old Black Joe" (1860). It was inspired by a black man who worked for the Foster family but did not live to see himself immortalized in song.

Outside the genre of minstrel-show music, Foster was a prolific composer of nonethnic sentimental ballads and nostalgic songs. The most significant of these are: "Sweetly She Sleeps, My Alice Fair" (1851); "Old Dog Tray" (1853); "Jeanie With the Light Brown Hair" (1854); "Hard Times Come Again No More," "Some Folks" and "Come Where My Love Lies Dreaming" (1855); "Gentle Annie" (1856); and "Under the Willow She's Sleeping" (1860).

With the outbreak of the Civil War in 1860, sentimental tunes about the Negro became less popular, and Foster's output of songs about home, mother, love or lost love, and death was prodigious. Among these were "Slumber, My Darling" (1862) and "Beautiful Dreamer" (1864). He also wrote war songs—"We Are Coming, Father Abraham," "Was My Brother in the Battle?" and "We've a Million in the Field" in 1862, and "We Still Keep Marching On" and "When This Dreadful War is Ended" a year later.

In 1860, with his wife and daughter, Foster moved to New York City, probably because he wanted to be closer to the popular-song publishing market. By now he was hard pressed to make a living, for the audience for his music had dwindled. To make any money at all he was reduced to hackwork, churning out inferior imitations of his classics, which earned him a pittance. He lived in squalor in a room on the Bowery, and often did not know from whence his next meal would come. Moreover, he suffered fevers that were symptomatic of tuberculosis, and sought release from despair and self-pity in drink.

Unable to tolerate Foster's disintegration, his wife and daughter returned to Pittsburgh. Now he began to drink with self-destructive fervor. One day, his friend George Cooper "found him lying in the hall, blood oozing from a cut in his throat and with a bad bruise on his forehead. . . . The doctor who had been sent for . . . started to sew up the gash in Stephen's throat, and I was horrified to observe that he was using black thread. . . . I decided the doctor was not much good and I went downstairs and got Stephen a big drink of rum which . . . seemed to help him a lot."

Foster was admitted to New York's Bellevue Hospital, where he died in early January 1864, at the age of 37. In his pocket were found three pennies, scrip worth 35 cents and a tattered piece of paper on which was scrawled the phrase, "dear friends and gentle hearts," probably the idea for a ballad. Funeral services were held in Pittsburgh on January 21, with a brass band playing "Old Folks at Home" and "Come Where My Love Lies Dreaming."

"Foster," as this author wrote in *Great Men of American Popular Song*, "was one of the greatest melodists America has produced. Though he was no trained musician, he brought to his best writing the taste, the . . . song structure and at times the inevitability of lyric line that are the fruits of sound musicianship. His creative world was a limited one, but within that world he was lord and master. Writing in a popular vein for a popular form of theatrical entertainment, he tapped veins of emotion and beauty the popular song had not known up to that time.

"His personal tragedy was that he dissipated his great talent as recklessly as he did his energy and his future. . . . He could write a masterpiece with one hand and a potboiler with the other, often without recognizing the value of either. . . . He was incapable of exploiting his talent the way it deserved. Ingenuous, impractical, maladjusted to his environment, given to dreams and fancies that carried him from reality, he was unable to look after himself. He wasted his life and he wasted his talent."

The screen dramatized Stephen Foster's life three times. Douglass Montgomery portrayed him in *Harmony Lane* (1935); Don Ameche in *Swanee River* (1939), in which Al Jolson was starred as Ed Christy; and Billy Shirley in *I Dream of Jeanie* (1932).

ABOUT: Ewen, D. Great Men of American Popular Song, 1970; Howard, J. T. Stephen Foster, America's Troubadour, 1962; Milligan, H. V. Stephen Collins Foster, 1977. *Periodicals*—Stereo Review January 1967; Musical Quarterly April 1944.

FREED, ARTHUR. *See* **BROWN, NACIO HERB** and **FREED, ARTHUR**

FRIML, RUDOLF (December 7, 1879–November 12, 1972), was, with Victor Herbert and Sigmund Romberg, one of the triumvirate who dominated the American operetta in the first decades of the 20th century. Between 1912 and 1930, Friml composed the music for 33 operettas, three of which are considered classics, *The Firefly, Rose-Marie* and *The Vagabond King.*

He was born in Prague. the son of Frank and Marie Slavinska (Kremenak) Friml. His father, a baker who loved music, played the zither and the accordion, and Rudolf was encouraged to play the piano when he was quite young. At the age of ten, he had one of his compositions published, a *Barcarolle* for the piano. Four years later, friends of the family and relatives raised the money to pay for his musical training. He did so well on the Prague Conservatory's entrance examinations that he was admitted to the third year of a six-year course. He studied composition with Antonín Dvořák, theory with Josef Foerster and piano with Josef Juranek.

After graduating from the Conservatory in 1896, Friml was engaged by the violinist Jan Kubelik to appear with him in recitals throughout Europe. While touring with Kubelik for the next decade, Friml won renown as a virtuoso pianist.

In 1901 Kubelik made a concert tour of the United States. When his accompanist fell ill, the violinist hired Friml who served as Kubelik's accompanist for the duration of the tour, and after that in Europe. Friml returned, alone this time, to the United States in 1904 to advance his career, and on November 17, 1904 he made his American debut as a pianist-composer at Carnegie Hall, introducing, with orchestra, his *Concerto in B-flat,* which he followed with a solo performance. He ended the concert by improvising a composition on a theme suggested to him by a member of the audience.

Once again as Kubelik's accompanist, Friml toured the United States in 1906. That fall, Friml was again heard at Carnegie Hall, this time as soloist with the New York Symphony Society, Walter Damrosch conducting, in a repeat performance of his *Concerto in B-flat.* That year Friml appeared in recitals and as a soloist with other orchestras, the enthusiastic response of American audiences convincing him to remain in the United States permanently. Over the next few years, Friml taught piano and composed songs and piano pieces, many of which were published by G. Schirmer Inc.

Chance rather than design dramatically altered the course of Friml's life. In 1911 Arthur Hammerstein, the distinguished Broadway producer, was preparing to mount a new Victor

RUDOLF FRIML

Herbert operetta, *The Firefly,* starring Emma Trentini. But Trentini, who had become a star in Victor Herbert's *Naughty Marietta* in 1910, was no longer on speaking terms with Herbert; and Herbert announced that Trentini would never again appear in any of his operettas. Because Otto Harbach's book for *The Firefly* had been tailored expressly for Trentini, Gustave Schirmer recommended Friml as Herbert's replacement, even though Friml had never composed for the stage. Another leading New York publisher, Max Dreyfus of Harms Inc., agreed that Friml's demonstrable melodic gifts would make for a graceful transition to the composition of operettas, and Hammerstein decided to take the gamble.

The Firefly opened at the Lyric Theatre in New York on December 2, 1912 and ran for 120 performances. Trentini appeared as Nina, a street singer who disguises herself as a boy and becomes a stowaway on a Bermuda-bound ship so she can be near the man she loves. He is Jack, a playboy millionaire who has thus far ignored her. When, years later, Nina has become a famous prima donna, Jack realizes that he has been in love with her all along. For Emma Trentini, Friml composed the most lyrical songs in the score (lyrics by Harbach): "Giannini Mia," "The Dawn of Love," "When a Maid Comes Knocking at Your Heart," and "Love is Like a Firefly." Another pleasing number from the operetta was "Sympathy," a duet for Audrey Maple and Melville Stewart. In 1912 "Sympathy" was recorded by Helen Clark with Walter Van Brunt, and "When a Maid Comes Knocking at Your Heart" by Olive Kline.

The Firefly was revived on Broadway in 1931, and six years later was made into a movie starring Jeanette MacDonald and Allan Jones. The story line and characterizations were altered almost beyond recognition, but Friml's score was untouched, though he added a new song, "The Donkey Serenade," for Allan Jones. Jones's recording sold more than a million discs, making it one of the biggest hit songs of 1937. The melody came from a piano piece, *Chanson,* which Friml had composed in 1920 and whose melody Sigmund Spaeth had used for a song called "Chansonette" in 1922. In 1937 George "Chet" Forrest and Robert Wright wrote new lyrics for it while Herbert Stothart helped make a musical adaptation and this was the version used in the movie version of *The Firefly.* Since 1937, stage revivals of *The Firefly* have included "The Donkey Serenade." This song reappeared in the 1943 movie *Crazy House,* starring Olsen and Johnson. In *Anchors Aweigh* (1944), starring Frank Sinatra and Gene Kelly, it was performed by the piano virtuoso José Iturbi.

Between 1912 and 1924, Friml composed music for about a dozen operettas. His best songs of this period were heard in *High Jinks* (December 10, 1913; 213 performances), *Katinka* (December 23, 1915; 220 performances), *You're in Love* (February 6, 1917; 167 performances) and *Sometime* (October 4, 1918; 283 performances). In *High Jinks*, with Otto Harbach's lyrics, Mana Zucca introduced "Love's Own Kiss"; she also sang, with Emile Lea and Burrell Barbetto, "The Bubble"; and Burrell Barbetto and Elaine Hammerstein and a male chorus performed "Something Seems Tingle-Ingling." From *Katinka* (lyrics by Harbach) came "Allah's Holiday," introduced by Edith Day; the title song, introduced by Samuel Ash and a male chorus; "My Paradise," assigned to Franklyn Ardell; and "Rackety Coo," which was recorded in 1916 by May Maudain. On stage, "Rackety Coo" featured not only the singing of Adele Rowland and chorus but a group of trained pigeons, fluttering and cavorting to the strains of Friml's music. The title song of *You're in Love* (lyrics by Harbach and Edward Clark) was assigned to Lawrence Wheat, Marie Flynn and chorus, and was recorded by Harry MacDonough and the Lyric Quartet. In *Sometime* (lyrics by Rida Johnson Young), Mae West, then an unknown, delivered "Any Kind of Man," the type of provocative song for which she would become famous in the 1930s cinema. Francis Larrimore, star of this opera, was heard in the title song.

Friml's most successful operetta was *Rose-Marie* (September 2, 1924), which had a Broadway run of 550 performances while four road companies toured the country. The libretto,

by Otto Harbach and Oscar Hammerstein II, was set in the Canadian Rockies. The story deals with two lovers, Jim Kenyon and Rose-Marie. When Jim is falsely accused of murder, Rose-Marie is prepared to marry another man to save Jim's life. The Royal Mounted Police clear Jim of the murder charge, making Rose-Marie's sacrifice unnecessary. Mary Ellis, who had been a Metropolitan Opera star, and Dennis King were the leads. For them, Friml composed the score's main love song, "Indian Love Call," while for Ellis alone he wrote "Door of My Dreams." The title song was a duet for Dennis King and Arthur Deagon. The bountiful score (lyrics by Harbach and Hammerstein) also included "The Mounties," a stirring march for chorus, and "Totem Tom-Tom," a production number in which chorus girls were made up to resemble totem poles.

In 1924 "Indian Love Call" was recorded by the orchestras of Leo Reisman and Paul Whiteman and by Virginia Rea, and "Rose-Marie" was recorded by the Okeh Syncopators and by the orchestra of Carl Fenton. Edith Day recorded "Door of My Dreams" and "Indian Love Call" in 1925.

In addition to a brief, second Broadway run in 1927, *Rose-Marie* was filmed three times. The first was a 1928 silent film starring Joan Crawford. With the story radically altered, the first sound version, starring Jeanette MacDonald and Nelson Eddy, was released in 1936 under the title *Rose-Marie,* but was shortly renamed *Indian Love Call.* Eddy and MacDonald sang "Indian Love Song"—their recording of it was a bestseller—while Eddy sang "Rose-Marie." In the second movie version, titled *Rose-Marie* (1954), Ann Blyth and Fernando Lamas sang "Indian Love Call" and Howard Keel sang "Rose-Marie."

In addition to Jeanette MacDonald and Nelson Eddy's version, "Indian Love Call" was recorded by Artie Shaw and his orchestra and by Fritz Kreisler in a transcription for violin. In 1951 the song was revived by Slim Whitman's bestselling recording. Whitman's recording of "Rose-Marie" revived that song in 1954.

After *Rose-Marie,* Friml composed the music for two more popular operettas, each set in the France of the *ancient régime.* The central character of *The Vagabond King* (September 21, 1925; 511 performances) was François Villon, the 15th-century vagabond poet. The book and lyrics by Brian Hooker and W. H. Post were based on J. H. McCarthy's romance, *If I Were King.* In the course of the single day on which Louis XI, on a whim, makes Villon king, the poet makes love to Katherine de Vaucelles, and helps save Paris and the French throne from the Burgundians. Throughout, his peasant sweetheart,

Huguette, remains faithful to him, even ready to sacrifice her life to save his. Dennis King, as Villon, introduced the rousing "Song of the Vagabonds"; King recorded it, as did Vincent Lopez and his orchestra. King shared "Only a Rose" and "Love Me Tonight" with Carolyn Thomson, who introduced "Some Day" and recorded "Only a Rose." Jane Carroll introduced the "Huguette Waltz."

In addition to periodic stage revivals in the popular musical theater, including returns to New York in 1943 and 1961, *The Vagabond King* was mounted by the Houston Grand Opera. The two film versions starred Dennis King and Jeanette MacDonald in 1930 and Kathryn Grayson, Oreste and Rita Moreno in 1956. In the first version, Jeanette MacDonald sang "Only a Rose"; Dennis King and chorus, "The Song of the Vagabonds"; Lillian Roth, "Huguette Waltz"; and King and MacDonald, "Some Day." The second film, with a greatly truncated stage score, had Oreste and chorus sing "Song of the Vagabonds" and Kathryn Grayson "Some Day." In 1950 "The Song of the Vagabonds" was revived by John Raitt's recording.

Friml's last successful operetta was *The Three Musketeers* (March 13, 1928), which ran for 319 performances. William Anthony McGuire adapted the famous Dumas romance and Clifford Grey and P. G. Wodehouse wrote the lyrics. Dennis King portrayed D'Artagnan, who falls in love with Constance Boncieux and teams up with his fellow musketeers to perform heroics in London and Paris for their king and queen. Dennis King introduced the score's principal ballad, "Heart of Mine." Another ballad, "Ma Belle," was sung by Joseph Macauley. "All For One" was the musketeers' song in the robust manner of "Song of the Vagabonds." Despite its box-office success when first mounted on Broadway, *The Three Musketeers* was never made into a motion picture and not until November 4, 1984 was it revived in New York.

Friml's last two musicals were failures, *Luana* (1930), a play with a Hawaiian setting, and *Music Hath Charms* (1934), neither of which survived a month of the Broadway stage. Friml was never again represented on Broadway with a new production, inasmuch as the vogue for old-fashioned operettas was over. He told an interviewer in the 1930s: "I like books with charm to them. And charm suggests the old things—the finest being things that were done long ago. I like full-blooded librettos with luscious melody, rousing choruses and romantic passion. . . . I can't write music unless there are romance, glamour and heroes."

Besides the songs from his operettas, Friml is remembered for a concert song composed in 1922, "L'Amour, toujours l'amour—Love Everlasting." Richard Crooks and Lily Pons each recorded it and, in 1944, it was sung by Susanna Foster in the movie *This is the Life*.

In 1934 Friml moved to Hollywood, where over the next 15 years he helped adapt his operettas for the screen. He also contributed songs to two films, *Music for Madame* (1937) and *Northwest Passage* (1939), starring Spencer Tracy and Walter Brennan. After that he composed concert music, most of which was never performed or recorded. However, as a pianist-conductor he appeared often in concert in the United States and Europe, performing his own popular compositions.

As he got older Friml maintained his vitality by adhering to a rigorous program of exercise, jogging and bicycling. His spectacular home in the Hollywood hills had been previously owned by Alexander Korda, and it was later purchased by Ginger Rogers. Its interior decoration scheme was Oriental, reflecting not only Friml's many travels to the Orient but also his marriage on April 16, 1957 to a young Chinese woman, Kay Ling, who had been his secretary. This was his fourth marriage. The first, to Mathilde Baruch, took place on May 26, 1909. Six years later, she divorced him and named as correspondent Emma Trentini. Friml then married Blanche Betters, whom he divorced in 1918, and one year later married Elsie Lawson. Rudolf Friml Jr., from the marriage to Lawson, became an orchestra conductor. Friml had two other children, a son and a daughter, both from his first marriage.

Friml's 90th birthday was celebrated in Manhattan by ASCAP on December 7, 1969. With Friml present, numbers from his successful operettas were sung, and Ogden Nash contributed a set of verses which ended: "I trust that your conclusion and mine are similar/'Twould be a happier world if it were Frimler."

A Rudolf Friml library was established at the University of California at Los Angeles in 1970, comprising 100 of his manuscripts as well as numerous tapes and recordings. In commemoration of the centenary of Friml's birth, New York City Mayor Edward Koch proclaimed December 7, 1979 as "Rudolf Friml Broadway Day."

ABOUT: Rigdon, W. (ed.) The Biographical Encylcopedia & Who's Who of the American Theatre, 1966. *Periodicals*—High Fidelity/Musical America November 1972; Music Business April 1946.

GERSHWIN, GEORGE (September 26, 1898–July 11, 1937). While George Gershwin was still alive, Isaac Goldberg, his first biographer, described him as a Colossus bestriding the world of music, with one foot planted in Carnegie' Hall and the other in Tin Pan Alley. He was a prolific composer for Broadway and Hollywood musicals, collaborating most often with his brother, Ira, who provided clever and witty lyrics. He also composed an opera and works for the concert hall, and his music in all genres was unusual for its time because of its sophisticated use of harmonic and rhythmic devices drawn from the newly discovered jazz and the blues. His songs were extremely popular during his lifetime and many of them have continued to be the favorites of well-known popular singers and jazz artists.

George Gershwin (originally Jacob Gershvin) was born at 242 Snedicker Avenue in Brooklyn. He was the second of four children of Morris and Rose (Bruskin) Gershvin who had emigrated from Russia; his older brother, Ira, later became his lyricist. At the time of George's birth, Morris Gershvin was a designer of fancy uppers for women's shoes; he soon opened a small stationery store in Brooklyn, from which he progressed to owning and running restaurants, Turkish baths, bakeries, rooming houses, a pool parlor, a summer hotel and a booking establishment at the Belmont racetrack. Because Morris Gershvin·liked living near the base of his business operations, the family was always on the move; they occupied 28 different apartments between 1900 and 1917. While George was still an infant, the Gershvins settled on the East Side of Manhattan, and it was there that George spent most of his childhood.

None of the Gershwins were musical, and in his early years, George gave little indication of being an exception. He was a child of the city streets, where he played punch ball, street hockey and "cat." He attended P. S. 20, and later P. S. 25, both on the East Side, but unlike his brother, Ira, he was no scholar—he avoided books and homework and frequently disrupted the class. On several occasions, Ira was called upon to "straighten out" George's classroom problems. It was only with difficulty that George achieved passing grades.

Yet there had been signs that George was musical. When he was about six, a rendition of Anton Rubinstein's *Melody in F* emanating from an automatic piano in a penny arcade made a deep impression: "The peculiar jumps in the music held me rooted," he later recalled. "To this day, I can't hear the tune without picturing myself outside the arcade." At about the same time, Gershwin would sit for hours outside Baron

GEORGE GERSHWIN

Wilkin's club in Harlem and listen to Jim Europe's jazz band and the sounds of spirituals, the blues and rags. Four years later, while he was playing ball outside the school, he heard the strains of Dvořák's *Humoresque.* "It was a revelation," he recalled. George befriended the performer, fellow schoolmate Maxie Rosenzweig, who later became famous as the virtuoso violinist Max Rosen. Through Maxie, George learned about the world of concert music for the first time, and inspired by their conversations, George began to fashion little tunes of his own on a friend's piano. When he played one of these pieces for Maxie, the young violinist told him firmly: "You haven't got it in you to be a musician, George. Take my word for it, *I know.*"

In 1910, the Gershwin family acquired an upright piano, which George monopolized (much to the relief of Ira, for whom it had been intended). He sought out a neighborhood teacher, Miss Green, who, for 50 cents a lesson, coached him through Beyer's exercise book. He also studied with two other local teachers, when, in 1912, a friend introduced him to Charles Hambitzer, a composer and pianist. After George played for him, Hambitzer remarked wryly, "Let's hunt out that guy [who taught you to play this way] and shoot him." But Gershwin's seriousness impressed Hambitzer, who accepted him as a pupil without asking any fee. Hambitzer, a splendid musician, had a profound effect on Gershwin's musical development. He introduced the young Gershwin to the piano literature, including works by the moderns; he made Gershwin aware of harmony, theory and instrumentation; he encouraged him to go to concerts. And Hambitzer was well aware of Gershwin's talent: "I have a new pupil," he wrote to his sister, "who will make a mark in music if anybody else will. The boy is a genius, without a doubt; he's crazy about music and can't wait until it's time to take his lessons."

Though Hambitzer was able to instill in Gershwin his own admiration for the masterworks of the great composers, he could not lure him away from popular music. Time and time again, George attempted to convince Hambitzer of the artistic validity of Tin Pan Alley, particularly of the songs of Irving Berlin and Jerome Kern. He also insisted that his own ambitions lay in the direction of writing music such as theirs and not in the music of the concert hall. Though Hambitzer felt Gershwin was a "genius," he also remarked: "He wants to go in for the modern stuff, jazz and what not. But I'm not going to let him for a while. I'll see that he gets a firm foundation in the standard music first."

In 1912, Gershwin enrolled in the High School of Commerce to prepare for a career as an accountant. That year, he also made his first public appearance as a pianist at the school, performing tunes from Tin Pan Alley. The following summer, he played piano at a Catskills resort for a weekly salary of $5. He also composed his first songs (to lyrics by Leonard Praskins), "Since I Found You" and "Ragging the *Träumere*"; neither was published.

Convinced that his destiny lay in popular music, Gershwin found a job as staff pianist and song plugger for the Tin Pan Alley publishing house of Jerome H. Remick, at a salary of $15 per week. He began to learn the business from the inside, and he became acquainted with the great composers such as Irving Berlin and Jerome Kern; his seriousness about music was evident when he continued to study the piano with Hambitzer. In 1915, Gershwin became Edward Kilenyi's pupil in harmony, theory and orchestration. According to Kilenyi, "He had an extraordinary facility or genius to absorb everything and to apply what he learned to his own use."

Gershwin's colleagues in Tin Pan Alley soon came to regard him as someone quite special. Lyricist Irving Caesar said of Gershwin's piano playing: "His rhythm had the impact of a sledgehammer. His harmonies were years ahead of their time. I never heard such playing of popular music." Harry Ruby, a song plugger who subsequently became an eminent song composer, remarked: "Sometimes, when he spoke of the artistic mission of popular music we thought he was going 'highfalutin'. . . . We just didn't understand what he was talking about." Sophie

Tucker, already a star in vaudeville, became so interested in young Gershwin that, in 1916, she used her influence to persuade Harry Von Tilzer to release Gershwin's first published song, "When You Want 'Em You Can't Get 'Em; When You Got 'Em, You Don't Want 'Em" (lyrics by Murray Roth); the only income it generated was the five dollars Gershwin had been given as an advance. Sigmund Romberg, a successful Broadway composer, incorporated one of Gershwin's songs, "The Making of a Girl" (lyrics by Harold Atteridge) into his score for *The Passing Show of 1916*. From this, Gershwin earned a total of seven dollars in royalties from sheet music sales.

In 1916, Gershwin also began to make piano rolls for the Perfection Music Company and for the Universal Company, at a fee of $25 for six rolls; some of these were released under pseudonyms. At the same time, Gershwin collaborated with Will Donaldson in composing a piano rag, *Rialto Ripples*, which Remick published in 1917.

In March 1917, Gershwin left Remick's to broaden his horizons. Irving Berlin offered him a job as arranger and musical secretary at the considerable salary of $100 a week. But Berlin added: "The job is yours if you want it, but I hope you don't take it. You are much too talented to be somebody else's arranger. You are meant for big things." Deciding to make his own way, Gershwin declined Berlin's offer. He replaced Chico Marx as pianist at Fox's City Theatre on 14th Street for $25 a week. He then became the rehearsal pianist for the Jerome Kern–Victor Herbert musical, *Miss 1917*, where his piano-playing and improvisations attracted the attention of Jerome Kern. Though the show closed after only 48 performances, "this young man is going places," Kern said. Gershwin then began to accompany the Sunday evening concerts at the Century Theatre. On the evening of November 18, 1917, Broadway star Vivienne Segal sang Gershwin's "You-oo, Just You" and "There's More to the Kiss Than X-X-X" (lyrics by Irving Caesar); soon after, Adele Rowland sang "You-oo, Just You" on Broadway in *Hitchy-Koo of 1918*.

In February 1918, Gershwin was hired as staff composer by the publishing house of T.B. Harms, Inc., headed by Max Dreyfus. "He was the kind of man I like to gamble on," Dreyfus said, "and I decided to gamble." Gershwin was paid $35 a week to write songs for possible publication. Harms's first published song by Gershwin was "Some Wonderful Sort of Someone" (lyrics by Schuyler Greene) issued in September 1918 and later placed in the Broadway musical *The Lady in Red* (1919).

On October 24, 1918, "The Real American Folk Song" became Gershwin's first song with lyrics by his brother, Ira, to be heard on the stage; it was introduced by the well-known actress and vaudeville star Nora Bayes in *Ladies First*. Through the influence of Max Dreyfus, he was assigned to compose the complete score for *Half-Past Eight*, a revue that opened in Syracuse, New York (December 19, 1818) and closed four evenings later. But he was able to place "There's More to the Kiss Than X-X-X" and "I Was So Young, You Were So Beautiful" (lyrics by Irving Caesar and Alfred Bryan) in the English musical, *Good Morning, Judge* (1919), which had come to Broadway.

Gershwin's first complete Broadway musical score was for producer Alex A. Aaron's *La, La, Lucille* (May 26, 1919), which ran at the Henry Miller Theatre for 104 performances. The action takes places in the bridal suite of a Philadelphia hotel, where John Smith, a dentist, and his wife, Lucille, pretend to be unfaithful and divorce. When they separate, John will inherit two million dollars. Complications ensue, and in the end, it is revealed that John's aunt was only testing the strength of their vows and the couple passes the test with flying colors. The Gershwin score (lyrics by Arthur Jackson and B. G. De Sylva) included songs previously composed for Tin Pan Alley, "There's More to the Kiss Than X-X-X" (retitled "There's More to the Kiss Than the Sound") and "Nobody But You," which was introduced by Helen Clark, Lorin Baker and chorus. Among the new numbers were "Tee-Oodle-Um-Bum-Bo" and "From Now On."

The year of 1919 brought Gershwin not only his first Broadway musical, but also "Swanee," (lyrics by Irving Caesar), his first hit song. It was heard in New York for the first time on October 24, 1919 in the stage show devised by Ned Wayburn for the opening of the Capitol Theatre, a motion-picture palace. Accompanied by Arthur Pryor's band, "Swanee" was sung by 60 chorus girls dancing to its strains with electric lights on their slippers. At the time, the song made little impression and few customers bought the sheet music being sold in the lobby. Had it not been for Al Jolson, the history of "Swanee" might have ended then and there. Jolson incorporated it into his Winter Garden extravaganza, *Sinbad* (1919), and although it had been released by the All-Star Trio and the Peerless Quartette, it was Jolson's 1920 recording that became a giant seller. By the end of the year, more than two million records and one million copies of sheet music had been sold, bringing Gershwin and Caesar substantial royalties of $10,000 each. It also continued to be a hit for Jolson, who later sang it in the motion pictures *The Jolson Story* (1946), *Jolson Sings Again* (1949) and in the Gershwin screen biography, *Rhapsody in Blue* (1946); his new recording in 1945 sold over one million copies. Judy Garland also made a successful recording of it in 1939 and sang it in the film, *A Star Is Born* (1953).

In 1919, George White made his debut as a Broadway producer with *Scandals of 1919*, modeled on Ziegfeld's *Follies*. For the second edition, Gershwin was engaged to write the complete score; contracts for the four successive editions followed. The second most important revue on Broadway, it was a prestigious showcase for the 45 songs contributed. The best were "I'll Build a Stairway to Paradise" (lyrics by B. G. De Sylva and Ira Gershwin) from the *Scandals of 1922* (August 28, 1922) and "Somebody Loves Me" (lyrics by De Sylva and Ballard MacDonald) from the *Scandals of 1924* (June 30, 1924), both introduced by Winnie Lightner, accompanied by the Paul Whiteman orchestra in the pit. They have been recorded by such artists as Sarah Vaughan, June Valli, Marion Harris, Tom and Isabelle Patricola, Eddie Fisher, Jane Froman, Aileen Stanley and the orchestras of Sam Lanin, Ray Miller and Paul Whiteman, and were also heard in the motion pictures *Broadway Rhythm* (1944), *Rhapsody in Blue* (1945), *Lullaby of Broadway* (1951) and *An American in Paris* (1951).

In addition to the songs, Gershwin also composed music for a one-act jazz opera, *Blue Monday Blues* (libretto by B. G. De Sylva) which was included in the opening-night presentation of the *Scandals of 1922*. It was subsequently removed from the program because White felt it was too somber for a Broadway revue. But it has not been forgotten—renamed *135th Street*, it has been revived in concerts, and was televised on the "Omnibus" program (1953).

Between 1920 and 1925, Gershwin also contributed individual songs to other Broadway productions. "Innocent Ingenue Baby" (music written with William Daly, lyrics by Brian Hooker) was introduced by John Merkyl in *Our Nell* (1922); Irene Bordoni introduced "Do it Again" (lyrics by B. G. De Sylva) in *The French Doll* (1922) and "I Won't Say I Will, But I Won't Say I Won't" (lyrics by De Sylva and Ira Gershwin) in *Little Miss Bluebeard* (1923). "Do it Again" remained little known and rarely heard for some years, as it could not be broadcast over the radio because of the sexual overtones of its double entendres. When it finally was permissible to play it on the air, it became a Gershwin song favorite and was recorded by Helen Morgan, Sarah Vaughan, Jaye P. Morgan and others. It was also revived in the films *Rhapsody in Blue* and *The Helen Morgan Story*, and Liza Minnelli sang it in *A Matter of Time* (1976).

The inventiveness of the rhythmic, harmonic and melodic writing in Gershwin's best songs also found admirers in the world of concert music. In an interview on September 6, 1922, Beryl Rubinstein, the piano virtuoso, then a faculty member at the Cleveland Institute of Music, called Gershwin "a great composer," adding that "this young fellow has the spark of musical genius . . . the fire of originality. . . . With Gershwin's style and seriousness he is not definitely from the popular-music school, but one of the really outstanding figures in the country's musical efforts. . . . I really believe that America will on a distant date honor [him] for his talent." Gilbert Seldes, apostle of the seven lively arts, wrote in the literary journal *The Dial* (August 1923) that "Delicacy, even dreaminess, is a quality he [Gershwin] alone brings into jazz music. And his sense of variation in rhythm, of an oddly placed accent, of emphasis and color is impeccable." On November 1, 1923, the celebrated concert singer, Eva Gauthier, gave a recital in Aeolian Hall, New York, in which she presented vocal masterpieces of the past and of the twentieth century. Her final group was composed of American popular songs, including three by Gershwin, "I'll Build a Stairway to Paradise," "Swanee," and "Innocent Ingenue Baby"; Gershwin was at the piano. This was the first time Gershwin's music had been heard in a concert hall, an occasion which writer and critic Carl Van Vechten considered to be "one of the very most important events in American musical history."

Though Gershwin was already held in high esteem by eminent writers and musicians, he continued to study music. He hired orchestral musicians to teach him to play the different instruments of the orchestra, and, in 1923, he studied composition with Rubin Goldmark, who was also one of Aaron Copland's teachers. In later years, he continued these studies with Henry Cowell, Joseph Schillinger and Wallingford Riegger.

One of those who had been strongly impressed by the new vistas opened up by *Blue Monday Blues* was Paul Whiteman, the orchestra leader who had conducted the opera in the *Scandals*. Whiteman was planning a concert of American music at Aeolian Hall, New York, and for this event he urged Gershwin to write an extended serious work for orchestra in a jazz idiom. The composition Gershwin produced for Whiteman was *Rhapsody in Blue*, introduced on February 12, 1924. It was an overwhelming success, eliciting an ovation that lasted several minutes. The

next day several critics hailed it as one of the most significant works in twentieth-century music. There were several dissenting voices—notably those of Lawrence Gilman and Pitts Sanborn—but nonetheless *Rhapsody in Blue* immediately established itself as "the foremost serious effort by an American composer," according to one critic. It was performed extensively in Europe and America; it was transcribed for every possible instrument or combination of instruments; it was the inspiration for several ballets; its initial recording by Paul Whiteman was a bestseller; it was sold to the movies. *Rhapsody in Blue* brought Gershwin international fame and wealth as well as the admiration of the entire music world.

Gershwin also continued to write for Broadway, and 1924 was an important year in his songwriting career. He composed the scores for *Sweet Little Devil* (January 21, 1924) to lyrics by De Sylva, the highly successful *Lady, Be Good!* (December 1, 1924), with a book by Guy Bolton and Fred Thompson. *Lady, Be Good!*, which had a run of 330 performances, starred Fred and Adele Astaire as Dick and Susie Trevors, a brother and sister who have come upon hard times. Dick considers marrying a rich girl he does not love, but Susie saves the day when she becomes involved in a Mexican scheme and falls in love with a man, who, unbeknownst to her, is extremely wealthy. *Lady, Be Good!* was the first of Gershwin's musicals to which his brother, Ira, contributed all of the lyrics. The delightful title song, "Oh, Lady, Be Good!" was introduced by Walter Catlett, was later recorded by Fred Astaire, Cliff Edwards, Jane Froman and Ella Fitzgerald, and it also served as title song for a motion picture starring Ann Sothern (1941). Though the story line was completely changed in the film adaptation of *Lady, Be Good!*, the score retained two of the principal songs from the stage production, "Fascinating Rhythm" and "The Half Of it, Dearie, Blues." On Broadway, "Fascinating Rhythm" was introduced by Fred and Adele Astaire with Cliff Edwards, and "The Half Of It, Dearie, Blues" was written for Fred Astaire, whose delivery of it with Kathryn Martyn was followed by his first performance of a tap dance solo.

The Gershwins had written "The Man I Love" for Adele Astaire but the song was deleted during the Philadelphia tryouts. Efforts were made to place it in several other shows, but it never enjoyed the benefit of a Broadway showcase. Nevertheless, it has become one of Gershwin's most celebrated and frequently sung love ballads. It first caught on in Paris and in London, where, in 1924, the distinguished composer of concert music, John Ireland, called it "a masterpiece. . . . Perfect. . . . It will live on as long as a Schubert lied or a Brahms waltz." In the United States, it was introduced in 1925 by Eva Gauthier at a concert in Derby, Connecticut with Gershwin again serving as her accompanist; the song was then recorded by Marion Harris, Helen Morgan, Jane Froman, Sophie Tucker, Frances Langford, Billie Holiday, Lena Horne, Sarah Vaughan, Ella Fitzgerald, and with a slight alteration of the lyrics, by Frank Sinatra. "The Man I Love" has also been heard in many motion pictures: Doris Day, accompanied by Harry James and his orchestra, sang it in *Young Man with a Horn* (1950); Liberace performed it in *Sincerely Yours* (1955), as did Eddie Duchin and his orchestra in *The Eddie Duchin Story* (1956); more recently, Diana Ross sang it in the screen biography of Billie Holiday, *Lady Sings the Blues* (1972) and Liza Minnelli used it in *New York, New York* (1977); "The Man I Love" also provided the title song for a film starring Ida Lupino.

After *Lady, Be Good!*, all of George Gershwin's important musicals on Broadway and in Hollywood featured lyrics written by Ira Gershwin. They became the most celebrated team of brothers in American popular music and were back on Broadway with the unsuccessful *Tell Me More!* (April 13, 1925). However, *Tip-Toes* (December 28 1925) fared better with 192 performances. In a text by Guy Bolton and Fred Thompson, Queenie Smith appeared as Tip-toes Kaye, a dancer in a down-on-its-luck vaudeville trio that connives to marry her off to a millionaire who has made his fortune in glue. As the fates would have it, she falls in love with him and succeeds in winning his heart. The score brought three important songs: "Looking for a Boy," introduced by Queenie Smith; "That Certain Feeling," a duet for Smith and Allen Kearns; and "Sweet and Low-Down," sung by Andrew Tombes, Lovey Lee, Jeanette MacDonald and Amy Revere. The first recordings of "Looking for a Boy" and "That Certain Feeling" were made by the Arden-Ohman orchestra, which had been in the pit during the production. *Tip-Toes* was revived at the Goodspeed Opera House in Connecticut in 1979 and, later that year, was brought to the Helen Care Playhouse in Brooklyn, New York.

Next came *Song of the Flame* (December 30, 1925), an operetta with book and lyrics by Otto Harbach and Oscar Hammerstein II; Gershwin and Herbert Stothart each contributed a part of the score. It did moderately well at the box office with a run of 194 performances. The action takes place in czarist Russia, where Aniuta, a noblewoman known as "The Flame," incites the peasants to revolt. Prince Volodyn, unaware of her

activities, falls in love with her, and after the revolution, they meet again in Paris and all resolves happily. Gershwin's best song was the title number, introduced by Tessa Kosta, Greek Evans and the Russian Art Choir. In 1926 it was recorded by Kosta with the Russian Art Choir, and by the Ipana Troubadours and the orchestras of Vincent Lopez and Sam Lanin; Kosta also recorded the "Cossack Love Song (Don't Forget Me)."

The collaboration of George and Ira Gershwin resumed with *Oh, Kay!* (November 8, 1926). It ran for 256 performances and was, according to Percy Hammond, "an event bordering upon the phenomenal. Mr. Gershwin's score is a marvel of its kind." The book was the work of Guy Bolton and P. G. Wodehouse: Kay, an English duchess, and her brother are in financial difficulties and are forced to use their yacht for rumrunning. Pursued by federal agents, they take refuge in the palatial home of Jimmy Winters, whose cellar has become the hiding place for their illicit cargo, where it is carefully guarded by Shorty McGee (memorably portrayed by Victor Moore). After extricating themselves from entanglements with the law, Jimmy and Kay predictably discover their love for one another.

Oh, Kay! produced many hits. The ballad, "Someone to Watch Over Me" was introduced by Gertrude Lawrence (in her first appearance in a Broadway musical) and has since found a permanent place in the popular song repertory. Lawrence recorded it, as did many others including Virginia Rhea, the Ohman-Arden orchestra, Lena Horne, Frances Langford, Dorothy Kirsten, the Revelers and Jaye P. Morgan. In motion pictures it was sung by Frank Sinatra in *Young at Heart* (1954); by Marge Champion (with dancing by Gower and Champion) in *Three for the Show* (1955); by Vera Miles in *Beau James* (1957); and by Julie Andrews in the Gertrude Lawrence screen biography, *Star!* (1968). The score also included "Clap Yo' Hands," introduced by the chorus, "Fidgety Feet," and the charming "Do, Do, Do" and "Maybe," both duets for Gertrude Lawrence and Oscar Shaw. When *Oh, Kay!* was revived Off Broadway on April 16, 1960, the Gershwin songs continued to hold center stage: Lewis Funke of the *New York Times* described the score as "rich, melodic, lovely, rhythmic, out of the ordinary and unforgettable."

The Gershwins' next musical, *Funny Face* (November 22, 1927), was composed for the opening of the Alvin Theatre on 52d Street in New York; the show remained there for 244 performances. Paul Gerard Smith and Fred Thompson wrote the book, and Fred and Adele

Astaire starred as Jimmy Reaves and his ward, Frankie. Eager to gain possession of the pearls her guardian was holding for her, Frankie enlists her boyfriend to help her steal them. Two blundering jewel thieves (one played by Victor Moore) attempt to thwart his efforts, but in the end, Frankie retrieves her pearls and wins her man.

Funny Faces's best numbers were "'S Wonderful," introduced by Adele Astaire and Allen Kearns, "My One and Only (What Am I Gonna Do)," "He Loves and She Loves," "Let's Kiss and Make Up" and "The Babbitt and the Bromide," a satirical patter song, all introduced by Fred and Adele Astaire.

In the motion picture adaptation starring Fred Astaire and Audrey Hepburn, *Funny Face* acquired an entirely new plot and set of characters, but three of the original stage numbers were retained: the title song, "'S Wonderful" and "He Loves and She Loves," all performed by Astaire and Hepburn; songs from other Gershwin musicals were also used.

The 1927–28 season also brought *Rosalie* (January 10, 1928), the longest-running Gershwin musical to that time (335 performances). *Rosalie* was a Ziegfeld production starring Marilyn Miller, with a book by Guy Bolton and William Anthony McGuire; credit for the show's songs was shared by the team of Sigmund Romberg and P.G. Wodehouse and also the Gershwins. "How Long Has This Been Going On?" a ballad which had been cut from *Funny Face*, became extremely popular after it was introduced by Bobbe Arnst. The following season, out of the short-lived *Treasure Girl* (November 8, 1928), came "I've Got a Crush on You," introduced by Clifton Webb and Mary Hay. It became quite successful in recorded performances by Gertrude Lawrence, Lee Wiley, Sarah Vaughan, Ella Fitzgerald, and Frank Sinatra, who recorded it three times.

Show Girl (July 2, 1929) was also a lavish Ziegfeld production. It starred Ruby Keeler as a show girl who pushes her way in to see Ziegfeld and succeeds in becoming a star in the *Follies*. The book was based on a novel by J. P. McEvoy and adapted by William Anthony McGuire. The score's showstopping number was "Liza" (lyrics by Ira Gershwin and Gus Kahn), sung by Nick Lucas with dancing by Keeler. Keeler had recently married Al Jolson, and when the show tried out in Boston and opened in New York, he sang "Liza" to her from his seat in the audience before leaping up to the stage to serenade her. He recorded it in 1929 and later sang it on the soundtrack of *The Jolson Story* (1946).

Strike Up the Band (January 14, 1930), a bit-

ing satire on war and the profiteering it produces, as well as on diplomacy and big business, was a striking departure from the earlier Gershwin musicals. Audiences found the book by George S. Kaufman so strong and uncompromising that the show closed out-of-town in 1927; it came to Broadway two years later with a revised text by Kaufman and Morrie Ryskind. In the new version, the Swiss are protesting a tariff on their chocolates. In his dreams, Horace J. Fletcher, an angry American chocolate maker, encourages the country to declare war. The Americans win the war when they decode the Swiss yodeling system. But everyone has won, including the Swiss hoteliers, who have made huge profits while boarding the troops. However, Fletcher, whose use of Grade B milk is exposed in the course of events, awakens with a completely new outlook on the situation.

The satire of the text was mirrored in Ira Gershwin's lyrics and George Gershwin's music. The title song was a march mocking military pomp and circumstance, introduced by Jim Townsend, Jerry Goff and chorus (accompanied in the pit by the Red Nichols orchestra) which Nichols recorded in 1930, and it was later recorded by the Revelers, Bing Crosby, Tom Patricola, Dinah Shore, Ella Fitzgerald and the Pickens Sisters. It was also heard in the motion picture (1940) carrying the song's title. In 1936, Ira Gershwin prepared new lyrics ("Strike Up the Band for U.C.L.A.") for an official football fight song of the University of California at Los Angeles, and during World War II, the melody was used to promote several war agencies. More recently, the song was revived on Broadway as a stirring finale for *My One and Only* (1983). Other numbers in the score such as the patter song "A Typical Self-Made American" and "Entrance of the Swiss Army" also had a satiric edge. But Gershwin, the composer of incomparable ballads, was not absent. "Soon " and "I've Got a Crush on You" (from *Treasure Girl*) quickly became standards.

Strike Up the Band ran on Broadway for 191 performances, and a revival was mounted on June 27, 1984 at the American Music Theatre Festival in Philadelphia. Because the text of the 1930 Broadway production proved irretrievable, the Kaufman text of 1927 was reconstructed by Eric Salzman, and several numbers, including "The Man I Love," were added to the 1930 score.

Girl Crazy (October 14, 1930) was a conventional musical comedy, and in it, Ginger Rogers made her first Broadway appearance, and Ethel Merman made a sensational debut. The cast also included comedian Willie Howard as a Jewish taxicab driver, and in the orchestra pit were such still unrecognized jazz greats as Benny Goodman, Glenn Miller, Red Nichols and Gene Krupa. *Girl Crazy* remained on Broadway for 272 performances.

In the book by Guy Bolton and John McGowan, Danny, a Park Avenue playboy, is sent by his father to the one-horse town of Custerville, Arizona; he arrives by way of a taxi driven by Gieber Goldfarb. Once there, Danny transforms a dude ranch into a hot spot filled with girls, liquor, gambling and music. But when Danny falls in love with the local postmistress, he realizes the error of his profligate ways.

As Kate Fothergill, wife of the man who runs the saloon, Ethel Merman introduced "I Got Rhythm," "Sam and Delilah" and "Boy! What Love Has Done to Me." Through the years, "I Got Rhythm" has been recorded more than 300 times, including releases by Mary Martin, Kate Smith, Ella Fitzgerald and the Merry Macs; a rock version by The Happenings in 1967 reached the top of the bestseller lists for several weeks running.

Ginger Rogers introduced "But Not for Me," which Willie Howard repeated in singing styles of various performers including Maurice Chevalier. This song later provided the title for a film (1958) starring Clark Gable, where it was heard as a recurrent theme and sung on the soundtrack by Ella Fitzgerald, whose recording won a Grammy in 1959. With Allen Kearns, Rogers was also heard in the show's principal ballad, "Embraceable You," which has since become one of Gershwin's best-loved and most frequently performed ballads. Through the years, it has been favored by such respected singers as Billie Holiday, Jane Froman, Mary Martin, Judy Garland, June Valli, Ella Fitzgerald, Dorothy Kirsten and Helen O'Connell. The score of *Girl Crazy* also included the novelty "Bidin' My Time," a parody of hillbilly songs. Delivered by "The Foursome," who accompany themselves on the harmonica, jew's harp, ocarina and tin flute, the song is heard throughout the production during each scene change, when the quartet reappears.

The Gershwins returned to satire with George S. Kaufman and Morrie Ryskind's *Of Thee I Sing* (December 26, 1931). In an examination of the political scene in Washington, John P. Wintergreen (William Gaxton), a candidate for President of the United States, and Alexander Throttlebottom (Victor Moore), his running mate, are campaigning on the issue of love. Wintergreen sponsors a beauty contest in Atlantic City to choose his First Lady, but after he is elected he marries simple Mary Turner, who

won his heart with her corn muffins. The jilted winner of the contest is of French extraction, and President Wintergeeen is threatened with impeachment when an international scandal ensues. He is rescued when his wife becomes pregnant—no expectant President has ever been impeached—and the dilemma is neatly solved when the Vice President is called upon to step in for the President and marry the contest winner.

Unlike the Gershwin musicals of earlier years, *Of Thee I Sing* placed a strong emphasis on the book and lyrics, in which political campaigns, Senate debates, Supreme Court hagglings and the innocuous office of vice president are closely scrutinized. One of the score's innovations was the extensive use of recitative, and consequently, individual songs, whose main interest was derived from the context, and which did not stand out as prominently as they had in previous musicals. The Gershwin touch never failed to provide the corresponding musical nuances for the wit and malice of the text. "Wintergreen for President," made sport of the jingoism of presidential campaigns by quoting tidbits from "Tammany," "A Hot Time in the Old Town Tonight" and Sousa's *The Stars and Stripes Forever,* while suggesting Irish and Jewish melodic strains to underline the tolerance of the presidential candidate for both   these ethnic groups. In "Posterity is Right Around the Corner," a tongue-in-cheek suggestion of a Salvation Army hymn is heard. For the stuffy proceedings in the Senate, Gershwin's music parodies grand opera conventions, and a sentimental waltz was used for the announcement of the First Lady's imminent motherhood.

Most of the musical numbers in *Of Thee I Sing* are so thoroughly integrated into the text that apart from the play, their meaning is lost. Nevertheless, three songs had melodic interest and a life apart from the show. The title song, "Who Cares?" and "Love is Sweeping the Country" were recorded by such artists as The Knickerbockers, the Arden-Ohman orchestra, Sarah Vaughan and Ella Fitzgerald.

According to George Jean Nathan, *Of Thee I Sing* was "a landmark in American satirical musical comedy." It enjoyed the longest run on Broadway of any Gershwin musical (441 performances), then toured the country, and became the first musical comedy to win the Pulitzer Prize in drama and to have its libretto published as a book. *Of Thee I Sing* was revived on Broadway on May 5, 1952 and again on March 7, 1969, and it is often mounted by amateur and regional stock companies during presidential election years; on September 24, 1972, a television special starring Carroll O'Connor was broadcast by CBS.

Gershwin's last two Broadway musicals failed. *Pardon My English* (January 20, 1933) which included "Isn't It a Pity?," "My Cousin Milwaukee" and "Lorelei," ran for only 46 performances. *Let 'Em Eat Cake* (October 21 1933) was an unhappy attempt (90 performances) to duplicate the success of *Of Thee I Sing* in a sequel in which Wintergreen and Throttlebottom are defeated and a successful revolution follows. "Their hatreds have triumphed over their sense of humor," wrote Brooks Atkinson about the authors. Nevertheless, Gershwin's songs provided a measure of compensation. The principal song was "Mine," introduced by William Gaxton and Lois Moran and was recorded by Dorothy Kirsten. *Let 'Em Eat Cake* was revived in concert performances at Lincoln Center in New York in May 1978 and at the University of Miami in 1981.

The decade in which George Gershwin proved so productive on Broadway was also one in which he enlarged his horizons as a composer of concert music with a series of works skillfully combining American popular music and jazz idioms with the forms and techniques of art music. The success of *Rhapsody in Blue* in 1924 brought a commission for a piano concerto from the New York Symphony Society and its conductor, Walter Damrosch. Gershwin himself was the soloist when the *Concerto in F* was introduced in Carnegie Hall on December 3, 1925; a year later, he introduced his five preludes for solo piano at Hotel Roosevelt in New York on November 4, 1926. The tone poem, *An American in Paris*, composed while Gershwin was visiting Paris early in 1928, was given its first hearing on December 13, 1928 in a performance by the New York Philharmonic, conducted by Damrosch; the *Second Rhapsody*, for piano and orchestra (1931), was premiered by the Boston Symphony under Serge Koussevitzky on January 29, 1932. *Cuban Overture*, inspired by a holiday in Havana, was first performed on August 16, 1932 at the Lewisohn Stadium in New York, Albert Coates conduting. For a 28-city tour with the Leo Reisman orchestra in 1934, Gershwin composed *Variations on I Got Rhythm* for piano and orchestra; the world premiere of the *Variations* took place in Boston on January 14, 1934.

Gershwin's last and greatest contribution was his folk opera, *Porgy and Bess*, which opened in Boston on September 30, 1935, starring Todd Duncan and Anne Brown in the title roles and John Bubbles as Sportin' Life; it opened in New York on October 10. Only a modest box-office and critical success, *Porgy and Bess* went on to become the most internationally celebrated and most often performed American opera in history. A motion picture version (1959) was produced by Samuel Goldwyn with a cast that included Sidney Poitier, Dorothy Dandridge, Sammy Davis, Jr., Pearl Bailey and Diahann Carroll, and in recent years, *Porgy and Bess* has become part of the repertory of major opera companies, including the Houston Grand Opera (1976) and the Metropolitan Opera (1985). Music from the opera was widely recorded by various artists including Paul Robeson, Sarah Vaughan, Leontyne Price and Bing Crosby with the Leo Reisman orchestra, and numbers such as "Summertime," "Bess, You is My Woman Now," "I Got Plenty o' Nuttin'" and "It Ain't Necessarily So" are still familiar standards.

In 1936, the Gershwins returned to Hollywood, where, in 1931, they had composed songs, including "Delishious" and "Blah, Blah, Blah," for *Delicious,* starring Janet Gaynor and Charles Farrell. They now began to work on scores for two new screen musicals starring Fred Astaire. In *Shall We Dance* (1937), Astaire was reunited with Ginger Rogers. She introduced "They All Laughed," and Astaire was heard in the title song and "They Can't Take That Away From Me," which was Gershwin's only song to be nominated for an Oscar; together they sang "Let's Call the Whole Thing Off." For *A Damsel in Distress* (1937), the Gershwins composed "Nice Work if You Can Get It" and "A Foggy Day" for Astaire; both were recorded by him, and the latter became a staple in the repertory of Frank Sinatra.

The last film musical by George and Ira Gershwin was *The Goldwyn Follies* (1938). George Gershwin did not live to complete the project, but what he did write was pure gold. Kenny Baker introduced "Love is Here to Stay" (completed by Vernon Duke) and "Love Walked In," which was Gershwin's only song to be heard on *Your Hit Parade*, where it appeared four times in first position.

During the last months of his life, George Gershwin suffered from excruciating headaches and frequent bouts of melancholia; his doctors diagnosed an oncoming nervous breakdown. On July 9, 1937, he collapsed and was rushed to the Cedars of Lebanon Hospital, where a tumor on the right temporal lobe of the brain was discovered. Gershwin's condition was inoperable, and he died in hospital on July 11.

Many of Gershwin's songs were heard in several films released after his death. Robert Alda portrayed the composer in a screen biography, *Rhapsody in Blue* (1945), and in 1947, Kay Swift and Ira Gershwin prepared the score for *The*

Shocking Miss Pilgrim from George Gershwin's sketches and manuscripts. One of its songs, "For You, For Me, For Evermore," is a gem. Gershwin composed it while in Hollywood, but had never found an appropriate place for it; in *The Shocking Miss Pilgrim*, it was introduced by Betty Grable and Dick Haymes. Several years later, *An American in Paris* (1951), the winner of an Oscar, featured some of Gershwin's songs, and the symphonic poem from which the film's title was taken served as background music for an elaborate ballet danced by Gene Kelly (who was also the choreographer) and Leslie Caron. For the Woody Allen motion picture, *Manhattan* (1979), selections from Gershwin's music were assembled to create the complete soundtrack.

Through the years, many collections of Gershwin's song have been released. The most significant of these, which includes some of the less familiar songs as well as the classics, is the five-album collection (Verve) by Ella Fitzgerald; *The Gershwin Years* (Decca) is a chronological anthology of Gershwin's songs from "When You Want 'Em You Can't Get 'Em" (1916) to "Love is Here to Stay" (1937); *The Popular Gershwin* (RCA Victor) has been assembled from masters in the RCA Victor archives; *George Gershwin Revisited* (Painted Smile) and *Gershwin Rarities* (Walden) revive many of Gershwin's little known and rarely heard songs. Many other albums of Gershwin's songs have also been released; among them are those by Jane Froman, Dorothy Kirsten, Fred Astaire, Bing Crosby, Joan Morris, Frances Gershwin, the orchestras of André Kostelanetz and Percy Faith, and the Cincinnati Pops Orchestra.

Since Gershwin's death, there have been a number of tributes to him, both on radio and television. In 1957, there was the 80-minute program on NBC radio featuring a galaxy of stars that included Eddie Cantor, Fred Astaire, Jimmy Durante, William Gaxton and Victor Moore; in 1969, a 90-minute show of Gershwin songs was broadcast throughout Europe by BBC in London: "The total impression," wrote Scottish composer and critic Ronald Stevenson in *The Listener*, "was a prodigality of melody matched only by Schubert and Johann Strauss." On a CBS-TV special hosted by Richard Rodgers in 1961, Gershwin's songs were performed by Frank Sinatra, Maurice Chevalier, Ethel Merman and others; *'S Wonderful, 'S Marvelous, 'S Gershwin* (NBC-TV) with Jack Lemmon as master of ceremonies, earned an Emmy, and is available on record; and the Tony Awards ceremony on June 5, 1983 was a salute to the theater songs of George and Ira Gershwin that concluded with renaming the Uris Theatre in New York the Gershwin Theatre.

Gershwin music has also inspired ballets. His songs were used by Léonide Massine for *The New Yorkers*, introduced in New York by the Ballets Russes de Monte Carlo in 1940, and by George Balanchine for *Who Cares?*, introduced by the New York City Ballet. In 1982, the New York City Ballet introduced *The Gershwin Concerto* with choreography by Jerome Robbins, based on the score of the *Concerto in F.*

Gershwin was a man consumed by his passion for making music, but he had other interests and talents as well. He was a gifted painter, whose work was favorably reviewed when it was exhibited posthumously in New York in 1937 and again in 1963. His golf game was in the 80s and he was equally proficient at tennis, ping-pong, tap dancing and photography. He enjoyed social affairs—he was usually the center of attention, the parlor games amused him, and he invariably performed his own music or improvised at the piano.

Since his death, Gershwin has been remembered in many ways. His name is borne not only by a New York theater but also by a college at the State University of New York at Stony Brook on Long Island, an auditorium at Brooklyn College and a junior high school in Brooklyn, New York. Gershwin weeks were proclaimed in New York in 1957 and in 1968, and in 1973, an eight-cent stamp bearing his likeness was issued by the Postal Service. The following year, he became the first composer to be inducted into the Entertainment Hall of Fame, and the Goodspeed Opera House in Connecticut presented its first annual Award of Excellence in the Musical Theatre to George and Ira Gershwin in 1981. A large collection of Gershwin memorabilia is housed by the Museum of the City of New York.

ABOUT: Ewen, D. George Gershwin: His Journey to Greatness, 1970; Goldberg, I. George Gershwin, 2d ed. 1958; Jablonski, E. and Stewart, L. B. The Gershwin Years, 2d ed. 1973; Kimball, R. and Simon, A. (eds.) The Gershwins, 1973; Rosenberg, D. The Brothers Gershwin, 1986. Schwartz, C. George Gershwin: His Life and Music, 1973; Schwartz, C. George Gershwin; A Selective Bibliography and Discography, 1974.

GERSHWIN, IRA (December 6, 1896–August 17, 1983). Ira Gershwin was one of the preeminent lyricists of his time and is known for his intelligent and clever verses for both Broadway and Hollywood musical scores. Though the majority of his work was done in collaboration with his brother, George, he also worked successfully with Harry Warren, Harold Arlen, Burton Lane and Kurt Weill.

He was born Israel Gershvin on Manhattan's

IRA GERSHWIN

lower East Side. He was the oldest of four children of Morris and Rose (Bruskin) Gershvin; brother George was two years younger. From his early boyhood, Ira was the family bookworm. He also had a passion for movies and the theater, and he spent his allowance and the extra money he earned by doing household chores at the Nickelodeon on Grand Street (the first movie house on the East Side), the Grand Street Theatre (live plays) and at the variety houses in Union Square.

After graduating from P.S. 20 on the East Side in 1910, Ira entered Townsend Harris Hall, a high school affiliated with the College of the City of New York that offered a three-year curriculum for gifted students. His mother hoped he would become a schoolteacher. At Townsend Harris, he revealed talents for both writing and drawing, and he served as art editor and cartoonist of the *Academic Herald* and also wrote a humorous column, "Much Ado," with classmate E. Y. Harburg.

Gershwin entered the College of the City of New York in February of 1914. At CCNY, he continued to pursue his literary endeavors, among them a weekly column (with Harburg), "Gargoyle Gargler" for *The Campus*, and humorous pieces and poems for the college monthly, *Cap and Bells*, and New York newspapers. But he found mathematics so difficult that he decided to drop out after two years, putting to rest any thoughts of becoming a teacher.

After leaving CCNY, Gershwin found employment in various occupations, including that of cashier at a carnival, two hotels and Turkish bathhouses owned and operated by his father. In

1916, to satisfy his literary urges, he began keeping a journal, "Everyman His Own Boswell," in which he meticulously reported the day's events and his ruminatons about them. The following year, he sold a satirical sketch to *Smart Set*, a monthly magazine, edited by H. L. Mencken and George Jean Nathan, for which he was paid one dollar, and he earned free theater tickets by reviewing vaudeville shows for *The Clipper*, the theater trade paper that preceded *Variety*.

He first turned to writing song lyrics in 1917 with a parody, "You May Throw All the Rice You Desire," which Don Marquis published in his newspaper column in the New York *Sun*. He also wrote words for several tunes by his brother George, who was breaking into the business in Tin Pan Alley, but in order not to capitalize on George's blossoming career, Ira adopted the pseudonym "Arthur Francis" (a combination of his other brother and his sister's names). Gershwin and "Francis's" first big break came when Nora Bayes introduced "The Real American Folk Song," in *Ladies First* at the Trent Theatre, New Jersey, in the fall of 1918; she also took it on tour, but it was cut soon after the show came to New York. Early in 1920, the Gershwins wrote "Waiting for the Sun to Come Out" for Helen Ford in *The Sweetheart Shop* which opened in New York on August 31, 1920. This song became Ira Gershwin's first work to be published and recorded; from it, he earned a total of $1,293.42, at that time, a small fortune.

The following year, Ira Gershwin wrote lyrics to five of George's songs for *A Dangerous Maid*, a musical that expired out of town. Ira was also working with other composers including Lewis Genzler, Raymond Hubbell and Milton Schwartzwald, but with no great rewards. Success finally arrived with *Two Little Girls in Blue*, with which Vincent Youmans was making his debut as a Broadway composer. Ira continued to use the name Arthur Francis on his contributions; the best one was "Oh, Me, Oh, My, Oh, You" The recognition he had earned in his own right for these songs persuaded Gershwin to discard the pseudonym and assume his own name. He did so for the first time on lyrics for the Broadway musical *Be Yourself* (September 3, 1924), for which George S. Kaufman and Marc Connelly wrote the book and Milton Schwartzwald composed the music. Three of these songs were published.

With the Broadway musical, *Lady, Be Good!* (December 1, 1924), the collaboration of Ira and George Gershwin went into high gear. Here, Ira came into his own as a skilled lyricist with such songs as the title number, "Fascinating Rhythm," "The Half of it Dearie, Blues," and "The Man I

Love," which was composed for the show but deleted before the Broadway opening. With each successive musical for which George was his musical collaborator, Gershwin displayed a continuing growth in technique and sophistication, with neat turns of phrase and rhyme. As the young Lorenz Hart, already an acclaimed lyricist and partner of Richard Rodgers, wrote to Ira Gershwin in 1925: "Your lyrics . . . gave me as much pleasure as Mr. George Gershwin's music. . . . I have heard none so good this many a day. . . . Such delicacies as your jingles prove that songs can be both popular and intelligent."

Ira Gershwin married Leonore Strunsky on September 14, 1926 and they spent their honeymoon in Philadelphia, where they attended an out-of-town tryout of *Oh, Kay*. Their first home was on the fourth floor of the Gershwin family house on 103d Street near Riverside Drive; George lived on the fifth floor. After that, the Gershwin brothers continued to live in close proximity, first at 33 Riverside Drive, and then on East 72d Street; while they were working on motion pictures, the three Gershwins rented a house on North Roxbury Drive in Beverly Hills.

After *Lady, Be Good!*, the Gershwins continued to pen a number of popular musicals. Many of the songs from these productions were big hits: "Looking for a Boy," "That Certain Feeling" and "Sweet and Low-Down" from *Tip-Toes* (December 28, 1925); "Clap Yo' Hands," "Fidgety Feet," "Do, Do, Do" and "Someone to Watch Over Me" from *Oh, Kay!* (November 8, 1926); "'S Wonderful," "He Loves and She Loves" and "My One and Only" (memorable for its sparkling lyrics), "The Babbitt and the Bromide" and the title song from *Funny Face* (November 22, 1927); "Soon," and "I've Got a Crush on You" from *Strike Up the Band* (January 14, 1930); "I Got Rhythm," "Embraceable You," "But Not for Me," "Bidin' My Time" and "Sam and Delilah" from *Girl Crazy* (October 14, 1930); "Who Cares?," "Love is Sweeping the Country," "Wintergreen for President" and the title song from *Of Thee I Sing* (December 26, 1931), which won the Pulitzer Prize for drama. Ira Gershwin also wrote some of the lyrics for his brother's opera, *Porgy and Bess* (1935), sometimes in collaboration with librettist DuBose Heyward.

George and Ira Gershwin also wrote original scores for a number of motion pictures. The most important songs from these were "Delishious" and "Blah, Blah, Blah" from *Delicious* (1931); "They Can't Take That Away From Me," "Let's Call the Whole Thing Off," and "They All Laughed" from *Shall We Dance* (1937); "Nice Work if You Can Get It" and "A Foggy Day"

from *A Damsel in Distress* (1937); and "Love Walked In" and "Love is Here to Stay" from *The Goldwyn Follies* (1938).

During the 13 years between the production of *Lady Be Good!* and the film *The Goldwyn Follies*, Ira Gershwin also worked with composers other than his brother. Collaborating with old school chum E. Y. Harburg on lyrics for Vernon Duke's first popular song composed in America, he wrote "I'm Only Human After All" for the *Garrick Gaieties of 1930*. With Billy Rose as co-lyricist and Harry Warren as composer, Gershwin wrote "Cheerful Little Earful," introduced in the Broadway revue *Sweet and Low* (1930). He also worked with Warren and Harburg on songs for the Winter Garden revue *Life Begins at 8:40* (August 27, 1934), from which comes "Fun to Be Fooled," "Let's Take a Walk Around the Park," "You're a Builder-Upper" and "What Can You Say in a Love Song?" In the *Ziegfeld Follies of 1936*, Ira Gershwin contributed the words to Vernon Duke's hit song, "I Can't Get Started."

When his brother George died in 1937, Ira withdrew from songwriting for four years. In 1941, he was persuaded to return to his work table to write lyrics for the Broadway musical, *Lady in the Dark* (September 1, 1941), with a book by Moss Hart and music by Kurt Weill. For Gertrude Lawrence, he wrote "The Saga of Jenny," and for Danny Kaye (in his Broadway debut), "Tschaikowsky," a tongue-twisting patter song made up of the names of 48 Russian composers—both were showstoppers. The score also included "My Ship," which recurred throughout the show, "Oh, Fabulous One" and "Princess of Pure Delight." *Lady in the Dark* was an impressive success not only at the box office, but also in the critics' columns.

In 1943, Gershwin collaborated with Jerome Kern on songs for the motion picture *Cover Girl*, starring Rita Hayworth. One of these songs, "Long Ago and Far Away," became the biggest commercial success of Ira Gershwin's career, with sales of recordings and sheet music exceeding all others. That same year, Aaron Copland, the renowned composer of American concert music, provided music to Gershwin's lyrics for the film *North Star*, a World War II story concerning the Soviet Union, with screenplay written by Lillian Hellman. Next, with Kurt Weill, Gershwin composed songs for *Where Do We Go From Here?* (1945), a whimsical romp through American history, starring Fred MacMurray.

Ira Gershwin wrote a second Broadway musical with Kurt Weill entitled *The Firebrand of Florence* (March 22, 1945). The book recounted the amorous escapades of Benvenuto Cellini, and in songs such as "Alessandro the Great" and "Sing Me Not a Ballad," Ira Gershwin's wit was rarely sharper and his verbal virtuosity rarely more scintillating. However, the show limped through only 43 performances. *Park Avenue* (November 4, 1946) with a book by George S. Kaufman and Nunnally Johnson and music by Arthur Schwartz was also a failure.

After 1946, Ira Gershwin turned exclusively to motion pictures in Hollywood. On the film *The Barkleys of Broadway* (1949), which starred Fred Astaire and Ginger Rogers, he worked with Harry Warren; on *Give a Girl a Break* (1953), starring Debbie Reynolds, with Burton Lane; and on *The Country Girl* (1954), based on a drama by Clifford Odets, starring Bing Crosby, and *A Star Is Born* (1954), starring Judy Garland, he collaborated with Harold Arlen. The most successful song from these productions was "The Man That Got Away" from *A Star Is Born*.

Ira Gershwin's last offering was a book, *Lyrics on Several Occasions* (1959). This is not only an anthology of Ira Gershwin's best lyrics (and, by the same token, a collection of some of the best lyric writing in the years from 1924 to 1954), but also a witty and sometimes trenchant analysis of these lyrics with asides describing how they came to be written.

After 1960, Ira Gershwin retired and from 1970, he was confined to his home because of an illness that left him incapacitated. However, he remained an active consultant concerning all Gershwin interests and he occasionally revised his lyrics for new productions.

Though he was unable to attend, Ira Gershwin was aware of the many tributes to his work offered by his colleagues. On July 27, 1975, a benefit for the Reiss-Davis Center, entitled "Lyrics by Ira Gershwin: Who Could Ask for Anything More?," was given in his honor at the Dorothy Chandler Pavilion in Los Angeles; in 1981, the Goodspeed Opera House in Connecticut presented its first annual Award for Excellence in the Musical Theater to George and Ira Gershwin; early in 1983, ASCAP and the Jean and Louis Dreyfus Foundation established a scholarship at the City University of New York in the name of George and Ira Gershwin; and on June 5, 1983, the Tony Awards ceremony included a salute to the Gershwins that ended with the rechristening of the Uris Theatre as the Gershwin Theatre.

Ira Gershwin died peacefully at his home in Beverly Hills on August 17, 1983. A memorial service, whose participants included collaborators Harold Arlen, Arthur Schwartz and Burton Lane, was held in New York on August 23. For the benefit of a scholarship fund at the Universi-ty of California at Los Angeles, "A Tribute to Ira Gershwin" was given in Los Angeles on November 19.

Though George and Ira Gershwin were of one mind as they worked on songs, their personalities were diametrically opposed. While George was outgoing and gregarious, a dynamo of energy who thrived on continuous activity and work and enjoyed being in the limelight, Ira was shy, introspective, even-tempered, sedentary and bookish. He preferred to remain a spectator on the sidelines, and work was something he did not relish. He found an inordinate delight in taking chances and preferred to go to the races, play poker with his cronies or try his luck at the casinos of Las Vegas. But what he really enjoyed most was spirited conversation with friends to which he brought an encyclopedic knowledge of the musical theater and a vast wealth of information gleaned from a lifetime of omnivorous reading through the night, and always, his lively sense of humor.

ABOUT: Current Biography, 1956; Ewen, D. George Gershwin: His Journey to Greatness, 1970; Gershwin, I. Lyrics on Several Occasions, 1959; Jablonski, E. and Stewart, L. B. The Gershwin Years, 2d ed., 1973; Kimball, R. and Simon, A. (eds.) The Gershwins, 1973; Rosenberg, D. The Brothers Gershwin, 1986. *Periodicals*—ASCAP Today January 1972; New York Times December 5, 1976.

GORDON, MACK. *See* **REVEL, HARRY** and **GORDON, MACK**

GORNEY, JAY (December 12, 1896–), composer, was born in 1896 to Jacob and Frieda (Perlstein) Gornetzky. In the wake of a pogrom in 1906, the family fled from Russia to settle in Detroit, where Jacob Gorney earned his living as a mechanical engineer for the Ford Motor Company. When Jay was 10, he was given lessons on a newly acquired second-hand piano. At Cass Technical High School Gorney organized and conducted the school orchestra; on weekends, he played the piano for silent films, an experience that helped him develop his ability to improvise.

Aspiring to a law career, Gorney attended the University of Michigan, where he received a bachelor of arts degree in 1917. While attending the university, he studied harmony, counterpoint and orchestration with Earl V. Moore, head of the School of Music. Gorney also organized and led a jazz band that performed at school functions.

During World War I, Gorney served with the

JAY GORNEY

U. S. Navy as bandleader at the Great Lakes Training Center. After the war, he returned to the University of Michigan, completing his law degree in 1919. He practiced law for a year, then decided to become a professional musician. He went to New York, where he wrote songs while earning a living in Tin Pan Alley. On November 14, 1922 Gorney married Edelaine Roden, whom he had met at the University of Michigan, and with whom he raised a son. The marriage ended in divorce in 1942.

Gorney was able to place "I've Been Wanting You" (lyrics by Harold Atteridge) in the Broadway musical, *The Dancing Girl* (1923). He continued to serve an apprenticeship on Broadway through the 1920s: his songs were interpolated into revues such as the *Greenwich Village Follies of 1924*, *Artists and Models of 1924*, and *Earl Carroll's Sketch Book* (1929), including "Kinda Cute" and "Like Me Less, Love Me More" (lyrics by E. Y. Harburg), and Earl Carroll's *Vanities of 1930*. He also provided complete scores for *Vogues of 1924*, composed with Herbert Stothart to lyrics by Clifford Grey, and *Merry-Go-Round* (1927), written with Henry Souvaine to lyrics by Morrie Ryskind and Howard Dietz; Libby Holman's performance of "Hogan's Alley" (lyrics by Howard Dietz) in the latter became her stepping stone to stardom.

Gorney also began to write songs for motion pictures at Paramount Studios (New York). In 1929, Gertrude Lawrence introduced "When I'm Housekeeping With You" and "What Makes My Baby Blue?" (lyrics by Howard Dietz) in *The Battle of Paris*. From 1929 to 1930, he served as music consultant and, in 1931, on the studio's ed-

itorial board. While at Paramount, he also composed "What Wouldn't I Do for That Man?" (lyrics by Harburg), which Helen Morgan sang in *Applause* (1929) and *Glorifying the American Girl* (1929); she also sang "It Can't Go on Like This" (lyrics by Harburg), the featured song in *Roadhouse Nights* (1930).

During this period, Gorney remained active and continued to collaborate frequently with lyricist E.Y. Harburg, with whom he also contributed songs to the *Ziegfeld Follies of 1931* and *Shoot the Works* (1931). Harburg also wrote the lyrics for Gorney's most celebrated song, one with which the Depression of the early 1930s is always associated: "Brother, Can You Spare a Dime?" Rex Weber and a male chorus introduced it in *Americana* (1932), an intimate Broadway revue; it was recorded by Al Jolson, Bing Crosby and Rudy Vallee, and was later heard in the film, *Embarrassing Moments* (1934).

In 1933, Gorney moved to Hollywood and went to work for the Fox Studio. His most important contributions to the screen were "Ah, But is it Love?" (lyrics by Harburg) from *Moonlight and Pretzels* (1933); "You're My Thrill" (lyrics by Sidney Claire) from *Jimmy and Sally* (1933); "Love at Last" (lyrics by Don Hartman) from *Romance in the Rain* (1934); "Song of a Dreamer" (lyrics by Hartman) and "It's Home" (lyrics by Jack Yellen) from *Marie Galante* (1934), the latter introduced by Helen Morgan. Gorney is also credited with the discovery of four-year-old Shirley Temple. For her, he composed "Baby, Take a Bow" (lyrics by Lew Brown), which she sang in *Stand Up and Cheer* (1934).

In California, Gorney enjoyed his greatest success in the musical theater with the topical revue, *Meet the People*. With a modest investment of $3,600, it opened in Hollywood on December 25, 1939, with a cast of unknowns and the barest of sets, but also with a wealth of youthful vitality, freshness and wit. It sardonically depicted current political, social and even musical issues through sketches and songs (book and lyrics by Edward Eliscu and Henry Myers) that lampooned the bigoted South, left-wing politics, torch songs, "borrowing" music from the classics, and so forth. This production was "the big break" for a number of its cast members, including Jack Gilford and Nanette Fabray, and from later editions, Jan Clayton, Betty Garrett, Joey Fay, June Haver and Virginia O' Brien. In addition to the satirical numbers, which included a parody of Latin songs, "In Chi-Chi-Castenango," the score boasted the fine ballad, "The Stars Remain," and a musical setting of "The Bill of

Rights," later designated the official song for the Bill of Rights Day by the U. S. Department of Education.

Meet the People ran for a year in Hollywood. Several performances were given in Chicago, and it arrived in New York on December 25, 1940 for a run of 20 weeks. A two-year road tour followed and editions were subsequently mounted in Hollywood in 1943 and 1944; however, travel restrictions during World War II prevented these later editions from touring.

From 1942 to 1945, Gorney worked as songwriter and producer for films including *Hey, Rookie!* (1944) and *The Gay Señorita* (1945) at Columbia Pictures. During the war years he also wrote songs and sketches for films and broadcasts for the armed forces, sponsored by the Hollywood Writers Mobilization Committee. On January 27, 1943, Gorney married Sondra Karyl, an associate editor for *PIC* magazine; they have a son, Daniel, and a daughter, actress Karen Lynn Gorney.

After the war, Gorney returned to Broadway with two musicals. *Heaven on Earth* (September 16, 1948) was a book musical that survived only 12 performances; its best musical numbers were "You're the First Cup of Coffee" and "You're So Near and Yet So Far," (lyrics by Barry Trivers). *Touch and Go* (October 13, 1949), a revue, did somewhat better (176 performances); from this production came "Funny Little Old World" and "It'll Be Alright in a Hundred Years" (lyrics by Walter and Jean Kerr).

In 1948, Jay and Sondra Gorney were invited to create the Music-Play department of the Dramatic Workshop at the New School for Social Research in New York. Chartered by the New York State Board of Education, it provided instruction and laboratory courses in all phases of show business. Its first student productions were a revival of *Meet the People*, and a new revue, *These Are the Times*, directed by the Gorneys. During their three years as chairmen, the Gorneys produced a total of five student musicals.

In 1952, the Gorneys joined the faculty of the American Theatre Wing professional training program, where in 1954, they produced an original student musical, *On the Wing*. In 1962, in recognition of years of outstanding teaching in the musical theater, Jay Gorney was the recipient of a special Tony award.

Thoughout the 1950s Gorney gave numerous lectures on the musical theater to various educational organizations and he composed music for CBS-TV specials. In 1959, he collaborated with Henry Myers on two musical fantasies for children, *The Georgrafoof* and *Kris Kringle Rides*

Again for the NBC-TV series, *Frontiers of Faith*, and in 1961, he wrote a series of original musicals (lyrics by John W. Bloch).

Also that year, his final Broadway venture was marked with *The Happiest Girl in the World*, (April 3, 1961) starring Cyril Ritchard and Janice Rule. The show was a modern adaptation of Aristophanes's *Lysistrata* with music by the 19th-century operetta composer, Jacques Offenbach, adapted by Gorney for lyrics by Harburg. At one time, Gorney was an avid tennis player and crossword puzzle addict. He now lives in retirement at his apartment on West End Avenue in New York.

ABOUT: Notable Names in the American Theatre, 1976.

GREEN, ADOLPH. *See* **COMDEN, BETTY** and **GREEN, ADOLPH**

GREEN, JOHNNY (October 10, 1908–). Composer John ("Johnny") Green was born in New York City on October 10, 1908, the son of Vivian I. Green and Irma (Jellenik) Green. His father was a well-to-do realtor and banker, and the Green household was a gathering place for musicians, writers and theatrical people. Though the father was interested in the arts, he was intolerant of his son's entering any profession but business, notwithstanding John's interest in music from his earliest years. When he was three, he heard a band concert in Central Park. "When I saw a man standing in front of the band waving his arms around," Green later wrote, "I knew even then what I wanted to do was to lead a band and write the music it was playing." At four, Green began to attend concerts and at five he heard his first stage musical, a production of the Gilbert and Sullivan comic opera, *The Gondoliers.* "After that, I was hooked. Nobody has ever been hooked on dope more than I was hooked on the theater and the concert hall."

Green began taking piano lessons with his mother's former teacher at the age of five. He attended the prestigious Horace Mann School between 1914 and 1924, studying the piano and elementary music theory with Clifton J. Furness. By the time he was 13, Green had taught himself the fundamentals of orchestration.

The precocious Green was only 15 when he matriculated at Harvard College. There he took courses in theory and music history from Walter Raymond Spalding, Clair Leonard and Edward Ballantyne, among others. At the same time he continued to study the piano privately with

JOHN GREEN

Hans Ebell. At Harvard, he and a classmate (the late Charles E. Henderson, the noted choral arranger for Fred Waring and others) formed a dance band called The Harvard Gold Coast Orchestra for which Green was the principal arranger. The band was good enough to cut two recordings for Columbia which came to the attention of Guy Lombardo. Impressed by the arrangements, he invited the 18-year-old Green to Cleveland during his 1927 summer vacation to work for his renowned orchestra, the Royal Canadians, at a fee of $125 an arrangement. Through Lombardo, Green met Gus Kahn, who was already a famous lyricist. With Kahn writing the words, and with saxophonist Carmen Lombardo (Guy's brother) as musical collaborator, Green composed the song "Coquette" that summer. Though it bore the same title as the play starring Helen Hayes, "Coquette" had no connection with the Broadway show. The song was introduced as an instrumental by Guy Lombardo and His Royal Canadians at the Blossom Heath Inn in Lakewood, Ohio, and the Guy Lombardo recording later in 1927 became a bestseller—Green's first hit as well as his first publication. The song, now a jazz standard, was interpolated into the nonmusical motion picture *Cockeyed Cavaliers* (1934) and was sung by Tony Martin in the film *Easy to Love* (1953).

Green graduated from Harvard with a B.A. degree in economics in 1928. Before his 20th birthday, Green moved to New York City, where he studied piano with Herman Wasserman and worked as a clerk in his uncle's Wall Street brokerage house. Green recalls: "One Thursday night, lying alone in bed, I got intro-

duced to myself. What are you doing there? I asked. You're a musician. The next morning, I walked into my uncle's office and told him I would not be back after lunch." Thereafter, Green's involvement with music was to be total.

He found employment as an arranger and composer at the Eastern studios of Paramount in Astoria, Long Island. Working there from 1930 to 1932, he arranged music for 12 films. At the studios he received some instruction in conducting from Frank Tours, the studio music head, but Green was primarily self-taught in both conducting and orchestration. Between film assignments, he conducted the orchestra at the Brooklyn Paramount Theater, and Victor Young, the music director of the Atwater Kent radio program, employed Green as an orchestrator for his broadcast. From 1931 to 1933 Green also worked as an accompanist for Gertrude Lawrence, Ethel Merman and James Melton.

Meanwhile Green continued writing songs. "I'm Yours" (lyrics by E. Y. Harburg) was recorded by the orchestras of Bert Lown and Lloyd Keating, and was interpolated for Ruth Etting into the Broadway musical, *Simple Simon* (1930). "Hello, My Lover, Goodbye" (lyrics by Edward Heyman) was introduced by Ethel Merman in a 1930 Paramount short and was brought into the Broadway musical theater by Frances Langford in *Here Goes the Bride* (1931). "Out of Nowhere" (lyrics by Heyman) was introduced as an instrumental by Guy Lombardo at New York City's Hotel Roosevelt Grill in 1930 and as a vocal by Bing Crosby in his recording debut as a solo vocalist. This song was interpolated into the nonmusical film *Dude Ranch* (1931) and was sung by Helen Forrest in the film *You Came Along* (1945), in which it was a recurring theme. Both Charlie Parker and Fats Navarro performed "Out of Nowhere" as a bebop number. "I Wanna Be Loved" (1932, lyrics by Heyman and Billy Rose) was introduced by Russ Columbo in public appearances, and the Saxon Sisters sang it in the Billy Rose nightclub revue at the Casino de Paris. In 1950, through recordings by the Andrews Sisters and by Dinah Washington, "I Wanna Be Loved" became one of the biggest hits of the year, receiving ten hearings on *Your Hit Parade*. It was again revived in the early 1960s in a recording by Jan and Dean, the pop singing duo from Southern California.

"Betty Boop" (1932, lyrics by Heyman) was the theme song for the popular animated cartoon character, Betty Boop. "Rain, Rain, Go Away" (1932, lyrics by Heyman and Mack David) and "You're Mine, You!" (1933, lyrics by Heyman) were recorded by numerous performers in the early 1930s. "I Cover the Waterfront" (lyrics by Heyman) was composed in 1933 for a motion picture of that title starring Claudette Colbert. The filmmakers decided not to use the song, but when it became popular through radio performances by Ben Bernie and his orchestra, the film was rescored to include Green's melody as the recurring theme on soundtrack. Eddie Duchin and his orchestra, Frank Sinatra, Billie Holiday and Artie Shaw all made memorable recordings of "I Cover the Waterfront." "The Same Time, the Same Place, Tomorrow Night" (1933, lyrics by Benny Davis and Mack David) became Jack Smith's radio theme song. "Easy Come, Easy Go" (lyrics by Heyman) was introduced as an instrumental on the soundtrack of the nonmusical motion picture *Bachelor of Arts* (1934). In 1969 it was used as a recurrent theme in the motion picture *They Shoot Horses, Don't They?*, starring Jane Fonda.

The popularity of these songs, some of which have become standards, was dwarfed by the success of "Body and Soul" (lyrics by Heyman and Robert Sour), a classic in popular song literature as well as in jazz. Green composed this ballad in 1930 for Gertrude Lawrence, who introduced it on the BBC in London. Recordings in London by Bert Ambrose and his band and by the orchestra of Jack Hylton helped popularize it in England and on the Continent. Composer Arthur Schwartz heard "Body and Soul" in London and recommended it to Max Gordon as a featured song for Libby Holman in *Three's a Crowd,* the Broadway revue he was producing. Gordon imported the song to the United States in 1930 and it immediately became one of the highlights of the show as sung by Holman and danced to by Clifton Webb and Tamara Geva. Although "Body and Soul" was banned from American radio for almost a year because of its sexually suggestive lyrics, and though the song was unusually structured in its key changes, cadences and releases, it acquired a vogue in the United States through recordings by Leo Reisman and his orchestra (with Eddie Duchin at the piano), Paul Whiteman, Ruth Etting, Frances Langford, Helen Morgan, Dinah Shore, Gertrude Niesen, Libby Holman, Ozzie Nelson and Billie Holiday, among others. A recording by Coleman Hawkins in 1930 became a jazz classic almost overnight. With its unusual changes in key and tempo, "Body and Soul" offered more improvisational freedom than most pop songs to jazz artists like Louis Armstrong, the Benny Goodman Trio, Art Tatum, John Coltrane and Thelonius Monk, all of whom recorded it and made it a staple of the live performance repertory. On the screen the song has been sung by Ida Lupino in *The Man I Love* (1946) and by Gogi Grant on the soundtrack of *The Helen Morgan Story* (1957).

"Body and Soul" provided the title for and was heard in a 1947 dramatic film starring John Garfield, and it was performed by Carmen Cavallero on the soundtrack of *The Eddy Duchin Story* (1956).

While writing popular songs, Green was also producing music in more ambitious formats. *Poem,* an orchestra piece, was recorded on the RCA Victor label in 1931. In 1932 Green was commissioned by bandleader Paul Whiteman to write *Night Club: Six Impressions for Three Pianos and Orchestra,* which Whiteman and his orchestra popularized. It was performed at Boston's Symphony Hall in 1932 and the following year was performed by the New York Philharmonic. It was subsequently played by the BBC Orchestra in London and by the CBS Symphony in performances conducted by André Kostelanetz and Bernard Herrmann. In each of these performances Green played first piano. In 1939 Green composed *Music for Elizabeth,* for piano and orchestra. It was performed by the CBS Symphony, with Vera Brodsky as soloist and Green conducting, and by the Eastman School Symphony Orchestra, conducted by Howard Hanson, in Rochester, New York. His later concert works were *Combo* (1967), commissioned and introduced by the San Diego Symphony, and *Mine Eyes Have Seen,* commissioned by the Denver Symphony and its conductor, Brian Priestman, for the opening of Denver's Boettcher Concert Hall in March 1978.

Between 1933 and 1940, Green toured the country with his own dance band, called Johnny Green, His Piano and His Orchestra. For a time in the mid-1930s he studied piano with Ignace Hilsberg. At this time Green became a familiar presence on the radio as the conductor on such coast-to-coast programs as the Packard Show, starring Fred Astaire, the Jell-O Hour, starring Jack Benny, and a Sunday evening CBS program called *Music in the Modern Manner,* among others.

In 1942 Green was the music director for *By Jupiter,* the last Broadway musical by Rodgers and Hart. That year Green was also represented on the Broadway stage with a score of his own for the musical *Beat the Band* (October 14, 1942), which had a four-month run and was then made into a motion picture. Its most popular song was "The Steam is on the Beam" (lyrics by George Marion, Jr.).

In November 1942 Green signed a contract with MGM to work as a composer-conductor-arranger in Hollywood. This affiliation began with the musical films *Broadway Rhythm* and *Bathing Beauty,* both released in 1944. In 1947 Green earned his first Oscar nomination, for his original dramatic score for *Fiesta*. It was for this film that, with Aaron Copland's blessing, Green adapted *El Salón México* as a rhapsody for piano and orchestra; entitled *Fantacia Méxicana,* it was published under the byline, Copland-Green. Seventeen-year-old André Previn played the piano solo part on the soundtrack, with Green conducting the MGM Symphony Orchestra. The culmination of Green's career in Hollywood came in 1948 with *Easter Parade,* which Green scored and conducted for, and which won him his first Oscar. Non-MGM productions for which Green composed music in the 1940s were *Something in the Wind* (1947), starring Deanna Durbin, and *The Inspector General* (1946), starring Danny Kaye. Green's score for the latter brought him a Golden Globe Award.

From 1949 to mid-1958, Green was General Music Director and Executive in Charge of Music for MGM Studios, gathering around him such brilliant screen composers as André Previn, Miklós Rózsa, Bronislaw Kaper and Adolph Deutsch, among others. Thus, Green's contributions to the so-called Golden Era of MGM musicals were considerable, especially in such outstanding productions as *Summer Stock* (1950); *The Royal Wedding, The Great Caruso* and *An American in Paris,* (all 1951); *Because You're Mine* (1952); *Brigadoon* (1954); and *High Society* (1958). As co-music director, conductor and arranger, Green earned his second Oscar for *An American in Paris.* For *Meet Me in Las Vegas* (1956), Green composed *Frankie and Johnny,* an extended sequence of ballet music for Cyd Charisse. For the dramatic film *Raintree County* (1957) Green and lyricist Paul Francis Webster composed "The Song of Raintree County," which was sung on the soundtrack by Nat King Cole, who also recorded it, and "Never Till Now," recorded by Mario Lanza. Green adapted some of the material from this score into a symphonic suite entitled *Raintree County—Three Themes for Symphony Orchestra,* which has been performed by the Los Angeles Philharmonic, the Chicago Symphony Orchestra, the Dallas Symphony Orchestra, the Indianapolis Symphony and the Boston Pops Orchestra.

Working for other studios, Green collected two more Oscars: for his score for *West Side Story* (1960) and for *Oliver!* (1968): the soundtrack recording of the latter earned a gold record.

For the decade that he was MGM General Music Director, Green produced several short subjects under the overall title *The MGM Concert Hall,* for which Green served as conductor of the MGM Symphony Orchestra. One of these, *The Merry Wives of Windsor* (1953), brought

him yet another Oscar. Green served as the music director and orchestra conductor for the Academy Awards ceremonies ten times. He also produced and directed the Academy's last radio broadcast of the Oscar awards and its first telecast.

In 1947–48 Green was composer and musical director of *The Man Called X,* a weekly radio program. In 1958–59 he produced several television specials, including *Music U. S. A.* and *A Diamond for Carla.* He was the associate producer of the acclaimed motion picture *They Shoot Horses, Don't They?* The film's score included seven of Green's standards from the Jazz Age.

Since 1958 Green has many times been the guest conductor of America's leading symphony orchestras. For three decades, he has conducted the Los Angeles Philharmonic each season at the Hollywood Bowl, and for several years after 1958 he was the musical director and permanent conductor for that orchestra's series of Promenade Concerts.

From 1966 to 1968 Green served on the California Committee on Public Education to which he had been appointed by the governor. He also held the post of president of the Screen Composers Association from 1965 to 1972, and has been a member of the Board of Governors of the Performing Arts Council of the Los Angeles Music Center. In 1973 the John Green Music Awards were established at the University of Southern California. Green himself was a lecturer and artist-in-residence at Harvard University in 1979 and, in 1981, he was elected to ASCAP's Board of Directors. Green was awarded an honorary doctorate of law by Pepperdine University in Los Angeles in 1981.

Green lives on North Bedford Drive in Beverly Hills with his wife Bonnie (Bunny) Waters Green, a former swimming champion, whom he married on November 20, 1943. They have three daughters, Barbara, Kim, and Kathe. He had been married twice before, to Carol Falk and to Betty Furness. His hobbies are cooking, experimenting with electronics and cinematography. The dapper and urbane Green is a natty dresser, with the carnation he always wears in his lapel his sartorial emblem.

ABOUT: Ewen, D. All the Years of American Popular Music, 1977; Wilder, A. American Popular Song: The Great Innovators 1900–1950, 1972.

GUTHRIE, WOODY (July 14, 1912–October 3, 1967), the composer-lyricist and folksinger, wrote or adapted nearly 1,000 songs in the years 1932 to 1952. Most were songs about the poor,

WOODY GUTHRIE

the exploited and working classes, the impact of the Great Depression on common people, the plight of migrant workers, and the victims of the Dust Bowl. He also wrote paeans to left-wing political causes and songs of antifascist solidarity. Other songs were ballads romanticizing the American outlaw, or children's songs, or Whitmanesque homages to America, its diversity, its immensity.

"His songs," wrote Louis Adamic, "are made out of what he sees and knows and feels; they are the living folk songs of America." Guthrie's music was embraced by millions, who heard him on recordings and on network radio and in concert. Guthrie paved the way for the folk-music revivalists of the 1950s and early 1960s, especially the young protest singer Bob Dylan, who emulated Guthrie and, like him, became an American folk hero.

He was born Woodrow Wilson Guthrie in the small town of Okemah, Oklahoma, the third of the five children of Charles Edward and Nora Belle (Tanner) Guthrie. The father had served as a District Court clerk from 1907 to 1912 and then became a land speculator. For the first few years after Woody was born, the family was in comfortable financial circumstances.

Guthrie was introduced to music by his mother, who sang folk tunes and children's songs, and by his father, who sang blues numbers while accompanying himself on the guitar. Guthrie received no formal musical training and his academic schooling did not go beyond the tenth grade. "Our family was sort of divided into two sides," he recalled. "Mama taught us kids to sing the old songs and told us long stories about each

ballad; and in her own way she told us over and over to always try to see the world from the other fellow's side. Meanwhile, Papa taught us all kinds of exercising rods and stretches and kept piles of kids boxing and wrestling out in the front yard, and taught us never but never to allow any earthly human to scare us or bully us or run over us." As a child he sold newspapers, earned pennies by performing jigs, and played the class clown in school.

As Guthrie was growing up, his family was beset by one disaster after another. Two of the Guthries' houses were destroyed by fire, and a third by cyclone. Woody's older sister was killed in 1919 when an oil stove exploded. His father's land-trading business went bankrupt and by 1923 he was destitute. The mother, a victim of Huntington's chorea, the disease that would claim her son too, became mentally disturbed. In 1927, when she set fire to the house and caused her husband to be severely burned, she was committed to an asylum.

When Guthrie was 13, his father left Okemah to look for work in Pampa, Texas. Now on his own, Guthrie found temporary shelter with a family of 13 who lived in a two-room house. He earned his living any way he could—shining shoes, delivering milk, soliciting business for the local hotel, washing spitoons, and playing the harmonica in barber shops and pool halls. He took to the road in 1929, traveling around the Gulf of Mexico and earning money by moving garbage cans, cleaning cars and doing farm work. Returning to Okemah, he found a five-dollar-a-week job in a service station, but later in 1929 he joined his father, now the manager of a rooming house, in Pampa.

It was in Pampa that Guthrie came upon a battered guitar. A relative taught him some basic chords, and that was the last musical instruction he was to receive. The self-taught Guthrie was soon proficient enough on guitar to perform with a dance band. At this time he sporadically attended high school before dropping out. Though a derelict student, he was a compulsive reader who devoured books at the local library on religion, Eastern philosophy and psychology. Kahil Gibran's narrative poem, *The Prophet*, introduced him to mysticism.

On October 8, 1933, Guthrie married Mary Esta Jennings at the Holy Souls' Catholic Church in Pampa. They had three children.

A talented sign painter, Guthrie earned a decent living as a painter of store murals and as a cartoonist. He was, however, looked upon as the town eccentric. He was the bag-of-bones minstrel who sang with a grating, nasal twang and preferred singing and playing at Saturday night dances, and spending the rest of the week making up songs, to following his trade. In 1935 Guthrie gathered 14 of his own compositions in a typewritten songbook which he called "Alonzo M. Zilch's Collection of Original Songs and Ballads."

On April 14, 1935 a dust storm struck Pampa, a disaster that provided Guthrie with the subject of his first successful song, "Dusty Old Bowl." (The melody for the verses was taken from Carson Robison's "Ballad of Billy the Kid," but the music of the chorus was his own.) This tune is now famous as "So Long, it's Been Good to Know Ya," the first line of the chorus. It was recorded under that title by the Weavers, after which the song became a classic in the folk-song literature of the 1950s. In 1940, Guthrie recorded it for inclusion on one of the two *Dust Bowl Ballads* albums released by RCA Victor. Most of those songs were inspired by *The Grapes of Wrath*, the John Ford film based on John Steinbeck's novel. The ballad "Tom Joad," said Guthrie, was written "because people back in Oklahoma haven't got two bucks to buy the book or even 35 cents to see the movie."

In 1936 Guthrie abandoned his family and went off on the road, rambling about the West and Southwest. He traveled by foot and in boxcars, spending some nights in jail on vagrancy charges and others in flophouses. He earned some money by painting signs, but mainly supported himself by singing songs and playing guitar in saloons and at rodeos, carnivals and dances. Most of his repertory consisted of songs he had written about the blighting of lives during the Great Depression. Guthrie wrote simply and from the heart about the suffering he had seen in his travels as a "hobo-vagrant."

Guthrie arrived in California in 1937. He was heard on various small radio stations before getting his own program, *The Oklahoma and Woody Guthrie Show*, which began its run on KFVD in Los Angeles on July 19, 1937. For two hours each day he performed some folk standards but mainly played his own songs, such as "Stalking Dust Bowl," "Philadelphia Lawyer," "Do Re Mi," and "Oklahoma Hills." This program quickly caught on and the following November he signed a one-year contract with the Standard Broadcasting Company of Los Angeles.

Financial stability enabled Guthrie to bring his family to Los Angeles for the first of several reconciliations, each of which proved short-lived. Before long, in 1939, he again left wife and children and set off with the actor/activist Will Geer, performing for labor unions and striking workers, and at camps for Dust Bowl migrants. In 1940 Guthrie made his way to New York, first living among Bowery derelicts, then at a fleabag hotel on 43d Street and Sixth Avenue. It was there on February 23, 1940 that he composed his celebrated song, a hymn to America, "This Land is Your Land." The melody was borrowed from two tunes made famous by the Carter Family, "When the World's on Fire" and "Little Darling of Mine." The Weavers introduced "This Land is Your Land" in public appearances and recorded it. A classic in American popular music, it has been recorded by Peter, Paul and Mary, Harry Belafonte, Bing Crosby, Connie Francis, the New Christy Minstrels, the Brothers Four, the Kingston Trio, and Glen Yarborough, among many others. Bruce Springsteen, who considers it "probably the greatest song ever written about America," performed "This Land is Your Land" before millions on his worldwide "Born in the USA" tour of 1984–85. Largely on the income from this song, Guthrie was earning annual royalties of $50,000 by the mid-1960s. The Ford Motor Company and United Airlines have used "This Land" in commercials, and in 1972 Senator George S. McGovern used it in his campaign for the presidency.

In March 1940 Guthrie went to Washington, D. C. to record interviews and songs at the Library of Congress, though these discs were not released for another 25 years. In New York he was making guest appearances on such network radio programs as *The Pursuit of Happiness* and *Cavalcade of America*. Beginning on November 25, 1940, he was the regular host of a CBS radio show, *Pipe Smoking Time*. Guthrie also gave well-attended concerts at Carnegie Hall and Madison Square Garden.

Guthrie was now earning more than $300 a week, in spite of his now-explicit affiliation with the political left. Though not a member of the Communist Party, he began writing a column for *The Daily Worker*. His radicalism was expressed in his music. "Union Maid" (melody borrowed from the folk song "Red Wing") was inspired by a union meeting Guthrie attended in Oklahoma City in 1940. Hired thugs were brought in to disrupt the proceedings but were kept from violence by the presence of women and children. Guthrie's verses, written the following morning, were from the point of view of a young girl who refused to be intimidated by "goons and ginks."

"You've Got to Go Down" (based on the spiritual, "You've Got to Walk That Lonesome Valley"), "Union Train a-Comin'" and "I'm Stickin' With the Union" all exhorted workers to join the union movement. "Hard Traveling" and "Blowing Down the Old Dusty Road" described the plight of migratory workers.

In May 1941 The Bonneville Power Administration engaged Guthrie to work for one month on a documentary about the Federal Power Agency's two giant projects in Washington and Oregon, the Bonneville Dam and the Grand Coulee Dam. Though he did neither the narration nor the dialogue, he did compose for that film 26 songs, including "The Grand Coulee Dam," "Roll on Columbia" and "The Biggest Thing That Man Has Ever Built." The documentary project was shelved during World War II but was completed in 1949.

Later in 1941, Guthrie returned East, joining Lee Hays, Pete Seeger and Millard Lampell to form the Almanac singers, who toured the United States performing in union halls and factories, on street corners and on college campuses. The Almanac Singers also made notable recordings. One of their albums, *Dear Mr. President (1942)*, contained "Round and Round Hitler's Grave," words by Pete Seeger, music by Guthrie and Millard Lampell. The melody had been adapted from a traditional square-dance tune, "Old Joe Clark." The Almanac Singers performed it on the CBS radio network when the United States declared war against the Axis powers, and the song was broadcast again on CBS to celebrate V-E Day.

In 1943 Guthrie published his autobiography, *Bound for Glory*. That same year he joined the merchant marine. Twice in an eleven-month period ships he was working on were torpedoed. On May 8, 1945 (V-E Day) he was drafted by the U.S. Army, but after a few months he was given a dependency discharge. After leaving the military, Guthrie briefly attended Brooklyn College on the G. I. Bill. Having divorced his wife, on November 13, 1945 Guthrie married Marjorie Greenblatt Mazia, a dancer with the Martha Graham company and an instructor at the Graham School of Dance. Of their four children, only Arlo Guthrie, born in Brooklyn on July 10, 1947, followed in his father's footsteps, becoming a noted folksinger and composer in the 1960s.

Clifton Fadiman wrote in *The New Yorker* in the 1940s, "People are going to wake up to the fact that Woody Guthrie and the 10,000 songs that leap and tumble off the strings of his music box are national possessions, like Yellowstone and Yosemite, and part of the best stuff this country has to show the world." Some of Guthrie's best-known compositions from this period are: "Reuben James"; "Pretty Boy Floyd"; "Vigilante Man"; "Hobo's Lullaby"; "Hard, Ain't it Hard"; "Pastures of Plenty"; "Get Thee Behind Me, Satan"; "This Train is Bound for Glory"; "I Got No Home in the World Anymore"; "Billy the Kid"; "John Hammer John"; "Sharecropper Song"; and "Someday."

Guthrie's attitude towards music and its relation to the condition of humanity was conveyed in a statement he made for a booklet accompanying the Woody Guthrie Library of Congress recordings. "I hate a song that makes you think that you're not any good. I hate a song that makes you think that you are a loser. . . . Songs that run you down or songs that poke fun at you on account of your bad luck or your hard traveling. I am out to fight those kinds of songs to my very last breath of air and my last drop of blood. I am out to sing songs that will prove to you that this is your world. . . . I am out to sing the songs that make you take pride in yourself and in your work. And the songs I sing are made up for the most part by all sorts of folks just about like you."

After Guthrie's second marriage was dissolved, he married the 22-year-old Anneke Van Kirk in December 1953. They had a daughter, but were divorced in 1956. About that time, Guthrie's second wife, Marjorie, returned to take care of him, for he was now suffering from Huntington's chorea, a rare hereditary disease afflicting the nervous system. By 1957 Guthrie was bedridden, and spent the next decade in hospitals. In his last years he could not move his body or his arms and was unable to speak or read. It was early in 1961 that the young Bob Dylan made his first pilgrimage to Guthrie's bedside. Presenting himself as the older man's successor, Dylan sought Guthrie's blessings, and received them. He cared for the dying man but more important, he played music for him. Many of the songs were Guthrie's own; some were Dylan's first compositions, including "Song to Woody," the tribute Dylan recorded for his first album. Guthrie is reported to have taken Dylan as, if not a surrogate son, then certainly as his anointed successor.

His affliction having ended Guthrie's career, his colleagues formed the Guthrie Children Trust Fund in 1956 to provide for Guthrie's children and to promote the heritage of his musical and literary works.

A benefit concert for Guthrie was held at Pythian Hall in New York on March 17, 1956. Millard Lampell prepared a script combining passages from Guthrie's writings and from his lyrics. The Almanac Singers, among others, performed. The concert ended with the entire cast singing "This Land is Your Land." Years later, Pete Seeger called this event the rebirth of the folk-song revival that swept America in the late 1950s and early 1960s.

California to the New York Island, a collection of Guthrie's songs with Lampell's commentary, was published in 1960. Four years later the Library of Congress released a three-record set of

Guthrie recordings. A volume of Guthrie's poetry, *Born to Win*, was issued in 1966.

A year and a half before his death, Guthrie received a letter from Steward L. Udall, the Secretary of the Interior, informing Guthrie that the department was presenting him with its Service Award and that the Bonneville Power Administration had named a substation after him. This, Udall wrote, was "in recognition of the fine work that you have done to make our people aware of their heritage and their land."

Woody Guthrie died at Creedmoor State Hospital in Queens, New York on October 3, 1967. All three television networks carried the news of his death on that evening's broadcast. His body was cremated, and a week after his demise the canister containing his ashes was dropped into the ocean near Coney Island in Brooklyn, where Guthrie had spent his last years. A memorial concert in which Bob Dylan participated was given at Carnegie Hall a few months later. Proceeds were contributed to the Committee to Combat Huntington's disease. On the two-disc live LP of that concert, Will Geer read a testamonial to Guthrie and Dylan performed "Grand Coulee Dam" and "Dear Mrs. Roosevelt," a moving tribute that Guthrie had written in the aftermath of the President's death.

"He was as simple and homespun as his songs," said the obituary in *The New York Times*. "His grammar was often atrocious. But his vision of America was bursting with image upon image of verdant soil, towering mountains and the eventual goodness and character of its people." Alan Lomax, the folklorist who had supervised Guthrie's recordings at the Library of Congress, described him as "slight of build, windburnt, Apache-eyed, thin-lipped, wiry and with a curly bush of dusty hair under his semi-Stetson." To Millard Lampell "part of him remained forever six years old." Guthrie's biographers, Joe Klein among them, have demonstrated that he was a genius with a towering ego. Guthrie was capable of being an obstreperous, ungenerous man, and his treatment of women could be cruel.

In 1976, when his film biography, *Bound for Glory*, was released, David Carradine portrayed Guthrie in episodes, based on Guthrie's autobiography, spanning the years from 1936 to 1940. Excerpts from Guthrie's songs punctuated the story, while Guthrie's raspy voice could be heard on the soundtrack singing under the end titles. The film won critical acclaim and was nominated for best picture in that year's Oscar sweepstakes. A soundtrack recording was released as were numerous LP compilations of Guthrie's songs, including the albums *A Tribute to Woody Guthrie* and *The Greatest Songs of Woody*

Guthrie, on which the performers included Bob Dylan, Joan Baez, Odetta, the Weavers and others, as well as Guthrie himself. Still in 1976, *Seeds of Man: An Experience Lived and Dreamed,* a collection of autobiographical writings, and *The Woody Guthrie Song Book*, edited by Harold Leventhal and Marjorie Guthrie, were published. A week in February 1977 was proclaimed Woody Guthrie Week by the governor of Oklahoma.

Woody Guthrie, a solo drama developed by Tom Taylor, staged by George Boyd and starring Taylor as Guthrie, was produced Off Broadway in November 1979. In 1984 a television documentary, *Woody Guthrie: Hard Travelin'*, featuring his son Arlo, was telecast on the network of the Public Broadcasting Service.

ABOUT: Guthrie, W. Bound for Glory, 1943, Seeds of Man: An Experience Lived and Dreamed, 1976; Klein, J. Woody Guthrie: A Life, 1980; Scaduto, A. Dylan: An Intimate Biography, 1971.

HAGGARD, MERLE (April 6, 1937–). Composer-lyricist Merle Haggard was described in *Newsweek* by Pete Axthelm as "the outstanding symbol of the trouble genre of country music." Haggard's best songs, especially his autobiographical ballads, provide a glimpse into an American Lower Depths, into lives afflicted by alcohol and drug abuse, crime, gambling, prison terms, vagrancy, loneliness and the torment of failed marriages.

Merle Ronald Haggard was born in a converted Santa Fe Railroad boxcar near Bakersfield, California on April 6, 1937. His forebears were Oklahomans, and his paternal grandfather had been one of the state's best hillbilly fiddlers. Merle's father, James Francis Haggard, had also been an excellent fiddler as well as the leader of a country band. Haggard's life as a bandleader ended when he married Flossie Mae Harp, a devout member of the fundamentalist Church of Christ, who scorned music-making in "drinkin' and fightin' bars." After his marriage, James Haggard played the fiddle privately at home or with his friends. For a living he turned to farming, but with the coming of the Dust Bowl storms of 1935 he and his family joined the westward exodus of the "Okies" to California. In Bakersfield, Haggard found work as a carpenter for the Santa Fe Railroad. He made his home in a converted boxcar near the railroad mainline, and it was there that Merle was born.

He attended elementary school in Bakersfield through the eighth grade, the level at which his formal education ended. In the classroom he was

MERLE HAGGARD

a daydreamer who, already interested in music, passed the time by making up melodies in his head. Introduced to country music by his father, Haggard grew to love it by listening to radio broadcasts of Jimmie "the Singing Brakeman" Rodgers, Bob Wills, and the Grand Ole Opry. As a child, he received violin lessons, but the instrument failed to hold his interest. When he came into possession of a guitar in his tenth year, his mother showed him some chords and he easily taught himself how to play. "For a boy who was shy . . . that guitar gave me a new and exciting way of saying something," he recalled in his autobiography, *Sing Me Back Home.*

James Haggard died when Merle, to whom he had been close, was nine. The mother went to work as a bookkeeper to support her family, but Merle, always a rebellious boy, began drifting toward trouble with the law. By the age of 14, by his own admission, he was "a general screw up," in and out of the Fred C. Nelles School for Boys or the Preston School of Industry, both reform schools, from which he ran away seven times. Then, escaping from home and school, he traveled around the West and Southwest for several years, hitching rides or traveling in boxcars. He worked odd jobs—driving trucks, pitching hay, working in oil fields, serving as a short-order cook—and occasionally played the guitar in roadhouses.

Haggard was constantly in and out of jail. The first incarceration came on August 15, 1951 when he was wrongly charged with having committed armed robbery of a liquor store. When the real felons were apprehended five days later, he was released. After that he was legitimately

jailed, once for ten months for car theft, another time for 90 days for having raided a scrap-metal yard, and several more times for passing bad checks. "I was just trying to grow up," he explained. "Wild hair is all it was. . . . Like the first time I got to jail. I felt I'd finally become a man. . . . Crime [was] almost an adventure. Hell, I had actually enjoyed being a criminal, took a certain pride in it. It was exciting and I felt alive."

All this while Haggard was making appearances as a guitarist and singer in clubs and bars in the Bakersfield area. In 1956 he filled a three-week stint on *The Smilin' Jack Tyree Radio Show* in Springfield, Missouri. Earlier in the 1950s he had married Leona Hobbs, with whom he had four children. They were divorced a decade later, ending a marriage that had been turbulent from the beginning.

In 1957 an intoxicated Haggard was caught trying to burglarize a roadhouse and was confined to the Bakersfield county jail. When he tried to escape, he was transferred to San Quentin, a maximum security prison where he remained almost three years. After a week in solitary confinement for getting drunk on cell-brewed beer, he decided to reform and make a new life for himself. He became a model prisoner and joined San Quentin's country band. Released on parole in February 1960 with $15 and a bus ticket in his pocket, he was a new man: "I'm one guy the prison system straightened out. I know damned well I'm a better man because of it."

Returning to Bakersfield, Haggard went to work for his brother, an electrical contractor, digging ditches and wiring houses. He performed regularly as a guitarist for singer Wynn Stewart in some of Bakersfield's leading night spots. With that city slowly becoming the West Coast capital of country music—it has been called "Nashville West"—Haggard was able to grow as an artist. Fuzzy Owen, one of the city's leading country musicians, became his manager. Owen was operating a small record company in his garage, Talley Records, and there Haggard cut his first disc, in 1963. It had sales of about 200 copies. Later that year he recorded "Sing Me a Sad Song" (by Wynn Stewart), which made the national charts. "Sad Song" was followed by "You Don't Have Very Far to Go," written for Haggard by Red Simpson, and "From Now on All My Friends are Gonna Be Strangers" (by Liz Anderson), with the latter reaching the top ten in the country charts.

Haggard now signed a contract with Capitol Records and in 1965 formed the Strangers to serve as his backup band in recording sessions.

His first album, *Strangers* (1957), included five of his own songs, the most important of which was "I'm Gonna Break Every Heart I Can." Between 1966 and 1968, Capitol released several bestselling singles which featured Haggard as both composer and performer. Written when he was a San Quentin parolee, "Branded Man" told of Haggard's experiences as an ex-convict, and "Sing Me Back Home" looked back on life in prison. "The Bottle Let Me Down" and "Swinging Doors" were bar-room ballads. "Loneliness is Eating Me Alive" reflected his sense of isolation, and in "I Take a Lot of Pride" Haggard said, "Things I learned in a hobo jungle were things they never taught me in a classroom." "Mama Tried" (which was featured in the 1969 motion picture, *Killers Three*) recalled the heavy burden his mother had shouldered after his father died, and "Hungry Eyes" evoked his father and mother's quiet courage in raising a family during hard times.

On June 28, 1965, in Mexico, Haggard married Bonnie Owens, the former wife of Buck Owens, the noted country music singer. That year Haggard and his wife recorded the album *Just Between the Two of Us*. The Academy of Country and Western Music honored them as the best vocal group of the year and singled out Haggard as the most promising male vocalist. Haggard and Bonnie repeated as best vocal group in 1966 and 1967.

Haggard's most popular song, the one that launched him to stardom, fell outside the autobiographical framework of his best work, which is soulful, gritty, and rough-hewn, anything but slick and calculated. "Okie From Muskogee" originated in 1969 while Haggard and his band were traveling by bus in eastern Oklahoma, in the vicinity of the small town of Muskogee. One of his entourage joked that "they [probably] don't smoke marijuana in Muskogee." About 20 minutes later, Haggard and his drummer, Roy Burris, had written a song enumerating the many vices of the hippie counterculture that the patriotic citizens of Muskogee scorned—taking LSD, men wearing long hair and the burning of draft cards. In Muskogee, said the song, such things were not done. There Old Glory and college deans were still respected. Haggard proclaimed himself "proud to be an Okie from Muskogee."

Haggard first sang this number at Fort Bragg, North Carolina before an audience of Green Berets, who responded with such rousing enthusiasm that they almost broke up the place after Haggard had finished. Both the single and the album titled after "Okie From Muskogee" became bestsellers, the LP earning a gold record in 1970. The Academy of Country and Western Music chose it in 1969 as the song of the year and in 1970 Haggard was named entertainer of the year by both the Academy and the Country Music Association.

"Okie From Muskogee" made Haggard a hero to the political right, which in the late 1960s was frightened and repelled by the rebellious "youth culture" that was in the vanguard of the anti-Vietnam War movement. The song's anthemic thrust helped get Haggard a political pardon for his past crimes from Governor Ronald Reagan of California in 1972. The song endeared him to Presidents Nixon and Reagan, both of whom invited him to perform for them and their guests: for Nixon at the White House in March 1973, for Reagan at the Sierra Grande Ranch north of Los Angeles in March 1982.

However, the song also aroused considerable resentment among liberals, many of whom had admired Haggard's slice-of-life ballads about the underdogs of American society. Progressives lamented that "Okie From Muskogee" contributed to the polarization of American political life during the Vietnam War era, and they deplored Haggard for what was viewed as using patriotism as the coin with which to purchase great success. Embarrassed by the controversy, Haggard insisted that his song "was not meant to mock the hippies. I feel it just covered the subject of being an Okie and being put down for years and years." Nevertheless he soon produced another divisive patriotic ballad, "The Fightin' Side of Me," which in 1971 provided the title of an album that won Haggard another gold record. The lyrics included the lines: "When you're running' down my country/You're walkin' on the fightin' side of me."

Haggard collected two more gold records for his albums *The Best of Merle Haggard* (1972) and *The Best of the Best of Merle Haggard* (1974). In 1975 his single "Things Aren't Funny Anymore" became one of the year's most popular country songs and the LP *Merle Haggard Presents His 30th Album* was a bestseller.

In 1973 Haggard starred in a television special, *Let Me Tell You a Song*, which was nationally syndicated. On March 25, 1975, he made his debut as an actor, playing the part of the Duke in a production of *Huckleberry Finn* which was televised on the ABC network. On October 7, 1976 he portrayed a country singer on an episode of *The Waltons*, the popular CBS series about a family in the rural South during the Depression.

Throughout the 1970s Haggard toured America making appearances with his wife at colleges, campuses, in nightclubs and at civic auditoriums, including the Hollywood Bowl. His New York City debut in 1974 filled the 4,600-seat Felt Forum of the Madison Square Garden twice in one evening. After those two performances, John Rockwell wrote in *The New York Times:* "The most important reason for his success is the quality of his songs. [His] concerns range far beyond the kind of small-town patriotism that won him his widest repute. Mr. Haggard is a contemporary populist, a singer of white rural America in the same spirit as Woody Guthrie, Bob Dylan, Kris Kristofferson . . . and his sentiments no doubt reflect that spirit more accurately these days than those of his hipper contemporaries."

With his earnings trom composing and performing and from his two publishing houses (Shade Tree Music, founded in 1970, and Hag Productions, formed three years later), Merle Haggard has gone from rags to riches. He owns a 300-acre estate outside of Bakersfield; it is landscaped with a private lake and equipped with a recording studio and a $50,000 model railroad. Here, for several years, he lived with his second wife and three of his children from his previous marriage. After divorcing Bonnie, Haggard married Leona Belle Williams on October 7, 1978. She had been a backup singer who occasionally collaborated on songwriting with Haggard. When they married, Haggard sold his Bakersfield estate and acquired a Spanish-style home on 23 acres outside of Redding, California. They were divorced in 1983.

Among Haggard's later albums are several released in the early 1980s: *Big City*; *Merle Haggard and Willie Nelson*: *Pancho and Lefty*; *Going Where the Lonely Go*; and *That's Where the Love Goes.* The *Pancho and Lefty* album brought him and Nelson the Country Music Association award in 1983 as best vocal duo. *That's Where the Love Goes* (1983) was his 52d album in 18 years. Four songs from that LP made the Top 100 country music charts: "Big City" (written with Dean Holloway), "Leonard," "My Favorite Memory" and "Rainbow." One of Haggard's earlier standards, "I Started Loving You Again" (written with Ronnie Haggard), brought him a Million Performance Award from BMI in 1983. Also that year, "Are the Good Times Really Over?" was named as song of the year by the Academy of Country Music.

ABOUT: Current Biography, 1977; Haggard, M. and Russell, P. Sing Me Back Home, 1981; Hemphill, P. The Nashville Sound, 1970; Shestack, M. Country Music Encyclopedia, 1974; Stambler, I. and Landon, G. Encyclopedia of Folk, Country, and Western Music, 1983. *Periodicals*—Atlantic September 1971; Look July 13, 1971; Time May 6, 1974; Washington Post August 13, 1974.

HAMLISCH, MARVIN (June 2, 1944–   ). The only composer to capture three Oscars in a single evening and the composer of the score for *A Chorus Line,* the most successful musical in Broadway history, is Marvin Frederick Hamlisch. He was born in New York City on June 2, 1944, the only son and the younger of two children of Max and Lily (Schachter) Hamlisch. The father was an accordion player who headed a band that specialized in music his son characterized as "very Continental, the Viennese Ball and like that." As an infant Hamlisch is said to have hummed the tunes his father played. When he was only four, Marvin demonstrated that he had perfect pitch by playing on the piano tunes he had heard on radio. Three years later he auditioned for a piano scholarship at the Juilliard School of Music by playing "Good Night, Irene" and smoothly transposing it into different keys on demand. Aged seven, he became the youngest student ever admitted to Juilliard. At eight, Hamlisch composed his first song, "What Did You Give Santa for Christmas?"; the lyrics were written by Howard Liebling, who later married Hamlisch's sister. "I had no style of my own," Hamlisch explained. "Whatever I heard, I imitated."

The first of Hamlisch's own compositions to be performed in public were heard at a girls' camp in Lake Geneva, New York, where the Juilliard student was employed as a music counselor one summer. His first hit song, "Sunshine, Lollipops and Rainbows" (lyrics by Howard Liebling), which had been composed when he was 15 was recorded by Leslie Gore in a version that reached the number 13 spot on *Billboard*'s Top 100 chart in 1965.

While attending Juilliard School (1951–64) Hamlisch received his academic education at P. S. 9 and at the Professional Children's School, both in New York City. He later completed the requirements for a B.A. degree in music from Queens College.

A prodigy, Hamlisch gave several piano recitals at Town Hall and elsewhere in Manhattan before he was 13. He might have become a concert pianist but, as he confided to *Newsday*, "The nerves got to me. Before every recital, I would throw up violently, lose weight, the veins in my hands would stand out. By the time I was 13 or 14 it become obvious it was going to kill me." Then and there he decided to channel his musical talent into composition.

From 1962 to 1965, while attending Queens College, Hamlisch was employed as a rehearsal pianist for the *Bell Telephone Hour,* on television. In 1964 he was hired as the musical assistant and vocal arranger for two Broadway

MARVIN HAMLISCH

musicals, *Fade Out—Fade In* and *Funny Girl.* Hamlisch later said of this period, when he was enrolled in college and getting started in the music business, "Because of all of my activities, I had a wild absentee record. But the teachers bent over backwards not to make it difficult for me. My first movie score was accepted by [one of my teachers] as a class project in place of the required string quartet. I'll always be grateful, because I couldn't have done both."

Hamlisch's first movie score was for *The Swimmer* (1968), starring Burt Lancaster and based on a short story by John Cheever. Hamlisch had been hired to play the piano at a party for the film producer Sam Spiegel. Hamlisch thus learned that Spiegel, who had enjoyed the way Hamlisch performed the Rodgers and Hart song, "Blue Moon," was in need of music for his new film. Spiegel made an appointment for an audition in which Hamlisch could play anything he might want to submit for *The Swimmer.* Three days later, Hamlisch appeared with the theme music that Spiegel accepted.

When *The Swimmer* was released, Hamlisch's music, unlike the movie, drew so much praise that he was at once engaged to score other films. Moving to Hollywood in 1968, he wrote the theme music for two of Woody Allen's first films, *Take the Money and Run* (1969) and *Bananas* (1971). Two other films with Hamlisch's music were vehicles for Jack Lemmon: *The April Fools* (1969) and *Save the Tiger* (1973). From *Kotch* (1971), starring Walter Matthau, the song "Life is What You Make It" (lyrics by Johnny Mercer) became Hamlisch's first to receive an Oscar nomination.

In addition to Hollywood assignments in the early 1970s, Hamlisch did the dance arrangements and wrote incidental music for *Minnie's Boys* (1970), a short-lived Broadway play about the career of the Marx Brothers. In 1973 he toured the nightclub circuit as pianist and straight man for Groucho Marx. Hamlisch also made special musical arrangements for stars who were close personal friends—Liza Minnelli, whom he had known since he was a high school student, Ann-Margret, and Joel Grey.

Hamlisch seized the national limelight on April 2, 1974, when he leaped to the stage three times to accept Oscars at the Academy Awards ceremonies. One came for the title song of *The Way We Were* (1973), a romantic drama starring Barbra Streisand and Robert Redford. Streisand introduced "The Way We Were" (lyrics by Alan and Marilyn Bergman) on the soundtrack, and received gold records both for the single and for the album that was titled after the song. The soundtrack LP recording also went gold. Streisand had originally refused to sing this number—one of the most popular ballads of recent years—for the film, because she found it too simple for her sophisticated singing style. "I had to beg her to sing it," Hamlisch recalled. "Everybody in the picture had to vote before she'd sing it. We all outvoted her." In 1975 "The Way We Were" won the Grammy for the song of the year.

Hamlisch's second Oscar that evening came for the best original dramatic score for the Streisand-Redford film. (A year later he received a Grammy for the best album of an original screen score.) The third Oscar was earned for Hamlisch's adaptation of Scott Joplin's ragtime music for the motion picture, *The Sting* (1973), starring Paul Newman and Robert Redford. Hamlisch's *The Entertainer,* an LP consisting of his Joplin adaptations and named after Joplin's ragtime classic, "The Entertainer," captured two more Grammys in 1975, one for the best pop instrumental performance and another for Hamlisch as the year's best new artist. Hamlisch's album also earned a gold record.

In 1975, for television, Hamlisch composed the theme music for two series, *Hot L Baltimore,* a 30-minute comedy on ABC, and *Beacon Hill,* a 60-minute drama on CBS. Neither show ran for more than a single season. More durable was the music he composed that year for the ABC-TV wake-up show, *Good Morning, America.* In 1976 Hamlisch composed the score for a made-for-TV movie, *The Entertainer,* starring Jack Lemmon as Archie Rice—a role Laurence Olivier had played years before—in an Americanized adaptation of John Osborne's play of the same name. Of the eight new Hamlisch songs, the best was "The Only Way to Go" (lyrics by Tim Rice). Since the mid-1970s Hamlisch has often been a guest on network talk shows and on such TV specials as Bell Telephone's *Jubilee* (March 26, 1976).

Hamlisch thought he was making a modest debut in the musical theater when he composed an ambitious score for *A Chorus Line*, for which he was initially paid only $900. For all involved with *A Chorus Line*, this production was a labor of love: bold, innovative musical theater planned for a small Off Broadway auditorium. The entire project was the brainchild of Michael Bennett, who conceived, directed and choreographed it. Joseph Kirkwood and Nicholas Dante contributed the book and Edward Kleban the lyrics. The setting is the backstage of a theater. It is devoid of any scenery, but revolving mirrors on the back wall reflect the action. The place is identified in the program as "Here" and the time as "1975." A one-day audition for a Broadway show is taking place with a group of dancers in rehearsal dress contesting for eight openings in the cast. Each dancer's audition is a 32-bar number in which his or her life story is told. The story line and the costuming are reduced to essentials. There are no central characters. An unseen director puts the auditioners through their paces with his questions.

The score comprises 13 autobiographical numbers which allow the dancers to emerge from their anonymity and reveal the sacrifices and frustrations of being a professional dancer on Broadway while providing glimpses into the pathos of their private lives. Music, lyrics, dance and dialogue are cohesively blended to make for a fast-moving tour de force which, having no intermission, does not allow the audience to catch its breath. "The problem is to find superlatives to convey something of the enjoyment and excitement of *A Chorus Line*," reported the critic for *Variety*. "It is one of the best musicals in recent years. . . . The basic idea is original, the story is engrossing, funny and frequently touching, and the characters are identifiable, colorful, and unpretentiously gallant. There is spectacular dancing, enjoyable music, lively pace . . . plus a finale that brought the consistently responsible opening-night audience to its feet, cheering."

A Chorus Line opened Off Broadway as a Joseph Papp production at the Public Theatre on May 21, 1975. That fall it moved to the Shubert Theatre on Broadway, where it remained a decade, celebrating its 3,389th performance on September 29, 1983 to become the longest running production in Broadway history. By then it had played to 22,300,000 theatergoers in the

United States alone, accumulating a worldwide gross of 260 million dollars for a net profit of 37.4 million dollars. It received the Pulitzer Prize in drama and nine Tony awards, including one as the season's best musical and another going to Hamlisch for the season's best musical score. The original cast recording received a gold record. It was adapted for the screen in 1985.

In composing the songs for *A Chorus Line*, Hamlisch tailored the music for each of his numbers to suit the character performing it, giving no consideration to melodies or musical ideas that might make for hit songs. "The problem," he observed, "was to write theme songs . . . so that you'd know the lives of every chorus gypsy in two bars. If I had written hit songs, the audience would root only for the people with hit songs, and it would throw the show off balance. I sacrificed like hell for the sake of the show." Nevertheless a standard did emerge, "What I Did for Love," which was introduced by Priscilla Lopez and chorus. "Two weeks before we opened," Hamlisch told the columnist Rex Reed, "there was pressure to cut the song because it was such a standout." Johnny Mathis included "What I Did for Love" in his bestselling album, *Too Much, Too Little, Too Late,* and successful recordings were made by Tony Bennett and Andy Williams, among others. "One," introduced by the company, was the other song that was widely performed outside the context of the stage musical. More rooted in characters' lives, and thus less effective when divorced from the text, were "Hello 12, Hello 13, Hello Love," a song about adolescence; "Nothing," about an actress who is unable to relate to the Stanisalavsky method; and "Dance: Ten; Looks: Three," describing how silicone injections improved a dancer's chances at an audition.

Hamlisch returned to the Broadway musical theater with his music for *They're Playing Our Song,* (February 11, 1979), book by Neil Simon, lyrics by Carole Bayer Sager. The protagonists were an egocentric pop composer, Vernon Garsh, and his eccentric lyricist-collaborator, Sonia Walsk, a younger woman who is also romantically involved with Vernon. These characters were modeled after Hamlisch himself and the noted lyricist Carole Bayer Sager, their romantic and professional involvement, their conflicts of temperament, their separations and reconciliations. "Mr. Hamlisch does far better as composer than subject matter," reported Richard Eder in *The New York Times*. The principal musical numbers were the title song, a duet by Robert Klein and Lucie Arnaz, and "If He Really Knew Me" and "I Still Believe in Love," each sung by Lucie Arnaz, with "Believe in Love" reprised in the show through a recording by Johnny Mathis. After a successful Broadway run, *They're Playing Our Song* toured the country with Lorna Luft and Richard Ryder taking over the leads.

After *The Way We Were,* Hamlisch continued to be a prolific contributor of songs and background music to motion pictures. "Nobody Does it Better" (lyrics by Sager) was composed for *The Spy Who Loved Me* (1977), a James Bond movie in which it was introduced on the soundtrack by Carly Simon, who also made a hit recording of it. "The Last Time I Felt Like This" (lyrics by Alan and Marilyn Bergman) was heard in the Alan Alda–Carol Burnett film *Same Time Next Year* (1979), in which it was sung on the soundtrack by June Oliver and Johnny Mathis. "Looking Through the Eyes of Love" (lyrics by Sager) appeared in *Ice Castles* (1979) and "One Hello" (lyrics by Sager) in *I Oughta Be in Pictures* (1982). Other films to which Hamlisch contributed either songs or background music were: *Chapter Two* (1979), *Seems Like Old Times* (1980), *The Devil and Max Devlin* (1980), *Sophie's Choice* (1982) and *Romantic Comedy* (1983). The music for "Maybe," from the last-named film, was composed in collaboration with Burt Bacharach; lyrics were written by Carole Bayer Sager.

Hamlisch has been the star of a popular nightclub act in which he combined the performance of his own compositions with charming between-songs chatter. He has also appeared as a conductor-pianist with such leading American symphony orchestras as the Cleveland Orchestra, the Minneapolis Symphony and the Los Angeles Philharmonic in programs including renditions of his hit songs. In 1983 a Marvin Hamlisch scholarship fund was established at Queens College's Aaron Copland School of Music. That year he announced that he was planning to concentrate on stage musicals at the expense of public appearances on either the classical concert stage or in nightclubs. By then he had completed the scores for two stage musicals. Based on a 1975 motion picture, *Smile* is a take-off on teen beauty pageants; Neil Simon has written the book and Carolyn Leigh the lyrics. With book by Julian Barry and lyrics by Christopher Adler, *Jean Seberg* is based on the life and death of the celebrated American film actress. "Both musicals are about the American dream," Hamlisch commented, "but they're as different from each other as my scores for *They're Playing Our Song* and *A Chorus Line. Smile* is homespun and middle-class America, a very funny slice of life with a sharp under bite, while *Jean Seberg* is very moody with a lot of big ballads."

Jean Seberg had originally been planned as an opera before it was reshaped into a musical play. It opened at the National Theatre in London on December 1, 1983 in what was planned as a Broadway tryout, but it failed to generate enthusiasm among either critics or the audiences.

Despite his often prolonged stays in Beverly Hills, Hamlisch has remained at heart a New Yorker. He grew up on the Upper West Side and now makes his home in a large apartment on Park Avenue. Like Woody Allen, he finds life in Manhattan a source of artistic inspiration.

Hamlisch has been little changed by his enormous success. He describes himself as a square because he does not smoke, never has used drugs, avoids alcohol, and is uncomfortable at lavish parties. He still regularly attends Friday evening religious services, often in the company of his parents. His weakness is desserts, the richer the better, and malted milks, but is forced to constraint because he once suffered from bleeding ulcers. Hamlisch is a driven worker who relaxes by playing ping pong and going to the movies. Despite his many romantic interludes, he has remained a bachelor. His wry sense of humor, which always spices his conversations, is often self-deprecatory.

ABOUT: Current Biography, 1976.
Periodicals—Newsday June 16, 1974; New York Times Magazine May 3, 1976; Stereo Review September 1978; Time June 3, 1974; Variety November 19, 1975.

HAMMERSTEIN, OSCAR (II) (July 12, 1895–August 23, 1960). The librettist, lyricist and producer Oscar Hammerstein II was the most influential and successful writer working in the Broadway theater during the Golden Age of the American musical, whose characteristics he did much to shape in a series of collaborations with the most talented composers of his day: Romberg, Youmans, Kern and, especially, Rodgers, with whom he wrote *Oklahoma, Carousel, South Pacific, The King and I,* and *The Sound of Music.* With Kern, in *Showboat* (1927), he rejected the customs of operetta and revue to create the first American musical play; with Rodgers, in *Oklahoma* (1943), he evolved a style of musical drama in which all the elements of musical theater, song, dance, choruses, and spectacle, served the aesthetic and dramatic demands of a text. Hammerstein's unrivalled gift consisted in an ability to write simple, eloquent lyrics that closely resemble common speech and arise naturally from the spoken dialogue.

Hammerstein was born in New York City, the son of William Hammerstein, manager of the

OSCAR HAMMERSTEIN (II)

Victoria, the city's leading vaudeville house, and Alice Nimmo. His German immigrant grandfather, Oscar Hammerstein, had used a fortune gained by inventing machinery to became a theatrical impresario and founder of the Manhattan Opera. His uncle, Arthur Hammerstein, was a notable Broadway producer. Despite the theatrical achievements of his family, Hammerstein originally intended to become a lawyer. He entered Columbia Law School in 1917, and at the same time worked as a process server for a city law firm at a weekly salary of $5. His literary talents had been evident while he was still a schoolboy, however, and as a Columbia undergraduate he had performed in and written Varsity Shows, collaborating with fellow students Lorenz Hart, Howard Dietz and Morris Ryskind.

When, during his first year in law school, Hammerstein met his future wife, Myra Finn, a distant relative of Richard Rodgers, and asked his employer for a raise, he was turned down. "If they had given me twenty dollars a week," he recalled later, "I would have stayed on, and probably become a lawyer. But they didn't. So I had to look for a job elsewhere." He found it with his uncle, Arthur Hammerstein, who employed him as assistant stage manager for a Rudolf Friml operetta, *You're in Love*, at a weekly salary of 20 dollars. That summer (1917) he married Myra Finn, whom he later divorced. They had two children, one of whom, William, followed the family theatrical tradition by becoming a producer.

After being a stage manager for his uncle's production of *Sometime* in 1918–1919, Hammerstein resigned (at his uncle's suggestion) to write a play. *The Light* closed in New Haven after six performances. Hammerstein's next writing project, *Always You* (January 5, 1920), became the first musical for which he wrote both book and lyrics, with Herbert Stothart composing the music. It stayed on Broadway for 66 performances. A critic for *The New York Times* praised Hammerstein's lyrics, saying they were "more clever than those of the average musical comedy." The Stothart musical that followed, *Tickle Me* (August 17, 1920), was the first of many collaborations with Otto Harbach in writing book and lyrics, though on this occasion they were assisted by Frank Mandel. This show stayed on Broadway for 207 performances before going on tour, giving Hammerstein his first taste of success. One of its songs, "If a Wish Could Make It So," had a million-copy sale in a Paul Whiteman recording, though this was only because the flip side was "Whispering" (words and music by Richard Coburn, Vincent Rose and John Schonberger), one of the leading hit songs of 1920.

Several box-office failures followed. In one of these, *Queen o' Hearts* (October 10, 1922), which closed after 40 performances, Nora Bayes and Arthur Uttry introduced "You Need Someone, Someone Needs You" (music by Lewis E. Gensler). Hammerstein's reputation was solidly established on Broadway with two box-office successes, in both of which he was Harbach's collaborator as librettist-lyricist. *Wildflower* (February 7, 1923) had a score by Vincent Youmans and Herbert Stothart in which "Bambalina" and the title number were hit songs. Rudolf Friml was the composer of *Rose-Marie* (September 2, 1924) which became a classic of the operetta theater. The former had an impressive run of 477 performances; the latter topped it by 80 performances. The top songs from *Rose-Marie* were the title number, "Indian Love Call" and "The Door of My Dreams."

It was not long after Hammerstein first met Jerome Kern in 1924, at Victor Herbert's funeral, that they planned working together on a Broadway musical. Since in 1924 Kern was already one of Broadway's most prestigious composers, any musical for which he was engaged as composer was likely to become a box-office attraction. This proved true of the first Hammerstein-Kern musical, *Sunny* (September 22, 1925) which ran for 517 performances. The main songs in *Sunny* were the title number "D'Ya Love Me?" and "Who." In the last of these, Hammerstein neatly solved a technical problem posed by Kern's music. The melody of the refrain began with a single note sustained for nine beats (two and a quarter measures). Feeling that only a single word could serve such a melodic phrase,

Hammerstein seized upon the word "Who." According to Kern, Hammerstein's use of this one-syllable word for the opening measures was the reason for the song's success in and out of the theater.

In 1925, Hammerstein also worked with George Gershwin. With Harbach as co-librettist and co-lyricist and Herbert Stothart as Gershwin's partner as composer, they wrote an operetta, *Song of the Flame* (December 30, 1925). Its musical interest lay mainly in two songs, "Cossack Love Song" and the title number.

Sigmund Romberg was the next composer with whom Hammerstein and Harbach realized further success on Broadway, first with *The Desert Song* (November 30, 1926), then with *The New Moon* (September 19, 1928). In the former, the most celebrated songs were the title song (sometimes called "Blue Heaven"), "One Alone," and "The Riff Song"; "Lover Come Back to Me," "Softly, as in a Morning Sunrise," "One Kiss" and "Stouthearted Men" were from *The New Moon*. Between these two productions, Hammerstein (this time working as librettist and lyricist) and Kern opened new horizons for the American musical with *Show Boat* (December 27, 1927) which made stage history by avoiding the long-accepted stereotypes and clichés of musical comedy to aspire for an integration of all the elements of the musical theater into a single artistic concept. From this score came many fine songs: "Ol' Man River," "Can't Help Lovin' Dat Man," "Why Do I Love You?," "Only Make Believe" and "You Are Love." Hammerstein was justifiably proud when, during World War II, Winston Churchill quoted from the lyrics of "Ol' Man River" when referring to the alliance between the U.S. and Great Britain: "The British Empire and the United States . . . together . . . No one can stop it. Like the Mississippi, it just keeps rolling along."

The Broadway collaboration with Kern continued with *Sweet Adeline* (September 3, 1929), *Music in the Air* (November 8, 1932) and *Very Warm for May* (November 17, 1939), for all three of which Hammerstein wrote the books and lyrics. *Sweet Adeline* brought "Why Was I Born?"; *Music in the Air*, "The Song is You" and "I've Told Ev'ry Little Star"; and *Very Warm for May*, "All the Things You Are," which had 11 representations on *Your Hit Parade* in 1939, twice in first position.

Among other Broadway musicals in which Hammerstein participated during the years before he teamed up with Richard Rodgers were *Rainbow* (November 21, 1928) and *May Wine* (December 5, 1935). For the first, Hammerstein wrote lyrics and was co-librettist with Lawrence

Stallings, while Youmans was composer. Hammerstein was the lyricist to Romberg's music in the second.

Hammerstein married Dorothy Blanchard on May 14, 1929. She was Australian by birth and had been on the stage in minor parts; she had been Gertrude Lawrence's understudy in *Charlot's Revue* in 1924. Hammerstein and Dorothy met in 1928 during a transatlantic voyage. Several years after marrying Hammerstein, Dorothy established an interior decorating business that she operated successfully until 1942. The Hammersteins had one child, James, who also became involved with the theater.

In 1930, Hammerstein came to Hollywood to work for Warner Brothers under a four-picture contract at $100,000 a picture. He completed work on only two of these projects, *Ballyhoo* and *Viennese Nights*, both in 1930; both were failures. Warner Brothers cancelled the contract for a $100,000 settlement. In *Ballyhoo*, Hammerstein's lyrics (written with Harry Ruskin) were set to Louis Alter's music for "I'm One of God's Children Who Hasn't Got Wings." For "You Will Remember Vienna" in *Viennese Nights*, Hammerstein wrote lyrics to Romberg's music. A few of Hammerstein's subsequent films were successful and two of his later film songs appeared on *Your Hit Parade*: "When I Grow Too Old to Dream," music by Romberg, from *The Night Is Young* (1935) and "I Won't Dance," lyrics written with Harbach to Kern's music, for the screen adaptation of *Roberta* (1935). Several of Hammerstein's finest screen songs during the next half-dozen years had music by Kern: the title song in *Reckless* (1935); the title song, "Can I Forget You" and "The Folks Who Live on the Hill" in *High, Wide and Handsome* (1937), for which he also wrote the screenplay; the title song in *I'll Take Romance* (1937); and "The Last Time I Saw Paris," inspired by the Nazi occupation of the French capital, written independently of any screen production but interpolated into the film, *Lady, Be Good* (1941), where it captured an Oscar. In addition, Hammerstein wrote the lyrics for "Mist Over the Moon" (music by Ben Oakland) for *The Lady Objects* (1938) and assisted in writing the screenplay for *The Story of Vernon and Irene Castle*, starring Fred Astaire and Ginger Rogers (1939).

On Broadway, except for *Music in the Air* and *May Wine*, Hammerstein was harassed by a long series of box-office disasters. "I kept going only through inner conceit," he said. When this streak of bad luck finally ended so decisively in 1942 with *Oklahoma!*, his first collaboration with Richard Rodgers, Hammerstein placed an advertisement in *Variety* carrying the following headline: "I'VE DONE IT BEFORE AND I CAN DO IT AGAIN." Under it, came a listing of his recent Broadway failures: *Very Warm for May* (seven weeks), *Ball at Savoy* (five weeks), *Sunny River* (six weeks), *Three Sisters* (nine weeks), *Free for All* (three weeks), *The Gang's All Here* (three weeks), *East Wind* (three weeks), *Gentleman Unafraid* (one week).

Hammerstein first met Richard Rodgers in 1915 at Columbia University when Rodgers, aged thirteen, was brought by his older brother backstage at a Varsity Show in which Hammerstein was a performer. Rodgers and Hammerstein did not meet again until 1919 when Rodgers himself entered Columbia University. That year, Hammerstein wrote the lyrics for two Rodgers songs, "Can It?" and "Weakness," heard in an amateur production. Hammerstein was on the committee that accepted Rodgers's score for the Columbia Varsity Show, *Fly with Me*, in 1920 when, once again, Hammerstein wrote the lyrics for a Rodgers song, "Room for One More." Though their paths often crossed during the next two decades, since they moved in the same social and theatrical circles, the subject of collaboration did not surface until 1942, by which time each had achieved considerable eminence in the theater.

When the long-standing partnership of Rodgers and Hart ended in 1942, and Rodgers needed a new collaborator for *Oklahoma!* he called on Hammerstein. Thus began the age of Rodgers and Hammerstein in the musical theater which brought about, as Cole Porter once said, "the most profound change in forty years of musical comedy," and in which several classics were born. The Rodgers and Hammerstein epoch lasted 16 years (terminated by Hammerstein's death) when nine Broadway musicals, and one each for motion pictures and television, were created, for all of which Hammerstein served as librettist-lyricist. *Oklahoma!*, which opened on March 31, 1943, was followed on Broadway by *Carousel* (April 19, 1945), *Allegro* (October 10, 1947), *South Pacific* (April 7, 1949), *The King and I* (March 27, 1951), *Me and Juliet* (May 28, 1953), *Pipe Dream* (November 30, 1955), *Flower Drum Song* (December 1, 1958), and *The Sound of Music* (November 16, 1959). *Oklahoma!* had the longest run of any musical on Broadway up to then (2,212 performances) and received a special award from the Pulitzer Prize committee. *South Pacific*, which ran on Broadway for 1,925 performances, won the Pulitzer Prize in drama and a Donaldson Award as the season's best musical. *Oklahoma!, Carousel, South Pacific, The King and I, Flower Drum Song* and *The Sound of Music* all became successful motion pictures. *State Fair* (1945) was the only motion picture for which Rodgers and Hammerstein created an original score, and *Cinderella* (March 31, 1957), their only original production for television.

From these productions came a parade of song hits, many of which became standards: "Oh, What a Beautiful Mornin'" and "People Will Say We're in Love" (*Oklahoma!*); "If I Loved You," "June is Bustin' Out All Over" and "You'll Never Walk Alone" (*Carousel*) "A Fellow Needs a Girl" and "The Gentleman is a Dope" (*Allegro*); "Some Enchanted Evening," "Bali Ha'i," "Younger Than Springtime" and "I'm in Love With a Wonderful Guy" (*South Pacific*); "Hello, Young Lovers," "Shall We Dance?" and "Getting to Know You" (*The King and I*); "No Other Love" (*Me and Juliet*); "Everybody's Got a Home But Me" (*Pipe Dream*); "I Enjoy Being a Girl" and "Love Look Away" (*Flower Drum Song*); the title song, "Climb Ev'ry Mountain," "My Favorite Things" and "Do Re Mi" (*The Sound of Music*). "It Might as Well Be Spring" from *State Fair* won an Oscar. "People Will Say We're in Love" was heard 30 times on *Your Hit Parade*; "If I Loved You," 19 times; and "It Might as Well Be Spring," 14 times. Each achieved the first position three times.

(For further information about songs and productions mentioned in the preceding pages, consult the biographies of Rudolf Friml, George Gershwin, Jerome Kern, Richard Rodgers, Sigmund Romberg and Vincent Youmans.)

Apart from his collaboration with Rodgers, Hammerstein created on his own another "memorable milestone in the upward and onward course of the Great American Showshop," in the words of the critic Robert Garland. This happened eight months after *Oklahoma!* had opened when, on December 2, 1943, *Carmen Jones* began a run on Broadway of 502 performances. Here, Hammerstein updated and Americanized the libretto of Bizet's opera, *Carmen*, for an all-black cast, while retaining Bizet's arias virtually intact (fashioning new Americanized lyrics for them). Within the American-Negro setting of a Southern American city during World War II, Carmen Jones, an employee in a parachute factory, seductively steals Joe, an army corporal, from Cindy Lou. She induces Joe to come with her to Chicago where he loses her to Husky Miller, a boxer. Realizing he has lost Carmen Jones, Joe murders her outside the sports arena on the night of Husky Miller's championship bout.

Thus the operatic role of Carmen became Carmen Jones; Don José, Joe; Escamillo, Husky Miller; and Micaëla, Cindy Lou. Hammerstein's lyrics transformed the well-known opera arias into Broadway songs: the "Habanera" became "Dat's Love"; the "Toreador Song," "Stan' Up and Fight"; the "Seguidille," "Dere's a Café on de Corner"; the "Flower Song," "Dis Flower"; and "Micaëla's Air," "My Joe." Muriel Smith and Muriel Rahn, alternating as Carmen Jones, introduced "Dat's Love" (with chorus) and "Dere's a Café on de Corner" (with Napoleon Reed and Luther Saxon, alternating as Joe). Reed and Saxon introduced "Dis Flower"; Glenn Bryant, as Husky Miller, "Stan' Up and Fight"; and Carlotta Franzell and Elton J. Warren, alternating as Cindy Lou, "My Joe." The entire score was issued in an original cast album.

The motion-picture adaptation of *Carmen Jones* (1954) starred Dorothy Dandrige as Carmen Jones and Harry Belafonte as Joe, with Marilyn Horne and Le Vern Hutcherson respectively dubbing the voices of Dandridge and Belafonte on the soundtrack which was released in a record album.

In *Carmen Jones*, as in his texts with Rodgers, Hammerstein avoided virtuoso versification in favor of a simplified vocabulary, dialect, colloquialisms and everyday catch phrases. His verses flowed easily, as did his dialogue. "A rhyme should be unassertive," he once wrote, "never stand out too noticeably. . . . The job of the poet is to find the right word in the right place, the word with the exact meaning and the highest quality of beauty and power. The lyric writer must find this word, too, but it also must be a word that is clear when sung and not too difficult for the singer to sing on the note which he hits when he sings it."

Hammerstein's lyrics generally preceded the composition of Rodgers's music. Hammerstein expended much time and effort on each song. Some took him weeks to write as they underwent painstaking selection and revision. When working on his verses, he stood in front of an erect, old-fashioned bookkeeper's desk given to him by Jerome Kern. When Hammerstein finished the first draft of a lyric he would devise a functional dummy tune, tunes so awful, his wife once remarked, that they want to make you cry. When writing dialogue he used a dictating machine, with his secretary then transcribing his material for revision. Hammerstein liked to act out a scene aloud in his study to hear how it sounded to the ear.

His friends called him "Ock." He was, as this writer described him in his biography of Richard Rodgers, "a large and bulky man with broad shoulders and gangling movements that are usually slow and sedate. His sensitive blue eyes register kindliness and tolerance, and his forehead seems to be contracted into a frown. A shy smile creeps across his lips frequently as he talks, touching his round, rugged and pockmarked face with a gentleness that are duplicated in his speech and manner. He always speaks in a softly modulated voice, rarely loses his temper, and is never temperamental. There is about him the air of a poet and a dreamer—but, as Rodgers hastens to add, 'a very careful dreamer,' whose head might sometimes be up in the clouds but whose feet are always firmly on the ground."

The Hammersteins maintained two residences. In New York, they occupied a five-floor brick house on East 63d Street off Fifth Avenue, the ground floor of which served as the office for Hammerstein's business ventures. Since Hammerstein had little appreciation for the visual arts, the walls of his living quarters were decorated not by famous paintings but by family photographs. The Hammersteins also owned "Highland Farm," on a seventy-three acre parcel of land in Doylestown, in Bucks County, Pennsylvania.

"Highland Farm" was where Hammerstein preferred to be whenever he started working on a musical. And "Highland Farm" was where he chose to die when he became afflicted with stomach cancer. He died on August 23, 1960. A few days later, on September 1, all the theater lights on Broadway and in London were blackened for a minute and a half as a memorial. In 1931, the Hammerstein family contributed a million dollars to Columbia University to help create an Oscar Hammerstein II Center for Theatre Studies.

ABOUT: Ewen, D. Richard Rodgers, 1957; Fordin, H., Getting to Know Him: A Biography of Oscar Hammerstein II, 1986. *Periodicals*—New Yorker May 12, 19, 1951.

HANDY, W. C. (November 16, 1873–March 28, 1958), composer-lyricist, was the self-proclaimed "father of the blues." Although the blues had been developed in New Orleans and the Mississippi Delta region long before Handy composed "Mr. Crump" in 1909, Handy wrote the first commercially successful blues numbers, songs that started the trend in Tin Pan Alley for popular songs in a blues idiom.

William Christopher Handy was born in Florence, Alabama to former slaves, Charles Bernard and Elizabeth (Brewer) Handy. His grandfather and father had been Methodist ministers and it was expected that William too would enter the ministry. He was, however, more interested in music, especially the music of brass bands, but

W. C. HANDY

his father considered instrumental music sacreligious, and it was forbidden in the Handy household.

By working at odd jobs, Handy saved enough money to buy a guitar. Calling it "one of the devil's playthings," his father forced him to return it to the store in exchange for an unabridged dictionary. "I'd rather see you in a hearse, son, than have you a musician," his father said, though he did allow him to play hymns and devotional music on an old Estey organ.

Determined to learn to play the trumpet after hearing a visiting musician perform with a local Baptist choir, Handy purchased a trumpet from a circus musician for $1.75, paying 25¢ down and the rest in installments. Furtively he taught himself to play the instrument. When he was 15, Handy joined a brass band, and after that he played the trumpet with a traveling minstrel show. While on the road, the troupe went bankrupt, and Handy returned home by jumping a freight car.

Deciding to become a teacher, Handy enrolled in the Agricultural and Mechanical College, an all-black school in Huntsville, Alabama, receiving his teacher's license in 1892. But because he did not want to support himself on a teacher's minuscule salary, Handy rejected the classroom for a day-laboring job as a molder's assistant at the Howard and Harrison Pipe Works in Bessemer, Alabama. There he also formed and directed a brass band. When the 1893 depression forced the closing of the foundry, Handy traveled to Chicago and then St. Louis, supporting himself by working as a bricklayer but also enduring periods of unemployment.

From 1896 to 1900, he was cornetist, arranger and minstrel for Mahara's Minstrels, eventually becoming the troupe's bandmaster. Now gainfully employed, he was able to marry Elizabeth V. Prince, his childhood sweetheart, on July 19, 1898. They had six children.

From 1900 to 1902, Handy taught music at Huntsville's Agricultural and Mechanical College. In 1903 he joined Mahara's Minstrels in Clarksdale, Mississippi, where he directed the Knights of Pythias Band, an all-black group that played the popular music of whites. With this band he toured the South for the next 25 years. While in Clarksdale, Handy was introduced to the music of Charley Patton, one of the pioneers of rural, Delta blues.

One day, at a deserted railroad station, Handy heard a black man singing a "sorrow song," Handy's introduction to the melancholy blues melody. Later, in Cleveland, Mississippi, he attended a performance of racial folk music and popular melodies by a local black band who elicited from their audience a shower of coins as well as an ovation. "This had the stuff people wanted," he wrote later. "It touches the spot. Their music wanted polishing, but it contained the essence. Folks would pay money for it. . . . That night, a composer was born, an American composer."

Handy had been composing ballads and up-tempo tunes in the popular styles favored by Tin Pan Alley, but now he began to infuse his compositions with racial identity. "In the Cotton Fields of Dixie" (1907, lyrics by Harry Pace) was his first published song; two years later he composed his first blues.

In Handy's autobiography, *Father of the Blues*, he told how he went about writing a blues: "The primitive southern Negro as he sang was sure to bear down on the third and seventh tone of the scale, slurring between major and minor. Whether in the cotton fields of the delta or on the levee up St. Louis way, it was always the same. Till then, however, I never heard this slur used by a more sophisticated Negro, or by any white man. I tried to convey this effect . . . by introducing flat thirds and sevenths (now called blue notes) into my song, although its prevailing key was major, and I carried this device into my melody as well. . . . This was a distinct departure, but as it turned out, it touched the spot. In the folk blues the singer fills up occasional gaps with words like 'Oh Lawdy' or 'Oh, Baby' and the like. This meant that in writing a melody to be sung in the blues manner, one would have to provide gaps or waits. In my composition, I decided to embellish the piano and orchestral score at these points. This kind of business is called a 'break' . . . and 'breaks' became a fertile source of the orchestral improvisation which became the essence of jazz. . . . I used a plagal cadence to give 'spiritual' effects in the harmony. Altogether, I aimed to use all that is characteristic of the Negro from Africa to Alabama."

Handy's first blues originated as a campaign song in a mayoralty race in Memphis in 1909. Each of three candidates had a brass band promoting his campaign, and for the candidate running on a reform ticket, Edward H. Crump, Handy was asked to compose a campaign song. He complied with "Mr. Crump," appropriating the folk style that was indigenous to the black population of Memphis. The song caught on instantly, and it is thought to have brought Crump enough black votes to have insured his election.

After the election, Handy adapted "Mr. Crump" as an instrumental piano piece called "Memphis Blues." Issued at his own expense, it became the first blues song ever published. In 1912, the Theron A. Bennet Company, a New York publisher, acquired the rights for $50. Reissued as a song with lyrics by George A. Norton, it also became the first blues to come from Tin Pan Alley, and proved to be an instant commercial success. It has been recorded by Marion Harris, Johnny Marvin and Dinah Shore, and was quoted in a production number called "The Birth of the Blues" in George White's *Scandals of 1926*. Bing Crosby sang it in the motion picture *The Birth of the Blues* (1941).

Having failed to realize any of the profits from "The Memphis Blues," Handy decided to compose another blues whose royalties would match those of "Memphis Blues." Searching for a suitable subject, as he recalled in his autobiography, Handy was suddenly inundated by "a flood of memories. . . . First there was a picture I had of myself, unshaven, wanting even a decent meal, and standing before a lighted saloon in St. Louis without a shirt under my frayed coat. There was also from that same period a curious and dramatic little fragment that till now seemed to have little or no importance. While occupied with my own memories during the sojourn, I had seen a woman whose pain seemed even greater. She had tried to take the edge off her grief by heavy drinking, but it hadn't worked. Stumbling along the poorly lighted street, she muttered as she walked, 'My man's got a heart like a rock cast in the sea'. . . . By the time I had finished all this heavy thinking and remembering, I figured it was time to get something down on paper, so I wrote 'I hate to see de evenin' sun go down.' If you ever had to sleep on the cobbles down by the river in St. Louis, you'll understand the complaint." (When

he first visited St. Louis in the mid-1890s, Handy, unable to find work, had slept on city streets and on the banks of the Mississippi River.)

Thus did Handy write his masterpiece, "The St. Louis Blues." Despite the popularity of "The Memphis Blues," Handy's new composition failed to interest even a single publisher. In 1913, to issue "The St. Louis Blues," Handy formed a publishing partnership with Harry Pace, the Memphis-based Pace and Handy Music Company. His song was released in 1914, but it initially failed to attract any attention. Over the next few years Handy wrote new blues numbers, most notably the "Yellow Dog Blues" (1914), "Joe Turner Blues" (1915) and "Beale Street Blues" (1916). The hero of "Joe Turner Blues" is the man assigned by his brother, the governor of Tennessee, to escort gangs of convicts from a Memphis jail to a penitentiary in Nashville. "Beale Street Blues" was recorded first by Ladd's Black Aces, then by Marion Harris and by Lena Horne before becoming a signature for Jack Teagarden, the celebrated jazz trombonist. Mitzi Gaynor sang it in Eva Tanguay's screen biography, *The "I Don't Care" Girl* (1953), starring George Jessel, and it was interpolated into Handy's screen biography, *St. Louis Blues* (1958), starring Nat King Cole and Eartha Kitt.

In 1917 Handy and Pace moved their publishing firm from Memphis to New York City. Denied an office in the Gaiety Theatre Building on Broadway because they were black, Handy and Pace bought a small building at 232 West 46th Street.

Before the end of the decade, "St. Louis Blues" had emerged from obscurity. Sophie Tucker sang it in vaudeville, and at the Winter Garden in 1919 Gilda Gray created a sensation by singing "The St. Louis Blues" while doing a shimmy. The 1925 recording by Bessie Smith with Louis Armstrong has become a classic item for collectors of jazz records. Numerous vocal and instrumental recordings have been made, notably by Mildred Bailey, Marion Harris, Paul Robeson, Bing Crosby, Lena Horne and the orchestra of Ted Lewis. It was performed by Ted Lewis's orchestra in the movie *Is Everybody Happy?* (1929) and in Lewis's screen biography, *Is Everybody Happy?* (1943), and it served as a recurring theme in the 1935 movie *Baby Face*, starring Barbara Stanwyck. In later films it was sung by Ruby Elzy in *The Birth of the Blues* (1941) and by Louis Armstrong in *Jam Session* (1944). In *The Glenn Miller Story* (1954), starring James Stewart and June Allyson, it was adapted as an instrumental called the "St. Louis Blues March," and it provided the title for Handy's screen biography in 1958.

"St. Louis Blues" made Handy an immortal in American popular music. In 1931 a public park and a square in Memphis were named after him, as were a school and theater. In 1940 Handy was honored for his contribution to American culture at the New York World's Fair, where he conducted a performance of his most famous song.

Shortly after World War I Pace withdrew from the firm, and Pace and Handy was renamed the Handy Bros. Music Company. Based on a folk blues, Handy's "Aunt Hagar's Blues," also known as "Aunt Hagar's Children" (lyrics by Jim Brymn), was introduced in 1920 as a jazz instrumental by Erskine Tate's orchestra; it was recorded in 1921 by Ladd's Black Aces and years later by Lena Horne. "Loveless Love" (1921) was derived from the folk song, "Careless Love," and was recorded by Noble Sissle and his orchestra. Handy followed these numbers with, among others, "Joe Henry Blues" (1922), "Atlanta Blues" (1923), and "East of St. Louis" (1937), which Lena Horne popularized in nightclub and concert performances. Handy also composed more than 100 nonblues songs, spirituals, and such instrumentals as "Hail to the Spirit of Freedom" (1915), for band, and "Afro-American Hymn" (1916), for band and chorus. Handy's symphony, *Blue Destiny*, was inspired by the Gettysburg Address. This symphony consisted largely of melodies from Handy's most famous blues, including "The St. Louis Blues," "Memphis Blues" and "Beale Street Blues."

When the orchestra of Vincent Lopez gave its first jazz concert at the Metropolitan Opera House in 1924, the second half of the program was devoted entirely to the evolution of Handy's blues. On April 27, 1928 Handy himself conducted a concert at Carnegie Hall that surveyed all styles of black music—spirituals, work songs, cakewalks, blues and jazz. Handy's 60th birthday in 1933 was celebrated in New York with a testimonial dinner and concert at Carnegie Hall, and in Hollywood with 15 performances of the "St. Louis Blues" by 15 different bands at a musical jamboree of the American Federation of Musicians.

In 1943 Handy fell from a subway platform, suffering a fracture of the skull that caused total blindness. In spite of this handicap, he continued to run his publishing house, to compose music by dictating it to an amanuensis, to appear on radio and television, and to play the trumpet in concert appearances. On January 1, 1954 Handy married his secretary, Irma Louise Logan (his first wife, Elizabeth, had died in 1937). During his last years Handy was confined to a wheelchair. He died in a hospital in New York City, less than two weeks before his screen biography

St. Louis Blues, starring Nat King Cole as the composer, opened in St. Louis. After Handy's death, the management of his publishing firm, now renamed the W. C. Handy Music Company, was taken over by his son and daughter.

In 1960 a statue of Handy was unveiled on Beale Street in Memphis. A six-cent stamp with his image was issued by the U. S. Post Office in 1969, and ten years later 52d Street between Seventh Avenue and Sixth Avenue was named after Handy under the authorization of New York City Mayor Edward Koch. For a salute to Handy at Carnegie Hall on March 6, 1981, his Carnegie Hall concert of 1928 was recreated.

Handy was the editor of *Blues: An Anthology* (1926); *Book of Negro Spirituals* (1938); *Negro Music and Musicians* (1944) and *A Treasury of the Blues* (1949).

ABOUT: Ewen, D. Great Men of American Popular Song, 2d ed. 1972; Handy, W. C. Father of the Blues, 1985; Montgomery, E. R. William C. Handy: Father of the Blues, 1968.

HARBACH, OTTO (August 18, 1873–January 24, 1963). For a quarter of a century, Otto Harbach was one of Broadway's most prolific librettists and lyricists, working with composers such as Rudolf Friml, George Gershwin, Karl Hoschna, Jerome Kern, Sigmund Romberg and Vincent Youmans. He was involved in 37 stage productions and was represented by as many as five Broadway shows in a single season. Though the critics sometimes found his libretti to be slow-moving and heavy, to Jerome Kern, Harbach was "second to no dramatic author in his understanding of musical values."

Harbach was born Otto Abels Hauerbach on August 18, 1873 in Salt Lake City, Utah, one of eight children of Adolph Julius and Hansina (Olsen) Hauerbach. His father had emigrated from Denmark in 1863 and had driven an ox team to Salt Lake City, where he settled and earned his living as a jeweler and watchmaker.

While attending the Collegiate Institute in Salt Lake, Otto contributed to the family finances by working as a delivery boy, a shoeshine boy in a barber shop and, later as a violinist in a theater orchestra. Following his graduation in 1891, Harbach entered Knox College in Galesburg, Illinois. He received a bachelor of arts degree in 1895, also won an interstate prize in oratory that year, and a master of arts degree in English three years later. From 1898 to 1901, he was professor of English at Whitman College in Walla Walla, Washington, where he participated in the school's dramatic programs.

OTTO HARBACH

In 1901, Harbach went to New York to pursue a doctorate in English literature at Columbia University. A problem with his eyesight and lack of funds forced him to abandon this plan after a few months. He then worked as a reporter for the New York *Daily News*, and from 1903 to 1910, he was employed as a copywriter at the George Batten Advertising Agency.

In 1902, Harbach met Karl Hoschna, a musician employed at the house of M. Witmark & Sons as arranger and as Isador Witmark's assistant in selecting songs for publication. Harbach and Hoschna decided to work on an operetta; Harbach would provide the libretto and lyrics, and Hoschna the music. Their first effort, *The Daughter of the Desert*, though given several options, was never produced. *The Belle of the West* (1905), their first production, failed, as did their next two operettas. Success came with *The Three Twins* (June 15, 1908), an adaptation by Charles Dickson of Mrs. Romualdo Pacheco's farce *Incog*, with lyrics by Harbach and music by Hoschna. It ran for 288 performances and established the team on Broadway. The "three twins" of the title were two brothers and a third man, Tom Stanhope, who disguises himself as one of the brothers to woo the girl he loves. Alice Yorke, in the role of that girl, introduced one of the show's most enduring songs, "Cuddle Up a Little Closer, Lovey Mine" in "a unique chorus setting representing the seven ages of lovers from infancy to old age." Hoschna had originally composed this song for a vaudeville sketch, but with new lyrics by Harbach, it was incorporated into *The Three Twins* while the operetta was in rehearsal. This song was often heard in motion pictures, from *The Story of Vernon and Irene Castle* (1939), *The Birth of the Blues* (1941), *Coney Island* (1943), and *On Moonlight Bay* (1951) to *Tall Story* (1960).

Madame Sherry (August 30, 1910) was Hoschna and Harbach's next operetta. It, too, was a great success at the box office with 231 performances on Broadway, followed by a national tour. In addition to writing the lyrics for it, Harbach also contributed a text (advertised as "a French vaudeville") loosely based on George Edwardes's London production. The story focuses on Edward Sherry, who has deceived his rich uncle into believing that he has a wife and family. When Uncle Theophilus pays a surprise visit, Edward coerces his housekeeper into posing as Madame Sherry. Suddenly, no relationship is what it seems to be, but the deception is eventually uncovered by the wily Theophilus. Florence Mackie, as Lulu (modeled on Isadora Duncan), introduced the provocative recurring theme of the operetta, the waltz "Every Little Movement (Has a Meaning All its Own)." In motion pictures, this waltz again became popular in the 1940s, when it was heard in such films as *Shine On, Harvest Moon* (1944), *The Al Jolson Story* (1946), *April Showers* (1948), and *On Moonlight Bay* (1951).

After Hoschna's early death in 1911, Harbach began to work with composer Rudolf Friml. He wrote the libretto and lyrics for Friml's first operetta, *The Firefly* (December 2, 1912). Though the critics found the libretto to be somewhat heavy, the score included the lovely "Sympathy," "Giannini Mia" and the fresh "Love is Like a Firefly." Because of the success of the 1936 film version of Friml's *Rose-Marie*, *The Firefly*, which also starred Jeanette MacDonald, was released in 1937. Harbach then wrote the text with Leo Ditrichstein and lyrics for Friml's *High Jinks* (December 10, 1913), a hit of the 1913–14 season which included "Love's Own Kiss" and "Something Seems Tingle-Ingling." Next came the also popular *Katinka* (December 23, 1915), from which comes the classic "Allah's Holiday."

In the teens, Harbach also composed two important musicals with Louis A. Hirsch. For *Going Up* (December 25, 1917) Harbach (with Hirsch and James Montgomery) adapted Montgomery's play, *The Aviator*. The main character is the author of a bestselling book about aviation, though he has never actually been in a plane. He soon finds himself in the position of having to compete in an air race with a veteran flier to win the girl he loves. After futile attempts to extricate himself from the situation, he goes on to meet the challenge. Edith Day, as Grace, the heroine, introduced the hit song, "The Tickle Toe." The show was extremely popular and achieved a run of 351 performances.

Hirsch's *Mary* (October 18, 1920) was already a success by the time it reached Broadway, where it ran for 259 performances. Frank Mandel collaborated with Harbach on the libretto and lyrics for the homespun. sentimental musical produced by George M. Cohan. The show's principal song and biggest hit, "The Love Nest" (introduced by Jack McGowan and Janet Velie), was inspired by the fact that the hero builds "portable houses" or mobile homes, known as "love nests." The song was recorded by both Frank Crumit and John Steel in 1920, and many years later, "The Love Nest" became the signature music of Burns and Allen; it was also heard in the film *June Bride* (1943), and was sung by Gogi Grant in *The Helen Morgan Story* (1957).

In 1923, Harbach and William Anthony McGuire were co-librettists for Ziegfeld's *Kid Boots* (December 31, 1923), a vehicle for Eddie Cantor with a score by Joseph McCarthy and Harry Tierney. While the show itself was unexceptional, Cantor and Mary Eaton carried it during a run of 479 performances.

The following year, Harbach renewed his collaboration with Friml, and together with Oscar Hammerstein II (the nephew of producer Arthur Hammerstein) he wrote the book and lyrics for *Rose-Marie* (September 2, 1924), commercially the most successful show of the 1920s. The show starred Mary Ellis and Dennis King in a romance with an Indian flavor set in the Canadian Rockies. The score was one of Friml's best, and included "Indian Love Call," "Tramp, Tramp, Tramp," and "The Song of the Mounties." The operetta was extremely popular, running for 557 performances before four companies toured the country; long runs were also achieved in London, Paris and other European cities. Three motion picture versions were made in 1928, (starring Joan Crawford), 1936 (in which Jeanette MacDonald and Nelson Eddy's rendition of "Indian Love Call" is a classic), and 1954 (starring Ann Blyth and Howard Keel).

Harbach and Hammerstein also worked with composer Vincent Youmans. To *Wildflower* (February 7, 1923), they contributed the book and lyrics, including the popular "Bambalina." Harbach went on to write the libretto (with Frank Mandel) and contribute lyrics to Youmans's *No! No! Nanette* (September 16, 1925); however the lyrics for many of the show's hit songs were written by Irving Caesar. But the team was reunited for Jerome Kern's *Sunny* (September 22, 1925), whose score included "Who?" and "D'Ya Love Me?" and for *Song of*

the Flame (December 30, 1925), with a score by George Gershwin and Herbert Stothart. They also contributed the libretto and lyrics (with Frank Mandel) for Sigmund Romberg's operetta, *The Desert Song* (November 30, 1926).

In 1931, Harbach went to Hollywood to write lyrics to music by Jerome Kern for the motion picture, *Men in the Sky* (1931), but in the final version, the songs were discarded and Kern's score was used as background music. Kern and Harbach then returned to Broadway with the highly successful (395 performances) *The Cat and the Fiddle* (October 15, 1931); among its songs were "The Night Was Made for Love" and "She Didn't Say Yes." One of Kern's last musicals, *Roberta* (November 18, 1933), followed; the score, which included "Smoke Gets in Your Eyes," "Yesterday" and "The Touch of Your Hand," compensated for the shortcomings of Harbach's libretto. The show ran for 295 performances and a motion picture version (which included Harbach's new "I Don't Dance") was released in 1935.

Harbach's career on Broadway ended with an operetta by Romberg, *Forbidden Melody* (November 2, 1936), a production which lasted for only 32 performances. It failed because both the book and the score were thought to be old-fashioned. In the mid-1930s, Harbach assumed executive duties at ASCAP: he had become a charter member in 1914 and he served as vice-president from 1936 to 1940 and as president from 1950 to 1953.

On December 4, 1918, Harbach married Eloise Smith and they made their home and raised two sons in New York. For diversion, he went horseback riding, yachting, and played golf. He was a member of the Lamb's Club and the author of several plays, including the highly successful farce, *Up in Mabel's Room* (1919), written with Wilson Collison. In 1934, he received an honorary doctorate of literature from his alma mater, Knox College.

Otto Harbach died at the age of 89 in New York.

ABOUT: Craig, W. Sweet and Lowdown: America's Popular Song Writers, 1978; Current Biography, 1950; Ewen, D. Great Men of American Popular Song, 2d ed. 1972.

HARBURG, E. Y. (April 8, 1896–March 5, 1981). One of the most eminent librettists and lyricists for the Broadway theater and motion picture screen, E. Y. Harburg was the partner of some of America's most distinguished composers of popular music: Harold Arlen, Vernon Duke,

E. Y. HARBURG

Sammy Fain, Jay Gorney, Jerome Kern, Burton Lane, Arthur Schwartz and Jule Styne. "Writing with different composers is always a different psychological experience," he told Max Wilk in *They're Playing Our Song*. "Each one has his own approach to creation. To know their idiosyncracies and to be able to get the best out of each one is fascinating. Each composer brings out a different aspect of your work. . . . It's diplomacy, it's psychology, it's psychiatry—it's knowing the person you are dealing with, and the sensitivities of the two of you." In both his books and lyrics, Harburg deftly treated subjects ranging from romance to satire, from the banal to the poetic. In addition, he was one of the few professionals on Broadway and in Hollywood who, in defiance of the establishment, often carried his strong political and social consciousness into his work: "I think I'm a rebel by birth," he has said. "I contest anything that is unjust, that causes suffering in humanity. My feeling about that is so great that I don't think I could live with myself if I weren't honest. . . . If they wanted me, they would have to endure my politics."

E. Y. ("Yip") Harburg was born Edgar Harburg in New York City, one of two sons of Lewis and Mary (Ricing) Harburg. The "Y" comes from a nickname he acquired in boyhood when his friends called him "Yipsel the squirrel" because he was always scampering about. Harburg's parents had emigrated from Russia, making their home on New York's East Side, where his father was employed as a garment worker in a sweatshop. Growing up in poverty, watching his father age prematurely as he eked out a meager living for the family, seeing eco-

nomic injustice and exploitation all around him, set the stage for Harburg's lifelong social consciousness. But his boyhood was not unhappy. He played baseball with a team that won the New York State championship, and he discovered his love of the theater when his schoolteacher took his class to a performance of *Peter Pan*, starring Maude Adams. Before long, he was acting in school productions, at a local settlement house, and in productions of a literary dramatic club to which he belonged. While attending P.S. 64, he contributed amusing pieces to the school newspaper which he sometimes was called upon to read in class to the delight of his peers. He was always creating witty parodies of current songs: "I found I had the ability to act and write my own stuff," he told Max Wilk. "Scrounging around for costumes, putting on shows—it was great. We were poor, always out on the street with our furniture, and never knowing if the next rent would be paid. But I had an excellent time."

Because he was an excellent student, in 1913, Harburg was admitted to Townsend Harris Hall, a high school for superior students offering an accelerated three-year curriculum. He helped to support himself by selling newspapers and working at night for the Edison Company for $3.06 a week, turning the street lamps on at dusk and off at 3:00 in the morning. At Townsend Harris, Harburg was co-editor (with classmate Ira Gershwin) of a literary column for the school paper. In 1914, both Harburg and Gershwin went on to the College of the City of New York with which Townsend Harris was affiliated. Gershwin remained for only two years, but during that time, he and Harburg wrote a column, "Gargoyle Gargler" by "Yip" and "Gersh" for *The Campus*, the college paper. Harburg contributed light verses and other pieces (for which he was paid $10 or $15 each) to humor magazines such as *Judge* and *Life*, and also to the famous column of Franklin P. Adams, "The Conning Tower," in the New York *World*, for which the sole compensation was being recognized. He and Gershwin also contributed special material to amateur shows produced at the Christadora House, a settlement house in lower Manhattan.

One day, at the Gershwin home, Harburg heard a Victrola recording of the Gilbert and Sullivan operetta, *H. M. S. Pinafore*. Harburg had previously read, and admired Gilbert's verses, but this was the first time he was hearing them set to Sullivan's music: "I was starry-eyed for days. I couldn't sleep at night. It was that music—and the satire that came out with all the emotion that I never dreamed of before when I read the thing in cold print." It was after listening to *Pinafore* that Harburg first considered the possibility of becoming a song lyricist.

But the impracticality of trying to earn a living by writing verses drove Harburg into the business world when he graduated from City College with a Bachelor of Science degree in 1918. He found a job as a South American representative of an American firm that soon went bankrupt. Harburg remained in South America three years, holding various jobs including one as journalist in Montevideo, Uruguay. Returning to New York in 1921, he and a former classmate formed the Consolidated Electrical Appliance Company, and on February 23, 1923, he married Alice Richmond with whom he had two children. Though the business thrived, Harburg did not enjoy it, and he continued to scribble verses and humorous pieces for magazines. His song lyrics were heard on the Broadway stage for the first time in 1926: "Brother, Just Laugh it Off," with music by two other fledglings, Arthur Schwartz and Ralph Rainger, was interpolated into the score (by Lew Gensler and B. G. De Sylva) of the highly successful musical, *Queen High.*

The stock market crash of 1929 and economic depression that followed spelled ruin for Harburg's prosperous business. "I was penniless—in fact, I owed a lot of money. I was left with a pencil, and finally had to write for a living. . . . I had my fill of this dream abstract thing called business and I decided to face reality and write lyrics."

He called on his friend, Ira Gershwin, for help. Gershwin introduced him to Jay Gorney, a young composer who had already gathered some impressive credits on Broadway. They joined their respective talents and placed six songs in Earl Carroll's *Sketch Book* (1929), the best of which was "Kinda Cute"; several songs in *Earl Carroll's Vanities of 1930* which included "One Love" and "I Came to Life"; "Mailu" in the *Ziegfeld Follies of 1931*; and three songs, including "Muchacha" (music written with Vernon Duke) in *Shoot the Works* (1931). Soon after Gorney started writing music for films at the Paramount studios in Astoria, Harburg also signed a contract. Together, they wrote "What Wouldn't I Do for That Man?" for Helen Morgan in *Applause* (1930) which she repeated in *Glorifying the American Girl* (1930); she also sang their "It Can't Go on Like This" in *Roadhouse Nights* (1930). For the screen adaptation of *Queen High* (1930), Harburg wrote "I Love the Girls in My Own Peculiar Way" (music by Henry Souvaine), and he also contributed songs to *The Count of Monte Cristo* (1934).

Harburg continued to collaborate with Vernon Duke on Broadway, notably on "I Am Only Human After All" (lyrics written with Ira Gershwin) and "Too, Too Divine" for the *Garrick Gaieties of 1930.* With Lew Gensler, he wrote the score for *Ballyhoo* (September 6, 1932) before working again with Duke on the revue, *Walk a Little Faster* (December 7, 1932), which starred Beatrice Lillie, Bobby Clark and Paul McCullough. In it, Evelyn Hoey introduced the lush "April in Paris," which quickly and firmly established the songwriting reputations of both Duke and Harburg.

Harburg's sympathy for the underprivileged and the downtrodden came to the fore in "Brother, Can You Spare a Dime?" (music by Jay Gorney), written for the modest, intimate revue, *Americana* (October 5, 1932); the song henceforth became identified with the Depression of the early 1930s. "It was a terrible period," Harburg told Wilk. "You couldn't walk along the street without crying, without seeing people standing in bread lines, so miserable. Brokers and people who'd been wealthy, begging. 'Can you spare a dime?' . . . a dime could keep you alive for a few days. When Jay played me the tune he had, I thought of that phrase, 'Can you spare a dime?' It kept running through my mind. . . . I thought that lyric out very carefully. I didn't make it a maudlin lyric of a guy begging. I made it into a commentary . . . It was about a fellow who works, the fellow who builds, who makes the railroads and the houses—and he's left empty-handed. How come? How did this happen? . . . This is a man proud of what he's done, but he's bewildered that his country could do this to him. I think the lyric first of all hits you emotionally, directly. And this did it because of the music, and because the fellow wasn't being petty or small or complaining."

Harburg also collaborated with Burton Lane and Vernon Duke on *Americana,* but particularly fortuitous was his meeting with the young composer, Harold Arlen; the two were soon to form one of the most successful partnerships in the musical theater and motion pictures of the 1930s. For *Americana,* they composed "Satan's Li'l Lamb" (lyrics written with Johnny Mercer). Next came "If You Believe in Me," composed as incidental music for the Broadway play, *The Great Magoo* (1932); it was then heard in the motion picture *Take a Chance* (1933) under the new title of "It's Only a Paper Moon," the first of the Harburg-Arlen standards. With Ira Gershwin as his co-lyricist, Harburg provided the words to Arlen's music for the Broadway revue, *Life Begins at 8:40* (August 27, 1934) which starred Bert Lahr and Ray Bolger; its best songs were "What Can You Say in a Love Song?", "You're a Builder-Upper," "Fun to Be Fooled" and "Let's Take a Walk Around the Block." For the Broadway revue, *The Show Is On* (December 25, 1936), the team composed "Song of the

Woodman" which became a tour-de-force for Bert Lahr. The next complete Harburg-Arlen Broadway score was *Horray, for What?* (December 1, 1937), starring Ed Wynn, which included "Moanin' in the Mornin'" and "I've Gone Romantic on You."

In 1935, Harburg and Arlen went to Hollywood, where they wrote "Last Night When We Were Young" for the Metropolitan Opera baritone, Lawrence Tibbett. Though it was cut from the final print of the motion picture, *Metropolitan*, in which Tibbett starred, it became one of their most successful ballads, and Harburg always regarded this as one of his best lyrics.

Harburg and Arlen were prolific in writing songs for the screen during the late 1930s. "You're the Cure for What Ails Me" and "I Love to Sing-a" appeared in *The Singing Kid* (1936), starring Al Jolson; "Fancy Meeting You" and "In Your Quiet Way," in *Stage Struck* (1936); and "Let's Put Our Heads Together" and "Speaking of the Weather," in *Gold Diggers of 1937*. In 1939, they reached the apex of their Hollywood careers, with "Over the Rainbow," from *The Wizard of Oz*. This song won an Oscar and was heard in first position on *Your Hit Parade* and Judy Garland, who introduced it in the film, adopted it as her musical signature. Harburg is modest about his role in creating one of the greatest successes of his career: "You're talking about a big giant of a composer writing a hell of a great tune . . . and I happened to take a hitchhike on his coattails."

Harburg and Arlen temporarily (and briefly) changed writing partners, after writing "Two Blind Loves" and "Lydia, the Tattooed Lady" for the Marx Brothers extravaganza, *At the Circus* (1939). Harburg and Burton Lane composed the score to *Hold on to Your Hats*, (September 11, 1940) starring Al Jolson in his last appearance on the Broadway stage in which "There's a Great Day Coming Mañana," "The World is in My Arms" and "Don't Let it Get You Down" were sung; the book was by Guy Bolton, Matt Brooks and Eddie Davis. For Hollywood, they composed songs for *Babes on Broadway* (1942), *Ship Ahoy* (1942) and *Meet the People* (1944), the last for which Harburg also served as producer. For several other films, starring Ethel Waters, the Harburg-Arlen team was revived, most significantly for the screen adaptation of the musical *Cabin in the Sky* (1943), which included the Academy Award-winning song, "Happiness is a Thing Called Joe."

Harburg and Arlen made a triumphant return to Broadway with *Bloomer Girl* (October 5, 1941). Its book, set during the Civil War, deals with racial prejudice, women's liberation and man's right to be free. Highlights included "Right as the Rain," "I Got a Song," "Evelina," "T'morra, T'morra," and "The Eagle and Me."

Harburg continued working for motion pictures until 1945. His most important assignment was *Can't Help Singing* (1944), starring Deanna Durbin. Jerome Kern composed the score, and their "More and More" was heard on *Your Hit Parade*. Harburg also wrote lyrics for *Centennial Summer* (1946).

By 1947, Harburg's open espousal of left-wing politics and organizations caused him to be blacklisted by Hollywood producers; failure to find work in Hollywood compelled him to turn once more to Broadway. But Hollywood's loss was Broadway's gain. With Burton Lane as composer, Harburg collaborated with Fred Saidy on the book and wrote the lyrics for the musical fantasy *Finian's Rainbow* (January 10, 1947). Setting the story in the mythical town of Missitucky, Harburg expressed his social philosophy wittily and sardonically by satirizing Southern politics, bigotry, the plight of sharecroppers, labor exploitation, avarice and the poll tax. In their score, Harburg and Lane combined such touching ballads as "How Are Things in Glocca Morra?" and "Look to the Rainbow" with the iridescent "When the Idle Poor Become the Idle Rich," "When I'm Not Near the Girl I Love" and "Something Sort of Grandish." The show was extremely successful and ran for 725 performances. *Flahooley* (October 31, 1957), with a book and lyrics by Harburg and music by Sammy Fain, was a satire on big business; it was a box-office disaster. Harburg resumed his winning stride with *Jamaica*, which starred Lena Horne; Fred Saidy wrote the book and Harold Arlen, the music. "Take it Slow, Joe," "Coconut Sweet," "Little Biscuit," and "Savannah" were memorable songs in a score that also included the political "Leave the Atom Alone" and "Napoleon."

The Happiest Girl in the World (April 3, 1961) proved to be an unhappy attempt to update Aristophanes's *Lysistrata* with a score by Gorney adapted from the music of Offenbach. It was short-lived on Broadway, as was *Darling of the Day* (January 27, 1968), with music by Jule Styne. Harburg (returning to Hollywood for the first time) and Arlen contributed songs to two Judy Garland films, first "Little Drops of Rain" to *Gay Purr-ee* (1962), an animated feature in which her voice was heard, and then the title song to *I Could Go On Singing* (1963).

In December 1970, Harburg inaugurated the annual series "Lyrics and Lyricists" at the YMHA in New York, to which he returned in

1972 and 1977. (Posthumously, he was honored with a program called "Harburg Back in Hollywood" in February 1982.) Four years later, *I Got a Song*, described in the program as "a view of life and times through the lyrics of E. Y. Harburg," with a book by Fred Saidy was mounted in Buffalo, New York. Harburg's last stage musical, *What a Day for a Miracle* (1977) is about the Children's Crusade of 1212, with a book (with Henry Myers) and lyrics by Harburg and music by Jeff Alexander and Larry Ornstein. It was produced by the American Playwrights Co. and has been presented on college campuses.

Commenting on Harburg's lyrics, Fred Saidy has written: "His rhymes see contemporary life as endlessly menacing but ultimately hopeful. They sing of man's foolishness but do not condemn him to it for life. If they sting while they sing, it is only to pry 'genus homo' off his rump and get him headed for the stars. This poet, you see, is too fond of the human race not to scold it now and then. That the scolding is couched in humorous strophes is a mark of his affection and a promise of your entertainment."

Harburg's first marriage ended in divorce in 1929; he married Edelaine Roden on January 18, 1943. They maintained a large apartment on Central Park West in New York, a home in California, and a summer retreat on Martha's Vineyard. Harburg was described by *The New York Times* (March 7, 1981) as "a slight, ebullient man with a puckish manner and eyes that were constantly twinkling with laughter." His favorite pastimes were golf, tennis and swimming, and he also kept fit by adhering to a diet of natural foods.

Harburg died in a head-on collision while driving on Sunset Boulevard in Los Angeles on March 5, 1981. He was en route to a meeting concerning a television tribute to him, and the following week, he was scheduled to receive the Johnny Mercer Award from the Songwriters Hall of Fame (into which he had been inducted in 1973) in New York.

In 1950, Harburg received the Townsend Harris Award as an outstanding alumnus of the College of the City of New York. He was awarded an honorary doctorate in literature from the University of Vermont (1971), an honorary Doctor of Fine Arts from Columbia College in Chicago (1978) and an honorary Doctor of Arts from the City University of New York (1979).

He was the author of two collections of light verse, *Rhymes for the Irreverent* (1965) and *At This Point of Time* (1976).

ABOUT: Current Biography, 1980; Engel, Lehman, Their Words Are Music, 1975; Wilk, Max, They're Playing Our Song, 1973; Notable Names in the American Theatre, 1976. *Periodicals*—New York Times, March 16, 1977, June 26, 1977.

HARRIGAN, ED. *See* BRAHAM, DAVID and HARRIGAN, ED

HARRIS, CHARLES K(ASSELL) (May 1, 1865–December 22, 1930), one of the most significant composers of sentimental ballads in the 1890s, was born in Poughkeepsie, New York, the son of Jacob and Rachel (Kassell) Harris. His father emigrated to the United States from Germany in 1853, and while Charles was still a boy, the family moved to East Saginaw, Michigan, where Jacob Harris operated a tailor shop. Many of his free hours were spent watching entertainers from variety and minstrel shows rehearse their acts in a nearby hotel, and he was inspired to construct a banjo from an empty oyster can and some strands of wire. An actor observing Charles singing and strumming along on his "banjo," presented him with the real thing and taught him several chords.

The family moved to Milwaukee when Harris was 14. There, in 1881, inspired by a frustrated love affair, he composed his first ballad "Can Hearts So Soon Forget?" which he published himself a decade later. In Milwaukee, Harris worked as a hotel bellhop and as a clerk in a pawnshop. In addition, he had become proficient enough on the banjo to take on several pupils and to secure occasional engagements in clubs and small variety theaters as a singer accompanying himself on the banjo. He also began teaching himself to play the piano.

After attending a performance of *The Skating Rink*, starring Nat Goodwin in 1881, Harris was encouraged by his friend, Charles Horwitz (later of the vaudeville team, Horwitz and Bowers) to write a skating song for the show. Goodwin was induced to use "Since Maggie Learned to Skate," (lyrics by Horwitz), and it was Harris's first success. Harris's other early efforts included "Creep, Baby, Creep," "Kiss and Let's Make Up," "When the Sun has Set," and his first published song, "Thou Art Ever in My Thoughts," issued by the Milwaukee publisher, William H. Rohlfing. By 1883, his reputation had begun to grow and David Henderson, manager of The Chicago Opera House, invited Harris to contribute three songs to the new edition of *Sinbad the Sailor*, a popular extravaganza starring Eddie Foy.

Harris soon came to believe that songwriting

CHARLES K. HARRIS

might be a more lucrative profession if he published his own songs. He borrowed a thousand dollars from two friends and opened a one-room publishing office on Grand Avenue in Milwaukee in 1885. The rent was $7.50 a month, and operating expenditures an additional $2.50. Outside of his office, he hung a shingle reading: "Charles K. Harris, Banjoist and Song Writer. Songs, Written to Order," and the firm's motto was "Never Out of Print." By the end of his first year in business, he had accumulated a profit of $3,000, which enabled him to repay his debts and move to a larger office in the Alhambra Building. Soon he opened a small branch in Chicago.

During a visit to Chicago, where he attended a dance, Harris noticed a young couple quarreling before going their separate ways. When he mused that "many a heart is aching, after the ball," Harris knew he had a subject for a sentimental ballad. Upon returning to Milwaukee, he composed a waltz, "After the Ball," designating it a "song story" because an extended narrative unfolds through three verses. It tells of an old man who had never married because many years earlier, he had found his only sweetheart kissing a stranger; only much later did he learn that the stranger was her brother.

Harris published "After the Ball" in 1892. When Sam Doctor, an aspiring singer (and Harris's tailor), introduced the song that year in a Milwaukee theater, it was a fiasco since midway in his rendition, Doctor forgot the words and inspired laughter rather then sentiment. But Harris was able to place the song with J. Aldrich Libby, the popular musical-comedy performer

who was starring in *A Trip to Chinatown* at the Bijou Theatre. For his cooperation, Libby received $500 and a small percentage of the royalties from the sheet music sales (an early example of "payola"). Dressed incongruously in evening clothes for a scene set in San Francisco's Chinatown, Libby sang this ballad even though it had no possible relevance to the plot of the musical or to any of its characters. At the end of the first verse and chorus "not a sound was heard," Harris later recalled in his autobiography, *After the Ball.* "I was ready to sink through the floor. He then went through the second verse and chorus, and again complete silence reigned. I was making ready to bolt, but my friends . . . held me tightly by the arms. Then came the third verse and chorus. For a full minute the audience remained quiet, and then broke loose with applause. . . . The entire audience arose and, standing, wildly applauded for five minutes." Harris declined Julius Witmark's immediate offer of $10,000 for the rights to the song, believing it would be more profitable to publish it himself. A few days later, the Boston music publisher, Oliver Ditson, ordered 75,000 copies of sheet music; to fill the order, Harris had to buy his own printing press. Before the year was over, it was being sung in saloons, restaurants and everywhere. In vaudeville, May Irwin took it to New York, and it became the *tour de force* of Helene Mora, "the female baritone." John Philip Sousa featured it prominently in a band arrangement at the World's Fair in Chicago in 1893, where it enjoyed such acclaim that, henceforth, he rarely gave a concert anywhere without performing it. That year, Harris earned $25,000 a week from "After the Ball," and he rented every available press in the city to fill the avalanche of sheet music orders. In time, "After the Ball" sold about five million copies, which was unprecedented in Tin Pan Alley, and in all, Harris earned more than 10 million dollars in profits.

In 1914, "After the Ball" was dramatized in a silent film produced by the Photo Drama Moving Picture Company. It brought Harris the highest fee paid for a scenario by the industry thus far. Magnolia, the heroine of Jerome Kern's *Show Boat* (1927) (first played by Norma Terris) sings it in a scene taking place in the Trocadero Music Hall at the Chicago World's Fair. It was also featured in films such as *Lillian Russell* (1940), *The Jolson Story* (1946), and *A Girl in My Heart* (1950).

At the height of his success, Harris married Cora Lehrberg on November 15, 1893; they raised two daughters. He continued to be a prolific writer of the fashionable ballads that brought tears to the eyes of listeners. Though none repeated the triumph of "After the Ball," two are of particular interest. "Break the News to Mother" (1897) was inspired by a scene in *Secret Service,* a stage melodrama starring William Gillette in which a wounded drummer boy in the Confederate army whispers to the plantation's black butler to "break the news to mother." The day after he had attended the play, Harris completed the first verse and chorus of a ballad but "how to end the song with a punch puzzled me," he wrote in his autobiography. "While still in the barber's chair a thought came to my mind in a flash, and I cried out, 'I have it! I'm going to kill him!' The barber who was shaving me at the time became very much startled when he heard this remark and thought I had lost my reason." When he tried out the ballad on his brother, the response was negative. His brother reminded him that America had not been at war since 1865 and that another was not imminent. This being the case, there could hardly be a market for a war song. However, the Spanish-American War made the ballad timely, and it became popular with both soldiers and their loved ones back home. There was a revival of interest in it during World War I; it was recorded in 1940 by the Mills Brothers and interpolated into the film, *Wait Till the Sun Shines, Nellie* (1952).

Harris's second greatest success was the heart-wrenching "Hello, Central, Give Me Heaven" (1901), in which a little girl tries to contact her recently deceased mother for comfort and consolation. It was one of the first Tin Pan Alley songs featuring the telephone. Charles Horwitz introduced it in vaudeville.

Among Harris's many ballads, the following, though unfamiliar now, enjoyed a measure of popularity in their own time: "Fallen by the Wayside" (1892), "You Never Spoke to Me Like That Before" (1893), "There'll Come a Time" (1895), "All for the Love of a Girl" (1896), "I've Just Come Back to Say Goodbye" (1897), "Mid' the Green Fields of Virginia" (1898), "One Night in June" (1899), "I've a Longing in My Heart for You, Louise" (1900), "What is a Home Without Love?" (1900), and "Always in the Way" (1903). Though Harris continued to compose throughout his life, his sentimental, narrative ballads no longer appealed to a public whose tastes had changed.

In 1903, Harris moved the Charles K. Harris Publishing Co. to New York, where he became the first composer-publisher in Tin Pan Alley without partners. He also wrote several plays, which were unsuccessful, and scenarios for silent films. In 1906, he published *How to Write a Popular Song,* which includes tips about the music business, as well as songwriting, and in 1926,

an autobiography, *After the Ball: Forty Years of Melody.* He died in New York City, where he had lived since 1903, in late 1930.

ABOUT: Dictionary of American Biography, 1932; Hamm, C. Yesterdays: Popular Song in America, 1979; Whticomb, I. After the Ball, 1972.

HART, LORENZ. *See* **RODGERS, RICHARD** and **HART, LORENZ**

HENDERSON, RAY (December 16, 1896–December 31, 1970). Composer Ray Henderson was the third member of the songwriting triumvirate, De Sylva, Brown and Henderson, who were the rage of Broadway in the later 1920s and whose hit numbers enriched the soundtracks of motion pictures from the late 1920s through the early 1950s.

Ray Henderson was born Raymond Brost in Buffalo, New York, the son of William Brost and the former Margaret Baker. The stage and music were family traditions, with three of Ray's uncles being professionals in the theater: Julius Baker, a manager of road shows; George Baker, a performer in circuses and vaudeville; and Frank Brost, a vaudevillian. Ray's father was a proficient flutist, violinist and pianist, and Margaret Brost played the piano.

As a boy, Ray Henderson sang in the choir of the local Episcopal Church, where he also played the organ and made his first attempt at composition. He studied harmony, counterpoint and organ in Buffalo in the years before World War I, and found work as an accompanist for local music teachers, as a pianist in dance bands, and he taught the piano himself. Later study of composition took place for one year at the Juilliard School of Music with Vittorio Giannini.

During World War I Henderson played in a band promoting the sale of Liberty bonds. On October 10, 1918 he married Florence Hoffman; they raised a son and two daughters. Henderson moved to New York City after the war, working in Tin Pan Alley as a song plugger for the publishing firm of Leo Feist Inc., as a staff pianist and arranger for the Fred Fisher publishing house, and as a song plugger and arranger for Shapiro-Bernstein. Louis Bernstein also helped Henderson get jobs as a piano accompanist for several vaudeville performers.

Because Henderson had for some time been writing songs, without recognition, in 1922 Bernstein introduced him to Lew Brown, an experienced lyricist. Their first hit song was

RAY HENDERSON

"Georgette," which Shapiro-Bernstein published that year. Ted Lewis and his band introduced it in the *Greenwich Village Follies of 1922*; they also recorded it as did Ruth Roye. In 1922 Henderson and Brown also composed "Humming," with "Annabelle," interpolated into the *Ziegfeld Follies of 1923*, and "Counterfeit Bill From Louisville" coming the next year. In 1924 they wrote "Why Did I Kiss That Girl?" (music written with Robert King), and in 1925, "Don't Bring Lulu" (lyrics written with Billy Rose), which the team of Van and Schenck popularized in vaudeville. The last of these was revived in the 1948 motion picture *When My Baby Smiles at Me* and was sung by a children's choir in the film *Bells on Their Toes* (1952).

All this time Henderson worked with other lyricists. With Bud Green he wrote "I Thought I'd Die" (1922). Billy Rose and Mort Dixon were the lyricists for "That Old Gang of Mine" (1923), which was interpolated for Van and Schenck into the *Ziegfeld Follies of 1923* and recorded that year by Bennie Krueger, by Billy Murray with Ed Smalle and by Les Stevens. Dixon and Rose were also the lyricsts in 1924, for "Follow the Swallow," which Al Jolson recorded, and "I Wonder Who's Dancing With Her Tonight?" Henderson and Dixon wrote "You're in Love With Everyone But the One Who's in Love With You" (1924) and "Bye, Bye, Blackbird" (1926). The latter was popularized in a recording by Eddie Cantor, and became Georgie Price's theme song. On the screen it was sung by Frankie Laine in *Rainbow 'Round My Shoulder* (1952); by Marilyn Monroe in *River of No Return* (1954);

by Eddie Cantor on the soundtrack of *The Eddie Cantor Story* (1954); and Jason Robards in *Melvin and Howard* (1981). In *Julia* (1977), starring Jane Fonda and Vanessa Redgrave, it was performed orchestrally.

For two of Henderson's hit songs of 1925 the lyricists were Sam M. Lewis and Joe Young. "Five Feet Two, Eyes of Blue" was much-performed in vaudeville and in 1925 it was recorded by the orchestras of Fred Rich and Art Landray. Later recorded by Guy Lombardo and His Royal Canadians, it was revived in 1948 in a recording by Art Mooney, and in 1949 it was heard twice on *Your Hit Parade*. Subsequently, "Five Feet Two, Eyes of Blue" was interpolated into the motion picture *Has Anybody Seen My Gal* (1952), was danced to by Doris Day in *Love Me or Leave Me* (1955), and was heard on the soundtrack of *The Great Gatsby* (1974). "I'm Sitting on Top of the World" was an Al Jolson specialty which he introduced and popularized at the Winter Garden. He recorded it in 1925 and sang it in the motion picture *The Singing Fool* (1929) and on the soundtrack of *The Jolson Story* (1947). In 1925 the song was also recorded by the orchestra of Roger Wolfe Kahn and in 1926 by the Trix Sisters.

Henderson's first important collaboration with B. G. De Sylva took place in 1925, when they composed "Alabamy Bound" (lyrics written with Ray Green). It was introduced and popularized by Al Jolson at the Winter Garden. Jolson recorded it, as did Aileen Stanely. It was further popularized by Eddie Cantor, who interpolated it into his Broadway musical *Kid Boots* in 1925 and also recorded it. Nora Bayes, too, was identified with this number. She sang it at her last performance, a benefit concert in New York just four days before her death. A jazz recording was made by the Goofus Five in 1925. In later performances "Alabamy Bound" was sung by the Ink Spots and danced to by the Nicholas Brothers in the film musical *The Great American Broadcast* (1941). Eddie Cantor sang it in the film, *Show Business* (1944), and Jane Froman performed it on the soundtrack of her screen biography, *With a Song in My Heart* (1952), starring Susan Hayward.

Henderson and De Sylva became a threesome when Lew Brown joined them to compose "It All Depends on You," which Jolson introduced in the 1925 extravaganza, *Big Boy*. Recordings by Al Jolson, Harry Richman, and the orchestras of Paul Whiteman and Fred Rich made the song a standard. Ruth Etting made "It All Depends on You" one of her specialties and in her screen biography, *Love Me or Leave Me* (1955), it was sung by Doris Day. Gordon MacRae and Eileen

Wilson dubbing for Sheree North sang it in *The Best Things in Life Are Free* (1956). Frank Sinatra recorded the song three times. Songs for the Broadway show *George White's Scandals of 1925* (June 22, 1925) followed the newly formed team.

From the start, De Sylva, Brown and Henderson had a unique working arrangement. Henderson was the composer and De Sylva and Brown the lyricists, but each always provided the other two valuable suggestions. Their songs were so much a three-way collaboration that in sheet-music publications, who had written the music and who the words was not identified. Their debut as composers for the *Scandals*, succeeding George Gershwin, was not auspicious. Except for "I Want a Lovable Baby," introduced by Helen Morgan, the 1925 production score lacked distinction and the show ran for just 171 performances.

Their songs for *George White's Scandals of 1926* (June 14, 1926), which had a 424-performance run, moved them into the front rank of Broadway's songwriters of the 1920s. "Lucky Day" was introduced by Harry Richman and was sung by Dan Dailey in De Sylva, Brown and Henderson's film biography, *The Best Things in Life Are Free* (1956). "Black Bottom," which featured Ann Pennington in a high-voltage dance routine devised by George White, helped make the so-called Black Bottom a popular dance in 1926. The orchestras of Lou Gold and Howard Lanin recorded the song. In *The Best Things in Life Are Free*, it was sung by Eileen Wilson (dubbing on the soundtrack for Sheree North). A segment of this song was quoted in Judy Garland's famous "Born in a Trunk" routine in *A Star Is Born* (1954). "The Girl is You" was introduced by Harry Richman, who also sang "The Birth of the Blues" in a production number pitting the blues against classicism and arriving at a compromise with a quotation from George Gershwin's *Rhapsody in Blue*. "Birth of the Blues" was recorded by Harry Richman, the Revelers, Jack Smith and the orchestra of Leo Reisman. In the 1941 film entitled *The Birth of the Blues* it was sung by Bing Crosby. Dan Dailey sang it in a production-number sequence in *When My Baby Smiles at Me* (1948); Danny Thomas in the remake of *The Jazz Singer* (1953); and Gordon MacRae in *The Best Things in Life Are Free*, in which it was danced to by Sheree North. The song was also interpolated into the film musical *Painting the Clouds with Sunshine* (1951).

In 1927–28, De Sylva, Brown and Henderson wrote three songs not originally planned for stage presentation—"Broken-Hearted" (1927),

"Just a Memory" (1927) and "Together" (1928) —but "Broken-Hearted" was interpolated into the Broadway revue *Artists and Models of 1927* for Jack Osterman, and it was popularized in vaudeville by Belle Baker. It was recorded by the Arden-Ohman orchestra, by Paul Whiteman and by Nick Lucas, and was used as a recurrent theme in the movie *Roxie Hart* (1943). In the late 1950s "Broken-Hearted" was revived by Johnnie Ray in a bestselling recording. "Just a Memory" was interpolated into the Broadway musical *Manhattan Mary* (1927) and was recorded by Paul Whiteman. It was again heard in *Penny Serenade* (1941), starring Cary Grant and Irene Dunne; in Marilyn Miller's screen biography *Look for the Silver Lining* (1949); and in *The Best Things in Life Are Free* was sung on the soundtrack by Eileen Wilson (dubbing for Sheree North) and a female chorus. "Together" was revived in the nonmusical film *Since You Went Away* (1944) and was recorded by Wayne King and his orchestra and by Dick Haymes with Helen Forrest. In 1944 it enjoyed such a renewal of popularity that it had 12 appearances on *Your Hit Parade*. Dan Dailey and Phyllis Avery sang it on *The Best Things in Life Are Free* and Connie Francis's 1961 recording was a bestseller.

Because there was no edition of *George White's Scandals* in 1927, De Sylva, Brown and Henderson found time to write their first Broadway book musical, *Good News* (September 6, 1927), libretto by Lawrence Schwab and De Sylva. The setting is Tait College, where the football stadium is vastly more important than the classroom. The hero, Tom Marlowe, captain of the football team, is coached in astronomy by his girlfriend, Constance, so that he will be eligible to play in the season's big game. Saved from making a fatal fumble, he remains the college hero while retaining Constance's love.

The entire production was alive with a sis-boom-bah spirit. Ushers dressed in college jerseys led patrons to their seats. Before the rise of the first-act curtain, the George Olsen orchestra trooped down the aisles, attired in college sweaters, yelling college rah-rahs as they took their place in the pit. Moreover there were songs like "The Girls of Pi Beta Phi," sung by a female chorus, and "The Varsity Drag," presented by a quartet headed by Zelma O'Neal and later recorded by George Olsen. The title song was introduced by Zelma O'Neal, recorded by George Olsen, and sung by Gordon MacRae, Dan Dailey and Ernest Borgnine in *The Best Things in Life Are Free*. The production's hit song was the ballad, "The Best Things in Life Are Free," introduced by John Price Jones and Mary Lawlor and recorded by Jack Smith and the orchestras of George Olsen and Frank Black.

There were two motion picture adaptations of *Good News,* one released in 1930, the other in 1947. In the first "The Varsity Drag" was sung by Penny Singleton and Billy Taft to the accompaniment of Abe Lyman and his orchestra, and by June Allyson and Peter Lawford. The title song was performed by Dorothy McNulty in the first screen version and by Joan McCracken in the second. "The Best Things in Life Are Free" was sung in the 1930 adaptation by Mary Lawlor and Stanley Smith and later by June Allyson and Peter Lawford. In *The Best Things in Life Are Free* the title number was presented before the opening titles and was reprised in a closing sequence in which it was sung by Borgnine, MacRae, Dailey and, on the soundtrack, Eileen Wilson dubbing for Sheree North.

A box-office attraction, *Good News* had an initial Broadway run of 557 performances. With text newly adapted by Garry Marshall, *Good News* returned to Broadway on December 23, 1974 after touring the country for almost a year. On Broadway, it starred Alice Faye and Gene Nelson, but critics felt that the show's prime asset was its 16 songs, 11 of which came from the original stage production, the others having been lifted from the repertory of De Sylva, Brown and Henderson standards.

In 1927 the publishing house of De Sylva, Brown and Henderson was formed. Over the next few years, as De Sylva, Brown and Henderson produced a string of hit songs, the company flourished. *George White's Scandals of 1928* (July 2, 1928), their last score for this revue as a songwriting trio, brought "I'm on the Crest of a Wave," introduced by Harry Richman, and "What D'Ya Say," a duet for Richman and Frances Williams. Richman recorded both songs. This edition of the scandals had a run of 240 performances.

Hold Everything (October 10, 1928) was the songsmiths' second book musical, and their second to have a Broadway run of more than 400 performances. Where *Good News* dealt with football, *Hold Everything,* book by De Sylva and John McGowan, lampooned the boxing game. As the veteran pugilist Gink Schiner, Bert Lahr emerged from this production as a star of musical comedy. The love story revolves around Sonny Jim Brooks, a welterweight champion, and Sue Burke. When Brooks fears he has lost Sue's love, he loses interest in his upcoming bout. However, his fighting spirit is revived when he discovers that his opponent has insulted Sue, and Sonny Jim goes on to win both the bout and his girlfriend's love. Jack Whiting and Ona Munson, as Sonny Jim and Sue, introduced "You're the Cream in My Coffee," and Alice Boulden, Buddy Harak and Harry and Anna Locke sang "Don't Hold Everything." The former was recorded by the King Cole Trio and by Carmen Cavallero. "You're the Cream in My Coffee" was interpolated into the 1929 motion picture *The Cockeyed World,* and "Don't Hold Everything" was sung by Dailey, Borgnine and MacRae in *The Best Things in Life Are Free.* The so-called film adaptation of *Hold Everything* (1930) had a completely rewritten text and the De Sylva, Brown and Henderson score was jettisoned in favor of new songs by Al Dubin and Joe Burke.

In 1928 De Sylva, Brown and Henderson received their first assignment for motion pictures, when Al Jolson asked them to write a song for his film, *The Singing Fool.* This musical number was crucial to the story of a singer-composer who is desolated by the death of his three-year-old son. Since shooting on the film was about to begin, De Sylva, Brown and Henderson had literally to produce their song overnight. They sang the finished number to Jolson over the telephone the morning after they had received the commission. That song, "Sonny Boy," is believed to have been written as a tongue-in-cheek parody of sentimental balladry, using the clichés in melody and lyric traditionally identified with such songs. To substantiate this belief is the fact that De Sylva, Brown and Henderson dispatched the sheet music to Hollywood under the pen name "Elmer Colby." Jolson performed the song without irony, presenting it with the appropriate vocal throbs and lachrymose sentimentality. Winning over the moviegoing public, "Sonny Boy" was largely responsible for the film's enormous popularity. Jolson recorded it twice, in 1928 and in 1946, and each recording sold more than a million copies. In *The Best Things in Life Are Free,* "Sonny Boy" was sung by Norman Brooks impersonating Jolson in blackface.

In 1929 De Sylva, Brown and Henderson were contracted to write their first complete score for motion pictures, a backstage story called *Sunny Side Up,* starring Janet Gaynor and Charles Farrell. The film's hit song was "If I Had a Talking Picture of You," done as a production number sung by Gaynor and Farrell and then reprised by a chorus of kindergarten children. Equally memorable in this score were "I'm a Dreamer, Aren't We All?" which Gaynor performed to her own zither accompaniment, and the title song, also introduced by Gaynor. Both "Dreamer" and "Sunny Side Up" were recorded by Paul Whiteman. "Sunny Side Up" was also heard on the soundtrack of *Paper Moon* (1973), the Peter Bogdanovich film set in the Midwest during the Great Depression. In *The Best Things in Life Are Free,* Byron Palmer and Eileen Wilson sang "If I Had a Talking Picture of You" (Wilson dubbing on the soundtrack for Sheree North), and the song was included on the soundtrack of *Lucky Lady* (1975), starring Liza Minnelli. "I'm a Dreamer, Aren't We All?" was interpolated into the motion picture *Holy Terror* (1931) and "Sunny Side Up" was revived in Woody Allen's *Zelig* (1983), which is set in the 1920s and 1930s.

For Jolson's 1930 film *Say It With Songs,* De Sylva, Brown and Henderson attempted unsuccessfully to duplicate the success of "Sonny Boy" by writing a similar sentimental ballad called "Little Pal." In this film Jolson also introduced "I'm in Seventh Heaven." For the 1930 film *Just Imagine* De Sylva, Brown and Henderson wrote "Old-Fashioned Girl" and "You Are the Melody," both introduced by John Garrick, the latter as a duet with Maureen O'Sullivan. "You Are the Melody" was also heard in *Holy Terror* and the trio's "Come to Me" was sung by Gloria Swanson in *Indiscreet* (1931). "You Try Somebody Else" was popularized in 1931 in a recording by Russ Columbo. It was revived in *The Best Things in Life Are Free,* sung on the soundtrack by Eileen Wilson.

Follow Thru (January 9, 1929) was the third straight De Sylva, Brown and Henderson book musical to run on Broadway for more than 400 performances. With a text by Guy Bolton and Eddie Davis, *Follow Thru* exploited golf and the country-club milieu for songs and humor, and the climax of the plot involved a golf match. "Button Up Your Overcoat," "My Lucky Star" and "I Want to Be Bad" were the show's principal songs. The first of these was introduced by Zelma O'Neal and Jack Haley and was sung by Nancy Carroll in the 1930 film adaptation, and by MacRae, Dailey and Eileen Wilson in *The Best Things in Life Are Free.* This song was also interpolated into the nonmusical cinematic remake of the Ben Hecht–Charles MacArthur classic from 1931, *The Front Page* (1974), starring Jack Lemmon and Walter Matthau. "My Lucky Star" was sung by John Barker, and "I Want to Be Bad" by Zelma O'Neal, in the stage musical. "Button Up Your Overcoat" and "My Lucky Star" were initially recorded by Helen Kane, Fred Waring's Pennsylvanians and Paul Whiteman. Helen Kane also recorded "I Want to Be Bad."

On June 23, 1984 *Follow Thru,* in an adaptation by Alfred Uhrey, was revived at the Goodspeed Opera House in East Haddam, Connecticut, adding five earlier De Sylva, Brown and Henderson songs to "Button Up Your Overcoat," from the 1929 production. The critic for *Variety* described *Follow Thru* as "a little gem," and in *The New York Times* Stephen Holden called it "a frothy entertainment that is more than a period piece."

Flying High (March 3, 1930), whose subject was air flight, was the last time the three men worked together. In a text by De Sylva and Jack McGowan, Bert Lahr was starred in the comic role of Rusty, who breaks all records for keeping an airplane in the air because he does not known how to land it. Oscar Shaw and Grace Brinkley played the romantic leads and performed the ballads "Wasn't it Beautiful While it Lasted?" and "Thank Your Father." A third number, "Without Love," was introduced by Grace Brinkley and the song was reprised by Oscar Shaw and Kate Smith. Eileen Wilson sang it on the soundtrack of *The Best Things in Life Are Free.* Another pleasant number from the show was "Good for You, Bad for Me," which was introduced by Pearl Osgood and Russ Brown. *Flying High* had a Broadway run of 357 performances. When it was made into a film in 1931 the stage score was discarded in favor of songs by Jimmy McHugh and Dorothy Fields.

When the partnership of De Sylva, Brown and Henderson was dissolved in 1931, they also disposed of their publishing firm. One of its last publications was the De Sylva, Brown and Henderson song "You Try Somebody Else" (1931), which, issued independently of any stage or screen production, was popularized in recordings by Russ Columbo and Kate Smith. The song was revived in *The Best Things in Life Are Free* by Eileen Wilson.

After 1931, De Sylva became a successful producer of both motion pictures and Broadway musicals. For a time, Henderson continued to work with Lew Brown as his lyricist. Their score for *George White's Scandals of 1931* (September 14, 1931) boasted no less than five important songs. "Life is Just a Bowl of Cherries" was introduced and recorded by Ethel Merman. "This is the Missus" was sung by Rudy Vallee; "My Song," by Merman and Vallee; "The Thrill is Gone" and "That's Why Darkies Are Born," by Everett Marshall. Rudy Vallee recorded "Life is Just a Bowl of Cherries," "This is the Missus," "The Thrill is Gone" and "My Song"; Ben Selvin and his orchestra, "My Song" and "This is the Missus"; Paul Robeson, "That's Why Darkies Are Born." That year these five songs were recorded by Bing Crosby and the Boswell Sisters on a 12-inch disc, the first time the score of any musical was marketed as a single release. "Life is Just a Bowl of Cherries" was interpolated into the film musical *George White's Scandals of 1945* as a duet for Jack Haley and Joan Davis. "This is the Missus" was performed on *The Best Things in Life Are Free,* soundtrack by Eileen Wilson. "My Song" was interpolated into the 1944 motion picture *Chip Off the Old Block* (1944), starring Donald O'Connor. The 1931 *Scandals* ran for 202 performances on Broadway.

Lew Brown collaborated with Henderson and Mark Hellinger to write the book for *Hot-Cha* (March 9, 1932), for which Brown was the lyricist and Henderson the composer. Bert Lahr was starred as Alky Schmidt, who flees from the Mexican speakeasy where he had been a waiter when it was raided. The comic device was that Alky is promoted throughout Mexico as a great bullfighter. Though it was lavishly produced by Ziegfeld, *Hot-Cha* ran for only 118 performances. Buddy Rogers and June Knight introduced "You Can Make My Life a Bed of Roses."

Brown and Henderson produced, wrote the book and composed the songs for the revue *Strike Me Pink* (March 4, 1933). Carolyn Nolte and Milton Watson introduced the production's leading song, "Let's Call it a Day," which the Arden-Ohman orchestra recorded. Though it had Jimmy Durante and Lupe Velez in the cast, *Strike Me Pink* survived for just 122 performances.

After Brown decided in 1934 to write mainly for Hollywood, Henderson began working with new lyricists. With Ted Koehler providing the lyrics and Jack McGowan the text, Henderson composed the songs for the Broadway musical, *Say When* (November 8, 1934), starring Bob Hope and Harry Richman. The action takes place on board a trans-Atlantic liner. Two show people fell in love with young women whose rich, snobbish parents disapprove of the budding romance. Harry Richman introduced and recorded the title song. Though favorably reviewed by critics, *Say When* lasted only 76 performances.

Jack Yellen was Henderson's lyricist for *George White's Scandals of 1936* (December 25, 1935), which ran for 110 performances. Gracie Barrie sang "I've Got to Get Hot." Irving Caesar and Yellen wrote the lyrics of "Nasty Man," which Alice Faye introduced in the film version of the *Scandals of 1936* in the role that made her a star. Ted Koehler and Irving Caesar were Henderson's lyricists for "Animal Crackers in My Soup." Edward Heyman was the lyricist for "When I Grow Up" and Ted Koehler for "The Simple Things in Life." All three songs were written for Shirley Temple in *Curly Top* (1935).

Henderson's last Broadway score was for the *Ziegfeld Follies of 1943* (April 1, 1943). This was the edition of the *Follies* with the longest Broadway run, 553 performances. Ilona Massey introduced the ballad "Love Songs are Made in the Night" (lyrics by Jack Yellen).

With "An Old Sombrero," published independently of any stage or screen production in 1947, Henderson collaborated once more with Lew Brown. Henderson, however, ceased to be a pro-

ductive songwriter after the late 1940s. The last two decades of his life were spent in retirement in Greenwich, Connecticut where for a time he worked on a never-completed opera. In suburban Connecticut he was able to pursue his favorite hobbies, gardening, fishing and hunting. In *The Best Things in Life Are Free* Henderson was portrayed by Dan Dailey. Henderson died at home of a heart attack on New Year's Eve 1970.

ABOUT: Craig W. Sweet and Lowdown: America's Popular Song Writers, 1978; Ewen, D. Great Men of American Popular Song, 1970.

HERBERT, VICTOR (February 1, 1859–May 26, 1924), was one of America's earliest and best-loved operetta composers. His works have remained viable in the repertory, and many of his songs have become classics in American popular song literature. To his writing, which was strongly rooted in the German tradition, he brought the gift of melody, spontaneity and a personal charm that set his songs apart from those of his predecessors and contemporaries. For every situation in an operetta, he was able to find the musical *mots justes*, which invariably were tunes that capture the ear and heart today as they did in his own time. A prolific composer, he produced music for approximately 50 operettas during a span of four decades; he also composed special numbers for musical comedies and revues, as well as ambitious works for the concert hall.

Victor Herbert, the only son of Edward and Fanny (Lover) Herbert, was born in Dublin, Ireland. Edward Herbert, a lawyer, died when Victor was three and Fanny and her infant son went to live with his grandfather at The Vine, his country house at Seven Oaks, a town not far from London. Samuel Lover was a novelist, poet and dramatist, and the author of the popular *Handy Andy*. At his home, distinguished writers, musicians, artists and people from the theater gathered for musicales, conversation and the best the culinary arts had to offer.

As an impressionable child, Victor learned early to appreciate culture and the refinements of living well. This environment also nurtured Herbert's talent for music: when he was two, he could hum perfectly the Irish songs his mother sang to him; when, at seven, he showed further interest in music, his mother, a well-trained musician, gave him his first piano lessons. Performances at The Vine by visiting musicians found the child an avid listener: "The music . . . filled my soul with deep peaceful satisfaction," he later recalled. Victor was particularly fascinated by

VICTOR HERBERT

Alfred Carlo Patti, a cellist. "Ah, his music was the supreme thing for me! Nobody in all the universe seemed quite as wonderful as he; nothing quite as glorious as his cello. . . . The longing to play the cello was lodged then and there in my soul."

In 1865, Herbert's mother married Dr. Wilhelm Schmid, a German physician she had met in London; the following spring, the family settled in Stuttgart, Germany. Herbert's stepfather planned a career in medicine for him, and at the local school he struggled with Greek, Latin and the sciences. At the same time, he learned to play the flute and piccolo and joined the school orchestra. By the time he was 15, he had displayed such a great musical talent that his parents allowed him to drop out of high school to devote himself completely to music. From 1874 to 1876, Herbert studied the cello with Bernhard Cossmann, and he received a comprehensive academic musical education at the Stuttgart Conservatory, where his studies were supervised by Max Seifriz. The following five years were spent playing in various orchestras throughout Europe under the direction of such renowned masters as Brahms, Anton Rubinstein and Saint-Saëns. In 1881, Herbert joined the court orchestra in Stuttgart, which was conducted by Seifriz. Seifriz encouraged him to become a composer, and on October 23, 1883, Herbert made his first appearance as composer-soloist when he performed his *Suite* for Cello and Orchestra, with the court orchestra; it was so well received that one of its movements had to be repeated. At Christmastime in 1885, Herbert gave the first performance of his *Concerto No. 1* for

Cello and Orchestra. A Stuttgart critic reported: "From the talented young musician we have already received many pearls of his exquisite art. We are happy to assert that the work he performed yesterday can be counted among the best compositions in violoncello literature."

When a new school of music opened in Stuttgart in the fall of 1885, Herbert joined its faculty as professor of cello. Later that year, he became a vocal coach and accompanist for Theresa Förster, a newly appointed dramatic soprano at the Stuttgart Royal Opera. A suave, well-traveled sophisticate with courtly manners, who was appealing to the eye and stimulating to the mind, Herbert attracted her attention, and they were married in Vienna on August 14, 1886. Two months later, they sailed to the United States, where Förster made her debut at the Metropolitan Opera on November 8, 1886 in Karl Goldmark's *The Queen of Sheba*. She remained at the Metropolitan Opera for one full season and a single performance during the following one, and Herbert was engaged to play the cello in the opera orchestra.

On January 8, 1887, Herbert appeared as soloist with the New York Philharmonic in his first cello concerto. Later that year, he founded and conducted an orchestra which gave concerts of light music in Boston and New York and he also played the cello in the New York String Quartet. In 1889, he joined the faculty of the National Conservatory in New York, founded by Jeannette Thurber in 1885, and from 1889 to 1891, he was also one of the conductors of the Worcester Music Festival in Massachusetts where, in 1891, he introduced *The Captive*, his cantata for solo voices, chorus and orchestra. In 1893, he succeeded Patrick S. Gilmore as conductor of the renowned 22d Regiment Band in New York, for which he composed *An American Fantasy*, a work based on America's patriotic melodies culminating with a richly orchestrated setting of "The Star-Spangled Banner"; Herbert introduced the work on November 26, 1893.

Herbert composed music for his first operetta, *La Vivandière*, in 1893 at the request of Lillian Russell. It was not produced at the Casino Theatre in New York as planned, and the score has been lost. The following year, William MacDonald, director of the Bostonians, a light-opera company, contracted Herbert to write the music for *Prince Ananias*, to a text and lyrics by Francis Neilson (who later distinguished himself as a political writer), set in 16th-century France. Produced in Boston on November 20, 1894, *Prince Ananias*, particularly its music, was well received by the critics, and Herbert's biographer, Edward N. Waters, has singled out "Amaryllis" (which was sung by Jessie Bartlett Davis) as "one of the gems of all light opera."

Herbert's next operetta was *The Wizard of the Nile* (November 4, 1895). The libretto and lyrics by Harry B. Smith were created to highlight the comedic talents of Frank Daniels, who appeared as Kibosh, a Persian magician who tries to use his magic powers to relieve a drought in ancient Egypt. When he fails, he is sentenced to be buried alive in a sealed tomb. The king is also trapped accidentally, and upon being rescued, the king is so delighted that he pardons Kibosh. "Am I a Wiz?", a phrase used by Kibosh throughout the play, quickly became a popular expression of the day. The best moments in Herbert's score, which was tinged with Oriental colors, were Kibosh's song, "Pure and White is the Lotus" and a lilting waltz, "Star Light, Star Bright," the show's biggest hit. With a run of 105 performances at the Casino Theatre followed by a tour, *The Wizard of the Nile* was Herbert's first success, and it made his name in the theater.

The Serenade, which the Bostonians brought to New York on March 16, 1897 with book and lyrics by Harry B. Smith, also did well with the critics. Alice Nielsen became an overnight success when Herbert's wife selected her from the chorus line to replace Hilda Clarke as Yvonne, a ballet dancer in love with a baritone at the Madrid Opera who, like all others, is temporarily infatuated with the fair Dolores, the Duke's ward. "[Harry B. Smith's text] is all a farrago of nonsense," says Edward N. Waters in his biography of Herbert, "but for it, Herbert supplied music brilliantly picturesque, clever, adroit and extremely melodious." The serenade, "I Love Thee, I Adore Thee," introduced as a love duet by Jessie Bartlett Davis and W. H. MacDonald, recurred throughout the operetta in varied forms and styles—as a ballad, a parody of opera arias, a monk's chant, a parrot's call and a song of a brigand.

For Alice Nielsen's new opera company, Herbert composed the operetta *The Fortune Teller*, with a libretto and lyrics again by Harry B. Smith. Though its initial New York run was only 40 performances, this operetta is still remembered through occasional revivals. After a tryout in Toronto, *The Fortune Teller* came to New York on September 26, 1898. Nielsen was cast in the dual role of Musetta, a gypsy fortune teller and her look-alike, Irma, a ballet student. Musetta is in love with Sandor, a gypsy violinist, while Irma, in love with a Hungarian Hussar, is attempting to avoid marrying the Count. Musetta is recruited to extricate her, and much confusion of identities follows until each of the two women is matched with the man she loves. Herbert

brought both the sensuousness of melody and the rhythmic verve of Hungarian gypsy music to "Romany Life" and "Czardas," both sung by Alice Nielsen, and particularly to the score's most memorable song, "Gypsy Love Song" ("Slumber On, My Little Gypsy Sweetheart"), with which Sandor (Eugene Cowles) serenades Musetta.

With *The Fortune Teller*, Victor Herbert became recognized as one of America's most successful and sought-after composers of operettas. Rupert Hughes said of him: "The music of Herbert dignifies the American stage. It reaches the highest level of European comic opera. Then too, it is learnedly humorous. He sprinkles his score with Attic salt." Following its run in New York, *The Fortune Teller* toured the east coast, played in Chicago and was mounted in London on April 9, 1901. It was revived on Broadway in 1919 and 1929, and songs from it have been recorded by Bing Crosby, Connie Boswell, Frances Langford, Charles Kullman and Andre Kostelanetz.

Herbert's involvement with operetta did not keep him away from the concert hall. In New York, *Serenade* for string orchestra was introduced on December 1, 1888, and his *Concerto No. 2* for Cello and Orchestra on March 9, 1894; the concerto lay dormant for nearly a century before being given a second time in New York on January 28, 1980.

Herbert was also the conductor of the Pittsburgh Symphony from 1898 to 1904, and at their concerts, he introduced several of his new works for orchestra, among them *Episodes amoureuses* in 1900, *Hero and Leander* and *Woodland Fancies* in 1901, and *Columbus* in 1903.

While serving as conductor in Pittsburgh, Herbert was subjected to a series of attacks by Marc A. Blumenberg, editor of the *Musical Courier* in New York. It was generally believed that this onslaught had begun because Herbert had refused to advertise in the journal. Blumenberg maintained that Herbert was not qualified to conduct the Pittsburgh Symphony and that he was a bad composer who often resorted to plagiarism. "Everything Herbert wrote is copied," wrote Blumenberg on July 17, 1901. "There is not an original strain in anything he has done, and all his copies are from sources that are comic or serio-comic." Herbert sought redress on October 12, 1902 in a libel suit lasting six days. Walter Damrosch and other celebrated musicians testified on Herbert's behalf. When attempts by Blumenberg and his witnesses to show similarities between Herbert's melodies and those of others crumbled under cross-examination, the defense lawyer argued that a journal has the right to publish unfavorable criticism. "I know of no law," the presiding judge advised the jury, "that gives the publisher of a paper the right to say an untruthful thing about a private individual or a public individual." The jury returned a verdict in favor of Herbert, granting him damages of $15,000 which were subsequently reduced to $5,000. At the victory dinner given by his friends, Damrosch described Herbert as "the courageous man who with one blow defeated this dragon, this Hydra." After the music critic, Henry E. Krehbiel, repeated in his speech Blumenberg's assertion that Herbert's music was not even popular enough to get played on hand organs, a hand organist behind the scenes began pumping out some of Herbert's tunes to the amusement of the guests.

In 1902, Herbert became an American citizen. A year later, he composed music for a new operetta, *Babes in Toyland* (October 13, 1903). This was a childhood fantasy-extravaganza with a book and lyrics by Glen MacDonough, emulating *The Wizard of Oz*, which had been produced in New York a year earlier. In it, little Jane and Alan are running from a miserly, autocratic uncle, and they reach Toyland, where characters from their storybooks are real. The loosely constructed plot was embellished with arresting scenes and spectacles: "The songs, the dances, the processions, the fairies, the toys, the spiders and the bears!" exclaimed James Gibbons Huneker in the *Sun*. "Think of them all set in the midst of really amazing scenery, ingenious and brilliant, surrounded with light effects which counterfeit all sorts of things from simple lightning to the spinning of a great spider's web, with showy women and costumes which show them, costumes rich and dazzling as well as tasteful, and all accomplished with music a hundred times better than is customary in shows of this sort. What more could the spirit of mortal desire?" The music included the songs "Toyland" and "Never Mind, Bo-Peep," introduced by Bess Wynn; "I Can't Do the Sum," sung by Mabel Barrison with a chorus of children tapping out the rhythm of the song with chalk on slates; and also "March of the Toys." According to Henry T. Finck of the *Evening Post*, "In song and ensemble [Herbert] has added greatly to his reputation. Every bar is melodious, while some of the incidental and melodramatic music betrays Mr. Herbert's position among the leading American composers."

Babes in Toyland ran on Broadway for 192 performances and several companies toured the country; it has since been revived many times in professional and amateur productions for children at Christmas. New productions were mounted on Broadway in 1905, 1929 and 1930, and two motion-picture versions were released,

the first starring the comedy team of Laurel and Hardy (1934) and the second with Ed Wynn and Ray Bolger heading the cast in a Walt Disney production (1961); both retained the essence of the stage score. *Babes in Toyland* was also presented as a television "Spectacular" in 1960.

Herbert resigned as conductor of the Pittsburgh Symphony in 1904, following a disagreement with the management over salary and improvement of the orchestra. He was now able to devote more of his time and energy to operettas, and during the ensuing decade, he completed 18. The best-known of these are *Mlle. Modiste* (December 25, 1905), *The Red Mill* (September 24, 1906), *Naughty Marietta* (November 7, 1910) and *Sweethearts* (September 8, 1913).

Henry Blossom wrote the libretto and lyrics for *Mlle. Modiste*, which starred Fritzi Scheff, the opera diva who had come from the Metropolitan Opera earlier to star in Herbert's operetta, *Babette* (November 9, 1903). In *Mlle. Modiste*, she was Fifi, an employee in a Parisian hat shop who is in love with Capt. Etienne de Bouvray; his family finds her humble social position unacceptable. Financed by a wealthy American, Fifi becomes a celebrated prima donna at the opera, and as Mme. Bellini, she wins the approval of the Captain's family.

One of Herbert's most famous waltzes, "Kiss Me Again," comes from *Mlle. Modiste*, and it was the number with which Fritzi Scheff was identified for the remainder of her career. The waltz had been composed but not used two years earlier, and it was incorporated into "If I Were on the Stage," in which Fifi demonstrates her vocal versatility by singing numbers in the style of a gavotte, a polonaise, a waltz, etc. For the waltz parody, Herbert decided to use the sentimental melody he had written in 1903, and when this part of the number stopped the show, he wrote new verses for it and presented it as an independent number within the show. In *The Century Girl* (November 6, 1916), a Broadway musical on which Herbert collaborated with Irving Berlin, "Kiss Me Again" was quoted during a witty scene in which Herbert was portrayed at the piano playing his most popular song while Berlin composed a counter melody for it. In 1931, a motion picture version of *Mlle. Modiste* was released as *Kiss Me Again*, and the song has been recorded by Lily Pons, Beverly Sills, Kate Smith, Risë Stevens and Deanna Durbin.

The score of *Mlle. Modiste* also included "Mascot of the Troop," introduced by Fritzi Scheff; the comedy number "I Want What I Want When I Want It," sung by William Pruette; and "The Time and The Place and The Girl," introduced by Walter Percival. The show ran on

Broadway for 202 performances and was revived in 1913 and 1929.

The Red Mill (September 24, 1906), with a book and lyrics by Henry Blossom, was written to highlight the comedic talents of Fred Stone and David Montgomery. In the operetta, they are Americans named Con Kidder and Kid Conner who are stranded penniless in an inn in a small port in Holland. To pay their bill, they work at the inn as an interpreter and a waiter, and in these capacities, they use their wiles to disrupt the wedding of Gretchen, daughter of the burgomaster, to the Governor of Zeeland, whom she does not love, in order to further her romance with the Capt. Van Damm. As the lovers, Augusta Greenleaf and Joseph W. Ratliff sang the romantic "Moonbeams" and "The Isle of Our Dreams"; Fred Stone and David Montgomery, the nostalgic "The Streets of New York"; and Neal McCoy, the amusing "Everyday is Ladies' Day To Me."

The Red Mill enjoyed the longest original Broadway run of any Herbert operetta (274 performances), but this was surpassed during its Broadway revival on October 16, 1945 (531 performances). More recently, productions have been mounted by the Bel Canto Opera (1978) and the Light Opera of Manhattan (1985).

Naughty Marietta (November 7, 1910), with book and lyrics by Rida Johnson Young, featured two grand opera stars, Emma Trentini in the title role and Orville Harrold as Capt. Richard Warrington; Oscar Hammerstein I, formerly the impresario of the Manhattan Opera Company, served as producer. *Naughty Marietta* takes place in New Orleans in 1780, while Louisiana is still under Spanish rule. Marietta is a Neopolitan lady of noble birth who comes to New Orleans to escape a failing marriage. She has been hearing a fragment of a song in her dreams, and she stands ready to marry anyone who can complete the melody. When Capt. Richard Harrington is able to do so, he wins Marietta from his rival, Etienne, son of the lieutenant governor.

The melody that seals the fate of Marietta and Richard is Herbert's most celebrated love ballad, "Ah! Sweet Mystery of Life," introduced by Orville Harrold; he was also heard in the equally appealing "I'm Falling in Love With Someone," and in "Tramp, Tramp, Tramp." Emma Trentini sang "Italian Street Song," a nostalgic reminiscence of Marietta's home, and Marie Duchene introduced "'Neath the Southern Moon." A screen adaptation of *Naughty Marietta*, starring Jeanette MacDonald and Nelson Eddy was released in 1935, and the score's songs have been recorded by many artists, including Connie Boswell, Bing Crosby, Risë Stevens, Richard Crooks, James Melton, Beverly Sills, Allan Jones and André Kostelanetz. *Naughty Marietta*, following its initial New York run of 136 performances, was revived on Broadway in 1929, 1931 and 1964.

Sweethearts (September 8, 1913) was Herbert's last successful operetta (136 performances). The libretto was written by Harry B. Smith and Fred de Gresac, and Robert B. Smith was the operetta's lyricist. Christie MacDonald starred as Sylvie, a foundling raised in ancient Bruges by the proprietress of a laundry. The Prince of Zilania falls in love with her, but because their social positions are worlds apart, their romance is doomed until it is discovered that Sylvie is actually of royal station. When the intrigue at court is resolved, Sylvie and the Prince vow to rule together. The show's finest songs, the title waltz and the prayer "The Angelus," were introduced on the stage by Christie MacDonald, and "Pretty as a Picture" was an appealing number for the chorus. Nelson Eddy and Jeanette MacDonald starred in the 1938 film version, and the show was revived on Broadway in 1929, in 1947 with an updated book (288 performances), and in 1986 by the Light Opera of Manhattan.

In addition to his music, Herbert made a permanent contribution to American music as a driving force behind the founding of the American Society of Composers, Authors and Publishers (ASCAP). He was one of eight who gathered at Luchow's Restaurant in New York in the fall of 1913 to discuss ways and means of protecting the financial interests of American composers and publishers; 100 participants took formal action at the Hotel Claridge in New York on February 13, 1914. When Herbert was offered the presidency, he declined. As Raymond Hubbell, ASCAP's first treasurer, once noted: "Through all the ups and downs of turbulent years, of adverse court decision and victories, of distracting internal dissensions . . . there stood Victor, 100 percent American Society, every minute of every day. . . . Never could it have been done without him—he just didn't recognize setbacks. The cause, which he knew was just, became a dominating part of him. He just simply forced it through a cloud because he didn't see or feel the cloud."

Herbert was also a pioneer in the composition of film scores. In 1916, he became the first American to create an original screen score for *Fall of a Nation*, which opened in New York on June 6 of that year. Herbert's score was played by orchestras in the theaters during the running of the silent film. "He has not merely written an orchestral accompaniment with a series of 'motifs,'" *Musical America* reported. "His score is interesting and worthwhile from a purely musical standpoint. . . . There are typical Herbert melodies, light and buoyant in his most characteristic style. . . . There is a beautiful theme for strings for the love scenes, and many other original touches too numerous to mention."

But for Herbert, there were defeats as well as victories. His two grand operas were failures and are currently unknown. *Natoma* was introduced in Philadelphia by the Philadelphia-Chicago Opera Company on February 25, 1911, with Joseph Redding's libretto based on an American Indian story. *Madeleine*, with a libretto by Grant Stewart set in Paris in 1914, received its unhappy world premiere at the Metropolitan Opera on January 24, 1914. During World War I, the loyalty of many musicians with German ties was questioned, and Herbert was viewed with suspicion when, as guest conductor, he frequently programmed music by German composers. "What have Beethoven and Wagner to do with the war?" he asked. Nevertheless, he did yield to public pressure by withdrawing the German works from a concert of the New York Orchestra.

What upset him most in the last decade of his life was the loss of box-office magic of his operettas and other contributions to the musical stage. Victor Herbert remained a prolific composer until the end of his life. Though his operettas were no longer successful at the box office, he was still capable of creating infectious, buoyant, and sweetly sentimental melodies. "Thine Alone" (lyrics by Henry Blossom) from *Eileen* (March 19, 1917), which Herbert regarded as one of his best scores, belongs among his finest ballads; *Orange Blossoms'* "A Kiss in the Dark" (lyrics by B. G. De Sylva) was written for Edith Day in the operetta (September 19, 1922). Both shows were commercial failures—*Eileen* closed after 61 performances and *Orange Blossoms* after 75. "My day is over," Herbert lamented to a friend. "They are forgetting poor, old Herbert."

Yet he remained productive, composing scores for seven operettas; all were unsuccessful. He also wrote songs and special material for the *Ziegfeld Follies* (1917; 1920–23) and was called upon to write music for the silent films *The Great White Way* (1922), *Little Old New York* (1923), *Star of the North* (1923) and *Under the Red Robe* (1923).

Despite persistent setbacks at the box office, Herbert remained a jovial, effervescent man with an omnipresent twinkle in his eye, who loved to laugh and relished playing pranks. His zest for living never diminished: he enjoyed the fellowship of friends, good conversation, fine literature (which he read in four languages) and

art, and his affluence enabled him to live well. He was a gourmet for whom eating well demanded his full attention; he never permitted conversation to interrupt his concentration on the meal. When Prohibition threatened to deprive him of fine wine and spirits, Herbert seriously contemplated returning to Europe permanently. In time, he acquired a huge and portly frame that led his friends to describe him as a Franz Hals cavalier. At his summer home in Lake Placid, he was an enthusiastic participant in water sports, particularly swimming and boating. Through the years, he owned several boats, and he always treasured the modest trophy won by the *Handy Andy II* in 1905.

Three months before his death, Herbert attended the world premiere of his most recent work for orchestra, *A Suite of Serenades*, which had been commissioned by Paul Whiteman for his concert of American music at Aeolian Hall on February 12, 1924, an occasion on which Gershwin's *Rhapsody in Blue* was also introduced. H. O Osgood of the *Musical Courier* remarked: "It proved that neither Victor's creative genius nor his orchestrating had lost their cunning."

On May 26, 1924, Herbert had a modest lunch at the Lambs Club in New York City. Feeling ill, he decided to consult his friend, Dr. Emanuel Barauch. The physician was momentarily out of the office, and as Herbert went out to take a short walk he suffered a heart attack and collapsed—his heart condition had been a closely guarded secret.

On May 28, the funeral procession began at the offices of ASCAP and proceeded to St. Thomas Episcopal Church, where services were held. Herbert was buried in Woodlawn Cemetary, and on June 10, 1925, his remains were transferred to a mausoleum; his widow is buried beside him.

Upon learning of Herbert's death, the composer and critic Deems Taylor dispatched the following message to be read at the funeral service: "He was the last of the troubadours. His musical ancestor was Mozart and the family of which he was so brilliant a younger son numbered Offenbach, Delibes, Bizet, the Strausses and Arthur Sullivan among its elders. What he had was what they all had, the gift of song. His music bubbled and sparkled and charmed, and he brought the precious gift of gaiety to an art that so often suffers from the pretentiousness and self-consciousness of its practitioners. The thirty years of his too-short career have left us with two grand operas and over 40 operettas and musical comedies, all distinguished by an unending flow of melodic invention, harmonic and rhythmic individuality and brilliant instrumentation. Above all, he had perfect taste. . . . He is not dead, of course. The composer of *Babes in Toyland, The Fortune Teller, The Red Mill . . .* and *Mlle. Modiste* cannot be held as dead by a world so heavily in his debt."

Victor Herbert received many honors posthumously. In 1924, he was awarded the David Bispham medal for his contribution to American opera, and three years later, a bust by Edward T. Quinn was unveiled by his daughter in Central Park. The United States Postal Service issued a three-cent stamp bearing his image in 1940, and, in 1945, a Victory ship carried his name. Herbert was once again in the public eye when, in 1938, Al Dubin wrote lyrics to a 1908 piano piece. "Indian Summer" was popularized by Frank Sinatra and was heard 14 times on *Your Hit Parade* in 1939. That same year, a screen biography, *The Great Victor Herbert*, was released with Allan Jones in the role of the composer.

Since Herbert's death, his beloved melodies have been recorded by many artists, among them André Kostelanetz, the Paul Lavalle Orchestra, Dorothy Kirsten, Jan Pearce with Thomas L. Thomas, Wilbur Evans with Eileen Farrell and Beverly Sills.

ABOUT: Ewen, D. American Composers: A Biographical Dictionary, 1982, Great Men of American Popular Song, 2d ed. 1972; Waters, E. N. Victor Herbert, 1955. *Periodicals*—New York Times November 18, 1979, May 31, 1981.

HERMAN, JERRY (July 10, 1933–   ), is one of the most successful composers for the Broadway theater in our time, one whose music represents a return to old values. He has been accused of being old-fashioned and formulaic because he has shunned the concept musical, and resisted the influence of rock music. Herman, like the masters of the 1920s, 1930s and 1940s, places his faith in richly melodious tunes that leave the audiences humming: "To me, the powerful tune has always been the meat and potatoes of the American musical theater." In the grand tradition of the musical comedy of yesteryear, each of his most successful musicals has had a show-stopping tune, and he is not timid about pulling out the stops for rousing production numbers. His scores are reminders that there is a place for magic and glamour within the musical theater.

He was born Gerald Herman in New York City. His father, Harry Herman, owned a children's summer camp; his mother, Ruth (Sachs) Herman was a professional musician who taught

JERRY HERMAN

voice and piano. While Jerry was still a child, his family moved to Jersey City, New Jersey, where, at the age of six, he learned to play the piano by ear. As a youngster, he saw his first show, Irving Berlin's *Annie Get Your Gun*, starring Ethel Merman. "I was absolutely dazzled," he later recalled in an interview. "I have one of those retentive ears, and when I came home I sat down at the piano and played about five of the songs. My mother was amazed. I was bit by that bug and I was bit by that man–Irving Berlin."

Following graduation from Henry Snyder High School in Jersey City, Herman enrolled in the Parsons School of Design in New York for training as an interior decorator. While there, he wrote his first song, which he sold for $200. From that moment on, songwriting has been his primary interest.

Herman left the Parsons School to attend the University of Miami in Coral Gables, Florida, where he majored in drama and became involved in all aspects of the school's stage productions. He initiated the University's annual Varsity Show, won the Snarks award for playwriting, and contributed pieces to the college newspaper. Because of such varied extracurricular activities, he was elected to the school's principal honor society and was listed in *Who's Who in American Colleges*.

In 1953, Herman received his B.A., and after a year in military service, he went to New York, where he supported himself by playing the piano in cocktail lounges and writing special material for Jane Froman, Ray Bolger, Garry Moore, Tallulah Bankhead, Polly Bergen, and Hermione Gingold. On October 18, 1954, he made his

Off Broadway debut with an intimate musical, *I Feel Wonderful* (October 18, 1954), which had first been produced at the University of Miami. For it, Herman not only wrote text, lyrics and music, but also served as its director. In the New York *World-Telegram and Sun*, William Hawkins wrote: "It is safe to say that this twenty-two-year old will be heard from in the future. He has a genuine comic feel and can turn out a song that is gay and hummable."

On May 15, 1958, Herman's new revue *Nightcap* opened in New York at the nightclub where he was playing. It ran for 400 performances and was referred to as an "Off Broadway miracle." *Parade*, an Off Broadway revue starring Dody Goodman, followed on January 30, 1960; it was also mounted in Hollywood (1961) and at the Purple Onion in San Francisco (1963). Though the critics were disapproving, the shows were quite popular with the public.

In 1961, Herman and a young playwright, Don Appell, discussed the possibility of writing a show set in Israel. The popularity of *Parade* brought financial backing from producer Gerard Oestreicher, and Herman spent a five-week period doing research in Israel. *Milk and Honey* (October 10, 1961) tells of the experiences of three American tourists in Israel. Ruth (Mimi Benzell), a middle-aged widow, becomes involved in a bittersweet romance with Phil (Robert Weede), an unhappily married businessman. In contrast, Clara (Molly Picon), also a widow, has come to Israel to find a husband and ultimately is successful in her comic search. But most compelling was the way in which *Milk and Honey* captured the soul and spirit of the young nation. Vivid use was made of local traditions, including a Yemenite wedding ceremony, the celebration of Israeli Independence Day, and indigenous dances, such as the hora. *Variety* described the musical as "fresh and skillful with something of the vigor and positive quality of a new land." Two songs were prominent in a score that brought Herman a Tony nomination: the title song (introduced by Tommy Rall and Juki Arkin) and "Shalom," sung by Mimi Benzell and Robert Weede. "Jerry Herman," reported Howard Taubman in *The New York Times*, "has provided songs that range from the functional to the exultant." The show ran for 543 performances.

Herman's next musical was *Madame Aphrodite* (December 29, 1961), with a Pulitzer prize-winning book by playwright Tad Mosel, based on his own television play. Produced Off Broadway, it lasted only 13 performances.

Herman rebounded from this failure with one of the greatest triumphs in theater history: *Hello, Dolly!* (January 16, 1964). The show was produced by David Merrick, and Michael Stewart adapted Thornton Wilder's play, *The Matchmaker*. The heroine is Dolly Levi, a New York marriage broker in 1898, who snares one of her clients for herself. With Gower Champion's brilliant direction and choreography, Oliver Smith's sets and Carol Channing to light up the theater with her portrayal of Dolly, *Hello, Dolly!* was a magnificent production. Though the success of the title song inevitably overshadowed the others, Herman's score boasted a number of fine songs, including "So Long, Dearie," "Before the Parade Passes By," "Put on Your Sunday Clothes," and "Ribbons Down My Back." In *The New York Times*, Howard Taubman praised it for its "qualities of freshness that are rare in the run of our machine-made musicals. It transmutes the broadly stylized mood of the mettlesome farce into the gusto and colors of the musical stage."

Hello, Dolly! captured ten Tonys, including one for the year's best musical and another for Herman as composer-lyricist. It also received the New York Drama Critics Circle Award and captured the first place for Herman as composer and lyricist in polls conducted by both *Variety* and the New York drama critics.

Hello, Dolly! made stage history on several counts. By the time it closed on Broadway on December 27, 1970, it had accumulated the greatest number of consecutive performances (2,844) of any musical in Broadway history up to that time. During its Broadway run of six years and eleven months, it grossed $27 million with worldwide revenues reaching $60 million. Five stars had appeared as Dolly following Carol Channing during the original run: Ginger Rogers, Martha Raye, Betty Grable, Phyllis Diller and Ethel Merman. When Merman assumed the role on Broadway (March 30, 1970), Herman reinstated two numbers composed especially for her: "World, Take Me Back" and "Love, Look in the Window"; these had been replaced with new songs when Carol Channing was signed for the part. National companies with some of the stars named above established box-office records in city after city. *Hello, Dolly!* became the only musical in recent history to have two productions running simultaneously on Broadway. The second, with a black cast headed by Pearl Bailey and Cab Calloway, opened on November 12, 1967. A lavish screen production of *Hello, Dolly!* was released in 1969 with Barbra Streisand as Dolly. Herman wrote the film score, contributing two new songs, and in his opinion, the film is "the definitive statement of this musical," adding that "in years to come [it] will be the one that everybody will remember." But when *Hello, Dolly!* with Carol Channing returned to

Broadway on March 5, 1978, neither the production, nor its star, had lost their spectacular appeal.

The show's title number, "Hello, Dolly!," became one of the biggest hit songs of the decade. In composing this song for Channing, David Hartman and company, Herman had no idea he was writing anything more than a functional, stylized, turn-of-the-century song, such as those Lillian Russell performed. But Louis Armstrong recorded it and the unexpected happened: "I went to a cast party where they had the first cut of the recording," Herman recalled. "Before that I never expected it would have any popular market, but the way the other members of the company loved it, I began to realize that it was going to be something special." Armstrong's performance earned a gold record and won Grammys as song of the year and best male vocal performance. Since then, 72 versions of the song have been recorded in America and 35 in Europe. The sheet music sales number in the hundreds of thousands. During the presidential campaign of 1964, Barry Goldwater's forces tried to adopt a paraphrase of it, "Hello, Barry!" as his campaign song, but were denied permission by Merrick, who opposed Goldwater's political ideology. Soon after, "Hello, Lyndon" was introduced by Carol Channing and Jerry Herman at the Democratic National Convention in Atlantic City.

Herman enjoyed another box-office and critical triumph on Broadway with *Mame* (May 24, 1966); it remained at the Winter Garden on Broadway for 1,508 performances. Based on Patrick Dennis's novel, it had been dramatized as *Auntie Mame* by Jerome Lawrence and Robert E. Lee who later wrote the book for the musical. Mame, magnificently played by Angela Lansbury, is an eccentric, uninhibited, boisterous *grande dame* whose unusual philosophy of life is revealed through the way she raises her orphaned nephew in a period spanning from 1928 to 1946. The musical closes as Mame is taking her nephew's son on a trip around the world so that he might experience the same individualized way of life to which his father had been exposed. In the finale, the audience is told: "And so, if you read tomorrow that a glamorous American widow won a race on a mad water ox, then went on to a party for the Egyptian ambassador where she served cheese blintzes, it will be Mame."

In addition to the appeal of the heroine, *Mame* boasted several effective satirical episodes, including a parody of the production numbers to which Broadway had been partial in the 1930s, and a mocking picture of Southern chivalry. Here, too, the principal song was the title number, which was introduced by Charles Braswell; bestselling recordings of it were made by Louis Armstrong, Bobby Darin, and Herbert Alpert and the Tijuana Brass. "If He Walked Into My Life," introduced by Angela Lansbury, was also quite popular; Eydie Gorme's recording won a Grammy in the best female vocal category.

Mame received a Tony as the year's best musical and a Grammy for the best original cast album. In addition to performances by road companies throughout the United States, *Mame* was mounted in London starring Ginger Rogers in 1969; others who have assumed the title role since Lansbury include Rosalind Russell, Dolores Gray, Beatrice Lillie, Greer Garson, Eve Arden, Sylvia Sidney and Juliet Prowse. A motion picture adaptation starring Lucille Ball was released in 1974, and on July 24, 1983, with Lansbury re-creating her original role, *Mame* was back on Broadway.

Blockbusting successes like *Hello, Dolly!* and *Mame* eluded Herman during the next 17 years. *Dear World* (February 6, 1969) was a musical adaptation of Jean Giraudoux's *The Madwoman of Chaillot*, with a book by Jerome Lawrence and Robert E. Lee. Though Angela Lansbury gave what *Variety* described as "a spectacular performance" in the title role, the show survived for only 132 performances. Its two best songs, delivered by Lansbury, were "I Don't Want to Know" and "Kiss Her Now."

In *Mack and Mabel* (October 6, 1974), Michael Stewart's text attempted to re-create the era of silent films by focusing on the turbulent romance of Mack Sennett and Mabel Normand, and Normand's subsequent deterioration. Despite the stellar performances of Robert Preston and Bernadette Peters in the leads, and Gower Champion's innovative staging, which made effective use of films, *Mack and Mabel* closed after eight weeks. "I Won't Send Roses," introduced by Preston, and "Time Heals Everything," sung by Peters, were the cream of the score.

The Grand Tour (January 11, 1979) also had a brief stay on Broadway (61 performances). Based on Franz Werfel's *Jacobowsky and the Colonel*, a farcical World War II play adapted for the American stage by S. N. Behrman, the story joins an aristocratic Polish colonel (Louis Calhern) with a wily Polish Jew (Joel Grey). Both are trying to escape from Nazi-occupied France, and in "You I Like," they sing a pleasing ode to their newfound friendship.

Herman's third blockbuster on Broadway came with the opening of *La Cage aux Folles* (August 21, 1983). The book, by Harvey Fierstein, was based on the French play by Jean Poi-ret and the French film version released in 1979. The story takes place in the south of France, where Georges (played by Gene Barry), owner of Le Club, a homosexual nightclub in Saint-Tropez, has been living for 20 years with his companion, Albin (George Hearn), a transvestite who, as Zaza, is the star of the club's show. When Georges's son, who was conceived during a single uncharacteristic moment, appears with his fiancée and her bigoted parents, Georges banish-es Albin in an effort to make his household ap-pear respectable and proper. Albin expresses his reaction to this indignity in "I Am What I Am"; chaos ensues, and Georges is heard in the roman-tic ballads, "Song on the Sand" and "Look Over There." But a rousing production number, "The Best of Times," is the show's most popular song and has becomes a favorite at sing-alongs in pi-ano bars.

La Cage aux Folles is the first Broadway musi-cal to portray a homosexual relationship, and ac-cording to *Variety*, "it does so with dignity, pathos, humor and honesty. . . . The single un-revolutionary theme is the importance of human commitment, loyalty and self-pride." About the score, which to Frank Rich of *The New York Times* "gives the charge to every genuine senti-ment in the show," Herman has said "[it] just poured out of me because I was so in love with the characters and the material. It was the easiest score I've written and with fewest changes." *La Cage aux Folles* won six Tony awards, including those for the season's best musical and best musi-cal score. The original cast album was a bestsel-ler.

A cavalcade of Herman's show tunes—all of the hits and some of the misses from productions ranging from the early *Nightcap* to the current *La Cage aux Folles*—have been assembled in *Jerry's Girls*. First offered in New York as a cab-aret revue in 1981, the show toured before open-ing on Broadway (December 18, 1985), with a cast starring Dorothy Loudon, Leslie Uggams and Chita Rivera.

When working on a musical, Herman is, as he told an interviewer, "first and foremost . . . faithful to the character, setting and style of the play. The greatest challenge is getting into a character's head. I am not representing myself in my songs. The stage is not a soapbox for me." He works on both the lyrics and the music simul-taneously, fitting them together "like pieces in a jigsaw puzzle." When his ideas for both gel, he sings them into a tape recorder; they are then transcribed by others.

In describing his own work, Herman has also said: "I'm very dedicated to trying to keep the

theater song alive." And he is unconcerned about those who find his scores "corny," if that means "sentimental, simple [and] melodic": "Those are all the attributes I aim for in my work. Hearing people humming my songs as they leave a show gives me my greatest satisfaction."

Herman maintains residences on Central Park West in New York (where he feels he does his best work) and in California. Among his extra-curricular interests are painting, reading and swimming. In 1970, he was awarded the Order of Merit from his alma mater, the University of Miami.

ABOUT: Current Biography, 1965; Dramatists Guild Quarterly Winter 1966; Green, S. The World of Musi-cal Comedy, 4th ed., 1980; Laufe, A. Broadway's Greatest Musicals, 2d ed., 1977; Notable Names in the American Theatre, 1976.

HEWITT, JOHN HILL (July 11, 1801– October 7, 1890). Though he pursued a career as a journalist, John Hill Hewitt composed more than 500 songs. He was America's favorite song composer until the late 1840s, when Stephen Foster appeared on the scene, but many of his songs retained their popularity through the end of the 19th century.

John Hill Hewitt, the oldest son of James and Eliza (King) Hewitt, was born in New York City in 1801. His father emigrated from England in 1792, distinguishing himself in America as a vio-linist, organist, impresario, publisher, and com-poser of songs, piano music and ballad operas; his most significant work was the opera *Tammany: or, The Indian Chief* (1794), a con-troversial anti-Federalist piece that was one of the first to treat an Indian subject. His brothers and sisters also became active in the music busi-ness as teachers, publishers and composers.

When John was 11, his family moved to Bos-ton, where he attended the public schools. He was then apprenticed to a sign painter, but found the work so distasteful that he ran away from home and supported himself by working in a commission house. In 1816, he was back in New York. Two years later, he was appointed to the Military Academy at West Point, where he studied music with Richard Willis, the conduc-tor of the Academy band.

Hewitt left West Point in 1822 before gradua-tion and married Estelle Mangin, with whom he had seven children. He then joined a theatrical company organized by his father; when the troupe went bankrupt in Augusta, Georgia, Hewitt stayed on in that city as a teacher of mu-sic. In 1825, he settled in Greenville, South Caro-

JOHN HILL HEWITT

lina where he studied law and founded and edited *The Republican,* a newspaper later renamed *The Mountaineer.*

Hewitt composed one of his first ballads, "The Minstrel's Return'd From the War," in Greenville in 1825; it was published by his reluctant brother two years later. In fact, his brother thought so little of it that he failed to register it for copyright protection. But as Hewitt later wrote on his autograph copy of the song, " . . . It was eagerly taken up by the public, and established my reputation as a ballad composer. It was sold all over the world—and my brother, not securing the right, told me that he missed making at least $10,000." The song was widely distributed by a number of firms, becoming one of the most widely known popular songs in America at the time; it also retained its popularity for more than half a century.

In 1828, the year after his father's death, Hewitt went to Baltimore. For many years, he engaged in the editing of various newspapers and journals, including Charles F. Cloud's literary weekly, *The Baltimore Saturday Visitor.* When the *Visitor* sponsored a literary contest, Hewitt entered one of his own poems ("The Song of the Wind") under a pseudonym. It captured first prize, winning over a contribution submitted by Edgar Allan Poe ("The Coliseum"). Though Poe had been awarded first prize in the short-story category, he accused Hewitt of using his influence as editor. In 1839, Hewitt became the editor and part owner of *The Baltimore Clipper,* a daily newspaper.

Some of the songs Hewitt composed during this period were modeled after English ballads.

The best of these were "O! Soon Return" (1829), "Farewell, Since We Must Part" (1829), "I'll Meet Thee Love" (1831), and the successful "The Mountain Bugle" (1833). Still others such as "Wilt Thou Think of Me?" showed the influence of Italian opera, which was immensely popular in America in the 1830s.

In 1840, Hewitt sold his interest in *The Baltimore Clipper* and moved to Washington, D. C. where he became the founding editor of *The Capitol.* In the late 1840s, he contributed songs to several minstrel shows, and for nine years, he taught music at the Chesapeake Female College in Hampton, Virginia.

With the outbreak of the Civil War, Hewitt served as drillmaster for Confederate recruits in Richmond, Virginia. In 1863, he went to Savannah, where he edited *The Evening Mirror* and married his second wife, Alethia Smith, who bore him four children. He also continued to contribute to the Confederate war effort by writing and producing war songs such as "Dixie, the Land of Cotton," "The Soldier's Farewell," and "The Young Volunteer." Because "Somebody's Darling" (lyrics by Marie Revenel De La Coste) typified these songs, Margaret Mitchell quoted it in *Gone With the Wind* (1936), her epic novel about the Civil War.

Hewitt's most celebrated war ballad was "All Quiet Along the Potomac Tonight." Authorship of the lyrics (the poem "The Picket Guard") has never been proven, but Major Lamar Fontaine claimed credit for them. According to Fontaine, he was inspired to write the poem by an incident in which a friend on guard duty stirred the coals of the campfire for warmth and was shot by an enemy picket on the opposite bank of the Potomac. When Fontaine found his friend, he also noticed a newspaper nearby with the headline, "All Quiet Along Potomac." When Hewitt set "The Picket Guard" to music, he dedicated his song "to the unknown dead of the present revolution." During the war, the song grew so popular, not only in Southern, but also in Northern camps, that it caused some commanding officers to prohibit campfires on guard duty.

Hewitt composed numerous ballads after that, the most successful of which were "The Knight of the Raven Black Flame," "Take Me Home Where the Sweet Magnolia Blooms," "Our Native Land," "Rock Me to Sleep, Mother" and "Carry Me Back to Sunny South."

About John Hill Hewitt, Charles Hamm wrote in *Yesterdays*: "His 300-odd songs are the product of an extremely skillful composer. He was a craftsman of the highest order, within the modest framework of the sort of music he chose to write. His accompaniments, for example, are idiomatic for the keyboard, richer than those of any of his contemporaries, easy to play, yet graceful to the ear. Many of his songs sound better today than those of some of his peers who achieved more popularity."

In addition to the songs, Hewitt composed several oratorios, cantatas and ballad operas, and he wrote poems, short stories and plays, sometimes under pseudonyms. He also published a book of reminiscences, *Shadows on the Wall; or, Glimpses of the Past* (1877).

ABOUT: Dictionary of American Biography, 1959; Hamm, C. Yesterdays: Popular Song in America, 1979; Harwell, R. B. Confederate Music, 1950; *Periodicals*—Musical Quarterly January 1931.

BILLY JOEL

JOEL, BILLY (May 9, 1949–). The music of performer and composer-lyricist Billy Joel is decidedly eclectic, an engaging blend of rock, which had been a powerful influence on his early musical development, and the popular Broadway and Tin Pan Alley ballads of the 1940s. "I like all kinds of music," he once explained, "jazz, country, rock, you name it. If I write a soft ballad, the next song I write will be a hard rock 'n' roll tune. I don't want to keep writing the same things. I want to interest *myself*." In so doing Joel has been, since the mid-1970s, one of the most prestigious songwriters in the music industry, producing a succession of gold and platinum albums which contain such popular numbers as "Piano Man," "Just the Way You Are," "Movin' Out," and "Scenes From an Italian Restaurant."

Born William Martin Joel in the Bronx, he was the elder of two children of Howard Joel, an Alsatian-born electrical engineer, and Rosalind (Nyman) Joel. His father had been trained as a pianist in the classical music that was favored by Joel's mother, who sang in choral groups, and his sister, who also played the piano. From them, Billy acquired a love of music while his maternal grandfather instilled in him an appreciation of literature. Joel was two when he began pounding on the piano, and four when he started taking lessons. He continued piano study, on and off, for the next decade, initially with dedication but later lackadaisically. Once, while practicing he gave a boogie-woogie treatment to a Beethoven piano sonata and was roundly punished by his father. At other times, while practicing, instead of mastering the notes of the music in front of him, he improvised music of his own in the style of the composer he was supposed to be studying.

When he was seven, his father returned permanently to Europe. Billy and his sister were supported by their mother on the meager salary she earned from clerical jobs. "I was," Joel remembers, "brought up by women—my mother and my sister—who were tender and loving." They lived in a middle-class community in Hicksville, Long Island, where Billy attended elementary and high school. He spent time in nearby Levittown, a largely Italian-American suburb, which may be the reason that his music is that of a streetwise Italian kid, though he was of Jewish-English ancestry. Becoming interested in popular music through records and the radio, he was 13 when he first heard James Brown perform at the Apollo Theater in Harlem. Brown's rhythm and blues introduced Joel to rock and, in the middle 1960s, the Beatles, with their new sound and memorable melodies, turned him on even more. "If there's anybody I've modeled on," he told *The New York Times,* "it's Paul McCartney."

At 14 Joel formed the Echoes, a rock band with whom he played the electric organ at teen parties. The income helped support his family, and Joel dropped out of school to concentrate on music, working during the day painting houses or dredging oysters and contributing rock criticism to *Changes* magazine to earn extra money. In 1965 he became the pianist for the Hassles, a popular Long Island bar band that recorded two albums which attracted no interest. When the Hassles disbanded, its drummer and Joel formed Atilla, a duo whose 1970 album did little to advanced Joel's career.

It seemed to have come to a dead end and in combination with a failed loved affair, this cast him into a deep, self-pitying, almost suicidal depression. He voluntarily entered a psychiatric ward, remaining there three weeks. Exposed to the truly ill, he decided he was well enough to resume his interrupted career. Moving in with his friend Elizabeth and her son from a previous marriage, and beginning to write songs, he accepted a five-year recording contract from Family Productions, assigning to them all music publishing rights in exchange for an advance and rent money.

His first solo album, *Cold Spring Harbor*, issued in 1972 on the Paramount label, was a disaster. Mastered at the wrong speed (33 2/3 rpm instead of 33 1/3), Joel's singing sounded shrilly high-pitched and the overly lush backing music would have better suited a Tony Bennett recording. In spite of a six-month promotional tour with a band, for which Joel and his musicians received little payment, the album failed to sell.

While trying to extricate himself from his ill-advised contract with Family Productions, Joel left New York for Los Angeles where, under the name of Billy Martin, he worked for a year and a half as a pianist at the Executive Lounge. At that time, a tape he had made with his band, "Captain Jack," about a young suburban heroin addict, was getting airplay on several FM radio stations. This song, and seeing Joel perform at a rock festival, prompted Clive Davis, the influential recording executive at Columbia Records, to sign Joel to his label. Joel's first Columbia single, the narrative ballad "Piano Man," descriptive of his own experience as a lounge pianist, was released on November 2, 1973 and was followed a month later by his first Columbia album, *Piano Man*. In addition to the title song, it included Joel's narrative ballad "The Entertainer" about a rock performer who is top-of-the-heap one day, a has-been the next. As Joel explained, "I was trying to stick a pin in the whole rock-star-as-god bit." Steven Gaynes described "The Entertainer" in *The New York Sunday News* (September 29, 1974) as "easily the best song written about modern show business, its meat-racking marketing techniques and the fickleness of the public."

By 1974, Joel was a rock star himself, and in small auditoriums and nightclubs he was establishing his performing identity as a rousing, raucous, energetic entertainer who, sometimes seated and sometimes standing, banged out vigorous self-accompaniments on the piano. Following one of his nightclub appearances in February 1974, John Rockwell wrote in *The New York Times* (February 23, 1974), "He plays it both versatilely and virtuosically. His backup quartet is similarly proficient: tight and subtle. But what is important is Mr. Joel's songs and the way he sings them. There is an overt theatricali-

ty in his work. The texts are deliberately rhetorical in their language—even the frequent bits of rather grubby, day-to-day detail are used theatrically. The tunes and arrangements court the bombastic. . . . Words are inflected melodramatically; his voice—an orotund, high baritone—has a melodramatic, throbbing vibrato."

In 1975 Joel left Los Angeles, spending several months in the upstate New York town of Highland Falls. There he composed the music for his next album, *Turnstiles* (1976), before settling down in Manhattan. For that record, Joel was his own producer, and for the first time used his own band as backup. Though sales were comparatively modest at first, by 1980 *Turnstiles* had gone platinum. Three of its numbers were autobiographical. "Say Goodbye to San Francisco," "Summer, Highland Falls" and "New York State of Mind." The success of these songs was enhanced through bestselling cover recordings by Barbra Streisand and Peter, Paul and Mary, among others.

In 1977, Joel's wife became his manager and she arranged for Phil Ramone to become his producer. The first Ramone-produced album was *The Stranger* (1977), which marked Joel's ascent to superstardom. Its central theme was the pain of leaving home, and home was in an urban Roman Catholic setting. Within a year, *The Stranger* was a platinum record, ultimately selling in excess of four million copies and becoming the most successful Columbia album since Simon and Garfunkel's *Bridge Over Troubled Water* (1970). Four of Joel's numbers became top ten singles: "Just the Way You Are," which in 1974 received two Grammys for best song of the year and best record of the year; "Moving Out"; "She's Always a Woman"; and "Only the Good Die Young."

The perversity of big city life was the subject of Joel's follow-up album, *52nd Street* (1978). This, too, went platinum and in 1979 won two Grammys for album of the year and best male performance. In *Rolling Stone,* Stephen Holden wrote: "Whereas in *The Stranger*—particularly in its centerpiece, 'Scenes from an Italian Restaurant'—captured the texture of urban neighborhood life in an Edward Hopperlike light, *52nd Street* evokes the carnivalesque neon glare of nighttime Manhattan, using painterly strokes of jazz here and there to terrific effect. The characters in Joel's new compositions—a Puerto Rican street punk ('Half a Mile Away'), a social climber ('Big Shot'), a sexual bitch ('Stiletto'), a barfly sports fan ('Zanzibar') and a Cuban guitarist ('Rosalind's Eyes')—comprise a sidewalk portrait gallery of midtown hustlers and dreamers." Other superlative numbers are "My Life";

"Honesty," a ballad; and "Until the Night," a Phil Spectorish soul song about teenage sex in the city.

On the heels of such phenomenal successes, Joel undertook the most ambitious concert tour of his career in 1978. In a two-and-a-half-month period, he appeared in major auditoriums in 46 cities, climaxed by three sold-out concerts in Madison Square Garden in New York City beginning on December 14, 1978. "The big surprise," wrote John Rockwell in *The New York Times*, "was Mr. Joel's personal restraint. Normally, he runs about with real ebullience, and peppers his between-song remarks with engaging wisecracks. He seemed nervous . . . and even his most energetic ramblings about the stage with a cordless microphone looked a little labored. Without his customary cocky wit, his demeanor was unduly somber, and that had the unfortunate effect of reinforcing the bitter, angry tingle to many of his songs. . . . In the end, Mr. Joel's concert reaffirmed his stature as a talented, craftsmanlike pop composer with a good deal more sophistication and range than most middle-of-the-road rockers or adult popsters."

In the first cultural exchange between Cuba and the United States since 1959, Joel accompanied a troupe of popular American musicians to Havana in March 1979 to participate in the "Havana Jam '79." "Over the past twenty years," wrote Jim Jerome of *People*, "the only other living person who has moved an audience with such charismatic intensity in the same venue (to use this rock term) has been Fidel Castro."

In the late 1970s the now wealthy Joel bought an estate at Cove's Neck on Long Island Sound with a 12-room house, and he and his wife also maintained a Manhattan apartment on 57th Street near Second Avenue. By late 1979 his wife Elizabeth had ceased to be his manager and soon thereafter their personal relationship ended as well.

With Phil Ramone remaining his producer, Joel's next platinum album was *Glass Houses* (1980), which contained the hit single "It's Still Rock 'n' Roll to Me." In 1981 he released *Songs in the Attic*, a live album, and in 1981 an anthology of his most popular songs from the 1970s. On *The Nylon Curtain* (1982), Joel sounded more somber strains, singing of the Vietnam War in "Goodnight Saigon"; of an unemployed steelworker in "Allentown"; of anxiety in "Pressure"; of the guilt feelings a parent instills in a child in "Laura." He has, indeed, "shifted gears," wrote Stephen Holden in *The New York Times*. "With its use of sound effects, aural montage, exotic orchestration and thickly overdubbed vocals, *The Nylon Curtain* is a far cry from the pared-down

rock of *Glass Houses* and harks back to the late sixties psychodelia of The Beatles. . . . *The Nylon Curtain* transcends Mr. Joel's earlier albums in the richness of its music and the depth of its perceptions."

His 1983 album, *An Innocent Man,* represented still another change of pace. A reviewer in *High Fidelity* described it as "an ebullient valentine to the pop, rock and soul styles the songwriter grew up with. In place of the previous album's pensive social concerns are the time-honored romantic issues, while the music turns from an eclectic, stylistic sweep to lovingly precise recreations of individual songs forged two or more decades ago." Among its superior cuts are the Frankie Valli-esque "Uptown Girl," "The Longest Time," "Tell Her About It" and the title song. The hit singles "Tell Her About It" and "Allentown" were acknowledged in 1983 to be among the most frequently performed songs in the BMI catalog.

On April 15, 1982, while riding on his motorcycle near his home in Long Island, Joel crashed into a car that had run a red light. He suffered a broken wrist and his other hand was so completely crushed that it had to be rebuilt. A few months later, though, he was able to tour in promotion of *The Nylon Curtain,* showing no sign that the accident had impaired his robust piano playing. In 1983, Joel composed the title song for the motion picture *Easy Money.*

Steven Gaines described Joel as having "deepset brooding eyes [that] add to his appearance of a street punk. He tries to be hard and tough, but he only looks vulnerable and cute. He has what people call 'street smarts,' backed by an uncanny ability to cut through hype and pretense."

Joel keeps fit by working out and boxing in a gymnasium in the house on his Long Island estate. He is a baseball fan (New York Yankees) and a voracious reader. On March 23, 1985, in New York, Joel married Christie Brinkley, a model.

In the summer of 1986 Joel released the critically acclaimed *The Bridge*, his first nonconcept LP since *52nd Street* (discounting the live *Songs in the Attic*). Among the album's infectious pop numbers were "A Matter of Trust," "Modern Woman" and "The Bridge."

ABOUT: Gambaccini, P. Billy Joel: A Personal File, 1979. *Periodicals*—High Fidelity February 1978, February 1983; Newsweek December 11, 1978; People March 19, 1979, January 10, 1983, April 8, 1985; Rolling Stone September 11, 1986.

JONES, TOM. *See* **SCHMIDT, HARVEY** and **JONES, TOM**

KAHN, GUS (November 6, 1886–October 8, 1941). In his heyday lyricist Gus Kahn averaged six hit songs a year over a period of two decades, both in Tin Pan Alley and Hollywood. He was born Gustav Gerson Kahn in Coblenz, Germany on November 6, 1886, the son of Isaac and Theresa (Mayer) Kahn. His father was a cattle rancher. In 1891 the Kahn family immigrated to the United States, settling in Chicago, where Gus attended public schools until he dropped out and went to work as a clerk in a hotel supply firm. But, having a gift with words, he was soon supporting himself by writing special material for vaudevillians while also producing song lyrics.

Kahn published his first song in 1906, "My Dreamy China Lady," with music by Egbert Van Alstyne, and a year later, to Grace Le Boy's music, he wrote and published "I Wish I Had a Girl." Kahn's career gained momentum after 1910 through his continuing collaboration with Van Alstyne, the New York-based composer who was seeking a replacement for the wordsmith partner, Harry Williams, he had lost to the West Coast. Kahn and Van Alstyne's "Sunshine and Roses" appeared in 1913; "Memories" in 1915; "Pretty Baby" in 1916; "Sailin' Away on the Henry Clay" in 1917; and "Your Eyes Have Told Me So" in 1919. Each profited from solid sheet-music sales. During this period Kahn also wrote lyrics for other composers including Grace Le Boy, with whom he wrote "On the Good Ship Mary Ann" in 1914 and who became his wife on August 18, 1915. They raised a son and a daughter in New York City.

Among Kahn's other hit songs in that decade were "Come Sunday Morning" and "Where the Morning Glories Grow" (both in 1917), with lyrics cowritten by Raymond Egan to music by Richard A. Whiting. "I'll Say She Is" and "You Ain't Heard Nothin' Yet" were written in collaboration with B. G. De Sylva and Al Jolson with Jolson performing them on Broadway in his Winter Garden Theatre extravaganza, *Sinbad*, in 1918.

Two Kahn songs of 1921 became standards: "Ain't We Got Fun?," words written with Egan and music composed by Whiting and "Toot, Toot, Tootsie," with music by Ernie Erdman and Dan Russo. The latter was introduced into the Winter Garden extravaganza *Bombo* in 1922 by Jolson, whose subsequent recording made it one of his evergreens. Jolson sang it again in the first film version of *The Jazz Singer (1927), The Rose of Washington Square* (1939) and on the soundtracks of his two film biographies, *The Jolson Story* (1946) and *Jolson Sings Again* (1949). His re-recording in 1946 made "Toot, Toot, Tootsie" a bestseller again. This song was interpolated for Doris Day in the romanticized screen

GUS KAHN

biography of Gus Kahn, *I'll See You in My Dreams* (1951), in which Danny Thomas played Kahn and Day his wife.

In the early 1920s, Kahn moved from Chicago to New York. A new era of hit songs was now initiated by his collaboration with the Broadway composer Walter Donaldson. In 1922 they produced "My Buddy" and "Carolina in the Morning"; in 1923 "Beside a Babbling Brook"; and "Mindin' My Business." "Yes, Sir, That's My Baby," "I Wonder Where My Baby is Tonight?," "My Sweetie Turned Me Down," "The Midnight Waltz," and "That Certain Party" were all produced in 1925.

In 1928 Donaldson and Kahn composed their only score for Broadway, *Whoopee* (December 4, 1928), a box-office success with 379 performances starring Eddie Cantor. Three songs came from that production: "Makin' Whoopee," "I'm Bringing a Red, Red Rose" and "Love Me or Leave Me."

Even while Kahn was Donaldson's successful collaborator in the 1920s, he also contributed lyrics to the music of numerous other composers. To the music of Isham Jones, Kahn wrote the words for "Broken-Hearted Melody" (1922); "Swingin' Down the Lane" (1923); and "It Had to Be You," "The One I Love Belongs to Somebody Else," "Spain" and "I'll See You in My Dreams" (all in 1924). All were introduced and first recorded by Isham Jones and his orchestra.

Three decades after Isham Jones had introduced "Swingin' Down the Lane" in a vaudeville theater in Pittsburgh in 1923, and it had been recorded by Ben Bernie and his orchestra, by the Columbians and by the Isham Jones orchestra,

Doris Day sang it in *I'll See You in My Dreams*. "It Had to Be You" was recorded in 1924 by Marion Harris and by the orchestras of Paul Whiteman and Sam Lanin, subsequently by Cliff Edwards and by Kay Thompson. In the 1940s and 1950s, this song was revived in motion pictures. It was sung by Nan Wynn in *Is Everybody Happy? (1943)*; by Betty Hutton in *Incendiary Blonde* (1945); and by Danny Thomas in *I'll See You in My Dreams*, where it was heard in the background as the movie's theme. In 1947 "It Had to Be You" was appropriated as the title for a film starring Ginger Rogers and Gene Kelly and later that same year Marie Mac-Donald danced to it in the movie *Living in a Big Way*.

"The One I Love Belongs to Somebody Else" was recorded by Al Jolson, by Sophie Tucker and by the Tommy Dorsey orchestra with vocal by Frank Sinatra. "Spain" was recorded by Van and Schenck and by the orchestras of Paul Whiteman and Leo Reisman. Doris Day sang "I'll See You in My Dreams" in Kahn's screen biography (and it was reprised by the chorus in the final scene). The song was crooned by Bob Crosby in the motion picture *Pardon My Rhythm* (1944) and Jeanette MacDonald sang it in *Follow the Boys* (1944). It also inspired the plot of the film *Margie* (1946).

Another popular bandleader of the 1920s who both composed music to Kahn's lyrics and introduced the finished song with his band was Ted Fiorito. In 1923 Fiorito and his band popularized "No, No, Nora" (music written in collaboration with Ernie Erdman), which Abe Lyman and his orchestra recorded, and "Why Lights Are Low" (lyrics written with Ted Koehler). In 1924 Fiorito and band introduced "Charlie My Boy," recorded and popularized by Eddie Cantor, and "Little Old Clock on the Mantle"; in 1925, "I Never Knew That Roses Grew," recorded by Ross Gorman and his orchestra, "Sometime" and "When I Dream of the Last Waltz With You"; in 1928, "I'm Sorry, Sally"; and, in 1930, "Hangin' on the Garden Gate."

With Ernie Erdman, Brill Meyers, and Elmer Schoebel as composers, Kahn wrote the lyrics for "Nobody's Sweetheart" in 1923 which was first heard in a performance by Ted Lewis and his orchestra in the Broadway revue, *The Passing Show of 1922*. Rudy Vallee featured it in *The Vagabond Lover* (1929), with which he made his screen debut, and the Mills Brothers recorded it in 1930. In motion pictures, it was also sung by Constance Moore in *I'm Nobody's Sweetheart* (1940); by Belle Baker in *Atlantic City* (1944); and by Doris Day in *I'll See You in My Dreams*.

Some of the other composers who worked

with Kahn in the 1920s were: Richard A. Whiting, with whom Kahn wrote "Ukulele Lady" in 1925; Charles N. Daniels, "Chlo-e" and "Persian Rug," both 1927; John Green, who collaborated with Carmen Lombardo on the music for "Coquette" (1928); Joe Sanders, "Beloved" (1928), which was introduced by Coon-Sanders' Original Night Hawks Orchestra and recorded by Guy Lombardo and His Royal Canadians; and Harry Warren, "Where the Shy Little Violets Grow," (1928), "Guilty" (1931) and "Someone to Care for Me" (1932). "Chlo-e" was given a burlesque treatment in a recording by Spike Jones and the City Slickers in 1928 and so successfully was "Guilty" revived by Margaret Whiting that, in 1947, the song received 11 representations on *Your Hit Parade*.

In 1929 Gus Kahn joined Ira Gershwin in writing words to George Gershwin's music for *Show Girl*, a Ziegfeld production in which "Liza," "So Are You" and "Do What You Do!" were heard. It opened on July 2, 1928 and ran for 111 performances.

Between 1930 and 1932, Kahn worked with still other composers. "Around the Corner" (1930) was introduced by Art Kassel, who composed the music, and his orchestra. "Was I to Blame for Falling in Love With You?" (1930, lyrics written with Chester Conn, music by Victor Young) became the theme music for Glen Gray and the Casa Loma Orchestra. "Goofus" (written with Wayne King and Will Harold) was introduced by Wayne King and his orchestra in 1930. Introduced in 1931 by Wayne King and his orchestra, "Dream a Little Dream of Me" (music by Wilbur Schmidt and Fabian Andre) was popularized by Kate Smith on the radio and in a recording. Also in 1931, Mildred Bailey introduced—and Heny Busse and his orchestra recorded—"I'm Through With Love" (music by Matt Malneck and Fred Livingston). In the motion picture *The Affairs of Dobie Gillis* (1953) it was sung by Bobby Van, and in *Some Like It Hot* (1959) by Marilyn Monroe. In 1932 "I'll Never Be the Same" (music by Matt Malneck and Frank Signorelli) was introduced by Mildred Bailey and, under the title "Little Buttercup," was recorded by Joe Venuti and his orchestra. This song later became a favorite in Ruth Etting's repertory and was recorded by Benny Goodman.

When Gus Kahn became affiliated with the motion-picture industry in 1933, he and his family moved permanently to Los Angeles. His first important assignment was *Flying Down to Rio* (1933), starring Fred Astaire and Ginger Rogers in their screen debut as a song-and-dance team. For that film Kahn wrote the words for

"Carioca" and "Orchids in the Moonlight" (lyrics written with Edward Eliscu, music by Vincent Youmans) and the title number (lyrics by Eliscu, music by Burton Lane). That same year Marion Davies introduced "Sweetheart Darlin'" (music by Herbert Stothart) in *Peg o' My Heart.*

With Victor Schertzinger as composer, Kahn wrote the title song of *One Night of Love* (1934), the movie which popularized operatic music in sound films and made the singer Grace Moore a star (she also recorded the song). With Richard A. Whiting providing the music, Kahn wrote "Waitin' at the Gate for Katie," which John Boles and chorus introduced in *Bottoms Up* (1934). Irene Dunne introduced "Tonight is Mine" (music by W. Franke Harling) in *Stingaree* (1934). Resuming his collaboration with Donaldson, Kahn wrote "An Earful of Music," "Okay Toots," and "When My Ship Comes In" for *Kid Millions* (1934), starring Eddie Cantor; "Sleepy Head" for *Operator 13* (1934); and "I've Had My Moments" for *Hollywood Party* (1934). Arthur Johnson was his composer for the film *Thanks a Million* (1935); its title song and "I'm Sitting High on a Hilltop," both introduced and recorded by Dick Powell, were each heard nine times on *Your Hit Parade.* Paul Whiteman and his orchestra also recorded "Thanks a Million" and "Sitting High." In *Thanks a Million* Dick Powell also sang "I've Got a Pocket Full of Sunshine," which he recorded; Ann Dvorak and Patsy Kelly sang "Sugar Plum"; and Paul Whiteman and his orchestra performed "New Orleans."

For Grace Moore's starring role in *Love Me Forever* (1935), Kahn and Schertzinger contributed the title song which she recorded and which became a six-time entry on *Your Hit Parade.* Introduced by Lorraine Bridges in *Escapade* (1935) and recorded by the Dorsey Brothers orchestra, "You're All I Need" (music by Bronislaw Kaper and Walter Jurmann) was heard nine times on *Your Hit Parade.* Other Kahn songs represented on that program were "Footloose and Fancy Free" (music by Carmen Lombardo), introduced in 1933 by the Dorsey Brothers orchestra; the title number for *Let's Sing Again* (music by Jimmy McHugh), introduced by Bobby Breen in his 1936 screen debut; "Tomorrow is Another Day" (music by Kaper and Jurmann), introduced by Allen Jones in the Marx Brothers movie *A Day at the Races* (1936); "Blue Love Bird" (music by Kaper), introduced by Alice Faye and Don Ameche in *Lillian Russell* (1940) and recorded by Kay Kyser and His College of Musical Knowledge, and by Mitchell Ayres and his orchestra; "You Stepped Out of a Dream" (music by Nacio Herb Brown) in the movie *Ziegfeld Follies* (1941); and "Stay Dreaming" (music by Jerome Kern), introduced in a recording by Bing Crosby.

Other screen songs by Kahn include the title number of *San Francisco* (1936, music by Kaper and Jurmann) which Jeanette MacDonald introduced and which was recorded by Ben Bernie and his orchestra and by Vicki Carr; "With All My Heart" (1936, music by Jimmy McHugh) from *Her Master's Voice* (1936); two songs in addition to "Tomorrow is Another Day" for *A Day at the Races* (music by Kaper and Jurmann), "All God's Chillun Got Rhythm," introduced by Ivie Anderson, and "A Message From the Man in the Moon," introduced by Allen Jones. "Who Are You to Say?" (music by Sigmund Romberg) was sung by Nelson Eddy in *Girl of the Golden West* (1938) and "Waltzing in the Clouds" (music by Robert Stoltz) was introduced and later recorded by Deanna Durbin in *Spring Parade* (1940).

Gus Kahn died suddenly of a heart attack at his home in Los Angeles on the morning of October 8, 1941. Between 1927 and 1930 he had served on the board of directors of ASCAP. As Kahn explained in 1927, his gift as a lyricist lay in his ability to "express colloquially something that every young person has tried to say—and somehow can't."

ABOUT: Burton, J., The Blue Book of Tin Pan Alley, 1950; Stambler, E., Encyclopedia of Popular Music, 1965; James, E. T. (ed.) Dictionary of American Biography, 1973. *Periodicals*—American Magazine June 1927; New York Times October 9, 1941.

KALMAR, BERT. *See* **RUBY, HARRY** and **KALMAR, BERT**

KANDER, JOHN (March 18, 1927–   ) and **EBB, FRED** (April 8, 1935–   ). For more than two decades, composer John Kander and lyricist Fred Ebb have been leading songwriters for the stage, screen, television and for nightclub performers.

John Harold Kander was born in Kansas City, Missouri, the son of Harold and Bernice (Aaron) Kander. His father was in the poultry business, and the family had no musical heritage. Nevertheless John began trying to play the piano when he was four. Noting his interest, an aunt taught him a few basic chords and, at six, he began formal piano studies. An opera performance he attended when he was ten—*Aida*, by the San Carlo opera—"was perhaps the most exciting event of my life," John recalled. "From that day on, I became an opera 'nut'."

While attending Westport High School, Kander studied piano with Wiktor Labunski, who exerted the first significant influence on

FRED EBB   JOHN KANDER

Kander's musical development. "I always had a wonderful time with music," Kander said. "I was always thinking about it. It gave me my greatest pleasure." Kander's senior year of high school was completed at Pembroke Country Day School, where he wrote the school show, one of whose numbers became the senior class song.

About 1946 Kander enrolled in Oberlin College in Ohio, where he combined an academic education with study at the school's conservatory. He composed music for two college productions, *Second Square Opus Two* and *Requiem for George*, with James Goldman writing the texts for both. Kander had met Goldman and his brother William at a boys' summer camp in 1937, where they became friends. In pursuing literary careers, both of the Goldman brothers were to become Kander's sometimes collaborators and, much later, both became eminent screenwriters.

After graduating from Oberlin with a B. A. degree in 1951, Kander moved on to Columbia University, studying composition with Jack Beeson, Otto Luening and Douglas Moore and earning an M. A. in composition in 1954. During this period, Kander dabbled in chamber music composition and wrote a one-act opera, but Douglas Moore convinced him to pursue a career in the popular musical theater.

After leaving Columbia, Kander served in the U. S. Army and the U. S. Merchant Marine Corps, and began working in the theater when he was out of uniform. He served as choral director and conductor of the Warwick (Rhode Island) Musical Theatre in the summers of 1955 and 1957, and in 1956 was pianist for a musical,

The Amazing Adele, during its pre-Broadway run, and for *An Evening with Beatrice Lillie* in Florida. In 1957 he conducted the orchestra for *Conversation Piece,* produced Off Broadway. He prepared the dance arrangements for the Broadway musicals *Gypsy,* in 1959, and *Irma la Douce,* in 1960.

With *A Family Affair* Kander made his debut as a composer of Broadway musicals. Starring Shelley Berman, and with text and lyrics by the Goldman brothers and Harold Prince making his bow as a producer, *A Family Affair* opened on January 27, 1962, but lasted only six performances. Its principal songs were "Beautiful," introduced by Shelley Berman; "There's a Room in My House," by Larry Kert and Rita Gardner; "Harmony," by Bibi Osterwald, Gino Conforti, Linda Lanvin and Jack De Lon; and the title song, introduced by the chorus. Later that year Kander composed the incidental music for the Broadway play *Never Too Late.*

In 1962 Kander's publisher, Tommy Valando, introduced him to a lyricist in his employ, Fred Ebb, suggesting that they collaborate. At that time, Ebb longed for a successful career in the theater.

Fred Ebb was born in New York City in 1936, the son of Harry and Anna Evelyn (Gritz) Ebb. He received a B.A. degree from New York University in 1955 and an M. A. degree in English literature from Columbia University two years later. He then wrote material for nightclub acts, revues, and for the satirical television show, *That Was the Week That Was,* working, as he put it, "for anybody who would work with me, if there was a dollar to be made." About the time he met

Kander, *Morning Sun,* an Off Broadway production for which Ebb wrote the lyrics, had closed after eight performances. "We came to each other fresh from our failures," Ebb recalled. Describing his first meeting with Kander, he said, "Our neuroses complemented each other. It was a case of instant communication and instant songs."

Before the year 1962 ended, and after one or two preliminary efforts, they enjoyed their first success, the song "My Coloring Book." Though introduced by Kaye Ballard, it became popular when Sandy Stewart sang the song on Perry Como's television show and then recorded it. Bestselling records by Kitty Kallen and Barbra Streisand followed. In 1963 Kander and Ebb wrote and published "I Don't Care Much," which Barbra Streisand introduced and popularized in a recording.

Collaborating with Richard Morris, Kander and Ebb wrote *Golden Gate,* which was scheduled to open in San Francisco on April 18, 1963, the 57th anniversary of the earthquake. It never opened, but the musical's material induced Harold Prince to contract Kander and Ebb to write songs for a Broadway musical then in the planning stages, *Flora, the Red Menace.* With book by George Abbott and Robert Russell, and based on Lester Atwell's novel, *Love is Just Around the Corner, Flora* was a satire on 1930s radicals and Greenwich Village bohemianism, starring Liza Minnelli in her first Broadway appearance. She portrayed Flora, a department store fashion designer who was induced by her boyfriend to join the Communist Party, and than nearly lost him to a sexy comrade. "The great merit of Flora," reported one reviewer, "is that its effervescent score is kept bubbling along by a lively and skillful troupe of singers with the proper talents to make the most of Ebb and Kander songs." With the ballads "A Quiet Thing," and "All I Need is One Good Break," and with "Sing Happy," a bluesy number, Liza Minnelli revealed her star potential. The complete score was recorded in an original cast album.

Flora, the Red Menace opened on May 11, 1965, and, in the main, received poor reviews. Though aware that his show was doomed to fail—it lasted only 87 performances—Prince summoned Kander and Ebb to his office to discuss his new musical, *Cabaret,* an adaptation for the musical stage by Joe Masteroff of John van Druten's play, *I Am a Camera,* which had been based on Christopher Isherwood's *Berlin Stories* (1935), about the social, moral and political decay of Berlin in the late 1920s. Much of the action took place in a night spot favored by the demimonde, the Kit Kat Club, where Joel Grey

played the role of the wickedly sly master of ceremonies. Jill Hayworth (as Sally Bowles) was the club's star singer and Lotta Lenya (as Fräulein Schneider) was the proprietess of the boardinghouse where Sally lives. *Cabaret,* wrote Walter Kerr in his review, "has elected to wrap its arms around all that was troubling and all that was intolerable with a demonic grin, an insidious slink, and the painted charm that keeps revelers up until midnight making false faces at the hangman." The critic for *Variety* found that the "ugliness, decadence and combination of hysteria and moral lethargy . . . of Berlin . . . are luridly reflected."

Despite its offbeat subject, *Cabaret* (November 20, 1966) was a major critical and box-office success. It had a Broadway run of 1,166 performances, and captured the Tony and the Drama Critics Award as the season's best musical; the New York drama critics chose Kander as composer of the year, and the original cast recording won a Grammy. A national company toured the United States for several years, and the show was produced throughout Europe. An Academy Award-winning motion picture adaptation of 1972 starred Joel Grey and Liza Minnelli, and it too produced a popular soundtrack LP.

The song "Cabaret" became a hit in 1966–67, popularized through bestselling recordings by Marilyn Maye and by Herbert Alpert and the Tijuana Brass. Jill Hayworth introduced the song in the stage production and Liza Minnelli sang it in the movie. Minnelli also recorded "Cabaret" and made it a staple of her repertory. In both the stage and screen productions, Joel Grey sang "Willkommen" and "If You Could See Her Now." "Tomorrow Belongs to Me," ostensibly a moving, nostalgic hymn to Germany that in fact chillingly portends the Nazis' rise to power, was performed by Joel Grey and the Kit Kat Club waiters in the stage production and by Mark Lambert (dubbing for Oliver Collignon, who signifies youthful Aryan perfection, on the soundtrack) on the screen. For the screen, Kander and Ebb composed "Money, Money" and "Mein Herr," production numbers sung by Joel Grey and staged by Bob Fosse, who directed the film.

Though *The Happy Time* (January 18, 1968) lasted only 285 performances on Broadway, it featured stellar performances by Robert Goulet and David Wayne, the imaginative choreography of Gower Champion and superb songs, issued in an original cast recording. *The Happy Time* was an adaptation by N. Richard Nash of Samuel Taylor's Broadway play of the same name. It portrayed a French-Canadian family—a lovable, somewhat lecherous grandfather,

Bonnard, who adores his 14-year-old grandson, Bibi, and the boy's uncle, Jacques Bonnard, who visits the family in time to sort out its problems and to fall in love with a village teacher, Laurie. In the staging, photographic backdrops were used ingeniously to provide transitions from scene to scene and to suggest the passage of time. "Life of the Party," in which the grandfather (David Wayne) recalls the amatory indiscretions of his youth, was a showstopper. Other distinctive songs were "A Certain Girl," introduced by Wayne, Goulet and Mike Rupert, and the title number and "I Don't Remember You," both sung by Goulet. On April 16, 1982 *The Happy Time* was revived by the Lyric Opera of Kansas City, Missouri.

In 1967 Ebb produced *Liza with a Z,* a television special starring Liza Minnelli. For it, Ebb and Kander composed the tongue-twisting "Liza With a Z (Not Lisa With an S)" theme song. The telecast won an Emmy and its soundtrack LP a Grammy. Ebb had earlier prepared special material for Minnelli, for her nightclub act at the Shoreham Hotel in Washington, D.C., in September 1965, which helped to make her a star.

When first produced on Broadway, *Zorba* (November 17, 1968) was a box-office disappointment, its run exceeding *The Happy Time*'s by just 19 performances. This musical was Joseph Stein's adaptation of the bestselling novel, *Zorba, the Greek,* by Nikos Kazantzakis. Set in the Greek city of Piraeus and in Crete, the plot concerns the unsuccessful effort by a man named Nikos to rebuild an abandoned mine he has inherited. For this task, he finds an ally in the earthy and vigorous Zorba. But Zorba goes carousing and squanders the money Nikos had given him to procure supplies. When the mine turns out to be unfit for opening, Nikos, disenchanted, returns to Athens. With the protean creativity that enabled Kander to catch the nuances of German popular music of the late 1920s in *Cabaret* and of the French-Canadian popular song in *The Happy Time,* he now captured the sound of Greek music in *Zorba.* The songs and dances, recorded in an original cast album, vividly suggested the rural culture of Greece, especially "Life Is," a frenetic dance with which the production opened, accompanied by bouzoukis, and a subsequent dance by Zorba and Nikos. Clive Barnes noted in *The New York Times* that "the ethnic element in the music and the cheerfully philosophical note struck by the lyrics endowed the production with most of its fire and spirit." "Grandpapa," sung and danced to by Herschel Bernardi, had an authentic Greek identity, as did the music Kander composed for the Greek dances. Herschel Bernardi was also heard espousing Zorba's hedonistic view of life

in "I Am Free" and "The First Time." Carmen Alvarez introduced the ballad "Why Can't I Speak" and Maria Karnilova introduced "Only Love." With some structural changes, *Zorba* was revived on Broadway on October 16, 1983, with Anthony Quinn, who had played Zorba in the nonmusical 1965 film, in the title role. For Quinn, Kander and Ebb composed a new number, "Woman."

The next Kander-Ebb musical, *70, Girls, 70,* opened on Broadway on April 15, 1971 and expired after 36 performances, in spite of which an original cast album was issued. The book, by Fred Ebb and Norman L. Martin, was based on a play which had become a British film, *Make Mine Mink,* about a group of female septuagenarians, residents of a small West Side Manhattan hotel, who try to bring excitement into their lives by becoming shoplifters. The songs, reported Douglas Watts in the *Daily News,* "are mainly brisk and mindless pieces, intermixed with sentimental terms." Despite its rejection by critics and audiences, *70, Girls, 70* remained a particular favorite of Ebb's. After the show closed he rewrote it for motion pictures, then for television, though it was never produced in either medium. "It taught me something about dealing with failure," Ebb said. "Forget your successes. Forget your failures. Keep working. Get on with it."

Fred Ebb "got on with it" in 1972 by serving as a producer for *Ole Blue Eyes is Back,* a television special starring Frank Sinatra. Also, with Kander as composer, he wrote the score for the stage musical, *Chicago* (June 3, 1975), which ran on Broadway for 923 performances before touring the country. *Chicago*'s score was recorded in an original cast album.

Chicago was a musical stage version of Maurine Watkin's 1924 Broadway play of that title which, in 1942, became the nonmusical movie *Roxie Hart,* starring Ginger Rogers. Fred Ebb and director-choreographer Bob Fosse prepared the text. All versions provided a colorful picture of the Roaring '20s, in corrupt and crime-ridden Cook County, Illinois. The leading character, Roxie Hart, is a honky-tonk entertainer who murders her husband, is jailed and then, pretending she is pregnant, wins her release with the help of a wily lawyer. Described in the program as "a musical vaudeville," *Chicago* was studded with Fosse-conceived vaudeville and nightclub routines. In *The New York Times* Clive Barnes called the show "easily one of the best musicals of the season; it is brassy, sassy, raunchy. . . . There is a great deal of glossiness to admire. . . . The show seems to be stuffed with virtues. Take the music by John Kander and the lyrics (perhaps especially the lyrics) by Fred Ebb. They . . . remain bright and clever pastiches of '20s music."

"All I Care About," sung by Jerry Orbach and a chorus of fetching young women, was a takeoff on the kind of ballad Al Jolson and Bing Crosby had favored. Redolent of a Helen Morgan song, "Funny Honey" was sung atop a piano by Gwen Verdon in the role of Roxie Hart. Verdon was also heard in an autobiographical number called "Rosie" and, with Chita Rivera, in "My Own Best Friend." "Razzle Dazzle" was a production number introduced vocally by Orbach, and "I Can't Do it Alone," a satire on operetta, was sung by Rivera. During the 1975 Broadway run of *Chicago,* when Gwen Verdon became indisposed, Liza Minnelli replaced her.

In 1975 Kander and Ebb contributed five new songs to the film *Funny Lady,* starring Barbra Streisand as Fanny Brice in the sequel to *Funny Girl.* Here Streisand introduced, and subsequently recorded, "How Lucky Can You Get" and "Let's Hear it for Me." In 1976 Kander and Ebb wrote songs for another film starring Liza Minnelli, *A Matter of Time.* One year later the score of the film *New York, New York* (1977), directed by Martin Scorcese and starring Liza Minnelli and Robert De Niro, brought older standards by other composers together with new Kander-Ebb numbers. The title number, by Kander and Ebb, was introduced by Minnelli and popularized both by her and by Frank Sinatra. In recent years the number has become something of an unofficial theme song for New York City. ("New York, New York" should not be confused with another song of the same title composed by Leonard Bernstein for the 1944 Broadway musical *On the Town.*) Soundtrack recordings for both *Funny Lady* and *New York, New York* were released.

2 by 5, a musical cabaret, was produced Off Broadway in October 1976 at the Village Gate Downstairs, in Greenwich Village. The "2" in the title referred to Kander and Ebb, and the "5" to the cast of performers. This was a showcase for songs from earlier Kander-Ebb musicals. But for *The Act* (October 29, 1977) Kander and Ebb composed 13 new numbers for the show's star, Liza Minnelli, who was heard in every number. The book was vaguely reminiscent of the story of *New York, New York,* depicting Minnelli as a one-time movie star who achieves new recognition as a nightclub performer; flashbacks offers glimpses into her troubled past and her years as a Hollywood actress. *The Act* was, wrote one critic, "essentially a one-person show tied together with a plot that is so sketchy and episodic as to be dreamlike." The best songs, which were re-

corded, were "The Money Tree," "There When I Need Him" and "Turning."

Woman of the Year (March 28, 1981) was a tour de force for Lauren Bacall, who, together with her successors, Raquel Welch and Debbie Reynolds, kept the production on Broadway for 771 performances. Peter Stone's book carried to the musical stage the 1942 motion picture of the same name in which Spencer Tracy portrayed a sportswriter and Katherine Hepburn a political columnist of international renown. In the musical the heroine's profession was changed to that of a television news commentator and the hero to that of a cartoonist. The protagonists "meet cute"—she angers him when she broadcasts a scathing denunciation of his cartoons—and their romance culminates in a marriage which turns out to be a continual battle of puffed-up egos. Eventually, she learns to subdue her dynamic personality, and the marriage endures. *Woman of the Year* earned four Tony Awards, including one for Bacall and another for Kander and Ebb. "The score," wrote Frank Rich in *The New York Times,* "is flush with melodic ballads and showbiz brio." One of its best songs and a particular favorite of both Kander and Ebb, was a comedy number, "The Grass is Always Greener," a duet for Bacall and Marilyn Cooper. Harry Guardino introduced "Sometimes a Day Goes By," and Bacall "I Wrote the Book" and "One of the Boys." The complete score was released in an original cast album.

With *The Rink* (February 9, 1984), whose score was also recorded in an original cast album, Kander and Ebb wrote again for Liza Minnelli. She was costarred with Chita Rivera in a text by Terence McNally about a mother-daughter relationship. Minnelli played a former hippie, long separated from her mother (Rivera), who is the proprietess of a decrepit roller-skating rink on the boardwalk of a disintegrating seaside resort. The reconciliation of mother and daughter ultimately comes about, though not easily. For Minnelli, Kander and Ebb composed a ballad, "The Colored Lights," and for Rivera and Minnelli, a duet, "The Apple Doesn't Fall." The title song, presented by a male chorus, became a second-act dance routine performed on roller skates.

In the 1980s Kander has contributed music to two nonmusical films, the Oscar-winning *Kramer vs. Kramer* (1980), starring Dustin Hoffman and Meryl Streep, and *Still of the Night* (1982).

Both Kander and Ebb live in Manhattan. Kander, who is married and has two children, occupies a townhouse on the Upper West Side. Ebb lives in an apartment five streets away on

Central Park West. They like working in the morning, usually at Ebb's apartment. "We are both very loose creatively," said Kander. "We talk a lot. We both can improvise almost instantly. We can write a lot of junk and throw it away. We're not long on ego. We don't get embarrassed in front of each other. If either of us gets a block, the other can jolt him out of it."

Songs are written phrase by phrase, stanza by stanza, like the working out of a jigsaw puzzle. Unlike other words-and-music collaborators, they do not begin with a completed Kander melody, but Ebb does not show up for work with a finished lyric calling for a melody either. "I'm very careful not to write a whole lyric because it would commit John to a form," Ebb has explained.

Kander's passion, apart from writing songs, is opera. He travels frequently, but primarily to attend foreign opera performances.

In 1975 Ebb received an honorary doctorate in Theater Arts from Emerson University in Boston. A year later he and Cy Coleman coproduced the Emmy-winning television special *Gypsy in My Soul,* starring Shirley MacLaine. He produced two television specials in 1980, *Goldie* [Hawn] *and Liza Together* and *Baryshnikov on Broadway.*

ABOUT: Green, S. The World of Musical Comedy, 4th ed. 1980 *Periodicals*—Stereo Review September 1977.

KERN, JEROME (January 27, 1885– November 11, 1945). For four decades, Jerome Kern's creative personality dominated American popular music. His songs were heard both on the Broadway stage and in Hollywood musicals. Of these songs, approximately 100 have become standards, and 15 belong among the greatest commercial successes in the history of American popular music.

Jerome David Kern was born in New York City, the youngest of nine boys (only three survived) of Henry and Fanny (Kakeles) Kern. Henry Kern was a prosperous entrepreneur; he owned a number of retail stores and as president of the Street Sprinklers's Association, he held the lucrative contract to clean the streets. Fanny Kern was an excellent pianist who brought not only concert music into the Kern household, but also the love of books, theater and culture.

Jerome spent his early childhood in a house on East 74th Street and attended the local public schools. When he was five, his mother began teaching him to play the piano for which he immediately revealed an aptitude and a consuming interest. He satisfied his musical interests further

JEROME KERN

by attending choir practice at a nearby Episcopal church. His first exposure to musical theater occurred at the age of 10, when he saw Victor Herbert's *The Wizard of the Nile*; upon returning home he was able to play the principal tunes on the piano from memory.

In 1895, the Kern family moved to Newark, New Jersey, where the father became the proprietor of a merchandising house. At Newark High School, Kern's musical gifts were recognized and admired; he was often referred to by his teachers as "the little genius." He composed music for school productions and played the piano and organ at school assemblies.

Upon graduating from high school in 1902, Kern spent the summer working for his father, who expected his son would enter the business on a permanent basis. An almost disastrous business deal soon convinced his father otherwise. Sent to a New York factory to purchase two pianos, young Kern was so magnetized by the hospitality and salesmanship of the factory owner, who plied Kern with wine, that Kern purchased not two pianos but 200. This deal would have ruined Henry Kern's business had he not been able to devise a profitable plan of selling pianos on installments.

In the fall of 1902, Kern enrolled at the Normal College in New York City (later called the Hunter College Training School) to prepare for a career as a teacher. At the same time, he continued to attend the New York College of Music where he studied piano with Alexander Lambert and Paolo Gallico and harmony with Austin Pierce and Albert von Doenhoff. Kern was also composing popular tunes which he sent in large bundles to Tin Pan Alley publishers; the first to be taken was *At the Casino*, a piano piece issued by Lyceum Music Publishing Company on September 5, 1902.

Late that year, Kern went to Europe, the first of several trips made during the next few years. In Berlin, he bought tickets for all of the shows, and for a brief period, he studied composition and harmony in Heidelberg. He then spent some time in London, a city with which he fell in love instantly.

But Kern returned to New York in 1903. In Tin Pan Alley he found a job as a song plugger at Lyceum Music for a salary of seven dollars a week; his duties there included a daily stint at Wanamaker's department store. His performance at Wanamaker's came to the attention of vaudevillian Marie Dressler, who asked to "borrow" Kern to accompany her. He was delighted, and at her request, wrote several songs for her. As a result, he was also asked to write for the comedy team of Joe Weber and Lew Fields. He went on to the Shapiro-Remick Company where, with an increase in pay to nine dollars, he worked as a song plugger.

From there, Kern went to work for the publishing house of T. B. Harms, first in the billing department, and then as a sheet music salesman, arranger and song plugger. Max Dreyfus, the president, recalled Kern's first interview: "He said he wanted to imbibe the atmosphere of music. I decided to take him on, and to start him off by giving him the toughest job I know, selling music. . . . He was full of youthful spirit, and with it a certain charm. He sold music."

But Kern was becoming more and more interested in selling his own music, and he was anxious to return to England. By the end of 1903, he had found employment in the London office of Charles K. Frohman, a Broadway producer who was also active in London's West End. At a salary of £2 a week, Kern wrote "openers" for Frohman productions; these were heard at the start of each performance to consume time while fashionably late patrons were seated. His first such contributions were for *The School Girl*, (May 9, 1903), which had opened at the Pavilion Music Hall, starring Edna May; on this occasion Billie Burke (later Mrs. Florenz Ziegfeld) made her singing début. Kern's songs were also interpolated into Frohman productions starring the well-known actor, Seymour Hicks, at the Aldwych Theatre. At about this time, the last of producer-director Edward E. Rice's shows, *Mr. Wix of Wickham* was being prepared for a Broadway run to begin on September 19, 1904. Hicks suggested that Kern might be called upon to "Americanize" the score. Kern agreed, and trav-

eled to New York with the show. In addition to bringing fresh harmonizations and orchestration to some of Herbert Darnley and George Everard's songs, Kern added four songs of his own, one of which, "Waiting for You," was introduced by the star, Harry Corson Clarke. Kern's efforts attracted the attention of Alan Dale, critic for the New York *American*: "[The] music by Jerome D. Kern towers, in such an Eiffel way, above the average hurdy-gurdy, penny-in-the-slot, primitive accompaniment to the musical show that criticism is disarmed."

After *Mr. Wix*, Kern went back to work at Harms and took occasional assignments as rehearsal pianist for Broadway musicals. At Harms, he ran into Edward Laska, a fellow student at the New York College of Music, now a budding lyricist. They collaborated on Kern's first hit in America, "How'd You Like to Spoon With Me?" They sold it to the Shuberts, who interpolated it in their production of the British musical, *The Earl and the Girl*, which opened at the Casino Theatre on November 4, 1905. It was introduced by Georgia Caine and Victor Morley and a chorus of six girls floating on flower-decorated swings. The *Dramatic Mirror* called "Spoon with Me" "the most successful number ever introduced here; it was demanded again and again."

In 1905, Kern again returned to London. Seymour Hicks was seeking topical songs for one of his shows, and he hired P. G. Wodehouse, a young columnist and lyricist, to write the words and suggested Kern for the music. Kern and Wodehouse's first meeting took place during a rehearsal at the Aldwych Theatre, where Wodehouse found Kern playing poker with the actors. "When I finally managed to free him from the card table and was able to talk with him," Wodehouse later recalled, "I became impressed. Here, I thought, was a young man supremely confident of himself, the kind of person who inspired people to seek him out when a job must be done."

Wodehouse and Kern conceived a timely political song called "Mr. Chamberlain," after Joseph Chamberlain, statesman and leader of the Liberal Unionists and father of Prime Minister Neville Chamberlain. Hicks introduced "Mr. Chamberlain" (with two other Kern numbers) in *The Beauty of Bath*, scoring such a success that during the year that followed, "Mr. Chamberlain" was continually heard throughout London.

The distinguished British actor, George Grossmith, first met Kern that year also and described his impressions in his autobiography, *G. G.* (1933): "I knew him as Jerry Kern and liked him immensely. He came often to my house and played to us. He played divinely . . . with a tremendous gift of 'tune'. He was the only one I could detect in a barren field likely to fill the shoes of [Lionel] Monckton, Paul Rubens, and Leslie Stuart. In my dressing room at the Gaiety was a tiny yacht piano. . . . on which Rubens had composed his first song that was sung in a London Theatre . . . 'Give me a lyric,' one night asked Jerry, 'and let me try what I can do on the same instrument'; and together we wrote and composed 'Rosalie,' which I sang in, I think, *The Spring Chicken* [1905]."

Because of Kern's growing reputation and the English mannerisms he affected, Frohman (who felt the British were better composers) invited him to go to America with him to work on Broadway. Kern's ruse did not continue for long, but between 1905 and 1912, almost 100 of his songs were interpolated into 30 Broadway musicals. By 1910, his assignments were bringing him an annual income in five figures and he continued to shuttle back and forth between New York and London. Very much the suave man of the world, he established bachelor quarters on West 68th Street to which he brought his bride, Eva Leale, an English girl he married on October 25, 1910. They had one child, a daughter, Betty.

Kern continued to make forward strides on Broadway. The Shuberts had been watching Kern since "How'd You Like to Spoon With Me?" and they asked him to write the score (with Frank Tours) for *La Belle Paree* (March 20, 1911) for the opening of their new Winter Garden Theatre; the show also featured the newcomer, Al Jolson.

In 1912, Kern was honored by a request from producer Florenz Ziegfeld to write a song ("Call Me Flo") for *A Winsome Widow* (April 11, 1912). This marked the beginning of an association which, in time, would make theater history. Meanwhile, Kern composed his first complete Broadway musical score; however, *The Red Petticoat* (November 13, 1912) was a failure (61 performances). This was followed by the score for *Oh, I Say!* (October 30, 1913), whose unusual orchestration (namely, the use of saxophones, later a mainstay of the Broadway orchestra) provoked wide comment. Kern also continued to provide single songs for interpolation into other scores; one of the most successful of these was "You're Here and I'm Here," introduced by Venita Fitzhugh and Nigel Barrie in *The Laughing Husband* (February 2, 1914).

Kern's next major venture was *The Girl From Utah* (August 24, 1914), a Frohman production imported from England which ran for 120 performances. Its heroine, who flees from London to Utah to avoid becoming a wife of a Mormon polygamist, was played by the beautiful Julia Sanderson. To this musical, Kern contributed eight songs, one of which, "They Didn't Believe Me" (with witty lyrics by Herbert Reynolds), introduced by Julia Sanderson, was Kern's first masterpiece. Its unusual structure, subtle change of key, introduction of a new musical idea near the end of the chorus, made this song a far cry from the routine efforts usually heard on Broadway and in Tin Pan Alley. "They Didn't Believe Me" was recorded in 1915 by Grace Kerns with Reed Miller; significant recordings were also made by André Kostelanetz, Artie Shaw, Risë Stevens, Dick Haymes, Julia Sanderson, Dinah Shore and Margaret Whiting.

The year 1915 was a turning point in Kern's career because it brought the first of his collaborations with the English writer Guy Bolton. Their first effort was *Ninety in the Shade* (January 25, 1915), produced at the Knickerbocker. Though Kern produced a delightful score, it could not compensate for the show's many problems. But it did bring the team to the attention of agent Elizabeth Marbury and F. Ray Comstock, the manager of the Princess Theatre. Together, they opened new vistas for the American musical.

The Princess Theatre was a small house on the edge of the theater district which would accommodate an audience of only 299. Marbury (who was part-owner) and Comstock were searching for viable productions to mount there, when Marbury conceived the idea of an intimate musical with a limited budget of $7,500, written expressly for the Princess. When operetta composer Victor Herbert was unavailable, Marbury commissioned Kern and Bolton to write the show.

Nobody Home (April 20, 1915), the first of four "Princess Theatre Shows," was a loose adaptation of the English musical comedy, *Mr. Popple of Ippleton*. In addition to a modest cast, it called for a chorus line of nine, an orchestra of ten, and sparing sets. The emphasis was placed on the wit and charm in telling the amusing experiences of an Englishman in the United States with an American show girl. The songs were as sprightly as the dialogue and lyrics. "The Magic Melody" (lyrics by Schuyler Greene), introduced by Adele Rowland and chorus, was of sufficient musical value to draw the praise of the distinguished musicologist Carl Engel, who termed it "the opening chorus of an epoch . . . a change, a new regime in American popular music . . . a relief, a liberation." Another fine song was "You Know and I Know" (lyrics by Greene) sung by Alice Dovey and George Anderson.

When *Nobody Home* (135 performances)

turned a small profit, a successor, *Very Good, Eddie* (December 23, 1915), was planned. The book was written by Bolton and Philip Bartholomae, the lyrics by Schuyler Greene, and it was highly successful (341 performances), turning a profit of more than $100,000. Like *Nobody Home*, *Very Good, Eddie* was a modest yet refined production, and it represented a sharp departure from the lavishly mounted musicals then in vogue, while stressing elegance, sophistication and wit. It was different from its Broadway predecessors and counterparts in that the music and lyrics were calculated to grow naturally from the characters and the events; it was also thoroughly American in its story, setting, characters and dialogue. *Very Good, Eddie* was a comedy of errors: two honeymoon couples, about to board the Hudson River Day Line's *Catskill*, become separated, and one bride sails off with the other groom. Aboard ship, they attempt to maintain the appearance of being married to one another, with embarrasing and humorous consequences. The show "depended upon the ease and credibility of the acting and characterization," wrote Cecil Smith in *Musical Comedy in America* (1950). "Scarcely any previous musical comedy had been favored with a plot and dialogue so coherent, so neatly related to those of well-written nonmusical plays . . . the 'intimate' musical comedy became established as a suitable and successful genre." The hit of the show was "Babes in the Wood," introduced by Oscar Shaw and Anna Orr, but the score boasted many fine songs, including "Some Sort of Somebody," "Nodding Roses," and "Size 13 Collar."

Very Good, Eddie was revived on Broadway on December 21, 1975. Clive Barnes (*The New York Times*) called it "an absolutely enchanting old musical. . . . It takes off. It flies. And it lands in a territory of innocence that we all think we ought to remember. . . . What a fantastic composer Kern was! . . . The musical texture of the score, its sheer sense of fun and liveliness, its attentiveness to the story, its variations of pace and mood are pure delight."

More successful still was *Oh, Boy!* (February 20, 1917) which ran for 463 performances. Bolton and P. G. "Plum" Wodehouse (whom Bolton had met at the opening of *Very Good, Eddie*) wrote the book and Wodehouse supplied the lyrics. This was a merry escapade in which a young lady, fleeing from the police, is forced to hide in the hero's apartment and assumes various disguises in order to escape discovery by the hero's new bride and their respective families. One of Kern's most celebrated ballads, "Till the Clouds Roll By," was introduced in the show by Anna Wheaton and Tom Powers, and three decades later it became the title song for Kern's film bi-

ography. The score also contained such gems as "You Never Knew About Me" and "Nesting Time in Flatbush."

Oh, Boy! was revived in 1979 by Gerald Bordman's New Princess Theatre Company, and at the Goodspeed Opera House in East Haddam, Connecticut in 1983. In a review of the latter, *Variety* said: "Kern is magnificent, and even in as early a show as this, he was already casting a potent spell. It is loaded with melody, elegance, sheer fun, not to mention charm." For the Kern centennial in 1985, *Oh, Boy!* and *Oh, Lady! Lady!!* were produced by John McGlinn at Carnegie Recital Hall in New York.

Kern's last "Princess Theatre Show," *Oh, Lady! Lady!!* (February 1, 1918), was another romantic comedy of the Long Island country club set, with a book by Bolton and Wodehouse and lyrics by Wodehouse. The show starred Carl Randall and Vivienne Segal, who introduced "Before I Met You," "Little Ships Come Sailing Home," and "You Found Me and I Found You". One of Kern's song classics, "Bill," (about which more will be said later), originally written for Miss Segal, was cut when she insisted it was not suited to her voice (ten years later, it found a home in *Show Boat*). Though *Oh, Lady! Lady!!* had a shorter run (219 performances) than *Very Good, Eddie* and *Oh, Boy!*, it nevertheless proved to be a profitable venture.

The urbane style and the simplicity and economy of the "Princess Theatre Shows" had a far-reaching effect in setting the stage for the smart, intimate revues of the 1920s and the unconventional, sophisticated shows of Rodgers and Hart. "Those smallish musicals inaugurated the American musical," says Alan Jay Lerner in his autobiography, *The Street Where I Live (1978).* "They were American because the music was American. Kern was writing genuine, eighteen karat American popular theatre music, and elegantly, discreetly but distinctly the music had a beat. . . . The books were light and amusing, and the music in the popular voice range, and Wodehouse wrote lyrics that were appropriate to both: clever, graceful, and wittily rhymed. Picking up the light verse tradition of W. S. Gilbert, he became the pathfinder for Larry Hart, Cole Porter, Ira Gershwin and everyone else who followed."

Even while Kern was working for the Princess Theatre, he was also composing music for the more formal, the more elaborately mounted musicals favored elsewhere on Broadway. One such was *Leave It to Jane* (August 28, 1917), based on George Ade's play, *The College Widow*, with book by Bolton and Wodehouse and lyrics by Wodehouse. Its run extended to 167 performances. A satire on life in an Indiana college town, the story revolves around Jane, the daughter of the college president, who uses her feminine wiles to prevent the star halfback from defecting to a rival school. Edith Hallor, as Jane, introduced "The Siren's Song" and the title song, and Georgia O'Ramey was heard in the score's principal comedy number, "Cleopatterer." In 1959, *Leave It to Jane* was revived Off Broadway and enjoyed a run of 928 performances before touring the country in 1961. In a review of the revival, Richards Watts, Jr. wrote of Kern's songs: "I have remembered the Kern score with delight, recalling five of the songs in particular. And hearing them again last night I was happy to find that not only was the score as a whole as charming and freshly tuneful as memory has made it, but my quintet came off easily as the best of a gloriously melodious lot. "

In 1918, the Kerns acquired an estate in Cedar Knolls near Bronxville, New York, which remained their home for two decades. Livestock was raised on the grounds and in addition, the family was devoted to its many pets. In the 1920s, Kern became the *grand seigneur* with a chauffeur-driven Rolls Royce, a speed boat for cruising on Long Island Sound and a houseboat for seasonal travel to Palm Beach. He was always fashionably dressed and was a gourmet of fine food. Kern loved being surrounded by those he admired and those of whom he was fond, and invariably the Kern home was filled with friends who engaged in conversation, music, parlor games and pranks; Kern was always an enthusiastic participant. He also derived considerable pleasure from playing poker, betting on horses, and attending baseball games. But such diversions did not preclude intellectual pursuits; he was an avid reader on a great many subjects: literature, art, world affairs, American politics, architecture, even home decoration. His love of books led him to collect first editions, rare editions and manuscripts, and he sold his collection in 1929 at an auction for more than two million dollars. He then went on to accumulate stamps, coins and old silver.

Between 1920 and 1924, Kern's music was heard in 14 Broadway musicals, 11 for which he composed the complete scores. The most successful were full-scale, star-studded productions faithful to the existing rituals of the musical theater; two of these were written to order as showcases for Marilyn Miller. *Sally* (December 21, 1920), a Ziegfeld production with a book by Bolton and lyrics by B. G. De Sylva and Clifford Grey, ballet music by Victor Herbert and sets by Joseph Urban, ran for 570 performances. Marilyn Miller portrayed the heroine, a dishwasher in an inn on Long Island who passes herself off

as a Russian dancer. Her triumph is complete when she appears in the *Ziegfeld Follies* and marries a socialite. Though it had been written for a musical which was never produced and not specifically for her, Marilyn Miller (with Irving Fisher) introduced another of Kern's durable ballads, "Look for the Silver Lining" (lyrics by De Sylva). In 1921, this song was recorded by Marion Harris. Later recordings included those by Bing Crosby, Judy Garland, Margaret Whiting, Dick Haymes with Helen Forrest, Connie Boswell, Risë Stevens, and André Kostelanetz. It was also heard in the screen adaptation of *Sally* (1929), in Marilyn Miller's film biography (1949) whose title borrowed that of the song, and *The Great Ziegfeld* (1936).

The score of *Sally* also included a title song (lyrics by Clifford Grey), introduced by Irving Fisher, then recorded by Joe Schenck, "Whip-poor-will" (lyrics by De Sylva), a duet for Marilyn Miller and Irving Fisher, "Little Church Around the Corner" (lyrics by P. G. Wodehouse), and "The Wild Rose" (lyrics by Grey), sung on the stage by Marilyn Miller.

Sunny (September 22, 1925), the second vehicle for Marilyn Miller produced by Ziegfeld, was another box-office success with a run of 517 performances. The book and lyrics were written by Otto Harbach and Oscar Hammerstein II, collaborating with Kern for the first time. Marilyn Miller now appeared as Sunny Peters, an American performing with a circus in England. She falls in love with an American and stows away on the ship on which he is returning home and captures his heart. Marilyn Miller and Peter Frawley introduced "Who?," the show's smash hit whose success was attributed to the young Hammerstein's effective lyrics and use of the monosyllabic word of the title as well as to Kern's melody. With Lawrence Gray, Marilyn Miller repeated her performance of it in the first screen adaptation of *Sunny* (1930); Anna Neagle and John Carroll sang it in the second (1941). When George Olsen and his band recorded "Who?" using a vocal trio for the chorus, it became fashionable for bandleaders to use vocal trios. Recordings were later made by Tommy Dorsey (with Frank Sinatra) and the orchestras of Guy Lombardo, André Kostelanetz and Al Goodman. In the original stage production of *Sunny*, Marilyn Miller also introduced "D'Ya Love Me?" which Margaret Whiting recorded.

After the opening of *Good Morning, Dearie* (November 1, 1921), Kern found himself in legal trouble over one of the show's songs, "Ka-lu-a," (lyrics by Anne Caldwell), which had been introduced by Oscar Shaw. Songwriter Fred Fisher filed a suit against Kern maintaining that he had plagiarized Fisher's repetitive rolling bass in "Dardanella." During the court action, celebrated musicians such as Leopold Stokowski, Walter Damrosch, Artur Bodanzky and Victor Herbert testified that this bass figure was not unique to Fisher's "Dardanella," but could be found throughout classical literature. Kern himself proved to be a sarcastic and hostile witness, and the court ruled in favor of Fisher, setting damages at $250.

In the 1920s Kern also wrote two musicals for the song-and-dance family of Fred Stone, his wife, Allene, and their daughter, Dorothy. *Stepping Stones* (November 6, 1923) was a modernized version of the Little Red Riding Hood fairy tale in which Dorothy Stone, as Roughette Hood, made her debut; "Once in a Blue Moon" and "In Love With Love" (lyrics by Anne Caldwell) were the score's best songs. *Criss Cross*, set in exotic places and whose score includes "You Will, Won't You?" (lyrics by Anne Caldwell and Otto Harbach), followed in 1926.

In 1927, Kern began to conceive of Edna Ferber's novel, *Show Boat*, as a stage musical. He had been fascinated by her story of life aboard the showboats on the Mississippi River in the 1880s which brought entertainment to towns and hamlets along the route. When he first broached the subject with Edna Ferber, she was skeptical because she envisioned the traditional musical comedy. But, as Kern explained to Ferber, he had in mind a new type of musical whose concerns would be character portrayal, logical plot line, authentic backgrounds, and credible motivations. Every element of the production would spring naturally from the dramatic events: production numbers contrived solely for their own sake would be avoided, as would a chorus line, synthetic humor, and songs not germane to the story or characters. When Ferber had been won over, Kern enlisted Oscar Hammerstein II to write the text and lyrics, Joseph Urban to design the sets, and Flo Ziegfeld to produce the show.

Show Boat takes place on the *Cotton Blossom*, owned by Cap'n Andy (Charles Winninger). His daughter, Magnolia (Norma Terris), falls in love and elopes with a gambler, Gaylor Revenal (Howard Marsh), and they go to Chicago. When his gambling debts mount, he leaves her to raise their daughter, even though he still loves her. Magnolia finds work as a singer at the Trocadero Music Hall, but Cap'n Andy induces her to return to the *Cotton Blossom*, where she finds a repentant Ravenal and their daughter becomes the singing star of the boat's show.

When *Show Boat* opened at the Ziegfeld Theatre in New York on December 27, 1927 with its innovative procedures it was universally acclaimed by the critics. *Show Boat* was called "a triumph, a beautiful example of musical comedy, "and Robert Garland described it as "a wonder and a wow . . . an American masterpiece." The show was also a box-office success, and after 572 performances on Broadway, *Show Boat* toured the country for nearly a year. In addition, three screen versions have been produced starring Laura La Plante and Joseph Schildkraut (1929), Irene Dunne and Allan Jones (1936), and Kathryn Grayson and Howard Keel (1951).

Show Boat is a veritable treasure house of riches; never before or since was Kern so abundantly melodic within a single score. If a single number stands out from the others, it is, perhaps, "Ol' Man River," a spiritual hymn to the Mississippi River lamenting racial oppression, sung by Joe, the black workhand. In her autobiography, *A Peculiar Treasure*, Edna Ferber describes her reaction when Kern first sang it for her: "The music mounted, mounted, and I give you my word my hair stood on end. The tears came to my eyes, and I breathed like a heroine in a melodrama. This was great music, this was music that would outlast Jerome Kern's day and mine. I have never heard it since without the emotional surge." Jules Bledsoe sang "Ol' Man River" in the original production and in the first screen version; it was sung in the two later screen adaptations by Paul Robeson (1936) and William Warfield (1951). In 1928, it was recorded by Paul Whiteman and others; subsequent recordings were made by Bing Crosby, Frank Sinatra, Paul Robeson and Robert Weede.

The show's other songs also became tremendously popular. "Make Believe," "You Are Love," and "Why Do I Love You?" are duets for Magnolia and Ravenal, and "Can't Help Lovin' Dat Man," was introduced by Helen Morgan, as Julie, a mulatto. The score also incorporated the biggest hit of the 1890s, Charles K. Harris's "After the Ball" for Magnolia to sing at the Trocadero, and "Bill" (lyrics by Wodehouse), which had been dropped from *Oh, Lady! Lady!!* at the Princess Theatre, and then from *Sally* (it was unsuitable for Marilyn Miller's voice) before finding its way to Helen Morgan in *Show Boat*, and a new song, "I Still Suits Me," added for Paul Robeson. All of the songs from *Show Boat* were widely performed and recorded by many, including the cast members, Willard Robison, Don Voorhees, Grace Moore, Paul Whiteman, Tommy Dorsey, André Kostelanetz, Guy Lombardo, Frances Langford, Artie Shaw, Ella Fitzgerald, Frank Sinatra, Lena Horne, Risë Stevens, Margaret Whiting and Dinah Shore.

Through the years, *Show Boat* has continued

to be extremely popular attaining the status of a classic. In 1946 it was revived on Broadway for a run of more than 400 performances followed by a national tour; for it, Kern composed a new song (and his last), "Nobody Else But Me" (lyrics by Hammerstein). *Show boat* was back on Broadway in 1948, at the New York City Opera in 1954 (and later at the Houston Grand Opera), at Lincoln Center in 1966 and on Broadway again in 1982. Since the late 1920s, there has hardly been a year when *Show Boat* has not been performed somewhere in the United States.

After *Show Boat*, Kern's next show was the musical comedy, *Sweet Adeline* (September 2, 1929), a "musical romance" about the Gay Nineties, with a book and lyrics by Hammerstein. It stayed on Broadway for 234 performances even though theatergoers suddenly found themselves ruined by the stockmarket crash in October. Helen Morgan starred as Addie, daughter of a beer garden owner, who becomes a success on the stage and marries the show's star. For Helen Morgan, Kern composed two fine ballads, "Why Was I Born?" and "Don't Ever Leave Me," both of which she recorded; Irene Dunne sang them in the movie version (1935).

But Kern had not abandoned the notion of musical plays. His next two shows continued to stress the integration of songs with the text and dramatic action. *The Cat and the Fiddle* (October 15, 1931), was "a musical love story" with book and lyrics by Otto Harbach, whose protagonists are composers: a Rumanian named Victor Florescu, who is engaged in writing an opera and an American, Shirley Sheridan, who is crazy about jazz. Intolerance towards each other's musical tastes must be broken down before their romance can flourish. Though it is set in Brussels and Kern's score is reminiscent of European operetta, *The Cat and the Fiddle* represented an innovation in the American musical theater by dispensing with the chorus, production numbers and gratuitous comedy; its four principal songs are basic to the plot development. The canzonetta, "The Night Was Made for Love," introduced by George Meaders, recurs throughout; Bettina Hall introduced "She Didn't Say Yes" (Jeanette MacDonald sang it in the screen adaptation, 1934); "Poor Pierrot," and the tearful "Try to Forget" rounded out the score. The show was highly successful and remained on Broadway for 395 performances.

Music in the Air (November 8, 1932), again in collaboration with Hammerstein, came next. It had settings and the love intrigues frequently encountered in operettas: Sieglinde, daughter of a village music teacher in Bavaria, and Karl, the village schoolmaster, are in love. They go to Mu-

nich to market a song Sieglinde's father has composed; each finds a new romantic interest: Karl, a prima donna, and Sieglinde, a composer who writes an opera for her. When the prima donna tires of Karl and Sieglinde fails on the stage they reconcile and return home. But in his review in *The New York Times*, Brooks Atkinson recognized the new direction in which Kern had been developing: "Mr. Kern and Mr. Hammerstein have discovered how musical plays can now be written as organic works of art. . . . At last, musical drama has been emancipated."

Though in places Kern's score is reminiscent of German folk songs and beer-hall tunes, the principal songs had the unmistakable identity of American hit songs. Of particular note are "I've Told Ev'ry Little Star," inspired by the song of a finch that Kern heard one summer night in Nantucket, "And Love Was Born" and "I'm Alone."

The initial run of *Music in the Air* was 342 performances. When it made a return visit to Broadway in 1951, the text was found wanting, described by the critics as "hackneyed," "dated" and "incredible corn." But the Kern score stood up well—as Brooks Atkinson wrote in *The New York Times* in his review of the revival, "The immortal songs . . . still flow through it [the play] like enchanted improvisations. They are part of the theater's richest treasures."

With *Roberta* (November 18, 1933), Kern returned to musical comedy. This was Otto Harbach's adaptation of *Gowns by Roberta*, a novel by Alice Duer Miller. John Kent, an all-American fullback goes to Paris to assume management of his aunt's modiste shop; he falls in love with Stephanie, its chief designer. Highlights of the production were a fashion parade and the Kern score. The "Smoke Gets in Your Eyes," introduced by Tamara Geva, regularly stopped the show. In the first screen adaptation of *Roberta* (1935) it was sung by Irene Dunne with dancing by Fred Astaire; in the second, entitled *Lovely to Look At* (1952), it was sung by Kathryn Grayson with dancing by Gower and Marge Champion. "Yesterdays" was introduced by Fay Templeton, "The Touch of Your Hand," a duet for Tamara Geva and William Hain, was recorded by Leo Reisman and his orchestra in 1933, and Bob Hope and Tamara Geva introduced "You're Devastating" on stage. Although the Broadway run of *Roberta* reached 295 performances, it was less successful than its predecessors because the houses were rarely full.

For the first screen version of *Roberta* (1935), two songs not heard in the original stage production were inserted: "Lovely to Look At" (lyrics by Dorothy Fields) and "I Won't Dance" (lyrics by Harbach and Hammerstein). "Lovely to Look At" was introduced by Irene Dunne, then became the title song for the remake in 1952. Recorded by George Hall and by Smith Ballew among others, this song grew so successful in 1935 that it rose to first position on *Your Hit Parade*, a rare honor for a song from the theater. The lively "I Won't Dance" was borrowed from *Three Sisters*, a failure produced in London in 1934.

Kern's last musical, *Very Warm for May* (November 17, 1939), was a failure (59 performances), but it is remembered for the masterpiece, "All the Things You Are." This ballad was introduced by Hiram Sherman, Frances Mercer, Wallace Shaw and Ralph Stewart, and was regarded as one of Kern's greatest songs by Richard Rodgers, Arthur Schwartz and Harry Warren. In *Broadway Rhythm* (1944), the motion picture adaptation of *Very Warm for May*, it was performed by Ginny Simms, and was the only song retained from the stage score. Successful early recordings of this song were made by Tommy Dorsey and Guy Lombardo and His Royal Canadians, and later by Frank Sinatra, Kenny Baker, Hildegarde, Tony Martin, Risë Stevens, Helen Traubel, Margaret Whiting, John Charles Thomas and Glenn Miller.

In 1937, Kern moved to Beverly Hills, and though his first experience with motion pictures had been frustrating (in 1929, the songs he wrote for *Men of the Sky* were deleted at the last minute), he now devoted his full energies to the screen. Between 1935 and 1946, his music was heard in nine major films: *I Dream Too Much* (1935), starring the soprano Lily Pons; *Swing Time* (1936), starring Fred Astaire and Ginger Rogers ("The Way You Look Tonight" and "A Fine Romance," lyrics by Dorothy Fields); *High, Wide and Handsome* (1937), starring Irene Dunne; *When You're in Love* (1937), starring Grace Moore; *Joy of Living* (1938), starring Irene Dunne ("You Couldn't Be Cuter," lyrics by Fields); *You Were Never Lovelier* (1942), starring Fred Astaire and Rita Hayworth ("Dearly Beloved," lyrics by Johnny Mercer); *Can't Help Singing* (1944), starring Deanna Durbin ("More and More," lyrics by Harburg); *Cover Girl* (1944), starring Gene Kelly and Rita Hayworth ("Long Ago and Far Away," lyrics by Ira Gershwin); and *Centennial Summer* (1946), starring Jeanne Crain ("All Through the Day," lyrics by Hammerstein and "In Love in Vain," lyrics by Leo Robin).

In 1936, Kern received his first Oscar for "The Way You Look Tonight" from *Swing Time*. Though it has become a celebrated love ballad, it was introduced by Fred Astaire as a comedy number in which he teased Ginger Rogers about her appearance while shampooing her hair.

"The Last Time I Saw Paris" (lyrics by Hammerstein) brought a second Academy Award. Inspired by the Nazi occupation of Paris in June 1940 during World War II, it is the only song in which the writing of the lyrics preceded Kern's music; it is also one of his rare independent numbers. The song was introduced in 1940 by Kate Smith on her radio program. Hildegarde, Sophie Tucker and Noël Coward helped to popularize it further in nightclub appearances as did the many recordings of the song. It was interpolated into the motion picture, *Lady, Be Good!* (1941), where it was sung by Ann Sothern and earned the Oscar. With his characteristic honesty, Kern objected to winning the award on the grounds that the song had not been composed for the screen and that Harold Arlen's "That Old Black Magic" was more deserving of this honor. Kern then used his influence to change the rules of the Academy Award so that only songs written expressly for the screen would be eligible.

In addition to receiving the Oscars, Kern's songs continued to be immensely popular across the country. Many of them were featured a number of times on *Your Hit Parade*, and "Long Ago and Far Away" and "All Through the Day" reached the top position. His songs were recorded by many artists too numerous to mention who represented a variety of styles; let it suffice to say that rarely does one encounter a performer who has not used one of Kern's songs. Anthologies of his songs have been made by Bing Crosby, Risë Stevens, Irene Dunne, Margaret Whiting, André Previn, George Byron, Joan Morris, and the orchestras of André Kostelanetz and Paul Weston.

In the 1940s, Kern turned his sights in the direction of the concert hall and, for the Cleveland Orchestra, he composed *Scenario*, a suite of tunes from *Show Boat*. It was first performed on October 23, 1941 under the baton of Artur Rodzinski. Several months later, André Kostelanetz commissioned him to write *Mark Twain: A Portrait for Orchestra*; Kostelanetz conducted the premiere, given by the Cincinnati Symphony on May 14, 1942. With Charles Miller, Kern transcribed a number of his songs for string quartet which were recorded by the Gordon String Quartet. His songs have also inspired orchestrator and composer Robert Russell Bennett to write *Symphonic Study* and *Variations on a Theme by Jerome Kern*, the latter based on "Once in a Blue Moon" from *Stepping Stones*.

In 1944, Kern was elected to the National Institute of Arts and Letters. From December 11 to 17 of that year a Jerome Kern Jubilee was celebrated throughout the United States with performances of his music in theaters, nightclubs and on the radio.

In October 1945, Kern went to New York to coproduce with Hammerstein a revival of *Show Boat* and to discuss with the new producing firm of Rodgers and Hammerstein a new Broadway musical, *Annie Get Your Gun* (for which Irving Berlin was destined to write the score). Kern arrived in New York with his wife on November 2, and on November 4, he collapsed outside the American Bible Society on Park Avenue at 57th Street. He died of cerebral hemorrage in Doctor's Hospital on November 11; funeral services were held the following day at the Ferndale Crematory in Hartsdale, New York.

"Genius is surely not too extravagant a word for him," said the New York *Herald Tribune*. "He left us rare treasures." On November 15 NBC broadcast a coast-to-coast radio tribute to Kern, which was folllowed on December 9 by another on the CBS radio network. On March 26, 1946, J. Philip Philbin of Massachusetts delivered a eulogy to Kern at the House of Representatives in Washington, D. C. in which he said in part: "In the life of our country we have had few such talented and gifted artists as Jerome Kern. . . . Americans will continue to sing the beautiful, touching songs, the joyous melodies, the appealing tunes which he wrote, and many of his works will be written in the folklore of American music."

When composing, Kern worked at the piano which had a desk attached to the keyboard so he could write down a tune and immediately try it out on the piano. If he was pleased with results he would rub his hands excitedly, and when a song was finished, he sometimes played it for his lyricist on the telephone, but more often, he recorded it and sent the disc to his collaborator.

In his thought processes, Kern was always precise, methodical and systematic, but paradoxically, he was often haphazard, even careless in his habits as a composer. In spite of the ever-present pressure of deadlines, he worked only when he was in the mood: "You might visit him on a certain afternoon all ready to pitch into work and find that he was in the mood to dawdle," Hammerstein once recalled. "He might have a new puzzle to work out, or he might feel like calling up a bookmaker and make bets on the races that day." But he never missed a deadline.

Once he became involved with the process of composition, Kern was a fastidious workman who was continually revising; he never submitted anything that he regarded as inferior. He would write more songs than were needed, alter-

nate numbers for an important scene, and make his final selection during rehearsals. Discarded numbers often re-emerged in subsequent productions. "Composing," he said, "is like fishing. You get a nibble, but you don't know whether it's a minnow or a marlin until you reel it in. You write twenty tunes to get two good ones, and the wastebasket yearns for the music."

In preparation at the time of his death, a lavish film biography of Jerome Kern, *Till the Clouds Roll By*, was released in 1946. Robert Walker portrayed Kern, Dorothy Patrick, Kern's wife, Eva, and Van Heflin, Oscar Hammerstein. It included a scene from *Show Boat*, and many of Kern's songs were performed by a stellar cast that also included Angela Lansbury, Dinah Shore, June Allyson, Ray McDonald, Judy Garland, Frank Sinatra, Lena Horne, Kathryn Grayson, Cyd Charisse, Gower Champion and Virginia O'Brien. The score was issued in a soundtrack recording.

Since Kern's death, his songs have remained quite popular with recording artists and the public, and they are often used in contemporary films. In 1958, Bob Hope revived *Roberta* as a television special, and a dozen of Kern's songs were used in *You Are Love*, produced in 1971 by the New York City Ballet featuring Jacques D'Amboise and Melissa Hayden. To celebrate the centenary of his birth, the United States Postal Service issued a Jerome Kern commemorative postage stamp in January 1985. Most recently, a revue entitled *Jerome Kern Goes to Hollywood* (January 23, 1986) opened at the Ritz Theatre in New York.

ABOUT: Bordman, G. Jerome Kern, His Life and Work, 1980; Ewen, D. The World of Jerome Kern, 1960; Freedland, M. Jerome Kern: A Biography, 1978. *Periodicals*—High Fidelity/Musical America January/February 1985; New York Times January 27, 1985.

KING, CAROLE (February 9, 1941–). A noted composer-lyricist of soft rock and a highly regarded performer of her own songs, Carole King created *Tapestry*, one of the most popular record albums of all time. Before that, she and her first husband, Gerry Goffin, were enormously successful Brill Building composers of rhythm-and-blues-derived easy-listening rock, which appealed to teenagers in the years before the Beatles transformed the pop music scene.

Carole King was born into a middle-class family in Brooklyn, on February 9, 1941. Her father was an insurance salesman, her mother a schoolteacher. While attending Madison High School

CAROLE KING

in Brooklyn, she heard the seminal rock music of Bill Haley, Elvis Presley and Fats Domino. By the time she graduated, King was composing pop songs in a rhythm and blues idiom. At Queens College she was a classmate of Neil Diamond and Paul Simon. At this time she dated Neil Sedaka, a friend since childhood. She dropped out of college after her freshman year to marry Gerry Goffin, who planned to become a chemist but whose avocation was writing song lyrics.

Through Sedaka, Carole King and her husband were introduced to Don Kirshner, a music publisher and co-owner of Alden Music. According to Kirshner Goffin was "torn between songwriting and chemistry. He was working in a laboratory in Brooklyn and when I drove out to see him, he was wearing a long white coat. I was determined to sign the both of them. They were brilliant. I drove out to Brooklyn and gave them a deal, but I told Gerry he had to quit the lab. He was really torn." Carole impressed Kirshner not only with her talent for composition but also with the infectious quality in her singing and piano playing.

Kirshner instructed the Goffins to produce rhythm and blues numbers slanted for the white teenaged pop market. The songwriters were assigned an office in the Brill Building on Broadway, where they daily churned out songs, as if on an assembly line. The office was a mere cubby hole, as King told an interviewer for *The New York Times* (November 29, 1970), "with just enough room for a piano, a bench and maybe a chair for the lyricist—if you were lucky. You'd sit there and write and you could hear someone

in the next cubbyhole composing some song exactly like yours. The pressure was really terrific." When the first of their two daughters was born, the Goffins took her along to the office, where a playpen was set up and a secretary kept a watchful eye on her while the songwriters worked.

Goffin and King had their first hit in 1960 with "Will You Still Love Me Tomorrow?" which was recorded in a bestselling release by the Shirelles. It remained on the *Billboard* pop charts for 19 weeks and climbed to first position during the week of January 30, 1961.

In 1961 Goffin and King numbers recorded by leading performers seemed always to be on the bestseller charts. Bobby Vee recorded "Take Good Care of My Baby"; the Drifters, "Some Kind-a Wonderful"; Tony Orlando, "Halfway to Paradise"; Gene Pitney, "Every Breath I Take." By the end of the year, Carole King and Gerry Goffin were established as one of the most successful songwriting teams in the soft-rock industry.

In 1962 Carole King made a demonstration record for Kirshner's Dimension Records, singing her own "It Might as Well Rain Until September." Realizing that King's ability to interpret her own material made her a potential recording star, Dimension executives released the demo as a single. While "It Might as Well Rain Until September" achieved only the 22nd spot on the *Billboard* Top 100, it soared to the top of the charts in England. However, King refused to cut any more records, preferring instead to concentrate on composing. "It Might as Well Rain Until September" was also recorded by Bobby Vee.

Over the next half-dozen years, Carole King was busily producing hit songs with her husband, setting his catchy lyrics to irresistible music. In 1962 they composed "The Loco-Motion," a dance tune, for their housekeeper who, using the name Little Eva, made it into a bestselling recording that year. Also in 1962, "Chains" was recorded by the Cookies (and, in 1964, by the Beatles) and "Don't Ask Me to Be Friends" by the Everly Brothers. In 1963 Steve Lawrence had one of the year's two bestselling records with "Go Away, Little Girl," which he introduced, which the Happenings recorded three years later and which Donny Osmond revived in 1971. Freddie Scott recorded "Hey, Girl"; The Cookies, "Don't Say Nothin' Bad (About My Baby)"; The Chiffons "One Fine Day"; and The Drifters, "Up on the Roof." Among the Goffin-King song hits of 1964 were "Oh, No, Not My Baby" and "I'm Into Something Good," recorded respectively by Maxine Brown and Herman's Hermits.

The Righteous Brothers recorded the soulful "Just Once in My Life" in 1965. Bobby Vinton, the Byrds and Dusty Springfield were among the artists who performed King's songs in mid-decade.

According to Jon Landau, the editor of *Rolling Stone* magazine, the songs of Goffin and King were "finely honed to meet the demands of the clients who commissioned them, and written with the requirements of AM Radio always in mind." Yet Goffin and King "still managed to express themselves in a rich and personal way . . . , and in the process created something of their own pop vision."

When, in the mid-1960s the soft rock of the Brill Building was eclipsed by the harder and more sophisticated rock 'n' roll of the Beatles, the Rolling Stones and other first-wave British invasion groups, the market for the Goffins' music crumbled. In 1967, though, there was a temporary reprieve from their failures with "A Natural Woman," a major hit for the Queen of Soul, Aretha Franklin.

The Goffins ended both their writing collaboration and their marriage in 1968. At that time, King took her two daughters to Los Angeles, where she organized the City, a musical group for whom she played the piano and sang. The City performed an album of Goffin-King songs called *Now That Everything's Been Said,* but it was not a commercial success. The City's bass player was Charles Larkey, who became King's second husband. They acquired a house in Laurel Canyon and reared a child of their own.

In the late 1960s King wrote several songs with Larkey as lyricist, and others for which she provided both lyrics and music. But her main activity at this time was in building her self-confidence through live performance. She played the piano on an album recorded by the not-yet-famous singer-songwriter, James Taylor, with whom she also toured. Encouraged by Taylor, Carole King began increasingly to sing in public, initially in an assortment of California nightclubs. Released in 1970, her first solo album, *Carole King Writer,* was praised by critics but had poor sales.

In March and April of 1971, she performed vocal backups for James Taylor on his nationwide tour. On June 15, 1971 she headlined as a singer-pianist in concert at Carnegie Hall, her first solo appearance in New York City. She established herself for the first time as a star performer in her own right with renditions of her old favorites together with several of her songs from the post-Goffin period. Of the latter, the most important were: "Child of Mine," "No Easy Way," "Smackwater Jack" and "You've Got a Friend." "Hers is far from a great natural voice," wrote a *New York Times* critic, "but it has the deceptive strength of a whip antenna. Its basic hue is a Canarsie twang. . . . The hue is one thing and the cry another, as proved by Carole's pile-driving thrust in a number called 'Smackwater Jack'."

Early in 1971, Lou Adler's Ode Records label issued King's second solo album, *Tapestry.* On songs like the title number, "Beautiful," "Way Over Yonder," "It's Too Late" and "You've Got a Friend," the emphasis was on the words as much as the melody, as Carole King sang pop hymns to such subjects as friendship, home, lost youth, erotic love and the pain of geographical separation from one's loved ones. *Tapestry,* wrote Robert Christgau in *Newsday,* "contained a true and sentimental standard about friendship and a true and ironic standard about breaking up. . . . But most of all, it established Carole King's individuality as a woman."

Tapestry was an unexpected bombshell. For 13 weeks, it topped the nation's charts, and for more than 250 weeks it remained on the *Billboard* bestseller lists. By May 1973 ten million copies of the album had been sold, and 14 million copies by 1976. In 1972 it won the Grammy for the year's best album with additional Grammys going to King for "You've Got a Friend" as the best song, for "It's Too Late" as the best single, and "Tapestry" as best female vocal performance. On her 1971 album *Barbra Joan Streisand,* Streisand included "Beautiful" and "You've Got a Friend." James Taylor's version of "You've Got a Friend" on his *Mud Slide Slim* LP helped make that song a standard.

King's next three albums were gold records. On *Music* (1971) and *Rhymes and Reasons* (1972), King continued to write from her personal experiences in songs such as "Going Away From Me" and "Carry Your Load" (from *Music)* and "Stand Behind Me," "Goodbye Don't Mean I'm Gone," and "Come Down Easy" (from *Rhymes and Reason).* *Fantasy,* released in mid-1973, was her first concept album. "In fantasy," she said, "I can be black or white," and she looked outward instead of inward in several songs about drugs, the struggle for racial and sexual equality, and the universal need of human understanding. The tenderly romantic "You Light Up My Life"; "Believe in Humanity"; "You've Been Around Too Long"; "Directions"; "Fantasy Beginning"; and "Fantasy End" were the album's principal numbers.

Two more gold records were earned by the albums *Wrap Around Joy* (1974) and *Carole King—Her Greatest Hits* (1978). Her subsequent albums were *Thoroughbred* (1976), *Simple Things (1977), One to One* (1983) and *Speeding Time* (1983). On these LPs can be found such stellar numbers as "Change of Mind, Change of Heart," "You Go Your Way, I'll Go Mine" and "There's Space Between Us." *Really Rosie* was an animated television cartoon of 1975, adapted from the writings and drawings of Maurice Sendak, for which Carole King provided the music to Sendak's lyrics. The soundtrack was released as a record album. Reviewing this album, John Rockwell said in *The New York Times*: "Mr. Sendak's words have a piquancy that has obviously given Miss King an inspirational boost, as has the Brooklyn basis of the story, so close to her own growing up. The whole record is sweet in the best sense imaginable." Greatly expanded, *Really Rosie* became an Off Broadway production in 1980.

In August 1977, having divorced Charles Larkey, King married her manager, Rick Evers. Evers died less than a year later from a drug overdose. In 1982 Carole King married Rick Sorenson.

Twenty-six of Carole King's most celebrated songs were gathered into a stage production called *King's Tapestry,* presented by the Cape Playhouse in Dennis, Massachusetts on July 13, 1981. "The show reflects the mores and moods of the 1960s and 1970s," one reviewer observed, adding that "King's ballads are the outstanding spots of the show."

For relaxation, Carole King practices yoga, stitches samplers, and putters in her kitchen, cooking and baking. A very private individual, she rarely grants interviews.

ABOUT: Current Biography, 1974; Stambler, I. Encyclopedia of Pop, Rock and Soul, 1976. *Periodicals*—Life May 19, 1972; Newsday November 5, 1972; New York Times November 29, 1970; Stereo Review May 1973; Washington Post May 24, 1973.

KRISTOFFERSON, KRIS (June 22, 1936–), composer-lyricist and performer of country-rock music, has been described as a leading exponent of the Nashville progressive style, along with Waylon Jennings and Willie Nelson. His songs, many autobiographical, provide glimpses into the mind of one who has known loneliness and despair too well, but who refrains from the empty solace of self-pity. He has combined the simplicity of country music with the poetic and the sensual, and with a sophisticated awareness of modern complexities. His songs have brought him gold and platinum records either for his own recordings or for those that have been cov-

KRIS KRISTOFFERSON

ered by distinguished country and rock performers. Indeed, more than 450 artists have recorded music composed by Kristofferson.

He was the oldest of the three children of an Air Force officer stationed in Brownsville, Texas. In his childhood Kristofferson taught himself to play the guitar by ear. After graduating from high school, where he had been an "A" student and a star athlete, he entered Pomona College in California. Besides being an honor student, he was a reporter for the school paper, a football hero and a Golden Gloves boxer. He also won four prizes in a national collegiate short story contest conducted by the *Atlantic Monthly*, and worked on a novel.

Receiving his B. A. degree and graduating Phi Beta Kappa in 1958, he studied English literature at Oxford on a Rhodes scholarship. In England, he started to work on a second novel and, inspired by the country blues of Hank Williams, began composing songs. A London promoter landed him a television appearance as a rock performer under the name "Kris Carson." However, after a couple of publishers had rejected his novels, he left Oxford in 1960, returned to the United States and married his childhood sweetheart. He also joined the Army that year, remaining in uniform until 1965, rising to the rank of captain and some of that time serving in Germany as a helicopter pilot. He described his experience in the military to an interviewer: "I was drinking all the time, doing all kinds of reckless things because I was so down on myself. I totalled two cars and had four motorcycle accidents." Eventually he started writing songs again, and began to perform with a band in clubs for military personnel.

In 1965 he was hired as an English literature teacher by West Point. En route, he stopped off in Nashville, never reaching West Point, resolved now to make his way in music. After receiving his discharge from the service, he tried marketing his songs. One of them, "The Vietnam Blues," for which he wrote both words and music, was published in 1965 and, a year later, recorded by country singer Dave Dudley.

For the next four years, while writing songs, he supported his family by working at part-time jobs such as ditch-digging and tending bar. For two weeks each month, between 1968 and 1970, he flew helicopters for oil-rig outfits outside of New Orleans. Those were difficult times, for Kristofferson's son had been born with a defective esophagus and needed regular medical attention. Moreover, Kristofferson's marriage was on the rocks; there were two separations before the final break, when his wife took their two children (a son, Kris, and a daughter, Tracy,) to California and sued for divorce. His parents, highly critical of his way of life, practically disowned him. "They called me a dope fiend, and a hippie and a Communist," he said. When in 1970 he finally recorded his first album, *Kristofferson*, it did so poorly that the label (Monument) removed it from its lists.

Nevertheless, Kristofferson's breakthrough as a songwriter had come in 1969, the year he published "Me and Bobby McGee." Written in collaboration with Fred Foster, that standard— with its refrain, "Freedom's just another word for nothin' left to lose"—was first recorded by Roger Miller in mid-1969, and it became a bestseller on the country charts. Soon afterwards, Janis Joplin released it as a single and as a cut in her last album, *Pearl*, and the song instantly became one of the standards of the 1970s. By 1972 more than 50 artists had recorded it.

At the Columbia Records studio in Nashville, where Kristofferson worked as a part-time janitor in the later 1960s, he had met Johnny Cash. Through Cash's intervention, Kristofferson was invited to perform at the Newport Folk Festival in the summer of 1969. Cash invited him to appear as a guest artist singing his own songs on Cash's television program in 1969 and 1970. Cash also recorded the Kristofferson ballad, "Sunday Mornin' Comin' Down," in 1970, when the Country Music Association chose it as song of the year. Kristofferson formed his own band and made his nightclub debut at the Troubadour Club in Los Angeles on June 23, 1970. Other personal appearances followed both in night spots and on college campuses, including his first performance in New York in August 1970 at the Bitter End, a popular Greenwich Village club. Before the year was over, Sammi Smith's record-

ing of Kristofferson's "Help Me Make it Through the Night" had popularized that country ballad.

On the strength of his mounting success, in 1970 Monument re-released Kristofferson's first album, renaming it *Me and Bobby McGee*. It sold well, and in time brought Kristofferson a gold record. In addition to the title song, the album's principal numbers were "Help Me Make it Through the Night," "The Other Side of Nowhere," "For the Good Times," and "To Beat the Devil." Those numbers were covered by other artists, and Ray Price's version of "For the Good Times" was a bestseller. In 1971, and again in 1974, Kristofferson was named songwriter of the year by the Nashville Song Writers' Association, and "Help Me Make it Through the Night" received an award from BMI as one of 1972's most frequently performed country songs.

Kristofferson's film career began in 1971, when he wrote songs for, and sang them in, the Dennis Hopper film, *The Last Movie*. One of these songs was "The Pilgrim: Chapter 33," in which, speaking in the autobiographical third person, he said: "He's a poet, he's a picker/he's a prophet, he's a pusher/He's a pilgrim and a preacher/and problem when he's stoned/He's a walking contradiction, partly truth, partly fiction/Taking every wrong direction/on his lonely way back home." Kristofferson sang "Help Me Make it Through the Night" on the soundtrack of *Fat City* (1972), directed by John Huston, and in *Cisco Pike* (1972) he made his debut as an actor. In 1972–73, in concert, he shared the stage with a country-blues singer, Rita Coolidge, whom he married on August 19, 1973.

He was awarded gold records for the single "Why Me?" and the albums *The Silver Tongued Devil and I* and *Jesus Was a Capricorn* in 1973. He and Coolidge recorded the album *Full Moon*, a collection of their country, pop and folk numbers, in 1974, and it too went gold. His LP *The Songs of Kristofferson* went gold in 1978, and *Willie Nelson Sings Kristofferson* earned a gold record in 1980. To Nelson, Kristofferson is "the best songwriter I know. Of all the contemporary artists, he's the most prolific. He's a poet."

In 1973 and again in 1976, he and Coolidge won Grammys as the best duo country performers. In 1983, in special ceremonies, Kristofferson was awarded five BMI citiations for songs that had received more than a million broadcast performances: "Me and Bobby McGee," "Lovin' Her Was Easier," "Why Me?" "Help Me Make it Through the Night," and "For the Good Times." Other bestselling Kristofferson albums include *Border Land* (1973), *Big Sur Festival* (1973), *Breakaway* (1974), *Surreal Things* (1976), *Who's to Bless and Who's to Blame*

(1978), *Easter Island* (1978), *Shake Hands with the Devil* (1979) and *To the Bone* (1980), the last of which dealt with the breakup of his marriage to Rita Coolidge in 1980. Of his later songs, the most notable have been "The Things I Might Have Been"; "Nobody Wins"; "Stranger"; "Give it Time to Be Tender"; "It's Never Gonna Be the Same Again"; "Please Don't Tell Me How the Story Ends"; "Josie"; "When I Loved Her"; and "Here Comes That Rainbow." Several of his songs have launched the recording careers of country artists: "Please Don't Tell Me How the Story Ends," for Ronnie Milsap; "Stranger," for both Johnny Duncan and Janie Fricke; and "Lovin' Her Was Easier," for the Tompall Glaser Brothers.

Apart from his musical career, Kristofferson is so popular an actor that he commands a million dollars for a movie role. He has starred in *Pat Garrett and Billy the Kid* (1973), in which he played Billy and Bob Dylan was a featured extra; *Blume in Love* (1974), directed by Paul Mazursky; Sam Peckinpah's *Bring Me the Head of Alfredo Garcia* (1974); Martin Scorsese's *Alice Doesn't Live Here Anymore* (1974); *The Sailor Who Fell From Grace With the Sea* (1976); *A Star is Born* (1976), in which he was costarred with Barbra Streisand; *Vigilante Force* (1976); *Semi Tough* (1977), costarring Burt Reynolds and Jill Clayburgh; *Convoy* (1978); Michael Cimino's *Heaven's Gate* (1980); *Rollover* (1981), costarring Jane Fonda; *Flashpoint* (1983); *Songwriter* (1984), in which he was costarred with Willie Nelson and for which he composed several songs; and *Trouble In Mind* (1985), a noirish cult film directed by Alan Rudolph.

Kristofferson lives in a hilltop house in Malibu which also houses a menagerie of animals and an assortment of plants. Once a heavy drinker, he has been abstaining from alcohol since 1976. To keep fit, he maintains a rigorous daily exercise regimen, running several miles, swimming about 50 laps in his pool and working out on a punching bag and a rowing machine. Sally Quinn, in *Newsday*, described him as "a series of contradictions. He's totally open and completely inaccessible. He's shy and gregarious, honest and devious, rude and polite, smart and dumb." His singing voice is a gravelly, unpretty baritone. On February 10, 1983, in Malibu, Kristofferson married Lisa Meyers, an attorney.

ABOUT: Current Biography, 1974; Shestack, M. The Country Music Encyclopedia, 1977; Stambler, I. Encyclopedia of Pop, Rock and Soul, 1976. *Periodicals*—Newsday September 11, 1971; New York Times August 24, 1977.

LANE, BURTON (February 2. 1912—). Burton Lane is a successful Broadway and Hollywood composer whose scores include *Finian's Rainbow* and *On a Clear Day You Can See Forever*, as well as songs for more than 30 motion pictures. He collaborated with such well-known lyricists as E.Y. Harburg, Alan Jay Lerner and Harold Adamson. He received two Oscar nominations and a number of his songs were heard on *Your Hit Parade*.

Burton Lane was born Burton Levy in New York City on February 2, 1912. His father, Lazarus Levy, was a successful realtor, and his mother, Frances (Fink) Levy, an amateur pianist. Burton began studying the piano seriously when he was 11; while attending the High School of Commerce in New York, he played viola and cello in the school orchestra and composed two marches for the school band, which were published by the Al Piantidosi Music Co. Some of his music came to the attention of Harold Stern, music director for the Shuberts, who arranged for the young Lane to audition for the Broadway producer, J. J. Shubert. Though only 14, Lane was commissioned by Shubert to write songs for a new edition of the *Greenwich Village Follies*. Unfortunately, James Barton, the star of that production, became ill, and the project never left the drawing board. Consequently none of Lane's songs were heard or published.

In 1927, while still a high school student, Lane was hired as a staff composer for J. H. Remick, where he stayed a year. He dropped out of high school after a year and a half to concentrate on writing songs, receiving encouragement and advice from some of Tin Pan Alley's most successful composers, including the former Remick employee, George Gershwin. Gershwin also suggested that Lane study with Simon Bucharoff, the noted pianist and composer, which Lane did from 1930 to 1933.

Lane's career on Broadway began when, in 1929, he met Howard Dietz, the lyricist working with Arthur Schwartz on songs for the Broadway revue, *Three's a Crowd* (1930). Dietz used two of Lane's melodies in the show: "Forget All Your Books" and "Out in the Open Air." The next year, "Say the Word" (lyrics by Harold Adamson), was introduced by Beatrice Lillie in *The Third Little Show* (1931) and, with Adamson as lyricist, Lane composed most of the score for the ninth edition of the *Earl Carroll Vanities* (August 22, 1931). Its best songs were "Have a Heart," sung by Lillian Roth and Woods Miller and "Love Came Into My Heart," introduced by Milton Watson and Woods Miller.

The Depression brought Lane's career on Broadway to a standstill, though he was able to

BURTON LANE

publish a number of songs, including the popular "Look Who's Here" and "Tony's Wife" (lyrics by Adamson). But in Hollywood screen musicals were in vogue, and the demand for songs and songwriters insatiable. In 1933, the Irving Berlin publishing house dispatched Lane and Adamson to Hollywood for a six-week trial period; Lane remained there for 21 years and became one of the most highly marketable composers.

From 1933 to 1936, Lane worked as a freelance composer (usually with lyricist Adamson) for several studios, among them MGM, RKO, and 20th-Century Fox. "Tony's Wife" was placed in the nonmusical film, *Turn Back the Clock* (1933), and *Dancing Lady* (1933), in which Fred Astaire made his screen debut and from which Joan Crawford emerged as a star, featured three songs by Lane and Adamson: "Heigh Ho, the Gang's All Here" (borrowed from the score of *Vanities*) and "Let's Go Bavarian"; Art Jarrett introduced what was to become Lane's first standard, "Everything I Have is Yours," later recorded by Rudy Vallee. Other notable songs were: "Your Head on My Shoulder," sung by Ann Sothern and George Murphy in the Eddie Cantor film, *Kid Millions* (1934); "You're My Thrill" (lyrics by Ned Washington), which Ted Lewis introduced in *Here Comes the Band* (1935); and "You Took the Words Right Out of My Mouth," introduced by Maurice Chevalier in *Folies Bergère* (1935).

On June 28, 1935 Burton Lane and Marian Seaman were married; they raised a daughter. The following year, Lane signed a contract with the Paramount Studios, where he stayed until 1941. During the years at Paramount, he wrote

"Stop, You're Breaking My Heart" (lyrics by Ted Koehler) for Judy Canova and Ben Blue in *Artists and Models* (1937); and with Frank Loesser, the title song for *Swing High, Swing Low* (1937; lyrics by Ralph Freed), introduced and recorded by Dorothy Lamour; "How'd ja Like to Love Me?," a comic-song routine for Bob Burns and Martha Raye in *College Swing* (1938); "Says My Heart," a standard that Harriet Hilliard first presented in *Cocoanut Grove* (1938), which was then recorded by Mildred Bailey, George Hall and his orchestra, and the Andrews Sisters and which reached the top of *Your Hit Parade*; "The Lady's in Love With You," introduced by Bob Hope and Shirley Ross in *Some Like it Hot* (1939) and recorded by the orchestras of Bob Crosby and by Benny Goodman and also heard on *Your Hit Parade*; and "I Hear Music," which Peter Lind Hayes introduced in *Dancing On a Dime* (1941). In the early 1940s, one of Lane's best songs, "How About You?" (lyrics by Ralph Freed), introduced by Judy Garland and Mickey Rooney in *Babes on Broadway* (1941), brought him an Oscar nomination. It is one of several songs in which Lane effectively alternated a lyrical first phrase with a rhythmic second phrase, and Freed's lyrics are unique in that he pays tribute to another songwriter ("I like a Gershwin tune, how about you?"). "How About You?" was recorded by Tommy Dorsey and Dick Todd and was later sung by Dean Martin in *The Young Lions* (1959) and Richard Dreyfus in *The Goodbye Girl* (1977).

Now one of Hollywood's leading songwriters, Lane was called to Broadway in 1940 to compose his first complete stage score, *Hold On to Your Hats* (September 11, 1940). The assignment was an important one because it brought him together with the lyricist E. Y. "Yip" Harburg. Al Jolson, in his last appearance in a Broadway musical, was cast as a timid radio "cowboy" persuaded by his scriptwriter to capture a Mexican bandit, a feat which was accomplished only after a series of madcap adventures. The show's best songs were "There's a Great Day Coming, Mañana," "The World is in My Arms," and "Don't Let it Get You Down." *Hold On to Your Hats* closed after 158 performances when Jolson refused to appear any further because of New York's inclement weather.

In 1944 Lane was back on Broadway with *Laffing Room Only* (December 23, 1944), a musical extravaganza written by the vaudevillians Olsen and Johnson. It was the successor to their successful *Hellzapoppin'* (1938), in which incongruous and frequently outrageous events transpired both on stage and in the audience and were combined with the slapstick humor characteristic of burlesque. *Laffing Room Only* attempted to do more of the same, but with little of its predecessor's exuberance or spontaneity, and the show survived only 233 performances. One of the high points of the production was the song "Feudin' and Fightin'" (lyrics by Al Dubin and the composer), introduced by Pat Brewster and the chorus. But the song's success outside the theater did not come until two years after the show closed. From 1944 to 1947, it could not be played on the radio because the producers of *Laffing Room Only* were involved in a dispute in which ASCAP refused to release broadcasting rights for the show's songs. Without such exposure, the song remained unknown. But in 1947, Lane acquired the radio rights, and Dorothy Shay reintroduced it on the Bing Crosby radio program where it was such a success that it became one of the biggest hits of the year, with Shay's recording leading the parade. The song appeared in first position on *Your Hit Parade,* and it was used in the motion picture, *Feudin', Fussin' and Fightin'* (1948), starring Donald O'Connor.

Lane's most remarkable success on Broadway was achieved by *Finian's Rainbow* (January 10, 1947), now a classic. The versatility of Lane's rich melodic and rhythmic invention was matched by the supple, sometimes romantic, touching, and often satiric and witty words of E. Y. Harburg. The book (by Fred Saidy and Harburg) was a blending of fantasy and realism, Irish legends and modern social problems, romance and political commentary. This delightful Irish fantasy was set in Rainbow Valley, Missitucky, and involved a leprechaun, a deaf-mute who communicates by dancing, two visitors with a pot of gold from a mythical Irish town and a Senator who, upon turning black, becomes a victim of his own discriminatory laws. Yet this text, for all its recourse to Irish lore, was vibrantly contemporary, concerned with social and racial problems in the South, filled with allusions to the poll tax, discriminatory legislation, sharecropping, greed and social injustice. Two of the show's romantic ballads, "How Are Things in Glocca Morra?" and "Look to the Rainbow," introduced by Ella Logan, the second with Donald Richards, were instant successes; the recordings of "Glocca Morra" by Dick Haymes, Buddy Clarke and Tommy Dorsey were heard on *Your Hit Parade.* Mockery and social criticism were found in "When the Idle Poor Become the Idle Rich," "The Begat," "Something Sort of Grandish," and "When I'm Not Near the Girl I Love"; "The Great Come-and-Get-It Day" was inspired by black spirituals.

Finian's Rainbow did exceedingly well at the box office with a run of 725 performances and the original cast album was a bestseller. It was revived on Broadway in 1955 and again in 1960 after a brief run at the New York City Center was enthusiastically received. A lavish but commercially unsuccessful motion picture adaptation starring Fred Astaire and Petula Clark was made in 1968.

Though Lane was busy on Broadway during the 1940s he also found time to contribute melodies to *Ship Ahoy* (1942), *Panama Hattie (1942), Du Barry Was a Lady* (1943), *Thousands Cheer* (1943), *Hollywood Canteen* (1944) and other Hollywood motion pictures and musicals. By 1950, screen musicals were losing their popularity, but *Royal Wedding* (1951), starring Fred Astaire and Jane Powell, was an exception. Lane's score featured "Too Late Now" (lyrics by Alan Jay Lerner), which brought him a second Academy Award nomination, and a comedy number with what is probably the longest title in American songwriting history: "How Could You Believe Me When I Said I Love You When You Know I've Been a Liar All My Life" (lyrics by Lerner). He also contributed songs to the motion pictures *Give a Girl a Break* (1953, lyrics by Ira Gershwin) and *Jupiter's Darling* (1955, lyrics by Adamson) including "I Have a Dream," introduced by Esther Williams. In 1958, Lane turned to television with songs for a special, *Junior Miss* (lyrics by Dorothy Fields); here, David Wayne sang "I'll Buy It" and Don Ameche, "Junior Miss."

Lane was also engaged in activities other than songwriting in the 1950s and 1960s. From 1957 to 1967, he was president of the American Guild of Authors and Composers (AGAC), which presented him with the Sigmund Romberg Award for "extraordinary achievements on behalf of composers and lyricists" in 1966. In 1961, Lane divorced his wife, Marian, and on March 5 of that year, he married Lynn Baroff Kaye who had three daughters from a previous marriage.

In 1965, Lane returned to the Broadway stage for the first time in almost two decades with *On a Clear Day You Can See Forever* (October 17, 1965). Richard Rodgers was to have collaborated with Alan Lerner, but he withdrew from the project when artistic differences developed. Lerner brought his libretto and lyrics to Lane who composed a well-balanced, singable score. The highlight was the title song, introduced by John Cullum and later made popular by Robert Goulet. "Melinda" and "Come Back to Me," introduced by Cullum, and "What Did I Have That I Don't Have Now?" as sung by Barbara Harris, were also appealing. Barbara Harris, who emerged as a new star, was Daisy, a girl with extrasensory perception who undergoes psychiatric treatment to cure her addiction to tobacco. In the process she discovers during one of her sessions that she is the reincarnation of an 18th-century girl named Melinda. Her psychiatrist falls in love with Melinda, but eventually realizes that it really is the present-day Daisy he desires. At the box office, *On a Clear Day You Can See Forever* did only moderately well, with 280 performances, but the original cast recording received a Grammy. The film version (1970), starring Barbra Streisand and Yves Montand, gained a much wider popularity.

Ten years later, Lane and Lerner collaborated again on a stage musical, *Carmelina* (April 8, 1978). Lerner had found his subject in a newspaper account about an Italian widow raising a daughter. Having had three G. I.'s as lovers during World War II, she does not know who the girl's father is, and she is receiving child support from all three. This plot had also been used for a motion picture starring Shelley Winters, *Buona Sera, Mrs. Campbell* (1968). In both the motion picture and *Carmelina*, the simultaneous return of the three G. I.'s to Italy to visit their wartime paramour brings unexpected complications. The book, consistently banal and implausible, doomed *Carmelina* from the start. Its retreat from Broadway was so hasty that it threw some very fine songwriting as in "One More Walk Around the Garden," and "It's Time for a Love Song," into total obscurity.

Burton Lane and his wife reside in an apartment on West End Avenue in New York. He has always preferred New York to Hollywood as a place to live and write songs: "In Hollywood. . . . It's a practical way of making a living," he explained to an interviewer. "There are two ways to do it. You can be under contract to a studio and do what they ask you to do. You're given an assignment and you hope you like it. If you're a free-lance, it's a struggle. You write and hope to sell what you write. Once you've been paid, you've a certain time to deliver but you have no control." Control is something he finds in the New York theater where "the creators of the show are involved in every way from the beginning." But working on Broadway has its drawbacks: "It takes two years or more out of your life and the show may close in two nights."

Lane was elected director of Songwriters Hall of Fame in 1973. Most recently he composed 11 songs to Sammy Cahn's lyrics for *Heidi* (1979), an animated motion picture, notably the title song, "An Unkind Word," "Can You Imagine" and "That's What Friends are For." In 1983, Brent Wagner directed a revue of his songs entitled "Mighty Fine Music!" at the T.O.M.I. Theater in New York. Lanes's hobbies include golf, tennis and chess.

ABOUT: Current Biography, 1967; Craig, W. The Great Songwriters of Hollywood, 1980, Sweet and Lowdown; America's Popular Song Writers, 1978; The New Grove Dictionary of American Music, 1986; Wilder, A. American Popular Song, 1972.

LEIGH, CAROLYN. *See* **COLEMAN, CY** and **LEIGH, CAROLYN**

LERNER, ALAN JAY. *See* **LOEWE, FREDERICK** and **LERNER, ALAN JAY**

LIVINGSTON, JAY (March 28, 1915–) and **EVANS, RAY** (February 4, 1915–). During their long and successful careers as songwriters for motion pictures, Jay Livingston, composer, and Ray Evans, lyricist, have written featured songs for more than one hundred films. They have worked exclusively with one another, though on occasion they have served as lyricists for other composers. Their achievements include three Oscars, many hit songs, and total record sales exceeding 200 million copies.

Jay Harold Livingston was born in McDonald, a suburb of Pittsburgh, the son of Maurice Livingston, the proprietor of a shoe shop, and Rose (Wachtel) Livingston. Jay studied harmony and the piano with Harry Archer. He played in the school orchestra and, to earn extra money, he also appeared in a band at local nightspots and at parties on Saturday evenings. After graduating from McDonald High School in 1933, he attended the University of Pennsylvania, where he received a B. A. degree in 1937. While majoring in journalism, Livingston also studied music with Harl MacDonald and organized a dance orchestra which performed at college functions.

He met Ray Evans at the university during his freshman year. Evans was born in Salamanca, New York, the son of Philip Evans, a secondhand scrap paper, string and burlap dealer, and Frances (Lipsitz) Evans. He received some informal instruction on the saxophone and clarinet, which he played in the school orchestra. Evans graduated from high school in 1931, and then enrolled in the Wharton School at the University of Pennsylvania. In 1936 he received a B. S. degree in economics with a major in banking and finance, and was elected to the honorary society of Beta Gamma Sigma. While at the university, he earned a letter in football and numerals in track, supporting himself by selling advertising for campus magazines and playing in dance orchestras, including the one Livingston had led.

RAY EVANS

JAY LIVINGSTON

In 1934 the band in which Evans then played needed a pianist for a summer crossing of the Atlantic on the Cunard Line. Evans recommended Livingston and this became the first of a series of Easter and summer cruises during which they traveled throughout the world. When the leader left the band, Livingston took his place.

Following Livingston's graduation in 1937, he and Evans worked in a band on the *Rotterdam* during a summer Scandinavian cruise. Upon their return, they settled in New York City to pursue their ambition to break into show business by writing songs. Livingston would compose the melodies and Evans would supply the lyrics.

For the next few years the budding young songwriters made no headway. Livingston earned a living as a piano accompanist and musical arranger for NBC and as a rehearsal pianist for the Olsen and Johnson Broadway extravaganzas *Hellzapoppin'* (1938) and *Sons o' Fun* (1941). Evans was employed as an office boy, statistician, and then as an accountant in an aircraft factory. In 1938 they organized an orchestra to play on a South American cruise; the following year they contributed special material to the Lambs Club *Gambols* but received no payment for their effort.

Livingston and Evans finally made their debut as professional songwriters with "G'bye Now" (1941). Not only was it recorded by Horace Heidt and his orchestra and incorporated into *Hellzapoppin'*, but it was also featured four times on *Your Hit Parade* in 1941. However, their careers were briefly interrupted by the war. Livingston served in the army from 1942

to 1943 while Evans was employed in a defense plant. When Livingston was released from the service, he resumed playing the piano and arranging, and also did some vocal coaching; Evans found a job writing gags for radio programs on CBS.

Lured by an offer from Olsen and Johnson, the team moved to Hollywood, California, in 1944, and for the first time devoted all of their time to songwriting. When final plans for the new project failed to materialize, they placed "Stuff Like That There," composed several years earlier, with Betty Hutton. She recorded it, and it was then sung by the King Sisters in the screen musical *On Stage Everybody* (1945). They also wrote songs for Producers Releasing Corporation films, including *I Accuse My Parents* (1944) and "The Cat and the Canary" for *Why Girls Leave Home* (1945) which brought their first Oscar nomination.

In 1945 Livingston and Evans signed a contract with Paramount studios, where they remained until 1956. Their early assignments included composing songs for B. G. De Sylva's *The Stork Club* (1945, "A Square in the Social Circle"), starring Betty Hutton, and the Olivia de Haviland film *To Each His Own* (1946). The title song from the latter film thrust the songwriters into the limelight with their first commercial success. It was also the first big hit for the then unknown singer Eddy Howard. Other bestselling recordings were made by the Ink Spots, Freddy Martin and his orchestra, Tony Martin and the Modernaires. During the week of September 14, 1946, five Livingston-Evans recordings were listed in the Top Ten on the

Billboard charts. "To Each His Own" was heard 20 times, eight times in first position, on *Your Hit Parade,* and the sheet-music sale exceeded one million copies. Since then, this song has become a standard. It was revived by the Platters, a group of soul singers, in 1961, and by the country-and-western superstar Willie Nelson in his album *Without a Song* (1983).

Following this early success, both men were married in 1947: Livingston to Lynne Gordon on March 19 in Los Angeles and Evans to Wyn Ritchie on April 19 in Santa Monica. Both couples are childless. Their songwriting career at Paramount continued to bring new rewards. Recordings of their songs began to sell more than one million copies each and were heard regularly on *Your Hit Parade,* often in first position. They wrote lyrics to music by Victor Young for the title song of the Marlene Dietrich film *Golden Earrings* (1947), and won their first Oscar for "Buttons and Bows," introduced by Bob Hope in *The Paleface* (1948) and popularized in a recording by Dinah Shore that sold more than a million discs. It was also recorded by Bob Hope and by Gracie Fields and made 19 appearances on *Your Hit Parade,* ten times in first position. In a cameo appearance in Billy Wilder's brilliant *Sunset Boulevard* (1950), Livingston and Evans were briefly seen singing "Buttons and Bows." Bob Hope reprised the song in *Son of Paleface* (1952).

A second Oscar soon followed for "Mona Lisa," from *Captain Carey, U. S. A.* (1950), starring Alan Ladd. The award was somewhat unusual because in the film, "Mona Lisa" was heard only in fragments, sung in Italian by a blind street singer and accordionist who is warning the hero against the imminent approach of the Nazis. Like "Buttons and Bows," "Mona Lisa" was a favorite on *Your Hit Parade* (17 appearances, eight times in first position), and the classic recording by Nat King Cole sold approximately three million copies. The song was later heard on the soundtrack of *The Godfather* (1972) and was revived in the early 1980s in a recording by Willie Nelson in his album *Over the Rainbow.* The following year, the team wrote what was to become one of their best-loved songs, the Yuletide favorite "Silver Bells," from *The Lemon Drop Kid* (1951). In the film it was sung by Bob Hope and Marilyn Maxwell, but since then recordings by Bing Crosby and others have sold more than 80 million copies.

While under contract at Paramount, Livingston and Evans composed other notable songs. These include "My Love Loves Me" (*The Heiress,* 1949); title songs for *Song of Surrender* (1949, music by Victor Young, introduced by

Buddy Clark) and *Copper Canyon* (1949); "Just for Fun" (*My Friend Irma,* 1949, introduced by Dean Martin); "I'll Always Love You (Querida mia)" from the cinematic debut of Dean Martin and Jerry Lewis in *My Friend Irma Goes West* (1950), introduced by Dean Martin and the Guadalajara Trio with Dean Martin's recording becoming his first disc success; and "Home Cookin'" from *Fancy Pants* (1950), introduced by Bob Hope and Lucille Ball. Others include the title song for *A Place in the Sun* (1951, music by the film-score composer Franz Waxman), an adaptation of Theodore Dreiser's novel *An American Tragedy;* "Bonne Nuit, Goodnight," introduced by Bing Crosby in *Here Comes the Groom* (1951); songs for *Mister Roberts* (1954) and the tongue-in-cheek western *Red Garters* (1954); and "Never Let Me Go," introduced by Nat King Cole in *The Scarlet Hour* (1956). Recorded by Cole, it was later sung by Stella Stevens in the Elvis Presley film *Girls! Girls! Girls!* (1962).

Shortly after leaving Paramount to pursue other projects, Livingston and Evans received their third Academy Award for "Que Será, Será (Whatever Will Be, Will Be)." This was a crucial-to-the-plot lullaby sung by Doris Day in *The Man Who Knew Too Much* (1956), and was the first song to be interpolated into a film directed by Alfred Hitchcock. Her recording sold more than a million copies. She later reprised it in the nonmusical film *The Glass Bottom Boat* (1956) and used it as the theme song for *The Doris Day Show* which aired on CBS from 1968 to 1973.

In 1956 Livingston and Evans left Paramount to work for the major studios on a free-lance basis and to establish their successful publishing house in the following year. For the Warner Brothers documentary *The James Dean Story* (1957) they composed "Let Me Be Loved." They received Academy Award nominations for the hit "Tammy," introduced by Debbie Reynolds in *Tammy and the Bachelor* (1957), with her recording achieving the million mark, and "Almost in Your Arms," performed by Sam Cooke, the legendary gospel and blues singer, in the Cary Grant–Sophia Loren film *Houseboat* (1958). In addition, they contributed title songs to the motion pictures *Saddle the Wind* (1958), *Another Time, Another Place* (1958) and *Take a Giant Step* (1959).

Livingston and Evans also turned to the musical theater on February 4, 1958, when *Oh, Captain!* opened on Broadway. This was a stage adaptation of the British film *The Captain's Paradise* (1953) which starred Alec Guinness as the captain of a ferryboat crossing between Gibraltar and Algiers who maintains a household with a different wife in each port. Tony Randall, Abbe Lane and Jacqueline McKeever played the principal roles in the musical which included the songs "All the Time" (introduced by Randall and McKeever), "Femininity" (introduced by Abbe Lane), "Morning Music of Montmartre" (introduced by Susan Johnson) and "You're So Right for Me" (introduced by Lane and Edward Platt). *Oh, Captain!* failed to maintain the light tone of the film and had a run of only 192 performances. However, numerous recordings of individual songs and six albums of the complete score (including an original cast release) were issued.

Their second Broadway musical, *Let It Ride!* (October 12, 1961), was a new musical adaptation of the Holm and Abbott farce *Three Men on a Horse* (1935). Sam Levene recreated the role of Patsy, the horseplayer, which he had first played in the nonmusical version, and George Gobel starred as Erwin, the meek greeting-card poet who has a gift for picking winning horses. An earlier musical adaptation, *Banjo Eyes* (December 25, 1941) had depended on the drawing power of Eddie Cantor, but George Gobel lacked his magnetism, and the show closed after 68 performances. Gobel sang "Through Children's Eyes" and "His Own Little Island," and Ted Thurston, Stanley Simonds and company performed "Just an Honest Mistake."

During the 1960s Livingston and Evans continued to work in Hollywood, primarily as lyricists for other composers, notably Henry Mancini. This collaboration produced the title song for *Dear Heart* (1964), which brought another Oscar nomination; "We've Loved Before" from *Arabesque* (1966); "In the Arms of Love" from *What Did You Do in the War, Daddy?* (1966); and the title song for *Wait Until Dark* (1967). Other partners have included Neal Hefti, Percy Faith, David Rose and John Addison.

The work of Livingston and Evans has also been heard on television. They provided songs for *Satin and Spurs* (1954), an NBC special starring Betty Hutton, and also for *No Man Can Tame Me* (1959), a production of the General Electric Theatre (CBS) starring John Raitt and Giselle McKenzie. They have also composed theme songs for *Bonanza* (NBC, 1959–73), *Mr. Ed* (CBS, 1961–66; Livingston is the singer on the soundtrack), and for *To Rome with Love* (CBS, 1969–71). They have also written songs for the Walt Disney programs *The Ringtail Cat* and *The Pond.*

Most recently, Livingston and Evans have composed songs for the Disney Studio's film *A Tale of two Critters* (1977), featuring a cast of live animals, and "The Joke's on Me" (Henry Mancini) for *W. C. Fields and Me* (1974). They contributed "The Sugar Baby Bounce" to the Broadway musical *Sugar Babies* (October 4, 1979), starring Ann Miller and Mickey Rooney. Their "Warm and Willing," written some years earlier with Jimmy McHugh, was also heard in this show, sung by Ann Jillian.

Since the early 1950s, Livingston and Evans have written special material for nightclub performers and other entertainers, including Betty Hutton, Mitzi Gaynor, Eddie Fisher, Joel Gray, Cyd Charisse, Polly Bergen and Bob Hope. For charity benefits in California they have written special material besides performing with Hope, George Jessel, Carol Burnett, Helen Reddy, Milton Berle and other stars.

"Our general approach to writing," Jay Livingston has said, "is for Ray Evans to write lyrics—sometimes with many different titles—for a particular assignment. We then get together and I see what strikes me as something that would fit the situation best and lead into a good melody, sometimes using only a line or two from pages of lyrics, and then we both sit down and write a melody to a set lyric, as I find it too restricting. I can write a stronger melody if I am free to go on with it where I like. A good example is 'To Each His Own.' One line caught my eye: 'Two lips must insist on two more to be kissed.' This gave me the opening phrase of the song and I went on to write the melody from there. We then got together and wrote the lyrics for this melody. Often we take ideas or phrases from Ray's original lyrics if they fit the new melody. It gives him extra work to do, but it has proved successful and we still work more or less that way."

Livingston and Evans both continue to live in the Los Angeles area, Livingston on Tortuoso Way in Los Angeles and Evans on Angelo Drive in Beverly Hills. Each has retained interests of earlier years: Livingston for travel; Evans for travel and sports. In his later years, Evans has confined his athletic activities to tennis and soft ball.

In 1982 Livingston and Evans were presented an "Aggie" by the American Guild of Authors and Composers for their contributions to American music.

ABOUT: Stambler, I. Encyclopedia of Popular Music, 1965, Notable Names in the American Theatre, 1976; Craig, W. The Great Songwriters of Hollywood, 1980.

LOESSER, FRANK (June 29, 1919–July 28, 1969). Frank Loesser was among America's leading lyricists and composers for Hollywood and Broadway musicals. He was known for his wit and the ability to capture the essence of everyday life in both his words and music. Through Frank Music Corporation and his other business ventures, he published many of his songs while also encouraging such young hopefuls as Meredith Willson, Richard Adler and Jerry Ross. His own creative talents were rewarded by a long procession of hit songs together with Oscar and Tony awards and the Pulitzer Prize.

Frank Henry Loesser, the youngest of three children of Henry and Julia (Ehrlich) Loesser, was born in New York City on June 29, 1910. The Loessers were a musical family; Henry Loesser, who had emigrated to the United States from Germany in the 1880s, was a well-known piano teacher who had once served as accompanist for the world-famous diva, Lilli Lehmann, and Frank's older brother, Arthur, later distinguished himself as a piano virtuoso and music critic.

As a boy, Frank responded in his own way to the intellectually stimulating environment of the Loesser household. At the age of six he composed a piano piece called *The May Party,* but when he refused to practice technical exercises, piano lessons were discontinued. As a teenager he enjoyed picking out popular tunes on the piano, much to the dismay of his father; he also learned to play the harmonica, and won third prize in a contest held in Central Park. He never received formal instruction in harmony, theory or composition, preferring to rely on his own ear and to experiment. He also revealed a gift for drawing, but there, too, avoided technical instruction.

Loesser was educated at the Speyer School before attending Townsend Harris Hall, a high school for gifted students. Practical jokes interested him far more than his schoolwork, and he was disqualified from the swimming team because his grades were substandard. He then transferred to De Witt Clinton High School, graduating in 1924. The next year was spent unproductively at the College of the City of New York.

Loesser then pursued a newspaper career by serving as editor of knit goods for *Women's Wear Daily,* reporter and political cartoonist for the Tuckahoe *Record,* and finally as city editor of the short-lived New Rochelle *News.* When the *News* folded, more odd jobs followed: waiter, caricaturist, pianist at a Catskills resort, press agent, process server for nearly 100 lawyers at once, and food inspector for a chain of restaurants. "In those times," he later recalled, "I had a rendezvous with failure every day."

FRANK LOESSER

Loesser's career as a songwriter began when he provided lyrics such as "Secretary Albert Vincent, Read the minutes right this instant" for a dinner of the Tuckahoe Lions Club. He then contributed special material and song lyrics to the Keith vaudeville circuit. Some of his lyrics interested the Tin Pan Alley firm of Leo Feist Inc., which hired him for $50 a week. By 1931, Loesser was employed by RKO in New York to produce songs for films. Few of those songs were used and none was published.

Though Loesser was then no longer employed by Leo Feist, that firm finally issued his first published song in 1931. It was "In Love With a Memory of You," set to music by the young William Schuman. Schuman was later to become one of America's most distinguished composers of concert music as well as President Emeritus of the Juilliard School of Music and the Lincoln Center for the Performing Arts. "I gave Loesser his first flop," Schuman recalls.

Loesser continued to write song lyrics while occasionally working as an entertainer with Irving Actman at the Back Drop, a nightclub on New York's East 52d Street. In 1934 he enjoyed a modest success with two songs. "I Wish I Were Twins" (lyrics written with Edgar DeLange, music by Joseph Meyer) was introduced and plugged by Fats Waller. "Junk Man" (music by Joseph Meyer) was introduced and recorded by Mildred Bailey; it was also recorded by Isham Jones and his orchestra. Loesser also contributed lyrics to *The Illustrators' Show* (1936, music by Actman), a revue that closed after a four-day run on Broadway. "Someone from Universal Pictures came to see the show on its last (rainy) night and was drunk enough to offer Actman and me a Universal contract," Loesser said.

Loesser left for Hollywood in March 1936, making his home in a small apartment on Sunset Boulevard. In Beverly Hills he married Lynn Garland—née Mary Alice Blankenbaker; later, as Lynn Loesser, she became a Broadway producer—on October 19, 1936; they raised a son and a daughter. His stay at Universal studios was brief and unproductive; from there, he went to United Artists where he wrote his first hit songs. Dorothy Lamour introduced "The Moon of Manakoora" (music by Alfred Newman) in *The Hurricane* (1937). And "Lovely One" (music by Manning Sherwin) was featured in the film *Walter Wanger's Vogues of 1938* (1937). But it was at Paramount in the years preceding World War II that Loesser's reputation as lyricist began to grow. There he wrote one of his biggest hits of those years, "Says My Heart" (music by Burton Lane) for the film *Cocoanut Grove* (1938); he also worked with Lane on songs for *College Swing* (1938), *Some Like It Hot* (1939), and *Dancing on a Dime* (1941). Hoagy Carmichael was also a frequent collaborator; together they produced such hits as "Small Fry" for Bing Crosby in *Sing, You Sinners* (1938), "Two Sleepy People" from *Thanks for the Memory* (1948), the independent number "Heart and Soul" (1938), as well as songs for Walt Disney's *Mr. Bug Goes to Town* (1941).

By 1940, Loesser had established himself as one of Hollywood's most popular and successful lyricists. He was working with leading composers and rarely did a week pass when one of his songs was not featured on *Your Hit Parade,* often in first position. He returned briefly to Universal to write songs with composer Frederick Hollander for Marlene Dietrich. She introduced "The Boys in the Backroom" in *Destry Rides Again* (1939) and "I've Been in Love Before" in *Seven Sinners* (1940). At Paramount, he continued to compose lyrics for many musicals. Some of his biggest hits included "Dolores" (music by Louis Alter from *Las Vegas Nights,* 1941), which was recorded by Harry James and his orchestra; "Sand in My Shoes" (music by Victor Schertzinger) from *Kiss the Boys Goodbye* (1941); "I Don't Want to Walk Without You Baby" (music by Jule Styne) from *Sweater Girl* (1942); "Jingle, Jangle, Jingle" (music by Joseph J. Lilley), which was introduced by an ensemble on horseback in the Fred MacMurray–Paulette Goddard film, *The Forest Rangers* (1942), with Kay Kyser's recording becoming one of his biggest hits; "They're Either Too Young or Too Old" (music by Arthur Schwartz) from *Thank Your Lucky Stars* (1943); "Say It" from *Buck Benny Rides Again* (1940); "Let's Get Lost" from

Happy-Go-Lucky (1943); and "Can't Get Out of This Mood" from *Seven Days' Leave* (1942, music by Jimmy McHugh).

The attack on Pearl Harbor stirred Loesser into writing a lyric inspired by words attributed to the United States Navy Chaplain, William Maguire, during the Japanese bombardment: "Praise the Lord and pass the ammunition!" When Loesser completed the lyrics, he followed his usual practice of inventing a dummy to see if the words could be sung easily. Loesser's friends were so impressed with the freshness and accessibility of this melody that they insisted he retain it. Published in 1942, "Praise the Lord and Pass the Ammunition" marked Loesser's debut as both lyricist and composer. At the same time, it became the first hit song of World War II. Kay Kyser's recording sold more than a million records and that of the Merry Macs was also a bestseller; sheet music sales exceeded a million copies. During the first year of America's involvement in the war, "Praise the Lord" was heard everywhere so often that the Office of War Information asked radio stations not to play it more than once every four hours. About this song, Arthur Loesser wrote: "It refrains from modern, urban, musical slang; it avoids any suggestion that anyone might consider disreputable, anything Negroid, jazzy, Jewish, Broadwayish, or night-clubby. Instead, the melody has an affinity for that of 'The Battle Hymn of the Republic,' it tastes like school, church, grandma and biscuits, a master-stroke of diplomacy, aptness and good business."

After completing "Praise the Lord," Loesser enlisted in the Army and served in the Special Services Division from 1942 to 1945. In this capacity, he wrote soldier shows which were distributed to army camps and composed songs (music as well as words) for various branches of the service. These included "The WAC Hymn," "First Class Private Mary Brown," "Sad Bombardier" "Salute to the Army Air Force," as well as "gripe" songs such as "What Do You Do in the Infantry?" The last of these, popularized by Bing Crosby's recording, became only the unofficial song of the infantry because high-ranking officers objected to its sardonic allusion to the fact that all the men in the infantry did was march, march, march.

Loesser's most important war song after "Praise the Lord and Pass the Ammunition" was "Rodger Young," composed in 1945 at the request of the Army for a ballad glorifying the infantry. The hero of this ballad was an infantryman who, despite physical limitations, singlehandedly attacked a hidden Japanese machine gun in the South Pacific to save the lives of his comrades. For this heroic act, Private Rodger Young was posthumously awarded the Congressional Medal of Honor.

"Rodger Young" was introduced on Meredith Willson's radio program in 1945. Originally, a dramatic presentation by a large orchestra and chorus was planned, but during the rehearsals, at the suggestion of an usher named "Ernie" (Ernest Martin, later a Broadway producer), Willson decided that the ballad would be far more eloquent in a simple, unpretentious setting. And so it was first heard sung by Earl Wrightson with guitar accompaniment. After the broadcast, the publisher restricted its performance to folksingers and concert artists; recordings by Burl Ives, John Charles Thomas and Nelson Eddy were among the many released.

When the war ended, Loesser returned to Hollywood, now as a composer for his own lyrics. His "I Wish I Didn't Love You So" from *The Perils of Pauline* (1947), made popular by the recordings of Dinah Shore and Vaughn Monroe, and "Tallahassee," introduced by Dorothy Lamour and Alan Ladd in *Variety Girl* (1947) and later recorded by Bing Crosby with the Andrews Sisters, were bestsellers. Two independent songs, "Bloop, Bleep," first recorded by Danny Kaye and later by Alvino Rey, and "What Are You Doing New Year's Eve?," introduced by Margaret Whiting, were also extremely popular. But one of Loesser's greatest successes came from "Baby, It's Cold Outside," a novelty number he had composed for himself and his wife to perform at private parties. It was introduced by Esther Williams and Ricardo Montalban in the MGM film *Neptune's Daughter* (1949) and brought Loesser an Oscar for the year's best song.

In 1946 the new producing team of Cy Feuer and Ernest Martin had plans to bring to Broadway a musical version of Brandon Thomas's classic farce, *Charley's Aunt,* first performed in London in 1892. They asked Harold Arlen to compose the music and Loesser to write the lyrics, but when Arlen declined because of other commitments, Loesser offered to provide the music as well as the lyrics. George Abbott adapted the original script and directed, George Balanchine choreographed the dance numbers and Ray Bolger, starring as Charley, assumed what became his most memorable role. Only minor changes were made in Thomas's work; the twists of the plot depended on the central ploy of having Charley impersonate his aunt by donning women's clothes and assuming feminine mannerisms.

Though it opened on October 11, 1948 to a lukewarm reception, *Where's Charley?* gained momentum until it achieved a run of 792 performances. This was due in part, no doubt, to Ray Bolger's showstopping performance of "Once in Love With Amy." During a matinee performance, he forgot (or pretended to forget) the words and asked for assistance from Cy Feuer's seven-year-old son, who had attended rehearsals and was sitting in the front row. This inspired Bolger to invite the audience to join him in the refrain, which he taught line by line. The routine was received so enthusiastically that it was retained in the production, consuming sometimes as much as 15 minutes; Bolger also recorded it successfully. But Loesser's first Broadway score was solid throughout: "Everything new, everything a fresh concept, musically and lyrically," Feuer said of Loesser's songs. "He was just a natural show writer." "My Darling, My Darling," a love ballad introduced by Doretta Morrow and Byron Palmer, was the show's second big number. It was recorded by Doris Day (with Buddy Clark), Jo Stafford (with Gordon MacRae) and Freddy Martin and his orchestra, and appeared on *Your Hit Parade.* In 1952 a motion picture adaptation of *Where's Charley?*, starring Bolger, was released by Warner Brothers, and the musical was revived at the New York City Center in 1966 and Off Broadway in 1974.

In 1948 "On a Slow Boat to China," published as an independent number, became one of the year's major hit songs, when the recording of Kay Kyser sold more than a million copies and another bestselling recording was released by Freddy Martin and his orchestra. "On a Slow Boat to China" made 16 appearances on *Your Hit Parade* and earned Loesser the rare distinction of having two of his songs competing for first and second place, the other song "My Darling, My Darling."

Loesser's next venture on Broadway, *Guys and Dolls,* has become a classic of the American musical theater. Subtitled "A Musical Fable of Broadway," it had an initial run of 1,200 performances that began on November 24, 1950 and earned $12 million at the box office. Many more millions came from touring companies, from the Samuel Goldwyn motion picture adaptation (1955), starring Marlon Brando, Frank Sinatra and Jean Simmons, and from the sale of original cast and soundtrack recordings. The characters from Damon Runyon's stories, primarily *The Idyll of Miss Sarah Brown,* provided Abe Burrows with material for a racy musical, enlivened by colorful eccentrics rarely featured on the Broadway stage: cops, chronic gamblers, nightclub entertainers and Salvation Army dogooders. George S. Kaufman's briskly paced direction and Michael Kidd's innovative choreography (including a dance routine against the backdrop of a crap game in a sewer) were further assets. Loesser received a Tony for his score and the show won a Tony and the New York Drama Critics Circle Award as the year's best musical.

The principal characters are the flamboyant Guy Masterson (played by Robert Alda in the original production); Sarah Brown (Isabel Bigley), a Salvation Army lass; Nathan Detroit (Sam Levene), a tinhorn gambler and longtime fiancé of Miss Adelaide (Vivian Blaine), a nightclub entertainer. However, their romantic misadventures are secondary to the gamblers' need to find sanctuary for their floating crap game, and also to the portrayal of the seamy side of New York life.

Guys and Dolls was praised for its tight construction and successful integration of dialogue and musical numbers. In describing Loesser's score, Gerald Bordman, in *American Musical Comedy* (1982), has written: "No modern Broadway composer has surpassed Loesser's knack for injecting as much wit into his melodies as into his words or of capturing the rhythms and tensions of everyday drama in his musical phrases." "Adelaide's Lament," in which she explains she suffers from a persistent psychosomatic cold because of her failure to bring Detroit to the altar, has been considered by many, including Moss Hart, to be one of the wittiest song routines in American musical comedy. The show's most popular song was "A Bushel and a Peck", introduced by Vivian Blaine, who was also heard in the witty "Take Back Your Mink"; the former appeared on *Your Hit Parade*. Other favorites included the romantic ballads, "I've Never Been in Love Before" and "I'll Know," "Luck Be a Lady," and "Fugue for Tinhorns," a three-voice canon for the horseplayers picking their favorites for the day.

When *Guys and Dolls* was revived on Broadway in 1976 with a black cast, Clive Barnes wrote in *The New York Times*: "Yes, it still works. *Guys and Dolls* . . . remains as wry, as funny, as enchanting and as entrancing as ever. . . . The music and lyrics of Frank Loesser . . . have enormous charm. . . . There is rough jazziness to the score and a bitter dryness to the lyrics that go together like gin and vermouth and the New York skyline."

After *Guys and Dolls*, Loesser returned to Hollywood to write songs for *Hans Christian Andersen* (1952), a handsomely mounted Samuel Goldwyn production starring Danny Kaye in the title role. Moss Hart's screenplay, based on a story of Myles Connolly, was a "fairy tale" made to appeal to children. Contributing to the enchanting aura of the film were eye-arresting fantasy scenes, a ballet sequence choreographed by Roland Petit, and Loesser's score, which included "Thumbelina," "Anywhere I Wander," "The Inch Worm," and "Wonderful Copenhagen," all introduced by Danny Kaye.

Loesser returned to Broadway on May 3, 1956 with *The Most Happy Fella,* a project that playwright Samuel Taylor persuaded him to undertake. Here Loesser expanded his creative accomplishments, and was one of the first to do so, by writing the text as well as the music and lyrics for his adaptation of Sidney Howard's Pulitzer Prize-winning play, *They Knew What They Wanted* (1924). Its principal character, Tony, is a gentle, middle-aged winegrower in Napa, California. While corresponding with a San Francisco waitress, Rosabella, he proposes marriage, and to insure acceptance he sends her a photograph of his handsome foreman, Joey, in place of his own. When Rosabella arrives in Napa, she discovers she has been deceived; nevertheless, she consents to the marriage. Rosabella soon submerges her disappointment in an affair with Joey and conceives his child. Tony drives her from his house, but later convinces her he will be able to forgive her and accept the child as his own.

The Most Happy Fella was far more ambitious than any of Loesser's previous endeavors. Little dialogue was employed, allowing the plot to unfold through music. The score embraces about 30 numbers; arias, recitatives, duets, canons, choral pieces, folk hymns, parodies and instrumental interludes. Loesser was so anxious that the work be perceived as an artistic whole rather than the sum of its musical parts that individual songs were not listed in the program. Nevertheless, several songs became hits, including as "Standing on the Corner" and "Big D," a tribute to the city of Dallas, reminiscent of popular songs of the 1920s. Others, such as "Joey, Joey, Joey" and "My Heart is So Full of You," sung by Robert Weede as Tony, were more subtle, penetrating into the personalities of the characters. Though Loesser was criticized by some for what was considered as inconsistency, others felt the many shades of emotion in the text— love, gentleness, tenderness, humor and simple humanity—were well-served by the wide gamut of Loesser's musical styles. Lehman Engel who, in *The American Musical Theater* (1967) described *The Most Happy Fella* as a "Broadway opera," felt that it "pulls together all of the best elements to be found in a superb musical show and adds to them arias of enormous emotional intensity." And for Brooks Atkinson of *The New York Times*: "He has told everything of vital importance in terms of dramatic music. His music drama . . . goes so much deeper into the soul of its leading characters than most Broadway shows, and it has such an abundant and virtuoso score in it that it has to be taken on the level of theater." In addition to being a substantial box-office success (676 performances), *The Most Happy Fella* was voted the year's best musical by the New York Drama Critics Circle. On April 21, 1960, it began a successful run in London, while other companies presented it in Sweden ad Australia. It was revived in New York in 1955 and 1979, and also by the Michigan Opera Theatre.

During the run of *The Most Happy Fella* a major change occurred in Loesser's private life. He and his wife Lynn were divorced in 1957 and on April 29, 1959, he married Jo Sullivan (née Elizabeth Joseph Jacobs), who had first created the role of Rosabella. At their apartment on East 70th Street in New York City, which remained Loesser's permanent residence, they raised two daughters.

Back on Broadway, Loesser again served as his own librettist (with the help of Lesser Samuels) in adapting the novel *Greenwillow* (1956) by B. J. Chute for a musico-dramatic production of ambitious scope. *Greenwillow* concerns a young man who, fearing he has inherited his father's perpetual wanderlust, is reluctant to marry the girl he loves until be can assure himself of his own strength of character. *Greenwillow* opened on Broadway on March 8, 1960. *Variety* found in it "a Dickensian, old English flavor . . . [with] the quality of Pickwick and the suggestion of Dingley Dell to carry on the Christmas tone." Its best songs were "Summertime Love" and "Never Will I Marry," introduced by Anthony Perkins, and "Walking Away Whistling" and "Faraway Boy," sung by Ellen McCown. Though *Greenwillow* was a box-office failure (97 performances), it is a work of which the creator was proud. The show enjoyed a brief revival Off Broadway in 1970.

Loesser's career on Broadway was brought to a triumphant conclusion with his greatest success, *How to Succeed in Business Without Even Trying* (December 14, 1961), which brought him the Pulitzer Prize in drama in 1962. The book, by Abe Burrows, Jack Weinstock and Willie Gilbert, based on the 1952 novel by Shepherd Mead, is a satire on big business practices and the opportunism and ruthlessness that drive ambitious men to success. J. Pierpont Finch, first played by Robert Morse, is a young go-getter who, through guile, nerve, supreme self-confidence and the help of a guidebook, climbs the corporate ladder by gaining first the attention, then the admiration, of J. B. Biggley, the

company president, portrayed by Rudy Vallee. In the end, Finch becomes Chairman of the Board of Directors.

Loesser's songs for their show were not only his most satirical, but some of his best. In "I Believe in You," Finch expresses self-confidence to his own reflection in the mirror, "Brotherhood of Man" is a tongue-in-cheek hymn celebrating fraternity; "Grand Old Ivy" mocks college songs; and "The Company Way" lampoons the politics of big business.

In his review of *How to Succeed* in *The New York Times,* Howard Taubman wrote: "It belongs to the blue chips among modern musicals . . . and [it] arrives bearing precious gifts of an adult viewpoint and consistency of style." Richard Watts, Jr., in *The New York Post,* called it "a brilliant musical comedy in which everything works out . . . a triumph for many talented people." Its run of 1,417 performances was the longest in Broadway history up to that time. In addition to the Pulitzer Prize, it won the Tony and the Drama Critics Circle awards, and its original cast recording earned a Grammy. For the motion-picture adaptation released in 1967, Robert Morse and Rudy Vallee returned to recreate their original stage roles.

On March 11, 1965, Loesser's new "comic opera," *Pleasures and Palaces,* opened in the Fisher Theatre in Detroit. The book by Sam Spewack and Frank Loesser, based on Spewacks's play, *Once There Was a Russian* (1961), is set in Russia during the reign of Catherine the Great. This was Loesser's last musical; both book and songs lacked audience appeal, and the judicious decision was made to close the show in Detroit.

Frank Loesser, a chronic smoker, died of lung cancer at Mount Sinai Hospital in New York City. According to his wishes, there were no funeral services and his ashes were scattered at sea.

Loesser was an intense man with a volatile temperament; his moods fluctuated between exuberance and despair and he was driven incessantly by nervous energy. Though he cultivated the image of an uncultured fellow, beneath it was a penetrating mind with a total command of popular musical craft. He preferred the city to country life, and inactivity to physically taxing endeavors; thus his hobbies were indoor diversions, such as cabinet-making, painting and collecting gadgets. Requiring little sleep, he rose early and was at the worktable before dawn. "You are alone then with the birds–no telephone, no interruptions, and the world is yours," he told an interviewer. Ernest Martin, the producer, recalled Loesser's "strange work habits": "He'd be up at four-thirty or five A.M., have a martini, and go to work between five and eight in the morning. He wasn't a boozer, he merely oiled himself up. Then, after he wrote, he'd go to sleep, get up later, work some more. Napped during the day, for maybe three or four hours." While working during the early morning hours, Loesser used a silent piano and earphones. Of his work habits, he said: "I don't write slowly. It's just that I throw out fast. I write by sitting down and being miserable, looking straight at a spot on the wall."

Following Loesser's death, his widow, Jo Sullivan Loesser Osborne, ran Frank Music Corporation, later selling it to CBS. But she has maintained control of her husband's rights and has been the caretaker of a repository of his work (now at the New York Public Library) which includes much still unpublished material.

In 1980 a stage panorama of Loesser's music, the revue *Perfectly Frank*, featured nearly 60 of his songs with Jo Sullivan narrating. It opened in Hollywood on September 7, 1980 before coming to Broadway the following November 30. "His musical sophistication, avoidance of cliché, endearing romanticism and often hilarious lyrical wit are clearly demonstrated," reported a critic for *Variety*. Jo Sullivan also starred in *I Hear Music . . . of Frank Loesser and Friends,* an Off Broadway production staged by Donald Sadler which opened on October 29, 1984.

ABOUT: Ewen, D. Great Men of American Popular Song, 2d ed. 1972; Green, S. The World of Musical Comedy, 4th ed. 1980; Wilk, M. They're Playing Our Song, 1973. *Periodicals*—New Yorker December 9, 1944; New York Times Magazine May 20, 1956.

LOEWE, FREDERICK (June 10, 1904–), and **LERNER, ALAN JAY** (August 31, 1918– June 14, 1986). When composer Frederick Loewe and librettist and lyricist Alan Jay Lerner combined their talents the results included *My Fair Lady*, one of the most highly esteemed and successful musicals in the history of Broadway, and *Gigi*, one of Hollywood's lasting musical achievements. Though as a mature composer Loewe worked exclusively with Lerner, Lerner has participated in projects with other collaborators as well.

Frederick ("Fritz") Loewe was born to a theatrical family in Vienna, Austria in 1904. His father, Edmund Loewe, was a distinguished operetta tenor who sang the role of Prince Danilo at the premiere of Lehár's *The Merry Widow* (1905); his mother, Rose, was an actress. As a boy, Frederick attended the Berlin Military Academy. Piano lessons began when he was five, and at 13, he became the youngest pianist to appear as soloist with the Berlin Symphony. He

FREDERICK LOEWE

made his first attempts at composition at seven, and contributed several musical numbers to his father's variety act. When Frederick was 15, he composed "Katrina," a song which not only was performed and published, but which sold about two million copies of sheet music throughout Europe.

Loewe received a thorough musical training at the Stern Conservatory in Berlin and later studied the piano with Europe's highly acclaimed keyboard masters, Ferruccio Busoni and Eugène d'Albert, winning the Hollander Medal for piano in 1923. He also studied composition and orchestration with Nikolaus von Reznicek.

In 1924, Loewe accompanied his father to the United States to promote himself as a piano virtuoso. His New York début recital in Town Hall that year was ignored. Unable to interest any concert managers, he earned his living by playing in a Greenwich Village nightclub and at the Rivoli Theatre, a movie house on Broadway, and also by working as a busboy in a cafeteria. For the next few years, he led a nomadic existence, wandering across the United States, prospecting for gold, cowpunching in Montana, delivering mail on horseback. Returning East, he taught horseback riding at a New Hampshire resort, engaged in professional boxing bouts as a bantamweight at a Brooklyn athletic club for $5 a fight, (he won eight out of nine contests); and played the piano on cruise ships and in Yorkville beer halls. In 1931, Loewe married Ernestine Zerline, an Austrian who was the New York manager of the Hattie Carnegie enterprises; they were divorced 26 years later.

ALAN JAY LERNER

Loewe was now beginning to write popular songs, but in a style reminiscent of Vienna. In 1934, "Love Tiptoes Through My Heart" was interpolated into the Broadway play, *Petticoat Fever,* where it was sung by Dennis King. A year later, Loewe formed a partnership with Earle Crooker, a radio and Hollywood scriptwriter, who provided him with the lyrics for "A Waltz Was Born in Vienna," which was first used as background music for the dance team of Gomez and Winona in the revue, *The Illustrators' Show* (1936). Loewe and Crooker then wrote the score for *Salute to Spring,* a musical produced by the St. Louis Municipal Opera during the summer of 1937, into which "A Waltz Was Born in Vienna" was interpolated. The Broadway producer Dwight Deere Wiman was sufficiently impressed by *Salute to Spring* to offer Loewe and Crooker a contract to compose the complete score for a Broadway musical, *Great Lady* (December 1, 1938). The show ran for just 20 performances.

This failure seemed to signal the end of his career in the musical theater, so Loewe decided to return to the concert stage. But after an undistinguished recital in Carnegie Hall in 1942, he relinquished all hope he had in this direction, and happily accepted an offer from a stock company in Detroit to adapt Barry Connor's farce, *The Patsy.* It was renamed *Life of the Party,* and the collaboration of Frederick Loewe and Alan Jay Lerner was born.

Alan Jay Lerner was born to a wealthy family in New York in 1918, the second of three sons of Jospeh J. Lerner and Edith A. (Lloyd) Lerner. His father had founded the Lerner Shops, a pros-

perous chain of stores featuring women's clothing and accessories; he was also a *bon vivant* who spoke four languages fluently, a scholar of the English language and a devotee of musical theater and boxing. Alan was his favorite son, whom he took to practically every Broadway musical and every boxing match at Madison Square Garden from the time Alan was five. His mother, who had studied singing, broadened Alan's cultural horizons by taking him to concerts and museums and, during his adolescence, to Europe annually for foreign cultural experiences.

Alan began studying the piano when he was five and he wrote his first songs as a teenager. "To all of that my father paid no attention," Lerner reveals in his autobiography, *The Street Where I Live.* "He was not one of those who believed in encouraging children." Planning a diplomatic career for his favorite son, Joseph Lerner decided that Alan's education should take place abroad before he entered a foreign service school in Washington, D. C. Alan attended Columbia Grammar School in New York, and when he was 12, he was sent to the Bedale's School in Hampshire, England, and then to the Choate School in Connecticut in preparation for advanced studies in France, Spain and Italy. Just before he graduated from Choate in 1936, Lerner was disciplined for smoking a cigarette (a serious offense at that time), which so angered his father that he discontinued Lerner's training for the diplomatic service and entered him instead in a general education curriculum at Harvard University. There Lerner contributed material to the Hasty Pudding Club Shows in 1938 and 1939, from which two songs were published. With the young John F. Kennedy, he was coeditor of the school's yearbook; he also composed a fight song and several other college numbers.

While attending Harvard, Lerner found time for other activities as well. In winter, he attended every Broadway tryout in Boston, and during the summers of 1936 and 1937, he took courses at the Juilliard School of Music. He also learned to fly with the hope of joining the air corps if the threat of war became a reality; and he was a member of the college boxing team. One of his bouts left him with sight only in his right eye, a development that not only ended his boxing days, but also his hopes for military service during World War II.

When he graduated from Harvard with a B.S. in 1940, Lerner focused his energy on the theater, which, had in fact, been his principal interest from the time he was 12. He took up residence at the Lambs Club in New York, whose clientele consisted solely of people in the theater. There he met Lorenz Hart, famous on

Broadway as the collaborator of Richard Rodgers, and the first man to encourage him to become a lyricist.

Soon after, Lerner was hired by the advertising firm of Lord and Thomas to write for radio, and during the next two years, he produced approximately 500 scripts. At one point, he was writing five shows each week, including material for Victor Borge, the Raleigh Hour and the Philco Hall of Fame. He also contributed lyrics to the *Gambols,* the annual satirical revues produced by the Lambs Club. Said Lerner: "The only way I could make the schedule work was not to sleep on Monday night."

When he left Lord and Thomas in 1942, he was still busy as a scriptwriter for radio. He was having lunch at the Lambs Club one day in August when Frederick Loewe, coming upon Lerner in the dining room, introduced himself. Though he knew Lerner only through the lyrics used in the *Gambols,* to which he had also contributed, Loewe invited Lerner to work with him as librettist-lyricist on *Life of the Party* for the Detroit production. Lerner was then without either a composer or a stage assignment, and an agreement was quickly reached.

Life of the Party survived a single performance in October 1942, after which the Detroit. stock company closed shop permanently. But the new collaborators went on to produce the Broadway musical, *What's Up?* (November 11, 1943; libretto written with Arthur Pierson). Jimmy Savo starred as a potentate from India visiting the United States during an international conference at a women's college; the conferees suddenly find themselves quarantined when there is an outbreak of measles. *What's Up?*, as Lerner and Loewe did not hesitate to confess, was a disaster. It mixed such unassimilable ingredients as Indian characters, American college girls, and songs with a Viennese lilt. The show closed after 63 performances.

What's Up? was followed by *The Day Before Spring* (November 22, 1945), which had a modest Broadway run of 165 performances. Lerner's book concerned a ten-year college reunion during which an old college romance is rekindled. Some critics praised the novel manner in which the ballet sequences, choreographed by Anthony Tudor, embodied the reactions of the principal characters to the event that transpired. Also worthy of note was the fact that Loewe's music was beginning to shed its Viennese identity. "I Love You This Morning" and "You Haven't Changed at All," both introduced by Bill Johnson and Irene Manning, were beginning to reveal a Broadway accent.

Lerner's admiration for the writings of turn-of-the-century Scottish playwright and novelist Sir James Barrie inspired the next Lerner and Loewe musical, *Brigadoon* (March 13, 1947), which became their first success. Lerner took his subject from a casual remark Loewe made about faith moving mountains. Why not a town? With this thought in mind, Lerner created Brigadoon, a mythical Scottish town which disappeared in 1747 only to return to life for one day each century. During one such reappearance, two Americans come upon it and one, Tommy, falls in love with Fiona, a Scottish lass. Tommy soon discovers the legend and realizes that his romance would be an unfulfilled fantasy for another 100 years. Upon returning to America, Tommy is unable to forget Fiona, and his love for her enables him to bring Brigadoon to life again. "The plot works beautifully," Brooks Atkinson said. "[Mr. Lerner] does not get down to the details of the fairy story until the audience has already been won by the pleasant characters, the exuberant music, and the prim though fiery dances. After that, the incantation is complete and easy."

For this Scottish fantasy, Lerner and Loewe composed their first hit, "Almost Like Being in Love," which was introduced by David Brooks and Marion Bell; Mildred Bailey, Jo Stafford, and Mary Martin with Guy Lombardo and His Royal Canadians recorded it in 1947, and it appeared on *Your Hit Parade.* Other numbers had a Scottish flavor: "The Heather on the Hill," "From This Day On," "Come to Me, Bend to Me," and "Waitin' for My Dearie."

Brigadoon, which had a run of 581 performances, became the first musical selected by the New York Drama Critics Circle as the year's best play. The motion picture adaptation starred Gene Kelly, who sang "Almost Like Being in Love" and "Heather on the Hill," as well as Jimmy Thompson and Cyd Charisse. *Brigadoon* lost none of its pristine glow and enchantment when it returned to Broadway in 1980. As Frank Rich reported in the *New York Times,* it is "a miracle that is pure Broadway . . . It's the kind of magic that can happen when young talent, a great song and plain old sexual chemistry all spring up in the same theater at the same time." And in a review (*The New York Times*) of the New York City Opera production (1986), John Rockwell wrote, "[Brigadoon] is a wonderful epitomization of mid-century American optimism and romanticism. The idea that love can overcome any difficulties, can make anything real, was so much a part of the national mystique from the mid-40's into the 50's that it shaped the personality of anyone who grew up during that time."

The partnership of Lerner and Loewe was temporarily interrupted after *Brigadoon* when

Lerner collaborated with Kurt Weill on *Love Life* (October 7, 1948). He filled once again the dual role of librettist and lyricist; from this musical comes the standard, "Green-Up Time" and also "Here I'll Stay."

In 1949, Lerner was invited by Arthur Freed, the MGM producer, to come to Hollywood. Freed wanted Lerner to spend ten weeks becoming acquainted with the motion picture industry and to write something for Fred Astaire. Remembering Astaire's many appearances with his sister, Adele, Lerner conceived a screenplay revolving around a famous brother-and-sister dance team. *Royal Wedding* was released by MGM in 1951. Jane Powell costarred with Astaire, and Burton Lane composed music for Lerner's lyrics; "Too Late Now" was its leading song.

Lerner continued to work for Freed in Hollywood. His next assignment was the screenplay for *An American in Paris* (1951), which used songs by George and Ira Gershwin, and, for a 20-minute dance sequence, George Gershwin's tone poem, *An American in Paris*. Vincente Minnelli directed and Gene Kelly and Leslie Caron, who was making her screen debut, were the stars. *An American in Paris* won the Oscar for the year's best motion picture; another was also awarded to Lerner for his screenplay.

Following *An American in Paris,* Lerner signed a three-picture deal with Freed. First came the screen adaptation of *Brigadoon* (1954) and a film musical based on *Huckleberry Finn* (music by Burton Lane) was planned, but it never materialized.

In 1951, Lerner was reunited with Loewe for the Broadway musical *Paint Your Wagon* (November 12, 1951), which ran for 289 performances. Lerner's book, set in California during the gold rush of the early 1850s, tells of Ben Rumson, a farmer, and his daughter, Jennifer, who become wealthy when gold is found on their land. Jennifer falls in love with Julio Valveras, one of the miners, and to break up this relationship, Rumson sends her to school in the East. During her absence, the gold runs out, and the boom town is abandoned. Jennifer returns in time to be with her father at his lonely death and to resume her romance with Julio.

The production of *Paint Your Wagon* was rich with local color, enlivened by dances choreographed by Agnes de Mille and songs evoking images of the American West. "They Call the Wind Maria," introduced by Rufus Smith and a male chorus in the show, became quite popular in the early 1960s as a result of Robert Goulet's bestselling recording; two melancholy numbers, "I Still See Elisa," in which Rumson remembers

his wife, and "Wand'rin' Star," which is heard before his death, were sung by James Barton; and the beguine, "I Talk to the Trees," belonged to the lovers, portrayed by Tony Bavaar and Olga San Juan. Almost two decades passed before *Paint Your Wagon* came to the screen, and in spite of an expenditure of 17 million dollars and a star-studded cast which included Lee Marvin, Clint Eastwood, Jean Seberg and Harve Presnell, the 1969 adaptation was an artistic and box-office calamity.

In 1952, Gabriel Pascal, the Hollywood producer and director, discussed with Lerner the possibility of making George Bernard Shaw's *Pygmalion* into a film musical. At first, this notion presented seemingly insurmountable problems: Lerner inquired, could one make a musical out of a "non-love story?" For the next two years, other composers and lyricists, including Rodgers and Hammerstein, were also approached; they all declined. During the summer of 1954, Lerner was hospitalized with encephalitis and spinal meningitis, but following his recovery, he reconsidered *Pygmalion,* and with Loewe, began to perceive how a musical might be developed. Acquiring the rights introduced new problems; Pascal had died that year, and in addition to his estate, the estate of Shaw and the MGM studio, which owned the screen rights to the play, were also parties to the negotiations.

It took considerable time and effort to unravel the legal entanglements, but during that period, Lerner was not idle. Though he still did not own the rights, he had interested Herman Levin in producing the show, and had engaged Oliver Smith as scenic designer, Cecil Beaton as costume designer and Rex Harrison and Julie Andrews for the two leading roles. Lerner was also at work on the libretto and was beginning to fashion some of the songs with Loewe. The first songs, "Why Can't the English?" and "I'm an Ordinary Man" took six weeks to write. Later, "The Rain in Spain" was completed in just 10 minutes. When the rights finally cleared, CBS-Columbia agreed to finance the show, and with Moss Hart (stage director) and Hanya Holm (choreographer) completing the list of collaborators, production moved quickly towards the electrifying opening of *My Fair Lady* at the Mark Hellinger Theatre on March 15, 1956, where it remained for six and a half years (2,717 performances).

Lerner's text remained faithful to Shaw. Professor Henry Higgins, a phonetician, spurred on by a wager, transforms Liza Doolittle, an ignorant cockney flower girl he encounters at Covent Garden, into a grand lady with impeccable manners and speech. The final test takes place at the Grand Embassy Ball, where Liza successfully passes herself off as a grand duchess. Higgins, now through with her, is strangely disturbed by a lingering fear that Liza might marry Freddy, a rich but vacuous young man. Here, Lerner deviated from the Shaw play by introducing a happy ending: Liza returns to and is accepted by Higgins. Small changes in the dialogue made by Lerner were so true to the style and spirit of Shaw that it was often difficult to detect where Shaw ended and Lerner had begun, the total integration of all elements, songs, dances, production numbers, sets, costumes, acting, and stage direction, caused the critics to cheer unanimously. Brooks Atkinson described *My Fair Lady* as "one of the best musicals of the century . . . close to the genius of creation." William Hawkins called the evening "legendary."

Loewe's abundantly melodic score passed flexibly from Continental charm and touching sentiment to impish cockney humor. Two numbers were immediate hits: "I Could Have Danced All Night," introduced by Julie Andrews, and "On the Street Where You Live," sung by John Michael King. Two amusing cockney numbers for Liza's father, Doolittle, were introduced by Stanley Holloway: "Get Me to the Church on Time" and "With a Little Bit of Luck"; Rex Harrison gave urbane presentations of "Why Can't the English?" "I'm an Ordinary Man," "Hymn to Him" and "I've Grown Accustomed to Her Face"; and Julie Andrews was still very much the cockney flower girl in dreaming of a better life in "Wouldn't it Be Loverly?" "The Ascot Gavotte" and "The Embassy Waltz" drew upon the traditions of European operettas and "The Rain in Spain," in which Liza reveals her mastery of her diction lessons, was a tango for which Moss Hart concocted a fandango routine and a pantomime simulating a bullfighter swinging his cape at a bull.

My Fair Lady dominated the Tony Award ceremonies that year by capturing one-third of the awards. Its original runs on Broadway and in London were the longest of any production in either city up to that time, and two national companies toured America for several years; it was also produced in 21 countries, including the Soviet Union, in translations. Its worldwide gross was about $80 million. The original cast album sold more than five million copies (the soundtrack recording of the film adaptation was also a bestseller) and 50 other record albums in several different languages brought the total sale to about 18 million copies. The film rights were sold for $5.5 million and a percentage of the gross, at that time, an arrangement without precedent. In all, the total revenue from *My Fair Lady* has been estimated at $800 million, a commercial success in a class by itself. From its investment of $400,000, Columbia Records earned more than $42 million.

In the attractively produced motion picture adaptation of *My Fair Lady* (1964), which won eight Oscars including one as best film, Rex Harrison and Stanley Holloway repeated their stage roles. Julie Andrews was replaced by Audrey Hepburn, whose singing was dubbed by Marni Nixon, and Jeremy Brett (dubbing by Bill Shirley) replaced John Michael King. Twenty-five years after its triumphant opening, *My Fair Lady* returned to Broadway in 1981 with banners flying. Rex Harrison again assumed the role of Higgins, and the musical according to Mel Gussow (*New York Times*), "endures as a paragon of wit, romance and musicality. Every song is a winner."

During the Philadelphia tryouts of *My Fair Lady* in 1956, Arthur Freed flew in from California to attend one of its performances and to bring Lerner a screen project with which to complete his three-picture deal. It was Freed's idea to anticipate the motion picture adaptation of *My Fair Lady* by several years with a screen version of Colette's novella, *Gigi. Gigi*, like *My Fair Lady*, also used a variation on the story of Pygmalion and Galatea: at the turn of the century, an awkward Parisian girl is taught to become a sophisticated courtesan. Lerner found the subject appealing, but Loewe, prejudiced against composing for the screen, agreed reluctantly and only after considerable persuasion.

With Vincente Minelli directing and Leslie Caron, Louis Jourdan and Maurice Chevalier starring, *Gigi* (1958) opened to a shower of critical praise and it grossed $16 million from a $3 million investment. *Gigi* became the first motion picture to win nine Oscars, including one for the picture itself, another for the title song, and a third to Lerner for his screenplay. The title song, described by Lerner as "one of the most rapturous [Loewe] ever composed" was written in a single hour except for the last two lines for which Lerner needed an additional two days; Louis Jourdan introduced it in the film. The score also boasted "Thank Heaven for Little Girls" and "I'm Glad I'm Not Young Anymore" introduced by Chevalier, and "I Remember It Well," a duet for Chevalier and Hermione Gingold. The soundtrack recording sold more than two million copies.

When *Gigi* opened, Loewe was being hospitalized for a massive coronary, and his slow recovery delayed the writing of *Camelot*, based on T. H. White's Arthurian romance, *The Once and Future King*. In planning this musical, for which Lerner again provided the libretto as well as lyrics, the team assembled many of the ingredients that had contributed to the success of *My Fair Lady*. Moss Hart returned as director, Oliver Smith as set designer and Hanya Holm as choreographer. Julie Andrews was signed as Guenevere and Robert Coots, a featured player, and Franz Allers, its music director, were also re-engaged. Once again, CBS-Columbia provided the necessary $400,000 subsidy. To this corps from *My Fair Lady*, Richard Burton (King Arthur), Robert Goulet (in his Broadway debut as Lancelot), and Roddy MacDowell (Mordred) were added.

In spite of an auspicious beginning, the creation of *Camelot* was marred by a series of disasters. Lerner was tormented by marital discord and bleeding ulcers that required hospitalization, and during the show's tryout in Toronto, in the newly constructed O'Keefe Centre, the machinery malfunctioned and the acoustics were poor; as a result, the audience was unresponsive. Then Moss Hart suffered a heart attack that left him unable to continue as director. To compound these misfortunes was the fact that, after 18 years of fruitful collaboration, Lerner and Loewe found working with one another was no longer a source of creative joy, mutual respect and personal affection, but one of constant misunderstandings, acrimony and hostile silences. They parted after *Camelot* "with no formal farewells, no goodbyes, nothing to mark the end of a long voyage we had been on together," writes Lerner in his autobiography.

Camelot, when it finally arrived on Broadway on December 1, 1960, with a $3 million advance sale, was not even a close approximation of *My Fair Lady,* as the critics discovered: "Graceful and sumptuous though it is," reported Howard Taubman in *The New York Times,* "*Camelot* leans dangerously in the direction of old-hat operetta. It has intervals of enchantment . . . but it cannot be denied that [Lerner and Loewe] badly miss their late collaborator—Bernard Shaw." Richard Watts, Jr. noted that "there is a curious air of heaviness hanging over it, and it has an unfortunate way of getting lost from time to time between its fantasy, its satirical humor, and its romantic wistfulness."

Though *Camelot* had been plagued by problems, and the critics were unmoved, it remained on Broadway for 873 performances and toured for two years. Many of the show's songs, particularly the title song, introduced by Burton, and "If Ever I Would Leave You," sung by Goulet, have achieved widespread popularity and are probably *Camelot's* greatest asset. Other songs contributing to the show's charm were "How to Handle a Woman," "What Do the Simple Folk Do?," "The Lusty Month of May" and "The Sim-

ple Joys of Maidenhood." A sumptuously produced screen adaptation starring Richard Harris and Vanessa Redgrave was released in 1967; both the original cast album and the soundtrack recording sold well. In 1980, with Richard Burton again as the star, *Camelot* was revived on Broadway and again in 1981, with Richard Harris.

After *Camelot,* Lerner and Loewe remained apart for the next decade; meanwhile, their achievements were hailed in "Salute to Lerner and Loewe" (1961) on *The Ed Sullivan Show* on CBS-TV and *The Broadway of Lerner and Loewe* (1962) on NBC-TV.

During the 1960s, Lerner pursued his career independently of Loewe. He wrote screenplays for the motion picture adaptations of *My Fair Lady* (1964) and *Paint Your Wagon* (1969), as well as the book and lyrics for two Broadway musicals.

The first of the two new Lerner musicals on Broadway was *On a Clear Day You Can See Forever* (October 17, 1965). The show was originally to have been a collaboration with Richard Rodgers, but when they realized they could not agree on how the text should be developed, Rodgers withdrew from the project. Lerner then went to composer Burton Lane, with whom he found he could work productively. *On a Clear Day You Can See Forever,* starring Barbara Harris and John Cullum, had an unimpressive run of 280 performances, though it fared much better in the sale of original cast and soundtrack recordings as well as in the film version with Barbra Streisand (1970) for which Lerner provided the screenplay. The title song became a hit; the other songs in the score were "Melinda," "Come Back to Me," and "What Did I Have That I Don't Have Now?"

The second of the Lerner musicals was *Coco* (December 18, 1969), based on the life of the Parisian fashion designer, Gabrielle "Coco" Chanel. André Previn composed the music for Lerner's text and lyrics, and Katharine Hepburn assumed the title role, her first in the musical theater. Lerner's book concentrated on Chanel's late career when, in 1954, at the age of 71 she tried to reopen the House of Chanel, which had been closed since World War II. Chanel's first postwar fashion show was rejected by the French press, but she made a striking comeback when the leading American department stores came to her support. Glimpses into her past, related by her father and her lovers, were projected on a screen. In addition to a vibrant subject and a cherished star, *Coco* offered fashion parades of feminine gowns designed by Cecil Beaton. Hepburn introduced the title song, and "A Woman is How She Loves" and "When Your Lover Says Goodbye" were sung by David Holliday; the show ran for 332 performances.

Lerner and Loewe buried the hatchet in 1973 to adapt *Gigi* for Broadway (November 13, 1973). Though it brought the songwriters a Tony for their score, *Gigi* had become too familiar a commodity by 1973 to attract much public interest. An attempt to bring new life to this stage musical took place in New Haven in 1984, but it still proved to be, as *Variety* noted, "a pale echo of the MGM original. . . . [that] suggested that a revival of the film might be more appropriate than an inevitably watered-down stage version."

Lerner and Loewe's last collaboration was the screen adaptation of Antoine de Saint-Exupéry's fable, *The Little Prince* (1974). This, too, was a failure, after which Loewe went into permanent retirement. Lerner went on to collaborate with the composer and conductor, Leonard Bernstein, on a new musical, *1600 Pennsylvania Avenue* (May 4, 1976); the show was a disaster in its out-of-town tryouts and a catastrophe on Broadway, where attacks by the critics and public indifference forced it to close after seven performances. Lerner's two most recent Broadway ventures, *Carmelina* (1979; music by Burton Lane) based on the film, *Buono Sera, Mrs. Campbell,* and *Dance a Little Closer* (1983, music by Charles Strouse), based on Robert Sherwood's 1936 Pulitzer Prize-winning play, *Idiot's Delight,* were also unsuccessful.

"My own taste has always run toward the romantic (meaning larger than life, not operetta)," says Lerner in his autobiography. "I have no gift for satire and I instinctively look for humor in the antics of personality. I like to write stories that move me. This does not necessarily mean love stories, but it usually does. As a rule it is not sadness that brings tears to my eyes, but a longing fulfilled."

About their early days Loewe says, "[Lerner had] a precise, lyric goal in view. . . . With all the fears and confidence of youth I set out to try to combine the dramatic lyrics of Hammerstein with the wit and tenderness of Larry [Lorenz Hart]. In other words, to write musical plays in which the songs would be witty and tender because the characters were witty and tender, and dramatize, musically and lyrically, legitimate situations."

As this observer has pointed out in *Great Men of American Popular Song,* in many ways, Lerner and Loewe were opposites, particularly in their creative life and outlook: "Lerner was precise and analytical, exact in his facts, given to calm evaluations and understatements. At opening nights, his nervousness reaches such a pitch that he almost becomes a basket case. Loewe took opening nights with a calm stride and calm confidence. Otherwise, he could be effusive, exuberant, partial to exaggerations. Lerner was an artist who had to revise, rewrite and change and delete continually before he was satisfied . . . Loewe detested revising once he had captured a tune and put it down on paper; abhorred the necessity of having to rework an idea, a chore that nauseated him . . . And he was in horror of deadlines. To Lerner, to live means to create; to Loewe, to create meant the means by which he could pursue the good life."

Lerner and Loewe were reunited at the Winter Garden Theatre in New York on May 14, 1979 for a gala in their honor. At the close of the evening, Lerner read from his autobiography his tribute to his partner: "There will never be another Fritz. . . . Writing will never again be as much fun. A collaboration as intense as ours, inescapably had to be complex. But I loved him more than I understood and misunderstood him and I know he loved me more than he understood or misunderstood me."

In addition to his other activities, Lerner was a member of the Dramatists Guild of America, of which he served as president from 1958 to 1963, and in 1971, he was elected to the Songwriter's Hall of Fame. He had been married eight times, most recently to Liz Robertson in 1981. In his autobiography, Lerner said of his "marital misadventures," " . . . If I had no flair for marriage, I also had no flair for bachelorhood. Marriage, as someone said, is often like a besieged fortress. Everyone inside wants to get out and everyone outside wants to get in." Lerner died of lung cancer in New York City. He was survived by his wife and son and three daughters.

Loewe was awarded an honorary doctorate of music from the University of Redlands in California (1962) and a D.F.A. from New York University in 1967.

For their contributions to and achievements in the performing arts in America, Lerner and Loewe were recipients of Kennedy Center Honors, presented by President Reagan on December 8, 1985.

ABOUT: Current Biography, 1958; Ewen, D. Great Men of American Popular Song 2d ed. 1972; Green, S. The World of Musical Comedy, 4th ed. 1980; Lerner, A. J. The Street Where I Live, 1978. *Periodicals*—New York Times Magazine November 17, 1957, March 15, 1959; New York Times May 8, 1983, June 15, 1986; Time November 14, 1960.

MANCINI, HENRY (April 16, 1924–   ). By 1984 the prolific composer Henry Mancini had written music for approximately 80 films and had recorded some 60 albums. He has also composed the scores for made-for-TV movies and provided the musical themes for such prime-time television programs as *Peter Gunn*. A popular orchestra conductor as well, he has won four Oscars, 20 Grammy awards and seven gold records.

He was born in Cleveland in 1924. His parents, Quinto and Anna (Pece) Mancini, had emigrated from the province of Abruzzi in Italy to Ohio before settling in the industrial town of Aliquippa, Pennsylvania. There, Henry attended elementary school and Aliquippa High. His father, who worked in the steel mills, was an amateur flutist, and began teaching his son the flute and the piccolo when Henry was eight. Henry later played these instruments in the local Sons of Italy band in which his father also performed. "It was always Dad's prodding and persistence that make me practice," he recalled. "He made many sacrifices to send me to teachers and schools." Henry started learning to play the piano when he was 12, but his heart was more in sports, especially football, than in music. "[My father] held a club over my head—well, not literally, but if I didn't practice, I got it." The younger Mancini disliked practice so much that his father was forced to cajole Henry by only permitting him to play ball after completing his music lessons.

Nevertheless his enthusiasm for music was aroused through recordings by big-name jazz bands. When Artie Shaw became his idol, one of Mancini's hobbies was writing out Shaw's jazz arrangements after listening to his records, a practice he would continue in the classroom, where he was required to write out the arrangements from memory. Next Mancini discovered Glenn Miller and he soon became the flutist for a local jazz combo. In 1937 Mancini was named first flutist in the Pennsylvania All-State Band.

From 1938 to 1940, Mancini studied piano, theory and composition with Max Adkins, a conductor and arranger at the Stanley Theater in Pittsburgh, and, "A new world opened up for me." After graduating from high school, Mancini enrolled in courses at the Music School of the Carnegie Institute of Technology. One day, he sent some of his jazz arrangements to Benny Goodman, who purchased one of them and advised Mancini to come to New York to work for him. This apprenticeship did not work out, because Mancini was unprepared for such an assignment. Needing more training, Mancini enrolled in the Juilliard School of Music in 1942, but later that year was drafted and sent overseas,

HENRY MANCINI

where he served with both the U.S. Army Air Corps and the infantry.

When he was discharged from the military in 1945, Mancini was hired as pianist and arranger for the Glenn Miller band, which, since Miller's wartime death, had been led by Tex Beneke. Two years later, on September 13, 1947, he married Virginia (Ginny) O'Connor, a vocalist with the Beneke orchestra and a member of the Meltones, Mel Tormé's singing group. The Mancini's have three children, a son and two daughters.

In 1947 Mancini left Beneke's band, and for the next four years worked as a free-lance musician and arranger for singers and jazz groups. When his wife, Ginny, and the Meltones were signed to contracts with the Universal-International film studios, Mancini was called in to do the arrangements. Joseph Gershenson, the music director, gave him a two-week assignment to prepare music for an Abbott and Costello film, *Lost in Alaska* (1952). Mancini stayed with Universal-International six years, writing music for more than one hundred motion pictures. This was hack work, but it enabled Mancini to learn the motion picture business as well as the techniques for scoring films. "I had no control over what I did," he commented. "I learned all the stock situations. I did all the cliché things and got them out of my system."

However, two productions at Universal-International were superior films which provided Mancini his first opportunity to test his abilities as an arranger of jazz: *The Glenn Miller Story* (1954), which earned him his first Oscar nomination, and *The Benny Goodman Story* (1956). A third picture at Universal-

International, the noirish *Touch of Evil* (1958), directed by Orson Welles and now regarded as a minor masterpiece, demanded music that would enhance a smoky, sinister mise-en-scène.

A fellow employed at Universal-International was Blake Edwards, who, when promoted to director, asked Mancini to write the music for his productions. This began a close friendship and a long-standing artistic collaboration. After Mancini left Universal-International in 1958, Edwards engaged him to compose the innovative (for TV) background music for *Peter Gunn,* a half-hour television series about a private detective. Working on a limited budget, Mancini employed a small, 11-man ensemble, and composed a score in the jazz idiom that heightened the show's drama and suspense. The first telecast of *Peter Gunn* took place on August 22, 1958 on NBC, where it remained until September 1960, when it moved to ABC, staying there until September 21, 1961. This was the first time jazz had been prominently used in a prime-time series. Mancini was soon receiving a third of the show's fan mail, and the background music brought him an Emmy nomination. The *Peter Gunn* theme, in a recording by Ray Anthony, sold more than a million copies, and Mancini's own album, *Music from Peter Gunn* (1958), became his first LP to sell more than a million copies. The record also earned him his first two Grammys, as best album of the year and as the year's best arrangement.

Mancini's next assignment for Blake Edwards was to prepare music for the television series, *Mr. Lucky,* dramatic adventure fare about a Los Angeles gambler. Though the series lasted only one season (1959–60), Mancini and his orchestra recorded *Music from Mr. Lucky,* a bestselling LP which in 1960 brought Mancini two more Grammys, as best performance by an orchestra and as best arrangement. That year Mancini received a third Grammy, for best jazz performance by a large orchestra, for his album *Blues and the Beat.*

Now a leading popular composer, Mancini returned to motion picture work on a free-lance basis, composing the music for *High Time* (1960) and *Breakfast at Tiffany's* (1961), which starred Audrey Hepburn in a film adaptation of the Truman Capote novella. For *Breakfast,* Mancini composed his first hit song and his first standard: "Moon River" (lyrics by Johnny Mercer), which was sung under the titles by Andy Williams and on the screen by Hepburn. Andy Williams's recording, both as a single and as an album entitled *Moon River,* surpassed the million-mark in sales, and he used the song as theme music for his television variety series. There

have been some 500 recordings of "Moon River," including a bestselling version by Jerry Butler. The song, which sold more than a million copies of sheet music, was awarded Grammys for best record of the year (in a recording by Henry Mancini and his orchestra); best song; best performance by an orchestra; best soundtrack album; and best arrangement. "Moon River" also became Mancini's first song to capture an Oscar, winning for best song. He received a second Oscar that same year when *Breakfast at Tiffany's* won for best original score.

In 1962 Mancini became the first composer to win Oscars for songs in two consecutive years. The next one came for the title song from *Days of Wine and Roses* (1962, lyrics by Johnny Mercer), in which Jack Lemmon and Lee Remick were starred as chronic alcoholics. Performed chorally on the soundtrack, the song became a million-seller in releases by Henry Mancini, Andy Williams, and André Kostelanetz. "Days of Wine and Roses" collected Grammy Awards for best song, best recording (that of Mancini and his orchestra) and best arrangement.

Other memorable Mancini songs from films were "Charade" (lyrics by Mercer), the title song of a 1963 motion picture starring Audrey Hepburn and Cary Grant. Significant recordings were made by Mancini, Andy Willilams and Jack Jones. "Dear Heart" (lyrics by Jay Livingston and Ray Evans) was the title song of a 1965 motion picture starring Glenn Ford. Heard both chorally and orchestrally on the soundtrack, "Dear Heart," soon after the picture was released, was recorded by some 20 artists, including bestselling versions by Andy Williams, Jack Jones and Wayne King. "It Had Better Be Tonight" (lyrics by Mercer, music written with Franco Misliacci) was introduced by Fran Jeffries in *The Pink Panther* (1964), starring Peter Sellers and directed by Blake Edwards. "Moment to Moment" (lyrics by Mercer) was the title song of a 1965 film starring Jean Seberg in which it was sung chorally under the titles and in the final scene and was used as a recurrent theme. Frank Sinatra was one of the first to record it. "Sweetheart Tree" (lyrics by Mercer) was sung on the soundtrack of *The Great Race* by Jackie Ward (dubbing for Natalie Wood). In the film, Wood invited the audience in a movie house to sing along with her, while a bouncing ball on the screen followed "Sweetheart Tree's" lyrics. Among the dozen or so recordings was a bestseller by Johnny Mathis. "In the Arms of Love" (lyrics by Livingston and Evans), interpolated in *What Did You Do in the War, Daddy?* (1966), was recorded by Andy Williams. "All His Children" (lyrics by Alan and Marilyn Bergman) was heard in *Sometimes a Great Notion* (1971), starring Paul Newman, who also directed. Charlie Pride's recording of the song hit number one on the country-and-western charts. "It's Easy to Say" (lyrics by Carol Bayer Sager) was introduced in *10* (1979), directed by Edwards and starring his wife, Julie Andrews, and Bo Derek.

Among the films for which Mancini has composed the background music are: *Breakfast at Tiffany's* (1961); *Bachelor In Paradise* (1961); *Days of Wine and Roses* (1962); *Charade* (1963); *Soldier in the Rain* (1963); *Dear Heart* (1965); *A Shot in the Dark* (1964); *The Pink Panther* (1964) and all of its sequels; *Arabesque* (1966); *Wait Until Dark* (1967); *Darling Lili* (1970); *The Hawaiians* (1970); *Sunflower* (1970); *Sometimes a Great Notion* (1971); *The Great Waldo Pepper* (1975); *House Calls* (1977); *Alex and the Gypsy* (1977); *Who Is Killing the Great Chefs of Europe?* (1978); *10* (1979); *Change of Seasons* (1980); *Mommie Dearest* (1981); *S. O. B.* (1981); *Back Roads* (1981); *Victor/Victoria* (1982); *The Man Who Loved Women* (1983); and *That's Dancing* (1985). His *Victor/Victoria* score received an Oscar.

Mancini's motion picture scores overflow with instrumental passages that he has recorded and performed in public appearances as conductor of his orchestra. "Mancini's writing," this author said in *Great Men of American Popular Song*, "is vividly programmatic as he seeks out the precise music that does full justice to, or enhances, the scene being projected on the screen. In his search for the musical mot juste, in his insistence on musical realism, Mancini is not afraid to employ the most unusual effects and instruments, and he often does so with remarkable results. He used a calliope for a descriptive and amusing little tune to a boogie woogie rhythm as the background music for a scene in *Hatari!* in which a girl is being followed by a baby elephant; for the recurring theme in the same movie he made use of an untuned piano. He brought a homespun fascination to "Moon River" when it was played by an amplified harmonica. In *Experiment in Terror* he employed a leitmotif for the asthmatic villain, strummed on two autoharps which contributed to the atmosphere of terror being projected. In *Wait Until Dark*, he introduced into the orchestra an ancient instrument of the flute family, a Sho, whose haunting, exotic sounds were just what these episodes called for."

Before working on background music or film songs, Mancini views the movie four or five times, taking copious notes and keeping the action well fixed in his mind. Then, when he starts to write his music, he does not look again at the picture until the notes are down on paper. Composition primarily takes place at the piano.

Mancini has discussed his approach to writing background music: "Sometimes there'll be just a basic theme, like in *The Pink Panther*. It'll run all the way through in different settings. In other cases, you'll have various individual songs. Some of these we call source music because they're actually made by a band or singer, in other words, a source that you can see in the picture. In *Breakfast at Tiffany's*, there are four or five of these in the party scene alone. . . . When I approach a film, I always think cinematically. I want to do my job for the picture honestly. I always approach a score as to what is best for the picture—not what's best for a record album, or the shortest cut to a hit song. That's the reason why so many of my scores—however effective they might be as part of the film—are unsuitable in recordings, since they consist of fragments."

Nevertheless, after *Peter Gunn* and its successor, *More Music From Peter Gunn,* six Mancini albums of instrumental passages from films earned him gold records: *Breakfast at Tiffany's; The Pink Panther; The Best of Mancini; Love Theme from Romeo and Juliet; A Warm Shade of Ivory* and *A Merry Mancini Christmas*. Mancini's "Pink Panther" theme won Grammy awards in several categories, including that of best instrumental composition. He has also received Grammys for his recorded performances and for his arrangements of film music by other composers.

In addition to public performances with his own orchestra, Mancini has been guest conductor of world-renowned symphonic organizations. In 1966 he performed at the London Palladium at a Royal Family Command Performance. On June 7, 1969 as guest conductor of the Philadelphia Orchestra, he conducted the world premiere of his three-movement symphonic suite, *Beaver Valley—'37*, nostalgic tonal impressions of his adolescent years in Aliquippa. In 1976 he conducted the London Symphony at Royal Festival Hall in London. On several occasions he has been the conductor of the orchestra for the Academy Award ceremonies.

Mancini was twice the guest of President and Mrs. Richard M. Nixon at the White House. On May 15, 1971 the Alumni Association of the University of California at Los Angeles (UCLA) honored him in special ceremonies at the Los Angeles Music Center, when he became only the seventh individual to be named an honorary alumnus. His 25 years in show business were commemorated on February 13, 1982, when he was feted as "Star of the Year" in Mexico City. Mancini received an honorary doctorate from Duquesne University in Pittsburgh in 1977 and from Mount Saint Mary's college in Maryland in 1980.

In 1976 the Readers Digest Association released an eight-volume collection of 111 songs composed, conducted and arranged by Mancini under the title, *Moon River—The Many Moods of Henry Mancini.*

The Mancinis reside in the Holmby Hills section of Los Angeles. He is no habitué of the Beverly Hills cocktail party circuit or of other social gatherings of the motion picture industry elite. He enjoys sailing, skiing, swimming, collecting art, photography, drawing, talking shop with musicians, or just loafing around the house with his family.

He is the author of *Sounds and Scores: A Practical Guide to Professional Orchestration.* Mancini endowed a chair at UCLA in screen music competition so that young musicians might learn the techniques of what he considers a "very delicate craft." He has also established annual scholarships at the Juilliard School of Music.

ABOUT: Current Biography, 1964; Ewen, D. Great Men of American Popular Song, 1970. *Periodicals*—ASCAP Today Spring 1978; Hi Fi Stereo Review June 1965.

MARKS, EDWARD B. *See* **STERN, JOSEPH W.** and **MARKS, EDWARD B.**

McHUGH, JIMMY (July 10, 1896–May 23, 1969). For three decades, Jimmy McHugh was one of the most prolific and successful composers of songs for more than 50 motion pictures. Nearly 100 became hits and many of those have since become standards.

He was born James Frances McHugh in Boston, the son of James Andrew McHugh, a plumber, and Julia Anne (Collins) McHugh, a trained pianist who became her son's first teacher. Jimmy attended St. John's Preparatory School in Danvers and Holy Cross College; after graduating in 1913, he worked as his father's assistant. A year later, he turned down a scholarship at the New England Conservatory to work as an office boy at the Boston Opera Company, where he soon served as rehearsal pianist and often delighted opera stars and conductors with his improvisations on famous opera arias.

In 1916, though McHugh's father had wanted him to become a plumber, he was hired by the Boston branch of the Irving Berlin publishing house as pianist and song plugger at a salary of eight dollars a week. Using the bicycle provided by the company, he traveled around Boston, appearing in three or four theaters each evening plugging the firm's songs, and made the rounds

JIMMY McHUGH

of five-and-ten-cent stores promoting sheet music. He also composed "Caroline, I'm Coming Back to You" (lyrics by Jack Caddigan), his first song to be performed.

McHugh served in the U.S. Cavalry during World War I, then returned to New York in 1921, where he joined the musical staff of Jack Mills Inc., rising to the post of professional manager. There he wrote "Emaline" (lyrics by George A. Little), his first published song.

Between 1921 and 1928, McHugh composed songs and special musical material for revues mounted at Harlem's famous Cotton Club. Two of these songs were his earliest successes: "When My Sugar Walks Down the Street" (written with Gene Austin and Irving Mills), introduced there in 1924, was popularized by Gene Austin in a bestselling 1925 recording; "I Can't Believe That You're in Love With Me" (lyrics by Clarence Gaskill), introduced in 1926 by Aida Ward, was also sung that year by Winnie Lightner in the Broadway revue, *Gay Paree*; recordings were made by Bing Crosby, Frank Sinatra, Dinah Washington, and Louis Armstrong. Nearly 30 years later, it was heard as the theme in the motion picture, *The Caine Mutiny* (1954).

McHugh wrote a number of other songs that became popular in the early and mid-1920s. "When You and I Were Young Maggie Blues" (lyrics by Jack Frost), composed in 1922, was popularized in vaudeville and recorded by Van and Schenck, and "Hinky Dinky Parlay Voo" was written in 1924 in collaboration with Al Dubin, Irving Mills and Irwin Dash, inspired by the favorite song of American doughboys in World War I, "Mademoiselle From Armentières."

"Hinky Dinky Parlay Voo" was introduced and popularized on radio by Ernie Hare and Billie Jones ("The Happiness Boys") and was heard in the motion picture *The Cockeyed World* (1929). "The Lonesomest Gal in Town" (lyrics by Dubin, music written with Irving Mills in 1925) was introduced by Jimmy McHugh and Irving Mills on radio where they were featured as The Hotsy Totsy Boys; Kay Starr recorded it. "My Dream of the Big Parade" (lyrics by Dubin) was composed in 1926 to help promote the silent film, *The Big Parade.* That same year, the death of Rudolph Valentino, the romantic star of the silent film era, led to the writing of "There's a New Star in Heaven Tonight" (with J. Keirn Brennan and Irving Mills), which was recorded by Vernon Dalhart.

In 1927, McHugh discovered a new "growl" band and introduced it at the Cotton Club—this was the young Duke Ellington. That year McHugh also met Dorothy Fields, daughter of vaudevillian Lew Fields; she was then a 22-year-old school teacher hoping to become a lyricist. He invited her to contribute lyrics for some songs he was writing for the Cotton Club. But their first complete score was for Lew Leslie's *Blackbirds of 1928* (May 9, 1928), a black revue on Broadway starring Bill "Bojangles" Robinson, Adelaide Hall and Aida Ward. It enjoyed one of the longest runs of any Broadway revue up to that time (518 performances). Its top song was the standard, "I Can't Give You Anything But Love, Baby," which Aida Ward (in her Broadway début) introduced with Willard MacLean. The song's popularity was enhanced by the numerous recorded performances, including those of Benny Goodman, Fats Waller, Ethel Waters with Duke Ellington, Louis Armstrong, Billie Holiday, Ella Fitzgerald, Gene Austin, the Mills Brothers, Connie Boswell, Dinah Shore, Harry Richman, Peggy Lee and Judy Garland; by 1965, this song had been recorded more than 450 times. It was also sung in films by Katherine Hepburn in *Bringing Up Father* (1938), Lena Horne with Bill Robinson in *Stormy Weather* (1943), Louis Armstrong in *Jam Session* (1944), and Gogi Grant in *The Helen Morgan Story* (1957), in which McHugh made a cameo appearance.

There were several other memorable numbers in *Blackbirds of 1928.* "Digga, Digga, Doo," a number sung by Adelaide Hall (also in her Broadway début) with dancers in Zulu costumes, was recorded by Duke Ellington (1928) and the Mills Brothers (1932), and Lena Horne sang it in *Stormy Weather.* Adelaide Hall introduced "I Must Have That Man"; Bill Robinson danced to "Doin' the New Low Down"; and Aida Ward and the Hall Johnson Choir were heard in

"Porgy," a tribute to the recently published novel, *Porgy,* by DuBose Heyward, which served as the basis for Gershwin's *Porgy and Bess* (1935).

Hello, Daddy (December 26, 1928) was the second Broadway musical with a score by McHugh and Fields; it ran for 198 performances. In the book by Dorothy Fields's brother, Herbert, based on *The High Cost of Loving,* three middle-aged members of the Purity League (one played by Lew Fields) each secretly support the illegitimate son of a burlesque queen in the belief that the child is his, when in reality none of them is the father. "In a Great Big Way," introduced by Betty Starbuck and Billy Taylor, was a showstopping number. Other attractive songs were "Futuristic Rhythm," introduced by Wanda Goll and chorus; "Let's Sit and Talk About You," introduced by Allen Kearns, Mary Lawlor and the Giersdorf Sisters; and "Out There Where the Blues Begins," introduced by Billy Taylor.

In 1929, McHugh and Fields contributed songs to Florenz Ziegfeld's *Midnight Frolics,* which took place on the roof of the New Amsterdam Theatre each season. The revue starred Paul Gregory, Helen Morgan, and Lillian Roth; the sets were designed by Joseph Urban. Paul Whiteman's orchestra played McHugh and Fields's songs in arrangements by the young black composer, William Grant Still, now best-known for his music heard in the concert hall. Among the songs were "I Can't Wait," "Looking for Love," and "Because I Love Nice Things."

Lew Leslie's *International Revue* followed in 1930; the score included the popular "Exactly Like You" and "On the Sunny Side of the Street," each introduced (and recorded) by Harry Richman. Tommy Dorsey's recording of "On the Sunny Side of the Street" was particularly successful; Tommy Dorsey made it one of his specialties, and recordings were also made by the orchestras of Ted Lewis, Roger Wolfe Kahn and Louis Armstrong, as well as by Franke Laine (whose release sold more than one million discs), Billie Holiday and Judy Garland. "On the Sunny Side of the Street" has also been featured in motion pictures, including one of the same title (1951), *The Benny Goodman* Story (1955) and *The Eddy Duchin Story* (1956); it was also heard more recently in *The Way We Were* (1973), starring Barbra Streisand; *House Calls* (1978), starring Walter Matthau; and *The Rich and the Famous* (1981), starring Jacqueline Bisset.

To the short-lived *Vanderbuilt Revue* (November 5, 1930) the team contributed two fine songs. Though the show closed after two weeks, "Button Up Your Heart," introduced by Evelyn Hoey and Charles Barnes, deserves to be remembered, and "Blue Again" became popular after it was picked up by Guy Lombardo and His Royal Canadians.

The partnership of McHugh and Fields continued into the 1930s, when they went to Hollywood where they signed with MGM to write songs for motion pictures. To *Love in the Rough* (1930), they contributed "Go Home and Tell Your Mother" (introduced by Robert Montgomery and Dorothy Jordan) and "One More Waltz" for which they received $50,000. Approximately a dozen films followed. With Herbert Stothart they composed the title song for *Cuban Love Song* (1931), which Lawrence Tibbett sang as a duet with his character's ghost, a feat which reputedly produced the first multiple recording.

For Dinner at Eight (1933), the songwriters composed the title song, which was used only for promotion, and "Don't Blame Me." "Don't Blame Me" had first been heard in the Chicago revue, *Clowns in Clover* (1932), sung by Walter Woolf King. Recorded by Matt Denis, Rudy Vallee, Ethel Waters, the Andrews Sisters, and the Leo Reisman orchestra, it has since become a standard and has been featured in several films.

In 1935 McHugh and Fields contributed songs to *Every Night at Eight.* "I Feel a Song Comin' On" (lyrics written with George Oppenheimer) was introduced by Harry Barris and later recorded by Frances Langford and Judy Garland and interpolated into the film, *Follow the Boys* (1944). But Frances Langford introduced the film's biggest hit, "I'm in the Mood for Love"; she then sang it on the soundtrack of *Palm Springs* (1936) and recorded it. Recordings were also made by Adelaide Hall, Lanny Ross, Hildegarde, the King Cole Trio, and the orchestras of Louis Armstrong and Red Nichols, and it was McHugh's first song to be heard on *Your Hit Parade,* and the first to reach the top position. Through the years approximately 400 recordings of this song have been released with total sales of millions of copies. Gloria De Haven sang it in *The Big Clock* (1948) and the song was heard in *Ask Any Girl* (1939) and *The Misfits,* starring Marilyn Monroe and Clark Gable (1961).

In 1935, McHugh and Fields wrote lyrics for Kern's "Lovely to Look At" for a motion-picture adaptation of Jerome Kern's stage musical, *Roberta*; they also composed the title song for *Hooray for Love* (1935), introduced by Gene Raymond, and "Livin' in a Great Big Way," introduced by Bill Robinson and Jeni le Gon. Both were recorded by Benny Goodman.

In addition to these film songs, McHugh and Fields wrote the independent numbers, "Goodbye Blues" (1932), later the theme song of the Mills Brothers; for the Dorsey brothers, "Lost in a Fog," which was then heard in the film, *Have a Heart* (1934); and "Every Little Moment" (1935), which was heard on *Your Hit Parade.* They also contributed songs to several revues, among them *Clowns in Clover.* From it comes "Hey, Young Fella," which Fields sang (with McHugh at the piano) for the opening of Radio City Music Hall in 1932; the song was later included in *Dancing Lady* (1933). "Thank You for a Lovely Evening," was composed for Phil Harris and Leah Ray at New York's Palais Royale, and was also heard in *Have a Heart* and *The Girl from Missouri* (1934).

In 1935, McHugh began to work with lyricists other than Fields, and with them he continued to produce a series of popular songs, many of which were heard on *Your Hit Parade.* With Ted Koehler, he wrote songs for *King of Burlesque* (1935), including "I've Got My Fingers Crossed" (introduced by Dixie Dunbar and Fats Waller), "Whose Big Baby Are You?" (introduced by Alice Faye), and "I'm Shooting High"; for Shirley Temple in *Dimples* (1936), they composed "Picture Me Without You." He collaborated with Gus Kahn on the title song for *Let's Sing Again* (1936), and with Frank Loesser he wrote the songs for three Hollywood musicals; these songs include "Say It (Over and Over Again)" from *Buck Benny Rides Again* (1940), popularized in a recording by Tommy Dorsey (with Frank Sinatra), "Can't Get Out of This Mood," introduced by Ginny Simms in *Seven Days Leave* (1942), and "Let's Get Lost," which was introduced by Mary Martin in *Happy Go Lucky* (1943), and then reached first position on *Your Hit Parade* through recordings by Kay Kyser and Jimmy Dorsey. He also worked with Johnny Mercer on songs for *You'll Find Out* (1940), including the Oscar nominee, "I'd Know You Anywhere."

In 1939, McHugh returned to the Broadway stage with the revue, *The Streets of Paris* (June 19, 1939) which ran for 274 performances. The cast included Luella Gear and Bobby Clark, Budd Abbott, Lou Costello, and Gower Champion; Al Dubin was McHugh's lyricist. The show's most popular song was "South American Way," which catered to the country's craving for things Latin-American. It was introduced by Ramón Vinay (the opera tenor) with Carmen Miranda, the Hylton Sisters and Della Lind; Miranda's explosive rendition is generally credited with making her a star. She repeated her performance in the film, *Argentine Way* (1940), and both she and the Andrews Sisters recorded it. The following year, again with Dubin as lyricist, McHugh composed the score for another Broadway revue,

Keep Off the Grass (May 23, 1940). Though it boasted a constellation of stars that included Jimmy Durante, Ray Bolger, Jane Froman and José Limon, it was a failure that stumbled through 44 performances.

Though McHugh worked with other lyricists in the 1930s and 1940s, he also initiated what became a long and successful collaboration with Harold Adamson in the late 1930s. Together they wrote the songs featured in *Banjo on My Knee* (1936), *Top of the Town* (1937), *Hitting a New High* (1937), *That Certain Age* (1938), *Mad About Music* (1938), as well as the title song for *You're a Sweetheart* (1937), which reached the top of *Your Hit Parade*. Their songs were introduced by such well-known stars as Alice Faye, coloratura soprano, Lily Pons, Tony Martin, Gertrude Niesen, and Deanna Durbin, and became extremely popular through recordings by Bobbie Breen, the Red Norvo orchestra, Tommy Dorsey, Jimmy Dorsey, and Frank Sinatra. Among their biggest hits from this period were "My Own," which was nominated for an Oscar, "I Love to Whistle," "Where Are You?" and "There's Something in the Air."

During World War II, McHugh and lyricist Herb Magidson were inspired to write "Say a Prayer for the Boys Over There" and "Comin' in on a Wing and a Prayer." "Say a Prayer" was introduced by Deanna Durbin in *Hers to Hold* (1943), and received an Oscar nomination. "Comin' in on a Wing and a Prayer" was published as an independent number in the same year. Its subject was suggested to McHugh by a letter from an Air Force pilot describing a crash in North Africa narrowly escaped by sputtering in with "one engine and a prayer." Eddie Cantor introduced the song at an Air Force base, after which it appeared on *Your Hit Parade*; sheet music sales exceeded one million copies. For these war songs, and his success in promoting the sale of war bonds, at an Aquacade (1945) that raised $28 million in one evening, McHugh received a Presidential Certificate of Merit from President Truman in 1947.

McHugh's collaboration with Adamson continued during the war. They composed songs for *Higher and Higher* (1943), in which Frank Sinatra introduced the Oscar nominee, "I Couldn't Sleep a Wink Last Night," and in *Doll Face* (1945), Perry Como introduced "A Hubba-Hubba-Hubba (Dig You Later)" and "It's a Most Unusual Day."

McHugh also collaborated with Adamson on several more films, writing "It's a Most Unusual Day" for *A Date with Judy* (1948), as well as songs for *His Kind of Woman* (1951), and *The Legionnaire* (1954). In 1959, he wrote songs for

A Private's Affair with Livingston and Evans, including "Warm and Willing"; his last film song was "Reach for Tomorrow" (lyrics by Ned Washington) for *Let No Man Write My Epitaph* (1960).

In the 1950s McHugh made many public appearances performing his songs. In 1951, he gave a command performance in London before Queen Elizabeth and the Duke of Edinburgh, offering a medley of 15 hits. Queen Elizabeth told him: "You seem to have written all of my favorite songs." McHugh then toured American air bases in Germany, and the following year, as "Jimmy McHugh and His Singing Starlets," he appeared in American nightclubs and hotels in 1952–1953, including the Copacabana (New York), the Cocoanut Grove (Los Angeles), the Fairmont Hotel (San Francisco) and the Sands Hotel (Las Vegas). His act was also featured on the Ed Sullivan and Kate Smith television shows. In October 1953, McHugh was the subject of the NBC-TV program, *This Is Your Life* and, in 1958, he was guest of honor on the television programs of Patti Page and Perry Como; he also appeared at the Seattle Opera House in a production for the 1962 World's Fair "The Musical World of Jimmy McHugh."

In addition to his activities as a songwriter and performer, McHugh was also an avid swimming enthusiast. In 1947, he became a major sponsor of the annual Southern California Swimming and Diving Championships, and in 1949, he brought a Japanese swimming team to Los Angeles to compete in the Men's Outdoor Nationals for the first time since the 1932 Olympics. In 1951, he organized the Jimmy McHugh Polio Foundation (later renamed Jimmy McHugh Charities) to raise funds for the purchase of respirators for Los Angeles hospitals and medical centers. He also established music scholarships for students of three schools in the Los Angeles area in 1955; four years later, with Pete Rugolo, he formed his own publishing house, Jimmy McHugh Music. He was also interested in opera, and he collected French paintings and Georgian silver. One of his most prized possessions was a gray, modernistic piano, given to him by George Gershwin, on which he composed many songs.

McHugh received honorary doctorates from Holy Cross University, Los Angeles City College, Harvard University and Georgetown University. From 1962 until his death, he was vice president of ASCAP.

Jimmy McHugh died of a heart attack at his home in Beverly Hills on May 23, 1969. "When they talk about great composers," said Stanley Adams, then president of ASCAP, in his eulogy, "the talk is meaningless unless the name of Jimmy McHugh is mentioned among the elite, the royalty of singdom, the Titans of Tin Pan Alley." The following year, the University of Southern California established in his memory an annual award for composition students.

Many of McHugh's songs—some of the less well-known as well as the standards—were revived in *Sugar Babies* (1979), a long-run revue (1,208 performances) recalling the days of burlesque, which starred Mickey Rooney and Ann Miller. On May 23, 1969, at St. Peter's Church in Manhattan, a jazz-accented musical tribute to McHugh and many of his standards was given.

ABOUT: Rigdon, W. (ed.) The Biographical Encyclopedia & Who's Who of the American Theatre, 1966; Wilder, A. American Popular Song, 1972. *Periodicals*—New York Times May 24, 1969.

JOHNNY MERCER

MERCER, JOHNNY (November 18, 1909– June 25, 1976). Although Johnny Mercer composed some excellent and successful melodies, he is best remembered as a lyricist. He won four Oscars and earned the rare distinction of having 14 of his songs reach first position on *Your Hit Parade*. He was prolific, having written about 1,500 songs for more than 70 films and seven Broadway musicals; many have become standards. He was versatile, able to adapt to the varied musical styles of such well-known composers as Harold Arlen, Hoagy Carmichael, Henry Mancini, Jerome Kern, and others. He was also a founder and president of Capitol Records.

John H. Mercer, who was of Scottish descent, was born in Savannah, Georgia, the son of George A. Mercer, a real estate man, and Lillian Mercer. Johnny was said to have been able to repeat any tune his aunt sang to him when he was six months old. At four, he showed an interest in popular songs; at ten, he was writing verses. He learned songs by listening to recordings on the family phonograph, or by singing them with his family at the living-room piano. "By the time I was 11 or 12, I really knew most of the songs by heart. Knew the verses. . . . I remember that one of the songs was 'When It's Apple Time in Normandy.' A lot of songs made me cry."

He tried to play the trumpet and made an attempt to organize a band; both were soon abandoned. He never received any musical instruction and he remained unable to read music throughout his life.

From 1922 to 1927, he attended the Woodbury Forest Preparatory School in Orange, Virginia, where his hobby was writing poems in the style of Edgar Guest. As a high school student, he composed the words and music of his first song, "Sister Susie, Strut Your Stuff," already revealing his predilection for alliteration. After graduating from the Woodbury School, he worked in a real estate office in Savannah, using his free hours to act with the Savannah Little Theater. In 1927, the group went to New York to participate in the Belasco Cup competition, from which it emerged with first prize. Mercer decided to remain in New York, determined to be a professional actor. He made his Broadway debut in 1928 as Volpone's slave in Ben Jonson's *Volpone,* then played a minor role in *Houseparty* (1929) and appeared as an extra in Eugene O'Neill's *Marco Millions* (1930).

In 1930, Mercer auditioned for a singing role in the Broadway revue, *Garrick Gaieties of 1930.* He did not get the part, but did succeed in placing one of his songs in the show, "Out of Breath and Scared to Death" (music by Everett Miller), which was introduced by Sterling Holloway. "I tried to be a singer and failed," he later recalled. "I tried to be an actor and failed. So I just naturally fell into lyric-writing."

One of his lyrics, "Every Time I Shave I Cut Myself With a Razor," attracted the attention of Eddie Cantor who commissioned Mercer to write more verses for it. Though Cantor never performed it, his encouragement meant much to Mercer. Mercer went on to write lyrics for *Jazz City,* a revue which was never produced.

In spite of these professional setbacks, Mercer had married Ginger Meehan, a dancer from the *Garrick Gaieties of 1930,* on June 8, 1931. They rented a modest apartment in Brooklyn, and before long began raising a son and daughter.

Mercer soon discovered that he was unable to

support his family by songwriting. For a time, he worked as a runner on Wall Street while continuing to write and market his lyrics. "Satan's Li'l Lamb" (lyrics written with E. Y. Harburg, music by Harold Arlen) and "Would'ja for a Big Red Apple?" (lyrics written with Everett Miller, music by Henry Souvaine) were all placed in the Broadway revue, *Americana* (1932). The following year, Mercer collaborated with Hoagy Carmichael, producing his first big hit song, "Lazybones," which used a melody adapted from Carmichael's *Washboard Blues.*

Mercer entered Paul Whiteman's "Youth of America" contest for unknown singers, and in 1933, Whiteman asked him to organize a trio for a radio broadcast. A two-year affiliation ensued with the Whiteman orchestra during which Mercer served not only as vocalist but also as emcee and writer of special material. But Mercer was not idle as a songwriter. In 1933 and 1934, he wrote lyrics for "You Have Taken My Heart" (music by Gordon Jenkins), introduced by Lanny Ross and recorded by Joe Venuti and his orchestra; "If I Had a Million Dollars" (music by Matty Malneck), which was recorded by Eddie Stone, was sung by the Boswell Sisters in the film, *Transatlantic Merry-Go-Round* (1934); and "P. S. I Love You" (music by Jenkins), recorded by Rudy Vallee, Eddie Stone and Will Osborne, and revived in a hit recording by The Hilltoppers in 1953. Other songs of this period include "Here Come the British" (music by Bernard Henighen), "Pardon My Southern Accent" (music by Malneck), one of many lyrics inspired by Mercer's Southern background, and "Moon Country" (music by Carmichael).

On the strength of his mounting success as lyricist and recording artist (particularly in his duets with Jack Teagarden), Mercer received a songwriting and acting contract from the RKO Studios in Hollywood for two films, *To Beat the Band* and *Old Man Rhythm,* both released in 1935. With Matty Malneck as composer, Mercer wrote "Eeny, Meeny, Miney, Mo," which he himself introduced in *To Beat the Band*; it was popularized by Fred Astaire on radio and Mercer's recording of it with Ginger Rogers was heard on *Your Hit Parade.* "Have You Got Any Castles, Baby?" (music by Richard Whiting) from *Varsity Show* (1935) was also quite popular.

New hit songs followed in 1936: "I'm Building Up to an Awful Let Down" (music by Fred Astaire) was popularized in recordings by Astaire and Eddie Duchin, and was the first song for which Mercer wrote both the music and the words; "I'm an Old Cowhand" was interpolated into the film *Rhythm on the Range* for Bing

Crosby; it returned to the screen sung by Roy Rogers in the *King of the Cowboys* (1943). Also in 1936, "Goody, Goody" (music by Malneck) was the first of Mercer's 14 songs to reach first place on *Your Hit Parade.* Benny Goodman featured it at concerts, recorded it, and performed it in *The Benny Goodman Story* (1955); it was also recorded by Bob Crosby.

Subsequent hits to occupy first position on *Your Hit Parade* during the late 1930s were "Lost" (1936; written with Phil Ohman and Macy O. Teetor); "You Must Have Been a Beautiful Baby" (1938) and "Jeepers, Creepers" (music by Harry Warren), both written while under contract to Warner Brothers Studios (1937–39) and the latter introduced by Louis Armstrong in the film *Going Places* (1938); "Day In—Day Out" (1939), a song that enjoyed considerable circulation among the big bands of Tommy Dorsey, Bob Crosby, Artie Shaw and others during the 1940s; as well as "And the Angels Sing" (1939, music by Ziggy Elman). Originally a number for Elman, the trumpet player in Goodman's band, "Angels Sing" was later introduced with Mercer's superimposed lyrics by Goodman with singer Martha Tilton; it was recorded by the Mills Brothers, Kate Smith and Count Basie. Also popular in the late 1930s were "Hooray for Hollywood" from *Hollywood Hotel* (1937), and "Too Marvelous for Words," from *Ready, Willing and Able* (1939), the music for both composed by Richard Whiting, as well as "Bob White" (1937, music by Bernie Henighen) and "I Thought About You" (1937, music by James Van Heusen).

By 1940, Mercer was well-established as a jazz singer and songwriter, and his career began to branch out in many directions. He made many appearances on coast-to-coast radio programs, including the broadcasts of the Benny Goodman and Bob Crosby orchestras; the *Kraft Music Hall,* starring Bing Crosby, and *Paul Whiteman Presents*; on *Your Hit Parade,* he appeared as a singer, then costarred with Dinah Shore on *Call for Music*; he was also the star of *The Johnny Mercer Music Shop* (1945–46) and *The Johnny Mercer Show* (1953) on CBS.

In 1942, with B. G. De Sylva and Glenn Wallichs, Mercer founded Capitol Records. Its first release, on July 1, was Mercer's own "Strip Polka," for which he had written both music and lyrics and which was also recorded on other labels by the Andrews Sisters and by Alvino Rey and his orchestra with the King Sisters. As president of Capitol Records, Mercer promoted the careers of new artists, including Margaret Whiting, Jo Stafford, Peggy Lee and the King Cole Trio. He also helped the company to embark on innovative recording procedures, including a national transcription service for disc jockeys. By 1946, Capitol Records was earning nearly one million dollars a year in profits, and the company floated a three-million-dollar stock issue enabling it to acquire its own recording studios. Mercer later sold his interest in the company.

Mercer's prestige as a songwriter continued to grow in the 1940s; he renewed what became a particularly successful collaboration with Harold Arlen, and worked with Arlen and other distinguished composers on Hollywood musicals which produced a number of Oscar nominations: "The Love of My Life" (music by Artie Shaw) from *Second Chorus* (1940); "I'd Know You Anywhere" (music by Jimmy McHugh) from *You'll Find Out* (1940); the title song from *Blues in the Night* (music by Arlen); "Dearly Beloved" (music by Jerome Kern) from *You Were Never Lovelier* (1942) starring Fred Astaire; "My Shining Hour" (music by Arlen) from *The Sky's the Limit* (1943); and "Ac-cent-tchu-ate the Positive" (music by Arlen) from *Here Come the Waves* (1944). The elusive first Oscar was finally awarded in 1946 for "On the Atchison, Topeka and the Santa Fe" (music by Harry Warren) from *The Harvey Girls*. Other notable songs from the 1940s include "Mister Meadowbrook" (1940, music by Walter Donaldson); "That Old Black Magic" (music by Arlen) from *Star-Spangled Rhythm* (1942); "Tangerine" (music by Victor Schertzinger) from *The Fleet's In* (1942); "Dream" (1944, words and music by Mercer); and "Laura," from the Otto Preminger film of that title starring Gene Tierney. Soon after the release of the film, Mercer wrote lyrics for David Raskin's music; the new version was introduced by Johnny Johnson and the recording by Woody Herman sold more than one million copies.

Mercer returned to Broadway in the 1940s, this time as a lyricist. His first musical, *Walk With Music* (June 4, 1940), written with Hoagy Carmichael, was a failure. His next show, *St. Louis Woman* (March 30, 1946), an Arlen collaboration, starred Ruby Hill in an all-black cast that also featured Pearl Bailey; its finest songs were "Come Rain or Come Shine," and "Legalize My Name." Though *St. Louis Woman* was critically acclaimed, it, too, was a box-office disappointment. *Texas, Li'l Darlin'* (November 25, 1949) fared somewhat better with a modest run of 293 performances. The book was written by John Whedon and Sam Moore, the music by popular musician Robert Emmett Dolan. The plot revolved around Hominy Smith, a psalm-singing Texas politician with presidential aspirations. One musical number to achieve a certain popularity was "The Big Movie Show in the

Sky," a revival-meeting hymn introduced by Danny Scholl.

Top Banana (November 1, 1951) had a respectable run of 350 performances, but it also suffered a financial deficit. Both the book and the music were written by Hy Kraft. *Top Banana* was a satire on television, then in its infancy, and one of its top comics, reputedly inspired by Milton Berle. Jeffrey Biffle, a brash, loud, self-assured egomaniac, was boisterously portrayed by Phil Silvers. A warm ballad, "Only if You're in Love," introduced by Lindy Donerty and Judy Lynn, was one of the memorable songs from the score.

Mercer's greatest success on Broadway came with *L'il Abner* (November 15, 1956), which ran for 693 performances. The book by Norman Panama and Malvin Frank was based on the world of Dogpatch from Al Capp's cartoon strips. On Sadie Hawkins Day, Daisy Mae pursues bachelor L'il Abner, also sought after by Appassionata von Climax. They then learn the United States government plans to confiscate Dogpatch and use it as a testing ground for the atomic bomb. Dogpatch is saved when it is discovered that President Lincoln had once declared it a shrine. Gene de Paul composed the music and Michael Kidd was the choreographer; highlights of the show included the satirical "Jubilation T. Cornpone," a showstopper introduced by Stubby Kaye, and the sentimental "Namely You," introduced by Edith Adams and Peter Palmer. The 1959 screen adaptation of *Li'l Abner* adhered faithfully to the stage production and included many performers from the Broadway cast.

Mercer's last two Broadway musicals were box-office disasters. *Saratoga* (December 7, 1959), based on Edna Ferber's novel, with a score by Mercer and Arlen, survived only 80 performances. *Foxy* (February 16, 1964), a musical adaptation of *Volpone,* had an even shorter existence (76 performances). Robert Emmett Dolan composed music for Mercer's lyrics and a ballad, "Talk to Me, Baby," introduced by John Davidson and Julienne Marie, was made popular through a recording by Frank Sinatra.

While Mercer was not an unqualified success on Broadway, his popularity as a lyricist continued to grow during the 1950s. He wrote new lyrics for "The Bilbao Song" from Kurt Weill's *Happy End* (1929), which were sung by Andy Williams in 1951, and the following year his witty version of "Glow Worm" from Paul Lincke's operetta, *Lysistrata* (1902), was recorded by the Mills Brothers and sung by Janet Leigh in the film, *Walkin' My Baby Back Home* (1953). He also provided lyrics for "Satin Doll" (music by

Duke Ellington and Billy Strayhorn) in 1959, as well as for "Autumn Leaves" (music by Joseph Kosma). "Autumn Leaves" was a French instrumental piece recorded by Roger Williams in 1955; the following year it was sung with Mercer's new lyrics by Nat King Cole as the title song of a motion picture starring Joan Crawford, and it was later recorded by Duke Ellington. Mercer also had a hit from an unexpected source: in 1959, Sadie Vimmerstedt, a housewife, sent him a song idea, asking for his reaction. Mercer liked the idea so much that he decided to collaborate with Mrs. Vimmerstedt; Tony Bennett's recording of the finished product, "I Wanna Be Around," became a bestseller in 1963.

Mercer also continued to write songs for Hollywood motion pictures. In 1951, he won an Oscar for "In the Cool, Cool, Cool of the Evening" (music by Carmichael), introduced by Bing Crosby in Here Comes the Groom. He collaborated with Gene de Paul on songs for Seven Brides for Seven Brothers (1954), and wrote both words and music for "Something's Got to Give," sung by Fred Astaire in Daddy Long Legs (1955). In 1961, Mercer began a long and fruitful partnership with Henry Mancini. They received Oscars for "Moon River" from Breakfast at Tiffany's (1961), and for the title song from The Days of Wine and Roses (1962). Their collaboration also produced many other memorable songs, among them the title song from Charade (1963), "The Sweetheart Tree" from The Great Race (1965), and "Whistling Away the Dark" from Darling Lili (1969), winner of the Golden Globe Award. Mercer also wrote lyrics for "Emily" from The Americanization of Emily (1964), and the title song from Love With a Proper Stranger (1963; music by Elmer Bernstein).

Johnny Mercer described his work habits to Max Wilk in They're Playing Our Song: "I'm best when I get up. . . . I feel good. I work for about half a morning or half a day. If I get tired, I quit. Don't come back. Let my subconscious do the work; it's a remarkable instrument. I have a study—always have had a room where people will leave me alone. When I really start to work at it, I get a lot of paper and I go to the typewriter and I type dozens of alternative lines. Then I look at those lines, and I gradually weed out the poor ones until I think, 'Now I've got the best.'" About composing, Mercer said he would hear "the chords in my head and then I'll play [the melody] with one finger." He notated his music with the aid of an arranger employed by the film studio, a role later assumed by his son-in-law, a trained pianist: "Together we find the chords, and he writes them down for me."

Mercer maintained a home in Savannah, Georgia, and an apartment in New York, but his main residence was in Los Angeles. "John was an odd sort of a duck, cantakerous and kind, humurous and morose, a combination of poetry and bitterness," said Gene Lees in High Fidelity. Though difficult to believe in view of his prodigious output, Mercer was lackadaisical about meeting deadlines. He liked to swim (particularly in the ocean) and to paint in watercolor; he also enjoyed playing tennis and golf.

Johnny Mercer died at his home in Bel-Air on June 25, 1976, following surgery for a brain tumor the preceding October from which he never recovered. His ashes were buried in Savannah, and memorial services were held in July in the Green Room of the Music Box Theatre in New York.

In 1982, his widow donated a collection of Mercer memorabilia to Georgia State University in Atlanta. It included all of his published songs, photographs, letters, awards and an unpublished autobiography.

A Johnny Mercer retrospective, I Remember Johnny: The Magic of Mercer, was held at the YMHA in New York on June 3 and 4, 1984; Margaret Whiting and Julius La Rosa were among the participants.

ABOUT: Craig, W. The Great Songwriters of Hollywood, 1980, Sweet and Lowdown: America's Popular Song Writers, 1978; Wilk, M. They're Playing Our Song, 1973. Periodicals—American Film, December-January 1978; ASCAP Today September 1971; High Fidelity June 1967, October 1976; New York Times June 26, 1976; New Yorker February 17, 1973.

MERRILL, BOB (May 17, 1921–), composer-lyricist, was born Henry Robert Merrill Levan in Atlantic City, New Jersey to James Arthur Levan, a candy-maker, and Sadie (Abrahams) Levan. While he was young, his family moved to Philadelphia, where he was raised and educated. As a young man, he frequently traveled around the country, supporting himself with odd jobs such as loading boats, harvesting crops, and ushering in movie theaters. Between 1935 and 1941 he found engagements as singer and mimic in nightclubs and vaudeville. Upon graduating from Simon Gratz High School in 1938, he attended Temple University briefly, and in 1939 he joined the Bucks County Playhouse in Pennsylvania where he studied acting with Richard Bennett.

From 1940 to 1942, Merrill served as a sergeant, first in the Cavalry and then in Special Services, writing and producing radio shows for

BOB MERRILL

the armed forces. Upon leaving the army, he hitchhiked to California where he found employment at the NBC studios supervising writers (1943–44). From 1943 to 1948, he was dialogue director at Columbia Pictures; he also played minor roles in several films.

At Columbia Pictures, Dorothy Shay, "the Park Avenue Hillbillie," then employed as an extra in a Western film, suggested he write some songs for a comedy album she was planning. Merrill had had no musical training and also had harbored no ambition to be a songwriter. "She kept after me," he recalled, "and there was nothing else to do, so I finally wrote a few for her." A recording contract and a check for $500 for his contributions was sufficient encouragement to write more songs.

His first songs were romantic ballads. "Why Does it Have to Rain on Sunday?" (1947, written with Vi Ott) was introduced in a recording by Freddy Martin and his orchestra; "Lover's Gold" (1948), for which he wrote lyrics to Morty Nevins's music, was introduced by the Three Suns, recorded by Dinah Shore and appeared on *Your Hit Parade*; "Fool's Paradise," for which he wrote music as well as words, was introduced by Billy Eckstine in 1949. That year, with Terry Shand, he also composed a novelty number, "The Chicken Song," which was featured by Guy Lombardo and His Royal Canadians.

Between 1949 and 1956, Merrill worked as production consultant for the Cunningham-Walsh Agency and for the Liggett and Myers Tobacco Company. Merrill's first hit song, another novelty number, appeared in 1950. "If I Knew You Were Comin' I'd've Baked a Cake,"

was written in collaboration with Al Hoffman and Clem Watts. Eileen Barton's recording of it sold one million discs, and it appeared on *Your Hit Parade* in first position.

During the 1950s, Merrill began to serve as both composer and lyricist and produced a series of songs heard on *Your Hit Parade*: in 1950, "Candy and Cake" recorded by Arthur Godfrey and by Mindy Carson; in 1951, "Sparrow on the Treetop" and "My Truly, Truly Fair," each popularized in recordings by Guy Mitchell with Mitch Miller; in 1952, "How Much is That Doggie in the Window" (sales of the bestselling recordings by Patti Page and others exceeded five million copies); in 1953, a parody of it called "That Hound Dog in the Window," recorded by Homer and Jethro; in 1954, "Honeycomb," later recorded by Jimmie Rodgers in 1957; "Tina Maria," introduced by and the specialty of Perry Como; and "Make Yourself Comfortable," recorded by Sarah Vaughan.

Between 1950 and 1957, recordings of many of Merrill's other songs also became bestsellers. Among these were Mindy Carson performing "I'm Bashful" in 1950; the Fontaine Sisters, "Let Me In" in 1952; Guy Mitchell with Mitch Miller, "Red Feathers" in 1952 and "Pittsburgh, Pennsylvania" and "Feet Up" in 1953; Sammy Kaye and his orchestra, "Walkin' to Missouri" in 1953; Patti Page, "Butterflies," and Mahalia Jackson, "Rusty Old Halo" in 1954; Rosemary Clooney, "Mambo Italiano" and "Where Will the Dimple Be" in 1955; Teresa Brewer, "A Sweet Old-Fashioned Girl" in 1956. Though these songs made Merrill wealthy, "They're not the kind of songs I wanted to write," he claims. "But every time I brought a ballad to my music publisher he wouldn't even listen—he'd crumple it up and throw it away. It was that frustration that made me turn to the theater."

In 1956, Merrill signed the first four-way contract ever awarded by MGM: producer, composer, writer and publisher. His first assignment was to compose a score for a film musical based on Eugene O'Neill's somber Pulitzer Prize-winning drama, *Anna Christie* (1921). The film never materialized, but the idea to make *Anna Christie* into a musical comedy was born. George Abbott adapted the text, and Merrill prepared the score. Renamed *New Girl in Town,* it opened on Broadway on May 14, 1957, where it remained for 431 performances. Gwen Verdon played the heroine, a prostitute suffering from tuberculosis who has come to New York to seek her father's help. There, she falls in love with Mat, an Irish seaman, who eventually learns to accept her past. Merrill's songs brought him an award from the Drama Critics Circle; these included

"Sunshine Girl," a ballad introduced by Dale Anderson, Eddie Phillips and Mike Dawson; the showstopping "Flings," performed by Thelma Ritter; "Look at 'Er," sung by George Wallace; "Did You Close Your Eyes When We Kissed," and "It's Good to Be Alive." *New Girl in Town* was revived Off Broadway in 1975.

Merrill's success on Broadway continued with a second musical adaptation of an O'Neill play. With a book by Joseph Stein and Robert Russell, the nostalgic American comedy *Ah, Wilderness!* became *Take Me Along* (October 22, 1959). Walter Pidgeon starred as Nat Miller, a small-town newspaper editor in Connecticut at the turn of the century. Robert Morse played his adolescent son Richard, a victim of puppy love, and Jackie Gleason was Sid Davis, a reporter whose weakness for alcohol keeps him from marrying the Millers's neighbor, Lily, a woman devoted to him. "Since the story is moderately faithful to the original Eugene O'Neill comedy," wrote a critic for *Variety, Take Me Along* tends to be a quiet musical with little of the slam-bang rush and clamor of the usual Broadway song and dance fiesta . . . Mostly the tone is gentle and nostalgic." The title song, introduced by Jackie Gleason and Walter Pidgeon, to whose strains they then perform a soft-shoe, also became a hit song outside the theater. Puppy love found its voice in "I Would Die," a duet for Robert Morse and Susan Luckey; mature love in the ballads, "Promise Me a Rose," a duet for Jackie Gleason and Eileen Hurlie, and in "Staying Young," introduced by Walter Pidgeon. *Take Me Along* had an initial Broadway run of 448 performances; it was revived at Manhattan Community College and by the Goodspeed Opera House in East Haddam, Connecticut in 1984.

Carnival (April 13, 1961) was Merrill's greatest success on Broadway (719 performances). Based on the popular film, *Lili* (1953), *Carnival*'s book was written by Michael Stewart with material by Helen Deutsch, but it included a completely new musical score by Merrill. Anna Maria Alberghetti, in her Broadway debut, starred as Lili, the petite French waif enchanted by a southern European circus. She falls in love with its ill-tempered puppeteer, Paul Berthalet; the puppets, to whom Lili becomes attached, help to bring about the fulfillment of the romance. "*Carnival*," reported Richard Watts, Jr., "captures the quality of magic . . . Its charm, warmth and humor, abetted by a fresh and beautiful production, a delightful cast, a bright and attractive score by Bob Merrill, zestful dances, a colorful background and a pleasant romantic story make it a wonderfully winning and thoroughly enchanting entertainment." The Drama Critics Circle selected it as the year's best

musical and a poll of the New York drama critics named Merrill's score the best of the season. It included "Love Makes the World Go 'Round," introduced by Alberghetti and a recurring refrain throughout the show; the song rivalled the film's "Hi Lili, Hi Lo" in popularity. Alberghetti was also heard in "Mira," "Yes, My Heart" and "Beautiful Lady;" "Her Face" was introduced by Jerry Orbach.

Merrill expanded his songwriting experiences in the early sixties, first by writing both words and music for the Laurence Harvey film, *The Wonderful World of the Brothers Grimm* (1962). He then began a fruitful collaboration with Jule Styne by writing lyrics to Styne's music for the television specials *Mr. Magoo's Christmas Carol* (1962) and *The Dangerous Christmas of Red Riding Hood* (1965), starring Liza Minelli. Mercer and Styne also worked together on *Funny Girl,* which opened on Broadway (March 26, 1964) with Barbra Streisand as Fanny Brice. The show's principal songs were "People" and "Don't Rain on My Parade"; when *Funny Girl* was filmed in 1968, Merrill and Styne added several new numbers, including the title song.

Merrill's fortunes in the musical theater went into a sharp decline for several years. *Holly Golightly* (1966) was based on the motion picture derived from Truman Capote's story, *Breakfast at Tiffany's;* about this score, to which Merrill is particularly partial, he says: "The story gave me a marvelous opportunity to write some very sophisticated, urbane songs. For once I had a chance to be clever." But the production closed after out-of-town tryouts. *Henry, Sweet Henry* (October 23, 1967), for which Merrill also wrote both music and lyrics, opened on Broadway but lasted only 80 performances. The book, by Nunnally Johnson, was based on his daughter's novel, *The World of Henry Orient,* which had been recently released as a motion picture; the stage version starred Don Ameche.

In the 1970s, Merrill again collaborated with Jule Styne, first on *Prettybelle* (1971), a show which closed in Boston, and then on *Sugar* (April 9, 1972), a successful adaptation of the motion picture, *Some Like It Hot* (1959). His last theatrical venture was *The Prince of Grand Street* (1978), for which he wrote not only the songs (both words and music), but also a text that was a nostalgic recollection of Yiddish theater in New York in the early 1900s. It was never produced on Broadway.

Since 1978, Merrill has been writing screenplays for motion pictures such as *Mahogany* (1975), *W. C. Fields and Me* (1976), *Chu Chu and the Philly Flash* (1980) and *Portrait of a Showgirl* (1982). He has taught classes in the

American musical theater at the University of California in Los Angeles and has also served as Adjunct Professor in the Communication Arts Department at Loyola University in Los Angeles.

Merrill resides in Beverly Hills, California, and on December 13, 1976, he married Suzanne Reynolds, a radio newscaster in Hollywood. His hobbies include travel, fishing, and physical fitness programs.

We're Home, a revue featuring 37 songs by Bob Merrill, conceived and directed by Douglas Alabel, was produced Off Broadway on October 12, 1984.

ABOUT: Craig, W. Sweet and Lowdown: America's Popular Song Writers, 1978; Green, S. The World of Musical Comedy, 4th ed. 1980; *Periodicals*—New York Times October 12, 1984.

ROGER MILLER

MILLER, ROGER (January, 2, 1936–). Roger Dean Miller, a noted composer-lyricist of country music, was born in Fort Worth, Texas in 1936. When he was a year old, his father died and the Miller family moved to Erick, Oklahoma. Because his mother couldn't work *and* raise a family of three boys, he was brought up by E. D. and Armella Miller, his uncle and aunt, while his brothers and sisters were dispatched elsewhere to find homes.

His uncle was a poor farmer, and Miller helped out by doing chores at five in the morning before walking three miles to school. "The school I went to," he recalled," had 37 students, me and 36 Indians. . . . During recess, we used to play cowboy and Indians."

He remained in school through the eighth grade while taking whatever odd jobs were available. He worked as a ranch hand, herded cattle, dehorned bulls and rode in rodeos, yet found the time to learn to play guitar, an instrument bought with money he earned by picking cotton. His inspiration in music had been Hank Williams, the soon-to-be-legendary country blues singer and composer. About this time, Roger began writing songs, drawing from his own experience for numbers about the unsatisfied need for the love of an absent mother, loneliness and poverty. He entered local talent contests, capturing first prize more than once. With the money he won Miller bought a fiddle which he taught himself to play.

When war broke out in Korea, Miller enlisted in the U.S. Army. For a time, he drove a truck in Korea, but was soon reassigned to Special Service as a member of a country western/bluegrass band which entertained the troops. With this group, he played the guitar, fiddle and drums, and occasionally performed songs he had written.

Following his discharge after three years of military service, Miller found a job as a fireman in Amarillo, Texas. He was dismissed after two months. "There were only two fires during the time I was with them," he recalled. "The first was a chicken coop. I slept through the second one; that was when they fired me." Set on becoming a professional musician, Miller traveled to Nashville, arriving with just enough cash for a single night's lodging. He worked as a bellboy at the Andrew Jackson Hotel while peddling his songs to publishers, performers and record company executives. The head of one label eventually gave him a contract, but Miller's first three releases failed so dismally that the contract was allowed to lapse. The recording artist Ray Price then hired him to sing in his traveling show, and recorded Miller's "Invitation to the Blues."

In 1958 the popular country singer Ernest Tubbs recorded Miller's "Half a Mind," which sold moderately well, and two years later Miller began recording his own songs for RCA Victor. Among his earliest releases were "You Don't Want My Love," "Sorry Willie" and "Teardrops" (all 1960). Other performers, moreover, were beginning to record his songs: Andy Williams covered, "You Don't Want My Love"; Jim Reeves, "Billy Bayou"; Faron Young, "A World So Full of Love" (written in collaboration with Young); Jaye P. Morgan, "A World I Can't Live In"; Hawkshaw Hawkins, "Much Too Well" (written with Hawkins).

Although Miller, like most popular country

and western and rock songwriters, could not read or write music, others performed this chore for him, and he was becoming an increasingly prolific composer. In 1961 Miller himself recorded "The Moon is High and So Am I"; "It Takes All Kinds to Make a World"; "Every Which-a-Way" and "When Two Worlds Collide." The last of these, written in collaboration with Bill Anderson, was Miller's first song to reach the top-ten charts. In 1962 Miller recorded "Hitch-Hiker," "Hey, Little Star," "I'll Pick Up My Heart" and "I Catch Myself Crying," while Kitty Wells recorded "A Heartache for Keepsake" and Jimmy Elledge released "Golden Tear." That same year Miller played drums for the country star Faron Young's band and appeared as a guest artist on Tennessee Ernie Ford's popular television variety show. Miller's last recording for RCA Victor, "Lock, Stock and Barrel," was released in 1963.

It was about this time that Miller, who has a colorful personality and a quick, droll wit, moved to Hollywood, where he joined an actor's workshop. However, this ambition to succeed in the theater was abandoned when "Dang Me," Miller's first record on the Smash label, soared on both the pop and country charts in 1964. Miller's first record to sell a million discs, "Dang Me" also brought him his first Grammy Awards, for the year's best country song, best country single and best country performance. Miller's follow-up single, "Chug-a-Lug," quickly earned him his second gold record.

Miller's greatest song success came in 1965 with "King of the Road," his autobiographical number which has become a standard. "King of the Road" sold half a million discs in the first 18 days of its release, ultimately passing the two-million mark. Receiving royalties as performer, composer and lyricist, Miller earned more than $150,000 from the song in one year. "King of the Road" has been recorded by more than 125 artists and translated into 30 languages. It brought Miller five Grammys in 1965, for best country song, best country single, best country performance, best rock 'n' roll single and best rock 'n' roll performance by a man. A sixth Grammy came for his album, *The Return of Roger Miller* (1965). In 1970 BMI presented the song with its award for being one of the most often-performed country tunes over a five-year period. Exploiting the song's enormous popularity, a songwriter named M. Taylor prepared a new set of lyrics for Miller's melody and titled it "Queen of the House." It was introduced and popularized by Jody Miller (Roger Miller's first wife) in a bestseller that received a Grammy in 1965 as the best country female vocal performance. Another Miller-composed-and-recorded hit at this time was "Do Wacka Do."

In 1965 Miller composed and recorded "Engine, Engine, Number Nine," "England Swings" (inspired by a visit to London on his first trip to Europe), "Kansas City Star (That's What I Are)" and "One Dyin' and a-Buryin'." That year Eddie Arnold had a bestseller with his recording of Miller's "The Last Word in Lonesome is Me." In 1966 came Roger Miller's successful recording of his song "Husbands and Wives," and Andy Williams's recording of Miller's "In the Summertime" sold two million copies.

Between 1965 and 1967, four of Miller's albums each sold in excess of a million copies: *Roger Miller/Dang Me; The Return of Roger Miller; Roger Miller/Golden Hits* and *Roger Miller, The Third Time Around.* Now a superstar, he appeared as a guest performer on Andy Williams's television program late in 1965, which led to a half-hour Roger Miller special on NBC on January 19, 1966. Miller's weekly television variety show premiered in the fall of 1966. That the series was a failure—and that Miller's went into decline at this time—can in part be attributed to his having been a "party animal," which seems to have led to his problem with amphetamines. "Before I knew it," he told an interviewer, "I was in a kind of snake pit. Pills were all I ever took." Miller said of his decision to quit drugs in 1969: "I decided one day I was going to be a man or a vegetable. . . . Only after my performance fell below par, my ability to concentrate declined, and my attitude towards people began to worsen, did I face the truth that you can't function with pills." In 1967, during this difficult period, he composed and recorded "Walking in the Sunshine." In 1968 he had a bestselling recording in his version of "Little Green Apples," which had been written by Bobby Russell. The album *Roger Miller: 1970* included only one of Miller's own songs, "I Know Who it Is."

For the remainder of the 1970s, Miller's career, as he remarked, "just got quiet, real quiet." With his recordings and public appearances reduced to an absolute minimum, he lived in virtual retirement in Los Angeles with his third wife, Mary Arnold, whom he married on February 14, 1978, and their son. They left Los Angeles about a year later for a remodeled adobe house outside Santa Fe, New Mexico. In 1981, after recent years of playing on the nightclub circuit, Miller signed a contract with Elektra Records, his first release, a single composed by Miller, coming the same year, "Everyone Gets Crazy Now and Then." In 1982 he recorded *Old Friends,* a duet album with Willie Nelson, for which he composed all the songs and whose title song became Miller's first in years to make the charts. Miller also returned to the public performing circuit, having signed a new management contract with Scotti Brothers of Los Angeles in 1982.

Miller's comeback was no longer a tentative one when *Big River; The Adventures of Huckleberry Finn* (April 25, 1985), with libretto by William Hauptman and score by Miller, was named the best musical of 1985. Miller himself received his first Tony Award, for best music and lyrics. In the 18-song score, Miller's best-received numbers were the folk ballad "River in the Rain," "Guv'ment," the gospel-like "How Blest We Are," and Jim's anthem, "Free at Last," inspired by the epitaph on Martin Luther King Jr.'s gravestone.

Beyond his activities as composer and performer, Miller has been the president of Dang Me Products and the proprietor of the King of the Road Motor Hotel in Nashville.

ABOUT: Current Biography, 1986; Stambler, I. and Landon, G. Encyclopedia of Folk, Country and Western Music, 1983. *Periodicals*—New Yorker March 1, 1968; New York Times May 5, 1985, June 23, 1985.

MONACO, JIMMY (January 13, 1885–October 16, 1945), composer, was born in Genoa, Italy on January 13, 1885. In 1891, his family immigrated to the United States, settling in Chicago. Monaco learned to play the piano without instruction, and at 17, he began earning a living playing ragtime at the Savoy and other Chicago night spots where he became known as "Ragtime Jimmy." In 1910, he moved to New York, where, he found employment performing piano rags at the Bohemia Club on West 29th Street and in several Coney Island saloons.

His songwriting career began in 1911 with "Oh, Mr. Dream Man," which was recorded that year by Walter Van Brunt. The following year, he composed his first song to be published, "Oh, You Circus Day" (lyrics by Edith Maida Lessing); it was introduced on Broadway by Florence Moore and Billy Montgomery in the musical extravaganza, *Hanky-Panky* (August 5, 1912). Two subsequent hits that year established Monaco's reputation in Tin Pan Alley. The first, "Row, Row, Row" (lyrics by William Jerome), was introduced by Lillian Lorraine in the *Ziegfeld Follies of 1912* and recorded that year by Ada Jones. It later made several important appearances in motion pictures, including *The Story of Vernon and Irene Castle* (1939), *The Eddie Cantor Story* (1954) and *The Seven Little Foys (1955)*.

The second, "You Made Me Love You" (lyrics by Joseph McCarthy), was introduced by Al Jolson in *The Honeymoon Express* (February,

1913) at the Winter Garden Theater. In his delivery, Jolson initiated a gesture to which he remained partial throughout his career: sinking to one knee and stretching his arms out to the audience. He recorded the song in 1913 and 1946, and performed it in the films *The Jolson Story* (1946) and *Jolson Sings Again* (1949). Fanny Brice also featured it in her vaudeville routine, and the young Judy Garland revealed her potential as a singer when she sang the song for the first time at a birthday party for Clark Gable, with additional lyrics written for the occasion by Roger Eden. Louis B. Mayer was so taken with her performance that he insisted she repeat it in the film, *Broadway Melody of 1938*. Ruth Etting, Grace La Rue and Bing Crosby also performed this ballad, and it was featured in many films of the 1930s, 1940s, and 1950s.

During the teens, Monaco added new hit songs to his credits. In 1913, "I Miss You Most of All" and "I'm Crying for You" (lyrics by McCarthy) were recorded by Edna Brown and Ada Jones with Billy Murray respectively. These were followed by "Pigeon Walk," (1914), and "If We Can't Be the Same Old Sweethearts" (1915; lyrics by McCarthy). In 1916, two of his songs were heard on Broadway: "You're a Doggone Dangerous Girl" (lyrics by Grant Clarke) was incorporated into the Jolson vehicle, *Robinson Crusoe, Jr.* (February 17, 1916), and "What Do You Want to Make Those Eyes at Me For?" (lyrics by McCarthy) was sung by Henry Lewis to Anna Held in the musical *Follow Me* (November 29, 1916). The latter was recorded by Ada Jones with Billy Murray, and popularized in vaudeville by Emma Carus; subsequently, it was interpolated into several films in the mid-1940s. "Honolulu Blues" (lyrics by Clarke) was also written that year, a time when songs about exotic places were in demand in Tin Pan Alley; it was recorded by the Peerless Quartette.

Monaco's achievements of the 1920s were equally impressive. "Caresses," for which he wrote his own lyrics, was introduced by the internationally known Alice Delysia in the Broadway musical, *Afgar* (November 8, 1920), and recorded by the Carl Fenton orchestra. In 1922, "You Know You Belong to Somebody Else" (lyrics by Eugene Westlyn) was popularized in vaudeville and later recorded by Nora Bayes. "Dirty Hands, Dirty Face" (lyrics by Edgar Leslie and Grant Clarke) was recorded the next year by Ben Selvin and his orchestra and by Joe Raymond; it became popular when Al Jolson sang it in *The Jazz Singer* (1927) from which he emerged as the first singing star of talking pictures in addition to his Broadway successes. Monaco also contributed to *Delmar's Revels* (November 28, 1927), a revue in which Bert

Lahr made his Broadway debut; "I Love a Man in Uniform" (lyrics by Billy Rose and Ballard MacDonald), was sung by Winnie Lightner while the Chester Hale Girls danced. Other successes of the twenties include "Me and My Boyfriend" (lyrics by Sidney Clare) and "The Only, Only One" (composed with Harry Warren, lyrics by Bud Green) from 1924; "Red Lips, Kiss My Blues Away" (1927, composed with Pete Wendling, lyrics by Alfred Bryan); "Me and the Man in the Moon" (1928, lyrics by Leslie); and "Through" (1929, lyrics by McCarthy), which was introduced by Glen Gray and the Casa Loma Orchestra and recorded by the Ted Lewis orchestra.

After 1930, Monaco composed songs for approximately 16 motion pictures. The most noteworthy of these early screen songs was "Crazy People" (lyrics by Leslie), introduced by the Boswell Sisters in *The Big Broadcast* (1932). In 1936, Monaco signed a contract with Paramount. There, working with Johnny Burke as lyricist, he composed songs for six films starring Bing Crosby. All were introduced and recorded by Crosby, and those featured on *Your Hit Parade* included "On the Sentimental Side," sung with Mary Carlisle in *Doctor Rhythm (1928);* "I've Got a Pocketful of Dreams" from *Sing, You Sinners* (1938); "An Apple for Teacher" (sung with Linda Ware and revived by Gene Autry in *The Last Round-Up* [1947]); "A Man and His Dreams," and "Go Fly a Kite" from *The Star Maker* (1939); "Too Romantic," sung with Dorothy Lamour in *The Road to Singapore* (1940); and "Only Forever," from *Rhythm on the River* (1940).

Monaco's songs continued to be heard on *Your Hit Parade* during the 1940s, among them "Six Lessons From Madame La Zonga" (1940, lyrics by Charles Newman), popularized in a recording by Jimmy Dorsey (vocals by Bob Eberle and Helen O'Connell) and sung by Lupe Velez in the film of the same title; "I'm Making Believe" (lyrics by Mack Gordon), introduced in *Sweet and Low-Down* (1944), and recorded by Ella Fitzgerald with the Ink Spots; and "I Can't Begin to Tell You" (lyrics by Gordon), introduced by John Payne and reprised by Betty Grable in *The Dolly Sisters* (1945).

Monaco has composed a number of other memorable songs. These include "That Sly Old Gentleman" from *East Side of Heaven* (1939); "That's for Me" (lyrics by Johnny Burke), sung by Bing Crosby and Mary Martin in *Rhythm on the River;* "Ev'ry Night About This Time" (1942; lyrics by Ted Koehler), recorded by the Ink Spots and by Kay Kyser; "We Mustn't Say Goodbye" (lyrics by Al Dubin), introduced by the Vaughn Monroe orchestra in *Stage Door Canteen* (1943); "Once Too Often," and "Time Will Tell" (lyrics by Gordon) from *Pin-Up Girl* (1944), which were both introduced by Charlie Spivak and his orchestra, the former with Betty Grable; it was also recorded by Ella Fitzgerald. Monaco's last successful song, "Crying for Joy" (lyrics by Billy Rose), was introduced and popularized by Dinah Shore in 1948, three years after Monaco's death.

Jimmy Monaco died of a heart attack in Beverly Hills, California.

ABOUT: Craig, W. Sweet and Lowdown: America's Popular Song Writers; 1978. *Periodicals*—New York Herald Tribune October 18, 1945.

NEWMAN, RANDY (November 28, 1943–). In the late 1960s composer-lyricist Randy Newman gained a cult following among the pop-rock cognoscenti with ironic, wryly observed songs that were often written from the ambiguous point of view of all-American grotesques—a rogues' gallery of disreputable characters unlike anything in American writing since the heyday of Flannery O'Connor. A decade later Newman's sophisticated, appealing melodies were reaching a much larger audience while he continued to address such subjects as loneliness, sexual maladjustment, cruelty, poverty, bigotry, chauvinism, the silence of God, middle-class distress, marital boredom, old age and death. "I've always been interested in things that are faintly abnormal, slight aberrations one way or another," he told Susan Lydon in *The New York Times Magazine.* "I write nonheroic things." Newman has been called "Stephen Foster with a lobotomy," and in *The New York Times* (June 25, 1972) Don Heckman wrote that Newman is "carving out an area of expression for popular song that hasn't been rivaled for lyric sophistication and musical complexity since the salad days of Cole Porter. [His music] is a brilliantly realized amalgam of Americana—one hears minstrel shows and marching bands, blues singers and jazz players."

He was born in Los Angeles, the older of two sons of Irving Newman, a physician, and his wife Adele. Three of Randy's uncles were successful composers and conductors for motion pictures—Alfred, Emil and Lionel Newman. (Al Newman had approximately 200 screen credits and received nine Academy Awards.) Between 1944 and 1946, while Irving Newman served in the armed forces, the family lived in New Orleans, Mobile, Alabama, and Jackson, Mississippi. Randy was seven when his father's military ser-

RANDY NEWMAN

vice came to an end and Irving Newman moved to Los Angeles to begin a successful practice in internal medicine. Encouraged by his father, an amateur musician, Randy began studying the piano when he was seven and theory five years later. By the time he was 15, Newman was composing songs. He regularly visited the film studios where his uncles were employed—"I know my uncle Al's music the way I know Brahms," he once told an interviewer—and was encouraged by Lenny Waronker, the son of the founder of Liberty Records. Lenny Waronker would later produce Newman's albums and himself become an influential executive with the Warner Brothers recording label.

In addition to his early involvement with music, Newman was a voracious reader and a diehard baseball fan. He devoutly memorized the statistics of the baseball greats who became his heroes. And although his eyes were badly crossed, Newman was an ace pitcher on his Little League baseball team. Newman's father believes Randy was an introverted loner in adolescence because he was "shattered, crushed" when a series of operations by eminent specialists failed to correct his eyes, even cosmetically.

While attending University High School in Los Angeles, he continued to write songs, one of which was recorded by Gene McDaniels. When Newman was 17, Lenny Waronker helped him get a job as a composer for Metric Music, a Liberty Records subsidiary, at a salary of $150 a month. Upon graduating from high school, Newman entered the University of California at Los Angeles, majoring in music and receiving intensive training in composition and theory.

Though he completed all the courses needed for graduation, he was never an enthusiastic student. "I'd drive to school," he recalled, "and if I couldn't find a place to park, I'd just drive home." Newman failed to get a diploma only because he did not fulfill a performance requirement.

After leaving UCLA, Newman concentrated on songwriting, gaining some recognition when the noted folk singer Judy Collins did his "I Think it's Gonna Rain Today," a bluesy lamentation about loneliness, in concert and included it on her 1967 album *In My Life*. At least 30 other performers were to record the song, Peggy Lee among them.

In 1967 Newman married Roswitha Schmale, a German-born woman he had met four years earlier while she was sunbathing at a condominium swimming pool. "She was really pretty," he said. "It kind of threw me when I saw her. I jumped into the pool with my glasses on." While raising three sons, they made their home for almost a decade in Mandville Canyon in West Los Angeles before moving to Pacific Palisades.

Two Newman songs made the top-ten charts in 1969–70. Recorded by Peggy Lee, "Love Story" is an ironically titled number whose narrator describes to his lover a vision of their future together, foreseeing a dreary retirement together in a home for the aged in Florida, where they will play checkers in the sun until they quietly pass away. "Mama Told Me Not to Come," about a naive girl's nightmarish experience with LSD at a wild party, was recorded by the group Three Dog Night. Harry Nilsson, who had been singing Newman songs in concert, in 1970 recorded the album *Nilsson Sings Newman*, with Newman playing piano. Other artists featuring Newman's songs in concerts and on records in the early 1970s were: Blood, Sweat and Tears, Ella Fitzgerald, Dusty Springfield, the Everly Brothers, Joni Mitchell, Fats Domino, and Vicki Carr. Newman made his own recording debut in 1968 with the single, "It's Gonna Rain Today" (backed with "The Beehive State"). One month later his first album, *Randy Newman Creates Something New Under the Sun,* was released on the Reprise label. Recorded with lush string accompaniment, the LP, in addition to "Love Story" and "It's Gonna Rain Today," included several new numbers, the most interesting being "Davy, the Fat Boy," a pathos-riddled song about a carnival barker who promises a child's dying parents that he will look after their son and then exploits him as a sideshow freak. This album had modest sales, as did his second LP, *12 Songs* (1970). Here Newman introduced "Yellow Man," an off-beat number described by the composer as a "pinhead's view of China and the Chinese people"; "Old Kentucky Home," a country song written from the point of view of a Snopesian Southerner; and "A Lover's Prayer," in which a man petitions the Lord to send him an unforgettable one-night stand.

Encouraged by Reprise Records, in the later 1960s Newman began making concert appearances on college campuses and at intimate night spots. In addition to promoting his little-heard recordings, Newman wanted to sing his own songs in public because he was dissatisfied with the unimaginative interpretations other artists had given them. His own voice was raspy and extremely limited in range, but these shortcomings were compensated by his careful, sensitive phrasing, the range of complex emotions he distilled from his music, and his sense of comic irony. "In concert," one journalist wrote, "he ambles on the stage, squints at the spotlight (as if he is surprised they are going to illuminate him) then hunches over the black grand piano and begins. He is a reluctant celebrity. . . . Newman usually looks like he has just awakened from a nap. His slouchy posture, unruly brown hair and quaint spectacles give him a distinctly droll look, His normal stage attire is jeans, Hush Puppy shoes and the kind of dress shirt you can buy on sale for $7.99."

An appearance at the Bitter End in Greenwich Village in 1971 provided most of the material for his third album, *Randy Newman/Live* (1971). Describing his performance at the Bitter End, Tim Crouse of *Rolling Stone* (August 19, 1972) spoke of the "flat desolation" of Newman's voice bespeaking "a detachment beyond cynicism, a true case of *tristitia mundi.*" Crouse felt that his "trance-like performance" allowed Newman to become "a medium [through whom] a bunch of Charles Addams characters . . . communicate. . . . "

In July 1970 Newman appeared as a guest artist on a Liza Minnelli television special. That same year he conducted the music for the motion picture *Performance,* starring Mick Jagger, in which Newman sang, to his own piano accompaniment, "Let Me Go." He also composed the score for the Norman Lear film *Cold Turkey,* in which his bitterly ironic "God's Song (He Gives Us All His Love)" was a recurring theme.

Newman returned to the studio to record his fourth album, *Sail Away,* released in 1972. Quickly becoming his most commercially successful LP to date, *Sail Away* contained the title number, a sales pitch written from the point of view of a slave trader in Africa; "Political Science," for which Newman adopted the persona of a xenophobe whose approach to American foreign policy is summed up in the line "They all hate us anyhow/So let's drop the big one now"; and "God's Song," whose gentle melody is belied by God's view of humanity: "I burn down your cities—how blind you must be/I take from you your children and you say how blessed are we/You all must be crazy to put your faith in me/That's why I love mankind/You really need me." "Sail Away" was recorded by numerous artists, including Linda Rondstadt.

Newman's album *Good Old Boys* (1974) was a humorous, sympathetic, and complicated look at the American South and its cultural contradictions. Newman sang "Rednecks" from the point of view of an Alabama steelworker, and mocked both the "redneck" and the smugness of Northeastern liberalism. "The Kingfish Gonna Save This Land" was about Louisiana's populist Governor and U.S. Senator, Huey P. Long. "Every Man a King," written by Long himself in collaboration with Castro Carazo, was the Kingfish's share-the-wealth campaign song.

Because composing is an exceedingly difficult chore for Newman, he periodically contracts writer's block. For two and a half years after *Good Old Boys* he did little composing, except for writing a commercial jingle for the Dr. Pepper soft drink and a song called "Sigmund Freud's Impersonation of Albert Einstein in America." But in 1977 he returned to the concert stage and released a new album, *Little Criminals.* One of several provocative songs on *Little Criminals* was "In Germany Before the War," about an actual child murderer in Düsseldorf in 1925. The cut "Short People" became his first recording to make the pop top-ten charts and the first to stir nationwide controversy. Intended as a sardonic comment on prejudice, "Short People" is sung from the viewpoint of a misanthrope who not only dislikes short people but insists that they have "no reason to live." Many small individuals, however, took the lyrics literally and flooded radio stations with demands that the song be withdrawn from the air. The song "Baltimore," with its deprecating remarks about that city, also generated controversy. Other outstanding cuts on the LP were, "Kathleen (Catholicism Made Easier)" and "Sigmund Freud's Impersonation of Albert Einstein in America." In 1978 "Short People" and *Little Criminals* earned Newman his first gold records.

Writing about Newman's return to the New York concert scene in 1977 after a three-year absence, John Rockwell of *The New York Times* said that he was no different from the "old lovable Randy Newman of yore. He still sang his quirky, semibitter songs in his hoarse but affecting baritone, accompanying himself on the piano; he still dressed in jeans and a plaid shirt and made wry remarks between songs; and he still gave a performance that made him one of the very finest—if more idiosyncratic—performers in present-day popular music." About Newman's songs, Rockwell added: "There can be no doubt that Mr. Newman . . . is writing [some of] the finest art songs of the day, and his mastery of [a] deeper kind of humor is a perfect indication of that. In the alternation of his songs from overtly serious through all the shadings to overtly funny, Mr. Newman shows his ability to make us laugh without making us feel detached from our feelings. Even more miraculously, he can do it within a single song, shifting the mood in the lyrics from frighteningly farcical to deeply philosophical to off-handed, and underpinning even the most outrageous conceits with the undeniable honesty of music itself."

Newman's 1979 album, *Born Again,* was poorly received in the United States, though it was lavishly praised in West Germany. Critics felt that Newman's usually corrosive irony was undercut by heavy-handed parody, especially on "Mr. Sheep," about a dull businessman, and the title track, a caustic number based on Bob Dylan's conversion to fundamentalist Christianity.

But with *Trouble in Paradise* (1983), Newman's hardest-rocking LP, he returned to the good graces of critics and to the bestseller charts with the catchy hit tune, "I Love L.A." Other standout tracks were "The Blues" and "I'm Different." Paul Simon joined in singing "The Blues" and Linda Ronstadt sang background on "I'm Different."

Newman composed the score for *Ragtime* (1981), director Milos Forman's motion picture adaptation of E. L. Doctorow's bestselling novel, and for *The Natural* (1984), starring Robert Redford and based on a novel by Bernard Malamud. The music of the latter was recorded in a soundtrack album, with Randy Newman conducting.

In March 1981 a cabaret revue, *Maybe I'm Doing It Wrong: A Musical Celebration of the Songs of Randy Newman,* opened Off Broadway before moving, in an expanded version, to Astor Place Theatre on March 14, 1982. The setting was a Fourth of July party in which two couples, the revue's only performers, picnicked in front of a bandstand and performed 23 of Newman's songs. This production began another limited run at the Roxy Theatre in New York City on October 14, 1984.

In the 1970s Randy Newman quit smoking and taking amphetamines, on which he had relied when he was younger. "My only vice," Newman has said, "is that I'm boring." He still follows baseball games on television with his sons and reads voraciously. He usually composes his songs at the piano, with the melody coming before the lyric.

ABOUT: Current Biography, 1982; Marcus, G. Mystery Train, 1975; Pollock, B. In Their Own Words 1975; Stambler, I. Encyclopedia of Pop, Rock and Soul, 1976. *Periodicals*—High Fidelity April 1983; New York Times April 1, 1983, September 25, 1977; New York Times Magazine November 5, 1972; New Yorker December 9, 1974; Rolling Stone November 1, 1979, January 21, 1982.

PARISH, MITCHELL (July 10, 1900–   ), has written lyrics for more than 1,000 songs, many of them hits which have since become standards. Though he did work with new melodies, his most successful songs were produced by adding lyrics to instrumental compositions such as "Star Dust," or making American adaptations of foreign songs.

Mitchell Parish was born in Shreveport, Louisiana but was raised and educated in New York City. As a student, he wrote poems and short stories, but in spite of his interest in literature, he planned a career in medicine. He enrolled at Columbia University, where he edited the school magazine and worked as a hospital clerk after school hours. In 1919, his verses came to the attention of Irving Mills, who offered him a job as staff writer at the Tin Pan Alley firm of Jack Mills, Inc. Parish accepted, and his ambition to become a doctor was abandoned.

It was several years before Parish attracted attention as a lyricist. In 1927, he had published "Bells of Avalon" (music by Joseph Charney). But his first success came a year later with "Sweet Lorraine" (music by Cliff Burwell); it was first popularized by Rudy Vallee, then performed by several jazz groups, and recorded by Muggsy Spanier (1944) and Nat King Cole (1950). In 1944, the song appeared on *Your Hit Parade.* Following the success of "Sweet Lorraine," Mills asked Parish to write lyrics for Hoagy Carmichael's "Star Dust" in 1929. The song has since become a standard in both the popular music and jazz repertories.

In 1932, Parish prepared new lyrics for a popular German song by Frank Markush, "Take Me in Your Arms." Ruth Etting featured it in her nightclub and vaudeville acts and she also recorded it. That year he also wrote lyrics for "Sentimental Gentleman From Georgia" (music by Frank Perkins) and "The Scat Song" (music by Frank Perkins and Cab Calloway).

MITCHELL PARISH

In 1933, Parish made his debut in the musical theater by writing lyrics for "Christmas Night in Harlem" (music by Raymond Scott) for the revue *Blackbirds of 1933*; he also contributed songs (with music by Sammy Fain and Rube Bloom) to *Blackbirds of 1939*, in which Lena Horne made her Broadway debut, and also to *It Happens On Ice* (stage show on ice, 1941; music by Vernon Duke and Peter De Rose).

From 1933 to 1939, Parish's lyrics were heard in many of the period's leading song hits. "Sophisticated Lady" (lyrics written with Irving Mills, music by Duke Ellington) came in 1933 and was followed the next year by "Stars Fell on Alabama" (music by Frank Perkins), recorded by various jazz groups including the orchestras of Richard Himber, Guy Lombardo and Freddy Martin, and prominently featured by Jack Teagarden. In 1936, "Organ Grinder's Swing" (lyrics written with Irving Mills, music by Will Hudson) was introduced by the Hudson-De Lange Orchestra and popularized by the Chick Webb orchestra with Ella Fitzgerald; it was also heard on *Your Hit Parade*. In 1938, *Your Hit Parade* featured Benny Goodman and Edgard Sampson's "Don't Be That Way," with new lyrics by Parish, "Who Blew Out the Flame?" (music by Sammy Fain), and "It's Wonderful" (music by Stuff Smith), recorded by Benny Goodman.

In addition to "Star Dust," "Deep Purple" (1939) has become a classic; it was also Parish's first song to reach the top position on *Your Hit Parade*. Originally a piano piece composed in 1934 by Peter De Rose, it was orchestrated by Domenico Savino a year later and introduced on radio by Paul Whiteman. It was popularized

with Parish's lyrics by Larry Clinton and his orchestra (vocal by Bea Wain), then recorded by Bing Crosby and interpolated into the motion picture, *Hi Buddy* (1943).

Parish continued to write lyrics for instrumental pieces and in 1939, these were also heard on *Yout Hit Parade*: "Stairway to the Stars" (music by Matty Malneck and Frank Signorelli), from *Park Avenue Fantasy*, introduced by Paul Whiteman and later recorded with the new lyrics by the orchestras of Chuck Bullock and Sammy Kaye; "Lilacs in the Rain" (music by De Rose); "The Lamp is Low," a popular adaptation of Maurice Ravel's *Pavane pour une Infante défunte*, introduced by Larry Clinton and his orchestra and recorded by Glenn Miller; "Moonlight Serenade" (music by Glenn Miller), which became the theme music for both the Glenn Miller orchestra and its successor, led by Tex Beneke; "Blue Tango" (music by Leroy Anderson), recorded by Tony Bennett and revived in 1963 by Bobby Vinton.

Songs with lyrics by Parish continued to be featured on *Your Hit Parade* in the 1940s and 1950s. These included "The Starlit Hour" (music by De Rose), which was interpolated into the Broadway revue, *Earl Carroll's Vanities of 1940*, and recorded by Ella Fitzgerald and by Glenn Miller; "Orange Blossom Lane (1941, music by De Rose), recorded by Claude Thornhill; "All My Love," from the French popular song, "Boléro" (music by Paul Durand), popularized in 1950 by Patti Page; "Tzena, Tzena," an adaptation of an Israeli popular song (music by Julius Grossman and Issacher Miron based on a traditional Yiddish folk song), popularized with Parish's lyrics in 1950 in a recording by the Weavers with Gordon Jenkins and his orchestra; and "Ruby" (music by Heinz Roemheld), the theme from the motion picture, *Ruby Gentry* (1953).

During the 1940s and 1950s, Parish also contributed lyrics to these hits: "Orchids for Remembrance" (1940, music by De Rose), recorded by Eddy Howard and by Will Bradley; in 1942, "All I Need is You" (lyrics written with Benny Davis, music by De Rose), recorded by Vaughn Monroe and his orchestra and by Dinah Shore; in 1945, "The Blond Sailor," a German popular song by Jacob Pfeil which the Andrews Sisters recorded; "Dream, Dream, Dream" (1954, music by Jimmy McHugh); "Moonlight Love," Savio's adaptation of Debussy's *Clair de Lune*, recorded by Perry Como in 1956; and "Volare," an adaptation of "Nel Blu, Dipinto Di Blu" (music by Domenico Modugno) which received a Grammy Award for best song of the year in 1958 and was revived in 1960 by Bobbie Rydell. Between 1950 and 1953, Parish also provided words for several pieces by Leroy Anderson, among them *Sleigh Ride, Syncopated Clock, Belle of the Ball* and *Fiddle Faddle.*

Parish married in 1922 and raised two children, a son and a daughter. After more than 25 years away from the academic world, he enrolled at New York University, where he majored in English literature. In 1949, as a junior, he was elected to Phi Beta Kappa, and he graduated summa cum laude in 1950. He is the author of a book of poetry, *For Those in Love.*

ABOUT: Jablonski, E. The Encyclopedia of American Music, 1981; Stambler, I. Encyclopedia of Popular Music, 1965.

PORTER, COLE (June 9, 1891–October 15, 1964). Both as lyricist and composer, Cole Porter was a master. As Alec Wilder said in *American Popular Song,* Porter "added a certain theatrical elegance, as well as . . . sophistication, wit and musical complexity to the song form." At the peak of his creative powers, during the Jazz Age 1920s, the Roosevelt-era 1930s and on into the wartime 1940s, his songs animated, reflected and chronicled the decades between the two great wars. But he wrote best about what he knew, the high life of upper-crust cosmopolites, the life Porter himself had lived. In Porter's songs we encounter the well-bred modern man—with the refined sensibility and jaded sophistication of someone who has been everywhere, seen everything, and not denied himself wordly pleasures.

Porter's lyrics are literate and urbane, sprinkled with witty sexual allusions and metaphors. The setting of a Porter song is often an exotic locale. His sensuous songs—with their insistent, throbbing rhythms, sweeping melodies and strong, compelling endings—were the gift of an inspired and exquisite talent as well as that of an extensively trained musician.

Cole Albert Porter was born to considerable wealth in Peru, Indiana on June 9, 1891. His grandfather, J. G. Cole, had built a fortune estimated at seven million dollars through investments in coal and timber. Cole's father, Samuel Fenwick Porter, a former druggist who dabbled in writing poetic verse, ran the family business with his wife. Born Kate Cole, Mrs. Porter had been educated in exclusive private schools and had been trained as a pianist. Their home was a 750-acre ranch. As her only surviving child, the pampered and overprotected Cole was forbidden by Kate to play with other children and, from childhood on, he was groomed carefully for the social world into which he was born. He

COLE PORTER

began to ride horses when he was four and at six was given his own pony. He was educated by private tutors. Aged six he began studying the piano, then the violin, the latter lessons taking place in Marion, Indiana, some 30 miles away.

Cole began composing when he was ten, his first effort being "The Song of the Birds," which he dedicated to his mother, whom he adored. In 1902, listening to the song of a bobolink inspired him to compose *The Bobolink Waltz,* for piano, which his mother had published in Chicago at a cost of $100. Apart from music, Cole's childhood interests lay in going to the circus and in playing with a toy theater with which he mounted his own productions.

Insisting that Cole be professionally trained, his grandfather promised him an endowment of one-sixth of his fortune the day Cole received a law degree. In 1906 Cole was enrolled in the Worcester Academy, an elite private school in Massachusetts. Away from the classroom, he spent his time playing the piano and composing humorous songs about members of the faculty. In his last year at the academy, he was president of the mandolin club, editor of the school paper, an actor in a school play, pianist for the glee club, and a contestant in a public-speaking debate. He graduated in June 1909 class valedictorian.

Following a summer holiday in Europe, where his lifelong love of travel was born, he entered Yale. Academic studies were once again combined with membership in a glee club which he later conducted, with writing and producing college shows, and with composing songs. Two of Porter's football "fight" songs, "Bulldog" and

"Bingo Eli Yale," became fixtures in the repertory of Yale "fight" songs. "Bridget" was his first to be published when it was issued commercially by Jerome H. Remick in 1910. He was voted "the most entertaining" and the "second most original" man in his class.

Upon receiving his B. A. from Yale in 1913, Porter entered Harvard University as a graduate student, then enrolled in Harvard Law School. His lack of interest in law and his talent as a songwriter were noticed by Ezra Ripley Thayer, Dean of the Law School, who advised him to transfer to the Harvard School of Music. Without telling his grandfather, Porter spend the academic year of 1915–16 studying composition, music theory, orchestration and piano. In the fall of 1915, two of his songs were performed on Broadway. "Two Big Eyes" (lyrics by John Golden) was sung by Irene Bordoni in *Miss Information* (whose basic score was the work of Jerome Kern) and "Esmeralda" (words and music by Porter) was performed by Maurice and Florence Walton in *Hands Up* (for which Sigmund Romberg was the composer). Both shows closed after short runs.

Porter's first score for a Broadway musical was for *See America First* (March 28, 1916). Its text, by J. Lawrason Riggs, who also helped write the lyrics, satirized the patriotic musicals popularized by George M. Cohan. Starring Clifton Webb, making his debut in the Broadway theater, the show lasted only 15 performances. One of the songs, "I've a Shooting-Box in Scotland," was in the sophisticated manner of Porter's later lyrics. This song had been written for a 1914 production at Yale but was revived for *America First*. After that show closed, Fred and Adele Astaire kept it alive by performing it in vaudeville in 1915 and 1916. Fred Astaire revived it on his television special in 1968. The Joseph C. Smith orchestra recorded it in 1916.

"I honestly believed I was disgraced for the rest of my life," Porter said recalling the unambiguous failure of *America First*. "I sneaked back to the Yale Club, rushed through the lobby and hid in my room." He even considered leaving the country but remained in New York in an apartment on 19th Street. There he studied composition and threw parties and costume balls.

In the fall of 1917, despite the war in Europe, Porter sailed for France. There he worked with the Duryea Relief, which distributed supplies to war-stricken villages. In April 1918 he joined the so-called first foreign regiment of the French 32d Artillery. A year later he was transferred to the Bureau of the United States Military Attaché. (In later years, Porter regaled his listeners with the fictitious tale that he had served in the French Foreign Legion.)

Discharged from military duty in April 1919, he rented an apartment in the rue Gounod in Paris and enrolled in the Schola Cantorum, studying composition with Vincent d'Indy. His home became a lively gathering place for the haute monde of Paris, whom he entertained with his songs. He soon found himself attracted to one of the most beautiful women and most celebrated hostesses in Paris, Mrs. Linda Thomas, a wealthy divorcée from Kentucky who had been married to a newspaper publisher. Porter and Thomas were married in Paris on December 18, 1919. They acquired an elegantly appointed mansion at 13 rue Monsieur and became the darlings of Parisian society. However lavish their parties, not the least of the attractions were the smart, sometimes risqué, songs Porter wrote and performed for his guests. One of his friends, Elsa Maxwell, observed, "You are much too good. Your standards are too high. But one day you will haul the public up to your own level and then the world will be yours."

In 1920 Porter returned to the Broadway musical theater with ten songs for a revue, *Hitchy-Koo*, starring Raymond Hitchcock. A box-office failure, it closed after 71 performances. "Old-Fashioned Garden" from that score is remembered. In the revue it was sung and danced to by two native American Indians, Chief Eagle Horse and Princess White Deer. Revived in the Cole Porter screen biography *Night and Day* (1946), the song was performed by Cary Grant.

Porter composed songs for another Raymond Hitchcock revue, *Hitchy-Koo of 1922*, but it opened and closed in Boston. Five of his songs were used in the *Greenwich Village Follies of 1924* (September 16, 1924), in which the Dolly Sisters introduced "I'm in Love Again." That song was virtually forgotten until Jane Wyman sang it in *Night and Day*. In 1951 April Stevens recorded it in a bestselling release. Also from the *Follies*, "Two Little Babes in the Woods" was introduced by Julia Silvers and Georgia Hale and danced to by the Dolly Sisters. In 1934 Porter recorded it to his own piano accompaniment.

On May 12, 1928 several Porter songs were premiered in *In the Old Days and Today*, a nightclub revue mounted in Paris at Des Ambassadeurs. One of these numbers, "Looking at You," turned up on Broadway in Cole Porter's 1929 musical, *Wake Up and Dream*.

Porter's first complete score for a Broadway musical came with *Paris* (October 8, 1928), which ran for 195 performances. Irene Bordoni starred as Vivienne Roland, a Parisian actress who pursues Andrew Sabot over his Bostonian socialite mother's objections. Writing songs for a musical set in Porter's beloved Paris inspired him to write "Let's Do It," the song in which his musical sophistication came into full focus for the first time. A clever, provocative number about the similarities between the "natural" and amatory behavior of insect and animal life and that of people in exotic places, "Let's Do It" was introduced by Irene Bordoni and Arthur Margetson. Irving Aaronson's Commanders, who had appeared in the show, recorded it in 1928 as Rudy Vallee, Billie Holiday and Mary Martin did subsequently; Rudy Vallee's recording was heard on the soundtrack of the film, *City Heat* (1985). Noël Coward parodied this song in a recording and in public appearances. Ginny Simms sang it in the film *Night and Day* and Frank Sinatra and Shirley MacLaine performed it as a duet in the screen version of *Can-Can* (1960). In *Paris*, "Two Little Babes in the Woods" was a carry-over from the *Greenwich Village Follies of 1924*. "Let's Misbehave," which Irene Bordoni sang during out-of-town tryouts, was dropped by the time *Paris* opened on Broadway. This song was revived in the film *At Long Last Love* (1975), directed by Peter Bogdanovich. "No one else writing words and music knows so exactly the delicate balance between sense, rhyme and tune," wrote a critic for *The New Yorker* about the *Paris* score. "[Porter's] rare and satisfactory talent makes other lyricists sound as though they had written their words for a steam whistle."

His songwriting career now having gained momentum, Porter received his first assignment from Hollywood, to write two songs for *The Battle of Paris* (1929), starring Gertrude Lawrence. An English stage producer, C. B. Cochran, contracted him to write songs for *Wake Up and Dream*, a revue, which opened in London on March 27, 1929. This was followed in New York by *Fifty Million Frenchmen* (November 27, 1929), whose Broadway run was 254 performances. This was the second Broadway show for which Porter had composed both the lyrics and the music. Here Herbert Fields's book made it yet another Paris setting in which Peter Forbes, a wealthy American playboy, on a wager, seeks to win the love of Looloo, a French girl of simple origin. Irving Berlin delightedly purchased a full-page advertisement saying that *Fifty Million Frenchmen* was "worth the price of admission to hear Cole Porter's lyrics. One of the best collections of song numbers I have ever listened to."

William Gaxton and Genevieve Tobin introduced "You Do Something to Me" and Leo Reisman and his orchestra recorded it in 1929; later it was recorded by Eddy Duchin and his orchestra, Marlene Dietrich, Frank Sinatra, and

Perry Como. In motion pictures it was sung by Jane Wyman in *Night and Day*; Doris Day in *Starlift* (1951); Mario Lanza in *Because You're Mine (1952)*; Gogi Grant on the soundtrack of *The Helen Morgan Story* (1957); and Louis Jourdan in *Can-Can* (1960). In the nonmusical film, *The Sun Also Rises* (1957), it was heard without vocals. Jack Thompson and Betty Compton introduced "You've Got That Thing," which was recorded by Leo Reisman and his orchestra, and Evelyn Hoey introduced "Find Me a Primitive Man." The former was sung by a female chorus in *Night and Day*; the latter, a classic of the popular style of the day, was revived in *At Long Last Love*.

Wake Up and Dream, imported from England to Broadway on December 30, 1929, for a run of 136 performances, brought Americans their first hearing of "What is This Thing Called Love?" Tilly Losch and Toni Birkmayer danced to its strains and it was recorded by Billie Holiday, Mary Martin, Libby Homan and Lena Horne, among many others. It was featured in such films as *Night and Day, Young Man with a Horn* and *Starlift*.

"Love for Sale" was first heard in *The New Yorkers* (December 8, 1930), a Broadway revue starring Jimmy Durante which ran for 168 performances; the song was introduced by Kathryn Crawford with the help of June Shafer, Ida Pearson and Arline Judge. In his popular syndicated column, Walter Winchell heavily promoted "Love for Sale" which, because it dealt with prostitution, was banned from the radio in the early 1930s. It was circulated in recordings by Libby Holman, Eddy Duchin and his orchestra, and Fred Waring's Pennsylvanians.

In the 1930s seven Cole Porter musicals were mounted on Broadway, four of them among the best of the decade. *Gay Divorce* (November 29, 1932, text by Dwight Taylor) was a bedroom farce starring Fred Astaire on the stage for the first time without his sister. Its principal song was "Night and Day," Porter's classic. It was written for, and introduced by, Fred Astaire in a duet with Claire Luce. Astaire initially balked, fearing that the song's "exotic" melody was alien to his singing style. Porter is thought to have borrowed the repeated use of an insistent B-flat note in the verse from the distant sound of the tom-tom he had once heard in Morocco. The chorus drew its basic melody from a religious chant Porter had heard sung by an Islamic priest. However unorthodox its structure and style, "Night and Day" was an immediate hit in *Gay Divorce,* and was the reason for the show's turnaround. After a poor start at the box office, business improved and *Gay Divorce* had for that time the modestly successful run of 248 performances. In 1932, "Night and Day" was recorded by Leo Reisman and his orchestra and within the next three decades by such big-name bands as those of Tommy Dorsey (with Frank Sinatra, in his recording debut, doing the vocal), Paul Whiteman, Eddy Duchin, and Benny Goodman; it was also recorded by such famous vocalists as Bing Crosby, Billie Holiday, Ella Fitzgerald and Fred Astaire. The song provided the title for Cole Porter's film biography, in which it was heard as a Cary Grant–Alex Smith duet and used as a recurrent theme. Frank Sinatra sang it again in the film *Reveille with Beverly* (1943) and Deanna Durbin's rendition was heard in *Lady on a Train* (1945). When *Gay Divorce* became a motion picture starring Fred Astaire and Ginger Rogers (1934), its title changed to *The Gay Divorcee*, only "Night and Day" was retained from the stage score. *Gay Divorce* was revived Off Broadway in March 1979.

The Guy Bolton–P. G. Wodehouse book of *Anything Goes* (November 21, 1934) was originally set on a shipwrecked gambling liner. But the disastrous burning of a cruise ship off the coast of New Jersey on September 8, 1934, made the humorous treatment of a shipwreck a dark form of entertainment. Howard Lindsay and Russell Crouse rewrote the book of *Anything Goes*, in which a band of unlikely characters gathers on a luxury liner bound for Europe. Ethel Merman portrayed Reno Sweeney, an ex-evangelist turned nightclub singer who is in love with Billy Crocker, played by William Gaxton. Victor Moore was Public Enemy No. 13, a fugitive from the police disguised as a minister. Reno ultimately marries a titled Englishman while Billy returns to a former fiancée.

Anything Goes was the first Cole Porter musical to run more than 400 performances (420) and the first of several Porter musicals starring Ethel Merman, whose talent Porter much admired. For her robust vocal delivery Porter composed three songs which she introduced, two of them duets with William Gaxton. These numbers became gigantic hits as well as Merman trademarks—"Blow, Gabriel, Blow," "I Get a Kick Out of You" and "You're the Top." Merman performed all three in the first screen version of *Anything Goes* (1936), sharing "I Get a Kick Out of You" and "You're the Top" with Bing Crosby. In the second screen version (1956), "I Get a Kick Out of You" was sung by Mitzi Gaynor and Bing Crosby, and "You're the Top" by Crosby, Gaynor, Jeanmaire and Donald O'Connor. Ginny Simms sang "I Get a Kick" in *Night and Day* and the song was interpolated into *At Long Last Love.* "You're the Top" was sung by Cary Grant and Simms in *Night and Day*; Barbra Streisand sang it under the opening titles of *What's Up, Doc* (1972). "Blow, Gabriel, Blow" was interpolated into the film *Nobody's Darling* (1943).

The title number of *Anything Goes* was introduced on the stage by Ethel Merman. Another popular song from the show's score was "All Through the Night," a languorous ballad introduced by Bettina Hall and William Gaxton on the stage and sung by Bing Crosby in both screen versions. *Anything Goes* was produced for television by Jule Styne in 1957 and mounted Off Broadway in 1962, receiving the Outer Critics Award as the season's best revival.

Victor Moore was one of the stars, and Mary Martin made her Broadway debut, in Porter's next show, *Leave It to Me,* which opened on Broadway on November 8, 1938 and had a 291-performance run. The book, by Bella and Sam Spewack based on their own stage comedy, is a satire on communism and the Soviet bureaucracy. Moore appeared as Alonzo P. Goodhue, the hapless American ambassador to the USSR who, homesick for Topeka, Kansas, tries to get recalled by engineering diplomatic faux pas; instead of blundering, he emerges each time a hero. But when he decides to do his job properly and promote better relations between America and the Soviet Union, he fails, bringing his diplomatic career to a now unwanted end. The sterling cast included Sophie Tucker and William Gaxton, but the performer who nightly stole the show was Mary Martin, in the minor role of Dolly Winslow, performing Porter's "My Heart Belongs to Daddy" as a quasi-striptease. She sang it in the films *Night and Day* and *Love Thy Neighbor* (1940) and Marilyn Monroe revived it in *Let's Make Love* (1960). Mary Martin, Peggy Lee and Kitty Kallen recorded it. Another song in this score, "Get Out of Town," introduced on the stage by Tamara, twice found a place on *Your Hit Parade.*

Porter's score for *Du Barry Was a Lady* (December 6, 1939) helped that musical to have a prosperous run of 408 performances. In a book by B. G. De Sylva and Herbert Fields, Bert Lahr starred as Louis Blore, a washroom attendant in a nightclub where May Daley, played by Ethel Merman, is the star performer. In his dreams, Blore becomes a lecherous Louis XV, whose mistress is the lusty Madame Du Barry (none other than May Daley). Their duet, "Friendship," was one of the score's most popular numbers. In the 1943 film version of the musical it was performed by Red Skelton, Lucille Ball, Gene Kelly and others. The recording by Kay Kyser and his orchestra was a bestseller. It was also recorded by Mary Martin and by Judy Garland with Johnny Mercer. Merman regularly wowed audiences with the song "Katie Went to Haiti," which Gertrude Niesen recorded. In the screen adaptation it was performed by the Pied Pipers, Jo Stafford, Dick Haymes and the Tommy Dorsey orchestra. "Do I Love You?" was introduced on the stage by Merman and Ronald Graham and became on the screen a solo for Gene Kelly. This song was represented four times on *Your Hit Parade*. *Du Barry Was a Lady* was revived Off Broadway in 1972.

Other Cole Porter standards in the 1930s came from Broadway musicals that were box-office failures. *Jubilee* (October 12, 1935, 169 performances) was so soundly rejected by critics and the public that a score containing two Cole Porter song masterpieces was largely ignored at first. "Begin the Beguine," inspired by the rhythms of a native dance Porter had witnessed in the Dutch East Indies, was introduced by June Knight and initially recorded by Xavier Cugat and the Waldorf orchestra. This song classic was neglected until 1938, when Artie Shaw and his orchestra sold two million copies of a recording that helped make Artie Shaw famous. More than 200 recordings followed, including three by Frank Sinatra and others by Billie Holiday, Fred Astaire, Bing Cosby, Ella Fitzgerald, and the orchestras of Glenn Miller, Tommy Dorsey, Benny Goodman, Sammy Kaye and André Kostelanetz. Fred Astaire and Eleanor Powell performed it in the film musical *Broadway Melody of 1940* and Carlos Ramirez and Alexis Smith sang it in *Night and Day*.

The second Porter song classic from *Jubilee* was "Just One of Those Things," sung as a duet by June Knight and Charles Walters. Ginny Simms sang it in *Night and Day*; Doris Day in *Lullaby of Broadway* (1951); Peggy Lee in *The Jazz Singer* (1953); Frank Sinatra in *Young at Heart* (1954); and Maurice Chevalier in the film version of *Can-Can* (1960). Sinatra, Bing Crosby, Ella Fitzgerald and the orchestras of Eddy Duchin, Les Brown and Guy Lombardo recorded it.

Red, Hot and Blue! (October 29, 1936, 183 performances) co-starred Ethel Merman and Jimmy Durante and had Bob Hope in the cast. A too-complicated plot in a text by Howard Lindsay and Russel Crouse found Ethel Merman as a millionairess widow who launches a lottery for a charity conducted by a quick-witted ex-convict (Jimmy Durante). Somehow, through the lottery, the widow and her lawyer (Bob Hope) discover that they are in love. From this score came "It's De-Lovely." Merman and Hope introduced it, Donald O'Connor and Mitzi Gaynor later revived it, and Merman recorded it.

Clifton Webb introduced "At Long Last Love" in *You Never Know* (September 21, 1938), which lasted only 78 performances. Recorded by Frances Langford, it appeared ten times on *Your Hit Parade*, in first position on November 20, 1938. Its title was used for that of the 1975 Peter Bogdanovich movie.

"Miss Otis Regrets," a novelty number, did not originally emerge from a stage musical. Porter improvised it one evening in 1934 at a party honoring his friend, Monty Woolley, the actor and Broadway director. Dressed as a butler, Woolley delivered its lines to Porter's piano accompaniment. At parties, this routine became a Woolley favorite and he performed it in *Night and Day*. Ethel Waters's recording is considered definitive, and it was also recorded by the Mills Brothers.

In November 1935, Porter went to work in Hollywood. His first score for the sceen was for *Born to Dance* (1936), costarring James Stewart and Eleanor Powell. The ever popular "I've Got You Under My Skin," which became one of Sinatra's signature songs, was introduced by Virginia Bruce. It was recorded by many artists, including Sinatra, Virginia Bruce, Dinah Shore, Frances Langford and Fred Waring's Pennsylvanians, and was featured in at least three movie musicals, including *Night and Day*. "I've Got You Under My Skin" was heard eight times on *Your Hit Parade*. Another *Your Hit Parade* entry from *Born to Dance* was "Easy to Love," introduced by Jimmy Stewart in his only singing performance ever on the screen. Allen Jones, Dick Haymes, Frances Langford, Virginia Bruce and the orchestra of Artie Shaw are among the many who have recorded it and Lawrence Melchior, the Wagnerian tenor, sang it in the film, *This Time for Keeps* (1947).

Porter's second film score was for *Rosalie* (1937), which featured Eleanor Powell, Nelson Eddy and Ray Bolger. Porter composed five versions of the title number, none of which pleased the MGM head, Louis B. Mayer. Porter's sixth effort was a melody and lyric that derived entirely from popular love ballad clichés. This was the final version of this number and no one was more surprised than Porter when it became a hit. It was recorded by Bing Crosby, among others, and made 12 appearances on *Your Hit Parade*, twice in first position. A male trio sang it in *Night and Day*. "In the Still of the Night," also from *Rosalie*, was introduced by Nelson Eddy. Ginny Simms and chorus sang it in *Night and Day*. Della Reese had her first recording success with it in 1953. It was also recorded by Jo Stafford and the orchestras of Fred Waring and André Kostelanetz.

In the 1930s the Porters made the U. S. rather than Paris their permanent residence. Their life style did not change. In America they maintained three homes: a suite on the 41st floor of the Waldorf Astoria on Park Avenue for fall residence; a country cottage in Williamstown, Massachusetts for weekends; and a mansion at North Rockingham in Hollywood for the summer months. Their personal needs were attended to by a full household staff. Also on hand were Cole Porter's indispensable secretaries: first Margaret Moore and then, in the last 17 years of his life, Madeline P. Smith.

In America, as in Paris, he was the darling of the upper crust. His presence at exclusive parties and social events helped assure their success. He kept company with the titans of the social, business and artistic worlds. Cole Porter epitomized grace and charm. Exquisitely turned out, he was known for his sartorial elegance. He smoked incessantly and drank well but in moderation, usually a single dry martini before dinner and champagne. Though he was capable of working long, arduous hours, he was wont to indulge in play and in the pleasures of the table. "I like hunting, swimming, food, drink, cats and voyages," he told an interviewer. "I like everything as long as it is different. I *hate* boredom."

Tragedy struck in Porter's life in 1937. While staying with his wife as house guests of a Countess on Long Island, Porter, a skilled horseman, was thrown and the horse fell on him. "I was so stunned," he recalled, "that I was unconscious of any great pain. In fact, strange as it may sound, while pinned under the horse and waiting for help, my mind was busily concocting some lines for a new lyric."

Both of Porter's legs were smashed and he sustained a serious nerve injury. To save his legs, he had to endure 30 operations over the next few years. For more than 20 months after the accident he was hospitalized. For five years after that, he was confined to a wheelchair. Despite his impairment, neither Porter's social nor professional life suffered. He composed the scores for the Broadway musicals *You Never Know* and *Leave It to Me*, both in 1937, while suffering acute physical pain. And he was an invalid at the time he composed songs for the film musical *Broadway Melody of 1940*. He lived with pain for the rest of his life.

In *Broadway Melody of 1940* Fred Astaire and Eleanor Powell danced to "I Concentrate on You," and Sinatra, Perry Como and Dinah Shore recorded it. Also in this revue, Fred Astaire introduced "I've Got My Eyes on You," which was to have four hearings on *Your Hit Parade* and which Kathryn Grayson sang in the film *Andy Hardy's Private Secretary* (1941).

One of the highlights of that year's Broadway season, Porter's musical *Panama Hattie,* opened on October 30, 1940. It starred Ethel Merman and ran for 501 performances. B. G. De Sylva and Herbert Fields's book deals with foreign spies who plan to blow up the Panama Canal. Although Pearl Harbor was more than a year away, this conventional, frothy musical fantasy had a comical but war-related subplot. *Panama Hattie*'s hit song was "Let's Be Buddies," introduced and recorded by Merman and eight-year-old Jean Carroll. In the 1942 film version, "Let's Be Buddies" was sung by Ann Sothern and Buddy Clark. When *Panama Hattie* became a television spectacular on CBS in 1957, Ethel Merman was once again its star.

When *Let's Face It* opened on October 29, 1941 (547 performances), Americans had become war-conscious. *Let's Face It,* based on an earlier Broadway farce, *Cradle Snatchers,* adapted by Herbert and Dorothy Fields, concerned three soldiers stationed near Southampton in Long Island and their romantic involvement with three local married women. One of the soldiers was played by Danny Kaye. Porter's best songs were "Ace in the Hole," introduced by Nanette Fabray and others; "You Irritate Me So," sung by Nanette Fabray and Jack Williams; and "Everything I Love," performed by Danny Kaye and Mary Jane Walsh. When *Let's Face It* was filmed in 1943 the score was dropped and it was turned into a comedic vehicle for Bob Hope.

Something for the Boys (January 7, 1943) was concerned with life on the home front during the wartime. Herbert and Dorothy Fields wrote the book. Ethel Merman appeared as Blossom Hart, a former chorus girl who has taken a job in a defense plant in Texas. Her romantic interest is Sergeant Rocky Fulton. Blossom becomes a heroine when the fillings her dentist had given her transform her into a human radio: she overhears and then frustrates a plot to destroy the U. S. Army Air Force Fighter Squadron. The show's principal song, the title number, was introduced by Ethel Merman and recorded by Paula Stewart. *Something for the Boys* had a Broadway run of 422 performances.

The last of the quartet of Cole Porter Broadway successes in the early 1940s, with a run of 481 performances, was *Mexican Hayride* (January 28, 1944). The book, by Herbert and Dorothy Fields, is far removed from the battlefront. It takes place in Mexico where the main characters are Montana, a lady bullfighter; Joe Bascom, an American fugitive from justice; Lombo Campos, a shady speculator; and David Winthrop, an American chargé d'affaires. An outstanding ballad, "I Love You," introduced by June Havoc and Wilbur Evans, was recorded by Bing Crosby, Wilbur Evans, and the orchestras of André Kostelanetz, Jimmy Lunceford, and Percy Faith. This song was represented on *Your Hit Parade* 18 times, three times in first place.

Seven Lively Arts (December 7, 1944) was a revue that lasted only 179 performances, in spite of a cast that included Beatrice Lillie, Bert Lahr, and Benny Goodman. Only one of Porter's compositions for this production became popular: "Ev'ry Time We Say Goodbye," introduced by Nan Wynn and recorded by the Benny Goodman Quintet, Dorothy Kirsten and Fred Waring's Pennyslvanians.

Two enduring songs of the early 1940s were composed for the screen. "Since I Kissed My Baby Goodbye" was introduced by the Delta Rhythm Boys in *You'll Never Get Rich* (1941) and recorded by Fred Astaire. "You'd Be So Nice to Come Home To," introduced by Don Ameche and Janet Blair in *Something to Shout About* (1943), was recorded by Frank Sinatra and Dinah Shore and made 16 appearances on *Your Hit Parade*.

Porter's greatest commercial success came in 1944 with the release of "Don't Fence Me In." In the 1930s a poem titled "Don't Fence Me In," written by Bob Fletcher, a Montana cowboy, came to Porter's attention. He bought the rights for $150 and used the title and a couple of phrases from the poem for a "cowboy" song of his own for a motion picture *Adios, Argentina*. This was the first time Porter had ever borrowed from another writer for one of his lyrics. *Adios, Argentina* was never filmed, and the song lay neglected for almost a decade. In 1944 it was recorded by Roy Rogers and the Sons of the Pioneers, then reprised by the Andrew Sisters in the movie *Hollywood Canteen* (1944). When Kate Smith sang it on radio, "Don't Fence Me In" achieved instant popularity. Within a few months a recording by Bing Crosby and the Andrews Sisters had sold more than a million copies. Sheet-music sales also exceeded the million mark. Of its 16 appearances on *Your Hit Parade*, eight were in first position. Roy Rogers sang it again in a 1945 cowboy movie bearing the song's title, and it was interpolated into *Night and Day*.

With the release of *Night and Day* in 1945, in which Cary Grant played Porter and Alexis Smith costarred as his wife, and with a score made up of 14 Porter classics, the composer-lyricist won still greater popularity. But then, in the second half of the 1940s, Porter suffered a reversal of fortune. *Around the World in Eighty Days* (May 31, 1946), book adapted by Orson Welles from the Jules Verne novel, closed after 74 performances. The movie musical, *The Pirate*

(1948), was also poison at the box office, in spite of which a soundtrack recording was released. Porter's friends suspected that his many operations and recurrent pain had finally taken their toll. But it was at this crucial period that Porter composed the songs for *Kiss Me, Kate*, not only his best score in any medium, but one of the best of any composed for the American musical theater.

Based on *The Taming of the Shrew*, *Kiss Me, Kate* (December 30, 1948) enjoyed a run of 1,077 performances, the longest of any Porter musical. The librettists, Bella and Sam Spewack, transposed the Shakespeare comedy to a modern setting with contemporary American characters. In the Spewacks' book, a theatrical troupe presents *The Taming of the Shrew* in Baltimore. Its two principals, Fred and Lilli, though divorced, still care for one another. *Kiss Me, Kate* shifts nimbly from today's Baltimore to yesterday's Padua and from the changing moods of Fred and Lilli to the troubles of Petruchio and his shrewish wife, Kate. Since Fred is playing Petruchio and since Lilli has the role of Kate, they sometimes forget they are performing Shakespeare and openly express either pent-up anger about their shared past or repressed romantic longing for one another. Like Kate and Petruchio, they come to realize that they should be together.

Porter's songs were at their sophisticated, satirical best; the music was heartfelt, the lyrics wittily risqué. The leading love ballads were "So in Love," "Were Thine That Special Face," and "Always True to You in My Fashion." "So in Love" was introduced by Patricia Morison, reprised by Alfred Drake, and recorded by Alfred Drake, Bing Crosby, Dinah Shore, Gordon MacRae and Patti Page. It had a single appearance on *Your Hit Parade* and was sung by Kathryn Grayson and Howard Keel in the 1953 film version of the stage musical. "Were Thine That Special Face" was sung by Drake on the stage and by Keel in the film. "Always True to You," introduced by Lisa Kirk, was sung in the film by Ann Miller and Tommy Hall. Another Porter favorite from the score was "Wunderbar," a parody of Viennese operetta music, a duet for Drake and Morison on the stage and Grayson and Keel on the screen. Alfred Drake with Jane Pickens recorded it. The wittiest numbers were: "I Hate Men," sung by Morison on the stage and Grayson on the screen; "Brush Up Your Shakespeare," a duet for Harry Clark and Jack Diamond on the stage and for Keenan Wynn and James Whitmore on the screen; and "Too Darn Hot," sung by Lorenzo Fuller, Eddie Sledge and Fred Davis on the stage and heard as a solo by Ann Miller on the screen. The screen version of

Kiss Me, Kate included a Porter standard not found in the stage score, "From This Moment On," which had been written for and dropped from an unsuccessful Porter musical of 1950, *Out of This World.*

One of the most successful musicals in stage history up to that time, *Kiss Me, Kate* played to sold-out houses throughout the country in a touring company. The original cast recording sold more than a million album copies. The lavishly mounted motion-picture adaptation (1953), whose soundtrack recording was released as a bestselling LP, was pronounced by *The New York Times* film critic Bosley Crowther "one of the year's most magnificent films."

In 1955 *Kiss Me, Kate* was staged in Berlin, becoming the first all-German production of an American musical in the German capital. Later that year, it was produced in Frankfurt. In 1956 *Kiss Me, Kate* enjoyed the longest run of any musical production in the history of the Vienna Volksoper. That same year, *Kiss Me, Kate* was brought back to Broadway. It went on to become the first American musical ever to be mounted in Poland. Performances followed throughout Scandinavia as well as in Hungary, Turkey, Yugoslavia, Czechoslovakia, Iceland, Italy, Belgium, Switzerland, Israel, Japan and Brazil. It has been translated into more than 20 foreign languages.

In his last two Broadway musicals, both successes, Porter returned to Parisian settings for the first time in a quarter of a century. *Can-Can* (May 7, 1953), book by Abe Burrows, takes a nostalgic look at Bohemian Paris of 1893, where the police attempt to shut down a Montmartre night spot that features performances of the "shocking" can-can dance. When Aristide Forestier, a judge, visits the cabaret, he falls in love both with the place and its proprietess, La Mome Pistache, and through his efforts the can-can is made legal. *Can-Can* had an initial Broadway run of 892 performances.

Porter's best songs had a piquant Parisian flavor. His paean to his beloved city, "I Love Paris," was introduced by Lilo (in her American stage debut) and recorded by Bing Crosby, Tony Martin and the orchestras of Les Baxter and Michel Legrand. "C'est Magnifique," a duet for Lilo and Peter Cookson, was recorded by Gordon MacRae. Both songs appeared on *Your Hit Parade,* the former with three hearings, the latter with one. "Allez-Vous-En" was introduced by Lilo and recorded by Kay Starr. "It's All Right With Me," introduced by Peter Cookson, was recorded by Lena Horne and Sammy Davis, Jr. "Come Along With Me" was introduced by Hans Conried and Erik Rhodes and recorded by Sarah

Vaughan. "I Am in Love" was introduced by Cookson and recorded by Ella Fitzgerald. In the sumptuous motion-picture adaptation of 1960, which starred Frank Sinatra, Shirley MacLaine, Maurice Chevalier and Louis Jourdan, Sinatra and Chevalier sang "I Love Paris"; Sinatra, "C'est Magnifique"; Shirley MacLaine, "Come Along With Me" and "Allez-Vous-En"; and Sinatra and Jourdan, "It's All Right With Me." "I Am in Love" was used on the soundtrack as background music. Three Porter classics of an earlier period were included: "You Do Something to Me" (Jourdan); "Just One of Those Things" (Chevalier); and "Let's Do It" (Sinatra and MacLaine). The score of *Can-Can* can be heard on an original cast and a soundtrack recording. Starring Jeanmaire, *Can-Can* was revived on Broadway in 1981 but closed after five performances.

Porter's farewell to the Broadway theater, *Silk Stockings* (February 26, 1955), had a run of 478 performances. This was a musical adaptation of *Ninotchka,* a 1939 movie comedy starring Greta Garbo which satirizes Soviet bureaucracy in particular and communist dogma in general. In both the musical and the film, Ninotchka is a Soviet diplomat with an unwavering faith in communist ideology. Dispatched to Paris to bring back a Soviet composer who had overstayed his leave in the French capital, she discovers that love transcends ideology when she meets Steve Canfield, an American theater agent.

In the score of *Silk Stockings* "All of You" was a romantic ballad introduced by Don Ameche; in the 1957 film version it was sung by Fred Astaire and danced to by Cyd Charisse. Nick Apollo Forte sang it in the Woody Allen film comedy, *Broadway Danny Rose* (1983). "Paris Loves Lovers" was a duet for Don Ameche and Hildegarde Neff on the stage, and a solo for Astaire in the film. "Without Love" was performed by Neff on the stage and by Carole Richards (dubbing on the soundtrack for Charisse) and Astaire in the film. Original cast and soundtrack recordings were released.

Following *Silk Stockings,* Porter composed the scores for two films. *High Society* (1956) was a screen musical based on Philip Barry's play, *The Philadelphia Story.* In *High Society,* Bing Crosby and Grace Kelly introduced "True Love"; their million-selling record was to become Porter's last hit in his lifetime. *Les Girls* (1957), which starred Gene Kelly and Mitzi Gaynor, had "Ca C'est Amour," which was introduced by Taina Elg and recorded by Tony Bennett. Porter's career ended with a score for *Aladdin,* a television special that aired on CBS on February 21, 1958. Its best song was "I Adore You," introduced by Sal Mineo and Anna Maria Alberghetti. The scores of *High Society, Les Girls,* and *Aladdin* were made available in soundtrack recordings.

Porter's "winter of discontent" began in the early 1950s with the death of his mother, in 1952, and his wife, a year later. He was devastated, caught in the grip of loneliness and melancholia, afflictions his tour of the Greek islands on a chartered yacht in February 1956 did not relieve. Back in the United States, he underwent two more operations on his legs, the last of which, the 33d since his accident, took place in 1958. Thereafter he suffered chronic pain. When a bone tumor was diagnosed as life-threatening, his right leg had to be amputated on April 3, 1958. Refusing to use an artificial limb, he lived as a recluse in his apartment at the Waldorf Astoria and, during summers at his California mansion, was carried around by two valets. When awarded honors he refused to attend ceremonies, such as the "Salute to Cole Porter" at the Metropolitan Opera House in New York in May 1960. An honorary degree from Yale University the following June had to be given, for the first time in Yale's history, in absentia. His 70th birthday was celebrated by friends and theater colleagues at the Orpheum Theatre in downtown Manhattan without his presence.

At his California home, in October 1964, Porter underwent a routine operation for a kidney stone. Though no complications set in, he died in the hospital two days later, on October 15. When death came, he was alone. Following his wishes, there was neither a funeral nor a memorial service. He was buried in Peru, Indiana between the graves of his mother and his wife.

Porter once described his method of working thusly: "First I think of an idea for a song and then I fit it to a title. Then I go to work on a melody, spotting the title at certain times in the melody. Then I write the lyrics, the end first, that way it has a strong finish. It's terribly important for a song to have a strong finish. I do the lyrics the way I'd do a crossword puzzle. I try to give myself a meter which will make the lyric as easy as possible to write, but without being banal. . . . I try to pick up my rhyme words of which there is a long list . . . ."

Before writing lyrics whose subjects were specialized areas of knowledge such as zoology, botany or internal medicine, Porter undertook considerable research. When writing, he was surrounded by dictionaries, a thesaurus, and assorted writing equipment. Always compulsively neat, he insisted that the contents of his desk be always in their proper place. While working, he kept the sheets of his music and lyrics neatly arranged in looseleaf notebooks and manila folders.

Both Cole Porter's music and his personality have stayed alive in the public consciousness. *The Decline and Fall of the Entire World as Seen Through the Eyes of Cole Porter* was an Off Broadway revue in 1965 in whch the years of 1929–1945 were viewed through 33 Porter songs. *Words and Music by Cole Porter* was a musical tribute to Porter, telecast on NBC on November 25, 1965, starring Robert Goulet and Maurice Chevalier. In July 1970 the American Ballet Theatre revived, after 45 years of neglect, a ballet for which Porter had written the music in his earlier years. Titled *Within the Quota,* the Swedish Ballet had introduced it in New York and Paris in 1923. With new choreography and a scenario by Keith Lee, and retitled *Times Past,* it retained the original score. *Cole Porter in Paris* was a television special aired on NBC on January 17, 1973; it starred Diahann Carroll, Louis Jourdan, and Charles Aznavour. In Bogdanovich's mid-decade *At Long Last Love,* 16 Porter standards were featured, but the film was a box-office failure. *Happy New Year,* a Broadway musical that opened on April 27, 1980, was an adaptation of Philip Barry's Broadway comedy, *Holiday,* combined with 26 Porter songs. The film *Evil Under the Sun* (1982) used a repertory of Porter's song classics as its basic score; it was heard orchestrally as background music on the soundtrack.

Porter was remembered on the anniversary of his 90th birthday at the Algonquin Hotel in New York. That day, June 8, 1981, was proclaimed by Mayor Edward Koch as "Cole Porter Day" and all that week, at Macy's department store, Porter's music was played daily at 12:30 by visiting pianists.

Porter's standards, as well as many of his less famous songs, have been assembled in albums recorded by Ella Fitzgerald, Mary Martin, Risë Stevens, Allan Jones, Kiri Te Kanawa, Ben Bagley, and André Kostelanetz and his orchestra, among many others.

ABOUT: The Cole Porter Song Book, 1959; Eels, G. The Life that Late He Led: A Biography of Cole Porter, 1967; Kimball, R. (ed.) Cole, 1971; Kimball, R. The Complete Lyrics of Cole Porter, 1983; Schwartz, C. Cole Porter, 1977; Wilder A. American Popular Song, 1972. *Periodicals*—Harper's September 1959; New York Times December 9, 1973; New York Times Magazine October 10, 1971; New Yorker September 18, 1971.

RAINGER, RALPH (October 7, 1901–October 23, 1942), composer, was born on the East Side of Manhattan. His father was a dealer in rugs. Rainger began studying the piano when he was six, and theory and composition at 13 from texts his mother provided him. After his family moved to Newark, New Jersey, he played the piano at school dances while attending high school. In his senior year he was awarded a scholarship from the Institute of Musical Art in New York City. During the one year Rainger spent there he played the piano in a jazz orchestra.

Urged by his father and his uncle to give up the ambition to become a professional musician, Rainger left the institute to study law at Brown University. As a law student he supported himself as a salesman and by driving trucks and working on farms. After graduating from Brown with honors he worked for a New York law firm for $25 a week. Bored with the practice of law, he sought diversion, and additional income, by playing in jazz bands. In 1926 he turned his back on the legal profession to concentrate on playing popular music. That year he found work as a pianist in the pit orchestra and formed the two-piano team of Blair Fairchild and Ralph Rainger for the Broadway musical, *Queen High.* When that show closed, he and Fairchild played piano in the pit for the *Ziegfeld Follies of 1927.* After that Rainger served as a piano accompanist for the touring vaudeville act of Clifton Webb and Mary Hay. When the tour ended in Chicago, Webb and Rainger returned to New York to join the Broadway revue, the *Little Show* (1929), Webb as one of its stars, Rainger as a duo pianist with Adam Carroll in the pit orchestra.

While the *Little Show* was in rehearsal, music was needed for a dance performed by Webb. Rainger provided it with "Moanin' Low" (lyrics by Howard Dietz), the first Rainger song to be performed in a Broadway musical, his first to be published and his first to become a hit. With this one number, which became a standard, his career as a composer was established. "One of the most striking things in the revue," wrote one reviewer of the *Little Show,* "is . . . 'Moanin' Low,' which Libby Holman sings in that powerfully throbbing voice of hers while Clifton Webb dances with her in a mad grotesque." Holman recorded the song in 1929, as did Sophie Tucker, Lee Morse and Leo Reisman and his orchestra. Later, Lena Horne's jazzy rendition became one of her first recording successes. "Moanin' Low" was interpolated into the Humphrey Bogart–Lauren Bacall film, *Key Largo* (1948), and Harry James performed it in *Young Man With a Horn* (1950), the film biography of jazz great Bix Biederbecke.

Rainger's "Breakfast Dance" (lyrics by Ed-

RALPH RAINGER

ward Eliscu) was used in the short-lived *9:15 Revue* (1930). "Got a Man on My Mind" (lyrics by Dietz) was introduced and popularized by Libby Holman in 1930. "I'll Take an Option on You" (lyrics by Dietz) was introduced by Frank Fay in the Broadway revue *Tattle Tales* (1933) and was recorded by Paul Whiteman.

After 1930 Rainger wrote primarily for motion pictures, making his debut with "When a Woman Loves a Man" (lyrics by Billy Rose), which was written for Fanny Brice, who introduced it in *Be Yourself* (1930). For six years, working mainly with Leo Robin as lyricist, Rainger was employed by Paramount. Many of his songs were introduced in films starring Bing Crosby and popularized in Crosby's recordings, beginning with "Please," first heard in *The Big Broadcast of 1932,* in which Crosby made his debut as a leading man in a full-length film. In this screen revue, Crosby was joined by Arthur Tracy and the orchestra of Vincent Lopez in performing "Here Lies Love." Jack Oakie sang "Please" in *From Hell to Heaven* (1933).

Bing Crosby introduced many other Rainger songs (lyrics by Leo Robin unless otherwise specified) in movies. He sang "Love in Bloom" as a duet with Kitty Carlisle in *She Loves Me Not* two years before Jack Benny presented it in *College Holiday* (1936). Benny adopted "Love in Bloom" as his theme song on radio and television, and Crosby's recording of it was a bestseller. "Bloom" was also recorded in 1934 by Georgie Price, Arthur Tracy and the orchestras of Hal Kemp and Paul Whiteman. Lynn Overman sang it in the film *New York Town* (1941) and Judy Canova in *True to the Army* (1942).

"June in January" and "With Every Breath I Take," the latter a duet with Kitty Carlisle, were Crosby's principal songs in *Here Is My Heart* (1934). "June in January" was recorded by Harry Richman, Arthur Tracy and the orchestras of Guy Lombardo and Bob Grant, and it was Crosby's first release on the Decca label. This song was interpolated for Frank Sinatra in *The Joker Was Wild* (1957) and was heard in a recording on the soundtrack of *The Day of the Locust* (1975), based on Nathanael West's 1939 novel. "With Every Breath I Take" was recorded in 1934 by Harry Richman and Arthur Tracy.

"I Wished on the Moon" (lyrics by Dorothy Parker) was introduced in *The Big Broadcast of 1936*, recorded by Lanny Ross, and had seven appearances on *Your Hit Parade*. The song was heard on the soundtrack of *Day of the Locust*. In *Waikiki Wedding* (1937) Bing Crosby sang "Blue Hawaii," which Harry Owens and His Royal Hawaiian Orchestra had introduced in performance in Honolulu. It provided the title for the popular Elvis Presley movie, *Blue Hawaii* (1961). Presley sang the Rainger-Robin number, and the soundtrack LP is Elvis's bestselling album. Crosby also introduced "Sweet is the Word for You" in *Waikiki Wedding*. Both songs were represented on *Your Hit Parade*, "Blue Hawaii" seven times, "Sweet is the Word" twice.

"I Have Eyes" and "You're a Sweet Little Headache," both from *Paris Honeymoon* (1939), were also on *Your Hit Parade*, the former six times, the latter three. "I Have Eyes" was introduced by Bing Crosby, Shirley Ross and Franceska Gaal, and "You're a Sweet Little Headache" by Crosby.

In 1938 Rainger won an Oscar for "Thanks for the Memory" which Bob Hope (in his screen debut) and Shirley Ross introduced in the *Big Broadcast of 1938*. Since then, Hope has made the song famous as his musical theme. Shirley Ross and Hope recorded it in 1938, as did Isham Jones and his orchestra. "Thanks for the Memory" received ten hearings on *Your Hit Parade*, three times in the top position.

Among the Rainger songs heard on *Your Hit Parade* were: "I Don't Want to Make History" (two appearances), sung by Frances Langford in *Palm Springs* (1936) and recorded by Bob Crosby; "A Rendezvous With a Dream" (11 appearances), introduced by Rochelle Hudson in the film *Poppy* (1936) and recorded by Shep Fields and his orchestra; the title song of *Blossoms on Broadway* (1937, 11 appearances), performed by Shirley Ross and recorded by the orchestra of Jan Garber; the title song of *Ebb Tide* (1937, two appearances), recorded by Ozzie Nelson and by Bunny Berigan; "What Have You Got That Gets Me?" (two times), introduced by Jack Benny, Joan Bennett, Joyce Compton and the Yacht Boys in *Artists and Models Abroad* (1938); "What Goes on Here in My Heart?" (six times), introduced by Betty Grable and Jack Whiting in *Give Me a Sailor* (1938) and recorded by Henry Busse and his orchestra; "You Took the Words Right Out of My Heart" (three times), which Dorothy Lamour and Leif Erickson sang in the *Big Broadcast of 1938*; "Mama, That Moon is Here Again" (once) from the 1938 *Big Broadcast*; "Faithful Forever" (nine times), introduced by Jessica Dragonette and Lanny Ross on the soundtrack of *Gulliver's Travels* (1940), an animated film; and "Here You Are" (three times), from *My Gal Sal* (1942), recorded by the orchestras of Sammy Kaye and Freddy Martin.

In other films, hit songs by Rainger and Robin were: "In the Park in Paree," which Maurice Chevalier introduced in *A Bedtime Story* (1933), and which he sang again in *A New Kind of Love* (1963); "Give Me Liberty or Give Me Love," introduced by Claudette Colbert in *The Torch Singer* (1933), recorded by Bob Causer; "A Guy What Takes His Time" (lyrics by Rainger), written for and introduced by Mae West in *She Done Him Wrong* (1933); "Take a Lesson From the Larks," introduced by Ben Bernie and his orchestra in *Shoot the Works* (1934); "Why Dream?" (music written with Richard Whiting), introduced by Henry Wadsworth in the *Big Broadcast of 1936* (1935); "If I Should Lose You," introduced by Gladys Swarthout and John Boles in *Rose of the Rancho* (1936) and recorded by Richard Himber and his orchestra; "Then it Isn't Love," written for Marlene Dietrich in *The Devil is a Woman* (1935) but deleted from that production (which Dietrich considered her strongest performance), then introduced by Carole Lombard in *Swing High, Swing Low* (1937); "A Little Kiss at Twilight," introduced by Martha Raye in *Give Me a Sailor* and recorded by Henry Busse.

Ralph Rainger left the Paramount studios in 1938 to work for 20th Century-Fox. The last two films with Rainger songs, *Riding High* and *Coney Island*, were released posthumously in 1943. Rainger died in an airplane accident near Palm Springs on October 23, 1942.

ABOUT: Burton, J. The Blue Book of Tin Pan Alley, 1950; Craig, W. Sweet and Lowdown: America's Popular Song Writers, 1978.

REVEL, HARRY (December 21, 1905–November 3, 1958) and **GORDON, MACK** (June 21, 1904–February 28, 1959). The com-

HARRY REVEL   MACK GORDON

poser Harry Revel was born in London, England in 1905 to a middle-class family. He began studying the piano when he was nine, and later attended the Guildhall School of Music and Drama in London with the ambition of becoming a piano virtuoso. The death of his teacher ended his formal piano study.

When he was 17, Revel became the piano player for an ensemble that toured the Continent playing Hawaiian music. He later toured Europe with a group called the New York Jazz, whose members were two Englishmen, two Italians, three Russians, two Frenchmen and one Texan. In Berlin Revel composed the score for an operetta, *Was Frauen träumen*, his first stage musical. In 1925, as a pianist, he gave a command performance for the royal family of Italy, and in 1927 he contributed songs to a music hall revue in London. An admirer of American popular music, Revel at this time wrote words and music for several songs in that style. The best numbers were "I'm Going Back to Old Nebraska," which had sheet music sales of about 500,000 copies in London, and "Just Give the Southland to Me."

Revel came to the United States in 1929 on a visitor's visa, and provoked the immigration authorities when he tried to represent himself as a native-born American (he subsequently obtained American citizenship). Revel's European musical experiences generated little enthusiasm in Tin Pan Alley, where his American-style compositions were received with indifference. To support himself, he toured the vaudeville circuit as a piano accompanist for Mack Gordon, a singer and comedian whose avocation was writing

song lyrics, some of which had been published. The two men were soon writing songs together, and Revel persuaded Gordon to give up his vaudeville performances and concentrate on musical composition.

The lyricist Mack Gordon was born Morris Gittelson in Warsaw, Poland in 1904. While he was still a child, his family immigrated to New York, where Gordon attended elementary schools in Brooklyn and the Bronx. He dropped out of school to become a boy soprano in a minstrel show with which he toured for several years. That experience enabled Gordon to make the transition into vaudeville as a headliner. In his spare time Gordon was writing songs. To music by Max Rich, he composed the lyrics for "Ain'tcha," which Helen Kane introduced in the motion picture, *Pointed Heels* (1929). With Harold Adamson as co-lyricist he wrote the words for the Vincent Youmans standard, "Time on My Hands," first heard in the Broadway musical *Smiles* (1930), starring Marilyn Miller.

Gordon and Revel began their collaboration by contributing songs to the *Ziegfeld Follies of 1931*, the last edition which Ziegfeld produced. "Help Yourself to Happiness" was written with and introduced by Harry Richman, and "Cigarettes, Cigars!" was first performed by Ruth Etting. The former was recorded by Glen Gray and the Casa Loma Orchestra, the latter by Ruth Etting. For Etting, Gordon and Revel composed "Such is Life, Such is Love" in 1931. Later that year Gordon and Revel composed the score for *Fast and Furious* (September 9, 1931), an all-black revue that lasted on Broadway for just six performances. Two Broadway musicals for which they composed complete scores in 1932 did little better. *Marching By* (April 3, 1932) closed after 12 performances and *Smiling Faces* (August 8, 1932) after 31.

They recovered from these setbacks in 1932 with the song "I Played the Fiddle for the Czar," which Ben Bernie and his orchestra introduced, and with "Underneath the Harlem Moon," which was heard in vaudeville, recorded by Carmen Cavallero, and had respectable sheet-music sales.

Lured to California in 1933 by a Paramount contract, Gordon and Revel's first assignment was music for *Sitting Pretty* (1933). In this film Ginger Rogers and Art Jarrett introduced "Did You Ever See a Dream Walking?" Snooky Lanson, the Pickens Sisters, Vaughn Monroe and Guy Lombardo and His Royal Canadians recorded this song, and it was revived in the film *Pennies From Heaven* (1981). Ginger Rogers, Jack Haley, Jack Oakie, Art Jarrett and the Pickens Sisters sang "Good Morning Glory" in *Sitting Pretty* and Jack Oakie, Ginger Rogers, Jack Haley and Thelma Todd "You're Such a Comfort to Me." In 1933 Russ Columbo introduced, and Ruth Etting recorded, "You're My Past, Present and Future," and Frances Williams introduced "Doin' the Uptown Lowdown" in *Through a Keyhole* (1933). Both numbers were recorded by Isham Jones and his orchestra.

Over the next seven years, Gordon and Revel contributed songs to more than 30 movies. Three of these songs reached the number one spot on *Your Hit Parade*: the title song from *Paris in the Spring* (1935); "When I'm With You," introduced by Shirley Temple and Tony Martin, and reprised by Alice Faye, in *Poor Little Rich Girl* (1936); and "Good Night, My Love" introduced by Shirley Temple and reprised by Alice Faye in *Poor Little Rich Girl.*

Fourteen other screen songs by Gordon and Revel appeared on *Your Hit Parade*. They were: "From the Top of Your Head" and "Without a Word of Warning" (six appearances each); both were introduced by Bing Crosby in *Two for Tonight* (1935) and recorded by him.

"You Hit the Spot" (six appearances), introduced by Frances Langford, Jack Oakie and Mack Gordon in *Collegiate* (1936) and interpolated into the film *Scared Stiff* (1953).

"I Feel Like a Feather in the Breeze" (nine), sung by a female chorus in *Collegiate* and recorded by Jan Garber and his orchestra.

"A Star Fell Out of Heaven" (11), heard in *Poor Little Rich Girl* after it had been introduced by Bennie Fields.

"Afraid to Dream" (nine), introduced by Don Ameche and reprised by Alice Faye and Tony Martin in *You Can't Have Everything* (1937).

"Never in a Million Years" (ten), sung on the soundtrack of *Wake Up and Live* (1937) by Buddy Clark dubbing for Jack Haley.

"There's a Lull in My Life" (nine), introduced by Alice Faye in *Wake Up and Live* and recorded by Ruth Etting, Alice Faye and the orchestra of Teddy Wilson.

"Sweet Someone" (two), introduced by Simone Simon in *Love and Hisses* (1937).

"I've Got a Date With a Dream" (four), performed by Arthur Jarrett, Buddy Ebsen, Joan Davis and a female chorus in *My Lucky Star* (1938) and recorded by Benny Goodman.

"Sweet as a Song," introduced by Tony Martin in *Sally, Irene and Mary* (1938).

"Where in the World?" (twice), introduced by Don Ameche in *Josette* (1938).

The title song for *Thanks for Everything* (1938, seven appearances), introduced by Tony Martin.

"I Never Knew Heaven Could Speak" (five), introduced by Alice Faye in *Rose of Washington Square* (1939) and recorded by Bing Crosby.

The partnership of Harry Revel and Mack Gordon ended in 1939, with each going on to work with other composers. During World War II, Revel devoted himself to war-related activities, supervising a USO unit in Hollywood, organizing stage shows that toured hospitals and military bases and editing *At Ease*, a magazine for hospitalized veterans.

After the war Revel returned to the Broadway theater for the last time, writing the music for *Are You With It?* (November 10, 1945). The lyrics were by Arnold B. Horwitt, and the book by Sam Perrin and George Balzer was based on *Slightly Imperfect,* a novel by George Malcolm-Smith. *Are You With It?* had a moderate run of 266 performances. Its hero, William Haskins, loses his job with an insurance company, but finds another with a carnival, where he meets and falls in love with Vivian Reilly. "Here I Go Again," and "Slightly Perfect" were sung by Joan Roberts; the title song by Dolores Grey; "Just Beyond the Rainbow" by June Richmond; and "This is My Beloved" by Joan Roberts and Johnny Downs.

Working with other lyricists, Revel contributed songs to another dozen and a half films, but his greatest success was behind him. His best screen songs after 1939 were: "When There's a Breeze on Lake Louise" (lyrics by Mort Greene), which was sung by Joan Merrill in *The Mayor of 44th Street* (1942); "I'd Like to Set You to Music" (lyrics by Paul Francis Webster) from *Hit the Ice* (1943); and "Remember Me to Carolina" (lyrics by Webster) from *Minstrel Man* (1944).

Revel's last popular song was "Jet" (lyrics by

Bennie Benjamin and George Weiss), composed in 1949, when it was introduced as an instrumental in a recording by the orchestra of Les Baxter and was popularized as a vocal in a recording by Nat King Cole.

Under the sponsorship of Corday Perfumes, Revel composed *Perfumes Set to Music,* an orchestral piece introduced at a "pop" concert at Carnegie Hall in the spring of 1954. This work attempted, as the program explained, "to capture and reproduce with musical instruments and the human voice the 'sounds' of fragrance and scents." Revel also created *Music Out of the Moon* and *Music for Peace of Mind* for therapeutic purposes. *Perfumes, Moon,* and *Mind* were all recorded.

For many years Revel was the director of Realm Music Company, his own publishing house which he founded in 1949. A bachelor his entire life, Revel spent his last years in retirement at his apartment on Manhattan's Upper West Side. He died of a cerebral hemorrhage at his home.

Mack Gordon wrote the lyrics to a series of hit songs after his separation from Revel while working at the Fox studios with the composer Harry Warren. Among them were: the Oscar-winning "You'll Never Know" from *Hello, Frisco Hello* (1943); "Chattanooga Choo Choo" from *Sun Valley Serenade* (1941); "I've Got a Gal in Kalamazoo" from *Orchestra Wives* (1942); "My Heart Tells Me" from *Sweet Rosie O'Grady* (1943); "I Can't Begin to Tell You" from *The Dolly Sisters* (1945); "The More I See You" from *Diamond Horseshoe* (1945). All of those songs reached the top position on *Your Hit Parade.* Also represented on *Your Hit Parade,* though not in first place, were: "Down Argentina Way" and "Two Dreams Met" from *Down Argentina Way* (1940); "Serenade in Blue" and "At Last" from *Orchestra Wives;* "I Had the Craziest Dream" from *Springtime in the Rockies* (1942); and "I Wish I Knew" from *Diamond Horseshoe.*

Other Gordon-Warren screen songs of special interest are: "You Say the Sweetest Things" from *Tin Pan Alley* (1949); "I Know Why," from *Sun Valley Serenade* (1941); "Long Ago Last Night" from *The Great American Broadcast* (1941); "In Acapulco" from *Diamond Horseshoe* (1945); "If You Feel Like Singing, Sing" and "Friendly Star" from *Summer Stock* (1950).

Jimmy Monaco was another composer with whom Gordon worked after 1939. Monaco was the composer of "I'm Making Believe," from *Sweet and Low Down* (1944); "Time Alone Will Tell" and "Once Too Often" from *Pin-Up Girl* (1944); and from *The Dolly Sisters* (1945), "I Can't Begin to Tell You," which held the top position on *Your Hit Parade.*

(For additional information about Harry Warren and Jimmy Monaco consult their biographies.)

For a half dozen years after 1945, Gordon was the lyricist for the composer Josef Myrow. They wrote "You Make Me Feel So Young," introduced by Vera-Ellen and Frank Lattimore in *Three Little Girls in Blue* (1946), and recorded by Dick Haymes. "You Do" was introduced by Dan Dailey in *Mother Wore Tights* (1947), recorded by Vaughn Monroe, Margaret Whiting and Bing Crosby, and had 12 representations on *Your Hit Parade,* holding first position on October 11, 1947. "By the Way" and "What Did I Do?" were heard in *When My Baby Smiles at Me* (1948). "By the Way" was recorded by Perry Como, who also recorded "Wilhelmina," which was heard in *Wabash Avenue* (1950). Debbie Reynolds introduced "A Lady Loves" in *I Love Melvin* (1951).

With the composer Edmund Goulding, Gordon wrote "Mam'selle," which was used in the café scene of the nonmusical film, *The Razor's Edge* (1946), starring Tyrone Power. Art Lund recorded it and it was heard 14 times on *Your Hit Parade,* three times in first position. Alfred Newman (rock singer Randy Newman's uncle) composed the music for "Through a Long and Sleepless Night," which was interpolated into the nonmusical film *Come to the Stable* (1949).

Gordon's last successful song was "You Will Find Your Love in Paris." The melody came from a French popular song, music by Guy La Forge, which Gordon refurbished with new English lyrics in 1958.

Mack Gordon spent his last years in Manhattan where he made his home in an apartment on East 64th Street. Both his marriages ended in divorce. He died at New York's Roosevelt Hospital, and was survived by two sons and a daughter.

ABOUT: Burton, J. The Blue Book of Tin Pan Alley, 1950; Craig, W. Sweet and Lowdown: America's Popular Song Writers, 1978.

RICHIE, LIONEL (June 20, 1949–   ). In the romantic ballads that have brought composer-lyricist Lionel Richie Grammy, ASCAP, gold, platinum and multiplatinum awards, country music, gospel, soul and rock meet on common ground.

Lionel Brockman Richie Jr. was born in Tuskegee, Alabama. His grandfather, who had worked in the business office of Tuskegee Institute, was a colleague of Booker T. Washington, the school's founder. His grandmother, Adelaide

LIONEL RICHIE

Foster, taught classical piano at the college. His father, Lionel Richie Sr., a retired army captain, was employed as a systems analyst; and his mother, Alberta, was the principal of an elementary school. Lionel was raised in a cultivated Southern household that was relatively untouched by racial tensions. He and his sister and their parents lived with Lionel's grandmother on the Institute campus, where he was introduced to classical music by his grandmother. She tried to give him piano instruction but he resisted, preferring to go his own way in music without formal guidance, being what he called "a music lover, a listener, period." Richie taught himself to perform some James Brown riffs on a tenor saxophone which his uncle had given him. As a boy, Lionel sang in the choir of the Episcopal Church, where he was also an altar boy. Religion and gospel music were significant early influences, but so were British-invasion rock and the Motown soul of the Temptations and the Supremes.

Richie received most of his primary and secondary education in Tuskegee, but in 1968 he graduated from high school in Joliet, Illinois. He then entered Tuskegee Institute; majoring in economics with a minor in accounting, he aspired to a career in law rather than music. Too small to play football, too short for basketball, and too slow for the track team, he used his spare time to teach himself to play the saxophone. Thomas Clary, a fellow freshman who played the guitar, invited Richie to join him and another Tuskegee student in forming a band. With McClary on the guitar, William ("Wak") King on the trumpet, and Richie doubling as saxo-

phonist and vocalist, the trio became known on campus as the Mystics. When a local group called the Jays disbanded, a few of its members joined the Mystics, who now began calling themselves the Commodores (a name they selected from a dictionary). Their ambition, recalled Richie, was "to be *like* the Beatles . . . a household word, a musical legend."

During the summer of 1968, the Commodores went to New York City, where Benny Ashburn, a public relations man, became the group's manager and booked it to play at Small's Paradise in Harlem and at the Cheetah, a rock club in midtown Manhattan. With the band now comprising Milan Williams (piano), Walter ("Clyde") Orange (drums) and Ronald LaPread (bass), together with Richie (lead singer), McClary and King, the Commodores attracted the attention of Suzanne DePasse, a booking agent, who arranged for the group to appear as the opening act for the 1971 European tour of the Jackson Five. The Commodores toured with the Jacksons for two years, including appearances in the United States climaxed by a performance at the Hollywood Bowl in 1973. The Commodores also signed a contract with Motown Records, cutting four tracks with James Carmichael as producer. One of their first original songs was an instrumental called "Machine Gun," composed by Milan Williams, which became the title cut of their first album. From that 1974 LP came the Commodores' first nationwide hit, "The Bump," an instrumental which provided the name for a popular dance of the mid-1970s.

At Motown, Richie began to show an interest in songwriting. He picked up pointers by studying the methods of such Motown composers as Norman Whitfield, Stevie Wonder and the team of Holland, Dozier and Holland. "I sat in on some Stevie Wonder sessions," he told an interviewer for *Rolling Stone*, "and Stevie would sit there and sing 'da da da da' and then fill in the words. I said 'Wait a minute, you mean all I gotta do is fill in the 'da da's?' When I found that out, the ball game was over."

In 1975 Richie emerged as the principal composer for the Commodores with the ballad "This is Your Life," a cut on the album *Caught in the Act*. That year, "Just to Be Close to You" became Richie's first song to achieve gold status as a single. This ballad was soon followed by another, the million-selling "Easy," which was from the 1977 album *Commodores*, the group's first platinum LP. In 1978 "Three Times a Lady," became a triple-platinum single. Inspired by a party honoring the 37th wedding anniversary of Richie's parents, the ballad was a tribute to the three most important women in Richie's life—

his grandmother, his mother, and his wife. This became the first single by the Commodores to reach number one on three charts, soul, country, and pop. It also reached number one in five other countries and made the top five in another 25 countries. And it received a triple platinum certification. The Commodores next album, *Natural High,* was awarded a gold record in 1978.

Ranked the number one rhythm-and-blues group by *Billboard, Rolling Stone* and *Cashbox* in 1978, the Commodores toured the United States that year, giving 92 performances over a period of six months. A year later, the band's superstar status was confirmed when Richie and his confreres signed a new contract with Motown valued at 20 million dollars.

The Commodores' two prime song successes of 1979, songs composed by Richie and included on their triple-platinum *Midnight Magic* album, were "Still" and "Sail On." Composed by Richie, each was inspired by the breakup of friends' marriages. "Still" rose to the number one position on the *Billboard* charts on November 17, 1979

The 1980 Commodores album, *Heroes,* included such notable Richie songs as "Got To Be Together" and "An Old-Fashioned Love," while *In the Pocket* (1981), the group's most critically praised album since 1977, included Richie's "Lady, You Bring Me Up" (written with Harold Hudson) and "Oh, No."

The first time Richie worked apart from the Commodores as a songwriter was in 1980 with the mournful "Lady," which Kenny Rogers, the country singer, recorded. "The idea," Rogers said, "was that Lionel would come from rhythm and blues and I'd come from country and we'd meet somewhere in pop." It was with this recording that Rogers, already a superstar, became America's foremost male balladeer. On the top spot of the national charts for six weeks, "Lady" was Rogers's largest-selling single to date. Rogers also recorded Richie's "Goin' Back to Alabama" as a single, and four Richie songs were included on his platinum album, *Share Your Love* (1981), which Richie produced.

In 1981 Richie moved further from the Commodores when he wrote "Endless Love," the title song of a motion picture directed by Franco Zeffirelli and starring Brooke Shields. Zeffirelli originally called upon Richie to contribute an instrumental to be used on the soundtrack as a recurrent theme, but then decided a title song was preferable. Zeffirelli also suggested that a female voice—Diana Ross's, specifically—should be added to that of Richie. Their single, which Richie produced, became the most successful ever released by Motown, remaining nine weeks at

the number one spot on the charts. It was also the most successful soundtrack single to that date and the most successful duet performance on a single. Richie sang it at the 1982 Oscar ceremonies before an audience estimated at 360 million worldwide. "After that evening," he said "life changed."

Richie's decision to leave the Commodores to devote himself to his career as a solo performer was finalized when Benny Ashburn died of a heart attack in September 1982. Signed with Kenny Rogers's manager, Ken Kragen, Richie released his first solo album, *Lionel Richie,* later that year. He described the recording as a survey of his musical past, contending, despite his forays into country pop and his burgeoning popularity with MOR (Middle of the Road) audiences, that he was still faithful to the Commodores sound. Reviewing the LP in the New York *Daily News,* (October 29, 1982), Hugh Wyat expressed awe "at both the singing and songwritng powers of Richie, who has the kind of stuff Joe Williams and Marvin Gaye are made of: musical majesty, as this album so emphatically demonstrates." One of its cuts, "Truly," became Richie's first single as a solo performer to reach the top of the charts. In addition "Truly" brought Richie his first Grammy as the year's best male vocalist. Other successful album numbers are "You Are" (written in collaboration with his wife, Brenda) and "My Love" (in the performance of which Kenny Rogers sang harmony).

Richie's next solo album was *Can't Slow Down* (1983), which went multiplatinum, won a Grammy as album of the year and led ASCAP to designate Richie composer of the year. Here we find another of Richie's giant song successes, "All Night Long," a number influenced by a Jamaican chant whose lyrics include the incantatory gibberish words "Tom bo li de say di moi ya, yeah, jambo, jumbo." "If you go back and try to find what it means," Richie has explained, "it's like most . . . chants. They don't mean anything, but you know what they mean—you know what I'm saying." By the time *Can't Slow Down* was released, "All Night Long" was already one of the year's biggest singles, topping the charts and having a video that was extremely popular on MTV. When Richie was invited to perform at the closing ceremonies of the Olympic Games in Los Angeles in the summer of 1984, he responded with a performance of "All Night Long," which included a new verse honoring the athletes. His audience on television that day numbered more than two and a half billion viewers in 120 countries.

From *Can't Slow Down,* "Hello" became Richie's sixth chart-topping single. It had been intended for, but was discarded from, his first album. Stephen Holden in *The New York Times* (November 9, 1983) described "Hello" as "a simple country ballad" with a "19th-century Romantic feeling." Three other songs from this album deserve attention: the title track, "Running With the Night" and "Penny Lover," the last-mentioned written in collaboration with his wife.

Richie's first tour as solo performer took place in the fall of 1983, during which his position as a superstar solidified. A year later he was the host of the three-hour telecast of the American Music Awards. When he returned to host that telecast a year later, he marched away with six trophies. Meanwhile, in 1984, he signed a contract estimated at eight and a half million dollars to sing and write commercials for Pepsi-Cola. In 1985 he captured the three top ASCAP awards for "All Night Long," including that of most-often-performed song.

In 1985 Richie took part in a songwriting event of international scope and with no precedent in recording history when, with Michael Jackson, he wrote "We Are the World." Forty-five singers, each a celebrity, joined voices to record it. In this group, besides Richie, were such stars as Bruce Springsteen, Stevie Wonder, Michael Jackson, Bob Dylan, Willie Nelson, Harry Belafonte, Ray Charles, Kenny Rogers, Billy Joel, Paul Simon, Bette Midler, Diana Ross, Dionne Warwick and many others. Never before has such a collection of pop singers assembled to record a new song. That song had been written, and its recording was made, to raise funds for famine relief in Ethiopia. The writing of the song requried three days of preparation but only two and a half hours of actual work. As Richie told *Billboard*: "He [Michael Jackson] brought in an idea. I brought in an idea. We went back, we listened, and then we smashed both ideas together. The music came first. As for the lyrics . . . it just kind of flowed. . . . I'd throw out a line—the same one, with the words changed around differently—and I'd change his line and finally we got this wonderful line."

Song history was made yet again on Good Friday, April 5, 1985 at 3:50 p.m. when 5,000 radio stations throughout the world broadcast the song simultaneously. Eight days later, the record became number one on the charts. By May, the recording was the first single ever to be certified as a multiplatinum record. A few weeks more and 7,300,000 singles had been sold (together with four million albums on which it was the title song). The first royalty check presented by Columbia Records to the relief fund was in the amount of $6,500,000. Further royalties from the worldwide sale of the record and related products swelled the contribution to about 50 million dollars for food, clothing and medical supplies for stricken Africa.

The success of "We Are the World" and of "Do They Know It's Christmas," a recording by British rock stars, set into motion another project, one of even more colossal proportions, for raising more millions for famine relief. A worldwide Live AID concert was arranged in July 1985 in which the world's most famous rock musicians appeared in a day-long event, telecast throughout the world from London and Philadelphia. The Philadelphia show climaxed when, after Bob Dylan had finished his set, Richie came onstage to lead a multitude of musical celebrities in singing "We Are the World." The worldwide financial returns from Live Aid amounted to another 40 million dollars.

Richie introduced his song "Say You Say Me" on the soundtrack of the film *White Nights,* (1985), starring Gregory Hines and Mikhail Baryshnikov. He recorded the song for Motown later that year, and at the Academy Awards ceremonies in March 1986, "Say You Say Me" won the Oscar for best original song, and it was included on his 1986 LP *Dance on the Ceiling.* The song "Dance on the Ceiling" was a hit single for Richie in the fall of 1986. Another popular song on the LP was the country-inflected "Deep River Woman," which Richie performed with Alabama, the country-rock group.

Lionel and Brenda Richie reside in a house in Beverly Hills, California, and in an apartment in Tuskegee, in a housing complex which he owns. Brenda has not only been Richie's collaborator on several songs but has also worked as his production assistant. In spite of his success and his polished performance style, Richie is shy and introverted when he is offstage. And in spite of his wealth, his personal modesty is reflected in his unpretentious way of life. He once explained that he does not ever want to live so that he cannot walk into his kitchen in his bathrobe without passing 18 "folks" and also that he has learned "you can only drive one car at a time."

To Robert E. Johnson in an interview for *Ebony* (January 1985), Richie said: "I want to make more than music. I want to make statements and I also want to make changes in areas such as minority education. For a long time, I have had an interest in kids with no opportunities."

ABOUT: Current Biography, 1984; Nathan, D. Lionel Richie, 1985; Nite, N. N. Rock On, vol. 2 1978. *Periodicals*—Chicago Tribune December 12, 1982; Ebony May 1979, January 1985; Newsday October 10, 1982; New York Times November 9, 1983; Rolling

Stone October 13, 1981; Washington Post August 1, 1980.

ROBBINS, MARTY (September 26, 1925–December 8, 1982), wrote the music and lyrics of more than 500 country-and-western songs. As a performer 12 numbers of his own composition reached the top position in the country charts, as did eight of his recordings of other writer's songs.

Martin David Robinson was born in Glendale, Arizona, the son of Jack Joe and Emma (Heckle) Robinson. His first 12 years were spent in Glendale, where he attended school, watched silent cowboy movies, and played the games adolescent males play with their friends. Music was not a part of his childhood.

In 1937 the Robbins family moved to Phoenix, where Marty attended high school. He enlisted in the Navy in 1944, serving for four years. While on duty in the Pacific, he became interested in the guitar, which he learned to play without instruction by accompanying himself as he sang.

About 1948 he returned to Phoenix, supporting himself by working as a ditchdigger. He also sat in on guitar with local bands and occasionally a local nightclub with a small backup combo. His appearances in night spots, including performances with his band, began to increase gradually. In addition to two daily radio shows and a weekly television program on a local station in Phoenix, he now began to appear as a guest artist at the Grand Ole Opry in Nashville.

On June 16, 1945 Robbins married Marizona Baldwin. They had two children. In 1952 Robbins signed a composer-performance contract with Columbia Records, and a year later recorded "I Couldn't Keep From Crying," for which he wrote words and music. That same year his song "I'll Go on Alone," which Robbins recorded for Columbia, became a bestseller in a release by Webb Pierce. In 1953 Robbins became a permanent member of the Grand Ole Opry, where he became a country-and-western star.

In 1955 Robbins scored his first nationwide hit with his recording of "That'd Be All Right" (words and music by Arthur Crudup). Robbins's own song, "You Don't Owe Me a Thing," which he introduced on a Columbia recording, became a bestseller in a release by Ray Price. In 1957 Robbins recorded two of his own compositions, "Please Don't Blame Me" and "A White Sport Coat and a Pink Carnation." The latter, which he recorded with the Ray Conniff orchestra, was a hit with the emerging mass audience of teen-

MARTY ROBBINS

age rock and rockabilly fans, who helped the song to reach the number one spot on the pop charts. This recording became Robbins's first first to sell a million copies. He continued to appeal to the Elvis Presley–Jerry Lee Lewis market with "She was Only 17" and "Teen-Age Dream." Robbins was also recording the songs of other composers such as "Singing the Blues" (Melvin Endsley) in 1956–57, "Knee Deep in the Blues" (Melvin Endsley) in 1957, and in 1958, "Stairway of Love" (Sid Tepper and Roy C. Bennett). Robbins's first three albums were *Song of Robbins, Marty Robbins* and *Song of the Islands,* all of 1957–58.

Robbins's classic country-and-western number, "El Paso," a four-minute ballad about a cowboy who gets killed in a barroom shootout over a senorita named Maria, brought him a Grammy for best country performance, the first time the award was presented for a country song. "El Paso" had first appeared early in 1959 on Robbins's album, *Gunfighter Ballads and Trail Songs,* which earned a gold record in 1965. As a single, "El Paso" became Robbins's first million-selling disc, holding the number one position on the charts for 16 weeks in 1959.

In Nashville, in 1960, Robbins founded and became president of his own publishing firm, Maricana Music, and assumed the post of president of the Mariposa Bank. In 1965 he purchased a cattle farm in Franklin, Tennessee. He was also appearing frequently on television and on the concert stage, and he became one of the first country performers to be a headliner in Las Vegas.

Many Robbins songs made the country charts

in the 1960s. The most important were: "Don't Worry" and "Big Iron" (both 1960); "It's Your World" (1961); "Devil Woman" (1962); "Begging to You" and "The Cowboy in the Continental Suit" (both 1963); "One of These Days" (1964); and "Tonight, Carmen" (1965).

As an interpreter of country music by other writers, Robbins recorded such hit songs in the 1960s as: "Ruby Ann" (Roberts Bellamy), "Ribbon of Darkness" (Gordon Lightfoot), and "It's a Sin" (Zeb Turner and Fred Rose). Robbins's most successful albums were *More Gunfighter Ballads* (1960), *More Greatest Hits* (1961), *Marty Robbins* (1962), *Devil Woman* (1962), *Return of Marty Robbins* (1963), *Turn the Lights Down* (1967), *My Kind of Country* (1967), and *I Walk Alone* (1969).

In 1970 his songs "You Gave Me a Mountain" and "Camelia" received a BMI award as two of the most frequently performed country songs within the preceding five-year period. A year later, Robbins's "My Woman, My Man" brought him his second Grammy, when it was named the year's best country song.

On August 1, 1969, while touring in Ohio, Robbins suffered a heart attack. A nationally ranked stock-car racer, Robbins, to find out whether his heart condition would interfere with his avocation, went for tests at the St. Thomas Hospital in Nashville early in 1970. As a result, he had triple coronary bypass surgery at a time when this was still a new surgical technique.

Upon his recovery, Robbins participated in the National 500 at Charlotte, North Carolina on October 11, 1917, taking the wheel of a car for the first time in two years. In 1972 he narrowly escaped injury at the Daytona 500, when he crashed his car while traveling at 150 miles an hour.

Resuming his career as a concert performer and a Grand Ole Opry star, Robbins went on to compose and record such stellar numbers as "Among My Souvenirs," "Return to Me" and "Some Memories Just Won't Do." The last of his more than 50 albums was *Come Back to Me*, released in 1982. Robbins also appeared in 15 films, many of them westerns. His last screen performance was a minor role in *Honky Tonk Man* (1982), starring Clint Eastwood, for which Robbins composed the title song. Robbins had published a novel, *Small Man*, in 1966.

In 1980 Robbins suffered a second heart attack, but on July 4, 1981 he was able to perform for President and Mrs. Ronald Reagan. Robbins spent his last years in Brentwood, Tennessee. In 1982 he was named to the Country Music Hall of Fame. In December of that year he underwent quadruple bypass surgery, and died at the St. Thomas Hospital on December 8, 1982. In 1983 Columbia issued a two-record memorial album, *Marty Robbins: A Lifetime of Songs, 1951–1982.*

"He doesn't look much like his publicity pictures," said Al Reinert, describing Robbins in *The Country Music ncyclopedia.* "The boots he wears, with two-inch stacked heels, must boost him up to about five feet nine inches. He's short and wiry, [and has] hard muscles, like a lightweight wrestler or a welterweight boxer. [His] hair's getting longer now, mussed and matted and sun-bleached to a color that's almost strawberry roan; the moustache barely slips around the corners of his mouth in the hint of a handlebar, giving him the appearance altogether of a wizened Robert Redford, a Sundance Kid who's spent 20 years robbing banks. His eyes, even hidden behind bronze-tinted glasses, are open and honest, quick, flashing and dancing in all directions."

ABOUT: Shestack, M. The Country Music Encyclopedia, 1977; Stambler, I. and Landon, G. Encyclopedia of Folk, Country and Western Music, 1983.

ROBIN, LEO (April 6, 1895–December 29, 1984), ranks as one of Hollywood's most prolific lyricists. His songs were heard in more than 100 films, and he collaborated on the scores for Broadway musicals with Vincent Youmans, Jule Styne and Sigmund Romberg.

He was born in 1895 in Pittsburgh, to Max and Fannie (Finkespearl) Robin. Upon graduating from high school, he entered the University of Pittsburgh, where he studied law in 1915–16 until his interest in writing and the theater superseded his ambition to become an attorney. In 1917–18 he took courses in dramatics at the Carnegie Institute of Technology, and from 1916 to 1920 worked as a reporter for the Pittsburgh *Chronicle Telegraph.* From 1920 to 1923 Robin was a social worker for the Jewish Big Brothers Club. He became a professional songwriter in 1925, when two of his songs, "I've Found a Bluebird" and "Looking Around" (music by Richard Myers), were placed in *By the Way*, a British revue on Broadway.

In 1926 Robin was assigned to collaborate with Clifford Grey in writing lyrics to Vincent Youmans's music for *Hit the Deck.* Opening on April 25, 1927, this musical was a box-office bonanza, and one of its songs, with Robin's lyrics, was "Hallelujah," which became a Youmans standard.

Working with other composers, Robin wrote the lyrics for three other Broadway productions

LEO ROBIN

in 1927, all failures. Charles Rosoff composed the music for *Judy* (February 7, 1927), starring Queenie Smith; Richard Myers composed for *Allez Oop* (August 2, 1927), a revue starring Victor Moore; and Phil Charig and Joseph Meyer for *Just Fancy* (October 11, 1927). Robin's song "Give Trouble the Air" (music by Louis Alter) was interpolated into the revue *À la Carte* (1927) and his "I Want the World to Know" (music by Richard Myers) was introduced by Dorothy Lee in the Broadway musical *Hello, Yourself* (1928).

In 1928 Robin signed a contract with Paramount and moved to Hollywood, where he was to write hit songs for the screen for the next quarter century. The first important composer with whom he worked at Paramount was Richard Whiting. Their initial assignment was *Innocents of Paris* (1928), in which Maurice Chevalier made his American screen debut, and for Chevalier they composed "Louise" and "Wait Till You See Me Chérie." Whiting also served as Robin's composer for "I Have to Have You" from *Pointed Heels* (1929); "Beyond the Blue Horizon," "Give Me a Moment Please," "Always in All Ways" and "She'll Love Me and Like It" (music written in collaboration with W. Franke Harling) from *Monte Carlo* (1930); "My Ideal" and "It's a Great Life" (music written with Newell Chase) from *Playboy of Paris* (1930), starring Chevalier; and "I Can't Escape From You" from *Rhythm on the Range* (1936).

Robin's "True Blue Lou" (music by Sam Coslow) was introduced by Hal Skelly in *Dance of Life* (1929). "If I Were King" (music by Newell Chase and Sam Coslow) was composed for the 1930 motion picture adaptation of Rudolf

Friml's *The Vagabond King* in which it was sung by Dennis King, who also recorded it. "We Will Always Be Sweethearts" (music by Oscar Straus) was a duet for Maurice Chevalier and Jeanette MacDonald in *One Hour With You* (1932).

"Prisoner of Love" (music by Clarence Gaskill and Russ Columbo), another of Robin's popular songs of the early 1930s, did not come from a motion picture. Russ Columbo introduced it in a 1931 recording and it was revived in 1946 in a bestselling recording by Perry Como and again in 1963 in a release by the Godfather of Soul, James Brown and his Famous Flames.

As a lyricist for the screen, Leo Robin is probably best known for his work with the composer Ralph Rainger, which began in 1931 and lasted a decade. Their principal songs were: "Please" and "Here Lies Love" from the *Big Broadcast* (1939); the title number for *One Hour with You* (1932), which became Eddie Cantor's radio signature; "Give Me Liberty or Give Me Love" from *Torch Singer* (1933); Jack Benny's radio and television musical theme, "Love in Bloom," from *She Loves Me Not* (1934); "June in January" and "With Every Breath I Take" from *Here Is My Heart* (1934); "Here's Love in Your Eye" from the *Big Broadcast of 1937* (1936); "Blue Hawaii" and "Sweet is the Word for You" from *Waikiki Marriage* (1937); "Then it Wasn't Love" from *Swing High, Swing Low* (1937); Bob Hope's radio and television signature music, the Oscar-winning "Thanks for the Memory," from the *Big Broadcast of 1938*; "Faithful Forever," from the full-length animated cartoon, *Gulliver's Travels* (1939); "I Have Eyes" and "You're a Sweet Little Headache" from *Paris Honeymoon* (1939); and "Here You Are" from *My Gal Sal* (1942).

Other composers collaborated with Robin in the writing of screen songs. Frederick Hollander composed the music for "Moonlight and Shadows," "Whispers in the Dark" and "This is the Moment." The first of these was introduced by Dorothy Lamour in *Jungle Princess* (1936) before she recorded it; it received nine hearings on *Your Hit Parade*. Connie Boswell with André Kostelanetz and his orchestra introduced "Whispers in the Dark" in the film *Artists and Models* (1937). "Whispers" was recorded by the orchestra of Hal Kemp and was heard 12 times on *Your Hit Parade*, four times in first position. "This is the Moment" was introduced by Betty Grable in *That Lady in Ermine* (1948) and was recorded by Jo Stafford.

Harry Warren was the composer for "No Love, No Nothin'" from *The Gang's All Here* (1944) and "Zing a Little Zong" from *Just for You* (1952); David Rose composed the music for

"So-o-o-o-o in Love," which was introduced by Danny Kaye in *Wonder Man* (1945); Arthur Schwartz composed for "A Girl in Calico" and "Oh, But I Do" from *The Time, The Place and the Girl* (1946); Jerome Kern, for "In Love in Vain" from *Centennial Summer* (1946); and Harold Arlen, for "For Every Man There's a Woman" from *Casbah* (1948).

The first Robin song heard in a Broadway musical since the 1920s was "I'll Take an Option on You" (music by Rainger), which was interpolated into the short-lived revue, *Tattle Tales* (1933). With Jule Styne as composer, Robin prepared the score for the successful book musical, *Gentlemen Prefer Blondes* (December 8, 1949), starring Carol Channing, whose principal numbers were "Diamonds Are a Girl's Best Friend," "Bye, Bye, Baby" and "A Little Girl From Little Rock." Robin's last Broadway musical was *The Girl in Pink Tights* (March 5, 1954), music by Sigmund Romberg. "In Paris and in Love" and "Lost in Loveliness" were its main songs. In 1954 Jule Styne and Robin composed the songs for a television special, *Ruggles of Red Gap*, in which "A Ride on the Rainbow" was introduced.

(For additional information consult the biographies of Harold Arlen, Jerome Kern, Ralph Rainger, Sigmund Romberg, Arthur Schwartz, Jule Styne, Harry Warren and George Whiting.)

On March 3, 1947 Robin married Fran English, with whom he had a son. Robin's second wife was the former Estelle Clarke, an actress, with whom he had a daughter. Robin lived in retirement on North Maple Drive in Beverly Hills.

In June 1982 the 87-year-old Robin appeared in a performance of his best songs, "An Evening with Leo Robin" at the YMHA in Manhattan. On that occasion John S. Wilson described him in *The New York Times* as "a small, ebullient man with a shock of thick white hair" and as "an insistently modest man with an expansive and witty way of telling a story." Robin died of a heart attack at Woodlawn Hills, California.

ABOUT: Craig, W. Sweet and Lowdown: America's Popular Song Writers, 1978.

RODGERS, RICHARD (June 28, 1902–December 30, 1979) and **HART, LORENZ** (May 2, 1895–November 22, 1943). Richard Rodgers's career as composer for the musical theater spanned almost six decades, and for much of that time he dominated it as no one before or since. He composed the music for 43 stage musicals, ten film musicals and four television productions. Of the thousand or so songs he wrote for stage and screen more than a hundred

RICHARD RODGERS

have become firmly established as classics of American song literature. "Rodgers' song," wrote Wilder in *American Popular Song*, "have, over the years, revealed a higher degree of consistent excellence, inventiveness and sophistication than those of any other writer." Legend has it that there is never a time in America when a Rodgers song is not being heard somewhere, and it is certainly accurate to claim that there is rarely a time when a Rodgers musical is not being performed somewhere in the world. No American theater composer has been performed more often and in so many different places. His achievements were recognized by two Pulitzer Prizes; the Donaldson and Tony Awards, four times each; the New York Drama Critics Circle Award and the Emmy, twice each; an Oscar and a Grammy. Four of his musicals had runs exceeding 1,000 performances each, and one passed the 2,000 mark. One of his motion pictures earned more money at the box office than any cinema production up to that time. Nine albums of his music were awarded gold records. But this tells of only part of his accomplishments. More significant still is the fact that with his literary collaborators Hart and Hammerstein [Oscar Hammerstein II is discussed in a separate biography] he did more to change the destiny of the American musical than any other single person.

Richard Charles Rodgers was born on June 28, 1902 at Hammels Station, near Arverne, Long Island, where the Rodgers family was then spending the summer. He was the younger of the two sons of William Rodgers, a physician, and Mamie (Levy) Rodgers. He was brought up

LORENZ HART

in a five-storey brownstone on West 120th Street in Manhattan where his father maintained his office. Financial security in the family was combined with an appreciation for and an indulgence in the refinements of good living, as well as in culture in general. His father enjoyed books, the theater and music. Since he had an appealing baritone voice, he often entertained his family and friends on Sunday evenings by singing opera arias and songs from operettas. His piano accompanist was his wife, a trained musician.

When Rodgers was six, he attended the first theatrical production to leave a strong impression on him: a musical, *Pied Piper,* starring De Wolf Hopper, at the 125th Street Theatre. "The moment the curtain went up I was carried into a world of glamor and beauty I had never known existed," he later recalled. A few months later, he was brought downtown for a performance of Victor Herbert's operetta, *Little Nemo.* From this point on, he attended the theater regularly; it became the focal point of his existence or, as he himself put it, "Life for me began on Saturday at two-thirty."

He began showing interest in the piano when he was four, and two years after that began formal instruction that lasted about two years. Though he disliked practicing, he was frequently at the piano improvising melodies. At P. S. 10 in Manhattan, he performed at the assembly a potpourri of opera arias that he had learned by ear. When, in 1911, the family moved to West 86th Street where they would stay for the ensuing decade, Richard was transferred to P. S. 166. There one of his teachers encouraged him to per-

form regularly at assemblies and at his graduation exercises in 1916. At a boys' summer resort in Highmount, New York in 1914, the camp paper took note in verse of Richard's preoccupation with the piano. At a later summer camp in Harrison, Maine in 1916, Rodgers made his first attempt at writing a camp song, words as well as music, "Campfire Days." His second song, composed later that year, was "The Auto Show Girl."

While attending De Witt Clinton High School from 1917, Rodgers began going regularly to opera and symphony concerts. He was also continuing to write songs. He composed the complete score, words and music, for *One Minute Please,* an amateur musical mounted by the Akron Club, a boys' athletic organization of which his brother was a member. It was produced in the grand ballroom of Hotel Plaza on December 29, 1917. Twenty more songs by Rodgers (this time with words by other lyricists) were heard in a second amateur production, *Up Stage and Down,* at the Waldorf Astoria Hotel on March 18, 1919. On this occasion, Rodgers made his debut as conductor.

A friend of the family, convinced that Rodgers could profit from working with a skilled lyricist, brought him, one Sunday afternoon in 1918, to the home of Lorenz Hart. Hart, who was seven years older than Rodgers and had a wide grasp of theater, literature, music and language, was then working for the Shuberts as a translator of German plays. Rodgers and Hart spent that afternoon discussing the profession of songwriting, about which the older man had fresh ideas. "I heard for the first time," Rodgers recalled years later, "of interior rhymes, feminine rhymes, false rhymes. I listened with astonishment as he launched a diatribe against songwriters who had small equipment and less courage, the boys who failed to take every advantage of every opportunity to inch a little further into territory hitherto unexplored in lyric writing." Rodgers played and sang for Hart, and by the time the visit ended, Rodgers had found a lyricist with whom he would work exclusively for the next quarter of a century. "I acquired a career, a partner, a best friend—and a source of permanent irritation." Hart, for his part, had found a composer with whom he could work throughout his professional career.

Lorenz Milton Hart, the older of two sons of Max and Frieda (Eisenberg) Hart, was born in New York City. His father was a promoter in real estate, railroads and mines. Lorenz's younger brother, Teddy, became a successful actor. After 1904, and for the next quarter of a century, the Harts occupied a brownstone on 119th

Street in Harlem, a stone's throw from where the Rodgers family was living at the time. Lorenz received his elementary and secondary schooling mainly in private schools in New York, including the Weingart Institute and Columbia Grammar School, where he excelled in all subjects and was outstanding in language study. Even as a boy he devoured books, including the classics, was an opera enthusiast and a passionate theatergoer. His favorite plaything was a toy theater for which he wrote and produced plays for his friends.

Following a summer vacation with his family in Europe in 1913, Hart spent a year at Columbia University studying the regular academic curriculum before transferring to the school of journalism. He had a gift for witty poems and prose pieces. For the 1915 Columbia University Variety Show, he wrote a satirical skit about Mary Pickford in which he himself portrayed "America's sweetheart." A year later, he played the part of a flirtatious maid in another varsity show. He left Columbia University without a degree. For several summers, he wrote and produced shows at Brant Lake Camp, a boys' summer resort, where his collaborator was Arthur Schwartz, later famous as a popular song composer.

His meeting with the 16-year-old Rodgers was a turning point in Hart's life. In their first few weeks, they completed 15 songs. "Any Old Place With You" brought them for the first time within a Broadway theater when it was interpolated into the 1919 musical, *A Lonely Romeo,* sung by Eve Lynn and Alan Hale. This was also their first song to be published.

In the fall of 1919 Rodgers entered Columbia University. During his first year there, he and Hart wrote the songs for the Columbia Varsity Show, *Fly With Me* (even though Hart, no longer a Columbia University student, was not qualified to participate). The first varsity show to have its music composed by a freshman, and the first with a Rodgers and Hart score, *Fly With Me* was produced at the Hotel Astor on March 24, 1920, with Rodgers conducting. In the New York *Globe*, S. Jay Kaufman said: "We had not heard of Richard Rodgers before. We have a suspicion we shall hear him again." *Fly With Me* with a reconstructed text was revived at Columbia University on April 21, 1980.

The songs from *Fly With Me* impressed the veteran showman Lew Fields. He was planning to bring *Poor Little Ritz Girl* to Broadway. The book by George Campbell and Lew Fields was about a Southern belle who comes to New York to make her way in the theater but settles for marrying a wealthy bachelor instead. Its score

used eight numbers composed by Sigmund Romberg, already a veteran of Shubert-produced musicals and operettas. Fields contracted Rodgers and Hart to write seven more songs for this show. These marked the beginning of Rodgers and Hart on Broadway. *Poor Little Ritz Girl,* starring Eleanor Griffith and Charles Purcell, opened on June 28th, 1920 and ran for 119 performances. Rodgers's music drew the praise of H. T. Parker, the distinguished Boston music and drama critic. "He writes uniformly with a light hand; now and then with neat modulations or pretty turns of ornament; here and there with a clear sensibility to instrumental voice; and once again with a hint of grace and fancy." The song "Mary, Queen of Scots" received special attention from Heywood Brown, the drama critic of the New York *World,* who praised Hart's skillful versification and wit. But five years elapsed before Rodgers and Hart were heard again on Broadway. Unable to find either producers or publishers to promote their work, they turned to amateur productions by the Akron Club.

Feeling the need for further musical training, Rodgers put an end to his academic schooling at Columbia University in 1922 to begin a two-year period of musical training at the Institute of Musical Art in New York City. He studied harmony with Percy Goetschius, ear training with George Wedge and music history with Henry E. Krehbiel. At the Institute, he contributed to some of its productions. On a brief leave-of-absence from the Institute in 1922, he toured the vaudeville circuit as conductor of a tabloid musical.

Rodgers left the Institute in June 1923. Resuming his collaboration with Hart, he wrote songs for amateur shows mounted by schools, churches and synagogues. With Herbert Fields, the son of Lew Fields, as a third collaborator, Rodgers and Hart wrote *The Melody Man,* basically a nonmusical play that satirized Tin Pan Alley. It opened at the Ritz Theatre on May 13, 1924 and closed 55 performances later.

By now, Rodgers had begun to feel he had come to a dead end, and discouragement brought on persistent insomnia. He finally decided to abandon his ambitions in theater and popular music for a place in the business world, accepting a job as a salesman of children's underwear at a weekly salary of $50.

On the night before he was to begin work, he received a call from a family friend informing him that the younger members of the prestigious Theatre Guild were planning to mount an intimate, sophisticated revue to raise money for two tapestries for the Guild's auditorium on 52d Street, then under construction. The revue, which was called *The Garrick Gaieties*, required fresh material, and the friend suggested that Rodgers and Hart contribute some of their songs. All thought of becoming a salesman evaporated as, the following day, Rodgers went to work with Hart. By the time *The Garrick Gaieties* opened about two weeks later, they had completed a dozen songs for the show.

Originally, only two performances of *The Garrick Gaieties* had been scheduled—the matinee and an evening show on May 17, 1925. Alexander Woollcott called the revue "fresh, spirited and engaging . . . bright with the brightness of something [newly] minted," and Robert Benchley called it "the most civilized show in town." Such praise, and the enthusiasm of the audience, persuaded the Theatre Guild to put on four more performances, each of which sold out, then to start a regular Broadway run beginning on June 8 that would continue for 25 weeks. Rodgers and Hart were paid $50 a week each in royalties during the show's run, with Rodgers earning an additional $83 as conductor. Each was drawing additional income from the publication of two of the songs.

Those two published songs were the first hits by Rodgers and Hart, "Manhattan" and "Sentimental Me." "Manhattan" was sung by June Cochrane and Sterling Holloway and "Sentimental Me" by Holloway, Cochrane, James Norris and Edith Meiser. Both were recorded in 1925 by Arden-Ohman with the Regent Club Orchestra; an additional recording of "Manhattan" was made by Bob Haring. As the first Rodgers and Hart standard, "Manhattan" was later recorded by Ella Fitzgerald and heard in several motion pictures. It was sung by Mickey Rooney, Tom Drake and Marshall Thompson in the screen biography of Rodgers and Hart, *Words and Music* (1948), and by Bob Hope and Vera Miles in *Beau James* (1957). It was played on the soundtrack of *The Eddy Duchin Story* (1956) by Carmen Cavallero. The song was also interpolated into the nonmusical film, *All About Eve* (1950), and in the screen musical based on the life of Jane Froman, *With a Song in My Heart* (1952), whose title was taken from another, later song by Rodgers and Hart.

The first book musical produced with a complete Rodgers and Hart score was *Dearest Enemy* (September 18, 1925), with a libretto by Herbert Fields (286 performances). This was Broadway's first musical to come from the American history book. Specifically, it dealt with an incident in the Revolutionary War, in which Mrs. Robert Murray, at the request of General Washington, detained British officers in her home in New York with her feminine allure

to permit the Continental Army to make a strategic retreat. Discreetly salacious, the book and lyrics sparkled with wit and vivacity while Rodgers's musical score was a rich and varied amalgamation of solo numbers, duets, trios, as well as an 18th-century gavotte for orchestra. It boasted a hit song in "Here in My Arms," a duet for Helen Ford and Charles Purcell. Ella Fitzgerald recorded it.

The Girl Friend (March 17, 1926), book by Herbert Fields, had a substantial Broadway run of 409 performances. It starred Sam White as Leonard Silver, a cyclist who is induced by an unscrupulous promoter to enter a fixed six-day race. Despite the devious machinations of professional gamblers, Leonard Silver wins his race honestly and, at the same time, the love of Mollie Farrell (played by Eva Puck). The box-office strength of *The Girl Friend* lay not so much in the plot or in the performance as in two hit songs: the title number and "The Blue Room," both introduced as duets by Sam White and Eva Puck. In 1926 "The Girl Friend" was recorded by the orchestra of Fred Rich and "The Blue Room" by George Olsen's orchestra. Among the later recordings of "The Girl Friend" were those by the orchestras of André Kostelanetz and Richard Rodgers, and of "The Blue Room," by Ella Fitzgerald, Hildegarde the Revelers, the Singing Sophomores, and Eddy Duchin in a piano rendition with drums. Perry Como sang "The Blue Room" in *Words and Music* and *The Eddy Duchin Story* (1956), and that song was interpolated into *Young Man With a Horn* (1950) while "The Girl Friend" was given an instrumental treatment on the soundtrack of *Words and Music.*

During the run of *The Girl Friend,* the second edition of the *Garrick Gaieties* opened on May 10, 1926 (174 performances). Its principal Rodgers and Hart song was "Mountain Greenery," introduced by Bobbie Perkins and Sterling Holloway. At that time it was recorded by Roger Wolfe Kahn and his orchestra with later recordings by Ella Fitzgerald and Matt Dennis and Perry Como. Allyn McLerie sang it in *Words and Music.*

More radical in theme and treatment than *Dearest Enemy* was *Peggy-Ann* (December 27, 1926; 333 performances), the first American musical comedy to treat the subject of dream psychology. The plot of Herbert Fields's book was built around the dream fantasies of Peggy-Ann, who is bored with her humdrum existence and her unromantic boyfriend in Glens Falls, New York. Translating dreams into the language of the musical stage, Fields introduced the often incongruous, absurd material from which dreams are spun. To make such a theme and its adventurous development convincing, the long-accepted methodology of musical comedy had to be discarded. No song was heard nor was the chorus required to appear during the first 15 minutes, something without precedent for a musical on Broadway. The dancing reflected the quasi-surrealism of the text. Instead of a conventional ending with a large production number, *Peggy-Ann* closed with a slow comedy dance on a darkened stage. Rodgers's score comprised not only hummable songs but also orchestral episodes suitable for a dream world. Its best tunes were "A Tree in the Park," introduced by Helen Ford and Lester Cole, and "Where's That Rainbow?," which Helen Ford and Margaret Breen introduced, which Ann Sothern sang in *Words and Music*, and which the Singing Sophomores recorded.

Betsy, a Ziegfeld production with a book by Irving Caesar and David Freedman (December 28, 1926), was conventional musical comedy and it expired after 39 performances. Then, in a renewed search for fresh textual material, Rodgers and Hart, with Herbert Fields as librettist, turned to American literature—Mark Twain's *A Connecticut Yankee in King Arthur's Court,* the title of which was shortened to *A Connecticut Yankee.* Opening on November 3, 1927, it stayed on Broadway for 418 performances. In Fields's adaptation, Martin, a modern-day American, loses consciousness at a party after being hit by a champagne bottle. He dreams he is back in the sixth century as Sir Boss in Camelot. In this high station, he introduces some of the technical and industrial developments of 20th-century America: the telephone, radio, advertising, efficiency experts and big business. Slowly, Camelot is turned into a typical American city whose inhabitants begin speaking in American slang and whose king resembles Calvin Coolidge.

The anachronisms of the text were often carried over into songs combining Arthurian idiom with American slang. One such was "Thou Swell," a duet for Willim Gaxton and Constance Carpenter which was recorded by Ella Fitzgerald, Hildegarde, Margaret Whiting and the orchestra of Bix Beiderbecke and which June Allyson and the Blackburn Twins revived in *Words and Music.* In a few tongue-in-cheek love songs, Hart sprinkled acerbic wit on romance and sentiment. But this was not true of the score's principal ballad, "My Heart Stood Still." This Rodgers and Hart standard had not been written for *A Connecticut Yankee* but for an earlier musical produced in London, *One Dam Thing After Another* (1927), where it had been introduced by Jessie Matthews and Sonny Hale.

"My Heart Stood Still" became popular in London after the Prince of Wales requested the orchestra leader in the Café de Paris in London to play it for him, and then proceeded to sing the entire number. Convinced of its marketability in the United States, Rodgers and Hart, who had previously sold the rights, bought back the song for use in *A Connecticut Yankee* where, with new lyrics, it was sung by William Gaxton and Constance Carpenter. The numerous performers who have recorded it include Ella Fitzgerald, Margaret Whiting, Gladys Swarthout, Dennis Day, James Melton, Hildegarde, Perry Como, and André Kostelanetz. It has also often been heard in motion pictures: as a piano episode on the soundtrack of *Never Say Goodbye* (1946); as an interpolation into the background music of *Humoresque* (1947); sung chorally in *Words and Music;* and interpolated into *Parrish* (1951).

An updated production of *A Connecticut Yankee* was mounted on Broadway in 1943, for which Rodgers and Hart composed a few new songs, most importantly "To Keep My Love Alive." It was written for and introduced by Vivienne Segal, and was recorded by Ella Fitzgerald. A television special of *A Connecticut Yankee* was produced on the NBC network in 1955.

A Connecticut Yankee had the longest run of any Rodgers and Hart musical to date, but none of their next six Broadway musicals lasted longer than 155 performances. Interest in some of them rested exclusively on their songs. From *Present Arms* (April 26, 1928; 155 performances) came "You Took Advantage of Me," introduced by Joyce Barbour and Busby Berkeley. Morton Downey first popularized it at the Café de Paris in London before circulating it in the United States on radio and in a recording. In 1928, it was also recorded by the orchestra of Fred Rich and by Vaughn De Leath with Frank Harris, with subsequent recordings by Ella Fitzgerald, Lee Wiley, and the orchestras of Richard Rodgers and Bunny Berigan. It was revived in 1984 by Linda Ronstadt on her album *Lush Life.* The song was interpolated into the movie version of *Present Arms* which was renamed *Leathernecking* (1930) and was quoted in an extended song sequence, "Born in a Trunk," in *A Star is Born* (1953), sung by Judy Garland.

One of the most celebrated of all Rodgers and Hart love ballads, "With a Song in My Heart," came from *Spring Is Here,* which opened on March 11, 1929 for a 104-performance run. There the ballad was introduced by Lillian Taiz and John Hundley. Alexander Gray sang it in the screen adaptation of this musical, and Jack Hylton and his orchestra, André Kostelanetz, Ella

Fitzgerald, James Melton, Patricia Munsel and Jane Froman were among those who recorded it. This song became so closely identified with Froman that when her biography was filmed the song title was used for the movie's name, with Jane Froman singing it on the soundtrack, dubbing for Susan Hayward. Donald O'Connor and Susanna Foster sang it in *This Is the Life* (1945); Doris Day with Harry James and his orchestra in *Young Man with a Horn* (1948); Tom Drake in *Words and Music*; Dennis Morgan and Lucille Norman in *Painting the Clouds with Sunshine* (1951). Many years later, it was interpolated into the Italian-made film, *The Busileus Quartet* (1983). In the 1930s the song was used as the signature music for Major Bowes and the Capitol Family's weekly radio program.

"A Ship Without a Sail" was introduced by Jack Whiting in *Heads Up* (November 11, 1929), which ran for 144 performances. Charles "Buddy" Rogers sang it in the 1930 film version of this musical and Ella Fitzgerald and Libby Holman recorded it. "Ten Cents a Dance" was introduced (and recorded) by Ruth Etting in *Simple Simon* (February 18, 1930). In Ruth Etting's screen biography, *Love Me or Leave Me* (1955), it was sung by Doris Day. "Dancing on the Ceiling" was also composed for *Simple Simon* but dropped from the production before its Broadway opening. It was interpolated into a Rodgers and Hart musical in London, *Evergreen* (1930). In 1932 it was recorded by Jack Hylton and his orchestra and, later, by Ella Fitzgerald. *Simple Simon* had a run of 151 performances.

On March 5, 1930 Richard Rodgers married Dorothy Feiner. The first of their two daughters, Mary, was born in 1931. In time, she emulated her father by composing the score for the Broadway musical. *Once Upon a Mattress* (1959). A second daughter, Linda, arrived in 1935. Soon after his marriage, Rodgers, his wife and Lorenz Hart left for Hollywood to compose three songs for a First National production, *The Hot Heiress,* a failure in 1931. They returned to Broadway for a new stage musical, *America's Sweetheart* (February 10, 1931), which lasted for 185 performances. This was a satire on Hollywood with book by Herbert Fields and it starred Ann Sothern (then billed as Harriet Lake). "It is the songs which must be the standbys," said Gilbert Gabriel in his review, "excellent songs, happily phrased, insinuatingly clever and memorable." The finest number was "I've Got Five Dollars," a Depression-era song introduced by Ann Sothern and Jack Whiting. It was interpolated into the Broadway revue *The Show Is On* (1936), then was sung by Jane Russell and Scott Brady in the film *Gentlemen Marry Brunettes* (1955). Lee Morse and Ella Fitzgerald recorded it.

Rodgers and Hart returned to Hollywood in the spring of 1931 to fulfill the terms of a one-picture deal with Paramount but they remained more than three years, working on several films, both for Paramount and other studios. Their first Paramount assignment was *Love Me Tonight* (1932), starring Maurice Chevalier and Jeanette MacDonald. For it they composed "Mimi," a song Chevalier recorded in English and in French and repeated in the films *Pepe* (1960) and *A New Kind of Love* (1963). In *Love Me Tonight* "Isn't it Romantic?" was introduced by Chevalier and Jeanette MacDonald; it was recorded by Hildegarde, Jeanette MacDonald and Ella Fitzgerald. This song provided the title for a 1948 movie starring Veronica Lake wherein the ballad was featured prominently. A recording of "Isn't it Romantic?" was heard on the soundtrack of the nonmusical motion picture, *The Day of the Locust* (1975), based on the Nathanael West novel. Jeanette MacDonald also introduced *Love Me Tonight*'s title song, which she recorded in French and in English and she introduced and recorded "Lover." It was revived in 1952 in a bestselling recording by Peggy Lee, who then sang it in the film *The Jazz Singer* (1953). This song was performed by an orchestra on the soundtrack of the nonmusical film, *Sabrina* (1954), starring William Holden, Audrey Hepburn and Humphrey Bogart. It was also recorded by Hildegarde and by the New York Philharmonic, Rodgers conducting.

Other films with scores by Rodgers and Hart were *The Phantom President* (1932), in which George M. Cohan made his debut in talking picutes; *Hallelujah, I'm a Bum* (1933), starring Al Jolson; and *Mississippi* (1935), starring Bing Crosby. In *Mississippi* Bing Crosby introduced "It's Easy to Remember" and "Soon," both of which he recorded. Ruth Etting and Arthur Tracy also recorded "It's Easy to Remember." These two songs were represented on *Your Hit Parade* five times each. ("Soon" should not be confused with a song of the same name by George and Ira Gershwin.)

"Blue Moon," the most famous song Rodgers and Hart composed in Hollywood, was never introduced in a motion picture though it was intended for two films. Originally entitled "My Prayer," this song was written for a movie starring Jean Harlow, from which both the star and the song were dropped. It was rewritten with new lyrics as "The Bad in Every Man," which Shirley Ross sang in *Manhattan Melodrama* (1934), starring Clark Gable, William Powell and Myrna Loy. With still another set of lyrics, and the now definitive title of "Blue Moon," it became the only song by Rodgers and Hart to get published as an independent number. When released in 1934, it was recorded by Florence Richardson and by Benny Goodman, with later recordings by Vaughn Monroe with the Norton Sisters, Ella Fitzgerald, Frances Langford, Matt Dennis, Billy Eckstine and the orchestras of André Kostelanetz and Paul Weston. "Blue Moon" has often been heard in films. Mel Tormé sang it in *Words and Music*; Valentina Cortesa, in *Malaya* (1950); Jane Froman on the soundtrack of *With a Song in My Heart*. The song was also interpolated into *East Side, West Side* (1950), *Rogue Cop* (1954), *Beloved Infidel* (1959), *8 ½* (1963) and *F.I.S.T.* (1978).

One day in 1934, a question posed in a newspaper column convinced Rodgers it was time to return to Broadway. The columnist had inquired: "Whatever became of Rodgers and Hart?" Rogers recalled: "That really made my head jerk. I sat right down and wrote him a letter thanking him and telling him we were getting out of Hollywood as fast as we could. The day our contract was up, we climbed aboard the Chief and came back to the United States. I felt as if I had just been given my pardon."

Soon after their return to New York, they met Billy Rose, who was planning an extravaganza combining musical comedy and circus for which he wanted Rodgers and Hart to write the score. This musical came to be called *Jumbo* (November 16, 1935). It starred Jimmy Durante as the circus press agent for an elephant and it had a Broadway run of 253 performances. The book by Ben Hecht and Charles MacArthur tells of the rivalry between two circus proprietors, a competition that continues until the son of one proprietor marries the daughter of the other. This production provided for such circus accoutrements as clowns, jugglers, high-wire-walkers and animals. One reviewer described it as an "exciting compound of opera, animal show, folk drama, harlequinade, carnival, circus, extravaganza and spectacle." Rodgers and Hart composed three of their finest ballads for it. "My Romance" was introduced by Donald Novis and Gloria Grafton and was sung by Doris Day in the 1962 screen adaptation of the musical. Among those who have recorded it are Arthur Tracy, Margaret Whiting, Ella Fitzgerald, Patrice Munsel, Lee Wiley, Paul Whiteman and Donald Novis with Gloria Grafton. Gloria Graham presented "Little Girl Blue" on the stage and Doris Day in the film version, with recordings by Margaret Whiting, Ella Fitzgerald, and Paul Whiteman. "The Most Beautiful Girl in the World" was sung on the stage by Donald Novis and, in the screen adaptation, by James Joyce dubbing on the soundtrack for Stephen Boyd. Patrice Munsel, Carmen Cavallero and the New York Philharmonic conducted by Richard Rodgers

were some of those who recorded it. "Little Girl Blue" became a feature of Mable Mercer's performances in night spots. "The Most Beautiful Girl in the World" became the signature music for Ted Straeter and his orchestra. The music of *Jumbo* was recorded in a soundtrack album.

In spite of the excellence of its three top songs, for Rodgers and Hart *Jumbo* was a digression from the kind of stage musical they wanted to do. As Hart told an interviewer, he and Rodgers "had a vision of a new form of musical for Broadway. It will not be musical comedy and it will not be operetta. The songs are going to be part of the progress of the piece, not extraneous interludes without rhyme or reason." Rodgers said, "I should like to free myself for broader motifs, more extended designs—but within the framework of the theater, for that is where I belong." Seven of the nine musicals that Rodgers and Hart wrote between 1938 and 1942 were box-office successes, and each was a radical departure from the norm in the Broadway musical theater.

On Your Toes (April 11, 1936), which ran for 315 performances, was the first musical for which Rodgers and Hart wrote book as well as songs (assisted with the text by George Abbott). It was also the first Broadway musical whose characters and plot were taken from the world of ballet and in which ballet sequences were essential to the plot. Philip Dolan II, a young dancer, son of vaudevillians, joins a ballet company to be near Vera Baranova, one of its ballerinas. He is a failure as a performer in classic ballet but a success in modern jazz ballet, which he induces the company to produce as a way out of their financial problems. Of the two ballets, *Princess Zenobia* was a satire on the classic form. The other, *Slaughter on Tenth Avenue*, was a jazz ballet for which Rodgers conceived music of symphonic dimensions. The choreography for both ballets was by George Balanchine, the former director of the Ballet Russe de Monte Carlo, making his debut in the Broadway theater.

"There's a Small Hotel" was one of the songs that had special interest. It had been composed for, but was dropped from, *Jumbo*. In *On Your Toes* it was sung by Doris Carson and Ray Bolger, and recordings were made by the orchestras of Hal Kemp, Claude Thornhill, André Kostelanetz and Richard Rodgers; it was also recorded by Jack Whiting and Ella Fitzgerald. This song was represented four times on *Your Hit Parade*. Betty Garrett sang it in *Words and Music* and Frank Sinatra in *Pal Joey* (1957). *Slaughter on Tenth Avenue* was recorded by the New York Philharmonic, Rodgers conducting.

Both "There's a Small Hotel" and *Slaughter on*

Tenth Avenue were highlights when *On Your Toes* was adapted for motion pictures in 1939 and when the stage musical was revived on Broadway in 1954 and 1983. "A sizable number of jazz ballets have passed this way since *On Your Toes* first appeared," wrote Richard Watts Jr. about *Slaughter on Tenth Avenue* in 1954, "but it is still something of a classic in its field, and the music Mr. Rodgers wrote for it continues to seem one of the major achievements of his career." An original cast album of the 1954 revival was issued.

Rodgers and Hart wrote both book and songs for *Babes in Arms* (April 4, 1937), which had a run of 289 performances. Once again Balanchine was called upon to do the choreography. The cast was largely made up of teenagers. As children of touring vaudevillians, they had been left behind by their parents in Eastport, Long Island. Threatened by the local sheriff with transfer to a work camp, they put on a show to raise money to support themselves. The show proves an artistic success but a financial failure. Nevertheless the children are saved from the work camp when a French pilot, who had made a forced landing on their farm, helps straighten out their affairs to the sheriff's satisfaction.

Even more than in *On Your Toes,* a deliberate attempt was made in *Babes in Arms* to make each song a "plot number." Though each had a specific place within the plot structure, five songs, divorced from the stage, became standards. "Where or When" was introduced by Mitzi Green and Ray Heatherton and appeared eight times on *Your Hit Parade.* Frank Sinatra recorded it three times, and there are other recordings by Adelaide Hall, Lena Horne, Ella Fitzgerald, Dick Haymes and the orchestras of André Kostelanetz, Paul Kemp, Guy Lombardo and Richard Rodgers. It became a bestseller in a recording by Dion and the Belmonts in 1960. Judy Garland sang it in the film version of *Babes in Arms* (1939); Lena Horne in *Words and Music*; and Ellen Burstyn in *Alice Doesn't Live Here Any More* (1974), directed by Martin Scorsese. It was heard as a recurrent theme on the soundtrack of *Gaby* (1956). "My Funny Valentine," introduced by Mitzi Green, was sung by Jeanne Crain and Alan Young in *Gentlemen Marry Brunettes* and by Frank Sinatra in the film version of *Pal Joey.* Margaret Whiting, Mary Martin, Ella Fitzgerald, and Lee Wiley were among those who recorded it, and Judy Garland made it one of her specialties. "I Wish I Were in Love Again" was introduced by Grace MacDonald and Rolly Pickert, then sung by Mickey Rooney and Judy Garland in *Words and Music,* and recorded by Garland. "Johnny One Note" was sung by Wynn Murray in the stage

production, and by Judy Garland in *Words and Music* and was recorded by Ella Fitzgerald. "The Lady is a Tramp," which Mitzi Green introduced, was sung by Lena Horne in *Words and Music* and by Frank Sinatra in *Pal Joey.* Sinatra recorded it three times, and it was also recorded by Adelaide Hall, Lena Horne and Ella Fitzgerald.

In *I'd Rather Be Right* (November 2, 1937; 290 performances), a satire on American politics, Rodgers and Hart left the writing of the book to George S. Kaufman and Moss Hart. An actual American president—Franklin Delano Roosevelt—was one of the characters, portrayed by George M. Cohan. Names and issues in the news in 1937 were touched upon and satirized in dialogue and song. Fantasy was introduced when, in Phil Barker's dream, he and his fiancée, Peggy Jones, victims of the Depression, meet the President on a bench in Central Park. When they confide that they cannot get married until Barker receives a raise, and a raise would not be forthcoming until the national budget was balanced, the President promises to help. He urges the young couple to marry and have faith in themselves and their country.

Most of the songs were so topical and so embedded in the text that they lacked interest outside the theater. The single exception is "Have You Met Miss Jones?" It was introduced by Joy Hodges and Austin Marshall. Rudy Vallee and Sammy Kay and his orchestra recorded it in 1938, Ella Fitzgerald somewhat later. Jane Russell, Jeanne Crain, Alan Young, Scott Brady and Rudy Vallee sang it in *Gentlemen Marry Brunettes* (1955).

Fantasy returned in *I Married an Angel* (May 11, 1938), which has a book by Rodgers and Hart based on a play by John Vaszary and which ran for 338 performances. Count Willy Palaffi, a man of the world who is disenchanted with women, marries an angel who flies through his window. Being wed to a paragon of virtue is not the idyll the Count thought it would be. Only when the angel begins to assimilate human shortcomings does their faltering marriage become stable. With Vera Zorina, a graduate from the Ballet Russe de Monte Carlo, as the angel, and Balanchine as choreographer, emphasis was placed on ballet. But commercial songs were not neglected. The title number, introduced by Dennis King and recorded by the orchestras of Buddy Clark, Blue Barron and Larry Clinton, was sung by Dennis King and Jeanette MacDonald in the screen adaptation (1942) and interpolated into *Words and Music.* It was heard seven times on *Your Hit Parade* in 1938. "Spring Is Here," a duet by Dennis King and Vivienne Segal in the stage musical, was shared by Nelson Eddy and Jeanette MacDonald in the screen adaptation (1942) and sung by Mickey Rooney in *Words and Music*. It was initially recorded by the orchestras of Buddy Clark and Blue Barron, and later by Jo Stafford, Ella Fitzgerald and Carly Simon.

The Boys from Syracuse (November 23, 1938; 235 performances), based on Shakespeare's *Comedy of Errors*, book by George Abbott, was the first significant attempt to adapt Shakespeare to the musical theater. The setting is ancient Greece; the principal characters, a pair of twins, the long-separated Antipholus boys and Dromio boys. One Antipholus and one Dromio come from Ephesus to Syracuse where mistaken identity involves them with the Syracuse Antipholus and Dromio in amusing, irreverent and bawdy situations. "If you have been wondering all these years just what was wrong with *The Comedy of Errors*," wrote Richard Watts Jr., "it is now possible to tell you. It has been waiting for a score by Rodgers and Hart." The two principal songs were "Falling in Love With Love" and "This Can't Be Love." The former was introduced by Muriel Angelus and sung by Allan Jones in the 1940 film version and recorded by Allan Jones, Gladys Swarthout, Dennis Day, Risë Stevens, Fred Waring's Pennsylvanians and André Kostelanetz. "This Can't Be Love" was sung on the stage by Marcy Wescott and Eddie Albert and on the screen by Rosemary Lane. Doris Day sang it in *Jumbo*, and it was danced to by Cyd Charisse in *Words and Music*. In 1938 the song appeared ten times on *Your Hit Parade*. It was recorded by Rudy Vallee, Frances Langford, Johnny Desmond, Margaret Whiting, Ella Fitzgerald and Benny Goodman.

A new production of *The Boys from Syracuse* came to Broadway in 1963, "every bit as enchanting as I remembered it was," said Richard Watts Jr. From this production an original cast album was released. In 1984 this musical was revived at the Goodspeed Opera House in East Haddon, Connecticut.

Too Many Girls (October 18, 1939) and *Higher and Higher* (April 4, 1940) are each remembered as the showcase for a standard. "I Didn't Know What Time it Was," appeared in *Too Many Girls* (149 performances), introduced by Marcy Wescott and Richard Kollmar; it was recorded by Artie Shaw's orchestra, Hildegarde, Dinah Shore and Margaret Whiting and was represented seven times on *Your Hit Parade*. Frances Langford (dubbing for Lucille Ball), Eddie Bracken, Hal Le Roy and Desi Arnaz sang it in the 1940 film version of this musical, and Sinatra sang it in the film *Pal Joey*. "It Never Entered My Mind," from *Higher and Higher* (108 performances) was introduced by Shirley Ross and recorded by Shirley Ross, Larry Clinton and his orchestra, Ella Fitzgerald and Lee Wiley. Linda Ronstadt revived it on her *Lush Life* LP.

The concept of a musical as escapist theater was shattered by *Pal Joey* (December 25, 1940). John O'Hara's libretto, based on his own stories, was populated with unsavory characters. In Chicago's South Side, Joey (played by Gene Kelly) was a nightclub gigolo. He exploits his personal charm to the full, and is ready to prostitute himself to get financial support from Vera, a middle-aged socialite, for his own nightclub. At the same time he ruthlessly deserts Linda, the girl he loves. He ends up thoroughly discredited, losing both his nightclub and his faithful girlfriend. Although many critics reacted against the odiousness of the main character, *Pal Joey* initially survived 374 performances. When it was revived on Broadway in 1952, there was a complete turnabout in critical reaction. *Pal Joey* was now described as "handsome, vigorous, dynamic . . . very definitely a work of art" (Richard Watts Jr.); as "fast, funny, tough and tuneful" (John Chapman); as "one of the shrewdest, toughest and in a way the most literate book ever written for a musical comedy" (Walter Kerr). In 1952 it captured both the Donaldson and the New York Drama Critics Circle Awards as the season's best musical, and enjoyed the longest run (542 performances) of any Broadway musical revival up to that time. In 1957 it became a star-studded screen production, with Frank Sinatra, Rita Hayworth and Kim Novak in the leads. The 1952 revival and the 1957 motion picture yielded an original cast and a soundtrack recording.

The songs remembered from *Pal Joey* are "Bewitched, Bothered and Bewildered" and "I Could Write a Book." "Bewitched" was introduced by Vivienne Segal and in the film adaptation of the musical was sung by Jo Ann Greer (dubbing on the soundtrack for Rita Hayworth) and reprised by Frank Sinatra. When *Pal Joey* was first on Broadway, this song failed to gain popularity because it was banned from the airwaves during a dispute between ASCAP and the radio networks. After the show closed, the song turned up in a French translation in a Parisian nightclub and became a hit in that city. The song's circulation on radio in the United States in the late 1940s (and successful recordings in 1950 by Doris Day and Bill Snyder) brought it to *Your Hit Parade* 16 times, five times in first place. It was also recorded by Mel Tormé, Benny Goodman and his orchestra and Ella Fitzgerald. On the strength of the song's belated success, Columbia Records released the complete score in

1951, which in turn led to the Broadway revival in 1952. "I Could Write a Book" was a duet for Gene Kelly and Leila Ernst in the original stage production, while in the screen adaptation it was sung by Frank Sinatra and Trudy Ewen (the latter dubbing on the soundtrack for Kim Novak). Artie Shaw and his orchestra and Ella Fitzgerald recorded it.

With *By Jupiter* (June 2, 1942), the last Rodgers and Hart musical, Rodgers in conjunction with Dwight Deere Wiman, made his debut as a producer. The book by Rodgers and Hart was based on Julian F. Thompson's mythological *The Warrior Husband*, set in Pontus in ancient Asia Minor where the women were warriors and the men homemakers. In a war with invading Greeks, the women warriors of Pontus used their feminine charms as weapons. *By Jupiter* had a run of 427 performances which probably would have been greatly extended further. Its star, Ray Bolger, left the cast, going on a secret mission to entertain American troops in the South Seas, and because he was considered indispensable, the show had to close. "Careless Rhapsody" was introduced by Constance Moore and Ronald Graham, and recorded by Hildegarde, and "Nobody's Heart" by Constance Moore, reprised by Ray Bolger.

When writing songs, Rodgers invariably first composed the melody, to which Hart would fashion lyrics. Hart, who hated the routine of work and detested making revisions, had erratic work habits. Habitually, on bits of paper which he would stuff in his pockets, he would write down an ingenious turn of phrase, random ideas, a rhyme scheme. When he joined Rodgers to plan songs, he would take out these disordered bits of paper and try to find something serviceable. When this method did not serve, he would have to submit to the torture of sitting down and developing a tentative idea into a fully realized lyric.

They usually worked at Hart's house on West 118th Street until 1928 and after that at his apartment at the Hotel Beresford on Central Park West. Meetings anywhere else meant that Hart would arrive hours late, if at all. On those rare occasions when he was expected at the home of either Rodgers or Fields, he became a will-o-the-wisp. Arriving, he would excuse himself and go to the bathroom, or downstairs for a cigar, and then be gone for the rest of the day. "It was never wise to leave him alone," Rodgers recalled, "because he would simply disappear and have to be found all over again."

In contrast, Rodgers was sober-minded, disciplined, pragmatic, a methodical workman who stuck faithfully to a daily schedule, allowing nothing and no one to interrupt him during those hours that he had designated for work. He met deadlines punctually, never balked at making necessary revisions, and when a show was being whipped into shape was always on hand to keep a watchful eye during the long, grueling hours of rehearsal.

Where Rodgers was mild of manner, rarely given to displays of temperament, Hart was a bundle of nerves and neuroses. He was always restless, always on the move, his hands always active. His favorite gesture was to rub them vigorously when excited or pleased. On opening nights, he habitually paced the back of the auditorium rather than remain in his seat.

His hotel apartment was in a perpetual state of disarray, strewn with papers, books, magazines and cigarette butts. He had no set hours for eating or sleeping. Parties, often all-night affairs, were improvised. Details confused him. He never knew how much money he was earning or how much he was spending. He kept huge rolls of bills in his pocket, replenishing them frequently since he was always the one to pick up the check in restaurants and night spots.

By the late 1930s, Hart was an unhappy man who succumbed to bouts of despair. He was acutely sensitive about his small stature, regarding himself as a freak; he had not been able to find a woman who loved him enough to marry him. He had become dissatisfied with his work. His unhappiness intensified a lifelong disposition to be lackadaisical about his work habits, meeting deadlines or attending rehearsals. Having lost his one-time zest for living, for work, for the theater and for success, he tried to find stimulation in alcohol and solace in the companionship of disreputable individuals.

When, in 1942, the Theatre Guild proposed a new project for Rodgers and Hart, Hart bowed out. He claimed the project did not interest him, but in fact he had lost the will to create. At their publisher's office, Hart informed Rodgers that he was leaving for a holiday in Mexico and advised Rodgers to find another collaborator. When Hart left the office, Rodgers remarked sadly: "A long and wonderful partnership just went through the door."

Rodgers found a new collaborator in Oscar Hammerstein II. Seven years older than Rodgers, Hammerstein in 1943 was already a veteran of the musical theater. He and Rodgers had met for the first time at Columbia University in 1915 when Rodgers, then 13, attended a varsity show in which Hammerstein was a performer. They had written songs together for an amateur show in 1919. Since then, each had made his mark, and when their creative worlds became one, they made stage history.

The project the Theatre Guild had proposed to Rodgers and Hart, and which now fell to Rodgers and Hammerstein, was a musical adaptation of Lynn Riggs's *Green Grow the Lilacs*, an American folk play the Guild had produced. "What happened between Oscar and me was almost chemical," Rodgers said of their coalition. "Put the right components together and an explosion takes place. Oscar and I hit it off from the day we began discussing the show." They immediately agreed that, in making the musical adaptation of a folk play, they would have to strike out boldly in a new direction in the musical theater by working for total integration of text, songs and dances. The play and the play alone would have to dictate what kind of materials would be used. Lyrics had to become an essential part of the text—so essential that Rodgers and Hammerstein decided to write the lyrics before the melody, a practice they would henceforth pursue. Humor, character and dance had to be a natural extension of the plot. In addition, the dances had to be in complete harmony with the setting and characters: American folk ballet, rather than formal dance numbers. They had to be conceived by one of America's leading dancers and choreographers, Agnes de Mille.

The main action of their play concerns the romance of Curly and Laurey in Midwestern Indian country at the turn of the 20th century. Since Curly was too shy to tell Laurey how much he loves her, she punishes him by attending a picnic with Jud Fry, a disreputable character. At the picnic, the girls' lunch boxes are auctioned off to the boys, the buyer given the right to share the food with the girl who brought the box. By outbidding Jud for Laurey's box, Curly finally convinces her he is interested in her. Their love affair now moves swiftly to matrimony. The wedding ceremony is rudely interrupted by Jud's arrival. He is drunk and menaces Curly with a knife. In the ensuing scuffle, Jud falls on his own blade and is killed. Curley is exonerated by an improvised court that permits him to leave with his bride for their honeymoon in territory soon to become the state of Oklahoma.

The musical play, baptized *Oklahoma!*, with a book by Hammerstein, arrived in New York on March 31, 1943. It marked a new age for the musical comedy theater, and the opening-night audience sensed it. Lewis Nichols described *Oklahoma!* as "a folk opera." Burton Rascoe called it "fresh, lovely, colorful, one of the finest musical scores any musical ever had." John Anderson found it "as enchanting to the eye as Richard Rodgers' music is to the ear."

Oklahoma! remained on Broadway for five years and nine months, for the then unprecedented run of 2,248 performances. A national company toured 250 cities during a ten-year period, and was eventually supplemented by the original New York company covering seventy cities. *Oklahoma!* was also produced in Europe, Australia and South Africa, and for the American armed forces throughout the Pacific. The various stage productions grossed more than 100 million dollars. It captured a special award from the Pulitzer Prize committee. As the first musical to issue its entire score in an original cast recording, it sold over a million albums during the period before long-playing records. The 1955 movie adaptation, starring Gordon MacRae and Shirley Jones, was also a giant box-office attraction, and its soundtrack recording became another bestseller. *Oklahoma!* was revived on the New York stage in 1951, 1953, 1958 and 1963. Reviewing the 1958 revival, Walter Kerr suggested some changes in the staging, but he added with finality: "No one should touch the music though. All that incredible music."

However thoroughly the songs were integrated with the text, the love ballad, "People Will Say We're in Love" managed to achieve hit status outside the theater. Alfred Drake and Joan Roberts introduced it; Gordon MacRae and Shirley Jones sang it in the screen adaptation. It was recorded by Bing Crosby, Frank Sinatra with Joan Roberts, James Melton, Elanor Steber and John Charles Thomas. It had 30 hearings on *Your Hit Parade*, three times in first position. Several other songs from *Oklahoma!* have also become standards. "Oh, What a Beautiful Mornin'" opened the musical and was sung off-stage by Alfred Drake. It was recorded by Bing Crosby, Sinatra, Alfred Drake with Joan Roberts, Nelson Eddy, Helen Traubel, André Kostelanetz and, in a swing version, by Jimmy Dorsey. In the film version of the musical it was sung by MacRae. "The Surrey with the Fringe on Top" was introduced on the stage by Drake, Joan Roberts and Betty Garde; sung on the screen by MacRae, Shirley Jones and Charlotte Greenwood; and recorded by Nelson Eddy and the orchestras of André Kostelanetz and Morton Gould. The title number appeared as the show's closing number (followed by a reprise of "Oh, What a Beautiful Mornin'"). Drake, Roberts, Garde and others sang it in the stage version; MacRae, James Whitmore, Shirley Jones, Jay C. Flippen and chorus in the screen adaptation. It was recorded by the Boston Pops Orchestra and by André Kostelanetz.

Hart was present at the triumphant premiere of *Oklahoma!* and at the reception at Sardi's that followed: a sad, forlorn figure in both places, now unavoidably aware that he had been permanently replaced and that his day in the theater was at an end. Soon after that, he went on an alcoholic spree that led to a rest cure at Doctors Hospital in New York. He left the hospital to attend the first night of a revival of *A Connecticut Yankee* on November 17, 1943. A few days later, he was found unconscious in his hotel apartment. He never regained consciousness. He died of pneumonia at Doctors Hospital on November 22, 1943. Five years later, his biography, together with that of Rodgers, was brought to the screen in *Words and Music* (1948), starring Mickey Rooney as Hart and Tom Drake as Rodgers.

The success of *Oklahoma!* made it possible for Rodgers and Hammerstein in 1944 to form their own publishing house, Williamson Music Inc. (so called because the fathers of both men were named William). That year, they also founded a company to produce stage works of other writers as well as some of their own. This organization was forthwith put on a solid footing with the successful productions of James Van Druten's play, *I Remember Mama* (1944), and Irving Berlin's musical, *Annie Get Your Gun* (1945).

In 1944 Rodgers and Hammerstein came to Hollywood to work on a motion picture, *State Fair* (1945), screenplay as well as lyrics by Hammerstein, based on Phil Stong's novel. This was a remake with songs of a 1933 nonmusical film, starring Will Rogers and Janet Gaynor, in which a Western family attends the Iowa State Fair. There the daughter and son find romance. The new musical version starred Jeanne Crain and Dick Haymes. Louanna Hogan (dubbing on the soundtrack for Jeanne Crain) sang "It Might as Well Be Spring," which won an Oscar, and was recorded in 1945 by Dick Haymes, Margaret Whiting and the orchestras of Sammy Kaye and Ray Noble; it received 14 hearings on *Your Hit Parade*, three times in first position. "It's a Grand Night for Singing" was introduced by the ensemble and was recorded by Helen Traubel and James Melton. In the 1962 screen remake of *State Fair*, with the Rodgers and Hammerstein score, starring Ann-Margret, Pat Boone and Pamela Tiffin, both songs were sung on the soundtrack by Anita Gordon (dubbing for Tiffin). "That's for Me" (15 hearings on *Your Hit Parade*) was sung by Vivian Blaine in the 1945 version and by Pat Boone in the 1962 remake; it was recorded by Artie Shaw and his orchestra. Soundtrack recordings of both the 1945 and 1962 productions were issued.

On Broadway, *Oklahoma!* was followed by *Carousel* (April 19, 1945) in which the concept of the musical play was developed further. This was Hammerstein's adaptation of *Liliom* by Ferenc Molnar with settings transferred from Budapest to New England and the time from the early 20th century back to 1873. There were also some basic changes in the plot. In the musical play, Billy Bigelow is a shiftless, happy-go-lucky operator of a carousel in an amusement park. He falls in love with and marries Julie, a mill girl. When he discovers she is pregnant, his parental pride makes him determined to find money for the proper upbringing of his soon-to-be-born child. He becomes involved in a holdup, is caught and commits suicide. Doomed to spend fifteen years in purgatory, he is allowed to return to earth for a single day to redeem his soul. His unselfish love for his now grown daughter proves to be her salvation, through which Billy achieves his own redemption.

"Rodgers has contributed some of the most beguiling music of his career," said one reviewer. This score, released in an original cast album, begins with the symphonic "The Carousel Waltz," played by the orchestra under the opening scene, which depicts a whirling carousel. This number has often been heard at pop concerts and was recorded by the New York Philharmonic with Rodgers conducting. The principal song, "If I Loved," was introduced by John Raitt and Jay Clayton. In 1945 it was recorded by Raitt with Clayton, and by Perry Como, Bing Crosby and Frank Sinatra, with other recordings by the orchestras of André Kostelanetz, Leo Reisman and Harry James. In 1965 the song was revived in a bestselling recording by Chad and Jeremy. It was heard 19 times on *Your Hit Parade* in 1945, three times in first position. "Soliloquy," a nine-minute narrative in which Billy reveals his pride on learning he is to become a father, was introduced by John Raitt and recorded three times by Frank Sinatra; it was also recorded by James Melton. "June is Bustin' Out All Over" was introduced by Christine Johnson, Jan Clayton and ensemble, and was recorded by Hildegarde and by Guy Lombardo and His Royal Canadians. "You'll Never Walk Alone" was introduced by Christine Johnson and recorded by John Raitt with Christine Johnson, Jan Clayton and chorus, Judy Garland and Frank Sinatra.

Carousel has become a classic of the American musical theater, often revived throughout the country. Of all his own musicals, Rodgers was most partial to this one, and *The New York Times* critic Brooks Atkinson concurred when, after a revival in New York in 1954, he wrote: "This is the most glorious of the Rodgers and Hammerstein works." The initial Broadway run was 890 performances, when it received the Donaldson and the New York Drama Critics awards for Rodgers's music and Hammerstein's lyrics as well as for the season's best musical. Libretto and lyrics were published as a book by Random House. In addition to the production of

1954, *Carousel* was revived in New York in 1949, 1957 and 1966. In 1958, *Carousel* represented the American musical theater at the World's Fair in Brussels and in 1967 it was adapted as a television special starring Robert Goulet. *Carousel* was transferred to the screen in 1956, with Shirley Jones and Gordon MacRae singing "If I Loved You"; MacRae, the "Soliloquy"; Claramae Turner, Barbara Ruick and chorus, "June is Bustin' Out All Over"; and Claramae Turner, "You'll Never Walk Alone." The soundtrack recording received gold status in 1964.

Allegro (October 10, 1947) was an experiment in musical theater. Oscar Hammerstein's text traced the biography of a physician, Dr. Joseph Taylor Jr., through various stages of his career to his final renunciation of materialism. Episodes were depicted in ballets or extended vocal and choral sections. Lights and colors pointed up moods and emotions and much of the action took place on an empty stage. A kind of Greek chorus was employed as a commentary on what was transpiring, sometimes in song, sometimes in speech. Although Robert Garland described *Allegro* as a "stunning blending of beauty, integrity, imagination, taste and skill," *Allegro* was comparatively unsuccessful at the box office (315 performances), and it has never been revived or made into a motion picture; but its complete score was recorded in an original cast record album. Three songs are remembered: "The Gentleman is a Dope" was introduced by Lisa Kirk, and was recorded by Lisa Kirk, Jo Stafford and by Guy Lombardo and His Royal Canadians. "A Fellow Needs a Girl" was introduced by William Ching and Annamary Dickey and recorded by Guy Lombardo and His Royal Canadians. "So Far," introduced by Gloris Willis and recorded by Guy Lombardo and His Royal Canadians, was twice heard on *Your Hit Parade*.

South Pacific, one of the glories of the American musical theater and one of the greatest artistic and box-office successes Rodgers and Hammerstein experienced, followed on April 7, 1949. The text by Hammerstein and Joshua Logan was based on A. Michener's Pulitzer Prize winning volume of stories about World War II. In the musical, Emile de Becque, a middle-aged French widower, is a wealthy planter living on a South Pacific island. He and Ensign Nellie Forbush, an American nurse stationed on the island, fall in love. The island is also the base for American soldiers, Seebees and Marines. Bloody Mary, a Tonkinese, sees Lieutenant Joseph Cable as an ideal suitor for her daughter Liat, but the marriage is frustrated by their racial difference. De Becque and Nellie Forbush encounter problems of their own when she discovers that he is the father of two Eurasian children. Cable is killed in a war mission but de Becque, who had accompanied him, returns to find Nellie has had a change of heart. She decides that prejudice must never stand in the way of her happiness with the man she loves. Ezio Pinza, fresh from his triumphs in opera, here made his Broadway debut as de Becque, and Mary Martin was Nellie, one of her most triumphant roles.

The critics praised *South Pacific* unanimously. Howard Barnes described it as a "show of rare enchantment, novel in texture and eloquent in song." Ward Morehouse described it as "a thrilling and exultant musical play." Richard Watts Jr. said it was "an utterly captivating work of theatrical art . . . a work of great style and loveliness that is yet gay, vigorous and vital." Its run of 1,925 performances on Broadway and its gross profit of nine million dollars made stage history. The national company toured for several years; the sheet music sold more than two million copies; the original cast recording had a sale of more than a million albums and again earned a gold record in 1966 in an album by Eddie Arnold. The name "South Pacific" was licensed for cosmetics, dresses, coats, lingerie, hairbrushes and other commodities. *South Pacific* captured every award available, including the Pulitzer Prize in drama, the New York Drama Critics Circle Award as best musical, eight Tony Awards (including one for the best musical, another for Rodgers's music and a third for the book by Hammerstein and Logan), and nine Donaldson Awards (including those for best musical, best lyrics and best book). In addition to productions in foreign lands, it has been consistently revived in the United States, with performances in New York at the New York City Center in 1949, 1955, 1957, 1961 and 1965 and at the Lincoln Center in 1967. The score of the handsomely produced 1958 film version starring Rossano Brazzi and Mitzi Gaynor was issued in a soundtrack recording.

South Pacific contributed an important entry to *Your Hit Parade*: "Some Enchanted Evening," with 21 performances, ten times in first position. Ezio Pinza introduced it on the stage; Giorgio Tozzi sang it on the soundtrack of the motion-picture adaptation (dubbing for Rossano Brazzi); and Bing Crosby recorded it. "Younger Than Springtime" and "A Wonderful Guy" were also on *Your Hit Parade*, the former once on September 24, 1949, the latter, nine times. "Younger than Springtime" was sung by William Tabbert on the stage and, on the screen, by Bill Lee (dubbing on the soundtrack for John Kerr). Mary Martin introduced "A Wonderful Guy" in the stage production and Mitzi Green sang it on the screen. Another song favorite from *South Pacific* was "Bali Ha'i," introduced by Juanita Hall on the stage while in the film version Muriel Smith was heard on the soundtrack dubbing for her. Frank Sinatra, Perry Como, Peggy Lee and Bing Crosby recorded it.

Oriental exoticism entered the text, music and dance of *The King and I* (March 29, 1951), the Rodgers and Hammerstein production that followed *South Pacific*, with which the writers realized another artistic and financial success of the first magnitude. The Oriental subject posed, probably, the most difficult creative problems Rodgers and Hammerstein had ever encountered. Hammerstein's text was based on *Anna and the King of Siam*, a novel by Margaret Landon, which in 1946, had been made into the nonmusical motion picture starring Rex Harrison and Irene Dunne. Distant and exotic Siam in the 1860s is the setting, and most of the characters are Orientals. Anna is a prim London schoolteacher who comes to Siam to teach Western ways to Oriental people. Initially, she was treated high-handedly by the king, whose despotic ways repelled her. But she soon finds much to admire in him and also becomes attached and devoted to the princes and princesses she had come to teach. After her ingenuity saves the king and his country from a diplomatic disaster, she decides to leave Siam but changes her mind when the king dies and she realizes how much the royal children need her. For both Hammerstein and Rodgers, the Oriental setting was a challenge. Hammerstein had no intention of writing a text with the long-familiar stage clichés of "girls dressed in Oriental costumes and dancing out onto the stage singing 'ching-aling-aling' with their fingers in the air." And Rodgers knew little about Oriental music. "What I tried to do," he explained, "was to say what the Far East suggested to me musically; to write a score that would be analogous in sound to the look of a series of Siamese paintings by Grant Wood. I myself remained a Broadway character, not somebody in Oriental getup."

With Yul Brynner playing the king, and Gertrude Lawrence as Anna, *The King and I* had an initial run of 1,246 performances, winning Tonys as best musical and best musical score, together with five Donaldson awards. "It is an original, beautiful excursion into the rich splendors of the Far East," wrote Brooks Atkinson, "done with impeccable taste by two artists, and brought to life with a warm romantic score, idiomatic, and some exquisite dancing." The score, though basically Western in style, was sometimes lightly touched and sometimes permeated with an Oriental atmosphere. It overflowed with popular numbers. The ballad, "Hello, Young Lovers" was introduced by Gertrude Lawrence

who was also heard in "I Whistle a Happy Tune," "Getting to Know You," and (with Yul Brynner) "Shall We Dance." Doretta Morrow and Larry Douglas introduced "I Have Dreamed" and "We Kiss in a Shadow," the former also recorded by Lena Horne. The original cast recording was a bestseller.

The King and I returned to New York at the City Center in 1956, 1960 and 1963, and to Broadway with an 88-week run in 1977–78 that grossed more than 17 million dollars, in which Yul Brynner reappeared in the starring role. His farewell appearances took place in 1985 with the return of *The King and I* to New York.

The King and I became a pictorially attractive motion picture in 1956 starring Yul Brynner and Deborah Kerr. Here, Marni Nixon was heard on the soundtrack dubbing for Deborah Kerr in "Hello, Young Lovers," "I Whistle a Happy Tune" and "Getting to Know You," and, with Yul Brynner, in "Shall We Dance." To Rita Morena and Carlos Rivas were assigned "I Have Dreamed" and "We Kiss in a Shadow." The film was awarded six Oscars besides being selected by the Film Daily poll of critics as the year's best motion picture. The soundtrack recording was awarded a gold record in 1964.

Rodgers and Hammerstein digressed from the concept of the musical play to the more conventional methods of musical comedy with *Me and Juliet* (May 28, 1935) and *Pipe Dream* (November 13, 1955), both failures (358 performances and 246 performances respectively). In both cases, original cast albums were recorded. *Me and Juliet*, with a book original to Hammerstein, was a backstage and onstage story of people in the theater, their reactions both to their craft and their audiences during the run of a musical comedy. Its best number was the tango "No Other Love," whose musical theme was lifted out of Rodgers's score for the television series *Victory at Sea* (1952–1953). Isabel Bigley and Bill Hayes introduced it and Perry Como made it successful on records. It was represented 18 times on *Your Hit Parade*, three times in first place. *Me and Juliet* was revived Off Broadway by the Equity Library Theatre in 1970. *Pipe Dream* was Rodgers's child of sorrow, and for reasons far more grave than its failure at the box office. Before the show opened, Rodgers was stricken by a cancer of the mouth that was arrested by a major operation in which the left jawbone and glands in the neck were removed. The operation was a success, but for months he suffered intense pain, a speech defect and continual flow of saliva. Nevertheless, he did not miss rehearsals, out-of-town tryouts or the New York opening.

Pipe Dream was Hammerstein's adaptation of

John Steinbeck's *Sweet Thursday*, presenting an odd assortment of offbeat characters in Cannery Row in San Francisco. Rodgers's score included two ballads. "Everbody's Got a Home But Me," introduced by Judy Tyler, became a bestseller in Eddie Fisher's recording, and "All at Once You Love Her," sung by William Johnson, Judy Tyler and Jerzy La Zaare (and reprised by Helen Traubel), was recorded by Perry Como.

During the 1950–1960 decade, Rodgers— once with Hammerstein—was involved with television. In 1952, he composed thirteen hours of background music for a series of documentary films on World War II naval operations, collectively entitled *Victory at Sea*. The first of 26 weekly half-hour programs was telecast on NBC on December 26, 1952, and the last on April 26, 1953. For this music, Rodgers was awarded the United States Navy Distinguished Public Service Award and an Emmy. An abridged motion-picture adaptation was released for distribution in theaters in 1954. "Hardly enough can be said for the score of Mr. Rodgers," reported Jack Gould in *The New York Times*. "His work has a compelling beauty and vigor that adds incalculably to the emotional intensity of the series." Robert Russell Bennett adapted the best pages of this score into a nine-movement orchestral suite whose recording by the NBC Symphony, conducted by Robert Russell Bennett, earned a gold record in 1964. As has been noted previously, this score was used by Rodgers for his song "No Other Love" in *Me and Juliet*.

Earlier in 1952, on June 15 and 22, Ed Sullivan on his "Toast of the Town" television show honored Richard Rodgers on two consecutive Sunday evenings, the first devoted to Rodgers and Hart, the second to Rodgers and Hammerstein. Even more impressive was the tribute to Rodgers on March 28, 1954 with a four-and-a-half-hour program of his music, telecast simultaneously by the four principal networks comprising 245 stations. Neither before nor since has an entertainment received such coverage; it was estimated that almost half the population saw the production, in which the participants included Ezio Pinza, Mary Martin, Yul Brynner, Jack Benny, Groucho Marx and many other stars.

As a television special for CBS, Rodgers and Hammerstein wrote *Cinderella*, adapted from the famous fairy tale. It was telecast on March 31, 1957, starring Julie Andrews. It was produced, as Jack Gould wrote in *The New York Times*, "with characteristic skill, dexterity and lilt." A new television production of *Cinderella* was produced by CBS on February 22, 1965. The music on the soundtracks of both productions was released in record albums.

Rodgers's last contribution to television was the background music for another World War II documentary series. Called *The Valiant Years*, it was an epic about Churchill, telecast on the ABC network between November 27, 1960 and May 21, 1961. It brought Rodgers his second Emmy.

Early in the spring of 1957, Rodgers succumbed to a deep depression. A psychiatrist suggested that Rodgers remove himself from his family and spend that summer at the Payne Whitney Clinic in New York. Only his wife and Oscar Hammerstein were allowed to visit him. "After a self-imposed exile of twelve weeks," Rodgers wrote in his autobiography, "I returned to my family and worked as if nothing happened."

Refreshed physically and in spirit, Rodgers was able to embark on a new Broadway musical, *Flower Drum Song* (December 1, 1958), his return to success on the stage (600 performances). The book by Hammerstein and Joseph Fields was based on a novel by C. Y. Lee. It told about the rivalry in San Francisco's Chinatown between the old and new generations of Chinese and between Eastern and Western cultures. The contrast of the East and West was also present in Rodgers's songs, the most successful of which, "I Enjoy Being a Girl," was rooted in Broadway rather than Chinatown. It was introduced by Pat Suzuki in her Broadway debut. The original cast recording became a gold record in 1962. *Flower Drum Song* toured the country for a year and a half and was made into an entertaining motion picture (1961) where "I Enjoy Being a Girl" was sung on the soundtrack by B. J. Baker dubbing for Nancy Kwan with the soundtrack music released in a record album.

The Rodgers and Hammerstein era in the musical theater ended with their greatest financial success, the musical play, *The Sound of Music*, starring Mary Martin (November 16, 1959). The text, by Howard Lindsey and Russel Crouse, was based on the story of the Trapp family (as suggested by Maria Augusta Trapp's autobiography, *The Trapp Family Singers*). The Trapps were a singing family from Salzburg, Austria, who, when the Nazis seized Austria, toured the world giving choral performances. The musical play also traced the biography of Maria Rainer from the time she was a postulate at the Nonnberg Abbey in Austria through the period of her service as governess of the seven children of Captain George von Trapp. After becoming his wife, she was forced to flee with her family to avoid the Nazis. The words most used by the critics to describe *The Sound of Music* were "sweetness," "innocence," "sentimentality." "Do

Re Mi," a song built from the ascending notes of the diatonic scale, which Mary Martin sang with the children to teach them to sing notes, was introduced by Mary Martin in the stage version and, in the screen adaptation of this musical, by Julie Andrews. It had the largest sheet-music sale of any Rodgers song. "My Favorite Things" was sung by Mary Martin and Patrice Neway on the stage and by Julie Andrews in the film. Other songs carried nostalgic recollections of Austria. Noteworthy are "Eidelweiss," a duet for Mary Martin and Theodore Bickel on the stage, sung by Bill Lee (dubbing for Christopher Plummer) on the screen soundtrack. The eclectic score also included the title song introduced by Mary Martin and sung on the screen by Julie Andrews in the opening scene. "Climb Ev'ry Mountain," an inspirational number, was assigned to Patrice Neway and on the screen to Marjorie McKay (dubbing on the soundtrack for Peggy Wood).

After arriving on Broadway with the then-unprecedented advance sale of more than three million dollars, *The Sound of Music* went on to become the greatest financial bonanza Rodgers and Hammerstein had known. It played 1,443 times on Broadway and won six Tonys, including those for best musical and best musical score. It received more than 1,000 additional performances from a national company touring for two-and-a-half years. The financial returns from the beautifully produced film version starring Julie Andrews (1965) established at that time what was a record for receipts the world over, approximately half a billion dollars. The recordings of the original Broadway cast and the motion-picture soundtrack recordings sold more than twelve million albums. Since then, *The Sound of Music* has gathered many millions more from the television presentations of the film and intermittent stage revivals throughout the country, including its first return to New York since 1959 at the City Center in 1967. With *The Sound of Music*, the career of Oscar Hammerstein II ended on a note of triumph. He died of cancer at his summer home in Doylestown, Pennsylvania, on August 23, 1960.

Rodgers and Hammerstein evolved a working arrangement that proved ideal. Before a line was put down on paper, they spent countless hours, which often stretched to weeks and months, discussing every phase of the play, every piece of stage business, the types of songs that were required and where they would best fit, the kind of performance they would need and so forth. Except in rare instances, Hammerstein always wrote the lyrics before Rodgers wrote the music.

Once the play was written, rehearsals consumed twelve hours a day, seven days a week,

with Rodgers and Hammerstein always at hand to make necessary changes, to give valuable suggestions to various departments, and to ensure that details were not neglected. Hammerstein usually remained seated in the auditorium—to all outward appearances thoroughly detached—making numerous notes. Rodgers, on the other hand, was all over the theater, testing the acoustics, and checking the lighting. Then he would suddenly lapse into complete silence, withdrawing as if to isolate himself completely from the stage in order to gain objective impressions.

When working with other collaborators after Hammerstein's death, Rodgers was never again to reach the summits he had previously attained. Nevertheless, a few of these post-Hammerstein musicals have interest. In 1961, Rodgers planned to work with Alan Jay Lerner on a musical about extrasensory perception. They could not agree on how the subject should be developed and Rodgers withdrew from a project that eventually became *On a Clear Day You Can See Forever* with music by Burton Lane. Then, with Samuel Taylor as librettist and serving as his own lyricist, Rodgers composed the score for *No Strings* (March 15, 1962), starring Diahann Carroll and Richard Kiley. The musical was innovative on several counts. Its plot involved a love affair in Paris between Barbara Woodruff, a black American model, and David Jordan, a young, white American writer. In the end they must part, the writer to fulfill his literary destiny in America. Pairing white and black leading performers without a hint of racial consciousness represented a fresh approach. Rodgers's use of the orchestra was also innovative. In keeping with the title of the play, it was made up solely of wind instruments played not in the customary pit but in the wings of the stage. Now one instrumental player, now another drifted informally onto the stage to stand near a character or characters and provide a soft, musical commentary on what was happening. Equally unconventional was the way the performers were used to shift the scenery in full sight of the audience. "He is still a magician of the theater," said Howard Taubman in *The New York Times. No Strings* lasted 580 performances, received three Tonys including one for Rodgers's music, the Outer Circle Award as best musical and a Grammy for the original cast recording. The three principal songs were introduced by Diahann Carroll and Richard Kiley: "The Sweetest Sounds" (with which the production opened), "Nobody Told Me" and the title song.

Stephen Sondheim was Rodgers's lyricist for *Do I Hear a Waltz?* (March 18, 1965) for which Arthur Laurents's book was an adaptation of his own stage play, *The Time of the Cuckoo*. The setting is Venice, where Leona Smith, a plain-looking American tourist, has an affair with Renato de Rossi, a romantic Italian shopkeeper. This musical was a failure (220 performances). The title song, introduced by Elizabeth Allen, was the score's main song. The complete score was recorded in an original cast recording.

In November 1967 a musical adaptation for television of George Bernard Shaw's *Androcles and the Lion* with words and music by Rodgers was telecast on the NBC-TV network, and the score was issued in a soundtrack recording.

While working on *Two by Two* in 1969, Rodgers suffered a heart attack. He recovered sufficiently to be able to attend an all-star production of *The Heyday of Rodgers and Hart* at the Lincoln Center in New York on November 16, 1969. He then continued to work on *Two by Two*, in which Peter Stone's text was an adaptation of Clifford Odets's play, *The Flowering Peach*, with lyrics by Martin Charnin. It opened for a run of 343 performances on November 10, 1970. Danny Kaye, in his first appearance on the Broadway musical-theater stage in 30 years, starred as the Biblical Noah in a retelling of the story of the flood while reflecting on 20th-century social mores and political problems. Noah communicated with God through an ingenious series of masterwork paintings flashed on a background screen. Kaye's presence on the stage was the main attraction. Rodgers's score, released in an original cast album, had two attractive numbers: "Something Somewhere," introduced by Kaye and "I Do Not Know a Day I Did Not Love You," by Walter Willison.

Rodgers had to undergo a laryngectomy in April 1975. Following therapy he was able to master esophageal speech. Physical disability did not keep him from working. In May 1975, he assisted in the production of *Rodgers and Hart*, a musical celebration on Broadway, and that summer he had a hand in a revival of *Oklahoma!* at Jones Beach in New York. He completed his autobiography, *Musical Stages* (1975), and went to work on a new musical, *Rex* (April 25, 1976). *Rex* was based on the marital problems of Henry VIII, and had a book by Sherman Yellen and lyrics by Sheldon Harnick. It closed after 42 performances. Rodgers's last musical, *I Remember Mama* (May 31, 1979) was also a failure, lasting 108 performances. Its book, by Thomas Meehan, was based on John Van Druten's play of the same name which, in turn, had been derived from stories by Kathryn Forbes. Martin Charnin was Rodgers's lyricist.

Rodgers's most celebrated songs from his earlier musicals were collected in record albums by Ella Fitzgerald, Margaret Whiting, Lee Wiley,

Patrice Munsel with Vaughn Monroe, Matt Denis, Ben Bagley, André Kostelanetz and his orchestra and the New York Philharmonic conducted by Richard Rodgers among others.

Richard Rodgers died at his home on Park Avenue in Manhattan on December 30, 1979. On the evening of January 3, the lights of the marquees along Broadway were dimmed for a minute in his memory.

Rodgers and his wife lived in New York, first in an apartment in the East 70s, then in a fourteen-room duplex on Park Avenue. Between 1949 and 1965, they spent weekends and summers at their summer home, Rockmeadow, in Southport, Connecticut, and later in a newly built house in Fairfield.

As one of America's great men of the theater, he was often honored. In addition to awards given him for his musicals, he received the Medal of Excellence from Columbia University (1949), the Alexander Hamilton Award of Columbia University (1956), the Creative Arts medal from Brandeis University (1968), and the Entertainment Hall of Fame Award (1975). He was honored by President Carter at a White House reception in 1979 as one of the first recipients of the Kennedy Center Honors Awards for lifetime achievement in performing arts. On June 3, 1979 at the Tony Award presentation ceremonies, he was presented with the Lawrence Langner Award for distinguished lifetime achievement in the theater. Rodgers was also the recipient of honorary degrees from Drury College (1949), University of Massachusetts (1954), Columbia University (1954), University of Bridgeport (1962) and University of Maryland (1962). Between 1962 and 1969 he was president and production director of the Music Theatre at Lincoln Center in New York.

Rodgers was a benefactor to music and theater in New York. In 1970, he financed the building of a one-million-dollar recreation center and theater in Mount Morris Park in Harlem, the neighborhood in which he had lived as a boy. He established scholarships at the Juilliard School of Music, the American Theatre Wing and the American Academy of Dramatic Art, and various awards for composers, performing musicians and people of the theater. In 1979 he presented another million dollars for an endowment financing production of new musicals in New York. The annual Richard Rodgers/ASCAP Award for contributions to the American theater was initiated in 1983.

ABOUT: Ewen, D. Richard Rodgers, 1957; Green, S. The Rodgers and Hammerstein Story, 1963; Hart, D. Thou Swell, Thou Witty: The Life and Lyrics of Lorenz Hart, 1976.

ROMBERG, SIGMUND (July 29, 1887–
November 9, 1951). The Hungarian-born composer, whose universally popular ballads and
waltzes were modeled on the European theater
music of his youth, was the principal successor
to Victor Herbert, and the last composer of
American operetta, a form that was displaced by
the musical when Romberg was in mid-career.

Romberg was born in Nagykanizsa, the oldest
of four sons of Adam and Clara (Fells) Romberg.
His father, the manager of a chemical manufacturing plant, was a cultivated man, a proficient
pianist and composer. Clara Romberg contributed to Viennese periodicals and wrote stories and
juvenile literature under the pseudonym Clara
Berg. Sigmund, though educated in music from
the earliest age, was intended by his parents to
become an engineer, and attended technical
schools in Hungary and Vienna from 1905.

After completing elementary schooling in
Belisce in 1898, Romberg attended the Realschule in Osiek for preliminary studies. There
the professor of art, a music lover, kept his interest in music alive. When he heard Romberg play
the violin, he waived a rule forbidding students
to join the orchestra before their fifth school year
and permitted him to join the violin section during his first semester. He also taught him orchestration and presented him with a trumpet.

After five years at the Realschule, Romberg
was sent to two other preparatory schools. At
first, in Pecs, in 1901 Romberg was a member
of the school orchestra, played the church organ
and formed his own band. A year later, he transferred to a high school in Szeged where he wrote
his first piece for orchestra, a march dedicated
to the Grand Duchess, patroness of the local Red
Cross. She used her influence to have Romberg
conduct it with an orchestra formed for the
town's Red Cross celebration.

Romberg completed his engineering studies at
the Politechnische Hochschule in Vienna, but
also participated enthusiastically in the musical
life of the city. He studied composition and harmony with Richard Heuberger, visited the salon
of Albert Grünfeld, an eminent Viennese musician, and frequented the musical theater. He
was briefly employed as assistant stage manager
at the Theater-an-der-Wien.

After receiving his degree, Romberg began an
18-month period of military service with the
19th Hungarian Infantry Regiment stationed in
Vienna. By the time he had completed his military commitment he had become convinced that
his future lay not in engineering but in music.
He also felt that if he were to make his way in
music, it would have to be in a city offering less
competition from brilliant musicians than Vienna did. He chose New York.

SIGMUND ROMBERG

In 1909 Romberg arrived in the United States
with 300 dollars. His first job was in a New York
pencil factory where he was paid seven dollars
a week. While wandering the streets in search of
some musical opportunity, he found a job as a pianist at the Café Continental on Second Avenue,
where his salary was 15 dollars a week, two
meals a day, and a percentage of the tips. He
held this post one week and was then hired by
the Pabst-Harlem Restaurant to play the harmo-
nium in its small orchestra. Within a short period
his weekly earnings grew to 45 dollars.

In 1912 he was engaged by Bustanoby's, an elegant New York restaurant, where he was required to conduct an orchestra in European
salon and light music. One evening he played
popular American dance music. Although dancing was still virtually unknown in restaurants,
the diners began taking to the floor. The novelty
caught on and made Bustanoby's a favorite rendezvous for the fashionable. Romberg's weekly
salary rose to $150. Influenced by the music he
was conducting, Romberg began writing popular dance pieces. Three were published in Tin
Pan Alley by J. W. Stern & Company in 1913:
the one-steps, "Leg of Mutton" and "Some
Smoke," and the waltz, "Le Poéme."

When Louis Hirsch resigned as staff composer
for Jacob J. and Lee Shubert, promoters of revues and musical theater, Romberg was hired as
his replacement. His first score was for the Winter Garden revue, *The Whirl of the World* (January 10, 1914) starring Eugene and Willie
Howard and the Dolly Sisters. Harold Atteridge,
with whom Romberg eventually wrote 20 shows,
was his lyricist. Romberg and Atteridge then

wrote the songs for *The Midnight Girl* (February 23, 1914), *The Passing Show* (June 10, 1914), in which Marilyn Miller made her debut in the legitimate Broadway theater singing "Omar Khayyam"; *Dancing Around*, starring Al Jolson (October 10, 1914); and *Maid in America*, starring Nora Bayes (February 18, 1915). By 1917, Romberg had composed 275 numbers for seventeen musicals and revues.

Much of this work was undistinguished and quickly forgotten, but one production suggested Romberg's potential in the musical theater. It was *The Blue Paradise* (August 15, 1915), adapted by Edgar Smith from a Viennese operetta. Romberg was required to contribute four new songs to lyrics by Herbert Reynolds. "The Blue Paradise" is the name of a Viennese garden restaurant where Mitzi works as a flower girl. She is separated from Rudolf, the student she loves, when he has to leave for America. As a wealthy American, Rudolf returns to Vienna and visits a restored "Blue Paradise." There he meets Mitzi's daughter. Wearing her mother's dress, she reminds Rudolf of the girl he had loved and lost long ago.

As Mitzi, Vivienne Segal made her Broadway debut, and with Cecil Lean she introduced "Auf Wiedersehen," a waltz that became the first of many hit songs she would introduce and Romberg's first major success. Nelson Eddy and André Kostelanetz and his orchestra each recorded it and Helen Traubel revived it in the film biography of Romberg, *Deep in My Heart* (1954).

The Blue Paradise had what was then a very long run of 356 performances. Nevertheless, Romberg continued to compose functional music for revues and extravaganzas produced by the Shuberts until 1916, when he told his employers he was looking for more ambitious stage assignments. To keep him with the company the Shuberts turned over to him the text of an operetta by Rida Johnson Young and Cyrus Wood. Entitled *Maytime* (August 16, 1917), it became Romberg's second major stage success on Broadway (492 performances). It is set in Washington Square during the 19th century. The lovers Otillie and Richard pledge eternal devotion to each other, but Otillie's father compels her to marry Claude, a disreputable gambler. The happiness denied Otillie and Richard is fulfilled many years later by Otillie's granddaughter and Richard's grandson, who fall in love and marry.

The waltz, "Will You Remember?" (lyrics by Rida Johnson Young), introduced by Peggy Wood and Charles Purcell, was used as a recurrent melody in the operetta. In the film adaptation of *Maytime* (1937), in which only three of the stage songs were retained, it was sung by Jeanette MacDonald and Nelson Eddy. In *Deep in My Heart* it was sung by Vic Damone and Jane Powell. Nelson Eddy also recorded it with Jeanette MacDonald, as did Dorothy Kirsten with Felix Knight and the orchestras of Al Goodman and André Kostelanetz.

Maytime did so well at the box office that before its first year was over at the Shubert Theater a second company was formed to present it, simultaneously, across the street at the 44th Street Theatre. This was the first time in American stage history that a show had been played simultaneously by two companies on Broadway. When those runs ended, both companies toured the United States for several years.

Romberg became an American citizen in 1914. Four years later, during World War I, he was inducted into the Army and assigned to Military Intelligence. He was also called upon to entertain troops at various army camps. On his release from the military he broke with the Shubert organization, signing a long-term contract with the music publishing house of M. Witmark & Sons for the publication of his songs while forming the company Wilner and Romberg to produce his own shows. *The Magic Melody* (November 11, 1919) and *Love Birds* (March 15, 1921) were both failures. Between these two musicals, and under other producing auspices, he composed half the score for *The Poor Little Ritz Girl* (July 27, 1920), the other half of which was composed by Richard Rodgers and Lorenz Hart in their professional debut as songwriters for the Broadway theater.

Romberg's failures as producer brought him back into the Shubert fold. The Shuberts had then recently acquired the rights to a popular Viennese operetta, *Das Dreimaederlhaus*, a romanticization of the last years of Franz Schubert, whose score was derived from Schubert's music. *Das Dreimaederlhaus* opened in Vienna in 1916 and came to New York a year later in a German-language production. For the Shuberts, Dorothy Donnelly revised the libretto and wrote the lyrics and Romberg was asked to write a new score derived from Schubert's melodies. As *Blossom Time* it opened on Broadway on September 29, 1921 and remained for 592 performances. Within a few months of the Broadway opening, four companies toured the country. For many years thereafter *Blossom Time* was performed throughout the United States. It returned to Broadway six times between 1923 and 1943.

Dorothy Donnelly's libretto made no attempt to adhere to biographical truth. Franz Schubert suffers from a frustrating love affair with Mitzi, a fictitious character. To express his feelings for her he composes "Song of Love." Too shy to advance his own interests, he calls on Schober, his best friend, to sing his love song to Mitzi. Schober does so, and the two fall in love. Schubert's heartbreak at losing his beloved to his best friend destroys both his health and his will to create. He is incapable of completing the symphony on which he is at work and allows it to remain unfinished. When this symphony is performed in its unfinished state, Schubert was too sick to attend the concert. He dies soon after, composing a song, "Ave Maria" on his deathbed.

"Songs of imperishable longing. . . . illuminated *Blossom Time* like pictures in a Christmas book," wrote George S. Kaufman, then the critic for *The New York Times*. The principal ballad, "Song of Love," introduced by Bertram Peacock and Olga Cook, used for its melody the main theme from the first movement of Schubert's *Unfinished Symphony*. Recordings of "Song of Love" were made by Jeanette MacDonald with Nelson Eddy, Everett Marshall, and Carmen Cavallero with André Kostelanetz and his orchestra. Other successful songs include "Tell Me Daisy," introduced by Peacock and Cook, melody taken from the opening theme of the second movement of the *Unfinished Symphony*; "Three Little Maids," a trio for Olga Cook, Dorothy Whitmore and Frances Halliday, from *Rosamunde*'s ballet music; and "Serenade," introduced by Howard Marsh, from the Schubert *Ried* of the same title. Al Goodman and his orchestra with the Guild Choristers and vocal soloists recorded an album of the principal songs from *Blossom Time*.

Before he undertook another operetta, where he knew his talent belonged, Romberg continued providing songs for 13 Shubert productions: five in 1922, and four each in 1923 and 1924. None of their songs are remembered. During some of this time he was planning a new operetta, his first in which the score would be entirely his own. *The Student Prince* (December 2, 1924), book and lyrics by Dorothy Donnelly, was adapted from a German play, *Old Heidelberg*, which had twice been unsuccessfully produced on Broadway in English. *The Student Prince* remained on Broadway for 608 performances, was performed by nine touring companies, and has become a classic of the American musical theater. Innumerable revivals have included return visits to Broadway in 1931 and 1943, an Off Broadway production in 1961, and a performance by the New York City Opera in August 1980. In 1954 it was filmed with Edmund Purdom and Ann Blyth, with Mario Lanza dubbing for Purdom on the soundtrack. A silent film version had been made in 1927 by Ernst Lubitsch.

The setting is the picturesque German city of Heidelberg in the mid-nineteenth century. Prince Karl Franz, heir to the throne of Karlsberg, arrives in Heidelberg incognito with his tutor. At "The Golden Apple," haunt of university students, he meets Kathi, daughter of the innkeeper, with whom he falls in love. This romance is frustrated when the king of Karlsberg dies, compelling Karl to return home, ascend the throne, and marry Princess Margaret. But he cannot forget Kathi, and returns to Heidelberg for a brief reunion and final separation.

The score contains three of Romberg's most celebrated ballads, including "Deep in My Heart, Dear" (introduced by Howard Marsh and Ilsa Marvenga) which provided the title for Romberg's screen biography. It was recorded by Mario Lanza, Risë Stevens and Nelson Eddy; the orchestras of André Kostelanetz and Al Goodman; and, in a violin transcription, by Fritz Kreisler. "Serenade" was sung by Howard Marsh, Raymond Marlowe, Frederic Wolff, Paul Kleeman and chorus in the stage version and by Mario Lanza on the soundtrack. Recordings were made by Lanza, Nelson Eddy with Risë Stevens, Richard Crooks, Lauritz Melchior with Nadine Connor and Dorothy Kirsten with Felix Knight. William Olvis sang it in *Deep in My Heart*. "Golden Days," a duet for Howard Marsh and Greek Evans on the stage, became a solo for Lanza on the soundtrack; he also recorded it. The rousing "Drinking Song" was sung by a chorus in both the stage and screen versions and on the soundtrack with the assistance of Lanza. It was recorded by Mario Lanza with chorus and by Nelson Eddy with Risë Stevens.

On March 20, 1925, in a private ceremony in Paterson, New Jersey, Romberg married Lillian Harris, whom he had met at a party given by Al Jolson. The Rombergs established residence in a hotel apartment in New York City. Spurred on by his wife, Romberg now decided to foresake the kind of nondescript, functional music he had been producing so abundantly for the Shuberts and concentrate on operettas, his real creative strength. Some of his ensuing operettas were failures, but two became landmarks of the American musical theater. They were *The Desert Song* (November 30, 1926), book and lyrics by Otto Harbach and Oscar Hammerstein II, and *The New Moon* (September 19, 1928), book by Hammerstein, Frank Mandel and Laurence Schwab and lyrics by Hammerstein.

The idea for *The Desert Song* was inspired by a newspaper account of a revolt by the French Riffs against the French protectorate in Morocco. Red Shadow, a Moroccan bandit, is in love with Margot, but Margot is interested in Pierre, the Governor's son. She is abducted by the bandit to the harem of Ali ben Ali, where Red Shadow succeeds in winning her love. When the Governor and his troops arrive to rescue Margot, the Red Shadow offers no resistance, which his men interpret as a sign of cowardice. But this unexpected behavior is explained when he is discovered to be none other than Pierre in disguise.

The Desert Song, badly reviewed, began its Broadway career as a box-office failure but developed into a 465-performance run through the growing popularity of its songs outside the theater. After Broadway, *The Desert Song* was produced in cities throughout the United States, with revivals in New York in 1946 and 1973. It was adapted into films three times, in 1929, 1943, and 1953.

Two of the principal numbers in this score were romantic ballads. "Blue Heaven" (also known as "The Desert Song") was introduced by Vivienne Segal and Robert Halliday and recorded by Edith Day, Dennis Morgan and by the orchestras of Al Goodman and André Kostelanetz. In the first screen version it was sung by John Boles and Carlotta King; in the second, by Dennis Morgan and Irene Manning; and, in the third, by Gordon MacRae and Kathryn Grayson. "One Alone," introduced on the stage by Robert Halliday was heard in the three film adaptations respectively by John Boles, Dennis Morgan with Irene Manning and Gordon MacRae with Kathryn Grayson. Recordings were made by Dennis Morgan, Richard Crooks. Dorothy Kirsten with Felix Knight and the orchestras of Don Voorhees and Al Goodman. In contrasting mood was the vigorous "The Riff Song," introduced by Robert Halliday, William O'Neal and a male chorus in the operetta's opening scene. It was performed on the screen by John Boles in 1929, Dennis Morgan in 1943 and Gordon MacRae in 1953; it was recorded in 1926 by Don Voorhees and his orchestra and by the Revelers. In *Deep in My Heart*, Cyd Charisse and James Mitchell performed a provocative dance to this music.

In *The New Moon*, the librettists (one of whom was Oscar Hammerstein II) used New Orleans in 1788 as their setting. Robert Mission, a French aristocrat who has come to New Orleans disguised as a bondsman, falls in love with his master's daughter, Marianne. "The New Moon" is a ship bearing Captain Paul Duval, come to arrest Mission for his revolutionary activities in France. Mission is apprehended at a gala ball to which he comes to steal a kiss from Marianne. Shipped back to France on "The New Moon," Mission and his followers escape after a mutiny. They set up a new government on an island off the coast of Florida where Mission is soon joined by Marianne.

The New Moon ran on Broadway for 509 performances, then received the highest sum yet paid in Hollywood for screen rights. It was twice adapted as a film: in 1930 with the opera luminaries Grace Moore and Lawrence Tibbett, and a decade later with Nelson Eddy and Jeanette MacDonald. *The New Moon* was revived in New York's Carnegie Hall for a short run in 1942, at the New York City Center two years later, and at Lincoln Center by the New York City Opera in 1986. It is, perhaps Romberg's most inventive score, bringing as it did five standards. "Lover, Come Back to Me" (melody derived partly from Tchaikovsky's *June Barcarolle*, for piano) and "One Kiss" were introduced by Evelyn Herbert. The former was originally recorded by the Revelers and by Segar Ellis and popularized by Rudy Vallee, but later was also recorded by Lawrence Tibbett, Kenny Baker, Jeanette MacDonald, Billie Holiday, Risë Stevens, Nelson Eddy, and Eddy Duchin and his orchestra; the latter, by Jeanette MacDonald and the orchestras of Al Goodman and André Kostelanetz. "Softly, as in a Morning Sunrise" was introduced by William O'Neal and recorded by Neslon Eddy, Kenny Baker and by Al Goodman and his orchestra. "Wanting You," introduced by Robert Halliday and Evelyn Herbert, was recorded by Nelson Eddy, Lawrence Tibbett and Dorothy Kirsten with Felix Knight. "Stouthearted Men," introduced by Richard Halliday, William O'Neal and male chorus, was recorded by Nelson Eddy and John Raitt, and revived in 1967 in a recording by Barbra Streisand.

In the first motion picture version of the operetta, "Lover, Come Back to Me" was sung by Lawrence Tibbett and Grace Moore and in the second film version by Nelson Eddy and Jeanette MacDonald. "One Kiss" was sung by Grace Moore in the first film adaptation and by Jeanette MacDonald in the second. "Softly, As in a Morning Sunrise" was sung by Lawrence Tibbett in the first film and by Nelson Eddy in the second. "Wanting You," was a duet for Tibbett and Grace Moore in the first film, and for Nelson Eddy and Jeanette MacDonald in the second. "Stouthearted Men" was assigned to Tibbett in the first film and to Nelson in the second.

Though Romberg continued to compose music for operettas after 1930, none met with favor, for the vogue for operettas in the Broadway theater had been eclipsed by musical comedy. Most of Romberg's operettas did not exceed a 50-performance run. Romberg first came to Hollywood in 1929 to compose music for the film *Viennese Nights* (1930). His third motion picture, *The Night Is Young* (1934), again had a Viennese setting. For it he composed another of his distinguished waltzes, "When I Grow Too Old to

Dream" (lyrics by Hammerstein), introduced by Evelyn Laye and sung by José Ferrer in *Deep in My Heart*. Among the many who have recorded it are Arthur Tracy, Nelson Eddy, Allan Jones, Jane Pickens and the orchestras of Guy Lombardo, Al Goodman and André Kostelanetz.

Romberg recognized that professionally he was standing still. He said in the early 1930s: "I've got to get out of the rut I am in. I've got to get away from Vienna, for instance. That is all passé. European backgrounds! Maybe that's what is dating me. I've got myself stranded in Europe and I have to get out of it. I think I'll refuse anything from now on without an American identity."

He returned to the Broadway stage with *May Wine* (December 5, 1935), which had a 213-performance run. Though Vienna was still a setting, the story was a realistic treatment of a contemporary subject that carried *May Wine* out of operetta and into musical comedy. The book, by Frank Mandel, was based on *The Happy Alienist* by Wallace Smith and Erich von Stroheim; Oscar Hammerstein II provided the lyrics. The principal character, Professor Johann Volk, a psychiatrist, marries a baroness whose fidelity he soon begins to doubt. He turns to drink and, in a fit of rage, shoots a dummy figure he mistakes for his wife. When he is finally convinced that his suspicions had no basis in fact, the marriage is saved. Brooks Atkinson noted that here the "excrescences and stock appurtenances" of operetta had been avoided, but he also noted that *May Wine* had "certain plodding mannerisms that dull the fine edge of appreciation." On the other hand, Gilbert Gabriel described it as "one of those fragrant and tasty concoctions which, poured in one's ear, warms the affection and tickles the humor considerably, before it flies out of the other." Its principal songs were: "Just Once Around the Clock," introduced by Walter Woolf King, Vera Van and Leo C. Carroll; "Dance My Darling," and "Something New is in My Heart," by Nancy McCord; and "I Built a Dream One Day," by Walter Slezak, Walter Woolf King and Robert C. Fischer.

In the spring of 1936, separating themselves temporarily from Broadway, Romberg and his wife acquired a house on North Roxbury Drive in Beverly Hills (next door to George and Ira Gershwin). Working for the MGM studios, Romberg composed the music for his first American story: David Belasco's *The Girl of the Golden West*, which, at the turn of the 20th century, had been a successful Broadway stage play before Giacomo Puccini turned it into an opera. *The Girl of the Golden West* (1938) starred Jeanette MacDonald and Nelson Eddy. With Kahn again

as his lyricist, Romberg composed two songs for *They Gave Him a Gun*, starring Spencer Tracy (1939).

For several years after that, Romberg was unproductive. Early in World War II he toured camps, hospitals, battleships to entertain the troops with his famous melodies. He also embarked on a new career as the conductor of his own orchestra, with which he toured the United States giving concerts of light music billed as "An Evening with Sigmund Romberg." The first of several such tours began in Baltimore on October 10, 1942 and the fourth tour culminated in an appearance at Carnegie Hall on September 10, 1943 to a sold-out auditorium.

Romberg returned to the Broadway theater after a four-year absence with *Up in Central Park* (January 27, 1945), a musical comedy set in New York with book by Herbert and Dorothy Fields and lyrics by Dorothy Fields. It had a run of 504 performances. Several companies toured with the show, and a motion picture adaptation starring Deanna Dubin and Dick Haymes was released in 1948. Its plot involves New York politics in the 1870s. John Matthews is a reporter investigating the political machine headed by Boss Tweed. During his investigation, Matthews falls in love with Rosie Moore, daughter of one of Boss Tweed's ward heelers, a young girl with ambitions to become a singer. She deserts Matthews to marry a Tweed henchman who offers to finance her career. After the Tweed machine is destroyed through Matthew's revelations, he meets the widowed Rosie and their long interrupted romance is revived.

Romberg's songs, recorded in an original cast album, here had an American identity. The principal ballads were "Close as Pages in a Book" and "It Doesn't Cost You Anything to Dream," both introduced by Wilbur Evans and Maureen Cannon. "Close as Pages in a Book" was recorded by Bing Crosby, Frances Langford and Wilbur Evans with Eileen Farrell. "Carousel in the Park" was introduced by Maureen Cannon. In the film version Deanna Durbin and Dick Haymes sang "Close as Pages in a Book" and "Carousel in the Park."

On November 16, 1946 Romberg's music made its sole appearance on *Your Hit Parade* when "Zing Zing–Zoom Zoom" (lyrics by Charles Tobias) had a single representation. This song had been popularized in Perry Como's recording.

The last Romberg musical to be produced during his lifetime, *My Romance* (October 19, 1948) was once again haunted by the ghost of operetta. This was a musical adaptation of Edward Sheldon's *Romance*, a Broadway stage play produced in 1913. Its heroine was the famous prima donna, Lina Cavalieri, who sacrificed her love for Reverend Armstrong for the sake of both of their careers. But operetta had lost its audience and *My Romance* barely survived three months. Sigmund Romberg was working on a new musical comedy, *The Girl in Pink Tights*, when he died in a hotel suite in New York in 1951.

His last musical described the circumstances surrounding the production of *The Black Crook*, the sensational musical extravaganza that had been produced in New York in 1866. *The Girl in Pink Tights* came to Broadway on March 5, 1954, two and a half years after Romberg's death, and was a failure, expiring after 115 performances. Its score contained two fine ballads (lyrics by Leo Robin): "Lost in Loveliness," introduced by David Atkinson, and "In Paris and in Love," introduced by David Atkinson and Jeanmaire. These and the other songs were recorded in an original cast album.

Later in 1954, Romberg's screen biograpjy, *Deep in My Heart*, in which José Ferrer portrayed the composer and Doe Avedon the composer's wife, was released. All its music was issued in a soundtrack recording.

ABOUT: *Periodicals*—New York Times August 24, 1980, August 24, 1986.

HAROLD ROME

ROME, HAROLD, (May 27, 1908–), composer-lyricist, was born in Hartford, Connecticut, one of five children of Louis Rome, president of the Connecticut Coal and Charcoal Company and Ida (Aronson) Rome. Harold attended the Hartford public schools and learned to play the piano, and upon graduating from high school in 1924, he attended Trinity College (Hartford) for two years, supporting himself by playing the piano and writing music for dance bands. Wavering between careers in law or architecture, he attended the architectural school at Yale University (1926–29), earning a bachelor of arts degree, and then he went on to Yale law school (1929–30) and the Yale school of architecture, where he was awarded the degree of bachelor of fine arts in 1934. While at Yale, he took courses in music and was a member of the college band that toured Europe four times; he also played piano with the Yale Collegians at proms.

In 1934, he went to New York City to pursue a career as architect. During the ensuing years, he studied piano with Arthur Lloyd and Loma Roberts, and composition and orchestration with Joseph Schillinger, Lehman Engel, and Meyer Kupferman, among others. The economic depression of the 1930s offered few opportunities for young architects, so Rome worked for the Works Progress Administration (WPA) for a weekly salary of $23.80, which was supplemented by the few dollars he earned each week playing the piano. He was finally hired as draughtsman for a New York architectural firm; this provided him with experience but no pay. While holding this job, he wrote songs; Gypsy Rose Lee liked one of them and helped him market it. Another of his songs, "Horror Boys From Brooklyn," was eventually used in a motion picture *One in a Million* (1936), starring the Ritz Brothers.

Deciding in 1935 to abandon architecture for songwriting as a way to make a living, Rome worked for three summers at Green Mansions, an adult camp in the Adirondacks that mounted live shows each week in its little theater. In addition to playing the piano in the pit orchestra, he wrote about 90 songs and sketches in a futile attempt to attract the attention of publishers and producers, but they often found his frequent emphasis on social and political problems objectionable.

But his songs did attract the interest of Louis Schaeffer of the International Ladies' Garment Workers Union. The Union had acquired New York's Princess Theatre, which it renamed the Labor Stage, where it provided entertainment for the members. When an intimate, modest, topical revue (with a cast composed entirely of union members) was planned, Charles Friedman (who had been the producer of the Green Mansions shows) was engaged as director, and Harold Rome was invited to write the songs (both words and music).

Pins and Needles opened on November 27, 1937 for an anticipated run of several weekends. Because of popular demand the run was extended, with eight presentations a week, for an unprecedented 1,108 performances for a Broadway revue. Commenting on the success of *Pins and Needles, Variety* said: "The very people it mocked and ridiculed—the carriage trade—came in droves." Eleanor Roosevelt was so taken with it that she saw it four times and brought it to the White House. Rome was constantly present during this long run as he played piano in the pit orchestra, for a salary of $100 a week.

Because of its satirical commentary on the social and political scene (which was frequently revised to reflect current events) and its support of the young union movements, *Pins and Needles* was described by the New York *Post* as "Puckish proletarian romp." "Sing Me a Song With Social Significance," performed by the ensemble, set the tone for the entire production, and "Sunday in the Park," also an ensemble number, romanticize the simple pleasures of the working class; it won an ASCAP award in 1937. Both of these songs have been recorded by Rome. "Nobody Makes a Pass at Me," introduced by Millie Weitz, was the lament of a girl whose beauty was not enhanced by the well-advertised cosmetics she used. *Pins and Needles* was revived Off Broadway on July 6, 1978. "There are still moments of enjoyment to be had," said *Variety*, "thanks to Harold Rome's clever lyrics [and] occasionally melodious tunes."

Pins and Needles established Rome's reputation. Mills Music published the songs from the show, and in 1938, producer Max Gordon contracted him to contribute songs to another socially and politically conscious Broadway revue, *Sing Out the News* (September 24, 1939). Though some of the show's material was written by George S. Kaufman and Moss Hart, the revue had only the modest run of 105 performances. However, one of Rome's songs, "F.D.R. Jones," became successful; it won the ASCAP award that year, was recorded by Cab Calloway and was brought to Billy Rose's Casa Manana nightclub in New York. Rome also contributed two songs to Jimmy McHugh's score for the successful Broadway revue *Streets of Paris* (1939) and he tried his hand at three musical comedies, but these never got off the ground.

Soon after the attack on Pearl Harbor, Rome wrote material for a series of revues collectively entitled *Lunchtime Follies* to be given in defense plants. For the professional theater, he composed the score for the short-lived revue, *Let Freedom Sing*, and several of his songs were interpolated into two successful Broadway revues, *Star and Garter* (1942) and *Ziegfeld Follies of 1943*.

Rome was inducted into the United States Army in 1943. Stationed at the New York Port of Embarkation, in the office of Special Services, he wrote material for army shows as well as orientation songs. One of his productions, *Stars and Gripes*, toured the army camps in the United States and in combat areas in Europe. Another, *Skirts*, was produced for the armed forces in England.

After the war, Rome worked on material for a revue concerning the transition from military service to civilian life. *Call Me Mister* (April 18, 1946) remained at the National Theatre for 734 performances and while some of the songs and sketches featured the social and political overtones for which Rome had become famous, the most celebrated song from the production was a satire on Latin-American dance rhythms, "South America, Take it Away." Rome had written the song before the war, but had found no place for it. Betty Garrett introduced it in *Call Me Mister*, and both she and the song were big hits; Bing Crosby's subsequent recording with the Andrews Sisters in 1946 sold more than a million discs. In "The Face of the Dime," introduced by Lawrence Winters, Rome paid tribute to the memory of President Franklin D. Roosevelt. In 1951, a motion picture version of the show was released, starring Betty Grable and Dan Dailey.

Rome enjoyed another success in 1948. "The Money Song" had been written for *That's the Ticket*, a musical that never reached Broadway; it became popular in a recording by the Andrews Sisters and was also recorded by Rome. Two years later, he wrote the score for Mike Todd's *Bless You All* (December 14, 1950), a Broadway revue in which Pearl Bailey introduced "You Never Know What Hit You" and Mary McCarty sang "Little Things Meant so Much to Me."

Rome's first book musical on Broadway was *Wish You Were Here* (June 25, 1952), Rome's most successful venture on Broadway (598 performances) since *Call Me Mister*. This was a musical comedy adaptation by Arthur Kober and Joshua Logan of Kober's play, *Having a Wonderful Time*. *Wish You Were Here* takes place at Camp Karefree, an adult resort in the Berkshire Mountains, where Teddy Stern, a girl from the Bronx, and Chick Miller, a waiter working his way through law school, fall in love. A false rumor circulates that Teddy has spent the night with the camp Romeo, but the misunderstanding is resolved in the end. The show's title song, introduced by Jack Cassidy, was the best musical number. Eddie Fisher's recording of it sold more than a million discs and it was heard on *Your Hit Parade* 15 times, three in first position.

Fanny (November 4, 1954) was Rome's greatest success on Broadway (888 performances). The book by S. N. Behrman and Joshua Logan, based on a trilogy of plays, *Marius, César* and *Fanny*, by Marcel Pagnol set in Marseilles, which had been made into a film, *Port of Seven Seas* (1938). César (played by Ezio Pinza in his only return to Broadway after *South Pacific*) was the owner of a small waterfront café. His son, Marius (William Tabbert), is in love with Fanny, who is carrying his child but is driven to the high seas by his wanderlust. Fanny marries Panisse (Walter Slezak), the middle-aged proprietor of a sailmaking establishment, to legitimize her unborn child. When Marius returns to Marseilles as the child's first birthday is being celebrated, his father sends him away, reminding him that Panisse has actually been the loving husband and father. Years later, Panisse, on his deathbed, dictates a letter urging Fanny to marry Marius, now in nearby Toulon.

Brooks Atkinson described Fanny as "a musical drama," adding: "Fortunately it comes to us with an excellent score by Harold Rome. . . . Mr. Rome has avoided the emotional astringence of modernism and written a number of melodies with feeling and strength." The highlights of the score, which was Rome's most ambitious to date, were the title song, introduced by William Tabbert; "Love is a Very Light Thing" and "To My Wife," introduced by Ezio Pinza; and "Be Kind to Your Parents," a duet for Florence Henderson and Lloyd Reese.

In Munich on December 16, 1955, *Fanny* became the second American musical to be staged in Germany since World War II (the first was Cole Porter's *Kiss Me, Kate* in Frankfurt, several days earlier). *Fanny* was also made into a motion picture starring Charles Boyer, Maurice Chevalier and Leslie Caron (1960); unfortunately, all of the songs were deleted but "Fanny," which was heard as background music on the soundtrack.

Destry Rides Again (April 23, 1959), was a "Western musical," based on a story by Max Brand which had previously been made into a film starring Jimmy Stewart. In the cattletown of Bottleneck at the turn of the century, Thomas Jefferson Destry, Jr. (Andy Griffith), son of a famous gunfighter, is appointed sheriff so that law and order can be restored. He is a shy, mild-mannered young man with little affinity for guns, but in time he realizes that violence is best met with violence. In a gun battle, the outlaws are wiped out and Destry's life is saved by Frenchy, the girl to whom he has long been attracted. "Beginning with a razzle-dazzle overture," reported Brooks Atkinson, "Mr. Rome has written an entertaining score in the traditional mood of cowboy music with some ragtime flourishes for the saloon festivities." The most notable songs were "Anyone Would Love You," a duet for Andy Griffith and Dolores Gray, and "I Say Hello" and "Fair Warning," both introduced by Dolores Gray. The show was a box-office success with a run of 473 performances.

In *I Can Get It For You Wholesale* (March 22, 1962), which ran for 300 performances, Barbra Streisand, playing opposite Elliott Gould, made a Broadway debut in which she revealed her potential as a comedy star. In this musical adaptation by Jerome Weidman of his own novel about New York's garment industry in 1937, the hero, Harry Bogen, is a callous, ruthless, double-dealer who has fought his way to the top in the garment trade through dishonesty and exploitation. But in the end, he ends up bankrupt, with only his mother and his one-time sweetheart, whom he had rejected, at his side. The leading musical numbers were a love song between husband and wife, "Have I Told You Lately?" introduced by Bambi Lynn and later recorded by Tony Bennett and Ken Le Roy, and "The Sound of Money," rendered by Elliott Gould, Sheree North, Barbara Monte, William Reilly and Edward Verse.

Rome went far afield for the setting of his next Broadway musical, *The Zulu and the Zayda* (November 9, 1965), which ran for 179 performances; it takes place in Johannesburg, South Africa. Billed as a "comedy drama with music," *The Zulu and the Zayda* was an adaptation by Howard da Silva and Felix Leon of a story by Dan Jacobson about a touchingly sympathetic relationship transcending bigotry and cultural differences between a Jewish grandfather (the Zayda), whose favorite language is Yiddish, and a native servant who speaks only Zulu. Rome's score occasionally suggests ethnic African music and at other times assumes a Yiddish flavor. Of the musical numbers, *Variety* said that "they are invariably appropriate in situation, help clarify character and make pointed comment. The incidental music enhances the atmosphere and background." The integration of music and play precluded a listing of separate songs in the program. "Good to Be Alive" and "Zulu Love Song" were introduced by Louis Gossett and "May Your Heart Stay Young" and "Rivers of Tears" by Menasha Skulnick. "Like the Breeze Blows" was later recorded by Mahalia Jackson.

Rome composed songs for Horton Foote's musical adaptation of Margaret Mitchell's epic novel about the Civil War and the siege of Atlanta, *Gone With the Wind*, which had already been made into a landmark motion picture. As

Scarlett, Rome's musical was introduced in Tokyo with a Japanese cast on January 2, 1970 and
proved a huge success. This was the first time
that Japan had financed an American musical
production adopting American production
methods and recruiting the help of American
talent, including choreographer, costume designer and musical director. The details of the
history of this production were recorded by
Rome's wife, Florence, in the book *The Scarlett
Letters* (1971).

Gone With the Wind opened in London in
1972, in Los Angeles and San Francisco the following year and toured the United States in
1976. In spite of continual revisions, the music
failed to gain the approval of critics or audiences, and the show never reached Broadway.

In *The World of Musical Comedy,* Stanley
Green said of Rome's stage music: "When timely
revues were no longer in style, and Rome at last
began to write scores for book shows, he was able
to bring to them the same understanding and
natural warmth that he had shown in earlier
works. Moreover, to his already well-established
skill with words, Rome soon added a greater
richness of musical style. . . . The ability to express in songs the honest emotions of those who
are least articulate has been one of his most distinguishing characteristics. For Rome is, essentially, a people's composer and lyricist, one who,
without being sentimental or patronizing, provides the common man with uncommon musical
expressions."

In an interview with *ASCAP Today,* Rome described his working methods: "The all important
thing about songs is the idea itself. It doesn't
matter how good the music is . . . If a song is
communicating with the people who hear it, it
transmits a mood or expression of something, an
opinion or a feeling about something.

"What usually comes to me first is the necessity for doing the song. The first thing you do is
go over the book and find the high emotional
points. . . . You find out what the situation or
the scene has to say. You figure out the characters that are going to do it, and then you think
of a song that will convey that—in music and
lyrics. . . . I usually work on both of them at the
same time.

"I work at the piano. I work while I am walking on the street. I work while I'm sleeping at
night. I wake up in the middle of the night sometimes and start going over things. After a while,
you learn to let your unconscious work for
you. . . . Sometimes, I'll make a list of things
that have to be done and let them sit for a while.
Quite often, when I get up one morning, I find
that somewhere during the night the problem

has been solved for me, and I can go ahead and
work on the song because it seems to have a direction by then."

Rome has composed songs for a children's album, *Sing Song Man,* recorded by Frank Luther
on the Decca label, and he has recorded several
albums of his songs to his own piano accompaniment. Occasionally, he has written lyrics for other people's music, such as "My Heart Sings"
(music adapted from a French song by Herpin),
which was introduced by Kathryn Grayson in
the film *Anchors Aweigh* (1945).

Harold Rome and Florence Miles were married in New York on February 3, 1939 and they
reside in an apartment on Fifth Avenue. Rome
collects paintings and also owns one of the largest private collections of African sculpture in
America. Painting is his favorite hobby, and in
1964, he exhibited 40 of his works at the Marble
Arch Gallery in New York. The show was
unique because each of 12 paintings were hung
in a separate room, and while viewing the paintings, the gallery patrons heard, through loud-
speakers, special songs composed by Rome for
the occasion.

ABOUT: Ewen, D. Great Mean of American Popular
Song, 1972; Green, S. The World of Musical Comedy,
4th ed. 1980. *Periodicals*—ASCAP Today September
1971; New York Times Magazine June 4, 1978.

ROOT, GEORGE FREDERICK (August 30,
1820–August 6, 1895), composer of "The Battle
Cry of Freedom" and other Civil War songs, was
born in Sheffield, Massachusetts. His parents,
Frederick F. Root and Sarah (Flint) Root, were
both musical. When George was six, his family
moved to North Reading, Massachusetts, where
he was raised on a farm not far from Boston. Music was an early influence in George's life: as a
child, he was taught to play the flute, and by the
time he was a teenager, he had learned the rudi-
ments of performing on 13 instruments.

In 1838, Root went to Boston, where he met
the choirmaster and organist, A. N. Johnson.
Johnson hired Root as his assistant in return for
room and board, music lessons and a weekly salary of $3. Before long, Root began acquiring his
own pupils and assisting Johnson as organist at
churches on Winter and Park Streets. In Boston,
Root also studied singing with George James
Webb, and he met Lowell Mason, whom he assisted at the Boston Academy of Music and also
with the experimental introduction of singing
school methods in American public schools. In
addition, Root conducted two choirs.

In 1844, Root went to New York to teach sing-

GEORGE F. ROOT

ing at the Abbott School for Young Ladies. He also accepted appointments at the New York State Institute for the Blind, the Union Theological Seminary, the Rutgers Female Institute, and Miss Haines's School for Young Ladies, and he served as choirmaster at the Presbyterian Church on Mercer Street. On August 28, 1845, he married Mary Olive Woodman, an accomplished singer; their daughter, Mrs. Clara Louise Burnham, distinguished herself as a novelist and their son, Frederic Woodman Root, became a professional organist and composer.

After spending a year in Europe in 1850, where he studied voice in Paris with Giulio Alary and Jacques Potharst, Root and William Bradbury founded the New York Normal Institute in 1853 to train music teachers. Inspired by Mason (who often taught at Root's Institute) he organized conventions in various parts of the country which continued to meet periodically to promote new methods of music instruction.

Though he had composed small pieces and edited collections of music for pedagogical purposes, Root's first major work was a cantata, "The Flower Queen," composed in 1851 to verses by Fanny Crosby, a former pupil at the New York Institute for the Blind. A sacred cantata, "Daniel" (libretto written with Crosby), soon followed in 1853. These and other similar works were extremely successful and received many performances in the East and the Midwest. But the best known of Root's cantatas was "The Haymakers" (1857), composed at the suggestion of Lowell Mason. This, too, was frequently performed during Root's lifetime, particularly in Boston and Chicago, and a re-

cording of it was released on New World Records in 1978.

Buoyed by the success of "The Flower Queen," and the popularity of Stephen Foster's songs, Root also began to write popular songs under the pen name of G. Friedrich Wurzel ("Wurzel" being the German word for "root"). His first success was "The Hazel Dell" (1852), a sentimental ballad, written with Crosby, about a girl whose untimely death was mourned by her lover at her grave in the hazel dell; "There's Music in the Air" (1854; lyrics by Crosby) later became a college song at Princeton University, and in 1855, Root wrote "Rosalie, the Prairie Flower," a lament for a child who was carried to heaven by angels. Root offered to sell "Rosalie" to publisher Nathan Richardson for $100, but Richardson, predicting limited sales, preferred a royalty arrangement; this arrangement eventually brought $3,000 in royalties to the composer. Root also composed music for worship, and by 1855, he had written his most celebrated hymn, "The Shining Shore" (verses by Reverend David Nelson), whose evangelical tone pervaded much of Root's music.

While in New York, Root was associated with the firm of Mason and Bradbury, a well-known publisher of church music, and in 1859, he moved to Chicago, where his younger brother, E. T. Root, had founded a publishing venture with C. M. Cady one year earlier. He became a partner in Root & Cady, which was successful until the disastrous fire of 1871.

With the outbreak of the Civil War, Root composed "The First Gun is Fired," three days after the attack on Fort Sumter. It did not become popular, but Root's second war ballad, "The Battle Cry of Freedom," inspired by President Lincoln's second call for volunteers and published in 1863 was one of the war's most celebrated ballads. In spirited words and music, it exhorted everyone to "rally 'round the flag" while "shouting the battle cry of freedom." Soon after he had completed it, Root was approached by the Lombard Brothers, popular singers who regularly featured war songs, then in search of new material. Root showed them his freshly composed song, and they introduced it that day at a war meeting in front of the Chicago courthouse. When the famous Hutchinson Family Singers opened a war rally in Union Square (New York City) with this ballad, it aroused so much enthusiasm that they retained it in their repertory.

"The Battle Cry of Freedom" became a significant force in promoting and maintaining the morale of Union soldiers, who sang it as they marched into battle. A young, unidentified sol-

dier wrote: "The tune put as much spirit and
cheer into the army as a splendid victory. Day
and night you could hear it by every campfire
and in every tent. Never shall I forget how these
men rolled their lines." President Lincoln also
admired the song. He wrote Root: "You have
done more than a hundred generals and a thousand orators. If you could not shoulder a musket
in defense of your country, you certainly have
served through songs."

During the presidential campaign of 1864,
"The Battle Cry of Freedom," with the appropriate lyrics, and "Rally 'Round the Cause" promoted the candidacy of Abraham Lincoln. In 1867,
it was sung by 1,000 voices at the Republican
convention as part of a successful maneuver to
nominate General Ulysses S. Grant for president.
That the song had enormous power more than
30 years later was demonstrated in 1896, when
10,000 people gathered at the Coliseum in Chicago to hear the aging Jules Lombard sing the
ballad he had helped introduce, and to raise
funds for a monument to Root.

Root composed several other popular Civil
War ballads. Among these was "The Vacant
Chair" (1861; words by H.S. Washburn), inspired by the death of Lt. John William Grout
of the 15th Massachusetts Volunteer Infantry,
just before a Thanksgiving furlough. Washburn,
a friend of the Grout family, was moved to write
a poem, which appeared in the *Worcester Spy*,
and which several composers set to music.
Though Root's sympathies lay decidedly with
the North, "The Vacant Chair" also became
well-known in the South because it expressed so
poignantly the tragedy being experienced by so
many families. "Just Before the Battle, Mother"
(1863) describes the emotions of young soldiers
about to go into battle, and it denounces Northern "copperheads" who "in every battle kill our
soldiers by the help they give the foe." "Just Before the Battle, Mother" first appeared in the
Christmas issue of *The Song Messenger*, the
house organ of Root and Cady; the sheet music
is reputed to have sold more than one million
copies, and Will Oakland recorded it in 1909.

"Tramp! Tramp! Tramp!" also known as "The
Prisoner's Hope" (1864) expresses the feelings of
Union soldiers held captive in Southern prisons.
Root composed it in two hours for the Christmas
issue of *The Song Messenger*. When his brother
saw the manuscript, he did not regard it highly,
yet this ballad went on to become one of Root's
most widely circulated and beloved Civil War
songs. With new lyrics, it became the campaign
song of Ulysses S. Grant in his 1868 presidential
campaign. In 1864, Root wrote a sequel entitled
"Just After the Battle" and "On, On, On, the

Boys Came Marching"; both of these were failures.

After the Civil War, Root continued to work
for Root and Cady. When the firm was destroyed during the Chicago fire of 1871, the
John Church Company of Cincinnati acquired
its copyrights, plates and catalogue. Root continued to publish under the imprint of George F.
Root & Sons, and he also continued his activities
with the Normal Schools. He was awarded a D.
Mus. degree from the University of Chicago in
1872, and in 1886, Root traveled to Europe to
observe music classes.

Root made his last public appearance, singing
"The Battle Cry of Freedom," at a Civil War
memorial at The Auditorium in Chicago in February 1895. He died while vacationing on Bailey
Island, Maine in the summer of 1895.

ABOUT: Dictionary of American Biography, 1935; Howard, J. T. Our American Music, 4th ed. 1965; Root, G.
F. The Story of My Musical Life, 1891.

RUBY, HARRY (January 27, 1895–February
23, 1974) and **KALMAR, BERT** (February 10,
1884–September 18, 1947). Harry Ruby, composer, and Bert Kalmar, lyricist, were leading
songwriters for the Broadway stage in the 1920s
and for motion pictures in the 1930s.

Harry Ruby was born Harry Rubinstein on
the Lower East Side of New York. He was the
fourth of six children of Barnett Rubinstein, at
turns a furrier and a jeweler, and Tilly Rubinstein; Harry's older brother by four years, Herman, became a professional song lyricist.

Ruby's boyhood was spent in the city streets
and on sandlots playing baseball, the sport he
would always love. He despised school studies
and neglected them. Upon graduating from
P. S. 42 in the Bronx, he attended the High
School of Commerce for 30 days before being
dropped, and Mount Morris High School for just
two days. In a period of four months he attended
two different business schools and then decided
to forgo formal schooling altogether. "It is true
I was no scholar," he once told this author, "but
at the age of 19 I found out that there was such
a thing as books and I started to read like mad,
especially in the field of science." His music
training was equally slender. After a few piano
lessons, he dropped his teacher to learn what he
could by himself.

When Ruby was 16 he earned five dollars a
week and board by playing the piano in a trio
performing in a resort in Long Branch, New Jersey. In 1913 he was hired as a staff pianist and
song plugger in Tin Pan Alley for the Gus Ed-

BERT KALMAR   HARRY RUBY

wards Publishing Company. Sometimes he and Walter Winchell (then a song plugger himself) would visit department and five-and-ten-cent stores to demonstrate the firm's songs. Ruby later worked as a song plugger for the Harry von Tilzer publishing firm, demonstrating songs in restaurants and rathskellers. He also played the piano for silent films in nickelodeons, appeared on the Fox and Loew vaudeville circuits as a member of the Messenger Boys Trio, and was a member of a musical act called Edwards and Ruby ("Edwards" became better known as Harry Cohn, the head of Columbia Pictures).

After leaving the firm of Harry von Tilzer, Ruby worked as a song plugger in Tin Pan Alley for Kalmar and Puck, where he met Bert Kalmar.

On June 14, 1915, Ruby married Dorothy Herman, an entertainer. This marriage lasted 15 years and produced one child, a daughter.

Bert Kalmar was born in New York City on February 10, 1884. Like Ruby, Kalmar had almost no academic training. When he was ten he ran away from home and joined a tent show, performing as a magician. Later he took up songwriting as a hobby, and toured burlesque and vaudeville theaters as a dancing comedian. Kalmar's first hit song came in 1911 with "In the Land of Harmony" (music by Ted Snyder), which was recorded by the American Quartette. With Snyder as composer, he wrote "The Ghost of the Violin" in 1912, and Harry Puck composed the music for "Where Did You Get That Girl?" (1931), which became a favorite in vaudeville with singing comedians after having been introduced in a recording by Walter van Brunt.

In 1915 Kalmar's "I've Been Floating Down the Green River" (music by Joe Cooper) was interpolated into the Broadway musical Maid in America, starring Nora Bayes, who recorded and popularized "Hello, Hawaii, How Are You?" (lyrics by Kalmar and Edgar Leslie, music by Jean Schwartz).

Just before World War I, Kalmar and Puck formed their own Tin Pan Alley publishing house. When Kalmar's career as a dancing comedian was ended by a serious knee injury, he turned more seriously to songwriting. His first collaborations with Harry Ruby came in 1917 with "When Those Sweet Hawaiian Babies Roll Their Eyes" and "He Sits Around," the latter written for and introduced by Belle Baker. In 1918 their "What a Girl Can Do" was interpolated into the Broadway musical Ladies First, starring Nora Bayes.

For a brief interlude before the musical partnership of Ruby and Kalmar became permanent, each worked with other writers. In 1918 Ruby composed "Come on Papa" and "The Dixie Volunteers," both to lyrics by Edgar Leslie; in 1919, "And He'd Say Oo-La-La Wee-Wee" (lyrics by George Jessel) and "Daddy Long Legs" (lyrics by Sam M. Lewis and Joe Young). In 1919 Kalmar wrote "Oh, What a Pal was Mary" (lyrics written with Edgar Leslie, music by Pete Wendling), which became popular in vaudeville. "You Said It" (lyrics written with Eddie Cox, music by Henry W. Santly) and "Take Your Girlie to the Movies" (lyrics written with Edgar Leslie, music by Pete Wendling) were composed that same year.

The collaboration of Ruby and Kalmar resumed in 1920. "I'm a Vamp From East Broadway" was a tour de force for Fanny Brice when she introduced it in the *Ziegfeld Follies of 1920*. "We've Got the Stage Door Blues" was interpolated into the revue, *Broadway Brevities of 1920*, starring Eddie Cantor. In 1920 Ruby and Kalmar also wrote "So Long, Oh Long (How Long You Gonna Be Gone)," which Fred Astaire and Red Skelton revived in *Three Little Words* (1950), the film biography of Ruby and Kalmar. "Where Do They Go When They Row, Row, Row?" (1920) was introduced in vaudeville by George Jessel, and "Timbuctoo" (1920) was recorded by the Premiere Quartette, Aileen Stanley and Frank Crumit. In 1921 "My Sunny Tennessee" (lyrics written with Herman Ruby) was interpolated by Eddie Cantor into the Broadway revue *The Midnight Rounders* (1921) and revived by Astaire and Skelton in *Three Little Words*. "Memories" was interpolated into the revue *Snapshots of 1921*. That year they also composed "She's Mine, All Mine" and "Snoops the Lawyer." The latter was popularized in vaudeville in the early 1920s and became the song that helped launch Beatrice Lillie's career as a comedienne in England. She recorded it, as did Nora Bayes and Eddie Cantor. In 1922 came "Beautiful Girls," interpolated into the *Greenwich Village Follies of 1922*; "I Gave You Up Just Before You Threw Me Down," introduced in a recording by Joseph Knecht; and "Sheik of Avenue B." In 1923, "The Window Cleaners" was introduced on Broadway in *The Town Clown*, and was revived for Dick Powell and Frank McHugh in the film *Happiness Ahead* (1934).

Kalmar and Ruby wrote the lyrics for their first standard in 1923. With music by Ted Snyder they composed "Who's Sorry Now." It was introduced in vaudeville by Van and Schenck, was first recorded by the orchestra of Isham Jones and by Art Mooney, and Gloria De Haven sang it in *Three Little Words*. In 1957 "Who's Sorry Now" was revived in a recording by the then unknown Connie Francis, whose best-selling version gave the song six appearances on *Your Hit Parade* in 1958. It was interpolated into the Bob Fosse film *All That Jazz* (1979).

The first Broadway musical for which Ruby and Kalmar composed a complete score was *Helen of Troy, New York* (June 19, 1923), which had a run of 191 performances. George S. Kaufman and Marc Connelly wrote the text for a satire on the business world and the advertising industry. Elias Yarrow is the head of the Yarrow Collar Factory in Troy, but he can never remember his own collar size without consulting a memorandum book. Among the show's other characters are an effete, bumbling male model,

a blundering efficiency expert, and Helen, a stenographer at Yarrow who is in love with the boss's son. When Helen is fired, she designs a semisoft collar and sells it to a rival company. This forces Yarrow to merge with his rival and agree to his son's marriage to Helen. The better musical moments were provided by "Happy Ending," introduced by Helen Ford, and "It Was Meant to Be So," a duet for Queenie Smith and David Williams.

Ruby and Kalmar continued to compose scores for Broadway in the 1920s. After *No Other Girl* (August 13, 1924), a failure (59 performances), came *The Ramblers* (September 20, 1926), a musical farce with a text by Bert Kalmar and Guy Bolton which ran for 289 performances. The show's best song was "All Alone Monday," sung as a duet by Jack Whiting and Marie Saxon and recorded by Johnny Marvin and the Revelers. June Clyde and Hugh Trevor sang it in the film. *The Cuckoos* (1930) and Gale Robbins performed it in *Three Little Words*. It was also recorded by Leo Reisman and his orchestra.

For *Lucky* (March 22, 1927), book by Otto Harbach, Ruby and Kalmar shared credit for the score with Jerome Kern. Nevertheless, *Lucky* closed after 71 performances. Its principal songs were "Dancing the Devil Away," introduced by Mary Eaton, and "The Same Old Moon," introduced by Joseph Santley and Ivy Sawyer.

Described as "a fairy tale in modern clothes," *Five O'Clock Girl* (October 10, 1927), with book by Guy Bolton and Fred Thompson, had a 280-performance run. Patricia Brown, an employee in a cleaning establishment, enjoys a daily five o'clock telephone conversation with Gerald Brooks, a wealthy playboy she has never met face to face. When they finally meet, she pretends to be a society girl. This ruse is soon uncovered, but Brooks is already smitten. "Thinking of You" and "Up in the Clouds," both introduced by Mary Eaton and Oscar Shaw, were the most popular songs. The former became Kay Kyser and his orchestra's theme song, and "Up in the Clouds" was performed by the chorus in *Three Little Words*. "Thinking of You" appeared seven times on *Your Hit Parade* in 1950 following the success of *Three Little Words*, in which it was revived by Vera-Ellen. *Five O'Clock Girl* was revived unsuccessfully on Broadway in 1981, using other Ruby-Kalmar songs besides those from the original production.

Good Boy (September 25, 1928), book by Oscar Hammerstein II, Otto Harbach and Henry Myers, ran for 253 performances. Two country bumpkins from Buttersville, Arkansas arrive in the big city, where one of them, Walter Meakin, abandons his sweetheart to marry a chorus girl. She soon discards him, but has a change of heart when Walter strikes it rich by manufacturing toy dolls. Helen Kane, who became famous as the voice of the cartoon character Betty Boop, was in the cast, and for her girlishly pip-squeaked singing voice they wrote "I Wanna Be Loved by You," which has become a standard. Kane recorded it, and in *Three Little Words* she sang it on the soundtrack, dubbing for Debbie Reynolds. Rudy Vallee, Jane Russell and Anita Ellis (dubbing for Jeanne Crain) sang it in *Gentlemen Marry Brunettes* (1955) and Marilyn Monroe performed it in *Some Like It Hot* (1959). In 1950, because of the popularity of *Three Little Words*, "I Wanna Be Loved by You" was heard ten times on *Your Hit Parade.*

For *She's My Baby* (January 3, 1928), Ruby and Kalmar wrote only the libretto, leaving the songwriting to Rodgers and Hart, but the music of Ruby and Kalmar returned in *Animal Crackers* (October 25, 1928). With book by George S. Kaufman and Morrie Ryskind, *Animal Crackers* was a classic Marx Brothers extravaganza, with Groucho playing a famous African explorer who is invited to the mansion of the wealthy Mrs. Rittenhouse (Margaret Dumont). There he and Chico try to retrieve a stolen painting, while Harpo Marx chases every female in sight and steals everything that is not nailed to the floor. In this score was born "Hooray for Captain Spaulding," introduced by Groucho Marx, Robert Grieg, Margaret Dumont and ensemble. Years later it became famous as the signature music for the Groucho Marx television quiz show, *You Bet Your Life.* The stage performers also sang it in the 1930 motion picture adaptation of the stage musical, and Astaire and Skelton performed it in *Three Little Words.* The main ballad in the stage production of *Animal Crackers* was "Watching the Clouds Roll By," introduced by Bernice Ackerman and Milton Watson. *Animal Crackers* had an initial run of 191 performances, and was revived in Washington, D. C. in 1982.

Top Speed (December 25, 1929), which Ruby and Kalmar produced with Guy Bolton, in addition to writing its songs, closed after 13 weeks.

Beginning in 1930, the most important Ruby and Kalmar songs were written for the screen. Their first assignment was *Check and Doublecheck* (1930), starring Amos 'n' Andy of radio fame. For that film Ruby and Kalmar composed their most famous song, "Three Little Words," introduced by Bing Crosby, who was backed by Duke Ellington and his orchestra. The song was first recorded by Crosby and Ellington, and later by Nick Lucas, by the Ipana Trouba-

dours and by Rudy Vallee. "Everybody predicted the song would lay an egg," Ruby recalled. "It was nearly dropped from the movie. But it was an overnight hit." The song provided the title for Ruby and Kalmar's screen biography, in which Astaire and Skelton sang it. It was heard as background music in the nonmusical films *From This Day Forward* (1948) and *This Earth of Mine* (1950).

Harry Ruby and his wife were divorced in 1930. The following year he married the performer Cleo Carter. Their marriage lasted three years, and on May 2, 1936 he wed the screen actress Eileen Percy, with whom he raised a son. They occupied a house on North Rodeo Drive in Beverly Hills until 1962, when they moved to Pacific Palisades.

These were Ruby and Kalmar's most important screen songs of the 1930s: "I Love You So Much," introduced by Bert Wheeler in *The Cuckoos* (1930) and recorded by the Arden-Ohman orchestra and by Leo Reisman.

"Ev'ryone Says 'I Love You,'" introduced by the Marx Brothers in *Horse Feathers* (1932) and recorded by Isham Jones.

"Just a Perfect Combination" (lyrics written with Irving Caesar, music by Harry Akst) was introduced by Eddie Cantor in *The Kid from Spain* (1932) and recorded by Ozzie Nelson.

"Keep on Doin' What You're Doin'," introduced by Bert Wheeler, Robert Woolsey, Dorothy Lee and Thelma Todd, and "Keep Romance Live" and "Tired of it All," introduced by Ruth Etting in *Hips, Hips Hooray* (1934).

In addition to their songwriting efforts, Ruby and Kalmar also wrote the screenplays for several films, including *The Kid from Spain*, the Marx brothers' *Duck Soup* (1933), and *Look for the Silver Lining* (1949), the screen biography of Marilyn Miller.

"Nevertheless" was a Ruby-Kalmar song issued in 1931 independent of any screen or stage production. It was popularized on radio and in recordings by both Bing Crosby and Rudy Vallee. Fred Astaire, Red Skelton and Anita Ellis (the last mentioned dubbing for Vera-Ellen on the soundtrack) sang it in *Three Little Words.* In 1950 it was revived in recordings by the Mills Brothers and by Paul Weston and his orchestra and received 12 hearings on *Your Hit Parade*, holding first position on November 4, 1950. The Barry Sisters revived it again in a recording in 1961. When *Five O'Clock Girl* was revived in 1981, "Nevertheless" was interpolated into the score and sung by Sherry Rooney and John Remme.

The only Broadway musical by Ruby and Kalmar of the 1930s, and their last, was *The High*

Kickers (October 31, 1941), starring Sophie Tucker and George Jessel. This was a project that had originated with Jessel, who helped write both the book and the lyrics. The "High Kickers" were a burlesque troupe playing at Piner's Burlesque in 1910. Thirty years later, this company is still intact. When the cast is arrested in Chamberville, Ohio for mounting a pornographic show, Sophie Tucker (playing herself) gains its release by reminding the mayor that his wife had once been a "High Kicker" herself. This show survived for 171 performances.

In 1947, two days after he had signed the contract for *Three Little Words*, in which he was portrayed by Astaire, Bert Kalmar died in Los Angeles. After his death, "A Kiss to Build a Dream On," which Ruby and Kalmar had written in 1935, became successful when, with lyrics revised by Oscar Hammerstein, it was interpolated for Kay Brown and Louis Armstrong in the film *The Strip* (1951) and was recorded by Louis Armstrong.

Before Kalmar's death, Harry Ruby wrote lyrics to Rube Bloom's music for "Give Me a Simple Life," introduced by John Payne and June Havoc in *Wake Up and Dream* (1945) and recorded by the orchestras of Benny Goodman and Sammy Kaye. In 1949 Ruby wrote the lyrics for "Maybe it's Because" (music by Johnnie Scott), which was interpolated into the Broadway revue *Along Fifth Avenue* (1949) and was represented on *Your Hit Parade* nine times.

After 1950 Ruby made guest appearances on network television programs starring Perry Como, Steve Allen, Groucho Marx and Danny Thomas. Ruby composed the theme music for the ABC television series *The Real McCoys*, which was first telecast on September 20, 1957. In 1961 Ruby was the subject of the television show, *This Is Your Life*.

By 1960 Ruby was in retirement. Apart from songwriting, his interests included astronomy and baseball. He attended every home game of the Los Angeles Dodgers, who voted him "the world's greatest fan." He also visited the spring training camps of major league teams. His prize possessions were his library and a collection of baseball uniforms presented to him by various teams.

Because of his lifelong fear of modern machinery Ruby never learned to drive, and his typing was so inept that he acquired a rubber stamp for the heading of his personal letters that read: "Please excuse the typing." He even took his typewriter to a repair shop just to have the ribbon changed. "Machines hate me," he often remarked.

Harry Ruby died in the Motion Picture and Television Hospital in Woodland Hills, California. In *Three Little Words* he was portrayed by Red Skelton. The film's music was released in a soundtrack recording.

Harry Ruby was the author of *Songs My Mother Never Sang to Me* (1943). Twenty-two highlights from this volume were collected into a three-man revue, *Harry Ruby's Songs My Mother Never Sang*, which was conceived by Michael S. Roth and Paul Lazarus and produced Off Broadway in June 1981.

ABOUT: Craig, W. Sweet and Lowdown: America's Popular Song Writers, 1978; Ewen, D. The Life and Death of Tin Pan Alley, 1964. *Periodicals*—ASCAP Today March 1971.

SCHMIDT, HARVEY (September 12, 1929–) and **JONES, TOM** (February 17, 1928–). Harvey Schmidt, composer, and Tom Jones, lyricist, are best known for writing the songs for *The Fantasticks,* the world's longest-running musical, and for *I Do! I Do!*

Harvey Lester Schmidt was born in Dallas, Texas, the son of Reverend Emmanuel Carl Schmidt, a Methodist minister, and Edna (Wieting) Schmidt. Schmidt attended the University of Texas, in Austin, where he majored in art, having a gift for painting and drawing. Music was a secondary interest and he learned to play the piano by ear. At the university he befriended a fellow student, Tom Jones, who specialized in stage direction and aspired to a career in the professional theater.

Tom Jones, son of W. T. and Jessie (Bellamy) Jones, was born in Littlefield, Texas. He entered the University of Texas in 1945, after graduating from Coleman High School. Jones aroused Schmidt's interest in the musical stage, and in 1951 they initiated their collaboration with *Hippsy-Boo,* a college show, with Schmidt contributing the music for the title number and Jones providing the sketches. They continued to work together, writing words and music for several songs and for the complete score of another college show, *Time Staggers On.*

Tom Jones graduated from the University of Texas with an M. F. A. degree in 1951; Schmidt earned his M. F. A. a year later. Jones then served in the United States Army, stationed in Baltimore in intelligence (1951–53) and, from 1953 to 1955, with a field artillery unit in Texas, where his duties consisted mainly of painting latrine signs. Schmidt and Jones continued their collaboration by mail, accumulating a sizable repertory of songs.

Following his release from the armed services,

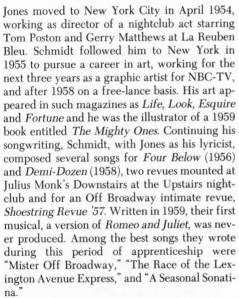

HARVEY SCHMIDT   TOM JONES

Jones moved to New York City in April 1954, working as director of a nightclub act starring Tom Poston and Gerry Matthews at La Reuben Bleu. Schmidt followed him to New York in 1955 to pursue a career in art, working for the next three years as a graphic artist for NBC-TV, and after 1958 on a free-lance basis. His art appeared in such magazines as *Life, Look, Esquire* and *Fortune* and he was the illustrator of a 1959 book entitled *The Mighty Ones.* Continuing his songwriting, Schmidt, with Jones as his lyricist, composed several songs for *Four Below* (1956) and *Demi-Dozen* (1958), two revues mounted at Julius Monk's Downstairs at the Upstairs nightclub and for an Off Broadway intimate revue, *Shoestring Revue '57.* Written in 1959, their first musical, a version of *Romeo and Juliet,* was never produced. Among the best songs they wrote during this period of apprenticeship were "Mister Off Broadway," "The Race of the Lexington Avenue Express," and "A Seasonal Sonatina."

At this time Schmidt and Jones discussed ways of turning Edmond Rostand's play, *Les Romanesques,* into a musical. In 1959 a fellow graduate from the University of Texas offered to produce and direct such a musical at Barnard College's summer theater if Schmidt and Jones could compress it into a single act. They complied with *The Fantasticks* which was introduced in its one-act version on August 3, 1959. Lorenzo "Lore" Noto, a young theater producer in search of new material, attended the premiere and persuaded Schmidt and Jones to do what they had always wanted: enlarge *The Fantasticks* into a full evening's entertainment

in an Off Broadway auditorium. It took the authors nine months to complete the necessary revision. On an investment of $16,500 and with a cast of eight, *The Fantasticks* opened at the Sullivan Street Playhouse in Greenwich Village on May 3, 1960. The reviews were mixed, hardly the kind to bring queues to the box office, although Henry Hewes of *Saturday Review* called it "one of the happiest Off Broadway evenings in a season that has been happier Off Broadway than on. . . . Jones and Schmidt have worked with professional expertness equalling the best Broadway has to offer with a degree of artistic taste that Broadway seldom attains anywhere."

Despite Hewes's praise, *The Fantasticks,* seemed doomed and it was ready to bring down the final curtain after its second month. Suddenly, however, a change of fortune unparalleled in the history of the musical theater took place. News spread by word of mouth that this was a musical full of charm, warmth, and appealing, even magical, entertainment, original both in the writing and the production. The small theater began to draw capacity houses especially after receiving the Vernon Rice Prize as year's the outstanding Off Broadway production.

In the text by Tom Jones, a free-wheeling adaptation of the story of Pierrot and Columbine, two young lovers are separated by a wall built by their fathers who play out a charade of Montague and Capulet-like enmity and opposition to bring the young couple together. The ruse works, particularly after the fathers contrive to have a bandit attempt to rape the girl, setting the stage for a heroic rescue by the girl's lover. But once the two young people discover they have been duped by their scheming parents, they break up. Once again the fathers erect a separating wall. In the end, the couple reconciles and romance triumps.

Much of *The Fantasticks'* charm lay in the simplicity of the commedia del l'arte staging. A single set was used together with the most fundamental props, such as a stick to represent a wall or a cardboard moon attached to a pole to suggest nighttime. "The simpler you do something the better off it's going to be," Tom Jones declared. Simplicity also characterized the dialogue, which is more poetic and whimsical than realistic, and the action of the plot, which at times is ingenious.

It seems that the enchantment of *The Fantasticks* is universal, transgenerational and transcultural, and that the Sullivan Street production might run forever. On May 13, 1984, after a run of 24 years, it celebrated its 10,000th performance at the Sullivan Street Playhouse, the longest consecutive run of any play in history. In the past quarter of a century there have been more than 8,000 professional, semiprofessional, amateur and school productions in the United States alone. Fifteen production companies have toured the United States and performed at U. S. Army bases in the Pacific and in Europe. In 66 foreign countries, 453 productions have been mounted, including five in Saudi Arabia and seven in New Zealand. In Scandinavia there has been an annual production since 1962. A taped presentation of a live performance of the stage production was seen on NBC-TV's Hallmark Hall of Fame on October 18, 1964. By 1984 the financial return to initial investors stood at 7,624 percent, or a profit of $76,240 on an investment of $1,000. Among the 86,820 actors and musicians who have appeared in productions worldwide have been Liza Minnelli, Richard Chamberlain, Anna Maria Alberghetti, Stephen Douglass, John Gavin, Elliott Gould, John Raitt, and Howard Keel. The *Fantasticks'* Off Broadway run came to an end on June 8, 1986, after its 10,864th performance.

The score, recorded in an original cast album, yielded a standard in "Try to Remember," which was introduced by Jerry Orbach. It was popularized in 1965 in recordings by Ed Ames and by The Brothers Four. Rita Gardner introduced "Much More," which in 1963 became a bestselling recording for Barbra Streisand, who also popularized "Soon It's Gonna Rain," which Rita Gardner and Kenneth Nelson had introduced. The same pair introduced "I Can See It" and "They Were You."

Schmidt and Jones graduated from Off Broadway to Broadway proper with two musi-

cals: *110 in the Shade* (October 24, 1963), which had a run of 330 performances, and *I Do! I Do!* (December 5, 1966), which stayed on Broadway for 560 performances. Each of these scores was recorded in an original cast release. *110 in the Shade* was N. Richard Nash's musical-stage version of his own play, *The Rainmaker*, which is set in a Western plains state, with the action taking place between dawn and midnight of a summer day during a drought. A stranger convinces the townspeople that he is a "rainmaker," capable of relieving the drought. The rains do come by the time the play ends, but not before the stranger has fallen in love with the heroine, Lizzie, a shy, introverted, plain-looking girl who has long since despaired of finding a husband. In the *Saturday Review*, Henry Hewes found that this musical's "integrity, its simplicity and its tenderness, are endearing without being the least bit sentimental," and that the songs "sustain the simplicity and tenderness of the story." As Lizzie, Inge Swenson (in her Broadway debut) introduced the principal musical numbers: "Love, Don't Turn Away"; with Robert Horton, "Is it Really Me?"; and with Will Geer, "Raunchy." George Church, Scooter Teague, Lesley Warren and chorus sang "Everything Beautiful Happens at Night."

Winner of the Tony award as the year's best musical, *I Do! I Do!* was the first Broadway musical with a cast of only two characters (performed by Mary Martin and Robert Preston). Like the play on which it was based (Jan de Hartog's *The Four Poster*), the musical, which was adapted by Tom Jones, traces the history of a marriage, beginning with the wedding night and encompassing the vicissitudes of marital fortune until the couple's old age. By then they have at last come to terms with each other and with life. The husband, designated simply as "He," is a successful writer, whose increasing popularity not only with his reading public but also with the ladies causes problems throughout the years. The songs were woven seamlessly into the text, heightening its sentiment, humor, and pathos. Mary Martin and Robert Preston introduced "My Cup Runneth Over," which in 1967 became a bestselling disc in a performance by Ed Ames, and "I Love My Wife," to which they performed a barefoot tap dance.

In *Celebration*, a musical fable for which Jones served as director as well as author of the text and lyricist, Schmidt and Jones returned to the fantasy and offbeat theater of *The Fantasticks*. *Celebration* opened on Broadway on January 22, 1969. Potemkin, the protagonist, is a cynic who believes that the only value in the world is survival. With the Revelers (a mask-wearing chorus of 12), he initiates a ritual, "Celebration," in which the characters include an orphan and an angel, symbolic of youth and old age, innocence and corruption, optimism and futility. *Time* described the play's music as charming "for sophisticates who have never quite foresaken the magic realm of childhood." Otis L. Guernsey Jr. selected it as one of the ten best plays of the season in his theater yearbook. *Celebration* closed after only 109 performances. The most appealing musical numbers, all recorded in an original cast album, were "Mr. Somebody in the Sky" and "My Garden," introduced by Michael Glenn-Smith; "Where Did it Go?" by Ted Thurston; and "Love Song," by Glenn-Smith and Susan Watson.

In 1967 the songwriters founded Portfolio Studio at 141 West 47th Street for the production of intimate, experimental, and relatively low-budget productions. Produced there in December 1974, *Portfolio Revue* was a collection of the best songs by Schmidt and Jones, the ones dropped from their shows as well as the popular numbers. The music was performed at the piano by the composer. Mel Gussow said in *The New York Times* that this was "an eminently engaging way for all of us to get acquainted with [the songs]."

Schmidt and Jones's *Philemon* opened Off Broadway on April 8, 1975. Set in ancient Rome, it was a chamber musical whose hero is a clown coerced by the authorities into impersonating Philemon, the spiritual leader of the oppressed Christians. The clown is supposed to operate as an informer, but he ends up as a saint. *Philemon* ran for only 48 performances.

Colette Collage, produced Off Broadway in April 1983, was a final attempt by Schmidt and Jones, after more than 12 years of work, to bring the biography of the French writer Colette to the musical theater. Their first effort had been a play with music (the play was written by Jones's wife). Transformed into a fully realized musical with book by Tom Jones, *Colette* opened in Seattle on February 10, 1982 and closed before reaching New York. The final version, now titled *Colette Collage*, condensed the text into the presentation of Colette as a young woman married to an older man who helps her launch her literary career, then as an older woman married to a younger man. "Mr. Jones and Mr. Schmidt have managed to give dramatic validity to their view of Colette," reported John S. Wilson in *The New York Times*. "Their score's charming and rhythmic songs provide color, detail and character in compact cameos." Wilson was especially impressed by the song "Come to Life," introduced by Timothy Jerome.

Schmidt and Jones contributed the score for *A*

Texas Romance, 1909, an art film that won first prize at the San Francisco Film Festival. Schmidt composed the background music for *Bad Company* (1972), a commercial film, and the score for a ballet, *Texas Fourth* (1973), produced by Agnes de Mille's Heritage Dance Theatre.

Tom Jones married Elinore Wright on June 1, 1963. They live in an apartment on New York's Upper West Side about a mile from Schmidt's residence. Schmidt is the coauthor of *In and Out Book* (1959) and *The Worry Book* (1962).

ABOUT: Green, S. The World of Musical Comedy, 4th ed. 1980; Rigdon, W. (ed.) The Biographical Encyclopedia and Who's Who in the American Theatre, 1966.

SCHWARTZ, ARTHUR (November 25, 1900–September 3, 1984) and **DIETZ, HOWARD** (September 8, 1896–July 30, 1983). Composer Arthur Schwartz was born in Brooklyn, the younger of two sons of Solomon and Dora (Grossman) Schwartz. His father was a successful lawyer who wanted Arthur to follow him in the legal profession. Though the older brother received musical training, Arthur was not allowed to study music. Nonetheless he would blow tunes through the teeth of a comb, play the harmonica, and tried to teach himself to play the piano. His only formal training was a course in harmony that he took in college, but while attending elementary school he had provided piano accompaniment for silent films at a moviehouse in Flatbush.

After graduating from Brooklyn's Boys High School in 1916, Schwartz enrolled in New York University, where he majored in English. There he composed marches for the band and a football "fight" song, and wrote for the school newspaper. He received his B.A. in 1920 and an M.A. in literature from Columbia University in 1921. From 1921 to 1924 he studied law at NYU, supporting himself by teaching high school English. Composing remained a hobby, and in 1923 Schwartz published "Baltimore, Maryland, You're the Only Doctor for Me" (lyrics by Eli Dawson); its royalties brought him eight dollars. He was admitted to the New York bar in 1924.

Schwartz spent the summer of 1924 working as a counselor at the Brant Lake Camp for boys, in the Adirondack Mountains. Lorenz Hart, then still an unknown, also worked there, and with Hart as his lyricist, Schwartz composed songs for camp shows. Their "I Know My Girl By Her Perfume" was sold for $75 to the vaudeville act, Besser and Amy, and "I Love to Lie Awake in Bed" became successful on Broadway with new

ARTHUR SCHWARTZ   HOWARD DIETZ

words by another lyricist and the title changed to "I Guess I'll Have to Change My Plan."

Schwartz open a law office in New York that fall, and kept up the practice for four years. But he also continued to compose songs, and in 1925 he played some of them for George Gershwin, including one that paid sentimental tribute to Gershwin's *Rhapsody in Blue*. "I sat down at the piano," Schwartz later recalled. "As he stood behind me patiently, I played a long, aimless introduction and cleared my throat much more than was necessary. Suddenly I wished I had never asked for this preposterous audition, for I began to realize the full extent of my audacity in writing this lily-gilding song. . . . How *dared* I? I could go no further, in spite of George's friendly insistence. When I told him I was withdrawing my composition then and there, he didn't quarrel with my decision. Mercifully changing the subject, he asked me to play some of my other tunes. I found his reactions the warmest, most encouraging I had yet received."

Working with other lyricists, Schwartz placed some of his songs in 1925 and 1926 in *The Grand Street Follies*, a sophisticated intimate revue mounted in downtown Manhattan, and in 1927 in a Broadway revue, *The New Yorkers* (not to be confused with the later, similarly titled musical production with Cole Porter's music).

In 1928 Hart encouraged Schwartz to take a year off from his now-successful legal practice to write songs. Heeding this advice, Schwartz closed his office, and had soon attracted the interest of Tom Weatherly, a young producer who was planning a sophisticated Broadway revue for which he wanted Schwartz's music. Weath-

erly suggested that Schwartz work with Howard Dietz as lyricist.

One of the four children of Herman and Julia (Blumberg) Dietz, lyricist Howard Dietz was born in New York City. His father was a jeweler, and the Dietz's moved frequently, forcing their children to attend various public schools in neighborhoods throughout New York. From the time he was a boy, Dietz was drawn to show business. He regularly attended nickelodeon shows, and later, vaudeville and Broadway musicals.

In 1911 he entered Townsend Harris, a high school for gifted students which compressed a four-year curriculum into three. After school and during the summer, Dietz worked as a copy boy for the New York *American*, and published a neighborhood magazine. Securing some small financial independence, he left home to live in a rooming house owned by John Philip Sousa.

In 1913 Dietz dropped out of Townsend Harris, and for the next year worked full-time for the New York *American*. Convinced he wanted to become a reporter, he passed the entrance examinations for the School of Journalism at Columbia University, entering the class of 1914, a fellow student of Lorenz Hart and Oscar Hammerstein II. There Dietz edited the college comic magazine, *The Jester*; wrote a column for the school's daily newspaper, the *Spectator*; earned $20 a week by serving as the Columbia correspondent for the *American*; and throughout his college years contributed articles and verses to magazines and newspapers, including the renowned "F. P. A." column in the New York *World*. His passion for the theater made him an avid reader of plays, his favorite playwrights being Shaw, Ibsen and W. S. Gilbert.

Upon leaving Columbia in 1917, Dietz worked for a small advertising firm headed by Philip Goodman, who later became a Broadway producer. One of the firm's clients was Samuel Goldwyn, then a film producer based in Fort Lee, New Jersey. When Goldwyn asked for a company logo, Dietz conceived the roaring "Leo Lion" over the Latin slogan, "Ars gratia artis." Since then it has served as the trademark for Goldwyn Pictures Corporation and later for MGM.

During the war in Europe, Dietz enlisted in the U. S. Naval Reserve. On September 15, 1917, while waiting to be called to service, he married Elizabeth Hall, a former Barnard College student then employed as a secretary for *Judge* magazine. They found dwellings in a converted barn.

Dietz wrote the lyrics for *Behind the Forest*, an operetta with music by Carl Engel which was performed in preparatory and high schools, and the lyrics for a song, "Philopena" (music by Victor Arden), Dietz's first song to be theatrically performed when it was introduced at the Palace Theatre in New York by Lina Abarbanell.

Dietz served in the Navy from 1917 to 1919, stationed at Hampton Roads, Virginia, where he edited *Navy Life*. After receiving his discharge, he went to work as director of advertising and publicity for Samuel Goldwyn Pictures at a starting salary of $50 a week. He also contributed verses to magazines and, in 1923, published *Judy Goes Down Town: A Story for City Children*.

In 1923, when Philip Goodman produced *Poppy*, a Broadway musical starring W. C. Fields, he called on Dietz to contribute some material for Fields. For this production, Dietz also wrote the words of "Alibi Baby" (music by Arthur Samuels), which was introduced by Louella Geer.

The following year Goodman produced on Broadway the musical *Dear Sir* (September 23, 1924), and he arranged for Dietz to serve as lyricist for the show's composer, Jerome Kern. *Dear Sir* closed after just 15 performances. At this point, Dietz corresponded for the first time with Arthur Schwartz, who had written to Dietz suggesting that they become collaborators. "I think," Schwartz wrote, "you are the only man in town to be compared with Larry Hart and, from me, that's quite a compliment because I know almost every line Larry has written. " Dietz replied: "As I have written a first show in collaboration with a well-established composer . . . I would suggest that you collaborate with an established lyric writer. In that way we

will both benefit by the reputation of our collaborators. Then when we both get famous we can collaborate with each other."

In 1924 Samuel Goldwyn merged with Metro Pictures Corporation and Louis B. Mayer Pictures Corporation to form Metro-Goldwyn-Mayer (MGM). Dietz was named director of publicity and advertising, and his weekly salary rose to $200. He retained this post until 1957, having served as vice president from 1942. He combined these duties, which he performed with imagination and occasional flamboyance, with theatrical assignments. With Jay Gorney as composer he wrote the lyrics for a revue, *Merry-Go-Round* (May 31, 1927), which was a minor success and introduced the song "Hogan's Alley."

Dietz's next assignment brought him together with Arthur Schwartz. It was *The Little Show*, a Broadway revue produced by Philip Goodman. "Arthur and I got along very well," wrote Dietz in his autobiography, *Dancing in the Dark*. "Sometimes I would suggest a title and even a rhythm with a melody. But more often he would write a tune first. We weren't touchy about criticism. I would say, 'The tune stinks.' He would say, 'The lyric is lousy.' We aimed to please each other. We figured that if we succeeded there were a lot of people like us. Schwartz was a great judge of lyrics. He had an editorial mind and an ear for the fitness of sound."

The Little Show, with Schwartz's music and Dietz's lyrics, starred Clifton Webb, Libby Holman and Fred Allen; sketches were contributed by Dietz and George S. Kaufman, among others. Opening on April 30, 1929, it did so well both at the box office (321 performances) and with critics that it helped to create a vogue for sophisticated revues on Broadway. "I Guess I'll Have to Change My Plan" was one of the show's hit songs, introduced by Clifton Webb. (This was the number that originated at Brant Lake Camp as "I Love to Lie Awake in Bed," words by Lorenz Hart.) Johnny Mercer recorded it and so did Eddy Duchin and his orchestra. Fred Astaire and Jack Buchanan sang "I Guess I'll Have to Change My Plan" in the movie musical *The Band Wagon* (1953), and Marsha Mason and Kristy McNichol performed it in the nonmusical Neil Simon film, *Only When I Laugh* (1981). It was also heard as an instrumental on the soundtrack of *The Breaking Point* (1950), starring John Garfield and Patricia Neal, and as a recurring theme on the soundtrack of *Goodbye My Fancy* (1951) starring Joan Crawford. However, *The Little Show*'s standout song was not by Schwartz and Dietz but an interpolation,

"Moanin' Low" (music by Ralph Rainger, lyrics by Dietz), written for Webb and Holman.

The success of *The Little Show* led to a sequel, *The Second Little Show* (September 2, 1930), the score once again by Schwartz and Dietz. It included "Lucky Seven," introduced by Joey Ray. This revue closed after only 63 performances, but Schwartz and Dietz rebounded with *Three's a Crowd* (October 15, 1930), a revue which ran for 272 performances. The "three" in the title were the stars of the first edition of *The Little Show*—Clifton Webb, Libby Holman and Fred Allen. Schwartz and Dietz's standout song from *Three's a Crowd* was "Something to Remember You By" which Holman introduced and recorded and was later recorded by Helen Morgan, Dinah Shore, and Dick Haymes. The melody had been written originally for a London musical in which it was used for a comedy number, "I Have No Words," lyrics by Desmond Carter. When it was brought into the *Three's a Crowd* score with Dietz's lyrics, Schwartz and Dietz still intended it as a comic number. The torch singer Libby Holman, however, recognized its potential as a ballad and prevailed on the songwriters to change the mood and tempo. Janis Paige sang it in the nonmusical film, *Her Kind of Man* (1946), and Betsy Drake in the screen musical *Dancing in the Dark* (1950). Another noteworthy Schwartz-Dietz song in *Three's a Crowd* was "The Moment I Saw You," introduced by Clifton Webb. But the show's most popular song was once again an interpolation by other writers, "Body and Soul" (music by Johnny Green, lyrics by Frank Eyton, Edward Heyman and Robert Sour), a standard.

The Band Wagon (June 3, 1931) was the first musical for which Schwartz and Dietz composed the complete score. This revue, which starred Fred and Adele Astaire and had sketches by Dietz and George S. Kaufman, prompted the critic Brooks Atkinson to say: "After the appearance of *The Band Wagon* . . . it will be difficult for the old-time musical to hold up its head. . . . It is both funny and lovely; it has wit, gaiety and splendor." To enhance the visual beauty of the production, Hassard Short devised twin revolving stages, the first time a Broadway musical used a revolving stage for anything more than a change of scenery. From this score came Schwartz and Dietz's most celebrated song, "Dancing in the Dark," introduced by John Barker and danced to by Tilly Losch on a mirrored stage. Ben Selvin and his orchestra and Fred Waring's Pennsylvanians recorded it in 1931 and, in 1941, a recording by Artie Shaw's orchestra sold a million copies. The orchestras of André Kostelanetz, Percy Faith, Guy Lombardo and Morton Gould, also recorded it. In 1950 this song provided the title for a movie musical starring William Powell and Betsy Drake, who performed the song. In the film *The Band Wagon*, it was used as background music for a dance routine by Fred Astaire and Cyd Charisse. The title *Dancing in the Dark* was used by Dietz for his autobiography and for an Off Broadway revue featuring Schwartz-Dietz songs.

Some of the other outstanding songs in *The Band Wagon* were "New Sun in the Sky," introduced by Fred Astaire and recorded by the orchestra of Leo Reisman. In the film version of *The Band Wagon*, it was sung on the soundtrack by India Adams (dubbing for Charisse) and in *Dancing in the Dark* by Betsy Drake. "I Love Louisa" was used for a production number in the first-act finale featuring a merry-go-round in a Bavarian setting. Reisman's orchestra recorded it. In the stage revue, "Confession" was heard chorally; "Hoops" as a duet for Fred and Adele Astaire; and "High and Low" as a duet for John Barker and Roberta Robinson. *The Band Wagon* had a Broadway run of 260 performances.

More Schwartz-Dietz song treasures came from *Flying Colors* (September 15, 1932) and *At Home Abroad* (September 19, 1935), though neither revue did well at the box office. *Flying Colors* ran for 188 performances, *At Home Abroad* for 198. The first of these had been conceived of as a successor to *The Band Wagon*, but it turned out to be little more than a faint carbon copy. "A Shine on Your Shoes" was introduced by Vilma and Buddy Ebsen, Monette Moore and Larry Adler; was sung and danced to by Fred Astaire in the movie, *The Band Wagon*; and was recorded by the orchestras of Roger Wolfe Kahn and Leo Reisman. "Alone Together" was sung by Jean Sargent and danced to by Clifton Webb and Tamara Geva and recorded by Leo Reisman and by Carmen Cavallero. "Louisiana Hayride" was introduced as a production number featuring Webb, Geva, chorus and dancers, and was recorded by the Raymond Paige orchestra and by Carmen Cavellero. In the *The Band Wagon* it was sung by Nanette Fabray.

In *At Home Abroad,* starring Beatrice Lillie and Ethel Waters, the following songs were heard: "Farewell, My Lovely," introduced by Woods Miller and the Continentals and danced to by Paul Haakon and Nina Whitney; "Love is a Dancing Thing," sung by a male chorus; "What a Wonderful World," introduced by Eleanor Powell, Woods Miller and the Continentals; and "Got a Bran' New Suit," sung by Ethel Waters before it was danced to by Eleanor Powell.

Book musicals with scores by Schwartz and Dietz were less successful than their best revues. The two they composed for in the 1930s both failed: *Revenge With Music* (November 26, 1934) had a run of 158 performances, and *Between the Devil* (December 22, 1937) lasted only 93; Dietz wrote the book as well as lyrics for both. *Revenge With Music*, adapted from Pedro de Alarcón's novel *The Three-Cornered Hat*, produced two Schwartz-Dietz standards: "You and the Night and the Music" and "If There is Someone Lovelier Than You." Both were introduced on radio by Conrad Thibault before being heard on the stage. In *Revenge With Music*, "You and the Night and the Music" was introduced by Libby Holman and George Metaxa and "If There is Someone Lovelier Than You" by Metaxa. The former, one of Schwartz's personal favorites, was recorded by Holman and was used as background music in *The Band Wagon*.

In *Between the Devil*, "I See Your Face Before Me" was introduced by Jack Buchanan, Evelyn Laye and Adele Dixon; it was recorded by Kay Thompson and by André Kostelanetz, and had a single hearing on *Your Hit Parade* on March 12, 1938. "By Myself" was introduced by Buchanan, was sung by Fred Astaire in *The Band Wagon*, and by Judy Garland in the 1963 movie *I Could Go On Singing*.

In 1936 Schwartz and Dietz wrote all the songs—94, which they composed over a period of two weeks—for *The Gibson Family*, a weekly musical comedy series on radio. "In that period," Dietz recalled, "it seems to me, I never came out of the shower without a new lyric. And Arthur always had a tune for it." One of the memorable songs from the series was "How High Can a Little Bird Fly?"

After *Between the Devil* Schwartz and Dietz did not work together again for 11 years. In that time, Schwartz married Katherine Carrington, an actress, on July 7, 1934. They had a son, and made their home in an apartment in Manhattan. Dietz, now divorced, married Tanis Guinness Montague on January 16, 1937, with whom he had his only child, Liza. Until 1960, the Dietz family resided in a brownstone, which they owned on West 11th Street in Greenwich Village.

Even before Schwartz and Dietz had temporarily gone separate ways, Schwartz had worked with other lyricists. In 1933 he composed "After All You're All I'm After" (lyrics by Edward Heyman), which was sung by John Beal in the Broadway play with music, *She Loves Me Not*. With Heyman again his lyricist, Schwartz composed songs for the 1936 movie *The Girl from Paris*, starring Lily Pons, who sang "Seal it With a Kiss" and "Love and Learn," the latter appearing on *Your Hit Parade* on January 6, 1937. Even while working with Dietz on *Between the Devil*,

Schwartz was writing music to lyrics by Albert Stillman and Laurence Stallings for *Virginia* (September 2, 1937), a musical set in colonial Williamsburg and mounted at New York's Radio City Center Theatre but which lasted only 60 performances. From *Virginia*, "You and I Know" was introduced by Anne Booth and Ronald Graham, recorded by the orchestra of Claude Thornhill and heard on *Your Hit Parade* on November 6, 1937. "An Old Flame Never Dies," also from this score, was sung by Anne Booth before being reprised by her, Ronald Graham and Mona Barrie. It was recorded by Claude Thornhill's orchestra.

For the Broadway musical *Stars in Your Eyes* (February 9, 1939), starring Ethel Merman and Jimmy Durante, Schwartz first worked with the celebrated lyricist Dorothy Fields. In J. P. McEvoy's text, Merman was cast as Jeanette Adair, a Hollywood starlet who has an affair with John Blake, a leftist screenwriter. Durante played the part of a studio troubleshooter who sometimes complicates their lives, but eventually sets things right for Jeanette and John. Despite the array of writing and performing talent, *Stars in Your Eyes* ended its run after 127 performances. Merman introduced "This is It" which was recorded by the orchestras of Tommy Dorsey and Jan Garber and had two hearings on *Your Hit Parade*. "A Lady Needs a Change," "I'll Pay the Check" and "Just a Little Bit More" were introduced and recorded by Merman. From this score "It's All Yours" was recorded by the orchestra of Artie Shaw.

From 1936 to 1946 Schwartz worked in Hollywood both as a composer and a producer. "They're Either Too Young or Too Old" (lyrics by Frank Loesser), the lament of home-front women during World War II, was introduced by Bette Davis in *Thank Your Lucky Stars* (1943) and recorded by Hildegarde and by Jimmy Dorsey. It was interpolated into Jane Froman's screen biography, *With a Song in My Heart* (1952) and was represented on *Your Hit Parade* a dozen times. For *Thank Your Lucky Stars* Schwartz also composed, to Loesser's lyrics, "How Sweet You Are" (three hearings on *Your Hit Parade*) and "The Dreamer," both introduced by Dinah Shore. For *The Time, The Place, The Girl* (1946), Schwartz composed "A Gal in Calico" (lyrics by Leo Robin). Introduced by Jack Carson, Dennis Morgan and Martha Vickers, it was recorded by the orchestras of Tex Beneke and Benny Goodman and had 14 hearings on *Your Hit Parade*, once in first position. "Oh, But I Do," introduced by Dennis Morgan, recorded by Harry James and his orchestra and by Nat King Cole, had 11 representations on *Your Hit Parade*; "A Rainy Night in Rio" was introduced by Carson, Morgan, Vickers and Janis Paige; and "Through a Thousand Dreams," introduced by Morgan and Vickers, was played on the soundtrack by Carmen Cavallero. Schwartz produced the Jerome Kern movie musical, *Cover Girl* (1944), starring Gene Kelly and Rita Hayworth, and Cole Porter's screen biography, *Night and Day* (1946), starring Cary Grant and Alexis Smith.

In the late 1930s Dietz was too busy with his duties as MGM's publicist to be engaged in extracurricular writing. In 1939–41 he served as publicity director for the U. S. Treasury, producing *The Treasury Hour* for radio. During World War II he wrote the lyrics (to Vernon Duke's music) and sketches for *Tars and Spars*, a U. S. Coast Guard revue starring the then unknown Sid Caesar.

With Vernon Duke as his composer, Dietz endured successive stage failures. *Dancing in the Streets*, starring Mary Martin, closed out of town in 1943. *Jackpot* came to Broadway on January 13, 1944, but closed after 67 performances. *Sadie Thompson* (November 16, 1944), was based on the play *Rain* by John Colton and Clemence Randolph—which had been based on the Somerset Maugham short story "Miss Thompson." With Rouben Mamoulian, Dietz was the author of the libretto, and he and Duke composed the score. Although it closed after just 60 performances, Sadie Thompson yielded a hit song, "The Love I Long For."

Before the collaboration of Schwartz and Dietz was revived, Schwartz composed the score for a book musical, *Park Avenue* (November 4, 1946), with Ira Gershwin as his lyricist. Despite a book by George S. Kaufman and Nunnally Johnson, the show proved to be not very lively and it closed after 72 performances.

What Schwartz and Dietz apparently needed for a successful return to the musical theater was each other. They were reunited with *Inside U. S. A.* (April 30, 1948), a revue for which Moss Hart, among others, wrote the sketches and which Schwartz produced. It starred Beatrice Lillie and Jack Haley and ran for 339 performances. John Tyers introduced "Haunted Heart," which Schwartz and Dietz had composed in 1940 but never used, and "Rhode Island is Famous for You" was sung by Jack Haley and Estelle Loring. "Haunted Heart" was recorded by Bing Crosby and by Guy Lombardo and His Royal Canadians.

The Band Wagon came to the screen in 1953 as a book musical instead of a revue. For the movie Schwartz and Dietz wrote a new song, "That's Entertainment," which has since become one of the standards that eulogize show business.

Fred Astaire, Nanette Fabray and (on the soundtrack dubbing for Cyd Charrisse) India Adams introduced it. The song's title was used for a 1972 Off Broadway revue made up of Schwartz-Dietz standards. It also became the title of two screen musicals offering choice extracts from MGM musicals: *That's Entertainment* (1974) and *That's Entertainment Part II* (1976).

The last two Schwartz-Dietz Broadway musicals were box-office flops, in spite of which original cast recordings were released. *The Gay Life* (November 18, 1961; 113 performances) was an adaptation by Fay and Michael Kanin of Arthur Schnitzler's comic play, *Anatol*. *Jennie* (October 17, 1963; 82 performances), starring Mary Martin, was a stage book by Arnold Schulman, and was inspired by Marguerite Courtney's biography of the actress Laurette Taylor. In *The Gay Life*, "Magic Moment" and "Something You Never Had Before" were introduced by Barbara Cook, and "For the First Time" was sung by Walter Chiari. In *American Popular Song* Alec Wilder described "For the First Time" as a "marvelous, modest, romantic ballad in the best possible taste," and called "Something You Never Had Before" as "refined and distilled and in as high style as any great Kern song." In *Jennie* there were two excellent ballads, "I Still Look at You That Way" and "Before I Kiss the World Goodbye," each introduced by Mary Martin. "Waitin' for the Evening Train" was a duet for Mary Martin and George Wallace.

In his biography, Dietz wrote: "There is no way of being sure that a show will be a hit, a failure, artistic, or crude. Too many factors enter into it. The timing of things . . . the mechanics. Many a scene that was funny in print and rehearsal laid the well-known Broadway egg when dressed up and presented. Many a dance that was exciting when the girls did it in practice clothes lost something when the wide skirts were put on. If the music is good perhaps overorchestration will cloud the melody; perhaps the lyrics will not be heard, perhaps they will be. The big effect that was to startle and amaze might not work right. So often audiences are a failure. Many an audience has been so bad it should have been panned by the reviewers."

Dietz went on: "The best lyric writers are the ones who write the most singable words. They need not be fancy words . . . but words you can lean on, which is to say solid substantial words you can put your teeth in. . . . A good lyric writer can put words to music and have it come out as though he'd put music to words. Every song that has a popular quality is not necessarily a popular success, but every success that is a popular success must have popular quality."

In *High Fidelity* Gene Lees called Dietz "a member of an elite group of literate people who chose song lyrics as their form of expression and wrote them with consummate skill and felicity. All his lyrics have the natural order of speech. He never inverts sentence structure to get a rhyme. . . . He has maintained a dazzling quality in the use of language, particularly rhyme. When Dietz is after laughter . . . he is almost incomparable. . . . For all the strictures imposed by our language, Dietz never seems constrained in either imagination or diction. It is this quality of ease, of beauty, or cleverness attained effortlessly, that makes his lyrics a perfect match for Schwartz's music. Their combined work is urbane, intelligent, warm, witty, lovely and above all civilized."

In the 1950s Schwartz again collaborated with Dorothy Fields, this time on two modestly successful Broadway musicals starring Shirley Booth. *A Tree Grows in Brooklyn* (April 19, 1951) was adapted by George Abbott and Betty Smith from her bestselling novel of the same name. The principal characters are members of the Nolan family, who live in the Williamsburg section of Brooklyn, at the turn of the century. The head of the household, Johnny, is an amiable, carefree singing waiter with a weakness for unrealistic daydreams and alcohol, and he becomes increasingly vulnerable to both after the birth of his daughter, Francie. He is killed while working as a sandhog, leaving behind only enough money to pay for the flowers for Francie's school graduation. Shirley Booth was cast as Francie's Aunt Cissy, a fast-living, lovable and loving character. She introduced "Love is the Reason." "Make the Man Love Me" was a duet for Marcia Van Dyke and Johnny Johnston, and "Look Who's Dancing" a duet for Booth and Van Dyke. Johnston introduced "I'll Buy You a Star." *A Tree Grows in Brooklyn* remained on Broadway for 270 performances and its score was recorded in an original cast album.

By the Beautiful Sea (April 8, 1954), too, cast a nostalgic glance at dawn-of-the-century Brooklyn. With a book by Herbert and Dorothy Fields, it ran for 270 performances. Shirley Booth played Lottie Gibson, a one-time vaudevillian who runs a Coney Island boardinghouse for show people called "By the Beautiful Sea." The plot revolved around her romance with Dennis Emery, a Shakespearean actor, and the efforts of his young daughter to break them up. Lottie, however, manages to win the child's affection. Booth and Wilbur Evans introduced the score's principal ballad, "Alone Too Long" (Fields served as Schwartz's lyricist). Evans also introduced "More Love Than Your Love," and an original cast recording of the score was released.

Discussing Schwartz's career as a composer for the musical theater, Alec Wilder wrote: "[He] wrote some splendid songs. They have the character and sinew of the best of theater music. None of these songs concern themselves with anything but the American musical atmosphere of the time. Schwartz never looked over his shoulder at Europe or operetta or the concert hall. He wrote with total self-assurance and high professional skill and never lingered by the wayside to gaze with longing at the musically greener grass of [high] culture. He rolled up his sleeves and went to work. . . . His published record contains some of the finest American songs in existence. He remains stylistically as mysterious and as elusive as Irving Berlin. And so, one can say only that quality was his style. And that's plenty."

Schwartz also composed for television. He produced and wrote the music for *Surprise for Santa*, a CBS production of 1945 which became the first 90-minute television special. For CBS in 1956 he composed the score for Maxwell Anderson's *High Tor*, which was recorded in a soundtrack album. That year, with Dietz, he wrote the songs for the television production of John Hersey's *A Bell for Adano*.

After his wife's death in 1954, Schwartz that year married Mary O'Hagen, an actress and ballet dancer. In 1969 they moved to London from which Schwartz would travel to New York once a month to attend ASCAP board meetings. In London, where he did broadcasts for BBC and Thames Television, Schwartz began writing lyrics to his own music. His first such effort was for a musical adaptation by his wife of Dickens's *Nicholas Nickleby*. His wife also revised the text of *A Tree Grows in Brooklyn*, which, with eight new Schwartz songs and the new title of *Look Who's Dancing*, was later produced at Stockbridge, Massachusetts in the summer of 1978. In 1976 *From the Pen of Arthur Schwartz*, an album of Schwartz's hit songs performed by the composer himself, had been released on the RCA label. Schwartz's last song was "The World is Turning Fast" (lyrics by George Balanchine). The victim of a stroke, he died at his home in Kintnersville, Pennsylvania, on September 3, 1984.

Schwartz was a director of ASCAP from 1958 to 1983. For three years beginning in 1967 he served on the governing board of the Dramatists Guild. Schwartz was elected by drama critics to the Theatre Hall of Fame in 1981. Three years later, he shared with Harold Arlen the second annual ASCAP/Richard Rodgers Award for significant achievement in the musical theater.

Without Schwartz, Dietz wrote a hit tune in

1947, "The Dickey Bird Song" (music by Sammy Fain). Dietz prepared new English lyrics for the librettos of *Die Fledermaus* and *La Bohème*, produced by the Metropolitan Opera in 1950 and 1952 respectively.

On July 31, 1951 Dietz married Lucinda Davis Goldsborough Ballard, a costume designer. With his daughter and Lucinda's two children, they lived at Dietz's house in Greenwich Village until 1960 before moving to a house in Sands Point, Long Island that Dietz had acquired in 1936. They lived there for 13 years, and then returned to an apartment in Manhattan.

On September 15, 1954 Dietz contracted paralysis agitana, which developed into Parkinson's disease and left him a chronic invalid. Despite his infirmity he continued to work with Schwartz on musicals and to write his autobiography. By 1968 he was in constant pain and barely able to walk. Earlier pastimes had to be curtailed if not altogether eliminated—painting and drawing, golf, tennis, table tennis and bridge. In the last-mentioned activity, he was an expert who devised a two-hand game that bears his name.

In October 1972 an exhibit, "Dancing in the Dark: The Career of Howard Dietz," was held at the Museum of the City of New York. In 1983 Dietz became the first recipient of the ASCAP/ Richard Rodgers Award. He died at his apartment near Lincoln Center on July 30, 1983. A tribute to Dietz was held at the Imperial Theatre in New York the following September.

ABOUT: Dietz, H. Dancing in the Dark, 1974; Ewen, D. Great Men of American Popular Song, 2d ed. 1972; Green, S. The World of Musical Comedy, 4th ed. 1980; Wilder, A. American Popular Song, 1972. *Periodicals*—High Fidelity September 1976; New York Times March 19, 1983; Show January 1962.

SCHWARTZ, JEAN (November 4, 1878– September 30, 1956), was a prolific songwriter for Tin Pan Alley and the Broadway stage in the early years of the 20th century. He was born in Budapest, Hungary late in 1878. As a child, he received piano instruction from his sister, who had studied under Liszt. Schwartz was about 13 when his family immigrated to the United States, settling on New York's Lower East Side where they lived in poverty. To help make ends meet, Jean worked throughout his teenage years, holding down such jobs as night cashier in a Turkish bath, pianist with a Coney Island ensemble, demonstrating popular songs in the first sheet-music department to be opened in a New York department store (Siegel-Cooper), and ulti-

JEAN SCHWARTZ

mately as staff pianist and song plugger for the Tin Pan Alley publishing firm of Shapiro-Bernstein.

Schwartz's first publication was a piano cakewalk, *Dusky Dudes*, issued in 1899. Two years later he became a friend of William Jerome, a lyricist with whom he launched a songwriting partnership that was to last 13 years. In their first year of collaboration, Schwartz and Jerome composed "I'm Tired," which Eddie Foy introduced on Broadway in *The Strollers* (1901); "When Mr. Shakespeare Comes to Town," heard in the Weber and Fields burlesque, *Hoity Toity* (1901); and "Rip Van Winkle was a Lucky Man," introduced by Harry Bolger in *The Sleeping Beauty and the Beast* (1901).

Schwartz became an American citizen in 1902. Later that year the Schwartz-Jerome song "I'm Unlucky" was introduced by Eddie Foy in *The Wild Rose* and "Mister Dooley," inspired by Finley P. Dunn's Irish stories, *Mr. Dooley*, was introduced by Thomas Q. Seabrooke in *A Chinese Honeymoon*. On December 30, 1902 Eddie Foy introduced "Hamlet was a Melancholy Dane" at the Iroquois Theatre in Chicago just hours before the theater caught fire and burned to the ground. Foy brought this song to New York on January 21, 1903 for *Mr. Bluebeard*, and it was recorded by the Knickerbocker Serenaders.

Schwartz and Jerome's greatest song success to date came in 1903 with "Bedelia," which helped make Blanche Ring, who sang it in *The Jersey Lily* in her first starring role, a star overnight. She made the song so popular that it gained wide circulation in variety theaters and enjoyed a sheet-music sale of some three million copies. A half century later, it was revived in the film, *The Eddie Cantor Story* (1954). An early recording was made by the Knickerbocker Serenaders, and a later one by the orchestra of Jan Garber.

Schwartz and Jerome's first complete score for the Broadway musical stage was for *Piff, Paff, Pouff* (April 2, 1904), starring Eddie Foy. The text, by Stanislaus Stange, dealt with the efforts of August Melon to marry off his four daughters and thereby satisfy the provisions of his deceased wife's will and inherit her fortune. Though each daughter has her own capricious idea of the kind of man she wants, all four eventually find desirable husbands. The score's principal song was "The Ghost That Never Walked," introduced by Foy. With a 264-performance run at the Casino Theatre, *Piff, Paff, Pouff* was a box-office success.

Their popularity as songwriters brought Schwartz and Jerome to the vaudeville circuit, where they were headliners for many years. Schwartz also played piano for the Dolly Sisters when they performed on the vaudeville circuit.

Schwartz and Jerome composed the scores for three Broadway musicals in 1905. From *Lifting the Lid* (June 5), a roof-garden vaudeville show starring Fay Templeton, came the hit song "Oh, Marie." In the early 1950s it was revived in a recording by Alan Drake. *The Ham Tree* (August 28) starred the black-faced comedians, McIntyre and Heath, and its principal number was "Goodbye Sweet Old Manhattan Isle." In *Fritz in Tammany Hall* (October 16) Ada Lewis regularly stopped the show with "East Side Lil."

Other successful Schwartz-Jerome songs from the years 1905 to 1913 were either interpolated into musicals or published as independent numbers. Blanche Ring introduced "My Irish Molly-O" in *Sergeant Brue* (1905). "Chinatown, My Chinatown," written in 1906 and published as an independent number, found a place in the Broadway revue, *Up and Down Broadway* (July 18, 1910), for which Schwartz and Jerome had written the basic score. Ernest Hare and chorus introduced it in that revue. In later years it was recorded by Art Gillham, the Merry Macs, the Mills Brothers and Louis Prima and his orchestra. "My Irish Molly-O" has been heard in numerous movies, including *Bright Lights* (1931), *Nob Hill* (1945), *Is Everybody Happy?* (1949) and *Young Man With a Horn* (1950). Al Jolson sang it on the soundtrack of *Jolson Sings Again* (1949) and Bob Hope performed it in *The Seven Little Foys* (1955).

"Handle Me With Care" was one of the most popular numbers in the first edition of the *Ziegfeld Follies* (1907), as was "When the Girl You Love is Loving" in the second edition (1908). "Meet Me in Rose Time, Rosie" was introduced by Will Oakland in a 1909 production of the Cohan and Harris Minstrels. "The Hat My Father Wore on St. Patrick's Day," composed in 1909, was recorded that year by the Billy Murray-Hayden quartette, who recorded "I'll Make a Ring Around Rose" one year later. Al Jolson introduced "Rum Tum Tiddle" in *Vera Violetta* (1911), the first musical for which he received top billing. This is also the song with which he made his recording debut on an Edison release in 1911. "Row, Row, Row" was introduced by Lillian Lorraine in the *Ziegfeld Follies of 1912* and recorded that year by Ada Jones. It was sung by Barbara Hutton in the film *The Incendiary Blonde* (1945), by Eddie Cantor on the soundtrack of *The Eddie Cantor Story* and by Bob Hope in *The Seven Little Foys.* It was also interpolated into the *The Story of Vernon and Irene Castle* (1939), starring Fred Astaire and Ginger Rogers, and into *Two Weeks With Love* (1950).

The collaboration of Schwartz and Jerome ended in 1913, after which Schwartz worked with several different lyricists. Harold Atteridge was the lyricist for Schwartz's scores for *The Honeymoon Express* (February 16, 1913), and *The Passing Show of 1913* (July 24, 1913), neither of which yielded any memorable tunes. For *When Claudia Smiles* (February 2, 1914) Anne Caldwell wrote the lyrics to Schwartz's music. The musical highlight of that production was "Bedelia," introduced by Blanche Ring.

In these years Schwartz's most successful numbers were those published individually in Tin Pan Alley rather than songs from his stage scores. Al Jolson had a hit recording in 1914 with "Back to the Carolina You Love" (lyrics by Grant Clarke). In 1915 Nora Bayes popularized "Hello, Hawaii, How Are You?" (lyrics by Bert Kalmar and Edgar Leslie) both in her public appearances and on a recording, and Willie and Eugene Howard featured it in vaudeville. This song started a vogue for numbers about Hawaii in Tin Pan Alley that lasted several years. "All Bound Round With the Mason-Dixon Line" (lyrics by Sam Lewis and Joe Young) was recorded in 1917 by Al Jolson. "When the Girls Grow Older They Grow a Little Bolder" (lyrics by Lewis and Young) was interpolated for Harry Tighe in *Follow Me* (1917).

Three hit songs by Schwartz, Lewis and Young, were popularized and recorded by Al Jolson in 1918. He interpolated "Rock-a-Bye Your Baby to a Dixie Melody" into the Winter Garden extravaganza, *Sinbad* (1918), with that now-standard song the showstopper. Thereafter,

"Rock-a-Bye" a staple of the Jolson repertory. He recorded it again in 1946 in a release that sold more than a million copies and he sang it in the film, *The Rose of Washington Square* (1939), and on the soundtracks of *The Jolson Story* (1946) and *Jolson Sings Again.* "Rock-a-Bye" was also recorded by Vernon Dalhart in 1918 and interpolated into the musical films *The Show of Shows* (1929) and *The Merry Monahans* (1944).

Jolson introduced "Hello Central, Give Me No Man's Land" in *Sinbad* and recorded it in 1918, the year it was also recorded by Edna Brown. In *Sinbad* Jolson also introduced the comedy song, "Why Do They All Take the Night Boat to Albany?"

With Harold Atteridge as his lyricist Schwartz composed the scores to several Broadway musicals in the 1920s. The most significant were: *The Passing Show of 1921* (December 29, 1920), starring Willie and Eugene Howard; *Make It Snappy* (April 13, 1922), starring Eddie Cantor and in which J. Harold Murray, Dolly Hackett and Conchita Piquer introduced "Tell Me What's the Matter Lovable Eyes"; *Artists and Models* (August 20, 1923), starring Frank Fay; and *A Night in Spain* (May 3, 1927), starring Phil Baker. The last Broadway production with a Schwartz score was *Sunny Days* (February 8, 1928); it starred Jeanette MacDonald and featured Clifford Grey as Schwartz's lyricist.

Schwartz's most successful songs of the post–World War I era were "Au Revoir, Pleasant Dreams" (lyrics by Jack Meskill) of 1931 and "Trust in Me" (lyrics by Ned Wever, music written with Milton Ager) of 1937. The former was recorded in 1931 by Ben Bernie and his orchestra and became their signing off theme on the radio. Mildred Bailey and the orchestra of Abe Lyman each recorded "Trust in Me" in 1937, the year it had five appearances on *Your Hit Parade.*

In the late 1930s, Jean Schwartz retired. He spent his last years in Los Angeles with his wife, Rozika, who had been one of the Dolly Sisters.

ABOUT: Burton, J. The Blue Book of Tin Pan Alley, 1950; Craig, W. Sweet and Lowdown: America's Popular Song Writers, 1978.

SEDAKA, NEIL (March 13, 1939–). Composer-lyricist Neil Sedaka became a bestselling pop star in the years between Elvis Presley's induction into the U. S. Army in 1958 and the first appearance of the Beatles on the *Ed Sullivan Show* in 1964. For a decade he lapsed into obscurity, but in 1974 made a triumphant comeback, achieving even greater commerical success than in the early 1960s, when his trademark songs

NEIL SEDAKA

about the agony and ecstasy of puppy love had included "Breaking Up is Hard to Do," "Calendar Girl," and "Happy Birthday, Sweet 16."

He was born in Brooklyn, one of the two children of Mac and Eleanor (Appel) Sedaka, both of whom had immigrated to the United States from Turkey. Neil's grandmother had been a concert pianist, and his father, a taxicab driver, also played the piano well. At a very early age, Sedaka showed so much musical promise that one of his teachers at P. S. 253, in the Brighton Beach section of Brooklyn, convinced his parents to give him private piano study. When Sedaka was nine he attended on scholarship the preparatory division of the Juilliard School of Music, where he trained for the next eight years to become a concert pianist. Meanwhile he attended elementary school and Abraham Lincoln High School in Brooklyn.

In music, Sedaka found a refuge from the rejection he suffered at the hands of his neighborhood peers, who ridiculed him because he was short, wore braces and eyeglasses, had a high-pitched voice and showed a preference for practicing the piano over playing boys' games in the streets. At Abraham Lincoln High he won several awards for tunes he composed for school productions. Having been drawn to pop music since 1954 when he heard the Penguins' hit "Earth Angel," Neil, aged 16, formed a rock combo called the Tokens. During the summers he worked as a music director at resorts and through popular music slowly gained social acceptance. "Not only was I invited to parties," he told an interviewer for *After Dark* (September

1976), "but I was suddenly the life of every party I attended."

Sedaka had been 13 when he composed his first song. At that time, living in the same apartment building, was Howard Greenfield, a 16-year-old poet and lyricist who suggested that Sedaka set one of his (Greenfield's) poems to music. "We had to wait until my mother left for shopping because it would have blown her mind, I was so into classical music," Sedaka recalled. Sedaka and Greenfield quickly composed "My Life's Devotion," and for the next three years they wrote about a song a day. Some were ballads modeled after hits sung by such pop artists as Patti Page and Johnny Ray while others were in a soft early rock idiom. Sedaka and Greenfield even managed to sell a few songs to rhythm and blues performers like LaVern Baker, the Clovers, and Dinah Washington.

In 1956 a jury of musicians that included Jascha Heifetz and Artur Rubinstein selected Sedaka as one of 15 young artists to perform classical music on the New York radio station WQXR, in a competition sponsored by *The New York Times* for local high school students. When Sedaka graduated from Abraham Lincoln High in 1956, he entered the college division of the Juilliard School on a piano scholarship and studied with Adele Marcus.

He was permanently deflected from a career as a concert pianist in 1958 when "Stupid Cupid," a song he had written with Greenfield, became a bestselling record for Connie Francis. Sedaka left Juilliard that year to collaborate with Greenfield. They were soon signed to produce songs that would appeal to the growing market of teenaged record buyers by Don Kirshner, a young publisher who operated the Aldon Music firm and who consigned Sedaka and Greenfield to a cubicle in the Brill Building on Broadway. A recording in which Sedaka, as vocalist, demonstrated one of his own songs so impressed Kirshner that he persuaded Sedaka to become a performer in his own right. Steven Sholes, an executive at RCA Victor, agreed and signed Sedaka to a contract. Sedaka debuted as a composer-performer with a single titled "The Diary" which was backed by "The Vacancy," with lyrics by Greenfield. For some months in early 1959 it stayed on the "Hot 100" list of *Billboard* magazine. Sedaka followed with "I Go Ape," a modestly successful soft-rock number, and then with "Oh! Carol," which made the top ten. Both of these songs he had written with Greenfield, the latter a tribute to Carole King, a young songwriter who was then Sedaka's girlfriend. "I became the king of King's Highway," he said, "riding up and down in my convertible,

picking up girls, with 'Oh! Carol' blasting on the radio."

In the next three years Sedaka's recordings of songs he had written with Greenfield became some of the hottest properties in the so-called bubble-gum market, which catered to the lucrative teenage trade. "Stairway to Heaven" appeared in 1960, and in the following year came "Calendar Girl," "Little Devil," and "Happy Birthday, Sweet 16." (A recording of the last-named song was heard on the soundtrack of the George Lucas film, *American Graffiti* in 1973.) "Breaking Up is Hard to Do" and "Next Door to an Angel" were hits in 1962, and "Let's Go Steady Again" was released in 1963. "I Go Ape," "Oh! Carol," and "Breaking Up is Hard to Do" became the first Sedaka recordings to earn him gold records while his first two albums, *Little Devil and Others* (1961) and *Neil Sedaka* (1963), were also bestsellers. By 1963 his records had sold more than 25 million copies bringing him an annual income of several hundred thousand dollars.

In addition, Sedaka and Greenfield had composed songs for *Where the Boys Are* (1961), in which Connie Francis made her motion picture debut. Introduced by Francis, the title song became a bestseller in her recording. Sedaka's fame was enhanced by his concert performances in the United States and England and on such network television programs as the *Ed Sullivan Show* and Dick Clark's *American Bandstand*. For his stage and screen appearances he was backed by the Tokens, a quartet that later had a number one hit in "The Lion Sleeps Tonight."

On September 11, 1962, Sedaka married Leba Margaret Strassberg, with whom he had two children (Dara Felice and Marc Charles) and who has helped to manage his business affairs. They met at Esther Manor in the Catskill Mountains, where her mother was the proprietress and Sedaka and his band performed.

By 1964, Sedaka's career both as composer and performer was in decline, with poor radio exposure and plunging record sales. "I overdid it," he later explained in *Rolling Stone* (December 4, 1975). "I overdid the sound. Plus there were the record executives. They said, 'You've got a winning formula and you have to stay with it.'" But in addition to the formulaic nature of Sedaka's singles, his music and that of the other "teen" stars of the early 1960s was eclipsed by the new wave of British bands, especially the Beatles, the Rolling Stones and the Kinks, and the hard-rock styles that flourished in their wake.

During the next few years Sedaka supported himself by appearing in small night spots in the

United States and in England, where he still had a small but loyal following. His program was made up of standards—"golden oldies" for younger listeners—and at one point Sedaka was reduced to performing Eddie Cantor songs in blackface. But Sedaka's understanding of the pop music market was shrewd, and he and Greenfield tailored some of their newer material to fit specific performers, providing hit tunes for Andy Williams ("One Day of Your Life"), Tom Jones ("Puppet Man"), Eydie Gormé ("My World Keeps Getting Smaller"), Peggy Lee ("One More Ride on the Merry-Go-Round"), Johnny Mathis ("The World I Threw Away") and the Fifth Dimension ("Working on a Groovy Thing").

In 1970 Sedaka and his family moved to London to try and rehabilitate his career there, touring the country and appearing in small nightclubs with a repertory consisting of a medley of his old hits and some of the new songs he was writing. A year later he put on a successful show at the Royal Albert Hall in London. When "Oh! Carol" was reissued in 1972 it became a hit in Britain again. A new album, *Tra-La Days Are Over,* was released in 1973 and it, too, reached the charts. British rock star Elton John, a longtime Sedaka fan, issued Sedaka's next album in the United States under John's own label, Rocket Records. Selecting the best tracks from some of Sedaka's London albums, John issued *Sedaka's Back* both in England and the United States in 1974. It became Sedaka's first album to receive a gold record. Within a few weeks of the release of this comeback LP, one of its cuts, "Laughter in the Rain" (lyrics by Philip Cody), reached the top spot on England's pop charts and came close to selling a million discs. Another cut, "Solitaire," was recorded in America by Andy Williams and by the Carpenters. In one year Sedaka's annual income leaped from about $27,000 to between three and four million dollars. With Philip Cody as lyricist, Sedaka recorded the album *The Hungry Years* in 1975. One of the record's songs was "Bad Blood," an up-tempo rocker which Elton John sang and which had lyrics that were racier than the usual Sedaka numbers. Both the album and the single earned gold records. A song from *Sedaka's Back,* "Love Will Keep Us Together" (lyrics by Greenfield), sold more than three million discs in 1975 for the wife-and-husband team of Captain and Tennille. This release won the Grammy award as Record of the Year in early 1976 and BMI honored the song with a plaque for being one of the most performed songs in its catalogue in the year 1975. Captain and Tennille soon followed this, their first national recording success, with "Lonely Night" (lyrics by Sedaka) from the *Hungry Years* LP; the single sold more than 600,000 copies within three weeks of release.

Now a star for the second time, Sedaka returned to the United States as the opening act for the Carpenters in August 1975 at Las Vegas's Riviera Hotel, where he became the headliner just three months later. Sedaka's 1975 tour of leading American nightclubs, casinos, and auditoriums was climaxed by two sold-out performances at the Lincoln Center in New York. On September 17, 1976, Sedaka was the host of his first television special, *Neil Sedaka: Steppin' Out,* on NBC. That year his album *Steppin' Out* was issued in the United States on the Rocket label to become Sedaka's third hit LP in a row. Its most popular cuts were "You Gotta Make Your Own Sunshine" and "Good Times, Good Music, Good Friends."

In 1977 Sedaka formed Neil Sedaka Music, a publishing firm managed by his wife with offices in Los Angeles and New York. At that time Sedaka paid the Kirshner Entertainment Corporation two million dollars for the acquisition of copyrights to more than 100 of his older songs. One of these, "Breaking Up is Hard to Do," was re-released by Sedaka in his own performance but in a new version, as a "torchy" ballad instead of soft rock.

Sedaka's 1977 album, *A Song,* was his first on the Elektra Asylum label, the company for which he also recorded the albums *All You Need Is Music* (1978) and *Now* (1981). From the 1978 record came the title song and the ballad "Should've Never Let Her Go"; from the latter, "Losing You," which he performed as a duet with his daughter, Dara, who also wrote this song in collaboration with her father. Reviewing *Now,* Peter Reilly wrote in *Stereo Review* "Neil Sedaka goes bubbling on like an inexhaustible bottle of seltzer. His voice and his performance still sound like those of someone who has to shave only twice a week, and, happily, his enthusiasm and vitality seem to erupt as genuinely natural result. . . . His sparkle comes from his ability to renew himself constantly plus a genuine delight in the way the public has responded over the years to his performances. Wisely ignoring the graybeards of the industry, who told him he was washed up years ago, Sedaka has gone on doing what comes naturally to him. Not the best, not the worst, of his era, he's still sailing along—a genial survivor."

"I'd like to think I'm a craftsman," Sedaka told Nik Cohn in an interview for *New York* magazine (August 4, 1975). "I sit at the piano and, more often than not, something comes to me. I try to make a song that's commercial . . . but I don't believe in making big gestures." To another interviewer for *BMI: The Many Worlds of Music* he said: "I wouldn't know how to tell someone how to write a song. I go about it sort of like a surgeon, carefully, artfully. There's mystery involved with the process. You don't know how something will turn out until you've almost worked your way through it. I still try to spend five days a week working on music, at least five hours of every day when I'm on tour."

The Sedakas reside in a large apartment in Manhattan and maintain houses in the Catskill Mountains and Westport, Connecticut. Still stimulated by practicing the classics on the piano, Sedaka sometimes speaks wistfully of conquering the concert stage. Apart from music, his main interests are playing tennis, skiing, giving and attending dinner parties comprising close friends, and spending time at home with his family. His daughter has sung with Sedaka both on records and on television.

ABOUT: Sedaka, N. Laughter in the Rain: My Own Story, 1982; Stambler, I. Encyclopedia of Pop, Rock and Soul, 1974. *Periodicals*—After Dark September 1976; BMI: The Many Worlds of Music no. 1, 1983; New York August 4, 1975; Rolling Stone November 20, 1975, December 4, 1975; Stereo Review September 1976.

SHERMAN, ROBERT B., (December 19, 1925–) and **SHERMAN, RICHARD M.** (June 12, 1928–). The Sherman brothers have collaborated on both music and words from the beginning of their careers as songwriters. The sons of Al and Rosa (Dancis) Sherman, they were born in New York City, Robert Bernard on December 19, 1925, Richard Morton on June 12, 1928. From an early age they were educated in classical music by their mother, an actress who had studied piano, and nurtured on popular music by their father, a prolific composer of tunes such as "No! No! A Thousand Times, No!," "You Gotta Be a Football Hero," "Now's the Time to Fall in Love," and "Save Your Sorrow," which were introduced by stars like Al Jolson, Eddie Cantor, Rudy Vallee and Maurice Chevalier.

The family moved to California in 1938, following Al Sherman, who had gone there on a film assignment the previous year. Robert studied the violin with private teachers for five years, until 1943, and Richard studied the piano and flute for 11 years until 1949. Both were graduated from the Beverly Hills School, Robert in 1943, Richard two years later. Robert briefly attended the University of California at Los Angeles in 1943 and Richard enrolled at the University of Southern California in 1945. During World War II Robert served in the Army as a

RICHARD SHERMAN

combat rifleman with the 86th Blackhawk Division, winning the Purple Heart and two battle stars in the European Theater of Operations (1943–45). Both brothers attended Bard College in upstate New York for three years, each receiving a B. A. degree in 1949. Richard afterward served in the Troop Information Branch of the Army as lecturer and education specialist (1953–55). He also organized entertainments for the troops in which he served as performer and master of ceremonies.

Richard had started writing music and lyrics in college, and his senior project was an original song score for a musical. His first professional production was *The Primitive Angel,* which ran for four months in Los Angeles in 1950. Robert created the sets and was the show's stage manager. He had originally aspired to be a writer, but his first novel, *The Best Estate,* was never published. The brothers' ambition to write songs together, in which they were encouraged by their father, was realized the year after they graduated from Bard. For several years, however, they encountered nothing but frustration. "It was miserable," Richard recalled. "Taking odd jobs; two-bit publishers that never should have been in the business would take our songs and lie to us and never let us have them back. Crooked publishers promised us advances and we never saw them again. It was a long, hard struggle."

In 1958 the Shermans made 1,500 pressings of a song called "Tall Paul" (which they had written with Bob Roberts) and distributed them among disc jockeys around the country. "Weeks went by," Robert reminisced, "and no response. We were despondent." But a radio show in New

ROBERT SHERMAN

Jersey picked up the song which was heard by Moe Preskell, an employee of the Disney Record Company. At that time Disney was planning to have one of the Mouseketeers, Annette Funicello, cut a record and Preskell suggested "Tall Paul." Annette's recording on the Disneyland label in 1959 made her an overnight recording star and brought the Shermans their first top ten hit.

In 1960 the Shermans composed several Hawaiian-sounding pop numbers for Annette. One was a novelty tune called "Pineapple Princess" which reached the top of the charts in 1960. The Shermans had another number one song on the national charts that year with "You're Sixteen," recorded by Johnny Burdette. Thirteen years later, "You're Sixteen" was featured on the soundtrack for the George Lucas film *American Graffiti* (1973). Recorded that same year by Ringo Starr, it became the number one song a second time. "You're Sixteen" has become a BMI-certified "One Million Performance Song," an honor given to numbers that have received more than 50,000 hours of air time.

In 1960 the Sherman brothers worked under contract as exclusive staff songwriters for Walt Disney Productions in Burbank, California. They hoped to be liberated from having to write rock numbers for the teenage market, but their first Disney assignment was *The Parent Trap* (1961), and for its star, Haley Mills, they were called upon to produce another pseudorock teen song, "Let's Get Together." Mills's recording became a smash hit. In *The Parent Trap* Maureen O'Hara introduced the Sherman ballad, "For Now, For Always."

In the eight years the Shermans worked for Disney they wrote the songs—very few of which were of the rock genre—for about two dozen films and as many television productions. The high point of this period was *Mary Poppins* (1964), the finest live-action film to be produced at the Disney studios. "One day," recalled Richard, "Walt [Disney] pulled a book out of his desk and asked, 'Have you fellas ever read this?' It was [author P. L Travers's] *Mary Poppins.* We'd read it, and it was a wonderful collection of stories that were not related to one another. But we felt that there was great magic and fun and visual possibilities, so we came up with two things. First, we thrashed out a tentative story line with a *need* for this flying nanny to appear. Then, to get just a little more magic going for it, we pushed the time frame back to the turn of the century, 1910." As the flying nanny, Julie Andrews made her screen debut in a performance that brought her an Oscar. The music and lyrics by the Shermans, which comprised 13 songs, earned them two Oscars, one for the overall score, another for the song "Chim Chim Cheree," which was introduced by Julie Andrews and Dick Van Dyke and recorded in bestselling releases by Arthur Fiedler and the Boston Pops Orchestra and by the New Christy Minstrels. It has also achieved BMI "One Million Performance" status. "Feed the Birds," a mood piece with which the motion picture opened and closed, was introduced by Julie Andrews, who was also heard in "A Spoonful of Sugar" and "Stay Awake." Dick Van Dyke sang "Jolly Holiday" and, with the Pearlies, "Supercalifragilisticexpialidocious." The soundtrack recording was a recipient of both a platinum record and a Grammy, selling over seven million copies in its first year of release. Its sheet music became the largest-selling film score in history.

Outstanding numbers from Sherman brothers song scores for Disney productions include: "Enjoy It!," introduced by Maurice Chevalier in *In Search of the Castaways* (1962); "The Ugly Bug Ball," introduced by Burl Ives in *Magic Summer* (1963); the title song of *That Darn Cat* (1965), introduced by Bobby Darin; the title song of *Winnie the Pooh* (1965); "Fortuosity," introduced by Tommy Steele in *The Happiest Millionaire* (1967), from which a soundtrack album was released; "I Wanna Be Like You," introduced by Louis Prima and Phil Harris in *The Jungle Book* (1967), whose soundtrack recording earned a gold record in 1968; and, from *The Family Pond* (1968), "Ten Feet Off the Ground," recorded by Louis Armstrong.

"It's a Small World" is something of a curiosity among the songs the Shermans composed for Disney. It was written as a theme song for a ride at the 1963–65 New York World's Fair and later became a musical fixture at Disneyland, Walt Disney World, and Tokyo Disneyland. Played while the ride is in operation, it is heard every 49 seconds; with 270,000 performances a year at Disneyland alone, it is the most performed song in the world. The Shermans also wrote the theme song, in addition to other numbers, for Walt Disney's *Wonderful World of Color,* the NBC-TV series telecast from 1961 to 1972.

Ending their exclusive affiliation with Disney Productions in 1968, the Shermans worked for various producers in Hollywood and England, including Disney. Their first film outside the Disney fold was *Chitty Chitty Bang Bang* (1968), a British production starring Dick Van Dyke and Sally Ann Howes. For it, the Shermans composed 11 songs recorded in a soundtrack album, including the title song, which was introduced by Van Dyke and Howes and became an international hit in a recording by Paul Mauriat and his orchestra, and "Hushabye Mountain," introduced by Van Dyke and Howes and recorded by Tony Bennett.

Maurice Chevalier came out of retirement (in what was to be his last performance) to record the Shermans' title song for the animated film, *The Aristocats* (1970). They composed song scores for two other animated features, *Snoopy, Come Home!* (1972) and *Charlotte's Web* (1973), but their major interest is in live-action musicals. For *Tom Sawyer* (1973), *Huckleberry Finn* (1974), *The Slipper and the Rose* (1977), and *The Magic of Lassie* (1978), the brothers not only composed the song scores but also wrote the screenplays. With *Tom Sawyer,* the Shermans became, in 1973, the only American composers ever to win first prize in music at the Moscow Film Festival. "The Age of Not Believing" was a song introduced by Angela Lansbury in *Bedknobs and Broomsticks* (1971). "River Song" was introduced by country-and-western singer Charley Pride on the soundtrack of *Tom Sawyer* and "Freedom" was the theme song of *Huckleberry Finn,* introduced by Roberta Flack. "The Slipper and the Rose Waltz" was performed by Richard Chamberlain and Gemma Craven in *The Slipper and the Rose,* the film version of the Cinderella story; and "When You're Loved" was introduced by Debby Boone in *The Magic of Lassie.* Their music from *Charlotte's Web, Tom Sawyer, Huckleberry Finn, The Slipper and the Rose* and *Bedknobs and Broomsticks* was recorded in soundtrack albums.

In 1970, the Shermans composed songs for, and were producers of, the NBC-TV special, *Goldilocks,* starring Bing Crosby and his family.

The first score by the Shermans for the Broadway stage was *Over Here!,* which opened on March 6, 1974, and starred Patty and Maxene Andrews, two members of the famous singing trio of the 1930s and 1940s, the Andrews Sisters (LaVerne was deceased.) Will Holt's book throws a backward glance at the early years of World War II, focusing on a trainload of soldiers en route to an embarkation center in New York. The two Andrews sisters appeared as a sister act which entertains the troops and is on the track of a German spy. The score (recorded by the original cast) was in the style, spirit, and sound of the music of the 1940s, as in the ballad "Where Did the Good Times Go?," introduced by Patti Andrews, and Janie Sell's showstopping performance of "Wait for Me, Marlene," a double-edged satire of the World War II German song "Lili Marlene" and of Marlene Dietrich. With a run of 341 performances—ending only when the management and the Andrews sisters failed to agree on a new contract—*Over Here!* was a modest box-office success.

In an interview with Mike Delamater for *Songwriter* (September 1980), the Sherman brothers revealed how they collaborated: "We just talk. Collaboration is just the exchange of ideas. Being brothers creates a lot of shortcuts. Sometimes we argue and chop each other, but it's all to the point of the song, not a personal affront. The key to our success . . . is that we both have to feel 100 percent about every word, every note, every concept, before we show it to a third party. When writing a song, don't be satisfied with your first shot. Don't get lazy; don't compromise with a word or a phrase; don't compromise with the melody. Make sure you love it and be certain of what you want it to say, musically and lyrically. Also, if you can't enjoy the song with just a voice and guitar or piano, you really don't have much of a song. Be your own toughest critic. Try to make believe that you had nothing to do with the song. It's not easy to set something aside and come back to it with a real critical eye, but this self-criticism helps you improve something you might have thought was absolutely perfect. And don't trust the opinions of your family or friends. You must hear a cold reaction, and the coldest reactions comes from people who have to pay money for it."

In addition to two Oscars and two Grammys, the Shermans have been awarded 15 gold or platinum records. In 1976, across from the Chinese Theater where many of their film musicals have premiered, the Hollywood Chamber of Commerce placed a bronze star bearing their names on The Hollywood Walk of Fame.

With the opening of EPCOT Center at Walt

Disney World in 1982, several new songs by the Sherman brothers were introduced, most notably "Magic Journeys," the theme song for a critically acclaimed 70mm 3-D film. In 1983, when Tokyo Disneyland opened, the Shermans were not only represented by their songs "It's a Small World" and "The Enchanted Tiki Room," but their theme song, "Meet the World," became a permanent part of the Japanese pavilion. In 1984, they wrote five songs, including the title song, for the children's album, *Cabbage Patch Dreams.*

Robert B. Sherman, who married Joyce Ruth Sasner on September 27, 1953, has four children. Richard M. Sherman, who married Ursula Gluck on July 6, 1957, has three. Both families reside one mile apart in North Beverly Hills. Among Richard's hobbies and diversions are helping to run the Society for the Preservation of Variety Arts, of which he is cofounder and a member of the board of directors, and long distance bicycle riding. At many charitable fund-raisers each year he plays and sings the songs that he and his brother and father have written. Robert's hobbies are oil painting, metal sculpture, archeology, and collecting classical recordings. Together, several times a year, the brothers speak at schools (elementary through college) as well as at charitable organizations.

ABOUT: Ewen, D. All the Years of American Popular Music, 1977. *Periodicals*—Songwriter September 1980.

SHIRE, DAVID (July 3, 1937–), composer of hit songs and scores for motion pictures and television, was born David Lee Shire in Buffalo, New York, the older of two sons. His father, Irving Daniel Shire, was the leader of a society dance band as well as a pianist and piano teacher. His mother, Esther Miriam (Sheinberg) Shire was a part-time teacher and geriatrics counselor. David Shire grew up, he has said, "saturated in the sounds of Gershwin, Kern, Rodgers and Cole Porter." While attending P. S. 56 and The Nichols School in Buffalo, between 1942 and 1955, he studied piano with Anita Frank, beginning in 1944, and with Warren Case from 1952 to 1955. His father taught him how to play popular music on the piano. Shire studied theory and composition with Stanley King in Buffalo in 1954–55. As a teenager, Shire also played with his father's band at weddings, bar mitzvahs and parties, worked as a cocktail pianist in Buffalo hotels and formed a combo that performed at school dances.

After graduating from The Nichols School in

DAVID SHIRE

1955, Shire entered Yale University, where he majored in English before switching to music. While at Yale, he led a progressive jazz group that performed at other eastern colleges. One of his classmates was Richard Maltby Jr., a writer with whom Shire collaborated on the writing of college musicals. From one of their undergraduate productions—a musical version of *Cyrano de Bergerac* produced by the Yale Dramatic Association in 1958 and subsequently mounted by the Williamstown (Massachusetts) Summer Theatre—came the song "Autumn," which Barbra Streisand included on her 1964 album *People.* In addition to his music courses at Yale, Shire studied theory and composition in Buffalo with Robert Hughes in 1958–59. (A decade later, he informally studied composition with Paul Glass in Los Angeles.)

From 1960 to 1963, while living in New York City, Shire served in the National Guard. In those years he supported himself by playing the piano, accompanying and coaching singers and arranging and conducting. For a year he was the pianist on Off Broadway for *The Fantasticks.* In 1961 he composed the songs for *The Sap of Life,* an Off Broadway musical, and in 1962 for *Graham Crackers,* a nightclub revue. From 1964 to 1966 he was the pit pianist, and for much of that time assistant conductor, for *Funny Girl,* which starred Barbra Streisand on Broadway.

In the later 1960s Shire worked for television. He composed his first dramatic television score for *The Final War of Ollie Winter,* the first production of the CBS Playhouse. Subsequently he served as assistant musical director and arranger for two Barbra Streisand television specials,

Color Me Barbra and *Belle of 14th Street*. He later composed the background music for the television series *The Virginian* and *McCloud*.

In the 1960s Shire was also active outside of television. "No More Songs for Me" (1964, lyrics by Richard Maltby) was introduced and recorded by Streisand. His first song to be heard in films was the title number for *I'd Rather Be Rich* (1964, lyrics by Maltby), in which it was sung by Robert Goulet and Andy Williams. Both Goulet and Pearl Bailey recorded it. With Maltby, Shire composed the scores for two musicals, though neither made it to Broadway, *How Do You Do, I Love You* (1968) and *Love Match* (1970). His incidental music and songs for Peter Ustinov's play, *The Unknown Soldier and His Wife* (1967), became Shire's first music to be heard in the Broadway theater.

In 1970 Shire was supervising the pre-Broadway tryout of his musical *Love Match* in Los Angeles (where it had a six-week run) when he was introduced to Stanley Wilson, head of the music department at Universal Studios. Wilson, who had been impressed by Shire's music for television, engaged him for Universal. This led to Shire's first motion picture score, for *One More Train to Rob* (1971). Over the next four years, Shire was hired by various studios to write the scores for eight films, culminating in his most important film assignment, the score for Francis Ford Coppola's ambitious mystery-drama *The Conversation* (1974), starring Gene Hackman.

Since *The Conversation,* Shire has been one of Hollywood's most prolific writers of background music. His most important films are: *The Taking of Pelham 1-2-3* (1974); *Farewell, My Lovely* (1975); *The Hindenburg Disaster* (1975); *All the President's Men* (1976); *Saturday Night Fever* (1977); *Norma Rae* (1979); and *2010* (1985).

For "It Goes Like it Goes" (lyrics by Norman Gimbel) Shire received an Oscar in 1979; it was introduced in *Norma Rae* by Jennifer Warnes. Notable Shire songs from other films are: "I'll Never Say Goodbye" (lyrics by Alan and Marilyn Bergman), introduced by Melissa Manchester in *The Promise* (1978) and recorded by Debbie Boone and by Judy Collins; "With You I'm Born Again" (lyrics by Carol Connors), introduced in *Fastbreak* (1978) and recorded by Billy Preston and by Johnny Mathis; the title song for *Only When I Laugh* (1981, lyrics by Maltby), recorded by Brenda Lee; and "Halfway Home" (lyrics by Carol Connors) from *The Earthling* (1981), recorded by Maureen McGovern.

Discussing his work for films, Shire has said: "Each movie has its own problems, and there aren't any pat solutions. I try, as any good film composer does, to service the picture—service the drama of the picture. If the score can be a nice concert suite away from the film, all the better. But basically the rule has to be to service what's there, and that can be like night and day from one movie to another. . . . There are places in a movie where you want the score to be heard—as in a montage, where the music can be as important as the photography, the effects or the action. Usually you want the main title to be heard. . . . Then there are cues that work almost subliminally . . . where many people would say 'What music?' if you said there was music in it. It was often working on a subconscious level. Almost every movie has a range of cues from one extreme to the other."

Apart from songs for the screen, Shire composed words and music for "What About Today?" which was recorded by Barbra Streisand and used as the title for one of her albums; and for "The Morning After" and "Starting Here, Starting Now," lyrics to both by Maltby and both recorded by Streisand. "With You I'm Born Again" (lyrics by Carol Connors) became one of Shire's most commercially successful songs when it was recorded by Billy Preston in 1980. It rose to number nine on the American charts and reached number one in England.

"Starting Here, Starting Now" provided the title for an Off Broadway musical that opened on May 7, 1977. This production was the result of a request by the Manhattan Theatre Club that Maltby serve as director for an evening of songs that he and Shire had written for theater projects that had been mounted but had failed or that had never been produced. "Probably no other songwriters alive could provide an evening of songs so generally unfamiliar and yet so delightful as these," reported Edwin Wilson in the *Wall Street Journal. Starting Here, Starting Now* presented 21 songs and the show's original cast album earned a Grammy nomination; two other cast albums were released following successful productions in South Africa and Denmark.

Shire made his debut as a composer for the Broadway theater with *Baby* (December 4, 1983), a musical comedy-drama. Sybille Pearson wrote the book, and Maltby doubled as lyricist and director. The subject was marriage and parenting in the lives of three couples—unmarried college undergraduates, a young couple recently married, and the middle-aged parents of three grown children. "Here," wrote Frank Rich in *The New York Times,* "is a modestly scaled entertainment that woos us with such basic commodities as warm feelings, an exuberant cast and a lovely score. . . . It often makes up in buoyancy and charm what it lacks in forceful forward drive. . . . Mr. Shire writes with sophistication over a range that embraces rock, jazz, and the best of Broadway schmaltz." *Baby*'s song highlights were "The Story Goes On," introduced by Liz Callaway; "Fatherhood Blues," shared by Todd Graff, James Congdon, Philip Hoffman and Dennis Warning; "I Chose Right," introduced by Todd Graff; "Patterns," introduced by Beth Fowler; and "And What if We Had Loved Like That?" a duet for James Congdon and Beth Fowler. An original cast recording was released.

Shire has admitted he works best when forced to meet strict deadlines, "I don't wake up each morning bursting with musical ideas. It's the deadline that produces the concentration and discipline that produce the work, and I know if I had eight weeks to do a picture I'd spend eight weeks on it; and if I had four weeks, I'd have it in four weeks. I don't know if the score would be any better for the eight weeks. There is a point of diminishing returns where, if you have too little time, you have to cut corners; but too much time can reduce the concentration, the intensity of the search for the solution."

On March 29, 1970 David Shire married Talia Rose Coppola, the actress-sister of the film director Francis Ford Coppola. They had a son, but were divorced in 1980. In 1984 Shire married Didi Conn, an actress in Hollywood.

Shire's favorite sport is running, and in 1980 he completed the New York City Marathon. He also enjoys travel, attending movies and the theater, and reading. His favorite retreat is the Esalen Institute in Big Sur, where he and his wife conduct a seminar, "Creating Musical Theatre." They make their home in Sherman Oaks, near Los Angeles.

ABOUT: BMI, The Many Worlds of Music, 1980.

SIMON, CARLY (June 25, 1945–   ), composer-lyricist and performer, emerged in the 1970s as a superstar of soft rock. Though having mastered the newer rock sounds as well, she has lost none of her ability to write and perform the intelligent, soulful and sometimes romantic, sometimes tough ballads that made her famous. "I don't write songs for the public," she has said. "I write them for myself. I write them out of the little ideas that come into my head. Most of my songs are about illusions and relationships; webs of half-spoken truths, things you can't say in time. The songs are an effort to figure it out or, at least, to free myself of the immediate dilemma." In so doing, she was not only autobiographical; she was also speaking for the society in which she has moved.

CARLY SIMON

The third of Richard and Andrea Simon's four children, she was born to wealth in New York City in 1945. Her father was the cofounder of the prestigious publishing house of Simon and Schuster. Three of her father's brothers earned distinction in the music world: George, as an authority on jazz; Henry, as a musicologist and book editor; and Alfred, as an authority on the musical theater and director of WQXR, the New York Times classical music radio station. Carly's older sister, Johana, whose exceptional musical talent was apparent in childhood, is a noted concert singer.

As a girl, Carly felt that she was neither as talented nor as attractive as her sisters. Her response to feelings of inadequacy took the form of rebellion and underachievement. A tomboy, she enjoyed playing baseball and became a rabid Brooklyn Dodgers fan, in part to gain the attention of her baseball-loving father. Unable to emulate her father in playing the masters on the piano, she learned to plunk out rock 'n' roll tunes instead. Realizing that her father's literary profession was not for her either, she did not become a voracious reader. In contrast to the cultivated atmosphere of her home, she became the family clown, the entertainer who made funny faces and imitated Al Jolson. "For a long time," Simon recalled, "I was feeling that the only way I could get someone's attention or love was by being the black sheep who wasn't making any money, didn't have a job, didn't fit."

Seeking a world apart from her family, she was drawn into the Greenwich Village folk music scene. An early influence was the folk singer, Pete Seeger, one of her teachers at a private elementary school in the village. Later on, while attending the Riverdale Girls' School in the Bronx, she was in thrall to Odetta, whose concerts and recording sessions she attended. Interest in folk music led Simon to take up the guitar. Her older sister, Lucy, had taught her how to form basic chords, and soon she was singing to her own accompaniment for her friends.

Upon graduating from the Riverdale Girls' School, she entered Sarah Lawrence College in 1961. During her sophomore year, she and Lucy formed a sister singing act to make money for a summer vacation. They found a job at a night spot in Provincetown, on Cape Cod, earning $50 a week and one free meal a day. They performed songs by Harry Belafonte and Peter, Paul and Mary, as well as "Winkin' Blinkin' and Nod," which Lucy had composed. Returning to New York, Carly dropped out of Sarah Lawrence. She and her sister played at the Bitter End, one of New York's showcases for folk, and appeared on the ABC folk-music television program, *Hootenany*. In 1964 the Simon sisters recorded "Winkin' Blinkin' and Nod," which made number 78 on the charts, and, in 1965, "Cuddlebugs" for Kapp Records. When Lucy married a physician in 1965, the act was broken up. Their album, *The Simon Sisters*, had been released in 1964.

Albert Grossman, Bob Dylan's manager, advised Carly Simon to go solo and become a "female Bob Dylan." But because she "couldn't sing like . . . Dylan", she turned her back on a career in music. For the next few years she worked in Manhattan as a secretary, then as an assistant coordinator for a television production company. She also gave guitar lessons at a summer camp and lived for a time in southern France with a boyfriend, an idyll that turned ugly when she developed tremors. After four years of psychoanalytic treatment it was discoverd that the malady had nothing to do with the diagnosis offered by her therapist but was caused by her allergy to French wine.

All this time Simon was writing songs, words and music. In 1969 she returned to professional performing by serving six months as a co-lead singer for a rock band called Elephant's Memory. In 1970 a friend, Jacob Brackman, asked her to perform her own songs at a party at his house which was to be attended by Jerry Brandt, manager of the Voices of East Harlem. Impressed, Brandt arranged for Simon to make a demo record which, in turn, brought her a recording contract from Elektra. Early in 1971 Elektra released her first album, *Carly Simon*, which was vigorously promoted and sold some 400,000 copies. "The woman in these songs," wrote Timothy

Crouse in his *Rolling Stone* review, "is at once passionately romantic and cynically realistic." One of the cuts became a top-ten hit, "That's the Way I've Always Heard it Should Be" (lyrics by Jacob Brackman), which reflected Simon's ambivalent-but-leaning-to-cynical feelings about marriage. "I guess," she explained, "I was trying to fight against the pattern established when we were children, growing up with bride dolls and having Mother say marriage is your goal in life." That single brought Simon a Grammy as the year's best new artist.

Through the influence of Elektra Records, Simon was booked for an April 6, 1971 engagement at the Troubadour, a popular night spot in Los Angeles. Chronically shy and nervous to the point of panic in her public appearances, Simon thereafter refused to perform in concert.

Her second album, *Anticipation*, released late in 1971, quickly sold more than 600,000 copies and earned Simon her first gold record. *Anticipation*'s best songs were the title number, "Three Days" and "Legend in Your Own Time," all written by Simon, and "I've Got to Have You" (words and music by Kris Kristofferson), and all were inspired by her love affair with Kristofferson. Simon received two more gold records in 1972, for the album *No Secrets* and for the single "You're So Vain (I'll Bet You Think This Song is About You)," a hard-hitting, sardonic rock song about the deficiences of a rich, self-absorbed lover. The glamorous Simon's acidulous lyrics invited speculation in the press as to the narcissitic lover's identity, and the names of Warren Beatty, James Taylor and Mick Jagger (who joined with Simon to belt out "You're So Vain's" chorus) were bandied about. Simon herself refused to say who it was about, because, as she said, "The song is so nasty."

Three more gold records followed, for "Mockingbird" (1973), a duet with James Taylor, the album *Hotcakes* (1974) and the 1975 LP *The Best of Carly Simon*. The most popular numbers from *Hotcakes*, in addition to "Mockingbird," were "Mind on My Man," "We Have No Secrets," and "Haven't Got Time for the Pain." For the last-mentioned song, the lyrics were by Jacob Brackman. Following the appearance of *Hotcakes*, Loraine Alterman wrote in *The New York Times*, "There can be no question about Carly Simon's artistic identity. Possessed of a rich and expressive voice that conveys positive energy charges, she also writes melodies that catch the ear easily. As a lyricist concerned with the subtleties in relationships between men and women, she can offer us insights into our own actions and reactions. Carly Simon is that rare artist who can express feelings that most of us have but don't take time to define."

In November 1971, Carly Simon attended a concert by singer-songwriter James Taylor, and later that evening spoke to him backstage. This was not their first meeting. When much younger, they had met casually while both their families were vacationing on Martha's Vineyard, and in April 1971 he had gone backstage to congratulate Simon after her performance at the Troubadour. But not until the night of Taylor's concert did they go out together. On November 4, 1972, they were married. A daughter, Sarah Maria, was born in 1974 and a son three years later. Taylor and Simon had a gray-shingled Cape house of their own design built in a secluded patch of woods on Martha's Vineyard. Here Simon indulged in her favorite sports, swimming, sailing and racing in speedboats. She and her husband also maintained an apartment on Central Part West in Manhattan.

The first few years of marriage and the birth of children brought emotional stability to both Simon and Taylor, enabling them to pursue their respective careers with a minimum of turbulence. Though for several years Carly Simon avoided solo appearances in public, she occasionally sang duets with Taylor at his concerts. They had performed "Mockingbird" together in the studio and he sang with Simon on *Hotcakes* and on her fifth album, *Playing Possum* (1975). The principal numbers on *Playing Possum* were, besides the title cut, "One-Man Woman," and "Look Me in the Eye." The song "Slave" was a clear expression of Simon's feminism. As she explained in her book, *Carly Simon Complete*, "I do feel . . . that I'm just another woman raised to be a slave; my conditioning is such that I am dependent upon another person, namely James. Yet I'm also quite aware of it and aware of trying to change the pattern." Simon's next three albums were *Another Passenger* (1976), *Boys in the Trees* (1978), which went platinum and *Spy* (1979). From *Boys in the Trees* came the hit single, "You Belong to Me," "Tranquillo (Melt My Heart)," "For Old Times' Sake" and "You're the One." *Another Passenger* included "You Keep Me Runnin'" and on *Spy* was "We're So Close."

Spy was Simon's last album for Elektra. On the Warner Brothers label she released *Come Upstairs* in 1982, Simon's hardest rocking album yet. In *Stereo Review* Peter Reilly described the title number as "either about passion suddenly lit between two people who've known each other for years, or about passion rekindled." "The Three of Us in the Dark" he described as "perhaps the memory of a past lover intruding upon a relationship, maybe about another, more critical self doing the same." He described "Jesse" as a "serio-comic ramble about a girl who is trying to swear off said Jesse's charms—but

she ends up obsessively chasing after him the moment she hears he is back in town." Reilly said of Simon: "She's moved away from her earlier intellectualized, girlish, even angry stance . . . to a softer, more cat-like subtlety, engaged but not committed." As a single, "Jesse" brought Simon another gold record.

On her next album, *Torch* (1982), Simon included her interpretations of song standards by Richard Rodgers, Hoagy Carmichael, John Green and Duke Ellington as well as her own compositions. Peter Reilly said in *Stereo Review*: "When Simon wraps herself in a great song like Rodgers and Hart's 'Spring Is Here' . . . or slithers through a pulsing, sequined 'Body and Soul,' you begin to sense that the change in her is more than a matter of repertoire. This is a woman singing, and singing in the matter of a High Romance—a style we all thought was going to disappear when such contenders as Frank Sinatra and Peggy Lee at long last get around to hanging up their gloves." As a single, Simon's own song, "Torch," was a bestseller.

Carly Simon continued to forge new musical directions for herself on the album *Hello, Big Man* (1983), on which she used reggae rhythms. Of this album, Reilly said: "Carly Simon is getting better and better. Her newest . . . release . . . is an exuberant, sexy, funny, sometimes poignant album with the vibrant gusto and earthiness that made her a star in the first place. . . . The songs . . . probably say more about the way life is lived in the '80s by an attractive, intelligent woman than any three weighty sociological treatises ever could." The title song told the story of how Simon's parents met and described their life together. "You Know What to Do" was, in Simon's words, "a sort of imagined macho-rape fantasy with overtones of Lady Chatterly and Mellors." "Menemsha" (written with Peter Wood) depicted a fishing village on Martha's Vineyard as it used to be and told of a boy she used to know.

Carly Simon composed the music for the theme song of the motion picture, *Torchlight* (1984), and wrote the lyrics with Tim Mayer. In 1980 Simon and James Taylor separated permanently; three years later their divorce was finalized. "It seemed impossible to stay together," Simon said. "James needs a lot more space around him—aloneness, remoteness, more privacy. I need more closeness, more communication. He's more abstract in our relationship. I'm more concrete. He's more of a poet, and I'm more of a reporter. What our personalities bring out in each other is quite fascinating and is what made us sometimes drive each other crazy. That phase of my life is over."

The new phase has been lived with her children and a housekeeper in the Martha's Vineyard house and the apartment on Central Park West. Her new companion is the musician Russ Kunkel. In an interview in *High Fidelity*, Simon called herself "the most undisciplined person imaginable. I have no schedule for anything. If I didn't have children, I don't know what I'd be like, because they keep me on some sort of schedule. I get up in the morning and just kind of see where the day takes me. Very often, it doesn't take me anywhere. But I don't take writing as seriously as I should. I've never had an office. I've never has a set time for working. I can't seem to ever say to the children, 'You have to stay out of here for two hours while I work.'"

ABOUT: Current Biography, 1976; Orloff, K. Rock 'n' Roll Woman, 1974; Simon, C. Carly Simon Complete, 1975. *Periodicals*—High Fidelity November 1983; Newsday September 3, 1972; New York Times June 12, 1977; Rolling Stone May 22, 1975; Saturday Review October 16, 1976.

PAUL SIMON

SIMON, PAUL (November 5, 1942–   ). The sensational success of the singing duo Simon and Garfunkel in the 1960s was due not only to their vocalizations (often accompanied by only a single acoustic guitar) but also to the elements of "arty" poetry, Dylan-influenced folk rock, urban sophistication, Tin Pan Alley cleverness and "soft" rock and roll that composer-lyricist Simon fused into a unique idiom. When Simon and Garfunkel went their separate ways in 1970, Simon continued to develop both as songwriter and performer, and by the middle of the decade he was established as one of popular music's most original and influential artists.

Paul Simon was born in Newark, New Jersey, the son of Louis and Belle Simon. The father played the double bass in a radio orchestra and later taught graduate courses in education at a branch of the City University of New York. The mother was an elementary school teacher. When Simon was very young, his family moved to Forest Hills, a pleasant middle-class community in the Queens section of New York, where he attended elementary and high school. In the sixth grade he played the White Rabbit in a P.S. 164 production of *Alice in Wonderland* in which Art Garfunkel, Simon's junior by three weeks, portrayed the Cheshire Cat. Walking home from rehearsals, they discovered a mutual interest in sports (especially baseball) and music, and began spending evenings together listening to early rock 'n' roll on the popular radio programs of Dick Clark and Alan Freed. To Simon's accompaniment on acoustic guitar, which he had learned to play without formal instruction, they began singing the popular rock numbers of the day, initially just for their own pleasure, but later on at school functions, club dates, and private parties. By this time Simon had begun writing and performing original material.

They cut a demonstration record which brought them a contract from Big Records, a small New York company specializing in rock. One of their first releases was "Hey, Schoolgirl" (1957) for which Simon composed the music and Garfunkel the words. They were billed as Tom and Jerry and the recording stayed on the Hot 100 of *Billboard* for nine weeks, reaching the 54th position and selling more than 100,000 copies by early 1958. As Tom and Jerry they cut several more records before Big Records went into bankruptcy, appeared on Dick Clark's popular television show, *American Bandstand*, and went on tour as the opening act of numerous rock 'n' roll groups.

In 1958 Simon and Garfunkel ended their musical partnership. For the next two years Simon worked as an instrumentalist and singer at various Manhattan recording studios. Upon graduating from Forest Hills High School in 1960 he enrolled at Queens College and majored in literature. After earning a B.A. degree, Simon entered Brooklyn Law School but, disenchanted, left after six months. At this time, Garfunkel was studying architecture at Columbia University. When both were college sophomores they reunited professionally. Stimulated by the music of Bob Dylan, the Kingston Trio, and Joan Baez, Simon and Garfunkel outgrew teenage rock and embraced folk music. In Greenwich Village they gave concerts in Washington Square Park, at the Gaslight, and at Gerde's Folk City.

During the summer of 1963 Simon made a number of solo folksinging appearances in Europe. While in Paris, he read of the murder in Mississippi of Andrew Goodman, a former classmate of Simon's at Queens, who had gone to the South as a civil rights activist. Deeply affected by this tragedy, Simon, as an emotional outlet, wrote a protest song, "He Was My Brother," the composition of which was a turning point in Simon's songwriting career. "I . . . reached the point of knowing I couldn't write dumb teenage lyrics," he later explained. "And I had just about finally decided that if I was going to be a failure as a songwriter, I would be a proud failure." This and other Simon ballads impressed an executive for Columbia Records who signed him to a contract. For his first Columbia recording, Simon suggested that Garfunkel be his singing partner. Though the company feared that their names made them sound like a law firm, their first album, *Wednesday Morning, 3 a. m.*, was released under their own names in October 1984. In addition to songs by others, including some by Bob Dylan, Simon and Garfunkel performed "He Was My Brother" and a few other Simon songs for which he wrote both words and music, including the title number, "Bleecker Street," and "Sounds of Silence."

In a market now dominated by hard rock, and principally by the Beatles, *Wednesday Morning, 3 a. m.* passed virtually unnoticed. A disc jockey for a rock station in Miami, however, noticed that whenever he played "Sounds of Silence," Simon's haunting song about the failure of people to communicate with each other, listeners deluged the station with requests for more airplay. This enthusiasm led Columbia to issue "Sounds of Silence" as a single (coupled with Simon's "We've Got a Groovy Thing Goin'") but with an electric guitar figure overdubbed (the LP version consisted of Simon and Garfunkel's voices and an acoustic guitar accompaniment). The record remained on the Hot 100 for three months, reaching the number one position on all charts and bringing Simon and Garfunkel their first gold record.

In February 1966 Columbia issued the second Simon and Garfunkel album, *Sounds of Silence*. This album earned them a gold record and it contained "I Am a Rock," whose theme was the rejection of emotional involvements, and which became a bestselling single. A third Simon and Garfunkel album followed in September of that year, *Parsley, Sage, Rosemary and Thyme,* another gold record. Here several more Simon song classics appeared: "Homeward Bound," a hit as

a single; "Scarborough Fair–Canticle"; "The Dangling Conversation"; and "59th Street Bridge Song (Feelin' Groovy)." "One glorious melody follows another, each brilliantly arranged and impeccably sung," wrote Stephen Holden of this album in *Rolling Stone* (August 3, 1972). "'The Dangling Conversation,' for all its literary self-consciousness, expresses better than any song before or since the pervasive *angst* of the affluent collegiate." One of the songs was less a song than it was a social and political document. Called "Seven O'Clock News—Silent Night," it juxtaposed a performance of the Christmas carol "Silent Night" with the murmuring background of radio or television newscasts of events in Vietnam and the civil rights movement. The volume of the newsman's voice grew increasingly audible until it eventually overwhelmed the singing and ended with the announcement of the death of comedian Lenny Bruce.

In the late 1960s Simon and Garfunkel became popular performers on the college and university circuit. They also made guest appearances on such network television programs as the *Kraft Music Hall,* the *Fred Astaire Show,* and the *Ed Sullivan Show,* and performed in such distinguished concert auditoriums as Carnegie Hall in New York. They also toured Europe and on November 30, 1969, they were hosts of their own one-hour CBS special, *Simon and Garfunkel.*

Meanwhile, impressed by "Sounds of Silence," Mike Nichols asked Simon and Garfunkel to provide music for *The Graduate* (1967), a film he was directing. For that story of youthful alienation and 1960s affluence, Simon and Garfunkel sang three Simon songs, "Sounds of Silence," "Scarborough Fair–Canticle" and a new number, "Mrs. Robinson." These songs underscored the conflicts in the life of Benjamin Braddock (played by Dustin Hoffman), a recent college graduate whose future is uncertain, and they played a significant role in making *The Graduate* into a cinematic icon of the 1960s rebellion against stifling middle-class mores. As Simon explained in *The New York Times* (January 21, 1968), "A song like the 'Sounds of Silence' is really Benjamin talking about his life and his parents and where he lives and what he sees around him." "Mrs. Robinson," about Benjamin's older lover, became a gold record as a single and won the Grammy for record of the year. The soundtrack album also went gold and captured a Grammy as the best original motion-picture score.

The songs on their next album, *Bookends* (1968, also a gold record), included "Mrs. Robinson" and new numbers like "Old Friends," "Save the Life of My Child," "A Hazy Shade of Winter," and "America." In "Old Friends," a view of old age from the perspective of youth, Simon poignantly described the emptiness of life in a home for the aged.

Simon and Garfunkel's greatest success came in 1970 with the album *Bridge Over Troubled Water,* which went gold on the day it was released, and eventually sold more than ten million copies. (With this album, Simon and Garfunkel became the first American performing artists to received gold discs for each of their first six albums.) The songs on *Bridge Over Troubled Water* included the title number and "Cecilia," each a gold record as a single, and "The Only Living Boy in New York." The LP won a Grammy as album of the year and the song "Bridge Over Troubled Water" won Grammys as record of the year and song of the year.

Reviewing *Bridge Over Troubled Water* for *The New York Times* (February 27, 1972), Don Heckman wrote, "Simon and Garfunkel continue to represent that rarity in the popular arts— talent that can appeal to wide audiences without sacrificing a whit of originality, complexity, skill or creativity. Quite simply, 'Bridge Over Trouble Water' is a stunningly beautiful song. Like all classic popular ballads, it has the virtue of instant identity." In *Rolling Stone,* Stephen Holden described 'Bridge,' which had become a standard, as having "one of Simon's greatest melodies—a long, soaring arch that perfectly carries forward the spirit of the lyrics, whose sentiments of hope and promise of comfort are universal."

Reviewing the Paul Simon songs of the Simon and Garfunkel era, Josh Greenfield noted in *The New York Times Magazine* (October 13, 1968) that Simon's message was "one of literate protest against the pangs of youth, the pathos of old age and the matter-of-fact hypocrisies of the middle age and the middle class in between." Greenfield declared that Simon's songs seem "to have transcended the communications breakdown, bridged the generation gap, broken through the usual establishment and anti-establishment lines." Discussing the musicianship of Simon and Garfunkel, Greenfield added: "Their sound—a soft and cool tenor and counter-tenor madrigal-like harmony to the accompaniment of a single guitar—has been acclaimed by . . . modern [musical authorities] as diverse as Leonard Bernstein . . . and the Beatles."

The annual income of Simon and Garfunkel had been estimated at $2,000,000, two-thirds of which went to Simon, because he wrote the songs. But despite his wealth Simon maintained a modest two-room apartment overlooking the

East River on Manhattan's Upper East Side in the years before he married Peggy Harper, his first wife. The small apartment's simple furnishings included a hobbyhorse, which Simon described as a "useless luxury," As he told one interviewer, " . . . I don't like to waste time on food, clothing, shelter, possessions. I don't even own a car. I don't have much relationship to my money." After his marriage Simon acquired a brownstone triplex on the Upper East Side and a country house in Bucks County, Pennsylvania.

When working, he rose about nine o'clock in the morning and started in right after breakfast. "Once I start on a project I never let up; I pace about the living room. I look over the river. I play some licks on the guitar, or else I'll just go off to the Cloisters and sit there and think." He composes the music first, then spends a considerable amount of time writing and polishing the lyrics. "I try to take an emotion or feeling I've had," he explained, "and capture it in one incident."

Simon and Garfunkel ended their professional partnership in 1970 with a farewell concert at Forest Hills Stadium in Queens. By then, Garfunkel had begun acting in films, having completed *Catch 22* (1970) and started on *Carnal Knowledge* (1971), both directed by Mike Nichols. For Simon, the breakup satisfied his need to be free of collaboration of any kind. "I didn't want to be half of something," he said. "You can't go for a long period of time as a partner, not anybody. . . . You've got to stop—and then it's traumatic." Nevertheless, in 1972 Simon and Garfunkel sang together at a McGovern-for-President rally at Madison Square Garden.

In their solo careers, both Simon and Garfunkel have been successful, especially Simon. Garfunkel has released four albums—*Angel Clare* (1973), *Breakaway* (1975), *Watermark* (1976) and *Scissors Cut* (1981). Simon's first solo LP was *Paul Simon* (1972), which he followed with *There Goes Rhymin' Simon* (1973); both records went gold. "Mother and Child Reunion," a hit single, "Papa Hobo," "Hobo's Blues" and "Paranoia Blues" were the superior cuts on *Paul Simon,* an album on which Simon explored blues-based motifs further than he had before and on which he experimented with reggae rhythms and sounds. Here he received musical support from the jazz violinist Stephane Grappelli and a Jamaican reggae unit. With *There Goes Rhymin' Simon,* which contained such superb cuts as "Kodachrome," "Tenderness," "Love Me Like a Rock," "Mardi Gras," and "American Tune," Simon clinched "his position as the top singer-songwriter-producer in contemporary music," wrote Lorraine Alterman in

The New York Times (May 6, 1973). "Simon has produced an album with lyrics, music and vocals that strike me emotionally and mentally as bursting with fresh ideas."

Simon made his first tour as a solo performer in 1973, an 11-city engagement that started in Hartford, Connecticut on May 4 and ended a month later at Carnegie Hall. Material from these appearances was used for his album *Live Rhymin'* (1974), a gold record.

On October 18, 1975, Simon appeared as a guest on the popular NBC comedy show, *Saturday Night.* Upon completing "Gone at Last," a duet with Phoebe Snow, he went to the wings to draw into camera range his old partner, Garfunkel. To the surprise and delight of the audience they sang a couple of their old favorites and introduced a new Simon number, "My Little Town," which he had included on his new album, *Still Crazy After All These Years,* as Garfunkel had on his own 1975 LP, *Breakaway.* For Simon, the critically acclaimed *Still Crazy After All These Years* meant another gold record and the winning of two Grammys, one for best album and another for leading male vocalist of the year.

In 1976 Simon had a bestselling single in "Fifty Ways to Leave Your Lover" and his *Greatest Hits* album (1978) eventually earned a platinum record. Simon's first collection of new songs in five years came in 1980 with *One-Trick Pony.* This was the soundtrack of a 1980 motion picture of the same title for which Simon wrote both the screenplay and the songs besides appearing in the starring role of Jonah Levin, a protest singer of the 1960s, whose entire success was based on a single hit, and that an accidental one. "One song after another demonstrates Simon's gift for seizing and holding up to the light these almost reflective emotional conclusions about a person, a time, a place or a relationship that any poetry, even on the pop level, must offer if it is going to communicate anything at all," wrote Peter Reilly in *Stereo Review* (December 1980) about this album. "Here again he illuminates those fugitive, fragmentary bursts of authentic feeling that contribute so much, plus or minus, to our perception of ourselves. . . . He is a master of mood and atmosphere, and he uses those means here to show us the calm, introspective maturity of a man for whom middle age is but another natural part of the life process." *One-Trick Pony* was not Simon's first work in popular cinema. He had composed the music for *Shampoo* (1975), directed by and starring Warren Beatty, and had played the bit part of a slick, name-dropping, "Hollywood-type" record producer in Woody Allen's *Annie Hall* (1977).

Simon and Garfunkel were again reunited on the evening of September 19, 1981, for a free concert in New York's Central Park which attracted an audience of about 500,000. That concert, and the gold record album of the performance, offered almost all of their most popular songs. In May 1982, they began a five-week tour of Europe, Japan, and Australia. In the middle of the summer of the following year they set off together again for a 19-city tour of the United States, opening in Akron, Ohio and closing in Boulder, Colorado. In addition to their familiar repertory, they featured several new Simon songs which were included on Simon's solo album *Hearts and Bones* (1983). In this record, as Stephen Holden noted in *The New York Times* (October 30, 1983), Simon "makes by far the most convincing case for rock and roll as the basis of mature artistic expression. . . . The lyrics dwell obsessively on the conflict between feeling and thinking while the music reflects Mr. Simon's abiding passion for the more refined expression." Principal numbers in this collection were the title song, "Allergies," "Think Too Much," and "The Late Great Johnny Ace."

Paul Simon married the actress Carrie Fisher, daughter of Eddie Fisher and Debbie Reynolds, on August 16, 1983, in a ceremony at Simon's duplex apartment on Central Park West. They spent their honeymoon the next evening at the Astrodome in Houston, where Simon and Garfunkel were performing. Simon and Fisher are now divorced. Simon had a son, Harper, by his first wife.

In the mid-1980s, in the wake of technopop, punk, and new wave, Simon's music had begun to sound dated, predictable and too middle of the road. His *Hearts and Bones,* for instance, was the first Simon LP to fail to earn a gold record. But with the release of his album *Graceland* in the summer of 1986, Simon entered a period of artistic renewal. His least "mainstream" record, but also his most joyful, *Graceland* was the product of Simon's immersion in the folk music of black South Africa. In *The New York Times* Stephen Holden described *Graceland* as "something new, an album that thoroughly blends various styles of acoustic black South African folk music with strains of stylistically related American rock and roll into songs that have unusual shapes and structures and that sound unlike anything familiar to most American ears. That is because about half the album was recorded in Johannesburg with many of the finest black South African musicians playing [their indigenous] music that was only later shaped [by Simon] into [popular] songs."

"My typical style of songwriting in the past,"

Simon told the *Times*, "has been to sit with a guitar and write a song, finish it, go into the studio, book the musicians, lay out the song and the chords, and then try to make a track. With these [South African] musicans, I was doing it the other way around. The tracks preceded the songs. We worked improvisationally. While a group was playing in the studio I would sing melodies and words, [most of them made up on the spur of the moment]—anything that fit the scale they were playing in." The album's principal cuts are "The Boy in the Bubble," about the "mystical connections between primitive magic and modern technology," and "Graceland," which Holden described as the transformation of "Elvis Presley's [hometown] shrine [into] a metaphor of salvation for 'poor boys and pilgrims with families,' as well as a personal symbol of healing for the songwriter's romantic wounds. Two hymn-like songs about the search for spiritual fulfillment are "Homeless" and "Under African Skies," whereas "Diamonds on the Soles of Her Shoes" takes a sardonic look at the neuroses of contemporary, urban life.

ABOUT: Cohen, M. S. Simon and Garfunkel: A Biography In Words and Pictures, 1977; Denisoff, R. S. Sing a Song of Social Significance, 1972; Humphries, P. Bookends: The Simon and Garfunkel Story, 1982; Leigh, S. Paul Simon: Now and Then, 1973; Marsh D. Paul Simon, 1978; Mathews-Walker, R. Simon and Garfunkel, 1982. *Periodicals*—High Fidelity May 1982; New Yorker May 4, 1968; New York Times January 21, 1968, February 27, 1972, February 28, 1982, August 24, 1986; New York Times Magazine October 13, 1968; Rolling Stone October 23, 1986; Saturday Review June 12, 1976.

SISSLE, NOBLE. *See* **BLAKE, EUBIE** and **SISSLE, NOBLE**

SONDHEIM, STEPHEN (March 22, 1930–). Since Rodgers and Hammerstein, no one has advanced the musical play or altered its destiny more than the composer-lyricist Stephen Sondheim. He has brought to Broadway a remarkable talent as a lyricist, a field in which his mastery is virtually unrivalled. A consummate musician, he has met the demands of the most complex texts, as he did in *Sunday in the Park with George,* which broke with the whole history of the Broadway musical and won the Pulitzer Prize for drama. Beyond his contributions to Broadway, as the artistic partner to unorthodox, formula-shattering texts, Sondheim is one of the leading innovators in contemporary American music.

STEPHEN SONDHEIM

Stephen Joshua Sondheim was born into upper-middle-class comfort in New York City. His father, Herbert Sondheim, was a dress manufacturer, and his mother, Janet (Fox) Sondheim, a dress designer and, later, an interior decorator. Precocious, Sondheim took an interest in the piano when he was four and, at five, began two years of piano study with a local teacher. His early education was at the Ethical Culture School, where he started reading *The New York Times* in the first grade.

When he was ten his parents divorced, and his mother enrolled him in the New York Military Academy, which he loved for its "rules and order" and because "the school had a large organ with lots of buttons." Two years later, mother and son settled on a farm in Pennsylvania, a few miles from the Doylestown summer residence of Oscar Hammerstein II, whose intimate friendship with the family brought young Sondheim into personal contact with the celebrated librettist-lyricist. When Sondheim composed words and music for *By George,* a production mounted at the George School in Newton, Pennsylvania, the 15-year-old brought his work to Hammerstein for objective criticism. "It's the worst thing I ever read," Hammerstein told him, then proceeded to deliver a point-by-point explanation of what was wrong. "We went on for a whole afternoon about it," Sondheim recalled. "I guess I learned most of the things about writing lyrics in that afternoon: 25 years of experience crammed into three hours. I gobbled it up." Sondheim continued to consult Hammerstein, who was to bequeath his legacy to the younger man. As Sondheim has said, "He got me into the theater, awoke a latent talent or a talent interest. . . . He'd been a second father to me since I was 13. . . . He taught me how to build songs, how to introduce characters, how to make a story relate to characters, how to tell a story, how not to tell a story, the interrelationships between lyrics and music—all, of course, from his own point of view.

When he was 17, Sondheim spent his vacation typing scripts and performing sundry menial tasks while the Rodgers and Hammerstein musical, *Allegro,* was being rehearsed. Later, he was a production assistant at rehearsals of *South Pacific* and *The King and I.* Meanwhile, in 1946, Sondheim was graduated from the George School and entered Williams College, where he planned to major in mathematics but finally decided on music. At college he wrote book, lyrics and music for two school productions, one of which was an adaptation of *Beggar on Horseback,* a 1924 Broadway fantasy-comedy by George S. Kaufman and Marc Connelly.

In 1950 Sondheim graduated from Williams College magna cum laude. The Hutchinson award for composition enabled him to spend the next two years studying composition with Milton Babbitt. About 1953 Sondheim wrote the words and music for *Saturday Night,* a musical which never reached Broadway because of the death of Lemuel Ayers, the producer. Having no immediate prospects for work on Broadway, Sondheim went to Hollywood, becoming co-scriptwriter for the half-hour TV series *Topper,* which premiered on NBC in October 1953. Sondheim's Broadway debut was the title song and incidental music for *Girls of Summer,* a short-lived play which opened on November 19, 1956. In 1959 Sondheim wrote for a CBS television series, *The Last Word,* discussions of the English language by a distinguished panel headed by Bergen Evans.

Impressed by the *Saturday Night* score, playwright Arthur Laurents introduced Sondheim to Leonard Bernstein. Bernstein, Laurents and the choreographer Jerome Robbins were preparing a dance musical that turned out to be *West Side Story.* After hearing some of Sondheim's lyrics, Bernstein invited him to become his lyricist. *West Side Story,* produced on September 26, 1957, became a major theatrical triumph as well as an acclaimed motion picture in 1960. Adapting his lyrics with brilliance and versatility to Bernstein's music for such now-standard ballads as "Tonight," "Maria," and "I Feel Pretty," and for comic songs like "Gee, Officer Krupke" and "America," the 27-year-old Sondheim secured his place in the professional American musical theater.

In 1958, while Laurents was working on the text for *Gypsy,* based on the life of stripper Gypsy Rose Lee, he asked Sondheim to serve as the musical's composer-lyricist. But *Gypsy's* star, Ethel Merman, demanded a more experienced composer and Sondheim ended up writing the lyrics to Jule Styne's score. Opening on May 21, 1959, *Gypsy* had a two-year Broadway run and was made into a motion picture in 1962. With such stellar Sondheim-Styne songs as "Everything's Coming Up Roses"; "Together"; "Let Me Entertain You"; "Small World" and "Rose's Turn," *Gypsy* has been called one of the most perfectly achieved of dance musicals. (The choreographer was Jerome Robbins.)

Sondheim composed incidental music for *Invitation to a March,* a Broadway play that opened in the fall of 1960. The first Broadway musical for which Sondhiem wrote both lyrics and music was the Harold Prince production, *A Funny Thing Happened on the Way to the Forum.* With a book by Burt Shevelove and Larry Gelbart loosely based on comedies by Plautus, *A Funny Thing Happened on the Way to the Forum* is a bawdy farce in the style of old-fashioned burlesque, with gags and routines set in ancient Rome. Zero Mostel played a slave trying to win his freedom by procuring for his owner a beautiful courtesan on whom a warrior has prior rights. Complicating the plot, the slave schemes to convince the warrior that his courtesan has died of the plague, and has another character, a male, appear as the corpse. The broad comic situations culminate in the slapstick of a Mack Sennett-like chase.

Opening on May 8, 1962, the show had a run of 964 performances, received a Tony as the season's best musical, was made into a motion picture in 1966, and was revived on Broadway on March 30, 1972. *A Funny Thing* stands as the most commercially successful of the eight musicals on which Sondheim and Prince have collaborated.

In preparing his score, Sondheim planned each song, as he explained, "to provide periods of respite from the restlessness of farce as one farcical situation piles upon another. . . . Though they're not used to develop character, [the songs] still had to be written for a specific personality since the characters are all prototypes." The score, recorded by the original cast, began with a rousing opening number, "Comedy Tonight," introduced by Zero Mostel and company. Sondheim's lyrics were at their most scintillating in the comedy number, "Everybody Ought to Have a Maid" (sung by Mostel, David Burns, Jack Gilford and John Carradine), and in a parody of sentimental ballads, "Lovely" (a duet by Brian Davies and Preshy Marker, and reprised by Mostel).

Sondheim's next two Broadway shows were failures. For *Anyone Can Whistle,* book by Laurents, which premiered on April 4, 1964, Sondheim again wrote both lyrics and music. This is a satire in which, to attract tourists, a small town promotes the hoax that water, gushing out of a rock, has miraculous curative powers. The title song and "See What it Gets You" were introduced by Lee Remick; Angela Lansbury was heard in "A Parade in Town" and Harry Guardino in "Everybody Says Don't." Though *Anyone Can Whistle* lasted only nine performances, an original cast recording was released and the musical was revived Off Broadway in 1980.

For *Do I Hear a Waltz?* (March 18, 1965) Sondheim served as lyricist for Richard Rodgers in a production based on a Laurents play, *The Time of the Cuckoo,* that had the shortest run of any Rodgers musical in a quarter of a century, 220 performances. Its best number was the title song, although Sondheim's lyrics sparkled in "What Do We Do? We Fly!", about the terrors of air travel, and "This Week Americans," about the follies and foibles of American tourists in Venice.

Sondheim was absent from the Broadway scene for the next five years, although in the interim he composed words and music for *Evening Primrose,* a musical play telecast by ABC-TV in 1966. With *Company* (April 26, 1970), Sondheim was reunited on Broadway with producer Harold Prince. *Company* was Sondheim's "concept musical"—an episodic, essentially plotless series of unromantic vignettes which owe as much to Brecht as to Hammerstein.

In this musical, both the librettist, George Furth, and Sondheim proved themselves innovators in the way they addressed the subject—a cold view of married and single life in the contemporary city without superfluous or meretricious trimmings—and in the way the songs commented on, rather than advanced, the action. The central character, Robert, is a bachelor whose well-meaning friends are trying to marry him off. In one song Robert observes: "It's the concerts you enjoy together/ Neighbors you annoy together/ Children you destroy together/ That keep marriage intact." But at play's end the bachelor here cries out for "Someone to hold you too close/ Someone to hurt you too deep/ Someone to sit in your chair,/ To ruin your sleep." "It is not a musical in the conventional sense," wrote one reviewer. "The singing and what little dancing there is melt into one integrated continuity

of action. The show is simply a collage of experiences. . . . So accurately does *Company* reflect New York life that the young in heart may want to rise up and scream about their anguish at the super-comfortable, super-impersonal environment our affluent fortyish swingers so unresistingly accept."

No less memorable for the supple, often sardonic lyrics and the expressive music are "The Ladies Who Lunch" and "The Little Things You Do Together," introduced by Elaine Stritch; "Barcelona," by Dean Jones and Susan Browning; "You Could Drive a Person Crazy," by Donna McKechnie, Charles Braswell, and Pamela Myers; "Being Alive," by Dean Jones and company; the chokingly poignant "Sorry-Grateful," by Dean Jones; and "Another Hundred People," by Beth Meyers. The original cast album contains the entire score. (Barbra Streisand revived "Being Alive" on her 1985 album, *Broadway.*) In the opinion of Arthur Laurents, Sondheim had now become a master of writing "a lyric which [can] only be sung by the character for which it is designed; [he] never pads with unnecessary fillers, . . . never sacrifices meaning or intention for a clever rhyme and . . . knows that a lyric is the shortest of one-act plays, with a beginning, a middle and an end."

With a run of 690 performances, *Company* was a box-office success. It won a Tony and the New York Drama Critics Circle Award as the season's best musical, while Sondheim received Tony awards for best lyrics and score. *Company* was revived Off Broadway in 1980.

More conventional, on the surface at least, in subject matter and musical form was the Prince-directed and -produced *Follies* (April 4, 1971), with lyrics and music by Sondheim, book by James Goldman and choreography by Michael Bennett. Though met with divided critical reaction, *Follies* stayed on the boards for 522 performances and won the awards of the New York Critics Circle and the Outer Critics Circle for the season's best musical, and Sondheim's music garnered a Tony.

Follies was ostensibly a nostalgic, sentimental show structured around traditional revue numbers which commented ironically on the complications of the lives of the four main characters, two unhappy married couples. The action took place on the naked stage of an old, about-to-be-demolished theater (presumably the New Amsterdam), once the auditorium of the famous *Ziegfeld Follies.* The producer, who called to mind Florenz Ziegfeld, gives a party for the now middle-aged and disenchanted stars of his chorus-girl productions. Old friendships are renewed and old romances remembered as numbers from old revues float in and out of the production like phantoms, and the characters must come to terms with this surreal Memory Lane after they are transported back to their youthful glory days in scenes staged with imaginative power.

In *The New York Times Magazine* (October 21, 1984) Frank Rich placed *Follies* within the context of Sondheim's attempts to advance beyond the formal limitations of the traditional, post-Hammerstein Broadway musical: "*Follies* was at once the seminal Sondheim-Prince musical and a dead end. The show's climactic phatasmagoric flashback sequence was a rite of exorcism. Sondheim filled it with songs in the style of old-time musical comedy numbers by Kern and Hammerstein and others; then, at the sequence's conclusion, he blended them all together in a nightmarish aural-visual spectacle of dissonance and chaos. Both in form and substance, *Follies* seemed to be saying that the musical theater's old traditions were as unsalvageable as the gutted, ghostly theater in which *Follies* was set. But, having made this statement, neither Sondheim, Bennett nor Prince seemed to know how to move beyond those traditions."

The original cast recording captures "Losing My Mind," the torch song that drew a nightly ovation for Dorothy Collins in the role of Lucy. "I'm Still Here," sung by Yvonne De Carlo in the role of the Gloria Swanson-like Carlotta Campion, is a masterpiece of combined thematic statement and character delineation. "Broadway Baby" was sung by Ethel Shutta; "Who's That Woman" by Mary McCarty and company; "The Story of Lucy and Jessie" by Alexis Smith (Jessie).

Sondheim had never been happy with the original cast recording, and late in 1985 he oversaw a new production of *Follies* which ran for only two nights in Los Angeles. That production's original cast recording, with Lee Remick as Jessie and Carol Burnett playing Lucy, was released in 1986.

With *A Little Night Music* (February 25, 1973), Sondheim became the first artist to receive Tonys as the year's top composer and lyricist for three years in succession. In *Stereo Review*, Rex Reed called this score Sondheim's "most ambitiously conceived and richly creative work to date." An enchanting idyll, though subtly ironic and consistently urbane, it was based on *Smiles of a Summer Night,* the classic, lighthearted Ingmar Bergman film. (The title of *A Little Night Music* was taken from Mozart's orchestral serenade, *Eine kleine Nachtmusik.*) Hugh Wheeler was the author of the book and

Harold Prince the director. The setting is Sweden; the time, the turn of the century; the plot, a tangled web of amatory involvements. A middle-aged lawyer is married to a child bride who has remained a virgin after eleven months of marriage. The lawyer's son is secretly in love with her, though he is the household maid's romantic interest. The lawyer finds sexual consolation with his ex-mistress, an actress, to the consternation of her hussar lover. These complications are eventually straightened out with the help of a dowager, the actress's mother.

Lightness of mood was sustained throughout this "waltz musical," all of whose musical numbers were in 3/4 waltz time. The score for the pit orchestra was for strings and woodwinds only. A five-voice chorus (three women and two men) sang the overture, and returned intermittently to comment on the action. Sondheim described his principal numbers as "inner monologue songs," because each expressed the innermost thoughts and emotions of the character in isolation from the other players. This show provided Sondheim's most successful song, "Send in the Clowns," an aging actress's lament for lost romantic possibilities. Introduced by Glynis Johns, it was awarded a Grammy as song of the year (a Grammy also went to the original cast album), and in 1977 "Send in the Clowns" became a top-ten hit record for Judy Collins. Barbra Streisand recorded it, with some new lyrics by Sondheim, in 1985. Two other outstanding songs from *Night Music* were "Liaisons," sung by Hermione Gingold, and "The Miller's Son," by D. Jamin-Bartlett.

Reviewing the show in *The New York Times,* John S. Wilson called Sondheim's lyrics "a body of work that has depth, range and consistency far beyond that of any previous lyric writer for the Broadway theater. . . . He is, in effect, a summation and an elevation of all the lyric writing that has gone before him." In recognition of the significance of the lyrics, the original cast recording contains a lyric sheet, the inclusion of which is a rarity for show albums.

With a run of 601 performances, *A Little Night Music* won a Tony for best score and received the New York Drama Critics Circle Award as the year's best musical. Since 1973 it has been revived throughout the country, including presentations by the Michigan Opera Theatre in 1983 and the Wolf Trap Opera in Virginia in 1984. The disastrous 1978 motion picture adaptation starring Elizabeth Taylor, who sang "Send in the Clowns," and with Len Cariou and Hermione Gingold from the stage production, was withdrawn soon after its premiere.

Recognition of Sondheim's eminence was made official by a testimonial at the Shubert Theatre, New York City, on March 11, 1973. Entitled *Sondheim: A Musical Tribute,* and staged for the benefit of the National Hemophilia Foundation, this was a four-hour performance of more than 40 Sondheim theater songs, 29 of which were released later in 1973 as a live LP.

About this time, Sondheim composed incidental music for *The Enclave,* a play by Laurents, which opened Off Broadway on November 15, 1973. He also composed the background music for the French director Alain Resnais's film, *Stavisky* (1974), whose soundtrack was released by RCA.

Sondheim's next Broadway musical, *Pacific Overtures* (January 11, 1976), departed even more from Broadway musical traditions than his previous efforts had. John Weidman's text (with additional material by Hugh Wheeler) attempted to merge the Broadway musical with Japanese Kabuki theater. It dealt with the Westernization of Japan following the arrival of Commodore Perry in 1853 on an American trade mission. The subject of the first act is Old World Japan, an isolated island, but proud of its ancient history, heritage and customs, and wary of the changes that might be wrought by Perry's arrival. In the second act Japan is transformed by Americanization. As in Kabuki, *Pacific Overtures* used an all-male cast (with men playing women), most of whom were either Asian or Asian-American. Also, a narrator of Kabuki tradition was employed, and supplementing the pit orchestra was a Japanese trio who performed native music. Haiku chants, Japanese choreography, Boris Aronson's screens and sets, and Florence Klotz's costuming all provided additional Oriental accents.

Sondheim's, and director Prince's, artistic ambitions received praise from critics, but opinion was sharply divided on the question of whether they had successfully reconciled the theatrical styles of different cultures. Clive Barnes of *The New York Times* said, "It tries to soar—sometimes it only floats, sometimes it actually sinks—but it tries to soar." Frank Rich wrote that "Sondheim and Prince didn't seem comfortable with the musical play form in *Pacific Overtures.* Aspiring to write a Rodgers-Hammerstein musical, they and the librettist John Weidman fractured the book's narrative to the point of confusing the audience. And as they floundered in dramatic limbo, they seemed to be scrambling for subject matter. How many times could they tell an audience that . . . everyday is a little death? In *Pacific Overtures* . . . they turned to political themes—cultural imperialism, class

warfare—but dramatized them with pessimistic variations on Rodgers and Hammerstein's old liberal bromides."

The Tony awards ignored *Overtures* completely, and public apathy forced a closing after 206 performances although the New York Drama Critics Circle chose it as the year's best musical. It was revived Off Broadway in 1984.

There was, however, virtually unanimous praise for the originality and daring of Sondheim's music. William Glover of the Associated Press found it to be "his most interesting [score] to date, combining Oriental tonal colors, rhythms and instruments that do not alienate the Western show-tune ear." Another critic wrote, "It is astonishing with what easy assurance he creates words and music in new, essentially experimental, and provocatively discussable forms." One of the outstanding numbers in the score, one that is a particular favorite of Sondheim's, is "Someone in a Tree," sung by a quartet. The entire score was recorded in an original cast album.

An interlude between Sondheim's musical plays, *Side by Side by Sondheim* (April 17, 1977) was a two-act revue, conceived by David Kernan, which had originated in London as an informal evening's entertainment. With the London cast of four, it brought to the Music Box Theatre in Manhattan 30 of Sondheim's theatrical numbers. All lyrics were by Sondheim, and so was most of the music. "This is a dream of a show," reported Clive Barnes. "It is the essential Sondheim. It places him—more confidently perhaps than any of the individual musicals—as the master lyricist of American popular music, and one of the two or three most interesting theater composers around."

For the Prince-directed *Sweeney Todd* (March 1, 1979), Sondheim wrote a score of operatic dimensions; in fact, he had originally conceived it as an opera. Based on Christopher Bond's 1973 version of an 1847 English melodrama, text by Hugh Wheeler, *Sweeney Todd* was of the Grand Guignol horror story genre, but its sardonic humor and elements of Dickensian social commentary reminded critics of Brecht and Weill's *Threepenny Opera.* The pseudonymous Sweeney Todd, once the "the demon barber of Fleet Street," returns to 19th-century London after 15 years in an Australian prison, to which he had been consigned by a lecherous judge who wanted Todd's wife. When the vengeful Todd fails in his attempt to decapitate the judge with his barber's razor, he enters into an arrangement with Mrs. Lovett, a baker of meat pies, whereby he can avenge himself on all humanity—slitting the throat of each of his clients and then dis-

patching the body by chute to the basement below where Mrs. Lovett grinds it for her meat
pies.

Three-quarters of this text was set to music
that was a complete network of recitatives, ballads, patter songs, set pieces, and choral numbers. The musical opened and closed with "The
Ballad of Sweeney Todd," sung by Len Cariou
with chorus and supplementary voices; it was
also heard intermittently as a theme. Other musical highlights were "Green Finch and Linnet
Bird," sung by Sarah Rice; "By the Sea," by Angela Lansbury; "Pretty Women," a duet for Len
Cariou and Edmund Lyndeck; "My Friends," a
Cariou solo; and "Johanna," a solo for Victor
Gerber. Richard Eder of *The New York Times*
found that "the musical and dramatic achievements of Stephen Sondheim's black and bloody
Sweeney Todd are so numerous and so clamor-
ous that they trample and jam one another in
that invisible but finite doorway that connects a
stage and its audience, doing themselves both
some harm in the process." But he concluded
that the failures were those "of an extraordinary,
fascinating and often ravishingly lovely effort."
Newsweek found *Sweeney Todd* to be "brilliant,
even sensationally so, but its effect is very much
a barrage of brilliancies, like flares fired aloft
that dazzle and fade into something cold and
dark."

At the box office, *Sweeney Todd* ran for 557
performances, and it won six Tony awards, including one for Sondheim for best musical score.
The Drama Desk, an association of New York
drama reporters, editors and critics, chose it as
the season's best musical. The two-disc original
cast album earned a Grammy. *Sweeney Todd*
was produced by the Houston Grand Opera in
June 1984 and by the New York City Opera the
following October.

Late in 1980, 16 Sondheim songs that had
been discarded from his musicals before reaching Broadway were assembled in an Off Broadway collage called *Marry Me a Little.* Three
songs from Sondheim's first musical, *Saturday
Night,* were resurrected, including the one that
provided this revue a title. After composing the
background music for *Reds* (1981), a film directed by and starring Warren Beatty, Sondheim
suffered a severe setback on Broadway with
Merrily We Roll Along (November 16, 1981),
which folded after just 16 performances. Directed by Prince, *Merrily We Roll Along* was George
Furth's musical stage adaptation of a 1935
George S. Kaufman-Moss Hart play. Told in re-
verse chronology, and thus beginning with emptiness and disenchantment and ending with
doomed youthful idealism, *Merrily* was about a

team of Broadway songwriters and the wages of
their success—moral corruption. Fortunately,
despite the show's early demise, an original cast
album was released, preserving three significant
Sondheim songs: "Old Friends," introduced by
Ann Morrison with two others; "Not a Day Goes
By," a ballad of unrequited love sung by Jim
Watson; and "Good Thing Going," sung by Lon-
ny Price.

Whereas *Merrily We Roll Along,* with its in-
gratiating show tunes, was fairly conventional
musical theater, *Sunday in the Park with
George*—which opened Off Broadway on July
6, 1983 and on Broadway on May 2, 1984, with
book and direction by James Lapine—was a concept musical. With a minimum of either plot or
characterization, and with little dance, *Sunday
in the Park with George* focused attention on the
creation of an epoch-making work of art:
Georges Seurat's *La Grande Jatte.* In the theater,
that impressionist canvas, through ingenious
lighting and staging, came to life piece by piece
and character by character before the eyes of the
audience at the end of Act I. The second act
leaps one century ahead to the career dilemma
of George, who may be Seurat's great-grandson,
a noted maker of multimedia conceptual artworks. An American artist, George is wracked by
self-doubt and pressured by the marketplace of
the current art scene, which is shown to be no
less ruled by Mammon than is Broadway.

"In his paintings a century ago, Georges Seurat demanded that the world look at art in a
shocking new way," wrote Rich. "In *Sunday in
the Park with George* . . . Stephen Sondheim
and . . . James Lapine demand that an audience radically change its whole way of looking
at the Broadway musical. [They] have created an
audacious, haunting and, in its own intensely
personal way, touching work. Even when it
fails—as it does on occasion—*Sunday in the
Park* is setting the stage for even more sustained
theatrical innovations yet to come." An original
cast recording was released, containing two
songs that may become Sondheim standards,
"Finishing the Hat," introduced by Mandy Pa-
timkin, and "Move On," by Bernadette Peters.
That recording was awarded a Grammy in 1985,
when the musical received the Pulitzer Prize in
drama. Previously, *Sunday in the Park* had been
the choice of the New York Drama Critics Circle
and the Drama Desk as the season's best musical.

Sondheim never composes a song until the
script for a musical is completed. "I like writing
within parameters," he told Samuel G. Freedman in an interview for *The New York Times
Magazine.* "I love for the playwright to create
the characters, and then for me to explore them

as if I were an actor. What I do is interpret and create simultaneously." Sondheim also elaborated on his compositional methods: "I take a huge amount of notes on songs, both musically and lyrically, so that by the time I start composing, I have so much to draw on. I always start with at least half a page of what the character should be talking about, or the things I want to bring out in the song. . . . Then comes the winnowing-down process of how much can this song take. . . . A refrain or an opening line will often suggest a melodic idea which I will then go the piano and test. About 40 percent of the time it's something somebody else has written. And then every now and then—the other 60 percent—it's something to build on. That's one way a song happens. The other way it happens is to sit at the piano with a page of dialogue that I'm trying to work the song into—along with any notes I may have—and just kind of read or hear music and start to fiddle at the piano until something occurs to me. It might be punctuation or some under-scoring. And often in those punctuations will come a suggestion of a whole musical atmo-sphere. And once you have a musical atmo-sphere—which could be anything from a running figure to a chord change—you have a way to start some melodic ideas. They're not re-lated to a conscious lyrical phrase, but it gives you a basic melodic rhythm and that can [be in-troduced] into other things."

Sondheim, a bachelor, resides in a townhouse on East 49th Street in New York. The walls of his study are lined floor-to-ceiling with book-shelves filled with phonographs records, which he collects. He owns about 10,000 recordings of all musical forms except opera, but confines his listening usually to 20th-century music. This room includes Sondheim's crowded but well-ordered desk, a recording apparatus, and a piano over which hangs a collection of happy birthday songs composed for him by Leonard Bernstein.

When he entertains friends, Sondheim uses his living room, at one end of which stands a grand piano. The furnishings also include such oddities as a skittle-billiard table, a verillon (which he de-scribes as looking "somewhat like a box of musi-cal beer glasses, and is") a chess set, and wall literally covered from floor to ceiling with dif-ferent kinds of games.

Sondheim's love of games verges on obsession and he has managed to collect a veritable muse-um, including the Games of the Goose, Transfor-mation Cards, Lotto Dauphin, Sky Jump and a musical game in which players move notes and clefs on a sheet of music. (Sondheim's apartment is thought to have inspired the Anthony Shaffer play *Sleuth*.) "I just like to play games," Sond-

heim has explained. "I don't really care about winning or losing." The game that absorbs him most is anagrams. Sondheim is also the creator of what have been described as "maddening, di-abolical crossword puzzles" which have been published in *New York* magazine. An aficionado of murder mysteries, he collaborated with his friend Anthony Perkins on the screenplay for *The Last of Sheila* (1973), a mystery thriller in which a parlor game aboard a yacht on the Rivi-era held clues for the solving of a murder.

Sondheim was elected to the Theatre Hall of Fame in New York in 1982 and to the American Academy and Institute of Arts and Letters in 1983. In 1983 RCA released a two-disc album, *A Stephen Sondheim Evening,* a collection of his most famous recorded music together with num-bers from shows never recorded and songs dropped from productions before they opened on Broadway.

ABOUT: Rockwell, J. All American Music: Composition in the Late Twentieth Century, 1983; Wilk, M. They're Singing Our Song, 1973; Zadan, C. Sondheim & Company, 1974. *Periodicals*—Atlantic December 1984; Newsweek, April 23, 1973, October 29, 1984; New York Times Magazine, April 1, 1984, October 21, 1984.

SPRINGSTEEN, BRUCE (September 23, 1949–). Composer-lyricist Bruce Springsteen achieved stardom in 1975, at a time when rock music had become both cynical and stagnant. Springsteen was, though, in the words of his bi-ographer, Dave Marsh, "the last of rock's great innocents." By the end of that decade, "The Boss," as he is affectionately called by fans and fellow musicians, had become rock and roll's foremost statesman. In the mid-1970s Spring-steen sang passionately about rock's traditional subjects—young love, cars, guitars and beating the trap of the nine-to-five grind. In doing so he paved the way for the "punk" and "new wave" musicians of the late 1970s who helped to revive the rock scene. His music, wrote James Will-werth in *Time* (October 27, 1975), represents "a regeneration, a renewal of rock. . . . [It] is pri-mal, directly in touch with all the impulses of wild humor and glancing melancholy, street tragedy and punk anarchy that made rock the distinctive voice of a generation." In the 1980s, however, Springsteen's music and lyrics deep-ened as he sang about the shattered dreams of common working people in post-industrial America, spinning naturalistic tales that have made him an American folk hero in the manner of Bob Dylan, Woody Guthrie and Hank Wil-liams.

BRUCE SPRINGSTEEN

Bruce Springsteen was born on September 23, 1949 in Freehold, New Jersey, 18 miles from Asbury Park, a once fashionable but now dismal beach town that Springsteen immortalized in songs like "Fourth of July, Asbury Park (Sandy)" and "Backstreets." He was the oldest of the three children (two girls and a boy) of Douglas and Adele (Zirelli) Springsteen. His father, whose ancestry is Irish and Dutch, through the years worked as a factory laborer and prison guard but was mainly a bus driver. He was often out of work, with the burden of supporting the family thrown on his wife, a secretary. Though close to his mother, Springsteen fought, sometimes bitterly, with his father throughout adolescence.

Bruce attended a local parochial school. He was a loner who had few friends and did poorly in his studies. "I lived half of my first 13 years in a trance or something," he has recalled. "People thought I was weird." Rock 'n' roll relieved the drabness of his typical small-town working-class upbringing. He was galvanized by Elvis Presley's first appearance on *The Ed Sullivan Show,* after which his mother purchased him a guitar. Detesting the formal lessons his mother insisted on, he abandoned the guitar until 1963, when he bought a secondhand $18 instrument. He learned to play by himself after a cousin taught him a few basic chords. He also taught himself to play the harmonica and the piano, and suddenly rock music became an all-absorbing passion. "If I hadn't found music, I don't know what I would have done," he said. As Springsteen told Marsh, the author of *Born to Run* (1979), "The first day I can remember looking in a mirror and being able to stand what I

was seeing was the day I had a guitar in my hand."

While in high school he formed his first band, the Castiles, who became good enough to play in a popular Greenwich Village nightspot, the Cafe Wha. The Castiles mostly covered pop hits like "My Generation" and "Double Shot of My Baby's Love," but Springsteen was already writing performable originals. When he graduated from high school, the Castiles broke up and he enrolled in Ocean City County Community College, dropping out after a few months to concentrate on music.

In 1969 his family moved to California, but Bruce stayed in Freehold, forming one band after another. Those bands, whose names changed as often as their personnel, played wherever they could—at parties, clubs and firemen's balls, trailer parks, drive-in movies during intermissions, in parking lots at shopping centers and at prisons. In 1969 he and his best-known group of this period, Steel Mill, appeared at Bill Graham's Fillmore West in San Francisco. But Springsteen was soon back East again in Greenwich Village cafés and jamming on weekends at the Upstage, a club and musician's hangout in Asbury Park.

For the development of his music, Springsteen's confinement to New York and the Jersey Shore was a blessing in disguise. According to Jon Landau, the former rock critic who eventually became Springsteen's producer and manager, "For 12 years, Bruce had the time to learn to play every kind of rock and roll. He has far more depth than most rock artists because he really had roots in a place—coastal Jersey, where no record company scouts ever went." As Marsh said, "Absorbing styles and influences that were too quickly forgotten in the music industry centers, Springsteen became not so much a human jukebox as a human synthesizer, with an enormous repertoire of songs, influences, bits and pieces picked up from almost anything heard on radio. He built his songs on guitar lines and hit records of vague memory, which gave his most original songs an immediately familiar quality."

In 1972 Springsteen was introduced to Mike Appel, a rock producer who became his manager. Appel, in turn, brought Springsteen to John Hammond, the legendary executive at Columbia Records who had discovered Billie Holiday, Aretha Franklin, and Bob Dylan. Springsteen's song, "It's Hard to Be a Saint in the City," which the composer performed for Hammond, won him over completely. "The kid absolutely knocked me out," Hammond told *Newsweek* (October 27, 1975). "I only hear somebody really good once every ten years, and not only was Bruce the best, he was a lot better than Dylan when I first heard *him*." Within a week, Columbia Records signed Springsteen to a contract. His first album, coproduced by Appel and Jim Cretecos, was *Greetings from Asbury Park, New Jersey* (1972), which contained "Saint in the City" and his first single, "Blinded by the Light."

A composer of poetic, narrative ballads, many of which, like "Growin' Up," were autobiographical, Springsteen was now carefully groomed by CBS Records in the folk-rock image of Bob Dylan. Largely because of that image-building, *Greetings* was badly misproduced. Although Springsteen had recruited a superb group of musicians—most of whom were to form the core of his famed E Street Band—for studio sessions, Appel and Columbia executives saw to it that the band sound was submerged. As a result the record was misconceived, making Springsteen sound like either a tentative rock 'n' roller or an earnest but musically confused singer-songwriter.

Though generally well received by critics, the album was at first a commercial failure. Many disc jockeys were turned off by CBS's "New Dylan" hype and refused to give the album air time. For lack of such exposure, all it could initially sell was some 35,000 copies.

Springsteen's second album, issued in the late fall of 1973, was *The Wild, The Innocent and the E Street Shuffle,* with solid backing by the E Street Band. Containing such Springsteen standards as "Sandy," "Rosalita," "E Street Shuffle," and "Incident on 57th Street," the record was lavishly praised by critics. *Rolling Stone* named it one of the best albums of the year, but it, too, did not sell at first. Regarded in some quarters as just another would-be New Dylan, Springsteen began making headway with live performances, touring almost nonstop for two years with the E Street Band and electrifying audiences in small auditoriums and clubs in Eastern seaboard cities. Slowly, he developed an intense cult following of fans who had been galvanized by his stage histrionics, his hortatory, high-voltage vocalizations, and his sweat-drenched two-and-a-half-hour shows. In Cambridge, Massachusetts in April 1974, he was heard by Jon Landau, the record review editor of *Rolling Stone,* who later wrote in a Boston paper: "*I saw rock and roll future and its name is Bruce Springsteen. . . .* He made me feel like I was hearing music for the first time."

It was rumored that CBS was not planning to renew Springsteen's contract but, encouraged by such an accolade, Columbia promoted Springsteen as "the future of rock 'n' roll." His first two albums now began to inch their way up the charts. Meanwhile, Springsteen went into the

studio to record his third, make-it-or-break-it, LP. It was an agonizing process, for Springsteen is a perfectionist, and the work he had started in early 1974 was not finished until the summer of 1975. One week before the album was released, Springsteen appeared at the Bottom Line, a prestigious club in Greenwich Village, drawing ecstatic crowds and rave reviews from the rock press. "It's the most exciting rock 'n' roll show I've ever seen," one disc jockey told his listeners after the performance. When released, this third album, *Born to Run,* was proclaimed "an instant [rock 'n' roll] classic," to quote Marsh.

It took Springsteen three months alone to record "Born to Run," the LP's top-20 single, a four-and-a-half-minute hard-rock narrative about the desperation, and the attempt to transcend it, of two young lovers in a big city which is a "death trap" and "suicide rap." The refrain declares that "tramps like you and me, baby, we were born to run." These pure rock numbers encompass a typical summer day in the life of a New Jersey man-boy, beginning with "Thunder Road," which introduces "the Kid," a leather-jacketed "punk" or romantic rebel in the mold of James Dean or young Marlon Brando. The other standout cuts were the anthemic "Backstreets,"; "Tenth Avenue Freeze-Out," a musical history of the E Street Band; "She's the One," a hybrid of Buddy Holly rock and Phil Spector's "wall-of-sound" production values; and "Jungleland," a miniaturized rock opera set in Harlem.

With Jon Landau now the coproducer with Appel and Springsteen, *Born to Run* had an advance sale of 350,000 copies, a figure that approached the million mark within a few months. Springsteen suddenly became a superstar when, on October 27, 1975, both *Time* and *Newsweek* ran cover stories on him. Success brought him his first home, a modest cottage overlooking the ocean near Asbury Park, which he shared with his two principal possessions, his record collection and a customized yellow '57 Chevrolet convertible.

To promote *Born to Run,* Springsteen and the E Street Band embarked on a two-month national tour. Now something of a rock legend, Springsteen insisted on playing only in comparatively small auditoriums where the intimacy and acoustics enhanced the band's hard-edged sound. This was followed by a four-city tour of Europe and, in 1976, by a jaunt through the American South and Midwest.

The three-year hiatus between Springsteen's third and fourth albums was the result of a lengthy, bitterly contested lawsuit which in the end enabled Springsteen to free himself permanently of Appel and allowed Landau to produce his albums and manage his career. Despite the rumors that the long layoff had damaged Springsteen's career, his album *Darkness On the Edge of Town* (1979) was a critical and commercial triumph, as was the 80-city cross-country tour that followed its release. The album's standout numbers include the title song, "Badlands," "Prove it All Night," "The Promised Land" and "Factory."

With *The River,* a two-disc LP issued in 1980, Springsteen reaffirmed his status as a rock superstar. As Sam Sutherland wrote in *High Fidelity:* "In *The River* he has done nothing less than summarize and extend the best features of his past work, fitting them into a brilliant conceptual framework. What makes that sense of formal purpose work is the seeming informality of the music. . . . These new songs often sound playful, off-the-cuff, or even relaxed. Yet underneath the restored exuberance of its up-tempo rockers and the spare, low-keyed ache of its introspective ballads lies a steady heartbeat. . . . *The River* is not only Bruce Springsteen's most persuasive gospel but one of the most satisfying and mature rock testaments in memory." The leading numbers were "Hungry Heart" "Cadillac Ranch"; "The Price You Pay"; "Something in the Night"; "Point Blank"; "Fade Away"; "Independence Day" and the title song, a ballad about an unemployed steel-worker whose marriage is falling apart. *The River* sold more than a million copies and "Hungry Heart" became Springsteen's first single to make the national top ten.

Following the first of four sold-out appearances at Madison Square Garden on November 27, 1980, John Rockwell wrote in *The New York Times:* "There are many things that make Mr. Springsteen the finest performer in rock music. Perhaps above all is the positive nature of what he conveys to his fans. His ultimate message is affirmative, a vision of the promised land right there just beyond his grasp. And the way he proposes to reach that land is through the joyous energy of rock and roll."

For *Nebraska* (1982) Springsteen temporarily foreswore the accompaniment of the E Street Band for an acoustic guitar and harmonica. Released at the peak of the 1981–82 recession, this starkly beautiful album is the bleakest of Springsteen's creations. It is a series of low-key country-folkish vignettes set in a small town populated by workers who must deal with complex father-son relationships, falling crop prices, faithless lovers, gambling debts, death and unemployment. *Nebraska's* finest cuts are "My Father's House"; "Open All Night"; "Atlantic City"; "Mansion on the Hill"; "Reason to Believe" and the title song.

Springsteen and the E Street Band addressed similar themes on *Born in the U.S.A.* (1984), which soared to the top of the LP charts. By the summer of 1985 this album had become Columbia's all-time bestseller with American sales of more than 7,500,000 units. The single "Dancing in the Dark" also hit number one on the charts. The album also contained five other singles that made the top ten: three rockers, "Cover Me," "Born in the U.S.A" and "Glory Days"; a spare, simple mid-tempo tune, "I'm on Fire," and the moving "My Hometown." Other gems on the album are the rollicking "I'm Goin' Down" and the rockabilly "Working on the Highway." The lyrical centerpiece, though, is "Born in the U.S. A.," the apotheosis of Springsteen's principal themes since *The River.*

As Stephen Holden wrote in *The New York Times,* this album "teems with characters and incidents related to a common theme—the decline of small-town working-class life in a post-industrial society. Mr. Springsteen's music, however, evokes not only the crushing humiliations and defeats of unemployment and a sense of economic hopelessness, it also suggests the courage and humor working people and laborers can muster in spite of the odds against them. Yet for all the exhilaration and energy in the album's songs about joy rides, high school memories and friendship, *Born in the U.S.A.* is a sad and serious album about the end of the American dream—of economic hope and security and of community—for a dwindling segment of our society. . . . Forged from the simple vernaculars of blues, folk, country and gospel, . . . hard Saturday night party music for the common people wasn't invented to help examine the hard realities of life but to find a release from those realities. [Springsteen] has transfused rock and roll and social realism into one another, and the compassion and the surging brawn of his music make his very despairing vision of American life into a kind of celebration."

In January 1985 "Dancing in the Dark" received the American Music Award as the year's most successful pop single. Its B side is "Pink Cadillac," one of Springsteen's more humorous songs, with its 1950s-sounding saxophone-dominated arrangement. "Shut Out the Light," about the experiences of a Vietnam veteran upon his return to home and wife, had been intended for, but was deleted from, *Born in the U.S.A.* It was released in 1984 as the flip side of the single version of the title cut.

Springsteen made an extensive tour of the United States in 1984 when he was heard by more than one million people. That fall, during the presidential campaign, Ronald Reagan said in Hammonton, New Jersey, "America's future rests in a thousand dreams inside your hearts. It rests in the message of hope in songs of a man so many young Americans admire, New Jersey's Bruce Springsteen." That many of Springsteen's best songs of the 1980s have been downbeat, reflecting the blighting of common people's lives in post-industrial America, imbued the president's words with a stark irony that was not lost on Springsteen's admirers. When Walter F. Mondale countered by saying he had won Springsteen's endorsement, Springsteen found himself embraced by both of the major presidential candidates.

In 1985 Springsteen was awarded a Grammy as best rock male vocalist. Later that year, on May 13, 1985, at Lake Oswego, a suburb of Portland, Oregon, he married Julianne Phillips, an actress and model.

ABOUT: Current Biography, 1978; Gambaccini, P. Bruce Springsteen, 1985; Marsh, D. Born to Run: The Bruce Springsteen Story, 1979. Periodicals—Commonweal August 12, 1983; Nation October 6, 1984; Newsweek October 27, 1975, June 15, 1984, August 27, 1984; People September 3, 1984; Rolling Stone August 2, 1984, August 16, 1984, December 6, 1984, February 28, 1985, March 14, 1985; Time October 27, 1975.

STERN, JOSEPH W. (January 11, 1870–March 31, 1934) and **MARKS, EDWARD B.** (1865–December 1944). Composer Joseph W. Stern and lyricist Edward B. Marks wrote some of the most successful sentimental ballads of the 1890s. In the first decades of the 20th century they ran one of the leading music publishing firms of the day. Neither man was musically trained. As Marks revealed in his autobiography, *They All Sang*, "Joe could play the piano with one hand and fake with the other like nobody's business, but he hadn't fooled around with the music end of the game. . . . I don't play any instrument and I can carry a tune a little farther than [the race horse] Equipoise can carry the Empire State Building."

Joseph W. Stern was born in New York City in 1870. His father was part owner of a prosperous necktie manufacturing company, and Joseph was born to affluence. He attended city public schools before taking a job as a traveling salesman for his father's company.

While on the road, he met Edward Bennett Marks, a salesman of hooks and eyes and whalebone. Born in Troy, New York in 1865, Marks attended public schools in Troy and New York City before enrolling in the College of the City of New York. From boyhood on, he had loved to compose in verse. "Where there was a wed-

JOSEPH W. STERN

ding or birthday party in the family I used to write rhymes for the occasion," he revealed. "Sometimes I even won little prizes for verses."

Marks wrote his first song lyrics in the early 1890s at the request of Polly Holmes, an Irish comedienne in vaudeville. His "Since McManus Went Down to the Track" (music by George Rosenberg), about a horse-playing bricklayer, was introduced by Holmes at Tony Pastor's Music Hall in Union Square. While working as a traveling salesman, Marks also wrote the lyrics for "Break the News to Mother, Gently" and "I'd Live Life Over in the Same Old Way" (music to both by Will H. Fox); both were published, both were failures.

Marks's first song success was "December and May" (music by William Lorraine), about the love of an elderly bachelor for a young girl. This was one of the earliest "December-May" songs in American popular music. Published in 1893, it was introduced that year by Lydia Yeamans at Tony Pastor's and acquired a permanent place in her repertory for the next quarter of a century.

Marks and Stern were marooned in a hotel in Mamaroneck, New York during a rainstorm when they chanced upon a news item about a lost child. Wandering the city streets, the child was found by a policeman who turned out to be her long-lost father. Their instincts telling them that this human-interest melodrama had the making of a salable song, Marks and Stern quickly wrote the words and music of "The Little Lost Child" on the piano in the hotel parlor. Once the ballad was committed to paper, Marks persuaded Stern to join him in forming a publishing firm

EDWARD B. MARKS

to issue the ballad. On an investment of $100 they rented an office basement in a building on 14th Street and Second Avenue in Manhattan, acquired a second-hand desk and chair, made a small deposit with a printing firm, and christened their venture Joseph W. Stern & Company. Though the two men were equal partners, Marks had omitted his name because he feared that his co-ownership of the company would put his job as a salesman in jeopardy.

The day the printer delivered the sheet music to their office, Della Fox, a vaudevillian, dropped in seeking new material for her act. She introduced "The Little Lost Child" in vaudeville, but the song was popularized by Lottie Gilson, who, in her vaudeville performance, was always compelled by audience enthusiasm to repeat the refrain again and again.

About this time a Brooklyn electrician developed a technique for flashing still pictures on a motion picture screen. With the help of William Fox, then running a slide exchange on 14th Street, slides were used at the Grand Opera House on 23rd Street to illustrate the story of "The Little Lost Child." The words of the song were shown beneath the photos so that audiences could sing along. This was the first time a song had been promoted in this manner, and it helped "Little Lost Child" become one of the most widely performed sentimental ballads of the decade. Millions of copies of sheet music were sold, assuring the success of Joseph W. Stern & Company and enabling the two partners to quit their jobs as salesmen and devote themselves full time to the writing and publishing of songs.

To promote their fledgling business, Stern and

Marks made use of their experience as salesmen by going on the road several times each year to market their ballads. They published the songs of other writers and issued their own compositions as well. In 1894 they composed and published "His Last Thoughts Were of You," which Minnie Schulte introduced at George Huber's Prospect Garden Music Hall and which later was featured prominently in vaudeville by Lottie Gilson. In 1895 they wrote another popular number, "No One Ever Loved More Than I."

One day in 1895 Stern and Marks dined at a German restaurant on 21st Street with Meyer Cohen, a popular singer of ballads. At a nearby table, two rude men insulted a waitress until she burst into tears and exclaimed, "My Mother was a lady! You wouldn't dare to insult me if my brother Jack were only here." Cohen told the songwriters that this episode was material for a ballad. In Marks's lyrics for "My Mother was a Lady" the rude salesman later discovers that the waitress is the sister of his best friend and, in atonement, offers to marry her. Lottie Gilson introduced the ballad at Proctor's 58th Street Theatre in 1896 and went on to popularize it in vaudeville theaters around the country. Several million copies of sheet music were sold, and the phrase, "My mother was a lady," became a popular expression of the day.

In 1896 Stern and Marks enlarged their operations, acquiring larger quarters for their firm at East 20th Street, where they now had a reception room in which songwriters could play compositions for performers in search of new material. Stern and Marks broke new ground by becoming the first publishers to issue their songs both in piano copies and in orchestrations, a practice that enhanced the opportunities for the performance of their songs. Among the most popular of their own ballads, which they also published, were "Games We Used to Play" and "I Don't Blame You, Tom," both introduced by Gilson. Among their other ballads in the 1890s were "Teacher and the Boy," "The Old Postmaster" and "Don't Wear Your Heart on Your Sleeve."

With the beginning of the 20th century, Stern and Marks abandoned songwriting to devote themselves to publishing. In 1920, Stern retired and Marks bought out his interest. Stern died at his home in Brightwater, Long Island 14 years later.

Marks remained active as a publisher, and renamed his firm, the Edward B. Marks & Company. In the 1930s he served on President Roosevelt's council for the coordination of industry in 1935 and 1936 and, later, on commissions for fair trade practice. He also completed two autobiographical books, *They All Sang* and *They All Had Glamour*. Marks spent his last year in retirement at his home in Great Neck, Long Island.

ABOUT: Ewen, D. The Life and Death of Tin Pan Alley, 1964; Marks, E. B. They All Had Glamour, 1944, They All Sang, 1934.

STROUSE, CHARLES (June 7, 1928–) and **ADAMS, LEE** (August 14, 1924–). Composer Charles Louis Strouse was born in New York City, the youngest of the three children of Ira and Ethel (Newman) Strouse. His father was an executive at a cigar-tobacco factory, and his mother was a trained pianist. After graduating from Manhattan's P. S. 87 in 1941, Strouse attended Townsend Harris High School for two years before transferring to De Witt Clinton High, from which he graduated in 1944. He took his first piano lesson when he was nine, but did not become interested in the instrument until a few years later when he studied jazz piano with Abraham Sokolow. Nevertheless by the time he was 14 Strouse was on his way to becoming an accomplished jazz pianist. He was 13 when he started writing songs, his first composition being "Welcome Home, Able-Bodied Seaman Strouse," honoring his brother who was home on leave from the Navy on the eve of World War II.

In addition to jazz, Strouse's main interests in high school, where he was an unexceptional student, were athletics (especially baseball) and girls. But he was also developing a yen to write music for the theater, and so entered the University of Rochester, where he could combine academic studies with musical training at the affiliated Eastman School of Music. Attending the Eastman School marked Strouse's transition from jazz to concert music. He studied harmony and composition, and graduated from Rochester with a bachelor of music degree in 1947. Strouse then sent samples of music he had composed to Aaron Copland, who arranged for Strouse to attend the Berkshire Music Center at Tanglewood, Massachusetts on a scholarship. There he spent the summers of 1950 and 1952 studying compositon with Copland, and some of his own compositions were performed for the first time.

At this time Strouse earned his living by playing the piano in a cocktail lounge and for the television series, *The Goldbergs*, providing the music for the show's characters when one of them was called upon to perform. He also scored and composed the background music for motion picture newsreels and composed music for dance bands.

LEE ADAMS

At Copland's suggestion Strouse spent the summer of 1951 in France studying composition with Nadia Boulanger. When he played some of his works for her, Boulanger suggested that he concentrate on popular music rather than concert compositions. Nonetheless Strouse returned to the United States and studied composition for two years with Arthur Berger and David Diamond. While studying with Berger and Diamond, Strouse became friends with Lee Adams, a young writer for radio whom he had met at a cocktail party in 1950, and they began playing popular music together.

Lyricist Lee Richard Adams was born in Mansfield, Ohio, the son of Dr. Leopold Adams, a physician who had emigrated from Germany as a child and Florence (Ellis) Adams. Adams has recalled that he "had a truly Norman Rockwell boyhood and youth." He graduated from Mansfield High School in 1942 and enrolled in Ohio State University, but left Columbus in 1943 to enlist in the Army. For the next three years Adams served in the 14th Armored Division, European Theater of Operations. After his discharge from the service he returned to Ohio State, earning a bachelor's degree in journalism in 1949. He then entered the School of Journalism at Columbia University and received a master's degree in 1950. That year Adams was hired as a copy editor for *Pageant* magazine. He also wrote articles for *Pageant* and contributed material to New York City radio programs.

Though Adams and Strouse had met in 1950, it was not until 1955 that they began writing songs together. Their collaboration took place at Green Mansions, an adult summer camp in the

CHARLES STROUSE

Adirondack Mountains where stage productions were mounted each week. Strouse had begun writing music for these shows the previous summer, and he secured a place for Adams on the entertainment staff in 1955. Consequently, they decided to become professional popular tunesmiths. They placed a song in the Broadway revue *Catch a Star!* (basic score by Sammy Fain), which lasted just 23 performances in 1955. A few of the numbers Adams and Strouse had written at Green Mansions were interpolated into two intimate revues, *The Shoestring Revue* in 1955 for which Strouse was music director, and *Shoestring '57* in 1956. Other Strouse-Adams songs were heard in *The Littlest Revue* (basic score by Vernon Duke) in 1956; in *Kaleidoscope*, an Off Broadway production of 1957; and in two London musicals, *Fresh Airs* (1954) and *From Here to There* (1955). Independent of Adams, Strouse had a hit song in "Born Too Late" (1958, lyrics by Fred Tobais), a bestseller in a recording by the Poni Tails. With Adams, Strouse composed the title song for the 1959 motion picture *The Mating Game*, introduced by its star, Debbie Reynolds.

Inasmuch as the writing and placing of songs in unsuccessful musicals was an unrewarding investment of his time, Strouse supported himself by writing music for a nightclub revue produced by George White at The Versailles, working with Irving Caesar and Jack Yellen as his lyricists. Strouse also played piano at nightclubs; served as a vocal coach and rehearsal pianist for Broadway shows; made vocal arrangements at recording sessions; and, with Adams, wrote special material for Jane Morgan, Dick Shawn and Carol Burnett, among others.

In the late 1950s the Broadway producer Edward Padula was planning a Broadway musical that satirized rock 'n' roll and the mass adulation of teenagers for Elvis Presley. Having heard the Strouse-Adams numbers in *Shoestring '57*, Padula asked them to write songs that could be used at auditions for raising money for his still-on-the-boards production. For a salary of $100 a month, Strouse and Adams wrote more than 40 songs which they performed at 75 auditions. Eventually Goddard Lieberson, the president of Columbia Records, arranged for the financing of Padula's production, *Bye Bye Birdie*, which opened on Broadway on April 14, 1960. Strouse and Adams dropped all but three of their original audition numbers, but wrote 13 other new songs to round out the score.

In addition to Strouse and Adams, *Bye Bye Birdie* introduced to Broadway such new faces as librettist Michael Stewart and, as a stage director, the choreographer Gower Champion. The Elvis Presley prototype was Conrad Birdie, a rock star whose imminent induction into the Army worries not only his multitude of teenage worshipers but his manager, Albert Peterson, as well. To raise the money he needs to get married, Peterson composes "One Last Kiss," which Birdie is to sing on Ed Sullivan's television show as his farewell, while kissing one of his grieving but star-struck female fans. The teenager chosen for the farewell kiss is Kim MacAfee from whose home Sullivan's program is to be broadcast. As a guest of Kim's family, Conrad creates turmoil both in the all-American town of Sweet Apple and within the MacAfee household.

The production abounded with the vitality and exuberance of youth, combining visual elements of cinematic montage, with the sounds of rock 'n' roll and traditional Broadway show tunes. *Bye Bye Birdie* had a run of 607 performances on Broadway, and the critic Kenneth Tynan declared that "Everything about the musical was filled with a kind of affectionate freshness that we have seldom encountered since Mr. Rodgers collaborated with Mr. Hart on *Babes in Arms*." *Bye Bye Birdie* received a Tony as the season's best musical and in 1963 was made into a laugh-filled movie starring Dick Van Dyke (reprising his stage role) and Janet Leigh as the parents of Ann-Margret (Kim).

The best of the Strouse-Adams songs were: "A Lot of Livin' to Do," introduced by Dick Gautier and the Teenagers on the stage and sung by Ann-Margret, Bobby Rydell and Jesse Pearson on the screen; "One Last Kiss," performed by Dick Gautier and company on the stage and Jesse Pearson on the screen; "Put on a Happy Face," by Dick Van Dyke on Broadway and Dick Van Dyke and Janet Leigh in the film; "Kids," by

Paul Lynde on the stage and Paul Lynde with Maureen Stapleton and Bryan Russell on the screen; and "Baby Talk to Me," by Dick Van Dyke and quartet on the stage. A recording of the original stage cast was released, as was a screen soundtrack.

When Edward Padula put together his next Broadway musical, *All American,* he once again enlisted Strouse as his composer and Adams as his lyricist. *All American* was originally planned as a satire on college football, but along the way it became a formulaic musical tailor-made to suit the gifts of its star, Ray Bolger. Bolger played Professor Fodorski, who teaches engineering at the Southern Baptist Institute of Technology, a small school that is not caught up in the craze for big-time college football—until Fodorski proves so successful as a coach that football hysteria seizes Southern Baptist. *All American,* despite a book by Mel Brooks, opened on Broadway on March 19, 1962, but survived only 90 performances. Its main attractions were Bolger's performance and a few of the Strouse-Adams songs. A rousing patriotic number, "What a Country!" was introduced by Bolger and chorus; "Once Upon a Time" and "If I Were You" were duets for Bolger and Eileen Herlie, with Bolger doing a tap dance to the former; and "Have a Dream" was sung by Fritz Weaver. An original cast album was released.

Strouse and Adams scored a modest Broadway success (569 performances) with *Golden Boy* (October 20, 1964), the musical adaptation of a play by Clifford Odets, updated by William Gibson's inclusion of subject matter related to the civil rights movement. In the Odets play the principal character, Joe Wellington, is an Italian-American who wants to become a violinist but turns to boxing for easy money and fame. In the musical he is a black man who uses the boxing profession as the means of gaining the respect of whites for American blacks. However, Joe falls for a white woman who is in love with his white manager. Joe is killed in an automobile accident the night he wins the title bout.

"One can have nothing but admiration for the snap, speed and professionalism of the [musical's] style," wrote Howard Taubman in *The New York Times.* "In two production numbers, *Golden Boy* is a knockout, not only for the whirling excitement of its action but also for the powerful punch in its comment." These production numbers were "Don't Forget 127th Street," featuring Sammy Davis Jr. and Johnny Brown, and "No More," featuring the company and Sammy Davis, Theresa Merritt and Lola Falana. Other noteworthy songs were: "Night Song" and "Can't You See It," introduced by Sammy Davis Jr.; "I

Want to Be With You," a duet for Davis and Paula Wayne; and "While the City Sleeps," a ballad for Billy Daniels. The score was released in an original cast album.

It's a Bird, It's a Plane, It's Superman!, which opened on Broadway on March 29, 1966 for a meager run of 129 performances, attempted to bring the Superman comic strip to the Broadway stage. The musical was not intended as a satire but, as Otis L. Guernsey Jr. noted in his *Ten Best Plays of 1965–66,* was "played [as] straight as possible for a good laugh at our secret longing for a hero who would solve all problems and defeat all enemies. The joke is not on Superman. . . . The joke is right where it should be— on us and our childish instincts." In the book by David Newman and Robert Benton, an evil scientist plots the destruction of the Man of Steel. But Superman rescues Metropolis from a missile attack, saves the woman who loves him from death by a 6,000-volt generator and causes the evil scientist's electrocution instead. The Strouse-Adams score of 16 songs, released in an original cast album, was so seamlessly woven into the text that no single number stood out prominently.

After *Superman,* Strouse and Adams wrote the songs for two films, *The Night They Raided Minsky's* (1968) and *There Was a Crooked Man* (1970), and Strouse composed the background music for *Bonnie and Clyde* (1967). The songs from *The Night They Raided Minsky's,* a comedy whose setting was New York City in the heyday of vaudeville, was released in a soundtrack album.

Strouse and Adams enjoyed another resounding success on Broadway with *Applause* (March 30, 1970). It ran for 896 performances, won a Tony as best musical of the year and Lauren Bacall, in her debut in the musical theater, won another as best actress. The show also produced a bestselling original cast album. Like the sources from which it was derived—Mary Orr's story "The Wisdom of Eve," which had been made into the celebrated film *All About Eve* (1950), starring Bette Davis—*Applause* swept away the surface glitter of show business to reveal the behind-the-scenes deceit, megalomania, and hypocrisy of so many who populate the theater world. Betty Comden and Adolph Green wrote a script that brimmed with what Clive Barnes called "a welcome and lovely cynicism about show business . . . preserved in the most astringent aspic." Margo (Bacall) is a now middle-aged and rather vain stage star who deceives herself into thinking that Eve Harrington, a young, adoring, apparently self-effacing admirer, is worthy of being her protege and confidante. Eve, as ruthless and scheming as she is ambitious, becomes Margo's secretary, then her understudy. Eventually she contrives to have Margo waylaid in the countryside so that she, the understudy, can make her stage debut. Eve next steals the coveted role away from Margo by having an affair with the author of the play.

The title song was so sensationally performed by Bonnie Franklin that, though appearing in a minor role, she became a star overnight. "Applause" was later recorded by Pearl Bailey. Other standout numbers were: "But Alive," sung and danced to by Lauren Bacall and a male group; "Good Friends," sung by Bacall, Ann Williams and Brandon Maggart; "One of a Kind," a duet for Bacall and Len Cariou; and "Best Night of My Life," introduced by Penny Fuller.

Separating himself temporarily from Adams, Strouse wrote the book, lyrics and music for *Six*, an offbeat production described in the program as "a musical trip." It opened Off Broadway on April 12, 1971, and quickly closed. The title was derived from the cast of six performers who, for about an hour, sang songs on such subjects as life and death, Adam and Eve, and the nature of good and evil.

Strouse and Adams composed "Those Were the Days," the theme song for one of the most popular situation comedies in television history, *All in the Family*, which made its debut on the CBS-TV network on January 19, 1971. "Those Were the Days" was sung by Carroll O'Connor (Archie Bunker) and Maureen Stapleton (Archie's wife, Edith). A year later, Strouse and Adams composed the score for *I and Albert*, a London musical. For the next six years Strouse and Adams worked independently of one another.

In 1974 and 1975 Adams conducted seminars in the American musical theater at Yale University. He was appointed adjunct professor at Columbia University in 1979, where he conducted annual theater seminars at the School of the Arts.

In the mid-1970s Strouse struggled to bring to Broadway a box-office blockbuster, *Annie* (April 21, 1977). Based on Harold Gray's enduring syndicated cartoon, *Little Orphan Annie*, it was the brainchild of the lyricist Martin Charnin. He conceived the idea for the musical during the Christmas season of 1971, when he purchased a copy of *Arf! The Life and Hard Times of Little Orphan Annie*. "I couldn't put it down," Charnin recalled. "I instantly saw in it all the material, characters, situations I thought would lend themselves to the musical theater." However, financial backers shied away from the project, thinking that its comic-strip subject matter would not appeal to sophisticated Broadway au-

diences. "It turned out they all believed, not so much that I had a screw loose, but that one couldn't make cartoon characters believable," said Charnin. "They all saw it as pure camp, high camp. Nobody could envision the flesh."

Charnin went into debt to keep his dream alive, spending more than $70,000 to retain the stage rights to *Little Orphan Annie*, to pay for office space and to hold parties and auditions for potential backers. "At one point in 1975," he said, "I literally had no money left. So I sent a letter to 25 friends, asking them each for $1,000 which I'd repay within five years come hell or high water. They did it on blind faith."

Charnin eventually persuaded Strouse to compose the music and Thomas Meehan to write a libretto. Charnin himself served as Strouse's lyricist, and by 1976 *Annie* was ready for tryout performances at the Goodspeed Opera House in East Haddam, Connecticut. But when Walter Kerr published an unfavorable review in *The New York Times*, *Annie* appeared to be doomed. However, Lewis Allen and the celebrated director Mike Nichols liked the show and volunteered to produce it on Broadway, where it stayed for six years. It grossed approximately 225 million dollars, captured the New York Drama Critics Circle Award as the season's best musical and won seven Tonys, including those for the season's best musical and, to Strouse, for the best score. *Annie* became the seventh longest-running musical in Broadway history on January 2, 1982 when the last of 2,377 performances was given. A record price of $9,500,000 was paid for the movie rights. Directed by John Huston, the 1982 film treatment of *Annie* was a critical and commercial disaster. The soundtrack recording, though, sold more than a million copies, and the original cast recording of the Broadway production earned both a gold record and a Grammy. *Annie* returned to Broadway for the Thanksgiving-Christmas holiday season of 1984, after having toured the country for the fifth time.

The libretto was the rags-to-riches story of Annie, an orphan, and her faithful companion Sandy the dog. After a futile search for her parents, she finds a benefactor in Oliver "Daddy" Warbucks, a tycoon who adopts her. The show was unabashedly sentimental and warmhearted, radiating optimism, sweetness and light. "To dislike . . . *Annie*," wrote the critic Clive Barnes, "would be tantamount to disliking motherhood, peanut butter, friendly mongrel dogs and nostalgia. It also would be unnecessary, for *Annie* is an intensely likable musical. You might even call it lovable; it seduces one [and] works on all levels. It is that . . . rare animal—the properly built, handsomely groomed Broadway musical."

Strouse's tuneful score produced a standard, "Tomorrow," which was introduced by Andrea McCardle, the first of several "Annies," and recorded by Barbra Streisand. "Maybe" was another ballad introduced by McCardle. In "I Think I'm Gonna Like it Here," McCardle was joined by Sandy Faison and Edwin Bordo. "You're Never Fully Dressed Without a Smile," was sung by Donald Craig and reprised by a chorus of orphans. "In *Annie*," wrote Peter Reilly in *Stereo Review*, "[Strouse] has hit an easy stride, composing music that is meant purely and simply to entertain."

On January 31, 1978 *By Strouse* opened Off Broadway. This revue showcased three dozen songs from produced and unproduced Strouse musicals. Before the year had ended, Strouse and Adams were reunited, composing the music and lyrics for *A Broadway Musical* (December 21, 1978), a backstage view of show business (book by William F. Brown) that closed after the premiere performance. Also of brief duration on Broadway were three subsequent Strouse musicals. *Charlie and Algernon* (September 14, 1980), with book and lyrics by David Rodgers, was based on the Daniel Keyes novel *Flowers for Algernon*. It consisted of 21 musical numbers and ran for just 17 performances. *Bring Back Birdie* (March 5, 1981) reunited Strouse and Adams with the librettist Michael Stewart. This sequel carried the *Bye Bye Birdie* story forward two decades, but closed after four performances. *Dance a Little Closer* (May 11, 1983) closed after the curtain rang down on opening night. With book and lyrics by Alan Jay Lerner, it was an attempt to make a musical update of Robert Sherwood's Pulitzer Prize-winning drama of 1935, *Idiot's Delight*.

Strouse composed the background music for the motion picture *Just Tell Me What You Want* (1980), and he has also composed of concert and operatic music, including a piano concerto. His opera *Nightingale*, to his own libretto based on a Hans Christian Andersen fairy tale, received its premiere at Wolf Trap Farm in Virginia in April 1982 and was produced in London in December 1983.

Both Strouse and Adams live in New York City, Strouse on 57th Street near Carnegie Hall, Adams on West End Avenue. Strouse married Barbara Simon on September 23, 1962; they have four children. Adam's first wife, with whom he raised a daughter, was Rita Reich. They were married on July 21, 1957 and divorced in 1978. Adams married Kelly Wood, an actress, on September 13, 1980.

In partnership with Edwin N. Morris, Strouse formed his own publishing company, Barbara

Music, in 1971. His main interest outside the theater is opera. Adam's favorite forms of recreation are reading, cooking, playing tennis and puttering about in his summer house in East Hampton, Long Island.

ABOUT: Green, S. The World of Musical Comedy, 4th ed. 1980; Rigdon, W., (ed.) The Biographical Encyclopedia and Who's Who of the American Theatre, 1966. *Periodicals*—New York Times March 3, 1978.

STYNE, JULE (December 31, 1905–), composer, has been one of Broadway's and Hollywood's leading songwriters for more than four decades. Working with some of America's foremost lyricists, Styne has composed some 1,500 songs for more than 80 motion pictures and about 20 Broadway musicals. At least 50 of his songs have become standards; 15 were heard on *Your Hit Parade*, eight in first position, and one brought him an Oscar for the year's best film song.

Born in London, England on New Year's Eve 1905, Julius Kerwin Stein was the oldest of the three children of Isadore and Anna (Kertman) Stein, émigrés from Russia. Isadore Stein was in the butter-and-egg business. Julius became interested in popular music when he was four by listening to Harry Lauder's recordings. One year later, taken to the Hippodrome to see Lauder, he spontaneously climbed onto the stage and sang "She's My Daisy" in imitation of Lauder's vocal style. Aged six, Stein was enrolled in the London Conservatory. Because his family did not own a piano he practiced daily in the back room of a music company. These lessons ended nine months later when, in 1912, the family immigrated to the United States. Four years later Julius Stein became a naturalized citizen.

Settling in Chicago, Stein resumed piano study with Esther Harris at the Chicago Musical College. Seven months later he won a silver medal in a competition of child pianists held by the Chicago Symphony. Within a year he had appeared as a soloist with the Detroit Symphony and the St. Louis Symphony. He also sang soprano in various synagogue choirs and intensively studied harmony and composition.

His ambition to become a virtuoso pianist was shattered when, aged 13, he was told by Harold Bauer, the piano virtuoso, that his hands were too small. While attending Tuley High School in 1916, Styne played the piano in an amateur band that performed popular music at school functions. At this time Stein composed his first song, "The Guy With the Polka-Dot Tie."

In 1917, after falsifying his age to gain admit-

JULE STYNE

tance into the Musicians Union, he was hired as a relief pianist at the Haymarket Burlesque Theatre. He also gained experience by playing piano with bands at school dances and social functions. When Stein was 16, at the request of the young Michael Todd, who was then preparing an act for vaudeville, he composed "The Moth and the Flame."

After Stein graduated from Tuley High in 1922, he spent the next few years playing the piano in pit orchestras for stage shows. He also led a band, in which Benny Goodman played clarinet, for several summers at the Hotel Bismarck, and played with the Arnold Johnson orchestra. With the last-named group in 1926, Stein composed the music for "Sunday" (lyrics by Ned Miller), his first published song (the sheet music also credited Chester Conn and Bennie Krueger as Styne's collaborators). The Williams Sisters introduced it at the Rendezvous Café in Chicago, after which it was recorded by Gene Austin, Cliff Edwards and, years later, by Frank Sinatra.

In 1926 and 1927 Stein worked with the Ben Pollack band, whose members included such jazz greats as Benny Goodman, Glenn Miller and Charlie Spivak. Stein also conducted several theater orchestras. On August 9, 1926 he married Ethel Rubenstein, with whom he had two sons. They were divorced in 1952. In 1932, after forming a band for a Chicago nightclub on East Superior Street, he changed his name to Jule Styne to avoid confusion with Jules Stein, head of the Music Corporation of America.

In 1934 Styne left Chicago for New York. For a few years he was employed as a vocal coach and arranger, as a writer of special material for the Ritz Brothers and others, and as the conductor of an orchestra accompanying Harry Richman on radio and on tour.

Styne was called to Hollywood in 1937 as a vocal coach at 20th Century-Fox, working with Alice Faye and Shirley Temple. For several of the studio's film productions, he composed songs to lyrics by Sidney Clare: "Limpy Dimp" for *Hold that Co-Ed* (1938); "Kentucky Opera" for *Kentucky Moonshine* (1938); "Let's Start Where We Left Off" for *Stop, Look and Love* (1939); and "Who'll Buy My Flowers" for *Pack Up Your Troubles* (1939).

In 1940 Styne went to work for the Republic studios, who engaged him to write five or six songs for each of its productions. He said: "I wrote country and western music. I wrote music for cattle and mules. I did just about everything I was asked to do." Additional chores included orchestrations, conducting orchestras and playing the piano. Out of these Republic pictures came several notable film tunes. "Who Am I?" (lyrics by Walter Bullock) was introduced by Frances Langford and Kenny Baker in *The Hit Parade of 1941* (1940). This was Styne's first song to be nominated for an Oscar. For *Youth on Parade* (1942), Styne began a songwriting partnership with lyricist Sammy Cahn. Their first collaboration was a winner, "I've Heard That Song Before," which was interpolated for Frank Sinatra who had introduced the number at Madison Square Garden in 1942. Harry James and his orchestra (vocal by Helen Forrest) made a bestselling recording which brought a Styne number to *Your Hit Parade* for the first time. "I've Heard That Song Before" had 15 hearings in 1943, four times in first position.

On loan to the Paramount studios, Styne composed "Conchita, Marquita, Lolita, Pepita, Rosita, Juanita Lopez" (lyrics by Herbert Magidson), which Johnny Johnston introduced and recorded and which was also recorded by Dinah Shore. To Frank Loesser's lyrics, Styne wrote the music for one of the outstanding ballads of World War II, "I Don't Want to Walk Without You Baby," which Betty Jane Rhodes introduced in *Sweater Girl* (1942) and which was recorded by Bing Crosby and by Harry James and his orchestra (vocal by Helen Forrest). With 12 appearances on *Your Hit Parade*, it occupied the first position on February 21, 1942. "Change of Heart" (lyrics by Harold Adamson) was introduce in Paramount's *Hit Parade of 1943*.

By 1944 Sammy Cahn had parted company with his songwriting partner Saul Chaplin. That year he teamed up with Styne, and they composed some of the most memorable tunes of the decade. Many of the songs they wrote for films over the next few years appeared on *Your Hit Parade*: "I'll Walk Alone" (21 appearances, eight in first position in 1944, four times more in 1952). Another memorable ballad of the war years, it was introduced by Dinah Shore in *Follow the Boys* (1944) and recorded by Shore, Sinatra and Louis Prima. In 1952 it was revived in a bestselling recording by Don Cornell.

"There Goes That Song Again" (12 appearances), introduced by Harry Babbitt with the orchestra of Kay Kyser in *Carolina Blues* (1944). It was recorded by Kate Smith and by Kay Kyser and was revived in the film *Cruisin' Down the River* (1953).

"And Then You Kissed Me" (one appearance), introduced by Frank Sinatra in *Step Lively* (1944).

"Five Minutes More" (16 appearances, four times in first position), introduced by Phil Brito in *Sweetheart of Sigma Chi* (1946). It was recorded by Sinatra and by the orchestra of Tex Beneke.

"Time After Time" (four appearances), introduced by Frank Sinatra in *It Happened in Brooklyn* (1947) and recorded by the orchestras of Jimmy Dorsey, Tommy Dorsey and Teddy Wilson.

"It's Magic" (16 appearances, twice in first position), introduced by Doris Day in *Romance on the High Seas* (1948). It was recorded by Day in a million-selling release and by Vic Damone and was revived in *Starlift* (1951).

"Fiddle Dee Dee" (four appearances), introduce by Doris Day in *It's a Great Feeling* (1949) and recorded by the orchestras of Sammy Kaye, Guy Lombardo and Jimmy Dorsey.

The title song of *It's a Great Feeling* (two appearances) introduced by Doris Day.

"Three Coins in a Fountain" (13 appearances, four times in first position), introduced by Frank Sinatra on the soundtrack of the 1954 motion picture of the same name. The winner of Styne's only Oscar, "Three Coins" was composed by Styne and Cahn in about half an hour, at the request of the film producer Sol C. Siegel, who needed a catchy song with that title so that he could change the name of a film then being made in Italy. Styne and Cahn had to write the song without having seen either the picture or the script. A demonstration record by Sinatra, which was later used on the soundtrack, overcame all resistance to changing the film's title. Sinatra's recording was a bestseller, as was the one by the Four Aces. This song contributed to *Three Coins in a Fountain*'s enormous earnings at the box office.

Other songs by Styne and Cahn that were heard on *Your Hit Parade* but not originally featured in films were: "It's Been a Long, Long Time" (heard 14 times, five times in first position). Written on V-E Day, it was introduced in 1945 on the radio by Phil Brito and initially recorded by Frankie Carle and his orchestra, then by Bing Crosby, the De Marco Sisters and the Harry James orchestra (vocal by Killy Kallen). Dan Dailey, June Haver and Gloria De Haven revived it in *I'll Get By* (1950).

"Saturday Night is the Loneliest Night in the Week" (ten times), introduced and popularized by Frank Sinatra in a bestselling recording.

"Let it Snow! Let it Snow! Let it Snow!" (13 times, twice in first position). Written in 1945, it was popularized in recordings by Vaughn Monroe, Connie Boswell and the Woody Herman band.

"Can't You Read Between the Lines" (two times), popularized in 1945 in recordings by the orchestras of Charlie Spivak and Kay Kyser.

"The Things We Did Last Summer" (11 times), popularized in 1946 in recordings by Frank Sinatra, Jo Stafford and Jimmy Dorsey and his orchestra.

Other screen songs by Styne and Cahn that never reached *Your Hit Parade*, but achieved considerable popularity were: "I Fall in Love Too Easily" and "The Charm of You," introduced by Sinatra in *Anchors Away* (1945) and recorded by him. Mel Tormé's Melitones (with Eugene Baird) also recorded "I Fall in Love Too Easily."

"Anywhere," introduced by Janet Blair in *Tonight and Everynight* (1945) and recorded by the orchestra of Horace Heidt.

"I'm Glad I Waited for You," introduced by Alfred Drake in *Tars and Spars* (1946) and recorded by Peggy Lee, Frankie Laine and Helen Forrest.

"I've Never Forgotten," introduced by Constance Moore in the film *Earl Carroll's Sketchbook* (1946) and recorded by Harry James.

"What Am I Gonna Do About You?" was introduced by Eddie Bracken and Virginia Weeles in *Ladies' Man* (1946) and recorded by both Bing Crosby and Perry Como.

"It's the Same Old Dream," introduced by Sinatra in *It Happened in Brooklyn* (1947) and recorded by Tommy Dorsey.

"I Believe," introduced by Sinatra, Jimmy Durante and Billy Roy in *It Happened in Brooklyn*, with recordings by Sinatra, Louis Armstrong and Ziggy Elman.

"Give Me a Song With a Beautiful Melody," introduced by Jack Carson in *It's a Grand Feeling* (1949) and recorded by Jack Carson, Helen Forrest and Guy Lombardo.

In 1944 Styne and Cahn composed the score for their first musical, *Glad to See You*. Though it expired in out-of-town tryouts, its score contained a standard, "Guess I'll Hang My Tears Out to Dry," recorded by Sinatra and by Ray Charles.

The first Styne-Cahn musical on Broadway was *High Button Shoes* (October 9, 1947), which ran for 727 performances. With a book by Stephen Longstreet (based on his own autobiographical novel) and direction by George Abbott, *High Button Shoes* starred Phil Silvers as Harrison Floy who, in 1913, arrives in New Brunswick, New Jersey. With Mr. Pontdue, his partner-in-crime, he defrauds the community with shady deals, including a real-estate scam in which the valuable property turns out to be a swamp. A repentant Floy tries to reimburse his investors by marketing the swamp mud as facial beauty clay. A ballet choreographed by Jerome Robbins, inspired by Keystone cop chases, was a showstopper. The song highlight from the Styne-Cahn score was a polka, "Papa, Won't You Dance With Me?"; it was introduced by Jack McCauley, Nanette Fabray and chorus. McCauley and Fabray also introduced the principal ballad, "I Still Get Jealous." In addition to the original cast recording, Doris Day and Guy Lombardo each recorded "Papa, Won't You Dance With Me?" and the orchestras of Guy Lombardo, Jimmy Dorsey and Harry James covered "I Still Get Jealous."

Except for a short-lived later reunion, the collaboration of Styne and Cahn ended in 1948 after eight years. Styne went on to achieve great success on Broadway rather than in Hollywood. With Leo Robin as lyricist, Styne had another Broadway hit with *Gentlemen Prefer Blondes* (December 8, 1949), which lasted 740 performances before being made into a film in 1953. The book by Anita Loos and Herbert Fields was based on Loos's short stories about two Jazz Age American "flappers" and their amatory adventures in Paris. As Lorelei Lee, Carol Channing became a star and her delivery of the score's two leading songs, "A Little Girl From Little Rock" and "Diamonds Are a Girl's Best Friend," were showstoppers. In the motion picture adaptation these were sung as duets by Marilyn Monroe and Jane Russell. "Bye Bye Baby" was introduced on the stage by Carol Channing and Jack McCauley and sung on the screen by Monroe. Besides the original cast and soundtrack recordings, Ethel Merman and Carol Channing each recorded "A Little Girl From Little Rock" and "Diamonds Are a Girl's Best Friend" while "Bye Bye Baby" was recorded by Sinatra and by Guy Lombardo.

Before his next box-office blockbuster, in the early 1950s Styne composed the scores for three lesser stage efforts. *Two on the Aisle* (July 19, 1951), a revue with sketches and lyrics by Betty Comden and Adolph Green, was directed by Abe Burrows and ran for 249 performances. It starred Bert Lahr and Dolores Gray; she introduced and recorded "Hold Me–Hold Me–Hold Me," which Marilyn Monroe sang in the film, *Niagara* (1952).

Hazel Flagg (February 11, 1953; book by Ben Hecht, lyrics by Bob Hilliard) was an unsuccessful attempt (190 performances) to make the film *Nothing Sacred* (1937), an enduring Carole Lombard comedy that had been written by Hecht and Charles MacArthur, into a stage musical. Styne's score contained two popular songs, "How Do You Speak to an Angel?" and "Ev'ry Street's a Boulevard in Old New York." Both were heard in the original cast album and in the 1954 film, *Living It Up*, in which Dean Martin sang "Ev'ry Street's a Boulevard."

For a Broadway revival of Sir James M. Barrie's *Peter Pan* (October 20, 1954), starring Mary Martin, Styne, with Comden and Green as lyricists, contributed six songs. The best were introduced by Martin: "Never-Never Land," "Wendy" and "Distant Melody." An original cast album was released, and in addition to a 152-performance run on Broadway this production was televised.

With *Bells Are Ringing* (November 29, 1956; 924 performances), Styne enjoyed his third Broadway triumph. In this musical with book and lyrics by Betty Comden and Adolph Green, Judy Holliday made her musical comedy debut as Ella Peterson, an operator for a telephone-answering service. She becomes personally involved with the problems she overhears and falls in love with one of her clients, Jeff. She also schemes to help two other clients realize their dreams, a dentist who wants to write songs and an actor manqué who wants to be a star. "Betty Comden and Adolph Green," wrote one reviewer, "have created characters that stick in the mind and Jule Styne has fashioned tunes that will make a jukebox rich. *Bells Are Ringing* bongs the golden gong." Three hit songs came from this score. "Just in Time" was introduced by Sydney Chaplin and Judy Holliday; "The Party's Over" by Holliday; and "Long Before I Knew You" by Sydney Chaplin. In the 1960 motion picture adaptation, the first two were sung by Dean Martin and the third by Holliday. Both original-cast and movie soundtrack LPs were released. Johnny Mathis's recording of "The Party's Over" was a bestseller, and Mel Tormé recorded "Just in Time."

Before Styne's next musical was mounted on Broadway, he worked in television and produced *The Best of Broadway* and two Cole Porter musicals, *Anything Goes* and *Panama Hattie*. Styne's songs (lyrics by Comden and Green) were heard in the Broadway musical *Say Darling* (April 3, 1958) and recorded on an original cast album. *Say Darling* was an unsuccessful comedy about the making of the noted musical, *Pajama Game*. Remembered from *Say Darling* are two songs, "Dance Only With Me," introduced by Vivian Blaine and Mitchell Gregg, and "Something's Always Happening on the River," introduced by David Wayne. *Say Darling* had a run of 332 performances at the ANTA Theatre and 16 more at the New York City Center.

Gypsy (May 21, 1959) had a run of 702 performances. Here Styne's lyricist was the young Stephen Sondheim. The book by Arthur Laurents was based on the autobiography of Gypsy Rose Lee, the burlesque star and stripper, which Ethel Merman cast unforgettably as the ruthless, singleminded Rose, the stage mother of two young promising performers, Gypsy Rose Lee (identified in the musical as "Louise") and June Havoc (called "June"). The story opens in Seattle in the 1920s and early 1930s. Louise and June become a vaudeville act touring the Orpheum circuit. When June sacrifices her show business career for marriage, Rose dedicates herself to making Louise a star, not in vaudeville but as a striptease artist in burlesque.

Gypsy was also made into an acclaimed motion picture starring Rosalind Russell and Natalie Wood in 1962, and it successfully returned to Broadway in 1974 with Angela Lansbury as Rose. Theater critic Clive Barnes said: "Everything about *Gypsy* is right. The Jule Styne score has a lilt and a surprise to it. The music bounces out of the pit, assertive, confident and cocky, and has a love affair with Stephen Sondheim's elegantly paced, daringly phrased lyrics."

The first act opened with "May We Entertain You," first sung by Karen Moore and Jacqueline Mayro as Baby Louise and Baby June. One act later, reprised as "Let Me Entertain You," it was sung by Sandra Church and company. The first act ended with the score's most famous song, "Everything's Coming Up Roses," with Ethel Merman memorably belted out. "Together, Wherever We Go" was a vocal trio for Merman, Sandra Church and Jack Klugman, and "Small World," a duet for Merman and Klugman. On the motion picture soundtrack Lisa Kirk dubbed for Rosalind Russell on "Everything's Coming Up Roses," "Together, Wherever We Go" and "Small World." Original-cast and soundtrack recordings were released, with the former winning a Grammy. Johnny Mathis recorded "Small World."

The hit song of Styne's next Broadway musical, *Do Re Mi* (December 26, 1960; book by Garson Kanin, lyrics by Comden and Green) was "Make Someone Happy," introduced by John Reardon and Nancy Dessault and popularized in a recording by Perry Como. Phil Silvers starred as Hubie Cram, a small-time con artist who aims to make it big in the jukebox business with the backing of three ex-mobsters. They bring about his corruption, and Hubie returns to the obscurity from which he came. "Cry Like the Wind" was a ballad introduced by Dessault and "I Know About Love" was introduced by Reardon. *Do Re Mi* had a run of 400 performances and an originalcast album was released.

Styne suffered setbacks on Broadway with the musicals *Subways Are for Sleeping* (December 27, 1961) and *Arturo Ui* (November 11, 1963), the latter adapted as a musical from a play by Bertolt Brecht. *Subways Are for Sleeping* managed to stay on the boards for 205 performances while *Arturo Ui* departed after just eight. The score of *Subways Are for Sleeping* (lyrics by Comden and Green), which was recorded by the original cast, yielded "Come Once in a Lifetime," introduced by Sydney Chaplin and Carol Lawrence, and "Be a Santa" and "I'm Just Taking My Time," both introduced by Chaplin, the latter with chorus.

Styne rebounded with *Funny Girl* (March 26, 1964), which, with 1,348 performances, had the longest Broadway run of any his musicals. In 1968 it was made into one of the great movie musicals. In both Barbra Streisand was starred as Fanny Brice, bringing her an Oscar for best actress in her screen debut. In Isobel Lennart's libretto and Bob Merrill's lyrics, Brice's career was traced from her beginnings as an awkward, unattractive teenager through her first successes in vaudeville and up to her triumph as a comedienne in the *Ziegfeld Follies*. Also depicted was her bittersweet love affair with Nick Arnstein, a professional gambler. "It's the authentic aura of show business arising out of Fanny Brice's luminous career that lights up *Funny Girl*," wrote Howard Taubman in *The New York Times*. "The true laughter in this musical comes from the sense of truth it communicates of Fanny Brice's stage world. And Fanny's personality and style are remarkably evoked by Miss Streisand. . . . Jule Styne, who has written one of his best scores, has provided [Streisand] with bluesy tunes . . . and she turns them into lyrical laments." Streisand's two principal songs were "People" and "Don't Rain on My Parade," with Streisand's recording of "People" becoming a bestselling single and earning her a Grammy for best female vocal performance. Streisand also sang "I'm the Greatest Star," "The Music That

Makes Me Dance" and, with Sydney Chaplin on the stage and Omar Shariff on the screen, "You Are Woman." For the film, Styne and Merrill composed four new numbers, most significantly the title song, which, as a single, was a bestseller for Streisand. The film score also consisted of songs not by Styne but long identified with Fanny Brice: "My Man," "Second-Hand Rose" and "Sadie Sadie." The original-cast and the soundtrack recordings of *Funny Girl* each earned a gold record.

Funny Girl was the high point of Styne's Broadway career. He continued to write for the musical stage, but his efforts were either very modest successes or outright failures. *Fade Out—Fade In* (May 26, 1964), with book and lyrics by Comden and Green, was a satire on Hollywood in which Hope, a plain chorus girl, becomes a star through a concatenation of mishaps and coincidences. Hope was played by Carol Burnett, whose withdrawal from the cast caused a premature closing after 271 performances. Burnett and Jack Cassidy introduced "I'm With You," while the title song was shared by Burnett and Dick Patterson. An original-cast album was released.

In *Hallelujah, Baby* (April 26, 1967), book and lyrics by Comden and Green, Leslie Uggams made her Broadway debut. This musical was intended as a panorama of cultural life in black communities and in black show business enterprises. The story begins in the early 1900s, but over the next six decades the characters never grow older. Georgina, played by Uggams, starts out as a 25-year-old who breaks into show business by playing black stereotypes. As the years pass, she progresses from one medium to another: nightclubs in the 1920s; the federal theater of the early Depression years; and a star in the theater of the 1940s and 1950s. En route, she tries to shed her black identity and so loses her lover, a civil rights activist. Several of Styne's songs were patterned after earlier styles. "Feet Do Yo' Stuff," in the style of the 1920s, was introduced by Uggams and a male chorus and was followed by a tap dance by Winston De Witt Hemsley and Alan Weeks. "Another Day," representing the songs of the 1930s, was sung by a quartet consisting of Uggams, Robert Hooks, Barbara Sharma and Allen Case. "Not Mine," introduced by Allen Case, was a 1950s-style ballad. *Halleluah, Baby* ran for less than 300 performances but it received a Tony as the season's best musical and its score was released in an original-cast album.

Several other stage failures followed. *Darling of the Day* (January 27, 1968) was a musical stage adaptation of Arnold Bennett's *Buried*

Alive. The author of the book was not identified and Styne's lyricist was E. Y. Harburg. In *Look to the Lilies* (March 29, 1970) Styne was reunited with Sammy Cahn, with Leonard Spiegelgass adapting William E. Barrett's novel, *Lilies of the Field*. *Darling of the Day* survived for only 32 performances, though an original-cast album was released. *Look to the Lilies* closed after 25 performances. *Pettybelle*, book and lyrics by Bob Merrill, closed during out-of-town tryouts in 1971.

The 505-performance run of *Sugar* (April 9, 1972) was a temporary respite from box-office failure. *Sugar* was adapted by librettist Peter Stone from *Some Like It Hot*, the 1959 Billy Wilder comedy starring Tony Curtis, Jack Lemmon and Marilyn Monroe. The stage adaptation remained faithful to the screen story, in which Jerry and Joe (Robert Morse and Tony Roberts) are two musicians who witness the St. Valentine's Day gang massacre in Chicago in 1931. Threatened by gangsters, they disguise themselves as women and join an all-female band bound for Miami. There complications set in when Jerry falls in love with Sugar Cane, the band's blonde vocalist, and Joe is courted by Osgood Fielding Jr., an aging millionaire swain. Styne's best songs (lyrics by Bob Merrill), released in an original cast LP, were "We Could Be Close," a duet for Morse and Elaine Joyce; "Tear the Town Apart," introduced by Steve Dondos and chorus; and "When You Meet a Man in Chicago," shared by Morse, Roberts, Joyce, Sheila Smith and chorus.

After *Sugar* come *Lorelei* (January 27, 1974), which was planned as a sequel to *Gentlemen Prefer Blondes* but turned out to be little more than a retread, with Carol Channing again as Lorelei Lee. Several of the original show's songs were repeated, but within the context of a new book by Kenny Solms and Gail Parent, and with a few new Styne songs with lyrics by Comden and Green. *Lorelei* lasted only 320 performances, but an original cast album was released. After that, a new *One Night Stand* folded during out-of-town tryouts in 1980.

Several Styne songs from the 1960s were composed outside the theater: the title song for the motion picture *All the Way Home* (1963), lyrics by Styne's son, Stanley; "What a Way to Go," lyrics by Comden and Green, inspired by the 1964 film of the same name; "Absent-Minded Me" (lyrics by Bob Merrill), introduced and popularized by Barbra Streisand in a bestselling recording of 1964. In 1982 Styne's song, "Hey, Look, No Crying" (lyrics by Susan Birkenhead) was introduced and popularized by Frank Sinatra.

On Broadway, Styne has produced or directed

about half a dozen shows. He was the producer of the 1952 return of the Rodgers and Hart musical, *Pal Joey,* which had the longest run of any musical revival in Broadway history up to that time.

For his contributions to the American musical theater and the American popular song, Styne has received many honors. A "Salute to Jule Styne" was held at the Hollywood Bowl in the early 1960s, and Styne performed both as conductor and pianist. Another Styne celebration was held on May 19, 1974 with "Jule's Friends at the Palace," in which stars from stage, screen, and the recording industry paid him tribute with performances of his hit songs. In 1981 Styne was elected to the Theatre Hall of Fame by the nation's drama critics, and he was one of four recipients of the New York Music Awards for excellence in music. In 1982 the National Music Council presented him with its first American Eagle Award for unique contributions to American popular music. In the early 1980s Styne taught a class in songwriting at New York University.

Styne rejects the idea that professional songwriters can rely on sudden inspiration to sustain their creativity over a long period. As he told an interviewer, "Only amateurs are inspired. Professionals perspire. The only time something happens is when you work. . . . The actual writing of the music is easy. It is knowing what to write, what you sing and don't sing about that is important. It is the talking over it in your mind that is difficult."

On June 4, 1962 Styne married his second wife, Margaret Ann Bissett Brown, a British-born actress and model professionally known as Maggi Brown They had a son and a daughter, and made their home in an apartment on the 16th floor of a Fifth Avenue building facing Central Park. Styne also maintains an office in the Mark Hellinger Theatre building. Aside from his involvement with the theater, film and television, his prime interests are playing golf and betting on horses.

ABOUT: Green, S. The World of Musical Comedy, 4th ed. 1980; Wilk, M. They're Playing Our Song, 1973.

TAYLOR, JAMES (March 12, 1948–), was one of the most influential singer-songwriters of the 1970s. His music is an amalgam of country and western, folk ballads, rock 'n' roll and the blues, characterized by gently seductive melodies and evocative lyrical imagery. In the early 1970s his songs drew their themes from his own troubled life, addressing the pleasure and the

JAMES TAYLOR

hellish pain of madness and drug addiction, doubt and confusion, and chronicling the discontents of a romantic in a materialistic world. But not all of Taylor's songs are dark evocations of a tortured sensibility. A yearning for simple pleasures and a feeling for the uncomplicated beauty of, say, a perfect Carolina day permeates Taylor's music. And since the mid-1970s his best songs—"Shower the People," "Mexico" and "Every Day" among them—have expressed a buoyant hopefulness and a strong faith in the basic goodness of humanity.

James Vernon Taylor was born to wealth and social position in Boston, Massachusetts in 1948. He was the second of the five children of Dr. Isaac M. Taylor, a medical intern at Massachusetts General Hospital when James was born, and Gertrude (Woodard) Taylor. Later, Isaac Taylor became the dean of the University of North Carolina Medical School; he was descended from a well-to-do Southern family. His wife had studied music at the New England Conservatory and was trained as an opera singer. Two of James's brothers, Livingston and Alexander, and his only sister Kate, also pursued careers in popular music in the 1970s. When James Taylor was four his family moved to Chapel Hill, North Carolina, where they lived in a beautifully landscaped ranch-house on 28 acres not far from the university campus. The Taylors spent their summers at a large house in Chilwork, on Martha's Vineyard. Dr. Taylor and his wife treated their children as "rather special beings," to quote *Current Biography.* "We quite consciously set out to raise our children free of the hang-ups we see in ourselves and our generation," Dr. Taylor told *Time* magazine. "We weren't going to use that cop-out of 'because the Bible tells you so.' Gertrude Taylor taught her children that the earth is a "beautiful, fragile place" and to "believe in people." "The basic orientation in my family," said James's younger brother, Livingston, "was that simply because you were a Taylor you should and could be able to accomplish anything."

Taylor received only elementary instruction in playing the violin, cello and piano, before he quit taking music lessons. When he was 12, he taught himself to play the guitar. He attended public schools in Chapel Hill until reaching eighth grade, when he was enrolled in the elite Milton Academy in Milton, Massachusetts. "James was a supersensitive boy," his mother recalled. "He worried over the Bible Belt religion he picked up in school. Though James never went to church or Sunday school, he often needed reassurance that he wouldn't burn in hell if he was bad."

Taylor's three and a half years at Milton Academy were troubled ones. Introverted and oversensitive, he experienced adolescence as a time of sheer misery. He has recalled: "Things were going on in my head other than what Milton people thought was right and proper." According to the school's dean, "We just weren't ready for him. James was more sensitive and less goal-oriented than most students. I'm sure James knew about drugs long before anyone else did." Music saw Taylor through this period. He enjoyed singing ballads, hymns or folk tunes while accompanying himself on the guitar. Aged 15, he and a friend, Danny "Kootch" Kortchmar, had won a hootenany contest, the prize being a one-week engagement at a local coffeehouse, Taylor's first public singing appearance. And while at Milton he dropped out of school for part of one term to join his brother Alex in the Fabulous Corsayers, a North Carolina rock band.

By the time of his senior year, when he had to choose a college, Taylor, as he said, "fell to pieces." On the advice of a psychiatrist, who feared that Taylor was showing suicidal impulses, he committed himself voluntarily in 1966 to a mental institution, the McLean Hospital in Belmont, Massachusetts. There Taylor graduated from the institution's high school and decided to become a professional musician. He took a course in musical therapy and began to compose songs, words as well as music. Among his compositions at McLean were "She Used to Be a Junkie" and "Knocking 'Round the School," the latter, about the darker side of life in an institution, was to be featured on his first album.

Taylor left McLean after nine months without waiting for an official discharge. In the summer of 1967 he moved to New York and became the guitarist and vocalist for the Flying Machine, a folk-rock band formed by Kootch Kortchmar. With such early Taylor compositions as "Night Owl" and "Rainy Day Man" in their repertory, the Flying Machine performed regularly at the Night Owl in Greenwich Village for $12 a night. Taylor lived hand-to-mouth in a tiny apartment far uptown, sleeping on a mattress on the floor. "He got hung up on taking in weird people— runaway teenagers and people like that," Kortchmar recalled. Taylor now became dependent on drugs, and what began as experimentation soon became an addiction.

In January 1968 Taylor left New York for London. There he made a demonstration record of several of his own songs that brought him a three-year contract from Apple Records, the company owned by the Beatles. Apple released *James Taylor* in the United States early in 1969. Despite its uniformly excellent reviews the album sold only 30,000 copies the first year. One of its numbers, "Carolina on My Mind," on which Paul McCartney played bass guitar, was released as a single and cracked the *Billboard* Top 40.

Taylor himself had returned to the United States in December 1968. His physical and mental health in a fragile condition, he spent the winter of 1969 in a hospital in New York and then entered Austin Riggs, a mental institution in Massachusetts where he overcame his addiction to heroin. There he also composed the song that would make him famous, "Fire and Rain," which was inspired by the suicide of a female patient with whom he had fallen in love.

In July 1969 Taylor performed at the Newport Folk Festival and was a sensation. Shortly thereafter, however, he had a motorcycle accident and broke both his hands and a foot. Reevaluating the business side of his career, he engaged Peter Asher, who had signed him to Apple and his first album, as his personal manager and producer. With help from Asher, who had been a member of the 1960s pop duo, Peter and Gordon, Taylor signed with Warner Brothers and recorded his second album, *Sweet Baby James*. Released early in 1970, its contents included "Fire and Rain" and the title song, a lullaby written for his eponymous nephew, and the arrangements were softer than on his debut recording, oriented more to the sound of an acoustic guitar than an electrical instrument. Reviewing the album in the *Saturday Review*, Burt Korall said: "Again the songs are delightful and enriching. Taylor remains at his best unraveling personal situations that are universal in application. . . . One senses he is endeavoring to solve his own problems and, in the process, to help lift the weight of ours." The singles "Fire and Rain," "Sweet Baby James" and "Country Road" all received extensive radio airplay, and within a year of its release the album had sold almost two million copies.

On the strength of the popularity of *Sweet Baby James*, sales of his first album soared and *James Taylor* dented *Billboard*'s pop chart for the first time in October 1970. Within a year, Taylor's status as a superstar, both as songwriter and as performer, was firmly established. A booking at New York's small Gaslight Café in March 1970 forced the club's managers to turn away thousands of would-be patrons each evening. The following June Taylor gave two concerts at Carnegie Hall. That winter he mounted a 27-city tour that climaxed in New York with sold-out concerts at Madison Square Garden and Lincoln Center. Reviewing the four concerts Taylor gave at Carnegie Hall in November 1971, Don Heckman wrote in *The New York Times*: "Mr. Taylor's. . . . stage presence . . . was that of a performer whose magic is so strong it virtually radiates out of his electric blue eyes. Every move he makes—gawky lopes to the piano, shy glances to the audience, awkward little bows of thanks—stamps him as an original. [He gave] a nearly perfect pop music concert."

Taylor's third album, *Mud Slide Slim and the Blue Horizon*, was released early in 1971 and became a gold record by April. By September, he had another gold record for the single, "You've Got a Friend," which was written by Carole King and has became a standard. Other notable songs on the album were the title track and "Hey Mister, That's Me Up on the Jukebox," both written by Taylor. The demos Taylor had cut after he moved to New York in 1967 were released in 1971 in an album entitled *James Taylor and the Original Flying Machine*. He made the cover of the March 1, 1971 issue of *Time*, and before the year was over Taylor had starred in a full-length motion picture, *Two-Lane Backtop*. In that counterculture "road" film that followed in the wake of *Easy Rider*, Taylor played an inarticulate knockabout who drives here and there in a 1955 Chevy hot rod looking for drag races.

In the years of 1972 and 1973 Taylor did not tour and recorded only one album, *One Dog Man*, and two singles, "Long Ago, Far Away" and "Don't Let Me Be Lonely Tonight," all of which were bestsellers. On November 4, 1972, Taylor married Carly Simon, the distinguished songwriter and pop singer. They built a modern house of their own design on Martha's Vineyard and maintained an apartment in New York, where they raised a son and daughter. In 1973

Carly Simon's single, "Mockingbird," was performed as a duet with her husband and earned a gold record. That same year Taylor, too, issued a bestselling single, "One-Man Parade."

Taylor's first tour since 1972, a one-month jaunt, began in early 1974 and climaxed on May 26 with a concert at Carnegie Hall. Marriage and the responsibilities of being a father seemed to give Taylor a stability he had never known before, and he released his second album in two years, *Walking Man*, which contained such hits as "Let it All Fall Down," "Me and My Guitar" and "Fading Away." Reviewing the LP in *The New York Times*, Loraine Alterman said that "*Walking Man* is the work of a musician who colors his perceptions about life with great sensitivity, humor and thoughtfulness. There's a warmth about this album based, I believe, on his own joy about the way his life has turned out. The quiet glow that permeates both his music and his vocals makes all the more winning the intimate quality Taylor has always achieved as a performer. Always Taylor makes each listener feel as if he's singing his songs just for her or him." This warmth and Taylor's newfound feelings of happiness and joy also permeated his 1975 album, *Gorilla*, on which "How Sweet it Is," "Love Songs," "Sarah Maria" and "You Make it Easy" can be found, and on his 1976 releases, the buoyant hit single "Shower the People" and the album *In the Pocket*, which became a gold record. Among this LP's best cuts were "A Junkie's Lament," which Taylor sang as a duet with Art Garfunkel, "Family Man" and "Woman's Got to Have It."

Taylor contributed several songs to Art Turkel's Broadway musical, *Working*, which opened on May 14, 1978. In 1977 he had left Warner Brothers for Columbia Records, and released the album, *J.T.*, which became a platinum record. To Sam Sutherland of *High Fidelity*, *J.T.* "is most convincing as a singer's record not as a collection of new songs. Taylor's conservatism as a composer has made his melodic development over the years rather minimal. That, coupled with his similar restraint as a lyricist, and an introspection now robbed of its disturbing force. . . . fill many of his newer songs with echoes of his earliest work. Only when his meditations turn toward an underlying desperation— as in the gentle alienation of 'Another Gray Morning'—does he approach the gravity of his best [songs]."

Though in *J.T.*'s "There We Are" Taylor had evoked a heartfelt sense of marital contentment, and though Carly Simon took the stage at his concerts to share a duet with him, their marriage began to unravel in the late 1970s. A separation became permanent in 1980; by 1983 they were divorced and there were rumors that Taylor was again using hard drugs. Nonetheless Taylor remained professionally active, releasing the album *Flag* in 1979 and, two years later, the album *Dad Loves His Work* and the single "Her Town Too."

By 1985 Taylor was fully rehabilitated. The album he released that year, *That's Why I'm Here*, was thought by critics to be his strongest collection of songs in years, and he had a hit single in his quietly joyous rendition of the Buddy Holly song, "Every Day."

"I think I'm probably much more guarded in my personal life than I am in song lyrics," Taylor said in an interview for *Stereo Review*. "But it's not really being open in a song; it's not like relating directly to someone. A song is a form, you know, it's something that you're putting in the air, and if it's a personal statement, that's okay—if that's the type of thing you're trying to do. In other words, if I were to explain myself to you, if would be as if to elicit some response from you. But you don't do that in a song. There is no interchange. It's just a statement."

ABOUT: Current Biography, 1972.
Periodicals—National Observer June 8, 1970; New York Times Magazine February 21, 1971; Time March 1, 1971; Stereo Review January 1978.

THORNTON, JAMES (December 5, 1861–July 27, 1938), composer-lyricist of popular sentimental ballads in the 1890s, was born in Livingston, England. His family immigrated to the United States when he was eight, settling in Boston where they acquired American citizenship. Thornton attended the Elliott School in Boston only briefly, dropping out to earn a living. Aged 17 he worked as a night watchman for a Boston printing plant and spent his free time reading, an activity in which he was encouraged and guided by Henry Wadsworth Longfellow.

Thornton's career in popular music began in Boston when he worked as a singing waiter. After moving to New York City, permanently as it turned out, he worked as a singing waiter at Bal Mabile, a saloon on Bleecker Street. There, he became known not only for his rendition of current ballads but for his fund of anecdotes and jokes, and his insatiable appetite for alcohol. One of his drinking companions was John L. Sullivan, the legendary heavyweight boxing champion. Thornton would entertain with his stories while they made the rounds of cafés and saloons on New York's East Side.

While working at Bal Mabile, Thornton fell in love with Lizzie "Bonnie" Cox, an entertainer at the same saloon. They were married in the late 1880s; the marriage survived, although Thornton's hard drinking, extravagance and carousing all night with his pals, sorely tried his wife's patience. Through the years, Bonnie was the inspiration for some of Thornton's greatest ballads and in 1889 she introduced his first published ballad, "Remember Poor Mother at Home," which he had sold for $2.50.

Thornton left Bal Mabile in 1889 to begin a new career as a vaudeville performer in an act with Charles Lawlor, the composer of the popular song "Sidewalks of New York." On stage, Thornton wore a clerical costume while singing ballads and interjecting jokes and mock serious dialogues. For his act Thornton wrote "Upper Ten, Lower Five" in 1889 and, in 1890, "The Irish Jubilee." Though he wrote both words and music for the former, it is thought that he wrote only the lyrics of "Irish Jubilee," with Lawlor probably composing the music.

Thornton's first successful ballad was "My Sweetheart's the Man in the Moon" (1892). One evening, when Thornton shrugged off his wife's entreaty that he come home after one of his performances instead of making the rounds of saloons, she asked, "Am I still your sweetheart?" Thornton answered flippantly: "My Sweetheart's the man in the moon"—a phrase too clever for him to resist using as the title for a ballad. Thornton himself introduced it at the Orpheum Theatre in San Francisco, but it was his wife, Bonnie who popularized it in cafés and theaters after having sung it at Tony Pastor's Music Hall in New York. This song was revived in recordings by Manual Romain, Will Oakland, and The Knickerbockers.

Other hit songs followed. "She Never Saw the Streets of Cairo" (1893) mocked Little Egypt, the hootchie-kootchie dancer at the Chicago World's Fair, and quoted a hootchie-kootchie melody. In 1894 Thornton wrote "She May Have Seen Better Days," a sentimental ballad which W. H. Widom popularized in a minstrel show production. Thornton wrote four notable songs in 1896: "Don't Give Up Your Old Love for the New," "On the Benches in the Park," "Going for a Pardon" and "It Don't Seem Like the Same Old Smile." "On the Benches in the Park" was recorded by Frank Luther. The idea for "It Don't Seem Like the Same Old Smile" probably came to Thornton when he was a patient in Bellevue Hospital where an attendant smuggled in for Thornton a brand of liquor that he considered ghastly. (The word "smile" was used at that time as a slang expression for a shot of alcohol.) Helene Mora introduced this song in vaudeville. In

1897 Thornton composed "There's a Little Star Shining for You" and "Curious Cures," the latter one of several songs Thornton wrote about the "cures" for drinking that had been foisted on him in clinics.

Thornton's most celebrated ballad was "When You Were Sweet 16," published in 1898. Asked one day by his wife whether she still loved her, Thornton replied, "I love you like I did when you were sweet 16." Bonnie Thornton introduced the song in vaudeville, and it quickly became a standard in the repertories of vaudeville ballad singers and barber-shop quartets. As was his wont, Thornton sold his rights to this ballad for a pittance. In fact he sold the song to two publishers: to Joseph W. Stern & Co. for $25 and to M. Witmark & Sons for $15. When Witmark realized sheet-music sales of over a million copies, J. W. Stern sued, claiming prior ownership. The matter was settled out of court with a payment of $5,000 to J. W. Stern.

"When You Were Sweet 16" was recorded by Manuel Romain in 1909 and revived by the Mills Brothers in a recording of 1940. In motion pictures, Shirley Temple and a male quartet sang it in *Little Miss Broadway* (1938), and it was heard on the soundtrack as a recurrent theme in *The Strawberry Blonde* (1941). Bing Crosby sang it on the soundtrack of *The Great John L* (1945) and in *The Jolson Story* (1946) it was sung by Scotty Beckett, appearing on the screen as the adolescent Al Jolson.

In 1900 Thornton composed "The Bridge of Sighs," inspired by a bridge in New York connecting the criminal court with the Tombs. His last successful ballad was "There's a Mother Waiting for You at Home, Sweet Home" (1903). With the public and Tin Pan Alley losing interest in the kind of sentimental ballad that had been popular in the Gay Nineties, Thornton abandoned songwriting for stage performance. He appeared in the 1927 Broadway musical *Sidewalks of New York*, and his last public appearance was in the cast of *Sweet Adeline*, the 1929 Broadway musical by Jerome Kern and Oscar Hammerstein II.

ABOUT: Ewen, D. The Life and Death of Tin Pan Alley, 1964; Spaeth, S. A History of Popular Music in America, 1948.

TIERNEY, HARRY (AUSTIN) (May 21, 1890–March 22, 1965), composer, was born in Perth Amboy, New Jersey into an Irish-American family of trained musicians. His father, Patrick Tierney, was a business executive who played the trumpet in a symphony orches-

HARRY TIERNEY

tra, and his mother, Catherine (Morrisey) Tierney, was a concert pianist. Harry Tierney's first piano teacher was his mother, and his uncle gave him his first instruction in harmony and composition. Tierney completed his training in music at the Virgil Conservatory of Music, New York City, from which he graduated in 1911.

From 1911 to 1913 Tierney toured the United States as a concert pianist. He moved to London in 1913 and worked as a staff composer for the publishing house of Francis, Day and Hunter. In London, some of his songs were published while several others were interpolated into *Keep Smiling* (1913) and *Not Likely* (1914), revues produced by André Charlot.

Tierney returned to the United States in 1916, the year his first hit song, "M-i-s-s-i-s-s-i-p-p-i" (lyrics by Bert Hanlon and Benny Ryan), was introduced by Frances White in Flo Ziegfeld's *Midnight Frolics* (1916); Tierney's song was popularized in 1917 in a recording by Anna Wheaton. Tierney's songs were now beginning to be interpolated into numerous Broadway musicals: "Sometime" (lyrics by William Jerome) was included in *Betty* (1916); "So This is Paris" (lyrics by Harold Atteridge) in *The Passing Show of 1916*; "It's a Cute Little Way of My Own" and "Oh, I Want to Be Good, But My Eyes Won't Let Me" (lyrics by Alfred Bryan) were introduced by Anna Held in *Follow Me* (1917); and "On Atlantic Beach" and "Honky Tonk Town" (lyrics by Joseph McCarthy) were introduced in the Hippodrome spectacle, *Everything* (1918).

In 1918 Tierney was hired as a staff composer by the Tin Pan Alley firm of Jerome H. Remick & Co. A year later he made the first of several contributions to the *Ziegfeld Follies* when "My Baby's Arms" (lyrics by McCarthy) was introduced in the *Ziegfeld Follies of 1919*. In 1919 Tierney's songs "Charming" and "A Wee Bit of Lace" (lyrics by McCarthy) were interpolated into the George M. Cohan musical *The Royal Vagabond*.

Tierney's greatest success on the Great White Way was his music for *Irene* (November 18, 1919), whose run of 670 consecutive performances was then the longest of any musical in Broadway history. With a book by James Montgomery and lyrics by Joseph McCarthy, *Irene* was a charming Cinderella story of Irene O'Dare, a shop girl from the New York slums who finds a patron, and eventually a husband, in Donald Marshall, who sponsors her career as a high-fashion model.

One of America's beloved waltzes, "Alice Blue Gown" (also known as "In My Sweet Little Alice Blue Gown") was introduced in *Irene* by Adele Rowland. (The color blue was fashionable in women's attire in 1919 after having been popularized by Alice Roosevelt Longworth, the daughter of President Theodore Roosevelt.) In the 1940 motion picture version of *Irene*, "Alice Blue Gown" was sung by Anna Neagle, who danced to it with Ray Milland. This song was recorded in 1920 by Edith Day and later on by Kenny Baker, Donald Novis and the orchestras of Eddie Duchin, Wayne King and Orrin Tucker. On April 13, 1940 it made its only appearance on *Your Hit Parade*. The title song was introduced (and recorded) by Edith Day, was sung in the film version of *Irene* by a chorus and was recorded by the orchestras of Orrin Tucker and Ted Straeter. "Castle of My Dreams" (melody was borrowed from Chopin's *Minute Waltz*) was introduced by Bernice McCabe and recorded by Edith Day. In the movie *Irene* it was sung by a chorus and used as a recurring theme.

Refurbished with a new book by Hugh Wheeler and Joseph Stein, *Irene* triumphantly returned to Broadway on March 13, 1973, directed by Gower Champion with Debbie Reynolds making her Broadway debut in the title role. It had a two-year run of 594 performances. Five songs from the first production were retained, and eight new numbers by various songwriters were added; the entire score was released in an original cast album.

Tierney and McCarthy provided two songs for the *Ziegfeld Follies of 1920*. That year Tierney went to London to assist in the production of *Irene* and to compose the score for *Afgar*, a comic opera produced by Charles Cochran. A year later Tierney was back on Broadway, contributing songs to *The Broadway Whirl*, starring

Blanche Ring (June 8, 1921), and, more important, the complete score for *Up She Goes* (November 6, 1922), a comedy which ran for 256 performances. The book by Frank Craven dealt with the problems confronting an about-to-be-married couple who are building a bungalow with the unhelpful assistance of the girl's family. The young lovers quarrel and separate but are reconciled when they happen upon one another unexpectedly at the bungalow. "Lady Luck, Smile at Me" was introduced by Donald Brian and "Let's Kiss and Make Up" by Brian and Gloria Foy (lyrics to both by McCarthy).

Tierney and McCarthy contributed songs to the ill-fated Broadway musical *Glory* (December 25, 1922), which closed after a savaging by the press. However, they scored a major success with *Kid Boots* (December 31, 1923), a Ziegfeld production which had a run of 479 performances. In the book by William Anthony McGuire and Otto Harbach, Kid Boots (Eddie Cantor) is a caddie at the Everglades Golf Club in Palm Beach who moonlights by selling bootleg whiskey and crooked golf balls that make golfers turn to him for lessons. The principal Tierney song in this score was "Someone Loves You After All," a duet for Cantor and Mary Eaton.

To the *Ziegfeld Follies of 1923*, Tierney and McCarthy contributed "Take O Take Those Lips Away," introduced by Brooke Johns. Their greatest success since *Irene* was *Rio Rita*, which began a 504-performance run on February 2, 1927. This lavish Ziegfeld production, with sets and costumes designed by Joseph Urban, opened the palatial Ziegfeld Theatre on Sixth Avenue because Oscar Hammerstein II and Jerome Kern did not have *Show Boat* ready in time. The book by Guy Bolton and Fred Thompson is set in Mexico, where Jim, a captain of the Texas Rangers, falls in love with a local girl, Rio Rita, while hunting for a Mexican bandit. The suspicion that the bandit is Rio Rita's brother is dispelled when the outlaw is captured, and Jim and Rio Rita are able to marry.

The title number, sung by J. Harold Murray and Ethelind Terry, became one of the hit songs of 1927 when it was recorded by Edith Day, by the Knickerbockers and by the orchestras of Sam Lanin and Nathaniel Shilkret. Bebe Daniels and John Boles sang it in the first film version of *Rio Rita* (1929) and John Carroll in the second (1942). "The Rangers' Song," introduced by Murray, Harry Ratcliff, Donald Douglas and chorus, was performed by John Boles in the first film version and by Kathryn Grayson, John Carroll and chorus in the second. John Raitt recorded it. "Following the Sun Around" was heard only in the stage musical, in which it was introduced by J. Harold Murray; it was recorded by Carl Fenton.

On February 21, 1928, Tierney married Ava Lowry. They had one child, a son. Tierney's last Broadway musical, *Cross My Heart*, opened later that year, on September 17, 1928, but closed after just 64 performances.

Tierney went to California in 1928 to help produce the film version of *Rio Rita*. In Hollywood, while working for the RKO studios, he wrote songs for two inconsequential films, *Dixiana* (1930) and *Half Shot at Sunrise* (1931).

Tierney's career went into decline after that. An operetta, *Omar Khaayam*, based on Arnold Kummer's novel *Forbidden Wine* (1932) was never produced. Another Tierney operetta, *Beau Brummel*, was produced in St. Louis in 1933, but it failed and has never been revived. Except for a return to Hollywood in 1939 to help produce a screen adaptation of *Irene*, and the composition of music for a ballet, *Prelude to a Holiday in Hong Kong*, Tierney was in retirement for the last three decades of his life. He lived with his wife in an apartment on East 79th Street in Manhattan. His hobbies were golf, art collecting and attending the ballet.

ABOUT: Rigdon, W. (ed.) The Biographical Encyclopedia and Who's Who in the American Theatre, 1966; ASCAP Biographical Dictionary, 4th ed. 1980.

TIOMKIN, DIMITRI (May 10, 1894–November 11, 1980), composer, provided the background music for some 160 nonmusical films together with numerous hit songs that were introduced in Hollywood movies, many of them Westerns, war movies or epic adventures. He received 24 Oscar nominations and won four Oscars.

He was born near St. Petersburg, Russia, the son of Dr. Zinovie Tiomkin, a physician who distinguished himself in Berlin as an assistant to Dr. Paul Ehrlich, who had discovered a cure for syphilis. Tiomkin's mother, Marie (Tartakovsky) Tiomkin, was a pianist and music teacher who gave her son piano lessons. He was also interested in mathematics and the stage, but his native musical talent convinced his mother that he should receive thorough training. In 1912 Tiomkin entered the St. Petersburg Conservatory, studying piano with Isabelle Vengerova and Felix Blumenfeld and composition with Alexander Glazunov. At the conservatory Tiomkin earned spending money by playing the piano for silent films, but also made appearances as a concert pianist.

Following the civil war, Tiomkin immigrated

DIMITRI TIOMKIN

to Berlin, where he lived from 1921 to 1924 and studied piano with Egon Petri and Ferruccio Busoni. In 1922 Tiomkin began his career as a concert virtuoso, giving piano performances throughout Europe and even appearing several times as a soloist with the Berlin Philharmonic. At this time Tiomkin and Michael Kariton formed a two-piano team that was enthusiastically received in Paris. They came to the United States in 1925 for a six-month tour, playing the Orpheum vaudeville circuit for a salary of $1,000 a week. This was Tiomkin's introduction to American popular music.

On May 28, 1925 Tiomkin married Albertina Rasch, a ballerina and choreographer. After completing the American tour, Tiomkin returned to Europe, giving concert tours and appearing as a solo pianist, often in programs featuring contemporary music. On May 29, 1928, at the Paris Opéra, he was heard in the European premiere of Gershwin's *Concerto in F*.

In 1930 Albertina Rasch was engaged by the MGM studios to supervise the performance of ballet sequences in Hollywood musicals. For four of these films Tiomkin provided the music. His first assignment to compose background music came with *Resurrection* in 1931, and for the next two years he gave piano concerts throughout the United States. In 1933 he composed the background music for *Alice in Wonderland*, working on his score more than 16 hours a day for 14 days, then conducting and recording it under conditions he described as "terrifying" and "fantastically stupid." Other assignments for minor films came after that, and it was not until he wrote the background music for *Lost Horizon* in 1937 that Tiomkin had his first score that was a popular success.

Tiomkin also became a naturalized American citizen in 1937. Established in the film industry, Tiomkin and his wife acquired a mansion on South Windsor Boulevard in Los Angeles. Over the next quarter of a century, he worked on assignment for every major studio in Hollywood. He composed the background music for the following films: *You Can't Take It With You* (1938); *Mr. Smith Goes to Washington*, (1939); *The Westerner* (1940); *Meet John Doe* (1941); *The Corsican Brothers* (1941); *The Moon and Sixpence* (1942); *The Bridge of San Luis Rey* (1944); *Duel in the Sun* (1946); *Champion* (1949); *Portrait of Jennie* (1949); *Home of the Brave* (1949); *The Happy Time* (1952); *High Noon* (1952); *I Confess* (1953); *Dial M For Murder* (1954); *The High and the Mighty* (1954); *Friendly Persuasion* (1956); *Giant* (1956); *The Young Land* (1957); *Gunfight at O. K. Corral* (1957); *The Old Man and the Sea* (1958); *The Alamo* (1960); *The Sundowners* (1960); *The Guns of Navarone* (1961); *Town Without Pity* (1961); *55 Days at Peking* (1963); *Circus World* (1964); *Fall of the Roman Empire* (1964); and *36 Hours* (1965).

Tiomkin received his first Oscar nomination for the background music to *Mr. Smith Goes to Washington*, starring James Stewart and Claude Rains. His first two Oscars came in 1952 for the background music and the title song for the classic Gary Cooper Western, *High Noon*. This was followed by two more Oscars, for the background music to *The High and the Mighty*, starring John Wayne and Claire Trevor in 1954, and to *The Old Man and the Sea*, starring Spencer Tracy as Hemingway's "old man," in 1958. When he was presented with the Oscar for *The High and the Mighty*, Tiomkin amused the audience when he expressed his gratitude not to his wife, producers or co-workers, but to Beethoven, Tchaikovsky, Brahms, and Wagner, without whose help, he observed, he could not have earned the statuette.

Although he was less than prolific in writing songs for films, Tiomkin's best numbers maintained the high standard of his finest background music. The song that brought him an Oscar became a standard—the title number for *High Noon*, also known as "Do Not Forsake Me"—and to hear its melody is to recall vividly the image of Gary Cooper facing down the outlaw Frank Miller and his gang of killers. The song was not part of the film when it was first screened for the producer, Stanley Kramer, and director, Fred Zinnemann. Both men felt that the picture needed an opening theme song to set

the mood for the story and to adumbrate the plot. Kramer called on Tiomkin and his lyricist, Ned Washington, to do the job. "The rule book says that in the movies you can't have singing while there's dialogue," Tiomkin noted in his autobiography. "But I convinced Stanley Kramer that it might be a good idea to have the song sung, whistled and played by the orchestra. A melody came to me. I played it on the piano at home and developed it until I thought it was right."

Tiomkin himself acquired the publication and recording rights to the theme song, and persuaded Frankie Laine to record it, a release that sold a million copies. By the time *High Noon* was released, months after Laine's recording had become a hit, the song had already generated widespread interest in the film, which is considered a classic Western. In the film, the song was introduced on the soundtrack by Tex Ritter, a performer of country-western and "cowboy" music. Ritter initially refused to record it, but following Frankie Laine's success, he relented and his version proved successful.

"Return to Paradise" (lyrics by Ned Washington) was the theme music for the 1953 movie of that title starring Gary Cooper. This song was popularized in a bestselling recording by the orchestra of Percy Faith.

"Friendly Persuasion," or "Thee I Love" (1956, lyrics by Paul Francis Webster), was the title song for another movie starring Gary Cooper, this one about a family whose son (Anthony Perkins) must come to terms with the question of physical violence during the Civil War. The film originally was to have been called *Thee I Love*, and when Perry Como turned down an offer to record the theme song the assignment went to Pat Boone, then a neophyte in show business, who received a flat payment of three thousand dollars. This recording had sales of a million and a half copies and made Boone a star.

"Wild is the Wind" (lyrics by Washington) was the title song of a 1957 movie about love, marriage and adultery starring Anna Magnani and Anthony Quinn. It was introduced on the soundtrack by Johnny Mathis, whose recording was a bestseller.

"Strange Are the Ways of Love" (lyrics by Washington) was introduced by Randy Sparks in *The Young Land* (1959), about racial prejudice in the Wild West.

"The Ballad of the Alamo" (lyrics by Webster) was introduced chorally on the soundtrack of *The Alamo* (1960), starring John Wayne and popularized in a recording by Marty Robbins.

"The Need for Love," or "The Unforgiven," was a song adaptation of the theme music from the *Unforgiven* (1960), starring Audrey Hepburn and Burt Lancaster and directed by John Huston. It was popularized as an instrumental in a recording by Don Costa's orchestra and as a vocal (lyrics by Ned Washington) in a recording by the McGuire Sisters.

"The Green Leaves of Summer" (lyrics by Webster) was introduced chorally on the soundtrack of *The Alamo* and recorded by the Brothers Four.

"They Call it Love" (lyrics by Washington), melody derived from an old Greek song, "Yala Yala," was introduced on the soundtrack of *The Guns of Navarone* (1961), starring Gregory Peck and David Niven, one of the greatest World War II action films. The movie's title song was an adaptation of the principal theme from Tiomkin's score with lyrics added later by Paul Francis Webster. As a vocal recording it was popularized by the orchestra of Mitch Miller and chorus.

"So Little Time" (lyrics by Webster) was introduced by Andy Williams on the soundtrack behind the end titles of *55 Days in Peking* (1963), starring Ava Gardner, David Niven and Charlton Heston. Williams's recording made the song famous.

"Town Without Pity" (lyrics by Washington) was introduced in the 1961 film of that title and was popularized by Gene Pitney's recording.

"A Heart Must Learn to Love" (lyrics by Webster) was the theme of *36 Hours* (1964), starring James Garner.

"The Fall of Love" (lyrics by Webster) was a song adapted from Tiomkin's orchestral theme for *The Fall of the Roman Empire* (1964), starring Sophia Loren and Alec Guinness.

"A Circus World" (lyrics by Washington) was the title song of a 1964 movie starring John Wayne. Introduced on the soundtrack, it was popularized in a recording by Andy Williams.

In 1958 Tiomkin composed the theme song for the popular CBS-TV Western series, *Rawhide*, featuring young Clint Eastwood as Rowdy Yates. With lyrics by Ned Washington, "Rawhide" was sung under the opening titles by Frankie Laine.

To an interviewer, Tiomkin vigorously denied the accusation that he composed for film solely for the enjoyment of financial benefits. "It isn't true that I do it only for money," he protested. "Writing film music lets me compose in as fine a style as I am capable of. I'm a classicist by nature, and if you examine my scores you will find fugues, rondos and passacaglias. I'm no Beethoven but I think if I devoted myself to concert composition I might have been a Rachmanioff. I'm not in sympathy with the harsh, atonal music of today. It's enough to lacerate your ears. Perhaps that is why I have done well in films—it was music for the masses."

Tiomkin's wife, Albertina, died in 1968; they were childless. His last ten years were lived in the Highgate section of London where, in 1972, he married Olivia Patch.

Tiomkin's last assignment in films was to serve as executive producer of *Tschaikowsky*, for which he did the scoring of that master's music. This Soviet-made film had its world premiere in Moscow on September 1, 1970, with Tiomkin attending.

During World War II, Tiomkin had worked with the Signal Corps as a music director, adviser and consultant, scoring the music for many of the armed service's training and orientation films. In 1960, in France, Tiomkin was named Chevalier of the Legion of Honor and in 1977 he was decorated Officier of the Legion of Honor.

He died at his home in London in 1980, two weeks after fracturing his pelvis in a fall. His friend, the songwriter John Green, said of Tiomkin: "Composing expresses his talent; the achievement of international fame fulfils his ego; successful negotiating gratifies his gamesmanship; the use of the epic dialect satisfies his comedic need; his gift for gracious hospitality gives him happiness."

ABOUT: *Periodicals*—Cue March 23, 1957; New York Times July 21, 1957.

VAN ALSTYNE, EGBERT (March 5, 1882– July 9, 1951), composer, was born in Chicago. At an early age he taught himself to play the organ by ear and, at seven, performed hymns in Sunday school at the Methodist church in Marengo, Illinois. His parents were devoutly religious and his father was a church director. On a scholarship Egbert studied piano at the Chicago Musical College while attending public schools in Chicago. He completed his academic education at Cornell College in Iowa.

After college, Van Alstyne, as pianist and musical director, went on tour with a repertory company playing one-night stands throughout the West and Southwest. Forced into bankruptcy, it disbanded in Nogales, Mexico, leaving Van Alstyne stranded. Working as pianist in a honkytonk he earned enough money to pay his way back to Chicago in 1898. There he found employment as a song plugger.

In 1900 Van Alstyne went to New York, where he became a song plugger for the Tin Pan Alley publishing house of Jerome H. Remick & Co. In 1903, with Harry Williams as lyricist, Van

EGBERT VAN ALSTYNE

Alstyne composed his first successful song, "Navajo." One of the first Tin Pan Alley songs about the American Indian, "Navajo" started a vogue that lasted for several years. Marie Cahill introduced it in the Broadway musical *Nancy Brown* (1903) and Emma Carus recorded it. A year later Alstyne and Williams composed "Seminole," another popular "Indian" song, and "Back, Back, Back to Baltimore," a comedy number that was much performed by vaudevillians and minstrel show entertainers done up in blackface.

"In the Shade of the Old Apple Tree," written and published in 1905, has become a standard. According to Van Alstyne, the idea for this song came to him and Williams one day during a stroll through Central Park, even though that park had no apple trees. A favorite of ballad singers in vaudeville, this number was recorded by the Sportsmen, was revived in 1937 in a recording by the Mills Brothers with Louis Armstrong, and was interpolated into the 1945 movie musical *The Stork Club*.

In 1905 Van Alstyne and Williams composed "Good-a-bye, John," which Remick & Co. published on October 7, 1905 and that same year was interpolated into the Broadway musical *The Belle of Avenue A*. In 1906 another "Good-a-bye, John," with almost identical lyrics and a similar melody, appeared in the operetta *The Red Mill* and was attributed to Victor Herbert. It is highly unlikely that Herbert would have resorted to plagiarism, but even if he had he would not have appropriated a song so recently published and performed. However, it is curious that neither Van Alstyne nor Williams

challenged Herbert's right to "Good-a-bye, John."

In 1906 and 1907, Van Alstyne and Williams composed two more American Indian songs—"Cheyenne" and "San Antonio"—as well as "Won't You Come Over to My House," "There Never Was a Girl Like You" and "I'm Afraid to Come Home in the Dark." In 1908 they wrote "It Looks to Me Like a Big Night," and over the next two years composed the complete scores for two Broadway musicals. In *A Broken Idol* (August 14, 1909), starring Alice Yorke with libretto by Hal Stephens, an English nobleman hires an American to teach him New World Manners so that he can better woo a wealthy American woman. The aristocrat loses all interest when he discovers that the woman's fortune has been dissipated. *Girlies* (June 13, 1910) starred Joseph Cawthorn and Ernest Truex in a libretto by George V. Hobart. Cawthorn appeared as a botany teacher at a small college who is in love with its directress. Because she is uninterested in anyone so ordinary, he tries to make himself out to be a hero. Both musicals had short runs and neither yielded any memorable songs.

With Williams as Van Alstyne's lyricist until 1913, they composed "What's the Matter With Father?" in 1910, and "Good Night, Ladies" and "When I Was 21 and You Were Sweet 16" in 1911. The last-mentioned song was an attempt to exploit the popularity of James Thornton's ballad of 1898, "When You Were Sweet 16." The Van Alstyne–Williams song was recorded in 1911 by Harry MacDonough with the American Quartette. While pursuing their trade as songwriters, Van Alstyne and Williams also toured the vaudeville circuit in an act featuring their songs.

Their partnership broke up when Williams left for Hollywood in 1913 to work as a director of silent films and Van Alstyne acquired a new lyricist, Gus Kahn. One of their earliest collaborative efforts was "Sunshine and Roses" (1913); their first standard, and Kahn's first hit song, was "Memories" (1915). It was recorded by the celebrated concert tenor John McCormack, and later by Bing Crosby with the Ken Darby Singers. McCormack's recording was heard on the soundtrack of Gus Kahn's screen biography, *I'll See You in My Dreams* (1951).

"Pretty Baby" (music written with Tony Jackson) is one of the most durable of the Van Alstyne–Kahn oeuvre. Composed in 1916, it was introduced by Dolly Hackett in *The Passing Show of 1916*. "Pretty Baby" then entered the repertory of the Dolly Sisters and became their signature. Jimmy Dorsey recorded it, and it has been heard in many motion pictures. Charles

Winninger sang it in *Broadway Rhythm* (1944);
Robert Alda and chorus in *April Showers* (1949);
Al Jolson on the soundtrack of *Jolson Sings Again*
(1949); Danny Thomas in *I'll See You in My
Dreams*; and Eddie Cantor on the soundtrack of
The Eddie Cantor Story (1950). "Pretty Baby"
provided the title for, and was briefly heard in,
Louis Malle's nonmusical film of 1978, starring
Brooke Shields.

"Sailin' Away on the Henry Clay" was the Van
Alstyne–Kahn hit song of 1917 and "Your Eyes
Have Told Me So" achieved popularity in 1919.
The first of these was introduced by Elizabeth
Murray in the 1917 Broadway musical *Good
Night, Paul* and was recorded that year by Har-
ry Kaufman. It was revived in the 1935 movie
The Littlest Rebel, starring Shirley Temple.
"Your Eyes Have Told Me So" (music written
with Walter Blaufuss) was popularized in vaude-
ville by Grace La Rue, and two decades later was
recorded by Kate Smith. In film, James Melton
sang it in *Sing Me a Love Song* (1938) and Doris
Day and Gordon MacRae in *By the Light of the
Silvery Moon* (1953). This song was also heard as
background music in *I'll See You in My Dreams*.

Van Alstyne's only popular song of the 1920s
was his last notable musical achievement: "Drifting and Dreaming" (1925, lyrics by Haven Gillespie, music written with Erwin R. Schmidt and
Loyal Curtis). In 1925 it was popularized in recordings by the orchestras of George Olsen and
Fred Rich; it was later appropriated by Orrin
Tucker and his orchestra as their theme song. He
spent the last two decades of his life in retirement, living most of that time in Chicago, where
his mother, then in her 80s, was the star of a
weekly radio program.

ABOUT: Burton, J. The Blue Book of Tin Pan Alley,
1950; Craig, Sweet and Lowdown: America's Popular
Song Writers, 1978.

*

VAN HEUSEN, JAMES (January 26,
1913–), composer, collaborated with Johnny
Burke in the 1940s, writing songs for some of the
leading movies of that period. Many of those
numbers are identified with Bing Crosby, who
introduced and popularized them. In the 1950s
he teamed with Sammy Cahn, writing hit songs
for films, many of which were introduced and
popularized by Frank Sinatra.

James Van Heusen was born Edward Chester
Babcock in Syracuse, New York, one of the two
sons of Arthur Edward Babcock, a building contractor, and Ida Mae (Williams) Babcock, who
is believed to have been a descendant of Stephen
Foster. Though Van Heusen's father played the

JIMMY VAN HEUSEN

cornet and initially allowed his young son to take
piano lessons, he insisted that the boy forego music for a solid academic education. But Van
Heusen's interest in classroom learning was minimal, preferring instead to spend his time inventing tunes on the piano. He was expelled
from Central High School in 1928 for perpetrat-
ing a prank—singing in the school assembly a
frivolous, mildly salacious song, "My Canary
Has Rings Under His Eyes," which he had heard
on the radio. A year later he was dismissed from
Czenovia Seminary, a boarding school near Syracuse, for being what school officials called "a
little bum hanging around poolrooms."

Aged 15, while still a high school student, Van
Heusen found a part-time $15-a-week job as an
announcer for radio station WSYR in Syracuse.
The station manager insisted that he change his
name, and "Van Heusen" was appropriated
from an advertisement for the Van Heusen
clothing manufacturer; "James" was chosen as
the prefix because it had the right sound. "The
manager was delighted with the name change
and I kept the job," he explained. "I liked it for
the reason that my parents did not know I was
skipping school." The name James Van Heusen,
though used professionally and in his personal
life, was never legally acquired; that of Edward
Chester Babcock appears on his passport and
other documents.

Following his expulsion from the seminary,
Van Heusen had his own popular-song program
on WFBL, a Syracuse radio station. His broadcasts included new songs by the top songwriters
of the day even before the sheet music had been
distributed. Van Heusen explained: "When I was

in high school I used to make it a point to listen to every orchestra which introduced a new song. I would take the lyrics down in Gregg shorthand, because I had learned 120 words a minute during a summer vacation. I would write down at least the main eight-bar strain of the music, which in many songs was repeated three times. Via shorthand I had the lyrics intact and correct, and that portion of the music that I didn't catch I would compose myself. This way I was able to sing on my own little radio programs brand new songs."

From 1930 to 1932, Van Heusen attended Syracuse University, where he studied piano and composition and formed a songwriting partnership with Jerry Arlen, Harold Arlen's younger brother. When, in 1933, Harold Arlen was called to Hollywood for a screen assignment and could not fulfill a songwriting commitment for Harlem's Cotton Club, he suggested that his brother and Van Heusen take over. "The show was a 'flop,'" Van Heusen recalled, "and the song ('Harlem Hospitality') [we contributed] was terrible."

Now living in New York City, Van Heusen supported himself by waiting on tables and by operating a freight elevator at the Park Central Hotel, while trying to market the songs he was writing. In 1943, "There's a House in Harlem for Sale" (lyrics by Jerry Arlen) was purchased by the Santly Brothers Music Publishing Co., becoming Van Heusen's first publication. This song was performed by the Park Central Hotel orchestra and it brought Van Heusen a short-lived job as staff pianist at Santly Brothers. Van Heusen went on to work as a staff pianist for other publishers, eventually landing a job with the firm of Jerome H. Remick & Co.

In 1938, while employed at Remick, Van Heusen met Jimmy Dorsey. They wrote "It's the Dreamer in Me" (1938), which was introduced that year by the orchestra of Jimmy Dorsey, who recorded it and popularized it in nightclub and radio appearances. With a sheet-music sale of 100,000 copies, "It's the Dreamer in Me" became Van Heusen's first hit song, bringing him a two-year contract from Remick as the company's staff composer for a weekly salary of $200.

In 1938 Van Heusen acquired a new lyricist in the bandleader Eddie de Lange. That year three of their songs were heard on *Your Hit Parade*. "So Help Me" was introduced by Lee Wiley on the radio program *Swing Session* and was recorded by the orchestra of Russ Morgan. "Deep in a Dream" was recorded that year by both Bob Crosby and Cab Calloway; it was popularized by Guy Lombardo and His Royal Canadians and had a sheet-music sale of 200,000

copies. "Good for Nothin'" was popularized by Guy Lombardo.

In 1939 Van Heusen and De Lange composed "Heaven Can Wait," which was introduced by Jimmy Dorsey's orchestra (vocal by Jack Leonard.) With 11 hearings on *Your Hit Parade*, twice in first position, it was one of the year's biggest hits. "All I Remember is You," which had a single hearing on *Your Hit Parade* in the summer of 1939, was introduced by Tommy Dorsey. "Can I Help It" (1939) was recorded by Horace Heidt and had two hearings on *Your Hit Parade*.

Van Heusen and Lange made their first contribution to the Broadway musical theater with the score for *Swingin' the Dream* (November 29, 1939) setting *A Midsummer Night's Dream* to swing music. Set in Louisiana in 1890, the cast was made up largely of black artists. Though Louis Armstrong appeared as Bottom and Benny Goodman's sextet provided the music, *Swingin' the Dream* closed after just 13 performances. But the score nonetheless yielded a hit, "Darn That Dream," introduced by Maxine Sullivan and Louis Armstrong. In 1939 it was recorded by Dinah Shore and by the orchestras of Tommy Dorsey and Paul Whiteman. In 1940 it was heard once on *Your Hit Parade*, and by the end of 1940 the song had accumulated sheet-music sales of some 200,000 copies.

Working with lyricists other than De Lange, Van Heusen had two more songs on *Your Hit Parade* in 1939, "Speaking of Heaven" (lyrics by Mack Gordon) had two hearings, and with "Oh, You Crazy Moon" (six hearings), Van Heusen's collaboration with the lyricist Johnny Burke began. This song was introduced by Tommy Dorsey and recorded by Bob Crosby and by the orchestras of Chick Bullock and Glenn Miller.

Van Heusen left the employ of Remick in 1939. A year later, three new Van Heusen entries were heard on *Your Hit Parade*. "You Think of Ev'rything" (lyrics by Billy Rose and Joseph McCarthy), which Van Heusen had composed for Billy Rose's Acquacade at the 1939 New York World's Fair. "All This and Heaven Too" (lyrics by De Lange), with six hearings on *Your Hit Parade*, was composed to promote the movie of the same title starring Bette Davis and Charles Boyer. The song was recorded by Tommy Dorsey's band (vocal by Frank Sinatra) and by the orchestra of Charlie Barnet. "Looking for Yesterday" (lyrics by De Lange), which had 15 *Hit Parade* hearings, was popularized in recordings by the orchestras of Glenn Miller, Kay Kyser, Woody Herman and Tommy Dorsey. "Imagination" (lyrics by Johnny Burke)—13 hearings, three times in first position—was introduced by Fred Waring's Pennsylvanians and popularized in recordings by Ella Fitzgerald, Dinah Shore, Kate Smith, Glenn Miller and the Tommy Dorsey orchestra (vocal by Frank Sinatra).

The success of "Imagination" took Van Heusen to Hollywood, where he enjoyed his greatest success. His first assignment was at the Paramount studios where, with the lyricist Johnny Burke, he wrote the songs for *Love Thy Neighbor* (1940), starring Jack Benny. Van Heusen and Burke remained collaborators for about 15 years, becoming the leading songwriters in Hollywood during that period. Their score for *Love Thy Neighbor* contained the following hit songs: "Do You Know Why?" and "Isn't That Just Like Love?" were introduced by Mary Martin and the Merry Macs, and "Dearest, Darest I?" was introduced by Eddie ("Rochester") Anderson. "Do You Know Why?" and "Isn't That Just Like Love" were recorded by the orchestra of Tommy Dorsey, the former with vocal by Frank Sinatra.

In 1940 Van Heusen and Burke composed "Polka Dots and Moonbeams," which was popularized that year not in any film but in recordings by the orchestras of Tommy Dorsey (vocal by Frank Sinatra), Glenn Miller and Glen Gray. "Humpty Dumpty Heart" was the best song from Van Heusen and Burke's second film, *Playmates* (1941), in which it was introduced by Harry Babbitt with the Kay Kyser orchestra. It was popularized in recordings by the orchestras of Glenn Miller, Kay Kyser and Art Jarrett, and had a single hearing on *Your Hit Parade* on January 31, 1942.

When Bing Crosby was contracted to star with Bob Hope in the first of their famous "road" films—*Road to Sinapore* (1941)—he asked Van Heusen and Burke to write the songs. This affiliation—Crosby introducing Burke–Van Heusen songs in popular movies—lasted a decade. And it was Crosby's performance of these songs, on the screen, on records and on radio, that brought them enormous popularity and made their composers famous. Indeed the list of Van Heusen–Burke songs introduced in films by Bing Crosby comprises some of the finest music to be heard in motion pictures in the 1940s and 1950s. The following are among the most significant: "It's Always You," "Ain't Got a Dime in My Pocket" and "Birds of a Feather" from *Road to Zanzibar* (1941). "It's Always You" was recorded by Tommy Dorsey's orchestra (vocal by Frank Sinatra), and had nine hearings on *Your Hit Parade*.

The title song and "Moonlight Becomes You" were introduced by Crosby in *Road to Morocco* (1942). "Moonlight Becomes You," had more than a dozen hearings on *Your Hit Parade*, twice in first position.

"Sunday, Monday or Always" and "If You Please" were sung by Crosby in *Dixie* (1943). The former had 18 hearings on *Your Hit Parade*, six times in first position, and both songs were recorded by Frank Sinatra.

"Swinging on a Star," "The Day After Forever" and the title song were first heard in *Going My Way* (1944), for which Crosby won an Oscar as best actor. "Swinging on a Star" also received an Oscar, Van Heusen's first, and was heard 19 times on *Your Hit Parade*. The writing of "Swinging on a Star" proved to be one of the most difficult assignments ever tackled by Burke and Van Heusen. They were at first stymied by the requirement that they compose a song for Crosby in which he, a priest, lectures a gang of juvenile troublemakers about the wisdom of heeding the Ten Commandments. Burke was at a loss for any suitable lyrics until one evening when he dined at Crosby's house. There, one of Crosby's sons misbehaved, and his father scolded him for acting "like a mule." Burke found the image of a child refusing to better himself because he was stubborn as a mule arresting, and he started wondering what an unruly child would be like if he behaved like a fish, or a pig, and so forth. The next morning the lyrics had been committed to paper, and though "Swinging on a Star" did not literally preach the Ten Commandments, it did so obliquely. More than 200 versions of the song have been recorded, with Crosby's enjoying the greatest successs with a sale of more than a million discs. The complete score of *Going My Way* was recorded in a soundtrack recording.

"Aren't You Glad You're You" was introduced in *The Bells of St. Mary's* (1946). It was also recorded by the orchestra of Les Brown and had ten representations on *Your Hit Parade*. The music from *The Bells of St. Mary's* was released in a soundtrack recording.

"Welcome to My Dreams," "It's Anybody's Spring" and "Put it There, Pal" were introduced in *The Road to Utopia* (1946). "Put it There, Pal" was a duet for Hope and Crosby.

"As Long as I'm Dreaming," "Smile Right Back at the Sun" and "My Heart is a Hobo" were sung by Crosby in *Welcome Stranger* (1947).

"But Beautiful," "Country Style" and "You Don't Have to Know the Language," the last sung with the Andrews Sisters, were introduced in *Road to Rio* (1948). "But Beautiful," which was recorded by Tex Beneke and his orchestra, was heard nine times on *Your Hit Parade*. "Country Style" was recorded by Crosby and by the orchestra of Tommy Tucker.

"You're in Love With Someone" was first heard in *Top o' the Morning* (1949), a comedy with Barry Fitzgerald and Ann Blyth.

"Once and for Always" and "When is Some-time?" were sung by Crosby in *A Connecticut Yankee* (1949), a lavish musical with Rhonda Fleming and Cedric Hardwicke.

"And You'll Be Home" came from *Mr. Music* (1950).

"Sunshine Cake," sung with Coleen Gray and Clarence Muse, was introduced by Crosby in *Riding High* (1950), directed by Frank Capra.

Several major film songs by Van Heusen and Burke were introduced by stars other than Bing Crosby . "Suddenly it's Spring" was performed by Ginger Rogers in *Lady in the Dark* (1944), and was recorded by Glen Gray and the Casa Loma Orchestra (vocal by Eugenie Baird).

"It Could Happen to You" was introduced by Dorothy Lamour and Fred MacMurray in *And the Angels Sing* (1944). It had 11 hearings on *Your Hit Parade*.

"Like Someone in Love" and "Sleigh Ride in July" were introduced by Dinah Shore in *Belle of the Yukon* (1944). The former was recorded by Bing Crosby, the latter by Crosby and by the orchestras of Tommy Dorsey and Les Brown. "Sleighride in July" made three appearances on *Your Hit Parade*.

"Personality" was sung by Dorothy Lamour in *Road to Utopia* (1946). It was recorded by Johnny Mercer and had ten hearings on *Your Hit Parade*.

"A Friend of Yours" was introduced by Lee Sullivan in *The Great John L* (1945). It was recorded by Bing Crosby and was heard twice on *Your Hit Parade*.

During World War II Van Heusen helped out with the U.S. war effort. He accompanied Bing Crosby on a tour of army camps on the West Coast in the summer of 1942. Three years later Van Heusen received a citation and plaque and, in 1946, a silver medal from the U.S. Treasury Department for helping to promote the sale of war and victory bonds. From 1942 to 1944, he was also a test pilot for the Lockheed aircraft company, while still working in the employ of the film studios. And he told this writer, "having two names now stood me in good stead. I was able to continue writing songs under the name of James Van Heusen and the 120 test pilots in the pilot house at Lockheed did not know for at least a year and a half that the Edward Babcock in their midst was the . . . James Van Heusen whose song 'Sunday, Monday or Always' was currently [in first place] on *Your Hit Parade*, and I was just 'one of the guys.' The fact that I was a test pilot was kept a secret from Paramount Pictures in the early days of my employment there because, as Johnny Burke warned me at the time, if they knew I was test-flying airplanes

at Lockheed they would not assign me to a picture in the middle of which I might be killed flying a sick airplane. The schedule at Lockheed was as follows: Four days running I would get up at 4 a. m. to start flying at 5 a. m. and I would be back home, or at the studio , by noon. Then after two and a half days, I would fly three days beginning at 1 p. m. and I could to to the studio in the mornings. Being young and able to survive without too much sleep I was able to juggle both occupations."

In 1944 Van Heusen and Burke formed their own publishing company, Burke & Van Heusen Inc., with Van Heusen serving as president. After the war, with Burke still his lyricist, Van Heusen returned to the Broadway musical theater with the score for *Nellie Bly* (January 21, 1946), which dealt with the adventures of Nellie Bly in her quest to better Phileas Fogg's 80-day record for circumnavigating the globe. "Just My Luck," introduced by Joy Hodges and William Gaxton, and "Harmony," introduced by William Gaxton and Victor Moore, were the show's principal, songs. *Nellie Bly* closed after just 16 performances, but "Harmony" survived by being interpolated into the movie *Variety Girl* (1947), in which it was performed by Bing Crosby, Bob Hope and Dorothy Lamour.

Carnival in Flanders (September 8, 1953), too, was a box-office failure on Broadway, its final curtain being lowered after the sixth performance. The noted director of screen comedies Preston Sturges wrote the text, basing it on a French motion picture of 1936 that was set in 17th-century Flanders. From this score came "Here's That Rainy Day," introduced by John Raitt, and "The Very Necessary You," a duet for Kevin Scott and Pat Stanley.

With *Carnival in Flanders*, the collaboration of Van Heusen and Burke ended. Burke's health was failing and he was unable to work in 1954 and 1955. Because a contractual agreement barred Van Heusen from working with anyone but Burke, Van Heusen for a time had to publish his songs under a pseudonym. When his exclusive contract with Burke was terminated, Van Heusen formed Maraville Music with Frank Sinatra and Henry Sanciola. Maraville's first publication was the title number of a movie starring Sinatra, *Not as a Stranger* (1955), in which the song (lyrics by Buddy Kaye) was used orchestrally for a dance episode, though Sinatra recorded it as a vocal.

In 1955 when new songs were needed for a planned film remake of *Anything Goes*, the Cole Porter stage musical, Bing Crosby, its star, suggested that Van Heusen team up with the lyricist Sammy Cahn to write the music. Cahn, who had just severed a songwriting awrrangement with the composer Jule Styne, was, like Van Heusen, in search of a partner. They teamed up for the first time to write the title song of *The Tender Trap* (1955), starring Frank Sinatra and Debbie Reynolds. Sinatra introduced it in the movie and his recording was a bestseller. Sinatra now began to play as important a role in promoting Van Heusen's songs as Bing Crosby had earlier.

Before *Anything Goes* was released in 1956 with three new songs by Van Heusen and Cahn, the two songwriters composed the score for a musical adaptation of Thornton Wilder's prize-winning play of 1938, *Our Town*, starring Frank Sinatra and Paul Newman when it made its debut on the NBC-TV network on September 10, 1955. One of the production's songs, "Love and Marriage," introduced and recorded by Sinatra, brought the songwriters their first Emmy (it was the first Emmy ever awarded to an individual song).

The Van Heusen–Cahn collaboration was now beginning to rival the achievements of the Van Heusen–Burke partnership. Van Heusen and Cahn collected three Oscars. The first was for "All the Way," which Sinatra introduced in *The Joker Is Wild* (1957), the screen biography of the nightclub entertainer Joe E. Lewis. "All the Way," Van Heusen has explained, was written so that Sinatra could depict Lewis's loss of voice. "The big jump musically at the end of the second to the middle of the third bar was especially designed to be difficult for [Sinatra] to sing, and he was supposed to break down dramatically." One of Sinatra's greatest bestsellers, "All the Way" was heard 11 times on *Your Hit Parade*, once in first position.

Their second Oscar came with "High Hopes," which Sinatra, singing with the young Eddie Hodges, introduced in *A Hole in the Head* (1959). In 1960, with revised lyrics, "High Hopes" was used to promote the presidential campaign of Senator John F. Kennedy.

In 1963 Van Heusen and Cahn won their third Oscar for "Call Me Irresponsible," which Jackie Gleason introduced in *Papa's Delicate Condition* (1963). This song had been composed in 1955 when *Papa's Delicate Condition* was being planned as a vehicle for Fred Astaire. After the movie version starring Gleason was released the song was popularized in recordings by Sinatra and by Jack Jones.

Other Van Heusen–Cahn screen songs were: The title song for *The Man with the Golden Arm* (1955), starring Frank Sinatra, which was recorded by the orchestras of Elmer Bernstein and Morris Stoloff.

"To Love and Be Loved," which was com-

posed for *Some Came Running* (1958), starring Sinatra, Dean Martin and Shirley MacLaine. It was popularized by Sinatra's recording.

"Indiscreet," which was based on the instrumental theme from the 1958 motion picture of the same name, starring Ingrid Bergman and Cary Grant. It was recorded by Sinatra.

"The Second Time Around," which was introduced by Bing Crosby in *High Time* (1960), and was recorded by Sinatra and by Shirley Bassey.

The title song of *A Pocketful of Miracles* (1961), starring Bette Davis, which was introduced on the soundtrack by Sinatra.

The title song of *The Boys' Night Out* (1962), which was popularized by Patti Page's recording.

"Warmer Than a Whisper," which was introduced by Dorothy Lamour in *The Road to Hong Kong* (1962).

"My Kind of Town," which was introduced by Frank Sinatra in *Robin and the 7 Hoods* (1964). It has become a kind of theme song for the city of Chicago, and was popularized by Sinatra's bestselling recording. With new verses it was used to promote Robert F. Kennedy's 1964 campaign for the U.S. Senate in New York.

The title song for *Where Love Has Gone* (1964), which was introduced on the soundtrack by Jack Jones, who also recorded it.

The title song for *Thoroughly Modern Millie* (1967), in which it was introduced by Julie Andrews, who recorded it.

Van Heusen and Cahn also wrote special musical material for nightclub and theatrical appearances by Paul Anka, Lena Horne, Nat King Cole and Sammy Davis Jr., among others. Van Heusen and Cahn also wrote the title songs for the Sinatra albums *Come Fly With Me* (1959), *Only the Lonely* (1958), *Come Dance With Me* (1959), *No One Cares* (1959), *Ring-a-Ding-Ding* (1961) and *September of My Years* (1965). Barbara Streisand introduced their song "Love is a Bore" in her bestselling recording of 1964.

Their contributions to television since *Our Town* have included the production of four spectaculars in 1959–60 for the *Frank Sinatra Show*; the songs for *Potomac Madness*, a 1960 television comedy starring Bob Hope; the title song for the popular NBC sitcom *Hazel*, starring Shirley Booth; songs for the television special *Jack and the Beanstalk* (1966), starring Gene Kelly, which earned Van Heusen and Cahn their second Emmy; and songs for the television specials *The Legend of Robin Hood* (1968) and *Journey Back to Oz* (1971).

Van Heusen and Cahn also composed the scores for two Broadway musicals. *Skyscraper* (November 13, 1965), starring Julie Harris, had a run of 241 performances. Peter Simon's book, loosely based on the Elmer Rice play *Dream Girl*, had as its heroine Georgina, a girl who escapes from everyday reality into romantic daydreams. She is the proprietress of an antique shop who stubbornly refuses to sell out to a construction company that plans to build a skyscraper next door. Her romantic yearnings are fulfilled when she meets a young architect who helps save her shop. "*Skyscraper* never lets up in its drive," reported Howard Taubman in *The New York Times*. "If it does not stop to charm, it always looks alive and is often funny. . . . Sammy Cahn and James Van Heusen have turned out several useful songs and one sure-fire romantic ballad." That ballad was "Everybody Has a Right to Be Wrong," introduced by Peter L. Marshall and Julie Harris and reprised by Harris. It was recorded by Sinatra and by Peggy Lee. Another memorable song from this score was "I'll Only Miss Her When I Think of Her," which Peter Marshall introduced and which was recorded by Sinatra, by Tony Bennett and by Nancy Wilson.

Walking Happy (November 26, 1966) lasted only 161 performances on Broadway. Roger O. Hirson and Ketti Frings derived their book from Harold Brighouse's play *Hobson's Choice*. In the musical Maggie Hobson, the daughter of a cobbler in Lancashire, falls in love with her father's meek, bumbling apprentice, whom she helps to become an expert shoemaker before leading him to the altar. In *The New York Times* Walter Kerr called it "an engaging, unpretentious, minor-league musical." The title song, the best in the score, was introduced by Norman Widom, Louise Troy and chorus. The scores of both *Skyscraper* and *Walking Happy* were released in original cast albums.

The partnership of Van Heusen and Cahn was dissolved in the early 1970s, and Van Heusen retired. During their productive years, they usually worked either at a Los Angeles apartment, maintained on Cahuenga Boulevard by Van Heusen as a pied-a-terre, or at Cahn's house in Holmby Hills. "The fun begins when Sammy comes bouncing into Jimmy's . . . apartment, or Jimmy into Sammy's house at noon, though Jimmy's idea of an early start is still 8 p. m.," wrote Robert Jennings in *Show* magazine. "Resplendent in his alpaca sweater, yellow slacks and uncommon eagerness, Sammy has, as someone remarked, the air of a troubled horseplayer looking for a lost ticket. Jimmy has just awakened, is slightly foggy."

Jennings went on to describe their method of writing songs. "Sammy thinks of the titles, Jimmy of the tunes, giving utmost consideration to its singability. . . . Then long, discursive discussions. Jimmy might interrupt for a mid-afternoon snack and a cup of coffee. Sammy charges ahead, 'embarrassed because lyric-writing comes so easily for me.' Sammy thinks of something and miraculously it molds into Jimmy's musical something. Sammy sings continually, hums, . . . flays the air with a jab of finger or a sweeping arm gesture. . . . After only eight bars, Sammy cracks: 'You know something? I think the song is finished.' . . . Or Jimmy might ask, 'And how are you gonna conclude the song?' And Sammy will answer, "I will let you know the conclusion whenever we come to the finish.' When they do, Jimmy seizes the king-sized Tanqueray martinis and 'we stagger away from each other happy.'"

Van Heusen once told an interviewer that "I dig chicks, booze, music and Sinatra—in that order." His list of preferences should have included his love of flying his own plane. He paid for his flying lessons with the royalties from his first hit, "It's the Dreamer in Me," and with the income from "Deep in a Dream" he bought his first plane, a Luscombe Silvaire which he flew from coast to coast five times. Since then Van Heusen has acquired many other small planes. His other interests include collecting manuscripts of famous composers, photography and the acquisition of well-appointed homes.

Van Heusen remained a bachelor until August 20, 1966, when he married Josephine Perlberg, who, years before, had been a member of the singing Brox sisters and had appeared in numerous Broadway musicals. Van Heusen maintains residences on a large horse ranch in California's Yucca Valley and at Lake Brant in upstate New York, as well as apartments in Los Angeles and Manhattan. In 1950 he founded Van Heusen Inc., a music publishing house.

ABOUT: Ewen, D. Great Men of American Popular Song, 1970; Wilder, A. American Popular Song, 1972. *Periodicals*—Show July 1963.

VON TILZER, ALBERT (March 29, 1878– October 1, 1956), was born Albert Gumm in Indianapolis, Indiana, one of six sons of Jacob and Sarah (Tilzer) Gumm. The family was quite musical; his older brother, Harry Von Tilzer, also became a successful songwriter, and three of his brothers were music publishers in Tin Pan Alley. Albert dropped out of high school and went to work in his father's shoe store; when he completed some lessons in harmony and learned to play the piano by ear, he found a job as music director for a vaudeville troupe. In 1899, he was hired as

ALBERT VON TILZER

staff pianist for the Chicago branch of Shapiro, Bernstein and Von Tilzer, of which his brother, Harry, was a member. At this time, Albert changed his name to Von Tilzer, which had been previously assumed by his brother. In 1900, Albert Von Tilzer's first publication appeared, a piano piece entitled *The Absent-Minded Beggar Waltz.*

Soon after the turn of the century, Von Tilzer went to New York, where, for a time, he worked as a shoe salesman in a Brooklyn department store. In 1903, his brother's publishing house, the Harry Von Tilzer Music Company, issued his song, "That's What the Daisy Said" (lyrics by Wilbur Gumm); also in that year, with his brother, Jack, Albert Von Tilzer formed the York Music Company which henceforth published his songs. "Teasing" (lyrics by Cecil Mack) and "Tell Me With Your Eyes" (lyrics by Arthur J. Lamb) were issued in 1905 and "Just for Auld Lang Syne" (lyrics by Edward Madden) in 1906. "I'm Sorry," interpolated into the Broadway revue, *About Town* (1906), starring Lew Fields, marked the beginning of a successful collaboration with vaudevillian Jack Norworth. They also composed "Honey Boy" (1907) as a tribute to minstrel George "Honey Boy" Evans, which Sophie Tucker performed in vaudeville and Beatrice Kay later recorded, and the hits "Good Evening, Caroline" and "Smarty" in 1908.

But it is for "Take Me Out to the Ball Game" (1908) that Von Tilzer and Norworth will always be remembered. Written some 20 years before Von Tilzer saw his first baseball game, he himself introduced this unofficial anthem of America's favorite sport in vaudeville, where it was

such a success that he was given a contract to tour the Orpheum vaudeville circuit. The song was further popularized by Nora Bayes (Jack Norworth's wife) and recorded by the Hoosier Hot Shots and by Ella Logan (1940). It was also heard in Nora Bayes's screen biography, *Shine On Harvest Moon* (1944), and became the title song of a motion picture (1949) starring Gene Kelly and Frank Sinatra.

Von Tilzer's next big success was "Put Your Arms Around Me, Honey" (lyrics by Junie McCree), published in 1910. It was first recorded that year by Arthur Collins with Byron G. Harlan and then became a staple of Blossom Seeley's vaudeville act. "Put Your Arms Around Me Honey" enjoyed a significant revival when Betty Grable sang it in the motion picture, *Coney Island* (1943); that year, it was heard 15 times on *Your Hit Parade*. Subsequently, it was interpolated into the film, *Louisiana Hayride* (1944) and Judy Garland sang it in MGM's *In the Good Old Summertime* (1949). In 1961, Fats Domino's bestselling recording initiated a new revival of interest in it.

With June McCree again serving as his lyricist, Albert Von Tilzer composed his first Broadway musical score, *The Happiest Night of His Life* (February 20, 1911); the show closed after three weeks. In 1912, Von Tilzer collaborated with vaudevillian Lew Brown on "I'm the Lonesomest Gal in Town," a popular ballad in the early 1910s. Kay Starr revived it in the 1940s in a recording with which she established her reputation; it was also recorded by Ella Fitzgerald and interpolated into the motion pictures, *Make Believe Ballroom* (1949) and *South Sea Sinner* (1950). At the same time, Von Tilzer and Brown composed "Kentucky Sue" and "Please Don't Take My Lovin' Man Away," which was introduced in vaudeville by Belle Baker. In 1914, Von Tilzer became a charter member of ASCAP.

Songs with a Hawaiian motif were very much in vogue in Tin Pan Alley at that time, so in 1916, Von Tilzer composed "Oh, How She Could Yacki, Hacki, Wicki, Wacki, Woo" (lyrics by Stanley Murphy and Charles McCarron). In 1916, Eddie Cantor used the song to audition for Florenz Ziegfeld and also sang it in his show stopping Broadway debut in Ziegfeld's *Midnight Frolic* on the roof of the New Amsterdam Theatre. After his opening-night appearance, Cantor received a telegram from Ziegfeld, who preferred addressing through wires rather than personally: "Enjoyed your act. You'll be here a long time."

In 1917, Von Tilzer and Lew Brown wrote several songs for the successful Broadway show, *Hitchy-Koo*. Grace La Rue introduced "I May

Be Gone for a Long, Long Time," a ballad inspired by World War I; the revue also included "Give Me the Moonlight, Give Me the Girl," which was recorded by Elsie Janis, and "Au Revoir, But Not Goodbye, Soldier Boy."

In 1919, "Oh, By Jingo!" (lyrics by Lew Brown), a nonsense song, was inserted into the show, *Linger Longer, Letty* for Charlotte Greenwood. That year, it was recorded by Margaret Young and subsequently by Ella Logan and by the Sam Lanin orchestra. It was later sung by Betty Hutton in the motion picture *Incendiary Blonde* (1945) and by Debbie Reynolds and Bobby Van in the screen musical *Skirts Ahoy* (1949).

Honey Girl (May 3, 1920), originally produced as *What's the Odds,* Von Tilzer's next complete score, achieved a Broadway run of 142 performances. In Edward Clark's text, based on the play *Checkers* by Henry Blossom, Honey Parker is in love with a horse player known as "Checkers." Her father, a banker, will consent to their marriage only when Checkers can produce assets of $25,000. Checkers pawns Honey's engagement ring to place a bet on a longshot; when the horse wins the race, Checkers wins Honey. The superior score, with lyrics by Neville Fleeson, included "Close to Your Heart" and a waltz, "I'm Losing My Heart to Someone," duets for the show's stars, Lynne Overman and Edna Bates, and "Racing Blues" for the chorus.

Written at the same time as *Honey Girl,* one of Von Tilzer's greatest song successes of 1920 was "I'll Be With You in Apple Blossom Time" (lyrics by Fleeson). It was recorded that year by Ernest Hare and by Charles Harrison and performed in vaudeville by Nora Bayes; two decades later, it could be heard in recordings by the Andrews Sisters and by Jo Stafford, and in the Abbott and Costello film comedy, *Buck Privates* (1941). Another hit of 1920 was the ballad, "I Used to Love You But It's All Over" (lyrics by Lew Brown) recorded by Frank Crumit and by the Nat Brandwyne orchestra. The following year, Von Tilzer and Brown composed "Dapper Dan, The Sheik of Alabam'" which was introduced by Eddie Cantor.

The Gingham Girl (August 28, 1922) was Albert Von Tilzer's greatest success on Broadway (322 performances). Eddie Buzzell and Helen Ford starred as Joe and Mary, lovers from Crossvile Corners, New Hampshire. Joe goes to New York to seek his fortune and, at first, is seduced by the glamour of the city; he soon comes to his senses. In the meantime, Mary, the "gingham girl" has followed Joe to New York to keep an eye on him, and has established a successful cookie business for the two of them to run. The show was appealing because of what the *World*

described as its "sweetness" and "simple charm"; its best song was "As Long as I Have You" (lyrics by Fleeson).

Von Tilzer wrote scores for two more Broadway musicals. *Adrienne* (May 28, 1923), with lyrics by A. Seymour Brown, starred Vivienne Segal; the songs for *Bye, Bye Bonnie* (January 13, 1927) were written with Louis Simon and Bide Dudley. Neither show ran for more than a few weeks.

In 1930, Albert Von Tilzer moved to Hollywood, where, during the next few years, he contributed songs to motion pictures, including the complete score (lyrics by Fleeson) for *Rainbow Over Broadway* (1933). He retired in the late 1930s, emerging briefly in 1950 to compose "I'm Praying to St. Christopher" to commemorate his 50th anniversary as a songwriter. It was recorded by the Tommy Tucker orchestra.

ABOUT: Burton, J. The Blue Book of Tin Pan Alley, 2d ed. 1962; Spaeth, S. A History of Popular Music in America, 1948.

VON TILZER, HARRY (July 8, 1872– January 10, 1946). Harry Von Tilzer was both a prolific composer and a successful and influential publisher in the early days of Tin Pan Alley. An astute businessman, he had rapidly mastered the technique of promoting songs, and in addition to publishing his own songs, he also issued those of Ernest R. Ball, Jean Schwartz, Fred Fisher, and the young Irving Berlin, George Gershwin (whose first published song carried the Von Tilzer imprint), and Jimmy Monaco. By his own estimates, he composed thousands of songs, some of which sold millions of copies during his lifetime. In 1914 Tilzer also became a charter member of ASCAP.

Born Harry Gumm in Detroit, Michigan, Harry Von Tilzer was the third of six sons of Jacob and Sarah (Tilzer) Gumm. His younger brother, Albert, also became a successful, though less prolific, composer of popular songs, and brothers Wilbur, Jules and Jack became publishers in Tin Pan Alley. Soon after Harry was born, the family moved to Indianapolis, where his father became proprietor of a shoe store. A theatrical stock company gave performances in a loft above the store and Harry fell in love with show business. He frequented hotel lobbies to catch glimpses of visiting performers, and when he had the price of admission, he attended minstrel and burlesque shows.

At 14, Von Tilzer left home to join the Cole Brothers Circus as an acrobat. A year later, he joined a traveling repertory company as pianist

HARRRY VON TILZER

(he had taken a few lessons and could play by ear) and also as an actor in juvenile roles. For the stage, he adopted the name of Von Tilzer, adding "Von" to his mother's maiden name to give it distinction.

In the early 1890s, Von Tilzer was a member of a burlesque troupe touring the midwest. In Chicago, he met Lottie Gilson, a comic opera star, who became interested both in him and the songs he was writing. Gilson persuaded Willis Woodward to publish "I Love You Both," for which he wrote both words and music in 1892. She also convinced the young composer to devote himself to songwriting rather than performing, and to go to New York to pursue his career.

In 1892, Von Tilzer worked his way to New York as a groom on a trainload of horses. He arrived with $1.65 in his pocket, with which he rented a furnished room near the Brooklyn Bridge. Soon he found a job as pianist and entertainer in a saloon for a salary of $15 a week. He traveled for a while with a medicine show, returning to New York in 1894 to appear with George Sidney in a "double Dutch" act at Tony Pastor's Music Hall. Meanwhile, he continued to write songs, completing more than 100 during his first few years in New York. Some were purchased by entertainers, including Tony Pastor, for $2 each. A few others were published; "The Swellest Gal in Town" (1897) achieved a modest sheet music sale after being introduced by minstrel George H. Primrose.

Von Tilzer was sharing a furnished room on the top floor of a building on 15th Street with lyricist Andrew B. Sterling; in 1898, they composed "My Old New Hampshire Home." While working, they had only the illumination from the street outside their window, as they had to keep the room dark to prevent the landlady from hounding them for the rent. They sold this new song for $15 to William C. Dunn, proprietor of Orphean Music Co., a small printing establishment. For another $15, Dunn also purchased a second song, "I'd Leave My Happy Home for You" (lyrics by Will A. Heelan). "My Old New Hampshire Home" soon became such a favorite with vaudevillians that its sheet music sales soared to two million copies. "I'd Leave My Happy Home for You" was introduced in vaudeville by Annetta Flagler and then made famous by Blanche Ring in her first big success at Tony Pastor's in 1899. It was later recorded by the Century Quartet and interpolated into the Abbott and Costello film comedy, *The Naughty Nineties* (1945).

The success of these songs led businessmen Maurice Shapiro and Louis Bernstein to purchase the Orphean Music Company in 1899. Recognizing the potential value of Harry Von Tilzer's songs, Bernstein and Shapiro, in spite of the fact that they already owned "My Old New Hampshire Home," paid him $4,000 as an advance on all future sheet music sales; they also made Von Tilzer a partner in their new venture, now Shapiro, Bernstein and Von Tilzer. In 1900, Von Tilzer provided the firm with a new hit: more than two million copies of "A Bird in a Gilded Cage" (lyrics by Arthur J. Lamb) were sold; it was one of the most widely sung sentimental ballads of the early 1900s. The central theme of the lyrics was that the girl who sold her beauty for an old man's gold, was just a bird in a gilded cage. In the first version of the lyrics, it was plain that the girl was not the old man's wife but his mistress. Though Von Tilzer insisted that the couple be married he had no scruples about trying out the ballad in a brothel. When the song brought tears to the girls' eyes, he knew he had a winner. "A Bird in a Gilded Cage" was widely performed by ballad singers in vaudeville in the early 1900s, and it was later recorded by Beatrice Kay with Ray Bloch's orchestra and interpolated into the motion pictures, *Ringside Maisie* (1941) and *Coney Island* (1943).

Harry Von Tilzer continued to compose songs for Shapiro, Bernstein, and Von Tilzer, including "When the Harvest Days Are Over, Jessie Dear" (1900; lyrics by Howard Graham) and "Down Where the Cotton Blossoms Grow" (1901, lyrics by Sterling); in 1901, "Oh, What a Dream!" was interpolated into the Broadway musical, *The Liberty Belles* (1901). In 1902, Von Tilzer left Shapiro, Bernstein and Von Tilzer to set up his own publishing house. During its first year in operation, the Harry Von Tilzer Music

Publishing Company, at 45 West 28th Street, issued many songs, three of them formidable hits which put the new firm on solid financial footing. "Mansion of an Aching Heart" (lyrics by Lamb) was a sequel to "A Bird in a Gilded Cage" and, like its predecessor, was widely circulated in vaudeville. "On a Sunday Afternoon" (lyrics by Sterling) sold two million copies of sheet music and was recorded by the Knickerbocker Serenaders; "Down Where the Wurzburger Flows" (lyrics by Vincent P. Bryan), a drinking song for a Broadway musical *Wild Rose* (1902) but never used, was introduced by newcomer Nora Bayes at the Orpheum Theatre in Brooklyn, in 1902. During her first performance there, she broke down. Seated in a box, Harry Von Tilzer arose spontaneously from his seat to complete the rendition. This met with such a delighted response from the audience that Von Tilzer and Bayes had to repeat the chorus separately and together 14 times. At the request of the management, Von Tilzer continued to serve as Nora Bayes's partner in delivering this song during her entire engagement. A staple in her repertory, Nora Bayes became so identified with it, that for many years she was known as "the Wurzburger Girl."

A success of equal dimensions was achieved in 1902 with "Mansion of an Aching Heart" (lyrics by Lamb). This became another one of the best-loved ballads of the early 1900s, and the young Irving Berlin sang it frequently in the streets and cafes of the Bowery district.

Another song from this period, "Please Go 'Way and Let Me Sleep," has been erroneously attributed to Harry Von Tilzer. When it was first published, R. C. McPherson was credited as the lyricist and J. Tim Brymn as the composer. Apparently Von Tilzer purchased the song for a flat fee and then plugged it in a unique way at the Chicago Opera House: as the song was being introduced by minstrel Arthur Deming, Von Tilzer, pretending to be asleep in the audience, disrupted the performance with raucous snoring; when the usher shook him vigorously, he responded in a lazy drawl with, "Please go 'way and let me sleep." Considerable publicity attended these performances, and when the song became successful, Von Tilzer appropriated it as his own composition. It continued to be popular as background music for silent films.

In the mid-19th century, most publishers of popular songs in New York were located near Union Square at 14th Street; by 1900, they had moved north to a short stretch on 28th Street between Broadway and Sixth Avenue. In 1903 Monroe H. Rosenfeld, a journalist and songwriter, was planning a series of articles on the popular song industry for *The World.* While searching for material, he paid a visit to the offices of the Harry Von Tilzer Music Publishing Company. There he heard the clanky sounds of the song pluggers' pianos, whose strings had been muted with strips of paper in order to pacify the neighbors. Inspired by these sounds and those emanating from the other nearby publishing houses, Rosenfeld entitled his articles "Down Tin Pan Alley Way," and the name stuck. Though Von Tilzer maintained that it was he who had suggested the sobriquet, Rosenfeld also claimed to be its inventor.

Harry Von Tilzer had become a giant in Tin Pan Alley, a position he continue to hold for the next two decades in his dual capacity as one of its most active composers and most successful publishers. With lyrics by Sterling, he composed the ragtime number, "Goodbye, Eliza Jane" (1903) and in 1904, "Under the Anheuser Bush," a sequel to "Down Where the Wurzburger Flows," and "Coax Me," which Lottie Gilson made successful by addressing herself provocatively to the men in the audience. "Alexander, Don't You Love Your Baby No More?" (1905), inspired by one of McIntyre and Heath's routines, was one of many songs intended for use by vaudevillians and minstrels in blackface; it may have stimulated Irving Berlin to compose "Alexander's Ragtime Band" (1911).

Von Tilzer decided to try his hand at a Broadway show, and his first attempt was *The Fisher Maiden* (October 5, 1903), an old-fashioned comic opera with a book and lyrics by Lamb; it closed after one month. *Heigh Ho!* and *A Jolly Baron* followed in 1905, and in 1910, *The Kissing Girl* closed after a two-week run in Chicago.

In spite of these setbacks, Von Tilzer's success in Tin Pan Alley was undiminished. In 1905 he composed "Wait 'Til the Sun Shines, Nellie" (lyrics by Sterling), whose sheet music sales surpassed one million copies. There are several stories of how Von Tilzer came to write this ballad, but it seems that he heard a young man in a hotel lobby consoling his new bride because their trip to Coney Island had to be postponed because of rain. Von Tilzer's daughter, appearing in vaudeville as Winona Winter, introduced this song, and it soon became a favorite of other singers and barber-shop quartets. In the 1940s there was a strong revival of interest in it: Bing Crosby and Mary Martin sang it in the film *The Birth of the Blues* (1941), and it was used in *Rhythm Parade* (1942), *In the Good Old Summertime* (1949) and served as the tittle song for a motion picture (1952) starring David Wayne; it was also recorded by the Harry James orchestra.

The popularity of Von Tilzer's songs was due, in part, to the fact that he wrote many for which there was already an established market, such as nostalgic "Where the Morning Glories Twine Around the Door" (1905). But he also had the ability to take the commonplace and turn it into something that would capture the public's fancy. For example, "What You Goin' to Do When the Rent Comes 'Round? (Rufus Rastus Johnson Brown)" (1905, lyrics by Sterling) is reputed to have been based on a chance remark overheard in a Miami railroad station. The song was picked up by minstrels and revived decades later by Jimmy Durante and more recently by George Segal in the film *California Split* (1974).

On August 1, 1906, Harry Von Tilzer married Ida Rosenberg, and after their marriage, he continued to be a prolific and versatile composer and an affluent publisher. "Take Me Back to New York Town" (1907; lyrics by Sterling) was recorded by the Knickerbocker Serenaders and later interpolated into the motion picture *The Story of Vernon and Irene Castle* (1939), starring Fred Astaire and Ginger Rogers. In 1909 the ragtime tune "The Cubanola Glide" (lyrics by Vincent P. Bryan) became one of the songs setting the stage for the craze dances such as the Grizzly Bear, the Turkey Trot and the Bunny Hug. An early recording of it was made by Arthur Collins with Byron G. Harlan, and though Sophie Tucker was to sing it in the *Ziefgeld Follies of 1909*, it was dropped before the show opened in New York; it was not introduced on Broadway until Harriet Hoctor sang it in the musical *The Girl from Rector's* (1910). It was susequently revived in *Fallen Angel* (1945), sung by Alice Faye.

Tributes to mothers were quite popular at this time, so in 1911, Von Tilzer contributed "I Want a Girl Just Like the Girl That Married Dear Old Dad" (lyrics by Will Dillon) to the repertoire; it was recorded that year by the American Quartette and later sung by Al Jolson in *the Jolson Story* (1946). Jolson subsequently introduced Von Tilzer's "Goodbye Boys, I'm Going to Be Married Tomorrow" (lyrics by Sterling and William Jerome) in *The Honeymoon Express* (1913), one of his extravaganzas at the Winter Garden. Other favorites in 1911 were "All Alone (Hello, Central, Give Me 603)" (lyrics by Dillon), an early song about the telephone; "They Always Pick on Me" (lyrics by Stanley Murphy), recorded by Ada Jones and revived by Alice Faye in *Hello, Frisco, Hello* (1943); and in 1912, "Last Night Was the End of the World" (lyrics by Sterling), which was featured by the glamorous opera prima donna Lina Cavalieri during her American concert tour in the season of 1912–1913. Because of the great demand, Von Tilzer composed many Irish songs; the most popular

among these were "A Little Bunch of Shamrocks" (1913; lyrics by Sterling and Jerome), which was recorded at the time by Arthur Clough, and also "That Old Irish Mother of Mine," (1920; lyrics by Jerome), recorded by the Nat Brandwyne orchestra.

Though it was some time before he was credited, Von Tilzer was one of the composers of "When My Baby Smiles at Me" (music composed with Ted Lewis, lyrics by Sterling and Bill Munro). It was introduced by the Ted Lewis orchestra in the *Greenwich Village Follies of 1919,* and it later became the orchestra's theme song. In the Hollywood musical *Sing, Baby, Sing* (1936) it was sung by Dan Dailey, and it also served as the title song of a 1948 motion picture.

After a series of failures, Von Tilzer produced a hit song, "Just Around the Corner" (lyrics by Dolph Singer), in 1925, inspired by a letter from Broadway producer Elizabeth Marbury telling him that "just around the corner the sun will shine for you." It was introduced and recorded by Ted Lewis and revived in Lewis's screen biography, *Is Everybody Happy?* (1943).

Harry Von Tilzer spent his remaining years in retirement at his home on Long Island and his residence at the Hotel Woodward in New York City, where he died on January 10, 1946.

ABOUT: Ewen, D. Great Men of American Popular Song, 2d ed., 1972, The Life and Death of Tin Pan Alley, 1964; Goldberg, I. Tin Pan Alley, 1930; Hamm, C. Yesterdays: Popular Song in America, 1979.

WALLER, FATS (May 21, 1904–December 15, 1943), composer, was born Thomas Wright Waller in Harlem, New York City, the youngest son of the five surviving children of Edward Martin and Adeline (Lockett) Waller. The paternal grandfather, Adolph Waller, had toured in the South as a violinist after the Civil War. Thomas's father owned a trucking company and was the deacon at the Abyssinian Baptist Church in Harlem, and his mother was an amateur musician who played the piano and organ. (Edward and Adeline had moved from Virginia to New York in the 1880s.) When Thomas was six, his family acquired a piano and his mother gave him rudimentary instruction. Organ lessons followed and, as a boy, Thomas played the organ in his father's church, as well as piano and violin in the orchestras of P.S. 89 and DeWitt Clinton High School. Despite his son's musical talent, Edward Waller was determined to have Thomas follow him into the ministry. He condemned his son's interest in popular music and was horrified whenever he heard his son improvise a rag treatment of hymns.

FATS WALLER

Nevertheless, Thomas pursued his musical interests. In 1918, while attending DeWitt Clinton, he substituted from time to time for the regular organist at the Lincoln Theatre, a combination movie and vaudeville house on 135th Street. Waller dropped out of high school that year, and for a time was employed in a jewel-box factory. But he was soon hired as permanent pianist-organist at the Lincoln Theatre for a weekly salary of $23 and one year later he won first prize in an amateur contest for pianists.

It was a meeting with pianist-composer James P. Johnson that introduced Waller into Harlem's jazz circles. Johnson began teaching Waller "stride piano," a technique of jazz performance which liberated the left hand rhythmically without sacrificing the melody-sustaining function of the right. Johnson also trained him in ragtime. While employed as a vaudeville pianist, Waller wrote his first composition in 1919, an instrumental titled "Boston Blues."

The death of his father in 1920 traumatized the 16-year old Waller and grief seems to have propelled him a year later into marriage with Edith Hatchett, a childhood friend. They lived first with her parents and then acquired a modest apartment of their own, where they raised a son. Their marriage lasted only a few years and its aftermath involved Waller in numerous legal imbroglios, including two jail sentences for failure to keep up his child support payments.

In 1921, Waller cut his first piano rolls for $100 a roll on the QRS recording label. Soon afterwards he was the piano accompanist for the singer Sara Martin, with whom he made his first phonograph recording at a payment of $250. His

first radio broadcast was in 1923 on a small station. All this while he played with various jazz performers—including a trio whose other members were James P. Johnson and William "Willie the Lion" Smith—at rent parties and fashionable white social gatherings, in cabarets and nightclubs. About this time he received piano instruction from Leopold Godowsky.

Recognition as a composer came with "Squeeze Me" (lyrics by Clarence Williams) which was published in 1925 but had been composed years earlier. This was a pastiche of two jazz tunes: "Boy in the Boat," a melody attributed to the legendary Buddy Bolden of New Orleans, and "St. Louis Tickler." As "Squeeze Me," it was first recorded by Clarence Williams's Blue Five. The 1928 recording by Louis Armstrong and his orchestra, with Earl Hines at the piano, helped make it a jazz classic. The Louisiana Rhythm Kings recorded it in 1930.

In 1925, another early Waller jazz tune was recorded by the Cat Happy Band, one of whose members was Sidney Bechet, the only jazz musician to become famous with the soprano sax: "In Harlem's Araby" (lyrics by Jo Trent). In 1926 Waller's "Georgia Bo-Bo" (lyrics by Jo Trent) was recorded by Lil's Hot Shots, and in 1927 "I'm Goin' Huntin'" (lyrics and music written with John C. Johnson) was recorded by Jimmy Bertrand's Washboard Wizards. Louis Armstrong performed in both groups.

In 1926, Waller toured the vaudeville circuit as pianist for an act called "Liza and Her Shufflin' Six." That year, he married Anita Priscilla Rutherford, with whom he had two sons. By mid-decade Waller's transition from the black middle class to life in the Prohibition-era speakeasy subculture was complete. He returned to the Lincoln Theatre in 1926, this time to head his own band. He also distinguished himself as a jazz organist in two Harlem clubs, the Lafayette and Connie's Inn. When in 1926 Lafayette mounted a revue, *Ten Town Topics,* Waller composed several songs that were set to Spencer Williams's lyrics. One of these was "Senorita Blues" (lyrics by Williams and Eddie Rector, music written with Clarence Williams). In 1928 he worked in Chicago with Louis Armstrong and with Earl Hines.

When a sequel to *Shuffle Along,* Eubie Blake's all-black musical of 1921, was being planned for Daly's 63d Street Theatre under the title *Keep Shufflin'* (February 27, 1928), Waller and James P. Johnson were engaged as co-composers with Andy Razaf and Henry Creams as co-lyricists, while Flournoy Miller and Aubrey Lyle returned as authors of the text. In *Keep Shufflin',* we are back in Jimtown, the locale of *Shuffle*

Along, where Flournoy Miller and Aubrey Lyle appeared as founders of an "Equal Got League" which is planning to blow up the local bank to achieve a more equitable distribution of wealth. Waller and Johnson, who appeared between acts as duo-pianists, introduced the show's leading musical number, "Willow Tree," (music by Waller, lyrics by Razaf) which they described as "a musical misery."

Hot Chocolates, an all-black revue with book and lyrics by Andy Razaf and music by Waller and Harry Brooks, opened on Broadway on June 29, 1929, and ran for 228 performances. Stage history was made when Louis Armstrong, in his Broadway debut, rose from the pit orchestra and took to the stage to perform a specialty number on the trumpet. Here, too, was born the song classic "Ain't Misbehavin'," whose origin Andy Razaf has recalled: "I remember one day going to Fats's house to finish up a number based on a little strain he thought up. The whole show was complete, but they needed an extra number for a theme and this had to be it. He worked on it for 45 minutes, and there it was—'Ain't Misbehavin'.'" In *Hot Chocolates*, "Ain't Misbehavin'" was introduced by Paul Bass, Margaret Simms and the Jubilee Singers, but during the run of the show Louis Armstrong took it over. Armstrong's recording became a classic and his orchestra performed it in the film *Atlantic City* (1955). The song was also recorded by Fats Waller (who made the number his theme), Bill Robinson, Mildred Bailey, the Mills Brothers, Ruth Etting, Kay Starr and Leo Reisman and his orchestra, among many others. Fats Waller sang it in the film *Stormy Weather* (1943); Dan Dailey in *You Were Meant for Me* (1948); and Alan Young and Jeanne Crain (with the voice of Anita Ellis dubbed in on the soundtrack) in *Gentlemen Marry Brunettes* (1955). The song received a comic treatment in Barbra Streisand's *Lucky Lady* (1975).

In addition to "Ain't Misbehavin'," the *Hot Chocolates* score included "What Did I Do to Be So Black and Blue?," introduced by Edith Wilson and popularized by Ethel Waters, and "Sweet Savannah Sue," introduced by Margaret Simms, Paul Bass and the Jubilee Singers and recorded by Louis Armstrong.

Besides his score for *Hot Chocolates* Waller composed two standards in 1928—"Honeysuckle Rose," "My Fate is in Your Hands" (lyries by Razaf)—and another in 1929, "I've Got a Feeling I'm Falling" (lyrics by Razaf, music written with Harry Link). "Honeysuckle Rose" was introduced as music accompanying a dance routine in *Load of Coal* (1928), a nightclub revue at Connie's Inn. This torch song was popularized

by Paul Whiteman and his orchestra on the radio and it later became a Benny Goodman specialty. It was also recorded by Waller himself, Mildred Bailey and Dinah Shore as well as by Goodman. In film it has been sung by Betty Grable in *Tin Pan Alley* (1949), by Lena Horne in *Thousands Cheer* (1943) and in the Martin Scorsese motion picture *New York, New York* (1972) by Diahanne Abbot.

"My Fate is in Your Hands" was also introduced in *Load of Coal* and has been recorded by the orchestras of Guy Lombardo, Nat Shilkret and Ted Wallace. "I've Got a Feeling I'm Falling" was introduced by Waller, who also recorded it. Other recordings were made by Gene Austin, Nick Lucas and Miff Mole, and the song was interpolated into the motion picture, *Applause* (1929).

However, Waller made little money from these songs. In 1929 he sold the copyrights of "Ain't Misbehavin'," "Honeysuckle Rose" and about two dozen other numbers to Irving Mills for $500. But in the 1930s he enjoyed both financial and artistic success through his appearances as jazz vocalist, pianist, and organist, as well as from his compositions. Throughout the decade he zigzagged across the country, playing one-night stands and performing in concert halls and nightclubs. He made his first tour of Europe in 1932 and was heard in the prestigious continental night spots. Waller was called "the only jazz organist of consequence in his lifetime" and in Paris he became the first jazz musician to play the organ at the Notre Dame Cathedral. In 1938, his second tour of Europe was highlighted by a one-week engagement at London's Palladium. Meanwhile, through a two-year engagement (1932–34) of *Fats Waller's Rhythm Club* on radio station WLW in Cincinnati and his appearances several times a week on the CBS radio network, he had become a broadcasting star in America. In 1934, Waller signed an exclusive recording contract with RCA Victor and within a year he was selling more records than any other black musician. In 1935 he toured, fronting a big band, and also performed in the motion pictures *Hooray for Love* (1934) and *King of Burlesque* (1936).

Waller's affluence enabled him to acquire a chauffeur-driven Lincoln limousine in 1935 and following his 1938 European tour he left the Harlem apartment he had been occupying with his family and purchased a large brick house in the Saint Albans section of Queens. He also acquired an office in the Brill Building on Broadway.

"Waller was a superb pianist," wrote Whitney Balliet in *The New Yorker*. "His touch was firm and clear, he rarely missed notes, and he had a nice sense of dynamics. His time was metronomic yet had the infinitesimal looseness that is part of swinging. Waller loved the organ. It gave him room for subtleties not possible on the piano and for his histrionic tendencies. . . . He could moon and whisper and make bird and wind and wave sounds; he could disport himself without saying a word. He was the first jazz organist. . . . Waller's endless vocal effects—mock English and West Indian accents, Bronx cheers, heavy Aeolian sighs, parlando, rubbery staccato diction—have been duly celebrated, but it should be said that he was a first-rate singer. He had an excellent light baritone, faultless diction (when he chose) and perfect intonation."

Waller's first popular song of the 1930s was "Blue Turning Gray Over You" in 1930 (lyrics by Razaf), which was first recorded by Louis Armstrong and his orchestra. In 1931 came "Concentratin'" (lyrics by Razaf), introduced and recorded by Waller, and "I'm Crazy About My Baby" (lyrics by Alex Hill), introduced and recorded by Ted Lewis and his band with Waller; in 1932 there were the songs "Keeping Out of Mischief" (lyrics by Razaf), introduced and recorded by Waller and also recorded by Louis Armstrong and his orchestra, and "Lonesome Me" (music written with Con Conrad, lyrics by Razaf) which was introduced by George Hall and his orchestra; in 1933, "Ain't Cha Glad" (lyrics by Razaf), introduced and recorded by Waller and also recorded by Benny Goodman and his orchestra; in 1937, "The Joint is Jumpin'" (music written with James C. Johnson, lyrics by Razaf), introduced and recorded by Waller; in 1938, "Patty Cake, Patty Cake" (music written with James C. Johnson, lyrics by Razaf), introduced and recorded by Waller.

Waller also composed a rich repertory of instrumental jazz pieces for the piano, many of which he himself recorded. These include: *Clothes Line Ballet, The Rusty Pail* and *Jitterbug Waltz.* Following his second European tour, he composed *London Suite,* which he recorded in 1939 but which was not released until the 1950s.

In 1943 Waller appeared in the motion picture *Stormy Weather* and, about that time, composed the score for the Broadway musical *Early to Bed* (June 17, 1943), which ran for 380 performances, with book and lyrics by George F. Marion, Jr. It used Martinique as its setting for a bordello disguised as a school institution for ladies which is run by a former school mistress. It is visited by a famous bullfighter who recognizes her as one of his former schoolmates, and his son, both of whom are duped by the establishment's

classy facade. *Early to Bed*'s show-stopping song was a satirical number, "The Ladies Who Sing With a Band," introduced by Muriel Angelus, Mary Small, Jane Deering and George Zoritch. "This is Nice" was a duet for Angelus and Richard Kollmar and "There's a Man in My Life," a solo for Angelus.

Though his health was poor in 1943, Waller maintained a rigorous performing schedule, including many one-night stands in theaters and nightclubs. Because this was the time of World War II, he also entertained on army bases and in hospitals. Having concluded an engagement at the Zanzibar Room in Los Angeles, and weakened by a recent attack of influenza, he boarded the Super Chief, returning to the East to spend the Christmas holidays with his family. He was found dead of bronchial pneumonia in his train compartment on December 15, 1943, when the Super Chief stopped at Kansas City. Funeral services were held at the Abyssinian Baptist Church in Harlem; Hazel Scott played "Abide with Me" on the organ and Reverend Adam Clayton Powell delivered the eulogy.

Fats Waller stood just under six feet tall and weighed about 285 pounds. Fun-loving, with a larger-than-life personality, he was also a devoted, generous-to-a-fault husband, father and friend. His prodigious appetite for food and liquor was legendary, and friends and acquaintances were wont to urge him on to exaggerated feats of consumption. While performing, his energetic showmanship endeared him to audiences, as did his clowning and witty, flippant comments. Indeed, Waller's deepest impulses were at once hedonistic and intensely spiritual. Despite his insatiable love of pleasure, Waller was a genuinely religious man who insisted that his sons attend Sunday school and who, in his dressing room between acts, would read passages from the Bible to his fellow performers and bandsmen.

"His attention span was that of a small boy," said his biographer, Joel Vance. "He wrote tunes as toys, forgetting them as quickly as they ceased to please him or to bring him quick money. He was constantly in search of adventure, but the adventures had to take place in comfortable and convivial surroundings—the company of his musical peers in Harlem, a backstage bash with cast and chorus girls, or a Gargantuan eating session. Waller's high-living was a succession of self-induced birthday parties. He never completed the emotional transition from childhood to maturity. At the price of preserving his childhood in alcohol, he managed to let his creative powers flow to the fullest."

A revival of interest in Waller and his music

began in 1975, when RCA issued the first of a multivolume series entitled *The Complete Fats Waller.* Subsequent volumes drew upon the 400 sides Waller had recorded for RCA during the last decade of his life. In 1977, two biographies of Waller were published and the following year, in February, the revue *Ain't Misbehavin'* opened Off Broadway at the Manhattan Theater Club. The score included Waller's own songs as well as works he had performed by other composers. Conceived and directed by Richard Maltby Jr. and Murray Horwitz, and with a cast of five black performers, *Ain't Misbehavin'* was lavishly praised by the critics and was transferred to the Longacre Theatre on Broadway on May 9, 1978 for a prolonged run. The original cast recording won a Grammy.

ABOUT: Davies, J. R. T. The Music of Thomas "Fats" Waller, 1953; Kirkeby, E. (ed.), Fats Waller: His Life and Times, 1977; Waller, M., and Calabrese, A. Fats Waller, 1977. *Periodicals*—New Yorker April 10, 1978; New York Times May 7, 1978.

HARRY WARREN

WARREN, HARRY (December 24, 1893–September 21, 1981). In the 1930s and 1940s Harry Warren was one of the leading composers in that golden era of screen musicals. Tony Thomas noted in his biography of Warren, "His primary claim to fame is his importance in the history of the motion-picture musical. No other composer can match his record for the 25-year period between 1932 and 1957, when he was consistently employed by four major studios." Heard in more than 75 film productions, over 100 of his songs achieved national popularity and many have become standards. Thirty-nine were represented on *Your Hit Parade,* with 12 in first position; three won Oscars, with eight others receiving Academy Award nominations.

Harry Salvatore Warren was born in Brooklyn, New York in a tenement under the Brooklyn Bridge, on Christmas Eve, 1893. He was the 11th of 12 children of Anthony and Rachel (De Luca) Warren. The father was a bootmaker whose name had originally been Anthony Guaragna, but who changed his name to Warren after he had emigrated from Calabria to the United States. For a year (1889–90), Harry Warren attended a Catholic school in Brooklyn, then, after graduating from P. S. 155, spent a short period at Commercial High School in Brooklyn. As a child, he earned money lighting stoves for Jewish families on the Sabbath for the fee of a penny a house.

Warren's interest in music was awakened by choir and organ performances at church. He sang in the boy's choir of Our Lady of Loretta Church and without instruction taught himself to play his father's accordion and then acquired a set of drums from a local barber. He soon found engagements with bands performing at local dances, weddings and funerals. "When I was a kid, I had a great craving for music," he told an interviewer. "Once I went to the Armory to hear the Boston Symphony and damned near died at the sound. I'd never heard an orchestra before." Warren dropped out of Commercial High School when he was 15 and joined a carnival where he played the drums with the John Victor Brass Band. With his savings he acquired a $70 secondhand piano which he learned to play without lessons.

During the next few years Warren supported himself at odd jobs. He played the piano in a Coney Island restaurant; worked as a pianist and drummer with touring carnivals; sold fruit in the Liberty Theatre in Brooklyn; and was a stagehand at Loewe's Theatre in the Brownsville section of Brooklyn. Eventually he was employed at the Vitagraph studios in Brooklyn as a pianist performing mood music and as assistant stage hand; then as extra; finally as an assistant director. Now earning $40 a week, he married Josephine Wensler on December 19, 1917. They moved into a Brooklyn apartment and had a son in 1918 (he died when he was 20) and a daughter in 1924.

During World War I, Warren enlisted in the Navy and was stationed in Long Island where he organized a band that provided entertainment for the troops. After leaving the service in 1918, he worked as a pianist in beer gardens and dance halls and in movie houses providing accompaniment for silent films. By now he had begun writing songs, one of which, "By the River Sainte Marie" (1921, lyrics by Edgar Leslie) had to wait a decade for publication. Meanwhile, in the 1920s, it was performed on radio by the concert baritone Reinald Werrenrath and by Lennie Haydon. Initially, no publisher would touch the song because of its religious subject matter. In 1931 one of Warren's friends persuaded the Robbins Music Corporation to publish it and Kate Smith introduced it on her first program on the CBS radio network on May 1 of that year. "By the River Sainte Marie" was later recorded by Tony Martin and by the orchestras of Gene Krupa, Russ Morgan, and Ray Benson; it was revived in the motion picture *Swing in the Saddle* (1944).

In 1922 Warren was hired as a rehearsal pianist and song plugger for the Tin Pan Alley publishers Stark and Cowan. This was the firm that issued Warren's first publication, "Rose of the Rio Grande" (1922, music written with Ross Gorman, lyrics by Edgar Leslie), introduced by Paul Whiteman and his orchestra and subsequently recorded by the orchestras of Eddie Condon, Bob Grant and Jan Savitt. Equally successful was "I Love My Baby" (1925, lyrics by Bud Green), which Fred Waring's Pennsylvanians introduced that year in a recording and which was later interpolated into the motion pictures *The Joker Is Wild* (1957) and *The Gene Krupa Story* (1959).

Warren's success brought him a job as staff composer for the publishing firm of Shapiro, Bernstein & Company, where he worked several years. In 1926 that company issued Warren's comedic "Where Do You Work a-John?" (lyrics by Mortimer Weinberg and Charley Marks), which was introduced in a recording by Fred Waring's Pennsylvanians and later recorded by the Dick Robertson Orchestra and the two-piano team of Fingerle and Schutt. This song was followed in 1927 by "Away Down South in Heaven" (lyrics by Bud Green), introduced by Fred Waring's Pennsylvanians and interpolated for Blossom Seeley into the Broadway show *Greenwich Village Follies of 1928*. "Nagasaki" (1928, lyrics by Mort Dixon) was introduced by the Friars' Society Orchestra of Paul Mares, was performed by Bill Robinson at the Cotton Club, and was recorded by the Mills Brothers, the Trix Sisters, and the orchestras of Benny Goodman, Fletcher Henderson, and Cab Calloway. Doris Day sang it in the film *My Dream Is Yours* (1949). Also in 1928 Warren composed and had published "Where the Shy Little Violets Grow" (lyrics by Gus Kahn, introduced by Guy Lombardo and His Royal Canadians, and eventually recorded

by Helen Morgan and by Basil Fomeen's orchestra) and "Old Man Sunshine—Little Boy Bluebird" (lyrics by Mort Dixon, recorded and popularized by Lee Morse). In 1929 appeared "Absence Makes the Heart Grow Fonder" (lyrics by Sam H. Lewis and Joe Young) which was recorded by Russ Morgan and his orchestra; "Here We Are" (lyrics by Gus Kahn, recorded by Ben Bernie and his orchestra); and "Where the Sweet Forget-Me-Nots Remember" (lyrics by Mort Dixon).

Two Warren songs found an important place in *Sweet and Low*, a Broadway revue produced in 1930 by Billy Rose and starring his wife Fanny Brice. "Cheerful Little Earful" (1920, lyrics by Ira Gershwin) was introduced by Hannah Williams and Jerry Norris and was soon recorded by Johnny Marvin, the High Hatters, and Ben Slavin and his orchestra. Introduced by Hannah Williams, Hal Thompson and a female chorus, "Would You Like to Take a Walk?" (1930, lyrics by Billy Rose and Mort Dixon), was recorded by Julia Sanderson with Frank Crumit and by Rudy Vallee, and was interpolated into the motion picture *You're My Everything* (1949).

In Billy Rose's next Broadway revue, *Crazy Quilt* (1939), "Would You Like to Take a Walk?" was repeated and an important new Warren song was interpolated: "I Found a Million Dollar Baby" (lyrics by Billy Rose and Mort Dixon), introduced by Ted Healy, Fanny Brice, Phil Baker, and Lew Brice. A standard, this song was recorded by Bing Crosby and by Sam Lanin and his orchestra and was interpolated into the motion picture *Million Dollar Baby* (1935). Four decades later Barbra Streisand revived it in *Funny Lady* (1975).

Warren's first complete score for a Broadway musical was for a revue, *The Laugh Parade* (November 2, 1931), with book by Ed Wynn and Ed Preble. Starring Ed Wynn, it ran for 231 performances and one of its songs became a Warren standard, "You're My Everything" (lyrics by Mort Dixon and Joe Young), introduced by Lawrence Gray and Jeanne Aubert and recorded by Russ Columbo and by the Arden-Ohmen Orchestra. This song provided the title for a 1949 motion picture in which it was sung by Dan Dailey. The song was also interpolated into the film *Painting the Clouds with Sunshine* (1951) and was played on the soundtrack of *The Eddy Duchin Story* (1956) by Carmen Cavallero. "Ooh that Kiss," in *The Laugh Parade*, a duet for Gray and Aubert, was recorded by the Arden-Ohmen Orchestra, and "The Torch Song" was introduced by Bartlett Simmons. The lyrics for all *Laugh Parade* songs were by Dixon and Young.

Warren first worked for motion pictures in 1930 by providing three songs (lyrics by Sam H. Lewis and Joe Young) for *Spring Is Here* (1930), a film adaptation of a Rodgers and Hart stage musical. Two of these numbers became popular. "Cryin' for the Carolines" was introduced by Lawrence Gray, popularized by Guy Lombardo and His Royal Canadians, and recorded by Belle Baker, Ruth Etting, Johnny Mervin, and Ted Straetter and his orchestra. "Have a Little Faith in Me," a duet for Lawrence Gray and Bernice Claire, was recorded by Russ Morgan and his orchestra.

Following a temporary lull in Hollywood in the making of film musicals in 1930 and 1931 in the wake of a Depression-era decline at the box office, Warren moved his family to a rented house in Beverly Hills. Establishing permanent residence in the movie capital and intending to devote his songwriting talent to the screen, he purchased the first of several houses in Beverly Hills in 1937. At this time he acquired a new lyricist in Al Dubin, who was then employed by Warner Brothers. Their collaboration began with "Three's a Crowd," which David Manners introduced in *The Crooner* (1932). For Warner, Warren and Dubin composed four songs for *Forty-Second Street* (1933), all of which became standards. The title song was introduced by Ruby Keeler, recorded in 1933 by the Boswell Sisters and by the orchestras of Hal Kemp, Art Kahn, and Don Bestor, and was interpolated into the motion-picture musical *The Jolson Story* (1946). "Shuffle Off to Buffalo," introduced by Ruby Keeler, Ginger Rogers, Clarence Nordstrom, and Una Merkle, was recorded by the Boswell Sisters and by the orchestras of Art Kahn and Don Bestor. It was revived for Jack Carson and Joan Leslie in the film *The Hard Way* (1942). Introduced by Bebe Daniels, "You're Getting to Be a Habit With Me," was recorded by Bing Crosby and sung by Doris Day (and danced to by Gene Nelson) in the film musical *Lullaby of Broadway* (1951). "Young and Healthy," introduced by Dick Powell, was recorded by Bing Crosby.

The box-office success of *Forty-Second Street* in 1933 restored the faith of Hollywood studio moguls in the mass popularity of screen musicals. Lavish dance-musical productions thrived in the next half-dozen years, and Warren and Dubin were among the genre's leading contributors of hit songs. Among the films in which their songs were introduced was the *Gold Diggers* series of 1933, 1935, 1937 and 1938. "Lullaby of Broadway" from *Gold Diggers of 1935* brought them an Oscar and their first song to be aired on *Your Hit Parade*, with nine appearances, twice in first position. It was introduced by Wini Shaw

and Dick Powell in one of Busby Berkeley's most famous production numbers. Dick Powell also recorded it, as did Little Jack Little and Richard Himber and his orchestra. It was interpolated into the movie musicals, *The Jolson Story* and *Young Man with a Horn* (1950). Doris Day sang it (and Gene Nelson danced to it) in a 1951 film entitled *Lullaby of Broadway*.

Other Warren and Dubin songs heard on *Your Hit Parade*, all introduced in films were:

"The Rose in Her Hair" (five appearances), was introduced by Dick Powell in *Broadway Gondolier* (1935). It was also recorded by Dick Powell and interpolated into the film *Cain and Mabel* (1936), starring Clark Gable. "Lulu's Back in Town" (seven appearances) was introduced by Dick Powell with the Mills Brothers in the *Broadway Gondolier*; it was also recorded by Dick Powell, and by the Mills Brothers, and in 1964 was revived in a recording by Jerry Vale.

"Don't Give Up the Ship" (six appearances) was introduced by Dick Powell in *Shipmates Forever* (1935) and recorded both by Dick Powell and Tommy Dorsey and his orchestra. The U.S. Naval Academy adopted it as one of its official songs.

"Where Am I?" (three appearances) was introduced and recorded by James Melton in *Stars Over Broadway* (1935). "September in the Rain" (14 appearances, five in first position) was introduced by James Melton in *Stars Over Broadway* and repeated by him in another movie, *Melody for Two* (1937). He also recorded it, and George Shearing enjoyed his first success as a recording artist with this song in 1949.

The title song of *Page Miss Glory* (six appearances, once in first position) was introduced by Dick Powell in *Gold Diggers of 1937* and recorded by Dick Powell, George Hamilton and the Ink Spots. Doris Day sang it in *My Dream Is Yours* (1949) and it was interpolated into another motion picture, *Working Her Way Through College* (1952).

"I'll Sing You a Thousand Love Songs" (12 appearances, once in first position) was introduced by Robert Paige in *Cain and Mabel* and recorded by radio's "Street Singer," Arthur Tracy, and by the team of Fingerle and Schutt.

"Remember Me?" (11 appearances, once in first position) was introduced by Kenny Baker in *Mr. Dodd Takes the Air* (1937). It was recorded by Bing Crosby and by the orchestras of Tommy Dorsey and Hal Kemp. Erroll Flynn and Eleanor Powell sang it in *Never Say Goodbye* (1946).

"Cause My Baby Says it's So" (one appearance) was introduced in *The Singing Marine* (1937) by Dick Powell who also recorded it. "I Know Now" (nine appearances) was introduced by Doris Weston in *The Singing Marine* and recorded by Dick Powell.

"How Could You?" (one appearance) was introduced by Ann Sheridan in *San Quentin* (1937).

The following are additional hit songs composed by Warren and Dubin for the screen:

"We're in the Money," also known as "The Gold Digger's Song," was introduced by Ginger Rogers in the *Gold Diggers of 1933*, recorded by Dick Powell and Hal Kemp and his orchestra, and interpolated into the motion picutres *The Jolson Story* and *Dillinger* (1973). "Pettin' in the Park" was introduced by Dick Powell and Ruby Keeler in the same film. Dick Powell and the orchestras of Ray Noble and Hal Kemp recorded it. Also from that screen musical were "Shadow Waltz" and "I've Got to Sing a Torch Song." The former was introduced by Dick Powell, and Ruby Keeler, recorded by Dick Powell and by the orchestras of Guy Lombardo, Russ Morgan and Hal Kemp, and was interpolated into the motion picture, *Cain and Mabel*. The latter was introduced by Dick Powell and recorded by Powell and by the orchestras of Paul Whiteman, Fletcher Henderson, Ray Noble and Hal Kemp.

"No More Love" was introduced by Ruth Etting in *Roman Scandals* (1933). Ruth Etting and Eddie Duchin and his orchestra each recorded it.

"Shanghai Lil," was introduced by James Cagney, Ruby Keeler and chorus in *Footlight Parade* (1933) and was recorded by Paul Whiteman and his orchestra. Introduced in that same film by Dick Powell and Ruby Keeler, "Honeymoon Hotel" was recorded by Dick Powell and by Freddy Martin and his orchestra.

"Muchacha" was introduced by Phil Regan (who also recorded it) and Dolores Del Rio in *In Caliente* (1933).

"Don't Say Goodnight" was introduced by Dick Powell and chorus (and danced to by Ricardo Cortez and Dolores Del Rio) in *Wonder Bar* (1934). Dick Powell recorded it. The title song of the film *Wonder Bar* was introduced by Al Jolson and recorded by Dick Powell, and "Why Do I Dream Those Dreams?" from the same film was introduced by Dick Powell and recorded by Bob Causer.

"The Boulevard of Broken Dreams" was introduced by Constance Bennett in *Moulin Rouge* (1934), recorded by Frances Langford, by Hal Kemp and his orchestra, and much later by Tony Bennett in a bestselling version. It was interpolated into the Paul Mazursky film *Harry and Tonto* (1974). In *Moulin Rouge*, "Coffee in the Morning" was introduced by Constance Bennett and Russ Columbo and recorded by the orchestras of Eddy Duchin and Hal Kemp.

"I'll String Along With You" was introduced by Dick Powell in *Twenty Million Sweethearts* (1934) and recorded by Dick Powell, Doris Day, and Jo Stafford with Gordon MacRae. Day sang it in *My Dream Is Yours*, Danny Thomas in *The Jazz Singer* (1953), and it was used as a recurrent theme in the nonmusical film *Battle Cry* (1959).

The standard "I Only Have Eyes for You," was introduced by Dick Powell and Ruby Keeler in *Dames* (1934) and was recorded by Georgie Price, Jane Froman, Al Jolson, Kate Smith, Lena Horne and Phil Regan. It was revived in a bestselling recording by The Flamingos in 1956 and by Art Garfunkel in the late 1970s.

"She's a Latin From Manhattan" was introduced by Al Jolson in *Go Into Your Dance* (1935), sung by Joan Leslie and Jack Carson in *The Hard Way* (1942) and interpolated into *The Jolson Story*. Gertrude Niessen recorded it in 1935. Out of the same screen musical also came "About a Quarter to Nine" and "The Little Things You Used to Do." The former was introduced by Jolson. John Green and his orchestra with Jolson recorded it, and Jolson sang it on the soundtracks of *The Jolson Story* and *Jolson Sings Again* (1949). "The Little Things You Used to Do" was introduced by Helen Morgan. Among those who recorded it were Helen Morgan and the orchestras of John Green and Henri Biagni.

"I'd Rather Listen to Your Eyes" was introduced by Dick Powell in *Shipmates Forever* (1935) and recorded by Chuck Bullock and his orchestra.

"Song of the Marines," or "We're Shovin' Right Off," was introduced in *The Singing Marine* (1937) by Dick Powell, who recorded it. The U.S. Marines adopted it as an official song.

After Warren and Dubin went their separate ways in 1937, Warren continued to produce popular songs for the screen. Working with lyricist Johnny Mercer he composed "Jeepers, Creepers," introduced by Louis Armstrong in *Going Places* (1938). Armstrong's recording was heard on the soundtrack of the John Schlesinger movie *Day of the Locust* (1975). "Jeepers, Creepers" was also recorded by the Mills Brothers and by Gene Krupa and his orchestra. This song was interpolated into the motion pictures *My Dream Is Yours* and *Onionhead* (1958). In 1938–39 it had 11 presentations on *Your Hit Parade*, five times in first position. "Daydreaming" was introduced by Rudy Vallee and Rosemary Lane in *Gold Diggers in Paris* (1938) and had a single hearing on *Your Hit Parade* on July 9, 1938. "You Must Have Been a Beautiful Baby" was introduced by Dick Powell in *Hard to Get* (1938), was recorded by Basil Fomeen and his orchestra, and was seven times represented on *Your Hit Parade*, three times in first position. Doris Day sang it in *My Dream Is Yours* and Eddie Cantor on the soundtrack of *The Eddie Cantor Story* (1953). Bobby Darin revived it in a bestselling recording in 1961. "In a Moment of Weakness" was introduced by Ann Sheridan and Gale Page in *Naughty but Nice* (1939). Six years later, with Mercer still writing the words, Warren won an Oscar for "On the Atchison, Topeka, and the Santa Fe," introduced by Judy Garland and ensemble in *The Harvey Girls* (1945). Garland recorded it, as did Bing Crosby and Johnny Mercer with the Pied Pipers. This song appeared 14 times on *Your Hit Parade*. "Wait and See," introduced by Kenny Baker in *The Harvey Girls,* had a single hearing on *Your Hit Parade* on January 19, 1946.

With songs for *Young People* (1940), starring Shirley Temple, Warren's fruitful collaboration with the lyricist Mack Gordon began. Warren and Gordon received an Oscar for "You'll Never Know," introduced by Alice Faye in *Hello, Frisco, Hello* (1943). Her recording was heard on the soundtrack of Bob Fosse's *Lenny,* the 1975 film about the life of comedian Lenny Bruce. Dick Haymens's recording sold more than a million copies and it was also recorded by Frank Sinatra. This song appeared 24 times on *Your Hit Parade,* nine times in first position. Alice Faye sang it again in *Four Jills in a Jeep* (1944) and Betty Grable in *Diamond Horseshoe* (1945).

Other Warren and Gordon songs represented on *Your Hit Parade* were:

"Down Argentina Way" (four appearances) was introduced in the 1940 film of the same name for an elaborate choreographed sequence and Dinah Shore recorded it. "Two Dreams Met" (one appearance) was also introduced in *Down Argentina Way,* performed by Don Ameche, Betty Grable and others. Kenny Baker and the orchestras of Tommy Dorsey and Mitchell Ayres recorded.

"Chattanooga Choo Choo" (13 appearances, twice in first position) was interpolated into *Sun Valley Serenade* (1941) after it had been introduced and popularized in a recording by Glenn Miller and his orchestra. It was also recorded by the Andrews Sisters and by Cab Calloway, Dan Dailey sang it in *You're My Everything* (1949), and it was interpolated into *Springtime in the Rockies* (1942), *The Big Lift* (1950), *Don't Bother to Knock* (1952), *Man on a Tightrope* (1953), and *The Glenn Miller Story* (1954). "Chattanooga Choo Choo" also provided the title for, and was heard in a 1984 comedy film.

"I've Got a Gal in Kalamazoo" (11 appearances, twice in first position) was introduced by Glenn Miller and his orchestra (vocal by Tex Beneke) in *Orchestra Wives* (1942). It was recorded by the orchestras of Glenn Miller and Benny Goodman. "Serenade in Blue" and "At Last" were also introduced in the same screen musical. "Serenade in Blue" (nine appearances) was introduced by Glenn Miller and his orchestra (vocal by Ray Eberle) and the Modernaires in *Orchestra Wives.* It was recorded by the orchestras of Glenn Miller and Benny Goodman and interpolated into the motion picture *You're My Everything.* "At Last" (seven appearances) was also introduced by Glenn Miller and his orchestra with the Modernaires. It was recorded by Ina Ray Hutton and Charlie Spivak and his orchestra, and in 1962 was revived in a bestselling release by Ray Anthony.

"There Will Never Be Another You" (four appearances) was introduced by John Payne in *Iceland* (1942), recorded by the orchestras of Woody Herman, Sammy Kaye, and Tommy Tucker, and interpolated into the film *I'll Get By* (1950).

"I Had the Craziest Dream" (15 appearances) was introduced in *Springtime in the Rockies* (1942) by Harry James and his orchestra. They recorded it as did Tony Martin.

"My Heart Tells Me" (19 appearances, nine times in first position) was introduced by Betty Grable in *Sweet Rosie O'Grady* (1944). It was popularized in a recording by Glen Gray and the Casa Loma Orchestra (vocal by Eugenia Baird).

"The More I See You" (16 appearances, once in first position) was introduced by Dick Haymes in *Diamond Horseshoe* (1945). It was recorded by Dick Haymes, Carmen Cavallero and the orchestras of Harry James and Sammy Kaye. "I Wish I Knew," also from *Diamond Horseshoe* (two appearances) was introduced by Dick Haymes and by Harry James and his orchestra.

After Mack Gordon, Warren maintained partnerships with other lyricists, producing many songs that were heard on *Your Hit Parade.* "Someone Like You" (lyrics by Ralph Blane), which had six hearings was introduced by Doris Day in *My Dream Is Yours.* With a single hearing on July 9, 1949, "My One and Only Highland Fling" (lyrics by Ira Gershwin) was introduced by Fred Astaire and Ginger Rogers in *The Barkleys of Broadway* (1949) and was recorded not only by Astaire with Rogers but also by Dick Haymes, Dinah Shore, and Jo Stafford with Gordon MacRae. "That's Amore" (lyrics by Jack Brooks) had 15 hearings and was introduced in *The Caddy* (1953) by Dean Martin, who also recorded it.

Several other Warren songs of the 1940s and 1950s deserve attention. Introduced by Alice

Faye in *The Gang's All Here* (1943), "No Love, No Nothin'" was popularized in a recording by Johnny Long and his orchestra (vocal by Patti Page) and represented ten times on *Your Hit Parade*. It was also recorded by Judy Garland and by Ella Mae Morse. "Someone Like You" (lyrics by Ralph Blane) was introduced by Doris Day in *My Dream Is Yours* and recorded by Day, Peggy Lee, Ella Fitzgerald, and Tommy Dorsey and his orchestra. "Zing a Little Zong" (lyrics by Leo Robin) was introduced by Bing Crosby and Jane Wyman in *Just for You* (1952). "An Affair to Remember," or "Our Love Affair" (lyrics by Harold Adamson and Leo McCarey), was introduced by Vic Damone on the soundtrack of *An Affair to Remember* (1957). Vic Damone's recording was a bestseller.

After an absence from the Broadway musical theater for a quarter of a century, Warren returned with *Shangri-La* (June 13, 1956), which stumbled through only 21 performances. The book by James Hilton, Jerome Lawrence, and Robert E. Lee was an unhappy attempt to adapt a musical version of Hilton's bestselling novel *Lost Horizon*. Jerome Lawrence and Robert E. Lee were Warren's lyricists. Warren also composed the theme music (to Harold Adamson's lyrics) for the ABC-TV Western series, *The Life and Legend of Wyatt Earp*, which aired for the first time on September 6, 1955.

Discussing the songwriting profession with Max Wilk, author of *They're Playing Our Song*, Warren said, "You can't be trained, you can't go to school and learn it. You get a script and read it, and then your subconscious mind goes to work. When I do a picture, I must write reams of melodies. I might write maybe 15, 20 tunes before I get the right one, the one that I like. . . . I always try to get the tune first, because they lyric writer can always fit the tune. If I don't get anything, I go away. Sometimes I get them away from the piano. Then, when I get the one I like I say, 'I think we'll use this!'"

With the shift in motion-picture music in the 1960s to rock-influenced pop sounds, Warren's previous flood of songs was reduced to a trickle. His last film assignments were *Satan Never Sleeps* (1962) and the title song for *Rosie* (lyrics by Johnny Mercer) in 1967. "The studios just stopped calling me," he said. "There just isn't a market for the kind of old-fashioned number I used to do, and which I still love to create." But he never ceased composing, publishing a *Mass* in 1962 and a set of piano vignettes seven years later.

Warren and his wife lived off Sunset Drive in Beverly Hills on a one-acre estate which he had acquired in 1956. His diversions were golf, a sport he had avidly played for decades, playing pool, good food, alcohol consumed in moderation, and "kibitzing with friends and fooling around at the piano." His wealth stemmed not only from his songs but from shrewd real-estate investments.

Harry Warren lived to see a revival of interest in the hits of his glory days when *Lullaby of Broadway*, a musical with 44 Warren songs, was produced Off Broadway with a small cast. Indeed, Warren's songs had stood the test of time so well that David Merrick decided to produce a stage version of the 1932 film *Forty-Second Street*. It opened on August 25, 1980 and has become one of the greatest box-office successes on Broadway in recent years. It won a Tony as the season's best musical and in 1984 was earning a combined weekly profit of $500,000 from the Broadway production and two touring companies—the greatest weekly profit ever recorded in the American theater for a single musical. The book by Michael Stewart and Mark Bramble, described in the program as "the song and dance fable of Broadway," retained the basic backstage film plot. Tammy Grimes and Jerry Orbach starred and the staging and choreography of Gower Champion (who died just hours before the show opened) was acclaimed as brilliant. The standards from the motion picture were supplemented by other songs from the Warren catalogue to provide 17 numbers in all, recorded in an original cast album. These songs, said Fred Rich in *The New York Times*, "are so good and plentiful that they make the story seem an unwanted intrusion. . . ."

Harry Warren died of kidney failure at the Cedars-Mt. Sinai Hospital in Los Angeles in 1981. Just before his death, 20th Century-Fox had contracted him to write a score for a new movie, *Manhattan Melody*.

ABOUT: Thomas, T. Harry Warren and the Hollywood Musical, 1982; Wilk, M. They're Playing Our Song, 1973. *Periodicals*—ASCAP Today March 1978; High Fidelity December 1975; New York Times December 7, 1979.

WASHINGTON, NED (August 15, 1901–December 20, 1976), lyricist and winner of three Academy Awards, was born in Scranton, Pennsylvania, one of nine children. He was educated at the Scranton Technical High School and the Charles Sumner School, and even as a young boy contributed poems to local newspapers. After his family moved to Norfolk, Virginia, he continued to publish his poems and prose in newspapers and even in national magazines.

NED WASHINGTON

His interest in show business brought him in 1922 to New York, where he found work in vaudeville, first as a booking agent, then as a master of ceremonies, and finally as a writer of special material for performers. He turned to lyric writing, placing two songs in the Broadway revue *Vanities of 1928*: "Getting the Beautiful Girls" and "My Arms Are Wide Open," both to music by Michael H. Cleary.

Washington went to California in 1928 to write songs for films. That year, "Singin' in the Bathtub" was introduced by Winnie Lightner in *The Show of Shows* and was recorded by Guy Lombardo and His Royal Canadians. Lupe Velez introduced "The Day You Fall in Love" in *Tiger Rose*. The lyrics for both songs were written in collaboration with Herb Magidson, and the music was composed by Cleary.

Washington returned to New York in 1930 and continued his career as a freelance songwriter. In 1931 "Can't We Talk it Over" (music by Victor Young), was popularized by Lee Wiley. Washington wrote his first standard in 1932, "I'm Gettin' Sentimental Over You" (music by George Bassman), which was recorded that year by the Dorsey brothers orchestra and later became the theme song of Tommy Dorsey's orchestra. Their version appeared on the soundtrack for the opening scene of *Carnal Knowledge* (1971). Other films using the song included *Keep 'Em Flying* (1941), *Du Barry Was a Lady* (1943) and *A Song Is Born* (1948). Benny Goodman and his orchestra recorded it, with vocals by Frances Langford in 1937, and the Ink Spots' version appeared in 1939.

Washington had other successes in 1932:

"Someone Stole Gabriel's Horn" (lyrics written with Irving Mills, music by Edgar Hayes) was introduced by the Mills Blue Rhythm Band and recorded by both the Jack Teagarden orchestra and the Washboard Rhythm Kings; "Waltzing in a Dream" (lyrics written with Bing Crosby, music by Victor Young) was popularized in Bing Crosby's recording; "Got the South in My Soul" (lyrics written with Lee Wiley, music by Victor Young), was recorded by Lee Wiley; "My Romance" (music by Young) was introduced on radio by Arthur Tracy, the "Street Singer," who also recorded it.

He continued his productivity in 1933; "Sweet Madness" (music by Victor Young) was interpolated into the Broadway musical *Murder at the Vanities*; "A Hundred Years From Today" (lyrics written with Joe Young, music by Victor Young) was introduced by Kathryn Perry in the Broadway revue *Blackbirds of 1933–1934,* then recorded by Glen Gray and the Casa Loma orchestra and by Ethel Waters with the Benny Goodman orchestra, and was interpolated into the film *Girl from Missouri* (1934); "Smoke Rings" (music by H. Eugene Gifford) was introduced by Glen Gray and the Casa Loma orchestra, which adopted it as its theme; "Love is the Theme" (music by Victor Young) was recorded by Ethel Waters and later by Richard Himber and his orchestra.

Washington returned to Hollywood in 1935, under contract to MGM. He lived from then on in Los Angeles, writing songs for movies, and realized the greatest successes of his career. *Here Comes the Band* and the Marx Brothers' *A Night at the Opera* (both 1935) were the first MGM films with Washington's songs. In the former, "Headin' Home" (music by Herbert Stothart) was introduced by Harry Stockwell and "You're My Thrill" (music by Burton Lane) by Ted Lewis; in the latter film, Allen Jones introduced "Cosi Cosa" (music by Bronislau Kaper and Walter Jourmann). "The Nearness of You" (music by Hoagy Carmichael), from *Romance in the Dark* (1938), was Washington's first song to appear on *Your Hit Parade*. The film *Pinocchio* (1940) brought him two Oscars, one for the complete score (music by Leigh Harling), the other for "When You Wish Upon a Star." This song, sung on the soundtrack by Cliff Edwards, was recorded by Frances Langford and by Kate Smith, and appeared on *Your Hit Parade* 14 times, five of them in first position. Washington won his third Oscar for "Do Not Forsake Me," also known as "High Noon," the title song of the 1952 Western with music by Dimitri Tiomkin.

Washington collaborated often with Tiomkin. "Return to Paradise" and "The High and the

Mighty" were theme songs for films of the same names (1953); "Wild is the Wind" was the title song of a film starring Anna Magnani and Anthony Quinn (1957); "Strange Are the Ways of Love" appeared in *The Young Land* (1959); "The Need for You," also called "The Unforgiven," came from a theme from *The Unforgiven* (1960); "Town Without Pity" was the title song of the Kirk Douglas film (1961); "They Call it Love" was introduced in *The Guns of Navarone* (1961); "A Circus World" was the title song of a 1964 film starring John Wayne and Rita Hayworth; "The Fall of Love" was adapted from a theme from the score of *The Fall of the Roman Empire* (1964). Washington and Tiomkin also composed the theme for the CBS television Western series *Rawhide* (1958).

Other songs from Washington's 35-year screen career include: "Baby Mine" (music by Frank Churchill), introduced in the Walt Disney animated film *Dumbo* (1941); "Saludos Amigos," an English adaptation of a popular Spanish song with music by Charles Walcott, introduced in the animated cartoon of the same name (1942); "Rio de Janeiro," another English adaptation of a popular Brazilian song with music by Ary Barroso, introduced in *Brazil* (1944); "Someday I'll Meet You Again" (music by Max Steiner), introduced in *Passage to Marseille* (1944), appeared once on *Your Hit Parade*; "Stella By Starlight" (music by Victor Young), the recurrent theme of the *The Uninvited* (1944), was recorded by Victor Young and his orchestra; "My Foolish Heart" (music by Victor Young), introduced by Susan Hayward in the film of the same name (1949), was recorded by Billy Eckstine and by Gordon Jenkins and his orchestra, and appeared 18 times on *Your Hit Parade*, three times in first position; "Sadie Thompson's Song," or "The Blue Pacific Blues" (music by Lester Lee), introduced in *Miss Sadie Thompson* (1953); "The Man From Laramie" (music by Lester Lee), title song of the 1955 film, was recorded by the Voices of Walter Schumann; "To Love Again" (music by Morris Stoloff and George Sidney adapted from Chopin's Nocturne in E-flat), the theme from *The Eddie Duchin Story* (1955), was introduced on the soundtrack by Carmen Cavallero and recorded by the Four Aces; "Song Without End" (music by Morris Stoloff and George W. Duning, melody based on Liszt's *Un sospiro*), was introduced in the film of the same name.

Washington served as director of ASCAP from 1957 to 1976 and was its vice president from 1964 to 1976. His hobby was riding, training, and exhibiting horses, and he won many trophies. He suffered from leukemia from about 1970, and died of a heart attack in Los Angeles in late 1976.

ABOUT: Stambler, I. Encyclopedia of Popular Music, 1965. *Periodicals*—ASCAP Today Spring 1978.

WEBSTER, PAUL FRANCIS (December 20, 1907–March 18, 1984). Few screen lyricists have matched Paul Francis Webster's achievements. His songs appeared in some 70 films, won three Academy Awards, and in addition received 16 Oscar nominations, more than any other lyricist. About 40 of his film songs have been hits, many of them standards, and ten were heard on *Your Hit Parade*.

Webster was born in New York City, the son of Myron Lawrence Webster, a manufacturer, and Blanche Pauline Stonehill Webster. He graduated in 1926 from the Horace Mann School in Riverdale, then attended Cornell University (1927–28) and New York University (1928–30). Leaving the latter without a degree, he found work as an instructor in a New York dance studio. His debut as a professional lyricist was "Masquerade" (music by John Jacob Loeb), a hit in 1932. This waltz-song, in Ferde Grofé's orchestration, was performed at the Lewisohn Stadium in New York by Paul Whiteman, who also recorded it. It was revived in 1963 as the title song of an album by the Melachrino Strings.

In 1933 "Virgins Wrapped in Cellophane" (music by Loeb) and "Sweet Madonna" (music by Victor Young) appeared in the Broadway musical *Murder at the Vanities*: they were Webster's first songs for the musical theater. The same year, "My Moonlight Madonna" (music by William Scotti) was introduced by Paul Whiteman and his orchestra in a recording; it was later recorded by Arthur Tracy, radio's "Street Singer," by Richard Crooks and by Jessica Dragonette. The song was further popularized by Rudy Vallee and was heard in the film *Stella Dallas* (1937). "Two Cigarettes in the Dark" (music by Lew Pollack) was introduced in the nonmusical Broadway play, *Kill that Story* (1934), was recorded by Bob Causer and by Frankie Parker, and won an ASCAP award. In 1934, "Got the Jitters" (music by Loeb) was introduced by Ben Pollack and his orchestra in a revue at the Casino de Paris, a New York nightclub.

A contract from 20th Century-Fox brought Webster to Hollywood in 1934. With Lew Pollack, he wrote songs for three films released that year by that studio: *Under the Pampas Moon, Dress to Thrill*, and *Our Little Girl*. The title song of *Rainbow on the River* (music by Louis Alter), an RKO production of 1936, was sung in the film by Bobby Breen, who recorded it. The song became the signature music for the dramatic series *Dr. Christian*, which premiered on the CBS radio network on November 7, 1937.

PAUL FRANCIS WEBSTER

While continuing to write for films, Webster wrote the lyrics for *Jump for Joy,* an all-black revue with music by Duke Ellington, which opened in Los Angeles in 1941. Featured were "I Got it Bad and That Ain't Good" as well as the title song. A year later, Webster wrote "Lily of Laguna" (music by Ted Fiorito), popularized in a recording by Bing Crosby with Mary Martin. In the early 1940s, Webster also began his collaboration with Hoagy Carmichael with "The Lamplighter's Serenade" and "Baltimore Oriole." They later wrote "Remember Me to Carolina" for *Minstrel Man* (1944), "Doctor, Lawyer, Indian Chief" for *The Stork Club* (1945) and "Memphis in June" for *Johnny Angel* (1945). They also published several numbers independent of any screen production: "No More Toujours l'amour" in 1945; "Bubble-boo, Bubble-boo" in 1948; "Follow the Swallow" and "The Three Sisters" in 1949; and "Watermelon Weather" in 1952.

"Black Coffee" (1948, music by Sonny Burke), one of Webster's best-known blues, was recorded by Ella Fitzgerald, by Sarah Vaughan and by Peggy Lee. In 1949, "How it Lies, How it Lies" and "You Was," (both to Burke's music) became Webster's first songs to appear on *Your Hit Parade,* each with a single performance; "How it Lies, How it Lies" was recorded by Connie Haines and "You Was" by Doris Day. "The Merry Christmas Polka" (music by Burke), also of 1949, was recorded by Dinah Shore and by the Andrews Sisters with Guy Lombardo and his Royal Canadians. "The Loveliest Night of the Year" (music by Irving Aaronson, adapted from Juventino Rosas' "*Sobre los olas*") was introduced

by Ann Blyth in *The Great Caruso* (1951) and recorded by Mario Lanza. This song received 23 performances on *Your Hit Parade.* "I'll Walk With God" (music by Nicholas Brodszky) was introduced in *The Student Prince* (1954) by Mario Lanza, who also recorded it. It has since become popular as a church hymn in the United States.

Webster's first Academy Award was won with composer Sammy Fain for "Secret Love" from *Calamity Jane* (1953). Their second Oscar came for the title song of *Love is a Many Splendored Thing* (1955), heard on *Your Hit Parade.* Other screen songs by Fain and Webster included: "A Little Love Can Go a Long, Long Way" from *Ain't Misbehavin'* (1955); the title song from *April Love* (1952), heard on *Your Hit Parade*; the title songs from *A Certain Smile* (1958), *The Gift of Love* (1958) and *Tender Is the Night* (1962); and "A Very Precious Love" from *Marjorie Morningstar* (1958). They also wrote several songs for the Broadway revues *Alive and Kicking* (1950) and *Catch a Star!* (1955), and the complete score for the Broadway musical *Christine* (1960), which closed after only a dozen performances. They collaborated on *Calamity Jane* (1961), a musical that never reached Broadway, which opened in Fort Worth and traveled to St. Louis, Pittsburgh, Kansas City, and Framingham, Massachusetts. Adapted for television, it appeared on CBS in 1962. Fain and Webster also wrote the score for another CBS special, *A Diamond for Carla* (1960).

Webster wrote, with Dimitri Tiomkin as composer, the title song for *Friendly Persuasion,* also known as "Thee I Love" (1956); "There's Never Been Anyone Else But You," adapted from one of the musical themes from *Giant* (1956); "The Green Leaves of Summer" and "The Ballad of the Alamo" from *The Alamo* (1960); the title song from *The Guns of Navarone* (1961); and "So Little Time" from *55 Days at Peking* (1963).

Other composers also worked successfully with Webster. "Honey-Babe" (music by Max Steiner based on a traditional melody) was the marching song from the nonmusical film *Battle Cry* (1955). Popularized in a recording by Al Mooney and his orchestra, it appeared ten times on *Your Hit Parade.* "Invitation" (music by Bronislau Kaper) was adapted from a theme from the motion picture of the same name (1956); it was recorded by Rosemary Clooney and by Jack Jones. The title song from *Anastasia* (1956, music by Alfred Newman) was derived from a theme from that score and was recorded by Pat Boone. "Twelfth of Never" in 1956 (music by Jerry Livingston, based on a Kentucky folk tune, "The Riddle Song") was recorded by Johnny Mathis in a popular release, and was also recorded by Andy Williams, by Bobbie Vinton, by Nina Simone and by the Fleetwoods. "The Song of Raintree County" (music by John Green) was composed for *Raintree County* (1957). "Padre" of 1957 was Webster's adaptation of a French song with music by Alain Romans; it was recorded by Tony Arden. "Shenendoah Rose" (music by Jerry Livingston), in 1957, was recorded in 1957 by John Desmond. "Like Young" (music by André Previn) was recorded in 1958 as an instrumental by André Previn and his orchestra and as a vocal by Ella Fitzgerald and Perry Como. "Bluebell" (music by Livingston) became a bestseller in 1958 in a recording by Mitch Miller and his orchestra and chorus. "The Falcon and the Dove" (music by Miklós Rózsa) was an adaptation of the love theme from *El Cid* (1961). "Follow Me" (music by Bronislau Kaper) was the love song from *Mutiny on the Bounty* (1962), where it was sung by a chorus. "The Seventh Dawn" (music by Riz Ortolani) was adapted from one of the melodies in the film of the same name (1964) and was recorded by Danny Williams.

Webster won his third Oscar for "The Shadow of Your Smile" (music by Johnny Mandel), the love theme from *The Sandpiper* (1965), where it was sung chorally on the soundtrack under the final credits. It won a Grammy award as song of the year, and was recorded by Tony Bennett. To Mandel's music, Webster wrote "A Time to Love" for *An American Dream* (1966), where it was sung by Jackie Ward (dubbing for Janet Leigh). Tony Bennett's recording was a bestseller. "Somewhere My Love," also known as "Lara's Theme" (music by Maurice Jarre), was adapted from the theme music for *Doctor Zhivago* (1965). The instrumental version was recorded by Roger Williams; the vocal one by the Ray Conniff Singers.

Webster also wrote the lyrics for the theme songs of two 1957 ABC television series, *Maverick* (music by David Buttolph) and *Sugarfoot* (music by Ray Heindorf and Max Steiner). He was also editor of a book, *Children's Music Box* (1945).

Webster, who lived for many years in Beverly Hills, died in 1984 of Parkinson's disease.

ABOUT: Craig, W. Sweet and Lowdown: America's Popular Song Writers, 1978; Rigdon, W. (ed.) The Biographical Encyclopedia and Who's Who of the American Theatre, 1966.

WEILL, KURT (March 2, 1900–April 3, 1950). In the 1930s and 1940s Kurt Weill was one of the Broadway musical theater's most prestigious and

KURT WEILL

prolific composers. Before immigrating to the United States, Weill was renowned for musico-dramatic works that integrated opera with the popular musical theater, especially in his collaborations with Bertolt Brecht. In New York, after successfully writing for the popular musical stage, he ended his career by fusing traditional elements of the Broadway musical with those of the post-Wagnerian opera.

Born in Dessau, Germany in 1900, Kurt Weill was the third of four children of Albert and Emma (Ackerman) Weill. Since the 15th century, the Weills had produced eminent rabbis. Albert Weill combined the rabbinate with the office of cantor and the writing of liturgical music. Kurt's mother was an amateur pianist. Because his parents expected Kurt to enter the rabbinate, he received a thorough religious training. But music was not neglected, and he received his first piano lessons from his mother. Drawn more to music than to religion, Kurt, though he had not had formal instruction in composition, tried writing an opera at ten, and at 14 composed songs which have survived. In Dessau he was "the wonder child" who was called upon to serve as rehearsal pianist and, occasionally, to give piano concerts at the ducal palace in Dessau.

When he was 15, Weill began piano study with Albert Bing, who also gave him his first instruction in composition. At Bing's suggestion, Weill left Dessau in 1918 to attend the Academy of Music in Berlin, where he studied composition with Engelbert Humperdinck and conducting with Rudolf Krasselt. At school he composed a tone poem for orchestra which was performed and earned him a scholarship. But after one semester, Weill decided to leave school to begin his professional career. In 1919 he was a coach at the Dessau Opera and, in 1920, a staff conductor at the Lüdenscheid Civic Opera in Westphalia.

Returning to Berlin later in 1920, he began a three-year period of composition study with Ferruccio Busoni, the noted progressive composer and pianist. Under Busoni's guidance, Weill composed concert works in the post-Wagnerian idiom then favored by young German modernists who had assimilated the innovations of Mahler and Strauss. A meeting with Georg Kaiser, the expressionist playwright, resulted in Weill's first opera, the one-act tragedy *Der Protagonist* (1926), with Kaiser's experimental text and Weill's music. It was introduced at the Dresden Opera on March 26, 1926 and Weill was at once established as a leader composer for the theater of the younger generation of modernists. In the next opera by Weill and Kaiser, a one-act comedy entitled *Der Zar lässt sich photographieren* (1928, The Czar has His Photograph Taken), Weill experimented for the first time with jazz and other popular idioms. Its premiere in Leipzig on February 18, 1928 proved so successful that it was eventually produced in 80 German theaters. "I want to reach the real people, a more representative public than any opera house attracts," Weill said at the time. "I write for today. I don't care about writing for posterity."

He now became a prominent musical voice of the German cultural movement known as *Zeitkunst*, which sought to reconcile and combine modern aesthetic techniques, such as "distancing effects," with popular forms of musical or dramatic expression and to treat contemporary themes that would appeal to the general public as well as the intelligentsia. For Weill, *Zeitkunst* meant the transformation of opera into a form of popular theater. Collaborating with Bertolt Brecht, the Marxist poet and modern dramatist, Weill helped to develop the epic theatrical form they called *Songspiel*, in which politically didactic parable comprised the text, which was augmented by songs written in a popular style that commented on, and sometimes criticized, the dramatic action.

Their first experiment with this format was *Mahagonny Songspiel* (also known as the *Little Mahagonny*) a dramatic satire of capitalism by Brecht that was set in an imaginary American city. Weill and Brecht's first stage success, though, came with *The Threepenny Opera*. This was a modern adaptation of John Gay's 18th-century ballad opera, *The Beggar's Opera*, but with an early 20th-century locale and the locale

transferred to Soho, an urban underworld populated by the demimonde. With a score made up of ragtime, jazz, blues ballads, ribald parodies and other popular forms, and a text that exposed the pervasive corruption of German society in the 1920, *The Threepenny Opera* was a sensation when introduced in Berlin on August 31, 1928. In its first year, the opera had been performed more than 4,000 times in some 100 German theaters; within five years of its premiere, the opera had been given 10,000 performances and been translated into 18 languages, and been made into a German-language motion picture directed by the noted expressionist G.W. Pabst.

The Threepenny Opera's first performance in America, on April 13, 1933 on Broadway, was a failure. But on March 10, 1954 it was revived Off Broadway with a text rewritten and updated by Marc Blitzstein—but with Weill's original music intact—and had a run of 2,500 performances. Its most successful ballad, "Moritat"—retitled "Mack the Knife" in America and introduced as such in the Blitzstein version by Scott Merrill—was recorded in the United States in more than 20 versions, including bestselling recordings by Dick Hayman and by Louis Armstrong. In 1956 "Mack the Knife" was heard nine times on *Your Hit Parade*. Bobby Darin's recording in 1959, which received a Grammy, sold more than two million copies and helped make him a star. Ella Fitzgerald's recording in 1960 brought her a Grammy, too. The complete score of Blitzstein's version of *The Threepenny Opera* was recorded in an original cast album.

The star of the world premiere of *The Threepenny Opera* in Berlin was Weill's wife, Lotte Lenya, who portrayed Jenny the Prostitute. Weill and Lenya had been married on January 28, 1926 and made their home in Berlin until 1933, when they fled to Paris. Two years later they immigrated to America. As one writer noted, "The marriage endured some shaky moments but survived to become one of the most creative of husband-and-wife partnerships." They had no children.

In the spirit of *Zeitkunst* was the Brecht-Weill opera *Happy End* (1929), whose plot was set in Chicago in 1915 and anticipated the story line in Frank Loesser's musical, *Guys and Dolls*, about gamblers and an innocent Salvation Army lass. Out of Weill's score came "The Bilbao Song," which, decades later and with new lyrics in English by Johnny Mercer, became a hit through a recording by Andy Williams. The American premiere of *Happy End* took place in New Haven, Connecticut on April 6, 1972.

Mahagonny Songspiel was expanded to epic

proportions when *The Rise and Fall of the City of Mahagonny* premiered in both Leipzig and Frankfurt on March 9, 1930. Its American premiere came in New York on March 4, 1970; it was revived by the Metropolitan Opera in 1979.

Weill's last production in Germany was *Der Silbersee* (Silverlake), with text by Georg Kaiser. It was scheduled to run concurrently at 11 different opera houses in early 1935, but in each instance the Nazis forced its closing soon after opening night. *Silverlake*'s American premiere came on March 20, 1980 in a performance by the New York City Opera.

Weill and Lenya left Nazi Germany on March 21, 1933, spending two years in Paris before arriving in New York in the fall of 1935. He had come to the United States to compose music for the Max Reinhardt production of *The Eternal Road* (text by Franz Werfel), a monumental depiction of the history of the Jews, but, delayed for two years, it did not open until 1937. Meanwhile, Harold Clurman's Group Theatre engaged Weill to compose music for *Johnny Johnson* (November 19, 1936), an antiwar satire with text and lyrics by Paul Green.

The Group Theatre became one of the American theater's most influential forces. In the late 1930s Clurman was surrounded by Lee Strasberg, Stella Adler, Morris Carnovsky, Clifford Odets, and Lee J. Cobb. Their aesthetics were advanced, influenced by Europeans like Stanislavsky, and their assault on the commercial American theater forever altered its shape. Weill was also sympathetic to their leftist-reformist politics. The program called *Johnny Johnson* a "fable" and the author a "legend." According to one reviewer, it comprised caricature, satire, musical comedy, polemical social drama and occasionally sentimental parable. The action takes place during World War I. Johnny Johnson, a pacifist, is infected with a kind of idealist war fever when World War I breaks out and he enlists in what he considers a crusade—the war to end all wars. A simple, naive and plain-spoken product of small-town America, he experiences the horrors of war at no small personal price—he loses the girl he loves and is himself briefly confined to an asylum—and returns as a pacifist once again. Years later, as he sees the world arming itself for yet another global conflict, his bitterness and disenchantment deepen. "The world," as Brooks Atkinson of *The New York Times* explained, "has slapped him with its ultimate indignity. It can no longer find room for a completely honest man, for it has surrendered to the charlatans, opportunists, and rogues who are captains and kings of destruction."

Weill composed 19 numbers for this production. "Though they were woven into Green's play, several songs stood out and demonstrated Weill's capacity to adapt his style to the American theater. "Oh, the Rio Grande," was a cowboy song introduced by Tony Kraber. "Johnny's Melody," or "Listen to My Song," introduced by Russell Collins, acquired a new set of lyrics in 1936 from Edward Heyman. Retitled "To Love You and To Lose You," it was first recorded by Ray Noble and his orchestra. "O Heart of Love" was a ballad introduced by Phoebe Grand.

With a run of just 68 performances, *Johnny Johnson* was a box-office failure. Two later revivals in New York, in 1936 and 1971, also had only brief runs.

With *Knickerbocker Holiday* (October 19, 1938), which had a 168-performance run, Weill established himself as a major new musical voice in the American musical theater. This production, which starred Walter Huston (father of the filmmaker John Huston) in a text by Maxwell Anderson, indicted dictatorial rule and was set in New Amsterdam in 1637. Peter Stuyvesant (Huston's role), the Governor General, rules New Amsterdam through his councilors, who, in turn, ruthlessly exploit the people for their own end but who actually are Stuyvesant's pawns. The freedom-loving, democratic Dutch are personified by Brom Broeck, who is in love with Tina, the young woman Stuyvesant plans to marry. The wedding ceremony is interruped by an Indian raid in which Brom fights courageously. Despite his heroism, he must face prison for having previously defied the Governor. However, reason is used to convince Stuyvesant to change his ways, and Brom is freed and allowed to pursue his love affair with Tina.

As the middle-aged man whose betrothed is many years younger than he, Huston introduced "September Song" (lyrics by Maxwell Anderson), a melancholy commentary on a May-December romance that is the most popular of the songs that Weill wrote in America. When he was composing it for Huston, Weill inquired as to the actor's vocal range. Huston replied, "No range—no voice." Later, when Huston appeared on a coast-to-coast radio broadcast, Weill urged him to sing any number so that he might better adapt his own song to the singer. Hearing Huston's rasping, nasal delivery, Weill fashioned his melody to suit Huston's style. Walter Huston, Bing Crosby, Frank Sinatra and Tony Martin recorded "September Song," as did the orchestras of Stan Kenton and Eddie Duchin. Charles Coburn sang it in the 1944 motion picture adaptation of the stage musical. In the film *September Affair* (1951), the song was used as a recurrent theme, with Walter Huston's recording heard on the soundtrack. Maurice Chevalier sang it in the film *Pepe* (1960).

Besides "September Song" there were other memorable numbers in the score, all with lyrics by Anderson. "Will You Remember Me?" was introduced by Richard Kollmar; "How Can You Tell an American?" by Kollmar and Ray Middleton; "There's Nowhere to Go But Up" by Kollmar and Clarence Nordstrom; "It Never Was You" by Kollmar and Jeanne Madden. Judy Garland sang "It Never Was You" in the film *I Could Go On Singing* (1963).

Lady in the Dark (January 23, 1941), with book by Moss Hart and lyrics by Ira Gershwin, represented, as did Rodgers and Hammerstein's *Oklahoma* (1943), an innovation in the format of the musical play by using the music and lyrics to advance the dramatic action and give psychological insight into the characters. Gertrude Lawrence, in a virtuosic performance, portrayed Liza Elliott, the editor of a fashion magazine (*Allure*), who undergoes psychiatric treatment for her "abnormal" behavior. The play moves in and out of Liza's real world as editor and woman and the interior world of her fantasies and recherché dreams of childhood and youth. In the process, her identity as a woman is established and her love life is happily resolved. The show ran for 467 performances, and Danny Kaye was catapulted to stardom in the role of *Allure* photographer Russell Paxton. He repeatedly stopped the show with "Tschaikowsky," a tongue-twisting patter song in which the names of 49 Russian composers were rattled off in 39 seconds.

Gertrude Lawrence's showstopping number was "The Saga of Jenny," in which the *Allure* editor was transformed into an earthy saloon singer doing bumps and grinds. She also introduced "My Ship," which was heard recurrently throughout the play. Because this is a tune the character had learned in childhood, Weill composed the melody in the style of turn-of-the-century ballads. "The Princess of Pure Delight" was sung by Gertrude Lawrence and a chorus of children; "One Life to Live" was a duet for Lawrence and Victor Moore. In the 1943 motion picture version "The Saga of Jenny," "One Life to Live" and "This is New" were all sung by Ginger Rogers. From "My Ship," which had been crucial to the plot development on the stage, only a few measures were retained, and "Tschaikowsky" was deleted entirely.

In addition to the original cast recording, "Saga of Jenny" and "My Ship" were recorded by Hildegarde; "My Ship" by Sammy Kaye and his orchestra; and "Tschaikowsky" by Danny Kaye. *Lady in the Dark* was produced for television production in 1954 in a version starring Ann Southern and Carleton Carpenter.

One Touch of Venus (October 7, 1943), a box-office attraction that ran for 567 performances, was for Weill a diversion from the musical play to musical comedy. The book, by S. J. Perelman and Ogden Nash (Nash also served as Weill's lyricist), was based on F. Anstey's 19th-century novella *The Tinted Venus*. Mary Martin was starred as the statue of Venus who comes to life, falls in love with a barber, Rodney Hatch, pursues him, much to his discomfort, and causes a breach between him and his girlfriend, Gloria. By the time Rodney falls hopelessly in love with Venus she is once again a statue in a museum.

Mary Martin introduced "Speak Low," the outstanding song in this Weill score. Guy Lombardo and His Royal Canadians recorded it. In the 1948 motion picture adaptation of the musical, "Speak Low" was sung on the soundtrack by Eileen Wilson (dubbing for Ava Gardner) as a duet with Dick Haymes, who played Rodney on the screen. On Broadway, Mary Martin also introduced "Foolish Heart." As "My Heart is Showing," and with new lyrics by Ann Ronell, this number was sung by Dick Haymes, Olga San Juan and Eileen Wilson (again dubbing for Gardner) in the film version. In the stage musical "West Wind" was introduced by John Boles and "How Much I Love You" by Kenny Baker. All these numbers were included on the original cast album.

Weill's next musical, *Firebrand of Florence* (March 22, 1945), lasted only 43 performances, Weill's most pronounced failure on Broadway. Its authors, Edwin Justus Mayer (librettist) and Ira Gershwin (lyricist), tried to translate Mayer's amusing 1924 Broadway comedy about Benvenuto Cellini into musical comedy. Three of Weill's songs, however, are noteworthy: "A Rhyme for Angels," introduced by Melville Coopera; "Sing Me Not a Ballad," by Lotte Lenya; and "You're Far Too Near to Me," by Earl Wrightson.

Firebrand of Florence was succeeded on Broadway by *Street Scene* (January 9, 1947), described in the program as a "folk play with music." This was a musical-stage adaptation by Elmer Rice of his realistic Pulitzer Prize-winning drama of the same name, which had first been produced in 1929. *Street Scene* described the elusive dreams, and blighted hopes of the down-and-out who live in an ordinary New York City tenement. Anna Maurant, a middle-aged woman neglected by her husband, finds consolation in the blandishments of the milkman. Finding her with the milkman one day, her husband, believing they are lovers, murders both of them. This tragedy convinces the daughter, Rosa Maurant, not to marry Sam Kaplan, a young idealist who is prepared to give up school and his ambitious plans for his future to take a mundane job and support Rosa in marriage. Refusing to accept responsibility for his self-defeating sacrifices, she escapes from him and the neighborhood, leaving to find a new life for herself.

Weill's music (with Langston Hughes's lyrics) reflected and intensified the surging elemental passions of Rice's play. "Not until *Street Scene*," Weill once said, "did I achieve a real blending of drama and music in which the singing continues naturally where the speaking stops, and the spoken word as well as the dramatic action is embedded in the overall musical structure." In *Theatre Arts*, Rosamund Gilder wrote that "Kurt Weill turned *Street Scene* into a symphony of the city. . . . His music reflects the hot nights, the chatter and gossiping housewives, the sound of children at play, the ebb and flow of anonymous existence."

Several musical numbers stood out from Weill's operatic score; "A Boy Like You," introduced by Polyna Stoska; "Moon-Faced, Starry-Eyed," a duet by Danny Daniels and Sheila Bond; and "Lonely House," introduced by Brian Sullivan. The entire score was recorded in an original cast album.

Though *Street Scene* ran for only 148 performances on the Broadway stage, it was introduced in Germany by the Düsseldorf Opera during the winter of 1955. It entered the repertory of the New York City Opera on April 2, 1959, at which time Howard Taubman wrote in *The New York Times*: "It is an American opera, if you emphasize the adjective more than the noun. For it is a congeries of musical idioms. It has some genuine operatic writing, in the sense that the music furnishes the emotional core of a scene, but it also has numbers that belong in a fast Broadway musical or an old-fashioned opera. The main point is that all these musical devices contribute to effective theater." A performance of *Street Scene* by the New York City Opera was televised nationally on October 27, 1979.

Love Life (October 7, 1948) was a Broadway musical comedy with a provocatively original text by Alan Jay Lerner, who also wrote the lyrics. It carries a couple, Sam and Susan Cooper, through a century and a half of marriage from 1791 to 1948. In that period, neither the hero nor the heroine ages. But as the years pass, their marriage withers and dies. From this musical came one of Weill's standards, "Green-Up Time," introduced by Nanette Fabray and recorded by Sammy Kaye and his orchestra. The duet "Here I'll Stay" was sung by Fabray and Ray Middleton, and "Mr. Right" by Fabray and Sylvia Stahlman. *Love Life* ran for 252 performances.

Weill's last Broadway musical was *Lost in the Stars* (October 30, 1949). This musical tragedy was an adaptation by Maxwell Anderson of Alan Paton's powerful novel of South Africa, *Cry the Beloved Country*. The musical play, like the novel, was deeply humanistic, eloquent in its plea for racial tolerance, and optimistic about the prospects for a better world. Absalom, the son of a humble parson, leaves his hometown in South Africa for Johannesburg. There, he falls in love with Irina, becomes involved in a robbery, is apprehended for the murder of a white man and sentenced to death by hanging. Just before his execution, the father of the murdered man visits Absalom's father. Through their common grief, a bond of understanding is forged.

Weill's music was so germane to the action, and so thematically ambitious, that some critics referred to it as an opera. His choral music provided a continuous emotional commentary on the stage action. Many of his songs (with lyrics by Maxwell Anderson) had the dramatic impact and operatic thrust of arias. The best of the choral numbers were "Cry the Beloved Country" and "Bird of Passage." Individual songs included "Big Mole," introduced by Herbert Coleman; "The Little Gray House" and "Thousands of Miles," by Todd Duncan; and "Stay Well" and "Trouble Man," introduced by Inez Matthews. An original cast album was released.

With a Broadway run of 273 performances, *Lost in the Stars* was produced by the New York City Opera on April 9, 1958 and was revived on Broadway in 1972. In his *New York Times* review of that revival, Clive Barnes wrote: "Kurt Weill was the greatest composer ever to write for Broadway, and his genius shone brightly . . . We will hear no better music on Broadway this season [or in the seasons following]. Weill was unique, a major composer who wanted to write for the popular theater, and not only wanted to, but could. . . . This is a tragic musical that extended the range of the musical theater. It brings dignity, passion and grand music to Broadway." A motion picture adaptation of *Lost in the Stars*, starring Brock Peters and Melba Moore, and using the basic stage score, was released in 1974.

"I believe," Weill wrote," that the musical theater is the highest, most expressive and most imaginative form of theater, and that a composer who has a talent and a passion for the theater can express himself completely in this branch of musical creativeness. Through my work for the theater, I have arrived at the conclusion that the distinction between 'serious' and 'light' music is one of the misconceptions of the Wagnerian period in music. The only distinction we should make is the one between good and bad music. I believe that new forms of musical theater can be developed in close connection with the living theater and the fundamental ideas of our time, and that these new forms can take the place of traditional opera or operetta. Most of my works for the theater in Europe and in this country have been experiments in different forms of musical theater. Broadway seems to me a perfect place to develop a musical theater which, in time, will become to this country what opera is to Europe."

In the 1940s Weill had composed *Down in the Valley,* a one-act American folk opera with libretto by Arnold Sundgaard, for a radio broadcast that was never made. In a revised version, it was given its world premiere at the University of Indiana, Bloomington, on July 15, 1948. In his score, Weill used five American folk songs: "Down in the Valley"; "The Lonesome Dove"; "The Little Black Train"; "Hop Up, My Ladies" and "Sourwood Mountain." This mini-opera was revived in a PBS telecast on April 16, 1984.

Weill also composed the music for three films, *Blockade* (1938), *You and Me* (1938) and *Where Do We Go From Here?* (1945). "The Right Guy for Me" (lyrics by Sam Coslow) was introduced by Carol Paige in *You and Me.* With Ira Gershwin as lyricist, Weill composed for *Where Do We Go from Here?* "All at Once," introduced by Fred MacMurray, and "If Love Remains," a duet for MacMurray and Joan Leslie.

In 1949–50 Weill was working with Maxwell Anderson on a musical based on *Huckleberry Finn.* Weill had composed the music for several numbers when he died of a heart attack at Manhattan's Flower–Fifth Avenue Hospital on April 3, 1950. In the New York *Herald Tribune* Virgil Thomson eulogized him: "Nothing he touched came out banal. Everything he wrote in one way or another became historic. He was probably the most original single workman in the whole musical theater, internationally considered, during the last quarter of a century. . . . He was an architect, a master of musico-dramatic design, whose structures, built for function and solidity, constitute a repertory of models that have not only served their original purpose but also had wide influence on composers as examples of procedure."

For the next three decades, until her death in 1981, Lotte Lenya indefatigably promoted Weill's music in concerts and theaters, recordings and television. Weill's music from the Broadway theater has been kept alive in other productions and recordings as well. His music was heard in *Whores, Wars and Tin Pan Alley,* which was mounted at the Bitter End in Greenwich Village in June 1969. Under the title "A Kurt Weill Cabaret," it toured nightclubs and college campuses for almost a decade before coming to Broadway in November 1979. A retrospective concert of Weill's American theater music was heard at New York's Lincoln Center on November 9, 1969. Another collection of Weill's theater songs, called *Berlin to Broadway with Kurt Weill* opened Off Broadway on October 1, 1972. In 1985 an LP featuring renditions of Weill numbers by new-wave rock musicians such as Sting and Marianne Faithful was released.

A three-day International Conference on Kurt Weill was presented by the Kurt Weill Foundation at Yale University, beginning on November 2, 1983. That same week the Foundation established in New York City the Weill/Lenya Research Center, a permanent repository of materials on Weill and his music.

Weill and his wife lived at Brook House, a 15-acre farm in New City, New York. In his leisure time he enjoyed art (Weill collected paintings) and reading anything, from the daily newspaper to Shakespeare.

ABOUT: Kowalke, K.H. Kurt Weill in Europe, 1979; Sanders, R. The Days Grow Short: The Life and Music of Kurt Weill, 1985. *Periodicals*—New York Times October 16, 1983, November 13, 1983; Opera News December 1, 1979.

WHITING, RICHARD (November 12, 1891– February 19, 1938), composer, was one of the dominant musical figures in Tin Pan Alley and Hollywood in the 1920s and early 1930s. Richard Armstrong Whiting was born in Peoria, Illinois, the son of Frank and Blossom (Leach) Whiting. His father, a real-estate broker, played several musical instruments and his mother was a trained pianist. Except for random lessons in harmony, Whiting had no formal instruction in music, but he taught himself to play the piano.

He spent his boyhood in Los Angeles, where he attended the Harvard Military School and devoted his spare time to writing songs and attending musical productions at local theaters. He found his first job in Santa Monica, working as a pianist for the actor Nat Goodwin. With Marshall Neilen (who later became a celebrated film director) he worked in vaudeville doing a song-and-patter act. Upon completing school, Whiting returned to Peoria, determined to make his way in popular music. A friend persuaded him

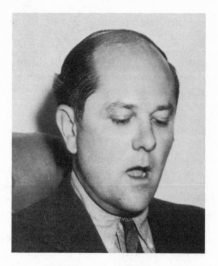

RICHARD WHITING

to move to Detroit and market his songs there, and Whiting sold three numbers for $50 each to the publishing house of Jerome H. Remick & Co. He was soon hired as the firm's copy boy, and eventually rose to the positions of song plugger and office manager. He also played piano with a Hawaiian orchestra in a Detroit hotel.

Whiting's professional songwritng career began when he and the lyricist Earle C. Jones composed "The Big Red Motor and the Little Blue Limousine" (1913) and "I Wonder Where My Lovin' Man Has Gone" (1914). In 1915 Remick published "It's Tulip Time in Holland" (lyrics by Dave Radford), Whiting's first song to reach a wide audience.

Whiting's ambition was to own a Steinway grand piano, and he thought himself both shrewd and fortunate to have bartered "Tulip Time" to Remick in return for a Steinway. But when the song sold more than a million and a half copies of sheet music a few months after it was recorded by Henry Burr, Whiting decided that henceforth he would sell his songs solely on a royalty basis. And between 1916 and 1917 Whiting produced five hit songs. "Where the Black Eyed Susans Grow" (lyrics by Dave Radford) was interpolated into the Winter Garden extravaganza *Robinson Crusoe Jr.* (1916), in which it was introduced and popularized by Al Jolson, who also recorded it. "Mammy's Little Coal Black Rose" and "They Called it Dixieland" (lyrics to both by Raymond Egan) became staples in the repertory of vaudevillian performers in 1916. "Where the Morning Glories Grow" (lyrics by Gus Kahn) and "Some Sunday Morning" (lyrics by Kahn and Egan) became popular

in 1917, when the former was recorded by Elizabeth Spencer and the latter by the orchestra of Joseph C. Smith. The royalties from these songs earned Whiting more than 30 thousand dollars.

America's entry into World War I inspired Whiting to compose the waltz "Till We Meet Again" (1918, lyrics by Egan), one of the most celebrated ballads of the war years. After being introduced in vaudeville by Muriel Window, it was recorded in 1918 by the Nicholas Orlando orchestra. It had sold more than three and a half million copies of sheet music before the war ended, and six million more copies by the middle of the next decade. When Whiting composed "Till We Meet Again" he thought it so inferior that he tossed the manuscript into a trash basket. It was retrieved by his wife who took it to Remick for publication. An instant standard, it was recorded by Helen Forrest with Dick Haymes and by the orchestras of Eddie Duchin and Al Goodman. Martha Eggerth sang it in the musical film *For Me and My Gal* (1942), and Gordon MacRae and Doris Day performed it in *On Moonlight Bay* (1951). It was interpolated into *The Eddie Duchin Story* (1956) and into the 1958 film version of *Auntie Mame*. "Till We Meet Again" is often sung in the halls of Congress when sessions of the House of Representatives are adjourned.

Having made his reputation in Tin Pan Alley, Whiting set out to conquer Broadway in 1919. His first stage score was for *Toot Sweet* (May 7; lyrics by Raymond Egan) a postwar revue starring Will Morrisey and Elizabeth Brice which closed after 42 performances. On June 2, 1919 Whiting wrote the score (lyrics by George White and Arthur Jackson) for the first edition of *George White's Scandals*. Despite an unimpressive run of 128 performances, the *Scandals* immediately established itself as a rival to the perennially popular *Ziegfeld Follies* in the lavishness of its production. Whiting's score was nondescript, and for the next edition the assignment to write the songs fell to young George Gershwin.

It was more than a decade before Whiting composed another score for Broadway. In the interim he continued to produce hit songs in Tin Pan Alley.

"The Japanese Sandman" (1920, lyrics by Egan) was popularized in vaudeville by Nora Bayes, who also recorded it, as did the orchestra of Paul Whiteman. "Sandman" sold more than a million copies of sheet music, and in motion pictures it was interpolated into *Rose of Washington Square* (1939) and sung by Pat Morita and Jack Soo in *Thoroughly Modern Millie* (1967). "When Shall We Meet Again" (lyrics by Egan) was introduced by the Duncan Sisters in the 1920 Broadway musical *Tip Top*.

In 1921 "Ain't We Got Fun?" (lyrics by Egan and Kahn) was introduced by George Watts in vaudeville, where it was popularized by Ruth Roye. The earliest recordings were made by Van and Schenck and Jack Norworth, later ones by Carmen Cavallero and Margaret Whiting. In motion pictures it was sung by Gordon MacRae and Doris Day in *On Moonlight Bay* and by Eddie Cantor on the soundtrack of *The Eddie Cantor Story* (1954). It was also interpolated into Gus Kahn's screen biography, *I'll See You in My Dreams* (1951).

"Sleepy Time Gal," (1925, music written with Ange Lorenzo, lyrics by Egan and Joseph B. Alden) was recorded by Nick Lucas, Cliff Edwards and the orchestras of Harry James and Ben Bernie. It was further popularized by Glen Gray and the Casa Loma Orchestra. Frances Langford sang it in the film *Never a Dull Moment* (1943), and it was interpolated into a 1942 movie bearing the song's title.

"Ukulele Lady" (1925, lyrics by Gus Kahn) was popularized in vaudeville by Nick Lucas and by Vaughn de Leath and was sung by a chorus in *I'll See You in My Dreams*.

"Breezin' Along With the Breeze" (1925, lyrics by Haven Gillespie and Seymour Simons) was popularized by Al Jolson. Among those who recorded it were Al Landry, Johnny Marvin, the Merry Macs, the Revelers and the Singing Sophomores. Danny Thomas sang it in the 1953 film *The Jazz Singer*, and Gogi Grant (dubbing for Ann Blyth on the soundtrack) sang it in *The Helen Morgan Story* (1957). It was interpolated into Nora Bayes's film biography, *Shine on Harvest Moon* (1944).

"Horses" (1926, lyrics by Byron Gay) was recorded by the Georgians and made popular by the orchestra of George Olsen.

"Honey" (1927, lyrics by Haven Gillespie and Seymour Simons) had a sheet-music sale of a million copies. It was introduced by Rudy Vallee in a bestselling recording and popularized in his performances in nightclubs and on radio. It was interpolated into the 1945 film *Her Highness and the Bellboy*.

"She's Funny That Way" (1928) was one of the few songs for which Whiting wrote the lyrics to somebody else's music, in this instance that of Neil Moret. It was recorded by Frank Sinatra, Connie Haines, the Benny Goodman Sextet and Eddy Duchin and his orchestra. Sinatra sang it in *Meet Danny Wilson* (1952) and Frankie Laine in *Rainbow 'Round My Shoulder* (1952). It was also interpolated into the nonmusical film *The Postman Always Rings Twice* (1945), starring John Garfield and Lana Turner.

Notwithstanding his stature in Tin Pan Alley,

Whiting achieved even greater success in his music for the screen. Having moved from Detroit to New York City in 1928, Whiting left for Hollywood a year later. He made his screen debut in 1929 by contributing songs to ten movies. In *Innocents of Paris* (1929), in which Maurice Chevalier made his American screen debut, "Louise" (lyrics by Leo Robins) was introduced by Chevalier, who also recorded it and made the song his signature. He sang it again in *A New Kind of Love* (1963). Jimmy Johnston and Betty Jane Rhodes sang it in *You Can't Ration Love* (1944) and Jerry Lewis in *The Stooge* (1952). It was recorded by Paul Whiteman's Rhythm Boys.

"Wait 'Til You See Me Chérie" (lyrics by Leo Robin) was introduced in *Innocents of Paris* by Chevalier, who also recorded it.

Other songs from his 1929 films included "True Blue Lou" (lyrics by Sam Coslow), which was introduced by Hal Skelly in *Dance of Life*, and "My Sweeter Than Sweet" (lyrics by George Marion Jr.), which was introduced by Nancy Carroll in *Sweetie*.

Whiting's songs were heard in 40 films after 1929. Five were represented on *Your Hit Parade*. "My Ideal" (one representation), lyrics by Leo Robin, was introduced by Maurice Chevalier in *Playboy of Paris* (1930) and sung by Buddy Rogers in *Along Came Youth* (1931). "When Did You Leave Heaven?" (twelve representations, twice in first position), lyrics by Walter Bullock, was introduced by Tony Martin in *Sing, Baby, Sing* (1936) and recorded by Tony Martin and by the orchestras of Ben Bernie and Charlie Barnet. "I Can't Escape From You" (eight representations), lyrics by Leo Robin, was introduced by Bing Crosby in *Rhythm on the Range* (1936). It was recorded by Bing Crosby and the orchestra of Jimmie Lunceford. "Have You Got Any Castles, Baby?" (ten representations), lyrics by Johnny Mercer, was introduced by Priscilla Lane in *Varsity Show* (1937). "Too Marvelous for Words" (six representations), lyrics by Johnny Mercer, was introduced by Ross Alexander and Wini Shaw in *Ready, Willing and Able* (1937). Bing Crosby and the orchestras of Harry James, Glen Gray and Shep Fields recorded it. With this number, Margaret Whiting began her singing career when she performed it on the Johnny Mercer radio show in 1940. Frankie Laine sang "Too Marvelous for Words" in *On the Sunny Side of the Street* (1951) and it was interpolated into *Dark Passage* (1947), starring Bette Davis.

The only Whiting song on *Your Hit Parade* which had not been written for and introduced on the screen was "Guilty" (lyrics by Gus Kahn and Harry Akst). It was recorded in 1931 by Gene Austin and by Russ Columbo. Revived in 1947 in a recording by Margaret Whiting, it received 11 hearings on *Your Hit Parade.*

Of the more than 50 other songs that Whiting composed for the screen, the most popular were: "Beyond the Blue Horizon" (music written with W. Franke Harling, lyrics by Leo Robin), which was introduced by Jeanette MacDonald in *Monte Carlo* (1930); she also recorded it and sang it again in *Follow the Boys* (1944). It was also recorded by Mary Martin.

"My Future Just Passed" (lyrics by George Marion Jr.) was introduced by Buddy Rogers in *Safety in Numbers* (1930) and was recorded by Rogers, by Margaret Whiting and by Harry James.

"One Hour With You" (lyrics by Leo Robin) was title song of a 1932 motion picture in which it was introduced by Maurice Chevalier and Jeanette MacDonald. Eddie Cantor used it as the signature song for his Sunday evening show on the NBC radio network, and he sang it again on the soundtrack of *The Eddie Cantor Story* (1954). Jeanette MacDonald recorded two versions of "One Hour With You," one in English, the other in French, and it was also recorded by Donald Novis.

"On the Good Ship Lollipop" (lyrics by Sidney Clare) was introduced by Shirley Temple in *Bright Eyes* (1934). Mae Questal, a child star known for her impersonations of Shirley Temple, recorded it, as did the orchestra of Nat Brandwyne and his orchestra. Dan Dailey and Shari Robinson revived it in *You're My Everything* (1949).

"Miss Brown to You" (music written with Ralph Rainger, lyrics by Leo Robin) was introduced by a chorus and the orchestra of Ray Noble, and danced to by Bill Robinson and the Nicholas Brothers, in *The Big Broadcast of 1936* (1935). This song became a signature for Billie Holiday, who recorded it.

"Double Trouble" (music written with Ralph Rainger, lyrics by Leo Robin) was introduced by Lyda Roberti, Jack Oakie and Henry Wadsworth in *Big Broadcast of 1936.*

"Why Dream?" (music written with Rainger, lyrics by Leo Robin) was introduced by Henry Wadsworth in *Big Broadcast of 1936.*

"Sailor Beware" (lyrics by Leo Robin) was introduced in the film version of *Anything Goes* (1936) by Bing Crosby, who also recorded it.

"Moonlight on the Campus" (lyrics by Johnny Mercer) was introduced in *Varsity Show* (1937) by Dick Powell, who also recorded it.

"You've Got Something There" (lyrics by Johnny Mercer) was introduced by Dick Powell

and Rosemary Lane in *Varsity Show* and recorded by Powell.

"Sentimental and Melancholy" (lyrics by Mercer) was introduced by Wini Shaw in *Ready, Willing and Able* (1937) and recorded by Glen Gray and the Casa Loma Orchestra.

"Hooray for Hollywood" (lyrics by Mercer) was introduced by Frances Langford, Johnny "Scat" Davis and Benny Goodman in *Hollywood Hotel* (1937). Sammy Davis Jr. sang it in *Pepe* (1960), and for many years Jack Benny used it as the signature music for his radio and television shows.

"Silhouetted in the Moonlight" (lyrics by Mercer) was introduced by Rosemary Lane in *Hollywood Hotel.*

"I've Hitched My Wagon to a Star" (lyrics by Mercer) was introduced by Dick Powell and the orchestra of Raymond Paige in *Hollywood Hotel* and was recorded by Powell.

"Ride, Tenderfoot, Ride" (lyrics by Mercer) was introduced in *Cowboy from Brooklyn* (1938) by Dick Powell, who also recorded it.

"I'll Dream Tonight" (lyrics by Mercer) was introduced by Dick Powell and Priscilla Lane in *Cowboy from Brooklyn.*

Whiting returned to Broadway with his scores for two stage musicals. *Free for All* (September 8, 1931), despite book and lyrics by Oscar Hammerstein II and Laurence Schwab, closed after just 15 performances. *Take a Chance* (November 26, 1932), however, had a 243-performance run. With book and lyrics by B. G. De Sylva and Laurence Schwab, and five interpolated songs whose music was composed by Vincent Youmans, *Take a Chance* dealt with the efforts of Kenneth Raleigh, a wealthy young Harvard graduate, to mount a Broadway musical. He becomes involved with Toni, an actress being promoted by two conmen. Though Raleigh suspects Toni of being a fraud, she becames the star of his show and wins her producer's love. From *Take a Chance*, "Eadie Was a Lady" (music written with Nacio Herb Brown, lyrics by B. G. De Sylva), as performed by Ethel Merman, was a showstopper. Merman recorded it, and Lillian Roth sang it in the 1933 motion picture adaptation of the stage musical. Another standout was "You're an Old Smoothie" (music written with Nacio Herb Brown, lyrics by De Sylva). It was introduced by Merman and Jack Haley, was recorded by Carmen Cavallero, became the theme song of Del Courtney's orchestra and was sung by Phyllis Shotwell in the Robert Altman film *California Split* (1974), starring Elliot Gould and George Segal.

Richard Whiting married Eleanore Youngblood, a theatre agent, on August 7, 1923. They had two daughters, Margaret, who became a celebrated popular singer, and Barbara, also a professional singer as well as an actress. In California the Whitings lived at South Beverly Glen in Los Angeles before moving to Beverly Hills. An excellent amateur golfer, Whiting won numerous tournaments, and was also a swimming enthusiast.

Whiting died of heart failure in 1938. Eleven years later "Sorry," a Whiting song set to Buddy Pepper's lyrics, was published posthumously and recorded by his now famous daughter Margaret Whiting.

ABOUT: Craig, W. Sweet and Lowdown: America's Popular Song Writers, 1978; Wilk, M. They're Playing Our Song, 1973.

HANK WILLIAMS

WILLIAMS, HANK (September 17, 1923–January 1, 1953). Called "the hillbilly Shakespeare" and "the king of western country music," composer-lyricist Hank Williams is one of the legends of American music. He was the first composer of country music to become popular in Tin Pan Alley, and his greatest songs—gospel numbers as well as the bluesy heartbreak ballads that were his signature—are standards, especially in the South, West, and Southwest United States. His influence on other musicians, especially that of his singing style, has been far-reaching, and the rags-to-riches story of this doomed musician's life continues to fascinate more than 30 years after his death at the age of 29.

He was born Hiram Williams in a two-room log cabin on a tenant farm in Mt. Olive, Alabama, one of two children of Elonzo and Lilly Skipper Williams. The father drove locomotives for the Alabama-based W. T. Smith Lumber Company and the mother was an amateur musician who played the organ at the Mt. Olive Baptist Church. When Hank was six, he learned to play the harmonica, and about this time he became the youngest member of the church choir.

In 1930 Hank's father, a World War I veteran suffering from the after-effects of gas or shell shock, entered the veteran's hospital in Biloxi. The burden of supporting the family during the Great Depression fell on Lilly Williams, who went to work in a factory and as a nurse and then as a proprietress of her own boardinghouses. To help out, Hank shined shoes and sold newspapers and peanuts in the streets of Georgiana, a fair-sized town near Mt. Olive, where the family had moved.

As a boy he was a loner with little interest in the pastimes of other boys except that he

dreamed of being a cowboy. Indeed, in 1940, he joined a rodeo but seriously injured his back in a fall from a bronco. (This back injury later required surgery, which introduced Williams to the pain-killing drugs that would contribute to his death.) In his biography, Roger Williams described Hank as "a tall, painfully thin boy with a shock of brown hair, a sad mouth, and sadder eyes, and ears that stuck out far too much; a quietly happy boy, but content to go his own way at his own pace." About 1930, as a gift from his mother, he had acquired a $3.50 guitar on which he taught himself the basic chords. Hank received coaching in singing from Tee-Tot, a black street singer in Greenville, Alabama.

In 1937 the Williams family moved to Montgomery, where Lilly became the proprietress of another boardinghouse. Dressed in boots and cowboy hat, her son entered an amateur contest at the local Empire Theatre. Singing one of his own songs, "W.P.A. Blues," he won first prize. Soon after, he was paid $15 to appear twice a week on Station WSPA in Montgomery as "The Singing Kid," a program that lasted more than a decade. About 1939, forming a group called Hank Williams and His Drifting Cowboys, he began performing, as he would for the next nine years, at square dances and barbecues and in honky-tonks. "It was the best of all possible schooling—and the roughest and toughest," wrote Henry Pleasants in *Great American Popular Singers*. "He was already an alcoholic . . . given to periodic and incapacitating benders succeeded by varying lengths on the wagon." As Hank himself said of honky-tonk audiences: "They didn't come to listen; they came to fight."

Williams's back injury kept him out of the Army during World War II. For a year and a half he worked at the Alabama Drydock and Shipbuilding Company, leaving that job in 1944 to reunite the Drifting Cowboys. In 1943, while playing at a medicine show in Banks, Alabama, Williams had met Audrey Shepard, a farm girl. In *The Country Music Story*, Robert Shelton described theirs as a "stormy courtship, in which he alternated between his need for the bottle and his need for her." But she joined the Drifting Cowboys and on December 15, 1944, Audrey and Hank were married in a ceremony held at a gas station outside Andalusia, Alabama. Their son, Hank Williams Jr., was born in 1949.

In 1946 Hank and Audrey moved to Nashville, where she began to promote her husband's career, arranging an audition for him with Fred Rose, who with the country singer Roy Acuff, had recently formed the Acuff-Rose publishing house. Rose had Williams record a couple of gospel songs and "Honky Tonk Blues," an original, autobiographical composition for a small label in New York. The record failed to sell, but in 1947 Williams became a regular on the "Louisiana Hayride," a popular radio show broadcast from Shreveport. In 1949 he signed an exclusive contract with the Acuff-Rose firm, which arranged for him to record for MGM Records.

Williams's first hit on the MGM label was "Move it on Over" (1948), an original composition which he followed with "Mansion on the Hill" (written by Williams and Fred Rose). In 1949, Williams caused a sensation when he sang "Lovesick Blues," his own adaptation of a popular song of 1922 by Irving Mills and Cliff Friend, at the Grand Ole Opry on June 11. He brought down the house and was called back for six encores. Becoming a regular with the prestigious Grand Ole Opry established him as a leading performer and composer of country music. And by the end of 1949 "Lovesick Blues" had been voted the year's best "hillbilly" record in a poll conducted by *Cash Box* and had reached number one on the *Billboard* country music charts.

Hank's bestsellers for MGM now came in rapid succession. "Mind Your Own Business" and "You're Gonna Change" were released in 1949. In 1950 "Long Gone Lonesome Blues," "Why Don't You Love Me?" and "Why Should We Try Any More?" reached the charts. His hit recordings of 1951–52 included "Baby We're Really in Love," "Hey, Good Lookin'," "Howlin' at the Moon," "I Can't Help It," "Ramblin' Man," and "Cold, Cold Heart." In 1953 his posthumously released bestsellers were "Weary Blues From Waitin'," "I Won't Be Home No More," "I'll Never Get Out of This World Alive" (written with Fred Rose), "Kawliga" (written with Rose),

"Jambalaya," and "Your Cheatin' Heart." Additionally, "Jambalaya" also became a giant seller for Jo Stafford and the version by Brenda Lewis marked her recording debut. "Cold, Cold Heart" became the first country song to cross over to the number one spot on the pop charts when it became a million seller for Tony Bennett in 1951. Other Williams compositions that have become much-covered standards are "I'm So Lonesome I Could Cry," "I Saw the Light," "Jambalaya," and "Kawliga."

"As a songwriter," Pleasants observed, "he was always more concerned with words than with melody. If he got the words he wanted, the melody seemed to take care of itself. He was not a distinguished or even a particularly inventive melodist. The tunes are simple, even primitive, as are the conventional tonic-subdominant-dominant chords that support them. One remembers them only in association with the words—and with the way he sang the words. That is what is remarkable about them. Hank's melodies were the music of language. His singing issued from the same linguistic source."

In the few years between Hank's emergence and his death, he became a symbol of country music and a hero to millions—even though as a singer he did not have much of a voice; as a composer he could neither read nor write musical notation; and as a "poet" he was ignorant of grammar and spelling (his reading was confined to comic books). Nevertheless in the simplicity of their structure, his songs had a beauty. His lyrics were almost always compelling and memorable, whether they conveyed a gospel blues or, as in "Jambalaya," a good-times message. What one critic described as "the mournful wail . . . nasal twang [and] choke" in his voice was the expression of country-western soul. Nor had nature endowed him with a striking personality. But as Allen Rankin, a columnist for the Montgomery *Advertiser* pointed out, when he was singing he was transformed. "He'd come slopping and slouching on stage, limp as a dishrag. But when he picked up the guitar and started to sing, it was like a charge of electricity had gone through him. He became three feet taller."

Hank Williams's life fell apart in the year before his death. His marriage had been unstable and in many respects unhappy—it inspired many of his "broken heart" songs—and it came to an end on New Year's Day, 1952, when Williams reportedly returned home drunk from a party and fired several shots at his wife. (Later that year he married a singer named Billie Jones in an onstage ceremony at the New Orleans Auditorium.) In August the Grand Ole Opry fired him, unable to tolerate any longer Hank's habitual drunkenness and erratic behavior. Williams's further immiserization came from the pills, pain-killing narcotics and liquor in which he sought solace. His death on January 1, 1953 in Oak Hill, West Virginia was the result of a heart attack brought on by liquor, drugs and a prolonged attack of insomnia. He had been riding in the back seat of his chauffeured Cadillac heading for an engagement in Canton, Ohio.

Twenty thousand admirers descended on Montgomery for Williams's funeral services at the Municipal Auditorium on January 4, provoking what has been called "the greatest emotional orgy in the city's history since the inauguration of Jefferson Davis." The "hillbilly Shakespeare" was laid out in a silver casket, and before 3,000 of the bereaved faithful, Ernest Tubb sang "Beyond the Sunset," Roy Acuff, "I Saw the Light" and Red Foley, "Peace in the Valley."

At the time of his death Williams was earning about $200,000 a year, but as the country singer Minnie Pearl said, "He was not prepared for sudden fame or money. Money was a big pressure on him. . . . Trying to cope with [Hank] was like riding a tiger; you couldn't ride it, and you couldn't get off." Contributing to the apotheosis of Williams were three biographies that have been published and the many hit recordings of his songs by other artists. In the 1960s MGM released several LP compilations of his greatest hits (he had written approximately 125 songs). Moreover, his son, Hank Williams Jr., became a popular country singer in the 1960s, best known for his interpretation of his father's songs. The son's most important album was *Songs My Father Taught Me,* a collection of Hank Williams songs that he had never recorded or published. They had been written at the end of the composer's life and were found in a shoebox. When the Country Music Association's new Hall of Fame was established in Nashville in 1961, Hank Williams was one of the first three performers elected to it. Williams's life story was made into *Your Cheatin' Heart,* a motion picture of 1964 in which Hank Williams Jr. sang his father's numbers on the soundtrack and George Hamilton played the part of the composer. The soundtrack recording became a bestseller.

In 1966 Fred Rose Music Inc. published several new Williams songs, one of which, "A House of Gold," received a Grammy as the season's best sacred recording. In 1969 *We Remember Hank Williams,* an MGM album, offered Williams standards in performances by three members of The Drifting Cowboys, among others. Two other Hank Williams albums that year received gold records: *Your Cheatin' Heart* and *Hank Williams' Greatest Hits.* In 1970 Williams's "Cajun

Baby" (as recorded by the Nashville Brass) received a Grammy as the best country-and-western instrumental performance. It also won an award from BMI for being one of the most frequently heard country music compositions of the preceding five-year period. BMI gave a similar award to "Your Cheatin' Heart."

So strong is the sense of time and place of Hank Williams's music that his songs contributed powerfully to the naturalism and richly evoked local color of *The Last Picture Show* (1972), a Peter Bogdanovich film set in a small Texas town in the early 1950s, with recordings by Hank Williams woven skillfully into the background of many scenes. A musical drama entitled *Hank Williams: The Show He Never Gave* tried to recreate a Hank Williams concert in St. Louis, what would have been, in the play, his last performance. This production, with book by Maynard Collins and a storehouse of Hank Williams songs, starred Sneezy Waters as the composer and four musicians who impersonated the Drifting Cowboys. It toured the cabaret circuit before opening at a theater in St. Louis on October 30, 1979. Hank Williams and his music received national television exposure on June 22, 1984, when a tribute called *Hank Williams, The Man and His Music* was telecast live on ABC-TV from the Grand Ole Opry. One year earlier, Williams and his songs were featured in *Living Proof,* a CBS dramatization of the autobiography of Hank Williams Jr. In 1986 the Country Music Foundation, Nashville, released *Hank Williams: The First Recordings,* a collection of 12 songs, "demos" that William had recorded in 1946.

ABOUT: Caress, J. Hank Williams: Country Music's Tragic King, 1979; Flippo, C. Your Cheatin' Heart: A Biography of Hank Williams, 1981; Goldblatt, B. and Shelton, R. The Country Music Story: A Picture History of Country and Western Music, 1966; Hemphill, P. The Nashville Sound: Bright Lights and Country Music, 1970; Koon, G. W. Hank Williams: A Bio-Bibliography, 1983; Krishof, R. K. Hank Williams, 1978; McCabe, P. and Rubenstein, R. Honkytonk Heroes, 1975; Pleasants, H. The Great American Popular Singers, 1974; Shestack, M. The Country Music Encyclopedia, 1974; Williams, H. Jr. Living Proof: An Autobiography, 1979; Williams, R. Sing a Sad Song: The Life of Hank Williams, 1973. *Periodicals*—Newsweek January 12, 1953, January 19, 1953; New York Times September 17, 1986.

WILLSON, MEREDITH (May 18, 1902–June 15, 1984), composer-lyricist, was born in Mason City, Iowa, the youngest child of John David and Rosalie (Reiniger) Willson. His father, a lawyer, played the guitar, and his mother,

MEREDITH WILLSON

the piano; from her, Meredith received his first piano lessons. While attending Mason City High School, he also learned to play the flute and piccolo.

Upon graduation from high school in 1919, Willson went to New York, where he studied with Julius Gold, Bernard Wagenaar, flute with Georges Barrère (1920–29) and conducting with Henry Hadley (1923–24) at the Institute of Musical Art (now the Juilliard School).

Willson played flute in the John Philip Sousa band from 1921 to 1923, with which he toured the United States, Europe, Mexico and Cuba. Then, after a brief stint in the orchestra of the Rialto Theatre, a plush New York movie house, Willson was appointed principal flutist of the New York Chamber Music Society and New York Philharmonic Symphony Orchestra (1924–29), where he played under such distinguished conductors as Arturo Toscanini, Wilhelm Furtwaengler and others.

In 1929, Willson moved to the West Coast, where he became music director, first of ABC's Northwest operations in Seattle (1929–30), then of radio station KFRC in San Francisco (1930–32) and, from 1932 to 1938, of the Western Division of NBC, where he directed *The George Burns and Gracie Allen Show* and *The Big Ten,* among others. Retaining this position at NBC, he settled in Hollywood in 1937, where he supervised as many as 17 major radio network programs each week, most importantly Maxwell House's *Good News Show, The Meredith Willson and John Nesbitt Show,* and *The Standard (Symphony) Hour.* He also appeared as guest conductor of the San Francisco and Seattle Symphony Orchestras and the Los Angeles Philharmonic.

In Hollywood, Willson also composed scores for the films *The Great Dictator* (1940), starring Charlie Chaplin, and Lillian Hellman's *The Little Foxes* (1941). In 1941, Willson emerged as a successful composer of popular songs, writing both lyrics and music. "Two in Love" was introduced by Tommy Dorsey with Frank Sinatra and was recorded by other jazz bands, including those of Gene Krupa and Bunny Berigan, and also by Bob Crosby and Vaughn Monroe. "You and I" was popularized in recordings by Kate Smith, Dick Jurgens and by Tommy Dorsey and Glenn Miller; it reached first position on *Your Hit Parade,* and Willson used it as signature music for the Maxwell House program.

During World War II, Willson served as a major in the United States Army (1942–45). He headed the music division of the Armed Forces Radio Service, for whose shows he composed "Mail-Call March," "America Calling" and "Centennial."

Following his discharge in 1945, Willson returned to Los Angeles and resumed his work on radio, conducting the music for network programs and starring in others as well, among them *The Ford Showroom,* where he distinguished himself not only as a conductor and composer, but also as a commentator and homespun philosopher. He initiated his own half-hour program on television, *The Meredith Willson Show,* broadcast during the summer of 1949. He then became music director of radio's last giant weekly variety program, *The Big Show,* a 90-minute production starring Tallulah Bankhead and featuring the greatest performers of the time. *Newsweek* called it "the biggest bang to hit radio since TV started." For the show, Willson composed "May the Good Lord Bless and Keep You" (1950), which was sung by that evening's performers, each presenting one of the lines at the close of the show. The popularity of the song, gained through weekly repetition, was enhanced by a bestselling recording by Frankie Laine, and more than 500,000 copies of the sheet music were sold during the first four months of publication. During the Korean War, this song and Willson's "I See the Moon" were among the selections most frequently requested by the American troops.

By 1948, Willson had begun writing what was to become his first stage musical, *The Music Man.* In spite of his total lack of experience in the theater, he assumed the task of writing the book as well as the lyrics and music, tapping his boyhood recollections of life in a small Iowa town in 1912. "I didn't have to make up anything for *The Music Man*," Willson said. "All I had to do was remember." The protagonist is Harold Hill, a swindler who travels from one town to another, selling the project of a boys' band, then absconding with the money entrusted to him for the purchase of uniforms and instruments. He arrives in River City, Iowa, where he falls in love with Marian Paroo, the local librarian. The town becomes infected with Hill's scheme and in time, even he becomes caught up in their enthusiasm. He remains to see the band parade through the streets in full regalia, and wins Marian's love.

The Music Man (December 19, 1957), starring Robert Preston in his Broadway debut, swept the opening night audience to its feet in an outburst of approbation; audiences remained enthusiastic for 1,375 performances. It won the Tony, the New York Drama Critics Circle Award and the Outer Circle Award as the year's best musical and the original cast recording won a Grammy and a gold record. A national company of *The Music Man* toured for several years, and in 1962, a handsomely produced and brilliantly acted motion picture starring Robert Preston was made by Warner Brothers. Walter Kerr in the New York *Herald Tribune* called *The Music Man* "easily the brightest, breeziest, most winning new musical to come along since *My Fair Lady* enchanted us all. . . . It was written to be enjoyed." The irresistible folksy, sentimental charm of the book was also present in the songs. One of the high points was "Seventy-six Trombones," introduced by Robert Preston and a chorus of youngsters. Willson also used this melody in "Goodnight My Someone," this time, romanticized and in a slow tempo. The tender love ballad, "Till There Was You" was sung by Robert Preston and Barbara Cook on the stage, and by Shirley Jones on the screen; Anita Bryant's recording of it in 1958 sold more than one million discs and launched her successful career. In 1963, a rock version became a bestselling recording by the Beatles; it was also recorded by Billy Eckstine.

The Music Man was produced by the Warsaw Operetka in Poland, and James Feron reported in *The New York Times* (October 17, 1972) "the show is a smash and could run for years." In 1965, and again in 1980, it was revived at City Center in New York, the first time with Bert Parks as Harold Hill, the second, with Dick Van Dyke. Since its first performance in 1957, there has hardly been a time when *The Music Man* was not being produced somewhere in the United States by a professional, semiprofessional or amateur organization.

Willson's second Broadway musical, *The Un-sinkable Molly Brown* (November 3, 1960), which enjoyed a run of 532 performances, again drew upon Americana for its background, characters and plot. On this occasion, Willson wrote the lyrics and music, while Richard Morris wrote the book. The heroine was an uninhibited, and uneducated girl from Hannibal, Missouri. Working as a singer in Colorado at the turn of the century, she meets and marries Johnny Brown whose mines bring them wealth. When she is snubbed by Denver's high society, she goes to Europe where she is treated like royalty. With the same indomitable spirit with which she conquers European society, she also survives the sinking of the *Titanic* on her return home from Europe by taking command of a lifeboat.

In this score, as in *The Music Man*, a spirited march tune, "I Ain't Down Yet," was a principal attraction; it was introduced by Tammy Grimes and Harve Presnell in the opening scene, and was later sung by Debbie Reynolds and Presnell in the film adaptation (1964). "Belly Up to the Bar, Boys" and "Colorado My Home" were also rousing numbers. The ballad, "Dolce far Niente," and "Are You Sure" were not included in the motion picture; in their place was a new production number, "He's My Friend."

For his third Broadway musical *Here's Love* (October 3, 1963) which ran for 334 performances, Willson again wrote the book, lyrics and music, using material based on the 1947 film, *Miracle on 34th Street*. Its principal character was Kris Kringle, a kindly old gentleman who embodies the Yuletide spirit. Hired by Macy's department store to play Santa Claus, he insists that he is Santa Claus and loses his job when skeptics believe him to be unbalanced. The true spirit of the season prevails when, during a court battle against the U.S. government, Kringle's friends rally to his support. Richard Watts, Jr. described *Here's Love* as "a very wholesome and good-hearted show, lavish in its merry Yuletide hospitality and cheerfulness"; to Howard Taubman it was "wholesome, with a scattering of laughs, a hint of tremulous emotion, the triumph of true love, a touch of fantasy, all appearing just where you anticipate them." The spirit of Christmas glowed in "Pine Cones and Holly Berries," introduced by Laurence Naismith, Janis Paige and Fred Gwynne; "Arm in Arm," introduced by Paige; "My Wish," a duet for Craig Stevens and Valerie Lee; and the title song, which was introduced by Naismith, Stevens and chorus. The score also incorporated "My State, My Kansas, My Home," which Willson had composed in 1961 for the State of Kansas centennial celebration.

Willson's last musical was *1491*, "a romantic

speculation," about Columbus and Queen Isabel-la. Produced by the Los Angeles Civic Light Opera in 1969, it was a failure.

In *The New York Times,* Tom Buckley described Willson as "a slim, straightbacked six-footer with a full shock of salt-and-pepper hair. He has sharp blue eyes, a long nose, astride which sits a pair of spectacles that he needs only for distance, and the sharp chin of a beardless Uncle Sam."

In addition to popular songs and scores for Broadway musicals, Willson also composed concert music. *Parade fantastique,* for orchestra, was performed at the Rialto Theatre in 1924; *Symphony No. 1 in f minor: San Francisco* was introduced by the San Francisco Symphony, conducted by the composer on April 19, 1936; and *Symphony No. 2: The Missions of California* was premiered by the Los Angeles Philharmonic under Albert Coates on April 21, 1940. Among his other concert works are *Radio City* (1934), *Nocturne* and *The Jervis Bay* (1940) for orchestra, *O. O. McIntyre Suite* for piano, *Mass of Bells,* for chorus, as well as many songs and marches.

Willson is the author of *And There I Stood with My Piccolo* (autobiography), *Eggs I have Laid* (memoirs), *But He Doesn't Know the Territory,* which recounts his experiences during the production of *The Music Man,* and a novel, *Who Did What to Fedalia?* (1950). He was awarded honorary doctorates from Parsons College in Fairfield, Iowa (1956), Coe College in Cedar Rapids, Iowa (1960) and the Indiana Institute of Technology in Fort Wayne (1963).

Willson was married three times. His first wife was Elizabeth Wilson, whom he married on August 29, 1920; the marriage ended in divorce in 1947. On March 13, 1948, he married singer Ralina Zarova. Following her death in 1966, Willson married his secretary, Rosemary Sullivan, on February 14, 1968. Willson's home was on El Camino Drive in the Brentwood section of Los Angeles; he had no children.

Meredith Willson died of heart failure in St. John's Hospital in Santa Monica on June 15, 1984. Funeral services were held on June 19 at St. Martin of Tours Roman Catholic Church in Brentwood, and Willson was buried in Mason City, Iowa.

ABOUT: Current Biography, 1984; The New Grove Dictionary of American Music, 1986; Notable Names in the American Theatre, 2d ed. 1976; Willson, M. And There I Stood with My Piccolo, 1948, Eggs I have Laid, 1952, But He Doesn't Know the Territory, 1959. *Periodicals*—New York Times June 5, 1980, June 17, 1984; Opera and Concert September 1948.

WONDER, STEVIE (May 13, 1950–   ), is one of the most influential and versatile composer-lyricists and performers of the latter part of this century. He was born Steveland Judkins Hardaway in Saginaw, Michigan, the third of Lulu Mae (Morris) Hardway's five children. A premature baby, Wonder was born blind. Nevertheless he led a normal and active childhood, playing games with other children and even riding a bicycle when he had someone to steer it. His parents separated when Wonder was a baby, leaving his mother with the responsibility of supporting the family. She moved to Detroit and raised the children there. As a child (his name now Steveland Morris), he played tunes on a four-hole harmonica and banged rhythms on toy drums. He was introduced to rhythm and blues by a program called "Sundown" on a black radio station and by the age of eight he could play the piano, a regular harmonica, the bongo and drums. He sang solo at the Whitestone Baptist Church, but was expelled from the choir when a church member caught him singing rock 'n' roll with some of his fellow choirboys.

In 1960 Ronnie White, a member of a soul group called the Miracles (soon to become famous as Smokey Robinson and the Miracles) discovered the musical prodigy and introduced him to Berry Gordy, the head of Hitsville, U.S.A., a black recording studio in Detroit soon to be renamed Motown. The ten-year-old boy was signed to a contract and his name changed to Little Stevie Wonder. Gordy's recording studio now became his second home, and its artists his surrogate family. The singer Clarence Paul remembers that Little Stevie would "come by at three every day after school and stay until dark. He'd play every instrument in the place. . . . " He was also encouraged by Gordy and his stable of artists to compose his own songs, the first of which, "Lonely Boy," was written when Wonder was ten.

In Gerri Hirshey's *Nowhere to Run,* Mary Wilson, one of the original Supremes, recalled the day in 1960 when Berry Gordy asked her to sit in on Wonder's audition: " . . . Stevie came up. . . . I think his mother was with him, and a couple of brothers. [Gordy asked the ten-year-old] 'Can you play this instrument?' So he played the piano. He played the organ. He played the drums, the congas. He played everything there. And Berry said, 'You are signed.'" Martha Reeves, of Martha Reeves and the Vandellas, who became his friend and surrogate sister, told Hirshey that Little Stevie "was truly a child genius. [He] seemed sometimes to be a spirit that's lived and is just here again."

In 1962 he recorded his first album, *Little Stevie Wonder: The Twelve-Year Old Genius,* on

STEVIE WONDER

the Tamla label (a subsidiary of Motown). Most of the songs were rhythm and blues numbers that had been written by others, but the multitalented Wonder sang and played the bongos, drums, piano, organ and harmonica. One of the cuts, "Fingertips" (music by Henry Cosby and Clarence Paul), a harmonica solo punctuated by Wonder's finger-snapping, growls and screams, sold more than 1,500,000 copies as a single and became Little Stevie's first number one hit. Released that same year, "Fingertips Pt. 2," by the same composers, earned Wonder his second gold record.

Now a member of Gordy's Motown "family," Wonder was assigned a court-appointed guardian, and the money he earned was placed in a trust to await his 21st birthday. For a time he continued to attend public school, but then enrolled in the Michigan School for the Blind in Lansing, where he studied classical piano. As a member of the Motown Revue, which performed in black theaters and nightclubs, he was on tour for two weeks of every month, but studied for three or four hours each day with a private tutor. In 1964 he appeared in two teen exploitation films, Bikini Beach and Muscle Beach Party.

While continuing to release hit songs written by others, by 1965 Wonder was beginning to collaborate on the composition of numbers that he was eager to record. "Uptight," written by Wonder, Sylvia Moy and Henry Cosby, was a bestseller in recordings in 1966 by Wonder and by the Ramsey Lewis Trio. Wonder's collaborators on "I Was Made to Love Her" (1967), a number one hit on the rhythm-and-blues charts, were Lula

Hardaway, Cosby and Moy, and he wrote "Shoo-Be-Doo-Be-Doo-Ba-Day" in 1968, "Yester-Me, Yester-You, Yesterday" and "Ma Cherie Amour," both in 1969, with Cosby and Moy.

By 1969 Wonder was one of the most popular black entertainers in America, and he had outgrown the label "Little." He performed at New York's prestigious Philharmonic Hall in September 1969 and at the Copacabana, his first supperclub engagement in Manhattan, the following April. He was, wrote Jack Slater in The New York Times Magazine, "all things to all who hear him: the child prodigy who made the transition to adulthood as a productive musician, the blind seer apocalpytically exposing America's injustices, the sightless man-child who still manages to smile, the musician who refused to accept the tyranny and paternalism of corporate recording interests, the black flower-child ruled by visions and astrological signs, the blind nature-boy telling us that the only thing that matters is to love and be loved in return, the black brother who 'made it,' who is still 'for real,' and finally—and perhaps most burdensome of all—the young man who has become, as some whites tell him, an example and inspiration for his people."

His 1970 LP Signed, Sealed and Delivered was the first to be produced by Wonder himself. His last album for Motown was Where I'm Coming From (1970), on which all the songs were written by Wonder and the singer-songwriter Syreeta Wright, whom he married in 1971. According to Current Biography, Where I'm Coming From was "a transitional work [that] struck an uneasy compromise between the Motown Sound and Wonder's own 'free-wheeling musical explorations.'"

Although his recordings had generated sales of more than 30 million, Wonder left Motown in 1971. Now aged 21, he wished to be free of Motown's paternalism and its restrictions on musical innovation. He invested $250,000 in a recording studio that he built in New York City. There he experimented with the sounds that could be produced by such new electronic instruments as the Moog and the ARP synthesizer. The first of his "one-man" albums, for which he wrote all the songs, made his own arrangements, sang and played most of the instruments, was Music Of My Mind (1972). In The New York Times Don Heckman wrote that "One-man recordings have been tried by other performers . . . but no one has brought off the complicated trick of playing most—or all—of the parts better than Wonder in this collection . . . . After a few minutes of the first track, one promptly forgets all about the technical legerdemain and settles down to hear a constantly provocative flow of musical ideas, good humor, artistic invention and solid swing."

Having negotiated a new contract that allowed him to be his own producer and gave him total artistic control over his recordings, Wonder returned to Motown in 1972. That year, on the Tamla label, he released *Talking Book*, which contained "You Are the Sunshine of My Life," now a standard, and "Superstition," both numbers million-sellers as single releases. One of the first commercially successful albums to make heavy use of the synthesizer, *Talking Book* stayed on the charts for 109 weeks.

In the spring of 1972 Wonder toured the United States with Wonderlove, a back-up group of three female vocalists which he had formed for concert performances. And in July and August of 1972 he was the opening act for the Rolling Stones on their much-ballyhooed North American tour. On February 7, 1973 he performed for the first time at New York's prestigious Carnegie Hall.

On August 6, 1973, while he was traveling to a concert, the car in which Wonder was riding crashed into a logging truck in Salisbury, North Carolina. Struck on the forehead by logs, Wonder lay in a coma for almost a week. For many weeks he was hospitalized, followed by months of slow recuperation. However, by February 1974 he was able to tour Europe, and he made his first American appearance since his accident at a Madison Square Garden concert on March 25, 1974.

In March 1974 Wonder received four Grammys, for "You Are the Sunshine of My Life" as best pop vocal by a male artist and as best rhythm and blues vocal; for "Superstition" as best rhythm and blues song; and for a new LP, *Innervisions* (1973) which he described as his "most personal album." The most popular numbers on *Innervisions* were "All in Love is Fair" (also recorded by Barbra Streisand), "Higher Ground" and the gritty, up-tempo radio hit "Living for the City."

In the aftermath of his near-fatal accident Wonder turned more closely than before to religion and mysticism and his music became more introspective. This side of his musical personality found its fullest expression in his *Fulfillingness' First Finale*, released in the summer of 1974. The following March he was awarded four more Grammys: for *Fulfillingness' First Finale* as album of the year and as best male vocal performance; for "Boogie on Reggae Woman" as best rhythm and blues vocal performance; and for "Living for the City" as best rhythm and blues song.

In 1975 Wonder signed a new, seven-year contract with Motown for $13 million dollars, the most lucrative in the history of the recording industry. Under the terms of that agreement, Wonder was required to produce only three new albums, but each was a significant artistic achievement and an unqualified commercial success. The first LP was *Songs in the Key of Life* (1976), Wonder's most ambitious project up to that time. Taking 26 months to produce at a cost of $300,000, it contained 21 new songs, the best of which were "I Wish"; "As"; "Love's in Need of Love Today"; "Knocks Me Off My Feet" and "Another Star." Reviewing this in *High Fidelity*, Stephen Holden wrote: "Wonder's attempt to Say it All results in the aural equivalent of a gigantic mural whose interlocking themes—God, the brotherhood of man, the black experience, love, and sex—encapsulate one man's total vision of human experience. . . . His best tunes have an elemental force that transcends any lack of sophistication. The depth of his spirituality renders irrelevant the feebleness of his attempts to verbalize it. And while Wonder often phrases syllables deliberately when he sings, his singing is so passionately urgent that one is carried along by the emotion of his delivery." More than 1,250,000 copies had been ordered in advance of the record's release, and it quickly attained multiplatinum status, with sales of more than two million before the end of 1976. Four more Grammys were awarded Wonder in February 1977: for *Songs in the Key of Life* as best album and as best pop male vocal performance; for best production; and for the song "I Wish" as best rhythm and blues vocal performance by a male artist.

On his 1979 LP *Journey Through the Secret Life of Plants,* Wonder used ethereal sounds to explore subconscious emotional, physical and intellectual exchanges between humans and plants. This album, which Wonder considers his best, was described by Stephen Holden in *The New York Times* as "a symphonic suite of songs, instrumentals and sound effects that represent pop-classical psychodelia at its most mystical."

Hotter than July (1980), though bereft of any overriding concept or theme, was rich in the kind of romantic balladry for which Wonder is famous. Its high points were "I Ain't Gonna Stand for It," "Do I Hear You Say You Love Me?" and "All Do." This album, said Zita Allen in *Stereo Review*, is "the first Wonder album entirely of the eighties. It is, typically, a prodigious (almost) one-man show. . . . This rewarding release should at least satisfy those doubting Thomases who were afraid Stevie Wonder had lost his touch. With *Hotter than July* the Wonder is definitely back."

In 1982 Wonder and Paul McCartney recorded the single "Ebony and Ivory," a plea for racial harmony, which earned a gold record.

Wonder also composed the songs for the 1983 movie *The Woman in Red* (1983), a comedy starring Gene Wilder. The soundtrack of that film was released in 1984, his first all-new studio album in four years. Many of the LP's cuts were sung as duets by Wonder and Dionne Warwick, and one of its tracks, "I Just Called to Say I Love You," reached the number-one position on the charts.

Among the honors conferred on Wonder are the 1977 American Music award for best male soul singer, an honorary doctorate of humane letters from Howard University in 1978, and the ASCAP Founder's Award in 1984 for "his achievements in creating and bringing an extraordinary range of musical expression to audiences far and wide."

Wonder explained how the creative process works for him in an interview with *Stereo Review* in 1980: "You hear this music in your mind first; that's the way it is for me, anyway. Then I go after getting it exactly the way I imagined it. If it doesn't come out the way it is in my mind, it has to come out either better than that or equivalent to it. If it's in a different fashion, it's got to be just as good."

Wonder and Syreeta Wright were divorced in 1974. He is now married to the former Yolanda Simmons, who had worked for Wonder as his secretary and bookkeeper. He owns a house in Los Angeles that is equipped with a state-of-the-art recording studio and maintains an apartment on Manhattan's Upper East Side. Though blind, he regularly attends movies and "watches" television. Wonder was a leader of the movement to have Dr. Martin Luther King's birthday proclaimed a national holiday, and wrote the song "Happy Birthday" in honor of the slain civil rights leader.

ABOUT: Current Biography, 1975; Haskins, J. The Story of Stevie Wonder; Hirshey, G. Nowhere to Run: The Story of Soul Music, 1984. *Periodicals*—New York Times Magazine February 23, 1975; Newsweek October 28, 1974; Stereo Review May 1980.

WORK, HENRY CLAY (October 1, 1832–June 8, 1884), composer-lyricist, was born in Middletown, Connecticut, the son of Alanson and Aurelia Work. His father was an abolitionist who helped thousands of slaves to escape by making his home part of the "underground railway." When Henry Work was three, his family moved to Quincy, Illinois. For his activity in the

HENRY CLAY WORK

underground railway Alanson Work was imprisoned. Released in 1845, he took his family back to Middletown, where Henry Work attended elementary school. Upon leaving school, he worked as a printer's apprentice in Hartford, Connecticut. In the printer's shop he found a melodeon which he learned to play and used to compose his first songs.

In 1854 Work moved to Chicago, where he was employed as a printer and pursued songwriting as a hobby. He achieved success with "We're Coming Sister Mary." Published in Chicago by Firth Pond & Co. in the early 1850s, it was popularized by the Christy Minstrels a decade later. Work's first song of enduring popularity was "Kingdom Coming," or "The Year of the Jubilo," a number composed in 1862 in Negro dialect. Following its publication by Root and Cady, it was introduced in Chicago by the Christy Minstrels on April 23, 1862, and soon became a minstrel-show staple, so popular it was often parodied. In 1863 Work wrote a sequel, "Babylon is Falling," inspired by the decision to recruit black soldiers into the Union Army. In the presidential election of 1864 the melody of "Kingdom Coming" was used as a campaign song for Abraham Lincoln. Part of "Kingdom Coming" was performed in the 1944 motion picture *Meet Me in St. Louis*, starring Judy Garland, but it was quoted in its entirety in Jerome Kern's Broadway musical, *Good Morning, Judge* (1921).

The success of "Kingdom Coming" brought Work a contract as songwriter for Root and Cady, enabling him to give up the occupation of printer and devote himself to composition. In

1862 he wrote "Grafted into the Army," a humorous number in which an Irish mother complains that her son has been "grafted" (instead of "drafted") into the Union Army. This was the most popular of the many songs of the Civil War years that satirized the draft, draft exemptions and war profiteers.

"Wake Nicodemus," of 1864, was a ballad about a black man, dead and buried in the hollow trunk of a tree, who begs to be aroused on the first Day of Jubilo following Emancipation. This song, too, became a minstrel-show standard.

"Come Home, Father," of 1864, is one of the most celebrated of all temperance songs. It is a child's plea that his father leave the saloon and come home to a dying son. The drunken father turns a deaf ear, and the boy dies begging for the absent father to kiss him goodnight. It was introduced in 1868 in *Ten Nights in a Barroom*, a melodrama by William W. Pratt based on a story by Timothy Shay Arthur. The popularity of "Come, Home, Father" spread rapidly. Heard at Temperance meetings everywhere, it was adopted by the National Prohibition Party as its official song when that party was organized in Oswego, New York.

One of Work's most famous ballads, "Marching Through Georgia," a classic among American patriotic songs, was written in 1865, during the closing months of the Civil War when General Sherman made his famous march to the sea. Southerners called it a "hymn of hate," and remained so hostile to it that in 1916 the Southern bloc temporarily walked out of the Democratic National Convention when the band thoughtlessly played Work's ballad. But in the Northeast, "Marching Through Georgia" never lost its popularity, and in World War II it was played by the bank when the Americans marched into Tunis.

After the Civil War, Work composed several sentimental ballads, the best of which were "The Lost Letter," "The Ship That Sailed" and his greatest commercial success, "Grandfather's Clock," whose sheet music sales exceeded 800,000 copies. Composed in 1876, it was introduced that year in New Haven, Connecticut by Sam Lucas of the Hyer Sisters Colored Minstrels. In the presidential campaign of 1886, its melody was borrowed for lyrics that satirized Benjamin Harrison.

Work continued to live in Chicago until 1871, working all the while at Root and Cady. But after the great fire of 1871 demolished that firm, Work moved to Philadelphia and then to Vineland, New Jersey, where he lost money on bad investments. Work returned to Chicago in 1875

when Root and Cady was reestablished and remained there the rest of his life. He died in Hartford in 1884 while visiting his mother. Work was buried next to his wife, whom he had married in Chicago in the early years of the Civil War. They had three children.

ABOUT: Howard, J. T. Our American Music; Spaeth, S. A History of Popular Music in America, 1948.

WRIGHT, ROBERT CRAIG. *See* FORREST, GEORGE and WRIGHT, ROBERT CRAIG

YELLEN, JACK (July 6, 1892–), lyricist, was born Jacob Selig Yellen in Razcki, Poland, to Abram Yellen, a merchant, and Bessie (Wallens) Yellen. The family immigrated to the United States in 1897. After attending public schools. Yellen received his B.A. degree at the University of Michigan in 1913. At college he earned pocket money by writing songs, both music and lyrics, one of the earliest being "I Used to be Lonesome" (1910). After his sophomore year, however, he concentrated on lyrics, collaborating with the composer George L. Cobb for the next few years. Their song "All Aboard for Dixieland" was interpolated into the Rudolf Friml Broadway operetta, *High Jinks* (1913), and was recorded that year by the American Quartette. They composed "Are You From Dixie?" in 1913, a song revived half a century later in a bestselling recording by the country singer Jerry Reed. "Alabama Jubilee" followed in 1915. Both "Are You From Dixie?" and "Alabama Jubilee" were recorded that year, by the Victor Band.

After college, Yellen worked as a sports editor for the Buffalo *Courier* before moving to New York City to advance his career as a songwriter. For a time he collaborated with the composer Albert Gumble, writing "How's Ev'ry Little Thing in Dixie?" (1916), which was recorded by the American Quartette, and "Southern Gal" and "Playmates" (both 1917).

During World War I Yellen served in the U. S. Army resuming his career as a songwriter in New York after 1919. "Peaches" (music by Gumble) was interpolated into the Broadway revue *Priorities of 1920*. "Down by the O-H-I-O" (1920, music by Abe Olman) achieved such popularity in Tin Pan Alley that Van and Schenck interpolated it into the *Ziegfeld Follies of 1920* and Lou Holtz included it in *George White's Scandals of 1920*.

A turning point for Yellen's career came in

JACK YELLEN

1920, when John Murray Anderson, planning a Broadway revue, engaged him to set lyrics to Milton Ager's music. The revue was *What's in a Name* (March 19, 1920) and it marked the beginning of the Ager-Yellen collaboration that yielded a rich harvest of hit songs in the 1920s. The most memorable number from their first revue was "A Young Man's Fancy."

Beginning in 1922, Ager and Yellen's songs were published by their own firm Ager, Yellen and Borenstein. Their best number from the years 1922–27 were: "Who Cares?" (1922); "Lovin' Sam, the Sheik of Alabam'" (1922); "Louisville Lou, the Vampire Lady" (1923); "Hard-Hearted Hannah, the Vamp of Savannah" (1924); "I Wonder What's Become of Sally?" (1924); "Ain't She Sweet?" (1927); "Forgive Me" (1927); and "Crazy Words, Crazy Tune" (1927).

For the musical theater they wrote the scores for *Zig Zag* (1922), the *Ted Lewis Frolic* (1923) and John Murray Anderson's *Almanac* (1929), all closed after brief runs. *Rain or Shine* (February 9, 1928), starring Joe Cook, was a box-office success. The title song and "Forever and Ever" were the show's principal songs.

With the advent of "talkies," Ager and Yellen were lured to Hollywood in 1928. For *Honky Tonk* (1929), starring Sophie Tucker, they wrote "I'm the Last of the Red Hot Mammas" and "He's a Good Man to Have Around"; to *King of Jazz* (1930), starring Paul Whiteman and his orchestra, they contributed "Happy Feet" and "A Bench in the Park"; and for *Chasing Rainbows* (1930) they wrote "Happy Days Are Here Again," a standard that the Democratic Party

adopted as its theme song during the years of President Franklin D. Roosevelt's leadership.

Yellen had a hit song in the 1920s independent of any help from Ager—"My Yiddishe Momme." He had written both the words and the music in 1924 as a tribute to his mother, who had recently passed away. Yellen had no intention of commercializing the song, and the manuscript remained unpublished until 1925, when he asked Lew Pollack to embellish the melody. Yellen took his finished version to Sophie Tucker, who burst into tears when Yellen sang it to her. She suggested that Yellen change the title to "Jewish" or "Hebrew" Momme instead of "Yiddishe," but Yellen not only refused, he also convinced Tucker to sing the chorus in Yiddish. She introduced it at the Palace Theatre in 1925 and brought down the house. It became one of her standard numbers, probably second in popularity only to her signature, "Some of These Days." She sang it in concert in Europe as well as the United States, and recorded both English and Yiddish versions. "I have found whenever I sang 'My Yiddishe Momme' in the United States or Europe," she recalled, "gentiles have loved the song [without needing] to understand the Yiddish words. They knew by instinct what I was saying." It has been recorded by Belle Baker, Connie Frances, Ella Logan, Johnny Desmond, Vic Damone, and by two black singers, Billy Daniels and Hazel Scott.

In 1930 Ager and Yellen dissolved their partnership, with Yellen selling his interest in their publishing firm. Over the next two decades both Ager and Yellen worked successfully with other songwriting partners. To Harold Arlen's music, Yellen wrote the lyrics for *You Said It* (January 19, 1931), a Broadway musical that ran for 192 performances and yielded the hit song "Sweet and Hot." With Ray Henderson as composer, Yellen wrote the lyrics for *George White's Scandals of 1936* (December 15, 1935), which produced the popular "I've Got to Get Hot."

In 1935 Yellen returned to Hollywood, where he wrote screenplays for 20th Century–Fox and only occasionally contributed lyrics to songs in movie musicals. The films he helped write the scripts for over the next three years were *George White's Scandals of 1935* (1935), *Sing, Baby, Sing* (1936), *Pigskin Parade* (1936), *Wake Up and Live* (1937), *Love Is News* (1937), *Submarine Patrol* (1938), and *Little Miss Broadway* (1938). For the *Scandals of 1935* he wrote the lyrics to "It's an Old Southern Custom" (music by Joseph Meyer) and "Nasty Man" (music by Ray Henderson). Lew Pollack was his composer for "The Right to Love," which Shirley Temple introduced in *Captain January* (1936).

Yellen returned to Broadway on August 28, 1939, teaming with composer Sammy Fain to write the songs for *George White's Scandals of 1939*, whose most memorable number was "Are You Havin' Any Fun?" With Fain he also prepared the complete scores for the Broadway musicals *Boys and Girls Together* (October 1, 1940; lyrics written with Irving Kahal) and *Sons o' Fun* (December 1, 1941). *Boys and Girls* ran for 191 performances, *Sons o' Fun* 742, the latter score produced the hit "Happy in Love." To Yellen's lyrics, Ray Henderson composed the music for the *Ziegfeld Follies of 1943* (April 14, 1943), which ran for 553 performances.

(For more information about the songs and stage musicals mentioned in this article consult the biographies of Milton Ager, Harold Arlen, Sammy Fain and Ray Henderson.)

In the 1950s Yellen wrote special material for Sophie Tucker and for revues mounted at Manhattan's Versailles nightclub. He served as the director of ASCAP from 1951 to 1969.

On September 13, 1944 Yellen married Lucille Hodgeman. They made their home in New York City before moving to a farm in Springville, in upstate New York. Yellen has a son and daughter from a previous marriage.

ABOUT: Burton, J. The Blue Book of Tin Pan Alley, 1950; Rigdon, W. (ed.) The Biographical Encyclopedia and Who's Who of the American Theatre, 1966.

YOUMANS, VINCENT (September 27, 1898–April 5, 1946). Facts and figures are poor yardsticks by which to measure the significance of Vincent Youmans as a composer for the musical theater of the 1920s and 1930s. When compared to the other giant figures of his day, Youmans's output is frugal. He left only 96 published songs, he composed scores for 12 musicals, only three of which were successful and he created music for only two films. Nevertheless, Youmans earned the right to belong to that elite group of songwriters that includes George Gershwin, Jerome Kern, Richard Rodgers) and Cole Porter, for what he lacked in quantity, he achieved in quality. A perfectionist, he rarely permitted anything but his best to leave the work table; he also reworked unused material for new shows. His publisher, Max Dreyfus (also the publisher of Gerswin, Kern, and Rodgers, once said that Youmans was the only composer he knew who could be expected to produce a standard with every song he submitted. A consummate craftsman who used his notes economically but always to full effect, and a magician in evoking moods with impeccable taste, Youmans left a rich and durable repertory of songs.

VINCENT YOUMANS

Vincent Millie Youmans Jr., the younger of two children of Vincent Miller and Lucy Gibson (Millie) Youmans, was born in New York City on a site now occupied by the Mayflower Hotel (to which a commemorative plaque was affixed in 1970). His father was the co-proprietor of prosperous establishments selling men's and women's hats. While the young Vincent was still a toddler, his family acquired a house in Larchmont, New York, where he was raised. As a child, Vincent revealed an alert, intelligent mind and a talent for drawing. He received his first piano lessons at the age of four from Charles André Feller, the church organist at the First Methodist Episcopal Church in New Rochelle. His education took place in private schools, first at Trinity School in Mamaroneck, New York, then at Heathcote Hall, in Rye. In spite of Youmans's interest and gifts in art and music, his father hoped he would become a businessman, while his mother insisted he be prepared for a profession. His mother prevailed, and preparations were made for him to enroll in the engineering program at Yale's Sheffield Scientific School.

Youmans never entered Yale. He left Heathcote Hall two months before graduation in 1916 to enter the world of finance. For two days, he was employed as a messenger for Guaranty Trust Company, in Wall Street, and also worked as a runner for another firm for a few weeks. He soon became convinced that his future lay not in finance, but in music, and found a job as a song plugger at the Tin Pan Alley publishing house of Jerome H. Remick, where the young George Gershwin was similarly employed.

When America became involved in World War I, Youmans enlisted in the U. S. Navy. For a year and a half, he was stationed with an entertainment unit at the Great Lakes Training Station, where he helped to produce shows, played the piano in a band, and wrote songs. One of these songs became popular with Navy bands and was frequently performed by the John Philip Sousa band. A decade later, Youmans used this melody for "Hallelujah," in the Broadway musical, *Hit the Deck!*.

After the war, Youmans returned to Tin Pan Alley, this time plugging songs for Harms Inc. at a weekly salary of $25. He also worked as rehearsal pianist and helped coach singers for several Victor Herbert operettas. Youmans's first published song, "The Country Cousin" (lyrics by Alfred Bryan), was issued by J. H. Remick in 1920; it was inspired by a silent motion picture of the same title.

George Gershwin recommended Youmans to producer Alex A. Aarons, who engaged him to share responsibility with Paul Lannin for the score of a Broadway musical, *Two Little Girls in Blue* (May 3, 1921), starring Oscar Shaw, Fred Santley and the Fairbanks Twins. (Aarons later sold his interest in the show to A.L. Erlanger, who produced it.) With a book by Arthur Jackson and lyrics by Ira Gershwin (pseudonymously identified as Arthur Francis), the plot concerned the efforts of the Sartori twins to reach India to claim an inheritance. Able to afford only a single steamship ticket, they take turns in the dining salon and stateroom without arousing suspicion. Aboard ship, each meets a desirable man, and the suitors pursue both girls, unaware they are two different people. Complications ensue, but once the twins reveal themselves, the romances progress smoothly. Among the show's best songs were "Dolly" and "Oh Me, Oh My, Oh You" (music by Youmans), which was recorded by Paul Whiteman and later was sung by Doris Day and Gene Nelson in the motion picture *Tea for Two* (1950) and by Kathryn Grayson in *So This Is Love* (1953). *Two Little Girls in Blue* had a summer run of 135 performances.

Youmans's next musical, for which he composed the score with Herbert Stothart, was a solid box-office success and the longest-running of his shows (477 performances). Entitled *Wildflower*, it opened on February 7, 1923 with book and lyrics by Otto Harbach and Oscar Hammerstein II. Its heroine, the volatile Nina, inherits a fortune, but in order to claim it, she must control her temper for six months. She succeeds, but only with great difficulty. The critic of the New York *World* called *Wildflower* "a musical comedy of delightful manner and really

gorgeous melodies . . . These song numbers not only are prepared with taste and understanding, but they seem a most essential part in the make-up of the whole. . . . Its music and tempo are extraordinary." With *Wildflower*, Youmans's reputation was established, and two of his songs from the show became popular: "Bambalina," which describes an eccentric fiddler who confuses the dancers with his sudden stops (introduced by Edith Day), and the title song, sung by Guy Robertson.

Herbert Stothart also collaborated with Youmans on the score of *Mary Jane McKane* (December 25, 1923), but for *Lollipop* (January 21, 1924), Youmans was solely responsible for the complete score for the first time. Both productions had only limited box-office appeal, the former running for 151 performances, the latter, with its weak libretto by Zelda Sears, for 152. However, Youmans reworked and used musical material from both productions in his next musical, *No, No, Nanette* (September 16, 1925), with which he reached the apex of his stage career. After a disastrous opening in Detroit, a new version of the show ran for a year in Chicago; a Broadway run of 321 performances and 665 in London followed. In addition, it became the first musical to circle the globe; 17 companies performed it in other parts of Europe and South America, New Zealand, the Philippines and China. The producer made a profit of two million dollars, while Youmans earned half a million dollars. *No, No, Nanette* later inspired three motion pictures: the first (1930) starred Alexander Gray and Bernice Claire; the second (1940) starred Anna Neagle; and the third, retitled *Tea for Two* (1950), starred Doris Day and Gordon MacRae. When *No, No, Nanette* returned to Broadway in 1971, it had the longest run of any musical revival in Broadway history (861 performances); it was also heard in 1986 in concert performances at Carnegie Recital Hall.

The book by Otto Harbach and Frank Mandel was an adaptation of *His Lady Friends*, a light stage comedy by Clifton Crawford produced in 1919. Billy Early, a publisher of Bibles, has a weakness for young ladies to whom he makes financial contributions in the name of career advancement. Nanette, his unconventional daughter, flirts with Jim, her father's friend and lawyer, arousing the jealousy of her boyfriend, Tom. Complications arise, but are resolved in Atlantic City, where Early's wife methodically disposes of her husband's amatory involvements and straightens out her daughter's romances.

Youmans (and lyricist Irving Caesar) composed four songs for *No, No, Nanette* including the popular title song and the standards "I Want to Be Happy" and "Tea for Two." Louise Groody (Nanette) and Charles Winninger (Jim) introduced "I Want to Be Happy" on the stage; Doris Day and Gordon MacRae sang it in *Tea for Two* and it has been recorded by Ella Fitzgerald, among many others. "Tea for Two" was introduced by Louise Groody and Jack Barker (Tom) and it has since been used in a number of films. Doris Day sang it again in *Young Man With a Horn* (1950), and Jane Froman (dubbing for Susan Hayward) sang it in *With a Song in My Heart* (1952); it was also interpolated into *Sincerely Yours*, starring Liberace (1955). There are also numerous recordings of "Tea for Two"; among them are those by Bing Crosby with Connie Boswell, Dinah Shore with Frank Sinatra, the Benny Goodman Quintet and Fats Waller. In 1958, "Tea for Two" received a cha-cha treatment in a recording by Warren Covington. As a young man, the distinguished Soviet composer, Dmitri Shostakovich, orchestrated "Tea for Two," calling his composition *Tahiti Trot* (1928); it was performed by the New York Philharmonic conducted by Gennady Roszhdestvensky in 1979.

The historic revival of *No, No, Nanette*, starring Ruby Keeler, came to Broadway on January 19, 1971, bringing nostalgic reminders of the 1920s. Burt Shevelove adapted the book and did the staging. "Time travelers of all ages will revel in the simplicity of Vincent Youmans' music," wrote Clive Barnes in his review in *The New York Times*. "It is music to hum and particularly music to dance to. Its rhythms suggest their own dancing feet and the melodies are light, cheerful and exuberant. . . . This is far closer to a musical of the twenties than anything New York has seen since the twenties, but it is seen through a contemporary sensibility." The revival received the Outer Critics Circle Award as one of the outstanding productions of the year, and its score was released in an original cast album. The history of this revival has been recounted by Donald H. Dunn in *The Making of No, No, Nanette*.

Though the two Youmans musicals that followed *No, No, Nanette* were box-office failures, they are not without musical interest. *A Night Out* (1925) folded in Philadelphia, but from it came "Sometimes I'm Happy," highlight of *Hit the Deck!* two years later. For *Oh, Please!* (December 17, 1926), a vehicle for Beatrice Lillie (79 performances), Youmans composed the lively standard "I Know That You Know" (lyrics by Anne Caldwell). It has been recorded by many, including Nat King Cole, the Revelers, the Benny Goodman Quintet and Lionel Hampton.

On February 7, 1927 Youmans married Anne Varley, a dancer in the company of *Oh, Please!*.

He soon discovered he could adjust neither to domesticity nor to matrimony. Though their home was in Greenwich, Connecticut, Youmans retained a residence in New York. Contact with his wife was maintained mainly by telephone and occasional visits, particularly after she gave birth to twins. Youmans persisted in his footloose ways for the remainder of his life, driven by both restlessness and his incapacity to accept permanent ties. He avoided taking root in any one home and had little interest in accumulating possessions.

With *Hit the Deck!* (April 25, 1927), Youmans's last success on Broadway, he became his own producer. This was "a nautical musical comedy" with a book by Herbert Fields, based on Hubert Osborne's play, *Shore Leave*, and lyrics by Clifford Grey and Leo Robin. Louise Groody starred as Loulou, the proprietess of a coffee shop in Newport, Rhode Island who falls in love with Bilge (Charles King), a sailor who frequents her establishment. When she inherits a fortune, Loulou follows Bilge around the world to persuade him to marry her. He refuses to marry an heiress, so she neatly solves her problem by signing away her fortune to their first child.

Two Youmans classics came from *Hit the Deck!*, though neither was originally composed for this score. The melody of "Halleluja" was composed while Youmans was in the Navy a decade earlier. In the show, it was introduced by Stella Mayhew; Ella Fitzgerald with the Chick Webb Orchestra, the Revelers, the Singing Sophomores and Hazel Scott later recorded it. "Sometimes I'm Happy" began as "Come on and Pet Me" (lyrics by Oscar Hammerstein II), intended for but deleted from *Mary Jane McKane*; it returned as "Sometimes I'm Happy" in *A Night Out*. In *Hit the Deck!* it was performed by Louise Groody and Charles King and subsequently recorded by Benny Goodman and by Jo Stafford with the Paul Whiteman Orchestra. Bunny Berigan's first success on records came with this song, Blue Barron and his orchestra adopted it as their signature music, and it also became a favorite in the repertory of Florence Mills. "If 'Sometimes I'm Happy' isn't sung all over the world until sometimes you're unhappy," wrote Alan Dale in his review for *The New York American*, "I'll eat my chapeau."

Hit the Deck! has continued to be popular through the years. Film versions were made in 1930 and 1955 and it was revived at the Jones Beach Marine Theatre on Long Island in 1960 and at the Goodspeed Opera House in East Haddam, Connecticut, in 1977.

After *Hit the Deck!* came an uninterrupted succession of stage failures for Youmans.

Rainbow (November 21, 1928), with dances staged by Busby Berkeley, closed after 30 performances; Great Day! (October 17, 1929), after 36; Smiles (November 18, 1930), produced by Florenz Ziegfeld, after 63; and Through the Years (January 28, 1932), after 20. For Great Day! (mounted in his own theater, renamed Youmans's Cosmopolitan) and Through the Years, Youmans was his own producer, and had assumed duties and responsibilities that he was not equipped to handle.

Although these shows failed, Youmans's songwriting remained on a high plane of excellence. "I Want a Man" (lyrics by Oscar Hammerstein II) from Rainbow, brought Libby Holman her first notices for the rendition in which she revealed her potential as a torch singer. "More Than You Know" (lyrics by Billy Rose and Edward Eliscu) was introduced by Mayo Methot in Great Day!, and was popularized in recordings by Benny Goodman, Perry Como, Helen Morgan, Billie Holiday, Johnny Mathis, Ruth Etting and Artie Shaw. It was also sung by Tony Martin in the second film version of Hit the Deck! and by Barbra Streisand in Funny Lady (1977). "Without a Song" and "Great Day" (lyrics to both by Billy Rose and Eliscu) were introduced in Great Day! by Lois Deppe and the Jubilee Singers. Paul Whiteman recorded both songs in 1929; "Without a Song" was recorded by Tommy Dorsey with Frank Sinatra and also by Paul Robeson. Marilyn Miller and Paul Gregory introduced "Time on My Hands" (lyrics by Harold Adamson and Mack Gordon) in Smiles. It, too, was widely used: recordings were made by Dick Todd, Vaughn Monroe and the orchestras of Guy Lombardo, Artie Shaw, Benny Goodman and Glen Gray; on radio, it became the theme song for the Chase and Sanborn Hour; and it was also sung by June Haver and Gordon MacRae in Marilyn Miller's screen biography, Look for the Silver Lining (1949) and by Gladys Swarthout in So This Is Love (1953).

But of all his songs, the title song of Through the Years (lyrics by Edward Heyman) was Youmans's favorite. Edward Heyman revealed to this author that writing the lyrics was "perhaps the most moving experience of my life. Youmans lived in a penthouse apartment in the West Forties and the night was a rare New York one in which moonlight actually filtered into the room. He turned out all the lights, opened the terrace door and sat me in a large chair facing the piano. For a little over half an hour he played the melody over and over without stopping. Then I asked him to stop because the lyric was finished. There was not one word ever changed in that lyric. Never again has such a thing happened to me." The song was intro-

duced on stage by Natalie Hall and Michael Bartlett and recorded by Gladys Swarthout, Nelson Eddy and Risë Stevens.

Youmans made his last contribution to the musical theater with several songs for Take a Chance (November 26, 1932); the remainder of the score was composed by Richard Whiting and Nacio Herb Brown. Youmans's "Rise 'n' Shine" was a spiritual introduced on Broadway by Ethel Merman and sung by Lillian Roth in the film adaptation of the musical (1933). "Should I Be Sweet" was introduced by June Knight, and "Oh, How I Long to Belong to You" and "So Do I" were duets for June Knight and Jack Whiting on the stage.

In 1930, Youmans composed songs for What a Widow, the first of two Hollywood musicals to which he contributed. The film starred Gloria Swanson, and Youmans's collaborators were the lyricists J. Russell Robinson and George Waggner. The second film was Flying Down to Rio (1933), the screen musical in which Fred Astaire and Ginger Rogers made their debut as a song-and-dance team. To lyrics by Gus Kahn and Edward Eliscu, Youmans composed three songs which are top drawer: "Carioca," "Orchids in the Moonlight" and "Music Makes Me." After Flying Down to Rio, Youmans's professional career as a songwriter ended. What he had composed up to that time never lost its appeal: "It is not hard to put one's fingers on the reasons that have kept the music of Vincent Youmans from ever going out of fashion," wrote Stanley Green in The World of Musical Comedy (1980). "There is never a wasted or false note, nor an awkwardly constructed phrase. More important, Youmans' songs have the rare knack of involving the emotions of their listeners; they are not only remembered, they are experienced. An insinuating phrase here, an intriguing use of syncopation there, give his melodies adhesive power and also endow them with the quality of deeply personal expressions."

Beginning in 1933, Youmans faced a number of serious personal and professional setbacks from which he never completely recovered. That year he divorced his wife, destroying once and for all the facade of domesticity he had erected. His business affairs went from bad to worse; the Vincent Youmans Company, his publishing firm founded in 1929, went into bankruptcy in 1934. The same year, he also lost the Cosmopolitan Theatre by defaulting on the mortgage. His health was also failing. Stricken by tuberculosis, Youmans moved to Colorado Springs in 1935, where he married Mildred Boots, a former Follies girl who served as his nurse, on October 31, 1935.

Youmans filed for bankruptcy in 1934, with liabilities exceeding $500,000 and only negligible assets. However, he managed to retain some of his zest for living. He still enjoyed staying up late with friends and going from one night spot to another. At other times, when his health allowed, he studied music in the hope he might one day write an opera or a symphony, and for a short period, he studied orchestration with Ferdinand Dunkley at the Loyola School of Music. He also continued to write songs, which he enjoyed performing for his friends on the piano while whistling the vocal part, but he made no attempt to market them.

After an eight-year absence, Youmans returned to New York in 1943 to make a comeback in the theater as a producer. His new project was not the usual musical, but a grandiose artistic project enlisting the services of world-famous dancers, choreographers and other artists as well as featuring the music of Cuban composer Ernesto Lecuona. *Vincent Youmans' Ballet Revue* opened in Toronto, Canada on January 20, 1944 to disastrous reviews. After several additional performances in Baltimore and Boston, the show closed permanently with a loss of $400,000.

When the tuberculosis now began to affect him to the point where he could speak only in whispers, Youmans and his wife returned to Colorado. Under the care of a physician, he rested all day, but at night, against his doctor's orders, he would go out on the town until early morning hours.

In January 1946, Youmans and his wife were divorced. He became a patient in a Denver sanatorium, but because he detested hospitals, he defied his physicians by leaving and moving into the nearby Park Lane Hotel one month later. Mrs. Mary Coyle Chase, the playwright who was often Youmans's companion, recalled: "Until . . . he was unable to get out of bed at all, he would delight Westerners by going to parties, sitting at the piano, playing over his old music

and much of his unpublished music–entrancing his audience but straining his strength cruelly."

Youmans died in his hotel suite in Denver on April 5, 1946. His body was brought back to New York, where funeral ceremonies were held in the St. Thomas Protestant Episcopal Church on Fifth Avenue on April 10. As he had requested, his ashes were scattered at Mud Hole, off Ambrose Light vessel, where he had fished as a boy.

Youmans's zest for living led F. Scott Fitzgerald to use him as the model for the character Abe North in *Tender Is the Night.* Youmans loved sailing, and he owned a boat, *The Carioca.* He also enjoyed fishing and driving expensive cars at high speeds. But for him life really began at midnight when he would enjoy the society of friends while, in earlier years, overindulging in alcohol. Once he was alone, he would become moody and depressed. At such times, he would sequester himself in his apartment for three or four consecutive days. "He had no self-discipline about his body," recalled lyricist Edward Eliscu. "His downfall. . . . was because he neglected his health."

In 1960, the *Bell Telephone Hour* presented *The Unforgettable Music of Vincent Youmans.* Four years later, Evergreen Records released an album of 36 Youmans songs covering his entire career on Broadway and Hollywood. The most recent tribute was the *Oh My, Oh Youmans,* conceived by Darwin Knight and Tom Taylor and staged by Knight; it was presented Off Broadway in 1981 and offered a cross-section of more than 40 Youmans songs including the unfamiliar as well as the classics. On May 9, 1983, Vincent Youmans was posthumously elected to the Theatre Hall of Fame in New York.

ABOUT: Bordman, G. Days to be Happy, Years to be Sad: The Life and Music of Vincent Youmans, 1982; Wilder, A. American Popular Song 1972; Wilk, M. They're Playing Our Song, 1973. *Periodicals*—ASCAP Today Spring 1975.

Photo Credits

AP/Wide World Photos, Betty Comden and Adolf Green, Bruce Springsteen; ASCAP, Lee Adams, Burt Bacharach, Ernest R. Ball, Leonard Bernstein, Chuck Berry, Eubie Blake, Lew Brown, Nacio Herb Brown, Johnny Burke, Irving Caesar, Johnny Cash, George M. Cohan, Cy Coleman, Con Conrad, John Denver, B. G. de Sylva, Neil Diamond, Howard Dietz, Walter Donaldson, Al Dubin, Bob Dylan, Gus Edwards, Ray Evans, Sammy Fain, Dorothy Fields, Fred Fisher, George Forrest, Arthur Freed, Rudolf Friml, Mack Gordon, Marvin Hamlisch, Oscar Hammerstein II, Otto Harbach, E. Y. Harburg, Lorenz Hart, Victor Herbert, Billy Joel, Tom Jones, Gus Kahn, Bert Kalmar, Jerome Kern, Carole King, Alan Jay Lerner, Frederick Loewe, Edward B. Marks, Johnny Mercer, Mitchell Parish, Cole Porter, Ralph Rainger, Harry Revel, Lionel Richie, Leo Robin, Sigmund Romberg, Harry Ruby, Harvey Schmidt, Arthur Schwartz, Jean Schwartz, Carly Simon, Noble Sissle, Stephen Sondheim, Charles Strouse, Harry Tierney, Egbert Van Alstyne, Albert Von Tilzer, Harry Von Tilzer, "Fats" Waller, Ned Washington, Paul Francis Webster, Kurt Weill, Richard A. Whiting, Stevie Wonder, Vincent Youmans; BMI Archives, Jerry Bock, "Fats" Domino, Fred Ebb, Merle Haggard, John Kander, Kris Kristofferson, Roger Miller, Marty Robbins, Neil Sedaka, Paul Simon, James Taylor, Hank Williams; from After the Ball, copyright renewed 1953 by James J. Geller, Charles K. Harris; Courtesy of The New York Public Library, Music Division, Reginald de Koven, Stephen Foster, Henry Clay Work.

SONG INDEX

473